Lecture Notes in Bioinformatics 12108

Subseries of Lecture Notes in Computer Science

More information about this series at http://www.springer.com/series/5381

Ignacio Rojas · Olga Valenzuela ·
Fernando Rojas · Luis Javier Herrera ·
Francisco Ortuño (Eds.)

Bioinformatics and Biomedical Engineering

8th International Work-Conference, IWBBIO 2020
Granada, Spain, May 6–8, 2020
Proceedings

Springer

Editors
Ignacio Rojas
University of Granada
Granada, Spain

Olga Valenzuela
University of Granada
Granada, Spain

Fernando Rojas
University of Granada
Granada, Spain

Luis Javier Herrera
University of Granada
Granada, Spain

Francisco Ortuño
University of Chicago and Fundacion
Progreso y Salud
Granada, Spain

ISSN 0302-9743 ISSN 1611-3349 (electronic)
Lecture Notes in Bioinformatics
ISBN 978-3-030-45384-8 ISBN 978-3-030-45385-5 (eBook)
https://doi.org/10.1007/978-3-030-45385-5

LNCS Sublibrary: SL8 – Bioinformatics

This Springer imprint is published by the registered company Springer Nature Switzerland AG
The registered company address is: Gewerbestrasse 11, 6330 Cham, Switzerland

Preface

We are proud to present the final set of accepted full papers for the 8th International Work-Conference on Bioinformatics and Biomedical Engineering (IWBBIO 2020) held in Granada, Spain, during May 6–8, 2020.

IWBBIO 2020 seeks to provide a discussion forum for scientists, engineers, educators, and students about the latest ideas and realizations in the foundations, theory, models, and applications for interdisciplinary and multidisciplinary research encompassing disciplines of computer science, mathematics, statistics, biology, bioinformatics, and biomedicine.

The aim of IWBBIO 2020 was to create a friendly environment that could lead to the establishment or strengthening of scientific collaborations and exchanges among attendees, and therefore IWBBIO 2020 solicited high-quality original research papers (including significant work in progress) on any aspect of bioinformatics, biomedicine, and biomedical engineering.

New computational techniques and methods in machine learning; data mining; text analysis; pattern recognition; data integration; genomics and evolution; next generation sequencing data; protein and RNA structure; protein function and proteomics; medical informatics and translational bioinformatics; computational systems biology; modeling and simulation; and their application in the life science domain, biomedicine, and biomedical engineering were especially encouraged. The list of topics accompanying the call for papers has also evolved, resulting in the following list for the present edition:

1. **Computational proteomics**. Analysis of protein-protein interactions. Protein structure modeling. Analysis of protein functionality. Quantitative proteomics and PTMs. Clinical proteomics. Protein annotation. Data mining in proteomics.
2. **Next generation sequencing and sequence analysis**. De novo sequencing, re-sequencing, and assembly. Expression estimation. Alternative splicing discovery. Pathway analysis. Chip-seq and RNA-Seq analysis. Metagenomics. SNPs prediction.
3. **High performance in bioinformatics**. Parallelization for biomedical analysis. Biomedical and biological databases. Data mining and biological text processing. Large scale biomedical data integration. Biological and medical ontologies. Novel architecture and technologies (GPU, P2P, Grid, etc.) for bioinformatics.
4. **Biomedicine**. Biomedical computing. Personalized medicine. Nanomedicine. Medical education. Collaborative medicine. Biomedical signal analysis. Biomedicine in industry and society. Electrotherapy and radiotherapy.
5. **Biomedical engineering**. E-Computer-assisted surgery. Therapeutic engineering. Interactive 3D modeling. Clinical engineering. Telemedicine. Biosensors and data acquisition. Intelligent instrumentation. Patient monitoring. Biomedical robotics. Bio-nanotechnology. Genetic engineering.

6. **Computational systems for modeling biological processes**. Inference of biological networks. Machine learning in bioinformatics. Classification for biomedical data. Microarray data analysis. Simulation and visualization of biological systems. Molecular evolution and phylogenetic modeling.
7. **Healthcare and diseases**. Computational support for clinical decisions. Image visualization and signal analysis. Disease control and diagnosis. Genome-phenome analysis. Biomarker identification. Drug design. Computational immunology.
8. **E-Health**. E-Health technology and devices. E-Health information processing. Telemedicine/E-Health application and services. Medical image processing. Video techniques for medical images. Integration of classical medicine and E-Health.

After a careful peer review and evaluation process (each submission was reviewed by at least 2, and on the average 3.2, Program Committee members or additional reviewer), 73 papers were accepted, according to the recommendations of reviewers and the authors' preferences, to be included in the LNBI proceedings.

During IWBBIO 2020 several Special Sessions were carried out. Special Sessions are a very useful tool in order to complement the regular program with new and emerging topics of particular interest for the participating community. Special Sessions that emphasized multidisciplinary and transversal aspects, as well as cutting-edge topics were especially encouraged and welcomed, and in this edition of IWBBIO 2020 the following were received:

– **SS1. High-throughput Genomics: Bioinformatic Tools and Medical Applications.**
  Genomics is concerned with the sequencing and analysis of an organism's genome. It is involved in the understanding of how every single gene can affect the entire genome. This goal is mainly afforded using the current, cost-effective, high-throughput sequencing technologies. These technologies produce a huge amount of data that usually require high-performance computing solutions and opens new ways for the study of genomics, but also transcriptomics, gene expression, and systems biology, among others. The continuous improvements and broader applications on sequencing technologies is producing a continuous new demand of improved high-throughput bioinformatics tools. In this context, the generation, integration, and interpretation of genetic and genomic data is driving a new era of healthcare and patient management. Medical genomics (or genomic medicine) is an emerging discipline that involves the use of genomic information about a patient as part of the clinical care with diagnostic or therapeutic purposes to improve the health outcomes. Moreover, it can be considered a subset of precision medicine that has an impact in the fields of oncology, pharmacology, rare and undiagnosed diseases, and infectious diseases. The aim of this Special Session was to bring together researchers in medicine, genomics, and bioinformatics to translate medical genomics research into new diagnostic, therapeutic, and preventive medical approaches. Therefore, we invited authors to submit original research, new tools or pipelines, as well as updated and reviewed articles on relevant topics, such as (but not limited to):

  - Tools for data pre-processing (quality control and filtering)
  - Tools for sequence mapping

- Tools for the comparison of two read libraries without an external reference
- Tools for genomic variants (such as variant calling or variant annotation)
- Tools for functional annotation: identification of domains, orthologues, genetic markers, and controlled vocabulary (GO, KEGG, InterPro, etc.)
- Tools for gene expression studies and tools for Chip-Seq data
- Integrative workflows and pipelines

Organizers: ***Prof. M. Gonzalo Claros****, Department of Molecular Biology and Biochemistry, University of Málaga, Spain.*

Dr. Javier Pérez Florido*, Bioinformatics Research Area, Fundación Progreso y Salud, Seville, Spain.*

Dr. Francisco M. Ortuño*, Bioinformatics Research Area, Fundación Progreso y Salud, Seville, Spain.*

- **SS2. Evolving Towards Digital Twins in Healthcare (EDITH).**
  Digital Twins is a very promising technique, as well as an ongoing research topic, imported from the industry domain in order to develop personalized healthcare around the behavior of either patient diseases or users' health profiles. It is clear that the positive advance in the treatment of the diseases improve the quality of life. The World Health Organization (WHO) characterizes a healthy life first of all with the prevention of diseases and secondly, in the case of the presence of disease, with the ability to adapt and self-manage. Smart measurement of vital signs and of behavior can help to prevent diseases or to detect them before they become persistent. These signs are key to obtain individual data relevant to contribute to this understanding of a healthy life. Here, the design of a Digital Twins appears in order to provide a frame of reference to analyze where the patient was previously versus after treatment has been given by a doctor. The objective of this session is to present and discuss the advances in this important topic, Digital Twins, in the generation of knowledge. We advocate that this session will proportionate an important meeting point among different and variate researchers.

  Organizers: ***Prof. Dr. Cecilio Angulo****, Full Professor in the Automatic Control Department at the Universitat Politecnica de Catalunya (UCP), Spain, and Director of the Intelligent Data Science and Artificial Intelligence Research Center (IDEAI-UPC), where he is leading the Knowledge Engineering Research Group.*

  Prof. Dr. Juan Antonio Ortega*, Full professor at the University of Seville, Spain, and Director of the Centre of Computer Scientific in Andalusia, Spain.*

  Prof. Dr. Luis Gonzalez*, head of the researcher group SEJ 442 at the University of Seville, Spain.*

- **SS3. Data Mining from UV/VIS/NIR Imaging and Spectrophotometry.**
  A wide range of information can be obtained via imaging and spectral analysis of bio-origin samples and environmental conditions. Not only spectrometry, but also imaging is nowadays used for color analysis. The capability of sensors allows multispectral analysis, development of smart devices, and advanced analysis. The

amount of measured datasets requires complicated mathematical models for features extraction, some could be performed by artificial intelligence, namely neural networks. The tasks consist of spectra evaluation, statistical analysis, comparisons, classification, etc. In this special section a discussion on novel development, implementation, and approaches in sensors, measurements, methods, evaluating software, and data mining focused on the spectral and color analysis. The topic covered practical examples, strong results, and future visions.

Organizer: ***Dr. Jan Urban****, Head of Laboratory of Signal and Image Processing, Institute of Complex Systems, South Bohemian Research Center of Aquaculture and Biodiversity of Hydrocenoses, Faculty of Fisheries and Protection of Waters, University of South Bohemia, Czech Republic.*

– **SS4. Intelligent Instrumentation.**
Instruments and devices are almost similar and used for different scientific evaluations. They have become intelligent with the advancement in technology and by taking the help of artificial intelligence. In our daily life, sensors are corporate in several devices and applications for a better life. Sensors such as tactile sensors are included in the touch screens and the computers' touch pads. The input of these sensors is from the environment that converted into an electrical signal for further processing in the sensor system. The sensor's main role is to measure a specific quantity and create a signal for interpretation.

Organizer: ***Prof. Dr. Barney****, Intelligent Instrumentation Division, USA.*

– **SS5. Image Visualization and Signal Analysis.**
Medical imaging is the technique and the process of creating visual representations of the inside of the body for clinical analyzes and medical interventions as well as the visual representation of the function of some organs or tissues (physiology). Medical images attempt to uncover internal structures hidden by skin and bones, as well as to diagnose and treat diseases. The medical images also create a database of normal anatomy and physiology to identify anomalies. Although imaging of harvested organs and tissues can be done for medical reasons, such procedures are generally considered part of the pathology rather than medical images.

Organizer: ***Prof. Dr. L.Wang****, University of California, San Diego, USA.*

– **SS6. Analysis of Protein-Protein Interactions.**
PPIs have been investigated using many methods and from different perspectives: biochemistry, quantum chemistry, molecular dynamics, signal transduction, etc. All this information allows for the creation of large protein interaction networks, similar to metabolic or genetic/epigenetic networks, which share current knowledge about the biochemical cascades and molecular etiology of diseases and the discovery of supposed protein objectives of therapeutic interest. Bioinformatics tools have been developed to simplify the difficult task of visualizing molecular interaction networks and complementing them with other types of data. For example, Cytoscape is

a generalized open source software for which there are currently many add-ons available. Pajek software is advantageous for viewing and analyzing very large networks.

Organizer: ***Dr. Yang****, University of Korea, South Korea.*

– **SS7. Computational Approaches for Drug Design and Personalized Medicine.** With continuous advancements of biomedical instruments and the associated ability to collect diverse types of valuable biological data, numerous research studies have recently been focusing on how to best extract useful information from the 'big biomedical data' currently available. While drug design has been one of the most essential areas of biomedical research, the drug design process for the most part has not fully benefited from the recent explosive growth of biological data and bioinformatics algorithms. With the incredible overhead associated with the traditional drug design process in terms of time and cost, new alternative methods, possibly based on computational approaches, are very much needed to propose innovative ways for effective drugs and new treatment options. Employing advanced computational tools for drug design and precision treatments has been the focus of many research studies in recent years. For example, drug repurposing has gained significant attention from biomedical researchers and pharmaceutical companies as an exciting new alternative for drug discovery that benefits from the computational approaches. This new development also promises to transform healthcare to focus more on individualized treatments, precision medicine, and lower risks of harmful side effects. Other alternative drug design approaches that are based on analytical tools include the use of medicinal natural plants and herbs as well as using genetic data for developing multi-target drugs. Keywords: Drug design, Drug repositioning/repurposing, Personalize medicine, Data-driven healthcare, Computational tools, Biomedical data analytics, Multi-target drugs.

Organizer: ***Prof. Dr. Hesham H. Ali****, Professor of Computer Science and Lee and Wilma Seemann Distinguished Dean of the College of Information Science and Technology at the University of Nebraska at Omaha (UNO), USA.*

The presented papers are classified under 14 chapters, and includes the contributions on:

1. Biomarker Identification
2. Biomedical Engineering
3. Biomedical Signal Analysis
4. Bio-Nanotechnology
5. Computational Approaches for Drug Design and Personalized Medicine
6. Computational Proteomics and Protein-Protein Interactions
7. Data Mining from UV/VIS/NIR Imaging and Spectrophotometry
8. E-Health Technology, Services, and Applications
9. Evolving Towards Digital Twins in Healthcare (EDITH)
10. High Performance in Bioinformatics
11. High-throughput Genomics: Bioinformatic Tools and Medical Applications

12. Machine Learning in Bioinformatics
13. Medical Image Processing
14. Simulation and Visualization of Biological Systems

This 8th edition of IWBBIO was organized by the Universidad de Granada. We wish to thank our main sponsor as well as the following institutions: Faculty of Science, Department of Computer Architecture and Computer Technology, and CITIC-UGR from the University of Granada for their support and grants. We also wish to thank to editors in charge of different international journals for their interest in editing special issues from a selection of the best papers of IWBBIO 2020. We would also like to express our gratitude to the members of the different committees for their support, collaboration, and good work. We especially thank the Local Organizing Committee, Program Committee, the reviewers, and Special Session organizers. We also want to express our gratitude to the EasyChair platform. Finally, we wish to thank Springer, in particular Alfred Hofmann and Anna Kramer, for their continuous support and cooperation.

May 2020

Ignacio Rojas
Olga Valenzuela
Fernando Rojas
Luis Javier Herrera
Francisco Ortuño

Organization

Steering Committee

Miguel A. Andrade	University of Mainz, Germany
Hesham H. Ali	University of Nebraska, USA
Oresti Baños	University of Granada, Spain
Alfredo Benso	Politecnico di Torino, Italy
Larbi Boubchir	LIASD, University of Paris 8, France
Giorgio Buttazzo	Superior School Sant'Anna, Italy
Gabriel Caffarena	University San Pablo CEU, Spain
Mario Cannataro	University Magna Graecia of Catanzaro, Italy
Jose María Carazo	Spanish National Center for Biotechnology (CNB), Spain
Jose M. Cecilia	Universidad Católica San Antonio de Murcia (UCAM), Spain
M. Gonzalo Claros	University of Malaga, Spain
Joaquin Dopazo	Bioinformatics Research Area, Fundación Progreso y Salud, Spain
Werner Dubitzky	University of Ulster, UK
Afshin Fassihi	Universidad Católica San Antonio de Murcia (UCAM), Spain
Jean-Fred Fontaine	University of Mainz, Germany
Humberto Gonzalez	University of Basque Country (UPV/EHU), Spain
Concettina Guerra	Georgia Tech, USA
Roderic Guigo	Pompeu Fabra University, Spain
Andy Jenkinson	Karolinska Institute, Sweden
Craig E. Kapfer	Reutlingen University, Germany
Narsis Aftab Kiani	European Bioinformatics Institute (EBI), UK
Natividad Martinez	Reutlingen University, Germany
Marco Masseroli	Politechnical University of Milano, Italy
Federico Moran	Complutense University of Madrid, Spain
Cristian R. Munteanu	University of Coruña, Spain
Jorge A. Naranjo	New York University Abu Dhabi, UAE
Michael Ng	Hong Kong Baptist University, China
Jose L. Oliver	University of Granada, Spain
Juan Antonio Ortega	University of Seville, Spain
Julio Ortega	University of Granada, Spain
Alejandro Pazos	University of Coruña, Spain
Javier Perez Florido	Genomics and Bioinformatics Platform of Andalusia, Spain
Violeta I. Pérez Nueno	Inria Nancy Grand Est, LORIA, France

Horacio Pérez-Sánchez	Universidad Católica San Antonio de Murcia (UCAM), Spain
Alberto Policriti	Università di Udine, Italy
Omer F. Rana	Cardiff University, UK
M. Francesca Romano	Superior School Sant'Anna, Italy
Yvan Saeys	Ghent University, Belgium
Vicky Schneider	The Genome Analysis Centre (TGAC), UK
Ralf Seepold	HTWG Konstanz, Germany
Mohammad Soruri	University of Birjand, Iran
Yoshiyuki Suzuki	Tokyo Metropolitan Institute of Medical Science, Japan
Oswaldo Trelles	University of Malaga, Spain
Shusaku Tsumoto	Shimane University, Japan
Renato Umeton	CytoSolve Inc., USA
Jan Urban	University of South Bohemia, Czech Republic
Alfredo Vellido	Politechnical University of Catalunya, Spain
Wolfgang Wurst	GSF National Research Center of Environment and Health, Germany

Program Committee and Additional Reviewers

Hisham Al-Mubaid	University of Houston, USA
Hesham Ali	University of Nebraska Omaha, USA
Cecilio Angulo	Universitat Politecnica de Catalunya, Spain
Rui Alves	Universitat de Lleida, Spain
Georgios Anagnostopoulos	Florida Institute of Technology, USA
Miguel Andrade	Johannes-Gutenberg University of Mainz, Germany
Saul Ares	Centro Nacional de Biotecnología (CNB-CSIC), Spain
Masanori Arita	National Institute of Genetics, Japan
Patrizio Arrigo	CNR-SCITEC, Italy
Hazem Bahig	Ain Sham University, Egypt
Oresti Banos	University of Granada, Spain
Ugo Bastolla	Centro de Biologia Molecular Severo Ochoa, Spain
Alfredo Benso	Politecnico di Torino, Italy
Paola Bonizzoni	Università di Milano-Bicocca, Italy
Larbi Boubchir	University of Paris 8, France
David Breen	Drexel University, Germany
Jeremy Buhler	Washington University in Saint Louis, USA
Dongbo Bu	Chinese Academy of Sciences, China
Gabriel Caffarena	CEU San Pablo University, Spain
Mario Cannataro	University Magna Graecia of Catanzaro, Italy
Francisco Carrillo Perez	University of Granada, Spain
Francisco Cavas-Martinez	Technical University of Cartagena, Spain
Rita Casadio	University of Bologna, Italy
Francisco Cavas-Martínez	Technical University of Cartagena, Spain
José M. Cecilia	Catholic University of Murcia, Spain
Keith C. C. Chan	The Hong Kong Polytechnic University, Hong Kong

Ting-Fung Chan	The Chinese University of Hong Kong, Hong Kong
Nagasuma Chandra	Indian Institute of Science, India
Bolin Chen	University of Saskatchewan, Canada
Chuming Chen	University of Delaware, USA
Jeonghyeon Choi	Georgia Regents University, USA
M. Gonzalo Claros	Universidad de Málaga, Spain
Darrell Conklin	University of the Basque Country, Spain
Bhaskar Dasgupta	University of Illinois at Chicago, USA
Alexandre G. De Brevern	Université Paris Diderot, France
Fei Deng	University of California, Davis, USA
Marie-Dominique Devignes	LORIA-CNRS, France
Joaquin Dopazo	Fundacion Progreso y Salud, Spain
Beatrice Duval	LERIA, France
Christian Esposito	University of Napoli Federico II, Italy
Jose Jesus Fernandez	Consejo Superior de Investigaciones Cientificas (CSIC), Spain
Gionata Fragomeni	Magna Graecia University, Italy
Pugalenthi Ganesan	Bharathidasan University, India
Razvan Ghinea	University of Granada, Spain
Oguzhan Gunduz	Marmara University, Turkey
Luis Gonzalez	University of Seville, Spain
Eduardo Gusmao	University of Cologne, Germany
Christophe Guyeux	University of Franche-Comté, France
Juan M. Gálvez	University of Granada, Spain
Michael Hackenberg	University of Granada, Spain
Nurit Haspel	University of Massachusetts Boston, USA
Morihiro Hayashida	National Institute of Technology, Matsue College, Japan
Luis Herrera	University of Granada, Spain
Ralf Hofestaedt	Bielefeld University, Germany
Vasant Honavar	The Pennsylvania State University, USA
Narsis Kiani	Karolinska Institute, Sweden
Dongchul Kim	The University of Texas at Rio Grande Valley, USA
Tomas Koutny	University of West Bohemia, Czech Republic
Istvan Ladunga	University of Nebraska–Lincoln, USA
Dominique Lavenier	CNRS-IRISA, France
José L. Lavín	CIC bioGUNE, Spain
Kwong-Sak Leung	The Chinese University of Hong Kong, Hong Kong
Chen Li	Monash University, Australia
Shuai Cheng Li	City University of Hong Kong, Hong Kong
Li Liao	University of Delaware, USA
Hongfei Lin	Dalian University of Technology, China
Zhi-Ping Liu	Shandong University, China
Feng Luo	Clemson University, USA
Qin Ma	Ohio State University, USA
Malika Mahoui	Eli Lilly, USA

Natividad Martinez Madrid	Reutlingen University, Germany
Marco Masseroli	Politecnico di Milano, Italy
Tatiana Maximova	George Mason University, USA
Roderick Melnik	Wilfrid Laurier University, Canada
Marianna Milano	University Magna Græcia of Catanzaro, Italy
Juan Carlos Morales	University of Granada, Spain
Enrique Muro	Johannes Gutenberg University of Mainz, Germany
Claudio Navo	CIC bioGUNE, Spain
Kenta Nakai	University of Tokyo, Japan
Isabel Nepomuceno	University of Seville, Spain
Dang Ngoc Hoang Thanh	Hue College of Industry, Vietnam
Anja Nohe	University of Delaware, USA
José Luis Oliveira	University of Aveiro, Portugal
Juan Antonio Ortega	University of Seville, Spain
Francisco Ortuño	Clinical Bioinformatics Area, Fundación Progreso y Salud, Spain
Motonori Ota	Nagoya University, Japan
Joel P. Arrais	University of Coimbra, Portugal
Paolo Paradisi	ISTI-CNR, Italy
Javier Perez Florido	Genomics and Bioinformatics Platform of Andalusia (GBPA), Spain
Antonio Pinti	I3MTO Orléans, Italy
Yuri Pirola	DISCo, Università degli Studi di Milano-Bicocca, Italy
Alberto Policriti	University of Udine, Italy
Hector Pomares	University of Granada, Spain
María M Pérez	University of Granada, Spain
Jairo Rocha	University of the Balearic Islands, Spain
Fernando Rojas	University of Granada, Spain
Ignacio Rojas	University of Granada, Spain
Jianhua Ruan	Utsa, USA
Gregorio Rubio	Universitat Politècnica de València, Spain
Irena Rusu	LINA, UMR CNRS 6241, University of Nantes, France
Michael Sadovsky	Institute of Computational Modelling of SB, RAS, Russia
Jean-Marc Schwartz	The University of Manchester, UK
Russell Schwartz	Carnegie Mellon University, USA
Daniel Secilla	University of Granada, Spain
Ralf Seepold	HTWG Konstanz, Germany
Xuequn Shang	Northwestern Polytechnical University, China
Wing-Kin Sung	National University of Singapore, Singapore
Prashanth Suravajhala	Birla Institute of Scientific Research, India
Yoshiyuki Suzuki	Tokyo Metropolitan Institute of Medical Science, Japan
Martin Swain	Aberystwyth University, UK
Sing-Hoi Sze	Texas A&M University, USA
Carolina Torres	University of Granada, Spain
Stephen Tsui	The Chinese University of Hong Kong, China

Renato Umeton	Massachusetts Institute of Technology, USA
Jan Urban	Institute of Complex Systems, FFPW, USB, Czech Republic
Lucia Vaira	Set-Lab, University of Salento, Italy
Olga Valenzuela	University of Granada, Spain
Alfredo Vellido	Universitat Politècnica de Catalunya, Spain
Konstantinos Votis	Information Technologies Institute, Centre for Research and Technology Hellas, Greece
Jianxin Wang	Central South University, China
Jiayin Wang	Xi'an Jiaotong University, China
Junbai Wang	Radium Hospital, Norway
Lusheng Wang	City University of Hong Kong, Hong Kong
Ka-Chun Wong	City University of Hong Kong, Hong Kong
Fang Xiang Wu	University of Saskatchewan, Canada
Xuanping Zhang	Xi'an Jiaotong University, China
Zhongmeng Zhao	Xi'an Jiaotong University, China
Zhongming Zhao	University of Texas Health Science Center at Houston, USA
Chiara Zucco	University Magna Græcia of Catanzaro, Italy

Contents

Biomarker Identification

Biomedical Engineering

High Performance in Bioinformatics

High-Throughput Genomics: Bioinformatic Tools and Medical Applications

Simulation and Visualization of Biological Systems

Biomarker Identification

Identification of Coding Regions in Prokaryotic DNA Sequences Using Bayesian Classification

Mohammad Al Bataineh(✉)

Yarmouk University, Irbid 21163, Jordan
mohamadfa@yu.edu.jo

Abstract. The identification of protein-coding regions in genomic DNA sequences is a well-known problem in computational genomics. Various computational algorithms can be employed to achieve the identification process. The rapid advances in this field have motivated the development of innovative engineering methods that allow for further analysis and modeling of many processes in molecular biology. The proposed algorithm utilizes well-known concepts in communications theory, such as correlation, the maximal ratio combining (MRC) algorithm, and filtering techniques to create a signal whose maxima and minima indicate coding and noncoding regions, respectively. The proposed algorithm investigates several prokaryotic genome sequences. Two Bayesian classifiers are designed to test and evaluate the performance of the proposed algorithm. The obtained simulation results prove that the algorithm can efficiently and accurately detect protein-coding regions, which is being demonstrated by the obtained sensitivity and specificity values that are comparable to well-known gene detection methods in prokaryotes. The obtained results further verify the correctness and the biological relevance of using communications theory concepts for genomic sequence analysis.

Keywords: Gene identification · Correlation · Maximal ratio combining · Period-3 filter · Bayesian classification

1 Introduction

The rapid pace of advancement in computational genomics and bioinformatics has led to several innovative engineering methods for data acquisition, interpretation, and analysis. Techniques from the information theory [1–3], communications [4–11], coding theory [12–15], signal processing [16–18], machine learning [19] and various statistical methods [20, 21] have been actively researched for use in gene detection, genomic sequence analysis and alignment.

Genes are the segments of DNA that contain the coding information required for protein synthesis. A considerable target of genomic research is to understand the nature and role of the coding and noncoding information embedded in the DNA sequence structure. A crucial step in attaining this target is the detection of the gene locations in the entire DNA sequence. Several diverse methods have been proposed in the literature for gene detection in prokaryotes. For example, probabilistic methods [22, 23], statistical methods [24–26], and other computational techniques including: machine learning [27], free energy calculations [28], support vector machine [29], Bayesian

I. Rojas et al. (Eds.): IWBBIO 2020, LNBI 12108, pp. 3–14, 2020.
https://doi.org/10.1007/978-3-030-45385-5_1

methods [16] information theory [30], hidden Markov model such GeneMark [20, 21, 31–34], and interpolated Markov model such as GLIMMER [35].

The design of a general gene identification algorithm is a compelling research problem. The gene identification method presented in this work utilizes a particular property of the DNA protein-coding regions, namely the period-3 property [36, 37] in a new novel approach using concepts from communications theory. The period-3 pattern generally gives a strong indication of the existence of coding regions. By mapping the DNA sequences to digital signals, standard digital signal processing (DSP) techniques can be implemented. The discrete Fourier transformation (DFT) [36], digital filtering [38, 39], wavelet transformations [40], Markov modeling [41] and Infinite Impulse Response (IIR) filtering [42] have shown fair performance in the detection of this period-3 behavior and, therefore, in identifying coding regions. In [17], we have proposed a novel algorithm for identifying protein-coding regions in the DNA sequences based on the period-3 property. The proposed algorithm in [17] identifies protein-coding regions by applying a digital correlating and filtering process to the entire genomic sequence under study. However, our proposed algorithm in this paper is both an enhanced and a generalized version of the work in [17] in terms of methodology, performance, and experimental validation.

This paper proposes a novel application of principles and techniques from communications theory and digital signal processing for the detection and identification of protein-coding regions in prokaryotic genomes. The proposed algorithm employs polyphase complex mapping to provide a numerical representation of the genomic sequences involved in the analysis and then uses basic concepts from communications theory and digital signal processing such as correlation, maximal ratio combining (MRC) algorithms and filtering to generate a signal whose peaks signify locations of coding regions and whose troughs signify locations of noncoding regions. The proposed gene detection algorithm investigates the complete genome sequences of several prokaryotes (e.g., MG1655 and O157H7 E. coli bacterial strains). Moreover, two Bayesian classifiers are designed to evaluate the performance of the proposed gene detection algorithm and compare it to well-known gene detection methods in prokaryotes. The conducted simulation show that the proposed algorithm can efficiently and accurately identify protein-coding regions, which is being demonstrated by the obtained sensitivity and specificity values that are comparable to the ones obtained by GLIMMER and GeneMark. The obtained results further verify the correctness and the biological relevance of using communications theory concepts for genomic sequence analysis.

The paper organization is as follows. Section 2 presents the mathematical description of the proposed gene detection algorithm. Algorithm 1 describes the method used for maxima (corresponding to coding regions) and minima (corresponding to noncoding regions) detection. Section 3 presents the simulation results and analysis. Finally, Sect. 4 concludes the paper.

2 The Proposed Gene Detection Algorithm

Figure 1 shows a schematic system-like representation of the proposed algorithm. The input parameter of the proposed detection algorithm is the genomic sequence under study, $\mathbf{g}$, of length L_x. The output parameters are three sequences: $f[n]$, $p[n]$ and $t[n]$

whose lengths are the same as the length of the input test sequence L_x. The sequence $f[n]$ represents the correlation of the genomic sequence **g** with twenty-four hypothetically generated period-3 based subsequences after passing through a maximal ratio combining module. The latter two sequences, $p[n]$ and $t[n]$, correspond to the detected peaks and troughs in the sequence $f[n]$, respectively. Detected peaks signify coding regions while detected troughs signify noncoding regions.

2.1 Mathematical Description

The following procedural steps describe the proposed gene detection algorithm:

1. Convert the input genome sequence **g** (of length L_x nucleobases) to a numerical representation $\boldsymbol{x}[\boldsymbol{n}]$ using polyphase complex mapping ($A = 1, C = +j, G = -1$, $T = -j$) [43, 44]. Such mapping will allow for performing signal processing operations, such as correlation in the following steps.
2. Generate all possible hypothetical sequences ($\boldsymbol{r_i}$) that exhibit a clear period-3 pattern. Each sequence is a periodic repetition of three different nucleobases out of the four possible genetic code alphabet letters $\{A, C, G, T\}$ [45]. This approach will result in twenty-four possible sequences ($\boldsymbol{r}_1, \boldsymbol{r}_2, \ldots, \boldsymbol{r}_{24}$) where each sequence is of a predefined length of ($3L_r$) nucleobases, where L_r is the number of repetitions used for each sequence.
3. Convert the hypothetical sequences ($\boldsymbol{r_i}$) obtained in step 2 to their corresponding numerical representations, $s_i[n]$, using the polyphase complex mapping described in step 1.
4. Correlate the signal, $x[n]$, with each one of the 24 hypothetical sequences, $s_i[n]$. The correlation of two signals measures how similar they are. Hence, this step will help detect the portions of the input genomic sequence that have a period-3 pattern like anyone of the twenty-four sequences, $s_i[n]$. The twenty-four corresponding correlation outputs denoted as $y_i[n]$, are the convolution of the input sequence, $x[n]$, with the time-reversed version of each of the twenty-four sequences, $s_i[n]$, as

$$y_i[n] = \sum_{m=0}^{3L_r-1} x[m]s_i[m-n], \tag{1}$$

   where each signal $y_i[n]$ is of length $(L_x + 3L_r - 1)$.
5. Truncate the first $\lfloor (3L_r - 1)/2 \rfloor$ and the last $\lceil (3L_r - 1)/2 \rceil$ elements of each sequence, $y_i[n]$. Such a step will force the latter sequences to be of a length equal to the length of the input genomic sequence, $x[n]$, which is L_x. The integer numbers $\lfloor (3L_r - 1)/2 \rfloor$ and $\lceil (3L_r - 1)/2 \rceil$ are equal if $(3L_r)$ is odd and different by one if $(3L_r)$ is even. Here, the symbol $\lfloor \cdot \rfloor$ is the largest integer not greater than the argument, while $\lceil \cdot \rceil$ is the smallest integer not less than the argument.
6. Pass the sequences, $y_i[n]$, obtained in step 5 into a maximal ratio combining (MRC) module. This combining technique multiplies each of the twenty-four signal branches by a weight factor, (α_i), that is proportional to the signal amplitude in each branch. That is to say; the combining technique further amplifies the branches with

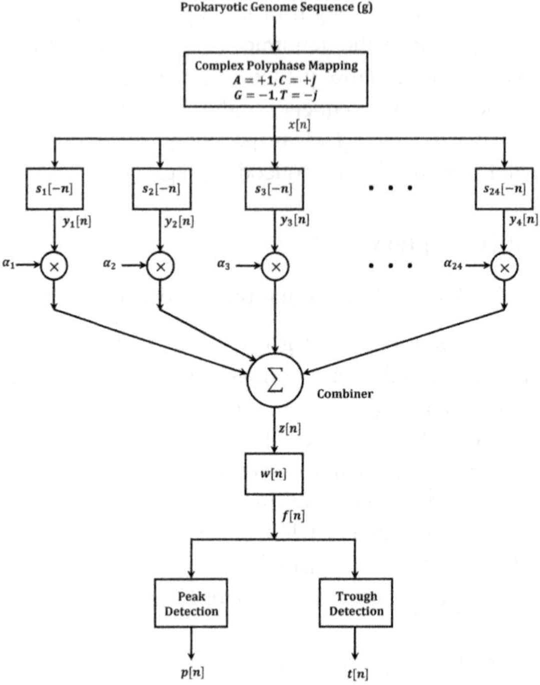

Fig. 1. The proposed gene detection algorithm

strong signals (high amplitude), while attenuating weak signals (low amplitude). The resulting signal at the output of the MRC module is given by

$$z[n] = \sum_{i=1}^{24} \alpha_i y_i[n], \tag{2}$$

where the factors (α_i), are defined by

$$\alpha_i = \frac{|y_i[n]|}{\sum_{j=1}^{24} |y_j[n]|}. \tag{3}$$

7. Pass the resulting sequence, $z[n]$, obtained in (6) through a period-3 bandpass filter of length N with about 13 dB minimum stopband attenuation like the one described in (3). The passband center is $(\omega_0 = 2\pi/3)$. Hence, the response of the period-3 filter is given by

$$f[n] = \sum_{m=0}^{N-1} w[m] z[n-m], \tag{4}$$

whose length is $(L_x + N - 1)$.

8. Truncate the first $\lfloor (N-1)/2 \rfloor$ and the last $\lceil (N-1)/2 \rceil$ elements of $f[n]$ to force its length to be L_x elements.

The peaks of the sequence $|f[n]|$ correspond to a high correlation between $z[n]$ and $w[n]$, while troughs correspond to a low correlation. A high correlation in this context corresponds to the occurrence of a period-3 structure, and vice versa. Hence, peaks of $f[n]$ signify coding regions in both forward and reverse strands of the genomic sequence, **g**, while troughs signify noncoding regions. Algorithm 1 describes the detection method of maxima and minima. The detection of maxima (peaks) and minima (troughs) utilizes a sliding a window of length L_p for maxima and L_t for minima through the whole correlation sequence, $f[n]$, obtained in step 8. At each alignment instant, maxima and minima are kept while setting all other values to zero. This step continues to generate the detected peak and trough sequences, $p[n]$ and $t[n]$, respectively.

Algorithm I: Peaks and Troughs Detection Algorithm

Input: The period-3 filter output sequence, $f[n]$, obtained in (4), whose length is L_x(after being truncated); the peaks detection window length, L_p; and the troughs detection window length, L_t.

Output: The detected peaks sequence, $p[n]$, and the detected troughs sequence, $t[n]$.

Initialization: $p[n]^{(0)} = \{0,0,\dots,0\}$, $t[n]^{(0)} = \{0,0,\dots,0\}$ where $0 \le n \le L_x$.

Peaks Detection Algorithm:

For $i = 1, 2, \dots, L_x - 2L_p$, **do**

- **If** $(i > L_p)$ and $(i < L_x - L_p)$ **then**
  - Set max to the maximum of the subsequence $f[i - L_p, i - L_p + 1, \dots, i + L_p]$

    If $f[i] \neq max$ **then**
    - Set $p[i]$ to zero,

    Else (i.e. if $f[i] = max$)
    - Set $p[i]$ to max,

Troughs Detection Algorithm:

For $i = 1, 2, \dots, L_x - 2L_t$, **do**

- **If** $(i > L_t)$ and $(i < L_x - L_t)$ **then**
  - Set min to the minimum of the subsequence $f[i - L_t, i - L_t + 1, \dots, i + L_t]$

    If $f[i] \neq min$ **then**
    - Set $t[i]$ to zero,

    Else (i.e. if $f[i] = min$)
    - Set $t[i]$ to min.

---

3 Simulation Results and Analysis

To demonstrate the fidelity and biological significance of the proposed gene detection algorithm, several prokaryotic genome sequences are investigated. For example, the complete genome sequence of Escherichia coli bacterial strains MG1655 and O157:H7 are used as input test sequences. Such sequences are available at the NCBI [46].

The length of each one of the 24-hypothetical period-3 based subsequences, $s_i[n]$, is selected to be 1950 (i.e., the number of repetitions, L_r, is 650). The length of the period-3 filter, $w[n]$, is selected as $N = 221$. The peaks detection window length, L_p, and the troughs detections window, L_t, are selected as 300 and 800, respectively.

Figures 2 and 3 show the simulation result obtained by applying the proposed gene detection algorithm to test sequences extracted from the complete genome sequences of the E. coli MG1655 and O157:H7 bacterial strains, respectively. In both figures, the red-colored regions (second row of rectangles) correspond to the $5'-3'$ genome sequence (forward strand), while the green-colored regions (the upper group of rectangles) correspond to the coding regions of the $3'-5'$ genome sequence (reverse strand). The blank regions in the latter two sequences correspond to the noncoding regions in both forward and reverse strands. It can be noticed that the proposed algorithm using the peaks and troughs detection method, described by Algorithm 1, is able to detect the coding regions (signified by the blue-colored lines with closed circles on top) and the noncoding regions (signified by the green-colored lines with cross signs on top) in both forward and reverse strands. The detected peaks/troughs indicate the existence of a coding/noncoding region in either the forward or reverse strands, respectively.

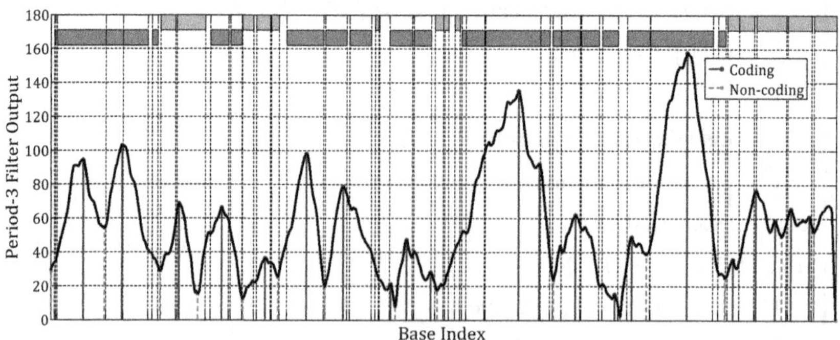

Fig. 2. Period-3 filter output with peaks and troughs identified (applied to MG1655) (Color figure online)

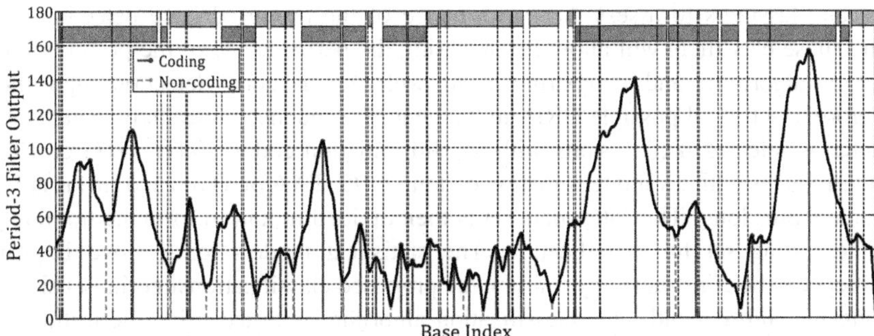

Fig. 3. Period-3 filter output with peaks and troughs identified (applied to O157:H7). (Color figure online)

A closer look at Figs. 2 and 3 shows that there are some peaks detected in the noncoding regions of the $5'-3'$ genome sequence (forward strand) that do not correspond to coding regions in the latter strand. This can be justified by the fact that there are coding regions (that also possess a period-3 structure) in the complementary $3'-5'$ sequence (reverse strand), that happen to coincide with noncoding regions in the $5'-3'$ sequence (forward strand). This remark is also being confirmed by the fact that the forward and reverse strands are totally complementary and statistically symmetric [47]. Therefore, the existence of a period-3 structure in the forward strand would imply the existence of a period-3 structure in the reverse strand as well, and vice versa. However, it can be observed that such ambiguous detected peaks have smaller amplitudes than the ones that do not coincide with coding regions in the complementary strand. In other words, the peaks with larger amplitudes most likely correspond to coding regions in the genomic sequence under study (and that is the forward strand here).

The obtained results of simulation verify that the algorithm proposed here is successful in detecting the period-3 structure embedded in the prokaryotic genomic sequence under study. However, due to the ambiguity of whether the detected peaks (with small amplitudes) correspond to coding regions in either the forward or reverse strands, the proposed gene detection method can be integrated with other detection methods, so that the areas between neighboring red lines can be utilized to identify the coding regions. This may also be confirmed with the blue lines that point out the locations of the coding regions. The proposed algorithm will significantly increase the efficiency of coding region detection.

For the prokaryotic genome sequences (MG1655 and O157:H7), the length of the peaks detection window, (L_p), can be selected by compromising the correctness and resolution. A smaller L_p will result in more peaks and hence, better resolution. However, decreasing L_p will also produce more fake peaks that are not real maximization points that correspond to real coding regions. In a similar way, L_t can be selected as well.

It is evident that the previous simulation results are basically visual and do not always provide a sharp decision of where coding and noncoding regions precisely lie in the entire genome sequence. Due to this uncertainty in detection, we have designed two

Bayesian classifiers to assess the performance of the proposed gene detection algorithm. These classifiers will allow for assessing the performance of the proposed gene detection algorithm and comparing it to well-known gene detection algorithms. Therefore, a set of all possible ORFs in the genome sequence understudy is generated. An ORF is selected if (i) it starts with a valid initiation codon (ATG, GTG or TTG), (ii) it terminates with a valid termination codon (TAG, TAA or TGA) and (iii) is at least 99 nucleobases long. This latter data set is then divided in half to form the training set and the testing set for classification. The statistical models for the two Bayesian classifiers can be constructed by training the proposed classification algorithm using the training set. Subsequently, the classification algorithm is tested using the testing data set to verify its performance in detection. Table 1 shows the obtained results of the two Bayesian classifiers when applied to the E. coli MG1655 bacterial strain being compared to the GLIMMER and GeneMark gene-finding software. The performance of the two Bayesian classifiers is assessed using the True Positive Rate (TPR, also referred to as sensitivity), the False Positive Rate (FPR, also known as fall-out), the True Negative Rate (TNR), also referred to as specificity, and the False Negative Rate (FNR). The four performance rates are defined by [48].

$$TPR = \frac{TP}{TP+FN} \times 100\%, \quad (5) \quad FPR = \frac{FP}{FP+TN} \times 100\%, \quad (6)$$

$$FPR = \frac{FP}{FP+TN} \times 100\%, \quad (7) \quad TNR = \frac{TN}{FP+TN} \times 100\%. \quad (8)$$

where TP, FP, FN, TN correspond to True positives, False Positives, False Negatives, and True Negatives, respectively.

The sensitivity or the TPR measure is the proportion of coding nucleotides that have been correctly predicted as coding. Additionally, the specificity (or the TNR) measure is the proportion of noncoding nucleotides that have been correctly predicted as noncoding. Both sensitivity and specificity range independently over [0, 1]. However, neither sensitivity no specificity alone constitutes good measures of global accuracy. Alternatively, in the gene structure prediction literature, the preferred measure of global accuracy has traditionally been the Correlation Coefficient (CC) defined as

$$CC = \frac{(TP \times TN) - (FN \times FP)}{\sqrt{(TP+FN) \times (TN+FP) \times (TP+FP) \times (TN+FN)}}. \quad (9)$$

Another performance measure is the Approximate Correlation Coefficient (AC), which approximates the behavior of the Correlation Coefficient (CC). It has been observed that $|AC| \geq |CC|$. In consequence, the AC measures the association between prediction and reality appropriately and can thus be used as an alternative to the CC. Unlike the CC, the AC has a probabilistic interpretation, and it can be computed in any circumstance. The AC, introduced in [48], is defined as

$$AC = (ACP - 0.5) \times 2, \quad (10)$$

where ACP is the Average Conditional Probability defined as:

$$ACP = \frac{1}{4}\left(\frac{TP}{TP+FN} + \frac{TP}{TP+FP} + \frac{TN}{TN+FP} + \frac{TN}{TN+FN}\right). \quad (11)$$

Since at least two of the conditional probabilities in (20) are always defined, ACP can always be calculated as the average of the one defined. CC and AC range over [−1, 1] and usually are close to each other whenever CC is defined.

Of the two Bayesian classifiers, Classifier 1 with equal prior probabilities seems to perform the best in terms of sensitivity (or TPR) and FNR. Hence, Classifier 1 outperforms both GLIMMER and GeneMark in both TPR and FNR. However, GLIMMER and GeneMark provide better performance in terms of FPR and TNR. Classifier 2 performs better than Classifier 1 in terms of specificity. Moreover, about both CC and AC, Classifier 1 slightly performs better than Classifier 2. Overall, Classifier 1 is performing better than Classifier 2.s claimed earlier, the proposed gene detection algorithm can efficiently extract the period-3 component and hence effectively identify protein-coding regions in the whole genomic sequences of prokaryotes. Also, it can effectively suppress the background $1/f$ noise with no added computational complexity. For a computer with an Intel (R) Core (TM) i7-4770 CPU @ 3.40 GHz and 3.40 GHz, on a genomic test sequence of 40,386 nucleotides long, the proposed gene detection algorithm takes about 9.7 s computational time to obtain the results.

Table 1. Performance evaluation of Classifier 1 and Classifier 2 compared to both GLIMMER and GeneMark with equal/unequal prior probabilities.

Classifier	(P_{w_1}, P_{w2})	TP (TPR)	FP (FPR)	FN (FNR)	TN (TNR)	CC	AC
GLIMMER	–	3561 (85.99%)	915 (0.21%)	580 (14.01%)	434618 (99.79%)	0.8254	0.8260
GeneMark	–	3683 (88.94%)	694 (0.16%)	458 (11.06%)	434839 (99.84%)	0.8638	0.8641
Classifier 1	(0.5, 0.5)	3858 (93.17%)	110387 (25.35%)	283 (6.83%)	325146 (74.65%)	0.1494	0.3556
	(0.43, 0.57)	3712 (89.64%)	97264 (22.33%)	429 (10.36%)	338269 (77.67%)	0.1546	0.3543
Classifier 2	(0.5, 0.5)	3384 (81.72%)	101803 (23.37%)	757 (18.28%)	333730 (76.63%)	0.1321	0.3067
	(0.43, 0.57)	3100 (74.86%)	73446 (16.86%)	1041 (25.14%)	362087 (83.14%)	0.1477	0.3088

4 Conclusions

This paper proposes a novel application of principles and concepts from communications theory and digital signal processing for the detection of protein-coding regions in prokaryotic genomes. The proposed gene detection algorithm employs polyphase complex mapping to provide a numerical representation of the genomic sequences involved in the analysis, and then uses basic concepts from communications theory and digital signal processing as correlation, maximal ratio combining (MRC) algorithms and filtering to generate a signal whose peaks signify locations of coding regions and whose troughs signify locations of noncoding regions. The proposed gene detection algorithm is applied to the complete genome sequences of several prokaryotes (e.g., MG1655 and O157H7 E. coli bacterial strains). Two Bayesian classifiers are designed for the performance evaluation of the proposed gene detection algorithm. Especially, the performance of the proposed algorithm is compared to the well-known ab initio gene detection methods: GLIMMER and GeneMark. The results verify that the algorithm can accurately and efficiently identify protein-coding regions with sensitivity and specificity values that sometimes outperform GLIMMER and GeneMark gene detection methods. The gene detection algorithm does not require any prior information about the coding regions, as does the DFT method described in [36]. Moreover, the proposed algorithm outperforms traditional methods as it puts off the need to apply a variable-length discrete Fourier transform.

References

1. Atkins, G.: Information Theory and Molecular Biology, vol. 327, no. 1. Cambridge University Press, New York (1993)
2. Battail, G.: Information theory and error-correcting codes in genetics and biological evolution. In: Barbieri, M. (ed.) Introduction to Biosemiotics, pp. 299–345. Springer, Dordrecht (2008). https://doi.org/10.1007/1-4020-4814-9_13
3. Weindl, J., Hanus, P., Dawy, Z., Zech, J., Hagenauer, J., Mueller, J.C.: Modeling DNA-binding of Escherichia coli sigma(70) exhibits a characteristic energy landscape around strong promoters. Nucleic Acids Res. **35**(20), 7003–7010 (2007)
4. Al Bataineh, M., Al-qudah, Z.: Cognitive interference channel: achievable rate region and power allocation. IET Commun. **9**(2), 249–257 (2015)
5. Al Bataineh, M., Huang, L., Atkin, G.: TFBS detection algorithm using distance metrics based on center of mass and polyphase mapping. In: 2012 7th International Symposium on Health Informatics and Bioinformatics, no. 1, pp. 37–40 (2012)
6. Al Bataineh, M.: Analysis of genomic translation using a communications theory approach. Illinois Institute of Technology, Chicago (2010)
7. Al Bataineh, M., Alonso, M., Wang, S., Zhang, W., Atkin, G.: Ribosome binding model using a codebook and exponential metric. In: 2007 IEEE International Conference on Electro/Information Technology, pp. 438–442 (2007)
8. Al Bataineh, M., Huang, L., Muhamed, I., Menhart, N., Atkin, G.E.: Gene expression analysis using communications, coding and information theory based models. In: 2009 International Conference on Bioinformatics & Computational Biology, BIOCOMP 2009, pp. 181–185 (2009)
9. Al Bataineh, M., Huang, L., Alonso, M., Menhart, N., Atkin, G.E.: Analysis of gene translation using a communications theory approach. In: Arabnia, H. (ed.) Advances in Computational Biology, vol. 680, pp. 387–397. Springer, New York (2010). https://doi.org/10.1007/978-1-4419-5913-3_44

10. Huang, L., et al.: Identification of transcription factor binding sites based on the Chi-Square (X^2) distance of a probabilistic vector model. In: 2009 International Conference on Future BioMedical Information Engineering (FBIE 2009), pp. 73–76 (2009)
11. Weindl, J., Hagenauer, J.: Applying techniques from frame synchronization for biological sequence analysis. In: IEEE International Conference on Communications, pp. 833–838 (2007)
12. Reiss, D.J., Schwikowski, B.: Predicting protein-peptide interactions via a network-based motif sampler. Bioinformatics **20**(Suppl. 1), i274–i282 (2004)
13. Dawy, Z., Hanus, P., Weindl, J., Dingel, J., Morcos, F.: On genomic coding theory. Eur. Trans. Telecommun. **18**(8), 873–879 (2007)
14. Rosen, G.L., Moore, J.D.: Investigation of coding structure in DNA. In: 2003 IEEE International Conference on Acoustics, Speech, and Signal Processing (ICASSP 2003), vol. 2, pp. 361–364 (2003)
15. MacDonaill, D.A.: Digital parity and the composition of the nucleotide alphabet. Shaping the alphabet with error coding. IEEE Eng. Med. Biol. Mag. **25**(1), 54–61 (2006)
16. Crowley, E.M.: A Bayesian method for finding regulatory segments in DNA. Biopolymers **58**(2), 165–174 (2001)
17. Huang, L., Bataineh, M.A., Atkin, G.E., Wang, S., Zhang, W.: A Novel gene detection method based on period-3 property. In: Conference Proceedings - IEEE Engineering in Medicine and Biology Society, vol. 2009, pp. 3857–3860 (2009)
18. Kakumani, R., Devabhaktuni, V., Ahmad, M.O.: Prediction of protein-coding regions in DNA sequences using a model-based approach. In: ISCAS 2008, vol. 18, no. 21, pp. 1918–1921 (2008)
19. Uberbacher, E.C., Mural, R.J.: Locating protein-coding regions in human DNA sequences by a multiple sensor-neural network approach. Proc. Natl. Acad. Sci. U. S. A. **88**(24), 11261–11265 (1991)
20. Henderson, J., Salzberg, S., Fasman, K.H.: Finding genes in DNA with a hidden Markov model. J. Comput. Biol. **4**(2), 127–141 (1997)
21. Eddy, S.R.: Hidden Markov models and genome sequence analysis. FASEB J. **12**(8), A1327–A1327 (1998)
22. Yada, T., Totoki, Y., Takagi, T., Nakai, K.: A novel bacterial gene-finding system with improved accuracy in locating start codons. DNA Res. **8**(3), 97–106 (2001)
23. Besemer, J., Lomsadze, A., Borodovsky, M.: GeneMarkS: a self-training method for prediction of gene starts in microbial genomes. Implications for finding sequence motifs in regulatory regions. Nucleic Acids Res. **29**(12), 2607–2618 (2001)
24. Walker, M., Pavlovic, V., Kasif, S.: A comparative genomic method for computational identification of prokaryotic translation initiation sites. Nucleic Acids Res. **30**(14), 3181–3191 (2002)
25. Hannenhalli, S.S., Hayes, W.S., Hatzigeorgiou, A.G., Fickett, J.W.: Bacterial start site prediction. Nucleic Acids Res. **27**(17), 3577–3582 (1999)
26. Nishi, T., Ikemura, T., Kanaya, S.: GeneLook: a novel ab initio gene identification system suitable for automated annotation of prokaryotic sequences. Gene **346**, 115–125 (2005)
27. Hayes, W.S., Borodovsky, M.: How to interpret an anonymous bacterial genome: machine learning approach to gene identification. Genome Res. **8**(11), 1154–1171 (1998)
28. Osada, Y., Saito, R., Tomita, M.: Analysis of base-pairing potentials between 16S rRNA and 5′ UTR for translation initiation in various prokaryotes. Bioinformatics **15**(7), 578–581 (1999)
29. Zien, A., Rätsch, G., Mika, S., Schölkopf, B., Lengauer, T., Müller, K.-R.: Engineering support vector machine kernels that recognize translation initiation sites. Bioinformatics **16**(9), 799–807 (2000)

30. Schneider, T.D.: Measuring molecular information. J. Theor. Biol. **201**(1), 87–92 (1999)
31. Besemer, J., Borodovsky, M.: GeneMark: web software for gene finding in prokaryotes, eukaryotes and viruses. Nucleic Acids Res. **33**(Suppl. 2), W451–W454 (2005)
32. Raman, R., Overton, G.C.: Application of hidden Markov modeling in the characterization of transcription factor binding sites. In: Proceedings of the Twenty-Seventh Annual Hawaii International Conference on System Sciences, vol. 5, pp. 275–283 (1994)
33. Krogh, A., Mian, I.S., Haussler, D.: A hidden markov model that finds genes in Escherichia-Coli DNA. Nucleic Acids Res. **22**(22), 4768–4778 (1994)
34. Eddy, S.R.: Hidden Markov models. Curr. Opin. Struct. Biol. **6**(3), 361–365 (1996)
35. Delcher, A.L., Bratke, K.A., Powers, E.C., Salzberg, S.L.: Identifying bacterial genes and endosymbiont DNA with Glimmer. Bioinformatics **23**(6), 673–679 (2007)
36. Vaidyanathan, P.P.: Genomics and proteomics: a signal processor's tour. Circuits Syst. Mag. IEEE **4**(4), 6–29 (2004)
37. Al Bataineh, M., Al-qudah, Z.: A novel gene identification algorithm with Bayesian classification. Biomed. Signal Process. Control **31**, 6–15 (2017)
38. Guan, R., Tuqan, J.: IIR filter design for gene identification. In: Gensips Processing, Baltimore, Maryland (2004)
39. Vaidyanathan, P., Yoon, B.: Gene and exon prediction using allpass-based filters. In: Workshop on Genomic Signal Processing and Statistics, vol. 3 (2002)
40. Murray, K.B., Gorse, D., Thornton, J.M.: Wavelet transforms for the characterization and detection of repeating motifs. J. Mol. Biol. **316**, 341–363 (2002)
41. Borodovsky, M., Ekisheva, S.: Problems and Solutions in Biological Sequence Analysis. Cambridge University Press, Cambridge (2006)
42. Vaidyanathan, P.P., Yoon, B.: Digital filters for gene prediction applications. In: Proceedings of the 36th Asilomar Conference on Signals, Systems, and Computers. Monterey, CA (2002)
43. Sharma, S.D., Shakya, K., Sharma, S.N.: Evaluation of DNA mapping schemes for exon detection. In: 2011 International Conference on Computer, Communication and Electrical Technology, ICCCET 2011, pp. 71–74 (2011)
44. Anastassiou, D.: Genomic signal processing. IEEE Signal Process. Mag. **18**, 8–20 (2001)
45. Rangel, P., Giovannetti, J.: Genomes and Databases on the Internet: A Practical Guide to Functions and Applications. Horizon Scientific Press, Wymondham (2002)
46. Pruitt, K.D., Tatusova, T., Maglott, D.R.: NCBI reference sequences (RefSeq): a curated non-redundant sequence database of genomes, transcripts and proteins. Nucleic Acids Res. **35**(Suppl. 1), D61–D65 (2007)
47. Baisnee, P.F., Hampson, S., Baldi, P.: Why are complementary DNA strands symmetric? Bioinformatics **18**(8), 1021–1033 (2002)
48. Burset, M., Guigó, R.: Evaluation of gene structure prediction programs. Genomics **34**(3), 353–367 (1996)

Identification of Common Gene Signatures in Microarray and RNA-Sequencing Data Using Network-Based Regularization

Inês Diegues[1], Susana Vinga[1], and Marta B. Lopes[2,3](✉)

[1] INESC-ID, Instituto Superior Técnico, Universidade de Lisboa, R. Alves Redol 9, 1000-029 Lisboa, Portugal

[2] NOVA Laboratory for Computer Science and Informatics (NOVA LINCS), FCT, UNL, 2829-516 Caparica, Portugal

marta.lopes@fct.unl.pt

[3] Centro de Matemática e Aplicações (CMA), FCT, UNL, 2829-516 Caparica, Portugal

Abstract. Microarray and RNA-sequencing (RNA-seq) gene expression data alongside machine learning algorithms are promising in the discovery of new cancer biomarkers. However, even though they are similar in purpose, there are some fundamental differences between the two techniques. We propose a methodology for cross-platform integration, and biomarker discovery based on network-based regularization via the Twin Networks Recovery (`twiner`) penalty, as a strategy to enhance the selection of breast cancer gene signatures that have similar correlation patterns in both platforms. In a classification setting based on sparse logistic regression (LR) taking as classes *tumor* from both RNA-seq and microarray, and *normal* tissue samples, `twiner` achieved precision-recall accuracies of 99.71% and 99.57% in the training and test set, respectively. Moreover, the survival analysis results validated the biological relevance of the signatures identified by `twiner`. Therefore, by leveraging from the existing amount of data for microarray and RNA-seq, a single biological conclusion can be reached, independent of each technology.

Keywords: Microarray · RNA-sequencing · Machine learning · Biomarkers · Network-based regularization

1 Introduction

Cancer is the second leading cause of death worldwide. Over 9.6 million people were estimated to die due to this malignancy in 2018 [2]. Tumors are the fast

Partially funded by the Portuguese Foundation for Science and Technology (UIDB/50021/2020 (INESC-ID), UIDB/00297/2020 (CMA), UIDB/04516/2020 (NOVA LINCS), and PTDC/CCI-CIF/29877/2017).

I. Rojas et al. (Eds.): IWBBIO 2020, LNBI 12108, pp. 15–26, 2020.
https://doi.org/10.1007/978-3-030-45385-5_2

growth of abnormal cells that are no longer able to perform apoptosis, which is the programmed death of the cell. These cells can later invade the adjacent tissues creating metastasis. To better manage cancer, it is crucial to understand its signaling pathways and find the gene signatures associated with each type of tumor.

Most of the cell functions depend on proteins and on the biochemical pathways they are on. The transcriptome is dynamic and a good representation of the cell's environment [22]. It is the link between encoded DNA and phenotype. Hence, by measuring it, it is possible to quantify the transcript abundance in a specific tissue at a given time and under different conditions. DNA microarray and RNA-sequencing (RNA-seq) are two technologies that quantify the transcripts abundance. Despite similar in purpose, their workflow is very different, leading to distinct expression values outcomes.

In this study, the target disease is the breast invasive carcinoma (BRCA), which is a very heterogeneous disease. We aim to find the biomarkers associated with the Estrogen Receptor positive (ER+) BRCA subtype irrespective of the technology (microarray or RNA-seq) used, by leveraging from cross-platform integration, since for many diseases the volume of available DNA microarray data is far higher than that for RNA-seq [13]. Thus, we can take advantage of well-validated microarray data and analyze it together with the newer data generated from updated technologies like RNA-seq. Besides their divergences, it has been proven that microarray and RNA-seq have some level of correlation [14].

1.1 Background

High-throughput genomic and proteomic technologies play a fundamental role in cancer research. They generate an enormous quantity of data, contributing to the so-called "Big Data" era [7]. However, this type of data is characterized by its high dimensionality, where the number of genes is far bigger than the number of samples. One of the biggest challenges of high-dimensional data is the *curse of dimensionality*, which describes the exponential increase in volume associated with adding extra dimensions in the Euclidean space. It is responsible for the break down of the optimal statistical model fitting [9]. Hence, techniques of Feature Selection (FS) have been developed to identify the biologically relevant genes involved in the cancer cell pathways [4].

FS aims to improve the accuracy of the models by eliminating irrelevant and noisy features. Since only a subset of the original set is used, the algorithms become faster [3]. One state-of-the-art approach to perform FS is the incorporation of regularizers in the classification process, such as the Ridge, LASSO, and Elastic Net (EN) penalties.

In this context, Algamal and Lee [4] proposed a regularized logistic regression (LR) with adjusted adaptive elastic net (AAElastic) that expands the existing adaptive EN regularization. Instead of using the EN estimations as the initial weights, in the adaptive version, the authors incorporate a new initial weight inside the l_1-norm term. The method was applied for gene selection in high dimensional cancer classification.

Other methods add network information in the regularization term to take advantage of the relationship between data points. Zhu et al. [24] proposed a network-based Support Vector Machine (SVM) to identify gene signatures that allow for cancer diagnostic classification and prognostic assessment. The authors incorporate a penalty term that takes into account pairwise gene neighbors. Another approach, named network-constrained SVM was developed in Chen et al. [6]. It integrates both gene expression data and protein-protein interaction data.

Zhang et al. [23] employs a Laplacian graph regularization with LR classification to classify and discover the pathways related to the disease status. In Butte et al. [5], relevance networks are used to find functional relationships between RNA expression and chemotherapeutic susceptibility by computing comprehensive pair-wise correlations between gene expression and measures of agent susceptibility.

To answer the research questions here formulated, particularly, what breast ER+ gene signatures can be extracted from combined microarray and RNA-seq data and, therefore, conclude on their independency on the platform used for data acquisition, we use a network-based regularizer. `Twiner` is a penalty term recently proposed by Lopes et al. [17] to find common gene signatures in breast and prostate cancers since both diseases are hormone-dependent and lead to bone-relapse. In the present study, sparse LR through the `twiner` regularizer, discriminating between *tumor* from both RNA-seq and microarray, and *normal* tissue samples, is used to disclose putative ER+ biomarkers with a similar correlation-based network profile across microarray and RNA-seq platforms.

2 Methodology

2.1 Data Sources

The microarray expression values for BRCA were collected from two different studies extracted from *Gene Expression Omnibus* (GEO) [11] using *GEOquery* package [10]. GEO data was obtained with Affymetrix HG-U133A Plus 2.0 microarrays. The first GEO study has 121 samples from which 67 are ER+ and 17 normal. The second GEO study accounts for 178 samples that include 59 ER+ and 11 normal (Table 1). The TCGA RNA-seq data was imported from *brca.data* R package [1]. The gene expression values for BRCA are Fragments Per Kilo base per Million (FPKM). The data is composed by 1222 observations from 1097 individuals. From those samples, 1102 are primary solid tumor, 7 metastasis and 103 normal breast tissue.

2.2 Data Preparation and Preprocessing

ER+ observations from the GEO and TCGA studies were selected for further analysis. From the TCGA study, only primary solid tumor samples were considered, leading to the exclusion of 7 metastatic samples. Also from the TCGA

Table 1. Data summary regarding the source, platform, the number of ER+ and normal samples used, and the number of transcripts considered.

Source	Platform	ER+	Normal	Transcripts
GEO1 (GSE42568) [8]	Affy U133a Plus 2.0	67	17	23788
GEO2 (GSE65194) [18]	Affy U133a Plus 2.0	59	11	22975
TCGA RNA-seq [1]	Illumina Hi-Seq	802	79	57251

study, only normal samples taken from ER+ patients, *i.e.* 79, were considered (Table 1). The gene set was filtered to account only with the protein coding genes accordingly to Ensembl genome browser and the Consensus Coding Sequencing (CCDS) projects [20]. A gene-probe mapping was applied to GEO studies to transform the probe IDs into HUGO gene nomenclature. The two microarray platforms were submitted to between-array normalization with the quantile method. GEO and RNA-seq TCGA studies were log_2 transformed.

2.3 Data Integration

In order to merge all data sets, a cross-platform integration was performed to correct for batch effects. By making use of ComBat from *sva* R package [16], microarray data was corrected for systematic errors. Then, this data was used as a target distribution in Quantile Normalization (QN) to transform RNA-seq into comparable microarray data (Fig. 1).

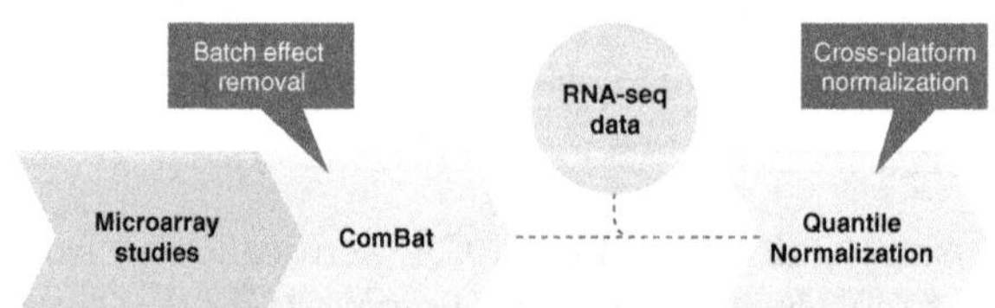

Fig. 1. Cross-platform integration. Microarray studies are first combined using QN and ComBat and then used as a target distribution to RNA-seq cross-platform integration using QN.

2.4 Sparse Logistic Regression

The relationship between one or more independent variables and a binary outcome, zero (*normal*) or one (*tumor*), is given by the logistic function:

$$p_i = P(Y_i = 1|\mathbf{X}_i) = \frac{\exp\left(\mathbf{X}_i^T\beta\right)}{1 + \exp\left(\mathbf{X}_i^T\beta\right)}, \tag{1}$$

where, $\mathbf{X}$ is the design matrix $n \times p$ (n and p are respectively the number of observations and features), p_i is the probability of success ($Y_i = 1$) for observation $i = 1, ..., n$, and $\boldsymbol{\beta} = (\beta_1, \beta_2, \dots \beta_p)$ are the regression coefficients associated to the p independent variables. These parameters are estimated by maximizing the log likelihood function of the LR defined as

$$\sum_{i=1}^{n} \{y_i \log p_i + (1 - y_i) \log (1 - p_i)\} + R(\boldsymbol{\beta}), \tag{2}$$

where $R(\boldsymbol{\beta})$ is a regularization term that is added.

The EN penalty [25] incorporates both l_1- and l_2-norms. Thus, it will not only promote sparsity but also encourages group selection. Thus, the regularization term that is added to the objective function is given by

$$R(\boldsymbol{\beta}) = \lambda \left[\frac{1}{2}(1 - \alpha)||\boldsymbol{\beta}||_2^2 + \alpha||\boldsymbol{\beta}||_1 \right], \tag{3}$$

where $\alpha \in [0, 1]$ shifts the penalty term towards Ridge or LASSO regularization, and is usually determined by cross-validation out of a grid of values. In fact, when $\alpha = 1$, the problem is reduced to a l_1-norm or LASSO, while $\alpha = 0$ means Ridge regression or squared l_2-norm. As for λ, it is the tuning parameter that controls the strength of the penalty term and is also selected by cross-validation.

The `twiner` regularizer [17] introduces a network penalty based on the angular distance between instances. It is a strategy to ensure that similarly correlated gene features across different data sets are less penalized during FS procedure within the learning model. The pairwise correlations between variables are obtained computing the correlation matrices using the Pearson correlation factor.

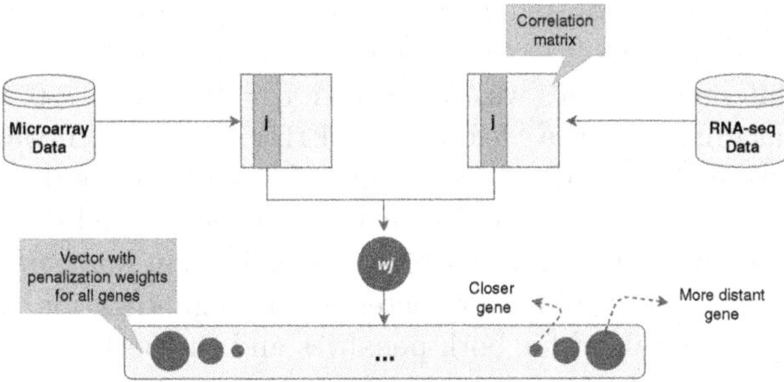

Fig. 2. The `twiner` penalty. To obtain the `twiner` penalty terms, the correlation matrices are first computed for both microarray and RNA-seq and then the angular distances between genes are calculated. The weight vector is obtained from those distances. The closer the gene in the two platforms, the smaller the corresponding weight associated with that gene.

Denoting A and B as two different profiling technologies, then the correlation matrices can be formulated as $\Sigma_A = \left[\boldsymbol{\sigma}_1^A, \dots, \boldsymbol{\sigma}_p^A\right]$ and $\Sigma_B = \left[\boldsymbol{\sigma}_1^B, \dots, \boldsymbol{\sigma}_p^B\right]$, where each column $\boldsymbol{\sigma}_j \in \mathbb{R}^p$ represents the correlation of each gene, $j = 1, \ldots, p$, with the remaining ones. Then, the dissimilarity measure of gene j between A and B is given by the angle of the corresponding vectors given by

$$d_j(A,B) = \arccos \frac{< \sigma_j^A, \sigma_j^B >}{\|\sigma_j^A\| \cdot \|\sigma_j^B\|}. \tag{4}$$

The angle is used because similar patterns will have the same proportionality between the entries of the two data sets regardless of the magnitude of the vectors. The weights for the penalty term, $\mathbf{w} = (w_1, ..., w_j, ..., w_p)$, are the distance normalized to the maximum value as follows:

$$w_j = \frac{d_j(A,B)}{\max_k d_k(A,B)}, \quad j,k = 1, \ldots, p. \tag{5}$$

Hence, for a given gene j, the smaller the distance between σ_j^A and σ_j^B is, the more similar the techniques are regarding the overall correlation pattern for gene j (Fig. 2). The twiner penalty is given by

$$R(\boldsymbol{\beta}) = \lambda \left\{ \alpha \|\mathbf{w} \circ \boldsymbol{\beta}\|_1 + (1-\alpha)\|\mathbf{w} \circ \boldsymbol{\beta}\|_2^2 \right\}. \tag{6}$$

2.5 Learning Process

Before starting the learning process, features with standard deviation equal to zero were removed because they did not change across samples and, therefore, were not relevant for classification purposes. Therefore, for the downstream analysis the data set accounts for 17001 genes and 1035 observations (Table 1).

For the classification model, two different penalties were used, EN and `twiner`, that were incorporated in a sparse LR classifier implemented using *glmnet* R package [15]. To find the optimal value of α (Eq. 3), a 10-fold cross-validation to different α values was performed, $\alpha = 0.1, 0.2, \ldots, 0.9$. The chosen α is the one that minimizes the Mean Square Error (MSE). Afterward, 100 bootstrap samples were generated, where training (75% of the total data) and test sets were randomly drawn with replacement from the merged data, microarray and RNA-seq together. Moreover, 10-fold cross-validation was performed to find the best λ, which is the tuning parameter of the regularization term. Finally, the gene signatures obtained for both penalties and the performance evaluation metrics for both EN and `twiner` were evaluated.

2.6 Differential Gene Expression Analysis

In parallel with the learning procedure, a Differential Gene Expression Analysis (DGE) was performed to evaluate whether the genes selected were under- or over-expressed in microarray and RNA-seq data when *normal* and *tumor* status are compared.

2.7 Survival Analysis

Survival Analysis (SA) was performed based on the biomarkers selected by `twiner` penalty, for the GEO1 microarray and RNA-seq TCGA studies, for which survival data were available. SA was intended to validate the gene signatures found by evaluating the statistical significance in the separation between low- and high-risk patients, which is achieved by a log-rank test. The code is freely available at https://github.com/inesdiegues/twiner.

3 Results and Discussion

Data Preprocessing and Integration. DNA microarray data were merged and batch corrected, and then used as a target distribution to approximate RNA-seq data. Figure 3 shows the results by the Principal Component Analysis (PCA) as a tool to visualize samples grouping in a reduced dimensional space.

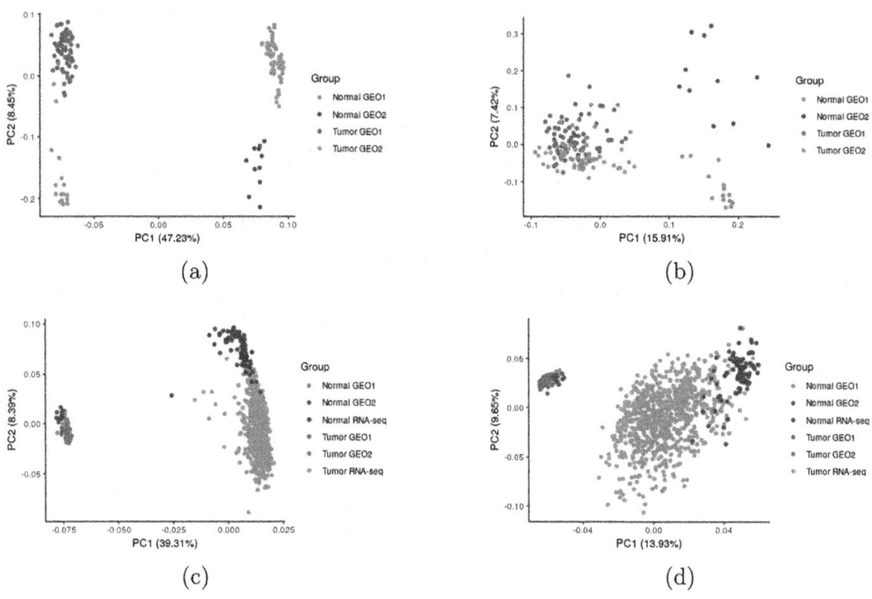

Fig. 3. PCA for microarray studies before (a) and after ComBat (b) and for all data merged before (c) and after (d) quantile normalization on RNA-seq data.

From Figs. 3(a) and (b), it can be seen that the batch effects were largely reduced according to the decreased variability in PC1 from 47.23% to 15.91%. When merging the three studies (Fig. 3(a)), the inter-variability between RNA-seq and microarray studies ($PC1 = 39.31\%$) is higher than between the *normal* vs. *tumor* status ($PC2 = 8.39\%$). After applying QN to RNA-seq and ComBat to microarray and scale the merged data, a more homogeneous data cloud is obtained, even though some inter-variability between studies remains (Fig. 3(d)).

Learning Process. The learning phase started by finding the optimal value of α, which was 0.9. Afterward, a 100-bootstrap classification was done. The results presented include the gene signatures found for each penalty and the performance evaluation measures (Table 2), including the number of misclassifications, MSE, and Area Under the Precision-Recall Curve (PR-AUC).

Table 2. Median accuracy values obtained for the 100-bootstrap runs performed in microarray and RNA-seq merged data using EN and `twiner` penalties.

	EN penalty		`twiner` penalty	
	Training	Test	Training	Test
# misclassifications	3	2	3	1
MSE (%)	4.349×10^{-3}	7.574×10^{-3}	4.699×10^{-3}	7.686×10^{-3}
PR-AUC (%)	99.705	99.569	99.706	99.569
# variables selected	54		47	

Both regularization methods performed well, achieving PR-AUCs always above 99%. `twiner` obtained 99.71% for training and 99.57% in the test set. Both the performance and number of features selected are comparable between the penalty terms.

In the 100 iterations, some features were always selected by the algorithm. For EN these were *ADAMTS5*, *CACNA1D*, *CLEC3B*, *COMP*, and *LAMP5*, while for `twiner` they were *CACNA1D*, *LAMP5*, and *WISP1*. Figure 4 illustrates that `twiner` selects features with lower weight compared to EN, as expected.

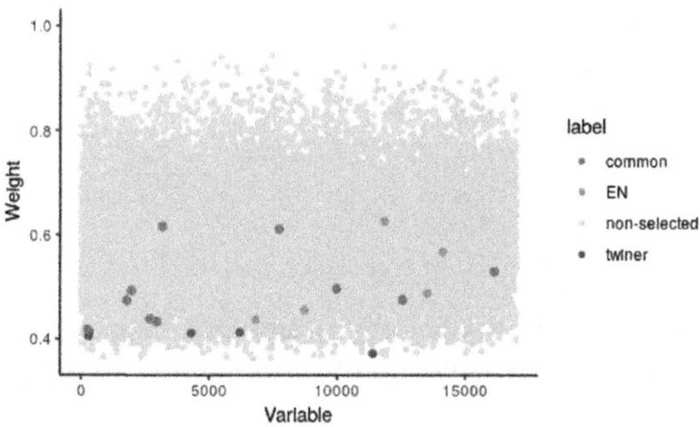

Fig. 4. Weight distribution of the features selected by `twiner` (orange), EN (green) or both (blue). (Color figure online)

Differential Expression Analysis. In order to identify the Differentially Expressed Genes (DEGs), the Benjamini-Hochberg adjusted p-values were obtained, which were corrected for the huge number of features in the data set. Hence, in microarray 64 DEGs were identified, while in RNA-seq there were 599.

Our analysis shows that the majority of the genes are consistently expressed in the same way, either up- or down-regulated, independently of the platform used. Figure 5 shows the distribution of the expression values in *normal* and *tumor* samples of the genes exclusively selected by `twiner` in the merged data, microarray and RNA-seq.

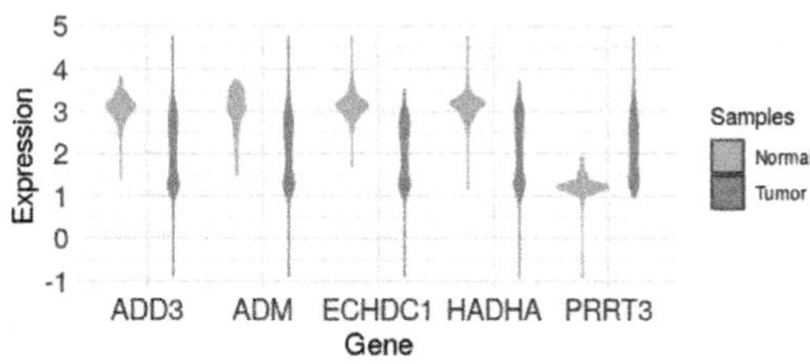

Fig. 5. Expression for the genes found exclusively by `twiner` in the merged data set, microarray and RNA-seq.

Genes Selected. Over the 100 iterations, in 75% of the times, EN and `twiner` selected ten genes in common: *ADAMTS5*, *C22orf39*, *CACNA1D*, *CES1*, *CLEC3B*, *COMP*, *LAMP5*, *OLFML2A*, *S100P*, and *WISP1*. From those, two are part of the group that was always selected, *CACNA1D* and *LAMP5*. From our DGE analysis, both genes are over-expressed in *tumor* samples.

One of the goals of this study was to identify the common biomarkers between the two profiling technologies. Thus, it is important to debate the features that were exclusively selected by `twiner`, which is the penalty that favours the selection of similarly correlated genes in the gene network in microarray and RNA-seq. These genes were: *ADD3*, *ADM*, *ECHDC1*, *HADHA*, and *PRRT3*. From Fig. 5, and based on our DEG analysis, all these genes were down-regulated, excluding *PRRT3*, which is over-expressed in *tumor* samples.

Some of the genes above were previously studied as being associated with breast or other types of cancer [12,19,21]. *ADD3* is part of membrane skeletal proteins family and is linked to the spectrin-actin network. *ADM* is involved in the promotion of angiogenesis, vasodilatation and regulation of hormone secretion such as oxytocine. *ECHDC1* encodes a metabolism related protein while *HADHA* is part of the mithocondrial β-oxidation process. *PRRT3* encodes a transmembranar protein. Therefore, although these techniques have different workflows and consequently distinct expression values, `twiner` is able to extract the gene features that are similarly expressed and connected in the gene correlation network, and play a role in the disease.

Survival Analysis. The aim of the SA was to evaluate the significance of the gene features discovered by `twiner` in the survival outcome. It is expected that suitable biomarkers can clearly distinguish between high and low-risk groups, where high risk refers to patients that have a considerable probability of facing the event of interest, which is, in this situation, death.

Figure 6 represents the Kaplan-Meier curves obtained by using the variables selected by EN (a and b) and `twiner` (c and d) for microarray GEO1 and RNA-seq TCGA studies, from which survival data was available. The p-values for `twiner` were always below 0.001, indicating that the gene signatures found by this network-based regularizer are statistically significant and associated with BRCA survival outcomes. Furthermore, in the microarray data, `twiner` showed a superior performance it selected variables that can clearly distinguish between the two groups, high- and low-risk patients.

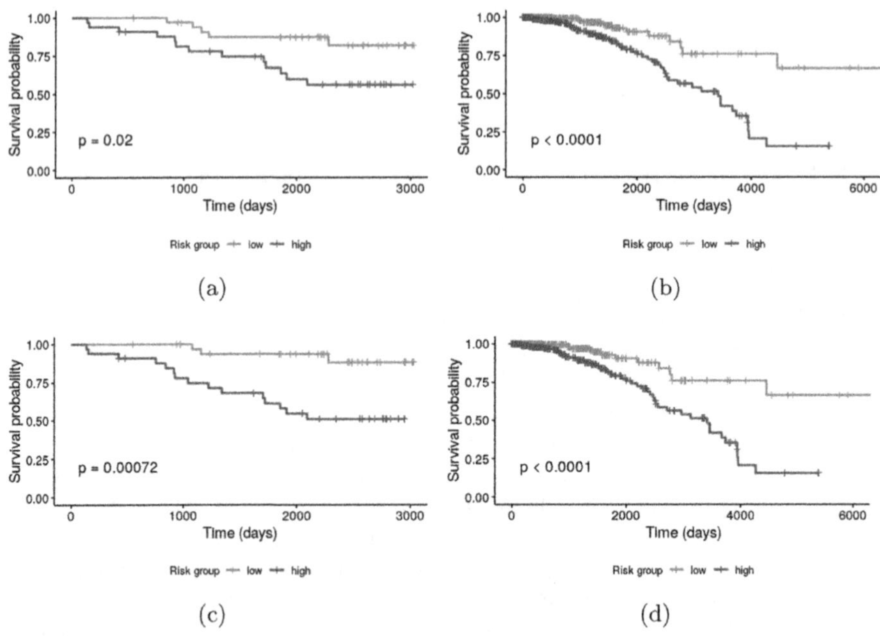

Fig. 6. Kaplan-Meier curves obtained for the microarray GEO1 (a and c) and RNA-seq TCGA (b and d) survival data, based on the biomarkers selected by EN (top figures) and `twiner` (bottom figures).

4 Conclusions

DNA microarray is a widespread technology that has been used for over the last decade. However, with the development of high-throughput NGS like RNA-seq, its use is slowly fading. Nonetheless, there is an excellent amount of validated microarray expression data available in public repositories like GEO. To leverage from this data that is invaluable for data mining purposes, we evaluated the level of concordance between these two profiling technologies and if different techniques lead to different outcomes. Thus, `twiner` was used as an embedded FS that promotes the selection of genes with a similar role in the gene correlation network in the two platforms through correlation-based information. Overall, `twiner` shows comparable performances regarding the EN penalty, selecting genes that were previously associated with cancer. SA enabled biological validation of the identified biomarkers, which could clearly distinguish between low and high-risk groups.

In summary, this study demonstrated that gene signatures found for breast cancer can be made independent of the platform by using `twiner` as a network-regularization method to approximate two realities, in our case, two different technologies. Lastly, the methodology proposed makes feasible integrating data from both microarray and RNA-seq platforms leveraging from the massive amount of data available.

References

1. TCGA data R package. https://github.com/averissimo/tcga.data/
2. World Health Organization. https://www.who.int/health-topics/cancer#tab=overview
3. Abeel, T., Helleputte, T., Van de Peer, Y., Dupont, P., Saeys, Y.: Robust biomarker identification for cancer diagnosis with ensemble feature selection methods. Bioinformatics **26**(3), 392–398 (2009)
4. Algamal, Z.Y., Lee, M.H.: Regularized logistic regression with adjusted adaptive elastic net for gene selection in high dimensional cancer classification. Comput. Biol. Med. **67**, 136–145 (2015)
5. Butte, A.J., Tamayo, P., Slonim, D., Golub, T.R., Kohane, I.S.: Discovering functional relationships between RNA expression and chemotherapeutic susceptibility using relevance networks. Proc. Natl. Acad. Sci. **97**(22), 12182–12186 (2000)
6. Chen, L., Xuan, J., Riggins, R.B., Clarke, R., Wang, Y.: Identifying cancer biomarkers by network-constrained support vector machines. BMC Syst. Biol. **5**(1), 161 (2011)
7. Clare, S.E., Shaw, P.L.: "Big Data" for breast cancer: where to look and what you will find. NPJ Breast Cancer **2**, 16031 (2016)
8. Clarke, C., et al.: Correlating transcriptional networks to breast cancer survival: a large-scale coexpression analysis. Carcinogenesis **34**(10), 2300–2308 (2013). https://doi.org/10.1093/carcin/bgt208
9. Clarke, R., et al.: The properties of high-dimensional data spaces: implications for exploring gene and protein expression data. Nat. Rev. Cancer **8**(1), 37 (2008)
10. Davis, S., Meltzer, P.S.: GEOquery: a bridge between the gene expression omnibus (GEO) and bioconductor. Bioinformatics **23**(14), 1846–1847 (2007)
11. Edgar, R., Domrachev, M., Lash, A.E.: Gene expression omnibus: NCBI gene expression and hybridization array data repository. Nucleic Acids Res. **30**(1), 207–210 (2002)
12. Fanale, D., Amodeo, V., Corsini, L., Rizzo, S., Bazan, V., Russo, A.: Breast cancer genome-wide association studies: there is strength in numbers. Oncogene **31**(17), 2121 (2012)

13. Franks, J.M., Cai, G., Whitfield, M.L.: Feature specific quantile normalization enables cross-platform classification of molecular subtypes using gene expression data. Bioinformatics **34**(11), 1868–1874 (2018)
14. Guo, Y., Sheng, Q., Li, J., Ye, F., Samuels, D.C., Shyr, Y.: Large scale comparison of gene expression levels by microarrays and RNAseq using TCGA data. PLoS ONE **8**(8), e71462 (2013)
15. Hastie, T., Qian, J.: Glmnet vignette (2014). http://www.web.stanford.edu/~hastie/Papers/Glmnet_Vignette.pdf. Accessed 20 Sept 2016
16. Leek, J.T., Johnson, W.E., Parker, H.S., Jaffe, A.E., Storey, J.D.: The SVA package for removing batch effects and other unwanted variation in high-throughput experiments. Bioinformatics **28**(6), 882–883 (2012)
17. Lopes, M.B., Casimiro, S., Vinga, S.: Twiner: correlation-based regularization for identifying common cancer gene signatures. BMC Bioinform. **20**(1), 356 (2019)
18. Maire, V., et al.: TTK/hMPS1 is an attractive therapeutic target for triple-negative breast cancer. PLoS ONE **8**(5), e63712 (2013)
19. Mamtani, M., Kulkarni, H.: Association of HADHA expression with the risk of breast cancer: targeted subset analysis and meta-analysis of microarray data. BMC Res. Notes **5**(1), 25 (2012)
20. Pruitt, K.D., et al.: The consensus coding sequence (CCDS) project: Identifying a common protein-coding gene set for the human and mouse genomes. Genome Res. **19**(7), 1316–1323 (2009)
21. Pugazhendhi, D., Sadler, A., Darbre, P.: Comparison of the global gene expression profiles produced by methylparaben, n-butylparaben and 17β-oestradiol in MCF7 human breast cancer cells. J. Appl. Toxicol. Int. J. **27**(1), 67–77 (2007)
22. Srivastava, A., George, J., Karuturi, R.K.: Transcriptome analysis. In: Ranganathan, S., Gribskov, M., Nakai, K., Schönbach, C. (eds.) Encyclopedia of Bioinformatics and Computational Biology, pp. 792–805. Academic Press, Oxford (2019)
23. Zhang, W., Wan, Y.w., Allen, G.I., Pang, K., Anderson, M.L., Liu, Z.: Molecular pathway identification using biological network-regularized logistic models. BMC Genomics **14**(8), S7 (2013)
24. Zhu, Y., Shen, X., Pan, W.: Network-based support vector machine for classification of microarray samples. BMC Bioinform. **10**(1), S21 (2009)
25. Zou, H., Hastie, T.: Regularization and variable selection via the elastic net. J. R. Stat. Soc. Ser. B (Stat. Methodol.) **67**(2), 301–320 (2005)

Blood Plasma Trophic Growth Factors Predict the Outcome in Patients with Acute Ischemic Stroke

Valeriia Roslavtceva[1(✉)], Evgeniy Bushmelev[2], Pavel Astanin[3], Tatyana Zabrodskaya[3], Alla Salmina[3], Semen Prokopenko[3], Vera Laptenkova[1], and Michael Sadovsky[2,3,4]

[1] I.S. Berzon Krasnoyarsk Interregional Clinical Hospital No 20, 12 Instrumentalnaya Street, 660123 Krasnoyarsk, Russia
roslavceva.valeriya@mail.ru, laptenkova.vv@gmail.com

[2] Institute of Computational Modelling of SB RAS, Akademgorodok, 660036 Krasnoyarsk, Russia
eugeny.bushmelev@gmail.com, msad@icm.krasn.ru

[3] Voino-Yasenetsy Krasnoyarsk State Medical University, 1 P. Zheleznyaka Street, 660022 Krasnoyarsk, Russia
med_cyber@mail.ru, ng286329@mail.ru, allasalmina@mail.ru, s.v.proc.58@mail.ru

[4] Siberian Federal University, 79 Svobodny Prosp., 660041 Krasnoyarsk, Russia
http://krasgmu.ru

Abstract. Stroke is an acute disorder of CNS being the leading factor of mortality and disability of the population. Dynamic assessment of trophic growth factors expression is a promising tool to predict the outcome of ischemic stroke. We investigated the concentration dynamics of the brain-derived neurotrophic factor (BDNF) and vascular endothelial growth factor (VEGF) in blood plasma of patients with acute ischemic stroke. 56 patients took part in the study. Venous blood was collected from all patients on the first, 7th and 21st day of their hospital stay. BDNF and VEGF plasma concentrations were measured using ELISA. Our study shows, that not single, but serial dynamic measures of BDNF plasma concentrations in the acute period of ischemic stroke have a prognostic significance. Increasing of the BDNF plasma concentration on day 7 in comparison to the concentration on day 1 was significantly associated with a better clinical outcome of acute ischemic stroke. Extremely high VEGF plasma concentrations (more than 260 pg/mL) on days 1 and 7 from the ischemic stroke onset were significantly associated with a worse clinical outcome on day 21 and a less favorable rehabilitation prognosis. Serial measurement of plasma concentrations of trophic growth factors in patients with ischemic stroke presents a rather simple, reliable and minimally invasive method of dynamic assessment of the clinical course of acute ischemic stroke and early outcome prediction.

Keywords: Brain-derived neurotrophic factor · Vascular endothelial growth factor · Ischemic stroke · Brain · Neurogenesis

I. Rojas et al. (Eds.): IWBBIO 2020, LNBI 12108, pp. 27–39, 2020.
https://doi.org/10.1007/978-3-030-45385-5_3

1 Introduction

Stroke is an acute disorder of the central nervous system (CNS) and one of the main causes of mortality and disability in the population. Ischemic stroke results from a transient or permanent occlusion of the cerebral arterial blood flow with an embolus or local thrombus, followed by an acute infarction of the brain tissue. Intracellular excitotoxicity, oxidative stress, apoptosis and inflammation are the main pathological mechanisms of ischemic brain damage. Cerebral ischemia triggers a number of biochemical and molecular mechanisms resulting in impaired functional activity of neurons through ruptures of intercellular connections. These pathological processes are mediated by excitotoxicity, glutamate-initiated signaling pathways, free radical reactions, ionic imbalance, etc. [1,2].

The evaluation of expression of trophic growth factors seems to be a promising approach to predict the outcome of ischemic stroke [1]. Both brain-derived neurotrophic factor (BDNF) and vascular endothelial growth factor (VEGF) play an in maintaining plasticity and stimulation of brain regeneration processes in the adult organism, taking part in the processes of angiogenesis and neurogenesis [3].

1.1 BDNF

Brain derived neurotrophic factor is the most common neurotrophin in the CNS [4]. BDNF belongs to the family of neurotrophins including nerve growth factor (NGF), neurotrophin3 (NT3) and NT4 [5]. The ability of this protein to cross the blood-brain barrier in both directions stands behind the correlation between circulating BDNF level and the concentration of BDNF in the CNS. Currently, it is not known for sure how strong this correlation is [6]. However, serum and plasma BDNF concentrations may be potential markers of the status of the brain (see [7–10] for details).

Current studies confirm the fact that the expression of BDNF increases in tissues surrounding the infarction zone during the first week after stroke (peracute period) [11]. BDNF effects were extensively studied in various stroke models [12,13]. In general, a positive effect of BDNF in the process of post-stroke rehabilitation is reported and a number of possible mechanisms are proposed: protection during acute ischemic damage [14], stimulation of angiogenesis [11] and neurogenesis [15], enhancement of brain tissue reparation mechanisms [11], and increased synaptic plasticity [13]. The above data show that BDNF is an endogenous factor in the post-stroke reparation of the brain tissue.

Studies of dynamics of BDNF plasma concentration in the acute period of ischemic stroke show controversial results. Paper [16] reports no significant changes in the BDNF plasma concentration in patients with ischemic stroke, thus claiming that this marker is of low practical value. However, this study included only 10 patients. Paper [17] also reported no significant change in the BDNF plasma concentration in a rat model of ischemic brain damage. However, the concentration of BDNF in plasma 4 h after embolization was positively correlated with the severity of the stroke. Paper [8] in their study of the effect of transient ischemia on rat plasma BDNF reported a peak increase in BDNF concentration 90 min after reperfusion.

Sun *et al.* [18] studied the effect of exercise intensity after ischemic brain damage in an animal model. An increase in rat plasma BDNF concentration has been reported in the group with a gradual increase in exercise intensity. Wang *et al.* [9] examined more than 200 patients in the acute period of ischemic stroke. They report that a low concentration of BDNF on admission to the hospital was associated with worse NIHSS and Rankin scores 3 months after a stroke. However, this study evaluated the concentration of BDNF in the blood serum of patients, not in plasma.

1.2 VEGF

Vascular endothelial growth factor (VEGF) was originally discovered in 1983 as the factor affecting the vascular permeability [19]. VEGF-A (the most widespread member of the VEGF family) is a homodimeric glycoprotein with a molecular weight of 36–46 kDa [20]. This protein plays a key role in the induction of angiogenesis in normal and pathological conditions [21].

The main angiogenic functions of VEGF-A (hereinafter VEGF) include promoting survival of endothelial cells [22], proliferation induction [23] and stimulation of migration and invasion of these cells [24]. Besides, VEGF is also involved in a number of other processes in the central nervous system, such as ontogenesis of the nervous system cells, including the processes of migration, differentiation, synaptogenesis, and myelination [25]; neuroprotection [26,27]; stimulation of neurogenesis in the adult organism [28,29]; post-ischemic reparation of the brain tissue [30] and blood vessels [31], stimulation of hippocampus-dependent memory formation [32]. VEGF is also involved in pathological processes such as atherogenesis [33] and cerebral edema [21,34,35].

In clinical practice, the minimally invasive and most common method of VEGF level assessment is the ELISA assay of the serum and plasma of patients with ischemic stroke [36,37]. Slevin *et al.* [37] showed a significantly increased level of serum VEGF in most patients in the acute period of ischemic stroke compared to healthy controls. The authors also found a correlation between the concentration of serum VEGF, the volume of brain tissue infarction and the residual neurologic deficit. These results were contradicted by authors of another study [36], who argued that the increased serum VEGF concentration indicates only the activation and destruction of platelets after the cerebrovascular accident. Other research groups have also reported elevated serum VEGF levels in patients with ischemic stroke and their correlation with stroke volume and post-stroke neurologic deficit [38,39].

In paper [39] the mean VEGF plasma concentration in patients with ischemic stroke was higher than in the control group: 249 and 50 pg/mL, respectively, which was consistent with the results of previous studies [40]. No significant increase or decrease of the VEGF level was observed in case of a progressive clinical course of ischemic stroke. In this study, no associations were found between the concentration of VEGF and the clinical variant of ischemic stroke classified according to the TOAST criteria [41]. Nevertheless, a high VEGF plasma concentration in the first 48 h of after ischemic stroke onset was associated with a less severe neurologic deficit at discharge [39]. A large screening study of biomarkers of angiogenesis, including VEGF, in the blood plasma of patients with ischemic stroke showed no correlation between the level of VEGF and the severity of the post-stroke neurologic deficit [42].

A study of serum VEGF levels in patients with ischemic stroke receiving treatment in the rehabilitation department found that the concentration of VEGF in the acute period correlates with NIHSS scores 3 months after the ischemic stroke. Patients with an initially higher level of serum VEGF showed worse results on scales evaluating the neurologic deficit at discharge from the rehabilitation department. These data suggest that an extremely high VEGF serum concentration in patients at admission to a rehabilitation institution may indicate a less favorable prognosis of recovery of motor functions [43].

Thus, we assume that there is a relation between the expression of VEGF and BDNF, hypoxia and brain tissue damage. The prognostic significance of VEGF in determining the outcome of ischemic stroke has been confirmed by several studies; data on BDNF are contradictory. Further studies are needed to answer the question of whether the change in plasma levels of BDNF and VEGF characterizes the clinical course of ischemic stroke. Also, a suitable methodology for examining patients has not been determined (the timing and number of measurements of plasma concentrations). It is also worth noting that the simultaneous study of VEGF and BDNF is found only in single studies. However, such an approach allows to characterize the individual course of angio- and neurogenesis, which are key processes in the recovery after ischemic stroke.

2 Materials and Methods

The study included 56 patients (21 men, 35 women) who were first admitted to the Primary Stroke Unit of I.S. Berzon Krasnoyarsk Clinical Hospital No 20 (Krasnoyarsk, Russia) with the diagnosis of acute ischemic stroke. The mean age of the patients was 63 years [39–85 years]. All patients were admitted within 24 h of the onset of stroke symptoms.

The clinical diagnosis of ischemic stroke was confirmed by computed tomography (CT), and a neurological examination of the patients was also performed. Medical history was obtained to identify risk factors (arterial hypertension, hypercholesterolemia, stenosing atherosclerosis of brachiocephalic arteries (more than 50 %), atrial fibrillation, smoking, diabetes mellitus). The severity of stroke was assessed on days 1, 7, and 21 after onset according to the following scales: National Institute of Health Stroke Scale, Brott T., Adams H.P., 1989; assessment of functional outcome according to The Modified Rankin Scale, UK-TIA Study Group, 1988; Rivermead Mobility Index, F.M. Collen, 1991. The stroke subtype was determined according to the TOAST classification criteria (Trial of Org 10172 in Acute Stroke Treatment, 1993). Computed tomography was performed in all patients on the first day of admission on a Bright Speed 16-slice CT scanner, GE Healthcare, USA. Ultrasound duplex scanning of the neck vessels was performed in all patients on the 1st day of hospital stay on an ultrasound scanner PHILIPS EnVisor C HD, USA.

The study was approved by the local ethics committee. Each participant gave written informed consent.

2.1 Sampling

Venous blood was collected from all patients on the first, 7th and 21st day of their hospital stay into a vacuum tube with EDTA (ethylenediaminetetraacetate) in a volume of 5 mL. Immediately after collection, the tube was centrifuged for 10 min at 3000 rpm and the plasma was separated from the precipitate with a dispenser into 4 eppendorfs of 200 μL each. The samples were kept at a temperature of −80 °C until measurement.

The BDNF plasma concentration was determined using a commercial ELISA kit according to the instructions for use set by the manufacturer of the test system (Cloud-Clone Corp., USA). The VEGF plasma concentration was determined using a commercial ELISA kit according to the instructions for use set by the manufacturer of the test system (Cloud-Clone Corp., USA). All patients also underwent a routine biochemical blood assay with the following measurements: blood glucose, total cholesterol, beta-lipoproteins, low-density lipoproteins, high-density lipoproteins, triglycerides.

2.2 Data Analysis

The data were processed both by routine methods of analysis (averages, standard deviations, correlations, etc.) and by modern methods based on the clustering of multidimensional data by various algorithms. Routine analysis was performed in MS Excel and Statistica, using built-in functions. Distinguishability of groups of patients was also checked by standard methods. The significance level of the criteria used in this study, which determines significant differences between the compared groups, was taken equal to 0.05.

It should be stressed that we followed two basically different approaches in analysis of the data. The first approach stipulates that groups of patients were divided by clinical indices and compared among themselves by classical methods of statistics; for example, patients on the admission day were compared with themselves on day 7 and day 21. It is important that here the division of patients into groups was carried out by the researcher in advance and groups of patients were compared, and it was known in advance who exactly they include.

The second approach opposes to the first one: all patients were merged into common database and clustering was carried out. We stress that clustering is carried out over the entire set of variables characterizing all patients enrolled in the database, with no exception. Clustering avoided any information whether a patient is sick (and at what stage) or healthy. Upon the cluster pattern implementation, we checked the composition of them: whether they comprise patients regularly, or randomly. It was found that each cluster comprises mainly the patients with the same character: for example, the patients with severe paresis, etc.

Two approaches were used to identify structuring in the data: the linear clustering method (K-means) and the nonlinear clustering method: elastic map technique. K-means is widely used and well presented [44,45]. The elastic map method is the most modern and powerful method of nonlinear statistics, based on the approximation of multidimensional data by manifolds of small (in our case, two-dimensional) dimension.

The method starts from implementation of the first and the second principal components, over the data set. All data are projected onto the plane determined by the components and then a minimum square containing all data projections is determined. Then each point of the initial data is connected to its projection by a mathematical spring; such a spring has infinite extensibility and its properties do not change as it stretches. At the third step, the initially rigid surface of the square is replaced with an elastic membrane (of the same size), that is able to bend and stretch; then the system is released to reach the configuration with minimum of total energy. An important constraint is the conservation of topology: the elastic membrane cannot be torn and glued.

At the fourth step, the position of each point on the jammed membrane is redefined: the orthogonal projection is determined. Finally, all the mathematical springs are removed so that the membrane gets back into original position and becomes a flat square. We used standard settings for a soft elastic map size 16×16 provided by freely distributed software *VidaExpert*.

3 Results

To begin with, we checked whether the patients with different NIHSS, Rankin, and Rivermead scales differ in VEGF and BDNF obtained on the 1st, 7th and 21st days. Since the data do not the normal distribution, we used Friedman and Wilcoxon criteria to compare them. On the contrary, the data of the observed groups did not differ in terms of the blood assay: the significance levels of the Friedman criterion for them were 0.509 (BDNF) and 0.703 (VEGF), respectively.

Next, we clustered all patients enrolled into the database with two methods: K-means and elastic map technique. K-means clustering failed to reveal any reliable cluster structure. A stable classification was observed for two classes. Despite the good stability of clustering, no clinically significant difference between the obtained classes has been observed. The clustering into three classes was unstable and also failed to reveal any clinically significant difference between the classes identified by this method.

Since the linear clustering methods failed to reveal any clinically significant pattern, we changed for the elastic map technique. This approach reliable identifies four clusters.

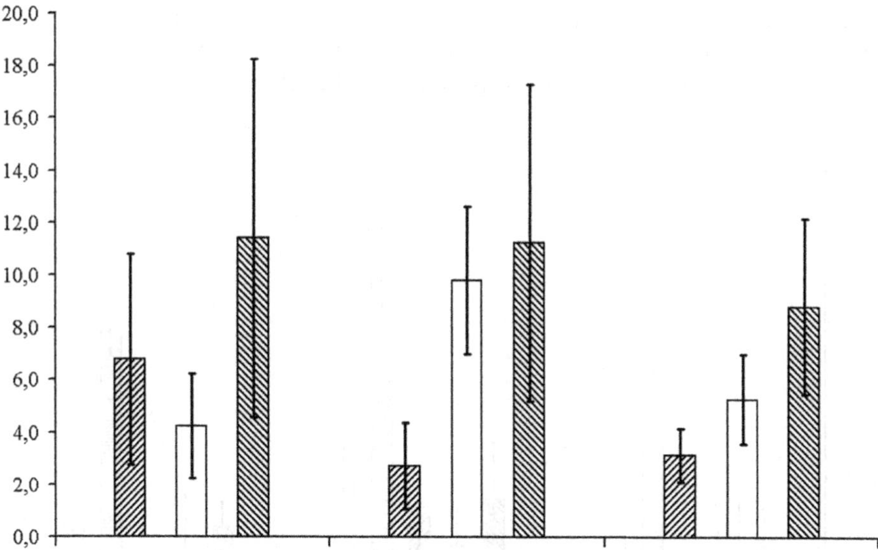

Fig. 1. The dynamics of BDNF plasma concentration in patients of Cluster 1 in comparison to patients of Clusters 2 and 3. Bars hatched right show Cluster 1, bars hatched left show Cluster 2, and white bars show Cluster 3. Vertical axis shows the concentration of BDNF in blood plasma, in ng/mL.

3.1 Cluster 1

Cluster 1 comprised 17 patients (5 men and 12 women). The mean age of the patients is 67 [39 to 85 years]. All patients of the cluster suffered from arterial hypertension and had either atrial fibrillation or stenosing atherosclerosis of brachiocephalic arteries as a risk factor for ischemic stroke; one patient had a combination of these risk factors. Two patients out of 17 were smokers. Atherothrombotic stroke prevailed among the ischemic stroke subtypes according to TOAST criteria, in this cluster.

The patients are characterized by a severe clinical course of ischemic stroke, in general. The neurologic deficit of the patients was estimated as mild (NIHSS score 8 to 10) in 2 patients, moderate (NIHSS score 13 to 18) in 3 patients, severe (NIHSS score 19 to 24) in 8 patients, extremely severe (NIHSS score 26) in 4 patients, upon the admission. At the 21st day, the neurologic deficit showed the following figures: mild (NIHSS score 10 to 12) in 3 patients, moderate (NIHSS score 14 to 16) in 5 patients, severe (NIHSS score 19 to 21) in 5 patients, extremely severe (NIHSS score 25 to 26) in 4 patients. Fatal outcome was recorded in 5 of 17 patients of this cluster. There was a tendency to a decrease or a slight increase in the BDNF plasma concentration in the patients of Cluster 1 on day 7 compared to day 1. The dynamics of BDNF plasma concentration in the patients of Cluster 1 in comparison to the patients of Cluster 2 is shown in Fig. 1.

VEGF plasma concentration in patients of Cluster 1 tended to increase from the 1st to the 7th day (the average value on the 1st day was 142.4 ± 58.2 pg/mL, on the 7th day it was 179.8 ± 110.0 pg/mL), see Fig. 2.

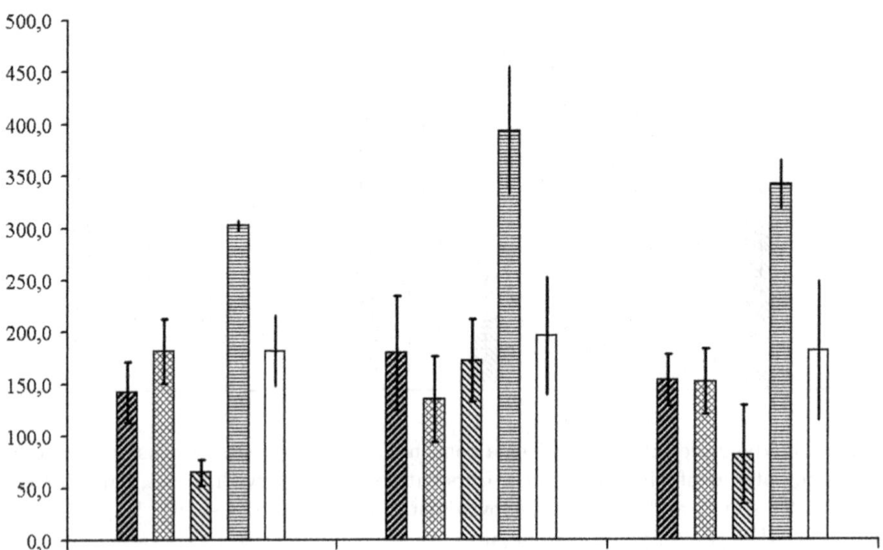

Fig. 2. The dynamics of VEGF plasma concentration in the patients. Bars hatched right show Cluster 1, bars hatched left show Cluster 2, bars hatched horizontally show Cluster 3, cross-hatched bars show Cluster 4 and white bars show the patients not included in any cluster. Vertical axis shows the concentration of VEGF in blood plasma, in pg/mL.

3.2 Cluster 2

Cluster 2 comprised 22 patients (13 men and 9 women) with an average age of 65 years [42–84 years]. All patients in the cluster, except one, suffered from arterial hypertension. Atrial fibrillation was diagnosed in 5 out of 22 patients; stenosing atherosclerosis of brachiocephalic arteries was also found in 5 patients. The number of smokers in Cluster 2 was significantly higher than in Cluster 1 (11 of 22 patients). Among the ischemic stroke subtypes according to the TOAST criteria, the atherothrombotic subtype also prevailed, however, the percent of lacunar ischemic stroke was also high (7 patients out of 22).

Cluster 2 patients were characterized by a milder course of ischemic stroke, a favorable outcome, and a good rehabilitation prognosis on the 21st day from the admission. Upon admission, the neurologic deficit was assessed as mild (NIHSS score 5–12) in 18 patients, moderate (NIHSS score 13–16) in 4 patients. On day 21, the neurological deficit was assessed as mild (NIHSS score 0–11) in all 22 patients. A remarkable fact is the peak growth of BDNF plasma concentration on the 7th day of hospital stay, with an increase of 194.56 to 269.11 % when calculated according to average indicators, compared with the concentration on the 1st day, see Fig. 1. VEGF plasma concentration in the patients of Cluster 2 tended to decrease from the 1st to the 7th day (average value on the 1st day was 181.3 ± 61.2 pg/mL, on the 7th day it was 135.5 ± 82.0 pg/mL), see Fig. 2.

3.3 Clusters 3 and 4

Cluster 3 and Cluster 4 included 4 and 3 patients, respectively, which casts discredit on their significance from a clinical point of view. Another possible reason for the small number of patients included in these clusters is the small initial database: expansion of the database can clarify the role of these clusters in the overall picture. However, there is a continuing trend in the correlation of the dynamics of BDNF concentration on day 7 in combination with extremely high VEGF plasma concentrations and the unfavorable course of ischemic stroke in patients from Cluster 4, see. Figure 2. Neurological symptoms were assessed as moderate stroke on admission (NIHSS score 12–18); on day 21 there was no significant regression of symptoms, as well as no change in the NIHSS score (12–20 points).

Also, 8 out of 56 patients were not included in any of the 4 clusters. All patients in this group suffered from arterial hypertension, 3 patients had stenosing atherosclerosis of brachiocephalic arteries, 2 patients were smokers. Neurological deficit on admission was assessed as mild in 5 patients (NIHSS score 3–11), moderate in 3 patients (NIHSS score 13–14). On day 21, all patients had a mild neurological deficit (NIHSS score 2–11). Among this group of patients, there was a relationship between the concentration of BDNF and VEGF and the clinical course of ischemic stroke: a decrease in the total NIHSS score by more than 4 (from 4 to 8 points) was observed only in those patients who showed an increase in BDNF concentration in combination with a simultaneous decrease in VEGF plasma concentration.

The clusters described above were revealed by nonlinear statistics, namely, by elastic map method [45]. Identified clusters had to be checked for distinguishability. There are various criteria of that latter [45]; we used the simplest but effective methods of linear statistics: these are the mentioned above Wilcoxon and Friedman criteria. The values of the significance levels of the Friedman criterion for all clusters for BDNF were 0.022, 0.050 and 0.174 on days 1, 7 and 21, respectively. The same values for VEGF were 0.039, 0.039 and 0.472, respectively.

Comparison of clusters by the Wilcoxon test revealed significant differences in VEGF values in patients included from Clusters 1 and 2 on the first day of the study (significance level was 0.033). Similar differences were observed on day 7 in patients of both Clusters 1 and 2, and Clusters 2 and 3; significance levels were 0.018 and 0.049, respectively. Conspicuous is the fact that on day 21 of the study, the indices in patients included in various clusters did not differ at all.

The BDNF indicator had different dynamics: on the first day of the study, no significant differences were found between the values in patients from all three clusters. However, on day 7, differences were found between patients from Clusters 1 and 2, the corresponding significance level was zero. Comparison of BDNF values on day 21 of the study also revealed differences between patients in Clusters 1 and 2 (significance level was 0.046).

4 Discussion and Conclusion

Studies of changes in the BDNF plasma concentration in the acute period of ischemic stroke present conflicting results [16,17]. Study data on the correlation degree of BDNF concentration with the severity of neurological deficit are different [17,20]. The role of BDNF in outcome prediction of ischemic stroke remains unclear.

We show that dynamic changes of BDNF concentration in the peracute and acute period of ischemic stroke (for example, on the day of admission) are of prognostic value, rather than their specific values. A growth of BDNF plasma concentration on the 7th day from stroke onset relative to the concentration on the first day was reliably associated with a better outcome of the acute period of ischemic stroke and lower scores on the NIHSS and Rankin scales.

VEGF is a powerful stimulator of angiogenesis, providing the development of new vascular collaterals to deliver oxygen and nutrients to the site of cerebral infarction. However, taking into account the ability of VEGF to increase vascular permeability and cerebral edema [21], one can hypothesize that an extremely high concentration of VEGF in the plasma of patients in the peracute period indicates a less favorable prognosis of motor function recovery.

An extremely high concentration of VEGF (more than 260 pg/mL) on days 1 and 7 from ischemic stroke onset was reliably associated with a worse outcome of ischemic stroke on day 21 and a less favorable rehabilitation prognosis. This is probably due to the predominance of the effects of increased vascular permeability over the effects of angiogenesis induction in conditions of high VEGF plasma concentration in the peracute period of ischemic stroke.

Thus, the serial measurement of the plasma concentration of trophic growth factors in patients with ischemic stroke is a rather simple, reliable and minimally invasive method for the assessment of dynamics of peracute and acute periods of ischemic stroke, as well as a tool for early prediction of the stroke outcome.

Acknowledgements. The work was supported by the State Assignment for Research issued by the Ministry of Public Health of the Russian Federation (2018–2020).

References

1. Kim, G., Kim, E.: The effects of antecedent exercise on motor function recovery and brain-derived neurotrophic factor expression after focal cerebral ischemia in rats. J. Phys. Ther. Sci. **25**(5), 553–556 (2013)
2. Skvortsova, V., Evzelman, M.: Ischemic stroke, p. 404 (2006). (in Russian)

3. Emanueli, C., Schratzberger, P., Kirchmair, R., Madeddu, P.: Paracrine control of vascularization and neurogenesis by neurotrophins. Br. J. Pharmacol. **140**(4), 614–619 (2003)
4. Huang, E.J., Reichardt, L.F.: Neurotrophins: roles in neuronal development and function. Annu. Rev. Neurosci. **24**(1), 677–736 (2001)
5. Roux, P.P., Barker, P.A.: Neurotrophin signaling through the p75 neurotrophin receptor. Prog. Neurobiol. **67**(3), 203–233 (2002)
6. Casoli, T., Giuli, C., Balietti, M., Giorgetti, B., Solazzi, M., Fattoretti, P.: Effect of cognitive training on the expression of brain-derived neurotrophic factor in lymphocytes of mild cognitive impairment patients. Rejuvenation Res. **17**(2), 235–238 (2014)
7. Sartorius, A., et al.: Correlations and discrepancies between serum and brain tissue levels of neurotrophins after electroconvulsive treatment in rats. Pharmacopsychiatry **42**(06), 270–276 (2009)
8. Gottlieb, M., Bonova, P., Danielisova, V., Nemethova, M., Burda, J., Cizkova, D.: Brain-derived neurotrophic factor blood levels in two models of transient brain ischemia in rats. Gen. Physiol. Biophys. **32**, 139–142 (2013)
9. Wang, J., et al.: Low serum levels of brain-derived neurotrophic factor were associated with poor short-term functional outcome and mortality in acute ischemic stroke. Mol. Neurobiol. **54**(9), 7335–7342 (2017). https://doi.org/10.1007/s12035-016-0236-1
10. Rodier, M., et al.: Relevance of post-stroke circulating BDNF levels as a prognostic biomarker of stroke outcome. Impact of rt-PA treatment. PLoS ONE **10**(10), e0140668 (2015)
11. Berretta, A., Tzeng, Y.C., Clarkson, A.N.: Post-stroke recovery: the role of activity-dependent release of brain-derived neurotrophic factor. Expert. Rev. Neurother. **14**(11), 1335–1344 (2014)
12. Madinier, A., et al.: Ipsilateral versus contralateral spontaneous post-stroke neuroplastic changes: involvement of BDNF? Neuroscience **231**, 169–181 (2013)
13. Clarkson, A.N., Overman, J.J., Zhong, S., Mueller, R., Lynch, G., Carmichael, S.T.: AMPA receptor-induced local brain-derived neurotrophic factor signaling mediates motor recovery after stroke. J. Neurosci. **31**(10), 3766–3775 (2011)
14. Schäbitz, W., et al.: Intravenous brain-derived neurotrophic factor reduces infarct size and counterregulates Bax and Bcl-2 expression after temporary focal cerebral ischemia. Stroke **31**(9), 2212–2216 (2000)
15. Schäbitz, W.R., et al.: Intravenous brain-derived neurotrophic factor enhances poststroke sensorimotor recovery and stimulates neurogenesis. Stroke **38**(7), 2165–2172 (2007)
16. Di Lazzaro, V., et al.: BDNF plasma levels in acute stroke. Neurosci. Lett. **422**(2), 128–130 (2007)
17. Béjot, Y., Mossiat, C., Giroud, M., Prigent-Tessier, A., Marie, C.: Circulating and brain BDNF levels in stroke rats. Relevance to clinical studies. PLoS ONE **6**(12), e29405 (2011)
18. Sun, J., Ke, Z., Yip, S.P., Hu, X.l., Zheng, X.x., Tong, K.y.: Gradually increased training intensity benefits rehabilitation outcome after stroke by BDNF upregulation and stress suppression. BioMed Res. Int. **2014**, 8 (2014). https://doi.org/10.1155/2014/925762. Article ID 925762. PMCID: PMC4090448. PMID: 25045713
19. Senger, D.R., Galli, S.J., Dvorak, A.M., Perruzzi, C.A., Harvey, V.S., Dvorak, H.F.: Tumor cells secrete a vascular permeability factor that promotes accumulation of ascites fluid. Science **219**(4587), 983–985 (1983)

20. Mărgăritescu, O., Pirici, D., Mărgăritescu, C.: VEGF expression in human brain tissue after acute ischemic stroke. Rom. J. Morphol. Embryol. **52**(4), 1283–1292 (2011)
21. Zhang, Z.G., et al.: VEGF enhances angiogenesis and promotes blood-brain barrier leakage in the ischemic brain. J. Clin. Investig. **106**(7), 829–838 (2000)
22. Gerber, H.P., et al.: Vascular endothelial growth factor regulates endothelial cell survival through the phosphatidylinositol 32-kinase/Akt signal transduction pathway requirement for Flk-1/KDR activation. J. Biol. Chem. **273**(46), 30336–30343 (1998)
23. Pedram, A., Razandi, M., Levin, E.R.: Extracellular signal-regulated protein kinase/Jun kinase cross-talk underlies vascular endothelial cell growth factor-induced endothelial cell proliferation. J. Biol. Chem. **273**(41), 26722–26728 (1998)
24. Hirashima, M.: Regulation of endothelial cell differentiation and arterial specification by VEGF and Notch signaling. Anat. Sci. Int. **84**(3), 95–101 (2009). https://doi.org/10.1007/s12565-009-0026-1
25. Sentilhes, L., et al.: Vascular endothelial growth factor and its high-affinity receptor (VEGFR-2) are highly expressed in the human forebrain and cerebellum during development. J. Neuropathol. Exp. Neurol. **69**(2), 111–128 (2010)
26. Svensson, B., et al.: Vascular endothelial growth factor protects cultured rat hippocampal neurons against hypoxic injury via an antiexcitotoxic, caspase-independent mechanism. J. Cereb. Blood Flow Metab. **22**(10), 1170–1175 (2002)
27. Yang, J., Yao, Y., Chen, T., Zhang, T.: VEGF ameliorates cognitive impairment in in vivo and in vitro ischemia via improving neuronal viability and function. Neuromolecular Med. **16**(2), 376–388 (2014). https://doi.org/10.1007/s12017-013-8284-4
28. Zhang, R., Zhang, Z., Zhang, L., Chopp, M.: Proliferation and differentiation of progenitor cells in the cortex and the subventricular zone in the adult rat after focal cerebral ischemia. Neuroscience **105**(1), 33–41 (2001)
29. Liu, F., Ni, J.J., Huang, J.J., Kou, Z.W., Sun, F.Y.: VEGF overexpression enhances the accumulation of phospho-S292 MeCP2 in reactive astrocytes in the adult rat striatum following cerebral ischemia. Brain Res. **1599**, 32–43 (2015)
30. Li, W.L., Fraser, J.L., Shan, P.Y., Zhu, J., Jiang, Y.J., Wei, L.: The role of VEGF/VEGFR2 signaling in peripheral stimulation-induced cerebral neurovascular regeneration after ischemic stroke in mice. Exp. Brain Res. **214**(4), 503 (2011). https://doi.org/10.1007/s00221-011-2849-y
31. Clayton, J.A., Chalothorn, D., Faber, J.E.: Vascular endothelial growth factor-a specifies formation of native collaterals and regulates collateral growth in ischemia. Circ. Res. **103**(9), 1027–1036 (2008)
32. Cao, L., et al.: VEGF links hippocampal activity with neurogenesis, learning and memory. Nat. Genet. **36**(8), 827 (2004)
33. Sluimer, J.C., Daemen, M.J.: Novel concepts in atherogenesis: angiogenesis and hypoxia in atherosclerosis. J. Pathol. J. Pathol. Soc. Gt. Br. Irel. **218**(1), 7–29 (2009)
34. van Bruggen, N., et al.: VEGF antagonism reduces edema formation and tissue damage after ischemia/reperfusion injury in the mouse brain. J. Clin. Investig. **104**(11), 1613–1620 (1999)
35. Li, Y.N., Pan, R., Qin, X.J., Yang, W.L., Qi, Z., Liu, W., Liu, K.J.: Ischemic neurons activate astrocytes to disrupt endothelial barrier via increasing vegf expression. J. Neurochem. **129**(1), 120–129 (2014)

36. Gunsilius, E., Petzer, A.L., Stockhammer, G., Kähler, C.M., Gastl, G.: Serial measurement of vascular endothelial growth factor and transforming growth factor-beta1 in serum of patients with acute ischemic stroke. Stroke **32**(1), 275–278 (2001)
37. Slevin, M., Krupinski, J., Slowik, A., Kumar, P., Szczudlik, A., Gaffney, J.: Serial measurement of vascular endothelial growth factor and transforming growth factor-β1 in serum of patients with acute ischemic stroke. Stroke **31**(8), 1863–1870 (2000)
38. Lee, S.C., Lee, K.Y., Kim, Y.J., Kim, S.H., Koh, S.H., Lee, Y.J.: Serum VEGF levels in acute ischaemic strokes are correlated with long-term prognosis. Eur. J. Neurol. **17**(1), 45–51 (2010)
39. Gonchar, I., Prudyvus, I., Stepanova, J.: Expression of vascular endothelial growth factor in patients with acute ischemic stroke. Zhurnal nevrologii i psihiatrii **113**(3), 25–29 (2013)
40. Gonchar, I., Stepanova, J.: Vascular endothelial growth factor in patients with non-cardioembolic brain infarction with mild atherosclerotic damage of cerebral arteries. Voennaya medicina **21**(4), 36–39 (2011)
41. Adams Jr., H.P., et al.: Classification of subtype of acute ischemic stroke. Definitions for use in a multicenter clinical trial. TOAST. Trial of org 10172 in acute stroke treatment. Stroke **24**(1), 35–41 (1993)
42. Navarro-Sobrino, M., et al.: A large screening of angiogenesis biomarkers and their association with neurological outcome after ischemic stroke. Atherosclerosis **216**(1), 205–211 (2011)
43. Okazaki, H., Beppu, H., Mizutani, K., Okamoto, S., Sonoda, S.: Changes in serum growth factors in stroke rehabilitation patients and their relation to hemiparesis improvement. J. Stroke Cerebrovasc. Dis. **23**(6), 1703–1708 (2014)
44. Fukunaga, K.: Introduction to Statistical Pattern Recognition. Academic Press, London (1990)
45. Gorban, A.N., Zinovyev, A.Y.: Fast and user-friendly non-linear principal manifold learning by method of elastic maps. In: 2015 IEEE International Conference on Data Science and Advanced Analytics, DSAA 2015, Campus des Cordeliers, Paris, France, 19–21 October 2015, pp. 1–9 (2015)

Analyzing the Immune Response of Neoepitopes for Personalized Vaccine Design

Iker Malaina[1(✉)], Leire Legarreta[1], Mª Dolores Boyano[2], Santos Alonso[3], Ildefonso M. De la Fuente[1,4], and Luis Martinez[1]

[1] Department of Mathematics, University of the Basque Country UPV/EHU, 48080 Bilbao, Spain
{iker.malaina, leire.legarreta, mtpmadei, luis.martinez}@ehu.eus

[2] Department of Cell Biology and Histology, University of the Basque Country UPV/EHU, Bilbao, Spain
lola.boyano@ehu.eus

[3] Department of Genetics, Anthropology and Animal Physiology, University of the Basque Country UPV/EHU, Bilbao, Spain
santos.alonso@ehu.eus

[4] Department of Nutrition, CEBAS-CSIC Institute, Espinardo University Campus, Murcia, Spain

Abstract. In the last few years, the importance of neoepitopes for the development of personalized antitumor vaccines has increased remarkably. This kind of epitopes are considered to generate a strong immune reaction, while their non-mutated version, which sometimes differs only in a single amino-acid, does not generate a response at all. In order to study if, regardless the immune tolerance, neoepitopes are quantitatively more immunogenic than the original strings, we have obtained samples of mutated and non-mutated epitopes of six patients with cutaneous melanoma in different stages, and then we have compared them. More precisely, we have used several bioinformatic tools to study certain properties of the epitopes such as the HLA binding affinity of classes I and II, and found that some of them are in fact increased in their mutated versions, which supports the hypothesis, and also reinforces the use of neoepitopes for cancer vaccine design.

Keywords: Neoepitope · Vaccine design · Bioinformatics · HLA immunogenicity

1 Introduction

In the last few years, personalized antitumoral vaccination has been increasingly proposed as a novel and encouraging approach to treat several types of cancers [1–4]. The main reasons for choosing personalized vaccination against cancer cells is that, on one hand, tumors contain a large amount of mutations, and on the other hand, it is that in a patient's tumor, approximately 95% of the mutations seem to be unique to that tumor [5]. Therefore, these mutations make ideal oncological targets for efficiently targeting individual tumors [6], and more precisely, for personalized vaccination.

I. Rojas et al. (Eds.): IWBBIO 2020, LNBI 12108, pp. 40–48, 2020.
https://doi.org/10.1007/978-3-030-45385-5_4

Nevertheless, even if the amount of mutations in tumors is considerable, in order to make an effective vaccine, first we need to distinguish between the mutations that only appear in the tumor, and the ones that happen in the rest of our non-oncogenic cells. Here is where we introduce the concept of neoepitope, which is a class of peptide which bounds to the Major Histocompatibility Complex (MHC, that in humans was denoted as HLA, referring to Human Leucocytic Antigen) and emerges from tumor-specific mutations [7]. This kind of epitopes have not been encountered before by the immune system, and as a consequence, the system will not apply the tolerance mechanisms against them [8].

However, even if targeting neoepitopes has resulted in clinical benefits [9, 10], when we consider the whole mutation spectrum of a tumor (known as mutanome), the amount of potential neoepitopes is too vast, and if we pick them blindly when we develop our vaccine, there is no guarantee of obtaining a highly immunogenic response. Generating an immune response against a mutated peptide depends directly on the capacity of the patient's HLA to bind the neoepitope and present it to lymphocytes [11], and therefore, selecting those epitopes which will bind more effectively the cells of the immune system seems like a reasonable first criterion.

In order to do this, and since the individual evaluation of every neoepitope in a tumor is too expensive in both time and cost, there have been developed several bioinformatic tools for *in silico* prediction of immunogenicity, HLA-1 and HLA-2 binding affinity, TAP transport, etc. [12–14]. These tools have been widely used to identify potential epitopes [15], but as a consequence an inevitable question arises: since a mutated peptide is capable of generating a strong immune response while their non-mutated version, which sometimes differs only in a single amino-acid (aa), does not generate a response at all, are these tools capable of quantitatively detect these differences? Or in other words, is it true that mutated versions of peptides are more immunogenic than the non-mutated ones, according to bioinformatic tools?

With the aim of giving response to this question, first, we have experimentally sequenced part of the mutanome of six patients affected with cutaneous melanoma. Cutaneous melanoma is a type of skin cancer that is located in the epidermis, and it arises from the pigment-containing cells known as melanocytes [16]. In Spain, the percentage of cases yearly increases by 7%, and happens more often in women (corresponding to the 2.7% of the cancers) than in men (where it represents the 1.5% of the male cancers). More importantly, besides being considered very invasive, and metastatic [17], this kind of cancer presents a lot of mutations, which makes it a good candidate for addressing our problem.

Secondly, after identifying the amino-acid sequence of the peptide corresponding to the detected DNA mutations, we have studied the predicted HLA binding affinity of classes I and II with the IEDB predicting tool [13] of the total of 152 potential neoepitopes, and their respective non-mutated versions.

Finally, we have compared both groups and our results have indicated that bioinformatic tools support the hypothesis indicating that neoepitopes are more immunogenic than the original strings, which as a consequence reinforces the use of neoepitopes for cancer vaccine design.

2 Methodology

In order to analyze *in silico* characteristics of potential neoepitopes, the first step was to obtain tumor samples of patients with cutaneous melanoma. Tumor biopsies of six patients from Cruces University Hospital and Basurto Hospital (Spain) were obtained, and sequenced. With the objective of obtaining sufficient mutational diversity (and therefore an advanced stage of tumor development), but also a heterogeneous staging sample (where different severities of tumor could be analyzed), we selected cases with several cancer stages, but without metastasis. Particularly, the stage of the studied cases was: one IB (up to 2 mm thick without ulceration), one IIA (from 1 to 2 mm thick with ulceration or from 2.01 to 4 mm thick without ulceration), two IIB (from 2.01 to 4 mm thick with ulceration or greater than 4 mm thick without ulceration), and two IIC (greater than 4 mm thick with ulceration) [18].

Next, since performing an analysis of the whole mutanome of patients was out of our scope, we targeted the regions with most variability in this kind of cancer, which is related to the regions which codify proteins such as BRAF, NRAS, MAP2K1 or MAP2K2 [19, 20]. In order to select only the mutations appearing in the tumor and discard the ones derived as mistakes of normal cellular division (and present in non-oncogenic cells), we also sequenced regular blood cells and studied their mutations, and afterwards, we only kept as mutation candidates the ones appearing solely in the tumor.

Once mutations that potentially could originate neoepitopes were detected, the next step was to define the length of the neoepitopes that we were going to consider, or in other words, the amount of amino-acids around the mutated base (and its respective amino-acid). There are several approaches regarding this issue, for example, Sharin et al. [3] used 27-mer peptides with the mutation in the center (i.e., in the 14th position), while Ott et al. [21] used variable lengths, ranging from 15 to 30, but maintaining the mutation in the center. One reason to maintain the mutation in the center and these range of lengths, is that class I MHC usually fit epitopes of 8-9-mer lengths while class II MHC attach epitopes of 12-15-mer lengths, and regardless the processing of the antigens presented by the Antigen Presenting Cells (APC) such as dendritic cells or macrophages [22], the mutation will likely be included in one of the presented peptides. In our case, we considered epitopes of length 17, with the mutation in the 8th amino-acid. This way, on one hand, if we perform a sliding window for peptides with length 9 (which has been used traditionally as standard length for HLA-I restricted T-cell epitopes [23]), the mutation will be included in all of them. On the other hand, this length is long enough to allow us to estimate computationally the HLA-II binding affinity.

After fixing the potential neoepitopes, and in order to evaluate the binding affinity of both classes, since HLA complexes are highly polymorphic and vary from each patient, we also sequenced the genes responsible for coding the MHC, which are located in the 6th chromosome [24], and identified the allele variants corresponding to each patient. In Tables 1 and 2, we depict, divided by patient, the obtained HLA alleles of class I and II respectively.

Table 1. In the first row, the patient number; in the second, the first or second allele (one obtained from the father and the other one from the mother); in the rest of the rows, the respective class I HLA alleles: HLA-A, HLA-B and HLA-C.

HLA-I	1st Patient		2nd Patient		3rd Patient		4th Patient		5th Patient		6th Patient	
	1st	2nd	1st	2nd	1st	2nd	1st	2nd	1st	2nd	1st	2nd
A	01:01:01	02:01:01	02:01:01	32:01:01	24:02:01	32:01:01	02:01:01	11:01:01	24:02:01	24:02:01	03:01:01	26:01:01
B	08:01:01	44:27:01	35:11:01	51:01:01	07:02:01	51:01:01	27:05:02	40:01:02	35:01:01	40:01:03	07:02:01	18:01:01
C	07:01:01	07:04:01	02:02:02	04:01:01	07:02:01	15:02:01	01:02:01	03:04:01	03:04:01	04:01:01	02:02:02	07:02:01

Finally, we estimated the MHC class I and II binding affinity predictions with the respective tools of the Immune Epitope Database Analysis Resource [13]. The prediction method used was "IEDB recommended 2.22", the selected species "human", and in length, for class I prediction we selected "all lengths" (which ranged from 8 to 14), while for class II we selected "default", (which fixed the epitope length to 15).

Table 2. In the first row, the patient number; in the second, the first or second allele (one obtained from the father and the other one from the mother); in the rest of the rows, the respective class II HLA alleles: HLA-DPA1, HLA-DPB1, HLA-DQA1, HLA-DQB1, HLA-DRB1, HLA-DRB3, HLA-DRB4 and HLA-DRB5.

HLA-II	1st Patient		2nd Patient		3rd Patient		4th Patient		5th Patient		6th Patient	
	1st	2nd	1st	2nd	1st	2nd	1st	2nd	1st	2nd	1st	2nd
DPA1	01:03:01	02:01:01	01:03:01	01:03:01	01:03:01	01:03:01	01:03:01	01:03:01	01:03:01	01:03:01	01:03:01	02:01:01
DPB1	02:01:02	14:01:01	02:01:02	04:01:01	--:01:--	--:01:--	04:01:01	06:01:--	04:01:01	04:01:01	02:01:02	11:01:01
DQA1	01:02:02	01:04:01	01:02:01	05:05:01	01:02:01	01:03:01	03:01:01	04:01:01	01:01:01	04:01:01	01:03:01	05:05:01
DQB1	05:02:01	05:03:01	03:01:01	06:02:01	06:02:01	06:03:01	03:02:01	04:02:01	04:02:01	05:01:01	03:01:01	06:03:01
DRB1	16:01:01	14:54:01	15:01:01	11:04:01	15:01:01	13:01:01	08:01:--	04:04:01	01:01:01	08:02:01	--:--:--	--:--:--
DRB3	02:02:01	--:--:--	02:02:01	--:--:--	01:01:02	--:--:--	--:--:--	--:--:--	--:--:--	--:--:--	01:01:02	01:01:02
DRB4	--:--:--	--:--:--	--:--:--	--:--:--	--:--:--	--:--:--	01:03:01	01:03:01	--:--:--	--:--:--	--:--:--	--:--:--
DRB5	02:02:--	--:--:--	01:01:01	--:--:--	01:01:01	--:--:--	--:--:--	--:--:--	--:--:--	--:--:--	--:--:--	--:--:--

3 Results

In order to compare the MHC binding affinity (correlated to the generated immune response [25]) of potential neoepitopes and their non-mutated version, we estimated the MHC class I and II binding affinity using the bioinformatic tools offered by IEDB [13] described in Methods section. After obtaining the estimations, following the recommendations from IEDB, we used the "percentile rank" variable to filter the potential binders from the ones that predictably would not be good binders. To cover most of the immune responses, IEDB recommends to select the strings with "percentile rank" of $\leq 1\%$ for MHC class I [26, 27], while for MHC class II the recommended "percentile rank" would be $\leq 10\%$. In Table 3, we depict the number of potential HLA-I and HLA-II binders, divided by patients, while in Fig. 1, we illustrate the distribution of these values in a box plot.

Table 3. Number of possible epitopes according to their predicted binding affinity, with "percentile rank" $\leq 1\%$ for MHC-I and $\leq 10\%$ for MHC-II, for both mutated (M) and non-mutated (NM) versions.

	1st patient	2nd patient	3rd patient	4th patient	5th patient	6th patient
HLA-I M	57	88	8	121	20	26
HLA-I NM	49	70	4	114	20	30
HLA-II M	51	229	26	144	47	21
HLA-II NM	45	193	22	118	33	22

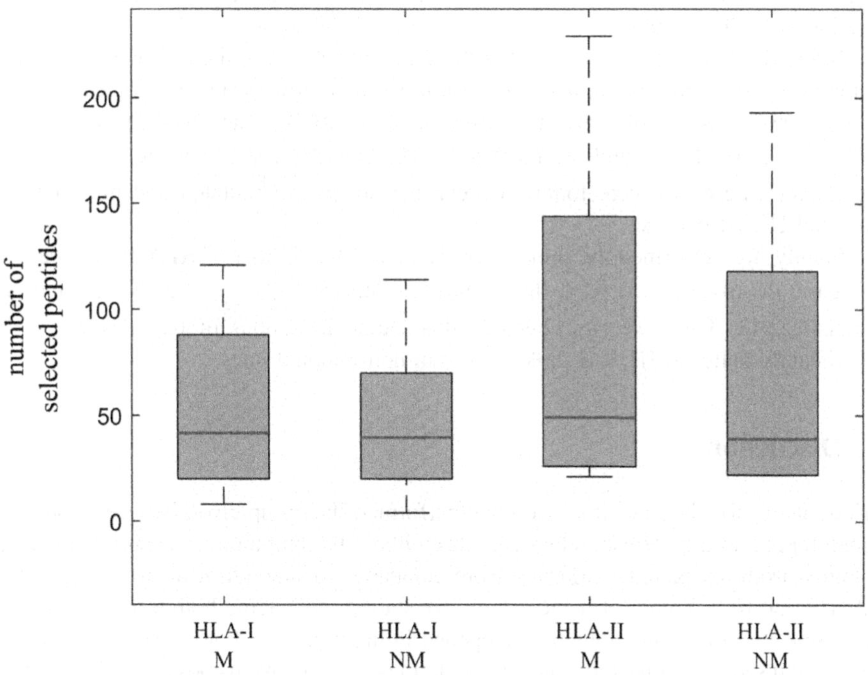

Fig. 1. Box plot of the number of peptides that pass the threshold. Box plot illustrating the distributions of the number of peptides that passed the respective cutoff points ($\leq 1\%$ for HLA-I and $\leq 10\%$ for HLA-II binding affinity). M indicates mutated peptides, while NM references the non-mutated ones. The maroon boxes represent the distribution of the central 50% of the values and the red lines represent the medians. The rest of the values are represented by the arms. (Color figure online)

Before studying the main hypothesis, we analyzed the relative percentages of each group. In the case of mutated peptides which would potentially bind HLA-I molecules, the average ± standard deviation was 0.69% ± 0.31%, ranging from 0.27% to 0.98%; for their non-mutated version, the results were 0.65% ± 0.36%, ranging from 0.14% to 1.13%; when HLA-II was analyzed, the mutated peptides were the 15.24% ± 2.96%, ranging from 10.63% to 19.88%; and finally the non-mutated ones were the 13.02% ± 2.93%, ranging from 9.38% to 16.75%.

Next, to verify the work hypothesis, i.e., to answer if is it true that the mutated versions of peptides are more immunogenic than the non-mutated ones, we performed two comparisons:

1. The first, studying if the number of predicted HLA-I mutated peptides is greater than the non-mutated amount.
2. The second, studying if the number of predicted HLA-II mutated peptides is greater than the non-mutated amount.

To make these comparisons, first we need to study if our variables are normally distributed. The p-values of the normality tests were 0.837, 0.978, 0.43 and 0.476, for HLA-I mutated, HLA-I non-mutated, HLA-II mutated and HLA-II non-mutated, respectively. Thus, normality was accepted in all cases, and we performed a paired T-test for each HLA couple.

Being the first null hypothesis that the difference between the average of mutated potential epitopes minus the average of non-mutated was greater than or equal to 0, with a significance of 5%, the p-value was 0.068, the confidence interval $CI^{0.95}_{\mu_1 \geq \mu_2} = (-0.74, \infty)$, and the t-statistic 1.78. Therefore, according to this data, no significant differences were found between the amount of mutated and non-mutated potential HLA-I peptides.

Finally, we performed the same comparison for the number of HLA-II peptides. In this case, the p-value was 0.03, the confidence interval $CI^{0.95}_{\mu_1 \geq \mu_2} = (2.44, \infty)$, and the t-statistic 2.43. Thus, we can conclude that mutated versions of peptides will bind significantly better to HLA-II molecules than non-mutated ones.

4 Discussion

In this work, for the first time, we have performed the comparison between potential neoepitopes and the corresponding peptides without the mutation, in experimental data obtained from six patients suffering from cutaneous melanoma in diverse stages (IB, IIA, IIB and IIC). To perform such study, we started sequencing both tumor and blood cells, selecting only mutations that happened in the tumor, and next, we identified the amino-acid sequence that surrounds the mutations, which gave us possible neoepitopes, for which we set the maximum length to 17aa. Then, we estimated the binding affinity for HLA classes I and II with the bioinformatic tools provided by IEDB, and for each case, enumerated the ones below the significance threshold.

Our results indicated that, even if the number of mutated strings (i.e., potential neoepitopes) presented higher binding affinity in almost every case, the difference was not significant when we compared HLA-I binding affinity (p-value: 0.068), while in the case of HLA-II, the number of mutated vs non-mutated was significantly bigger (p-value: 0.03). Thus, we consider that this study answers, at least partially, the question raised by the medical community, which considered that mutated versions of peptides are more immunogenic than the non-mutated ones.

However, we want to acknowledge that our sample size is relatively small (n = 6), and since the differences between the number of possible HLA binders are also small, we hypothesize that increasing the sample size would lead to more significance in the results, and even also to difference between HLA-I binding mutated and non-mutated candidates.

In summary, here, we have performed a comparison between potential neoepitopes and their respective original peptides, and found that the mutated ones have significantly more HLA-II binding affinity, which supports the hypothesis indicating that mutated strings are indeed more immunogenic than their more common versions.

Acknowledgements. This work was supported by Basque Government funding (IT1974-16, KK-2018/00090), and by the UPV/EHU and Basque Center of Applied Mathematics (US18/21)

References

1. Vormehr, M., Diken, M., Türeci, Ö., Sahin, U., Kreiter, S.: Personalized neo-epitope vaccines for cancer treatment. In: Theobald, M. (ed.) Current Immunotherapeutic Strategies in Cancer. RRCR, vol. 214, pp. 153–167. Springer, Cham (2020). https://doi.org/10.1007/978-3-030-23765-3_5
2. Vermaelen, K.: Vaccine strategies to improve anti-cancer cellular immune responses. Front. Immunol. **10**, 8 (2019). https://doi.org/10.3389/fimmu.2019.00008
3. Sahin, U., et al.: Personalized RNA mutanome vaccines mobilize poly-specific therapeutic immunity against cancer. Nature **547**, 7662 (2017)
4. Kakimi, K., Karasaki, T., Matsushita, H., Sugie, T.: Advances in personalized cancer immunotherapy. Breast Cancer **24**, 16–24 (2017)
5. Stratton, M.R.: Exploring the genomes of cancer cells: progress and promise. Science **331**, 1553–1558 (2011)
6. Kreiter, S., Castle, J.C., Türeci, Ö., Sahin, U.: Targeting the tumor mutanome for personalized vaccination therapy. Oncoimmunology **1**, 768–769 (2012)
7. Leclerc, M., et al.: Recent advances in lung cancer immunotherapy: input of T-cell epitopes associated with impaired peptide processing. Front. Immunol. **10**, 1505 (2019)
8. Vormehr, M., Türeci, Ö., Sahin, U.: Harnessing tumor mutations for truly individualized cancer vaccines. Annu. Rev. Med. **70**, 395–407 (2019)
9. Tanyi, J.L., et al.: Personalized cancer vaccine effectively mobilizes antitumor T cell immunity in ovarian cancer. Sci. Transl. Med. **10**, eaao5931 (2018)
10. Hu, Z., Ott, P.A., Wu, C.J.: Towards personalized, tumour-specific, therapeutic vaccines for cancer. Nat. Rev. Immunol. **18**, 168 (2018)
11. Fritsch, E.F., Rajasagi, M., Ott, P.A., Brusic, V., Hacohen, N., Wu, C.J.: HLA-binding properties of tumor neoepitopes in humans. Cancer Immunol. Res. **2**, 522–529 (2014)
12. Lundegaard, C., Lund, O., Nielsen, M.: Prediction of epitopes using neural network-based methods. J. Immunol. Methods **374**, 26–34 (2011)

13. Zhang, Q., et al.: Immune epitope database analysis resource (IEDB-AR). Nucl. Acids Res. **36**, 513–518 (2008)
14. Soria-Guerra, R.E., Nieto-Gomez, R., Govea-Alonso, D.O., Rosales-Mendoza, S.: An overview of bioinformatics tools for epitope prediction: implications on vaccine development. J. Biomed. Inform. **53**, 405–414 (2015)
15. Martínez, L., Milanič, M., Malaina, I., Álvarez, C., Pérez, M.B., Ildefonso, M.: Weighted lambda superstrings applied to vaccine design. PLoS ONE **14**, e0211714 (2019)
16. Malaina, I., et al.: Metastasis of cutaneous melanoma: risk factors, detection and forecasting. In: Rojas, I., Ortuño, F. (eds.) IWBBIO 2018. LNCS, vol. 10813, pp. 511–519. Springer, Cham (2018). https://doi.org/10.1007/978-3-319-78723-7_44
17. Miller, A.J., Mihm, M.C.: Melanoma. N. Engl. J. Med. **355**, 51–65 (2006)
18. Thompson, J.A.: The revised american joint committee on cancer staging system for melanoma. In: Seminars in Oncology, vol. 29, pp. 361–369. WB Saunders (2002)
19. Edlundh-Rose, E., et al.: NRAS and BRAF mutations in melanoma tumours in relation to clinical characteristics: a study based on mutation screening by pyrosequencing. Melanoma Res. **16**, 471–478 (2006)
20. Nikolaev, S.I., et al.: Exome sequencing identifies recurrent somatic MAP2K1 and MAP2K2 mutations in melanoma. Nat. Genet. **44**, 133 (2012)
21. Ott, P.A., et al.: An immunogenic personal neoantigen vaccine for patients with melanoma. Nature **547**, 217 (2017)
22. Mann, E.R., Li, X.: Intestinal antigen-presenting cells in mucosal immune homeostasis: crosstalk between dendritic cells, macrophages and B-cells. World J. Gastroenterol. WJG **20**, 9653 (2014)
23. Trolle, T., et al.: The length distribution of class I–restricted T cell epitopes is determined by both peptide supply and MHC allele–specific binding preference. J. Immunol. **196**, 1480–1487 (2016)
24. López-Martínez, A., Chávez-Muñoz, C., Granados, J.: Función biológica del complejo principal de histocompatibilidad. Revista de investigación clínica **57**, 132–141 (2005)
25. Sette, A., et al.: The relationship between class I binding affinity and immunogenicity of potential cytotoxic T cell epitopes. J. Immunol. **153**, 5586–5592 (1994)
26. Moutaftsi, M., et al.: A consensus epitope prediction approach identifies the breadth of murine T CD8 + -cell responses to vaccinia virus. Nat. Biotechnol. **24**, 817 (2006)
27. Kotturi, M.F., et al.: The CD8+ T-cell response to lymphocytic choriomeningitis virus involves the L antigen: uncovering new tricks for an old virus. J. Virol. **81**, 4928–4940 (2007)

A Data Integration Approach for Detecting Biomarkers of Breast Cancer Survivability

Huy Quang Pham[1,2(✉)], Luis Rueda[1], and Alioune Ngom[1]

[1] School of Computer Science, University of Windsor, Windsor, ON, Canada
{pham118, lrueda, angom}@uwindsor.ca
[2] University of Dalat, Dalat, Vietnam

Abstract. We introduce a network-based approach to identify subnets of functionally-related genes for predicting 5-year survivability of breast cancer patients treated with chemotherapy, hormone therapy, and a combination of these. A gene expression dataset and a protein-protein interaction network are integrated to construct a weighted graph, where edge weight expresses the predictability of the two corresponding genes in predicting the class. We propose a scoring criterion to measure the density of a weighted sub-graph, which is also an estimation of its predictive power. Thus, we can identify an optimally-dense sub-network for each seed gene, and then evaluate that sub-network by classification method. Finally, among the sub-networks whose classification performance greater than a given threshold, we search for an optimal set of sub-networks that can further improve classification performance via a voting scheme. We significantly improved the results of existing approaches. For each type of treatment, our best prediction model can reach 85% accuracy or more. Many selected sub-networks used to construct the voting models contain breast/other cancer-related genes including SP1, TP53, MYC, NOG, and many more, providing pieces of evidence for down-stream analysis.

Keywords: Breast cancer biomarkers · Survivability prediction · Network-based classification · Data integration · Sub-network selection · Sub-network biomarkers

1 Introduction

Breast cancer is a common disease in women. Approximately one in eight women commit with breast cancer over their lifetime [1]. According to SEER data for US female patients from 2007–2013 [2], the 5-year-survival rate was 99% for patients with tumors located only in the breast and the rate declined to 85% if the tumors spread to regional lymph nodes, and dropped to 26% if breast cancer becomes metastatic. In Canada, about 30% of women patients of earlier stages are prone to develop metastatic breast cancer [3]. Chemotherapy or hormone therapy can reduce the risk of distant metastases by one third, but still, 70–80% of patients receiving this treatment would have survived without it [4]. According to the authors of [5], more than 75% of breast cancers patients have ER+, but their responses to therapy vary significantly. This evidence suggests that diagnosis and prognosis factors still need to be improved for better treatments.

I. Rojas et al. (Eds.): IWBBIO 2020, LNBI 12108, pp. 49–60, 2020.
https://doi.org/10.1007/978-3-030-45385-5_5

Machine learning (ML) has been applied to predict the survivability of breast cancer patients or to define groups of patients who share some special characteristics. Some studies have used only clinical and histological information of the patients to learn a suitable classification model that achieves considerable high accuracy [6]. Others have relied on genomic data such as RNA or DNA sequencing, gene expression (GE), mutations, copy number variations (CNV) or copy number alterations (CNA). One of the challenges in this scenario is that the number of features in genomic data is usually far larger than the number of samples, though many of them are redundant. This problem, known as the curse of dimensionality, might prevent even the state-of-the-art algorithms from achieving good results. In this regard, feature selection approaches are usually applied to avoid over-fitting, and extract the most informative subsets of features [7, 8]. Then, the selected features are, in turn, considered as potential biomarkers.

In the last two decades, network-based machine learning approaches have gained a lot of interest in the research community, since they take existing relations among genes into account when selecting relevant biomarkers [9–13]. These methods often integrate primary data, e.g., GE, with one or more secondary network-based data expressing functional relationships among genes such as co-expression networks, cellular pathway maps, gene regulatory networks, protein-protein interaction networks or other "omics" data. They aim at identifying the most discriminative subset of interacting genes for prediction, called sub-network (or subnet, for short) biomarkers. Once integrating such useful knowledge into the learning process, the results might be more consistent with current known mechanism of the disease, or more robust to be considered as biomarkers. As the interaction network can involve thousands of nodes and millions of edges, searching for subnet biomarkers has been a computational challenge. Different scoring functions have been proposed to weight the nodes, edges, and subnets, and different data integration approaches have been proposed to identify relevant subnet biomarkers [11, 14, 15]. In the following paragraphs, we briefly summarize some network-based machine learning approaches that make use of the protein-protein interactions, as well as one of our previous studies on breast cancer survivability prediction.

In [9], a subnet is called a meta-gene, and its expression value for each patient is calculated as the average expressions of the genes in the subnet for that patient. They aim to transform the GE data into a meta-gene data and conduct the classification on the meta-gene data. The key is to identify the informative subnets. A subnet can be initialized by a seed gene, and then gradually extend it to its neighbors until some conditions based on the mutual information are met. As genes of a subnet might correlate to the response variable in opposite directions, the authors of [10] proposed the Direction Aware Average operator to compute meta-gene expressions and obtained better result than the method in [9].

In [12], the authors combined a protein-protein interaction network and a gene-gene co-regulation network, GGCRN, induced from brain tissue in EQTL data. A pair of genes is considered co-regulated if they share a significant proportion of common single-nucleotide polymorphisms. They applied a random walk with restart algorithm to find Alzheimer related candidate genes; 14 out of 29 known Alzheimer-related genes, have been used as source nodes and initialized with equal probabilities.

In [16], the authors developed classification models to predict the 5-year survivability of breast cancer patients treated with Paclitaxel under different circumstances, including combinations of hormone therapy and chemotherapy. A set of about 35 initial genes were selected by a machine learning method. Minimum Redundancy Maximum Relevance scores (mRMR [5]) were used to evaluate the subsets of genes, and random forest (RF) and support vector machine (SVM) with radial basis function kernel were used in a greedy search procedure to select a subset of informative genes among those 35 genes. That approach yielded fairly good accuracy in prediction for many cases. However, due to the imbalance of the classes in the datasets, the limited number of available genes, and other reasons, for some cases, the corresponding Matthews correlation coefficient (MCC) showed that the classifier was just slightly better than random, especially when RF was used.

In this paper, we introduce a network-based approach to identify subnet biomarkers for predicting 5-year survivability of breast cancer patients after treated with chemotherapy (CT), hormone therapy (HT), or at least one of them (chemotherapy or hormone therapy (CT_HT). GE and protein-protein interaction network data are integrated into a weighted interaction network, where the weights of the edges are computed via joint mutual information. We define a new density of a subnet in a weighted graph, which can also be interpreted as an estimation of the predictive ability of the subnet. Then, the true predictive power of the subnet is evaluated by SVM or RF. We also apply two techniques to reduce the effects of imbalanced data. The prediction results show that our approach outperforms the methods of [16]. Finally, we propose a greedy search to find a set of subnets that can even produce better prediction results than using the single best subnet. The MMCs for the best settings are about 0.68 or higher, while the accuracies are about 85% or higher. This implies that our model is effective in predicting breast cancer survivability while reducing the effect of imbalanced data.

2 Materials and Methods

GE datasets for the mentioned treatments were extracted from the breast cancer dataset used in [16] which contains GE of almost 2,000 patients with long-term clinical follow-up. The distribution of samples of the 5-year survivability for these datasets is given in Table 1. Protein-protein interactions were collected from the STRING database (version 10) and the Pathways Common database (version 9).

Table 1. Data distribution versus therapies

Dataset	Died before 5-years	Died after 5-years	# Samples	# Genes
CT	33	20	53	15293
HT	118	302	420	15293
CT_HT	169	335	504	15293

The protein-protein interaction network was converted to a gene-gene network (GGN) by mapping the proteins to their corresponding gene based on Entrez ID. After processing GGN is an undirected graph of 15,293 vertices and 290,328 edges.

We aim at searching for an optimal set of subnets of functionally-related genes that can result in better prediction than using any single subnet. Our proposed approach can be summarized as follows. First, we compute a weighted gene-gene network (WGGN), from the GGN and GE data, where the weight of the edge between two genes expresses the predictability of their combination. Second, we search for an optimally-dense subnet for each gene, based on the WGGN. The denser a subnet, the higher classification performance it may produce. Third, we evaluate the optimally-dense subnets by SVM and Random Forest and keep only the ones having MCC greater than a given threshold. Finally, we apply a greedy search to find a set of subnets that can together improve the classification results when voting for the survivability of the patients.

2.1 Generating the Gene-Gene Interaction Network

Given a gene expression dataset and a GGN, we can obtain a WGGN by assigning to each edge (X, Y) in the GGN a weight which is the join mutual information of (X, Y) and the class C [17], denoted as $I(X, Y; C)$. $I(X, Y; C)$ is calculated as in Eq. (1), based on gene expressions of X and Y, where, $I(Y; C)$ is the mutual information between Y and C and $I(X; C|Y)$ is the conditional mutual information between X and C given Y. The join mutual information expresses the ability of the combination of X and Y in predicting survivability. All edge weights are scaled to the range [0..1].

$$I(X, Y; C) = I(Y; C) + I(X; C|Y) \tag{1}$$

2.2 Searching for an Optimally-Dense Subnet for Each Seed Gene

In our approach, we assume that each gene in a subnet of n genes has, on average, $\sqrt{n-1}$ edges connecting to other genes in the subnet. Thus, given the class C, a subnet S of n genes ($n > 1$), which is a sub-graph of WGGN, and E, the set of edges in S, the density of S is calculated as in Eq. (2). This density function is an estimation of the predictive power of subnet S based on the weights of its edges. The denser the better. The numerator of Eq. (2) is the sum of the weights of the edges; while the denominator is the average number of edges in a subnet of n vertices.

$$density(S) = \frac{\sum_{(X,YB)\in E} I(Y, Y; C)}{0.5 \times n \times \sqrt{n-1}} \tag{2}$$

Practically, it is very difficult to find a polynomial-time function $f(n)$ ($f(n) \in O(n^m)$) that can fairly express the density of a sub-graph of n vertices in a weighted graph for different values of n, even if the edge weights are in the range [0..1]. When $m = 1$, the numerator of Eq. (2) and $f(n)$ increase linearly on the size of the subnet. However, the numerator tends to increase faster than the denominator if n gets large enough. Thus, the densest subnet for a seed gene tends to be the largest component of WGGN containing the seed gene. Meanwhile, when $m \geq 2$, $f(n)$ tends to increase much faster than the numerator when n gets larger. Thus, subnets of small size tend to be denser the subnets of large size. The function that we selected for the denominator of Eq. (2) speeds up the denominator slightly as compared to the case $m = 1$.

Algorithm 1. Finding an optimally-dense subnet for a seed gene

```
Input: a weighted graph GGN and a seed gene g.
Output: S, an optimally-dense subnet induced by g.
Begin
1. Initialize the subnet S by g.
2. Repeat step a and step b below to gradually extend
   S until its density cannot be improved:
   a. Identify the genes can be added to S which are
      the neighboring genes of any gene in S, according
      to the structure of GGN.
   b. Add to S the new gene that can improve the density
      of S the most.
End
```

We search for an optimally-dense subnet in WGGN for each seed gene as the Algorithm 1.

2.3 Evaluating the Predictive Power of a Subnet

For each subnet *S*, the GE data projected on the genes in *S* will be used to train and test a SVM (or RF) classifier, with a 5-fold cross-validation. The MCC of the classifier based on test sets is used to measure the quality of S, instead of the accuracy of the model. Because, MCC has been known to be a good measurement in evaluating the classifier learned from imbalanced data. We keep only the top subnets whose MCC is greater than or equal to the MCC obtained by the method of [16] for the same dataset.

To further deal with imbalanced data, we also implemented two other techniques. One of which is the Distribution Optimally Balanced Stratified Cross-Validation (DOB-SCV) technique proposed in [18]. It stratifies the "close-by" samples in the projected GE data into different folds, based on (the inverse of) the Euclidean distance between the projected GE profiles. The idea is to make the five folds as similar as possible, so that each fold can have the representative samples for different regions of the problem, hopefully. For this purpose, we take a sample and move it to the first fold. Then, we find its four nearest neighbors of the same class and move it to the four other folds. We also applied the heuristic called Synthetic Minority Oversampling (SMOTE) introduced in [19] to duplicate the minority class of the training set. For each sample in the minority class, denoted as x, SMOTE randomly picks one neighbor, denoted as y, among its k (say, $k = 5$) nearest neighbors of the same class. A synthetic sample is created by adjusting each coordinator of x by a random amount of the difference between the corresponding coordinators of x and y.

In our context, given a classification method, e.g., SVM, one subnet induce only one classifier and vice versa.

2.4 Searching for an Optimal Set of Subnets for Classification by Weighted Voting

The next step is to search for an optimal set of subnets from the remaining subnets (after evaluating and removing) such that the prediction based on the weighted voting results of those subnets can be more accurate than using any single subnet. The weighted voting scheme predicts the outcome for a new patient as simple as follows. Each classifier (i.e., subnet) predicts the survivability of the patient based on his/her GE profile. The final decision is assigned to the outcome that has the highest sum of weight, where the MCC of each model is used as its weight.

Algorithm 2. Finding an optimal set of subnets for weighted voting

```
Input: W, T, and MaxS, which are an initial set of
models/subnets along with their MCCs, a set of training
datasets, and the limited number of selected subnets.
Output: OS, a subset of W which can yield an optimal
MCC by the weighted voting scheme
Begin
1. Initialize OS by the best subnet based on MCC.
2. Repeatedly add to OS the new subnet that improves
   the average training MCC the most, based on the
   votes of the subnets in OS until OS cannot be im-
   proved or OS reaches the limited number of subnets.
End
```

The greedy search for such an optimized set of subnets is shown in Algorithm 2. For this algorithm, we randomly split the learning dataset into two datasets 500 times. The larger one will be used as a training dataset and the other will be used as a testing dataset. Then, the training MCC, in step 2, is the average MCC computed from the training datasets. After Algorithm 2 finishes, the reported MCC and other measures are computed based on the testing datasets and the optimal set of subnets extracted.

3 Results and Discussion

Using either SVM or RF, we ran our approach on the three datasets CT, HT, CT_HT (see Table 1), with different combinations of SMOTE and DOB-SCV. Thus, each experimental setting is given in the form of three letters SDV, where S, D, and V can be either “Y” (YES) or “N” (NO), indicating whether SMOTE and DOB-SCV and the voting scheme are applied or not, respectively. When V is “N”, we search for only one best subnet. For example, the setting YNY means that we use the voting scheme to find the optimal set of subnets where the five folds will be stratified randomly (without DOB-SCV), but the training set will be over-sampled by SMOTE. Meanwhile, the setting NYN means that we search for only one best subnet and only DOB-SCV is applied.

Tables 2, 3 and 4, respectively, show the classification performance in detail for each setting, using SVM and RF, for the three types of treatments. The measures for classification performance are recall, specificity (SPEC), accuracy (ACC), MCC, and area under the curve (AUC) of the receiver operating characteristics (ROC) curve. Due to limitations on space, we provided only the standard deviation for the MCCs obtained by the voting scheme. For comparison purposes, the three tables also contain classification performances obtained by the method of [16] which applied a wrapper feature selection approach using mRMR and SVM or RF. We denote the setting for this approach as "F1000". The comparison on MCCs obtained by SVM and RF for different settings are shown in Figs. 1, 2, and 3. In these figures, the results based on the single best subnet are shown in the first four groups (NNN, NYN, YNN, and YYN). The results based on the weighted voting scheme by the set of optimal subnets are shown in the last four groups (NNY, NYY, YNY, and YYY).

3.1 Classification Performances on CT

On CT, our approach produces much better results than F1000, and SVM yields better results than RF in all cases. Using the best subnet, the MCCs obtained by RF and SVM is 0.72 and 0.88, respectively, for the best setting. They are about three to four times larger than the MCC in F1000. As a result, the accuracies increase by about 20% and 26%, respectively. DOB-SCV contributes a smaller increase for SVM than for RF when applied alone; in contrast, SMOTE did not improve the results.

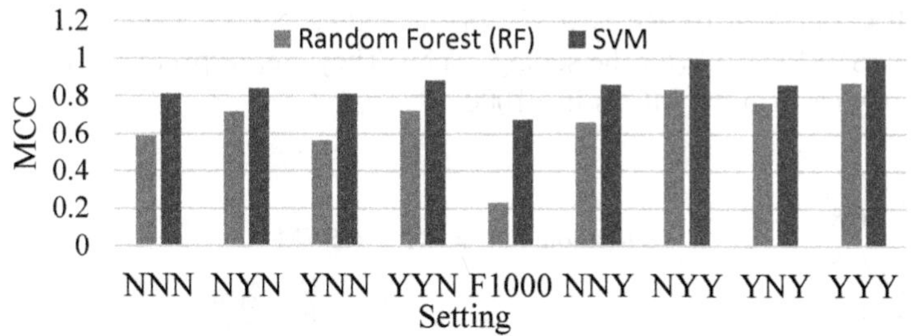

Fig. 1. MCCs obtained on patients treated with chemotherapy

When using the voting scheme based on the optimal set of subnets, the MCCs are further raised up by about 0.12 (or 6% accuracy, approximately), on average, as compared to similar settings based on the best subnet. The setting YYY results in the highest accuracy for RF and for SVM, 93.5% (±6%) and 99% (±0%), respectively.

Table 2. Classification results on patients treated with chemotherapy

Algorithm	Setting	Recall	SPEC	ACC	MCC	AUC	# Subnets/Genes
RF	F1000			66.0%	0.23	0.65	19
	NNN	0.65	0.88	79.3%	0.55	0.76	14
	NYN	0.80	0.91	86.8%	0.72	0.86	3
	YNN	0.65	0.91	79.3%	0.56	0.78	14
	YYN	***0.85***	***0.88***	***86.8%***	***0.72***	***0.86***	***21***
	NNY	0.70	0.93	82.9%	0.66 (0.21)	0.81	4
	NYY	0.80	1.00	91.3%	0.84 (0.11)	0.90	4
	YNY	0.78	0.96	88.4%	0.77 (0.19)	0.87	6
	YYY	**0.90**	**0.96**	**93.5%**	**0.87 (0.13)**	**0.93**	3
SVM	F1000			84.9%	0.68	0.82	10
	NNN	0.90	0.91	90.6%	0.80	0.90	25
	NYN	0.90	0.94	92.5%	0.84	0.92	15
	YNN	0.95	0.88	90.6%	0.81	0.91	15
	YYN	***0.95***	***0.94***	***94.3%***	***0.88***	***0.93***	***14***
	NNY	0.87	0.98	93.3%	0.81 (0.12)	0.92	9
	NYY	**0.99**	**1.00**	**99.1%**	**0.99 (0.0)**	**0.99**	**9**
	YNY	0.87	0.98	93.3%	0.86 (0.12)	0.92	9
	YYY	**0.99**	**1.00**	**99.1%**	**0.99 (0.0)**	**0.99**	**3**

3.2 Classification Performance on HT

Although the classification results on HT are not as high as the results on CT, we can still able to obtain good classification models (MCCs are about 0.5 or more). Figure 2 shows that our approach is still much better than F1000. Using the best subnet, the highest MCC obtained by RF is 0.37 (for the setting NYN), and the highest MCC obtained by SVM is 0.32 (for the setting YYN). They are, respectively, about six and two times higher than the MCCs in F1000.

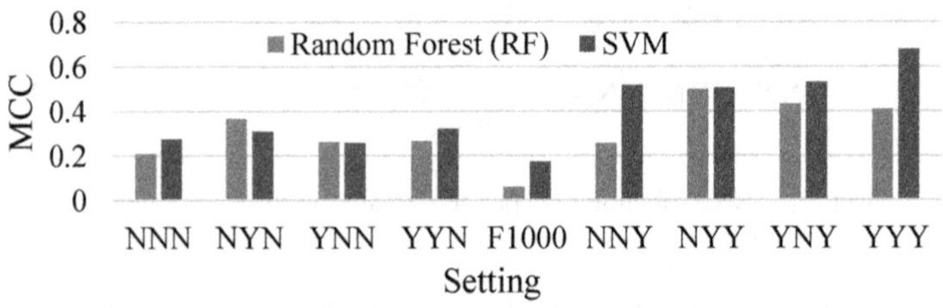

Fig. 2. MCCs obtained on patients treated with hormone therapy

The MCCs become the highest, 0.5 (±0.14) and 0.68 (±0.11), respectively, using the voting scheme with the similar combinations of DOB-SCV and SMOTE (i.e., the setting NYY for RF and YYY for SVM). They are about eight and four times better than the MCCs in F1000. In comparing the settings NYN and YNN against NNN (or NYY and YNY against NNY), DOB-SCV seems to deal with imbalanced data better than SMOTE and contributes more to the improvement in MCC. However, it is the voting scheme using the optimal set of subnets that brings about the most improvement. SVM often yields better results than RF, except for the setting NYN.

Table 3. Classification results on patients treated with hormone therapy

Algorithm	Setting	Recall	SPEC	ACC	MCC	AUC	# Subnets/Genes
RF	F1000			71.0%	0.06	0.63	9
	NNN	0.89	0.28	71.9%	0.21	0.59	4
	NYN	***0.92***	***0.38***	***76.9%***	***0.37***	***0.65***	***2***
	YNN	0.77	0.49	69.5%	0.26	0.63	8
	YYN	0.76	0.51	69.3%	0.27	0.64	2
	NNY	0.98	0.17	75.6%	0.26 (0.16)	0.57	4
	NYY	**0.98**	**0.39**	**81.7%**	**0.50 (0.14)**	**0.68**	**4**
	YNY	0.91	0.46	79.2%	0.43 (0.15)	0.69	6
	YYY	0.90	0.46	78.3%	0.41 (0.15)	0.68	4
SVM	F1000			72.9%	0.17	0.55	10
	NNN	0.87	0.37	73.1%	0.28	0.62	4
	NYN	0.89	0.38	74.5%	0.31	0.63	4
	YNN	0.88	0.34	72.9%	0.26	0.61	15
	YYN	***0.74***	***0.60***	***70.2%***	***0.32***	***0.67***	***4***
	NNY	0.99	0.37	82.1%	0.53 (0.14)	0.68	6
	NYY	0.98	0.39	80.8%	0.51 (0.14)	0.68	4
	YNY	0.99	0.40	80.2%	0.53 (0.14)	0.69	6
	YYY	**0.97**	**0.62**	**87.8%**	**0.68 (0.11)**	**0.79**	**7**

3.3 Classification Performances on CT_HT

On CT_HT, our approach yields almost similar MCCs as those obtained on HT. Figures 2 and 3 follow a similar trend. Using the single best subnet, the best MCC for RF is 0.328 (four times higher than F1000) and the best MCC for SVM is 0.33, 0.1 higher than F1000. DOB-SCV was still more efficiently than. For the voting scheme, SVM yields better results than RF. The combination of DOB-SCV and SMOTE produces the best MCC for RF, 0.52 (±0.16), and for SVM, 0.68 (±0.1), respectively.

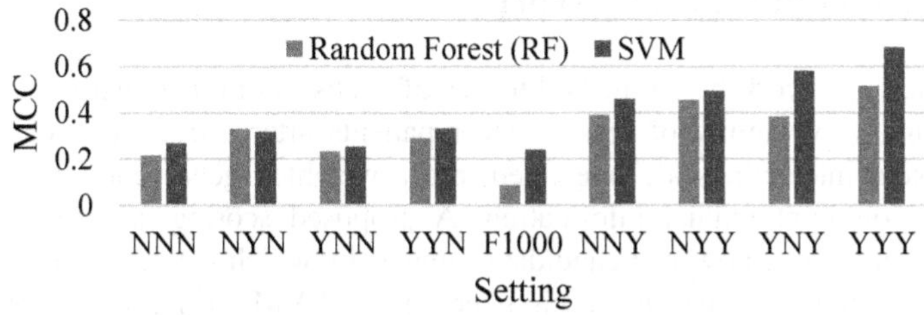

Fig. 3. MCCs obtained on patients treated with chemotherapy or hormone therapy

Table 4. Classification results on patients treated with chemotherapy or hormone therapy

Algorithm	Setting	Recall	SPEC	ACC	MCC	AUC	# Subnets/Genes
RF	F1000			65.3%	0.09	0.59	7
	NNN	0.89	0.28	68.5%	0.21	0.59	8
	NYN	***0.85***	***0.45***	***71.6%***	***0.33***	***0.65***	***2***
	YNN	0.70	0.53	64.7%	0.23	0.62	5
	YYN	0.72	0.58	67.1%	0.29	0.65	2
	NNY	1.00	0.21	73.7%	0.39 (0.13)	0.60	7
	NYY	0.98	0.35	77.0%	0.45 (0.14)	0.66	6
	YNY	0.87	0.48	74.1%	0.38 (0.13)	0.67	6
	YYY	**0.85**	**0.66**	**79.0%**	**0.52 (0.16)**	**0.75**	**6**
SVM	F1000			67.9%	0.24	0.61	11
	NNN	0.94	0.24	70.4%	0.26	0.59	4
	NYN	0.88	0.39	71.6%	0.31	0.64	10
	YNN	0.83	0.42	69.1%	0.27	0.62	23
	YYN	***0.74***	***0.60***	***69.3%***	***0.33***	***0.67***	***3***
	NNY	0.97	0.38	77.4%	0.46 (0.13)	0.67	6
	NYY	0.93	0.49	78.6%	0.49 (0.13)	0.71	4
	YNY	0.97	0.52	82.0%	0.58 (0.12)	0.74	8
	YYY	**0.90**	**0.77**	**85.9%**	**0.68 (0.10)**	**0.83**	**8**

There are 789 unique genes in 139 selected subnets for both SVM and RF for the three datasets. There are 414 unique genes for 46 subnets for CT, 272 unique genes for 42 subnets for HT, and 263 unique genes for 52 subnets for CT_HT. Among all selected subnets for the three treatments, there are very frequent genes including SP1 (69), NOG (45), IL6 (41), JUN (38), TP53 (32), MYC (30), GCLC (30), CLU (19) and some others, where their occurring times shown in parentheses. These genes play critical roles in pathways involving cell growth control, DNA repair mechanism, MAPK signaling pathway, etc. SP1, NOG, TP53, MYC, and CLU have been known as breast-cancer-related genes. For example, TP53 is a primary tumor suppressor gene that is situated as a critical signaling hub for such pathways and is targeted in many cancer therapies. NOG, a BMP inhibitor, provides metastatic breast cancer cells with the ability to colonize the bone [20]. Additionally, JUN, IL6, GCLC relate to other cancers.

4 Conclusion and Future Work

We introduce a network-based method to identify subsets of functionally related genes for predicting survivability of breast cancer patients after a treatment. GE data and protein-protein interactions are integrated into a weighted gene-gene interaction network based on joint mutual information. A proposed scoring criterion is used to estimate the predictive power of candidate subnets, by which we need to evaluate only one most predictive subnet for each gene, using SVM or Random Forest. Two heuristics, DOB-SCV and SMOTE, are applied to deal with class-imbalance in data.

We also propose a greedy method to select an optimal set of subnets for a better classification performance based on a weighted voting scheme.

In general, SVM yields better classification results than Random Forest, DOB-SCV always results in positive impact and higher performance than SMOTE, and the models based on the weighted voting scheme are much more accurate than those based on one single best subnet. Our approach significantly outperforms the approach of [16]. The MCCs show that our model can deal with imbalanced data while being effective to predict survivability of breast cancer patients. Many selected subnets contain breast/other cancer-related genes such as TP53, MYC, SP1, etc.

In the future, we plan to analyze the genes in the selected subnets with pathway data or cancer-related genes to reveal meaningful biomarkers and perform their corresponding biological validation using relevant literature. We would also like to try other functions that score the density of a subnet which can better estimate its predictive ability.

Acknowledgements. This work has been supported by the Natural Sciences and Engineering Research Council of Canada (NSERC).

References

1. DeSantis, C.E., Ma, J., Goding Sauer, A., Newman, L.A., Jemal, A.: Breast cancer statistics, 2017, racial disparity in mortality by state. CA Cancer J. Clin. **67**(6), 439–448 (2017). https://doi.org/10.3322/caac.21412
2. American Cancer Society: Breast cancer facts & figures 2017–2018 (2017)
3. O'Shaughnessy, J.: Extending survival with chemotherapy in metastatic breast cancer. Oncologist **10**(Suppl. 3), 20–29 (2005)
4. Van't Veer, L.J., et al.: Gene expression profiling predicts clinical outcome of breast cancer. Nature **415**(6871), 530 (2002). https://doi.org/10.1038/415530a
5. Pereira, B., et al.: The somatic mutation profiles of 2,433 breast cancers refine their genomic and transcriptomic landscapes. Nat. Commun. **7**, 11479 (2016). https://doi.org/10.1038/ncomms11479
6. Ferroni, P., Zanzotto, F.M., Riondino, S., Scarpato, N., Guadagni, F., Roselli, M.: Breast cancer prognosis using a machine learning approach. Cancers **11**(3), 328 (2019). https://doi.org/10.3390/cancers11030328
7. Peng, H., Long, F., Ding, C.: Feature selection based on mutual information: criteria of max-dependency, max-relevance, and min-redundancy. IEEE Trans. Pattern Anal. Mach. Intell. **8**, 1226–1238 (2005). https://doi.org/10.1109/TPAMI.2005.159
8. Huy, P.Q., Ngom, A., Rueda, L.: PAFS-an efficient method for classifier-specific feature selection. In: 2016 IEEE Symposium Series on Computational Intelligence (SSCI), pp. 1–8. IEEE, December 2016. https://doi.org/10.1109/ssci.2016.7850131
9. Chuang, H.Y., Lee, E., Liu, Y.T., Lee, D., Ideker, T.: Network-based classification of breast cancer metastasis. Mol. Syst. Biol. **3**(1) (2007). https://doi.org/10.1038/msb4100180
10. Allahyar, A., De Ridder, J.: FERAL: network-based classifier with application to breast cancer outcome prediction. Bioinformatics **31**(12), i311–i319 (2015). https://doi.org/10.1093/bioinformatics/btv255

11. Wang, X., Gulbahce, N., Yu, H.: Network-based methods for human disease gene prediction. Brief. Funct. Genomics **10**(5), 280–293 (2011). https://doi.org/10.1093/bfgp/elr024
12. Li, J., et al.: Mining disease genes using integrated protein–protein interaction and gene–gene co-regulation information. FEBS Open Bio **5**, 251–256 (2015). https://doi.org/10.1016/j.fob.2015.03.011
13. Amgalan, B., Lee, H.: WMAXC: a weighted maximum clique method for identifying condition-specific sub-network. PLoS ONE **9**(8), e104993 (2014). https://doi.org/10.1371/journal.pone.0104993
14. He, H., Lin, D., Zhang, J., Wang, Y.P., Deng, H.W.: Comparison of statistical methods for subnetwork detection in the integration of gene expression and protein interaction network. BMC Bioinform. **18**(1), 149 (2017). https://doi.org/10.1186/s12859-017-1567-2
15. van Dam, S., Vosa, U., van der Graaf, A., Franke, L., de Magalhaes, J.P.: Gene co-expression analysis for functional classification and gene–disease predictions. Brief. Bioinform. **19**(4), 575–592 (2017). https://doi.org/10.1093/bib/bbw139
16. Mucaki, E.J., et al.: Predicting outcomes of hormone and chemotherapy in the molecular taxonomy of breast cancer international consortium (METABRIC) study by biochemically-inspired machine learning. F1000Res. **5** (2016). https://doi.org/10.12688/f1000research.9417.3
17. Wyner, A.D.: A definition of conditional mutual information for arbitrary ensembles. Inf. Control **38**(1), 51–59 (1978). https://doi.org/10.1016/S0019-9958(78)90026-8
18. Moreno-Torres, J.G., Sáez, J.A., Herrera, F.: Study on the impact of partition-induced dataset shift on k-fold cross-validation. IEEE Trans. Neural Netw. Learn. Syst. **23**(8), 1304–1312 (2012). https://doi.org/10.1109/TNNLS.2012.2199516
19. Chawla, N.V., Bowyer, K.W., Hall, L.O., Kegelmeyer, W.P.: SMOTE: synthetic minority over-sampling technique. J. Artif. Intell. Res. **16**, 321–357 (2002). https://doi.org/10.1613/jair.953
20. Tarragona, M., et al.: Identification of NOG as a specific breast cancer bone metastasis-supporting gene. J. Biol. Chem. **287**(25), 21346–21355 (2012). https://doi.org/10.1074/jbc.P112.355834

Biomedical Engineering

Effects of the Distribution in Space of the Velocity-Inlet Condition in Hemodynamic Simulations of the Thoracic Aorta

Maria Nicole Antonuccio[1], Alessandro Mariotti[2(✉)], Simona Celi[1], and Maria Vittoria Salvetti[2]

[1] BioCardioLab - Heart Hospital, Fondazione Toscana G. Monasterio, Massa, Italy
m.nicole.antonuccio@gmail.com, s.celi@ftgm.it

[2] Dipartimento di Ingegneria Civile ed Industriale, University of Pisa, Pisa, Italy
alessandro.mariotti@for.unipi.it, mv.salvetti@ing.unipi.it

Abstract. In the present paper the effects of the spatial distribution of the inlet velocity in numerical simulations of the thoracic aorta have been investigated. First, the results obtained by considering *in-vivo* measured inlet velocity distribution are compared with the ones obtained for a simulation having the same flow rate waveform and plug flow condition at the inlet section. The results of the two simulations are consistent in terms of flow rate waveform, but differences are present in the pressure range and in the wall shear stresses, especially in the foremost part of the ascending aorta.

This motivates a stochastic sensitivity analysis on the effect of the distribution in space of the inlet velocity. This distribution is modeled through a truncated-cone shape and the ratio between the upper and the lower base is selected as the uncertain parameter. The uncertainty is propagated through the numerical model and a continuous response surface of the output quantities of interest in the parameter space can be recovered through a "surrogate" model. A stochastic method based on the generalized Polynomial Chaos (gPC) approach is used herein. The selected parameter appears to have a significant influence on the velocity distribution in the ascending aorta, whereas it has a negligible effect in the descending part. This, in turn, produces significant effects on the wall shear stresses in the ascending aorta, confirming the need of using patient-specific inlet conditions if interested in the hemodynamics and stresses of this region.

Keywords: Thoracic aorta · Hemodynamic simulations · CFD · *In-vivo* measured inlet velocity · Uncertainty quantification.

1 Introduction

Hemodynamic forces play an important role in the initiation and progression of cardiovascular diseases such as in case of ascending thoracic aortic aneurysms [1].

I. Rojas et al. (Eds.): IWBBIO 2020, LNBI 12108, pp. 63–74, 2020.
https://doi.org/10.1007/978-3-030-45385-5_6

The 3D flow magnetic resonance imaging (3D PC-MRI) technique has been proposed as a clinical tool able to provide, *in-vivo* in a non-invasive manner, hemodynamic information. However, MRI suffers of spatial and temporal resolution limitations and it is not able to provide quantitative flow descriptors, such as wall shear stresses, with a sufficient accuracy. In the last years, merging MRI with computational fluid dynamics (CFD) has been proposed to provide clinical information at patient-specific level. Indeed, CFD allows the flow and pressure fields to be investigated with a space and time resolutions that are not achievable by any *in-vivo* measurement. Nonetheless, the accuracy of CFD predictions strongly depends on modeling assumptions and computational set-up and different sources of uncertainties are present in CFD models. Among others, important critical aspects are represented by inlet/outlet boundary conditions, which must be correctly prescribed to reproduce the effect of organs and vessels outside the portion of the aorta that is actually simulated, and by the modeling of the properties of the vessel wall compliance. These uncertainties may affect the accuracy of the output quantities of interest (see e.g. [2–4]). *In-vivo* 3D PC-MRI data can be successfully used to obtain patient-specific boundary conditions for the simulations (see e.g. [5–8]) as well as for comparison against numerical results, providing a cross validation. A framework integrating *in-vivo* 3D PC-MRI data into the numerical simulation of a healthy thoracic aorta is presented in [9], whereas a comparison between numerical simulations and *in-vitro* data obtained from a fully controlled and sensorized circulatory mock loop for 3D-printed aortic models is provided in [10,11]. The integration is all in all successful, but some discrepancies among numerical results, although calibrated, *in-vivo* and *in-vitro* data are still observed.

We focus herein on inlet boundary conditions. The need of accurate inflow boundary conditions is particularly important in the thoracic aorta, because the complexity of the trileaflet aortic valve, along with its ring-like annulus, sinuses, and feeding coronary arteries, may lead to highly intricate flow patterns entering the ascending aorta [12], far from the idealized profiles widely used in numerical simulations. A common practice in hemodynamic simulations is indeed the imposition of a flow rate waveform, usually derived from patient-specific measured volumetric flow rate waveforms. The volumetric flow rate is generally imposed under the hypothesis of plug flow, i.e. flat velocity profiles, whereas, only in some cases, the distribution in space and in time is used as inlet velocity condition. A systematic sensitivity analysis to the shape of the inlet flow rate waveform, and, in particular, to the flow stroke volume and to the period of the cardiac cycle has been carried out in [3]. Plug flow is considered and the two input parameters show a deep influence on wall shear stresses, confirming the need of using patient-specific flow rate waveforms. On the other hand, only a few studies have investigated the effect of using patient-specific space-distributed inlet velocity profiles on CFD-simulated hemodynamics of the abdominal aorta [13] or carotid arteries [14]. Recent studies by [6,15] assessed the effect of inlet boundary conditions on the thoracic aorta of a healthy subject, and found that idealized boundary conditions can lead to misleading results.

In this work we first compare the results of a simulation carried out by considering an *in-vivo* measured inlet velocity distribution data with the ones obtained for a simulation having the same flow rate waveform and plug flow condition at the inlet section. The open-source code Simvascular [16] is used to carry out the numerical simulations and phase-contrast magnetic resonance imaging is used to provide temporally and spatially resolved velocity data, which has provided a reliable non-invasive method of acquiring patient-specific inflow boundary conditions (see e.g. [17]). Moreover, we carry out a stochastic sensitivity analysis on the effect of the distribution in space of the inlet velocity. This distribution is modeled through a truncated-cone shape and the ratio between the upper and the lower base is selected as the uncertain parameter. The uncertainty is propagated through the numerical model and a continuous response surface of the output quantities of interest in the parameter space is recovered using a stochastic method based on the gPC approach.

2 Problem Definition and Numerical Methodology

The considered aorta geometry and inlet flow rate are the same as in [9]. The procedure used to obtain patient-specific data are briefly recalled herein, together with the numerical approach and simulation set-up. The geometry of the ascending thoracic aorta, shown in Fig. 1(a), is obtained from MRI acquisitions performed on a healthy subject (28 years, male) with tricuspid aortic valve.

An isotropic voxel resolution of $2 \times 2 \times 2\,\text{mm}^3$ is adopted, together with an echo time of 3 ms, a repetition time of 5.32 ms and a flip angle equal 10°. The velocity encoding range (VENC) is properly set to $250\,\text{cm}\,\text{s}^{-1}$ after scouting on cross-sections positioned in the ascending aorta. The resulting flow rate at the inlet section of the considered region of the aorta is reported in Fig. 1(b). The MRI

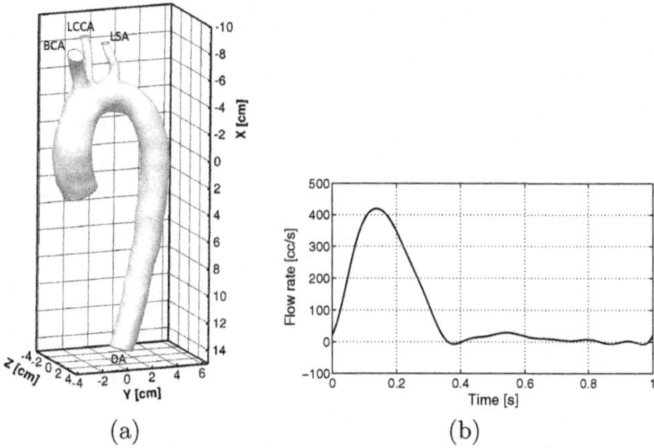

Fig. 1. Sketch of the healthy ascending aorta geometry (a) and flow rate waveform measured through 3D PC-MRI at the inlet section (b).

dataset volume is retrospectively reconstructed with phase contrast angiography (PC-MRA) technique. Informed consent was obtained from the patient. The study protocol conforms to the ethical guidelines of the 1975 Declaration of Helsinki as reflected in a priori approval by the institution's Human Research Committee.

The open-source code *SimVascular* is used to carry out the hemodynamic simulations (see e.g. [16]). In the simulations, blood is considered as a Newtonian and incompressible fluid with density and kinematic viscosity equal to $\rho = 1.06\,\mathrm{g\,cm^{-3}}$ and $\nu = 3.77 \times 10^{-2}\,\mathrm{cm^2\,s^{-1}}$. The three-dimensional Navier-Stokes equations for incompressible flows are thus considered as governing equations. A finite-element method, including SUPG/PSPG stabilizing terms, is used to discretize the governing equations. The stabilized formulation allows to choose P1-P1 elements, i.e. linear shape functions for both velocity and pressure. At the inlet section of the computational domain we impose the measured flow-rate waveform with different distribution in space, while at the outflow boundaries, we use the 3-elements Windkessel model. Finally, on the arterial wall we impose a no-slip condition between the fluid and the wall and the effect of wall compliance is not taken into account in the simulations herein.

3 Deterministic Results: Comparison Between *In-vivo* Measured Velocity Inlet and Plug Flow

This section focuses on the analysis and comparison between the results obtained by considering the *in-vivo* measured inlet velocity distribution and the ones obtained for a simulation having the same flow rate waveform and plug flow

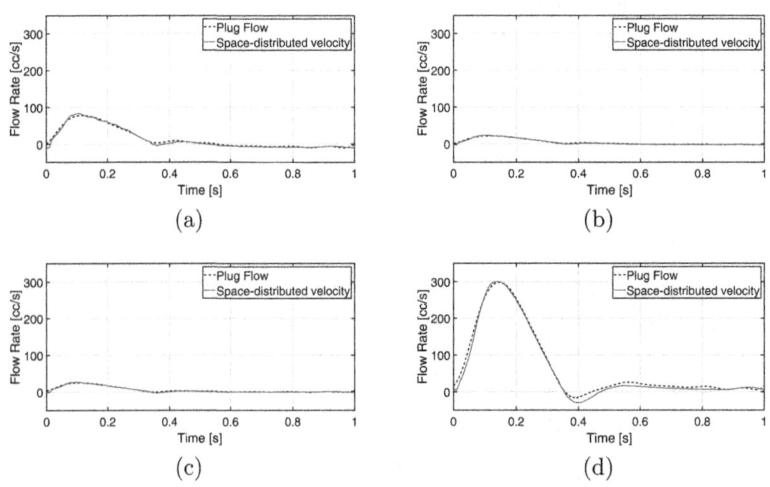

Fig. 2. Flow rate waveforms at the different outlet sections: (a) BCA, (b) LCCA, (c) LSA and (d) descending aorta. Comparison between *in-vivo* measured inlet velocity distribution and plug flow condition (from [9]).

at the inlet section. First, the flow rate waveforms at the outlet sections of the side branches and of the descending aorta are compared in Fig. 2, whereas the pressure waveforms are shown in Fig. 3. The flow rates present a perfect agreement between the two considered cases. Conversely, the pressure obtained for the simulation carried out with the *in-vivo* measured inlet velocity is uniformly reduced of approximately 10 mmHg, while maintaining the same shape of the waveforms.

In order to investigate the possible reasons for the decrease of pressure, the Time-Averaged Wall Shear Stresses (TAWSS) along the whole cardiac cycle are compared in Fig. 4(a, b). It is evident that a reduction of the wall shear stresses occurs in the simulation having the *in-vivo* measured inlet velocity distribution, especially in the foremost part of the ascending aorta, and this is probably due to a lower value of the velocity derivative near the wall. The reduction of the stresses, in turn, produces a global reduction of the pressure waveform. Moreover, the wall shear stresses averaged during only the systolic portion of the cycle and over the diastolic one are compared in Fig. 4(c, d) and in Fig. 4(e, f), respectively. The systolic phase is clearly the main responsible for the differences in TAWSS, while the stresses in the diastolic phase are very low and almost the same for both the considered inlet conditions.

The difference in the results for *in-vivo* measured inlet conditions and plug flow stresses the importance of a patient-specific space-distributed inlet conditions. Moreover, it motivates a systematic sensitivity analysis on the effect of the distribution in space of the inlet velocity, aimed at assessing whether the differences in TAWSS are limited to the foremost part of the thoracic aorta (ascending region) or to the whole thoracic aorta. To perform this analysis we

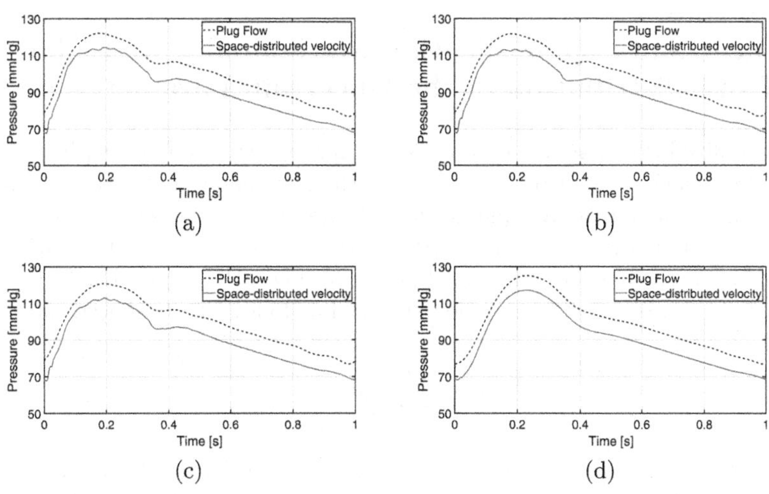

Fig. 3. Pressure waveforms at the different outlet sections: (a) BCA, (b) LCCA, (c) LSA and (d) descending aorta. Comparison between *in-vivo* measured inlet velocity distribution and plug flow condition (from [9]).

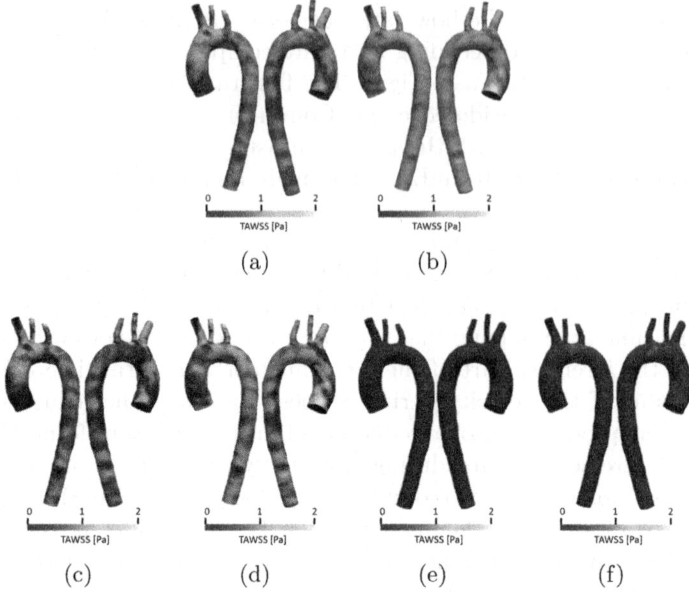

Fig. 4. TAWSS evaluated considering (a, b) the whole cardiac cycle, (c, d) only the systolic phase of the cardiac cycle and (e, f) only the diastolic phase of the cardiac cycle. (a, c, e) *in-vivo* measured inlet velocity distribution and (b, d, f) plug flow condition.

use the stochastic approach described in Sect. 4 and the main results are discussed in Sect. 5.

4 Uncertainty Quantification Methodology and Choice of the Distribution of the Uncertain Parameter

The generalized Polynomial Chaos (gPC) is the strategy used in the present work to obtain a continuous response surface in the parameter space starting from a few deterministic numerical simulations. We briefly recall here its main features. The gPC approach is based on the projection of a given stochastic response in terms of an orthogonal polynomial basis [18]. The gPC expansion for a given quantity of interest, say X, may be expressed as follows (term-based indexing):

$$X(\omega) = \sum_{k=0}^{\infty} a_k \Phi_k(\boldsymbol{\xi}(\omega)) \tag{1}$$

where ω is an elementary event, $\boldsymbol{\xi}(\omega)$ is the vector consisting of the independent random variables (i.e., the set of considered uncertain parameters), $\Phi_k(\boldsymbol{\xi})$ is the gPC polynomial of index k and a_k is the corresponding coefficient.

The response surface is obtained by a truncation of the expansion (1) to a finite limit T. Using the maximum polynomial order for all one-dimensional polynomials (i.e., full tensor-product polynomial expansion), T is obtained as follows:

$$T = \prod_{i=1}^{M} (P_i + 1) - 1 \tag{2}$$

where M is the number of the uncertain parameters and P_i is the maximum polynomial order for the ith parameter. The coefficient a_k can be computed as follows:

$$a_k = \frac{\langle X, \Phi_k \rangle}{\langle \Phi_k, \Phi_k \rangle} = \frac{1}{\langle \Phi_k, \Phi_k \rangle} \int_{\omega \in \Xi} X\, \Phi_{k\rho}(\boldsymbol{\xi})\, d\boldsymbol{\xi} \tag{3}$$

where $\langle \cdot, \cdot \rangle$ denotes the usual L_2 scalar product involving a weight function depending on the polynomial family chosen. The integrals in the scalar products are computed numerically by using Gaussian quadrature. The polynomial family, Φ_k, must be *a priori* specified and its choice affects the speed of the convergence of the gPC expansion: a suitable polynomial family is able to approximate the stochastic response by means of fewer degrees of freedom. When dealing with Gaussian quadrature, an optimal family has a weight function similar to the probability measurement of the random variables. The choice of the polynomial family thus depends on the Probability Density Function (PDF) shape of the uncertain parameters.

We aim at investigating the sensitivity of the output hemodynamic quantities of interest (velocity, pressure, TAWSS, ...) to the distribution in space of the velocity at the inlet section. For this purpose, we first have to define and analytic function for the distribution of the inlet velocity. Since from the previous analysis it was found that the systolic phase is mainly responsible of the differences in terms of pressure waveform and wall shear stresses, the velocity distribution at the systolic peak (see Fig. 5(a)) is considered. Its shape resembles a truncated cone and this shape is used for implementing the distribution in space of the inlet velocity. The shape of the truncated cone is function of the ratio between

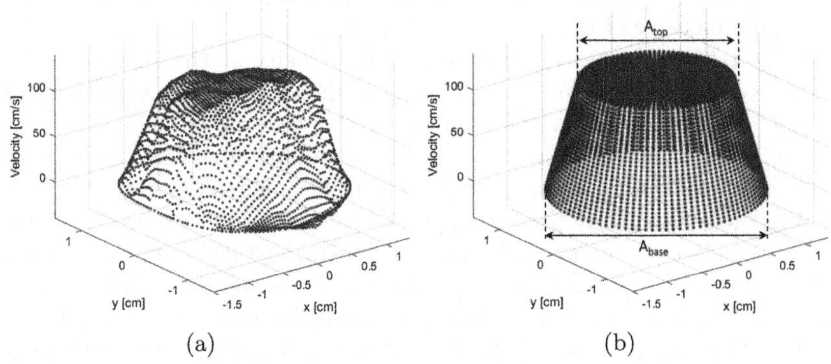

Fig. 5. Space-distributed inlet velocity: (a) patient-specific shape at systolic peak, (b) modeled truncated-cone shape.

the upper and the lower base, and thus the base ratio $r = A_{top}/A_{base}$ is chosen as the uncertain parameter. It varies in the range $A_{top}/A_{base} = [0.2 - 1]$, being $A_{top}/A_{base} = 1$ the plug flow condition. This parameter physically depends on the opening-time of the valve placed upstream of the ascending thoracic aorta. We assume a uniform Probability Density Function (PDF) on the given variation range because it is the least informative distribution with the highest variance in given intervals. The optimal polynomial family for the gPC basis in case of uniform PDF distribution of the input uncertain parameters is Legendre polynomials. The polynomial expansion is truncated to the third order for each dimension and thus four quadrature points for each random variable are needed to compute the coefficients of the expansion. These values are shown in Table 1 for all the parameters. Note that for all the considered values of A_{top}/A_{base}, the height of the truncated cone is calculated for each time instant in order to match the flow rate curve presented in Fig. 1(b).

Table 1. Quadrature points for the base ratio.

Random variable	1st	2nd	3rd	4th
(A_{top}/A_{base})	0.256	0.464	0.736	0.944

5 Analysis of the Stochastic Results

The flow rate waveforms at the outlet sections of the side branches and of the descending aorta for the four deterministic simulations having different base ratios A_{top}/A_{base} are compared with the one with plug flow (base ratio $A_{top}/A_{base} = 1$) in Fig. 6. As in Fig. 2, no significant differences are present among all the considered cases. On the contrary, for the pressure waveform, whose probability density functions is given in Fig. 7, the overall dispersion is of the order of $\Delta P \leq 4$ mmHg and a monotone decrease of the pressure values is found for the increase of the base ratio A_{top}/A_{base}.

The effect of the base ratio on the normal velocity at the systolic peak for different cross sections of the thoracic aorta is shown in Fig. 8. A section of the ascending aorta (S1), of the aortic arch (S2) and of the descending aorta (S3) are considered. Moreover, the related stochastic standard deviation of the normal velocity at the systolic peak is reported in the right panel of the same figure. The main differences are clearly present in the ascending aorta, i.e. the cross section closest to the inlet boundary, with an averaged stochastic standard deviation of the order of the 10% of the velocity magnitude. Consistently with the imposed distribution in space of the inlet velocity, a progressive increase of the velocity in the center of the aorta walls is found for increasing A_{top}/A_{base}. On the contrary, the variation of the velocity distribution is more limited for the cross-section at the aortic arch, despite some local high differences, and in the descending aorta. The averaged stochastic variation is of the order of 5% and lower than the

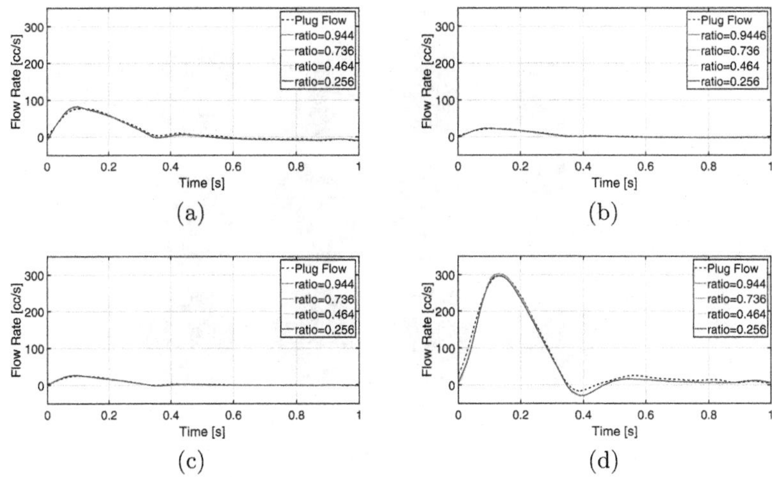

Fig. 6. Effect of the base ratio on the flow rate waveforms at the different outlet sections: (a) BCA, (b) LCCA, (c) LSA and (d) descending aorta.

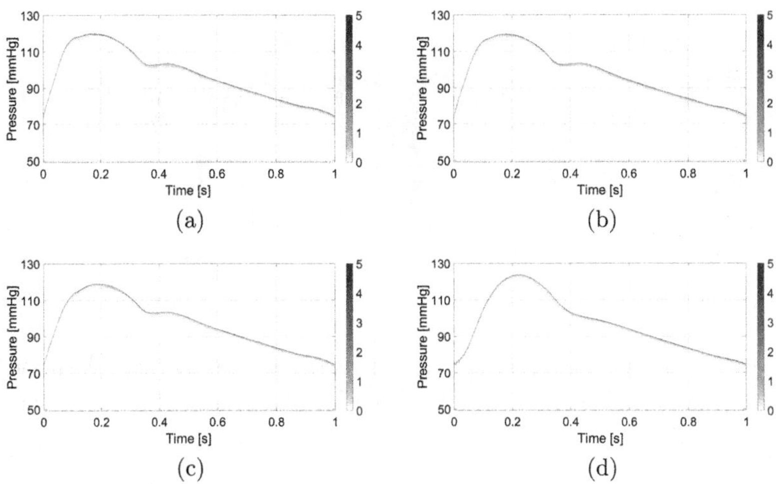

Fig. 7. Effect of the base ratio on the probability density function of the pressure waveforms at the different outlet sections: (a) BCA, (b) LCCA, (c) LSA and (d) descending aorta.

3% of the velocity magnitude for the two sections, respectively. In addition, the variations in space of the velocity field are not clearly related to the shape of the imposed velocity. Analogous results and trends are found for other time instants in the systolic part of the cardiac cycle, while in the diastolic phase differences are all in all very small (not shown here for the sake of brevity). This highlights how the space-distribution of the inlet velocity deeply affects the foremost part

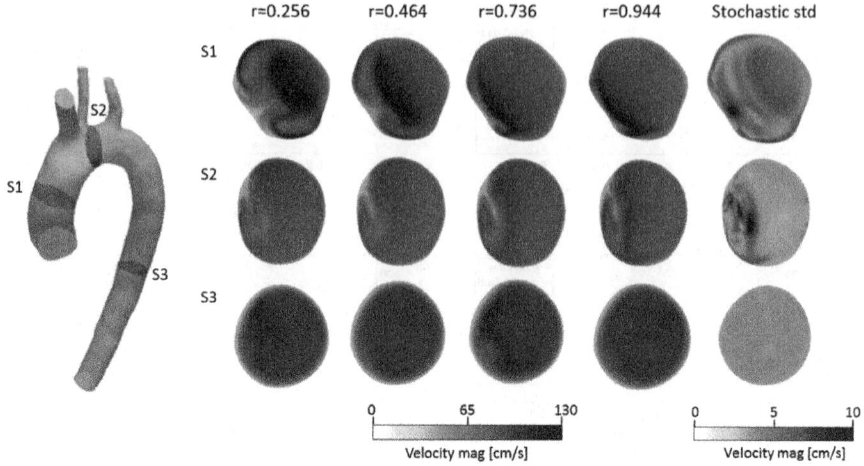

Fig. 8. Effect of the base ratio on the normal velocity at systolic peak for different cross sections of the thoracic aorta and stochastic standard deviation of the normal velocity at systolic peak.

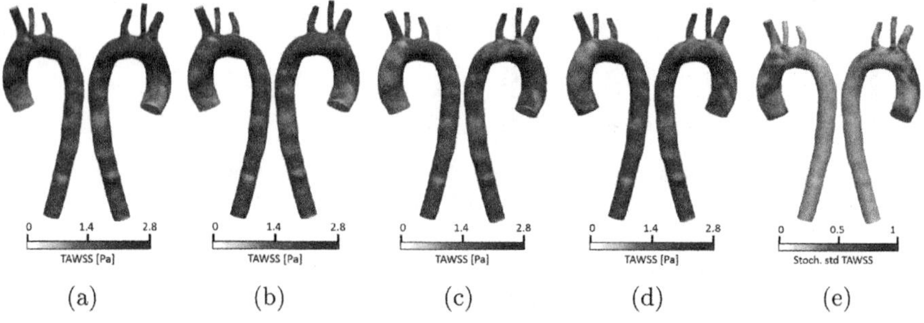

Fig. 9. Effect of the base ratio on the TAWSS: (a) $A_{top}/A_{base} = 0.256$, (b) $A_{top}/A_{base} = 0.464$, (c) $A_{top}/A_{base} = 0.736$ and (d) $A_{top}/A_{base} = 0.944$. (e) Stochastic standard deviation of the TAWSS.

of the thoracic aorta, i.e. the ascending aorta, while it tends to reduce its effect in the aortic arch and, even more, in the descending aorta.

TAWSS results confirm the importance of inlet condition in the ascending aorta. The distribution of TAWSS for the four deterministic simulations is shown in Fig. 9(a–d) and the related stochastic standard deviation is reported in Fig. 9(e). The region of maximum variability of TAWSS comprises the ascending aorta and the foremost part of the aortic arch, i.e. the green part in Fig. 9(e). In the foremost part of this region the stresses first increase and then decrease by increasing the parameter A_{top}/A_{base}.

6 Conclusions

The effects of the spatial distribution of the inlet velocity in numerical simulations of the thoracic aorta are investigated. The results of the simulations carried out with *in-vivo* measured inlet velocity distribution are compared with the ones obtained for a simulation having the same flow rate waveform and plug flow condition at the inlet section. Almost identical results are found in terms of flow rate waveform, while a general decrease of the pressure waveform and of the wall shear stresses are found with the *in-vivo* measured inlet condition, especially in the ascending aorta.

In addition to this, a stochastic sensitivity analysis is carried out on the effect of the parameter A_{top}/A_{base} of the truncated-cone shape that modeled the inlet velocity distribution. This parameter has a significant influence on the velocity distribution in the ascending aorta, whereas it has a negligible effect in the descending part. This, in turn, produces significant effects in the wall shear stress distribution in the ascending aorta, confirming the need of using patient-specific inlet conditions if interested in the hemodynamics and stresses in this region.

References

1. Capellini, K., Vignali, E., Costa, E., et al.: Computational fluid dynamic study for ATAA hemodynamics: an integrated image-based and radial basis functions mesh morphing approach. J. Biomech. Eng **140**(11), 111007 (2018)
2. Boccadifuoco, A., Mariotti, A., Celi, S., Martini, N., Salvetti, M.V.: Uncertainty quantification in numerical simulations of the flow in thoracic aortic aneurysms. In: Proceedings of the 7th European Congress on Computational Methods in Applied Sciences and Engineering (ECCOMAS Congress 2016), vol. 3, pp. 6226–6249 (2016)
3. Boccadifuoco, A., Mariotti, A., Celi, S., Martini, N., Salvetti, M.V.: Effects of inlet conditions in the simulation of hemodynamics in a thoracic aortic aneurysm. In: Proceedings of the 23rd Conference of the Italian Association of Theoretical and Applied Mechanics (AIMETA 2017), vol. 2, pp. 1706–1724 (2017)
4. Boccadifuoco, A., Mariotti, A., Celi, S., Martini, N., Salvetti, M.V.: Impact of uncertainties in outflow boundary conditions on the predictions of hemodynamic simulations of ascending thoracic aortic aneurysms. Comput. Fluids **165**, 96–115 (2018)
5. Gallo, D., et al.: On the use of *in vivo* measured flow rates as boundary conditions for image-based hemodynamic models of the human aorta: implications for indicators of abnormal flow. Ann. Biomed. Eng. **40**(3), 729–741 (2012). https://doi.org/10.1007/s10439-011-0431-1
6. Morbiducci, U., Ponzini, R., Gallo, D., Bignardi, C., Rizzo, G.: Inflow boundary conditions for image-based computational hemodynamics: impact of idealized versus measured velocity profiles in the human aorta. J. Biomech. **46**(1), 102–109 (2013)
7. Morbiducci, U., et al.: A rational approach to defining principal axes of multidirectional wall shear stress in realistic vascular geometries, with application to the study of the influence of helical flow on wall shear stress directionality in aorta. J. Biomech. **48**(6), 899 (2015)

8. Condemi, F., et al.: Fluid- and biomechanical analysis of ascending thoracic aorta aneurysm with concomitant aortic insufficiency. Ann. Biomed. Eng. **45**(12), 2921 (2017). https://doi.org/10.1007/s10439-017-1913-6
9. Boccadifuoco, A., Mariotti, A., Capellini, K., Celi, S., Salvetti, M.V.: Validation of numerical simulations of thoracic aorta hemodynamics: comparison with *in-vivo* measurements and stochastic sensitivity analysis. Cardiovasc. Eng. Technol. **9**(4), 688–706 (2018). https://doi.org/10.1007/s13239-018-00387-x
10. Mariotti, A., Vignali, E., Gasparotti, E., Capellini, K., Celi, S., Salvetti, M.V.: Comparison between numerical and MRI data of ascending aorta hemodynamics in a circulatory mock loop. In: Proceedings of the 24th Conference of the Italian Association of Theoretical and Applied Mechanics (AIMETA 2019) (2019)
11. Vignali, E., et al.: Development of a fully controllable real-time pump to reproduce left ventricle physiological flow. In: Proceedings of the 24th Conference of the Italian Association of Theoretical and Applied Mechanics (AIMETA 2019) (2019)
12. Sigovan, M., Dyverfeldt, P., Wrenn, J., Tseng, E.E., Saloner, D., Hope, M.D.: Extended 3D approach for quantification of abnormal ascending aortic flow. Magn. Reson. Imaging **33**(5), 695–700 (2015)
13. Chandra, S., et al.: Fluid-structure interaction modeling of abdominal aortic aneurysms: the impact of patient-specific inflow conditions and fluid/solid coupling. ASME J. Biomech. Eng. **135**(8), 081001 (2013)
14. Campbell, I.C., Ries, J., Dhawan, S.S., Quyyumi, A.A., Taylor, W.R., Oshinski, J.N.: Effect of inlet velocity profiles on patient-specific computational fluid dynamics simulations of the carotid bifurcation. J. Biomech. Eng. **134**(5), 051001 (2012)
15. Youssefi, P., Gomez, A., Arthurs, C., Sharma, R., Jahangiri, M., Figueroa, C.A.: Impact of patient-specific inflow velocity profile on hemodynamics of the thoracic aorta. J. Biomech. Eng. **140**(1), 1011002 (2018)
16. Updegrove, A., Wilson, N.M., Merkow, J., Lan, H., Marsden, A.L., Shadden, S.C.: SimVascular: an open source pipeline for cardiovascular simulation. Ann. Biomed. Eng. **45**(3), 525–541 (2016). https://doi.org/10.1007/s10439-016-1762-8
17. Efstathopoulos, E.P., Patatoukas, G., Pantos, I., Benekos, O., Katritsis, D., Kelekis, N.L.: Wall shear stress calculation in ascending aorta using phase contrast magnetic resonance imaging. Investigating effective ways to calculate it in clinical practice. Physica Med. **24**(4), 175–181 (2008)
18. Xiu, D., Karniadakis, G.: The Wiener-Askey polynomial chaos for stochastic differential equations. SIAM J. Sci. Comput. **24**, 619–644 (2003)

Coupled Electro-mechanical Behavior of Microtubules

Sundeep Singh[1] and Roderick Melnik[1,2(✉)]

[1] MS2Discovery Interdisciplinary Research Institute, Wilfrid Laurier University, 75 University Avenue West, Waterloo, ON N2L 3C5, Canada
rmelnik@wlu.ca

[2] BCAM - Basque Center for Applied Mathematics, Alameda de Mazarredo 14, 48009 Bilbao, Spain

Abstract. In this contribution, the coupled electro-mechanical behavior of the microtubules has been systematically investigated utilizing a continuum-based finite element framework. A three-dimensional computational model of a microtubule has been developed for predicting the electro-elastic response of the microtubule subjected to external forces. The effects of the magnitude and direction of the applied forces on the mechanics of microtubule have been evaluated. In addition, the effects of variation of microtubule lengths on the electro-elastic response subjected to external forces have also been quantified. The results of numerical simulation suggest that the electro-elastic response of microtubule is significantly dependent on both the magnitude and direction of the applied forces. It has been found that the application of shear force results in the attainment of higher displacement and electric potential as compared to the compressive force of the same magnitude. It has been further observed that the output potential is linearly proportional to the predicted displacement and the electric potential within the microtubule. The increase in the length of microtubule significantly enhances the predicted piezoelectric potential under the application of different forces considered in the present study. It is expected that the reported findings would be useful in different avenues of biomedical engineering, such as biocompatible nano-biosensors for health monitoring, drug delivery, noninvasive diagnosis and treatments.

Keywords: Electro-mechanical coupling · Microtubules · Piezoelectricity · Computational modelling

1 Introduction

Microtubules are one of the most fundamental structural elements within the cytoskeleton of biological cells that is involved in performing a variety of vital functions, such as providing major mechanical supports and strength to the cells for maintaining and organizing their shapes and facilitating cell division, migration, self-contraction and intracellular transport and signaling [1–3]. Microtubules represent a self-assembling polymer composed of heterodimers of α-tubulin and β-tubulin protein that stack head to tail forming the protofilaments. The lateral bonding of the number of protofilaments contributes to the construction of more stable, rigid and structurally

I. Rojas et al. (Eds.): IWBBIO 2020, LNBI 12108, pp. 75–86, 2020.
https://doi.org/10.1007/978-3-030-45385-5_7

intact microtubules in the form a cylindrical surface as shown in Fig. 1 [4]. Thus, microtubules are long hollow cylindrical shaped objects typically made up of 13 protofilaments, but those with 8 to 16 protofilaments have also been reported in the literature [5, 6].

Owing to the vital roles played by the microtubules in the biological cells, several studies have been reported in the literature for understanding the mechanics of microtubules in the last two decades [2, 6–12]. The accurate quantification of the mechanical properties and behavior of the microtubules will be extremely important in new biomedical developments, such as in the application of microtubules based novel non-invasive biosensors for disease diagnostics and therapies, and development of advanced biomimetic nanomaterials, e.g., the MT-graphene nanotubes [1, 8]. Although much of the initial work in this field was confined to experimental and theoretical studies, recently numerical modelling has also been extensively explored for capturing and understanding the mechanical behavior of the microtubules. The numerical modelling approaches are considered to have superiority at capturing the precise information at nano and microscales as compared to experimental studies due to associated limitations and complexities for conducting experiments at such scales [9, 10].

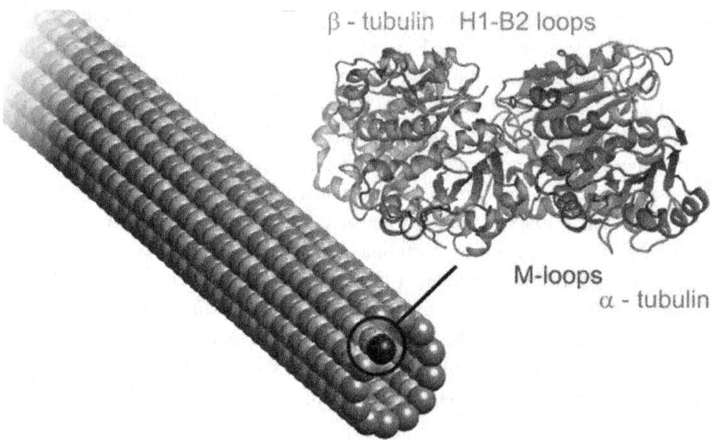

Fig. 1. (Color online). Schematic description of a single microtubule with 13 protofilaments along with the secondary protein structure of an α-β tubulin dimer [4]. (This image is reproduced under the terms of the Creative Commons Attribution 4.0 International License, http://creativecommons.org/licenses/by/4.0/, Copyright © 2019, Springer Nature Limited).

Most of the numerical studies reported till date are focused on evaluating the mechanical properties of the individual isolated microtubules utilizing only the mechanical coupling between the applied stress and the induced strains. It has also been reported that the microtubules possess piezoelectric properties as a result of electromechanical coupling [13], whereby an electrical charge is produced under the application of mechanical force or vice versa. These studies fall under the research in biomaterials which has received tremendous attention due to its importance in opening the new doors for different promising avenues in biomedical industries, viz., medical devices, wearable sensors, flexible actuators and energy harvesting devices [14]. Thus, the present study focuses on developing a three-dimensional coupled electro-mechanical model of microtubule for quantifying the piezoelectric behavior under the application of external forces. A parametric analysis has been conducted for evaluating the effects of length of the microtubule, along with the magnitude and direction of the applied forces on the electro-elastic response of the coupled electro-mechanical model.

2 Continuum Model with Piezoelectricity

A continuum-based three-dimensional model of individual isolated microtubule considered in the present computational study has been presented in Fig. 2. A 1 μm long microtubule with 15 nm inner diameter and 23 nm outer diameter has been modelled as a hollow cylindrical tube comprising of 13 protofilaments, as shown in Fig. 2 [15]. The modelling parameters considered in the present computational study are given in Table 1 [16–18].

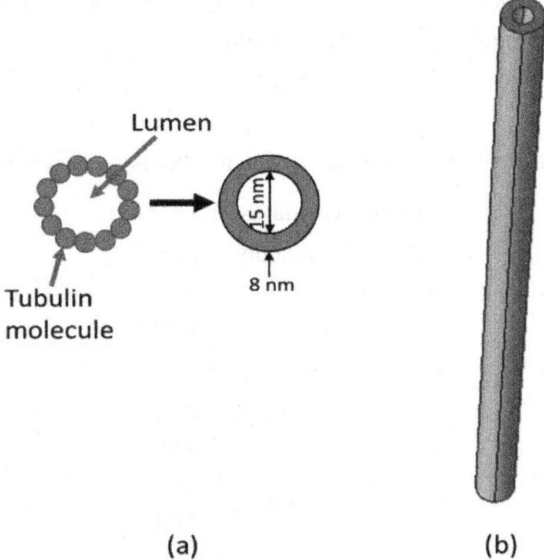

Fig. 2. (a) Reduction of the 13 protofilament microtubule to continuum-based model, and (b) schematic of single isolated hollow microtubule with 1 μm length considered in the present computational study.

The constitutive equations for a linearly coupled electro-mechanical model are given by [19–22]:

$$\sigma_{ij} = c_{ijkl}\varepsilon_{kl} - e_{ijk}E_k, \tag{1}$$

$$D_j = e_{jkl}\varepsilon_{kl} + \kappa_{jk}E_k, \tag{2}$$

where σ_{ij} are the components of mechanical stress tensor, ε_{ij} are the component of mechanical strain tensor, E_k are the components of electric field vector, D_j are the components of electric displacement vector, c_{ijkl} are the linear elastic coefficients, e_{ijk} are the linear piezoelectric coefficients and κ_{ij} is the dielectric permittivity coefficients, where subscript $i, j = 1, 2, 3$ and $k, l = 1, 2, 3, 4, 5, 6$. In this computational study, the piezoelectric coefficients of microtubules have been considered similar to that of collagen and have been adapted from [18]. Using Voigt's notation, piezoelectric strain coefficients are given as [18]

$$d_{ij} = \begin{bmatrix} 0 & 0 & 0 & d_{14} & d_{15} & 0 \\ 0 & 0 & 0 & d_{15} & -d_{14} & 0 \\ d_{31} & d_{31} & d_{33} & 0 & 0 & 0 \end{bmatrix}. \tag{3}$$

Further, since the present study is formulated using the stress form, thus accordingly the piezoelectric coefficients in strain form given in Eq. (3) have been converted into the stress form utilizing the following relation

$$e_{ijk} = c_{jklm} d_{ilm}, \tag{4}$$

where e_{ijk} are the piezoelectric stress coefficients, c_{jklm} are the components of the elastic tensor and d_{ilm} are the piezoelectric strain coefficients given in Eq. (3).

Table 1. Electro-mechanical characteristics of microtubules considered in the present study.

Material constants	Values
Elastic coefficients (GPa)	
c_{11}	2.5577
c_{22}	2.5577
c_{33}	2.5577
c_{12}	1.0962
c_{13}	1.0962
c_{44}	0.7308
c_{55}	0.7308
c_{66}	0.7308
Relative permittivity	
κ	40
Piezoelectric coefficients (pC/N)	
d_{14}	−12
d_{15}	6.21
d_{31}	−4.84
d_{33}	0.89

The relationship between the strain field and displacement field is given by the Cauchy representation

$$\varepsilon_{ij} = \frac{1}{2}\left(u_{i,j} + u_{j,i}\right). \tag{5}$$

Further, the electric field is related to the gradient of the electric potential as

$$E_i = -\phi_{,i}\,. \tag{6}$$

The constitutive equations are further subjected to the equilibrium condition and Gauss's law. Assuming that there is no body forces and no free charges, these governing equations are given by

$$\sigma_{ij,j} = 0, \tag{7}$$

$$D_{i,i} = 0. \tag{8}$$

The fully coupled electro-mechanical model of microtubule has been numerically implemented using a finite-element method (FEM) based commercial COMSOL Multiphysics 5.2 software [23]. The bottom face of the microtubule has been subjected to fixed and electrically grounded boundary conditions. A compressive and/or shear force has been applied at the top surface of the microtubule and accordingly, the induced stresses, strains, electric field and electric potential have been numerically computed. The initial displacement and electric potential within the computational domain of microtubule have been assumed to be 0 m and 0 V, respectively. All simulations have been performed in a stationary state regime. An optimum number of heterogeneous tetrahedral mesh elements obtained after conducting a mesh convergence analysis has been used for meshing the computational domain of a hollow cylindrical microtubule using COMSOL's built-in mesh generator. All simulations have been conducted on a Dell T7400 workstation with Quad-core 2.0 GHz Intel® Xeon® processors.

3 Results and Discussion

In the present computational study, the coupled electro-mechanical model of a microtubule has been modelled by adopting a similar mathematical framework utilized for modeling zinc oxide (ZnO) nanowires [19, 20]. Further, the numerical model fidelity and integrity have been evaluated by comparing the predicted results of the current model to those available in the literature, for e.g. [19]. The geometrical details of the nanowire (adapted from [19]) with a hexagonal cross-section considered for numerical validation has been presented in Fig. 3(a). Figure 3(b) presents the piezoelectric potential obtained in the previous study of Hao et al. [19] under the application of 100 nN compressive force along the z-axis at the top surface and the fixed bottom surface of the nanowire, as presented in Fig. 3(a). The piezoelectric potential (in V) obtained under the 100 nN compressive force from the present model utilizing similar geometrical detail and electro-mechanical parameter has been presented in Fig. 3(c). As evident from Fig. 3(c), the piezoelectric potential obtained from the present study completely matches with that obtained by [19] (see Fig. 3(b)) in the nanowire with the maximum absolute potential of 0.48 V. The maximum displacement (in nm) (refer to Fig. 3(d)) induced at the top surface of the nanowire under the application of 100 nN compressive force from the present model has been found to be 0.03 nm that is consistent with that obtained in [19]. Moreover, the developed model has also been validated with the applied compressive force of 85 nN at the top surface of the nanowire. Figures 3(e) and (f) presents the piezoelectric potential (in V) and displacement (in nm) distributions, respectively, obtained from the present model. As evident from Figs. 3(e)

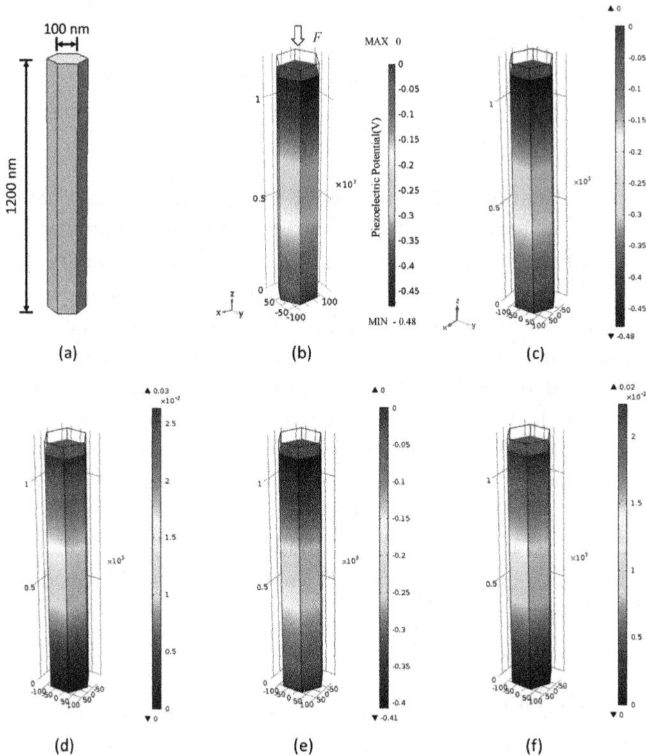

Fig. 3. (Color online). (a) Schematic illustration of the nanowire having a hexagonal cross-section, (b) piezoelectric potential distribution in the nanowire under a compressive force of 100 nN along the z-axis reported in [19], (c) piezoelectric potential (in V) predicted from the present model of the nanowire under a compressive force of 100 nN along the z-axis, (d) total displacement distribution (in nm) predicted from the present model of the nanowire under a compressive force of 100 nN along the z-axis, (e) piezoelectric potential (in V) predicted from the present model of the nanowire under a compressive force of 85 nN along the z-axis, and (f) total displacement distribution (in nm) predicted from the present model of the nanowire under a compressive force of 85 nN along the z-axis. (Figure 3(b) has been reproduced from [19] under the terms of the Creative Commons Attribution 4.0 International License, http://creativecommons.org/licenses/by/4.0/, Copyright © 1996-2019 MDPI, Basel, Switzerland).

and (f), the maximum electric potential and displacement have been found to be 0.41 V and 0.02 nm, respectively, that is in good agreement with those obtained in [19]. Thus, our developed model is consistent with the previous works and lends confidence in the results derived from the developed coupled electro-mechanical model.

The results obtained from the coupled electro-mechanical model of a single hollow cylindrical microtubule of 1 μm in length under the application of 0.1 nN compressive force uniformly applied at the top surface and fixed bottom surface have been presented in Fig. 4. The displacement distribution within the microtubule under the application of compressive force at the top surface has been presented in Fig. 4(a). As evident from Fig. 4(a), the top surface shows the maximum displacement of 0.09 nm under the applied force of 0.1 nN. It is worthwhile to mention that the displacements induced due to the compressive force lies within the range of that being induced in previous study reported in the literature, for e.g. [16]. In Fig. 4(b) the blue side is the negative potential side and the red side is the ground. As evident from Fig. 4(b), the maximum piezoelectric potential of 0.44 mV has been obtained under the compressive load of 0.1 nN. Further, the maximum stress induced in the microtubule under the compressive load has been found to be 0.23 MPa, as shown in Fig. 4(c). The displacement, electric potential and stress distributions predicted from the coupled electro-mechanical model under the application of 0.1 nN shear force at the top surface and fixed bottom have been presented in Fig. 5. The maximum displacement and maximum electric potential under the application of 0.1 nN shear force have been found to be 408.86 nm (see Fig. 5(a)) and 0.62 mV (see Fig. 5(b)), respectively. Accordingly, the maximum stress induced within the hollow microtubule under the application of shear force has been found to be 36.4 MPa and is concentrated at the bottom edges of the microtubule due to

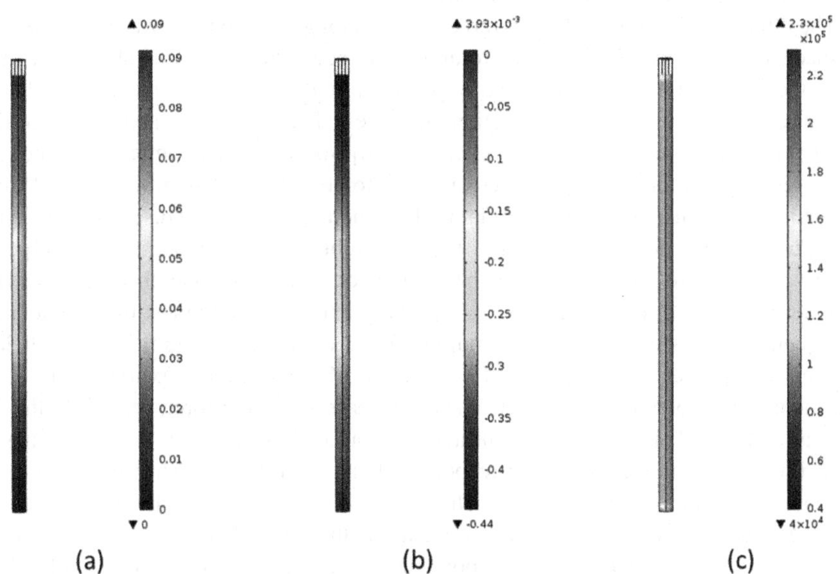

Fig. 4. (Color online). Electro-elastic response of a hollow cylindrical microtubule subjected to a compressive force of 0.1 nN at the top surface: (a) total displacement distribution (in nm), (b) electric potential distribution (in mV), and (c) stress distribution (in Pa).

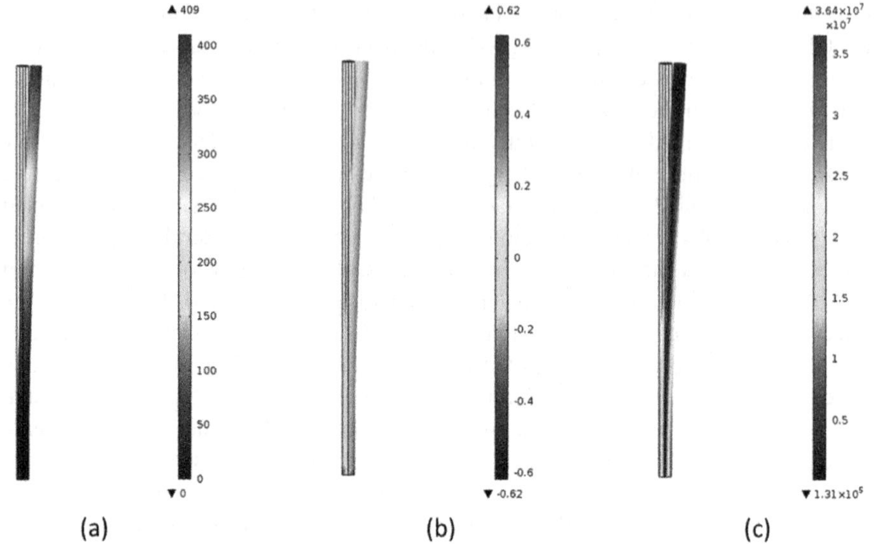

Fig. 5. (Color online). Electro-elastic response of a hollow cylindrical microtubule subjected to a shear force of 0.1 nN at the top surface: (a) total displacement distribution (in nm), (b) electric potential distribution (in mV), and (c) stress distribution (in Pa).

significant bending, as shown in Fig. 5(c). Thus, the application of shear force has a far more pronounced effect on the electro-elastic response of a microtubule as compared to the compressive force of the same magnitude.

The effect of direction of 0.1 nN force applied along the *x*-axis, *y*-axis and *z*-axis on the electro-elastic response of a microtubule has been presented in Table 2. In this table, the maximum predicted electric potential and the displacement have been summarized for a different combination of forces. The value of maximum electric potential has been presented in absolute values [20], so as to better compare the electro-elastic response of microtubule under different forces. As evident from Table 2, the application of 0.1 nN shear force results in the generation of bigger displacements and corresponding electric potential within the microtubule when compared to a perpendicular compressive force. This can be attributed to the fact that the piezoelectric coefficient in shear direction (e_{25}), i.e. along the y-axis, has the highest magnitude and subsequently results in the enhanced coupling between the strain and the electric field, resulting in a higher electric potential generation. Moreover, the maximum values of both the electric potential and displacements increase when the force applied in the *x*-axis was added to that of the *y*-axis. Further addition of the force in the *z*-direction has a trivial impact on the electro-elastic response of the microtubule. Therefore, the predicted results of the coupled electro-mechanical model of a microtubules demonstrate a coupling effect between the three components of the applied forces and the electro-elastic response, viz., induced electric potential and displacements. Consequently, this coupling effect should not be ignored for better predicting the behavior of microtubule subjected to external forces.

Table 2. Maximum displacement and electric potential obtained within a hollow cylindrical microtubule under the application of 0.1 nN force in different directions at the top surface.

Applied force (nN)			Displacement (nm)	Electric potential (mV)
x-axis	*y*-axis	*z*-axis		
0	0	0.1	0.09137	0.44
0	0.1	0	408.86	0.62
0.1	0	0	408.86	0.65
0.1	0.1	0	578.21	0.88
0.1	0	0.1	408.86	0.65
0	0.1	0.1	408.86	0.62
0.1	0.1	0.1	578.21	0.89

As mentioned earlier, one of our main motivations for the present computational study is to evaluate the effect of length of microtubule on the electro-elastic response under the application of external forces. Although microtubules can be up to 50 μm long, the typical length of microtubules ranges between 0.5 to 10 μm [15, 24, 25]. In what follows, we considered three effective lengths of the microtubule, viz., 1 μm, 5 μm and 10 μm, for evaluating the impact of microtubule length on their electro-elastic response under the influence of externally applied forces. Notably, the magnitudes of the force considered in our analysis have been varying from 0.02 nN to 0.1 nN, with the increment of 0.02 nN and have been adapted from [16]. The total displacements obtained under the application of different magnitude of compressive forces for the microtubule lengths of 1 μm, 5 μm and 10 μm have been presented in Fig. 6(a). It can be seen from Fig. 6(a) that the total displacement increases linearly as the externally applied force increases from 0.02 to 0.1 nN. However, the slope of increment increases with the increase in the microtubule length from 1 to 10 μm. Similar trends have been observed for the maximum electric potential generation within the different lengths of the microtubule considered in the present study when subjected to the varying magnitude of compressive forces. The effect of varying magnitudes of shear force on the maximum total displacement and the electric potential generated within the microtubule for different active lengths have been presented in Figs. 7(a) and (b), respectively. It has been observed that the trends of shear force are somewhat similar to that of compressive force. However, there is a significant variation in the magnitude of the respective values. For example, the maximum magnitude of displacement with compressive force has been found as 0.99 nm under the application of 0.1 nN force on a 10 μm long microtubule, whereas for shear force the predicted value of total displacement considerably rises to 407 μm. Similarly, the maximum electric potential generated within the 10 μm long microtubule under the compressive force of 0.1 nN has been found to be 4.39 mV in comparison to 6.13 mV under the application of shear force. Thus, the length of microtubules significantly influences the electro-elastic response as the coupled electro-mechanical model developed in the present study confirms.

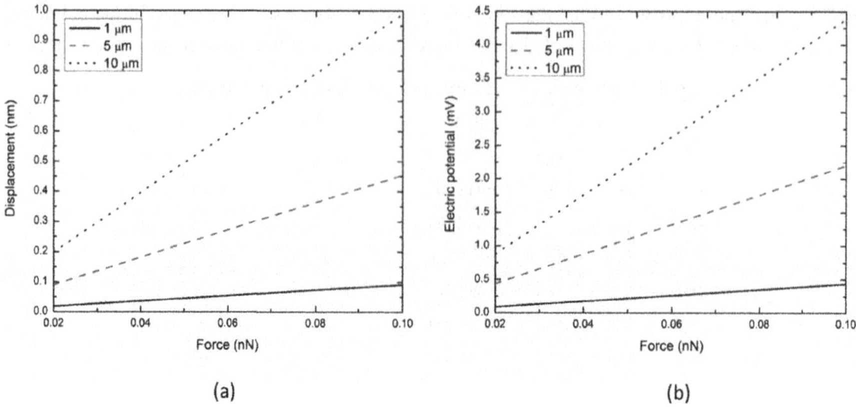

Fig. 6. Variation of (a) total displacement, and (b) electric potential with the applied compressive force at the top surface of hollow cylindrical microtubule for the active lengths of 1, 5 and 10 μm.

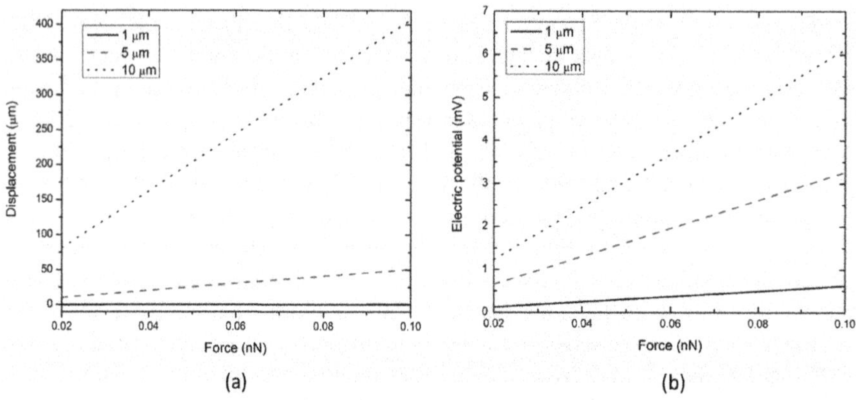

Fig. 7. Variation of (a) total displacement, and (b) electric potential with the applied shear force at the top surface of hollow cylindrical microtubule for the active lengths of 1, 5 and 10 μm.

4 Conclusion

In this work, a coupled electro-mechanical model of a microtubule has been developed for accurately quantifying its complex mechanics at a cellular scale under the influence of external stimuli. Important relations between the applied force and the displacement and applied force and the generated electric potential have been revealed. In particular, it has been observed that the application of shear force leads to both higher displacement and higher electric potential generation as compared to the application of compressive force. Moreover, the increase in the length of microtubules results in a significant rise in the predicted electric potential under the application of external forces. This work clearly demonstrates the importance of electro-mechanical coupling in our better understanding of the complex behaviors of microtubules exposed to external forces, which might be difficult to predict utilizing experimental studies. We expect a future extension of the proposed model for biomedical engineering and other related applications ranging from sensing to energy harvesting devices based on biological systems.

Acknowledgments. Authors are grateful to the NSERC and the CRC Program for their support. RM is also acknowledging the support of the BERC 2018-2021 program and Spanish Ministry of Science, Innovation and Universities through the Agencia Estatal de Investigacion (AEI) BCAM Severo Ochoa excellence accreditation SEV-2017-0718. Authors are also grateful to Prof. Jack Tuszynski as well as to Dr. Jagdish Krishnaswamy for useful discussions, valuable suggestions, and a number of important references.

References

1. Li, S., Wang, C., Nithiarasu, P.: Simulations on an undamped electromechanical vibration of microtubules in cytosol. Appl. Phys. Lett. **114**(25), 253702 (2019)
2. Kučera, O., Havelka, D., Cifra, M.: Vibrations of microtubules: physics that has not met biology yet. Wave Motion **72**, 13–22 (2017)
3. Melnik, R.V.N., Wei, X., Moreno-Hagelsieb, G.: Nonlinear dynamics of cell cycles with stochastic mathematical models. J. Biol. Syst. **17**(3), 425–460 (2009)
4. Havelka, D., Deriu, M.A., Cifra, M., Kučera, O.: Deformation pattern in vibrating microtubule: structural mechanics study based on an atomistic approach. Sci. Rep. **7**(1), 4227 (2017)
5. Li, S., Wang, C., Nithiarasu, P.: Three-dimensional transverse vibration of microtubules. J. Appl. Phys. **121**(23), 234301 (2017)
6. Tuszyński, J.A., Luchko, T., Portet, S., Dixon, J.M.: Anisotropic elastic properties of microtubules. Eur. Phys. J. E **17**(1), 29–35 (2005)
7. Jiang, H., Jiang, L., Posner, J.D., Vogt, B.D.: Atomistic-based continuum constitutive relation for microtubules: elastic modulus prediction. Comput. Mech. **42**(4), 607–618 (2008)
8. Liew, K.M., Xiang, P., Sun, Y.: A continuum mechanics framework and a constitutive model for predicting the orthotropic elastic properties of microtubules. Compos. Struct. **93** (7), 1809–1818 (2011)
9. Xiang, P., Liew, K.M.: Dynamic behaviors of long and curved microtubules based on an atomistic-continuum model. Comput. Methods Appl. Mech. Eng. **223**, 123–132 (2012)
10. Liew, K.M., Xiang, P., Zhang, L.W.: Mechanical properties and characteristics of microtubules: a review. Compos. Struct. **123**, 98–108 (2015)
11. Marracino, P., et al.: Tubulin response to intense nanosecond-scale electric field in molecular dynamics simulation. Sci. Rep. **9**(1), 1–14 (2019)
12. Civalek, Ö., Demir, C.: A simple mathematical model of microtubules surrounded by an elastic matrix by nonlocal finite element method. Appl. Math. Comput. **289**, 335–352 (2016)
13. Tuszynski, J.A., Kurzynski, M.: Introduction to Molecular Biophysics. CRC Press LLC, Boca Raton (2003)
14. Chae, I., Jeong, C.K., Ounaies, Z., Kim, S.H.: Review on electromechanical coupling properties of biomaterials. ACS Appl. Bio Mater. **1**(4), 936–953 (2018)
15. Thackston, K.A., Deheyn, D.D., Sievenpiper, D.F.: Simulation of electric fields generated from microtubule vibrations. Phys. Rev. E **100**(2), 022410 (2019)

16. Katti, D.R., Katti, K.S.: Cancer cell mechanics with altered cytoskeletal behavior and substrate effects: a 3D finite element modeling study. J. Mech. Behav. Biomed. Mater. **76**, 125–134 (2017)
17. Singh, S., Krishnaswamy, J.A., Melnik, R.: Biological cells and coupled electro-mechanical effects: a new model with nonlocal contributions (submitted)
18. Denning, D., et al.: Piezoelectric tensor of collagen fibrils determined at the nanoscale. ACS Biomate. Sci. Eng. **3**(6), 929–935 (2017)
19. Hao, H., Jenkins, K., Huang, X., Xu, Y., Huang, J., Yang, R.: Piezoelectric potential in single-crystalline ZnO nanohelices based on finite element analysis. Nanomaterials **7**(12), 430 (2017)
20. Cardoso, J., Oliveira, F., Proenca, M., Ventura, J.: The influence of shape on the output potential of ZnO nanostructures: sensitivity to parallel versus perpendicular forces. Nanomaterials **8**(5), 354 (2018)
21. Krishnaswamy, J.A., Buroni, F.C., Garcia-Sanchez, F., Melnik, R., Rodriguez-Tembleque, L., Saez, A.: Lead-free piezocomposites with CNT-modified matrices: accounting for agglomerations and molecular defects. Compos. Struct. **224**, 111033 (2019)
22. Krishnaswamy, J.A., Buroni, F.C., Garcia-Sanchez, F., Melnik, R., Rodriguez-Tembleque, L., Saez, A.: Improving the performance of lead-free piezoelectric composites by using polycrystalline inclusions and tuning the dielectric matrix environment. Smart Mater. Struct. **28**, 075032 (2019)
23. COMSOL Multiphysics® v. 5.2. www.comsol.com. COMSOL AB, Stockholm, Sweden
24. Adnan, A., Qidwai, S., Bagchi, A.: On the atomistic-based continuum viscoelastic constitutive relations for axonal microtubules. J. Mech. Behav. Biomed. Mater. **86**, 375–389 (2018)
25. Xiang, P., Zhang, L.W., Liew, K.M.: Meshfree simulation of temperature effects on the mechanical behaviors of microtubules. Eng. Anal. Boundary Elem. **69**, 104–118 (2016)

Comparison of Corneal Morphologic Parameters and High Order Aberrations in Keratoconus and Normal Eyes

Jose Sebastián Velázquez[1], Francisco Cavas[1](✉), Jose Miguel Bolarín[2], and Jorge Alió[3,4]

[1] Department of Structures, Construction and Graphic Expression, Technical University of Cartagena, 30202 Cartagena, Spain
francisco.cavas@upct.es

[2] Technology Centre for IT and Communications (CENTIC), Scientific Park of Murcia, 30100 Murcia, Spain

[3] Keratoconus Unit of Vissum Corporation Alicante, 03016 Alicante, Spain

[4] Department of Ophthalmology, Miguel Hernández University of Elche, 03202 Alicante, Spain

Abstract. The aim of this study is evaluating the influence of corneal geometry in the optical system's aberrations, and its usefulness as diagnostic criterion for keratoconus.159 normal eyes (normal group, mean age 37.8 ± 11.6 years) and 292 eyes with the diagnosis of keratoconus (keratoconus group, mean age 42.2 ± 17.6 years) were included in this study. All eyes received a comprehensive ophthalmologic examination. A virtual 3D model of each eye was made using CAD software and different anatomical parameters related with surface and volume were measured. Statistically significant differences were found for all anatomical parameters (all $p < 0.001$). AUROC analysis showed that all parameters reached values above 0.7, with the exception of the total corneal surface area (TCSAA-S). In conclusion, the methodology explained in this research, that bases in anatomical parameters obtained from a virtual corneal model, allow to analyze the diagnostic value of corneal geometry correlation with optical aberrations in keratoconus pathology.

Keywords: Ophthalmology · Corneal apex · Computer-Aided Design (CAD) · Computational modelling · Scheimpflug technology

1 Introduction

The human eye is an optical instrument that projects images from outside into the retina [1]. However, the eye is characterized by a lack of symmetry in its surfaces, as these do not present revolution symmetry because of their de-alignment and de-centration. This causes a degradation in the quality of image by means of aberrations of the optical system [2, 3]. This refractive anomaly can elicit the well-known astigmatism, myopia or hyperopia in patients.

I. Rojas et al. (Eds.): IWBBIO 2020, LNBI 12108, pp. 87–97, 2020.
https://doi.org/10.1007/978-3-030-45385-5_8

In keratoconus (KCN) disease, that is an affection in which the cornea acquires a conical structure as a result of a progressive corneal thinning [4], corneal thickness reduction causes optical aberrations.

There are different indices for the detection of KCN basing on astigmatism [5], like the AST or the SRAX index. Both quantify irregular astigmatism, but these indices are characterized for using only data of the anterior surface of the cornea. Other authors [6, 7] use wave-front based technologies to detect astigmatism, yet it has been demonstrated that aberrations are difficult to measure with these methods, as they do not cover the whole corneal surface. Consequently, it would be interesting to measure astigmatism from geometrical data obtained from the corneal topographies, as this data in fact register almost completely anterior and posterior corneal surfaces.

Our research group has validated a geometrical patient-specific virtual model for the diagnosis of KCN from a morpho-geometric point of view [2, 8–10]. This patient-specific model has been used in other fields, such as the Finite Elements one [11–14], in which it has been used to analyze the biomechanical behavior of the cornea to refractive surgeries or the response to the intra-stromal ring segment implantation in corneas with keratoconus [11, 13], and also to analyze the behavior of corneal tissue properties in different scenarios [14].

Also, there are many different approaches in which KCN classification can be based, usually relying in lens refraction, corneal thickness, keratometry data, corrected distance visual acuity (CDVA), internal astigmatism, root mean square, central keratometry, corneal asphericity at 8 mm, pachymetry and myopia, among others [5]. This study proposes using a classification based in high order aberrations (HOA), the one known as Alió-Shabayek [15].

Therefore, in this research work it is evaluated the influence of the corneal geometry in optical aberrations, and its usefulness as a criterion for the diagnosis of keratoconus.

2 Patients and Methods

2.1 Patients

A total number of 451 eyes of 451 individuals with ages ranging from 16 to 75 years were evaluated at Vissum Hospital (Alicante). All the procedures adhered to the tenets of the Declaration of Helsinki (Fortaleza, 2013) and were approved by the Ethical Board of the hospital. All patients were informed and authorized their inclusion in the study by signing an informed consent. These data are included in the "Iberia" database of KCN eyes created for the National Network for Clinical Research in Ophthalmology RETICS-OFTARED.

A thorough and detailed ophthalmic exam was made to all the subjects [10] and they were divided into two different groups (normal and keratoconus) according to the Alió-Shabayek grading system [15].

The first group did not present any ocular pathology and consisted in 159 healthy eyes of 159 patients (89 men/70 women, mean age 37.8 ± 11.6). Inclusion criterion was: any patient who did not present any ocular or corneal pathology. Exclusion criterion was: patient whose eyes had undergone any previous surgical procedure.

The second group corresponded to diseased eyes, and consisted in 292 eyes of 292 patients. (162 men/130 women, mean age 42.2 ± 17.6). Inclusion criterion was: presence of a localized corneal topography steepening and/or the presence of an asymmetric bow tie with or without topographical angulated principal meridians, and any microscopic keratoconic sign: Fleischer ring, Vogt striae, stromal thinning, protrusion apex or anterior corneal scars in the corneal stroma. Exclusion criterion was: any previous eye surgical procedure and any other eye pathology different from the keratoconus.

2.2 Methods

The procedure followed in our research work can be described by two main phases (see Fig. 1): a first phase of 3D corneal model generation and a second one of geometrical analysis of the 3D model.

First Phase. Systems based on the projection of a slit of light onto the cornea and on the principle of Scheimpflug photography [5] allow the exportation of data containing the geometrical readings of each specific patient. These data are known as "raw data" [8, 9], and are used to create patient-specific models [2, 8–10, 13, 14] in the fields of Finite Elements and Computer-Aided Design.

In our study, we have used Sirius tomographer (Construzione Strumenti Oftalmici, Italy), a device based in principle of Scheimpflug photography, that allows the characterization of the optical aberrations present in the patient's eye, as well as the exportation of geometrical data into a .CSV format file [14]. These data are transformed into Cartesian coordinates, as we are working with a set of spatial points (see Fig. 1), so our team has programmed an algorithm using Matlab® V R2014 software (Mathworks, Natick, USA), in order to:

- Transform the set of spatial data given in polar coordinates in the .CSV file to a set of spatial data in Cartesian format in a .TXT file (see Fig. 1, First Phase). We made this transformation because Rhinoceros® V 5.0 software (MCNeel & Associates, Seattle, USA) uses this set of spatial data in Cartesian format to generate the corneal surfaces.
- Validate those sets of spatial data that present invalid reading values of the corneal surface's geometry (see Fig. 2). Due to the existence of factors extrinsic to the patient while measures are being taken [5], like tear film stability, tabs that block the visual field or improper opening of the eyelids, data acquired by the Sirius device for determined points located in the peripheral zones can be not valid, getting in those cases a value of −1000 in the corresponding matrix cells. To avoid including these invalid cyphers, all the CSV files created for each cornea went through a filtering process, being selected for this research just those cases that held correct values in their first 21 rows (256 values per row; radii values ranging from 0 mm to 4 mm in reference to the normal corneal vertex), discarding from the research any cornea that included invalid −1000 values located within this range. This filtering procedure guaranteed that all data utilized for generating clouds of points was real, and interpolation was not used [8, 9, 16].

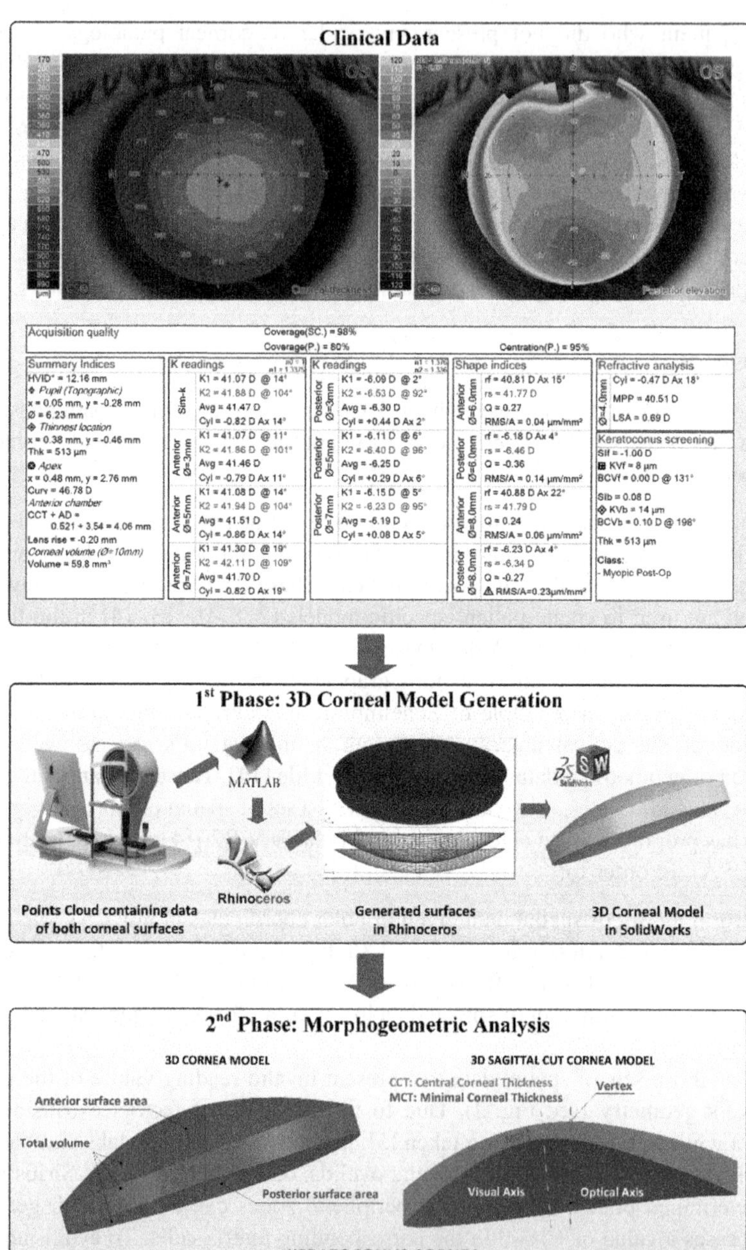

Fig. 1. Procedure followed for the 3D corneal model generation and later analysis. Data obtained from Sirius tomographer allow the generation of a personalized 3D model, in which several morphogeometric variables are studied.

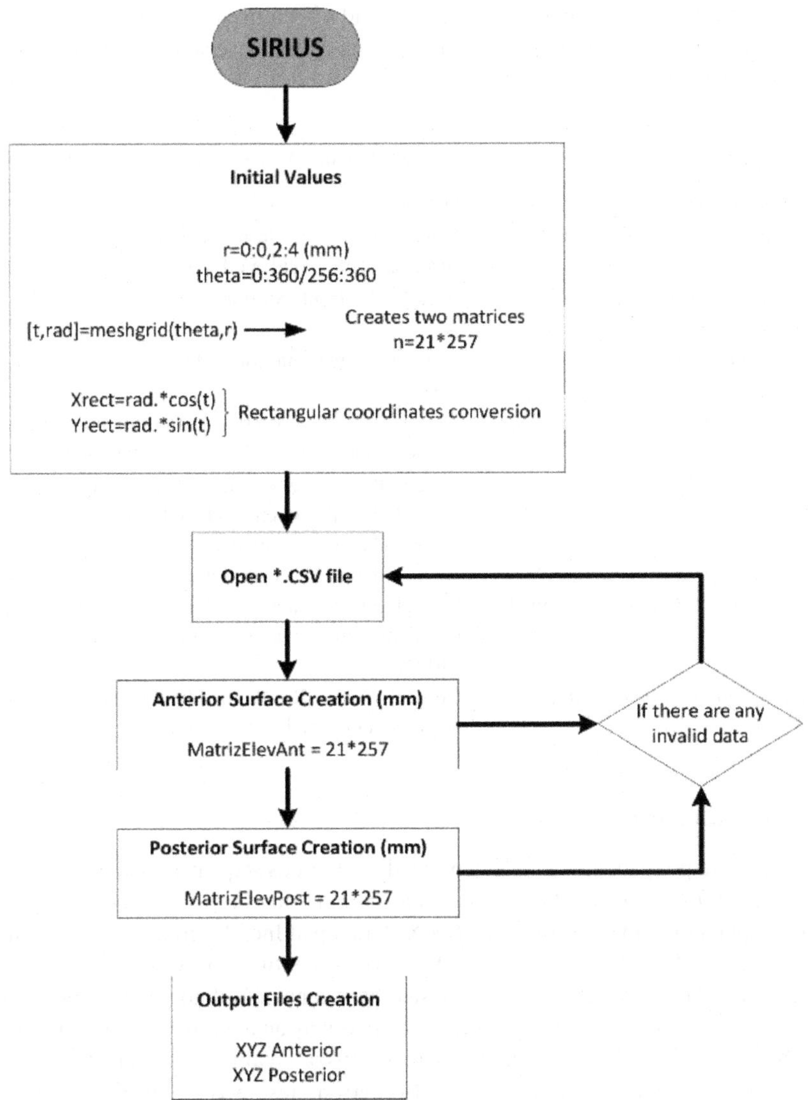

Fig. 2. Description of the algorithm followed for the coordinate transformation

Once anterior and posterior surfaces of the cornea have been generated in Rhinoceros®, they are both exported into SolidWorks V2017 software (Dassault Systèmes, Vélizy-Villacoublay, France) to create a complete 3D model of the cornea.

Second Phase. Over the 3D model and within the graphical environment of the modelling software, a structural characterization of the corneal morphology was done through a geometrical analysis of the model, that was made with the measurement tools integrated in the program. These tools allow the definition of a set of variables of superficial and volumetric nature that have already been used in previous works (see Table 1), although it is the first time that they are used to evaluate the influence of corneal geometry in optical aberrations.

Table 1. Set of geometrical parameters analyzed for the Alió-Shabayek classification [10].

Geometric variable	Description
Total corneal volume (TCV_{A-S}) [mm^3]	Volume limited by front, back and peripheral surfaces of the solid model generated
Anterior corneal surface area ($ACSA_{A-S}$) [mm^2]	Area of the front/exterior surface
Posterior corneal surface area ($PCSA_{A-S}$) [mm^2]	Area of the rear/interior surface
Total corneal surface area ($TCSA_{A-S}$) [mm^2]	Sum of anterior, posterior and perimetral corneal surface areas of the solid model generated
Sagittal plane apex area ($SPAP_{A-S}$) [mm^2]	Area of the cornea within the sagittal plane passing through the optical axis and the highest point (apex) of the anterior corneal surface
Sagittal Plane Area in minimum thickness point ($SPAMTP_{A-S}$) [mm^2]	Area of the cornea within the sagittal plane passing through the optical axis and the minimum thickness point (maximum curvature) of the anterior corneal surface
Corneal volume R-x (CV_{A-S} R-x) [mm^3]	Corneal volume R-x defined by the anterior corneal apex at radii 0.5, 1.0 and 1.5 mm

2.3 Statistical Analysis

Just a single eye per patient was selected in a dichotomous sequence (0 and 1), made by a computer software, to elude any potential correlations between eyes of the same patient Graphpad Prism v7.0 for MAC OS X (Graphpad Inc., La Jolla, USA) and SPSS 24.0 software (SPSS Inc., Chicago, USA) were the two software chosen for the analysis of the data. Data normality was tested by means of Kolmogovov-Smirnov test. Comparison between groups was performed by one-way analysis of variance (ANOVA) if variables were normally distributed, whereas Kruskal-Wallis non-parametric test was used for non-normally distributed ones. Bonferroni test was selected for post-hoc comparative analysis for the ANOVA when the variances were homogeneous and T2 Tamhane test was the option when variances did not show homogeneity. P-values < 0.05 were considered statistically significant for the differences. Lastly, receiver operating characteristic (ROC) curves were used to determine which parameters better characterized diseased corneas.

3 Results

This study comprised a total number of 451 eyes: 159 healthy eyes (35.25%) and 292 (64.75%) diagnosed as suffering from KCN according to the Alió-Shabayek grading scale, presenting High Order Aberrations (HOA) of third order.

With respect to the healthy eyes, 74 individuals were men (46.5%) and 85 were women (53.5%), being 82 right eyes (51.4%) and 76 left eyes (49.6%).

Clinical data that these individuals presented for optical aberrations were: Root Mean Square High Order Aberrations (RMS HOA) was 0.41 µm (range 0.23 to 0.73 µm); Spherical Aberration (SA) was 0.23 µm (range 0.07 to 0.43 µm); Root Mean Square Coma (RMS Coma) was 0.30 µm (range 0.03 to 0.69 µm); Root Mean Square Coma-like was 0.35 µm (range 0.09 to 0.72 µm) and Root Mean Square Spherical-like was 0.25 µm (range 0.10 to 0.50 µm).

Finally, regarding astigmatism, corneal asphericity was calculated at 4.5 mm and at 8 mm. In this respect, the one at 4.5 mm was −0.1 (range −0.62 to 0.87) and the one at 8 mm was −0.28 (range −0.70 to 0.17).

With respect to the eyes diagnosed as KCN, 125 subjects were men (42.8%) and 167 were women (57.2%), being 134 right eyes (45.8%) and 158 left eyes (55.2%).

Clinical data that these individuals presented for optical aberrations were: Root Mean Square High Order Aberrations (RMS HOA) was 2.6 µm (range 0.33 to 13.9 µm); Spherical Aberration (SA) was −0.19 µm (range −7.9 to 1.40 µm); Root Mean Square Coma (RMS Coma) was 2.1 µm (range 0.05 to 12.9 µm); Root Mean Square Coma-like was 2.34 µm (range 0.21 to 13.01 µm) and Root Mean Square Spherical-like was 0.89 µm (range 0.14 to 8.3 µm).

As with the healthy group, corneal asphericity was calculated at 4.5 mm and at 8 mm, being at 4.5 mm −0.6 (range −7.39 to 4.09) and at 8 mm −0.81 (range −3.0 to 2.85).

Analyzing descriptive values and their differences when comparing healthy and KCN eyes (see Table 2), all the geometrical variables ($p < 0.05$) showed good capability of discrimination between groups, without exceptions.

Table 2. Descriptive values and differences in the modelled geometric variables among the normal and keratoconus groups. SD: standard deviation. P: statistical test.

Measurement	Normal group (n = 159)				Keratoconus group (n = 292)				z	P
	Mean	SD	Min	Max	Mean	SD	Min	Max		
$TCV_{A\text{-}S}$ (mm^3)	25.55	1.58	25.51	25.61	23.91	1.89	23.85	23.96	25.08	<0.001
$ACSA_{A\text{-}S}$ (mm^2)	43.10	0.15	43.07	43.14	43.45	0.54	43.32	43.64	175.59	<0.001
$PCSA_{A\text{-}S}$ (mm^2)	44.27	0.30	44.22	44.32	44.82	0.87	44.69	44.99	151.62	<0.001
$TCSA_{A\text{-}S}$ (mm^2)	103.87	1.18	103.81	103.91	104.07	1.99	104.01	104.16	36.16	<0.001
$SPAP_{A\text{-}S}$ (mm^2)	4.28	0.26	4.22	4.34	3.96	0.33	3.91	4.00	34.46	<0.001
$SPAMTP_{A\text{-}S}$ (mm^2)	4.27	0.27	4.22	4.33	3.94	0.33	3.89	3.97	36.38	<0.001
$CV_{A\text{-}S}$ R-0.5 (mm^3)	0.41	0.03	0.35	0.45	0.36	0.05	0.23	0.40	221.38	<0.001
$CV_{A\text{-}S}$ R-1 (mm^3)	1.69	0.11	1.63	2.01	1.47	0.08	1.38	1.50	221.20	<0.001
$CV_{A\text{-}S}$ R-1.5 (mm^3)	3.86	0.25	3.80	3.91	3.43	0.37	3.36	3.46	73.39	<0.001

In addition, an area under the receiver-operator curve (AUROC) analysis was made for the nine geometrical studied variables (Fig. 3), with good values of area under the curve (above 0.7), for all variables except total corneal surface, as shown in Table 3.

Table 3. The area under the ROC results.

Measurement	Area	Sensitivity	Specificity	Standard error	95% confidence interval	
					Lower limit	Upper limit
$TCV_{A\text{-}S}$	0.751	60.6	78.0	0.023	0.706	0.796
$ACSA_{A\text{-}S}$	0.782	62.3	83.6	0.021	0.741	0.824
$PCSA_{A\text{-}S}$	0.754	47.6	90.6	0.023	0.710	0.799
$TCSA_{A\text{-}S}$	0.501	17.5	93.7	0.021	0.447	0.545
$SPAP_{A\text{-}S}$	0.781	50.3	94.3	0.021	0.739	0.823
$SPAMTP_{A\text{-}S}$ (mm^2)	0.781	48.3	95.0	0.021	0.739	0.823
$CV_{A\text{-}S}$ R-0.5 (mm^3)	0.860	70.2	89.9	0.017	0.826	0.894
$CV_{A\text{-}S}$ R-1 (mm^3)	0.853	72.3	85.5	0.017	0.819	0.887
$CV_{A\text{-}S}$ R-1.5 (mm^3)	0.836	61.6	91.8	0.018	0.800	0.873

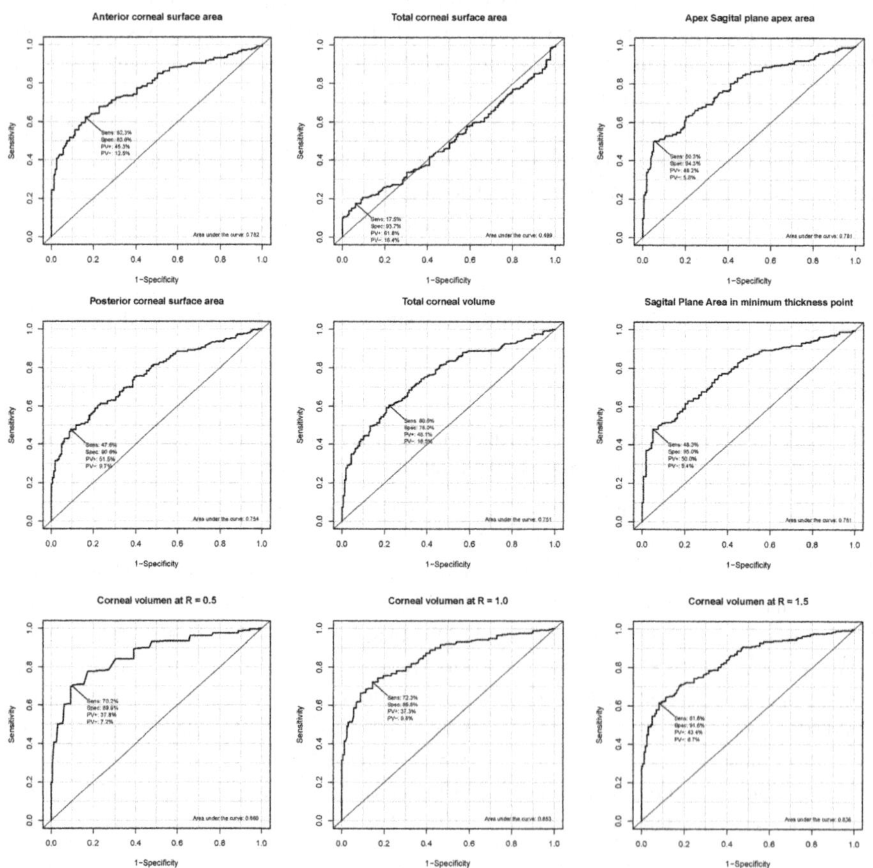

Fig. 3. Curves for modelled parameters detecting KC.

4 Discussion

Patients suffering from KCN present values in optical aberrations significantly higher than the ones of those with normal eyes [17]. This is caused by the deformation that the wave front suffers when it reaches the corneal surface, due to the de-centration of the point of maximum curvature in KCN. However, one of the aspects to which less attention has been paid is the potential diagnostic value of the optical aberrations correlated with corneal geometry in KCN pathology. This work develops a methodology that analyses the relationship between different anatomical parameters and optical aberrations.

For this study, a Sirius corneal tomographer (Construzione Strumenti Oftalmici, Italy) has been used. It is a device that provides consistent and repeatable measures for each patient [18]. In reference with the anatomical parameters studied in the virtual model, volume parameters and surface parameters should be considered separately. Regarding the first ones, total corneal volume ($TCV_{A\text{-}S}$) presented significant differences between the studied groups, but they were not remarkable, not coinciding this result with the ones reported in other previous studies. [16, 19, 20]. This can be explained by the fact that the KCN group includes an important amount of eyes with advanced KCN. In addition, this result is in line with the existence of significant differences in measured corneal volumes at $R = 0.5$, $R = 1$ and at $R = 1.5$, as the tendency of corneal structure is being more irregular or oblate (more curved) in central zone than in peripheral zone, in which it is more regular or prolate.

Regarding anatomical surface parameters, all variables presented statistically significant differences between groups, being these remarkable for anterior corneal surface area and posterior corneal surface area. This finding is in line with other studies that have used the same Sirius technology [20, 21]. Piñero et al. [20] proved that corneal curvature increases with disease progression, this is, the areas of both corneal surfaces grow as they become steeper. Also, Ishi et al. [21] demonstrated that a correlation between surfaces existed for the more advanced degrees of the disease. An explanation of the finding in our study can be that posterior surface curves, in proportion, more than the anterior one, because of the relation of mechanical feebleness that corneal tissues present [12]. Other less significant superficial parameters were also studied, such as the sagittal areas obtained from the apex and from anterior the minimum thickness point of the cornea, although these variables were not significant for the study. This can be caused by the fact that the local change inducted by the intra-ocular pressure in corneal surface is not representative in these areas for the study of a wave front (aberrometry). This has been reported by our research team in previous studies [8–10].

Sensibility analysis of the measured variables revealed that some variables presented values of AUROC > 0.7, more precisely $TCV_{A\text{-}S}$ AUC, $ACSA_{A\text{-}S}$, $PCSA_{A\text{-}S}$, $SPAP_{A\text{-}S}$, $SPAMTP_{A\text{-}S}$, $CV_{A\text{-}S}$ R-0.5, $CV_{A\text{-}S}$ R-1 and $CV_{A\text{-}S}$ R-1.5. Consequently, these variables can be used for diagnosing KCN.

5 Conclusion

Anatomical variables of surface and volume obtained from a virtual model of the cornea for each patient allow to characterize and discriminate, in a reliable way, healthy corneas from corneas with optical aberrations, diagnosed with KCN according to the Alió-Shabayek optical classification. These anatomical variables can be a helpful tool that may allow measuring the optical quality of vision of the patients. However, the discrimination power of several variables used conjointly has not been studied in this research work, and opens a new way to explore for future ones, using techniques such as logistic regression.

Funding. This publication has been carried out in the framework of the Thematic Network for Co-Operative Research in Health (RETICS), reference number RD16/0008/0012, financed by the Carlos III Health Institute–General Subdirection of Networks and Cooperative Investigation Centers (R&D&I National Plan 2013–2016) and the European Regional Development Fund (FEDER).

References

1. Hansen, E.D., Hartnett, M.E.: A review of treatment for retinopathy of prematurity. Expert Rev. Ophthalmol. **14**(2), 73–87 (2019). https://doi.org/10.1080/17469899.2019.1596026
2. Cavas-Martínez, F., Piñero, D.P., Fernández-Pacheco, D.G., Mira, J., Cañavate, F.J.F., Alió, J.L.: Assessment of pattern and shape symmetry of bilateral normal corneas by scheimpflug technology. Symmetry **10**(10) (2018). https://doi.org/10.3390/sym10100453
3. Giovanzana, S., Kasprzak, H.T., Pałucki, B., Ţălu, Ş.: Non-rotational aspherical models of the human optical system. J. Mod. Opt. **60**(21), 1899–1905 (2013). https://doi.org/10.1080/09500340.2013.865802
4. Salomão, M., et al.: Recent developments in keratoconus diagnosis. Expert Rev. Ophthalmol. **13**(6), 329–341 (2018). https://doi.org/10.1080/17469899.2018.1555036
5. Cavas-Martinez, F., De la Cruz, S.E., Nieto Martinez, J., Fernandez Canavate, F.J., Fernandez-Pacheco, D.G.: Corneal topography in keratoconus: state of the art. Eye Vis. (London, England) **3**, 5 (2016). https://doi.org/10.1186/s40662-016-0036-8
6. Maeda, N., et al.: Wavefront aberrations measured with Hartmann-Shack sensor in patients with keratoconus. Ophthalmology **109**(11), 1996–2003 (2002). https://doi.org/10.1016/s0161-6420(02)01279-4
7. Mihaltz, K., Kranitz, K., Kovacs, I., Takacs, A., Nemeth, J., Nagy, Z.Z.: Shifting of the line of sight in keratoconus measured by a hartmann-shack sensor. Ophthalmology **117**(1), 41–48 (2010). https://doi.org/10.1016/j.ophtha.2009.06.039
8. Cavas-Martínez, F., Bataille, L., Fernández-Pacheco, D.G., Cañavate, F.J.F., Alio, J.L.: Keratoconus detection based on a new corneal volumetric analysis. Sci. Rep. **7**(1) (2017). https://doi.org/10.1038/s41598-017-16145-3
9. Cavas-Martínez, F., Bataille, L., Fernández-Pacheco, D.G., Cañavate, F.J.F., Alio, J.L.: A new approach to keratoconus detection based on corneal morphogeometric analysis. PLoS ONE **12**(9) (2017). https://doi.org/10.1371/journal.pone.0184569

10. Velázquez, J.S., Cavas, F., Alió Del Barrio, J., Fernández-Pacheco, D.G., Alió, J.: Assessment of the association between in vivo corneal morphogeometrical changes and keratoconus eyes with severe visual limitation. J. Ophthalmol. **2019** (2019). https://doi.org/10.1155/2019/8731626
11. Carvalho, L.A., et al.: Keratoconus prediction using a finite element model of the cornea with local biomechanical properties. Arquivos Brasileiros de Oftalmologia **72**(2), 139–145 (2009). https://doi.org/10.1590/S0004-27492009000200002
12. Gefen, A., Shalom, R., Elad, D., Mandel, Y.: Biomechanical analysis of the keratoconic cornea. J. Mech. Behav. Biomed. Mater. **2**(3), 224–236 (2009). https://doi.org/10.1016/j.jmbbm.2008.07.002
13. Lanchares, E., Buey, M.A.D., Cristóbal, J.A., Calvo, B., Ascaso, F.J., Malvè, M.: Computational simulation of scleral buckling surgery for rhegmatogenous retinal detachment: on the effect of the band size on the myopization. J. Ophthalmol. **2016** (2016). https://doi.org/10.1155/2016/3578617
14. Pandolfi, A., Manganiello, F.: A model for the human cornea: constitutive formulation and numerical analysis. Biomech. Model. Mechanobiol. **5**(4), 237–246 (2006). https://doi.org/10.1007/s10237-005-0014-x
15. Alio, J.L., Shabayek, M.H.: Corneal higher order aberrations: a method to grade keratoconus. J. Refract. Surg. (Thorofare, NJ: 1995) **22**(6), 539–545 (2006)
16. Cavas-Martínez, F., et al.: Geometrical custom modeling of human cornea in vivo and its use for the diagnosis of corneal ectasia. PLoS ONE **9**(10) (2014). https://doi.org/10.1371/journal.pone.0110249
17. Wang, L., Dai, E., Koch, D.D., Nathoo, A.: Optical aberrations of the human anterior cornea. J. Cataract Refract. Surg. **29**(8), 1514–1521 (2003). https://doi.org/10.1016/S0886-3350(03)00467-X
18. Hernández-Camarena, J.C., et al.: Repeatability, reproducibility, and agreement between three different scheimpflug systems in measuring corneal and anterior segment biometry. J. Refract. Surg. **30**(9), 616–621 (2014). https://doi.org/10.3928/1081597X-20140815-02
19. Montalbán, R., Piñero, D.P., Javaloy, J., Alió, J.L.: Intrasubject repeatability of corneal morphology measurements obtained with a new Scheimpflug photography-based system. J. Cataract Refract. Surg. **38**(6), 971–977 (2012). https://doi.org/10.1016/j.jcrs.2011.12.029
20. Piñero, D.P., Alió, J.L., Alesón, A., Vergara, M.E., Miranda, M.: Corneal volume, pachymetry, and correlation of anterior and posterior corneal shape in subclinical and different stages of clinical keratoconus. J. Cataract Refract. Surg. **36**(5), 814–825 (2010). https://doi.org/10.1016/j.jcrs.2009.11.012
21. Ishii, R., Kamiya, K., Igarashi, A., Shimizu, K., Utsumi, Y., Kumanomido, T.: Correlation of corneal elevation with severity of keratoconus by means of anterior and posterior topographic analysis. Cornea **31**(3), 253–258 (2012). https://doi.org/10.1097/ico.0b013e31823d1ee0

Graph Databases for Contact Analysis in Infections Using Spatial Temporal Models

Lorena Pujante, Manuel Campos(✉), Jose M. Juarez, Bernardo Canovas-Segura, and Antonio Morales

AIKE Research Group (INTICO), Facultad de Informatica, University of Murcia, Campus Espinardo, 30100 Murcia, Spain
{lorenapujante,manuelcampos,jmjuarez,bernardocs,morales}@um.es
http://www.um.es/aike

Abstract. Infections acquired in healthcare settings (nosocomial infections) have become one of the main health problems in acute care centers. Some of epidemiologists' efforts are focused on studying patient's traceability and determining the main factors that lead to its appearance. However, specialists demand new technology to ease such analysis.

In this work, we explore the capacity of alternative technologies in information storage, like Graph databases (GDBs). GDBs, unlike the traditional (relational) databases present in Information Health Systems, have a remarkable expressiveness for modeling and querying highly interliked concepts in data-sets. In particular, we focus on the study of the advantages GDBs can offer in the analysis of contacts between patients diagnosed with a bacterial nosocomial infection in a hospital setting.

The contributions of our research are the following: a design and implementation of the domain has been carried out, with the ability to model any hospital architectural structure on several levels, as well as represent the clinical events associated with patients, thus contemplating a spatial and temporal modeling. Finally, we study the query expressiveness and performance for the analysis of contacts in infection spread.

Keywords: Graph datatabases · Spatial-temporal information · Analysis of contacts

1 Introduction

Nosocomial infections (NI) are those acquired in health care facilities, one of the main causes of deaths and morbidity in hospitalized patients [2] and its economic and human repercussions are increasingly significant. This has alerted the medical field of epidemiology, focusing part of its efforts on traceability and determining the main factors that lead to the appearance and spread of NI. However, the study of these diseases is a challenge due to the wide range of infections that can be classified as NI and the wide variety of causes for

I. Rojas et al. (Eds.): IWBBIO 2020, LNBI 12108, pp. 98–107, 2020.
https://doi.org/10.1007/978-3-030-45385-5_9

which they can appear and spread. In particular, the analysis of contact spread consist of studying the agents involved in the infection transmission, considering both direct contact (human-to-human) and indirect contact (e.g. contaminated objects). One important bottleneck of the data analysis of contacts is to extract a clear trace of the activity of patients from the Electronic Health Records (EHRs) stored in the Health Information System (HIS) databases. In general, commercial HIS are supported by relational databases (RDBs) making difficult to manage the complex relations between the different dimensions of study: clinical data and spatial-temporal information. The alternative is the use of non-relational databases, successfully used in areas where large volumes of data must be worked at high speed and at a reduced cost. Graph databases (GDBs) are a particular kind of non-relational database with network-like structure that allow them to work with highly connected data sets. Data are represented as the graph nodes and relationships between them as edges. Nodes and edges store direct links to other nodes and edges. These characteristics allow the optimal navigation through the information stored in the database and the use of graph theory algorithms.

In this preliminary work, we evaluate the capacity of GDB technology in the design of data queries for spread contact analysis for its use in the field of bacterial epidemiology to determine the origin of an epidemic outbreak and to perform analysis of contacts.

The contributions of this research work are the following:

- Review of GDB technology for spread contact analysis.
- Design a graph-based domain model considering spatial-temporal information of hospitals. The domain must be generalist enough to express: (1) a variety of levels any type of architectural structure of a hospital, (2) temporal dimension and (3) events recorded in the patients' clinical files.
- Translate epidemiological investigations into database queries that take advantage of the graph structure.

2 Related Work

In this work we review GDB technology as well as recent research advances of the use of GDBs.

From the technological point of view, we analyse three GDB management systems widely extended in both industry and the research field: Neo4J, OrientDB and Arango. Table 1 summarises their key aspects. OrientDB[1] is a multi-model database (based on graphs, documental and key-value). At present, it is one of the most extended approaches in Big Data scenarios since uses a totally object oriented approaches (Java). It is also worth mentioning its query language, OrientDB SQL with is a version of SQL with operations to traverse the graphs. Its open version, OrientDB Community, provides the widest number of

[1] OrientDB: https://orientdb.com/.

features, compared with the other two GDBs mentioned in this paper. Arango[2] is a C++ implemented platform for different non-relational databases, including graph models. Queries are defined using AQL, a variation of SQL allowing control flow commands from imperative language (e.g. for sentence). Finally, Neo4J[3] is a dedicated GDB management system. It is multiplatform using Java and is widely used in industry and academia. Unlike OrientDB or Arango, it provides a tailored language for graph querying called Cypher.

A relevant aspect is the underlying graph storage model. While Neo4j uses a triples store, OrientDB and ArangoDB are multi-model, and include a vertices-edges models. This latter, is *a-priori* more expressive than the others for our queries since it is more closed to a graph representation.

Recent research on bioinformatics proofs the suitability of GDB technologies to manage large amounts of data in life science. Maiers et al. [7] used Neo4J for matching and estimating genotypes. A number of studies in the medical informatics field focuses on GDBs. The authors of [3] propose to implement FIHR standards for storing clinical data in a Neo4J model. Similarly, an analysis of the advantages of representing medical health records with graphs is carried out in [8].

Regarding the study of infection diseases, researchers of [6] focus on Tuberculosis disease research from the biology perspective, representing biological entities in a labelled property graph using Neo4J. From the theoretical point of view, several models recently described the spread of disease [5]. However, little attention is paid on the use of GDBs for infectious diseases from an epidemiological perspective. Grande et al. [4] research on the epidemiological profile of HCV infection, using GDBs for modeling social network information for public health purposes. Researchers also explored the use of spatial information to improve contact tracing analysis. For example, the work of [1] used geographical information to analyse outbreaks for SARS diseases. As far as we know, there is not research on the literature of the use of GDBs for analysing infection spread in hospitals considering spatial and temporal information.

Table 1. Comparative analysis of GDB technologies

Features	Neo4J	OrientDB	ArangoDB
Query lang.	Cypher	OrientDB	AQL
Graph alg.	No	Dijkstra, Shortest path, A*	No
Interoperability	Cloud & drivers	Cloud & drivers	Cloud & drivers
Scalability	Query (horizontal) Write (vertical)	Horizontal in queries	Horizontal in queries
Graph model	Triples	Vertices and edges	Vertices and edges

[2] ARANGO: https://www.arangodb.com/.
[3] Neo4J: https://neo4j.com/.

3 Spatial and Temporal Models

In order to detect a possible infectious outbreak, it is essential to calculate an exhaustive traceability of each patient's events and their location. Therefore, by analysing the Electronic Health Record (EHR) of a patient, the physical path followed by a patient over time can be established. Therefore, a model of a physical (building elements) and functional distribution of the hospital (unit, departments) is required to extract this information.

We propose the following spatial model for representing the different hospital locations in a hierarchy that allows to represent different abstraction levels. First, we consider the basic physical distribution present in most hospitals: Bed (Furniture) → Room → Corridor → Floor → Building → Hospital Setting. Due to the specific requirements of spread analysis, we extend this hierarchy with two intermediate levels: area and zone. Areas are helpful to divide each floor into a logical instead of physical grid, dividing some floors into areas. Zones are used to divide floors with abstract shapes in which a grid does not match well. Figure 1 illustrates the different needs of grids and areas depending on the floor architecture. Finally, we also propose to combine this model with some logical aspects of physical space. In particular, we consider hospitalization units, services and nursing posts. These concepts represent the team of doctors and nurses who care for hospitalized patients in a specific area of the hospital. The taxonomy described in this section (from Bed to Hospital Setting) inherit from the abstract class *Location* and are included as nodes of the graph.

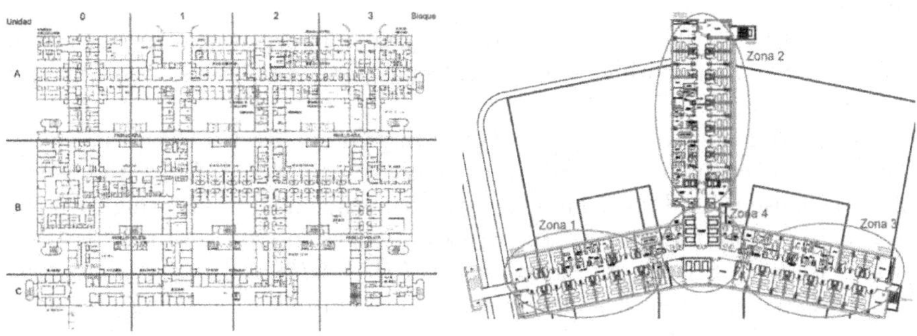

Fig. 1. Spatial model of the hospital (left: grid model of 1st floor, right: zone model of 6th floor).

In this work, we also assume that patient information can be represented as a sequence of events extracted from the EHR. In particular, regarding the problem of infection-spread analysis, we consider two key components for each event. First, we consider the type of infection associated to the event ($TypeInfection$). Second, we consider the nature of time information of the event. According of the duration of each event, we consider two types of events: *Point Events* (instant events with a time stamped mark) and *Interval Events* (with start and end information). In the graph, *Patient* nodes are linked to Events using the *hasHistoryOf* edge and *Events* are connected to Locations via *locatedAt* edge.

4 Case of Use

4.1 Epidemiology Queries

In order to study the capacity of GDBs to support contact-spread analysis we study 2 use cases in the form of queries. Each query illustrates common needs of epidemiologists to deal with this spread problem.

- The first, Q1, searches for all patients of a hospital service who have been diagnosed with a certain bacterial infection during a specified period of time.
- In the second query, Q2, given a set of patients P and a period of time, it searches for everything that patients of P have in common: the types of *Event*, the *unit* or *Service* where they stayed, and the hierarchy of *Locations* in which each *Event* is located. Note that this search focuses on objects and locations in contact to the group P and other patients will not be included.

4.2 Implementation and Results

A general assumption for implementing the queries described in Sect. 4.1 is that the information required must be extracted from a unique query in the most efficient manner.

The GDB was artificially populated with patient information using the model described in Sect. 3 and using the building topology of a public hospital university of Madrid, Spain.

The experiments have been carried out using OrientDB. For the query implementation two commands in OrientDB must be considered. First, the use of SELECT clause is used for defining a path from some nodes indicating with the functions *in*(), *out*() and *both*() the classes of edges to cross and the direction in which to do it. Second, given two nodes, *TRAVERSE* clause computes the edges used to connect such nodes given some constraints (e.g. max. number of steps, intermediate node conditions, etc.).

Query 1. The SELECT-based query extracts all patients diagnosed with the bacteria Staphylococcus Aureus between March 11th to 18th 2019. Figure 2 describes the syntax of this query. Figure 3 shows the outcome: two patients retrieved #34 and #35. Finally, we also depict why these patient were selected, calculating the subgraph of relations between them. As shown in the figure, *Patient*, *TimePointEvent* and a hierarchy of *Location* nodes are involved.

```
SELECT expand(DISTINCT(in('hasHistoryOf'))) FROM (
  SELECT expand(out('Comprende')) FROM (
    SELECT expand(in('has').in('associatedTo'))
                    FROM Service WHERE id='idService'
  ) WHERE ((inicio between 'startDate' and 'endDate')
              OR (fin between 'startDate' and 'endDate')
              OR (inicio <= 'startDate'
                  AND (fin IS NULL OR fin >= 'endDate')))
) WHERE description = ' Staphylococcus Aureus'
          AND out('isTypeOf').@class='InfectionType'
```

Fig. 2. Query 1: code.

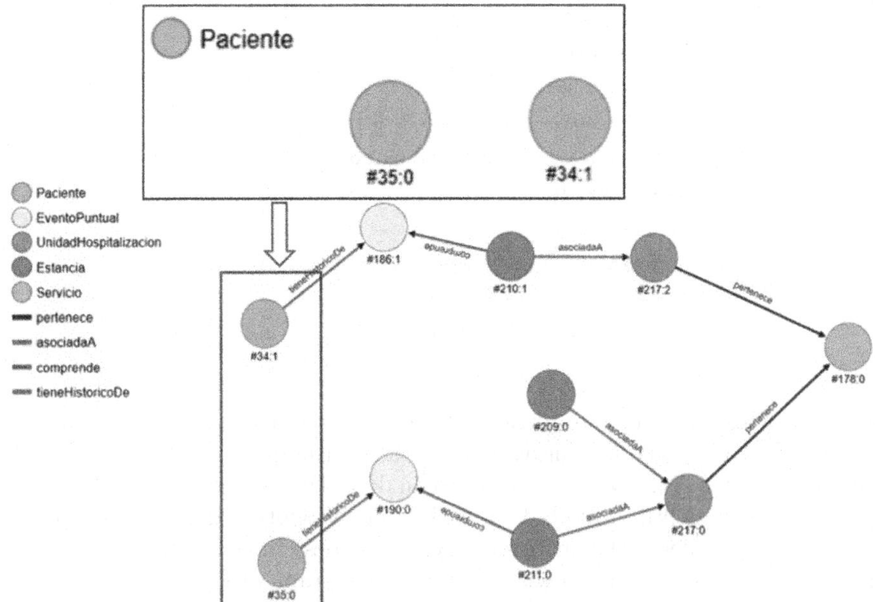

Fig. 3. Query 1: outcome and subgraph obtained.

```
TRAVERSE out('hasHistoryOf'), both('locatedAt', 'contains', 'doneBy')
FROM (
  SELECT FROM Paciente WHERE id IN ['idsPatient]
) WHILE (
 ((@class NOT IN ['Zone', 'Area', 'Block', 'Unit', 'Floor']
  AND NOT (@this instanceof 'Event'))
  OR (@class='Zone' AND $depth IN [5, 6, 7])
  OR (@class='Area' AND $depth IN [5, 7])
  OR (@class='EventPoint'
    AND ((date between 'startDate' and 'endDate')
      OR ((first(in('span')).inicio between 'startDate' and 'endDate')
      OR (first(in('span')).fin between 'startDate' and 'endDate')
      OR (first(in('span')).inicio <= 'startDate'
          AND (first(in('span')).fin IS NULL
            OR first(in('span')).fin >= 'endDate')))))
  OR (@this instanceOf 'EventInterval'
    AND ((start between ' startDate ' and ' endDate ')
      OR (end between ' startDate ' and ' endDate ')
      OR (start <= ' startDate ' AND (end IS NULL OR end >= ' endDate '))))
 ) AND ($depth<=11)
)
) /*WHERE @class instanceOf 'Event'*/
```

Fig. 4. Query 1: code.

Query 2. This query aims to retrieve all elements related to a group of patients using a TRAVERSE-based query. The syntax of the query is shown in Fig. 4, where *idsPatient* is the set of patients to analyse. Due to the complexity of the query, its search depth is limited up to 7 levels of depth regarding the spatial dimension. This query relates 7 events (yellow nodes) from the EHR related to 2 patients (pink nodes), as shown in the outcome graph of Fig. 5.

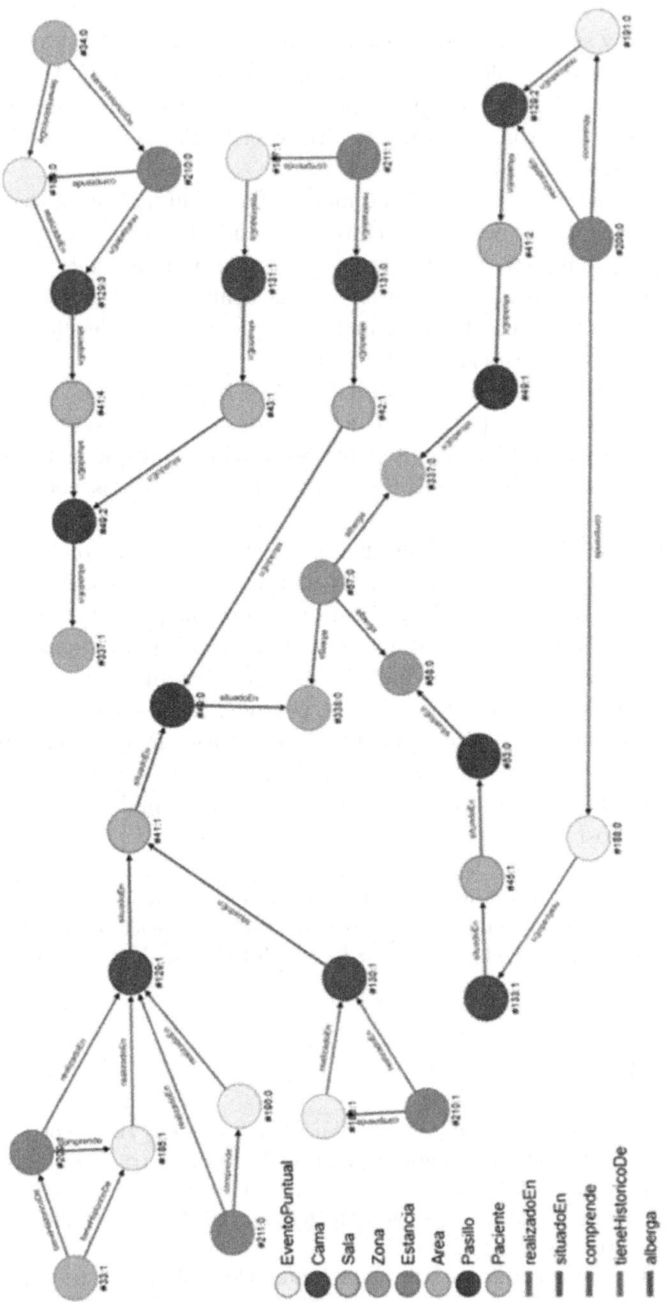

Fig. 5. Query 1: outcome and subgraph obtained. (Color figure online)

5 Conclusions

This preliminary study was undertaken to determine the capacity of GDB technologies to help epidemiologist to carry out contact-spread analysis. First, we analyse principal GDB technologies. Then, we propose a spatial temporal model to structure the GDB from electronic health records. Finally, we explore different query strategies, driven by two cases of use.

One key contribution is the spatial model. The combination of the real topological structure of the hospital architecture and the logical elements of the hospital setting makes the model more expressive. One advantage of the proposal is its extension to group spatial regions using a grid and zone divisions. This extension provides flexibility to include an intermediate level of abstraction when the topology of hospital is heterogeneous.

The use of SELECT-based or TRAVERSE-based queries is a key issue. Despite the complexity of specifying the conditions of a query with TRAVERSE, its outcome is a subgraph computed by calculating multiple paths from each source node. Therefore, we think the utility of such result is very valuable to carry out contact-spread analysis.

Regarding the efficiency of the queries or the possibility of being resolved is very dependent on the expressiveness of the language of the database. For example, OrientDB is a fairly optimal database to make paths through the graph stored in the database. However, it does not allow defining functions, so the graph resulting from one query cannot be used as input for another query. This fact quite reduces the possibility of developing complex results with this database.

Our experiments are limited to a few cases of use. Despite our preliminary results point out the principal pros and cons of GDBs in spread analysis, future studies will further investigate other queries and a formal evaluation of their computational cost.

Acknowledgments. This work was partially funded by the SITSUS project (Ref: RTI2018-094832-B-I00), given by the Spanish Ministry of Science, Innovation and Universities (MCIU), the Spanish Agency for Research (AEI) and by the European Fund for Regional Development (FEDER).

References

1. Chen, Y.-D., Tseng, C., King, C.-C., Wu, T.-S.J., Chen, H.: Incorporating geographical contacts into social network analysis for contact tracing in epidemiology: a study on Taiwan SARS data. In: Zeng, D., et al. (eds.) BioSurveillance 2007. LNCS, vol. 4506, pp. 23–36. Springer, Heidelberg (2007). https://doi.org/10.1007/978-3-540-72608-1_3
2. European Centre for Disease Prevention and Control: Point prevalence survey of healthcare-associated infections and antimicrobial use in European acute care hospitals 2011–2012 (2013). https://www.ecdc.europa.eu/en/healthcare-associated-infections-acute-care-hospitals. Accessed 22 Nov 2019

3. Fette, G., et al.: Implementation of a HL7-CQL engine using the graph database Neo4j. Stud. Health Technol. Inform. **267**, 46–51 (2019). https://doi.org/10.3233/SHTI190804
4. Grande, K., Stanley, M., Redo, C., Wergin, A., Guilfoyle, S., Gasiorowicz, M.: Social network diagramming as an applied tool for public health: lessons learned from an HCV cluster. Am. J. Public Health **105**, e1–e6 (2015). https://doi.org/10.2105/AJPH.2014.302193
5. Huang, Y., Ding, L., Feng, Y.: A novel epidemic spreading model with decreasing infection rate based on infection times. Physica A **444**, 1041–1048 (2016). https://doi.org/10.1016/j.physa.2015.10.104
6. Lose, T., van Heusden, P., Christoffels, A.: COMBAT-TB-NeoDB: fostering tuberculosis research through integrative analysis using graph database technologies. Bioinformatics (Oxford, England) (2019). https://doi.org/10.1093/bioinformatics/btz658
7. Maiers, M., et al.: GRIMM: GRaph imputation and matching for HLA genotypes. **35**(18), 3520–3523 (2018). https://doi.org/10.1101/323493
8. Yip, H.Y., Taib, N.A., Khan, H.A., Dhillon, S.K.: Electronic health record integration. In: Ranganathan, S., Gribskov, M., Nakai, K., Schönbach, C. (eds.) Encyclopedia of Bioinformatics and Computational Biology, pp. 1063–1076. Academic Press, Oxford (2019). https://doi.org/10.1016/B978-0-12-809633-8.20306-3

Window Functions in Rhythm Based Biometric Authentication

Orcan Alpar and Ondrej Krejcar(✉)

Faculty of Informatics and Management, Center for Basic and Applied Research, University of Hradec Kralove, Rokitanskeho 62, 500 03 Hradec Kralove, Czech Republic
orcanalpar@hotmail.com, ondrej.krejcar@uhk.cz

Abstract. Emerging new technologies and new threads entail additional security; therefore, biometric authentication is the key to protecting the passwords by classifying unique biometric features. One of the protocols recently proposed is the rhythm-based authentication dealing with the dominant frequency components of the keystroke signals. However, frequency component itself is not enough to understand the whole keystroke sequence; therefore, the characteristic of a password could only be analyzed by transformations providing the information of when which dominant frequency arises. In this paper, the biometric signal generated from keystroke data is divided into windows by various window functions and sizes for frequency and time localization. As a guide for signal processing in biometrics and biomedicine, we compared Hamming and Blackman widow functions with various sizes in short time Fourier transformations of the signals and found out that Blackman is more appropriate for biometric signal processing.

Keywords: Biometrics · Signals · Authentication · Security · Frequency · Window functions

1 Introduction

Biometric authentication is a branch of Biometrics discipline that deals with unique characteristics of users which could be physical, biological or behavioral like keystrokes. Behavioral biometrics, sometimes referred as habitual biometrics, basically deals with extracting unique features of the individuals in a moment or action which also represents self-evolving characteristics or predetermined deliberate traits. In keystroke authentication or similar protocols, the users enter their password numerous times, unintentionally making the inter-key times narrower than usual; however the users could decide to protect their passwords with an intentional entering style as well.

Either way, the data extracted from a password sequence is said to be unique to protect the main password with a hidden password which could be named as the biometric password or the ghost password. In recent years, time-domain solutions have been very popular and worth investigating, such as: [1–10] where the unique feature is the inter-key time data. However, considering unique password entering style, the inter-key times are not so sufficient to reveal the habits of the users, precisely. Therefore, we

I. Rojas et al. (Eds.): IWBBIO 2020, LNBI 12108, pp. 108–118, 2020.
https://doi.org/10.1007/978-3-030-45385-5_10

changed the kernel by neglecting time-domain and turning the biometric data into biometric signals using pre-processing techniques [11, 12], for analyzing the signals in frequency domain [13]. We also used this innovative approach in [14, 15] for online signature verification as well.

The basic tool for revealing the frequency component of a signal is Fourier transformations; however, ordinary Fourier could not provide time and frequency localization at the same time on the same graph; therefore, the most promising and trustworthy approaches are the short-time Fourier (STFT) and the continuous wavelet transformations (CWT). We already analyzed the differences between STFT and CWT to provide the scientists an insight on selection of the methods [16]. The main topic of that paper was comparing STFT and CWT spectrograms in keystroke authentication and signature verification. As a continuation of this study, we, in this paper, investigate windowing functions of STFT with various window sizes for better classification of the keystroke signals.

Rhythm-based keystroke recognition is firstly proposed in the work of Hwang et al. [17], where they proposed an improvement on keystroke authentication by fusion of rhythm of the users. We very recently proposed frequency spectrograms for keystroke authentication [13] by short time Fourier transformations using Blackman window function. We found out that, depending on the window size, the resulting spectrograms significantly vary for Blackman. Therefore, we, in this research, analyzed Blackman and Hamming window functions with various window sizes on the same training and testing sets using the identical SVM classifier and same pre-processing procedure for unbiased benchmarking. The main purpose of this paper is to show the differences between Blackman and Hamming in a technical way by providing experiments and performance results. We present this paper as a guide of STFT alternatives for researchers dealing with signal processing in biometrics and biomedicine, which is our main contribution.

2 Short-Time Fourier Transformations

The frequency component of a signal is extracted by transforming time domain into frequency domain mostly using Fourier transformations [18]; yet the regular transformations will only reveal the frequency component without time localization. Let's assume that $f(x)$ is the main signal in time domain and $F(u)$ is the frequency domain representation, the STFT is computed for continuous signals by

$$STFT_f^u(t', u) = \int_0^{N-1} \left[f(x)W\left(\dot{x} - \dot{x}'\right)\right] e^{-j2\pi ux} dx, u = 0, 1, \ldots, N-1 \tag{1}$$

or for discrete signals as:

$$STDFT_f^u(t', u) = \sum_{x=0}^{N-1} \left[f(x)W\left(\dot{x} - \dot{x}'\right)\right] e^{-j2\pi ux}, u = 0, 1, \ldots, N-1 \tag{2}$$

where $W(\dot{x}-\dot{x}')$ is the special window function. Although the STFT diagrams are not adequate for providing necessary information on the frequency localization, the spectrograms created by $\left|STDFT_f^u(t',u)\right|^2$ which are normally placed in a three dimensional space; while can be reduced to two-dimensional plane by coloring the surfaces.

2.1 Window Functions

The window functions are various; yet there are two major alternatives for dividing the signals in STFT: Hamming and Blackman. Despite the similarities between, they, however, are very different given the resulting frequency diagrams. The Hamming window function is represented as:

$$W_n\left(\dot{x}-\dot{x}'\right) = 0.54 - 0.46\cos\left(2\pi\frac{n}{N}\right) \tag{3}$$

where $0 \le n \le N$ while Blackman window function as:

$$W_n\left(\dot{x}-\dot{x}'\right) = 0.42 - 0.5\cos\left(2\pi\frac{n}{N-1}\right) + 0.08\cos\left(4\pi\frac{n}{N-1}\right) \tag{4}$$

where $0 \le n \le N-1$. The window function could be plotted by taking 64 samples and taking Fourier transformation of a sinusoidal signal; which are shown in Fig. 1.

Strictly depending on the window function, the outputs of frequency extraction certainly vary, which would be handled in experiments section.

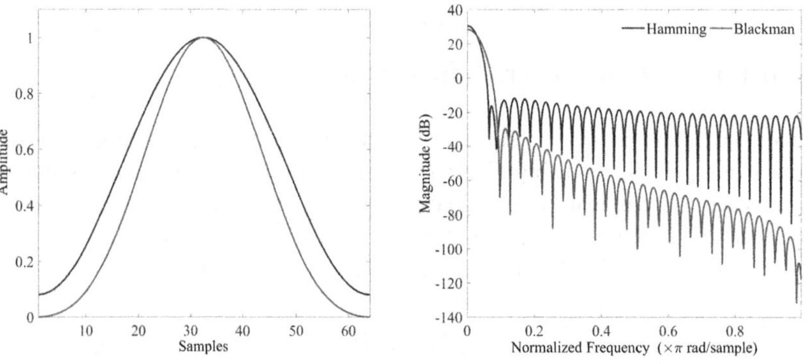

Fig. 1. Hamming and Blackman window functions (left) and corresponding frequency diagrams (right)

3 Experiments

This section includes the training set consisting of keystroke data in time-domain, preprocessing, optimal window size determination and postprocessing.

3.1 Training Set

The training set we are working on is consisting of 8 trials from the same user and created by entering the password "Orcanalpar90*". Despite the traditional approach, we didn't deal with inter-key times but only with the exact key-press times to form a signal regardless of keycodes (Table 1).

Table 1. Training data set

Attempt	1	2	3	4	5	6	7	8
O	0	0	0	0	0	0	0	0
r	0.29	0.33	0.34	0.33	0.33	0.23	0.41	0.3
c	1.34	1.3	1.22	1.25	1.3	1.15	1.35	1.41
a	1.58	1.53	1.5	1.59	1.64	1.46	1.69	1.67
n	2.03	1.88	1.8	2.07	2.11	1.79	2.04	2.08
a	2.19	2.04	1.95	2.24	2.31	1.96	2.21	2.25
l	2.28	2.13	2.03	2.33	2.38	2.03	2.27	2.33
p	2.47	2.3	2.23	2.5	2.58	2.23	2.46	2.55
a	2.72	2.58	2.46	2.79	2.83	2.45	2.69	2.75
r	2.95	2.72	2.63	3.02	3.03	2.64	2.86	2.97
9	3.16	2.94	2.83	3.21	3.24	2.82	3.09	3.16
0	3.35	3.11	3.03	3.44	3.44	3.01	3.24	3.37
*	3.61	3.4	3.25	3.69	3.68	3.25	3.52	3.63
↵	3.74	3.47	3.41	3.84	3.85	3.35	3.63	3.78

The timer initiates by entering the first digit of the password and terminates by "enter" button. While extracting the keystroke, the keycodes are also extracted as usual; however, deleted in preprocessing section.

3.2 Preprocessing

The time-domain data set could be prepared for spectrogram analysis by several preprocessing methods indeed; yet the first step always would be turning the data into a signal for further steps. Therefore, we converted the data arrays into imaginary signum signals continuously switching from −1 to 1 and to −1 as a new key is pressed until the enter command for termination. The original keycodes and corresponding signum step signal is shown in Fig. 2.

The imaginary signum signal is ready for extracting high frequency regions of the keystroke sequence; yet it is necessary to define the optimal window size.

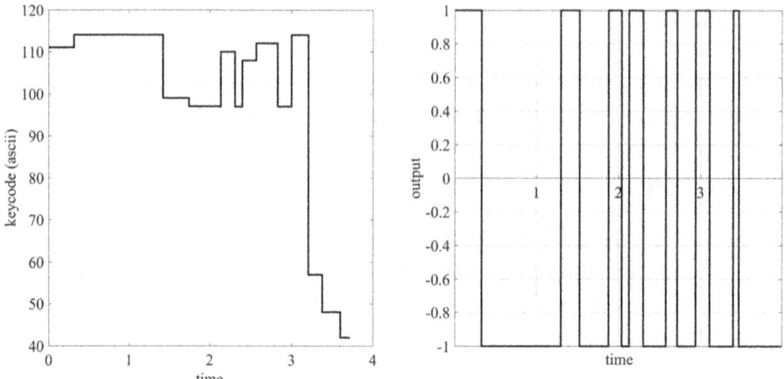

Fig. 2. Original signal and generated imaginary signum signal

3.3 Determining Optimal Window Size

The window size selection is very crucial; since shorter size reveals only the time localization; and larger sizes will only give the information of frequency component without time localization. As seen in Figs. 3 and 4, the spectrograms generated by 100 ms window size, which are very similar with the original signal in Fig. 2 left, only give the information of time; while 750 ms window size reveals that there are two major frequencies hidden in the signal; but no time localization.

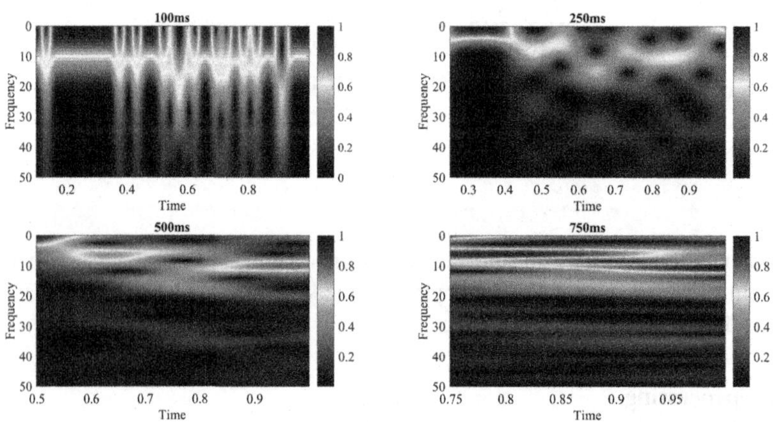

Fig. 3. Spectrograms with different window sizes (Blackman)

Given the spectrograms and differences between, the optimal scenario seems to be 500 ms for this case where the higher frequency regions stick to their appearance times. On the other hand, the experiments with the highest and the lowest window sizes conceal the difference between Blackman and Hamming window functions due to nonexistence of time and frequency localization.

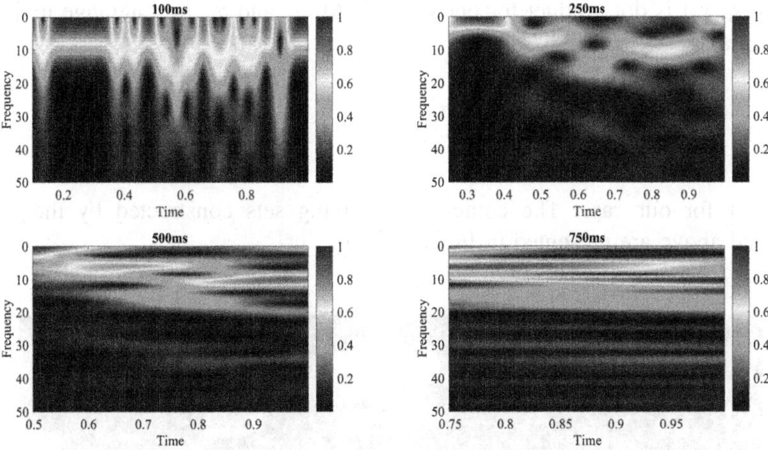

Fig. 4. Spectrograms with different window sizes (Hamming)

For these examples, there are no considerable differences between window functions that a human eye could catch. However, slight differences could cause significant classification inaccuracy; which will be investigated after post processing phase where the spectrograms are digitized.

3.4 Postprocessing

Postprocessing in this stage refers to digitization and binarization of the spectrograms for finding common features between real set and training set for differentiating fraud attempts. We firstly omit the color channels and fix the matrix size to 100 $\times$ 100 by reducing the spectrogram size and subsequent grayscaling. Afterwards, we extracted the spectrograms as figures from Matlab for training the SVM.

3.5 Training by One-Class SVM

Among all alternatives, there are two main classifiers we are working on, which are Neural Network based, such as back-propagated, Levenberg-Marquardt or Gauss-Newton optimized or even adaptive neuro-fuzzy optimized; or support vector machines to find a score instead of binary classification. Given any pixel $p_{i,j}$ on a binary image $I_{w,h}$, a spectrogram image could be mathematically denoted as

$$p_{i,j} \in I_{w,h}(i = [1:w], j = [1:h]) \tag{5}$$

where w is the width and h is the height of the image. The optimizer is stated for each element $x_u = p_{i,j}$ in the vector A_k derived from the matrix as

$$\max_{\alpha} \sum_{u=1}^{k} \alpha_u - \mu \sum_{u=1}^{k} \sum_{v=1}^{k} y_u y_v k(x_u, y_v) \alpha_u \alpha_v \tag{6}$$

where $k(x_u, y_v)$ is dot product for one-class SVM, α_u and α_v are Lagrange multipliers estimated as

$$\sum_{j=1}^{n} \alpha_j = n\nu \tag{7}$$

and $\mu = 1$ for our case. The contents of training sets constructed by the process mentioned above are presented in Figs. 5 and 6.

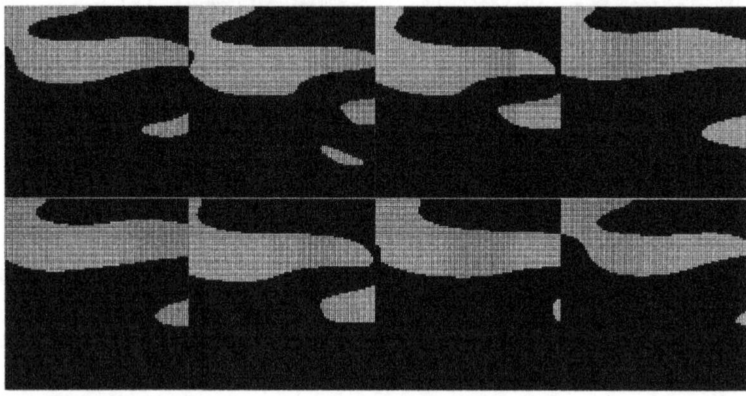

Fig. 5. Training images - Blackman

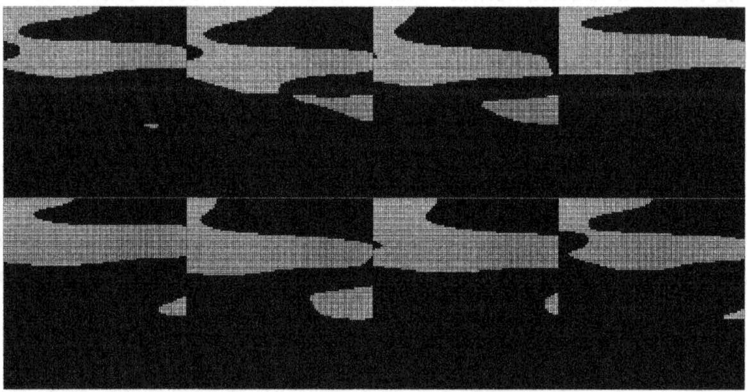

Fig. 6. Training images - Hamming

The digitized spectrograms are not alike, if we compare the images at same positions in Figs. 5 and 6. Not only the shapes vary; but also the areas and the location of filled pixels are entirely different. The initial observation about the training sets are intriguing since when we feed forward the algorithm using training set images, the following results are achieved (Table 2).

Table 2. SVM outputs

Trial	1	2	3	4	5	6	7	8
Hamming	64.94	99.42	94.85	106.73	117.17	126.21	156.46	64.09
Blackman	111.05	97.14	113.56	133.04	148.57	133.34	161.99	86.24

All of the values are above zero as expected; however, the average of the Blackman is greater than Hamming, which also means that the training set of the Blackman is more inter-consistent. These scores also represent how a member represent the whole set and gives the information of closeness of the digitized spectrograms. After training the SVM, the testing phase is executed by inserting the real and fraud data to the trained SVM as digitized spectrograms.

4 Results

The performance of the classifier is based on several indicators in biometric keystroke authentication; yet the most common one is the equal error rate (EER) calculated by finding false reject (FRR) and false accept rates (FAR). However FAR and FRR are strictly depending on any kind of thresholding or similar operation that will give a binary decision like accept or reject. The FAR rates are found as 5% and 10% and FRR rates as 3.75% and 11.25% for Blackman and Hamming respectively, for zero threshold as seen in Fig. 7. The EER points are linearly interpolated as 4.66% and 11.13% for Blackman and Hamming respectively, which are the intersection points of real and fraud curves.

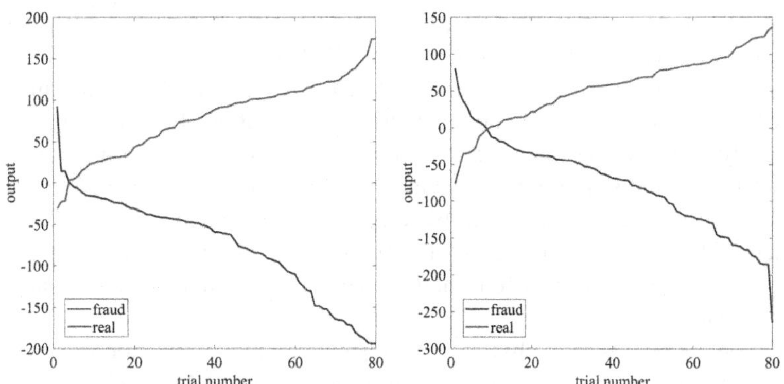

Fig. 7. EER diagrams: Blackman (left) Hamming (right)

The intersection points are still dependent on arbitrary thresholding which could be omitted by receiver operating characteristics ROC and detection error trade-off DET curve analysis. The Blackman window function in SFTF, however, seems more promising at first sight, considering the lowest EER. The ROC and DET curves are presented in Fig. 8.

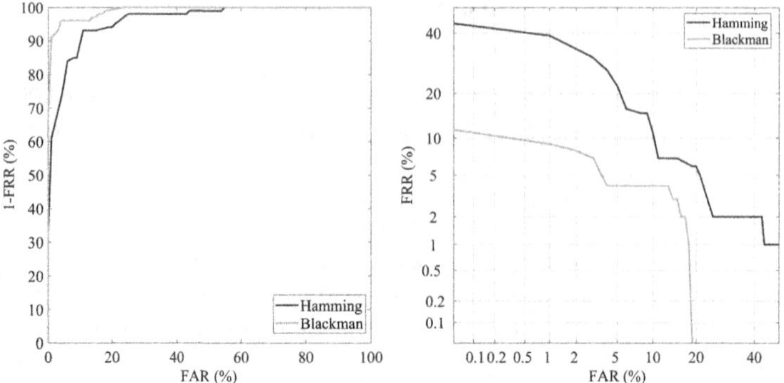

Fig. 8. ROC curve (left) DET curve (right)

Parallel with the results of EER, the area under the ROC curve is larger in Blackman window function regardless of arbitrary thresholding. Therefore, it could be stated that Blackman window function is more proper for signal processing of our keystroke dataset and for this framework.

Given the results, the main difference of the windowing equations is that the Blackman curve intersects the point of x = 0, y = 0 with steeper curve shape; while Hamming does not. Therefore, it could be considered that steeper curves provide better differentiation of high and low frequencies of a keystroke signal.

5 Conclusion and Discussion

This paper belongs to one of our major research areas which could be briefly described as frequency domain solutions in biometrics. Although we couldn't include every single step of our algorithm, the results would provide necessary information on window functions and their usage in biometric authentication. The first purpose of this paper briefly is enhancing the security of the passwords entered via a hardware keyboard; while the results are implementable to touchscreens as well. Although it was not our major concern, we also calculated EER values and presented ROC and DET curves for understanding the performance of the framework. The EER values presented in Table 3 are not comparable indeed; though these values could provide an insight for the performances.

Based on the results, it is obvious that Blackman window function provides better outputs with identical preprocessing, postprocessing and SVM training phases. Still depending on the training set and testing sets though; however according to the experiments, Blackman window function describes the training set better, provides inter-consistency between the elements of the set and discriminates the attempts better than Hamming for this case.

As a guide for signal processing in biometrics and biomedicine, there is no drawback of this paper since the main purpose is understanding the differences between Blackman and Hamming window functions and results. Despite the kernel of the paper,

Table 3. EER comparison

Authors (ref no)	Method	EER
This paper	*Blackman STFT + SVM*	*4.66%*
This paper	*Hamming STFT + SVM*	*11.13%*
Alpar [18]	mSTFT + SVM	1.40%–2.12%
Alpar [18]	mSTFT + SVM	2.01%–3.21%
Alpar [18]	STFT + SVM	6.93%–10.12%
Alpar [18]	STFT + SVM	7.49%–11.95%
Alpar [10]	Global Fuzzy Proximity	1.61%
Alpar [13]	GN-ANN	4.1%
Alshanketi et al. [4]	Random Forest	2.3%–9%
Roh et al. [19]	Statistical	6.93%–12.3%
Alpar [6]	RGB Histogram + LM	7.5%
Alpar [6]	ANFIS	2.5%
Alpar [6]	BP-ANN	8.75%
Alpar and Krejcar [8]	GN-ANN	31.8%
Alpar and Krejcar [8]	LM-ANN	14.75%
Alpar and Krejcar [9]	ANFIS	5.4%
Alpar and Krejcar [9]	LM-ANN	2.2%
Sae-Bae [20]	Statistical	5%–10%
Chang [21]	Statistical	6.9%–14.6%

which is biometrics, findings of this paper might shed light on new research areas in biomedical signal processing.

Acknowledgement. The work and the contribution were supported by the SPEV project "Smart Solutions in Ubiquitous Computing Environments", University of Hradec Kralove, Faculty of Informatics and Management, Czech Republic. We are also grateful for the support of Ph.D. students of our team (Ayca Kirimtat and Sebastien Mambou) in consultations regarding application aspects.

References

1. Sarier, N.D.: Multimodal biometric identity based encryption. Future Gener. Comput. Syst. **80**, 112–125 (2017)
2. Kroeze, C.J., Malan, K.M.: User authentication based on continuous touch biometrics. S. Afr. Comput. J. **28**(2), 1–23 (2016)
3. Mondal, S., Bours, P.: A study on continuous authentication using a combination of keystroke and mouse biometrics. Neurocomputing **230**, 1–22 (2017)
4. Alshanketi, F., Traore, I., Ahmed, A.A.: Improving performance and usability in mobile keystroke dynamic biometric authentication. In: Security and Privacy Workshops (SPW). IEEE (2016)
5. Alsultan, A., Warwick, K., Wei, H.: Non-conventional keystroke dynamics for user authentication. Pattern Recogn. Lett. **89**, 53–59 (2017)

6. Alpar, O.: Intelligent biometric pattern password authentication systems for touchscreens. Expert Syst. Appl. **42**(17), 6286–6294 (2015)
7. Alpar, O.: Keystroke recognition in user authentication using ANN based RGB histogram technique. Eng. Appl. Artif. Intell. **32**, 213–217 (2014)
8. Alpar, O., Krejcar, O.: Biometric swiping on touchscreens. In: Computer Information Systems and Industrial Management (2015)
9. Alpar, O., Krejcar, O.: Pattern password authentication based on touching location. In: Intelligent Data Engineering and Automated Learning–IDEAL 2015 (2015)
10. Alpar, O.: Biometric touchstroke authentication by fuzzy proximity of touch locations. Future Gener. Comput. Syst. **86**, 71–80 (2018)
11. Alpar, O., Krejcar, O.: Biometric keystroke signal preprocessing Part I: signalization, digitization and alteration. In: Benferhat, S., Tabia, K., Ali, M. (eds.) IEA/AIE 2017. LNCS (LNAI), vol. 10350, pp. 267–276. Springer, Cham (2017). https://doi.org/10.1007/978-3-319-60042-0_31
12. Alpar, O., Krejcar, O.: Biometric keystroke signal preprocessing Part II: manipulation. In: Benferhat, S., Tabia, K., Ali, M. (eds.) IEA/AIE 2017. LNCS (LNAI), vol. 10350, pp. 289–294. Springer, Cham (2017). https://doi.org/10.1007/978-3-319-60042-0_34
13. Alpar, O.: Frequency spectrograms for biometric keystroke authentication using neural network based classifier. Knowl.-Based Syst. **116**, 163–171 (2017)
14. Alpar, O., Krejcar, O.: Hidden frequency feature in electronic signatures. In: Fujita, H., Ali, M., Selamat, A., Sasaki, J., Kurematsu, M. (eds.) IEA/AIE 2016. LNCS (LNAI), vol. 9799, pp. 145–156. Springer, Cham (2016). https://doi.org/10.1007/978-3-319-42007-3_13
15. Alpar, O., Krejcar, O.: Online signature verification by spectrogram analysis. Appl. Intell. (2017). https://doi.org/10.1007/s10489-017-1009-x
16. Alpar, O., Krejcar, O.: Frequency and time localization in biometrics: STFT vs. CWT. In: Mouhoub, M., Sadaoui, S., Ait Mohamed, O., Ali, M. (eds.) IEA/AIE 2018. LNCS (LNAI), vol. 10868, pp. 722–728. Springer, Cham (2018). https://doi.org/10.1007/978-3-319-92058-0_69
17. Hwang, S.S., Lee, H.J., Cho, S.: Improving authentication accuracy using artificial rhythms and cues for keystroke dynamics-based authentication. Expert Syst. Appl. **36**(7), 10649–10656 (2009)
18. Alpar, O.: TAPSTROKE: a novel intelligent authentication system using tap frequencies. Expert Syst. Appl. **136**, 426–438 (2019)
19. Roh, J.H., Lee, S.H., Kim, S.: Keystroke dynamics for authentication in smartphone. In: International Conference on Information and Communication Technology Convergence (ICTC). IEEE (2016)
20. Sae-Bae, N., Ahmed, K., Isbister, K., Memon, N.: Biometric-rich gestures: a novel approach to authentication on multi-touch devices. In: CHI 2012 Proceedings of the 2012 ACM Annual Conference on Human Factors in Computing Systems, New York (2012)
21. Chang, T.Y., Tsai, C.J., Lin, J.H.: A graphical-based password keystroke dynamic authentication system for touch screen handheld mobile devices. J. Syst. Softw. **85**(5), 1157–1165 (2012)

Relationships Between Muscular Power and Bone Health Parameters in a Group of Young Lebanese Adults

Patchina Sabbagh[1,2], Pierre Kamlé[1,3], Antonio Pinti[4(✉)], Georgette Farah[1], Hayman Saddick[1,3], Eddy Zakhem[1], Boutros Finianos[1,5], Gautier Zunquin[5,6], Georges Baquet[2], and Rawad El Hage[1]

[1] Department of Physical Education, Faculty of Arts and Social Sciences, University of Balamand, El-Koura, Lebanon

[2] University of Lille, EA 7369 - URePSSS - Unité de Recherche Pluridisciplinaire Sport Santé Société, Ronchin, France

[3] I3MTO Laboratory, EA 4708, University of Orléans, 45067 Orléans, France

[4] DeVisu-Design, Visuel, Urbain, EA 2445, UPHF, Valenciennes, France
antonio.pinti@uphf.fr

[5] EA 7369 - URePSSS - Unité de recherche pluridisciplinaire sport santé société, Université Littoral Côte d'Opale, Dunkerque, France

[6] Laboratoire Mouvement, Equilibre, Performance et Santé (UPRES EA 4445), Département STAPS, Université de Pau et des Pays de l'Adour, Tarbes, France

Abstract. The aim of the current study was to explore the relationships between lower limb muscular power and bone variables (bone mineral content (BMC), bone mineral density (BMD), hip geometry indices and trabecular bone score (TBS)) in a group of young Lebanese adults. 29 young Lebanese men and 31 young Lebanese women whose ages range between 18 and 32 years participated in this study. Body weight and height were measured, and body mass index (BMI) was calculated. Body composition and bone variables were measured by DXA. DXA measurements were completed for the whole body (WB), lumbar spine (L2–L4), total hip (TH) and femoral neck (FN). Hip geometry parameters including cross-sectional area (CSA), cross-sectional moment of inertia (CSMI), section modulus (Z), strength index (SI) and buckling ratio (BR) were derived by DXA. Trabecular bone score was also derived by DXA. Horizontal jump (HJ), vertical jump, vertical jump maximum power, force-velocity maximum power and 20-m sprint performance were measured or calculated by using validated fitness tests. In men, fat mass percentage was negatively correlated to TH BMD, FN BMD, CSA, CSMI, Z and SI. In women, weight, BMI, lean mass and fat mass were positively correlated to WB BMC, CSMI and Z. Regarding physical performance variables, horizontal jump performance and force-velocity maximal power were positively correlated to TH BMD, FN BMD, CSA and Z in men. Vertical jump maximal power was positively correlated to WB BMC in women. 20-m sprint performance was negatively correlated to FN BMD, CSA, Z and SI in men. In conclusion, the current study suggests that force-velocity maximum power is a positive determinant of BMD and hip geometry indices in men but not in women.

I. Rojas et al. (Eds.): IWBBIO 2020, LNBI 12108, pp. 119–129, 2020.
https://doi.org/10.1007/978-3-030-45385-5_11

Keywords: Muscular performance · Peak bone mass · DXA · Gender differences · Hip geometry

1 Introduction

Bone strength is influenced by several components such as bone mineral density (BMD), bone geometry, bone texture and bone microarchitecture [1–5]. BMD, hip geometry indices and trabecular bone score are indices of bone strength and can predict fracture risk in the elderly [6–17]. BMD remains the strongest predictor of bone strength and fracture risk [1–4]. Peak BMD attained at the third decade is considered as a strong predictor of fracture risk later in life [9–13]. Implementing strategies to increase peak BMD are useful for the prevention of osteoporosis [9–13]. Identifying determinants of peak BMD is clinically important especially in the Lebanese population in which mean BMD values are lower than American/European subjects [17–24]. This may be in part explained by low daily calcium intake and serum vitamin D levels as well as inactivity [25–31]. We have previously shown several positive correlations between several physical performance variables and BMD in several populations [32–41]. However, it is unclear whether the positive correlations between muscular power and bone variables in young adults are gender-specific. The aim of the current study was to explore the relationships between lower limb muscular power and bone variables (bone mineral content (BMC), BMD, hip geometry indices and TBS) in a group of young Lebanese adults.

2 Materials and Methods

2.1 Subjects and Study Design

Sixty young Lebanese adults whose ages ranged from 18 to 32 years voluntarily participated in the present study. They were divided into 2 groups: 29 young men and 31 young women. All participants were nonsmokers and had no history of major orthopedic problems or other disorders known to affect bone metabolism or physical tests of the study. Women who were pregnant, amenorrheic and/or taking medications that may affect bone and calcium metabolism (corticosteroid or anticonvulsant therapy) were excluded from the study. Other inclusion criteria included no diagnosis of comorbidities and no history of fracture. An informed written consent was obtained from the participants. All participants completed an interview about medical history including menstrual history and medication use. The work described has been carried out in accordance with the declaration of Helsinki (regarding human experimentation developed for the medical community by the World Medical Association).

2.2 Anthropometrical Measurements and Body Composition

Height and body weight were measured using a mechanic scale (precision of 100 g) and a standard stadiometer (upright position to the nearest 1 mm). The participants were weighed wearing light clothing and had their shoes removed. BMI was calculated as body weight divided by height squared (kg/m^2). Body composition (lean mass, fat mass and bone mineral content) was evaluated by dual-energy X-ray absorptiometry (DXA; GE Healthcare, Lunar iDXA System, version 13.60).

2.3 Bone Variables

BMD measurements were completed for the whole body (WB), the lumbar spine (L2–L4), the total hip (TH) and the femoral neck (FN) using the instrument described earlier (DXA; GE Healthcare, Lunar iDXA System, version 13.60). Geometric indices of femoral neck (FN) strength [cross-sectional area (CSA), cross-sectional moment of inertia (CSMI), section modulus (Z), strength index (SI) and buckling ratio (BR)] were derived by DXA. Analyses of TBS based on gray level analysis of bidimensional DXA images were performed using the TBS iNsight software (version 2.1; Medimaps, Merignac, France). The same certified technician (holder of a Bachelor of Science in medical imaging sciences) performed all analyses using the same technique for all measurements. The coefficients of variation were <1% for BMC and BMD in our laboratory [32–41].

2.4 Physical Performance Variables

All subjects participated in a familiarizing session before evaluation. Testing was done on two non-consecutive days. All the assessments were performed in the following order. During day one, horizontal jump performance was assessed, vertical jump was measured by using the Sargent test and vertical jump maximal power was calculated by using the Lewis Formula [42], and lastly time of the twenty-meter sprint was measured by using photoelectric cells (BROWER Timing Systems) [43]. On the second day, the force-velocity test was performed on a cycle ergometer using a technique adopted from the study of Vandewalle et al. [44]. Force-velocity maximum power was accordingly calculated as previously described [44–46].

2.5 Statistical Analysis

The means and standard deviations were calculated for all clinical data and for the bone measurements. Comparisons between the 2 groups (men and women) were made after checking for Gaussian distribution. If Gaussian distribution was found, parametric unpaired *t*-tests were used. In other cases, Mann-Whitney *U*-tests were used. Correlations between clinical characteristics and bone data were given as Pearson correlation coefficients. Multiple linear regressions were used to test the relationships of BMD with age, force-velocity maximum power and fat mass, and r^2 were reported. Data were analyzed with Number Cruncher Statistical System (NCSS, 2001; NCSS, Kaysville, UT). A level of significance of $p < 0.05$ was used.

3 Results

3.1 Clinical Characteristics and Bone Data and Physical Performance Variables of the Study Population

Age, BMI, L2–L4 BMD, SI and BR were not significantly different between the two groups. Body weight, height, lean mass, WB BMC, WB BMD, TBS, TH BMD, FN BMD, CSA, CSMI, Z, horizontal jump, vertical jump, vertical jump maximum power and force-velocity maximum power were significantly higher in men compared to women. Fat mass and fat mass percentage were higher in women compared to men. 20-m sprint performance was significantly different between the two groups (Table 1).

Table 1. Clinical characteristics and bone variables of the study population.

	Men (n = 29)	Women (n = 31)
	Mean ± SD	Mean ± SD
Age (years)	20.7 ± 3.2	21.5 ± 2.9
Weight (kg)	75.966 ± 11.746***	60.132 ± 10.550
Height (m)	1.74 ± 0.06***	1.61 ± 0.05
BMI (kg/m^2)	24.4 ± 3.9	22.9 ± 4.3
Lean mass (kg)	52.390 ± 11.164***	34.739 ± 3.757
Fat mass (kg)	20.890 ± 9.513***	23.331 ± 7.530
Fat mass (%)	27.5 ± 8.1***	38.8 ± 5.6
WB BMC (g)	2676 ± 455***	2062 ± 192
WB BMD (g/cm^2)	1.165 ± 0.139**	1.077 ± 0.078
L2–L4 BMD (g/cm^2)	1.121 ± 0.488	1.135 ± 0.099
TBS	1.49 ± 0.09***	1.41 ± 0.06
TH BMD (g/cm^2)	1.077 ± 0.129***	0.925 ± 0.098
FN BMD (g/cm^2)	1.099 ± 0.149***	0.916 ± 0.102
CSA (mm^2)	178 ± 26***	133 ± 15
CSMI (mm^2)^2	14982 ± 3267***	8690 ± 2590
Z (mm^3)	864 ± 166***	562 ± 126
SI	1.57 ± 0.46	1.71 ± 0.46
BR	3.46 ± 1.72	3.05 ± 1.02
Horizontal jump (m)	1.92 ± 0.33***	1.48 ± 0.47
Vertical jump (cm)	53.5 ± 8.7***	35.5 ± 5.0
Vertical jump P max (watts)	1195 ± 156***	773 ± 128
Force-velocity P max (watts)	731 ± 134***	404 ± 95
20 m sprint performance (s)	3.59 ± 0.35***	4.46 ± 0.45

SD: standard deviation; BMI: body mass index; WB: whole body; BMD: bone mineral density; L2–L4: lumbar spine; TBS: trabecular bone score; TH: total hip; FN: femoral neck; CSA: cross-sectional area; CSMI: cross-sectional moment of inertia; Z: section modulus; SI: strength index; BR: buckling ratio; P max: maximum power; **$p < 0.01$; ***$p < 0.001$.

3.2 Correlations Between Clinical Characteristics and Bone Data in Men

Age was negatively correlated to FN BMD but positively correlated to BR. Weight was negatively correlated to SI. Height was positively correlated to WB BMC but negatively correlated to TBS. Lean mass was positively correlated to WB BMD, CSMI and Z. Fat mass was negatively correlated to SI. Fat mass percentage was negatively correlated to TH BMD, FN BMD, CSA, CSMI, Z and SI (Table 2).

Table 2. Correlations between clinical characteristics and bone data in men.

	WB BMC (g)	WB BMD (kg/m^2)	L2–L4 BMD (kg/m^2)	TBS	TH BMD (kg/m^2)	FN BMD (kg/m^2)	CSA (mm^2)	CSMI (mm^4)	Z (mm^3)	SI	BR
Age (years)	0.15	0.09	−0.13	0.10	−0.35	−0.39*	−0.25	0.12	−0.08	−0.36	0.54**
Weight (kg)	0.35	0.13	0.00	−0.05	−0.08	−0.09	−0.03	0.09	0.01	−0.42*	0.13
Height (m)	0.47**	0.18	0.00	−0.45*	0.00	0.09	0.25	0.37	0.27	−0.16	0.06
BMI (kg/m^2)	0.16	0.30	−0.02	0.08	−0.03	−0.06	−0.08	0.00	−0.05	−0.41	0.11
LM (kg)	0.34	0.38*	0.14	−0.07	0.21	0.25	0.34	0.43*	0.40*	0.00	0.09
FM (kg)	0.20	0.04	−0.16	−0.10	−0.17	−0.18	−0.24	−0.19	−0.23	−0.48**	0.16
FM %	−0.02	−0.21	−0.35	−0.18	−0.52**	−0.49**	−0.54**	−0.42*	−0.50**	−0.62***	0.22

WB: whole body; BMC: bone mineral content; BMD: bone mineral density; L2–L4: Lumbar spine; TH: total hip; FN: femoral neck; CSA: cross-sectional area; CSMI: cross-sectional moment of inertia; Z: section modulus; SI: strength index; BR: buckling ratio; BMI: Body mass index; LM: lean mass; FM: fat mass; FM %: fat mass percentage; *$p < 0.05$; **$p < 0.01$; ***$p < 0.001$

3.3 Correlations Between Physical Performance Variables and Bone Data in Men

Horizontal jump was positively correlated to TH BMD, FN BMD, CSA, Z and SI. Vertical jump was positively correlated to SI. Vertical jump maximum power was positively correlated to WB BMC. Force-velocity maximum power was positively correlated to WB BMD, L2–L4 BMD, TH BMD, FN BMD, CSA, CSMI and Z. 20-m sprint performance was negatively correlated to FN BMD, CSA, Z and SI (Table 3).

Table 3. Correlations between physical performance variables and bone data in men.

	WB BMC (g)	WB BMD (kg/m^2)	L2–L4 BMD (kg/m^2)	TBS	TH BMD (kg/m^2)	FN BMD (kg/m^2)	CSA (mm^2)	CSMI (mm^4)	Z (mm^3)	SI	BR
HJ (m)	−0.05	0.30	0.23	0.02	0.47**	0.42*	0.41*	0.29	0.40*	0.46*	−0.30
Vertical jump (cm)	−0.04	0.16	0.20	0.12	0.36	0.30	0.31	0.18	0.31	0.52**	−0.19
Vertical jump P max (watts)	0.39*	0.25	0.12	−0.03	0.12	0.08	0.17	0.24	0.22	−0.16	0.01
Force-velocity P max (watts)	0.27	0.47**	0.39*	−0.02	0.60***	0.58***	0.55**	0.38*	0.49**	0.13	−0.33
20 m sprint performance (s)	0.06	−0.27	−0.15	0.04	−0.25	−0.42*	−0.45*	−0.32	−0.40*	−0.46*	0.27

WB: whole body; BMC: bone mineral content; BMD: bone mineral density; L2–L4: Lumbar spine; TH: total hip; FN: femoral neck; CSA: cross-sectional area; CSMI: cross-sectional moment of inertia; Z: section modulus; SI: strength index; BR: buckling ratio; HJ: Horizontal jump; P max: maximum power; *$p < 0.05$; * $p < 0.01$; ***$p < 0.001$.

3.4 Correlations Between Clinical Characteristics and Bone Data in Women

Age was positively correlated to TBS, CSMI and Z. Weight was positively correlated to WB BMC, CSA, CSMI and Z. Height was negatively correlated to TBS but positively correlated to CSMI and Z. BMI was positively correlated to WB BMC, CSMI and Z. Lean mass was positively correlated to WB BMC, L2–L4 BMD, CSA, CSMI and Z. Fat mass was positively correlated to WB BMC, CSMI and Z. Fat mass percentage was positively correlated to WB BMC (Table 4).

Table 4. Correlations between clinical characteristics and bone data in women.

	WB BMC (g)	WB BMD (kg/m^2)	L2–L4 BMD (kg/m^2)	TBS	TH BMD (kg/m^2)	FN BMD (kg/m^2)	CSA (mm^2)	CSMI (mm^4)	Z (mm^3)	SI	BR
Age (years)	0.31	0.30	0.16	0.45*	−0.27	−0.25	0.19	0.53**	0.46**	0.29	0.01
Weight (kg)	0.61***	0.26	0.33	0.16	−0.04	0.01	0.36*	0.49**	0.46**	−0.30	0.06
Height (m)	0.30	0.04	−0.11	−0.52**	−0.06	−0.05	0.29	0.41*	0.39*	−0.03	0.06
BMI (kg/m^2)	0.44**	0.18	0.33	0.39	−0.04	0.04	0.27	0.37*	0.37*	−0.27	−0.07
LM (kg)	0.61***	0.21	0.38*	0.18	0.11	0.09	0.44*	0.49**	0.49**	−0.15	0.08
FM (kg)	0.55**	0.24	0.26	0.14	−0.10	−0.03	0.30	0.46**	0.42*	−0.31	−0.02
FM %	0.42*	0.17	0.10	0.04	−0.17	−0.06	0.19	0.34	0.30	−0.33	−0.08

WB: whole body; BMC: bone mineral content; BMD: bone mineral density; L2–L4: Lumbar spine; TH: total hip; FN: femoral neck; CSA: cross-sectional area; CSMI: cross-sectional moment of inertia; Z: section modulus; SI: strength index; BR: buckling ratio; BMI: Body mass index; LM: lean mass; FM: fat mass; FM %: fat mass percentage; *p < 0.05; **p < 0.01; ***p < 0.001.

3.5 Correlations Between Physical Performance Variables and Bone Data in Women

Horizontal jump was negatively correlated to CSMI and Z. Vertical jump maximum power was positively correlated to WB BMC but negatively correlated to SI. 20-m sprint performance was positively correlated to CSMI and Z (Table 5).

Table 5. Correlations between physical performance variables and bone data in women.

	WB BMC (g)	WB BMD (kg/m^2)	L2–L4 BMD (kg/m^2)	TBS	TH BMD (kg/m^2)	FN BMD (kg/m^2)	CSA (mm^2)	CSMI (mm^4)	Z (mm^3)	SI	BR
HJ (m)	−0.35	0.03	−0.06	0.00	0.00	0.10	−0.32	−0.42*	−0.37*	−0.10	0.01
Vertical jump (cm)	−0.18	−0.1	−0.04	0.16	0.18	0.20	−0.06	−0.33	−0.29	−0.07	−0.02
Vertical jump P max (watts)	0.57***	0.27	0.32	0.25	0.05	0.12	0.35	0.34	0.33	−0.37*	0.04
Force-velocity P max (watts)	0.30	0.12	0.01	−0.14	0.08	0.14	0.24	0.13	0.15	−0.33	0.17
20 m sprint performance (s)	0.37	0.11	0.10	0.05	−0.20	−0.16	0.17	0.42*	0.36*	0.04	−0.17

WB: whole body; BMC: bone mineral content; BMD: bone mineral density; L2–L4: Lumbar spine; TH: total hip; FN: femoral neck; CSA: cross-sectional area; CSMI: cross-sectional moment of inertia; Z: section modulus; SI: strength index; BR: buckling ratio; HJ: Horizontal jump; P max: maximum power; *p < 0.05; **p < 0.01; ***p < 0.001.

3.6 Multiple Linear Regression Models in Men

Force-velocity maximum power remained positively correlated to WB BMD, L2–L4 BMD, TH BMD and FN BMD after adjusting for age and fat mass (Table 6).

Table 6. Multiple linear regression models in men.

	Coefficient ± SE	*t*-value	*p*-value
Dependent variable: WB BMD (R^2 = 0.27)			
Constant	0.602 ± 0.223	2.69	p = 0.012
Age (years)	0.010 ± 0.008	1.17	p = 0.25
Force-velocity maximum power (watts)	0.000 ± 0.000	2.98	p = 0.006
Fat mass (kg)	−0.000 ± 0.000	−0.76	p = 0.45
Dependent variable: L2–L4 BMD (R^2 = 0.21)			
Constant	0.870 ± 0.250	3.43	p = 0.002
Age (years)	0.002 ± 0.009	0.26	p = 0.79
Force-velocity maximum power (watts)	0.000 ± 0.000	2.41	p = 0.02
Fat mass (kg)	−0.000 ± 0.000	−1.24	p = 0.22
Dependent variable: TH BMD (R^2 = 0.47)			
Constant	0.860 ± 0.170	4.87	p < 0.001
Age (years)	−0.007 ± 0.006	−1.10	p = 0.27
Force-velocity maximum power (watts)	0.000 ± 0.000	4.00	p < 0.001
Fat mass (kg)	−0.000 ± 0.000	−1.05	p = 0.30
Dependent variable: FN BMD (R^2 = 0.47)			
Constant	0.920 ± 0.200	4.50	p < 0.001
Age (years)	−0.011 ± 0.007	−1.41	p = 0.16
Force-velocity maximum power (watts)	0.000 ± 0.000	3.80	p < 0.001
Fat mass (kg)	−0.000 ± 0.000	−0.94	p = 0.35

SE: Standard error; WB: whole body; BMC: bone mineral content; BMD: bone mineral density; L2–L4: Lumbar spine; TH: total hip; FN: femoral neck.

3.7 Multiple Linear Regression Models in Women

Force-velocity maximum power was not correlated to BMD values after adjusting for age and fat mass (Table 7).

Table 7. Multiple linear regression models in women.

	Coefficient ± SE	*t*-value	*p*-value
Dependent variable: WB BMD (R^2 = 0.12)			
Constant	0.840 ± 0.140	6.01	p < 0.001
Age (years)	0.008 ± 0.006	1.36	p = 0.18
Force-velocity maximum power (watts)	0.000 ± 0.000	0.64	p = 0.52
Fat mass (kg)	−0.000 ± 0.000	0.17	p = 0.86
Dependent variable: L2–L4 BMD (R^2 = 0.07)			
Constant	1.084 ± 0.180	6.01	p < 0.001
Age (years)	0.000 ± 0.000	0.04	p = 0.96
Force-velocity maximum power (watts)	−0.000 ± 0.000	−0.52	p = 0.60
Fat mass (kg)	0.000 ± 0.000	1.23	p = 0.23
Dependent variable: TH BMD (R^2 = 0.08)			
Constant	1.085 ± 0.180	6.03	p < 0.001
Age (years)	−0.008 ± 0.007	−1.09	p = 0.28
Force-velocity maximum power (watts)	0.000 ± 0.000	0.31	p = 0.75
Fat mass (kg)	−0.000 ± 0.000	−0.10	p = 0.91
Dependent variable: FN BMD (R^2 = 0.08)			
Constant	1.060 ± 0.180	5.81	p < 0.001
Age (years)	−0.009 ± 0.007	−1.17	p = 0.25
Force-velocity maximum power (watts)	0.000 ± 0.000	0.39	p = 0.69
Fat mass (kg)	0.000 ± 0.000	0.21	p = 0.83

SE: Standard error; WB: whole body; BMC: bone mineral content; BMD: bone mineral density; L2–L4: Lumbar spine; TH: total hip; FN: femoral neck.

4 Discussion

The current study conducted on a group of young Lebanese adults mainly shows that maximum power calculated by the force-velocity test is a positive determinant of BMD and hip geometry indices in men but not in women. The study also shows that lean mass is a positive determinant factor of BMD and hip geometry indices in women. Fat mass percentage was negatively correlated to several bone variables in men. Fat mass excess seems to negatively influence bone variables in men. Fat mass excess is usually associated with lower testosterone and growth hormone levels in men; this may in part explain the negative correlations between fat mass percentage and bone variables. Lean mass was positively correlated to WB BMD, CSMI and Z. Our results confirm those of previous studies conducted on men [32–34]. Regarding physical performance variables, maximum power evaluated by the force-velocity test was the strongest factor associated with bone variables in men. Importantly, the positive associations between force-velocity maximum power and BMD values remained significant after adjustment for age and fat mass. Accordingly, implementing strategies to reduce fat mass percentage and to increase lean mass and maximum power in men would be interesting to prevent osteopenia and osteoporosis later in life. Sprint performance was significantly correlated to FN BMD, CSA, Z and SI in men. Our results are in line with those of two previous studies that studied the relationships between sprint performance and bone variables [43, 47]. Weight, BMI, lean mass and fat mass were positively correlated to WB BMC, CSMI and Z in women. These results are in accordance with those of several studies previously conducted on women [35–37]. Regarding physical performance variables, we noted only one positive association between vertical jump maximum power and WB BMC. Maximum power evaluated by the force-velocity test was not correlated to bone variables. This result is in contrast with those reported by Witzke et al. [48]. The reasons that may explain the different results obtained may be due to the age and characteristics of the studied population. Overall, lean mass was the strongest factor associated with bone variables in women. Consequently, implementing strategies to increase lean mass in women would be interesting to prevent osteopenia and osteoporosis later in life. The present study has several limitations such as its cross-sectional nature, the relatively low number of subjects, the two-dimensional nature of the DXA measurement, and the lack of measurement of many bone determinants (hormones, vitamin D and nutritional intakes). However, up to our knowledge, it is one of very few studies that aimed at studying the relationships between maximum power and bone health parameters in young Lebanese adults.

5 Conclusion

In conclusion, the current study suggests that lean mass is the strongest determinant of bone variables in adult women while maximum power evaluated by the force-velocity test seems to be the strongest determinant of bone variables in adult men. Physical training programs should be designed and executed accordingly in order to prevent the occurrence of osteopenia and osteoporosis later in life.

Conflicts of Interest. The authors state that they have no conflicts of interest.

References

1. Beck, T.J.: Extending DXA beyond bone mineral density: understanding hip structure analysis. Curr. Osteoporos. Rep. **5**(2), 49–55 (2007)
2. Friedman, A.W.: Important determinants of bone strength: beyond bone mineral density. J. Clin. Rheumatol. **12**(2), 70–77 (2006)
3. Ammann, P., Rizzoli, R.: Bone strength and its determinants. Osteoporos. Int. **14**(Suppl 3), S13–S18 (2003)
4. Fonseca, H., Moreira-Gonçalves, D., Coriolano, H.J., Duarte, J.A.: Bone quality: the determinants of bone strength and fragility. Sports Med. **44**(1), 37–53 (2014)
5. Rizzoli, R., Bonjour, J.P., Ferrari, S.L.: Osteoporosis, genetics and hormones. J. Mol. Endocrinol. **26**(2), 79–94 (2001)
6. Beck, B.R., Snow, C.M.: Bone health across the lifespan–exercising our options. Exerc. Sport Sci. Rev. **31**(3), 117–122 (2003)
7. Petit, M.A., Beck, T.J., Kontulainen, S.A.: Examining the developing bone: what do we measure and how do we do it? J. Musculoskelet. Neuronal Interact. **5**(3), 213–224 (2005)
8. Goltzman, D.: The aging skeleton. Adv. Exp. Med. Biol. **1164**, 153–160 (2019)

9. Min, S.K., et al.: Position statement: exercise guidelines to increase peak bone mass in adolescents. J. Bone Metab. **26**(4), 225–239 (2019)
10. Monge, M.C.: Optimizing bone health in adolescents. Curr. Opin. Obstet. Gynecol. **30**(5), 310–315 (2018)
11. Bonjour, J.P., Chevalley, T., Rizzoli, R., Ferrari, S.: Gene-environment interactions in the skeletal response to nutrition and exercise during growth. Med. Sport Sci. **51**, 64–80 (2007)
12. Bonjour, J.P., Chevalley, T., Ferrari, S., Rizzoli, R.: The importance and relevance of peak bone mass in the prevalence of osteoporosis. Salud Publica Mex. **51**(Suppl 1), S5–S17 (2009)
13. Bonjour, J.P., Chevalley, T.: Pubertal timing, bone acquisition, and risk of fracture throughout life. Endocr. Rev. **35**(5), 820–847 (2014)
14. El Hage, R., Jacob, C., Moussa, E., Jaffré, C., Baddoura, R.: Bone mass in a group of Lebanese girls from Beirut and French girls from Orleans. J. Med. Liban. **59**(3), 131–135 (2011)
15. El Hage, R., Baddoura, R.: Anthropometric predictors of geometric indices of hip bone strength in a group of Lebanese postmenopausal women. J. Clin. Densitom. **15**(2), 191–197 (2012)
16. El Hage, R., Jacob, C., Moussa, E., Baddoura, R.: Relative importance of lean mass and fat mass on bone mineral density in a group of Lebanese postmenopausal women. J. Clin. Densitom. **14**(3), 326–331 (2011)
17. Ayoub, M.L., et al.: DXA-based variables and osteoporotic fractures in Lebanese postmenopausal women. Orthop. Traumatol. Surg. Res. **100**(8), 855–858 (2014)
18. El Hage, R., Bachour, F., Sebaaly, A., Issa, M., Zakhem, E., Maalouf, G.: The influence of weight status on radial bone mineral density in Lebanese women. Calcif. Tissue Int. **94**(4), 465–467 (2014)
19. El Hage, R., et al.: Influence of age, morphological characteristics, and lumbar spine bone mineral density on lumbar spine trabecular bone score in Lebanese women. J. Clin. Densitom. **17**(3), 434–435 (2014)
20. Maalouf, G., et al.: Epidemiology of hip fractures in Lebanon: a nationwide survey. Orthop. Traumatol. Surg. Res. **99**(6), 675–680 (2013)
21. El Hage, R., Mina, F., Ayoub, M.L., Theunynck, D., Baddoura, R.: Relative importance of lean mass and fat mass on bone mineral density in a group of Lebanese elderly men. J. Med. Liban. **60**(3), 136–141 (2012)
22. El Hage, R., Theunynck, D., Rocher, E., Baddoura, R.: Geometric indices of hip bone strength in overweight and control elderly men. J. Med. Liban. **62**(3), 150–155 (2014)
23. El-Hajj Fuleihan, G., Baddoura, R., Awada, H., Salam, N., Salamoun, M., Rizk, P.: Low peak bone mineral density in healthy Lebanese subjects. Bone **31**(4), 520–528 (2002)
24. Arabi, A., et al.: Bone mineral density by age, gender, pubertal stages, and socioeconomic status in healthy Lebanese children and adolescents. Bone **35**(5), 1169–1179 (2004)
25. El Hage, R., Jacob, C., Moussa, E., Jaffré, C., Benhamou, C.L.: Daily calcium intake and body mass index in a group of Lebanese adolescents. J. Med. Liban. **57**(4), 253–257 (2009)
26. Salamoun, M.M., et al.: Low calcium and vitamin D intake in healthy children and adolescents and their correlates. Eur. J. Clin. Nutr. **59**(2), 177–184 (2005)
27. Gannagé-Yared, M.H., Chemali, R., Yaacoub, N., Halaby, G.: Hypovitaminosis D in a sunny country: relation to lifestyle and bone markers. J. Bone Miner. Res. **15**(9), 1856–1862 (2000)
28. Gannagé-Yared, M.H., Chemali, R., Sfeir, C., Maalouf, G., Halaby, G.: Dietary calcium and vitamin D intake in an adult Middle Eastern population: food sources and relation to lifestyle and PTH. Int. J. Vitam. Nutr. Res. **75**(4), 281–289 (2005)

29. Fazah, A., Jacob, C., Moussa, E., El-Hage, R., Youssef, H., Delamarche, P.: Activity, inactivity and quality of life among Lebanese adolescents. Pediatr. Int. **52**(4), 573–578 (2010)
30. Nasreddine, L., et al.: Dietary, lifestyle and socio-economic correlates of overweight, obesity and central adiposity in Lebanese children and adolescents. Nutrients **6**(3), 1038–1062 (2014)
31. Naja, F., Hwalla, N., Itani, L., Karam, S., Sibai, A.M., Nasreddine, L.: A Western dietary pattern is associated with overweight and obesity in a national sample of Lebanese adolescents (13-19 years): a cross-sectional study. Br. J. Nutr. **114**(11), 1909–1919 (2015)
32. El Hage, Z., et al.: Bone mineral content and density in obese, overweight and normal weight adolescent boys. J. Med. Liban. **61**(3), 148–154 (2013)
33. El Hage, R.: Geometric indices of hip bone strength in obese, overweight, and normal-weight adolescent boys. Osteoporos. Int. **23**(5), 1593–1600 (2012)
34. Khawaja, A., et al.: Does muscular power predict bone mineral density in young adults? J. Clin. Densitom. **22**(3), 311–320 (2019)
35. Berro, A.J., et al.: Physical performance variables and bone parameters in a group of young overweight and obese women. J. Clin. Densitom. **22**(2), 293–299 (2019)
36. Al Rassy, N., et al.: The relationships between bone variables and physical fitness across the BMI spectrum in young adult women. J. Bone Miner. Metab. **37**(3), 520–528 (2019)
37. Nasr, R., et al.: Muscular maximal strength indices and bone variables in a group of elderly women. J. Clin. Densitom. (2018). pii: S1094-6950(18)30014-3. https://doi.org/10.1016/j.jocd.2018.03.003
38. El Khoury, G., et al.: Bone variables in active overweight/obese men and sedentary overweight/obese men. J. Clin. Densitom. **20**(2), 239–246 (2017)
39. El Khoury, C., et al.: Physical performance variables and bone mineral density in a group of young overweight and obese men. J. Clin. Densitom. **21**(1), 41–47 (2018)
40. Zakhem, E., et al.: Performance physique et densité minérale osseuse chez de jeunes adultes libanais. J. Med. Liban. **64**(4), 193–199 (2016)
41. El Hage, R., et al.: Maximal oxygen consumption and bone mineral density in a group of young Lebanese adults. J. Clin Densitom. **17**(2), 320–324 (2014)
42. Harman, E.A., Rosenstein, M.T., Frykman, P.N., Rosenstein, R.M., Kraemer, W.J.: Estimation of human power output from vertical jump. J. Strength Cond. Res. **5**(3), 116–120 (1991)
43. Finianos, B., Sabbagh, P., Zunquin, G., El Hage, R.: Muscular power and maximum oxygen consumption predict bone density in a group of middle-aged men. J. Musculoskelet. Neuronal. Interact. **20**(1), 53–61 (2020)
44. Vandewalle, H., Peres, G., Heller, J., Panel, J., Monod, H.: Force-velocity relationship and maximal power on a cycle ergometer Correlation with the height of a vertical jump. Eur. J. Appl. Physiol. Occup. Physiol. **56**(6), 650–656 (1987)
45. Vandewalle, H., Pérès, G., Monod, H.: Standard anaerobic exercise tests. Sports Med. **4**(4), 268–289 (1987)
46. Driss, T., Vandewalle, H.: The measurement of maximal (anaerobic) power output on a cycle ergometer: a critical review. Biomed. Res. Int. **2013**, 589361 (2013)
47. Vicente-Rodriguez, G., Dorado, C., Perez-Gomez, J., Gonzalez-Henriquez, J.J., Calbet, J.A.: Enhanced bone mass and physical fitness in young female handball players. Bone **35**(5), 1208–1215 (2004)
48. Witzke, K.A., Snow, C.M.: Lean body mass and leg power best predict bone mineral density in adolescent girls. Med. Sci. Sports Exerc. **31**(11), 1558–1563 (1999)

Biomedical Signal Analysis

Thermal Behavior of Children During American Football Sports Training

Irving A. Cruz-Albarrán[1], Pierre Burciaga-Zuñiga[2], Ma. Guadalupe Perea-Ortiz[3], and Luis A. Morales-Hernandez[1(✉)]

[1] Mechatronics/Engineering Faculty, Autonomous University of Queretaro, Campus San Juan del Rio, San Juan del Rio, Queretaro, Mexico
{icruz, lamorales}@hspdigital.org
[2] National Center for Preventive Programs and Disease Control, Health Secretary, Mexico City, Mexico
pierre.burciaga@salud.gob.mx
[3] Nursing Faculty, Autonomous University of Queretaro, Queretaro, Mexico
direccion.fen@uaq.mx

Abstract. This paper shows the thermal behavior in the nose, the fingertips and lower limbs (right and left) before and after an American football training in fourteen children who are members of a private football academy. During the one-hour training, four different activities were carried out: warm-up, speed test at 40 yards, long jump tests and three-cone drill tests, in which each stage was developed in a time of fifteen minutes. For the statistical analysis of the thermal information, a methodology that allows to calculate the thermal matrix and thus obtain the thermal values of each point was developed. Once the analysis was carried out, significant changes (temperature decrease) were found in the analyzed regions of interest, except for the thumb. Subsequently, a temperature decrease index was obtained and it was found that the greatest temperature change is shown in the area of the lower extremities.

Keywords: Infrared thermography · American football · Sports training

1 Introduction

Nowadays, technology is quickly entering in the medical area. Medical devices are currently used to diagnose, prevent, control or relieve diseases [1]. Therefore, safety and reliability are of vital importance, since they influence the health and life of patients [2]. A medical tool that has experienced a great boom is infrared thermography (IRT), this because it works non-invasively, it does not generate radiation, and it is inexpensive [3]. Among the main medical applications of IRT we found the followings: breast cancer detection [4], psychophysiology [5, 6], gynecology [7], problems related to diabetic foot [8, 9], dental diagnoses [10] and medical-sports area issues [11].

When physical activity is performed, significant changes occur within the human body, one of the most important is the temperature variation, which in turn requires the activation of autonomic responses for temperature regulation and thus be able to maintain the proper body temperature human [12]. Hence, studies have been developed

I. Rojas et al. (Eds.): IWBBIO 2020, LNBI 12108, pp. 133–142, 2020.
https://doi.org/10.1007/978-3-030-45385-5_12

to analyze the thermal behavior of the human body on different sports activities. For example, those focused on football: Bouzas et al. [13] conducted a study to obtain the thermographic profile of the lower extremities of young elite players and obtained that they show contralateral thermal symmetry, where the temperature differences matched for each ROI was ≤ 0.2 °C. Rodriguez-Sanz et al. [14] studied thermographic changes in elite players in functional condition of the equine and non-equine ankle, thereby concluding that there is a higher temperature after exercising in those with the equine ankle than the non-equine. Menezes et al. [15] studied a group of soccer players and showed the thermal changes in healthy conditions and injuries, the result was that there were temperature gradients greater than 7 °C between healthy and injured athletes. Furthermore, important works have also been developed in cycling, such is the case of Ludwig et al. [16] who evaluated the temperature during a dynamic training of elite cyclists who showed a significant temperature decrease during the exercise followed by an increase after exhaustion. At the same time, work related to runners has been carried out, as an example of this, we look at Merla et al. [17], who analyzed temperature variations in well-trained runners during a graded exercise routine and it was obtained that body temperature decreased as the exercise began, and it increased during exercise recovery. Rodriguez-Sanz et al. [18] evaluated how the temperature of the skin is related to the activation of the gastrocnemius muscle, obtaining that the temperature is widely related to the activation of the muscular pattern of the lower limb. De Andrade et al. [19] monitored 12 youngers to obtain the temperature variation in different areas of interest of the body and concluded that depending on the activity and the area of analysis there are significant variations before and after exercising. As can be seen, a variety of studies focused on the thermal behavior of the human body when training distinctive sports, have been developed; however, these have been documented only for adults, not for children. Although it is known that everyone reacts differently. Additionally, these investigations only show the behavior of the muscles that become active during exercise, though it is known that the effects occur on the face after exercising, too.

This paper shows the thermal behavior of the lower extremities, the tip of the right-hand fingers and the tip of the nose before and after a football training in children of an academy. To this effect, the hues thermographic image was transformed to thermal values through obtaining the thermal matrix, subsequently the regions of interest (ROI's) were obtained, the information was extracted, and the statistical analysis was performed for each of them.

2 Materials and Methods

The general methodology that was carried out in this work is shown in Fig. 1. It comprises four stages: in the first stage the information is taken (thermographic images) to capture the baseline state, then the training plan is executed and once this is completed, the information is re-acquired. Finally, the analysis of the information obtained is performed and the results obtained are shown.

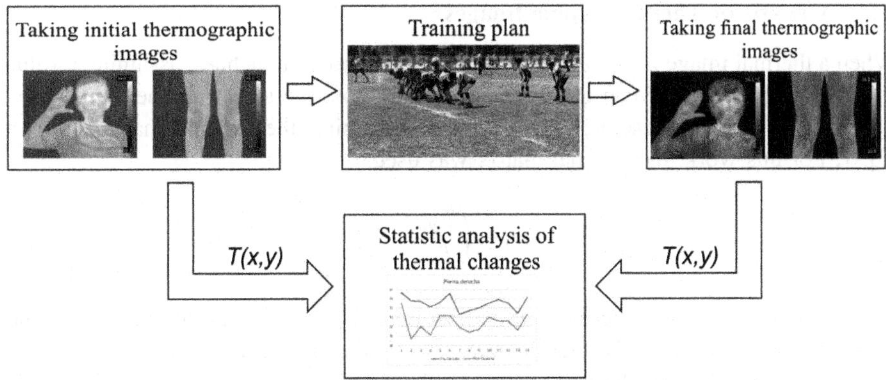

Fig. 1. General proposed methodology

2.1 Factors to Consider When Taking Thermographic Images

The study was carried out according to the factors that influence researches based on Infrared Thermography [3]. This was done in Mexico City, Mexico, in a 6 m long and 2.5 high cabin, with the lowest possible light incidence. The environmental conditions were temperature of 20 ± 2 °C and relative humidity between 45–60%. It was performed with 14 children, with an average age of 11.07 years and a standard deviation of 0.73. The Helsinki declaration was fulfilled [21] and the parents of each study subject signed the informed consent letter. The exclusion criteria for the study were: do not drink stimulating liquids or drinks, do not exercise (all the above at least 8 h before the study), do not use beauty products (cosmetics, creams, deodorants, among others), do not brush their teeth, be free of respiratory diseases and fast of two hours.

For the study, a FLIR A310 camera was used with a sensitivity of 0.05 at 30 °C, a spectral range between 7.5 and 13 μm and a resolution of 320 × 240 pixels, which was positioned in a tripod at a distance of 1.2 of the study subjects, the height was variable, depending on the height of each subject. The emissivity taken for this work was 0.98 [20].

2.2 Training Plan

The training plan that was carried out for the study was based on four main stages (Fig. 2). Each stage lasted 15 min. The first stage consisted in warming-up, to subsequently perform the speed test at forty yards, then the long jump was carried out and finally the three-cone drill test. At the beginning and at the end of the protocol, the thermographic images were taken.

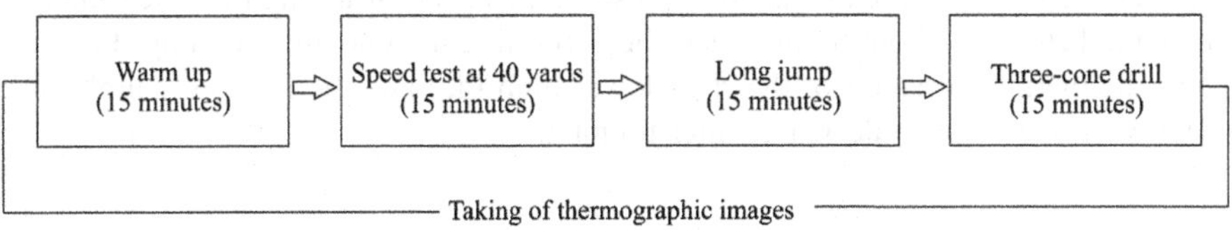

Fig. 2. Training protocol

2.3 Analysis of Thermographic Images

When a thermal image is obtained, it is represented based on its hues, assigning a value to each channel, (red, green and blue). It is only possible to extract the temperature values using the manufacturer's software or obtaining the thermal matrix through Eq. 1. For this work, the thermal matrix was used.

$$T_r(x,y) = T_{min} + \left(\frac{T_{gray}}{T_{mgv}}(T_{max} - T_{min})\right) \tag{1}$$

Where $T_r(x,y)$ is the thermogram temperature, T_{max} y T_{min} are the maximum and minimum temperature on the thermogram, T_{gray} is the gray level intensity of the point to be treated and T_{mgv} is the maximum gray level value.

The ROI's that were considered were the tip of the nose, the fingertips and the thighs, which are show in red in Fig. 3.

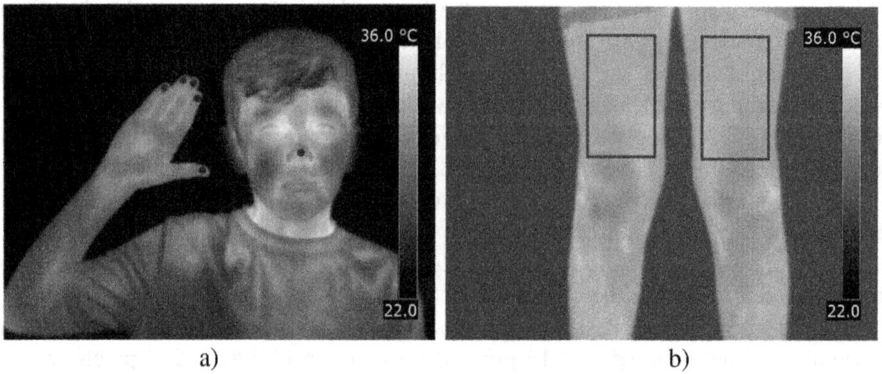

Fig. 3. ROI's. (a) Tip of the fingers and nose. (b) Lower limbs (Color figure online)

Once the temperature values of each region of interest were taken, the statistics analysis was carried out. This consisted in a Wilcoxon test to paired samples [22]. The level of significance to be used for this study was 95% [23].

3 Results

The statistical analysis was carried out by ROI and for each study subject, therefore, the individual behavior of each of them is presented. In each of the figures, the blue line shows the behavior before training and the green line the one after training. Figure 4 shows the thermal behavior of the right lower limb (4a) and the left lower limb (4b), where each one of them decreases after training.

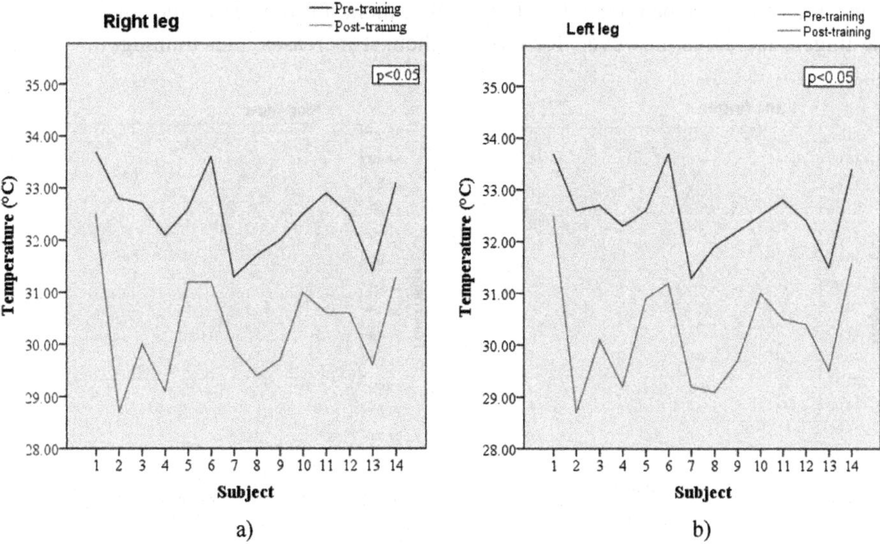

Fig. 4. Thermal behavior in the lower limb per subject. (a) Right lower limb. (b) Left lower limb. (Color figure online)

Figure 5 shows the behavior of the nose, which also decreases for 13 subjects, only increasing for one of them.

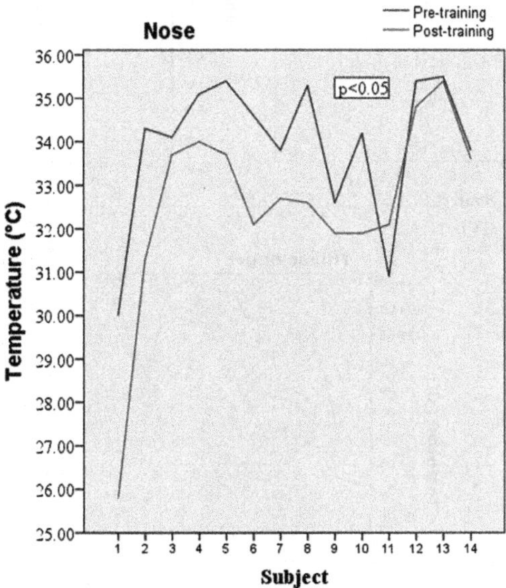

Fig. 5. Thermal behavior in nose per subject (Color figure online)

Figure 6 shows the thermal behavior of each of the fingertips of the right hand. In the 6a the little finger is presented, in 6b the ring finger, in 6c the middle, in the 6d the index and finally, in the 6d the thumb. For all of them, in some cases the temperature of the fingers increases, however, for most of them it increases after training.

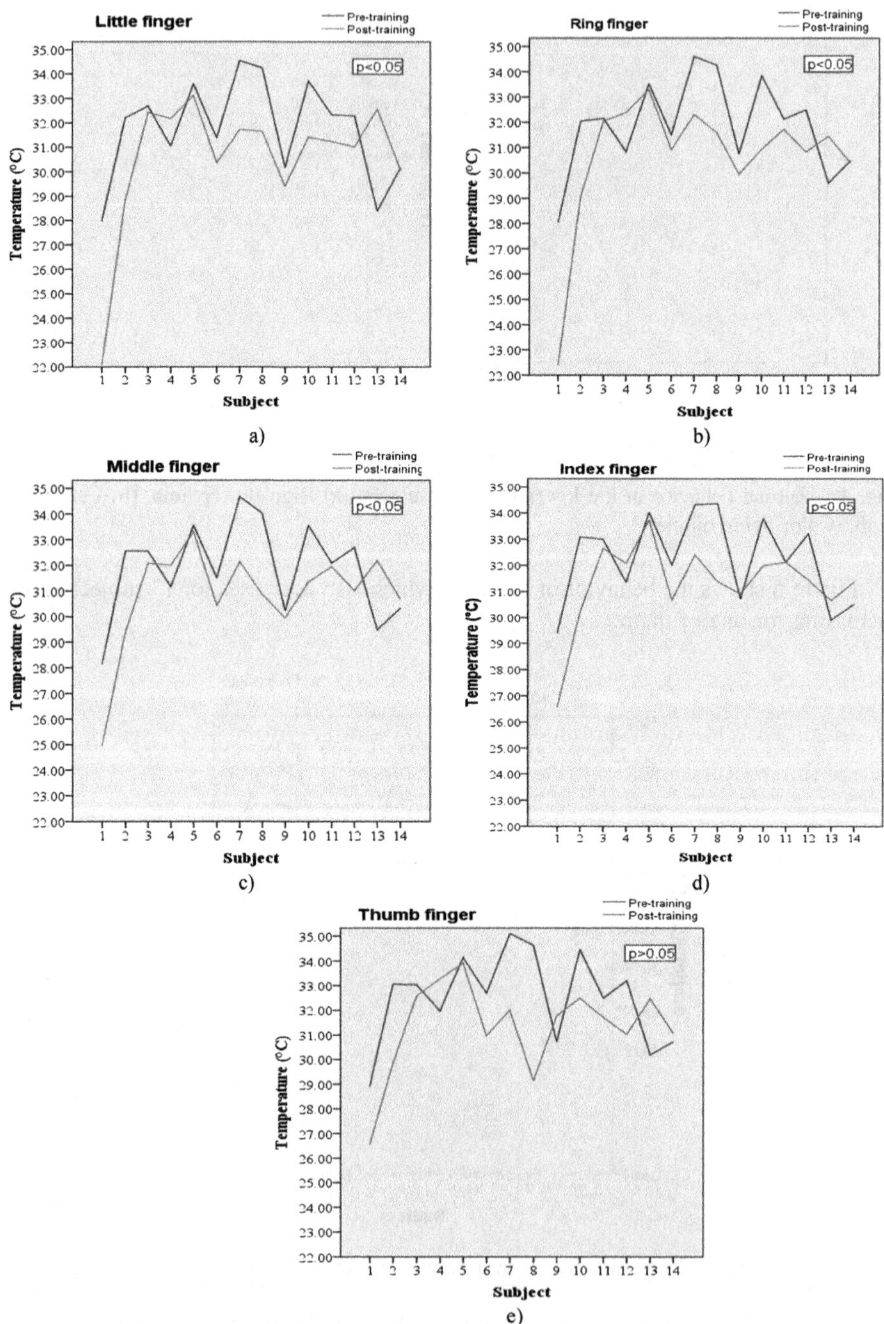

Fig. 6. Thermal behavior of fingers. (a) Little. (b) Ring. (c) Middle. (d) Index. (e) Thumb. (Color figure online)

Once the thermal values of each ROI had been extracted, the statistical analysis was carried out, which, as already stated, was based on the Wilcoxon test. The results obtained are shown in Table 1. There we can appreciate that there was a significant temperature decrease between ROI, except for the thumb.

Table 1. Statistical values by region of interest before and after training

	Pre-training (°C)	Post-training (°C)	ΔT (°C)	ρ
Right lower limb	32.492	30.342	−2.150	0.001
Left lower limb	32.492	30.257	−2.235	0.001
Nose	33.928	32.542	−1.386	0.005
Little finger	33.772	30.579	−3.193	0.041
Ring finger	31.879	30.663	−1.216	0.022
Middle finger	31.900	30.881	−1.019	0.048
Index finger	32.274	31.298	−0.976	0.041
Thumb finger	32.531	31.243	−1.288	0.064

Finally, Fig. 7 shows a series of thermograms where the temperatures in the different ROI's analyzed in this work can be seen qualitatively.

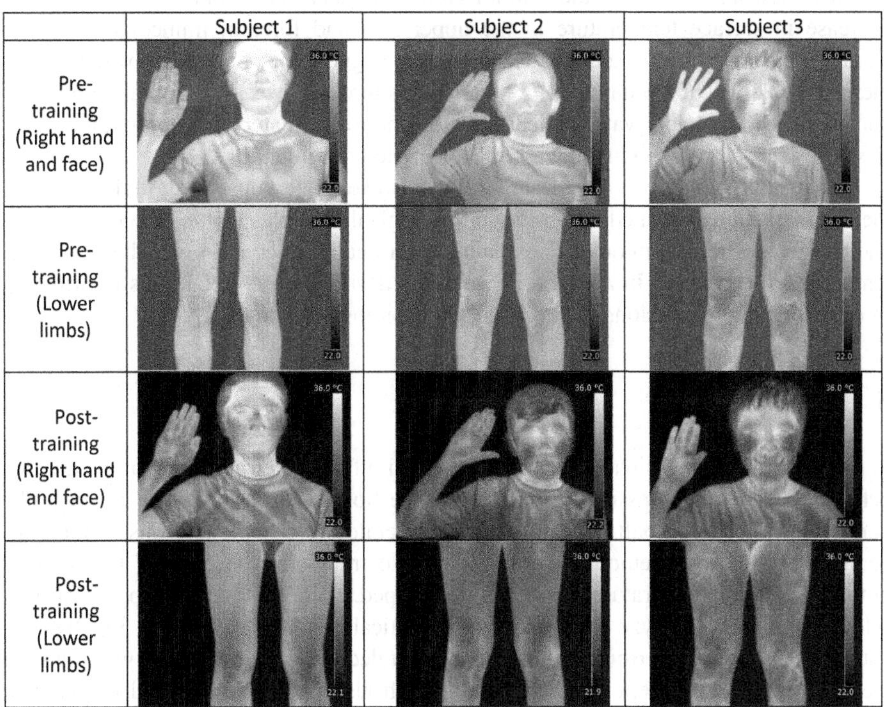

Fig. 7. Thermographic images of the ROI's pre-training and post-training.

4 Discussion

The thermo-regulatory system of the human body has the task of maintaining its proper temperature despite variations in environmental conditions or physical activity [24]. For this reason, any physical activity will produce temperature variations at the average values of the different regions of the human body, these average values in Mexican children have been previously documented [25]. This paper shows the temperature variations in children members of a private American football academy after a training, which has four stages, each stage lasting fifteen minutes. Once the analysis of the thermal information obtained was carried out, it was found that there is a significant temperature decrease in the ROI's analyzed, except for the thumb, which, although it presents a temperature decrease, it is not significant. In the case of the lower limbs a temperature decrease of 2.192 ± 0.042 °C was found, in the case of the fingers a decrease of 1.538 ± 1.654 °C and in the case of the nose there was a decrease of 1.385 °C, all of them, after training. These temperature decreases had already been previously documented by another author, for example Torri et al. [26] showed that there is a decrease in temperature during initial muscle work in a bicycle exercise, which did not depend on the amount of sweating. Merla et al. [17] mention a decrease in body temperature between 3 and 5 °C as the subjects performed the physical activity, which increased after the physical activity stopped. De Andrade et al. [19] obtained significant decreases after 10 min of activity, being the hands where the greatest decrease was achieved (2.5 °C for the back view and 2.4 °C for the anterior view). Chudeka and Lubkowska [27] found a decrease in surface temperature in the upper arm and forearm immediately after a handball training. These temperature decreases suggest that they are not due to the thermo-regulation of the human body that occurs through sweating, but rather to vaso-constriction. In the same way, it can be seen that there are greater temperature differences in studies carried out in adults than the ones carried out in children.

The results found show important findings. However, it would be desirable to relate the thermal values obtained with other physiological variables (for example, heart rate and oxygen saturation) in order to explain clearer and more concise way the reasons of temperature decrement. In addition, it would be desirable to correlate this information in order to find connections between these physiological variables.

5 Conclusion

In this work the analysis was carried out based on infrared thermography of the thermal behavior of the fingertips of the right hand, the tip of the nose and the lower limbs before and after a football training in fourteen children. For the analysis of the temperature behavior, a methodology that allows to transform the hues of the thermographic image to temperature values was developed. Also, this methodology allows to select the areas to analyze and shows the statistical result of each zone. Finally, statistical analyzes were performed and a significant decrease in temperature was found in the analyzed areas, except for the thumb, which also presented a global decrease in temperature, however, it was not significant. The temperature gradients of each area (lower limbs, hands and face) were obtained, concluding that the greatest decrease in temperature occurs in the frontal area of the lower limbs, both right and left.

Acknowledgements. The authors would like to thank the Nursing Faculty of the Autonomous University of Queretaro, for supporting part of this study.

References

1. Jamshidi, A., Rahimi, S.A., Ait-Kadi, D., Ruiz, A.: A comprehensive fuzzy risk-based maintenance framework for prioritization of medical devices. Appl. Soft Comput. **32**, 322–334 (2015)
2. Song, W., Li, J., Li, H., Ming, X.: Human factors risk assessment: an integrated method for improving safety in clinical use of medical devices. Appl. Soft Comput. **86**, 1–14 (2019)
3. Fernández-Cuevas, I., et al.: Classification of factors influencing the use of infrared thermography in humans: a review. Infrared Phys. Technol. **71**, 28–55 (2015)
4. Garduño-Ramón, M.A., Vega-Mancilla, S.G., Morales-Henández, L.A., Osornio-Rios, R.A.: Supportive noninvasive tool for the diagnosis of breast cancer using a thermographic camera as sensor. Sensors **17**(3), 1–21 (2017)
5. Cruz-Albarran, I.A., Benitez-Rangel, J.P., Osornio-Rios, R.A., Dominguez-Trejo, B., Rodriguez-Medina, D.A., Morales-Hernandez, L.A.: A methodology based on infrared thermography for the study of stress in hands of young people during the Trier Social Stress Test. Infrared Phys. Technol. **93**, 116–123 (2018)
6. Cruz-Albarran, I.A., Benitez-Rangel, J.P., Osornio-Rios, R.A., Morales-Hernandez, L.A.: Human emotions detection based on a smart-thermal system of thermographic images. Infrared Phys. Technol. **81**, 250–261 (2017)
7. Jo, J., Kim, H.: Comparison of abdominal skin temperature between fertile and infertile women by infrared thermography: a diagnostic approach. J. Therm. Biol **61**, 133–139 (2016)
8. Peregrina-Barreto, H., Morales-Hernandez, L.A., Rangel-Magdaleno, J.J., Avina-Cervantes, J.G., Ramirez-Cortes, J.M., Morales-Caporal, R.: Quantitative estimation of temperature variations in plantar angiosomes: a study case for diabetic foot. Comput. Math. Methods Med. **2014**, 1–10 (2014)
9. Silva, N.C.M., Castro, H.A., Carvalho, L.C., Chaves, É.C.L., Ruela, L.O., Iunes, D.H.: Reliability of infrared thermography images in the analysis of the plantar surface temperature in diabetes mellitus. J. Chiropr. Med. **17**(1), 30–35 (2018)
10. Zakian, C.M., Taylor, A.M., Ellwood, R.P., Pretty, I.A.: Occlusal caries detection by using thermal imaging. J. Dent. **38**, 788–795 (2010)
11. Priego Quesada, J.I. (ed.): Application of Infrared Thermography in Sports Science. BMPBE. Springer, Cham (2017). https://doi.org/10.1007/978-3-319-47410-6
12. Schlader, Z.J., Stannard, S.R., Mündel, T.: Human thermoregulatory behavior during rest and exercise - a prospective review. Physiol. Behav. **99**, 269–275 (2010)
13. Bouzas Marins, J.C., et al.: Thermographic profile of soccer players' lower limbs. Revista Andaluza de Medicina del Deporte. **7**(1), 1–6 (2014)
14. Rodríguez-Sanz, D., Losa-Iglesias, M.E., López-López, D., Calvo-Lobo, C., Palomo-López, P., Becerro-de-Bengoa-Vallejo, R.: Infrared thermography applied to lower limb muscles in elite soccer players with functional ankle equinus and non-equinus condition. PeerJ **2017**, 1–11 (2017)

15. Menezes, P., Rhea, M., Herdy, C., Simão, R.: Effects of strength training program and infrared thermography in soccer athletes injuries. Sports **6**, 148 (2018)
16. Ludwig, N., et al.: Thermography for skin temperature evaluation during dynamic exercise: a case study on an incremental maximal test in elite male cyclists. Appl. Opt. **55**, D126 (2016)
17. Merla, A., Mattei, P.A., Di Donato, L., Romani, G.L.: Thermal imaging of cutaneous temperature modifications in runners during graded exercise. Ann. Biomed. Eng. **38**, 158–163 (2010)
18. Rodriguez-Sanz, D., et al.: Thermography related to electromyography in runners with functional equinus condition after running. Phys. Ther. Sports **40**, 193–196 (2019)
19. de Andrade Fernandes, A., dos Santos Amorim, P.R., Brito, C.J., Sillero-Quintana, M., Marins, J.C.B.: Regional skin temperature response to moderate aerobic exercise measured by infrared thermography. Asian J. Sports Med. **7**, 1–8 (2016)
20. Fernandes, A.A., et al.: Validity of inner canthus temperature recorded by infrared thermography as a non-invasive surrogate measure for core temperature at rest, during exercise and recovery. J. Therm. Biol **62**, 50–55 (2016)
21. World Medical Association: World medical association declaration of helsinki: Ethical principles for medical research involving human subjects. JAMA **310**(20), 2191–2194 (2013)
22. Woolson, R.F.: Wilcoxon signed-rank test. In: D'Agostino, R.B., Sullivan, L., Massaro, J. (eds.) Wiley Encyclopedia of Clinical Trials, pp. 1–3. Wiley (2008). https://doi.org/10.1002/9780471462422.eoct979
23. Simon, R.: Confidence intervals for reporting results of clinical trials. Ann. Intern. Med. **105**, 429–435 (1986)
24. Formenti, D., Ludwig, N., Gargano, M., Gondola, M., Dellerma, N., Caumo, A., Alberti, G.: Thermal imaging of exercise-associated skin temperature changes in trained and untrained female subjects. Ann. Biomed. Eng. **41**, 863–871 (2013)
25. Kolosovas-Machuca, E.S., Javier Gonzàlez, F.: Distribution of skin temperature in Mexican children. Skin Res. Technol. **17**, 326–331 (2011)
26. Torii, M., Yamasaki, M., Sasaki, T., Nakayama, H.: Fall in skin temperature of exercising man. Br. J. Sports Med. **26**, 29–32 (1992)
27. Chudecka, M., Lubkowska, A.: Temperature changes of selected body's surfaces of handball players in the course of training estimated by thermovision, and the study of the impact of physiological and morphological factors on the skin temperature. J. Therm. Biol **35**, 379–385 (2010)

Positioning Algorithm for Arterial Blood Pressure Pneumatic Sensor

Viacheslav Antsiperov(✉) and Gennady Mansurov

Kotelnikov Institute of Radioengineering and Electronics (IRE) of RAS, Mokhovaya street 11-7, 125009 Moscow, Russia
antciperov@cplire.ru, gkmansurov@gmail.com
https://www.researchgate.net/profile/V_Antsiperov

Abstract. The paper is devoted to the algorithmic solution of quality control over the pneumatic blood pressure sensor positioning. Previously, this problem was solved by the operator based on his subjective assessment of the presence/absence of a pulse wave in the observed signal and its quality estimation. Recent studies have led us to a simple algorithm for automatically evaluating the accuracy of positioning. The algorithm is based on the value of the variability of the intervals of side peaks that the multiscale autocorrelation function can manifest as part of its structure. Since this value is closely related to such a characteristic of the signal as its quasi–periodicity, the algorithm essentially estimates the degree of periodicity of the signal, which is high in the presence of a pulse wave and small in its absence. In addition to the general principle of quasi–periodicity estimation much empirical information has been accumulated on the necessary preliminary normalization of the signal, the censorship of the side peaks to be considered, on the numerical values of the comparison thresholds, etc. The main ideas of the algorithm are illustrated by examples of processing real data obtained by positioning the developed pneumatic sensor.

Keywords: Pneumatic blood pressure sensor · Positioning problem · Arterial blood pressure signal analysis · Quasi–periodicity detection · Degree of quasi–periodicity

1 Positioning of ABP Pneumatic Sensor

The idea of a pneumatic sensor for measuring the arterial blood pressure (ABP) and the physical principle of local pressure compensation on which it is based were described in detail in the paper [1]. It was shown that the use of miniature measuring unit, its arrangement close to the working area and the possibility of processing digitized data in real time directly in the microcontroller of the sensor made it possible to carry out a unique cuffless method of ABP monitoring by

The work is supported by the Russian Foundation for Basic Research (RFBR), grant N 18-29-02108 mk.

I. Rojas et al. (Eds.): IWBBIO 2020, LNBI 12108, pp. 143–154, 2020.
https://doi.org/10.1007/978-3-030-45385-5_13

directly applying the sensor to the surface tissues of the human body. The technical details of the implementation of the sensor were patented at approximately the same time [2].

The practical implementation of local compensation method became possible thanks to the developed unique technique of pressure measurements on a very small working area (1 mm^2 or less) [3]. Due to the very small sensing contacts and, consequently, the ability to accurately position the sensor directly over the artery, it became possible to ensure high quality blood pressure measurement. However, since the artery itself is generally not visible, the correct positioning of the sensor is a non-trivial problem [4]. Therefore, the problem of pneumatic sensor positioning is an important part of the pressure measurement methodology. In Fig. 1 the sensor readings are presented in the process of its correct positioning above the radial artery before the start of pressure monitoring session.

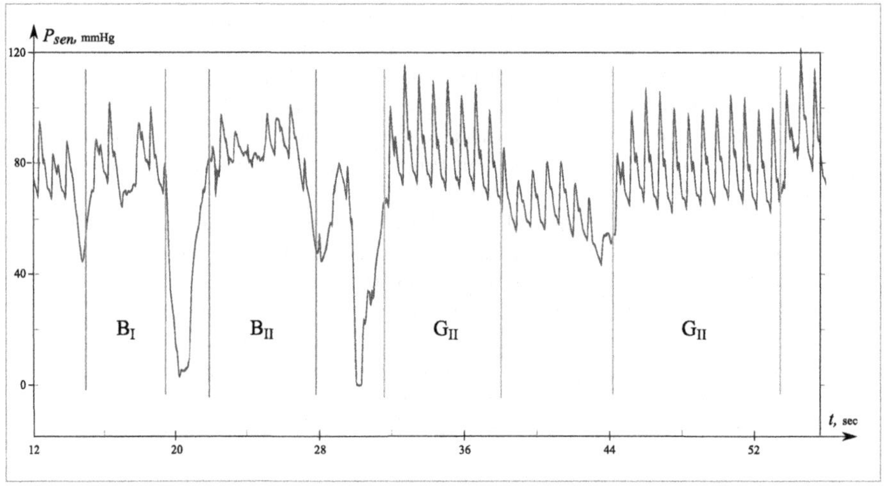

Fig. 1. Positioning the sensor before the start of ABP monitoring, based on operator subjective assessment of the current signal regularity (quasi–periodicity): from $B_I - B_{II}$ – bad regularity to $G_I - G_{II}$ – good quasi–periodicity

As a result of numerous recent experiments on ABP measuring, we have arrived at an estimation of the positioning quality based on the degree of quasi–periodicity of the specialized autocorrelation function (ACF), synthesied in frames of multiscale correlation analysis (MCA) approach. The foundations of the MCA were developed in [5], where we tried to combine the main ideas of two popular approaches – multiscale (wavelet) analysis and quadratic time-frequency representations to solve the maximum number of problems of non–stationary biomedical signals processing within the framework of a single general methodology. The implementation of such a synthesis was possible thanks to the adaptation of the analysis of the non–stationary signals containing the quasi–periodic fragments to biomedical problems. The main part of the next sections is devoted to MCA adaptation to ABP processing problems and to the results obtained in this line.

2 MCA Methodology for Estimating the Value of Quasi–periodicity of Biomedical Signal Patterns

From the 1990s active efforts were undertaken to solve the problem of estimating frequency characteristics of non–stationary signals [6], analogous to characteristics obtained by the classical spectral methods. One direction in this research was associated with the theory of quadratic time–frequency representations, generalizing the classical spectrograms, which were essentially developed at that time. The researchers of the other line began to use actively the wavelet analysis instead of the traditional Fourier analysis. The transfer from the frequency band to the scale space (wavelet transform coefficients) was justified by the fact that for the non-stationary signals the multiscale approach has a number of advantages over the fixed scale preset by the processing window. As noted above, we managed to combine the advantages of both approaches, but before discussing our (MCA) method, it's worth saying a few words about the paradigm of time-frequency representations synthesis, which was developed in the first decade of this millennium.

2.1 Cohen Class Time-Frequency Representations

To emphasize the essence of MCA, let us recall briefly the basic idea of the synthesis of quadratic time–frequency representations (TFR), following, for example, work [7]. The most popular and fairly broad TFR class is the so–called Cohen class, whose members $C_z(t, f, \Phi)$ have the following form:

$$\begin{aligned} C_z(t, f, \Phi) &= \int\int \Phi(t-u, f-\xi) W_z(u, \xi) du d\xi, \\ W_z(u, \xi) &= \int z(u+\tau, 2) z(u-\tau, 2) exp\{-2\pi\imath\tau u\} d\tau, \end{aligned} \tag{1}$$

where $z(u)$ is the signal analyzed, $W_z(u, \xi)$—Wigner distribution of $z(u)$, $\Phi(u, \xi)$ – any two–dimensional smoothing window, which determinates the preset properties to the Cohen class TFR $C_z(t, f, \Phi)$, $\imath$—imaginary unit. Formally, it follows from the first relation of (1) that $C_z(t, f, \Phi)$ is some smoothed version of Wigner distribution $W_z(u, \xi)$, which, in turn, can be presented in the following form:

$$\begin{aligned} W_z(u, \xi) &= \int R_i(u, \tau) exp\{-2\pi\imath\tau\xi\} d\tau, \\ R_i(u, \tau) &= z(u+\tau/2) z(u-\tau/2). \end{aligned} \tag{2}$$

Function $R_i(u, \tau)$ is usually called as the "instantaneous auto-correlation" function (instantaneous ACF) [7]. In this regard let us note that the name "instantaneous ACF unbiased estimator" would be more accurate for $R_i(u, \tau)$. Indeed, if we average out $R_i(u, \tau)$ (2) along the ensemble of realizations, then, in the stationary case, when the result depends on the arguments difference τ, the theoretical ACF determined by relation $R_z(\tau) = \langle z(u + \tau/2) z^*(u - \tau/2) \rangle$ will be obtained.

In the context of relations (2), Wigner distribution $W_z(u, \xi)$ is the Fourier transform of instantaneous ACF $R_i(u, \tau)$. It allows to interpret distribution $W_z(u, \xi)$ as the estimation of spectral density $N_z(\xi)$ of average signal power $\langle z(u)^2 \rangle$. Indeed, if in the stationary case to average out the first relation in (2) and use Wiener–Khinchin theorem connecting the ACF Fourier transform of $R_i(\tau)$ with $N_z(\xi)$, then we obtain $\langle W_z(u, \xi) \rangle = N_z(\xi)$. The problem of such interpretation, as known, is that estimated value $N_z(\xi)$ is principally positive, and its estimator $W_z(u, \xi)$ (2) can take on the negative values. In order to minimize this disadvantage, moving averaging of $W_z(u, \xi)$ is fulfilled with some $\Phi(u, \xi)$ window. So in non–stationary case, the $C_z(t, f, \Phi)$ (1) becomes the smoothed (locally averaged) estimation of time dependent spectral density $N_z(t, f) = \langle W_z(u, f) \rangle$.

Summarizing the above discussion, it is possible to formulate the main goal of synthesizing the quadratic TFR like the $C_z(t, f, \Phi)$ (1). It is the wish to construct such a time–dependent estimations of the spectral density $N_z(t, f)$, which would meet some additional requirements (positivity, validity, covariance regarding the frequency or/and time shifts, etc., see [6]). At that, it is supposed explicitly or implicitly that $N_z(t, f)$ shall have the pronounced, narrow maxima for some characteristic frequencies. The latter implies the narrow bands for each of the components corresponding to these frequencies. For such signals, sharp maxima of $C_z(t, f, \Phi)$ (1), corresponding to the signal components would have well–pronounced time trajectories in TFR, whose parameters can be controlled using the smoothing windows $\Phi(u, \xi)$.

It follows from the previous discussion that the question of how efficiently the TFR of type (1) can be used for the ABP quasi–periodicity analysis, is reduced to another question: to what extent it is appropriate to consider the ABP as a set of the narrow-band components. The last question was discussed in details in work [8]. In this work, based on the ABP waveforms analysis, the thesis was justified that the best model, to which ABP signal could be attributed, is the class of the wide-band pulse signals with the preset rhythm of the pulses. It is known that the analysis of such signals is more efficient within the time domain (variants of the correlation processing, in particular, matched filtering). That is why we have proposed the synthesis of ABP signal representations in the time domain instead of investigating its frequency content. This synthesis is fulfilled below basing on the methodology of the analysis of non–stationary signals containing quasi–periodic fragments, earlier proposed by the authors [5].

2.2 Synthesis of Specialized MCA Representation for Estimating the Value of Quasi–periodicity

The point of departure for the synthesis of the time–scale signal representations within MCA, as well as for the synthesis of the Cohen Class TFRs (1), (2), is some ACF estimation. However, the MCA uses the general (integrated over the signal realization) correlation function estimator, which takes into account some neighbourhood of time moment u, rather than single time instant u as for "instantaneous auto–correlation $R_i(u,\tau)$" (2):

$$R_{MCA}(u,\tau) = \frac{1}{|\tau|}\int_{u-|\tau|/2}^{u+|\tau|/2} z(u'+\tau/2)z(u'-\tau/2)du' \tag{3}$$

It can be easily shown that averaging $R_{MCA}(u,\tau)$ (3) along the ensemble of realizations in the stationary case gives exactly theoretical auto–correlation $R_z(\tau)$, i.e., (3) is its unbiased estimator. A number of properties including the signal support conservation property—vanishing of $R_{MCA}(u,\tau)$ beyond the support interval of the signal $z(u)$, important for the signal segmentation problems, was discussed in previous work [8]. An interesting feature of the representation (3) is that it can be expressed as convolution of the signals local past with respect to current time moment u and its local future. Indeed, let us define the signal local with respect to u past $z_{Pu}(u')$ and its local future $z_{Fu}(u')$ as follows:

$$\begin{aligned} z_{Pu}(u') &= \theta(u')z(u-u') \\ z_{Fu}(u') &= \theta(u')z(u+u') \end{aligned} \tag{4}$$

where $\theta(t)$ is an indicator of the positive semi–axis, the Heaviside step function.

It is now easy to deduce that for positive scale $\tau > 0$ the representation (3) with the definitions (4) can be rewritten as:

$$\begin{aligned} R_{MCA}(u,\tau) &= \frac{1}{\tau}\int_{-\infty}^{\infty} z_{Fu}(u')z_{Pu}(\tau-u')du' \\ &= \frac{1}{\tau}\int_{-\infty}^{\infty} z_{Fu}(\tau-u')z_{Pu}(u')du' \end{aligned} \tag{5}$$

It follows from (5), in particular, that if after a certain time moment u the signal became zero, i.e. $z_{Fu}(u') \equiv 0$, then $R_{MCA}(u,\tau)$ becomes also zero for all scales τ—the mentioned above property of signal support conservation. The same also applies to the past of time u, i.e. $z_{Pu}(u') \equiv 0$. It should be noted here that for negative scales $\tau < 0$ representation (5) becomes identically zero, i.e. it does not coincide with (3). However, there is no loss of information because of $R_{MCA}(u,\tau)$ (3) symmetry – its values at negative scales τ are equal to values at corresponding positive scales $-\tau$.

To determine the presence of the signal quasi–periodicity intervals, the following property of the theoretical ACF $R_z(\tau)$, the estimation of which is $R_{MCA}(u,\tau)$ (3), is usually used. It is known that the global maximum of each ACF is located at zero. If some signal $z(u)$ has period T, then $R_z(\tau)$ will have, by definition, the same period and, in particular, $R_z(kT) = R_z(0)$ for $k = 0, 1, 2, \cdots$. So, in the points divisible by kT, the (side) maxima will be located at ACF as well. If the estimation $R_{MCA}(u,\tau)$ (3) resembles the ACF behaviour at least approximately, then its side maxima will be also the indicators of period T and its multiples. The most estimations of the pulse repeats period are based on this property. Exactly in the same way as for the frequency analysis, in which it is possible to estimate the frequencies of the signal components by TFR $C_z(t, f, \Phi)$ (1) maxima, in the case of the scale–time signal representations $R_{MCA}(u, \tau)$ (3), it is possible to estimate the time scales of the signal pulse repeats – the local quasi–periodicity periods – by their maxima.

Based on the above discussion regarding the problem considered, it is worth concluding the following. Analysing the local quasi–periodic signal behaviour it is possible, having calculated MCA representation $R_{MCA}(u, \tau)$ (5), to concentrate efforts on detecting its side maxima – side peaks, instead of considering the signal dynamics itself.

2.3 Specialized MCA Representation Improvements for Analysing the ABP Signals

However, in practice, due to the coexistence of many maxima, part of which can be conditioned by the quasi–periodicity, and part—by the side effects, as well as due to the slow signal trends, additive uncorrelated interferences, etc., the estimation of the position of the specific ACF side maximum directly through $R_{MCA}(u, \tau)$ (3) is rather an unstable procedure. In order to increase stability to some extent, it is possible to apply to (5) some of the methods for improving the reliability of estimates, that are well–known in the digital signal processing.

The first, apparent step in this direction is $R_{MCA}(u, \tau)$ (5) emphasizing by means of some weighing window $w_{box}(\tau)$, which is non–zero only in the important for processing area:

$$H(u, \tau) = w_{box}(\tau) R_{MCA}(u, \tau) \tag{6}$$

If maximum of window $w_{box}(\tau)$ is located at some point T^*, and its left/right openings are $\delta 1$ and $\delta 2$, then this window outlines the region of interest $(T^* - \delta 1, T^* + \delta 2)$, rejecting everything not included in it. It is clear that the center of window T^* shall be located in the most probable position of the traceable peaks, and $\delta 1 + \delta 2$ shall exceed the span of their positions (but not to a high degree). For the problems considered in this work, the window having the form of the gamma distribution of the first order $w_{box}(\tau) = \tau exp(-\tau/\theta)/\theta^2$ was successful. Substituting this expression for $w_{box}(\tau)$ into formula (6) and using the (5), we will obtain the explicit expression for representation $H(u, \tau), \tau > 0$:

$$H(u, \tau) = \frac{1}{\theta^2} exp(-\frac{\tau}{\theta}) \int_{-\infty}^{\infty} z_{Fu}(u') z_{Pu}(\tau - u') du' \tag{7}$$

The next step is associated with the accentuation of the form of the specific peaks. For this purpose, the idea of the peculiar matched filtering was proposed – the procedure, which is similar to the Wigner's distribution smoothing for (1), but intended to smooth the weighted representation $H(u, \tau)$ (7). If, based on the matched filtering principles, we select the form of window $w_{pic}(\tau)$ modelling the form of the side peaks in some sense, then the relevant representation will be of the following type:

$$\begin{aligned} G(u,\tau) &= \int_0^{\infty} w_{pic}(\tau' - \tau) H(u,\tau') d\tau' \\ &= \frac{1}{\theta^2} \int_0^{\infty} w_{pic}(\tau' - \tau) \left[\int_{-\infty}^{\infty} z_{Fu}(u') z_{Pu}(\tau' - u') du' \right] d\tau' \end{aligned} \tag{8}$$

where the condition that the internal integral identically becomes zero at $\tau < 0$ is used.

Due to the fact that this representation is considered as the main tool for quasi–periodicity estimation, we emphasize, to avoid confusion, that although $G(u,\tau)$ (8) is a result of the matched filtering, but not of a signal $z(u)$, but of ACF $H(u,\tau)$ (7), obtained from the signal.

After testing several methods for constructing the window $w_{pic}(\tau)$, we proposed an indirect method for synthesizing the shape of the window, based on constructing the shape of its spectrum $W_{pic}(f)$. To justify the proposed method, we rewrite the representation of $G(u,\tau)$ (8) through $W_{pic}(f)$ and the Fourier transform $P(u,f)$ of $H(u,\tau)$ (7):

$$G(u,\tau) = \int_{-\infty}^{\infty} W_{pic}^*(f) P(u,f) exp\{2\pi\imath\tau f\} df \tag{9}$$

where, due to the reality of $w_{pic}(\tau)$, symmetry $W_{pic}(-f) = W_{pic}^*(f)$ is used. It follows from (9), that $W_{pic}^*(f)$, like the $w_{box}(\tau)$ window, have the meaning of the weighing window, but in the frequency domain. Hereof it follows the alternative interpretation of $W_{pic}^*(f)$ destination – to accentuate in $P(u,f)$ those features of behaviour, which can be associated with the quasi–periodicity (if available).

In its turn, $P(u,f)$, as the Fourier transform of the product of exponent and $z_{Pu}(u')$ – $z_{Fu}(u')$ convolution, can be written as follows:

$$P(u,f) = \frac{1}{\theta} \int_{-\infty}^{\infty} \frac{S_{Pu}(f') S_{Fu}(f') df'}{1 + 2\pi\imath(f - f')\theta} \tag{10}$$

where, by means of $S_{Pu}(f)$ and $S_{Fu}(f)$, the Fourier transforms are marked for the signals of local past $z_{Pu}(u')$ and local future $z_{Fu}(u')$ (4):

$$\begin{aligned} S_{Pu}(f) &= \int_{-\infty}^{\infty} z_{Pu}(u') exp\{-2\pi\imath u' f\} du' \\ &= \int_0^{\infty} z(u - u') exp\{-2\pi\imath u' f\} du' \\ S_{Fu}(f) &= \int_{-\infty}^{\infty} z_{Fu}(u') exp\{-2\pi\imath u' f\} du' \\ &= \int_0^{\infty} z(u + u') exp\{-2\pi\imath u' f\} du' \end{aligned} \tag{11}$$

The Fourier transforms $S_{Pu}(f)$ and $S_{Fu}(f)$ (11) have the same feature as those of Laplace transforms, they are determined with integrals only along the positive time semi–axis. It results, as in the case of the Laplace transform, in the possibility of their analytical continuation into the lower half plane of the complex frequencies. That is why they were named as the analytical spectra of the local past and local future of signal $z(u)$.

Using the analytical property of product $S_{Pu}(f)S_{Fu}(f)$, it is possible, based on the theory of residues, to calculate the integral in (10). Here, having closed the real axis with the infinite arc located in the lower half plane and considering the zero of the denominator at the complex frequency $f' = f - \imath/2\pi\theta$, we will obtain:

$$P(u,f) = \tfrac{1}{\theta^2} S_{Pu}(f - \imath/2\pi\theta) S_{Fu}(f - \imath/2\pi\theta) = S^{\theta}_{Pu}(f) S^{\theta}_{Fu}(f) \tag{12}$$

where the shifted analytical spectra $S^{\theta}_{Pu}(f)$ and $S^{\theta}_{Fu}(f)$ are introduced and the calculation of which, in accordance with (11), was fulfilled using the formulas:

$$\begin{aligned} S^{\theta}_{Pu}(f) &= \tfrac{1}{\theta} \int_0^{\infty} z(u-u') exp\{-u'/\theta\} exp\{-2\pi\imath u' f\} du' \\ S^{\theta}_{Fu}(f) &= \tfrac{1}{\theta} \int_0^{\infty} z(u+u') exp\{-u'/\theta\} exp\{-2\pi\imath u' f\} du' \end{aligned} \tag{13}$$

Substituting (12) into (9), we will finally obtain:

$$G(u,\tau) = \int_{-\infty}^{\infty} W^{*}_{pic}(f) S^{\theta}_{Pu}(f) S^{\theta}_{Fu}(f) exp\{2\pi\imath\tau f\} df \tag{14}$$

Shifted analytical spectra $S^{\theta}_{Pu}(f)$ and $S^{\theta}_{Fu}(f)$ (13) can be roughly approximated with the finite integrals with some upper limit w ($\sim\theta$). These integrals, in their turn, will be standard windowed Fourier transforms at intervals $(u-w,u)$ and $(u,u+w)$:

$$\begin{aligned} S^{\theta}_{Pu}(f) &\approx \tfrac{1}{w} \int_0^{w} z(u-u') exp\{-2\pi\imath u' f\} du' = exp\{-2\pi\imath u f\} S^{w\,*}_{u-w/2}(f) \\ S^{\theta}_{Fu}(f) &\approx \tfrac{1}{w} \int_0^{w} z(u+u') exp\{-2\pi\imath u' f\} du' = exp\{2\pi\imath u f\} S^{w}_{u+w/2}(f) \\ S^{w}_{u}(f) &= \tfrac{1}{w} \int_{u-w/2}^{u+w/2} z(u') exp\{-2\pi\imath u' f\} du' \end{aligned} \tag{15}$$

Therefore, for the product of the analytical spectra, we obtain simple relation $S^{\theta}_{Pu}(f)S^{\theta}_{Fu}(f) \approx S^{w\,*}_{u-w/2}(f)S^{w}_{u+w/2}(f)$. Considering all the spectra (15) on the intervals of signal quasi–periodicity, we note that the windowed spectrum modules change slowly $|S^{w}_{u-w/2}(f)| \approx |S^{w}_{u}(f)| \approx |S^{w}_{u+w/2}(f)|$, which gives us the approximate relationship $|S^{\theta}_{Pu}(f)S^{\theta}_{Fu}(f)| \approx |S^{w}_{u}(f)|^2$ within the boundaries of such fragments. It follows from this, that the absolute value of the product of the analytical spectra on the quasi–periodicity fragments under integral in (14) will have approximately the same frequency behaviour as spectrogram $|S^{w}_{u}(f)|^2$.

The proposed method of selection of form $W_{pic}(f)$ follows from the above analysis. Here, we form window $W_{pic}(f)$ so that it would model in form that of standard spectrogram $|S^{w}_{u}(f)|^2$, which is typical for the quasi–periodicity fragments. In particular, it can be set with several maxima located at some estimated main frequency F of the first maximum $|S_u^w(f)|^2$ and its subsequent harmonics $2F$, $3F$, ... etc. The geometrical parameters of each of the maxima – their width and height can remain either instrumental parameters of the procedure or be selected experimentally depending on the problem.

Having formed the spectral weighing window $W_{pic}(f)$ and while forming for the subsequent time moments u of shifted analytical spectra $S^{\theta}_{Pu}(f)$ and $S^{\theta}_{Fu}(f)$ (13), by means of the standard procedure of the inverse Fourier transform from the product of all three functions, the main instrument for the ABP quasi–periodicity estimation – representation $G(u, \tau)$ (14) can be found. Without getting into the details of the numerical algorithm of formation $G(u, \tau)$), suffice it to point out that as the analytical spectra are also formed by means of the standard procedure of the Fourier transform (13), the algorithm allows the fast realization based on known FFT (fast Fourier transform) algorithms.

3 Positioning Algorithm for Arterial Blood Pressure Pneumatic Sensor

As we mentioned at the beginning of the paper, numerous experiments on measuring blood pressure showed that the quality of sensor positioning is closely related to the degree of quasi–periodicity of the MCA autocorrelation function. Thus, on-line estimation of the current ABP signal quasi–periodicity degree by ACF $G(u, \tau)$ (14) gives us an instrument of both coarse and fine control of

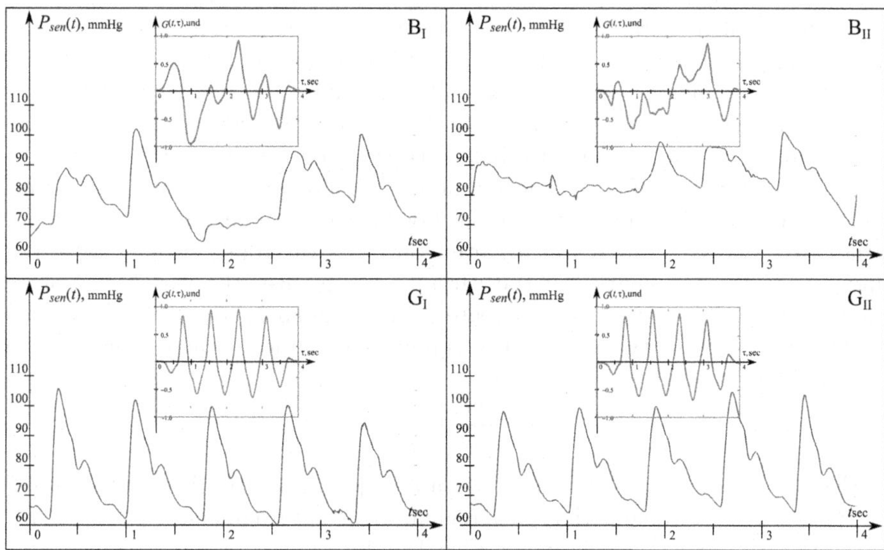

Fig. 2. Four ABP signal fragments from Fig. 1: $B_I - B_{II}$ – bad regularity and $G_I - G_{II}$ – good quasi–periodicity and corresponding to them ACF $G(u, \tau)$ (14) that demonstrates non–regular/regular side peak locations.

the location of the sensor over the artery. Figure 2 presents the calculated ACF $G(u,\tau)$ for the four fragments $B_I - B_{II}$ and $G_I - G_{II}$ of the signal shown in Fig. 1.

From the Fig. 2 it follows that even with time lags less than 4 s the ACF $G(u,\tau)$ (14) manifests a regular structure within the intervals of quasi–periodicity. The latter is quite enough to estimate the quality of positioning. Obviously, by increasing the maximum lag, due to the increase in the interval of correlation of signals of local past $z_{Pu}(u')$ and local future $z_{Fu}(u')$ (4), as it follows from (3), this structure can be made even more distinct. However, what is preferable for off-line ABP records analysis is undesirable during on-line ABP measurements. The fact is that in measuring the signal in real time, the real future is not known, therefore, instead of it, it is necessary to use the measured future and past of the signal in a certain previous time moment, which introduces a delay in estimating the current position of the sensor. Such a delay is exactly equal to half of the maximum lag used in the ACF $G(u,\tau)$ formation. The optimal compromise solution regarding the ACF size and the delay in its formation at the signal ABP sampling frequency in 250 Hz was experimentally determined as ~2 s, as shown in Fig. 2.

Obviously, for a person taking ABP measurements it is enough, in principle, to have an ACF shape $G(u,\tau)$ (like shown in Fig. 2) before one's eyes to evaluate the regularity of the signal measured structure. In the framework of the proposed approach, $G(u,\tau)$ contains all the necessary information about the degree of quasi–periodicity. However, if you want to have some kind of quantitative estimation of this degree, for example, in computer automation tasks, you need to use some numeric characteristics related to the form of the current ACF. One of such characteristics, used in our experiments and strongly related to the equidistant dislocation of $G(u,\tau)$ side peaks in quasi–periodic signals, is the reciprocal value of inter–peak intervals variability.

Namely, estimating the locations of k ACF's maximal side peaks (in our case $k = 4$) and calculating intervals $\{\delta_i\}$ between them, we can get a couple of simple characteristics of $G(u,\tau)$ form: inter–peak intervals mean and their standard deviation. The ratio of the standard deviation to the mean of any random variable is usually considered as a parameter of its variability – the greater the randomness, the irregularity of the variable, the greater the variability. Since in our methodology we strive for greater signal regularity, the reciprocal value of ACF side peak intervals variability is a good numeric characteristic ϱ of the quasi–periodicity degree:

$$\varrho = \frac{mean(\{\delta_i\})}{std(\{\delta_i\})} \tag{16}$$

Figure 3 illustrates graphically, and Table 1 quantitatively the dependence of the characteristic ϱ value with typical regular/irregular fragments $G_I - G_{II}/B_I - B_{II}$ of the ABP signal shown in the Figs. 1 and 2.

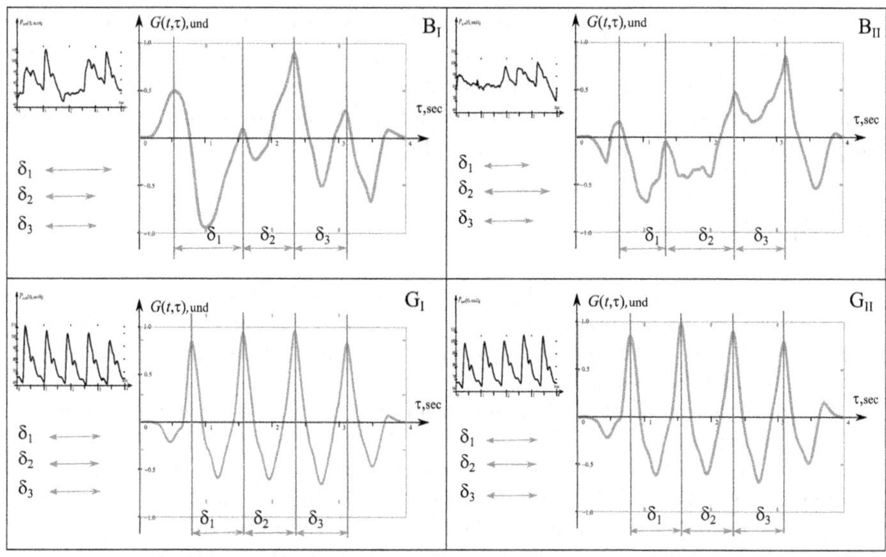

Fig. 3. Four ABP signal fragments from Fig. 1: $B_I - B_{II}$ – bad regularity and $G_I - G_{II}$ – good quasi–periodicity and corresponding ACFs $G(u, \tau)$ (14) with $k = 4$ maximal side peaks marked and inter–peak intervals compared.

Table 1. Correlation between regular/irregular ABP signal fragments $G_I - G_{II}/B_I - B_{II}$ shown in the Figs. 1 and 2 and the value of quasi–periodicity degree ϱ (16).

Fragment	Regular	δ_1 (sec)	δ_2 (sec)	δ_3 (sec)	ϱ
B_I	N	1.032	0.772	0.768	5.67
B_{II}	N	0.702	1.036	0.776	4.75
G_I	Y	0.772	0.780	0.784	127.44
G_{II}	Y	0.764	0.768	0.772	192.03

4 Conclusions

The testing results of the discussed algorithm, based on the reciprocal value of inter–peak intervals variability of the ACF $G(u, \tau)$ (14), turned out to be completely satisfactory. At least they are not worse than the methods based on popular versions of non-stationary spectral analysis [6]. Due to the fact that the calculation procedure of the algorithm allows fast realization, it is reasonable to expect that the instruments synthesized in the article will be important not only for the particular problem the work is dedicated to.

As for the actual problem of positioning the ABP sensor, it was found that in practice it is much more convenient to control the quality of positioning by the ACF $G(u, \tau)$ form dynamics (as shown in Fig. 2), rather than using some characteristics of the signal measured. In particular, this is due to the fact that the calculated $G(u, \tau)$ contains almost all the necessary information about the current state of the process in the sense of measured signal quasi–periodicity, regularity, etc. Moreover, the proposed approach opens up wide opportunities for the search for new procedures for automating the control of the correct sensor position, which seems today to be very relevant.

References

1. Antsiperov, V., Mansurov, G.: Wearable pneumatic sensor for non-invasive continuous arterial blood pressure monitoring. In: Rojas, I., Ortuño, F. (eds.) IWBBIO 2018. LNCS, vol. 10814, pp. 383–394. Springer, Cham (2018). https://doi.org/10.1007/978-3-319-78759-6_35
2. Mansurov, G.K., et al.: Pneumatic sensor for continuous non-invasive measurement of arterial pressure. Invention patent RU2638712 (C1), bull 35, 15 December 2017
3. Mansurov, G.K., et al.: Monolithic three-chamber pneumatic sensor with integrated throttle channels for continuous non-invasive measurement of arterial pressure Invention patent RU2675066 (C1), bull 35, 14 December 2018
4. Antsiperov, V., Mansurov, G.: Positioning method for arterial blood pressure monitoring wearable sensor. In: Rojas, I., Valenzuela, O., Rojas, F., Ortuño, F. (eds.) IWBBIO 2019. LNCS, vol. 11465, pp. 405–414. Springer, Cham (2019). https://doi.org/10.1007/978-3-030-17938-0_36
5. Antsiperov, V.: Multiscale correlation analysis of nonstationary signals containing quasi-periodic fragments. J. Commun. Technol. Electron. **53**(1), 65–77 (2008). https://doi.org/10.1134/S1064226908010099
6. Hlawatsch, F., Auger, F. (eds.): Time-Frequency Analysis: Concepts and Methods. ISTE and Wiley, London (2008)
7. Jeong, J., Williams, W.J.: Kernel design for reduced interference distributions. IEEE Trans. Signal Process. **40**(2), 402–412 (1992). https://doi.org/10.1109/78.124950
8. Antsiperov, V.E., Mansurov, G.K.: Arterial blood pressure monitoring by active sensors based on heart rate estimation and pulse wave pattern prediction. Pattern Recogn. Image Anal. **26**(3), 533–547 (2016). https://doi.org/10.1134/S1054661816030019

An Approach to Detecting and Eliminating Artifacts from the Sleep EEG Signals

Rym Nihel Sekkal[1(✉)], Fethi Bereksi-Reguig[1], Nabil Dib[1], and Daniel Ruiz-Fernandez[2]

[1] Biomedical Engineering Research Laboratory, Biomedical Electronics Department Science Engineering, University Aboubekr Belkaid, Tlemcen, Algeria
sekrym@yahoo.fr,
{fethi.bereksi,nb_dib}@mail.univ-tlemcen.dz

[2] Ingeniería Bioinspirada e Informática para la Salud, Department of Computer Technology, University of Alicante, Alicante, Spain
druiz@ua.es

Abstract. The objective of our ongoing work is to develop an algorithm for detecting and eliminating artifacts from the EEG polysomnographic signals thus helping practitioners in their diagnostic. The EEG signals play an important role in the identification of brain activity and thus in the sleep stage classification. However, it is well known that the recorded EEG signals may be contaminated with artifacts that affect the analysis of EEG signal. Our short paper proposes methods for detecting and eliminating non-physiological and physiological artifacts using filtering for the first and a mixed method based on ICA and wavelets for the second.

Keywords: Sleep analysis · Polysomnography · Artifact detection · Electroencephalogram · Independent component analysis

1 Introduction

People spend around a third of their lives sleeping, mostly during the night. Sleep quality is therefore essential for people's health. The consequences of poor quality sleep (reduced sleep, abnormal sleep patterns or desynchronized circadian rhythms) are numerous: lack of concentration, fatigue, and irritability [1]. They can also be severe ranging from sleep apnea to narcolepsy and neurodegenerative diseases).

The detection of the sleep disorders is therefore crucial for the human health. In this context, sleep stage classification is an important part of this detection process. Indeed, during sleep, one enters different stage defined by electrical activity recorded from sensors placed at different parts of the body [2]. Following the AASM, six sleep/wake stages are traditionally discerned in the human sleep: wakefulness, non rapid eye movement sleep (NREM) divided into sleep stages NI, NII, NIII and NIV, and rapid eye movement sleep (REM).

I. Rojas et al. (Eds.): IWBBIO 2020, LNBI 12108, pp. 155–160, 2020.
https://doi.org/10.1007/978-3-030-45385-5_14

These stages are identified by the variations in electrical potential corresponding to the eye movements measured by the electroculogram, the electrical activity of the muscles measured by the electromyogram and the specific brain activities recorded using the electroencephalogram and which play a central role in sleep stage processing.

However, the EEG signal is frequently contaminated by several signals (artifacts) which come from sources other than neuronal activity and which lower the quality of electroencephalography. Hence, it is necessary to eliminate such noises to obtain more accurate and appropriate results.

2 Sources and Nature of Artifacts

Artifacts can be distinguished according to their sources [3]:

- Non-physiological artefacts which may be environmental or experimental such as detachment of the electrode, interference from the electrical network centered on the 50 Hz frequency and its multiples, patient movements, sweating, etc. recordings often give rise to flat waves, abrupt slopes, etc. [4].

Environmental artifacts can often be removed using a simple filter. This is either because they move around a narrow frequency band (50/60 Hz), or because their frequency band does not overlap with that of the useful signal [3].

- Physiological artefacts which come from the contamination of the signals of the EEG in the first place by the movement of the eyes which appears especially in the frontal electrodes (near the eyes) measured by the EOG, then by the cardiac signals and by the muscle tension signals measured by the EMG. Ocular contamination is the most important and most studied artifact [5].

However, physiological artefacts do not have a specific frequency band and often overlap with the frequency band of useful signals so that simple filtering techniques are not applicable. Several methods have been proposed to remove these artifacts, but the research on physiological artifact removal continues to be an open problem.

3 Database

For our purpose, we utilize the Physionet Sleep-EDF Database Expanded. This database contains 20 whole-night polysomnographic sleep recordings, containing EEG, EOG, oro-nasal respiration, chin EMG, and event markers. Corresponding hypnograms are manually scored by well-trained experts. In Fig. 1, an example of recorded PSG signals of an epoch is given.

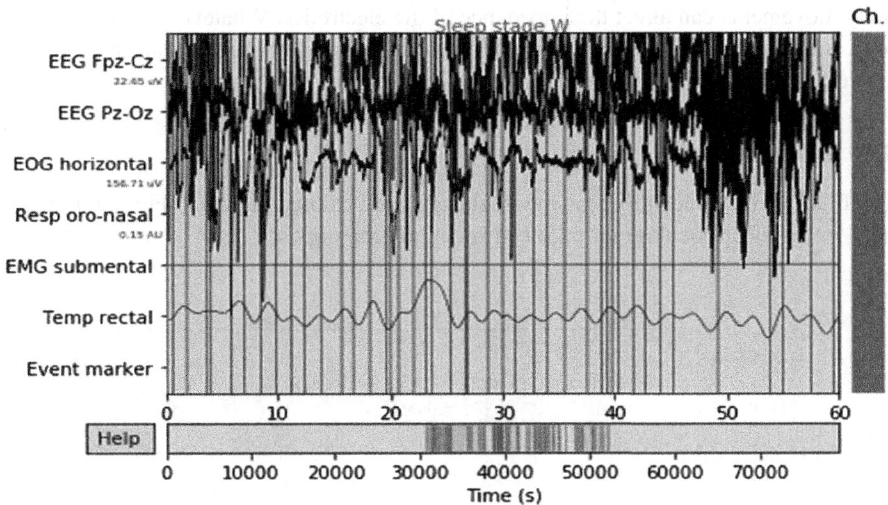

Fig. 1. PSG of the first patient in the database

4 Detection of Artifacts

4.1 DC Artifacts

This artifact results in a peak in the 50 Hz frequencies and its multiples. Figure 2 presents the power spectral density (PSD) of the two signals of the EEG (Fpz-Cz and Pz-Oz) of the first patient and a zoom on the frequency band: 30–50 Hz.

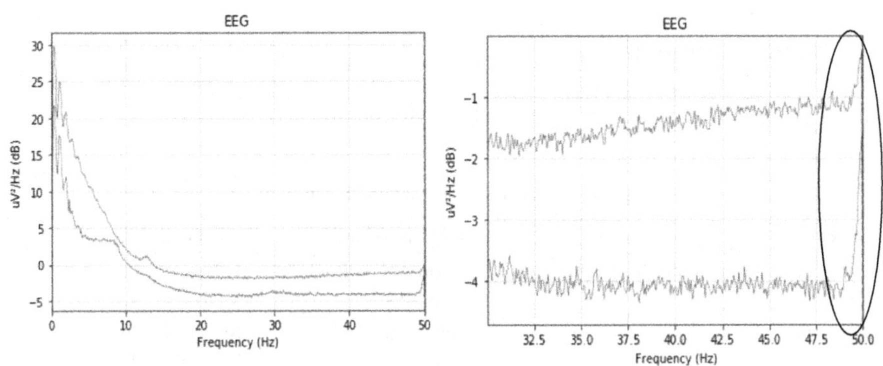

Fig. 2. DC artifact detection

4.2 Slow Ondulations Artifacts

These artifacts are the result of persistent source over time. The slow ondulations that appear on EEG signals are usually caused by breathing or sweating. When breathing, body movements can affect the impedance of the electrodes. Whatever the cause, these long waves are easily detected because their frequencies are lower than those of the slowest sleep waves (delta rhythm).

4.3 EOG Artifacts

The EOG artifact is identified by the frequency band colored in blue in Fig. 3 through a peak in the electrooculogram followed by an abrupt slopes.

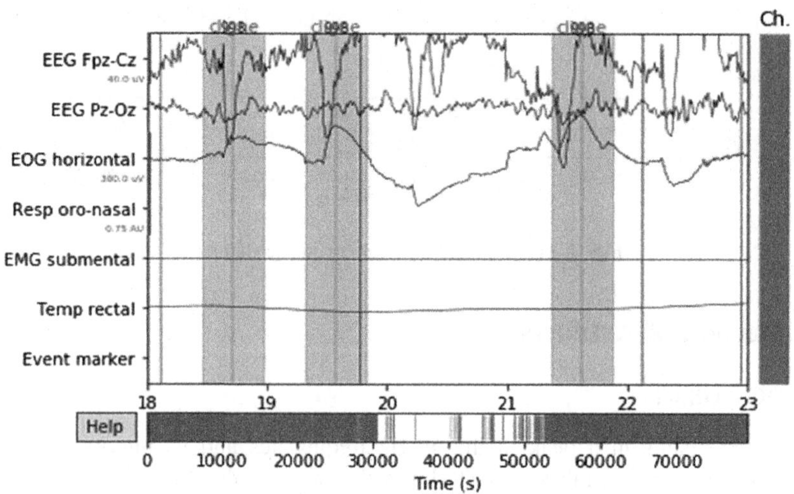

Fig. 3. EOG artefact detection (Color figure online)

5 Artifact Removal

Table 1 presents the approach used to eliminate the artifacts

Table 1. Approach for artifacts removal

Frequencies	Nature of artifacts	Artifacts removal
Cases where the artifacts frequency is known	Non-physiological artifacts	Filtering
Cases where the artifacts frequency is unknown or overlap with other signals	Physiological artifacts	Signal decomposition by ICA and Wavelets

1st Step: Treatment of Artifacts by Filtering

We apply a filter with a pass-band (0,5–45 Hz) with the results shown in the Fig. 4:

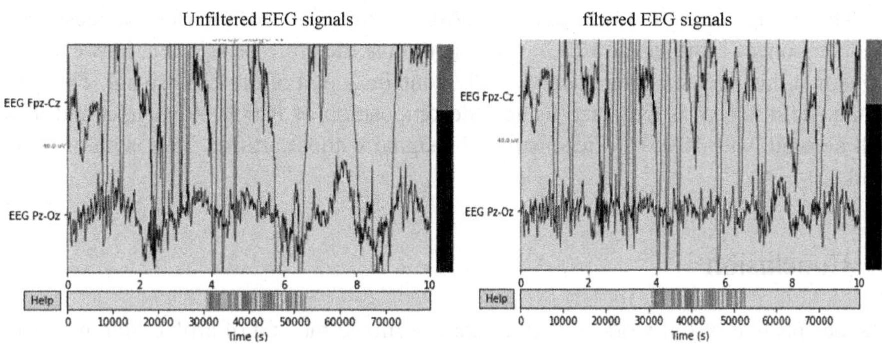

Fig. 4. Unfiltered and filtered EEG signals

We clearly see that the slow ondulations in the unfiltered EEG signals have been removed in the filtered signals. This filtering will be useful for ICA decomposition because a high pass filter improves the signal to noise ratio (SNR) and allows better separation of sources [6].

2nd Step: Treatment of Physiological Artifacts by ICA and Wavelets

Following state of the art, there is not one method but several approaches to eliminate physiological artifacts from the EEG signals [7]. We adopt an hybrid method that combines independent component analysis (ICA) with wavelets decomposition. We follow the following three stages:

- Decomposition of the signal by ICA
- Decomposition of the rejected component by wavelets and
- Reconstruction of the useful signal (ICA-W).

The result of this blind sources separation by ICA is shown in the following figure (Fig. 5):

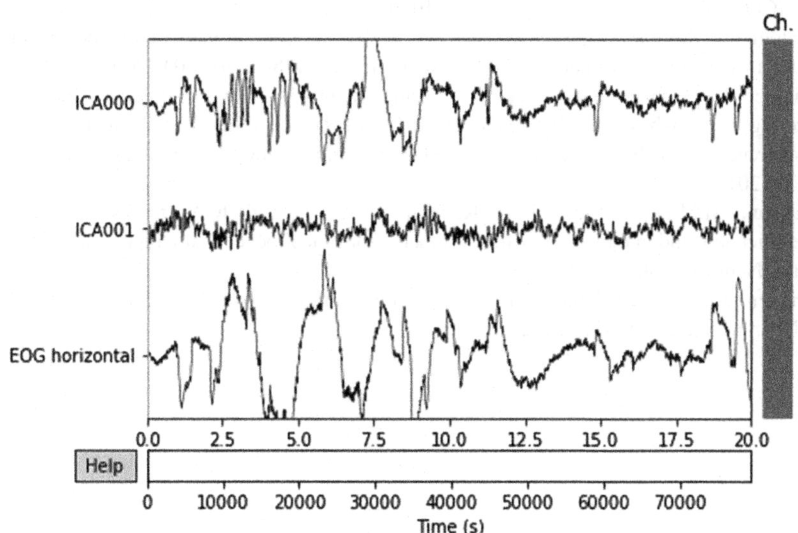

Fig. 5. Sources separation of EEG signals by ICA

The strong correlation between the ICA000 component and the EOG suggests that this component captures the EOG artifact and must therefore be rejected. However we argue that this rejected component actually contains a part of the EEG signal. This part of the useful signal is extracted using a decomposition of IC000 by wavelet and then will be used, with IC001, to reconstruct the signal without artifact. This is an ongoing work.

6 Conclusion

The perspective of our work is to compare this mixed method of artifact removal with simple methods such as ICA or linear regression. We hope to show the superiority of mixed methods and validate Urigüen and Garcia-Zapirain's hypothesis for whom 'the optimal method for removing artifacts from the EEG consists in combining more than one algorithm to correct the signal using multiple processing stages, even though this is an option largely unexplored by researchers in the area' [8].

References

1. Devuyst, S., et. al.: Automatic sleep spindles detection—overview and development of a standard proposal assessment method. In: Annual International Conference of the IEEE Engineering in Medicine and Biology Society. IEEE (2011)
2. Rechtschaffen, A., Kales, A. (eds.): A manual of standardized terminology, techniques and scoring system for skip stages of human subjects. Brain Information Service/Brain Research Institute, Washington, DC (1968)
3. Sweeney, K.T., Ward, T.E., Mcloone, S.F.: Artifact removal in physiological signals—practices and possibilities. IEEE Trans. Inf Technol. Biomed. **16**(3), 488–500 (2012)
4. Dora, C., Biswal, P.K.: Automated detection of nonphysiological artifacts in polysomnographic EEG using conventional signal processing techniques. In: Region 10 Conference, TENCON 2017, pp. 1568–1572. IEEE (2017)
5. Schlögl, A., Keinrath, C., Zimmermann, D., et al.: A fully automated correction method of EOG artifacts in EEG recordings. Clin. Neurophysiol. **118**(1), 98–104 (2007)
6. Winkler, I., Debener, S., Müller, K.R., Tangermann, M.: On the influence of high-pass filtering on ICA-based artifact reduction in EEG-ERP. In: 2015 37th Annual International Conference of the IEEE Engineering in Medicine and Biology Society (EMBC), pp. 4101–4105 (2015)
7. Mannan, M.M.N., Jeong, M.Y., Kamran, M.A.: Hybrid ICA—regression: automatic identification and removal of ocular artifacts from electroencephalographic signals. Front. Hum. Neurosci. **10**, 193 (2016)
8. Urigüen, J.A., Garcia-Zapirain, B.: EEG artifact removal—state-of-the-art and guidelines. J. Neural Eng. **12**(3), 031001 (2015)

Bio-Nanotechnology

New Genomic Information Systems (GenISs): Species Delimitation and IDentification

Sambriddhi Mainali[1(✉)], Max H. Garzon[1(✉)], and Fredy A. Colorado[2]

[1] Computer Science, University of Memphis, Memphis, TN 38152, USA
{smainali,mgarzon}@memphis.edu
[2] Biology, National University of Colombia, Bogotá, Colombia
facoloradog@unal.edu.co

Abstract. Genomic Information Systems (GenISs) have been recently proposed to provide a universal framework for feature extraction, dimensionality reduction and more effective processing of genomic data. They are based on methodologies more anchored in biochemical reality and exploit newly discovered structure of DNA spaces to extract and represent genomic data in compact data structures rich enough to answer critical questions about the original organisms, including phylogenies, species identification and, more recently, phenotypic information. They work *from just DNA sequence alone* (possibly including full genomes), in a matter of minutes or hours, and produce answers consistent with well-established and accepted biological knowledge. Here, we introduce a second family of GenISs based on further structural properties of DNA spaces and demonstrate that they could also be used to provide principled, general and intuitive solutions to fundamental questions in biology such as "What exactly is a biological species?" Current answers to these all important questions have remained dependent on specific taxa and subject to analyst choices. We further discuss other applications to be explored in the future, including universal biological taxonomies in the quest for a truly universal and comprehensive "Atlas of Life", as it is or as it could be on earth.

Keywords: Species definition and delimitation · noncrosshybridizing (nxh) · DNA chips · Genomic Information Systems · Biological taxonomies · Neural nets

1 Introduction

We continue the development of Genomic Information Systems initiated in Garzon and Mainali (2017b) to tackle a fundamental problem in our time, and particularly in bioinformatics, brought forth by our ability to generate enormous amounts of biological data through, for example, genomics (e.g., the human genome project, Next-Generation Sequencing (NGS)), proteomics and metabolomics. A GenIS for genomic information processing is analogous to a Geographic Positioning System (GPS) for positional information on planet earth. Methods developed for computer networks (such as the internet, the web, and wireless communication) have enabled billions of people on the planet to use a cell phone to communicate. This requires, in particular, the ability of the

I. Rojas et al. (Eds.): IWBBIO 2020, LNBI 12108, pp. 163–174, 2020.
https://doi.org/10.1007/978-3-030-45385-5_15

systems to determine the location of the phone anywhere on the planet so as to quickly establish paths to send messages through. That is similar to what biological organisms do (e.g., living cells and brains), where location, physical proximity and obstruction represent hard anchoring constraints that are exploited for biological function, such as cell membranes, organs and organisms. Without them, biological reality, in particular organs and living organisms as we know them, would be impossible. A GenIS is aimed at developing a similar system for biological information processing where planet earth is replaced by the *entire biome* on planet earth.

Garzon and Mainali (2017b) have described prototypes of such a system in order to achieve a truly universal Genomic Positioning System (GenIS) by using a set of noncrosshybridizing (nxh) oligonucleotides (technical definitions are given below in Sect. 2 below) that define universal data structures for arbitrary genomic data. To illustrate the power of this approach, we presented competitive solutions to two important problems in biology: phyologenetics and species IDentification. Here, we introduce a second family of GenISs based on further structural properties of DNA spaces and demonstrate that they could also be used to provide principled and general solutions to fundamental old questions in biology, such as "*What exactly is a biological taxon?*" In Sect. 2, we present the theoretical foundations of the system. In Sect. 3, we provide the precise definition of the new coordinate system, the pmeric system, that will serve as the foundation of the pmeric GenIS and provide an assessment of the quality of the definition by reference to standard biological taxonomies as the ground truth. In Sect. 4, we discuss further work that would be necessary to make the system practical and operational, as well as other applications to be explored in the future, including objective criteria to produce biological taxonomies to produce a truly universal atlas of life.

2 GenIS: A New Framework for Indexing Genomic Sequences

This section sketches the theoretical foundations of the underlying method, DNA indexing (DNI). We focus on the relevant novel methods to be used later in applications in the remainder of the paper. The framework was motivated by the field of DNA computing, inspired by the ideas of using DNA itself as a computational medium in Adleman (1994) and as smart glue for self-assembly applications in Seeman (2003) and (Winfree et al. 1998). These developments have stimulated the development and analysis of various techniques aimed at finding large sets of short oligonucleotides with noncrosshybridizing (nxh) properties by several groups, particularly the nxh bases described in Garzon (2014), Garzon et al. (2012), Deaton et al. (2004). They exploit the key property of Watson-Crick hybridization between homologous single strands of DNA, the fundamental characteristic property of the double helix. An nxh chip consists of a set B of n-mers (oligonucleotides of length n) that are noncrosshybridizing (nxh) for a certain set of reaction conditions determined by a hybridization threshold parameter τ, for a given small parameters n. Multiple copies of these strands and their WC-complements are affixed to the spots of a chip (they are the probes), with a fluorophore attached to them, as described in Fig. 1. The specific choice could be based on the Gibbs energy of duplex formation or on an approximation thereof, the so-called hybridization distance (h-distance) at a minimum threshold τ. On any such DNA chip, a unique hybridization pattern (the *genomic signature*) can be produced as follows. A given (possibly unknown) target is fragmented by sonication into shreds of (roughly) equal size, poured over the chip under appropriate reaction conditions enforcing τ, and given enough time so they hybridize to the probes on the chip.

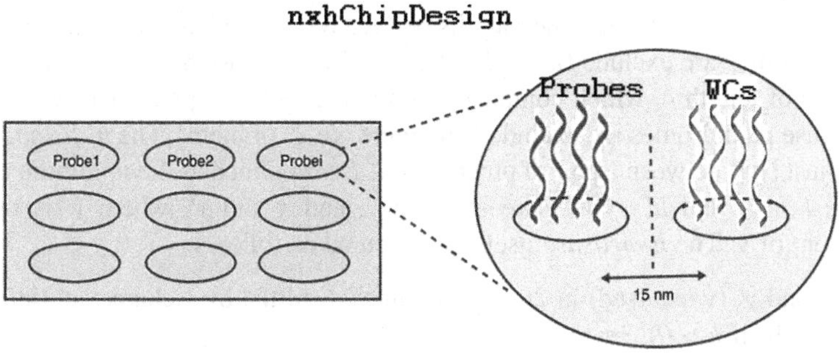

Fig. 1. Design of virtually noise-free nxh chips as proposed in Garzon and Mainali (2017a) based on a judicious selection of probes and consisting of a number of spots in 1-1 correspondence with the oligos in an nxh basis B. Digital genomic *signatures* can be obtained for arbitrary sequences x when shredded into fragments (also called *shreds* below) of comparable probe size (as would be obtained as output of a NGS sequencing of x.) The signature of x serves as a data structure to store x because a number of analyses of the original genome (perhaps bypassing the process in NGS), and even nongenomic information (such as very detailed and quantitative phenotypic information), can be extracted directly from these signatures (Mainali et al. 2020).

These genomic signatures capture a great amount of *biomic information contained in an original genome x.* For example, GenISs have been successfully used to demonstrate that phylogenies can be obtained by alignment-free methods with a universal set of biomarkers (the basis B) for arbitrary taxa (2017b). They have been further shown to contain enough information for certain Machine Learning (ML) models (such as deep neural networks and random forests) to predict phenotypic features to a fine level of detail, for example the area of the cephalic apotome and the postgenal cleft in blackfly (Simuliidae) larvae, as well as certain characteristic spot patterns on their apotome in the form of a Latin cross; likewise for the life span and rosette dry mass in *A. thaliana* (Mainali et al. 2020). These problems belong to the area of phenomics, the field of study in biology that deals with the relationship between the genome and the phenotype of an organism. This relationship is a very complex dependency and not clearly understood in biological morphogenesis, despite the several efforts made in the field (Valan et al. 2019; Weimann et al. 2016; Karr et al. 2012; Vinces 2011). These GenISs have also been used to introduce a genomic-based solution to the problem of species Identification of bacterial infections commonly found in Hospitals (Garzon and Pham 2018), an important problem in public health.

The purpose of this paper is to introduce another coordinate system (the *pmeric* system) for genomic sequences and show how this new GenIS can be used to solve two important problem in the field of biology, namely provide a tentative, but universal, definition of the concept of "species" that has proved elusive in biology and, as a consequence, a solution to the problem of species delimitation in biology. These systems are made possible by newly discovered structural properties of DNA spaces, as follows.

In the sequel, a DNA strand is referred to an n-mer of a given size n; a paired n-mer, or just, *pmer* x consists of an n-mer and its perfect WC–complement of the same length (WC-palindromes are excluded); the *DNA space* D_n refers to the collection of all possible pmers of length n, which contains roughly $4^n/2 = O(4^n)$ pmers (fewer when n is even because palindromes are excluded and there are 2^n of them). The *h-distance* $h(x,y)$ (denoted just $|xy|$) between a pair of pmers $x, y \in D_n$ is defined as the minimum of the *h-measures* $h(x,y)$ and $h(x,y')$ between x and y, and x and y', where y' is the WC-complement of y. The *h-measure* itself is computed as follows:

1. align x and y^r (y reversed) in $2n - 1$ alignments shifted by k characters (left shift if $k < 0$; right if $k > 0$), $-n < k < n$;
2. count the total number c_k of WC complementary mismatches between facing nucleotide pairs (single nucleotides are counted as mismatches);
3. compute the h-measure $h(x,y) = min_k\{c_k\}$.

The h-distance values range between 0 and n. An h-distance $|xy| = 0$ means that either x and y are identical as oligonucleotides, or they are perfect Watson-Crick (WC) complements of one another, i.e. they are the same pmers; on the other hand, an h-distance of $|xy| = n$ means that there is no pair of complementary nucleotides at all in x and y hybridizing with each other, as in *aaa* and *ccc*, or their complements. Thus, the h-distance induces the structure of a metric space (including the triangle inequality) in the space D_n. Moreover, there exist at least 16 isometries of the space, i.e., transformations that do not change the h-distance, such as the so-called *polar isometry* (that swaps elements in the pairs *a–c* and *t–g*) and the *reversal isometry* (that inverts the order of an n-mer, now being read from the 3′-end, without taking complementation.)

Definition 1 (*h-Centroid*)
Let S be a set of pmers in D_n of size $|S|$ and $w_z(z \in S)$ be a set of weights for its elements. The *(weighted) square error function* $SE_w : D_n \rightarrow R$, is defined as the average squared h-distance from z to a pmer in S, i.e. $SE_w(z) = \frac{1}{|S|}\sum_{x \in S} w_z|zx|^2$.

A pmer $z \in D_n$ is a *centroid* of S if and only if it minimizes $SE_w(z)$, i.e.

$$a = \arg min_z\{SE(z)\} \text{across all } z \text{ in } D_n.$$

The centroids of the full DNA spaces for the pmers of lengths up to 4 can be computed by an exhaustive method and they are shown in the Table 1. They can be used to provide a new *pmeric coordinate system* for arbitrary genomic sequences x.

Table 1. Centroids for the DNA spaces D_n of all pmers of length n (as given by their first lexicographical n-mers, e.g. ac stands for pmer ac/gt.)

n	Centroids
2	ac, ag, ca, ga
3	aca, aga, cac, ctc
4	acca, agga, caac, cttc

Definition 2 (*Pmeric signatures*)
Given a DNA sequence x and a shred size n > 1, let m be the number of centroids in D_n. The m-dimensional (*mD*) *pmeric signature* of x is defined as follows:

- shred x to nonoverlapping fragments of size n (ignoring any shorter leftover nucleotides, if necessary);
- for each centroid $z_i \in D_n$ and for each unique shred x_j, compute $y_{ij} = w_j|z_i x_j|$, where w_j is the fraction of the number of occurrences of x_j in x normalized to the total number of shreds in x;
- the ith component of a *pmeric signature* of x is given by the average of the y_{ij} cross all shreds x_j.

Intuitively, using a physical metaphor, the *pmeric signature* of x is a mass distribution on D_n obtained by placing "*genomic masses*" (i.e., the average weighted distance of the corresponding unique shreds across x, normalized by dividing by the total number of nonoverlapping shreds of length n in x, from left to right) at each centroid z_i.

3 A Molecular Definition of Biological "Species" and "Genus"

In this Section, we show how this pmeric coordinate system can be used to propose a definition of the biological concept of "species" with the following properties:

a. It is only based on genomic sequence (e.g., on the whole genome) of an organism;
b. It is largely consistent with current conventional taxonomies in biology;
c. It is universal, i.e., it can be used to classify an arbitrary genomic sequence in a species once a proper region defining a species in a given GenIS has been identified.

Ever since Linnaeus (1758) initial proposal to standardize, organize, and rank the biome (all living organisms on earth) into a universal system (known as a taxonomy) to catalog all the biodiversity of life, biologists have discovered that delimiting species boundaries is quite a difficult task that demands years of research to get a meaningful comprehension even of a relatively small group of organisms (Hebert et al. 2003). A general definition of the concept of *species* is currently a challenge in theoretical biology because it is the most relevant taxonomic category in areas such as conservation, genetics, evolution and phylogenetics. More than 25 definitions have been proposed in the last century (Valan et al. 2019; de Queiroz 2005; Van Valen 1976;

Sokal and Crovello 1970; Mayr 1942). Figure 2 illustrates the range of criteria that could be used. As a result, some taxonomists have reached the conclusion that the ideal of establishing a single species definition applicable to all (present and extinct) species that inhabit(ed) planet earth, as desirable as it may be, might be practically unattainable (de Queiroz 2007).

Species concept	Property(ies)
Biological	Interbreeding (natural reproduction resulting in viable and fertile offspring)
Isolation	*Intrinsic reproductive isolation (absence of interbreeding between heterospecific organisms based on intrinsic properties, as opposed to extrinsic [geographic] barriers)
Recognition	*Shared specific mate recognition or fertilization system (mechanisms by which conspecific organisms, or their gametes, recognize one another for mating and fertilization)
Ecological	*Same niche or adaptive zone (all components of the environment with which conspecific organisms interact)
Evolutionary	Unique evolutionary role, tendencies, and historical fate
(some interpretations)	*Diagnosability (qualitative, fixed difference)
Cohesion	Phenotypic cohesion (genetic or demographic exchangeability)
Phylogenetic	Heterogeneous (see next four entries)
Hennigian	Ancestor becomes extinct when lineage splits
Monophyletic	*Monophyly (consisting of an ancestor and all of its descendants; commonly inferred from possession of shared derived character states)

Fig. 2. A summary of alternative criteria for contemporary species concepts, extracted from a summary according to de Queiroz (2007).

The major aim of this paper is to present evidence that it is indeed possible to create a new atlas of the biome that would encompass the vastness of biological diversity in a *geometric* representation that groups together biological organisms by their molecular characteristics, as follows. Conventional methods classify different organisms by grouping them into a different taxa to illustrate the degree of difference between living organisms, i.e. "species", "genus", "family", "orders", "class", "phylum", "kingdom" or "domain", as in Henning (1966) or Woese and Fox (1977). Two organisms belonging to the same species level would share more similarities than organisms in different species. An organism will be represented by a DNA sequence (for example, its whole genome; more about this in the conclusion.) With the pmeric coordinate system in place, we propose the following definition of an Operational Taxonomical Unit (OTU) as the level of species (we will restrict ourselves to species and genus taxa.) *They are regions in ordinary Euclidean spaces defined by nearest neighbor distances from certain (hypothetical) prototype organisms (the so-called "centroids") of the*

OTU. This concept is well known in geometry as a Voronoi diagram and is probably the simplest and most natural way to define a region in Euclidean spaces. An example is shown in Fig. 3 below.

Definition 3 (*Voronoi diagram*)
In *dD* Euclidean space $\mathbf{R}^d$, *k* points (the *centroids*) define a nearest neighbor partition (classification) of the space into *k* classes, i.e. a random point *x* belongs to the class defined by its *nearest* centroid. This partition of $\mathbf{R}^d$ is called the *Voronoi diagram* determined by the *k* points.

Table 2. Sample data for estimating the taxon definition of several *species*.

ID	Taxa	(# Specimens)/Taxa	Type	Source
S20	Simuliidae	20/2 species	Partial COIs	Colorado-Garzón et al. (2017)
A17	*Arabidopsis*	17/3 species	rRNA, mt COIs	Weigel and Mott (2009)
B80	Bacteria	80/16 genera	Whole Genome	Garzon and Pham (2018)

In order to test the soundness of this definition, we selected genomic sequences representing a number of species, as shown in Table 2. We then reduced the dimension of the sequence and computed their genomic signatures on an nxh basis (referred to as 4mP3-3) and pmeric coordinates for 3-pmers and 4-pmers. Using them as predictor features, we trained the OTU using the unsupervised learning algorithm *k*-Means from Machine Learning (shown in Algorithm 1) in order to cluster specimens by their pmeric signatures similarity.

ALGORITHM 1 (*k-Means*) (Hartigan & Wong, 1979)
INPUT: a finite data set of points *D* in Euclidean space $\mathbf{R}^d$
OUTPUT: a set of *k* centroids defining a nearest neighbor clustering of *D*

1. Randomly choose *k* points in *D* as (tentative) centroids;
2. Assign each point in *D* to the cluster of the nearest centroid;
3. Calculate the new centroid (average) for each cluster based on the points in the cluster;
4. Repeat steps 2-3 until convergence.

We used the careful seeding of the centroids suggested by Arthur and Vassilvitskii (2007) to speed up the convergence. About only 40 iterations of the algorithm were sufficient to obtain convergence to a stable set of centroids for the samples described next. These centroids were used as a typical representative of the specimens in each species. Thus, ideally every taxon (e.g. a species) should be mapped to a Voronoi region that includes the coordinates of every specimen belonging to that species, be it past, present or future.

An assessment of the quality of the OTU was done using the standard biological taxonomy as ground truth. The predictions for each specimen in all samples by the models based on *k*-Means clustering were compared with the corresponding taxon in the standard biological taxonomy and the metrics were computed for the assessment of the maps of these OTUs in 3D and 4D spaces (which are not presented visually here due to the higher dimensions.) The results for the 20 specimens in data set S20 are shown in Table 3, using standard measures of accuracy, precision, recall and F1-score.

The quality appears relatively low for S20, probably because the COIs were probably too small to contain enough information about the specimens. The same procedure was applied to sample A17 consisting of 17 specimens of *Arabidopsis* distributed across 3 species *A. lyrate*, *A. helleri* and *A. thaliana*. Table 3 also shows the quality of the OTU species definitions. They appear to be much better, with perfect accuracy on 3pmers but above 0.9 overall for all metrics considered, including the F1 score.

Table 3. Quality assessment of the maps for the OTUs of the two species in S20, three species in A17 and 16 genera in B80

Size *n*	Sample	Accuracy	Precision	Recall	F1-score
3-pmers	S20	0.700	0.531	0.531	0.531
	A17	1.000	1.000	1.000	1.000
	B80	1.000	1.000	1.000	1.000
4-pmers	S20	0.500	0.438	0.406	0.405
	A17	0.941	0.952	0.933	0.937
	B80	1.000	1.000	1.000	1.000

Finally, the same procedure was applied to sample B80 for the definition of genus taxa consisting of 80 specimens of bacteria common in hospital acquired infection and distributed across 16 different genera. Table 3 also shows perfect the quality of the OTU definitions, in full agreement with the standard biological taxonomies for the samples.

These results lead to an interesting question – what are the precise locations of these organisms with respect to their centroids in an Euclidean space? Unfortunately, these spaces are 4D spaces and it is very difficult for a human eye to capture the sense of their locations graphically. So, we used the basis 4mP3-3 as introduced in Garzon and Mainali (2017b) to get their locations in 3D Euclidean space. Then, we rotated these signatures to fall onto a 2D plane. Figure 3 shows the graphical representation of the genomic signatures of these organisms and their arrangement with respect to their centroids defining genera for sample B80.

These findings raise another interesting question, namely whether the choice of the full set of *h*-centroids is better than any other set of pmers chosen randomly? In particular, would the *k*-mer method with a full set of *k*-mers produce better results? To address this question, we performed an experimental control for the samples on 3-pmers and 4-pmers. We randomly selected 32 different batches of *k*-pmers for each case of 3- and 4-pmers and repeated exactly the same procedure for k-Means clustering. Then, we averaged the scores for each batch consisting 32 batches of pmers for each of the three samples. The averages for S20 and A17 are reported in Table 4. There was a

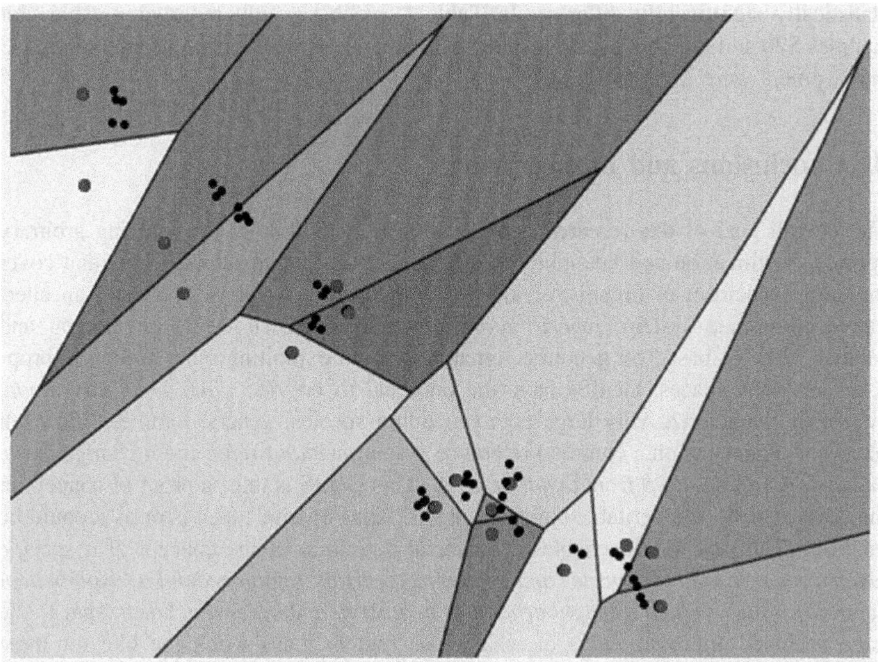

Fig. 3. 2D OTU map for genus definition from sample B80 containing specimens from the domain of bacteria across 16 different genera prevalent in hospital acquired infections on the nxh basis 4mP3-3 using genomic signatures.

huge difference with corresponding scores for the full set of *h*-centroids. To test the statistical significance of the difference, we ran a hypothesis *z*-test for each sample. In all cases, the results of the tests confirmed that the null hypothesis (equality between the average score and to the score for full *h*-centroids) should be rejected, i.e., the scores on OTUs obtained from the pmeric signatures on the full set of *h*-centroids are

Table 4. Comparison of quality scores for OTUs obtained from the pmeric signatures on the full set of *h*-centroids and those from random sets of k-mers of the same size. The choice of *h*-centroids is significantly better since the *p*-values obtained from hypothesis tests, with the rejected null hypotheses being equality between the pairs of scores (here C = e^{-10} and E = e^{-16}.)

n		S20				A17			
		A	P	R	F	A	P	R	F
3	pmeric	0.700	0.531	0.531	0.531	1.000	1.000	1.000	1.000
	pm-rand	0.502	0.267	0.209	0.227	0.415	0.400	0.300	0.271
	p-value	1.51C	<2.2E	<2.2E	<2.2E	<2.2E	<2.2E	<2.2E	<2.2E
4	pmeric	0.500	0.438	0.406	0.405	0.941	0.952	0.933	0.937
	pm-rand	0.325	0.248	0.135	0.168	0.638	0.496	0.492	0.493
	p-value	1.71C	<2.2E	<2.2E	<2.2E	<2.2E	<2.2E	<2.2E	<2.2E

statistically significantly different. In Table 4, we have only reported *p*-values for samples S20 and A17 but *p*-values on all performance scores for sample B80 on both 3 and 4-pmers were less than $2.2e^{-16}$.

4 Conclusions and Future Work

The overall goal of this research is to develop a methodology for enabling arbitrary species identification and taxonomy based on so-called universal nxh chips that cover the entire spectrum of organisms, known or unknown. We have presented an alternative coordinate system, *pmeric coordinates*, to a known GenIS in Garzon and Mainali (2017b) based on genomic signatures, again exploiting other structural properties of DNA spaces. GenISs have the potential to provide a *universal coordinate system* to characterize very large taxa (including species, genera, families, and even phyla) of organisms on a common reference system, *without requiring a change in the molecular markers used from taxon to taxon*. This GenIS is thus, a proof of concept in the development of a veritable comprehensive "Atlas of Life", as it is or as it could be on earth. The new GenIS enables a universal definition of the concept of *a specific taxon (demonstrated for species and genus) as a certain region around a (hypothetical centroid) prototype and a neighborhood of nearest neighbors in Euclidean space*. We have provided approximations of what those regions/maps would be like for three samples of genomic data ranging from partial COIs to whole genomes and from three representative clades (plants, bacteria and higher animals in blackfly.) The quality assessment of the definitions of the corresponding taxonomical units (OTUs) provide encouraging results that this goal may be scalable to a large segment of the biome and produce results largely consistent with standard biological taxonomies. The accuracy of the results appears to become better as we include larger taxa and more representative genomic sequences, such as whole genomes. Using higher dimensions (increasing the size of the shreds for genomic and for pmeric signatures), these scores are only expected to improve given that more information will be retained from longer shreds and additional room is available in higher dimensions to accommodate nuances in the diversity of the taxa involved. Furthermore, we have only explored the genomic sequences and the simplest type of regions determined by the Voronoi diagrams of a sample of the taxon. It would be interesting to see the performance of these diagrams at different level of granularity in the standard biological taxonomy, and on much larger samples.

Further steps to bring this program to fruition include at least two important choices. First, the specific selection of a common choice of genomic sequence for all organisms. The entire genome would appear to be an obvious candidate, but more common conserved sequences (such as COIs or 16 sRNAs) are also candidates. This choice, however, will require procedures to extract feature vectors in the pmeric signatures. Second, *the selection of specific neighborhoods that define a given taxon based on currently available knowledge on biological taxonomies*, which in turn may be determined by other factors (geographic and environmental, for example.) The Voronoi diagrams appears to be an obvious choice, but certainly other types of regions could potentially yield more accurate results.

Finally, regardless of the choices, it is truly remarkable that such as simple minded definition of a taxon (here species or genus), purely based on geometric distance of the feature vectors from the centroids afforded by pmeric coordinates, could capture so much of the complexity of the taxon, as given by the standard biological classification.

Acknowledgements. We would like to thank the labs of professors Nubia Matta and Fernando Garcia at the National University and Duy Pham at the University of Memphis for their work in collecting some of the sample data for blackfly used in this paper. Many thanks also go to the High Performance Computing Center (HPC) at the U of Memphis for the time to compute DNA space centroids, pmeric feature vectors and Voronoi diagrams.

References

Adleman, L.: Molecular computation of solutions of combinatorial problems. Science **266**, 1021–1024 (1994)

Arthur, D., Vassilvitskii, S: k-means++: the advantages of careful seeding. In: Proceedings of the Eighteenth Annual ACM-SIAM Symposium on Discrete Algorithms, pp. 1027–1035 (2007)

Colorado-Garzón, F.A., Adler, P.H., García, L.F., Muñoz de Hoyos, P., Bueno, M.L., Matta, N. E.: Estimating diversity of black flies in the simulium ignescens and simulium tunja complexes in Colombia: chromosomal rearrangements as the core of integrative taxonomy. J. Heredity **108**(1), 12–24 (2017)

de Queiroz, K.: Species concepts and species delimitation. Syst. Biol. **56**(6), 879–886 (2007)

de Queiroz, K.: Ernst Mayr and the modern concept of species. Proc. Nat. Acad. Sci. **102**(suppl 1), 6600–6607 (2005)

Deaton, J., Chen, J., Garzon, M., Wood, D.H.: Test Tube Selection of Large Independent Sets of DNA Oligonucleotides, pp. 152–166. World Publishing Co., Singapore (2004). (Volume dedicated to Ned Seeman on occasion of his 60th birthday)

Garzon, M.H., Mainali, S.: Towards reliable microarray analysis and design. In: The 9th BiCOB-International Conference on Bioinformatics and Computational Biology. International Society for Computational and their Applications ISCA (2017a). 6pp.

Garzon, M.H., Mainali, S.: Towards a universal genomic positioning system: phylogenetics and species IDentification. In: Rojas, I., Ortuño, F. (eds.) IWBBIO 2017. LNCS, vol. 10209, pp. 469–479. Springer, Cham (2017b). https://doi.org/10.1007/978-3-319-56154-7_42

Garzon, M.: DNA codeword design: theory and applications. Parallel Process. Lett. **24**(2), 1–21 (2014)

Garzon, M.H., Bobba, K.C.: A geometric approach to Gibbs energy landscapes and optimal DNA codeword design. In: Stefanovic, D., Turberfield, A. (eds.) DNA 2012. LNCS, vol. 7433, pp. 73–85. Springer, Heidelberg (2012). https://doi.org/10.1007/978-3-642-32208-2_6

Garzon, M., Pham, D.: Genomic solutions to hospital-acquired bacterial infection identification. In: Rojas I., Ortuño F. (eds) Bioinformatics and Biomedical Engineering. Proc. IWBBIO 2018. Lecture Notes in Bioinformatics, Part I, vol. 10813, pp. 486–497. Springer-Verlag (2018). https://doi.org/10.1007/978-3-319-78723-7_42

Hartigan, J.A., Wong, M.A.: Algorithm AS 136 A *k*-means clustering algorithm. J. Roy. Stat. Soc. Ser. C (Applied Statistics) **28**(1), 100–108 (1979)

Hebert, P.D., Cywinska, A., Ball, S.L.: Biological identifications through DNA barcodes. Proc. R. Soc. Lond. B Biol. Sci. **270**, 313–321 (2003)

Henning, W.: Phylogenetic Systematics. translated by Davis, D.D., Zangerl, R. University of Illinois Press, Urbana (1966)

Karr, J.R. et al.: A whole-cell computational model predicts phenotype from genotype. Cell **150** (2), 389–401 (2012)

von Linnaeus, C.: Systema Naturae, edition X, vol. 1 (Systema naturae per regna tria naturae, secundum classes, ordines, genera, species, cum characteribus, differentiis, synonymis, locis. Tomus I. Editio decima, reformata). Salvii Holmiae 1 (1758)

Mainali, S., Colorado, F.A., Garzon, M.H.: Foretelling the phenotype of a genomic sequence. IEEE Trans. Comput. Biol. Bioinform. (2020, under review)

Mayr, E.: Systematics and the Origin of Species. Columbia University Press, New York (1942)

Seeman, N.: DNA in a material world. Nature **421**, 427–431 (2003)

Sokal, R.R., Crovello, T.J.: The biological species concept: a critical evaluation. Am. Nat. **104**, 127–153 (1970)

Van Valen, L.: Ecological species, multispecies, and oaks. Taxon **25**, 233–239 (1976)

Valan, M., Makonyi, K., Maki, A., Vondráček, D., Ronquist, F.: Automated taxonomic identification of insects with expert-level accuracy using effective feature transfer from convolutional networks. Syst. Biol. **68**(6), 876–895 (2019)

Vinces, R.F.: Phenomics: genotype to phenotype. A Report of the USDA/NSF Phenomics Workshop (2011). https://www.nsf.gov/bio/pubs/reports/phenomics_workshop_report.pdf. Accessed March 2020

Winfree, E., Liu, F., Wenzler, L.A., Seeman, N.C.: Design and self-assembly of two-dimensional DNA crystals. Nature **394**, 539–544 (1998)

Weigel, D., Mott, R.: The 1001 genomes project for Arabidopsis thaliana. Genome Biol. **10**(5), 107 (2009)

Weimann, A., Mooren, K., Frank, J., Pope, P.B., Bremges, A., McHardy, A.C.:From genomes to phenotypes: traitar, the microbial trait analyzer.mSYstems **1**(6) 101–116 (2016). https://doi.org/10.1128/mSystems.00101-16

Woese, C., Fox, G.: Phylogenetic structure of the prokaryotic domain: the primary kingdoms. Proc. Natl. Acad. Sci. U.S.A. **74**, 5088–5090 (1977)

Production of 3D-Printed Tympanic Membrane Scaffolds as a Tissue Engineering Application

Elif Ilhan[1,2], Songul Ulag[1,3], Ali Sahin[4], Nazmi Ekren[1,5], Osman Kilic[1,6], Faik Nuzhet Oktar[1,2], and Oguzhan Gunduz[1,3](✉)

[1] Center for Nanotechnology & Biomaterials Application and Research (NBUAM), Marmara University, Istanbul, Turkey
ucemogu@ucl.ac.uk

[2] Department of Bioengineering, Faculty of Engineering, Marmara University, 38000, 34722 Istanbul, Turkey

[3] Department of Metallurgical and Materials Engineering, Faculty of Technology, Marmara University, Istanbul, Turkey

[4] Department of Biochemistry, School of Medicine/Genetic and Metabolic Diseases Research and Investigation Center, Marmara University, Istanbul, Turkey

[5] Department of Electrical and Electronics Engineering, Faculty of Technology, Marmara University, Istanbul, Turkey

[6] Department of Electrical and Electronics Engineering, Faculty of Engineering, Marmara University, Istanbul, Turkey

Abstract. In recent years, scaffolds produced in 3D printing technology have become more widespread tool due to providing more advantages than traditional methods in tissue engineering applications. In this research, it was aimed to produce patches for the treatment of tympanic membrane perforations which caused significant hearing loss by using 3D printing method.

Polylactic acid (PLA) scaffolds with Chitosan (CS) added in various ratios were prepared for artificial eardrum patches. Different amounts of CS added to PLA to obtain more biocompatible scaffolds. The created patches were designed by mimicking the thickness of the natural tympanic membrane thanks to the precision provided by the 3D printed method. The produced scaffolds were analyzed separately for physical, chemical, morphological, mechanical and biocompatibility properties. Human adipose tissue-derived mesenchymal stem cells (hAD-MSCs) were used for cell culture study to analyze the biocompatibility properties. 15 wt% PLA was chosen as the control group. Scaffold containing 3 wt% CS demonstrated significantly superior and favorable features in printing quality. The study continued with these two scaffolds (15PLA and 15PLA/3CS). This study showed that PLA and PLA/CS 3D printed scaffolds are a potential application for repairing tympanic membrane perforation.

Keywords: 3D printing · Biomaterials · Tissue engineering · Tympanic membrane patch

I. Rojas et al. (Eds.): IWBBIO 2020, LNBI 12108, pp. 175–184, 2020.
https://doi.org/10.1007/978-3-030-45385-5_16

1 Introduction

The eardrum or tympanic membrane (TM), which has both hearing-related tasks and acts as a barrier, is less than 100 μm thick and is located between the middle ear and the outer ear canal [1]. TM perforations usually occur due to trauma to the middle ear. While some eardrum perforations show spontaneous healing, the closing of chronic perforations requires surgical intervention (myringoplasty) [2]. These surgeries under anesthesia carry various complications and risks of infection. In many cases, multiple operations may be required to close the TM holes. Therefore, risk-free, safer alternatives are needed [3]. As a result, in the case of chronic and non-healing perforations, an artificial TM is required [4].

In tissue engineering, the repair of damaged tissues with biology and engineering principles is investigated. The scaffolds produced in tissue engineering are significant materials to provide mechanical support to the tissue and to interact with the cells and to increase tissue growth [5]. 3D printing method is a new generation tissue production technique that can provide precise control over the design of the scaffold, with greater precision in the spatial relationship between each printing method is a new generation tissue production technique that can provide precise control over the design of the scaffold, with greater precision in the spatial relationship between each element of the desired tissue [6]. 3D printing is based on the principle of layered manufacturing, in which materials are overlapped layer by layer [7]. In recent years, the development of 3D printed biocompatible scaffolds for tissue engineering applications is promising [8].

Natural and synthetic polymers are suitable materials in terms of their processability and applicability to produce biodegradable scaffolds in tissue engineering applications [9]. PLA is a synthetic polymer with high strength, stiffness hardness, thermoplasticity, biocompatibility [10]. These unique properties make PLA an ideal polymer in tissue engineering applications. Kozin et al. study, demonstrated that the mechanical properties required for the tympanic membrane scaffold can be achieved with PLA [11]. Chitosan, a natural polymer, is used in tissue engineering applications due to its cell compatibility, biodegradability, flexibility and non-toxic properties [12]. Patch et al. study has been reported that the eardrum produced using chitosan has good biocompatibility and nontoxic properties [13].

In the presented study, PLA and PLA/CS composite scaffolds are aimed to be produced using 3D printing technology. These scaffolds are intended to function as biocompatible and biodegradable patches that can repair damaged tissue in tympanic membrane perforations. Morphological, chemical and mechanical properties of 3D printing scaffolds were performed by characterization tests. Rheological properties such as density, viscosity and surface tension, which are very important parameters for 3D printing method, were examined. Furthermore, cell viability and cell proliferation analysis were performed to observe the biocompatibility properties of the fabricated scaffolds. The aim of this research is that the TM patch is produced with 3D printing technology that can make fine adjustments on the tissue and produce scaffolds with the desired pore size and thickness. This study contributes to the creation of composite materials with biocompatible and biodegradable polymers and to produce scaffolds with the properties required for TM patch using 3D printing.

2 Materials and Methods

2.1 Materials

Poly (L-lactic acid) (PLA) 2003D was purchased from Nature Works LLC. Chitosan (CS, MW = 50000–190000 Da). Chloroform was purchased from Sigma-Aldrich. Sodium hydroxide (NaOH), and Acetic acid (CH3COOH) were obtained from Yasin Teknik Company.

2.2 Preparation of the Solutions

Different concentrations of PLA and PLA/CS solutions were prepared and shown in Table 1. 15 wt% PLA was prepared by dissolving in chloroform with a magnetic stirrer (WiseStir®, MSH-20A, Germany) at room temperature and the first scaffold candidate was obtained. After that, binary blends of PLA were developed using different concentrations of CS. Different amounts of CS as 1 wt%, 3 wt% and 5 wt% were dissolved in 10 ml of distilled water and 0.2 ml of acetic acid for 30 min at room temperature. The fully dissolved PLA and each CS polymers were mixed in a 2:1 (PLA: CS) ratio to prepare the emulsion and kept in the magnetic stirrer for two hours. A 5% Sodium hydroxide solution was prepared as the crosslinking agent of chitosan so that the molecules could bind more tightly together.

Table 1. Content of solutions.

3D printed scaffold	PLA content (wt%)	CS content (wt%)
15PLA	15	0
15PLA/1CS	15	1
15PLA/3CS	15	3
15PLA/5CS	15	5

2.3 Design and Fabrication of the 3D Printed Scaffolds

The scaffold was designed to be 20 mm × 20 mm × 1 mm in size and was produced with an extrusion 3D printer (Hyrel 3D, SDS-5 Extruder, GA, USA). A 0.2 mm diameter needle was used and 3D printing was performed at a flow rate of 1 ml/h at a printing speed of 10 mm/s. The other parameters were set as follows: the infill density = 90%, the total layer = 7, and the infill pattern was rectilinear. After whole optimization studies, these parameters related to 3D printer were decided. After the printing process, samples printed with pure PLA were dried to remove chloroform, while crosslinking was performed by placing the PLA/CS scaffolds in sodium hydroxide solution for 3 min.

2.4 Characterization of the Physical Properties of Solutions

The density of the prepared solutions was calculated using standard density bottle (10 ml) DIN ISO 3507-Gay Lussac (Pipe Glass Inc., Turkey). The surface tension and the viscosity of the solutions were measured at room temperature using a force tensiometer (Sigma 703D, Caution, Germany) and a digital viscometer (DV-E, Brookfield AMETEK, USA) respectively.

2.5 Fourier Transform Infrared Spectroscopy (FT-IR)

The molecular structure and chemical characterization of the scaffolds were analyzed using a Fourier transform infrared spectroscopy (FTIR, 4700 Jasco, Japan) at a range of 450–4000 cm^{-1} and 4 cm^{-1} resolution.

2.6 Scanning Electron Microscopy (SEM)

Each scaffold was analyzed using scanning electron microscopy (SEM) (EVA MA 10, ZEISS, USA) for morphological features and pore size differences. Mean pore sizes of the scaffolds were measured using software (Analysis5, Olympus, USA).

2.7 Tensile Properties

The mechanical strength of the scaffolds was determined and evaluated using a tensile testing machine (SHIMADZU, EZ-LX, CHINA). The thickness of the scaffolds was calculated using a digital micrometer (Mitutoyo MTI Corp., USA).

2.8 MTT Test and Cell Attachment Analysis

Scaffolds were incubated in a humid 5% CO2 incubator (SANYO) at 37 °C for in growth medium (DMEM with 10% FBS and 0.1 mg/ml penicillin/streptomycin). 5×10^4 mesenchymal stem cells (hAD-MSCs) derived from human adipose tissue were added on scaffolds. The biocompatibility of the scaffolds was examined on days 1 and 7. A cytotoxicity detection kit (MTT from Glentham Life Sciences) was used to investigate cytotoxicity at a given time point. The absorbance value of the cytotoxicity test was measured at 560 nm wavelength (690 nm as Ref. value) in ELISA reader (Perkin Elmer, Enspire).

3 Results and Discussion

In this study, solutions were prepared by adding CS at different rates to the PLA concentration (Table 1). The prepared solutions were characterized in terms of their physical properties such as density, viscosity and surface tension. The viscosity of the solutions used in the 3D printer is very important. If the viscosity of the solution is too low, the printed wires tend to spread and cause the wires of the first layer to merge. On the other hand, high viscosity solutions can clog the tip of the dispensing needle and disrupt the next printing process. Therefore, the viscosity of the solutions should be well adjusted [14]. Another important parameter, the surface tension determines the shape of the drop coming out of the needle and its shape on the substrate. The surface tension values of the inks generally range from 28 to 350 mN m^{-1} [15]. The parameters of the physical properties of the solutions are given in Fig. 1(a, b, c). Low concentrations of CS and (1 wt% CS) diminished viscosity and density of solutions when mixed with 15 wt% PLA. The printed strands were spread so that the porous structure on the scaffold was broken. High concentrations of CS (5 wt% CS) increased viscosity and density. That's why the tip of the needle clogged and defected the structure of the scaffold. Finally, the optimal solution density and viscosity for the needle tip and the designed scaffold used were obtained by mixing 3 wt% CS with 15 wt% PLA (15PLA/3CS). The research was continued with these optimized data.

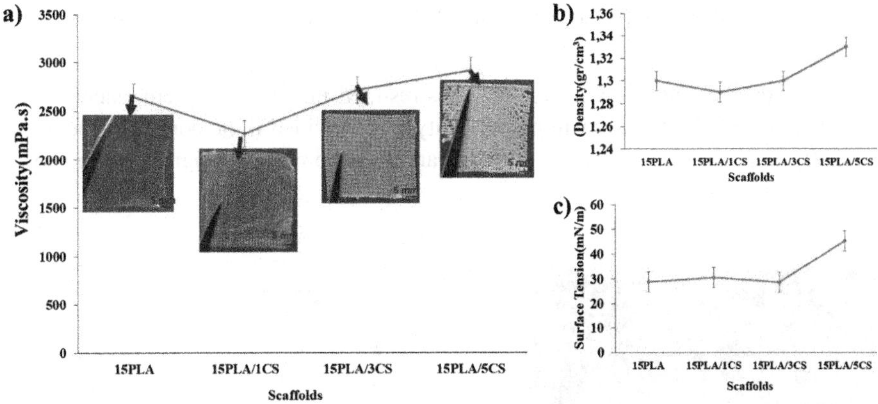

Fig. 1. Viscosity (a), Density (b) and Surface tension (c) of polylactic acid/chitosan solutions.

FTIR analysis was examined to analyze the chemical and molecular structure of the scaffolds (Fig. 2). From Fig. 2, characteristic bands of pure PLA were found C=O vibration peak at 1749 cm^{-1}, which can be recognized as a backbone ester group of PLA. A band, corresponding to bending vibration of CH_3 (asymmetric) was observed at 1452 cm^{-1}, C–O–C stretching at 1080 cm^{-1}, C–COO stretching peak at 867 cm^{-1}, C–O asymmetrical stretching and CH_3 twisting at 1181 cm^{-1}, C–CH_3 stretching at 1042 cm^{-1} [16, 17]. For pure CS in Fig. 2, related peaks were found at 3283 cm^{-1} representing the N-H stretching, C–H vibration at 2869 cm^{-1} and primary amide C=O stretching at 1589 cm^{-1} [18]. As can be seen in Fig. 2, the related peaks of PLA, and CS, are found in the produced 15PLA/3CS scaffold. The reason for the peaks of pure PLA to be more dominant than CS is because the amount of PLA in the prepared solution is higher.

The pore sizes of the scaffolds produced have an important place in tissue engineering applications. Appropriate and open pore size is important for cell nutrition, migration, permeability, and cell growth [19]. A porous surface provides mechanical stability and helps promote new tissue formation [19, 20]. Results indicated that average pore size distributions of pure PLA scaffold resulted in 141.20 μm. After the

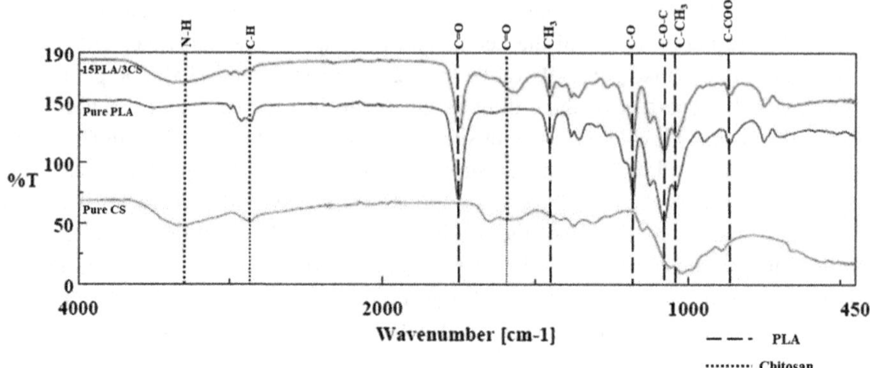

Fig. 2. FTIR spectrums of polylactic acid/chitosan scaffold

addition of the CS, the average pore size has resulted in 160.44 μm. Hutmacher et al. study demonstrated that sufficient permeability was provided if the pore sizes were less than 300 μm [21]. SEM images of scaffolds and their pore size histograms were shown in Fig. 3(a, b).

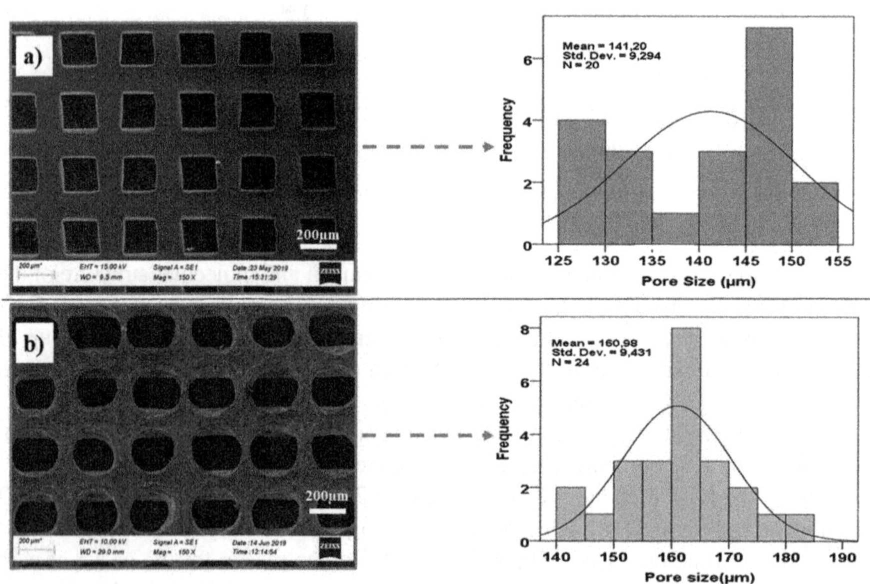

Fig. 3. SEM images and pore size histogram of pure PLA (a) and 15PLA/3CS (b) scaffolds.

A tensile test was performed on printed scaffolds to analyze the effect of pore sizes on mechanical properties [22]. Table 2 showed the tensile strength and elongation at break values of scaffolds. The results showed that the tensile strength of pure PLA had the maximum value (14.25 MPa) and strain values (6.41%). It was observed that with the addition of CS to the PLA, the tensile strength decreased to 4.72 MPa. The reason for the diminishing in mechanical properties is that CS is a natural polymers with micropores and its mechanical properties are very low. A similar decreasing pattern was numerically observed for the strain values of the scaffolds. When the effect of pore size on mechanical properties is analyzed, scaffolds with a pore size of 141.20 μm (PLA), 160.44 μm (15PLA/3CS), caused the important differences for tensile strength values. Although CS has attractive biological properties, its low strength and fragile behavior limit its availability [23]. Another important factor in the eardrum patch is to adjust the appropriate thickness. While the scaffold being too thin causes easy folding, very thick patches may not be well adapted to the natural eardrum [24]. In some areas, the thickness of the human natural eardrum varies from 20 μm, 80 μm, by digital micrometer, respectively. These data showed that the scaffolds produced were similar to the natural eardrum thickness.

Table 2. Tensile testing results for PLA, 15PLA/3CS scaffolds.

Scaffold	Tensile strength (MPa)	Elongation at break (%)
15PLA	14.25	6.41
15PLA/3CS	4.72	4.22

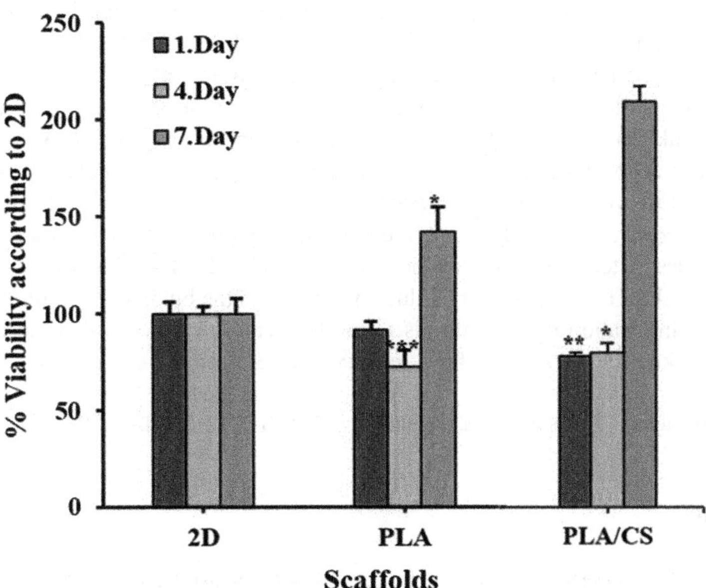

Fig. 4. Cell viability analysis of pure PLA and 15PLA/3CS scaffolds with their standard deviations (*p < 0,05, **p < 0,01, ***p < 0,001).

The MTT test was carried out to analyze the biocompatibility of the scaffolds produced. Mesenchymal stem cells were chosen because they can easily grow and differentiate into fibroblast cells [25]. The cell viability values of the scaffolds were shown in Fig. 4. When the viability graphic of the structures was compared, the highest viability value (91.3%) was seen in PLA scaffold. For day 4, the viability values of PLA scaffold was found to be 72.4%. On the other hand, the viability value of 15PLA/3CS scaffold increased from 81.3% to 83%. Cell viability in PLA and 15PLA/3CS samples increased to 141.9%, 217.8% after 7 days of incubation, respectively. Yaret et al. study observed that cell proliferation and adhesion increased with rising CS concentration in the PLA/CS composites compared to pure PLA [26]. MTT results were observed to be similar compared to the literature. Biological tests have shown that the results are consistent when compared with the literature and pure PLA and PLA/CS composites promote cellular activity and increase cell viability [27].

4 Conclusion

In this study, we developed novel scaffolds for the eardrum perforations using Polylactic acid (PLA) and Chitosan (CS) because of their significant properties such as biodegradability and biocompatibility. This novel eardrum patch can be as an alternative to paper patch graft technique or surgical treatment. In the presented study, 3D printed technology was used to overcome the problems of traditional surgical methods or the restrictions of the paper patch technique. Pure PLA and different concentrations of CS were used and the ideal concentration was chosen for printability. Fabricated tympanic membrane patches have been able to mimic the thickness of the natural eardrum thanks to 3D printing technique. The mechanical properties of PLA scaffold are observed at the high level but by adding CS we observed a decrease of tensile properties. However, the tensile properties of the scaffolds are similar to the natural eardrum. According to the MTT test, biocompatibility properties were observed at the desired values, after 7 days of incubation. Especially, 15PLA/3CS scaffold demonstrated the highest biocompatibility value and increased the binding and proliferation of MSCs. The innovation in this study is to produce eardrum patches with desired pore size and thickness thanks to the high sensitivity of 3D printed technology.

Acknowledgments. This study was supported by FEN-B-121218-0614 BAPKO project.

References

1. Kuypers, L.C., Decraemer, W.F., Dirckx, J.J.J.: Thickness distribution of fresh and preserved human eardrums measured with confocal microscopy. Otol. Neurotol. **27**, 256–264 (2006). https://doi.org/10.1097/01.mao.0000187044.73791.92
2. Laidlaw, D.W., Costantino, P.D., Govindaraj, S., et al.: Tympanic membrane repair with a dermal allograft. Laryngoscope **111**, 702–707 (2001). https://doi.org/10.1097/00005537-200104000-00025

3. Teh, B.M., Marano, R.J., Shen, Y., et al.: Tissue engineering of the tympanic membrane. Tissue Eng. Part B Rev. **19**, 116–132 (2012). https://doi.org/10.1089/ten.teb.2012.0389
4. Ghassemifar, R., Redmond, S., Zainuddin, C.T.V.: Advancing towards a tissue-engineered tympanic membrane: silk fibroin as a substratum for growing human eardrum keratinocytes. J. Biomater. Appl. **24**, 591–606 (2010). https://doi.org/10.1177/0885328209104289
5. Derakhshanfar, S., Mbeleck, R., Xu, K., et al.: 3D bioprinting for biomedical devices and tissue engineering: a review of recent trends and advances. Bioact. Mater. **3**, 144–156 (2018). https://doi.org/10.1016/j.bioactmat.2017.11.008
6. Bishop, E.S., Mostafa, S., Pakvasa, M., et al.: 3-D bioprinting technologies in tissue engineering and regenerative medicine: current and future trends. Genes Dis. **4**, 185–195 (2017). https://doi.org/10.1016/j.gendis.2017.10.002
7. Yeong, W.Y., Chua, C.K., Leong, K.F., et al.: Indirect fabrication of collagen scaffold based on inkjet printing technique. Rapid Prototyp. J. **12**, 229–237 (2006). https://doi.org/10.1108/13552540610682741
8. Gao, G., Cui, X.: Three-dimensional bioprinting in tissue engineering and regenerative medicine. Biotechnol. Lett. **38**, 203–211 (2016). https://doi.org/10.1007/s10529-015-1975-1
9. Yan, Q., Dong, H., Su, J., et al.: A review of 3D printing technology for medical applications. Engineering **4**, 729–742 (2018). https://doi.org/10.1016/j.eng.2018.07.021
10. Elsawy, M.A., Kim, K.H., Park, J.W., Deep, A.: Hydrolytic degradation of polylactic acid (PLA) and its composites. Renew. Sustain. Energy Rev. **79**, 1346–1352 (2017). https://doi.org/10.1016/j.rser.2017.05.143
11. Kozin, E.D., Black, N.L., Cheng, J.T., et al.: Design, fabrication, and in vitro testing of novel three-dimensionally printed tympanic membrane grafts. Hear. Res. **340**, 191–203 (2016). https://doi.org/10.1016/j.heares.2016.03.005
12. Akmammedov, R., Huysal, M., Isik, S., Senel, M.: Preparation and characterization of novel chitosan/zeolite scaffolds for bone tissue engineering applications. Int. J. Polym. Mater. Polym. Biomater. **67**, 1–9 (2017). https://doi.org/10.1080/00914037.2017.1309539
13. Patch, W.C., Chung, J.H., et al.: Tympanic Membrane Regeneration Using a water-soluble chitosan patch. Tissue Eng. Part A **16**, 225–232 (2010). https://doi.org/10.1089/ten.TEA.2009.0476
14. You, F., Wu, X., Chen, X.: 3D printing of porous alginate/gelatin hydrogel scaffolds and their mechanical property characterization. Int. J. Polym. Mater. Polym. Biomater. **66**, 299–306 (2017). https://doi.org/10.1080/00914037.2016.1201830
15. Guvendiren, M., Molde, J., Soares, R.M.D., Kohn, J.: Designing biomaterials for 3D printing. ACS Biomater. Sci. Eng. **2**, 1679–1693 (2016). https://doi.org/10.1021/acsbiomaterials.6b00121
16. Cesur, S., Oktar, F.N., Ekren, N., et al.: Preparation and characterization of electrospun polylactic acid/sodium alginate/orange oyster shell composite nanofiber for biomedical application. J. Aust. Ceram. Soc., 1–11 (2019). https://doi.org/10.1007/s41779-019-00363-1
17. Fernández-Cervantes, I., Morales, M.A., Agustín-Serrano, R., et al.: Polylactic acid/sodium alginate/hydroxyapatite composite scaffolds with trabecular tissue morphology designed by a bone remodeling model using 3D printing. J. Mater. Sci., 9478–9496. (2019). https://doi.org/10.1007/s10853-019-03537-1
18. Ulag, S., Kalkandelen, C., Oktar, F.N., et al.: 3D printing artificial blood vessel constructs using PCL/chitosan/hydrogel biocomposites. ChemistrySelect **4**, 2387–2391 (2019). https://doi.org/10.1002/slct.201803740
19. Loh, Q.L., Choong, C.: Three-dimensional scaffolds for tissue engineering applications: role of porosity and pore size. Tissue. Eng. Part B Rev. **19**, 485–502 (2013). https://doi.org/10.1089/ten.teb.2012.0437

20. Karageorgıou, V., Kaplan, D.: Porosity of 3D biomaterial scaffolds and osteogenesis. Biomaterials **26**, 5474–5491 (2005). https://doi.org/10.1016/j.biomaterials.2005.02.002
21. Hutmacher, D.W., Schantz, J.T., Lam, C.X.F., et al.: State of the art and future directions of scaffold-based bone engineering from a biomaterials perspective. J. Tissue Eng. Regen. Med. **1**, 245–260 (2007). https://doi.org/10.1002/term.24
22. Jian, Y.T., Yang, Y., Tian, T., et al.: Effect of pore size and porosity on the biomechanical properties and cytocompatibility of porous NiTi alloys. PLoS ONE **10**, e0128138 (2015). https://doi.org/10.1371/journal.pone.0128138
23. Miles, K.B., Ball, R.L., Matthew, H.W.T.: Chitosan films with improved tensile strength and toughness from N-acetyl-cysteine mediated disulfide bonds. Carbohydr. Polym. **139**, 1–9 (2016). https://doi.org/10.1016/j.carbpol.2015.11.052
24. Kim, J.H., Bae, J.H., Ki, T.L., et al.: Development of water-insoluble chitosan patch scaffold to repair traumatic tympanic membrane perforations. J. Biomed. Mater. Res. Part A **90**, 446–455 (2009). https://doi.org/10.1002/jbm.a.32119
25. Rahman, A., Von Unge, M., Olivius, P., Dirckx, J.: Healing time, long-term result and effects of stem cell treatment in acute tympanic membrane perforation **71**, 1129–1137 (2007). https://doi.org/10.1016/j.ijporl.2007.04.005
26. Torres-Hernández, Y.G., Ortega-Díaz, G.M., Téllez-Jurado, L., et al.: Biological compatibility of a polylactic acid composite reinforced with natural chitosan obtained from shrimp waste. Mater. (Basel) **11** (2018). https://doi.org/10.3390/ma11081465
27. Rodríguez-Vázquez, M., Vega-Ruiz, B., Ramos-Zúñiga, R., et al: Chitosan and its potential use as a scaffold for tissue engineering in regenerative medicine. Biomed. Res. Int. (2015). 821279. https://doi.org/10.1155/2015/821279

Controlled Release of Metformin Loaded Polyvinyl Alcohol (PVA) Microbubble/Nanoparticles Using Microfluidic Device for the Treatment of Type 2 Diabetes Mellitus

Sumeyye Cesur[1,2], Muhammet Emin Cam[1,3,4], Fatih Serdar Sayın[5], Sena Su[1,6], and Oguzhan Gunduz[1,7(✉)]

[1] Center for Nanotechnology and Biomaterials Application and Research (NBUAM), Marmara University, Istanbul, Turkey
ucemogu@ucl.ac.uk

[2] Department of Metallurgical and Materials Engineering, Institute of Pure and Applied Sciences, Marmara University, Istanbul, Turkey

[3] Department of Pharmacology, Faculty of Pharmacy, Marmara University, 34668 Istanbul, Turkey

[4] Department of Mechanical Engineering, University College London, Torrington Place, London WC1E 7JE, UK

[5] Department of Electrical and Electronical Engineering, Faculty of Technology, Marmara University, Istanbul, Turkey

[6] Department of Bioengineering, Institute of Pure and Applied Sciences, Yıldız Technical University, Istanbul, Turkey

[7] Department of Metallurgical and Materials Engineering, Faculty of Technology, Marmara University, Istanbul, Turkey

Abstract. Nowadays it became obvious that a relentless increase in Type 2 diabetes mellitus (T2DM), affecting the economically affluent countries, is gradually afflicting also the developing world. The currently used drugs in the treatment of T2DM have inefficient glucose control and carry serious side effects. In this study, nano-sized uniform particles were produced by microfluidic method by the explosion of microbubbles. Morphological (SEM), molecular interactions between the components (FT-IR), drug release test by UV spectroscopy measurement were carried out after production process. When microbubbles and nanoparticles, optical microscope and SEM images obtained were examined, it was observed that metformin was successfully loaded into nanoparticles. The diameter of the microbubbles and nanoparticles was 104 ± 91 μm and 116 ± 13 nm, respectively. Metformin was released in a controlled manner at pH 1.2 for 390 min. It is promising in the treatment of T2DM with the controlled release ability of metformin loaded nonoparticles.

Keywords: Diabetes mellitus · Microbubble · Nanoparticle · T-junction · Drug delivery

I. Rojas et al. (Eds.): IWBBIO 2020, LNBI 12108, pp. 185–193, 2020.
https://doi.org/10.1007/978-3-030-45385-5_17

1 Introduction

Diabetes Mellitus is a common disease that that occurs when insulin levels are too low to remove glucose from plasma or insulin is not used efficiently by the body [1]. The common type of diabetes called Type 2 which results from insulin resistance of the cells, is increasing rapidly throughout the world. The World Health Organization estimated that 425 million diabetic people are living all over the world and this figure will reach 629 million diabetic people by 2045 [2]. Type 2 diabetes can lead to chronically high blood glucose levels potentially leading to serious complications such as liver and heart diseases, neuropathy, ulcers, etc. The most preferred treatment of type-2 diabetes is using Metformin Hydrochloride which provides lowering glucose production in the liver and improving the sensitivity of hepatic insulin [3, 4]. However metformin must be taken two or three times per day and it may cause several symptoms like dizziness, muscle pain, chills, irregular heartbeat, etc. Drug delivery systems is one of the popular research area which aims at maximum therapeutic efficacy, drug-releasing stability, increased bioavailability with minimum side effects of the drugs.

Microbubbles and microparticles applications have increasingly gained attention in recent years due to their ability of encapsulation efficiency and direct delivery of drugs or bioactive molecules to targeted organs [5].

There are various methods for preparing polymeric microparticles such as spray drying, electrohydrodynamic techniques, precipitation, phase separation, etc. However uniform nanoscale particles can not be produced by these methods [6].

Microfluidic techniques ensure the formation of monodisperse microbubbles/particles due to its capabilities such as easy control of gas pressure and liquid flow [7, 8]. Moreover, this technique allows bubbles to be produced in a single step and more cost-effectively than other techniques. Several microfluidic methods with various device geometries have been researched in literature such as T-junctions, coflowing or crossflowing devices and flow-focusing capillaries. Among these methods, T-junction is one of the easiest methods to produce highly uniform and scalable bubbles. T-junction device forms the microbubbles in three stages: the growth, the necking and the pinch-off. When the polymer solution meets the gas, the bubbles form, expand and begin to fall. Gas pressure, flow rate, physical properties of the polymer solution are the main parameters to affect the bubble size and distribution [9].

Multifunctional particles can be made from natural and synthetic biopolymers for drug delivery field. Synthetic biopolymers is generally preferred by researches because of its biocompatible and good mechanical properties. Polyvinyl alcohol (PVA) is a a water-soluble synthetic polymer that has low toxicity, good chemical stability, excellent barrier properties, and good flexibility [5]. It is widely used biopolymer in biomedical and pharmaceutical field such as drug delivery systems, wound dressing and artificial blood vessels [10].

In this study, metformin loaded microbubbles/nanoparticles based on PVA biopolymers are produced using a T-junction microfluidic device. Solution properties such as density, viscosity and surface tension were studied. Morphological and chemical analysis conducted by optical microscope, scanning electron microscope and Fourier-transformed infrared spectrometer. The release behaviour of metformin from the particles were examined.

2 Materials and Methods

Materials
Polyvinyl alcohol (PVA, Mw = 89,000–98,000, 99% hydrolyzed), and metformin were purchased from Sigma Aldrich, USA.

Preparation of Solution
0.3 wt.% PVA was dissolved in 10 ml distilled water at 120 °C with magnetic stirrer (Wise Stir®, MSH-20 A, Germany) for approximately 1 h. Then, 1 mg/ml of metformin was added to the 0.3 wt.% PVA solution for the in vitro release study.

Characterization of Solution
Physical characterizations of solution were performed by using a viscometer, pycnometer and surface tension device. The density was quantified by using a standard 10 ml density bottle, DIN ISO 3507- (Boru Cam, Turkey). The surface tension values of the solution were measured with a force tensiometer (Sigma 703D, Attention, Germany) with a platinum ring. The viscosity was measured by a digital viscometer (DV-E, Brookfield AMETEK, USA). All the experiments were done at ambient temperature.

Device Design and Construction
In study, the T-junction device used to produce microbubbles/particles is shown in Fig. 1. The device was fabricated with poly(methylmethacrylate) (PMMA) using CNC machining. The device is designed to withstand high pressures during the microbubble process. Teflon FEP (fluorinated ethylene polypropylene) capillaries with internal diameter ID = 100 μm and outer diameter OD = 1.6 mm were embedded in the PMMA block (22 × 27 × 15 mm).

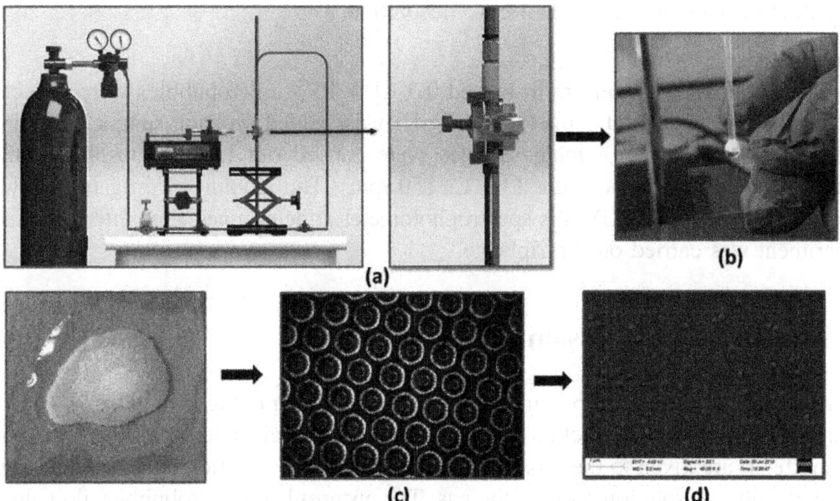

Fig. 1. Microfluidic system (a) Microbubble production stage (b) Optical microscope images of microbubbles produced using Polyvinyl Alcohol (PVA) polymer and metformin drug (c) Nanoparticles obtained by the explosion of bubbles (d)

Generation of Microbubbles

Teflon FEP tube (ID = 100 μm) was used to connect the inlets and outlet of the microchannels, which were supplied with gas and the solution. The top tube of the T-connecting device is connected to a pressure manometer providing N_2 under controlled pressure. The solution flow rate was controlled using a 10 ml plastic syringe mounted on a digitally controlled syringe pump (NE-300, New Era Pump Systems, Inc., USA). The solution and gas meet at the intersection between the two upright capillaries. Microbubbles are then produced from the outlet capillary under the T-junction. The bubbles are collected on glass slides.

Bubble and Particle Characterization

Some characterization tests have been carried out to examine the characteristics of the microbubbles and nanoparticles produced.

Optical Microscope

Size analysis, morphological distribution of microbubbles, whether they are uniform and their structures were analyzed by viewing under optical microscope (Olympus AnalySIS, USA).

Scanning Electron Microscope (SEM)

The bubbles collected on glass slides were dried under ambient conditions (23 °C). Scanning electron microscopy (SEM, EVO LS 10, ZEISS) was used to characterize the size and morphology of the nanoparticles produced. Before imaging, the nanoparticles were sprayed with gold palladium using a Quorum SC7620 Mini Spray Coater.

FTIR Spectroscopy

Fourier-transformed infrared spectroscopy (FTIR) was performed using a Jasco FT/IR-4700 model machine to examine the binding structures and functional groups of metformin-loaded PVA nanoparticles. All spectra were taken in absorbance mode at a resolution of 4000–400 cm^{-1} at 4 cm^{-1} resolution.

Drug Release Study

The certain amount of metformin loaded 0.3 wt.% PVA microbubbles were collected into Eppendorf tubes and 1 ml PBS (1.2 pH) were added on each sample. The drug release from PVA microbubble samples were carried out in 7.4 phosphate buffer solutions in a shaking incubator (37 °C, 150 rpm). The amount of drug release was measured at 232 nm by UV-Vis spectrophotometer at determined time intervals. Each experiment was carried out in triplicate.

3 Results and Discussion

Various near-monodisperse polymeric nanoparticles were produced by the explosion of microbubbles using a T-junction device. In order to obtain micro bubbles, two non-mixing feeds are given to the mixing area, one is polymer solution and the other is N2 gas. The polymer solution absorbs the gas. The encapsulated microbubbles flow down the outlet capillary channel and permanent bubbles form [11]. The sizes of the bubbles obtained are affected by the gas and liquid flow rate [12]. Bunun yanısıra viskozite ve yüzey gerilimi, monodisopers mikrobaloncuk oluşumunu etkileyen en hayati faktörlerdir. Polimer konsantrasyona bağlı olarak değişirler [13]. The surface tension of the polymer solution is 42.90 mN/m and its viscosity is 280 mPa.s.

Optical Microscope Results of Microbubbles

0.3% PVA solution was injected into the inlet 1 of the T-junction, N2 gas was pumped into the inlet 2. In the production of microbubbles, gas pressure was kept constant at 40 kPa and flow rates were increased from 40 to 100 μl/min. According to the optical microscope images of microbubbles (Fig. 2), the increase in flow rate reduced the diameter of the microbubbles from 115 ± 5 μm to 104 ± 91 μm. According to this result, microbubbles were observed to be more regular and monodisperse [14].

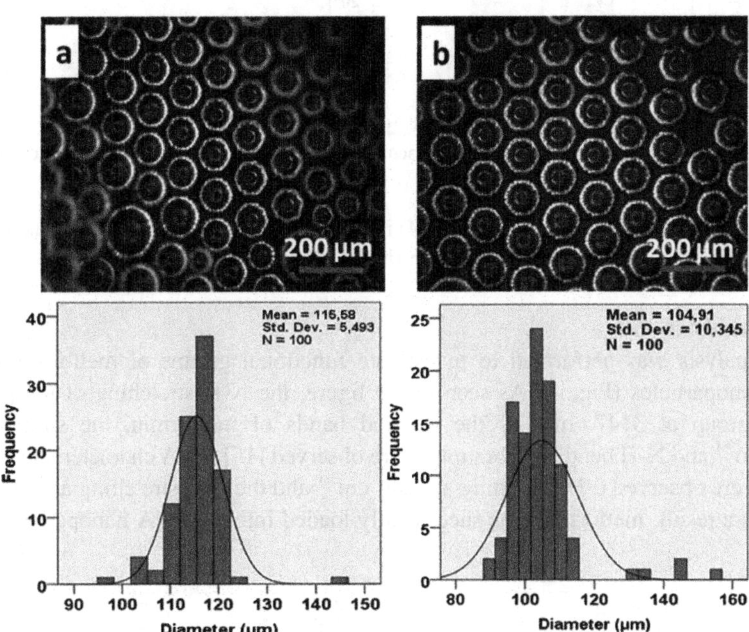

Fig. 2. Optical images and diameter distribution of microbubbles produced at different flow rate (a) 40 μl/min (b) 100 μl/min

SEM Results of Nanoparticles

According to the SEM images of the nanoparticles (Fig. 3) obtained by the explosion of microbubbles, their average diameters were 198 ± 35 nm for 40 μl/min at constant 40 kPa gas pressure and 116 ± 13 nm for 100 μl/min. According to this result, it was observed that increasing the flow rate decreased the nanoparticle size.

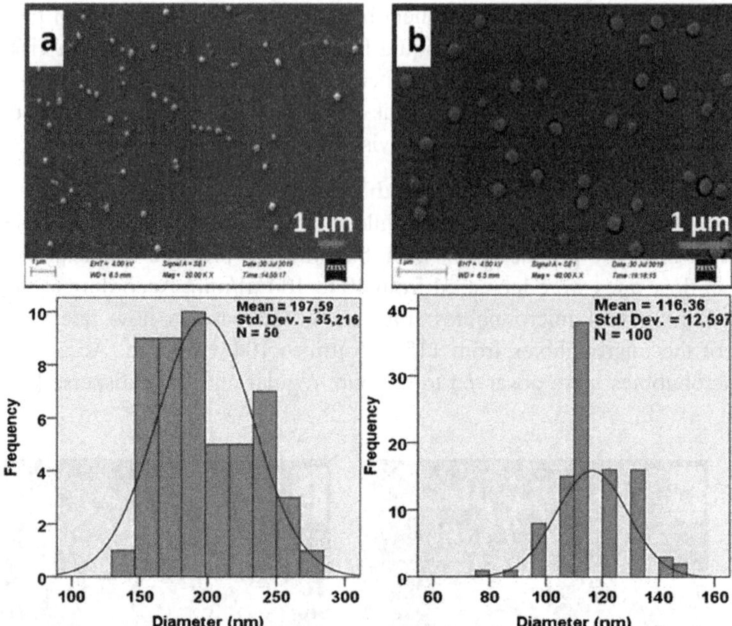

Fig. 3. Scanning electron microscopy (SEM) images and diameter distribution of nanoparticles produced at different flow rate (a) 40 µl/min (b) 100 µl/min

FTIR Analysis

FTIR analysis was performed to investigate functional groups of metformin-loaded PVA nanoparticles (Fig. 4). As seen in the figure, the N-H stretching of the primary amine group at 3147 cm^{-1} of the infrared bands of metformin, the stretching at 1577 cm^{-1} and N-H bending vibrations were observed [15]. PVA characteristic infrared bands were observed 0-H stretching at 3286 cm^{-1} and the C-O stretching at 1116 cm^{-1} [16]. As a result, metformin was successfully loaded into the PVA nanoparticles.

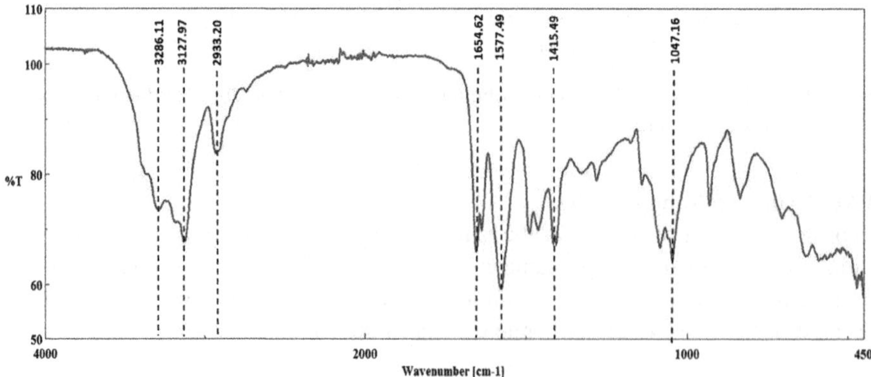

Fig. 4. FTIR Spectra of the resultant PVA/Metformin nanoparticles

Metformin Release Behaviour

A linear standard calibration curve was drawn according to the absorbance of metformin at 232 nm (R2 = 0.9978). In vitro drug release from nanoparticles was examined in gastric conditions (1.2 pH) at 37 °C along the 390 min. As illustrated in Fig. 5 burst release was observed (% 28.4) within the first 15 min. After that, the drug showed a controlled release profile for 240 min. On the other hand, the release amount reached nearly %100 within 390 min at pH 1.2. These results are consistent with previous studies in which controlled release drug delivery systems of metformin were produced [17].

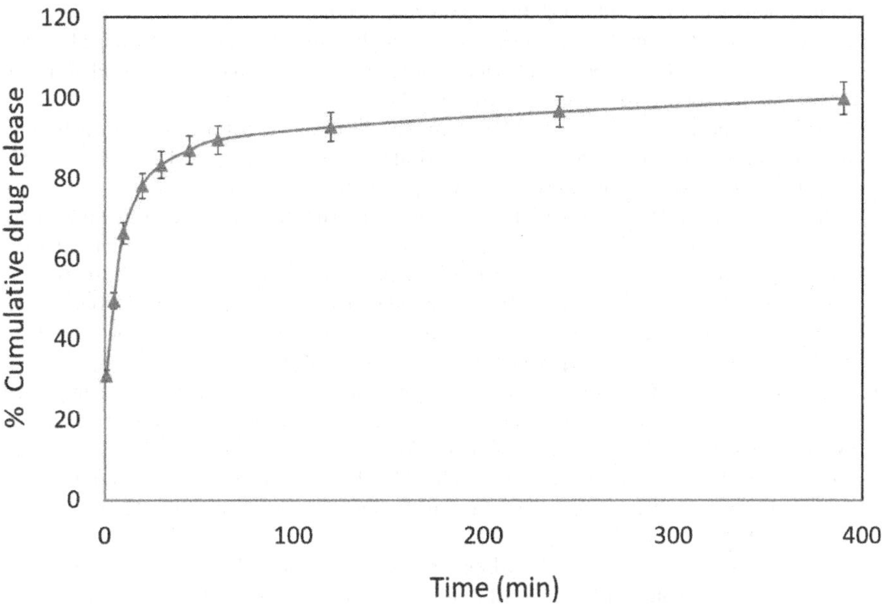

Fig. 5. The release profile of metformin in gastric fluid conditions (ph = 1.2)

4 Conclusions

In this study, microbubble and nanoparticles by using Polyvinyl alcohol (PVA) and metformin were generated through T-junction microfluidic device. It has been shown that these nanoparticles can be used as a nanocarrier for metformin drug. The flow rate of the solution has a significant effect on the nanocarrier diameter. When the microbubbles and nanoparticles, optical microscope and SEM images obtained were examined, 0.5 wt.% PVA solution was optimized with 40 kPa pressure and 100 μl/min flow rate. Metformin was successfully loaded into nanoparticles, and the diameter of microbubbles and nanoparticles was 104 ± 91 μm and 116 ± 13 nm, respectively. It is promising in the treatment of T2DM with the ability of controlled release of metformin loaded nanoparticles.

References

1. Cam, M.E., Hazar-Yavuz, A.N., Yildiz, S., et al.: The methanolic extract of Thymus praecox subsp. skorpilii var. skorpilii restores glucose homeostasis, ameliorates insulin resistance and improves pancreatic β-cell function on streptozotocin/nicotinamide-induced type 2 diabetic rats. J. Ethnopharmacol. (2019). https://doi.org/10.1016/j.jep.2018.10.028
2. Cho, N.H., Shaw, J.E., Karuranga, S., et al.: IDF diabetes atlas: global estimates of diabetes prevalence for 2017 and projections for 2045. Diabetes Res. Clin. Pract. **138**, 271–281 (2018). https://doi.org/10.1016/j.diabres.2018.02.023
3. Stumvoll, M., Goldstein, B.J., Van Haeften, T.W.: Type 2 diabetes: principles of pathogenesis and therapy. Lancet **365**, 1333–1346 (2005)
4. Patiño-Herrera, R., Louvier-Hernández, J.F., Escamilla-Silva, E.M., et al.: Prolonged release of metformin by SiO2 nanoparticles pellets for type II diabetes control. Eur. J. Pharm. Sci. (2019). https://doi.org/10.1016/j.ejps.2019.02.003
5. Martínez-Gómez, F., Guerrero, J., Matsuhiro, B., Pavez, J.: In vitro release of metformin hydrochloride from sodium alginate/polyvinyl alcohol hydrogels. Carbohydr. Polym. **155**, 182–191 (2017). https://doi.org/10.1016/j.carbpol.2016.08.079
6. Peltonen, L., Valo, H., Kolakovic, R., Laaksonen, T., Hirvonen, J.: Electrospraying, spray drying and related techniques for production and formulation of drug nanoparticles. Expert Opin. Drug Deliv. **7**(6), 705–719 (2010). https://doi.org/10.1517/17425241003716802
7. Garstecki, P., Gitlin, I., DiLuzio, W., Whitesides, G.M., Kumacheva, E., Stone, H.A.: Formation of monodisperse bubbles in a microfluidic flow-focusing device. Appl. Phys. Lett. **85**(13), 2649–2651 (2004). https://doi.org/10.1063/1.1796526
8. McEwan, C., et al.: Combined sonodynamic and antimetabolite therapy for the improved treatment of pancreatic cancer using oxygen loaded microbubbles as a delivery vehicle. Biomaterials **80**, 20–32 (2016). https://doi.org/10.1016/j.biomaterials.2015.11.033
9. Elsayed, M., Kothandaraman, A., Edirisinghe, M., Huang, J.: Porous polymeric films from microbubbles generated using a T-junction microfluidic device. Langmuir **32**(50), 13377–13385 (2016)
10. Jiang, S., Liu, S., Feng, W.: PVA hydrogel properties for biomedical application. J. Mech. Behav. Biomed. Mater. **4**(7), 1228–1233 (2011). https://doi.org/10.1016/j.jmbbm.2011.04.005
11. Kucuk, I., Yilmaz, N.F., Sinan, A.: Effects of junction angle and gas pressure on polymer nanosphere preparation from microbubbles bursted in a combined microfluidic device with thin capillaries. J. Mol. Struct. **1173**, 422–427 (2018). https://doi.org/10.1016/j.molstruc.2018.06.084
12. Gunduz, O., Ahmad, Z., Stride, E., Tamerler, C., Edirisinghe, M.: Bioinspired bubble design for particle generation. J. R. Soc. Interface **9**(67), 389–395 (2012). https://doi.org/10.1098/rsif.2011.0671
13. Parhizkar, M., Edirisinghe, M., Stride, E.: The effect of surfactant type and concentration on the size and stability of microbubbles produced in a capillary embedded T-junction device. RSC Adv. **5**(14), 10751–10762 (2015). https://doi.org/10.1039/c4ra15167d
14. Parhizkar, M., Edirisinghe, M., Stride, E.: Effect of operating conditions and liquid physical properties on the size of monodisperse microbubbles produced in a capillary embedded T-junction device. Microfluid. Nanofluid. **14**(5), 797–808 (2013). https://doi.org/10.1007/s10404-012-1098-0
15. Kim, D.W., Park, J.B.: Development and pharmaceutical approach for sustained-released metformin succinate tablets. J. Drug Deliv. Sci. Technol. **30**, 90–99 (2015). https://doi.org/10.1016/j.jddst.2015.09.019

16. Roberts, M.J., Bentley, M.D., Harris, J.M.: Chemistry for peptide and protein PEGylation. Adv. Drug Deliv. Rev. **54**(4), 459–476 (2002). https://doi.org/10.1016/S0169-409X(02)00022-4
17. Patiño-Herrera, R., Louvier-Hernández, J.F., Escamilla-Silva, E.M., Chaumel, J., Escobedo, A.G.P., Pérez, E.: Prolonged release of metformin by SiO2 nanoparticles pellets for type II diabetes control. Eur. J. Pharm. Sci. **131**, 1–8 (2019). https://doi.org/10.1016/j.ejps.2019.02.003

Patch-Based Technology for Corneal Microbial Keratitis

Songul Ulag[1,2], Elif Ilhan[1,3], Burak Aksu[4], Mustafa Sengor[1,5], Nazmi Ekren[1,6], Osman Kilic[1,7], and Oguzhan Gunduz[1,5](✉)

[1] Center for Nanotechnology and Biomaterials Application and Research (NBUAM), Marmara University, Istanbul, Turkey
ucemogu@ucl.ac.uk

[2] Department of Metallurgical and Materials Engineering, Institute of Pure and Applied Sciences, Marmara University, Istanbul, Turkey

[3] Department of Bioengineering, Institute of Pure and Applied Sciences, Marmara University, Istanbul, Turkey

[4] Department of Medical Microbiology, Marmara University School of Medicine, Maltepe, Istanbul, Turkey

[5] Department of Metallurgical and Materials Engineering, Faculty of Technology, Istanbul, Turkey

[6] Department of Electric and Electronic Engineering, Faculty of Technology, Istanbul, Turkey

[7] Department of Electric and Electronic Engineering, Faculty of Engineering, Istanbul, Turkey

Abstract. Corneal opacities, which happened mainly due to microbial keratitis, are the fourth cause of blindness worldwide. Antimicrobial therapy is an alternative solution for microbial keratitis caused by *Staphylococcus aureus and Pseudomonas Aeruginosa.* The aim of this study, to develop patches for the treatment of corneal keratitis which caused significant corneal blindness by using electrospinning method. Polyvinyl-alcohol (PVA) patches with Gelatine (GEL) studied in various ratios. Different amounts of gelatine added to PVA to resemble the collagen fibril structure of the cornea. To enable the patches to the antimicrobial effect against the bacterias, the special plant extract was used. The produced corneal patches were examined separately for chemical, morphological, and antimicrobial properties. Scanning electron microscope (SEM), Fourier-transform infrared (FT-IR) spectroscopy were performed to observe the surface morphology and chemical structure of the patches, respectively.

Keywords: Bacterial keratitis · Corneal distropy · Electrospinning · Nanofiber patches · Propolis

1 Introduction

Microbial keratitis is a common ocular infection that may be caused by bacteria, fungi, viruses, or parasites [1]. It is hard to distinguish microbial keratitis from other non-infectious conditions for the ophtalmologist. These noninfectious conditions can come from trauma and immune-mediated reactions. It is still not found specific clinical signs

I. Rojas et al. (Eds.): IWBBIO 2020, LNBI 12108, pp. 194–200, 2020.
https://doi.org/10.1007/978-3-030-45385-5_18

which can confirm the absolute bacterial caues. Therefore, more studies are required to determine the specific causative organism at laboratory. There should be formed a therapeutic plan based on clinical response and give tolerance of the antimicrobial agents [2]. The aim of this study is to fabricate the tissue-engineered artificial corneal patches which is bring new treatment for corneal microbial keratitis by using electrospinning method which allows mimicking the structure of the human cornea. These corneal patches contain polyvinyl alcohol (PVA) and gelatin (GEL) which are widely used in biomedical applications. PVA is a synthetic hydrophilic polymer, which is biocompatible and biodegradable. Its hydrogel form extensively used in the field of tissue engineering to repair and regenerate the tissues [3]. It has high availability for arterial phantom, heart valves, corneal implants, and cartilage tissues. Furthermore, it should be added that PVA is supportive for the development of oxygen permeability which is an essential property for corneal tissue engineering. GEL is a fibrous protein and was added to provide the collagen fibril structure of the cornea. Besides, it is non-toxic, biocompatible and has antibacterial activity [4]. In the present study, GEL was combined with PVA as a potential cornneal patch that can provide functional corneal stroma. Propolis was used as an additive material should give the antibacterial activity property to the PVA/GEL patches. Propolis has significant antibacterial activity due to its phenolic compounds [5, 6]. Besides propolis has antiviral, antifungal, and antioxidant properties [7–9]. Thus, it is generally used in biomedical field and wound healing.

2 Materials and Method

2.1 Materials

Polyvinyl alcohol (PVA, MW = 89000–98000) and Gelatin (GEL, MW=) were bought from Sigma Aldrich (USA).

2.2 Production of the 13% PVA/0.5% GEL Composites

In this study, 13% PVA was used as matrix polymer. 0.5% Gelatin was added into solution to provide the collagen fibril structure of the cornea layer. To decrease the surface tension, 3% Tween 80 was added into solutions. After preparation of the solutions, they were electrospinned to get nanofiber patches (Fig. 1). At the spinning stage, voltage, flow rate, and distance between the needle and collector were optimized.

2.3 Production of the 13% PVA/0.5% GEL/5%Propolis Composites

PVA solution (13%) were solved in deionized water at 90 °C at magnetic stirrer (300 rpm) for 1 h. 0.5% GEL was added into this PVA solution to provide the structure of the cornea fibril. To enable patches to antibacterial properties against the S.auerous and P. Aeruginosa which causes the corneal bacterial keratitis mostly, the propolis was added into the 13% PVA/0.5% GEL at 5% concentration.

2.4 Electrospinning Settings

In the electrospinning stage, 10 mL syringe was used to electrospun the 13% PVA, 13% PVA/0.5% GEL, and 13% PVA/0.5% GEL/5% Propolis solutions. The needle inner diameter was 0.25 mm and syringe pump was adjusted to range of 0.3 mL/h–0.5 mL/h. The collector was used to collect the electrospunned patches. The voltage values of the high power supply during the electrospinning process were the range of 23 kV–26 kV and electrospinnig was studied at room temperature.

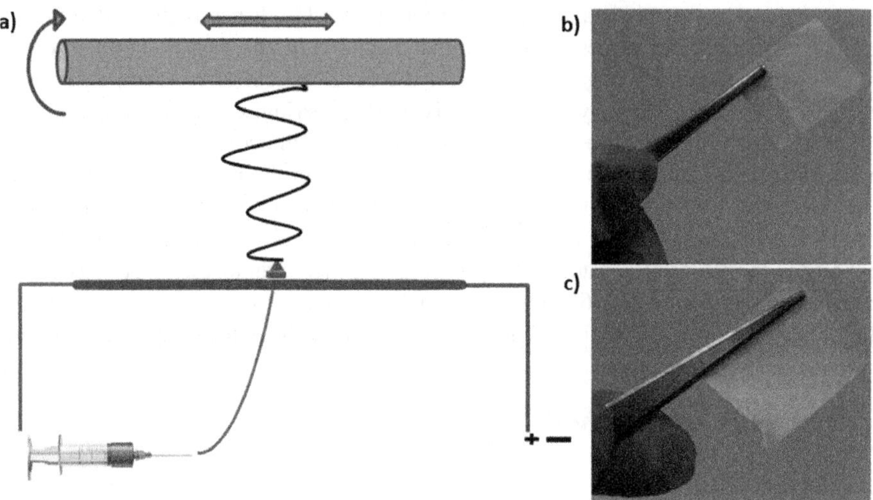

Fig. 1. The schematic view of the electrospinning setup (a), electrospunned 13% PVA/0.5% GEL (b), 13% PVA/0.5% GEL/5% Propolis (c).

2.5 Characterization of the 13% PVA/0.5% GEL Composites

To determine the chemical interactions and bonds between the components, Fourier Transform Infrared spectroscopy (FTIR, JASCO-4000) was performed. The scan range of the device is the range of 4000–400 cm^{-1} and it has 4 cm^{-1} resolution.

Scanning electron microscopy (SEM, ZEISS MA/EVO10) was used to examine the morphological properties of the patches. The pieces of patches were coated with Au for 60 s by using Quorum SC7620.

S.aureus and *P. Aeruginosa* in Mueller-Hinton broth were cultured overnight to get bacterial suspensions in the same broth. The 0.5 McFarland turbidity standard (1–2 × 10^8 CFU/mL) was adjusted. Automated plate inoculator was used to inoculate the resulting bacterial suspensions on Mueller-Hinton agar plates. Propolis containing patches were cut to have 5 mm in diameter. To sterilize the patches, they were hold under UV light (254 nm) for 1 h. Disks were put on the Mueller-Hinton agar plates which is inoculated with bacteria. 2 µg ampicillin added disks were used as positive control group for *S. Aureus* and *P. Aeruginosa*. After the disks in plates were incubated at 37 °C during the 18 h, the growth inhibition zones surrounding the disks were measured.

3 Results and Discussions

3.1 SEM Analysis

The morphology of the produced nanofiber patches were observed with SEM analysis in Fig. 2 with their diameter histograms. In Fig. 2a, the SEM image of the 13% PVA nanofiber patch had fine morphology without the existence of beads. and highly uniform distribution. Its fiber diameter was found to be 293 ± 53 nm. In Fig. 2b, the SEM image of the 13% PVA/0.5% GEL had highly uniform and more aligned structure than 13% PVA nanofiber. It had average 395 ± 119 nm which was taken from 100 measurements. By the addition of 5% Propolis, the diameter of the nanofiber patch

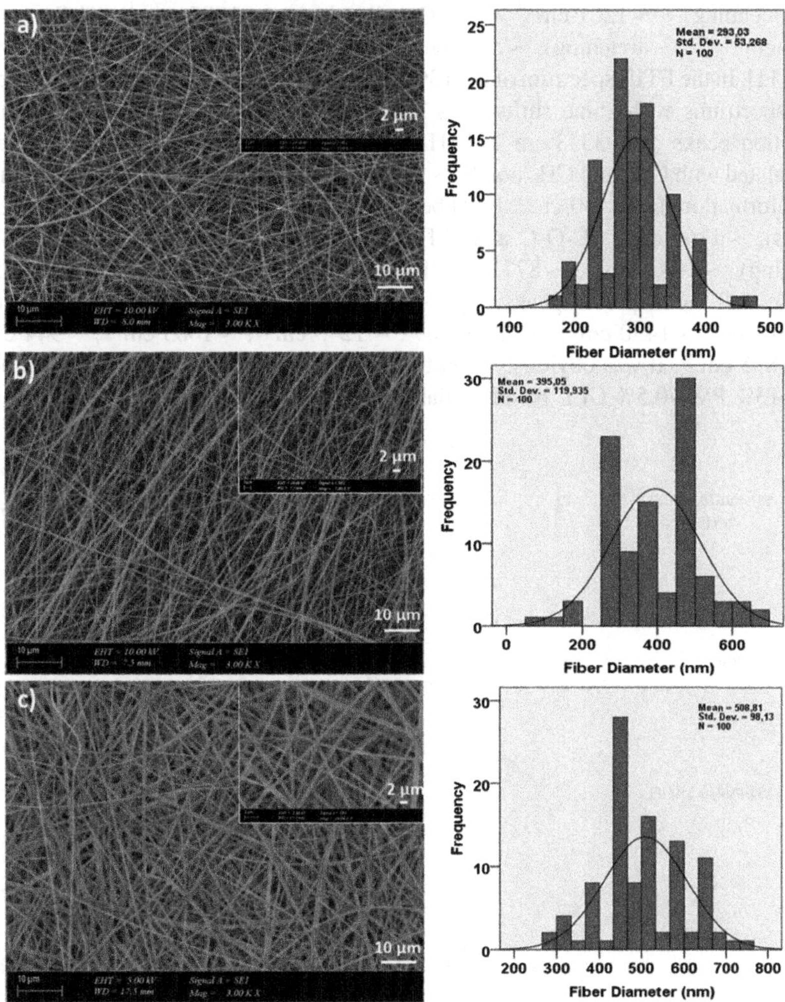

Fig. 2. SEM images of the 13% PVA (a), 13% PVA/0.5% GEL (b), 13% PVA/0.5% GEL/5% Propolis (c).

incerased to the 508 ± 98 nm (Fig. 2c). According to the images, it can be said that SEM images showed the quality of the nanofiber patches as an acceptable evidence. Since all of the electrospinned patches had nanoscale, it can be said that all nanofiber patches had a high surface areas which increase its usability in tissue engineering applications [10].

3.2 FTIR Spectroscopy

FTIR spectroscopy was used to confirm the interactions between the components. Figure 3 displayed the FTIR spectrums of the neat propolis and nanofiber patches. There were observed several absorption peaks at ~3268 cm^{-1} (O-H group, N-H amino group), ~2910 cm^{-1} (C-H stretch vibration), ~1646 cm^{-1}, ~1417 cm^{-1} (C-O), ~1326 cm^{-1} (C-H bending), ~1261 cm^{-1} (C = O vibration), ~1085 cm^{-1} (C-O group), ~917 cm^{-1} (C-C stretching), ~821 cm^{-1} (C-O stretching), for 13% PVA nanofiber patch [11]. In the FTIR spectrum of the 13% PVA/0.5% GEL, there were indicated nearly same spectrums with some shifts at ~1324 cm^{-1}, and ~833 cm^{-1}. PRP had main absorption peaks at ~3343 cm^{-1} (O-H stretching), ~2973 cm^{-1} and ~2927 cm^{-1} were related with CH_2 and CH_3 bonds, ~1637 cm^{-1} (C = C stretching, due to aromatic ring deformations), ~1450 cm^{-1} (C-H bending vibration), ~1270 cm^{-1} (C-O group of polyols), ~1164 cm^{-1} (C-O-C and C-F stretching), ~1085 cm^{-1} (C-O and C-O-C stretching), ~1043 cm^{-1}, ~877 cm^{-1} [12–14]. The 13% PVA/0.5% GEL/5% PRP had several absorption peaks at ~3301 cm^{-1}, ~2915 cm^{-1}, ~1731 cm^{-1}, ~1639 cm^{-1}, ~1430 cm^{-1}, ~1373 cm^{-1}, ~1243 cm^{-1}, ~1085 cm^{-1}, ~944 cm^{-1}, and ~835 cm^{-1}. It was obviously seen that PRP addition shifted the absorption peaks of the 13% PVA/0.5% GEL blend partially.

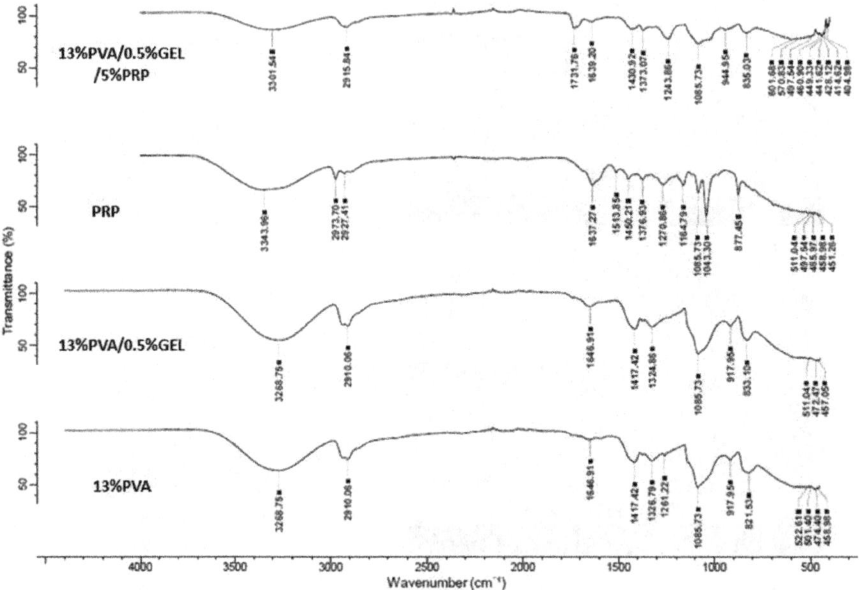

Fig. 3. FTIR spectrums of the pure PVA, Propolis and their blends.

3.3 Antibacterial Activity

Figure 4 demonstrated the results of the antibacterial activity of the both control and extract added nanofiber patches against *S.aeurous* and *P. Aeruginosa.* According to the disk diffusion assay, it was seen that nanofiber patches which had propolis showed the significant antibacterial activity against the *S. Aureous* with 7 mm inhibition zone (Fig. 4a). 2 μg ampicillin added disk showed 19 mm inhibition zone. The control groups (13% PVA, 13% PVA/0.5% GEL) didnt show any antibacterial activity against the S. Aureous (Fig. 4b). In Arıkan et al. study, it was found that propolis added mats showed antibacterial activity against the S.aureus (Gram-positive) bacteria [15]. Figure 4c displayed the antibacterial activity results of propolis added patches and ampicillin disk. It was seen clearly that propolis added patches and control groups didnt show any antibacterial activity against the *P. Aeruginosa.* It can be deduced from the results that propolis is a good extract for corneal microbial keratitis. To see the effect of *P. Aeruginosa* on the nanofiber patches, further studies are required.

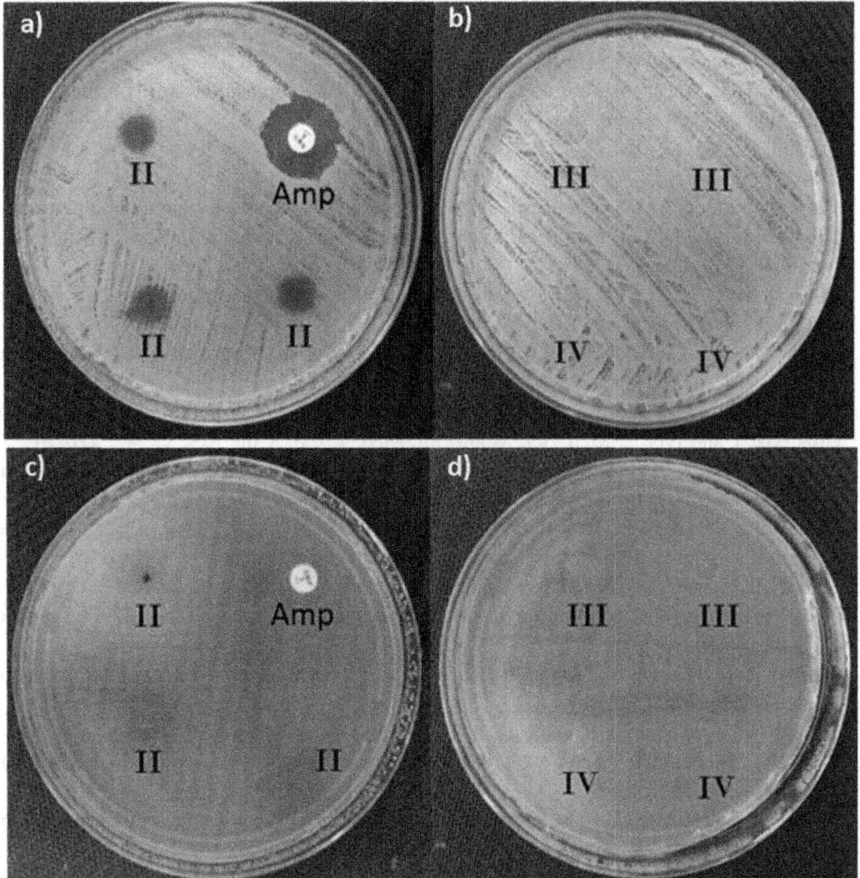

Fig. 4. *Staphylococcus aureus* tested by disk diffusion (a, b), *Pseudomonas aeruginosa* tested by disk diffusion (c, d). II: 5% propolis, Amp: 2 μg ampicillin disk, III: 13% PVA, IV: 0.5% gel containing disks.

4 Conclusions

Propolis added nanofiber patches were successfully fabricated by using electrospinning process. Propolis has potential for wound healing in tissue engineering. PVA, GEL and Propolis were combined to produce blends which had antibacterial activity against the Staphylococcus aureus and Pseudomonas Aeruginosa bacterias which cause the corneal microbial keratitis. FTIR analysis promoted the good interactions between the components. SEM showed the produced patches with highly homogeneous and beadless surfaces and their diameters at nanometer scale which is the important parameter for the tissue engineering applications. Antibacterial assay were examined against the two bacterias. The results promoted the antibacterial activity of propolis against the S.aureous. This gives the promises of propolis effect on corneal microbial keratitis.

References

1. Upadhyay, M.P., Srinivasan, M., Whitcher, J.P.: Diagnosing and managing microbial keratitis. Community Eye Health **28**(89), 3–6 (2015)
2. O'Brien, T.P.: Management of bacterial keratitis: beyond exorcism towards consideration of organism and host factors. Eye **17**, 957–974 (2003)
3. Yusong, P., Jie, D., Yan, C., Qianqian, S.: Mater. Technol. Adv. Perform. Mater. **31**(5), 266–273 (2016)
4. Mad-Ali, S., Benjakul, S., Prodpran, T., Maqsood, S.: Characteristics and gelling properties of gelatin from goat skin as affected by drying methods. J. Food Sci. Technol. **54**(6), 1646–1654 (2017)
5. Oliveira, R.N., et al.: PVA hydrogels loaded with a Brazilian propolis for burn wound healing applications. J. Appl. Polym. Sci. **132**(25) (2015)
6. Albayrak, S., Albayrak, S.: PROPOLIS: natural antimicrobial matter. Ankara Üniversitesi Eczacılık Fakültesi Dergisi **37**(3), 201–215 (2008)
7. Yildirim, A., et al.: Antiviral activity of hatay propolis against replication of herpes simplex virus type 1 and type 2. Med. Sci. Monit. Int. Med. J. Exp. Clin. Res. **22**, 422 (2016)
8. Kujumgiev, A., et al.: Antibacterial, antifungal and antiviral activity of propolis of different geographic origin. J. Ethnopharmacol. **64**(3), 235–240 (1999)
9. Mouhoubi-Tafinine, Z., Ouchemoukh, S., Tamendjari, A.: Antioxydant activity of some algerian honey and propolis. Ind. Crops Prod. **88**, 85–90 (2016)
10. Linh, N.T.B., Lee, B.-T.: Electrospinning of polyvinyl alcohol/gelatin nanofiber composites and cross-linking for bone tissue engineering application. J. Biomater. Appl. **27**(3), 255–266 (2011)
11. Anicuta, S.G., Dobre, L., Stroescu, M., Jipa, I.: Zootehnie si Tehnologii de Industrie Alimentară, 815–822 (2010)
12. Oliveira, R.N., et al.: FTIR analysis and quantification of phenols and flavonoids of five commercially available plants extracts used in wound healing. Matéria (Rio de Janeiro) **21**(3), 767–779 (2016)
13. Hussein, U., et al.: Ginger and propolis exert neuroprotective effects against monosodium glutamate-induced neurotoxicity in rats. Molecules **22**(11), 1928 (2017)
14. Martín-Ramos, P., et al.: Potential of ATR-FTIR spectroscopy for the classification of natural resins. BEMS Rep. **4**(1), 03–06 (2018)
15. Arıkan, H.K., Solak, H.H.: Propolis extract-PVA nanocomposites of textile design: antimicrobial effect on gram positive and negative bacterias. Int. J. Secondary Metabolite **4**(3, Special Issue 1), 218–224 (2017)

Computational Approaches for Drug Design and Personalized Medicine

MARCO Gene Variations and Their Association with Cardiovascular Diseases Development: An *In-Silico* Analysis

Kholoud Sanak[1,2], Maryame Azzouzi[1,3], Mounia Abik[2], and Fouzia Radouani[1(✉)]

[1] Chlamydiae and Mycoplasma Laboratory, Institut Pasteur du Maroc, 20360 Casablanca, Morocco
kholoud.sanak@gmail.com, maryame.azz@gmail.com, radouani@gmail.com

[2] IRDA Team, ENSIAS, Mohammed V University, 10112 Rabat, Morocco
mounia.abik@um5.ac.ma

[3] Laboratory of Microbiology, Pharmacology, Biotechnology and Environment, Faculté des sciences Aîn-Chock, 20100 Casablanca, Morocco

Abstract. Cardiovascular diseases (CVDs) represent the leading cause of morbidity and mortality in both developed and developing countries. They have complex etiology, influenced by several risk factors including the genetic component. The genetic variations were shown to be highly associated with different CVD forms, in this objective we proceeded to analyze the Macrophage Receptor with Collagen structure gene (MARCO), we performed an *in-silico* study with a genomic functional analysis, to evaluate the mutations' effects on the proteins' structures and functionalities. Indeed, we used dbSNP to retrieve single nucleotide polymorphisms (SNPs) of MARCO gene. We proceeded then to a filtration and a stability analysis using several bioinformatics tools to evaluate the most deleterious variations. Moreover we predicted the 3D structures of the encoded proteins by MARCO gene, which was validated using PROCHECK. Then we analyzed and visualize the proteins' 3D structures.

The extraction of the human MARCO gene SNPs revealed that dbSNP contains more than 14000 SNPs. The filtration process revealed the variations G241V and G262W to be the most deleterious SNPs, indeed, I-Mutant and DUET showed decreased protein stability. The validation using PROCHECK revealed a total of 89.9% MARCO protein residues to be in the favored region.

As conclusion, our results let suggesting that G241V and G262W variations can cause alteration in the proteins' structures and functions. Hence, to improve the health management, screening precariously these variants, can be useful as model for CVD diagnosis and helpful in pharmacogenomics.

Keywords: Cardiovascular diseases · Genomics · MARCO gene · Variations · *In-silico* study

I. Rojas et al. (Eds.): IWBBIO 2020, LNBI 12108, pp. 203–212, 2020.
https://doi.org/10.1007/978-3-030-45385-5_19

1 Introduction

Cardiovascular disease (CVD) is a major health problem [1]. According to the World Health Organization it's taking over than 17 million lives each year, with an estimated 31% of all deaths worldwide. CVD encloses a range of disorders including stroke, congenital heart disease, rhythm disorders, subclinical atherosclerosis, coronary heart disease, heart failure, valvular disease, venous disease and peripheral artery disease [2, 3].

CVDs have multifactorial etiology with several interacting risk factors (environmental, metabolic, pathological, behavioral and genetic) that can increase the disease susceptibility [4]. Therefore, the best way to address this problem is through prevention, which can be fulfilled by understanding the risk factors [5, 6]. It was shown that many genetic variations were associated with CVD development [7–11]. In our investigation, we targeted the gene of the Macrophage Receptor with Collagen structure (MARCO) [12–14]. The protein encoded by this gene is a type I membrane protein, it belongs to the class A receptor family [15, 16] and represents a part of the innate antimicrobial immune system. It is known that this protein is associated with the clearance of pathogens.

The MARCO gene variants are shown to be associated with many infectious diseases, including tuberculosis [17, 18] and respiratory virus diseases [19]. It is also associated with atherosclerosis [19–21].

In our research, we had as principal goal to explore the genetic variations of MARCO gene and their implication in CVD development. Hence, we performed an *in-silico* analysis with genomic and functional studies to evaluate the mutations' effects on the proteins' structures and functionalities.

2 Materials and Methods

2.1 Dataset for Genomic Analysis

The dataset of the single nucleotide polymorphisms (SNPs) and the human MARCO gene reference sequences were extracted respectively from NCBI database: dbSNP https://www.ncbi.nlm.nih.gov/SNP/snp_ref.cgi?locusId=8685 and https://www.ncbi.nlm.nih.gov/nuccore/XM_017005171.2.

2.2 SNPs Detection and Protein Sequence Extraction for Functional Analysis

The SNPs detection was performed by multiple sequences alignment using SEAVIEW tool which is based on ClustalW algorithm [22, 23].

The MARCO protein sequence was retrieved from UniProt database: https://www.uniprot.org/uniprot/Q9UEW3.

2.3 Selection and Analysis of the Nonsynonymous Single Nucleotide Polymorphisms (nsSNPs)

Extracting the variations from the databases revealed several types of variations. In the present investigation, we targeted the non-synonymous or missense variations, which affect the functionality of the protein encoded by the MARCO gene.

The functional impacts of the nsSNPs of MARCO were predicted using several tools such as, **SIFT** (https://sift.bii.a-star.edu.sg/), PolyPhen2 (http://genetics.bwh.harvard.edu/pph2/) [24], SNAP2 (https://rostlab.org/services/snap/) [25], SNP&GO (https://snps-and-go.biocomp.unibo.it/snps-and-go/) [26], PROVEAN (http://provean.jcvi.org/seq_submit.phps) [27], PANTHER http://pantherdb.org/), PhD-SNP (http://snps.biofold.org/phd-snpg).

Furthermore, I-Mutant 3.0 (http://gpcr2.biocomp.unibo.it/cgi/predictors/I-Mutant3.0/I-Mutant3.0.cgis) and DUET (http://biosig.unimelb.edu.au/duet/stability) were used to predict the stability of the proteins encoded by the nsSNPs.

2.4 Proteins' 3D Structure Modeling

The proteins' three-dimensional (3D) structure were constructed using MUSTER (https://zhanglab.ccmb.med.umich.edu/MUSTER/) because of the none availability in the Protein DataBase (PDB). The native protein structure was validated by PROCHECK (https://servicesn.mbi.ucla.edu/PROCHECK/), this validation evaluates the stereochemical quality of the modeled protein structure, analyzing its overall and residue-by-residue geometry based upon Psi/Phi angles in Ramachandran plots.

3 Results

3.1 nsSNPs Retrieval

More than 14 000 SNPs of the MARCO gene were extracted, among them 390 missense polymorphisms, 187 synonymous, 11223 intronics, 41 in 3′ untranslated region (UTR), 30 in 5′ UTR region, 424 upstream, 131 downstream and the rest not identified SNPs in the database. We subsequently targeted the nsSNPs (n = 390).

3.2 Computational Analysis of the Deleterious nsSNPs

The MARCO protein sequence in FASTA format was given as input data and computational algorithms were used separately. As result, many nsSNPs were revealed to be deleterious of the proteins' functionalities. The percentage of damaging nsSNPs varied according to the tool used. Indeed, SIFT predicted the most damaging nsSNPs in the MARCO gene (Fig. 1).

Both I-Mutant and DUET predicted the two variations rs147907250 (G241V) and rs202171758 (G262W) nsSNPs as affecting the protein stability, basing on their negative scores (Table 1).

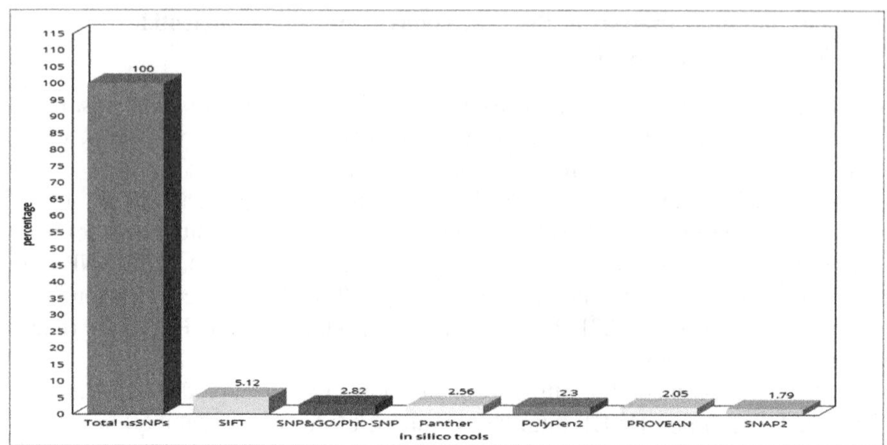

Fig. 1. Prediction of the most deleterious nsSNPs using *in-silico* approaches.

Table 1. Stability prediction results using I-Mutant et DUET

SNP ID	Amino acid variations	Variations	I-Mutant 2.0		DUET	
			ΔΔG < 0	Prediction	Score ΔΔG	Prediction
rs144036978	G163V	G > T	0.54	Stable	0.11	Stable
rs147907250	G241V	G > T	−0.38	Destabilizing	−0.528	Destabilizing
rs150412097	E323K	G > A	−0.78	Destabilizing	0.717	Stable
rs200889645	G151D	G > A	0.01	Stable	−2.731	Destabilizing
rs202171758	G262W	G > T	−0.21	Destabilizing	−1.406	Destabilizing

3.3 Homology Modeling

Using MUSTER, the 3D structure of the protein was modeled based on template PDB, Id: 1vt4I3 with the highest Zscore (28.207) and coverage (0.996), the resulted structure of the native encoded protein is shown in Fig. 2.

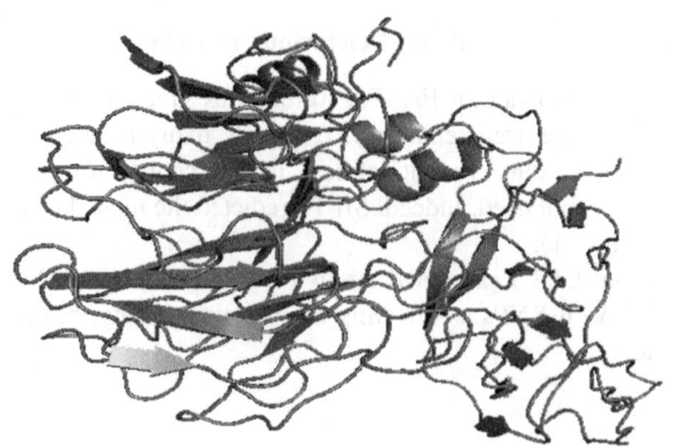

Fig. 2. 3D structure of the MARCO encoded protein

The validation by PROCHECK showed that the generated model by MUSTER had enough stereochemistry quality, due to the geometry of the Phi/Psi angles in the Ramachandran plot and most residues (89.9%) were located in the favored regions (Fig. 3).

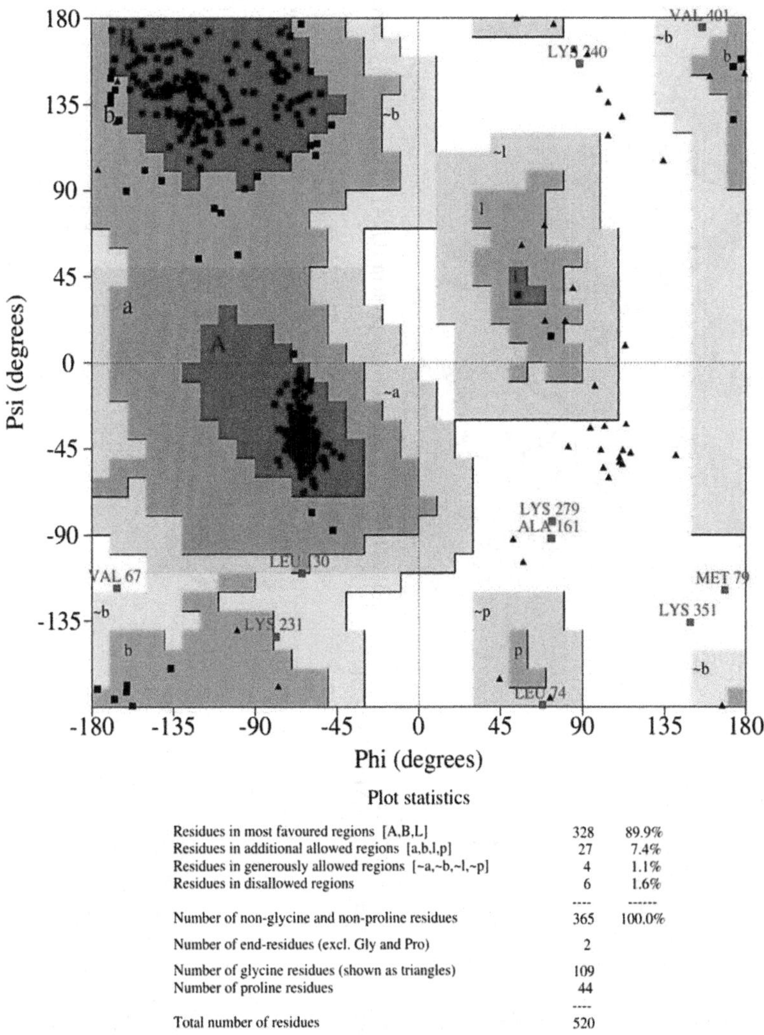

Plot statistics

Residues in most favoured regions [A,B,L]	328	89.9%
Residues in additional allowed regions [a,b,l,p]	27	7.4%
Residues in generously allowed regions [~a,~b,~l,~p]	4	1.1%
Residues in disallowed regions	6	1.6%
	----	------
Number of non-glycine and non-proline residues	365	100.0%
Number of end-residues (excl. Gly and Pro)	2	
Number of glycine residues (shown as triangles)	109	
Number of proline residues	44	

Total number of residues	520	

Fig. 3. Ramachandran plot of the native protein of MARCO

The functional and stability analysis revealed that only the two variations G241V and G262W are the most damaging which can change the protein structure and functionality (Table 2), the transition from G to T at position 319 of the nucleotides' sequence results the substitution guanine for valine at 241 in the protein's sequence. While the transition from C to T at 340 of the nucleotides' causes the amino acid guanine to pass into tryptophan at position 262 of the MARCO protein's sequence.

Table 2. 3D structure of the native and highly deleterious mutated MARCO proteins.

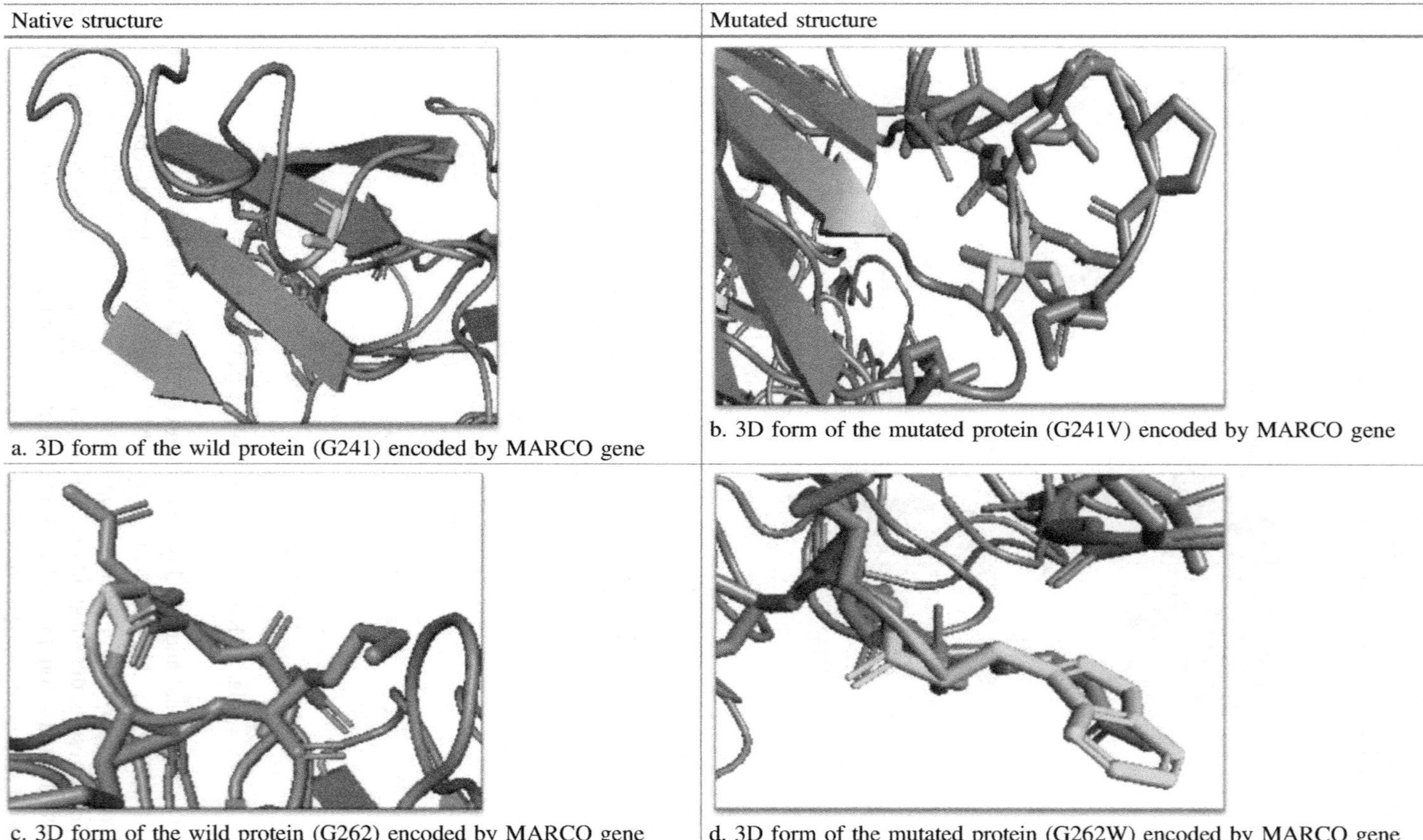

Native structure	Mutated structure
a. 3D form of the wild protein (G241) encoded by MARCO gene	b. 3D form of the mutated protein (G241V) encoded by MARCO gene
c. 3D form of the wild protein (G262) encoded by MARCO gene	d. 3D form of the mutated protein (G262W) encoded by MARCO gene

4 Discussion

It is known that the protein encoded by the MARCO gene is associated with the clearance of Lipopolysaccharide (LPS) and hydrophobic peptides of pathogens such as bacteria [12]. Most of these ligands bind to the Scavenger Receptor Cyteine-Rich domain (SRCR) of the MARCO molecule, which is a major ligand binding domain in MARCO, and it contains several binding sites [28]. The gene coding for this protein is located at chromosome 2, location 2q14.2 at coordinates 2: 118, 942, 166-118, 994, 660 (GRCh38) and contains 17 exons. Consequently, minor mutations in the SRCR domain can have negative effects on the binding of the MARCO receptor ligand, which are associated with the susceptibility of other major diseases. The nsSNPs of the MARCO gene has been associated with several infectious diseases such as tuberculosis, viral respiratory disease [17–19] and atherosclerosis [19–21]. In most human genetic diseases, polymorphisms of single nucleotides are considered to play an important role. The number of databases such as NCBI dbSNP and the Human Genome Variation Database (HGVbase) include approximately more than 4 million human SNPs [29]. Only 2% of SNPs associated with genetic disorders are found in coding regions called non-synonymous SNPs, which mainly contribute to functional protein changes in humans [30]. In addition, the mechanism of phenotypic change due to most of the polymorphism of the single nucleotide is still unknown. However, our *in-silico* analysis using powerful predicting nsSNPs and validating tools could prove the importance and usefulness to predict the phenotypic and functional effect of nsSNPs on the physicochemical properties of the protein in question and to better understand the genotype-phenotype correlation. In this objective, we set out the identification of the nsSNPs of MARCO gene which are able to alter the structure, function and expression of proteins.

Our results revealed two nsSNPs of MARCO gene, namely G241V and G262W which have been predicted to be the most deleterious SNPs by various computer tools. The transition from G to T at position 319 of the nucleotides' sequence results the substitution guanine for valine at 241 in the protein's sequence. While the transition from C to T at 340 of the nucleotides' causes the amino acid guanine to pass into tryptophan at position 262 of the MARCO protein's sequence. It seems that the genomic and functional analysis of the nsSNPs of the MARCO gene haven't been performed and/or evaluated previously. In comparison to the studies related to the genes associated with cancer such as BCL11A [31, 32], HBA1 [33, 34]. Our work represents therefore the first investigation in this term.

5 Conclusion

As conclusion, our results let suggesting that G241V and G262W can cause alteration in the proteins' structures and functions. Hence, for a good health management, we recommend to screen precociously these variants, this can be useful as model for CVD diagnosis and helpful in pharmaco genomics and precision medicine practice to improve the performance in public health especially cardiovascular diseases.

Acknowledgement. We acknowledge the h3ABioNet network (African Bioinformatics Network for H3Africa) for the scientific support.

References

1. Yusuf, S., Reddy, S., Ôunpuu, S., Anand, S.: Global burden of cardiovascular diseases: part II: variations in cardiovascular disease by specific ethnic groups and geographic regions and prevention strategies. Circulation **104**(23), 2855–2864 (2001). https://doi.org/10.1161/hc4701.099488
2. Roger, V.L., et al.: Heart disease and stroke statistics—2012 update: a report from the American Heart Association. Circulation **125**(1) (2012). https://doi.org/10.1161/CIR.0b013e31823ac046
3. Benjamin, E.J., et al.: Heart disease and stroke statistics—2018 update: a report from the American Heart Association. Circulation **137**(12) (2018). https://doi.org/10.1161/CIR.0000000000000558
4. Roca-Millan, E., González-Navarro, B., Sabater-Recolons, M.-M., Marí-Roig, A., Jané-Salas, E., López-López, J.: Periodontal treatment on patients with cardiovascular disease: systematic review and meta-analysis. Medicina Oral, Patologia Oral Y Cirugia Bucal **23**(6), e681–e690 (2018). https://doi.org/10.4317/medoral.22725
5. Perk, J.: Risk factor management: a practice guide. Eur. J. Cardiovasc. Prev. Rehabil. **16** (Suppl 2), S24–S28 (2009). https://doi.org/10.1097/01.hjr.0000359232.80893.77. Official Journal of the European Society of Cardiology, Working Groups on Epidemiology & Prevention and Cardiac Rehabilitation and Exercise Physiology
6. Van Camp, G.: Cardiovascular disease prevention. Acta Clinica Belgica **69**(6), 407–411 (2014). https://doi.org/10.1179/2295333714Y.0000000069
7. Heijmans, B.T., Westendorp, R.G.J., Knook, D.L., Kluft, C., Slagboom, P.E.: Angiotensin I–converting enzyme and plasminogen activator inhibitor-1 gene variants: risk of mortality and fatal cardiovascular disease in an elderly population-based cohort. J. Am. Coll. Cardiol. **34**(4), 1176–1183 (2015). https://doi.org/10.1016/S0735-1097(99)00337-X
8. Patel, N., Nadkarni, G.N.: Apolipoprotein L1, cardiovascular disease and hypertension. Cardiol. Clin. **37**(3), 327–334 (2019). https://doi.org/10.1016/j.ccl.2019.04.009
9. Urreizti, R., et al.: A CBS haplotype and a polymorphism at the MSR gene are associated with cardiovascular disease in a Spanish case–control study. Clin. Biochem. **40**(12), 864–868 (2007). https://doi.org/10.1016/j.clinbiochem.2007.04.008
10. Zhang, H., Mo, X., Hao, Y., Gu, D.: Association between polymorphisms in the adiponectin gene and cardiovascular disease: a meta-analysis. BMC Med. Genet. **13**(1), 40 (2012). https://doi.org/10.1186/1471-2350-13-40
11. Elomaa, O., et al.: Cloning of a novel bacteria-binding receptor structurally related to scavenger receptors and expressed in a subset of macrophages. Cell **80**(4), 603–609 (1995). https://doi.org/10.1016/0092-8674(95)90514-6
12. Elomaa, O., et al.: Structure of the human macrophage MARCO receptor and characterization of its bacteria-binding region. J. Biol. Chem. **273**(8), 4530–4538 (1998). https://doi.org/10.1074/jbc.273.8.4530
13. Kangas, M., et al.: Structure and chromosomal localization of the human and murine genes for the macrophage MARCO receptor. Genomics **58**(1), 82–89 (1999). https://doi.org/10.1006/geno.1999.5811

14. Mukhopadhyay, S., Varin, A., Chen, Y., Liu, B., Tryggvason, K., Gordon, S.: SR-A/MARCO-mediated ligand delivery enhances intracellular TLR and NLR function, but ligand scavenging from cell surface limits TLR4 response to pathogens. Blood **117**(4), 1319–1328 (2011). https://doi.org/10.1182/blood-2010-03-276733
15. Plüddemann, A., Neyen, C., Gordon, S.: Macrophage scavenger receptors and host-derived ligands. Methods (San Diego, Calif.) **43**(3), 207–217 (2007). https://doi.org/10.1016/j.ymeth.2007.06.004
16. Ma, M.-J., et al.: Genetic variants in MARCO are associated with the susceptibility to pulmonary tuberculosis in Chinese Han population. PLoS ONE **6**(8), e24069 (2011). https://doi.org/10.1371/journal.pone.0024069
17. Thuong, N.T.T., et al.: *MARCO* variants are associated with phagocytosis, pulmonary tuberculosis susceptibility and Beijing lineage. Genes Immun. **17**(7), 419–425 (2016). https://doi.org/10.1038/gene.2016.43
18. High, M., et al.: Determinants of host susceptibility to murine respiratory syncytial virus (RSV) disease identify a role for the innate immunity scavenger receptor MARCO gene in human infants. EBioMedicine **11**, 73–84 (2015). https://doi.org/10.1016/j.ebiom.2016.08.011
19. Chu, Y., Lao, W., Jin, G., Dai, D., Chen, L., Kang, H.: Evaluation of the relationship between CD36 and MARCO single-nucleotide polymorphisms and susceptibility to carotid atherosclerosis in a Chinese Han population. Gene **633**, 66–70 (2017). https://doi.org/10.1016/j.gene.2017.08.034
20. Katakami, N., et al.: Adiponectin G276T gene polymorphism is associated with cardiovascular disease in Japanese patients with type 2 diabetes. Atherosclerosis **220**(2), 437–442 (2012). https://doi.org/10.1016/j.atherosclerosis.2011.11.010
21. Moore, K.J., Sheedy, F.J., Fisher, E.A.: Macrophages in atherosclerosis: a dynamic balance. Nat. Rev. Immunol. **13**(10), 709–721 (2013). https://doi.org/10.1038/nri3520
22. Gouy, M., Guindon, S., Gascuel, O.: SeaView version 4: a multiplatform graphical user interface for sequence alignment and phylogenetic tree building. Mol. Biol. Evol. **27**(2), 221–224 (2010). https://doi.org/10.1093/molbev/msp259
23. Larkin, M.A., et al.: Clustal W and Clustal X version 20. Bioinformatics (Oxford, England) **23**(21), 2947–2948 (2007). https://doi.org/10.1093/bioinformatics/btm404
24. Ramensky, V., Bork, P., Sunyaev, S.: Human non-synonymous SNPs: server and survey. Nucleic Acids Res. **30**(17), 3894–3900 (2002). https://www.ncbi.nlm.nih.gov/pmc/articles/PMC137415/
25. Hecht, M., Bromberg, Y., Rost, B.: Better prediction of functional effects for sequence variants. BMC Genomics **16**(8), S1 (2015). https://doi.org/10.1186/1471-2164-16-S8-S1
26. Capriotti, E., Calabrese, R., Fariselli, P., Martelli, P.L., Altman, R.B., Casadio, R.: WS-SNPs&GO: a web server for predicting the deleterious effect of human protein variants using functional annotation. BMC Genomics **14**(Suppl 3), S6 (2013). https://doi.org/10.1186/1471-2164-14-S3-S6
27. Choi, Y., Sims, G.E., Murphy, S., Miller, J.R., Chan, A.P.: Predicting the functional effect of amino acid substitutions and indels. PloS ONE **7**(10), e46688 (2012). https://doi.org/10.1371/journal.pone.0046688
28. Stephen, S.L., et al.: Scavenger receptors and their potential as therapeutic targets in the treatment of cardiovascular disease. Int. J. Hypertens. **2010** (2010). https://doi.org/10.4061/2010/646929
29. Smigielski, E.M., Sirotkin, K., Ward, M., Sherry, S.T.: dbSNP: a database of single nucleotide polymorphisms. Nucleic Acids Res. **28**(1), 352–355 (2000). https://www.ncbi.nlm.nih.gov/pmc/articles/PMC102496/

30. Fredman, D., Siegfried, M., Yuan, Y.P., Bork, P., Lehväslaiho, H., Brookes, A.J.: HGVbase: a human sequence variation database emphasizing data quality and a broad spectrum of data sources. Nucleic Acids Res. **30**(1), 387–391 (2002). https://www.ncbi.nlm.nih.gov/pmc/articles/PMC99093/
31. Abdulazeez, S., Sultana, S., Almandil, N.B., Almohazey, D., Bency, B.J., Borgio, J.F.: The rs61742690 (S783N) single nucleotide polymorphism is a suitable target for disrupting BCL11A-mediated foetal-to-adult globin switching. PLoS ONE **14**(2) (2019). https://doi.org/10.1371/journal.pone.0212492
32. Abdulazeez, S.: Molecular simulation studies on B-cell lymphoma/leukaemia 11A (BCL11A). Am. J. Transl. Res. **11**(6), 3689–3697 (2019)
33. AbdulAzeez, S., Borgio, J.F.: In-silico computing of the most deleterious nsSNPs in HBA1 gene. PLoS ONE **11**(1) (2016). https://doi.org/10.1371/journal.pone.0147702
34. Minor, J.M., Rickey, L.M., Bergenstal, R.M.: Digital health care by in silico glycation of HbA1 blood cells. J. Diabetes Sci. Technol. **11**(5), 975–979 (2017). https://doi.org/10.1177/1932296817700920

Computational Approaches for Drug Design: A Focus on Drug Repurposing

Suyeon Kim, Ishwor Thapa, Farial Samadi, and Hesham Ali(✉)

College of Information Science and Technology, University of Nebraska Omaha, Omaha, NE 68182, USA
{suyeonkim,ithapa,fsamadi,hali}@unomaha.edu

Abstract. With the continuous advancements of biomedical instruments and the associated ability to collect diverse types of valuable biological data, numerous recent research studies have been focusing on how to best extract useful information from the Big Biomedical Data currently available. While drug design has been one of the most essential areas of biomedical research, the drug design process for the most part has not fully benefited from the recent explosive growth of biological data and bioinformatics tools. With the significant overhead associated with the traditional drug design process in terms of time and cost, new alternative methods, possibly based on computational approaches, are very much needed to propose innovative ways to propose effective drugs and new treatment options. Employing advanced computational tools for drug design and precision treatments has been the focus of many research studies in recent years. For example, drug repurposing has gained significant attention from biomedical researchers and pharmaceutical companies as an exciting new alternative for drug discovery that benefits from the computational approaches. Molecular profiling of diseases can be used to design customised treatments and more effective approaches can be explored based on the individuals' genotype. With the newly developed Bioinformatics tools, researchers and clinicians can repurpose existing drugs and propose innovative therapies and precision treatment options. This new development also promises to transform healthcare to focus more on individualized treatments, precision medicine and lower risks of harmful side effects. In particular, this potential new era in healthcare presents transformative opportunities to advance treatments for chronic and rare diseases.

Keywords: Computational approaches · Bioinformatics tools · Drug repurposing · Personalized treatments · Precision medicine

1 Introduction

From the nineteenth-century benches of microbiologists Louis Pasteur and Robert Koch to the recent success of the Human Genome Project, the development of modern medicine has seen remarkable advancements. The impact of such

I. Rojas et al. (Eds.): IWBBIO 2020, LNBI 12108, pp. 213–223, 2020.
https://doi.org/10.1007/978-3-030-45385-5_20

development on our quality of life has been significant. People are now healthier and living longer than their ancestors. In the past century, the discovery of *insulin*, *penicillin*, *cortisone*, and vaccines are paradigmatic of both experimental sciences and modern medical care. People with diabetes led shorter lives before *insulin* was discovered in 1921, and while minimal carbohydrate intake was the most effective treatment, these restricted diets in many cases lead to death from starvation. *Penicillin*, one of the world's first antibiotics, was accidentally discovered in 1928. It saved many lives from deadly infectious diseases. *Cortisone* appeared in the late 1940s and was used to treat patients with rheumatoid arthritis. It was also used to treat to cancer cases not within range of medical facilities suitable for surgery or radiotherapy. During this period, rigorous scrutiny and many refinements were implemented to make sure that approved drugs are safe and effective. In addition, preventive measures evolved as a critical part of improving healthcare.

However, scientific advancements are not the only major factor impacting the development of modern medicine. Cost associated with drug development and other business aspects play a non-trivial role in shaping current situation of healthcare. Rare diseases don't always attract the attention they deserve from pharmaceutical companies due to the lack of viable business models associated with the development of drugs for a small population. Developing effective drugs for rare conditions can be very expensive. In other words, a large number of potential patients or customers are needed to develop affordable drugs. How a rare is condition or disease falls into the rare or orphan diseases category is not always clear. Each country has its own official definition of orphan diseases and different thresholds are often used to make such determination. In the United States, a condition that affects fewer than 200,000 people is usually defined as an orphan disease. An example of an orphan disease is Young Onset Parkinson disease (YOPD), which occurs in individuals between the age of 21 and 45. Typically, most patients with Parkinson's Disease (PD) are much older. It has been observed that widely used treatments for typical patients are not as effective for YOPD patients and different treatments are much-needed.

2 Current Challenges in Drug Development

The drug development process usually has five steps: Discovery and development, preclinical research, clinical research, Food and Drug Administration (FDA) review, and FDA post-market safety monitoring. In the first step, researchers typically discover new drugs in the laboratory. These drugs undergo laboratory tests on animal models during the preclinical trial period to assess the basic impact and safety issues. After the preclinical trial, drugs are tested on a sample of individuals to make sure they are safe and effective. Prior to marketing, FDA teams thoroughly review all data related to the drug and trials, then decide whether to recommend approval of the developed drug. Once products are available for use by the public, FDA conducts post-market safety monitoring.

Drug development is a lengthy, complex, risky and costly process with a high degree of uncertainty as to a new drug will actually succeed in the marketplace.

It also comes with various challenges associated with potential unknown biological mechanisms and severe side effects that were not revealed during the trial periods. The process of identifying and recruiting suitably targeted cohort for clinical trials is yet another major challenge. There is also the lack of complete and seamless collaboration among academia, pharmaceutical industry, research institutes, and government pertaining to drug development.

The promise of precision medicine - delivering the right treatments, at the right time, every time to right person - led to an exciting potential paradigm shift in healthcare. Current conventional drugs are typically offered, designed and prescribed based on broad population averages. With many advances in experimental and computational tools as well as the new emerging technologies, it is more feasible than ever to uncover new indications or profiles that can lead to more efficient and precise treatments. Figure 1 illustrates the paradigm shift from the trial and error phase to the generic one-size-fits-all model to the potential precision medicine era.

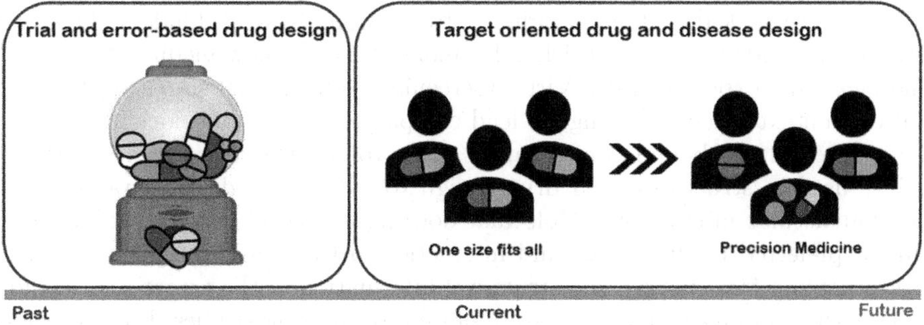

Fig. 1. Recent findings reveal that patient groups are often heterogeneous and there is desperate need to move towards precision medicine and personalized treatments.

3 Computational Approaches to Drug Design

With the continuous evolution of computing systems and Information technology techniques, the interest in the computational-aided drug discovery and design (CADD) techniques has increased. The combination of chemistry and high-throughput screening (HTS) techniques have played a major role in the discovery of new compounds. These techniques aim to increase the hit rate of novel drug compounds by reducing the number of compounds needed to be tested experimentally and to optimize the process of identifying the lead compounds obtained by the rationalization of a structure-activity relationship. Although CADD concepts encompasses many computational methodologies, the main CADD methods can be classified into ligand-based and structure-based approaches, depending on the availability of structural information.

The ligand-based computer-aided drug design (LBDD) method is employed in the analysis of compounds known to interact with targets of interest. The rationale of the method is based on the principle that structurally similar molecules are likely to have similar properties [17]. When a three-dimensional structure is not available, it is useful to identify indications based on a compound that has similar bio-chemical properties. Two approaches are fundamentally used in LBDD. The first approach is capable of selection of compounds based on chemical similarity to known activities. The other approach employs a quantitative structure-activity relationship (QSAR) model to predict biological activity of desirable compounds.

The structure-based computer-aided drug design (SBDD) method is capable of determining and analyzing 3D structures of biological molecules. SBDD is the design and optimization of a chemical structure used in identifying a drug candidate. It is based on the knowledge of the drug's three-dimensional structure, its shape and charge associated with the interaction with its biological target. Virtual screening (VS) is a powerful computational tool in screening a large number of compounds against one protein that can be tested experimentally. These small molecules are ranked by binding affinity, from strong to weak binders. The top list of compounds is usually enriched for molecules that show medium to strong binding affinity experimentally. Virtual screening is often a first step in a pharmaceutical context when searching for lead compounds. Molecular docking studies aim to predict the bound conformation of a protein-ligand complex, which is mainly used in structure-based drug design to gain detailed understanding of the biomolecular interactions. Molecular docking is used to predict the binding affinity, preferred binding pose, and interaction of the ligand-receptor complex with minimum free energy. The structural information of the target and ligand along with computer simulations are required for docking studies. Energy scoring function and a search algorithm are essential components to accomplish the docking task.

4 Drug Repurposing

The main concept behind drug repurposing or repositioning is to find a new clinical use for an approved drug. This is not an entirely new concept. However, many examples of success stories related to drug repurposing were largely the result of serendipitous discoveries. A well-known successful example of drug repurposing is *sildenafil (Viagra)* [27]. It was originally developed as an anti-angina pectoris medication, later found to be viable as an erectile dysfunction treatment by inhibiting a phosphodiesterase. Another example of drug repurposing is *thalidomide.* It was originally used as a medication for morning sickness, but later repurposed as a treatment for multiple myeloma and leprosy [27]. Discovering and developing a successful new medicine is time consuming, highly risky and incredibly difficult. From research and development to final introduction into the market, the process can take over 12 years and typically costs more than one billion dollars with high attrition rates. The pharmaceutical industry is facing intense pressure to reduce the cost of prescription drugs and to develop new medicines to treat unmet medical needs such as drugs for orphan diseases. The drug repurposing or repositioning approach has gained much attention recently as it can significantly reduce the time, cost, and risk associated with drugs development. It can also expand the usefulness of existing compounds as it aims at repurposing approved medicines for new applications.

The recent advances in computational methods and the growing access to publicly available large amount of data can play significant roles in novel drug discovery. In particular, with the advances in high-throughput sequencing technologies, bioinformatics researchers have access to massive amounts of very useful data. In addition to such valuable data, the rapid development of Bioinformatics tools and algorithms has enabled bioinformaticians and biomedical researchers to work together to advance the important drug discovery process. This could significantly improve the process and shorten the development timeline; thus, allowing newer (and hopefully better) medicines to be delivered to patients faster. Figure 2 shows an overview of the available databases along with *in silico* drug repurposing approaches. Different computational approaches utilize different types of datasets. Since different types of data could be interdependent, several approaches have been introduced to integrate heterogeneous datasets to optimize the repurposing pipeline.

As data types are dependent on each other, several integrated approaches have been introduced to integrate heterogeneous data sources to reduce trial and error for drug design. It can be argued that although Bioinformatics as a new discipline has evolved significantly in the last two decades, its impact on clinical and biomedical research remains somewhat limited. Employing advanced computational approaches to develop drug repurposing strategies provide exciting opportunities for the discipline of Bioinformatics and the growing research groups in biomedical informatics to finally make the much-anticipated influence on advancing biomedical studies and improving healthcare.

4.1 Transcription Signatures-Based Approaches

Due to the advances in genomic and transcriptomic (gene expression) technologies such as RNA Seq and SNP Arrays, transcriptional profiling can capture genomic and environmental effects within a complex biological living system. A signature is defined as the set of genes that is combined with a pattern of expression [16]. The signature of differential gene expression (SDE) can also be used to identify the summary of a compound's effects. Drug-induced SDEs and disease-associated SDEs can be compared and if they are negatively correlated, that could indicate the drugs ability to change the disease SDE and potentially counteract the disease phenotypes. A shared SDE among two drugs can indicate that the drugs may share therapeutic properties that may lead to common applications. Signature-based drug repurposing methods make use of gene expression signatures from omics data associated with diseases, drug treatment, or both. It can also be used in the discovery of unknown disease mechanisms and unknown off-targets. Such data are available in public databases such as Gene Expression

Omnibus (GEO) [12], Sequence Read Archive (SRA) [23], Connectivity Map (CMap) [22], Cancer Cell Line Encyclopedia (CCLE) [2], and the recent Library of Integrated Network-based cellular Signatures (LINCS) datasets [19].

The recent work by Sham et al. successfully employed a computational pipeline for drug repurposing for treating patients with psychiatric disorders [29]. In their study, Genome-wide association studies (GWAS) data was used to impute gene expression profiles for different disease conditions. Similar work by Kim et al. discovered potential drug candidates for patients with Ulcerative colitis (UC) [20]. In this study, the authors introduced a drug repurposing pipeline to propose new usages for candidate drugs with the help of the gene expression data. Several candidate drugs were identified to be repurposed and used for the treatment of UC patients. For validation, those drugs were found to be widely used in several experimental studies of colitis-induced animal models [20].

4.2 Text Mining-Based Approaches

Literature based discoveries can help researchers find new and hidden relationships between diseases and drugs. The basis of text mining in the field of drug repurposing stems from the ABC model, and based on this model, if A and C are both connected to B, then A and C have can have a possible relationship as well, despite the fact that there may be no published relationship between the two [11]. Medical information is now readily available to patients and researchers in various resource of the public domain. A vast amount of information related

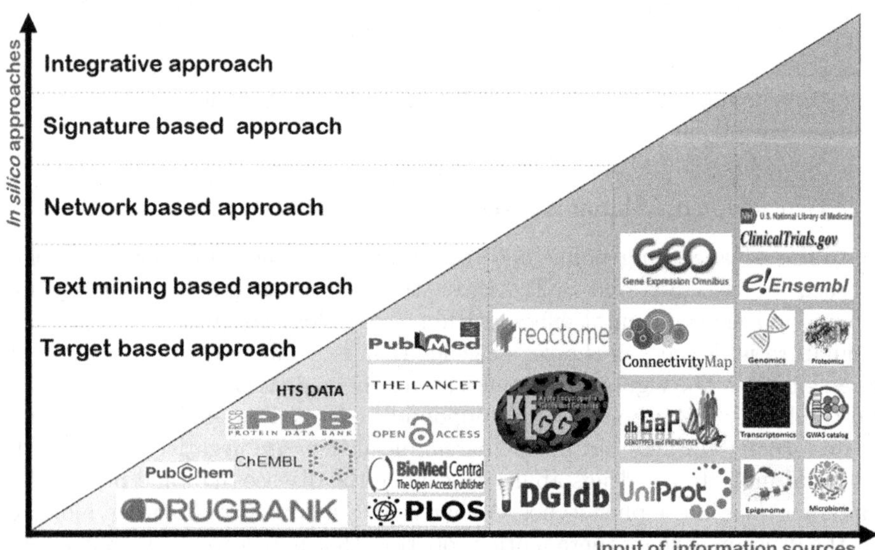

Fig. 2. 'The right drug for the right group of patients'. As massive amounts of information sources are increasing, the integrative approaches are proposed for drug design and development.

to biology and medicine is stored in various bioinformatics and cheminformatics databases. Databases of patients' records have also been radically transformed by the information revolution [28]. Text mining approaches with these massive amounts of data have been successfully utilized in drug repurposing applications [1,21,24]. These approaches make it possible to discover new potential applications for approved drugs through biomedical literature mining and ontologies. In [21], Kirk et al. employed text mining approaches along with pathway analysis to investigate potential new drug treatments for oral mucositis (OM). Genes related to both 'OM' and 'wound healing' were determined by text mining technique and enriched genes targetable by known drugs were further analyzed. A final enriched gene list was used to determine the interactions associated with known drugs using Drug Gene Interaction Database (DGIdb) [30].

4.3 Network-Based Approaches

The use of networks or graphs to represent biological systems has emerged as one of the most popular and effective methods to model the different, and sometimes complex, types of interactions and relationships associated with biological data. Using nodes to represent biological entities and edges to represent interactions, cooccurrences, or other types of relationships provide a simple yet powerful way to model the massive amount of data currently available to biomedical researchers [10]. Since Biology has a long history of new discoveries that are based on deductions from current related knowledge, new associations can be found by comparing network models obtained from related systems or from similar systems in different experimental conditions [10]. For example, this approach can be used to provide a viable path for obtaining useful relations associated with rare diseases. Shared biological processes, represented by network models, between rare and common diseases can be used to identify genes or gene products that could potentially be candidates as therapeutic targets.

Network-based approaches for drug repurposing [7], target identification [6,31] and drug combinations [8] for a specific disease have been utilized with the help of the massive amount of available data including omics data, known drug information, signaling or metabolic pathways, clinical trial information and other relevant drug phenotypic information [25]. In [6], Cheng et al. proposed a Network-Based Inference (NBI) method to infer new targets for known drugs using a drug-target bipartite network based on topological similarity. Through the NBI method using in vitro assays, two existing drugs namely *simvastatin* and *ketoconazole*, which were originally used to treat risk of several heart conditions and fungal infection respectively, were reported to have potential antiproliferative activities on human MDA-MB 231 breast cancer cell line.

Network-based approaches can also be used to predict potential drugs-target interactions. Guilt by Association (GBA) is an another useful concept that can benefit from network models and can be employed to suggest new benefits for existing drugs [9]. The main concept of this approach is based on the assumption that if two diseases share similar characteristics, then medications that are currently being used for one disease can also be used as potential therapy for the other. As a result, disease-disease network, developed based on the their similarities, can be constructed to predict novel drug-disease associations. In [9], more than 57,000 novel drug use suggestions were identified using 3,517 FDA-approved drugs and 2,022 off-label drugs with respect to 726 diseases. Based on the obtained results, several drug repurposing suggestions are currently being tested or going through various stages of clinical trials.

Many studies have implemented network-based methods by enriching gene expression data with metabolites information, chemical compounds data, and protein-protein interaction data in drug repurposing [3–5,13–15,18]. These studies illustrate how, network-based drug repurposing can serve as an effective tool for the identification of potential applications for existing drugs.

4.4 Integrative Approaches

Drug repurposing is a complex process that requires sophisticated computational methods along with the wealth of domain knowledge and omics data to propose new, safe and effective treatments. In many cases, this can only be achieved by integrating different types of data and/or incorporating multiple methods. Several computational methods attempt to employ multiple techniques and utilize different types of datasets in order to discover unknown mechanisms or drugs for repurposing. However, since such complex processes are not based on simple or direct drug-target interactions, they often require rigorous validation steps.

A recent study by Cheng et al. network proximity parameters were used to quantify the relationship between disease modules and drug targets in protein-protein interaction (PPI) network [7]. In this study, five heterogeneous networks were used and proposed repurposed drugs were validated with in vitro experiments. The study proposed *hydroxychloroquine* (HCQ) and *leflunomide* to be used for treating Coronary Artery Disease (CAD) patients. These two drugs were originally approved for the treatment of malaria and rheumatoid arthritis. As the result of in vitro experiments, although HCQ was found to be more effective than *leflunomide*, both drugs showed promising results in treating CAD patients.

In [26], Moosavinasab et al. created a database called 'Re: find Drugs' for users to interactively identify drug repurposing candidates. They used transitivity between drug-gene and gene-disease pairs to extract and prioritize drug candidates for various diseases. All relevant information was extracted from different data sources such as DrugBank, GWAS and Phenome-wide association studies (PheWAS). Gene-disease pairs were obtained from GWAS catalog and drug-gene target pairs were obtained from DrugBank. While users can search for drugs, diseases, and genes by prefixes, this interface also allows users to search for candidates by providing evidence from the literature or from clinical trial databases.

In another recent study, Cheng et al. developed network-based disease modules by integrating whole exome sequencing data and transcriptome data across 5000 tumor genomes into protein-protein interactome [8]. The study introduced the notion of Genome-wide Positioning System network (GPSnet), which was used to integrate large-scale patient DNA and RNA data with PPI networks. This method can predict the response of proposed drugs and prioritize their new applications for existing drugs. One of the proposed repurposed drugs was *ouabain*. This drug was originally approved for treating cardiac arrhythmia and heart failure. Using the proposed approach, along with experimental validation, it was shown that it can be used as an anti-tumor drug in lung adenocarcinoma. This work demonstrated the value of incorporating Bioinformatics tools and experimental validation in advancing drug repurposing.

5 Bioinformatics and the Future of Medicine

The incredible revolution in computing technologies and Informatics tools has been playing a major role in advancing many scientific disciplines. Although similar impact in the biomedical domain can be seen as evident in the recent growth in Bioinformatics, much more can be expected in the very near future. Advances in sequencing technologies, combined with progress in molecular analysis reveal the variations that make every human body unique. Variants can cause or contribute to specific disease and also give individuals' particular traits. Studying omics data helps us understand why and how certain people are susceptible to certain diseases. Moreover, such knowledge will also make it possible to explore new approaches to discover new treatments. The majority of current drug design approaches are developed generically without taking personalized traits into consideration. In precision medicine approaches, the goal is to customize prevention, diagnosis, and treatment to the patient's unique biochemical or genetic makeup, and in some cases, while considering environmental and lifestyle factors. For instance, researchers can now analyze the DNA of patient's cells rather than rely on particular population-based therapy. Similarly, genomics-driven approaches for therapeutic treatments are rapidly developing. Molecular profiling of diseases can be employed to develop targeted treatments for various diseases. Unfortunately, we can't ignore the business aspect of drug design. While it is critical to develop more effective and precise treatments, it is as critical to make sure that such treatments are affordable to all patients. The growing studies using drug repurposing approaches promise to play significant roles in developing more effective, yet more affordable, drugs. These new transformative approaches will surely lead to major advancements in healthcare, particularly in treating chronic and rare diseases.

References

1. Andronis, C., Sharma, A., Virvilis, V., Deftereos, S., Persidis, A.: Literature mining, ontologies and information visualization for drug repurposing. Brief. Bioinform. **12**(4), 357–368 (2011)
2. Barretina, J., et al.: The cancer cell line encyclopedia enables predictive modelling of anticancer drug sensitivity. Nature **483**(7391), 603–607 (2012)
3. Brown, A.S., Kong, S.W., Kohane, I.S., Patel, C.J.: ksRepo: a generalized platform for computational drug repositioning. BMC Bioinformatics **17**(1), 78 (2016)

4. Chavali, A.K., D'Auria, K.M., Hewlett, E.L., Pearson, R.D., Papin, J.A.: A metabolic network approach for the identification and prioritization of antimicrobial drug targets. Trends in Microbiol. **20**(3), 113–123 (2012)
5. Chen, H.R., Sherr, D.H., Hu, Z., DeLisi, C.: A network based approach to drug repositioning identifies plausible candidates for breast cancer and prostate cancer. BMC Med. Genomics **9**(1), 51 (2016)
6. Cheng, F., et al.: Prediction of drug-target interactions and drug repositioning via network-based inference. PLoS Comput. Biol. **8**(5), e1002503 (2012)
7. Cheng, F., et al.: Network-based approach to prediction and population-based validation of in silico drug repurposing. Nat. Commun. **9**(1), 1–12 (2018)
8. Cheng, F., et al.: A genome-wide positioning systems network algorithm for in silico drug repurposing. Nat. Commun. **10**(1), 1–14 (2019)
9. Chiang, A.P., Butte, A.J.: Systematic evaluation of drug-disease relationships to identify leads for novel drug uses. Clin. Pharmacol. Ther. **86**(5), 507–510 (2009)
10. Delavan, B., Roberts, R., Huang, R., Bao, W., Tong, W., Liu, Z.: Computational drug repositioning for rare diseases in the era of precision medicine. Drug Discovery Today **23**(2), 382–394 (2018)
11. Dong, G., Zhang, P., Yang, J., Zhang, D., Peng, J.: A systematic framework for drug repurposing based on literature mining. In: 2019 IEEE International Conference on Bioinformatics and Biomedicine (BIBM), pp. 939–942. IEEE (2019)
12. Edgar, R., Domrachev, M., Lash, A.E.: Gene Expression Omnibus: NCBI gene expression and hybridization array data repository. Nucleic Acids Res. **30**(1), 207–210 (2002)
13. Emig, D., et al.: Drug target prediction and repositioning using an integrated network-based approach. PLoS One **8**(4), e60618 (2013)
14. Folger, O., Jerby, L., Frezza, C., Gottlieb, E., Ruppin, E., Shlomi, T.: Predicting selective drug targets in cancer through metabolic networks. Mol. Syst. Biol. **7**(501), 1 (2011)
15. Fukuoka, Y., Takei, D., Ogawa, H.: A two-step drug repositioning method based on a protein-protein interaction network of genes shared by two diseases and the similarity of drugs. Bioinformation **9**(2), 89 (2013)
16. Iorio, F., Rittman, T., Ge, H., Menden, M., Saez-Rodriguez, J.: Transcriptional data: a new gateway to drug repositioning? Drug Discovery Today **18**(7–8), 350–357 (2013)
17. Johnson, M.A., Maggiora, G.M.: Concepts and Applications of Molecular Similarity. Wiley, Hoboken (1990)
18. Keane, H., Ryan, B.J., Jackson, B., Whitmore, A., Wade-Martins, R.: Protein-protein interaction networks identify targets which rescue the MPP+ cellular model of Parkinson's disease. Sci. Rep. **5**(1), 1–12 (2015)
19. Keenan, A.B., et al.: The library of integrated network-based cellular signatures NIH program: system-level cataloging of human cells response to perturbations. Cell Syst. **6**(1), 13–24 (2018)
20. Kim, S., Thapa, I., Zhang, L., Ali, H.: On identifying candidates for drug repurposing for the treatment of ulcerative colitis using gene expression data. In: Rojas, I., Valenzuela, O., Rojas, F., Ortuño, F. (eds.) IWBBIO 2019. LNCS, vol. 11465, pp. 513–521. Springer, Cham (2019). https://doi.org/10.1007/978-3-030-17938-0_45
21. Kirk, J., et al.: Text mining-based in silico drug discovery in oral mucositis caused by high-dose cancer therapy. Support. Care Cancer **26**(8), 2695–2705 (2018). https://doi.org/10.1007/s00520-018-4096-2
22. Lamb, J., et al.: The connectivity map: using gene-expression signatures to connect small molecules, genes, and disease. Science **313**, 1929–1935 (2006)

23. Leinonen, R., Sugawara, H., Shumway, M., Collaboration, I.N.S.D.: The sequence read archive. Nucleic Acids Res. **39**(suppl_1), D19–D21 (2010)
24. Li, J., Zheng, S., Chen, B., Butte, A.J., Swamidass, S.J., Lu, Z.: A survey of current trends in computational drug repositioning. Brief. Bioinform. **17**(1), 2–12 (2016)
25. Lotfi Shahreza, M., Ghadiri, N., Mousavi, S.R., Varshosaz, J., Green, J.R.: A review of network-based approaches to drug repositioning. Brief. Bioinform. **19**(5), 878–892 (2018)
26. Moosavinasab, S., et al.: 'RE: fine drugs': an interactive dashboard to access drug repurposing opportunities. Database **2016** (2016). https://doi.org/10.1093/database/baw083/2630453. https://academic.oup.com/database/article/
27. Shim, J.S., Liu, J.O.: Recent advances in drug repositioning for the discovery of new anticancer drugs. Int. J. Biol. Sci. **10**(7), 654 (2014)
28. Shore, N.: Accelerating the use of electronic health records in physician practices. N. Engl. J. Med. **362**, 192–195 (2010)
29. So, H.C., et al.: Analysis of genome-wide association data highlights candidates for drug repositioning in psychiatry. Nat. Neurosci. **20**(10), 1342 (2017)
30. Wagner, A.H., et al.: DGidb 2.0: mining clinically relevant drug-gene interactions. Nucleic Acids Res. **44**(D1), D1036–D1044 (2016)
31. Wang, R., Loscalzo, J.: Network-based disease module discovery by a novel seed connector algorithm with pathobiological implications. J. Mol. Biol. **430**(18 Pt A), 2939–2950 (2018)

Computational Proteomics and Protein-Protein Interactions

Comorbidity Network Analyses of Global Rheumatoid Arthritis and Type 2 Diabetes Reveal IL2 & IL6 as Common Role Players

Tuck Onn Liew[1], Rohit Mishra[2], and Chandrajit Lahiri[1](✉)

[1] Sunway University, 47500 Petaling Jaya, Selangor, Malaysia
chandrajitl@sunway.edu.my
[2] Guru Nanak Khalsa College, Mumbai 400019, Maharashtra, India

Abstract. Comorbidities are associated with harder clinical management, worse health outcomes and an overall increase in healthcare expenditure. Here, we present a novel method of finding the common key genes and pathways via comorbidity network analyses. Essentially, we deployed data from the RAvariome database and Type 2 Diabetes Knowledge Portal for mutually exclusive interpopulation RA and T2D susceptibility genes, respectively. Protein interactomes (PIN) are built by mapping direct interactions between the above gene products and their interacting partners, along with a comorbid network combining both RA and T2D PIN. Network centrality analyses of all PIN projected 18 overlapping proteins with IL-6 and IL-2 being the common key role players found in the comorbid PIN, despite being exclusive to our curated RA susceptible gene list. Subsequent pathway analyses revealed the involvement of cellular senescence, MAPK and AGE-RAGE signalling in diabetic complications. We conclude that RA and T2D susceptible genes do not necessarily translate into indispensable proteins in their induced individual or comorbid diseased networks, but those of RA can outcompete T2D susceptible genes despite the much larger T2D component in the comorbid network. Our method is a unique approach to find key genes/proteins and implicated pathways in disease comorbidities.

Keywords: Comorbidity · Protein interactome · Network analysis · Rheumatoid arthritis · Type 2 Diabetes

1 Introduction

It is estimated that 95.7% of the world population is affected by sequelae [1]. Numerous diseases that caused these sequelae are classifiable by eight criteria: (1) topographic, (2) anatomic, (3) physiological, (4) pathological, (5) etiologic, (6) juristic, (7) epidemiological, and (8) statistical [2]. Many of these sequelae are known to be complex and multifactorial, and some are known comorbidities of other diseases. For instance, many gene mutations can predispose one to type 2 diabetes, but one's diet and food choices in the immediate environment are amongst the other factors involved in prognosis [3]. Adding on, most rheumatoid arthritis cases are genetic but epigenetic and environmental factors such as smoking has been recognized to play a role in its pathogenesis as well [4].

I. Rojas et al. (Eds.): IWBBIO 2020, LNBI 12108, pp. 227–236, 2020.
https://doi.org/10.1007/978-3-030-45385-5_21

Due to the abundance of these diseases, a single gene can end up being a factor in a variety of diseases, such as APOE being a factor in atherosclerosis, Alzheimer's and emphysema [5]. The existence of such complexity between proteins and diseases enables one to determine the association mechanisms between them. By studying genes that are differentially expressed, implicated in genome wide association studies or found significant via other methods, common genes found between them can be used to infer a pathophysiological mechanism which they might share. An illustration of this has been done for autoimmune disorders, where Östensson et al. [6] proposed that chronic autoimmune diseases with an inflammatory component may share a mechanism involving a response of TGM2 overexpression to extracellular matrix degradation, against which the adaptive immune system develops antibodies.

Our attention is drawn to the association of diabetes with arthritis in patients, where Molsted et al.'s study revealed that diabetes patients have up to 71% higher risk of developing rheumatoid arthritis (RA) [7], whereas Jiang, Li & Li's meta-analysis showed RA patients to have 378% and 41% higher incidences of developing type 1 diabetes and type 2 diabetes (T2D) overall, respectively [8]. The latter association was an interesting find considering that RA and T2D is an autoimmune disease and a metabolic disease, respectively.

However, despite this, a molecular explanation for this is yet to be found. The only article to explore this to our knowledge is Niu et al.'s study [9], which hypothesized pathways leading to the activation of immune response to be the connecting mechanism. Moreover, acknowledging that there are no studies that have utilized centrality parameters to find key protein regulators in comorbidities, our aim for this study is to do a first-ever study to employ protein-protein interaction networks, also known as interactomes, to fulfil our aim as mentioned. Taking sets of data from two disease-specific databases, we have identified key comorbidity proteins interleukin-2 (IL2) and interleukin-6 (IL6) between two comorbidities, RA and T2D when there are no shared genes between them, using centrality measures analysis in network biology.

2 Materials and Methods

2.1 Collection of Susceptibility Genes

Two databases to Type 2 Diabetes Knowledge Portal and RAvariome databases were referred to for interpopulation genome-wide (GWAS) & candidate gene (CGAS) association studies for T2D and RA, respectively. In these studies, genetic variants with genetic risk ratios of 1.25 or above (and 0.8 or below) that meet the significance threshold of 1.0×10^{-5} and 0.05 for GWAS & CGAS respectively were selected and the corresponding genes compiled in two disease-specific lists.

2.2 Construction of Protein-Protein Interaction Network (Interactomes)

Our compiled gene lists for T2D and RA were fed as queries to STRING version 10.5 biological meta-database to obtain high-confidence (combined score of 0.7 or above) interaction information as well as neighbour proteins that directly interact with target protein counterparts, which will be visualized on Cytoscape [10]. Redundant interactions were removed by removing self-loops and duplicate edges from these networks. A comorbid interactome was built by combining resulting networks for both diseases in union.

2.3 Centrality Measure Analysis

The interactome was analysed to compute values for four network centrality parameters which are degree, betweenness, closeness and eigenvector centralities via the CytoNCA plugin [11]. Degree centrality (DC) ranks a protein with more interactions higher. Then, betweenness centrality (BC) ranks a protein that acted as a bridge between all possible protein pairs' shortest paths more often higher. After that, closeness centrality (CC) ranks a protein higher when it has more shorter paths between it and all other proteins in the network, hence being "closer" to all other proteins. Finally, eigenvector centrality (EC) ranks a protein higher when it has more connections to other highly-ranked proteins. For this study, we observe the proteins for each network when they are found among the top approximate fifteen rankers in 2 or more measures, believing them to be key proteins that connect these comorbidities. For our study, observed proteins in the comorbid network that were also found in the lists of susceptibility genes were noted, along with proteins that have a universal consensus among all four measures in a network.

2.4 Pathway Analysis of Implicated Genes

The resulting list of implicated proteins and subnetworks of observed proteins are fed as queries to ConsensusPathDB [12] to uncover pathways that these proteins will affect. BioCarta [13], Kyoto Encyclopedia of Genes and Genomes (KEGG) [14] and Reactome [15] are selected as pathway databases to be used for the analysis, and implicated pathways with p-values below 0.01 and a minimum overlap of 2 genes are considered to be significant.

3 Results

3.1 Interactome Construction from Lists of Susceptibility Genes

Using 6 project datasets from Type 2 Diabetes Knowledge Portal and data from 11 studies in RAvariome, we obtained a total of 312 susceptibility genes after filtering for genes that meet our criteria of risk ratios and significance thresholds. 300 of these genes belong to T2D and 12 belong to RA respectively. Our lists are mutually exclusive. The resulting disease-specific interactomes using these genes comprises of 6632 interactions between 1878 proteins for T2D and 376 interactions between 100 proteins for RA, whereas the combined interactome (T2DRA) comprises of 6966 interactions between 1932 proteins. Properties of their main components, the largest isolated network in the interactome, are as shown in Table 1.

Table 1. Properties of the main component of the disease-specific interactomes compared to the entire hypothesized human reference interactome.

Main component of network	Proteins	Interactions
T2D	1,323	5,160
RA	59	252
T2DRA	1,428	5,664
Homo sapiens	>20,000	>200,000

Table 2. Summary of implicated proteins found in the disease-specific and comorbid interactomes.

Interactomes analysed	Number of implicated proteins	Implicated proteins common among…		
		2 measures	3 measures	4 measures
T2D	16	ITGB1, MYC, TP53, CTNNB1, UBA52, HIST2H3A, CDC25B, MAPK14, FYN, SRC, CDC42, RHOA	TOP2A, CDK1, CCNA2	RAC1
RA	15	CTLA4, IFNG, IL5, IL2RB	IL2RG, FOS, CSF2, STAT5A, STAT5B	FOXP3, LCK, IL2, IL2RA, JAK3, JAK1
T2DRA	18	TOP2A, UBA52, CTNNB1, TP53, HIST2H3A, AKT1, FYN, IL6, CDC42, RHOA, IL2, GRB2	RAC1, MYC, CDK1, CCNA2, HRAS, JAK1	–

3.2 Centrality and Pathway Analysis

Analysis using DC, BC, CC and EC measures implicates 16, 15 and 18 proteins in the T2D, RA and T2DRA interactomes respectively (Table 2). We found no universal consensus proteins common among all four measures in the interactomes except for the T2D interactome, where Ras-related C3 botulinum toxin substrate 1 (RAC1) is found among the top rankers in all four measures (Fig. 1). Contrary to what was expected, we also found no protein counterparts of our procured T2D susceptibility genes in our implicated proteins for T2DRA despite the T2D interactome being a part of it. Instead, we found two of these from RA, which are interleukin-2 (IL2) and interleukin-6 (IL6) (Fig. 2).

Pathway analysis of these implicated proteins showed over-representation of the T2DRA ones in 449 pathways in total from the three databases, which includes 110 KEGG pathways. Implicated T2D and RA proteins are over-represented in 343 and 99

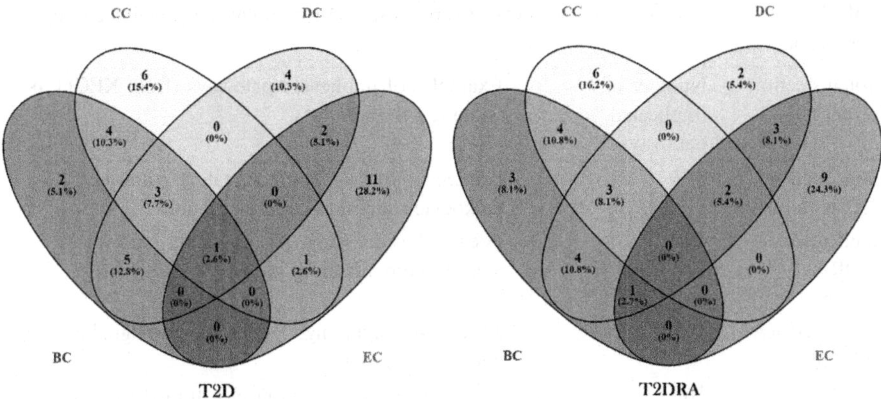

Fig. 1. Venn diagram representation for commonality between the top fifteen rankers of BC, CC, DC, and EC parametric analyses of the T2D and T2DRA interactomes.

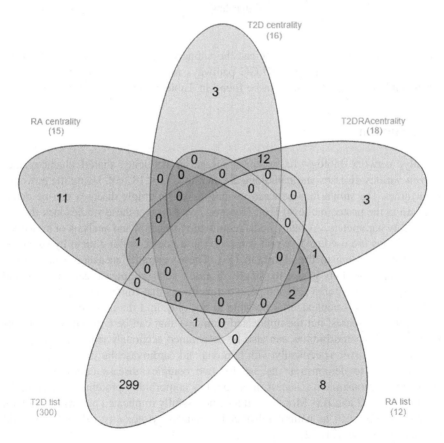

Fig. 2. Venn diagram representation for genes/proteins found in gene lists and observed through our centrality measures analysis respectively.

Table 3. Summary of implicated pathways overrepresented by implicated proteins and certain subnetworks.

Proteins sent for analysis	Number of implicated pathways	Examples of implicated pathways (from KEGG, p-value < 1.0×10^{-6})
Implicated T2D proteins	343	Adherens junction, Rap1 signaling pathway, leukocyte transendothelial migration
Implicated T2DRA proteins	449	Focal adhesion, PI3K-Akt signaling pathway, neurotrophin signaling pathway
Implicated RA proteins	99	JAK-STAT signaling, T-cell receptor signaling pathway, necroptosis
RAC1 subnetwork	165	Focal adhesion, regulation of actin cytoskeleton, MAPK signaling pathway
IL2 & IL6 subnetwork	410	JAK-STAT signaling, PI3K-Akt signaling, AGE-RAGE signaling in diabetic complications, IL17 signaling

pathways in total respectively, whereas the subnetworks of RAC1 and IL2/IL6 are over-represented in 47 and 119 KEGG pathways respectively. A summary of these with KEGG pathway examples can be found in Table 3.

4 Discussion

Recently, network biology has seen its usage in deducing shared characteristics between various diseases and pathological conditions [16, 18, 19]. Using the power of interactomes, the similarities between conditions and multiple diseases can be determined up to the proteomic level [16]. However, we find that these studies lack the use of centrality parameters. As many fields require the formation and analysis of networks, these measures are used to give real values to these nodes, ranking them by supposed importance according to the algorithm [17]. These centrality measures were mostly used to implicate hub genes of single diseases such as breast cancer [18] and nasopharyngeal carcinoma [19] and point out pathways that confers to its pathogenesis. Used in this study's context, it is possible to not only find the noteworthy regulators between these diseases, but the implicated pathways that can be targeted with patients exhibiting these comorbidities can also be determined accurately from these proteins. This has been proven specifically with hypoxia and cardiovascular diseases [20]. Our study, the first to demonstrate its use for two complex disease comorbidities has managed to demonstrate its success in finding key comorbidity proteins connecting the two cytokines IL2 and IL6. Moreover, it has successfully implicated pathways common in both diseases such as natural killer cell mediated cytotoxicity [9] and PI3K-Akt signalling pathways [21, 22].

The results that we have obtained is also in line with existing studies. Our list of RA susceptibility genes reflects the model of rheumatoid arthritis, with 10 out of 12 genes being involved in the regulation of immune system process (GO:0002682), and 6 involved in inflammatory responses (GO:0006954). Inflammation is known to be systemic and a common factor not only among all infectious diseases, but also in non-infectious diseases including T2D [23], hence the high involvement of IL2 and IL6, both inflammatory proteins in the comorbid network. They play significant roles in connecting the two diseases, namely RA and T2D. For example, RA patients have significantly higher plasma IL2 levels compared to their healthy counterparts [24]. In fact, the proposed theory that increased IL2 production is the first step of events leading to insulin resistance, including decreased bioavailability of IGF-1, is backed up by the significantly higher fasting insulin levels in these RA patients [24]. Moreover, resistin, a crucial protein in insulin resistance, strongly upregulates IL6 in the mouse model and is shown to preferentially accumulate in the inflamed joints of RA patients [25]. Conversely, inhibiting IL6 in RA patients improves their insulin sensitivity [26]. Thus, it is being suggested that IL6 causes insulin resistance via a pathway cascade. This stimulation activates JAK-STAT pathway which induces SOCS3 expression, leading to an induction of IRS1 through serine phosphorylation of IRS1 that impairs insulin signaling [26].

RAC1 is also found to be intricately involved in T2D; our PubMed search input ("RAC1" [Title/Abstract] OR "TC25" [Title/Abstract] OR "MIG5" [Title/Abstract]) AND ("Diabetes Mellitus, Type 2" [Mesh] OR "type 2 diabetes" [Title/Abstract] OR "insulin independent diabetes" [Title/Abstract] OR "non-insulin dependent diabetes" [Title/Abstract]) procured 38 articles showing the association between RAC1 and type 2 diabetes. This association can be summarized into the following: RAC1 plays a positive role before diabetes onset by playing important roles in glucose-stimulated insulin secretion in pancreatic ß-cells [27, 28], while facilitating GLUT4 translocation to skeletal muscle membranes [28, 29]. On the other hand, RAC1 has a negative role in diabetic complications by promoting overproduction of reactive oxygen species via RAC1/NOX2 signalling [30], and endothelial-to-mesenchymal transition via RAC1/PAK1 signalling [31].

We recognize a few limitations in our study. Firstly, highly studied genes/proteins will usually appear highly ranked within the human protein-protein interaction networks and vice versa, due to the lack of proven interactions of highly studied genes and vice versa. This is shown by the presence of TP53, IL6 and AKT1 in our centrality datasets, which are within the top 10 most studied genes [32]. We have minimized this effect by only using high confidence interactions from STRING-DB which are usually experimentally validated and making sure that the gene counterparts are also susceptibility genes themselves before selecting our implicated proteins as key comorbidity proteins. Secondly, there are currently no positive controls for validating our results. We consider this to be important as our method does not show the direction of effect, requiring such validation to confirm our results. Knowing this, we have noted that acquiring protein expression levels of patients or cell lines exhibiting molecular characteristics of these diseases should be one of our future targets for this project. Other targets include the use of other centrality parameters such as LAC and game-centric centralities. Alternatively, other network analysis methods such as k-core analysis can be used to further confirm our findings.

5 Conclusion

We hereby report the use of centrality measures on a comorbid network constructed from susceptibility genes of two diseases to find for key proteins that connect both comorbidities. For type 2 diabetes and rheumatoid arthritis, we find IL2 and IL6 to be the key proteins that connect them, while also implicating RAC1 as a key regulator in type 2 diabetes. We hope that our utilized method will be used to find other key comorbidity proteins in future.

Contributions. RM constructed the interactome and compiled the implicated proteins and pathways. LTO wrote the manuscript and corrected the analysis. CL checked and corrected the manuscript and headed the project. The authors declare no conflicts of interest.

References

1. Global Burden of Disease Study 2013 Collaborators: Global, regional, and national incidence, prevalence, and years lived with disability for 301 acute and chronic diseases and injuries in 188 countries, 1990–2013: a systematic analysis for the Global Burden of Disease Study 2013. Lancet **386**(9995), 743–800 (2015). https://doi.org/10.1016/s0140-6736(15)60692-4
2. Human disease - Classifications of diseases. https://www.britannica.com/science/human-disease/Classifications-of-diseases. Accessed 25 Nov 2019
3. Melmed, S., Polonsky, K.S., Larsen, P.R., Kronenberg, H.M.: Williams Textbook of Endocrinology, 13th edn. Elsevier/Saunders, Philadelphia (2016)
4. Smolen, J.S., Aletaha, D., McInnes, I.B.: Rheumatoid arthritis. Lancet **388**(10055), 2023–2038 (2016). https://doi.org/10.1016/S0140-6736(16)30173-8
5. Stolerman, I.P., Price, L.H. (eds.): Encyclopedia of Psychopharmacology. Springer, Heidelberg (2015). https://doi.org/10.1007/978-3-642-36172-2
6. Östensson, M., et al.: A possible mechanism behind autoimmune disorders discovered by genome-wide linkage and association analysis in celiac disease. PLoS ONE **8**(8), e70174 (2013). https://doi.org/10.1371/journal.pone.0070174
7. Molsted, S., Bjorkman, A.-S.D., Andersen, M.B., Ekholm, O.: Diabetes is associated with elevated risks of osteoarthritis, osteoporosis and rheumatoid arthritis. Diabetologia **61** (Supplement 1), S543–S544 (2018). https://doi.org/10.1007/s00125-018-4693-0
8. Jiang, P., Li, H., Li, X.: Diabetes mellitus risk factors in rheumatoid arthritis: a systematic review and meta-analysis. Clin. Exp. Rheumatol. **33**(1), 115–121 (2015)
9. Niu, X., et al.: The crosstalk of pathways involved in immune response maybe the shared molecular basis of rheumatoid arthritis and type 2 diabetes. PLoS ONE **10**(8), e0134990 (2015)
10. Su, G., Morris, J.H., Demchak, B., Bader, G.D.: Biological network exploration with cytoscape 3. Curr. Protoc. Bioinform. 8.13.1–8.13.24 (2014). https://doi.org/10.1002/0471250953.bi0813s47
11. Tang, Y., Li, M., Wang, J., Pan, Y., Wu, F.X.: CytoNCA: a cytoscape plugin for centrality analysis and evaluation of protein interaction networks. BioSystems **127**, 67–72 (2015). https://doi.org/10.1016/j.biosystems.2014.11.005

12. Kamburov, A., Pentchev, K., Galicka, H., Wierling, C., Lehrach, H., Herwig, R.: ConsensusPathDB: toward a more complete picture of cell biology. Nucleic Acids Res. **39**(SUPPL. 1) (2001). https://doi.org/10.1093/nar/gkq1156
13. Nishimura, D.: Biocarta. Biotech Softw. Internet Rep. **2**, 117–120 (2001)
14. Kanehisa, M., Furumichi, M., Tanabe, M., Sato, Y., Morishima, K.: KEGG: new perspectives on genomes, pathways, diseases and drugs. Nucleic Acids Res. **45**(D1), D353–D361 (2017)
15. Fabregat, A., et al.: The reactome pathway knowledgebase. Nucleic Acids Res. **44**(D1), D481–D487 (2016)
16. Paik, H., Heo, H.S., Ban, H.J., Cho, S.B.: Unraveling human protein interaction networks underlying co-occurrences of diseases and pathological conditions. J. Transl. Med. **12**(1), 1–8 (2014). https://doi.org/10.1186/1479-5876-12-99
17. Bonacich, P.: Power and centrality: a family of measures. Am. J. Sociol. **92**(5), 1170–1182 (2002). https://doi.org/10.1086/228631
18. Zhuang, D.Y., Jiang, L.I., He, Q.Q., Zhou, P., Yue, T.: Identification of hub subnetwork based on topological features of genes in breast cancer. Int. J. Mol. Med. **35**(3), 664–674 (2015). https://doi.org/10.3892/ijmm.2014.2057
19. Azodi, M.Z., Tavirani, M.R., Tavirani, M.R., Vafaee, R., Rostami-Nejad, M.: Nasopharyngeal carcinoma protein interaction mapping analysis via proteomic approaches. Asian Pac. J. Cancer Prev. **19**(3), 845–851 (2017). https://doi.org/10.22034/APJCP.2018.19.3.845
20. Wang, R.S., Oldham, W.M., Loscalzo, J.: Network-based association of hypoxia-responsive genes with cardiovascular diseases. New J. Phys. **16**(10), 105014 (2014). https://doi.org/10.1088/1367-2630/16/10/105014
21. Huang, X., Liu, G., Guo, J., Su, Z.Q.: The PI3K/AKT pathway in obesity and type 2 diabetes. Int. J. Biol. Sci. **14**(11), 1483–1496 (2018). https://doi.org/10.7150/ijbs.27173
22. Malemud, C.J.: The PI3K/Akt/PTEN/mTOR pathway: a fruitful target for inducing cell death in rheumatoid arthritis? Future Med. Chem. **7**(9), 1137–1147 (2015). https://doi.org/10.4155/fmc.15.55
23. Hunter, P.: The inflammation theory of disease. EMBO Rep. **13**(11), 968–970 (2012). https://doi.org/10.1038/embor.2012.142
24. Öncül, O., Top, C., Özkan, S., Cavuşlu, Ş., Danaci, M.: Serum interleukin 2 levels in patients with rheumatoid arthritis and correlation with insulin sensitivity. J. Int. Med. Res. **30**(4), 386–390 (2002). https://doi.org/10.1177/147323000203000404
25. Bokarewa, M., Nagaev, I., Dahlberg, L., Smith, U., Tarkowski, A.: Resistin, an adipokine with potent proinflammatory properties. J. Immunol. **174**(9), 5789–5795 (2005). https://doi.org/10.4049/jimmunol.174.9.5789
26. Schultz, O., et al.: Effects of inhibition of interleukin-6 signalling on insulin sensitivity and lipoprotein (A) levels in human subjects with rheumatoid diseases. PLoS ONE **5**(12), e14328 (2010). https://doi.org/10.1371/journal.pone.0014328
27. Ueda, S., Kitazawa, S., Ishida, K., Nishikawa, Y., Matsui, M., Matsumoto, H., et al.: Crucial role of the small GTPase Rac1 in insulin-stimulated translocation of glucose transporter 4 to the mouse skeletal muscle sarcolemma. FASEB J. **24**(7), 2254–2261 (2010)
28. Asahara, S., Shibutani, Y., Teruyama, K., Inoue, H.Y., Kawada, Y., Etoh, H., et al.: Ras-related C3 botulinum toxin substrate 1 (RAC1) regulates glucose-stimulated insulin secretion via modulation of F-actin. Diabetologia **56**(5), 1088–1097 (2013). https://doi.org/10.1007/s00125-013-2849-5
29. Kowluru, A.: Friendly, and not so friendly, roles of Rac1 in islet β-cell function: lessons learnt from pharmacological and molecular biological approaches. Biochem. Pharmacol. **81**(8), 965–975 (2011). https://doi.org/10.1016/j.bcp.2011.01.013

30. Newsholme, P., et al.: Insights into the critical role of NADPH oxidase(s) in the normal and dysregulated pancreatic beta cell. Diabetologia **52**(12), 2489–2498 (2009). https://doi.org/10.1007/s00125-009-1536-z
31. Lv, Z., Hu, M., Zhen, J., Lin, J., Wang, Q., Wang, R.: Rac1/PAK1 signaling promotes epithelial-mesenchymal transition of podocytes in vitro via triggering β-catenin transcriptional activity under high glucose conditions. Int. J. Biochem. Cell Biol. **45**(2), 255–264 (2013). https://doi.org/10.1016/j.biocel.2012.11.00332
32. Dolgin, E.: The most popular genes in the human genome. Nature **551**(7681), 427–431 (2017). https://doi.org/10.1038/d41586-017-07291-9

Variant Analysis from Bacterial Isolates Affirms DnaK Crucial for Multidrug Resistance

Shama Mujawar, Amr Adel Ahmed Abd El-Aal, and Chandrajit Lahiri(✉)

Sunway University, 47500 Petaling Jaya, Selangor, Malaysia
chandrajitl@sunway.edu.my

Abstract. Next-generation sequencing and associated computational analyses have become powerful tools for comparing the whole genomes and detecting the single nucleotide polymorphisms (SNPs) within the genes. In our study, we have identified specific mutations within the plausible drug resistant genes of eight multidrug resistant (MDR) bacterial species. Essentially, we have unearthed few proteins, involved in folding and enabling survival under stress, to be the most crucial ones from the network of the whole genome protein interactome (PIN) of these species. To confirm the relevance of these proteins to antibiotic resistance, variant analyses were performed on all the selected MDR species, isolated from patients' samples in PATRIC database, against their respective reference genomes. The SNPs found in the patient isolates revealed the nucleotide changes from C to A on DnaK, thereby altering a single amino acid change that might lead to misfolding of proteins. Thus, we propose DnaK to be the best characterized bacterial chaperone having implications in multidrug resistance. To this end, to provide an alternative solution to tackle MDR, docking studies were performed with a phenaleno-furanone derivative which revealed the highest binding energy and inhibition against DnaK.

Keywords: Multidrug resistance · SNP analysis · Whole genome sequence

1 Introduction

Multidrug-resistant pathogens complicate the infection control and lead to the significant morbidity and mortality worldwide [1–3]. Today, many health organizations recognize MDR infections as a multidimensional global challenge [4–6]. This complicated issue needs an extensive solution [7]. It was suggested that there should be efficient problem-solving strategies such as: (i) Identification and monitoring of infectious agents, (ii) Tracking resistance to antibiotics, (iii) Development of new antimicrobials, (iv) Providing a rational anti-microbial management program in healthcare organizations to prevent inappropriate or excessive use of antibiotics and (v) Developing unified tools and norms for effective global data management [7–9].

The increasing incidence of bacterial resistance in hospitals and communities to a wide range of antibacterial drugs is today a major public health threat and a compelling

I. Rojas et al. (Eds.): IWBBIO 2020, LNBI 12108, pp. 237–248, 2020.
https://doi.org/10.1007/978-3-030-45385-5_22

reason for the application of whole genome sequencing (WGS). WGS can be used in many ways to treat infectious diseases of MDR bacteria. WGS can be used as a primary tool for detection of multidrug sensitivity, evolution and transmission dynamics of MDR pathogens, diagnosis and control of MDR infections, monitoring MDR, discovering novel antibacterial drugs and therapeutics and analysis of their preventability.

Microbial species namely *S.* Typhimurium, *A. baumannii, E. coli, S. aureus, S. pneumoniae, P. aeruginosa and P. mirabilis* are known to be most virulent in causing acute and chronic infections in human community. These bacteria can flourish at low densities between 4 °C to 42 °C and have interactions with eukaryotic hosts [10, 11]. The interactions result in severe pathological conditions such as pneumonia, bacteremia, urinary tract infections and fatal diarrhea [12]. These bacterial species are intrinsically prevalent and shows resistance to many antibiotics.

NGS technology is becoming popular for analyzing omics data generated from genome, proteome and transcriptome sequencing. NGS is a fast and high-performance technique that allows conversion of complex biological data into scientific findings by implementing automated workflows. Using this technique, one-base pair mutations can be identified in the same bacterial species that can replace traditional molecular typing methods for bacterial pathogens [13]. WGS is also epidemiologically associated with the evolution and pathogen biology that provides insights into antibiotic resistance and virulence factors [14]. Identification of SNPs in bacterial genomes plays an important role in determining the connection between patient samples resistant to antibiotics and their evolutionary counterparts [15, 16].

The bioinformatics tools and genomic information has made it possible to distinguish the molecular pathways responsible for the diversity caused by MDR. For example, the other retrospective studies identified the exact unique genetic single nucleotide variations (SNVs) in the primary genetic factors associated with the epidemic infection in *P. aeruginosa* [17]. The increased resistance of emerging MDR *P. aeruginosa* to antibiotics was described by SNPs enrichment of the efflux pumps that effectively transports the toxic compound out of the bacterial cell to prevent contact with the target site [18, 19]. Revealed SNPs and SNVs may potentially be used as a molecular clock to predict new or potentially emerging/re-emerging strains of outbreak, proper tracking, alert system, and targeted infection control of pathogenic bacteria. Any genetic variations that alter the function of chromosome encoded genes and/or plasmid-resistant genes, collectively contribute to antibiotic-resistant mechanisms [20]. Current epidemiological typing methods such as pulsed-field gel electrophoresis (PFGE) and variable-number tandem repeat (VNTR) have facilitated the detection of these outbreak strains in hospital settings [21, 22]. These systems, however, have limited resolution, cost and complex workflow enabling batch mode typing in reference laboratories that impacts the attempts to sequencing in real-time. Furthermore, traditional typing techniques lack insights into the evolutionary significance of pathogens [23]. Multilocus sequence typing (MLST) has also been recorded as an efficient genotyping technique to detect specific genes in infected patient samples [24].

Besides conventional methods, the WGS approach would help in analyzing the most indispensable role players involved in different mechanisms that could be the cause of MDR across all species. This can be determined by analyzing the whole genome protein interaction network (GPIN) of all the selected species. Ideally, a determination of the number of interacting partners of a specific protein defines its degree centrality (DC), which correlates with its vital nature in the biological scenario [25]. However, in the global network of all proteins, a much deeper understanding of the vital nature of a specific protein arises from evaluating its interaction with other partners. In this study, we have discussed the relevance of other centrality measures for the genes and proteins involved in whole genome of aforementioned pathogenic strains [26]. This led us to conduct a deep probing of the whole genome analysis (WGA) of each species to identify the important proteins according to the degree centralities and compare with all other strains, to confirm the target protein.

In this study, we have examined genetic variations of selected strains of bacterial species within the antibiotic-resistant and susceptible patient samples, collected from PATRIC database restricted only to Malaysia. These SNPs found in bacterial resistant samples may potentially alter the sequence of amino acids and may influence the functional stability of the resulting protein expression. The sole objective of this study is to utilize whole genome-based approach to analyze and identify crucial role players of virulent strains and thus, to identify the SNPs in these identified protein candidates to propose their importance as potential drug targets.

2 Methods and Materials

2.1 Data Collection

2.1.1 Protein and Gene Sequences

The sequences of the 16S rDNA, genes and proteins, used in this study have been retrieved from NCBI genome and gene databases [27] and UniProt database [28], respectively. The genes and proteins are for the antibiotic resistance targets, anticipated to be involved in MDR, across all species and include chaperone proteins, multidrug efflux proteins and two-component signal transduction proteins (Table 1).

2.1.2 Bacterial Sequences from Infected Patients

The bacterial whole genome sequences, from the infected patient samples, were accessed from the PATRIC database (Pathosystems Resource Integration Center), that serves as the platform to provide integrated data and analysis tools to support biomedical research on bacterial infectious diseases [29]. In total, 30 genome samples, for each bacterial strain, restricted to Malaysian patients, were utilized for the further next generation sequencing data analysis.

2.1.3 Reference Genomes Protein Interaction Datasets

The interaction datasets of the curated reference genomes of the bacterial strains, used in this study, have been retrieved from STRING 10.5 (Functional protein association network) biological meta-database [30] with the default medium confidence of 0.4 and 50 interactors, where the interactors relate to the protein interactions present in the vicinity of the query (period of access: January to February 2019). These bacterial strains are known to be involved in MDR, such as *Salmonella Typhimurium* strain LT2/ATCC 700720, *Acinetobacter baumannii* AYE/ATCC 19606, *Escherichia coli* strain O157:H7, *Pseudomonas aeruginosa* strain PAO1/ATCC 15692, *Mycobacterium tuberculosis* strain H37Rv, *Staphylococcus aureus* strain ATCC 35556, *Streptococcus pneumoniae* ATCC BAA-255/R6, and *Proteus mirabilis* strain HI4320.

Table 1. Proteins, with their functions, used in this study

Protein	Name	Function
SicA	*Salmonella* invasion chaperone	Chaperone
DnaK	Heat shock protein 70	
SigE	Sigma factor SigE	
AcrA	Acridine resistance protein A	Efflux pump
AcrB	Acridine resistance protein B	
AcrD	Acriflavine resistance protein D	
MdtA	Multidrug transporter MdtA	MdtABC tripartite complex which is an RND-type drug exporter
MdtB	Multidrug transporter MdtB	
MdtC	Multidrug transporter MdtC	
OmpR	Transcriptional regulatory protein OmpR	Two- component system (TCS) signal transduction proteins
EnvZ	Osmolarity sensor protein EnvZ	
BaeS	Histidine kinase	TCS proteins related to MDR
BaeR	Response regulator	

2.2 Network Analyses

The constructed genome protein interaction network (GPIN) of all bacterial species mentioned above, were subsequently analyzed individually through the four common centrality measures applied to biological networks, namely EC, BC, DC and CC, as mentioned in approach 2 and 3 [31, 32]. This was done via Cytoscape [33] integrated java plugin CytoNCA [34]. The combined scores obtained from various parameters in STRING were taken as edge weights for calculating CytoNCA scores. The combined scores, varying from 0 to 1, were considered for reporting interactions in STRING to identify common proteins from each centrality measure. Further, these top 10 proteins were taken for drawing Venn diagrams through the online tool Venny 2.1 [35].

2.3 Phylogenetic Tree Reconstruction

The retrieved gene sequenced were further used to study its evolutionary relationship across the species. The Molecular Evolutionary Genetics Analysis (MEGA-X) software, is an integrated platform used for genome analysis of molecular sequences to evaluate the evolutionary distances for phylogeny reconstruction [36]. A maximum likelihood phylogenetic tree, for each of the proteins used in this study, was generated using the Jones, Taylor, and Thornton (JTT) model of nucleotide substitution. For each method, 100 iterations were performed to provide support for nodes on the tree.

2.4 Next Generation Sequencing Data Analysis

In order to identify genetic differences at the genome level, the aligned read sequences obtained from the infected patient samples for each bacterial strain were mapped on to their respective reference genome using an inbuilt application in Geneious Prime 2.0 licensed software [37]. This software uses following steps such as assembling chromatograms, de-novo assembly and mapping and SNP Calling. High- confidence data sets of SNP variants were produced by applying a series of filters. These identified SNPs were further annotated using this software to relate their impact to the genes that could be responsible for MDR.

2.5 Candidate Protein and Ligand Docking

The network analysis has revealed the top 10 interactors across all the bacterial strains. Molecular docking studies were performed for each of these proteins against XR770 [38]. The approximate binding affinities of the ligands were analyzed by molecular docking software AutoDock V4.2.6 [39]. The utilized docking protocol comprised 35 autonomous iterations per ligand and the dock results were recorded in kcal/mol. Docking studies were performed on the validated candidate protein against proposed molecule, XR770.

3 Results

3.1 Phylogenetic Analysis

Phylogenetic analysis was performed for all the genes listed in Table 1. These genes were analyzed for their clade matches across the species. These matches were identified while analyzing for the occurrence of horizontal gene transfer (HGT) events. According to the method of identifying sequence similarities to consider them in the same clade, BLAST (Basic local alignment search tool) [40] was performed that resulted in the highest scores. Therefore, the phylogenetic tree of the genes *dnaK, acrA, sicA* matches the clades as that of 16S rDNA tree. Whereas, the other genes *acrB, acrD, sigE, ompR, envZ, baeS, baeR, mdtA, mdtb* and *mdtC* did not reflect the same clades as the nearest hit to 16SrDNA tree. Therefore, to substantiate the probable event of HGT occurring in these genes, the transposable components (TEs) were also attempted to be detected in the genome of each strain of bacteria. No transposons, however, could be identified in the nearest vicinity of the respective genes (Fig. 1).

3.2 Network Analyses

The network analysis of the MDR bacterial strains has revealed 99287 interactions in *S.* Typhimurium, 575584 in *A. baumannii*, 481805 in *E. coli*, 15692 in *P. aeruginosa*, 419974 in *M. tuberculosis*, 35556 in *S. aureus*, 373153 in *S. pneumoniae* and 529507 in *P. mirabilis*. These interactions were filtered by highest centrality scores of EC, BC, CC and DC. This has resulted in top 10 interactors to be the most important ones. Among them, DnaK was observed to be present in 10 interactors of each bacterial strain, except P. aeruginosa. Many of the protein names, categorized as NA (Not available), were all reported as theoretical ones in UniProt database. Also, Cluster of Orthologous Groups (COG) analysis was done to identify similar groups of proteins having related functions. For the proteins categorized as NA, the COG analysis was not reported.

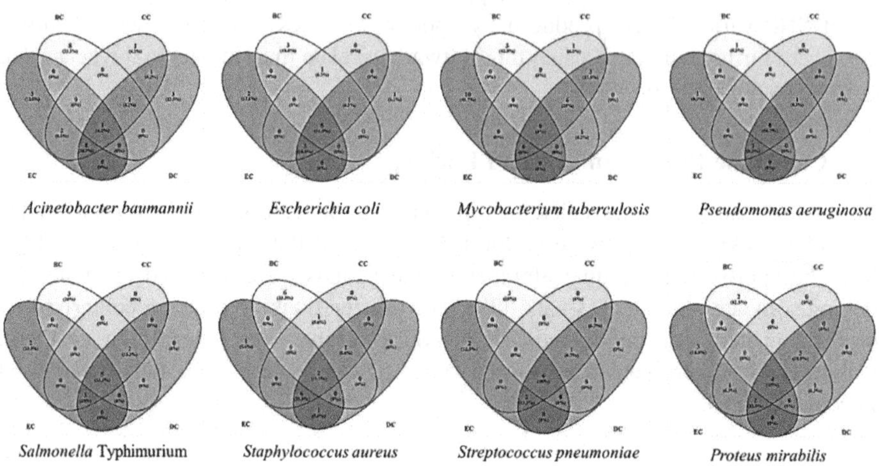

Fig. 1. Venn diagram representation for the top ten rankers of parametric analyses of individual GPIN of each species

3.3 Genomic Polymorphism

We have focused our analysis on identifying SNPs within the functional gene sequences that might result in amino acid changes. We have initially screened the SNPs from the sequences of MDR bacterial samples for infected patients against their reference genome. The number of SNPs identified in each sample, when compared to their reference genomes were 70 for *S.* Typhimurium, 8 for *baumannii*, 18 for *P. aeruginosa*, 29 for *S. aureus*, 14 for *P. mirabilis* could be plausibly be involved in different drug resistance mechanisms. Each bacterium represented DnaK protein to be the most indispensable and thus, the SNP change from C to A at position 723401 in *S.* Typhimurium lead to its amino acid change. Thus, the rigid structure of proline found in the close proximity of amino acid change can lead to misfolding of the target sites controlled by its chaperone activity. However, Table 2 showed the representative SNPs for each species with C to A at position 723401 for *S.* Typhimurium, T to G at position 758342 for *A. baumannii*, T to A at position 113303 for *P. aeruginosa*, T to A at position 747288 for *S. aureus* and T to A at position 535499 for *P. mirabilis*. These SNPs are mostly found in hypothetical proteins when mapped onto their reference genomes. Thus, each of these SNP sites, might be worth exploring to identify its relatedness to be involved in MDR.

Table 2. SNP prediction of each bacterial species

Species	SNP	Position	Genes
S. Typhimurium	C to A	723401	*dnaK*
A. baumannii	T to A	758342	*dnaK*
P. aeruginosa	T to A	113303	*guaB*
S. aureus	T to A	747288	*groL*
P. mirabilis	T to A	535499	*gltB*

3.4 Docking Analysis

Docking analysis was performed against the hypothesized molecule XR770 for the proteins *viz.* DnaK, GltB, GroL, RecA, GuaB, RecA, PhnB as revealed from network analysis. The docking results were evaluated based on the ranked conformations of compound with highest binding energy values as shown in Table 3. High affinity is associated with release of free energy upon binding. The inhibition pattern of XR770 against the list of marketed drugs were compared for their efficiency against other selected proteins efflux pump proteins i.e. AcrA, AcrB, AcrD, MdtA, MdtB and MdtC, two- component system signal transduction proteins i.e. OmpR, EnvZ, BaeS, BaeR and chaperone proteins i.e. SicA, DnaK and SigE. Based on the binding pattern of the aforementioned proteins, DnaK showed Thr11 and Gly197 as the most consistent residue for all the drugs with the highest binding energy being −10.11 kcal/mol in *S.* Typhimurium against XR770. It is to be noted that, the SNP that has led to the amino acid change, also falls under the same active site wherein the XR770 has bound. Importantly, XR770 also showed the relatively highest binding energy for DnaK in *A. baumannii* with −9.98 kcal/mol, and was the strongest binding affinity amongst all the proteins compared. Moreover, other proteins viz. GltB, GroL, RecA, GuaB, RecA and PhnB, showed consensus interaction pattern with efficient binding energies against XR770.

Table 3. Probable candidates inferred from genome network analysis across each species

Species	Candidate protein	Protein name	Binding energy (kcal/mol)
Salmonella Typhimurium	Q56073	**DnaK**	−10.11
Acinetobacter baumannii	V5VIH3	**DnaK**	−9.98
Proteus mirabilis	B4EXM7	GltB	−9.27
Staphylococcus aureus	Q5HEH2	GroL	−8.5
Escherichia coli	C3SY12	RecA	−9.03
Pseudomonas aeruginosa	Q9HXM5	GuaB	−9.36
Streptococcus pneumoniae	Q04IM6	RecA	−8.01
Mycobacterium tuberculosis	P9WI81	PhnB	−9.5

4 Discussion

Next generation sequencing promises insights into the repertoire of genetic polymorphism. This method can be used to evaluate the SNPs by altering a single amino acid. Herein, using comparative genomics on sequences generated by high- throughput sequencing technology, we have explored the genetic variation on the reported resistant genes in infected patients' samples. Based on their antibiotic resistant profiles, the samples included in this research were selected, that showed highest statistics for its occurrence by Centers for Disease Control and Prevention (CDC), 2017. In order to study the genomic variation between these samples with different characteristics of antibiotic resistance, we have analyzed their whole genome sequences and compared the data with the respective reference genome of the individual species of bacteria.

Several SNPs have been identified that might play a significant role in antibiotic resistance, with ideas to improve our present knowledge of the factors influencing the hospital based antibiotic resistance system. In this study, we initially performed the network analyses of each bacterial strain, known to be involved in MDR. This has revealed the top ten crucial proteins, wherein, DnaK is present in each of the ten rankers of individual species, except *P. aeruginosa*, which indicate the importance of the expression of *dnaK* in the continuous emergence of MDR intracellular pathogens. DnaK, being a chaperone protein, assists in the proper folding and refolding of proteins, prevents aggregation and mediates the degradation of misfolded proteins. Essentially, DnaK helps to resist the hostile environment including elevated temperature or/and antibiotic treatments [41]. Further, to see the evolutionary relatedness of each species, the 16S rDNA tree was constructed which showed that the few genes of the bacterial strains have co-evolved with the species.

Besides DnaK, other proteins revealed from SNP analysis viz. GltB, GroL, RecA, GuaB, RecA, PhnB were further considered for molecular docking studies. DnaK showed the highest binding energy for *S. Typhimurium* and *A. baumannii*. Several mechanisms such as alteration of porins, enzymatic modification of drugs and chromosomal mutations within regulatory genes were reported to be involved in antibiotic resistance [17, 42–45]. Again, efflux proteins contribute to aminoglycoside resistance and other regulatory proteins are known to impart resistance to aminoglycosides, β-lactams and fluoroquinolone [46]. Moreover, it has been revealed that any alterations in the *dnaK* gene reduce the growth of bacteria within the host [47]. On the other hand, it has been showed in many other studies that *dnaK* expression is drastically elevated in intracellular pathogenic bacteria such as *S. enterica* serovar Typhimurium, *Yersinia enterocolitica*, *Legionella pneumophila* and *Brucella abortus* growing within macrophage phagosomes after phagocytosis, where bacteria are threatened by oxidative or non-oxidative bactericidal mechanisms [48]. Thus, this phenomenon gives an insight into the essential regulatory mechanism of Hsp70 like Dnak and its role in controlling protein activity that contributes to its virulence and antibiotic resistance. Collectively, to attain multidrug antibiotic resistance, different species may use a combination of all these mechanisms.

To our knowledge, DnaK chaperone protein can be considered as a promising target for antibiotic therapies as it has been characterized in several pathogenic bacteria and due to its important roles not only in stress resistance and pathogenicity of continuously emerging MDR strains but also in many cellular processes, such as DNA replication of the bacterial chromosome, RNA synthesis, protein transport, cell division, and autoregulation of the heat shock response [49].

Drug resistance to multiple antibiotics may be due to a combination of mutations resulting in overexpression of different multi-drug efflux pumps, altered enzyme expression and structural elements engaged in the stabilization of mutations affecting aminoglycoside phosphotransferases and mutations influencing gyrase activity. In our research work, the genomic assessment of drug-resistant infected patient samples had mutations in at least one gene known to participate in antibiotic resistance. These are for instance, *pknA, pknB, amiC, ospR, dnaK, recA, rpoB* and *baeS*. The genes that carry these mutations, code for proteins that are involved in the permeability of the outer membrane, gyrases and enzyme-modifying drugs and multidrug pump. However, a limitation of this study is that the reported SNPs, containing the resistant genes, require further targeted evidence with site-driven genome analysis. Such analysis of the antibiotic resistant mechanism will provide future insights into the overall phenotype alteration and synergistic effect of these SNPs.

Through WGS and comparative genomic analysis of various bacterial infected patient samples, we have shown that even though all the samples on genetic background were distinct and the strains were diverse at the genomic level, it has still revealed the same chaperone system to be an important mechanism to explore as the effective drug targets. These strains revealed significant differences in their indel and SNP compositions, potentially correlated with antibiotic resistance. Further in-depth research is required on these variations and their associations with mechanisms of antibiotic resistance.

5 Conclusion

In conclusion, this study reveals the potential of high-throughput genome sequencing to compare the genetic variants between archived infected patient samples. Also, we have reported some important SNPs that may be the key role players in modifying resistant genes in bacteria leading to its genomic polymorphism. This should form the basis of our future research to study the spread and prevalence of such antibacterial resistance in developing countries. This technology can be used to analyze genetic variations and pathogen biology of "high-risk" bacterial species along with their epidemiological studies. Thus, the SNP variation from C to A was observed in *dnaK* gene at position 723401 in *S.* Typhimurium. This variation has also affected the single amino acid, that could mislead the protein function, thereby posing DnaK to be the new therapeutic target.

References

1. Kumar, S., Rizvi, M., Vidhani, S., Sharma, V.K.: Changing face of septicaemia and increasing drug resistance in blood isolates. Indian J. Pathol. Microbiol. **47**(3), 441–446 (2004)

2. Jain, A., Awasthi, A.K., Kumar, M.: Etiological and antimicrobial susceptibility profile of nosocomial blood stream infections in neonatal intensive care unit. Indian J. Med. Microbiol. **25**(3), 299 (2007)
3. Solomon, S.L., Oliver, K.B.: Antibiotic resistance threats in the United States: stepping back from the brink. Am. Fam. Physician **89**(12), 938 (2014)
4. US Department of Health and Human Services: Antibiotic resistance threats in the United States, 2013. Centers for Disease Control and Prevention, pp. 1–113 (2013)
5. World Health Organization: Antimicrobial resistance: global report on surveillance. World Health Organization (2014)
6. Chatterjee, A., et al.: Quantifying drivers of antibiotic resistance in humans: a systematic review. Lancet Infect. Dis. **18**, e368–e378 (2018)
7. Davies, S.C., Fowler, T., Watson, J., Livermore, D.M., Walker, D.: Annual Report of the Chief Medical Officer: infection and the rise of antimicrobial resistance. Lancet **381**(9878), 1606–1609 (2013)
8. Sydnor, E.R., Perl, T.M.: Hospital epidemiology and infection control in acute-care settings. Clin. Microbiol. Rev. **24**(1), 141–173 (2011)
9. World Health Organization: Annual report of the Regional Director for 2010 and progress reports (No. EM/RC58/R. 1) (2011)
10. Grisaru-Soen, G., Lerner-Geva, L., Keller, N., Berger, H., Passwell, J.H., Barzilai, A.: Pseudomonas aeruginosa bacteremia in children: analysis of trends in prevalence, antibiotic resistance and prognostic factors. Pediatr. Infect. Dis. J. **19**(10), 959–963 (2000)
11. Fujitani, S., Sun, H.Y., Victor, L.Y., Weingarten, J.A.: Pneumonia due to Pseudomonas aeruginosa: part I: epidemiology, clinical diagnosis, and source. Chest **139**(4), 909–919 (2011)
12. Snyder, L.A., et al.: Epidemiological investigation of Pseudomonas aeruginosa isolates from a six-year-long hospital outbreak using high-throughput whole genome sequencing. Eurosurveillance **18**(42), 1–9 (2013)
13. Metzker, M.L.: Sequencing technologies—the next generation. Nat. Rev. Genet. **11**(1), 31 (2010)
14. Sabat, A.J., et al.: Overview of molecular typing methods for outbreak detection and epidemiological surveillance. Eurosurveillance **18**(4), 20380 (2013)
15. Octavia, S., Lan, R.: Single-nucleotide-polymorphism typing and genetic relationships of Salmonella enterica serovar Typhi isolates. J. Clin. Microbiol. **45**(11), 3795–3801 (2007)
16. Lewis, T., et al.: High-throughput whole-genome sequencing to dissect the epidemiology of Acinetobacter baumannii isolates from a hospital outbreak. J. Hosp. Infect. **75**(1), 37–41 (2010)
17. Gooderham, W.J., Hancock, R.E.: Regulation of virulence and antibiotic resistance by two-component regulatory systems in Pseudomonas aeruginosa. FEMS Microbiol. Rev. **33**(2), 279–294 (2009)
18. Dettman, J.R., Rodrigue, N., Aaron, S.D., Kassen, R.: Evolutionary genomics of epidemic and nonepidemic strains of Pseudomonas aeruginosa. Proc. Natl. Acad. Sci. **110**(52), 21065–21070 (2013)
19. Jeukens, J., et al.: Comparative genomics of isolates of a Pseudomonas aeruginosa epidemic strain associated with chronic lung infections of cystic fibrosis patients. PLoS ONE **9**(2), e87611 (2014)
20. Lister, P.D., Wolter, D.J., Hanson, N.D.: Antibacterial-resistant Pseudomonas aeruginosa: clinical impact and complex regulation of chromosomally encoded resistance mechanisms. Clin. Microbiol. Rev. **22**(4), 582–610 (2009)

21. Turton, J.F., Turton, S.E., Yearwood, L., Yarde, S., Kaufmann, M.E., Pitt, T.L.: Evaluation of a nine-locus variable-number tandem-repeat scheme for typing of Pseudomonas aeruginosa. Clin. Microbiol. Infect. **16**(8), 1111–1116 (2010)
22. Robinson, E.R., Walker, T.M., Pallen, M.J.: Genomics and outbreak investigation: from sequence to consequence. Genome Med. **5**(4), 36 (2013)
23. Aguilar-Rodea, P., et al.: Identification of extensive drug resistant Pseudomonas aeruginosa strains: new clone ST1725 and high-risk clone ST233. PLoS ONE **12**(3), e0172882 (2017)
24. Martin, K., et al.: Clusters of genetically similar isolates of Pseudomonas aeruginosa from multiple hospitals in the UK. J. Med. Microbiol. **62**(7), 988–1000 (2013)
25. Jeong, H., Mason, S.P., Barabási, A.L., Oltvai, Z.N.: Lethality and centrality in protein networks. Nature **411**(6833), 41 (2001)
26. Mujawar, S., Mishra, R., Pawar, S., Gatherer, D., Lahiri, C.: Delineating the plausible molecular vaccine candidates and drug targets of multidrug-resistant acinetobacter baumannii. Front. Cell. Infect. Microbiol. **9**, 203 (2019)
27. Maglott, D., Ostell, J., Pruitt, K.D., Tatusova, T.: Entrez Gene: gene-centered information at NCBI. Nucleic Acids Res. **33**(suppl_1), D54–D58 (2005)
28. UniProt Consortium: UniProt: a hub for protein information. Nucleic Acids Res. **43**(D1), D204–D212 (2014)
29. Wattam, A.R., et al.: PATRIC, the bacterial bioinformatics database and analysis resource. Nucleic Acids Res. **42**(D1), D581–D591 (2013)
30. Szklarczyk, D., et al.: The STRING database in 2017: quality-controlled protein–protein association networks, made broadly accessible. Nucleic Acids Res. **45**, D362–D368 (2016). https://doi.org/10.1093/nar/gkw937
31. Ozgur, A., Vu, T., Erkan, G., Radev, D.R.: Identifying gene-disease associations using centrality on a literature mined gene-interaction network. Bioinformatics **24**(13), i277–i285 (2008)
32. Pavlopoulos, G.A., et al.: Using graph theory to 221ytosca biological networks. BioData Min. **4**(1), 10 (2011)
33. Cline, M.S., et al.: Integration of biological networks and gene expression data using Cytoscape. Nat. Protoc. **2**(10), 2366 (2007)
34. Tang, Y., Li, M., Wang, J., Pan, Y., Wu, F.X.: CytoNCA: a cytoscape plugin for centrality analysis and evaluation of protein interaction networks. Biosystems **127**, 67–72 (2015)
35. Oliveros, J.C.: Venny 2.1.0. An interactive tool for comparing lists with Venn's diagrams. BioinfoGP of CNB-CSIC (2015)
36. Kumar, S., Nei, M., Dudley, J., Tamura, K.: MEGA: a biologist-centric software for evolutionary analysis of DNA and protein sequences. Brief. Bioinform. **9**(4), 299–306 (2008)
37. Kearse, M., et al.: Geneious Basic: an integrated and extendable desktop software platform for the organization and analysis of sequence data. Bioinformatics **28**(12), 1647–1649 (2012)
38. Kitchen, D.B., Decornez, H., Furr, J.R., Bajorath, J.: Docking and scoring in virtual screening for drug discovery: methods and applications. Nat. Rev. Drug Discovery **3**(11), 935 (2004)
39. Trott, O., Olson, A.J.: AutoDock Vina: improving the speed and accuracy of docking with a new scoring function, efficient optimization, and multithreading. J. Comput. Chem. **31**(2), 455–461 (2010)
40. Altschul, S.F., et al.: Gapped BLAST and PSI-BLAST: a new generation of protein database search programs. Nucleic Acids Res. **25**(17), 3389–3402 (1997)

41. Bertelsen, E.B., Chang, L., Gestwicki, J.E., Zuiderweg, E.R.: Solution conformation of wild-type *E.coli* Hsp70 (DnaK) chaperone complexed with ADP and substrate. Proc. Natl. Acad. Sci. **106**(21), 8471–8476 (2009)
42. Poole, K.: Efflux-mediated antimicrobial resistance. J. Antimicrob. Chemother. **56**(1), 20–51 (2005)
43. Alekshun, M.N., Levy, S.B.: Molecular mechanisms of antibacterial multidrug resistance. Cell **128**(6), 1037–1050 (2007)
44. Hocquet, D., et al.: MexXY-OprM efflux pump is necessary for adaptive resistance of Pseudomonas aeruginosa to aminoglycosides. Antimicrob. Agents Chemother. **47**(4), 1371–1375 (2003)
45. Vogne, C., Aires, J.R., Bailly, C., Hocquet, D., Plésiat, P.: Role of the multidrug efflux system MexXY in the emergence of moderate resistance to aminoglycosides among Pseudomonas aeruginosa isolates from patients with cystic fibrosis. Antimicrob. Agents Chemother. **48**(5), 1676–1680 (2004)
46. Garneau-Tsodikova, S., Labby, K.J.: Mechanisms of resistance to aminoglycoside antibiotics: overview and perspectives. MedChemComm **7**(1), 11–27 (2016)
47. Arita-Morioka, K.I., Yamanaka, K., Mizunoe, Y., Ogura, T., Sugimoto, S.: Novel strategy for biofilm inhibition by using small molecules targeting molecular chaperone DnaK. Antimicrob. Agents Chemother. **59**(1), 633–641 (2015)
48. Takaya, A., Tomoyasu, T., Matsui, H., Yamamoto, T.: The DnaK/DnaJ chaperone machinery of Salmonella enterica serovar Typhimurium is essential for invasion of epithelial cells and survival within macrophages, leading to systemic infection. Infect. Immun. **72**(3), 1364–1373 (2004)
49. Lin, J., Ficht, T.A.: Protein synthesis in *Brucella abortus* induced during macrophage infection. Infect. Immun. **63**(4), 1409–1414 (1995)

Topological Analysis of Cancer Protein Subnetwork in Deubiquitinase (DUB) Interactome

Nurulisa Zulkifle(✉)

Cluster for Oncological and Radiological Sciences,
Advanced Medical and Dental Institute, Universiti Sains Malaysia,
13200 Bertam, Penang, Malaysia
nurulisa@usm.my

Abstract. Ubiquitination pathway regulates many cellular events that underlie the development of various cancer types. This led to tremendous interest in exploration of cancer therapeutics potential among the ubiquitination components, the E1, E2, E3 and deubiquitinase (DUB). Approximately 101 DUBs are encoded in human cell and often, studies on the DUBs were performed individually. Therefore, this study is conducted to observe the peculiarities of cancer protein subnetwork within DUB interactome, aiming to increase understanding on the relationship between DUBs and cancer from system biology point of view. To construct the DUB interactome, proteins associated with DUBs were extracted from IMEx consortium database and the interaction network were visualized in Cytoscape. Cancer protein nodes were identified according to the list from COSMIC Cancer Gene Census database and were extracted to form a subnetwork of 247 nodes and 326 edges. Some DUBs such as BAP1, TNFAIP3, USP6, CYLD and USP44 are observed to be the cancer proteins themselves and 78 DUBs have direct association with cancer related proteins. Topological analysis by NetworkAnalyzer and CentiScaPe suggested that OTUB1, COPS5 and USP7 have the strongest characteristics, indicating that these DUBs must have important roles in cancer-related pathways. Comparison with essential protein subnetwork suggested that the cancer protein subnetwork tends to have weaker clustering coefficient, lower betweenness centrality and higher closeness centrality. Overall, it could be said that the topological analysis of cancer protein subnetwork in DUB interactome interpreted from this study helps to provide a deeper understanding on the biological significance of DUBs in cancer.

Keywords: DUB · Cancer · Protein interaction network · Network topology

1 Introduction

Protein-protein interaction (PPI) plays a fundamental role in all biological processes and provides a framework for understanding cells function and behavior [1]. Perturbation in PPI network is believed to be the cause of many diseases such as cancers, neurodegenerative disorders and infectious diseases [2]. Therefore, understanding PPI network is very useful not only for comprehending the diverse biological processes but

I. Rojas et al. (Eds.): IWBBIO 2020, LNBI 12108, pp. 249–260, 2020.
https://doi.org/10.1007/978-3-030-45385-5_23

also for elucidating the molecular mechanisms of diseases and subsequently, identifying potential targets for therapeutic interventions [2–4].

Ubiquitination is a sophisticated protein post-translational modification process that mediates diverse functions in cellular pathways and biological processes, ranging from protein degradation, DNA repair, protein trafficking and so forth [5]. The canonical ubiquitination process involves the addition of ubiquitin molecule(s) to a target protein by enzymatic machinery comprising of E1 ubiquitin-activating enzyme, E2 ubiquitin-conjugating enzyme and E3 ubiquitin protein ligase that work in hierarchical manner [5, 6]. This process is reversible by the action of deubiquitinating enzymes (DUBs), a group of protein that belong to the superfamily of proteases and function to cleave the isopeptide or peptide bonds within polyubiquitin chain or between ubiquitin and its substrate [6]. Beside removing attached ubiquitin from specific target protein, certain DUBs could also function by preventing ubiquitin attachment to the substrate [7, 8]. Human genome encodes approximately 101 DUBs, categorized into seven families; USP[1], OTU[2], MJD[3], UCH[4], JAMM[5], ZUFSP[6] and MINDY[7] [9–13].

Many DUBs have been found to be associated with cancer [14]. For example, mutated TNFAIP3 gene results in malfunctioned A20 protein that failed to regulate NF-κB pathway. Beside mutation, alteration in DUBs expression level is also correlate with cancer. To name a few, increased expression level of OTUD6B, UCH37, VCPIP1, USP7 and COPS5 are detected in various types of breast cancer while USP6 is found to be overexpressed in primary aneurysmal bone cyst. Interestingly, some DUBs expression is differentially altered depending on the type of cancer. For instance, USP4 mRNA level is elevated in colon and thyroid cancers while its protein level is decreased in lung cancer. Another DUB known as USP2 is upregulated in prostate carcinoma, whereas in colon cancer, USP2 expression is downregulated [14].

Many other research works and reviews have highlight the DUBs' roles in cancer as well as their potential cancer therapeutics value. However, a deeper understanding of the exact role of DUBs in cancer is always difficult since DUBs have multiple substrates and often found in multiprotein complexes. Since it is assumed that these DUBs-associated proteins may regulate DUBs activities, analysis of DUBs protein interaction network could provide a better understanding of DUBs regulatory mechanism. Therefore, this study is conducted with the aim to preliminarily assess the topological characteristics of DUB interactome and its cancer protein subnetwork. The result from this study is expected to be important for comprehensive understanding regarding the relationship between DUBs and cancer in system biology point of view.

[1] Ubiquitin specific protease.

[2] Ovarian tumour protease.

[3] Machado-Josephin domain.

[4] Ubiquitin C-terminal hydrolase.

[5] Jab1/MPN/MOV34 metalloenzyme.

[6] Zinc finger with UFM1 specific peptidase domain.

[7] Motifs interacting with Ub-containing novel DUB family.

2 Methods

2.1 Construction of DUB Interactome

List of DUBs was identified from UniProt[8] database as well as published literatures [9–13] that were obtained from PubMed database using 'deubiquitin' as search query. PPI network was constructed by submitting the list of DUBs as queries in Cytoscape ver3.6.0 [15]. Through Cytoscape plugin PSICQUIC[9] client [16], the DUBs interaction partners were extracted from experimentally derived protein interaction databases IntAct [17], MINT[10] [18] and IMEx[11] consortium [19]. All nodes in the integrated PPI network were filtered to species *Homo sapiens* only. Redundant nodes and edges and self-interactions were removed to obtain a reliable human DUB interactome.

2.2 Extraction of Cancer Protein Subnetwork from DUB Interactome

To generate cancer protein subnetwork, list of cancer related protein with their detailed annotations was obtained from COSMIC[12] Cancer Gene Census database ver90 (downloaded on September 6, 2019) [20]. The list was integrated into the node table of DUB interactome and cancer related nodes were selected based on the annotation information. Meanwhile, nodes representing DUBs protein were all selected regardless of their 'cancer' or 'non-cancer' status. A subnetwork representing cancer protein in DUB interactome were formed by creating new network from all selected nodes.

Meanwhile, list of essential genes was retrieved from OGEE[13] ver2 database (downloaded on December 12, 2019) [21]. In this database, a total of 21,556 genes were tested for essentiality in 18 selected datasets. In our study, only genes that are considered essential in at least four datasets were included. The genes were mapped in the DUB interactome and a subnetwork of essential protein was generated by selecting the essential genes and DUBs nodes to form new network.

2.3 Networks Analysis

Topological analysis of DUB interactome, cancer protein subnetwork and essential protein subnetwork was performed using NetworkAnalyzer, a built-in tool in Cytoscape and CentiScaPe ver2.2 [22, 23]. As centralities are computed for connected networks, the isolated component in the networks were excluded during network analysis to avoid unreliable result. Five topological measures were applied to assess the networks: degree, network diameter and characteristic path length, clustering coefficient, betweenness centrality (BC) and closeness centrality (CC). Meanwhile, to predict

[8] UniProt: UNIversal PROTein (https://www.uniprot.org/uniprot/).

[9] PSICQUIC: Proteomics Standard Initiative Common QUery InterfaCe.

[10] MINT: Molecular INTeraction.

[11] IMEx: International Molecular EXchange.

[12] COSMIC: Catalogue of Somatic Mutations in Cancer (https://cancer.sanger.ac.uk/census).

[13] OGEE: Online GEne Essentiality database (http://ogee.medgenius.info/browse/).

the importance of individual nodes in cancer protein subnetwork, three centrality measures were used: degree, betweenness centrality and closeness centrality.

To test whether the observed cancer protein subnetwork is not random, Network Randomizer ver1.1.3 were applied to generate random network based on Erdős-Rényi model [24]. The average value of degree, clustering coefficient, characteristic path length and betweenness centrality were calculated and compared with cancer protein subnetwork.

3 Result and Discussion

3.1 Datasets

A total of 101 DUBs were retrieved from literature and data mining. A brief analysis on the proteins structure and sequence is performed to predict the protein activity. Several of the proteins (FAM105A, USPL1, USP39, USP50, PAN2, USP53, USP54, MINDY4B and COPS6) are predicted to be inactive due to the lack of necessary catalytic properties. Meanwhile, HIN1L and EIF3FP2 are annotated as pseudogenes hence they are probably not coding any proteins. Some DUBs; namely ALG13, USP9X, USP9Y and MINDY4; are 'putative' or 'probable' proteins, which means their recorded activities are based on prediction. Regardless of their activity status, all DUBs are submitted as queries for construction of DUB interactome.

3.2 The DUB Interactome

The PPI network of 101 DUBs and their immediate neighbors consists of 2328 nodes and 3409 edges (Fig. 1). Analysis on DUBs protein partners reveals that DUBs associated with various types of protein including E2 and E3 enzymes and the preference towards these proteins may not be conferred according to the DUBs family [25].

In network analysis, the simplest topological parameter is the degree or connectivity, which means the number of direct interaction one node has. Nodes with high degree number reflect that they are interacting with many proteins, suggesting a central role. In this network, average degree is 2.939, which means in average every node has approximately three interactors. The top 10 DUBs with the highest connectivity are OTUB1, ZRANB1, USP7, COPS6, COPS5, USP2, USP11, USP15, USP21 and EIF3F while the least connected DUBs are OTUD3, USP41, USP27X, MPND, MINDY1, USP29, USP26, USP37, IFP38 and MINDY4, which have at most three partners only. The worst one is USP51, which is observed without a partner. FAM105A has eight interactors but none of them are connected with any nodes from the core interactome, causing them to be isolated from the network.

The network diameter is 9 and characteristic path length is 4.097. Network diameter corresponding to the maximum shortest path length between two most distance nodes, therefore in this network, the node must go through nine other nodes before reaching its most distant neighbor. Meanwhile, characteristic path length means the average of shortest path length of every possible pairs in the network. Another parameter measured is the clustering coefficient, which calculates the connection among the node's immediate neighbors. Therefore, a high clustering coefficient suggesting a high-density network that is more likely to form a functional module. The clustering coefficient for DUB interactome is 0.090, which is not quite a high number. Meanwhile, the distribution of node degree approximately followed power law fit distribution with value of $R^2 = 0.632$, which is moderately robust and suggested that this network is most probably stable against random small elimination of some nodes. Detail analysis of network robustness under perturbation, most importantly the hub nodes removal or BC-based and CC-based perturbations could be performed to further evaluate the stability of the DUB interactome.

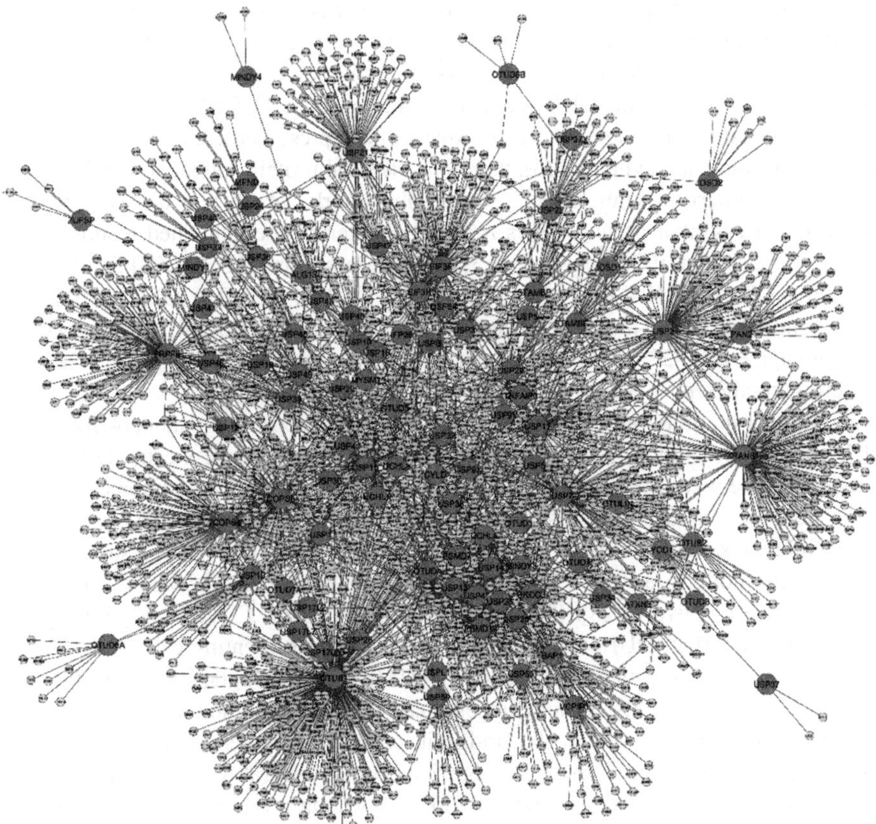

Fig. 1. The DUB protein-protein interaction network (without the isolated components). Red node denotes the DUBs while green node represents the proteins that have direct interaction with the DUBs. (Color figure online)

3.3 Cancer Protein Subnetwork

Figure 2 shows the cancer protein subnetwork with 247 nodes and 326 edges. This subnetwork suggests that approximately 10% of DUBs substrates are cancer-related protein. Some DUBs such as BAP1, TNFAIP3, USP6, CYLD and USP44 are cancer protein themselves. As many as 78 DUBs have direct association with at least one cancer protein. Some of the DUBs (USP18, USP30, USP33, USP41, USPL1, PAN2 and VCPIP1) and their partner(s) are disconnected from the network while some others (USP9Y, USP24, USP37, USP38, USP50, USP51, USP53, USP54, OTUD3, OTUD6A, OTUD6B, YOD1, ALG13, JOSD2, FAM105A, ZUFSP, MINDY1 and MINDY4) are single nodes. Without the isolated components, the average degree of cancer protein subnetwork is 2.977, network diameter is 9, characteristic path length is 4.120 and clustering coefficient is 0.090.

For the purpose of evaluating the characteristics of cancer protein subnetwork, another subnetwork within DUB interactome needs to be generated. Essential genes have been considered non-disease genes due to their presumed role in developmental defects and associated lethality [26], therefore essential protein subnetwork could serve as a good comparison with cancer protein subnetwork, which is a disease network. Extraction of essential protein nodes from DUB interactome generated a subnetwork with 655 nodes and 1025 edges (Fig. 3). There are several DUBs (ZUFSP, USPL1, OTUD6A, OTUB2, MINDY1, MYSM1, USP29, USP51, OTUD3, JOSD1, MINDY4, JOSD2 and FAM105A) that are isolated from the subnetwork. For this subnetwork, the average degree is 3.222, network diameter is 10, characteristic path length is 4.215 and clustering coefficient is 0.172.

To predict the importance of individual nodes in cancer protein subnetwork within DUBs interactome, the degree, betweenness centrality and closeness centrality of each individual node were measured. The node betweenness measures the number of times that a node acts as a bridge along the shortest path between two other nodes [27]. Meanwhile, closeness centrality is defined as the inverse of the average shortest path length of the node to all other nodes and reflects the closeness between a node and other nodes in a network [28]. Result suggests that OTUB1, COPS5 and USP7 could be the most important DUBs while TP53 and JUN are representing cancer proteins as the vital nodes in this subnetwork (Table 1). OTUB1 has the highest number of degree and betweenness centrality, which suggest that this protein communicates with many other proteins and may acts as the bridge in crosstalk between signaling pathways. Cancer protein TP53 and JUN show higher closeness centrality, which indicate that they are closer to most nodes in the network, suggesting a central role.

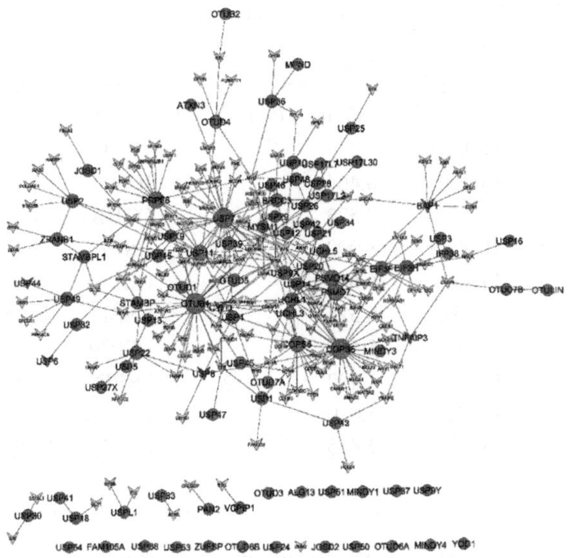

Fig. 2. Cancer protein subnetwork in DUB interactome.

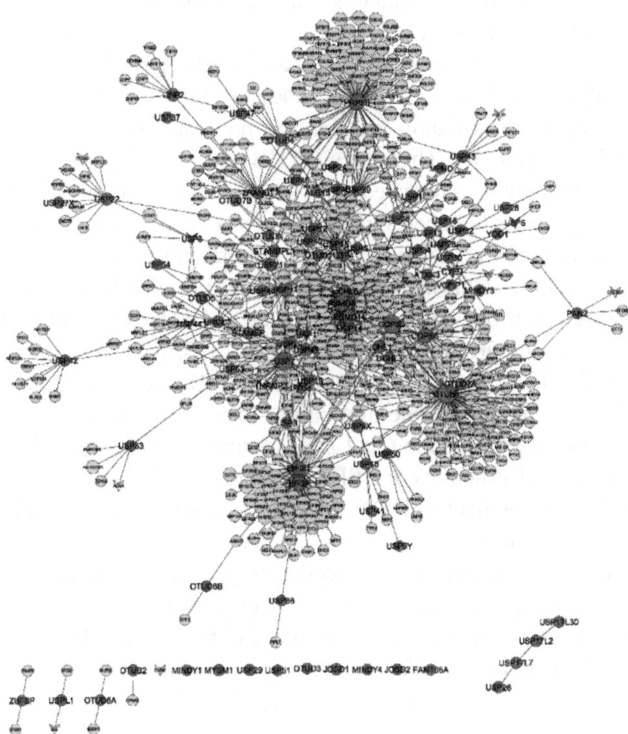

Fig. 3. Essential protein subnetwork in DUB interactome.

Table 1. Top 10 protein in cancer protein subnetwork based on connectivity, betweenness centrality and closeness centrality measures.

Protein	Degree	Protein	Betweenness centrality (10^3)	Protein	Closeness centrality (10^{-3})
OTUB1	31	OTUB1	13.087	TP53	1.730
COPS5	30	COPS5	10.464	JUN	1.724
USP7	28	USP7	9.523	OTUB1	1.692
PSMD7	18	JUN	8.099	USP7	1.658
PRPF8	17	PRPF8	6.661	COPS5	1.642
COPS6	14	TP53	6.326	USP11	1.605
USP11	13	PSMD7	5.507	USP39	1.603
PSMD14	13	USP11	4.422	PRPF8	1.555
TP53	12	BAP1	3.010	USP9X	1.541
JUN	11	MYC	2.815	COPS6	1.517

Figure 4 shows a plot of closeness centrality over betweenness centrality of each node in protein cancer subnetwork within DUB interactome. Proteins such as OTUB1, COPS5, USP7, JUN, TP53, PRPF8, PSMD7 and USP11 shows strong characteristics by having high values for both parameters. Thus, they are more likely to play a crucial regulatory role in the subnetwork.

OTUB1 is an unusually interesting DUBs due its ability to suppress ubiquitination independently of its catalytic activity. It does so by interaction with certain E2 enzymes, thus preventing ubiquitin transfer and non-catalytically inhibiting accumulation of polyubiquitin [29, 30]. The role of OTUB1 in cancer-related pathway has been established as many studies revealed the direct association of OTUB1 with the development of various malignancies including breast cancer, colorectal cancer, gastric adenocarcinoma, lung cancer, ovarian cancer, glioma and prostate cancer [31]. Similarly, COPS5 association with many types of cancer has also been established. Comprehensive studies confirmed that COPS5 lies at the intersection of many signaling pathways involved in tumorigenesis such as HER-2, EGFR, TGF-β, Wnt, NF-κB and PI3K/AKT signaling [32]. Importantly, the role of USP7 in cancer is also well-studied. This USP DUB plays important role in a various cancer-related mechanism including tumor invasion, apoptosis regulation and DNA damage response [33]. Several groups have reported the crystal structures of USP7 in complex with small molecule inhibitors, indicating that the development of USP7 inhibitor for cancer therapy is highly likely to be achieved in near future [33].

Interestingly, ZRANB1 that has the second highest connectivity in DUB interactome is nowhere to be seen in cancer protein subnetwork. In the subnetwork, ZRANB1 has only three cancer protein partners, thus it is predicted that ZRANB1 may not be significantly involved in cancer-related pathway.

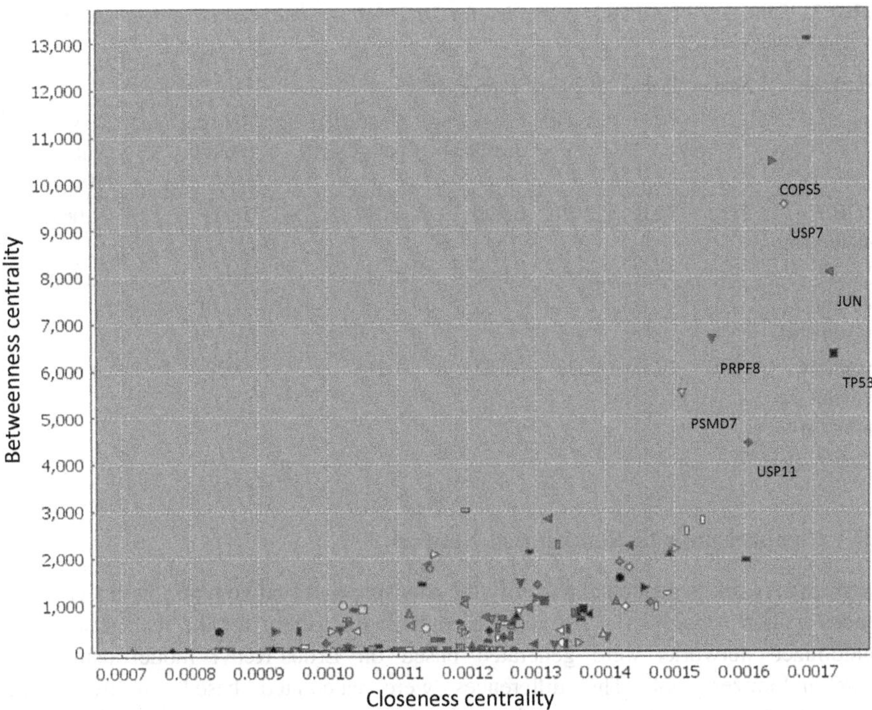

Fig. 4. Plot of closeness centrality over betweenness centrality of each node in protein cancer subnetwork extracted from DUB interactome.

3.4 Cancer Protein Subnetwork has Weaker Clustering Coefficient, Lower Betweenness Centrality and Higher Closeness Centrality

Relative to the essential protein subnetwork, analysis of network topology suggests that the cancer protein subnetwork tends to have a weaker clustering coefficient, lower betweenness centrality and higher closeness centrality (Table 2). Clustering coefficient of a node in a network measures how its direct interactors is well-connected among themselves. A higher clustering coefficient of a node indicates a higher density of its network connections. Therefore, relative to the essential proteins, the neighbors of the cancer proteins had less likelihood to connect with each other. The lower betweenness centrality may suggest that there are less signals passing through the cancer proteins compared to the essential proteins. This could suggest that in DUB interactome, there are more signaling activities occur in essential protein subnetwork compared to cancer protein subnetwork. Higher closeness centrality is observed in cancer protein subnetwork, indicating that the nodes in this subnetwork are much closer to each other compared to essential protein subnetwork. This could also mean that cancer protein subnetwork is more likely to form functional unit compared to essential protein subnetwork.

Table 2. Summary of network properties for DUB interactome, cancer protein and essential protein subnetworks.

Network	Nodes	Edges	Network properties[a]				
			Degree	Clustering coefficient	Characteristic path length	Betweenness centrality (10^3)	Closeness centrality (10^{-4})
DUB interactome	2314	3401	2.939	0.090	4.097	7.162	1.067
Cancer protein subnetwork	213	317	2.977	0.093	4.120	0.661	11.760
Essential protein subnetwork	630	1015	3.222	0.172	4.215	2.022	3.848

[a]Mean value

3.5 Comparison with Randomized Network

Random network is generated to verify the robustness of real network, in this case, the cancer protein subnetwork. To create a comparison pattern for the real network, 10 randomized networks were generated based on Erdős-Rényi model using NetworkRandomizer tool. The differences were calculated based on two-sample Kolmogorov-Smirnov test, which for each of the attributes used in each pair of real and random networks, the difference between their distribution is calculated. The result in Table 3 shows that the differences value between real and randomized network are acceptable and thus, it can be assumed that cancer protein subnetwork generated in this study is not random.

Table 3. Comparison of the topological characteristics between cancer protein subnetwork and randomized network.

Network properties[a]	Cancer protein subnetwork	Random networks[b]	Difference (Kolmogorov-Smirnov test)
Degree	2.977	2.977	0.28169
Clustering coefficient	0.093	0.011	0.21596
Characteristic path length	4.120	4.849	0.42254
Betweenness centrality (10^3)	0.661	0.726	0.37089
Closeness centrality (10^{-4})	11.760	95.982	0.30516

[a]Mean value
[b]Mean value of ten random networks

4 Conclusions and Future Perspectives

Analysis of cancer protein subnetwork within DUB interactome confirmed the close relationship between DUBs and cancer. Topological analysis suggested that OTUB1, COPS5 and USP7 are critical in the subnetwork topology, thus validate their capacity as potential cancer therapeutics target as reported in many research works, published elsewhere. The results also revealed that cancer proteins subnetwork has different topological properties compared to essential protein subnetwork by having weaker clustering coefficient, lower betweenness centrality and higher closeness centrality. In summary, preliminary topological analysis in this study helps to provide a deeper understanding on the biological significance of DUBs in cancer. Based on the data from this study, further analysis such as clustering analysis, link prediction and functional analysis could be executed to gain more information that can be interpreted to reveal the biological significance of cancer in DUB environment.

Acknowledgement. This work was supported by Universiti Sains Malaysia under Bridging Grant (304/CIPPT/6316203).

References

1. Stelzl, U., et al.: A human protein-protein interaction network: a resource for annotating the proteome. Cell **122**(6), 957–968 (2005)
2. Ryan, D.P., Matthews, J.M.: Protein-protein interactions in human disease. Curr. Opin. Struct. Biol. **15**(4), 441–446 (2005)
3. Harun, S., Zulkifle, N.: Construction and analysis of protein-protein interaction network to identify the molecular mechanism in laryngeal cancer. Sains Malays. **47**(12), 2933–2940 (2018)
4. Zulkifle, N., Che Rosli, A.F., Abdul Razak, S.R.: Bioinformatics analysis of differentially expressed genes in liver cancer for identification of key genes and pathways. Malaysian J. Med. Health Sci. **15**(SP2), 18–24 (2019)
5. Weissman, A.M.: Themes and variations on ubiquitylation. Nat. Rev. Mol. Cell Biol. **2**(3), 169–178 (2001)
6. Wilkinson, K.: Regulation of ubiquitin dependent processes by deubiquitinating enzymes. FASEB J. **11**(14), 1245–1256 (1997)
7. Komander, D., et al.: Breaking the chains: structure and function of the deubiquitinases. Nat. Rev. Mol. Cell Biol. **10**(8), 550–563 (2009)
8. Reyes-Turcu, F.E., et al.: Regulation and cellular roles of ubiquitin specific deubiquitinating enzymes. Annu. Rev. Biochem. **78**, 363–397 (2009)
9. Nijman, S.N.B., et al.: A genomic and functional inventory of deubiquitinating enzymes. Cell **123**(5), 773–786 (2005)
10. Abdul Rehman, S.A., et al.: MINDY 1 is a member of an evolutionarily conserved and structurally distinct new family of deubiquitinating enzymes. Mol. Cell **63**, 146–155 (2016)
11. Maurer, T., Wertz, I.E.: Length matters: MINDY is a new deubiquitinase family that preferentially cleaves long polyubiquitin chains. Mol. Cell **63**, 4–6 (2016)
12. Keusekkoten, K., et al.: OTULIN antagonizes LUBAC signaling by specifically hydrolyzing Met1 linked polyubiquitin. Cell **153**(6), 1312–1326 (2013)

13. Kwasna, D., et al.: Discovery and characterization of ZUFSP/ZUP1, a distinct deubiquitinase class important for genome stability. Mol. Cell **70**, 150–164 (2018)
14. He, M., et al.: Emerging role of DUBs in tumor metastasis and apoptosis: therapeutic implication. Pharmacol. Ther. **177**, 96–107 (2017)
15. Shannon, P., et al.: Cytoscape: a software environment for integrated models of biomolecular interaction networks. Genome Res. **13**(11), 2498–2504 (2003)
16. Millán, P.P.: Visualization and analysis of biological networks. Methods Mol. Biol. **1021**, 63–88 (2013)
17. Kerrien, S., et al.: IntAct–open source resource for molecular interaction data. Nucleic Acids Res. **35**(Database issue), D561–D565 (2007)
18. Chatr-aryamontri, A., et al.: MINT: the Molecular INTeraction database. Nucleic Acids Res. **35**(Database issue), D572–D574 (2007)
19. Orchard, S., et al.: Protein interaction data curation: the International Molecular Exchange (IMEx) consortium. Nat. Methods **9**(4), 345–350 (2012)
20. Sondka, Z., et al.: The COSMIC Cancer Gene Census: describing genetic dysfunction across all human cancers. Nat. Rev. Cancer **18**(11), 696–705 (2018)
21. Chen, W.H., et al.: OGEE v2: an update of the online gene essentiality database with special focus on differentially essential genes in human cancer cell lines. Nucleic Acids Res. **45**(D1), D940–D944 (2017)
22. Assenov, Y., et al.: Computing topological parameters of biological networks. Bioinformatics **24**(2), 282–284 (2007)
23. Scardoni, G., et al.: Analyzing biological network parameters with CentiScaPe. Bioinformatics **25**(21), 2857–2859 (2009)
24. Tosadori, G., et al.: Creating, generating and comparing random network models with NetworkRandomizer [version 3]. F1000Res. **5**, 2524 (2017)
25. Zulkifle, N., Zulkifli, N.W.: Understanding human deubiquitinases target specificity by network based analysis towards their development as therapeutics target. In: Proceedings of the 9th International Conference on Computational Systems Biology and Bioinformatics (CSBio 2018), pp. 1–5. ACM, New York (2018)
26. Vidal, M., et al.: Interactome networks and human disease. Cell **144**, 986–998 (2011)
27. Freeman, L.C.: A set of measures of centrality based on betweenness. Sociometry **40**(1), 35–41 (1977)
28. Beauchamp, M.A.: An improved index of centrality. Behav. Sci. **10**, 161–163 (1965)
29. Zulkifle, N.: Systematic yeast two hybrid analysis of human E2 ubiquitin conjugating enzyme and deubiquitin (DUB) protein interactions. Int. J. Biol. Chem. **7**(1), 1–14 (2013)
30. Juang, Y.C., et al.: OTUB1 co-opts Lys48 linked ubiquitin recognition to suppress E2 enzyme function. Mol. Cell **45**(3), 384–397 (2012)
31. Saldana, M., et al.: Otubain 1: a non-canonical deubiquitinase with an emerging role in cancer. Endocr. Relat. Cancer **26**(1), R1–R14 (2019)
32. Guohong, L., et al.: Jab1/COPS5 as a novel biomarker for diagnosis, prognosis, therapy prediction and therapeutic tools for human cancer. Front. Pharmacol. **9**, 135 (2018)
33. Wang, Z., et al.: USP7: novel drug target in cancer therapy. Front. Pharmacol. **10**, 427 (2019)

Graph Based Automatic Protein Function Annotation Improved by Semantic Similarity

Bishnu Sarker[1(✉)], Navya Khare[1,2], Marie-Dominique Devignes[1], and Sabeur Aridhi[1(✉)]

[1] University of Lorraine, CNRS, Inria, LORIA, 54000 Nancy, France
{bishnu.sarker,navya.khare}@inria.fr
[2] IIIT, Hyderabad, India
{marie-dominique.devignes,sabeur.aridhi}@loria.fr

Abstract. Functional annotation of protein is a very challenging task primarily because manual annotation requires a great amount of human efforts and still it's nearly impossible to keep pace with the exponentially growing number of protein sequences coming into the public databases, thanks to the high throughput sequencing technology. For example, the UniProt Knowledge-base (UniProtKB) is currently the largest and most comprehensive resource for protein sequence and annotation data. According to the November, 2019 release of UniProtKB, some 561,000 sequences are manually reviewed but over 150 million sequences lack reviewed functional annotations. Moreover, it is an expensive deal in terms of the cost it incurs and the time it takes. On the contrary, exploiting this huge quantity of data is important to understand life at the molecular level, and is central to understanding human disease processes and drug discovery. To be useful, protein sequences need to be annotated with functional properties such as Enzyme Commission (EC) numbers and Gene Ontology (GO) terms. The ability to automatically annotate protein sequences in UniProtKB/TrEMBL, the non-reviewed UniProt sequence repository, would represent a major step towards bridging the gap between annotated and un-annotated protein sequences. In this paper, we extend a neighborhood based network inference technique for automatic GO annotation using protein similarity graph built on protein domain and family information. The underlying philosophy of our approach assumes that proteins can be linked through the domains, families, and superfamilies that they share. We propose an efficient pruning and post-processing technique by integrating semantic similarity of GO terms. We show by empirical results that the proposed hierarchical post-processing potentially improves the performance of other GO annotation tools as well.

Keywords: Graph mining · Bioinformatics · Knowledge discovery · Protein function annotation · Network inference · GrAPFI

I. Rojas et al. (Eds.): IWBBIO 2020, LNBI 12108, pp. 261–272, 2020.
https://doi.org/10.1007/978-3-030-45385-5_24

1 Introduction

Thanks to advanced high throughput sequencing technologies, an ever growing number of protein sequences are accumulating into public databases [6]. These sequences should be annotated with functional properties to produce valuable information out of this huge quantity of data. Due to high costs and the time-consuming nature of manual function identification procedures, automated prediction of the functions of uncharacterized proteins is an important topic in the field of bioinformatics. This presents many challenges for biologists as well as computer scientists. A comprehensive knowledge about functional characteristics of proteins is central to understanding life at the molecular level, and is key to understanding human disease processes and drug discovery efforts [4]. The UniProt knowledgebase (UniProtKB), the most comprehensive publicly available protein database, consists of two parts: (i) the UniProtKB/Swiss-Prot database contains the manually reviewed protein sequences [6,12] and (ii) the UniProtKB/TrEMBL database is used for storing un-reviewed protein sequences [12]. According to the November, 2019 release of UniProtKB, some 561,000 sequences have received manually reviewed functional annotations, whereas over 150 million protein sequences lack reviewed functional annotations. In UniProtKB, proteins information includes primary sequence as well as some other attributes such as the structural domains and family information. These attributes can be explored to compute pairwise similarity among proteins. However, in TrEMBL, proteins lack other important information such as their function and cellular localization in contrast to Swiss-Prot proteins that are often annotated with functional attributes. This huge quantity of TrEMBL proteins calls for efficient and rapid procedures to annotate them automatically.

Gene Ontology (GO) [3] terms are such functional attributes that indicate the functions that the proteins and genes are performing in our body. In gene ontology, GO terms are arranged hierarchically in three different directed acyclic graphs (DAG) namely (1) Biological Process (BP), (2) Molecular Function (MF), and (3) Cellular Component (CC). Every node in a DAG represents a GO term; and two connected GO terms are linked by different types of edges indicating different relationships. The most commonly used relationships are "is a", "part of", and "regulates".

At present, two complementary systems are in action for automatic annotation of UniProtKB/TrEMBL sequences: (1) UniRule [15] is a rule-based system that uses manually engineered rules to assign appropriate annotation. Although rules in UniRule are generally very reliable, designing rules is a laborious and time consuming process as well as it performs with low coverage. (2) SAAS (Statistical Automatic Annotation System) [23] reduces the manual labour in UniRule system by automatically generating rules using the annotations of the Swiss-Prot sequences and C4.5 decision tree algorithm [36]. Many other approaches exist for predicting protein functions leveraging various attributes. For example, structural similarity of proteins is used in [14,33,39,46] for the purpose of function prediction. In [2,26,35,38,44,47], authors exploit sequence similarities i.e. homology relationships to annotate un-reviewed sequences. Various machine learning based techniques are extensively studied in [7–9,13,18,19,27–29,33,34,41,43,45,52].

Recently, the notion of network science has attracted great attention across many scientific communities [5]. Network science has become a multidisciplinary area of research due to its ability to describe complex intertwined systems. It has found applications in many real-world scenarios from banking and the internet routing to modeling the human brain and understanding complex biological process. Several approaches for annotating protein function have used network science, particularly neighborhood based techniques for protein-to-protein propagation of functional information using protein-protein interaction (PPI) networks and Gene Ontology terms [10,17,32,40,42,50]. The general belief is that interacting proteins share similar functional behaviours. A particular feature of biological networks is that they often require expert biological knowledge to fully understand and exploit the network.

We provide a brief overview of few state-of-the-art GO prediction tools that propose ensemble approaches and exploits different attributes such as sequence encoding, functional domain similarity and structural similarity, protein interaction network etc.

Blast2GO or B2G [11] is a sequence similarity-based functional annotation suite. By using BLAST [31], B2G retrieves all GO annotations for the hit sequences, together with their evidence codes which is interpreted as an index of the trustworthiness of the GO annotation. To find specific annotations with certain level of reliability, an annotation score (AS) is computed for each candidate GO, which is composed of two additive terms. The first direct term (DT), represents the highest hit similarity of this GO weighted by a factor corresponding to its evidence code. The second term (AT) of the AS provides the possibility of abstraction. This term multiplies the number of total GOs unified at the node by a user defined GO weight factor that controls the possibility and strength of abstraction. Finally, lowest terms per branch that lies over a user defined threshold are selected. Once GO annotation is available through B2G, the application offers the possibility of direct statistical analysis on gene function information.

GoFDR [16] is a sequence alignment-based algorithm that runs BLAST [31] or PSI-BLAST [1], for a query protein, to obtain multiple sequence alignment (MSA) over the query sequence. It then identifies all GO terms associated with the sequences in MSA, and determines the functionally discriminating residues (FDRs) for each GO term. These FDRs are used to generate a position-specific scoring matrix (PSSM) which is then used to compute the score between the query protein and a GO term, followed by a raw score adjustment step to convert the raw score into a probability.

DeepGO [25] uses deep learning to learn features from protein sequences as well as from a cross-species protein–protein interaction (PPI) network. It utilizes the dependencies between GO classes as background information to construct a deep learning model. Input to the model is amino acid (AA) sequence of proteins in the form of trigrams, which is represented as one-hot encoding vectors followed by a dense embedding layer. An 1D convolution is applied over protein sequence data and redundant information from the resulting feature map is discarded through temporal max-pooling. In addition, DeepGO uses PPI networks of multiple species, to generate knowledge graph embedding, which are with output of the max-pooling layer to form a combined feature vector. Finally, fully connected layers for each class in GO are used to create a hierarchical classification neural network model that encodes for transitivity of subclass relations. The main advantage of this approach is that it does not rely on manually crafted features, rather it is an entirely data-driven approach.

PANNZER [22,30] uses weighted k-nearest neighbours approach with statistical testing to predict protein functional annotation. It starts with a sequence search against sequence database, to obtain a Sequence Similarity Result List (SSRL). To avoid biases towards large sequence families due to locally similar but globally dissimilar sequences, there is a limitation on number of sequences taken for analysis. Focus is only on the sequences that obtained strongest results from sequence scoring and hence apply pre-set filtering thresholds on alignment coverage, identity percentage, sequence length and informative descriptions. Non-linear weighting of taxonomic distances is another source of information used in PANNZER, corrected with a non-linear similarity function between the descriptions of compared query and target sequence. The second step of the PANNZER pipeline is to re-score the sequence hits using a sparse regression model that combines various signals from sequence alignment and non-linear taxonomic distance score and the weighted sum of score functions obtained is optimized against weighted similarity. In the final regression model all terms that had negative correlation with predicted variable from the model are excluded and final score is obtained.

A structure-based protein function annotation is proposed in COFACTOR [39,48]. COFACTOR proposes a hybrid model combining information from structure and sequence homology, as well as protein–protein interaction (PPI) network for optimal protein function predictions focusing on three most widely-used and computationally amenable categories of function: Gene Ontology (GO) term, Enzyme Commission (EC) number and ligand-binding sites.

In this paper, we apply GrAPFI [40], a Graph-based Automatic Protein Function Inference approach for Gene Ontology (GO) annotation. We propose a pruning and hierarchical post-processing to eliminate the outlier annotations based on functional similarity discussed in GOGO [51]. More specifically, our contributions are the followings:

- We extend GrAPFI to perform Gene Ontology Prediction. GrAPFI is a neighborhood-based label propagation approach that works on a network of proteins connected using domains and family information. Originally proposed for Enzymatic protein function prediction using Enzyme Commission (EC) Number.
- We integrate semantic similarity to take into account the hierarchical nature of the Gene Ontology data and to prune outlier annotations based on their distance in semantic space. To find functional similarity, we used GOGO

[51] which is claimed to be a fast and efficient way of computing GO term similarity.
- We experimentally evaluate the performance of the proposed approach by annotating protein sequences with Gene Ontology (GO) terms and report a comparative understanding of the efficacy of the proposed pruning technique for GO term prediction.

The remainder of the paper is organized as follows. Section 2 presents a brief overview of GrAPFI and describes the proposed pruning and hierarchical post-processing technique. In Sect. 3, we describe our experimental evaluation and we discuss our findings.

2 Method

A graph is a collection of objects denoted as $G = (V, E)$, where V is a set of vertices/nodes and $E \subseteq V \times V$ is a set of edges.

2.1 Function Annotation Using GrAPFI

GrAPFI [40] is a neighborhood-based label propagation approach that works on a network of proteins connected using domains and family information. GrAPFI follows the following steps to perform function annotation:

1. First, we construct a graph using the protein information. Each node u of the graph represents a protein. An edge (u, v) between two nodes/proteins u and v means that the linked proteins share some attributes like, domains and functional sites. A node u may have a set of labels $L(u)$ (one or more annotations to propagate), has a set of neighbors $N(u)$, and for every neighbor $v \in N(u)$, it has an associated weight $W_{u,v}$. Jaccard similarity is used to compute the link weight and computed as $W_{P1,P2} = \frac{|D1 \cap D2|}{|D1 \cup D2|}$ for two protein P1 and P2 having sets of domains $D1$ and $D2$, respectively.
2. Then, a label propagation approach is applied to the protein graph in order to infer functional properties of the unlabeled nodes. Given a query protein, based on the domains and family information of it contains, all the neighboring proteins and their annotations are retrieved from the weighted graph. After having the neighbors, each of the labels of the neighbors are weighted with edge-weights that these neighbors exhibit with this query protein. When retrieving neighbors, it is possible to select only those neighbors which meet a certain similarity threshold. That means that the links can be filtered based on a predefined cut-off weight. For each candidate annotation, GrAPFI provides a confidence score, namely model score (MS) that is computed as:

$$MS(u, i) = \frac{\sum_{v \in N(u)} W_{u,v} \delta(v^i, i)}{\sum_{v \in N(u)} W_{u,v}} \tag{1}$$

where $MS(u, i)$ is the weighted score of the candidate function i for the query protein u. And $\delta(v^i, i)$ is 1 if the function v^i of the protein v is the same as function i, otherwise, 0.

2.2 Pruning Prediction Set Using Functional Similarity Score

We observed that the state-of-the-art tools in the field of GO annotation [20, 37] yield a large number of predictions. Due to the large number of predicted annotations for each protein, precision of the model declines and leads to an increase in recall. But results from these approaches raise a big concern on false positives in the predictions. Therefore we need a method that increases the precision of the model, and hence decreases false positives in the predicted set.

To reduce the number of false positive annotations, we adopted an naive pruning technique by identifying and eliminating the outlier annotations using semantic similarity. Measuring semantic similarity between GO terms has always been an essential step in functional bioinformatics research. In a set of predicted GO annotations for a protein, pairwise semantic similarity between GO terms can show how closely these terms are related to each other and not just to the protein. We used an open-source tool called GOGO [51] for calculating the functional similarity score between GO terms and thus used it to compute the membership score of each predicted GO terms.

GOGO is relatively fast method which does not need to calculate the information content (IC) from a large gene annotation corpus and it considers the number of children nodes in the GO DAGs when calculating the semantic contribution of an ancestor node toward its descendent nodes. GOGO is based on GO DAG topology instead of IC which means that it is comparatively stable.

Given, $DAG_g = (g, T_g, E_g)$ be the Directed Acyclic GO Graph of a term g and it's ancestors T_g, the weight of semantic contribution is calculated as,

$$w_e(t) = 1/(c + nc(t)) + d \tag{2}$$

Where, c and d are constants, $nc(t)$ is the total number of children of the term $t \in T_g$. And E_g is the set of edges of the links among the terms in T_g. The semantic contribution of each term in $DAG_g = (g, T_g, E_g)$ is defined as,

$$S_g(t) = \begin{cases} 1 & if\ \ t = g \\ max\{w_c(t) * S_g(t')|t' \in children(t)\} & if\ \ t \neq g \end{cases} \tag{3}$$

Therefore, the aggregated semantic value for the term g is computed as,

$$SV(g) = \sum_{t \in T_g} S_g(t) \tag{4}$$

In the case of two terms where $DAG_{g1} = (g1, T_{g1}, E_{g1})$ of term g1 and $DAG_{g2} = (g2, T_{g2}, E_{g2})$ of term g2, the semantic similarity between them is as follows:

$$SS(g1, g2) = \frac{\sum_{t \in T_{g1} \cap T_{g2}} (S_{g1}(t) + S_{g2}(t))}{SV(g1) + SV(g2)} \tag{5}$$

Finally, the functional similarity between a set of GO terms, A= g1, g1, g1, . . . , gm and a query GO term $g \notin A$ and is as follows:

$$SS(g, A) = max_{1 \leq i \leq m}(SS(g, g_i \in A)) \tag{6}$$

Once the semantic similarity between each pair of GO terms in the predicted set is calculated, we measure the membership of each annotation in the set. $SS(g, A)$ can be used to find the membership score of a particular GO term in a set of predicted GO annotations. Equation 6 is reused to compute the membership score as follows:

$$SS(g_i, A) = max_{1 \leq j \leq m}(SS(g_i \in A, g_j \in A \setminus \{g_i\})) \tag{7}$$

Where, $SS(g_i, A)$ denotes the membership score of term g_i in a set of terms A.

Instead of maximum, membership score can also be calculated as the average and Root Mean Square (RMS) score of each annotation in the set. For this study, we used RMS score as it gave the best results. We name this measure of membership as semantic similarity (SS) score.

2.3 Aggregation of Scores

In all state-of-the-art GO annotation models, used for experiments in this study, there is a prediction score associated to each predicted annotation for every protein. We refer to this as model score (MS).

For a protein, u with a set of predicted annotations A, each annotation $g \in A$ has two scores associated to it: (1) first, the Model Score (MS), defined as $MS(u, g)$, which shows the credibility with which the annotation was predicted by a particular annotation tool and (2) second, the Semantic Similarity (SS) score, defined as $SS_u(g, A)$, which shows the semantic similarity of each member annotation g to the predicted set A. Now, we need to combine these scores to find a combined prediction (CP) score, defined as $CP_u(g, A)$, for each annotation $g \in A$ of protein u. Joining the scores into a single score provides an overall assessment. A score should be able to distinguish between annotations that score average in both MS score and SS score, from those that score high in one scoring scheme and low in the other scheme. Therefore, instead of averaging the scores, we follow the following scheme:

$$CP_u(g, A) = \sqrt{\frac{(\frac{MS(u,g)}{max\_MS})^2 + (\frac{SS_u(g,A)}{max\_SS})^2}{2}} \tag{8}$$

Here, max_MS and max_SS denotes the maximal model score and semantic similarity score, respectively. Range for both the scores is from 0 to 1 and hence are bounded. Since this is a technique to prune an already predicted set, we take square root in the equation to increase the overall value of combined scores so as to increase threshold cutoff. Once we have the combined score, we can take a certain score as cutoff to filter the predicted set. Annotations with scores above the cutoff forms a new predicted set.

The final step of the process is hierarchical post-processing of predictions in the new predicted set. In the Gene Ontology DAGs, the GO terms holds different parent-child relations putting biologically closer GO terms hierarchically nearer in the graph. We implemented a methodology to include more reliable predictions by including the ancestors of target GO term in the new set of prediction. The ancestors of a GO term in the DAG that the term belongs to, have a very high semantic similarity with the term. Therefore, we first topologically sorted the DAG for each GO category and determined all possible paths from each GO term to the root of the corresponding category. Finally, we follow these paths from terms to the root, one by one and add corresponding ancestors to the set of predictions to obtain final prediction set.

3 Experiments and Result Analysis

3.1 Datasets

To experimentally validate the performance of the proposed technique, we have used a benchmark test set published in MetaGo [49]. For GrAPFI, we build the network using the training data from CAFA3[1]. CAFA3 is a well known competition that seek to annotate a list of protein sequences waiting for proper annotation. Along with target sequences, CAFA3 also published sequences that can be used as training data to develop model. In this study, to build the network, we have used CAFA3 training sequences and we have collected domain and family information for those proteins from UniprotKB. After that, we have built the graph of CAFA3 training proteins. This graph contains more than 65,000 nodes as proteins and an average 16 ground truth GO terms per protein. To prepare the test set, we have used MetaGO benchmark sequences and run InterProScan [21] to identify the domains and family information from sequence. Using the domains and family information of test proteins, we run GrAPFI and other annotation tools over all of the test proteins and annotated them with appropriate GO terms post-processed using proposed approach.

3.2 Result Analysis

In the Table 1, we show the annotation performance using standard evaluation measure namely precision, recall and F1 score. Among the top performing methods, only a few had their source code available to run experiments. Therefore, we focus on three easily available tools namely GrAPFI, PANNZER and DeepGOPlus [24], an improved version of DeepGO. DeepGoPlus learns models with less parameters than DeepGO. These tools are recently published and claimed to be high performing. We show that the semantic similarity improves the precision by many folds. However, the approach suffer from low recall as the number of predictions is much lower than the original predictions. This reduced number of predictions per protein essentially reduce the recall score and this ending up having lower f1-max score.

[1] https://www.biofunctionprediction.org/cafa/.

Table 1. The experimental results for cases when (1) No-post-processing: without post-processing and pruning (2) SS-max: post-processed using highest semantic similarity score as cut-off, (3) SS-5: post-processed using 5th highest semantic similarity (SS) score as cut-off and (4) SS-5-MS-max/2: post-processed using 5th highest semantic similarity and (maximum model score)/2 as cut-off

Method	Post-processing cut-off	Precision	Recall	F1-max
GrAPFI	No-post-processing	0.165	0.108	0.107
	SS-max	**0.573**	0.115	0.175
	SS-5	0.445	0.380	0.376
	SS-5-MS-max/2	0.440	**0.391**	**0.379**
Pannzer	No-post-processing	0.547	**0.942**	0.668
	SS-max	**0.637**	0.225	0.301
	SS-5	0.634	0.515	0.536
	SS-5-MS-max/2	0.603	**0.689**	**0.609**
DeepGOPlus	No-post-processing	0.053	**0.653**	0.095
	SS-max	**0.249**	0.120	0.138
	SS-5	0.186	0.182	0.160
	SS-5-MS-max/2	0.167	0.233	**0.1725**

We run the above mentioned annotation tools on MetaGo benchmark data and obtain results of annotation prediction. These predicted sets are further pruned using semantic similarity and hierarchical post-processing and results are mentioned below (Table 1). Semantic similarity score and hierarchical post-processing score is obtained for each prediction for each protein. Different cut-offs of these two scores along with the score obtained from the model is used for analysis. For each annotation tool, Table 1 shows the annotation outcome in four cases: (1) without any kind of pruning and post processing, (2) when highest semantic similarity score is the cutoff, (3) when 5th highest semantic similarity score is the cutoff and (4) when 5th highest semantic similarity score and half of the maximum model score are the cutoff. From the Table 1, it is evident that the proposed post-processing and pruning techniques that uses the semantic similarity of predicted GO terms improves the overal performance in most cases. In particular, it improves the precision by many folds. For example, the precision of GrAPFI is improved from 16.5% to 57.3% using maximum semantic similarity score as cut-off during post-processing. Similarly, the proposed combined scoring improves the precision of Pannzer and DeepGOPlus by many folds.

4 Conclusion

Automatic protein function annotation is an important topic in the field of bioinformatics because of the lack of annotation of proteins due to high costs and time-consuming nature of manual functional identification procedures. There are a number of tools exist to perform automatic protein function annotation using GO terms, EC numbers, ligand binding sites etc. These tools use various attributes and different methods to accomplish the task. Although they show higher performance based on F1 score, the high F1 score is coming from a higher recall as they predict a large number of candidate annotations. This, in turn, increases the number of false positive annotations. In this paper, (1) we present a graph based protein function inference method extended for GO term prediction, and (2) we propose an efficient pruning and hierarchical post-processing technique by integrating semantic similarity of candidate annotations. We experimentally validate that the proposed method can significantly improve the annotation outcome. In fact, in most cases, recall is significantly low as the number of annotations is fewer compared to the number of annotations from predicted by other tools. Nevertheless, the precision is improved by many folds as we select the highly coherent semantically close annotations.

Acknowledgement. We would like to thank INRIA for providing the doctoral funding for Bishnu SARKER with CORDI-S grant and a internship funding to Navya Khare.

References

1. Altschul, S.F., et al.: Gapped BLAST and PSI-BLAST: a new generation of protein database search programs. Nucleic Acids Res. **25**(17), 3389–3402 (1997)
2. Arakaki, A.K., Huang, Y., Skolnick, J.: EFICAz 2: enzyme function inference by a combined approach enhanced by machine learning. BMC Bioinformatics **10**(1), 107 (2009)
3. Ashburner, M., et al.: Gene ontology: tool for the unification of biology. Nat. Genet. **25**(1), 25 (2000)
4. Bakheet, T.M., Doig, A.J.: Properties and identification of human protein drug targets. Bioinformatics **25**(4), 451–457 (2009)
5. Barabási, A.L.: Linked: The New Science of Networks. Perseus Books Group. ISBN 9780738206677
6. Berger, B., Daniels, N.M., Yu, Y.W.: Computational biology in the 21st century: scaling with compressive algorithms. Commun. ACM **59**(8), 72–80 (2016)
7. Cai, C., Han, L., Ji, Z.L., Chen, X., Chen, Y.Z.: SVM-Prot: web-based support vector machine software for functional classification of a protein from its primary sequence. Nucleic Acids Res. **31**(13), 3692–3697 (2003)
8. Cai, C., Han, L., Ji, Z., Chen, Y.: Enzyme family classification by support vector machines. Proteins Struct. Funct. Bioinf. **55**(1), 66–76 (2004)
9. Cai, Y.D., Chou, K.C.: Predicting enzyme subclass by functional domain composition and pseudo amino acid composition. J. Proteome Res. **4**(3), 967–971 (2005)
10. Chua, H.N., Sung, W.K., Wong, L.: Exploiting indirect neighbours and topological weight to predict protein function from protein–protein interactions. Bioinformatics **22**(13), 1623–1630 (2006)
11. Conesa, A., Götz, S., García-Gómez, J.M., Terol, J., Talón, M., Robles, M.: Blast2GO: a universal tool for annotation, visualization and analysis in functional genomics research. Bioinformatics **21**(18), 3674–3676 (2005)

12. UniProt Consortium: UniProt: a hub for protein information. Nucleic Acids Res. **43**(Database issue), D204–D212 (2015)
13. De Ferrari, L., Aitken, S., van Hemert, J., Goryanin, I.: EnzML: multi-label prediction of enzyme classes using interpro signatures. BMC Bioinformatics **13**(1), 61 (2012)
14. Dobson, P.D., Doig, A.J.: Predicting enzyme class from protein structure without alignments. J. Mol. Biol. **345**(1), 187–199 (2005)
15. Gattiker, A., et al.: Automated annotation of microbial proteomes in SWISS-PROT. Comput. Biol. Chem. **27**(1), 49–58 (2003)
16. Gong, Q., Ning, W., Tian, W.: GOFDR: a sequence alignment based method for predicting protein functions. Methods **93**, 3–14 (2016)
17. Hishigaki, H., et al.: Assessment of prediction accuracy of protein function from protein–protein interaction data. Yeast **18**(6), 523–531 (2001)
18. Huang, W.L., Chen, H.M., Hwang, S.F., Ho, S.Y.: Accurate prediction of enzyme subfamily class using an adaptive fuzzy k-nearest neighbor method. Biosystems **90**(2), 405–413 (2007)
19. des Jardins, M., Karp, P.D., Krummenacker, M., Lee, T.J., Ouzounis, C.A.: Prediction of enzyme classification from protein sequence without the use of sequence similarity. Proc. Int. Conf. Intell. Syst. Mol. Biol. **5**, 92–99 (1997)
20. Jiang, Y., et al.: An expanded evaluation of protein function prediction methods shows an improvement in accuracy. Genome Biol. **17**(1), 184 (2016)
21. Jones, P., et al.: InterProScan 5: genome-scale protein function classification. Bioinformatics **30**(9), 1236–1240 (2014)
22. Koskinen, P., Törönen, P., Nokso-Koivisto, J., Holm, L.: PANNZER: high-throughput functional annotation of uncharacterized proteins in an error-prone environment. Bioinformatics **31**(10), 1544–1552 (2015)
23. Kretschmann, E., Fleischmann, W., Apweiler, R.: Automatic rule generation for protein annotation with the c4.5 data mining algorithm applied on SWISS-PROT. Bioinformatics **17**(10), 920–926 (2001)
24. Kulmanov, M., Hoehndorf, R.: DeepGOplus: improved protein function prediction from sequence. Bioinformatics **36**(2), 422–429 (2020)
25. Kulmanov, M., Khan, M.A., Hoehndorf, R.: DeepGO: predicting protein functions from sequence and interactions using a deep ontology-aware classifier. Bioinformatics **34**(4), 660–668 (2017)
26. Kumar, N., Skolnick, J.: EFICAz2.5: application of a high-precision enzyme function predictor to 396 proteomes. Bioinformatics **28**(20), 2687–2688 (2012)
27. Li, Y., et al.: DEEPre: sequence-based enzyme EC number prediction by deep learning. Bioinformatics **34**(5), 760–769 (2018)
28. Li, Y.H., et al.: SVM-Prot 2016: a web-server for machine learning prediction of protein functional families from sequence irrespective of similarity. PLoS ONE **11**(8), e0155290 (2016)
29. Lu, L., Qian, Z., Cai, Y.D., Li, Y.: ECS: an automatic enzyme classifier based on functional domain composition. Comput. Biol. Chem. **31**(3), 226–232 (2007)
30. Medlar, A.J., Törönen, P., Zosa, E., Holm, L.: PANNZER 2: annotate a complete proteome in minutes!. Nucleic Acids Res. **43**, W24–W29 (2018)
31. Altschul, S.F., et al.: Basic local alignment search tool. J. Mol. Biol. **215**(3), 403–410 (1990)
32. Nabieva, E., et al.: Whole-proteome prediction of protein function via graph-theoretic analysis of interaction maps. Bioinformatics **21**(suppl_1), i302–i310 (2005)
33. Nagao, C., Nagano, N., Mizuguchi, K.: Prediction of detailed enzyme functions and identification of specificity determining residues by random forests. PLoS ONE **9**(1), e84623 (2014)

34. Nasibov, E., Kandemir-Cavas, C.: Efficiency analysis of KNN and minimum distance-based classifiers in enzyme family prediction. Comput. Biol. Chem. **33**(6), 461–464 (2009)
35. Quester, S., Schomburg, D.: EnzymeDetector: an integrated enzyme function prediction tool and database. BMC Bioinformatics **12**(1), 376 (2011)
36. Quinlan, J.R.: Induction of decision trees. Mach. Learn. **1**(1), 81–106 (1986)
37. Radivojac, P., et al.: A large-scale evaluation of computational protein function prediction. Nat. Methods **10**(3), 221 (2013)
38. Rahman, S.A., et al.: EC-BLAST: a tool to automatically search and compare enzyme reactions. Nat. Methods **11**(2), 171 (2014)
39. Roy, A., Yang, J., Zhang, Y.: COFACTOR: an accurate comparative algorithm for structure-based protein function annotation. Nucleic Acids Res. **40**(W1), W471–W477 (2012)
40. Sarker, B., Rtichie, D.W., Aridhi, S.: Exploiting complex protein domain networks for protein function annotation. In: Aiello, L.M., Cherifi, C., Cherifi, H., Lambiotte, R., Lió, P., Rocha, L.M. (eds.) COMPLEX NETWORKS 2018. SCI, vol. 813, pp. 598–610. Springer, Cham (2019). https://doi.org/10.1007/978-3-030-05414-4_48
41. Sarker, B., Ritchie, D.W., Aridhi, S.: Functional annotation of proteins using domain embedding based sequence classification. In: Proceedings of 11th International Conference on Knowledge Discovery and Information Retrieval, Vienna, Austria, pp. 163–170 (2019)
42. Schwikowski, B., Uetz, P., Fields, S.: A network of protein–protein interactions in yeast. Nat. Biotechnol. **18**(12), 1257 (2000)
43. Shen, H.B., Chou, K.C.: EzyPred: a top-down approach for predicting enzyme functional classes and subclasses. Biochem. Biophys. Res. Commun. **364**(1), 53–59 (2007)
44. Tian, W., Arakaki, A.K., Skolnick, J.: EFICAz: a comprehensive approach for accurate genome-scale enzyme function inference. Nucleic Acids Res. **32**(21), 6226–6239 (2004)
45. Volpato, V., Adelfio, A., Pollastri, G.: Accurate prediction of protein enzymatic class by N-to-1 neural networks. BMC Bioinformatics **14**(1), S11 (2013)
46. Yang, J., et al.: The I-TASSER suite: protein structure and function prediction. Nat. Methods **12**(1), 7 (2015)
47. Yu, C., Zavaljevski, N., Desai, V., Reifman, J.: Genome-wide enzyme annotation with precision control: catalytic families (CatFam) databases. Proteins Struct. Funct. Bioinf. **74**(2), 449–460 (2009)
48. Zhang, C., Freddolino, P.L., Zhang, Y.: COFACTOR: improved protein function prediction by combining structure, sequence and protein–protein interaction information. Nucleic Acids Res. **45**(W1), W291–W299 (2017)
49. Zhang, C., Zheng, W., Freddolino, P.L., Zhang, Y.: MetaGO: predicting gene ontology of non-homologous proteins through low-resolution protein structure prediction and protein–protein network mapping. J. Mol. Biol. **430**(15), 2256–2265 (2018)
50. Zhao, B., et al.: An efficient method for protein function annotation based on multilayer protein networks. Hum. Genomics **10**(1), 33 (2016)
51. Zhao, C., Wang, Z.: GOGO: an improved algorithm to measure the semantic similarity between gene ontology terms. Sci. Rep. **8**(1), 15107 (2018)
52. Zhou, N., et al.: The CAFA challenge reports improved protein function prediction and new functional annotations for hundreds of genes through experimental screens, p. 653105. bioRxiv (2019)

Data Mining from UV/VIS/NIR Imaging and Spectrophotometry

Cancer Detection Based on Image Classification by Using Convolution Neural Network

Mohammad Anas Shah(✉), Abdala Nour, Alioune Ngom, and Luis Rueda

School of Computer Science, University of Windsor, Windsor, ON, Canada
{shahlag, noura, angom, lrueda}@uwindsor.ca

Abstract. Breast cancer starts when cells in the breast begin to grow out of control. These cells usually form a tumor that can often be seen on an x-ray or felt as a lump. The tumor is malignant (cancer) if the cells can grow into (invade) surrounding tissues or spread (metastasize) to distant areas of the body. The challenge of this project was to build an algorithm by using a neural network to automatically identify whether a patient is suffering from breast cancer by looking at biopsy images. The algorithm must be accurate because the lives of people are at stake.

Keywords: Image breast cancer · Malignant · Benign · Convolutional neural network · Algorithms · Prediction · Deep learning

1 Introduction

This report account for the development of the algorithm for Cancer detection based on Image classification by using a convoluted neural network (CNN). This project reports the use of Deep Learning methods to complete the task. This kind of learning facilitate to learn a feature automatically from the data. This report also deals with the problems where the input sample is very high dimensional like images and hence use of the CNN is required for a better understanding of the problem statement.

1.1 General Overview

Cancer has been characterized as a heterogeneous disease consisting of many different Subtype. The early diagnosis and prognosis of a cancer type have become a necessity in cancer research, as it can facilitate the subsequent clinical management of patients [3]. In this project, we are focusing on breast cancer and with the help of the CNN model, it can be detected from the sample images and report whether they are health images or malignant images. The sample of 10,000 images is used for training the CNN model in this report.

I. Rojas et al. (Eds.): IWBBIO 2020, LNBI 12108, pp. 275–286, 2020.
https://doi.org/10.1007/978-3-030-45385-5_25

1.2 Motivation

Breast Cancer is the most common type of cancer among women accounting for 25% of all cases. In 2018 it resulted in 2 million new cases resulting in 627,000 deaths across the world [1].

Screening mammography has been shown to reduce breast cancer mortality by 38–48% among participants. Many countries are planning to implement the screening program to diagnose and treat breast cancer at an early stage [2].

1.3 Importance

During a standard mammographic screening examination, an X-Ray image of the patient is captured from the 2 angles of each breast. These images are then inspected by specialists' physicians for malignancy. Research indicates that most experienced physicians can diagnose cancer with at most only 79% accuracy and this data comes from most experienced physician who won't be readily available at all local hospital, sometimes hard to find in states or maybe in-country and if that happens then with non-experienced physician this number may go far below 79%. This may lead to misinterpretation and might be to cause of death. Also, a human inspection of the mammographic report is length, tiring, costly and most importantly prone to error [2].

2 The Problem

In this project, we use a convoluted neural network or CNN to analyze histopathological images of breast cancer for prediction accuracy. We have a dataset of 10,000 images, where we will be running our CNN model by feeding these images into the algorithm and which will inform us whether the image is malignant or benign. Below is an example of histopathological images of breast cancer used in this report (Fig. 1).

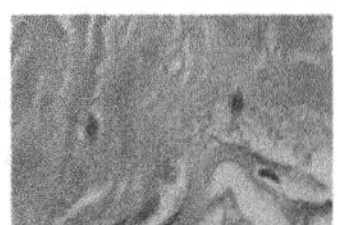

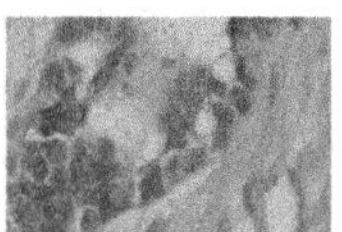

Fig. 1. Benign and malignant sample

The input to our CNN model will be the processed image obtained by 4 stages explained later in this report. The features of this image (xi) becomes input layer of neural network followed by hidden layer which is given by Rectified Linear Unit (ReLU) and lastly the output layer which is sigmoid, that gives the probability of the output i.e. percentage probability of image belonging to either one of class {0, 1} (Fig. 2).

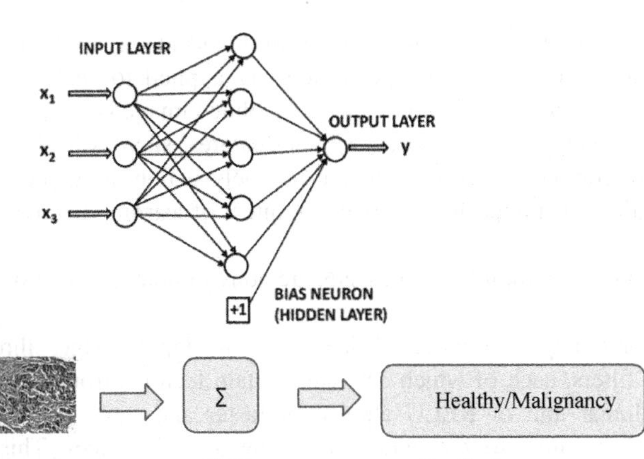

Fig. 2. Describing the problem

3 Materials and Methods

3.1 Input Data

The input data used in this project is courtesy of Robotic Vision and Imaging Laboratory [4] who originally used these images for their predication models [5]. The original dataset consisted of 162 whole mount slide images of Breast Cancer specimens scanned at 40x. From that 10,000 patches of size 50 × 50 were extracted. Each patch's file name is of the format: u_xX_yY_classC.png — > example 8863_idx5_x101_y1251_class0.png. Where u is the patient ID (8863_idx5), X is the x-coordinate of where this patch was cropped from, Y is the y-coordinate of where this patch was cropped from, and C indicates the class where 0 is non-IDC and 1 is IDC where Invasive Ductal Carcinoma (IDC) is the most common subtype of all breast cancers. For example (Fig. 3):

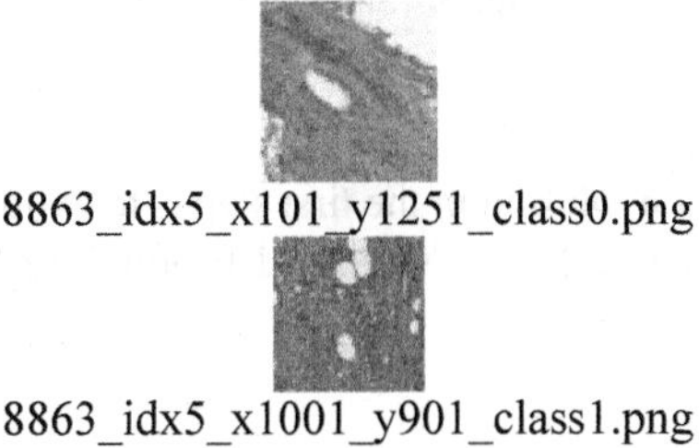

Fig. 3. Sample dataset

3.2 How Convolutional Network Works

A convolutional neural network can have tens of thousands of layers that each learns to detect different features of the image. Filters are applied to each training image at different resolutions, and the output of each convoluted image is used as the input to the next layer. The filters can start as very simple features, such as brightness and edges, and increase in complexity to features that uniquely define the object as these layers perform operations that alter the data with the intent of learning features specific to the data.

The three most common layers of CNN are convolutional, activation or RELU and pooling.

Convolutional Layer or moving filters puts the input images through a set of convolutional filters, each of which activates certain features from the images.

Rectified linear unit or RELU allows for faster and more effective training by mapping negative values to zero and maintaining positive values. This is sometimes referred to as activation because only the activated features are carried forward into the next layer [6].

Pooling or subsampling simplifies the output by performing nonlinear down-sampling, reducing the number of parameters that the network needs to learn [6].

The steps for processing of the image in a convolutional neural network are as below (Fig. 4)

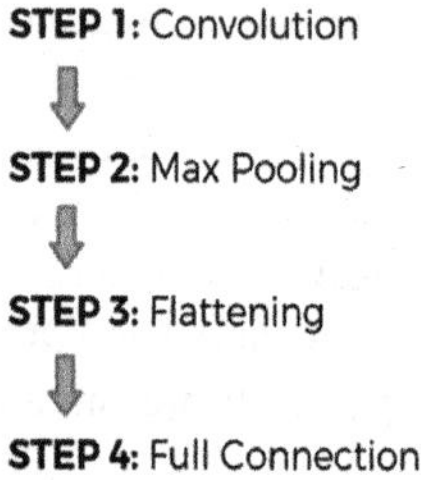

Fig. 4. Steps of CNN

Step1: Convolution

The primary purpose of Convolution in the first step is to extract features from the input image. The output matrix is called “Convolved Feature” or “Feature Map” or “Activation Map” (Fig. 5).

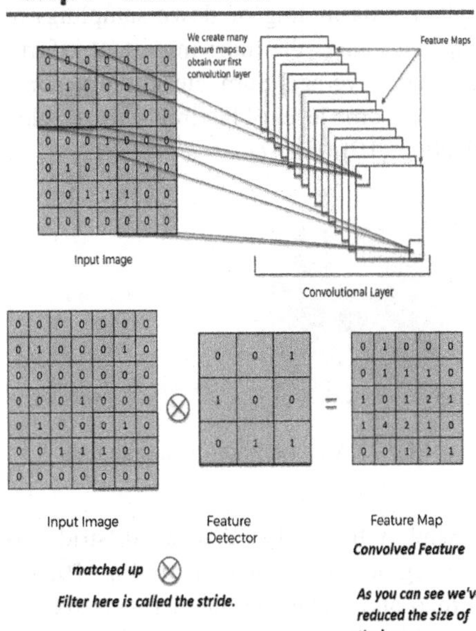

Fig. 5. Matched up filters from the sample image by convolution layer

We create multiple Feature Maps because we use different filters, and that's another way that we preserve lots of the information. we use different Feature Detectors to get different Feature Maps of the same image, therefore now we have lots of versions of a single image. The network decides through its training which features are important for certain types or certain categories. Also, Stride is the number of pixels by which we slide our filter matrix over the input matrix [7].

ReLU is a non-linear operation, acts as the function, to breaks up linearity. When the feature maps are applied, a risk that might create something linear, and therefore we need to break up the linearity. ReLU is applied per pixel and replaces all negative pixel values in the feature map by zero [8] (Fig. 6).

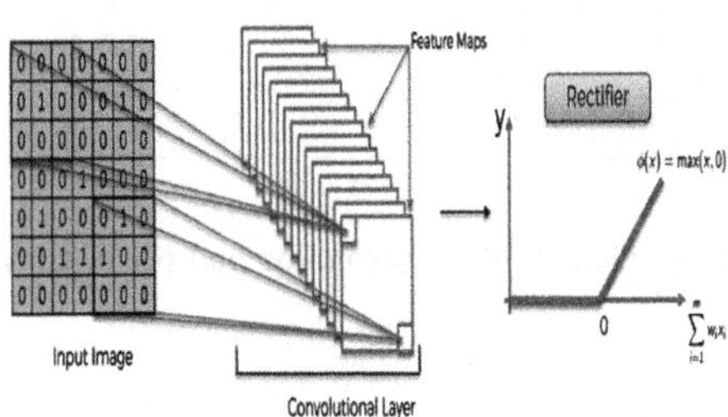

Fig. 6. ReLU activation function

Step2: Max Pooling

Spatial Pooling (also called subsampling or down-sampling) reduces the dimensionality of each feature map but retains the most important information. Spatial Pooling can be of different types: Max, Average, Sum, etc. If the feature itself is a bit distorted, our neural network must have some level of flexibility to be able to still find that feature and make some classification [10] (Fig. 7).

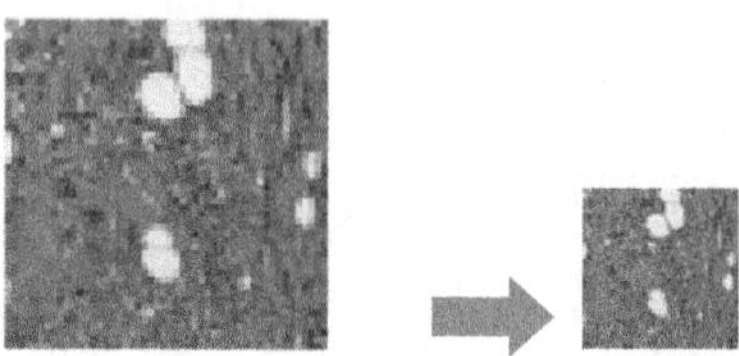

Fig. 7. Max pooling of sample data

We slide our 2 × 2 window by 2 cells (also called 'stride') on images and take the maximum value in each region. As shown in the Fig. 10, this reduces the dimensionality of our feature map and makes the input representations (feature dimension) smaller and more manageable, also reduces the number of parameters and computations in the network, therefore, controlling overfitting [9] (Fig. 8).

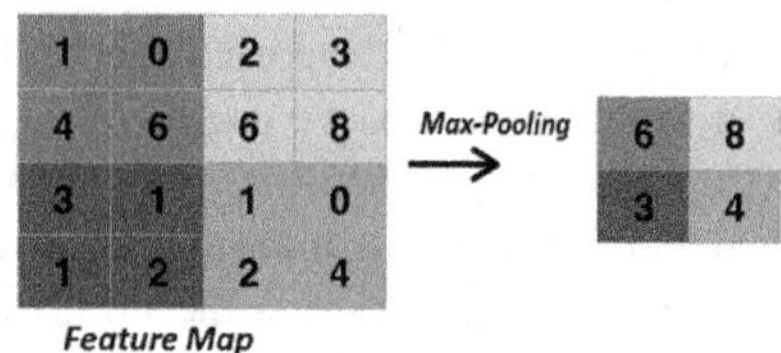

Fig. 8. Example of max pooling

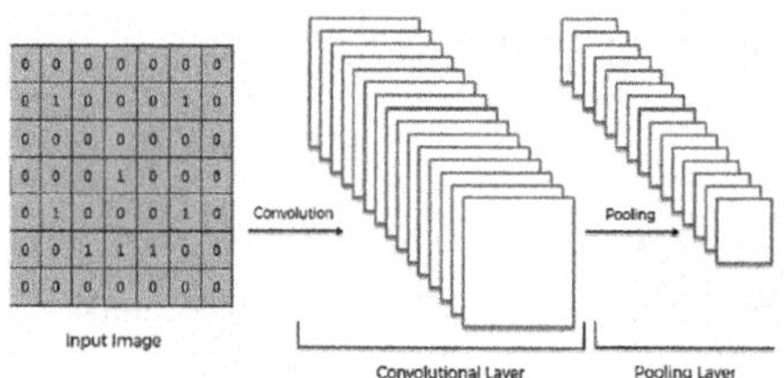

Fig. 9. Output after convolution and pooling layer

Step3: Flattening

As the name of this step implies, we are literally going to flatten our pooled feature map into a column as seen in Fig. 9. The reason we do this is that we're going to need to insert this data into an artificial neural network later [10, 11].

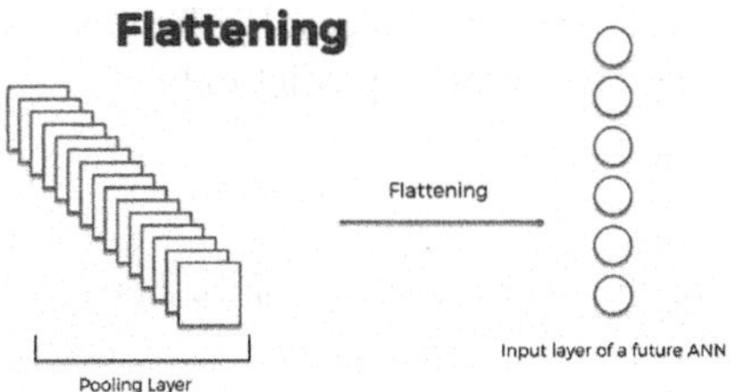

Fig. 10. Flattening of pooling layer

Step4: Fully Connected

In a fully connected layer, we flatten the output of the last convolution layer and connect every node of the current layer with the other nodes of the next layer. Neurons in a fully connected layer have full connections to all activations in the previous layer, as seen in regular Neural Networks and work in a similar way. Furthermore, this deal with a huge number of parameters (thousands and sometimes even millions), and hence may lead to overfitting [12].

Data Augmentation

Data augmentation is one method that we can use to reduce the problem of overfitting on models. Data augmentation is used to increase the amount of training data using information only in our training data. By this way of the increasing number of images present in the dataset lead to reduce overfitting [13].

In our model we deal with a form of data augmentation consists of generating image translations and horizontal reflections. We do this by extracting random (50,50,3) patches from the original 256_256 images. Therefore, we train our neural network on these extracted patches.

Example: datagen = ImageDataGenerator (featurewise_center = True, featurewise_std_normalization = True, rotation_range = 180, horizontal_flip = True, vertical_flip = True)

Use Dropouts

Dropout is one way to prevent the overfitting problem. So, the dropout technique is used to modify the network itself by keeping a neuron active with some probability P, and other neurons with probability Zero during the training dataset. The probability P is a Hyperparameter called dropout rate and usually takes a default value (0.5). Thus, in each iteration, we randomly select the neurons that we drop according to the assigned probability [14]. The different networks will overfit in different ways, so the net effect of dropout will be to reduce overfitting [15].

The Loss Functions

The loss function is a measure of the difference between the probability distribution of any given dataset. In our problem, the probability between 0 and 1 or benign and malignant is given by the loss function Binary Cross-entropy, because each of the values (0,1) belong to one of two complementary classes while making sure the dataset is i.i.d (independent, identical, and distributed). Furthermore, as classification function is given by C = {0 1} where we want to predict only

$$P(y = 1|\boldsymbol{x}; \boldsymbol{w})$$

because the probability for the negative class can be derived from it i.e.

$$P(y = 1|\boldsymbol{x}; \boldsymbol{w}) = p(\boldsymbol{x}; \boldsymbol{w}) \quad \text{and} \quad P(y = 0|\boldsymbol{x}; \boldsymbol{w}) = 1 - p(\boldsymbol{x}; \boldsymbol{w})$$

The Binary Cross-Entropy loss function can be given by the below formula:

$$L(f(\boldsymbol{x}; \boldsymbol{w}), y) = -\frac{1}{m}\sum_{i=1}^{m} y^{(i)} \log p\left(\boldsymbol{x}^{(i)}; \boldsymbol{w}\right) + \left(1 - y^{(i)}\right) \log\left(1 - p\left(\boldsymbol{x}^{(i)}; \boldsymbol{w}\right)\right)$$

Where m is the total number of the images in the dataset.

Summarized CNN Process

Step1: We initialize all filters and parameters/weights with random values
Step2: The network takes a training image as input, goes through the forward propagation step (convolution, ReLU, and pooling operations along with forward propagation in the Fully Connected layer) and finds the output probabilities for each class.
Step3: Calculate the total error at the output layer

$$L(f(\boldsymbol{x}; \boldsymbol{w}), y) = -\frac{1}{m}\sum_{i=1}^{m} y^{(i)} \log p\left(\boldsymbol{x}^{(i)}; \boldsymbol{w}\right) + \left(1 - y^{(i)}\right) \log\left(1 - p\left(\boldsymbol{x}^{(i)}; \boldsymbol{w}\right)\right)$$

Step4: Use Backpropagation to calculate the gradients of the error with respect to all weights in the network and use stochastic gradient descent to update all filter values/weights and parameter values to minimize the output error.
Step5: Repeat steps 2–4 with all images in the training set.

4 Solution to the Main Problem

The complete problem stated above for image classification pipeline can be formalized as follows:

- Our sample dataset of the histopathological image is a training data that consists of *N* images, each labeled with one of 2 different classes
- Then, we use this training data to train a classifier to learn what every one of the classes looks like
- In the end, we evaluate the quality of the classifier by asking it to predict labels for a new set of images (Test Data) that it has never seen before. We will then compare the true labels of these images to the ones predicted by the classifier

Our experiments are run for 100 epochs at the learning rate of 0.0001 using Adam Optimization. The highest test accuracy at all the epochs is reported as the best score. We used a batch size value of 32. Batch size is one of the important hyperparameters to tune in deep learning. We are also using sklearn model selection for the random split of our data in train and test for 80% and 20% respectively Below is the model summary we used for training our data and on test data with the parameters involved in each layer.

Hidden layer	Rectified Linear Unit (ReLU)
Output Layer	Sigmoid
Loss Function	Binary Cross-Entropy
Optimizer	KERAS's Optimizer ADAM
Learning rate	0.0001
sklearn.model_selection	train_test_split
Train Test Split	80-20
Epochs	100
Batch Size	32

Confusion Matrix

Confusion Matrix is a very important metric when analyzing misclassification. Each row of the matrix represents the instances in a predicted class while each column represents the instances in an actual class. The diagonals represent the classes that have been correctly classified [6]. The Neural network model can detect validation loss of about 0.28, where validation accuracy is 0.88 (Fig. 11).

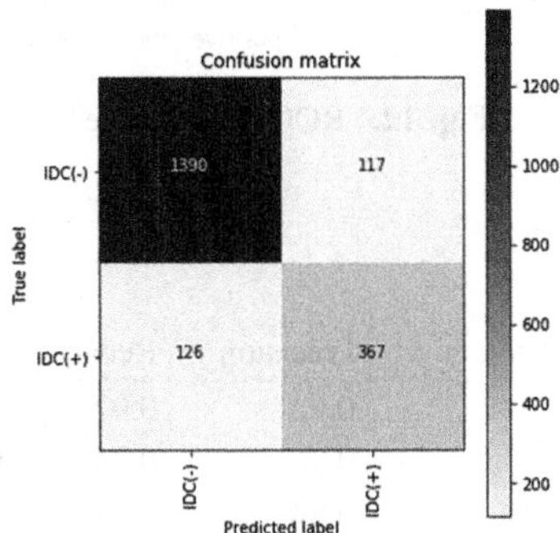

Fig. 11. Confusion matrix

Precision, Recall and F1-Score

For understanding the misclassification, the precision, recall, and F1-score metric is used for calculating various negative and positive values and even false negative can be calculated with these metrics [6].

Recall is the ratio of correctly predicted positive observations to all the observations in an actual class.

F1-Score is the weighted average of Precision and Recall [6].

$$F1 = \frac{2 * (Recall * Precision)}{(Recall + Precision)}$$

ROC Curves

The 45-degree line is the random line, where the Area Under the Curve or AUC is 0.83. The further the curve from this line, the higher the AUC and the better the model. The highest a model can get is an AUC of 1, where the curve forms a right-angled triangle. The ROC curve can also help debug a model. For example, if the bottom left corner of the curve is closer to the random line, it implies that the model is misclassifying at Y = 0. Whereas, if it is random on the top right, it implies the errors are occurring at Y = 1 [6] (Fig. 12).

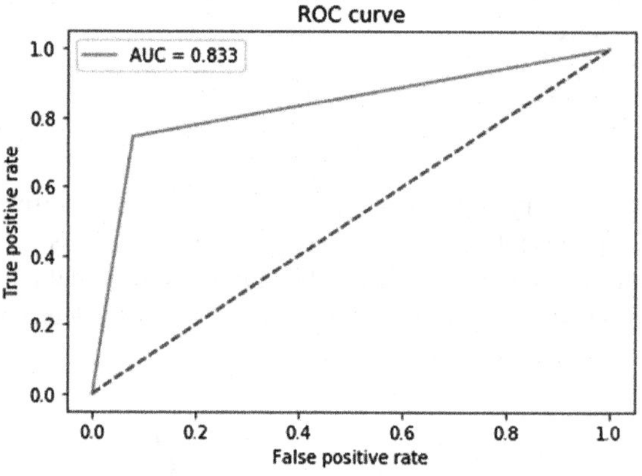

Fig. 12. ROC-AUC curve

Results

	Accuracy	Precision	Recall	F1 Score	Support
ID- (benign)		0.92	0.92	0.92	1507
ID+ (malignant)		0.76	0.74	0.75	493
Macro average	88%	0.84	0.83	0.84	2000
Weighted average	88%	0.84	0.88	0.88	2000

5 Conclusion and Future Work

It is very satisfactory to see that the accuracy rate obtained is 0.88 and the ROC (AUC-Area Under the Curve) value is also 0.83. The Recall value (0.74) calculates how many of the Actual Positives our model capture through labeling it as Positive (True Positive) and the Precision reflects how accurate model is out of those predicted positive (0.76) and based on this conclusion it shows how capable our model is for the problem.

The study was performed on Anaconda3 software product with TensorFlow on a system with configuration of 16 GB RAM, and GPU support. With this accuracy for the classification or prediction of different types of cancer, it is remarkable to see the success of the Convolution Neural Network in such varied real-world problems. This study has produced very successful results considering there is so much to improve upon with future studies like enhancing this model with other techniques of cross-validation Kfold algorithms and comparison to other approaches like ImageNet to find which model suits best on our dataset.

Acknowledgment. This research has been partially supported by NSERC, the Natural Sciences and Engineering Research Council of Canada. The authors would also like to thank the Office of Research and Innovation Services at the University of Windsor.

References

1. Bray, F., Ferlay, J., Soerjomataram, I., Siegel, R.L., Torre, L.A., Jemal, A.: Global cancer statistics 2018: GLOBOCAN estimates of incidence and mortality worldwide for 36 cancers in 185 countries. CA **68**(6), 394–424 (2018)
2. Riblil, D., Anna, H., Zsuzsa, U., Peter, P., Istvan, C.: Detecting and classifying lesions in mammograms with Deep Learning. Sci. Rep. **4165**(8), 2–6 (2018)
3. Kourou, K., Exarchos, T., Exarchos, K., Karamouzis, M., Fotiadis, D.: Machine learning applications in cancer prognosis and prediction. Comput. Struct. Biotechnol. J. **13**(10), 1–2 (2014)
4. Spanhol, F., Oliveira, L.S., Petitjean, C., Heutte, L.: A dataset for breast cancer histopathological image classification. IEEE Trans. Biomed. Eng. (TBME) **63**(7), 1455–1462 (2016)
5. Spanhol, F.A., Oliveira, L.S., Petitjean, C., Heutte, L.: Breast cancer histopathological image classification using Convolutional Neural Networks. In: 2016 International Joint Conference on Neural Networks (IJCNN), Vancouver, BC, pp. 2560–2567 (2016)
6. Kuo, C.C.J.: Understanding convolutional neural networks with a mathematical model, 3–14 (2016). arXiv: 1609(04112)
7. He, K., Zhang, X., Ren, S., Sun, J.: Delving deep into rectifiers: surpassing human-level performance on ImageNet classification, 6–7 (2015). arXiv: 1502(01852)
8. Cogswell, M., Ahmed, F., Girshick, R., Zitnick, L., Batra, D.: Reducing overfitting in deep networks by decorrelating representations **2**(4), 4–7 (2015)
9. Scherer, D., Müller, A., Behnke, S.: Evaluation of pooling operations in convolutional architectures for object recognition. In: Diamantaras, K., Duch, W., Iliadis, Lazaros S. (eds.) ICANN 2010. LNCS, vol. 6354, pp. 92–101. Springer, Heidelberg (2010). https://doi.org/10.1007/978-3-642-15825-4_10
10. SuperDataScience Team: Convolutional-neural-networks-cnn-step-3-flattening, 3–4 (2018). Accessed 17 Aug 2018
11. Caruana, R., Lawrence, S., Giles, C.: Overfitting in neural nets: backpropagation, conjugate gradient, and early stopping. In: Advances in Neural Information Processing Systems, vol. 13, pp. 402–408 (2000)

12. Perez, L., Wang, J.: The effectiveness of data augmentation in image classification using deep learning. **1**(1), 2–3 (2017)
13. Alex, K., Ilya, S., Geoffrey, E.: ImageNet classification with deep convolutional neural networks. **60**(6): 84–90 (2017)
14. Srivastava, N., Hinton, G., Krizhevsky, A., Sutskever, I., Salakhutdinov, R.: Dropout: a simple way to prevent neural networks from overfitting. J. Mach. Learn. Res. **15**(1), 1929–1958 (2014)
15. Martens, J.: Deep learning via Hessian-free optimization. In: ICML 2010 - Proceedings, 27th International Conference on Machine Learning, pp. 735–742 (2010)

Steps to Visible Aquaphotomics

Vladyslav Bozhynov[1(✉)], Oleksandr Mashchenko[1], Pavla Urbanova[1], and Zoltan Kovacs[2]

[1] Laboratory of Signal and Image Processing, Faculty of Fisheries and Protection of Waters, South Bohemia Research Center of Aquaculture and Biodiversity of Hydrocenoses, Institute of Complex Systems, University of South Bohemia in České Budějovice, Zámek 136, 373 33 Nové Hrady, Czech Republic
vbozhynov@frov.jcu.cz

[2] Faculty of Food Science, Department of Physics and Control, Szent István University, 14-16 Somlói str., Budapest 1118, Hungary
http://www.frov.jcu.cz/en/institute-complex-systems/lab-signal-image-processing

Abstract. This article discusses one of the most popular methods for studying water - spectrophotometry. Already known as a fact that water is strongly absorbing at most of the wavelengths in the electromagnetic spectrum. The water molecule, in the gaseous state, has three types of transition that can give rise to absorption of electromagnetic radiation: rotational transitions, vibrational transitions and electronic transitions. In liquid water the rotational transitions are effectively quenched, but absorption bands are affected by hydrogen bonding. In this paper, we mainly consider the behavior of the spectral characteristics of liquid water in the visible range of the spectrum. The results discussed in this article show the influence of the path length on the water spectral characteristics in the visible range.

Keywords: Spectrum · Aquaphotomics · Spectrophotometry · Biomonitoring · Measurement

1 Introduction

Water is the most common inorganic compound on Earth. A water molecule consists of two hydrogen atoms and one oxygen atom, which are interconnected by a covalent bond. And the first exceptional property of water is that such a compound, according to chemical laws, must be gaseous, but under normal conditions the water is liquid.

Early civilizations knew the importance of rain and annual flooding to avoid life-threatening drought and hunger. However, there has been surprisingly little enthusiasm to understand the unique properties of water until quite recently. So, for example, it has long been known that water exists in nature in three states: solid, liquid, and gaseous. But now it is already known about more than 20 states of water, of which 14 are frozen water [1].

I. Rojas et al. (Eds.): IWBBIO 2020, LNBI 12108, pp. 287–297, 2020.
https://doi.org/10.1007/978-3-030-45385-5_26

The beginning of scientific research of water can be considered the discovery of hydrogen by London scientist Henry Cavendish (1731–1810). He discovered water's composition (two parts hydrogen to one part oxygen) in about 1781. Since that time a lot of methods were developed for examination different characteristics and properties of water.

One of the most useful methods of quantitative analysis in various fields is spectrophotometry. Spectrophotometry is a method to measure how much a chemical substance absorbs light by measuring the intensity of light passes through sample solution. The basic principle is that each compound absorbs or transmits light over a certain range of wavelength. This measurement can also be used to measure the amount of a known chemical substance.

One of the modern methods of spectrophotometry, which is successfully used for the studying and systematizing knowledge about water-light interaction is Aquaphotomics. Aquaphotomics is a novel scientific discipline founded by Professor Roumiana Tsenkova at Kobe University, Japan, in 2005 [2]. The word 'aquaphotomics' is derived from the words 'aqua-water', 'photo-light' and 'omics-all about' since this new discipline studies water by using its interaction with the light [3]. The main objective of establishing aquaphotomics as a novel scientific discipline was to provide a common platform and strategy to lead to an improved general understanding of the water functionality by utilizing water-light interaction at every frequency of the electromagnetic spectrum.

The majority of aquaphotomics works so far have been done by using near infrared (NIR) spectroscopy, especially in the area of the 1st overtone of the OH stretching band (1,300–1,600 nm) where many water absorbance bands are identified and consistent with previously reported or calculated overtones of water absorbance bands in the infrared region [4–8]. What aquaphotomics research studies showed is that NIR spectroscopy, and in general water-light interaction over the entire electromagnetic spectrum, can significantly contribute to the field of water science and better understanding of water molecular systems [7].

Liquid water has weak light absorption in the visible region. Absorption coefficients for 200 nm and 900 nm are almost equal at 6.9 m^{-1} (attenuation length of 14.5 cm). An absolute minimum of water absorption is at 418 nm, at which wavelength the attenuation coefficient is about 0.0044 m^{-1}, which is an attenuation length of about 227 m. These values correspond to pure absorption without scattering effect.

2 Absorption Spectra of Liquid Water in VIS-NIR Region. Aquaphotomics Approach

The two major mechanisms by which light interacts with water are scattering and absorption. Scattering by water has been studied both theoretically and experimentally. Although there are some differences in the estimates of scattering by pure water. The connection between theory and experiment is well developed. In contrast, our theoretical and experimental understanding of absorption by water is quite limited. The lack of agreement on the structure of liquid water hampers the task of solving Schrodinger's equation, from which we might be able to get a theoretical handle on absorption [9].

Water absorbs over a wide range of electromagnetic radiation (Fig. 1) with rotational transitions and intermolecular vibrations, intermolecular vibrational transitions and electronic transitions. The water absorption spectrum is very complex. The water molecule may vibrate in several ways: symmetric stretch (v_1), asymmetric stretch (v_3) and bending (v_2) of the covalent bonds (Fig. 2). There is also a weak broadband absorption continuum that roughly follows the vibrational bands. This is due to interactions of the water molecules with each other and other atoms and molecules. The water molecule has a very small moment of inertia on rotation which gives rise to rich combined vibrational-rotational spectra in the vapor containing tens of thousands to millions of absorption lines [10,11]. In the liquid, rotations tend to be restricted by hydrogen bonds, giving the librations.

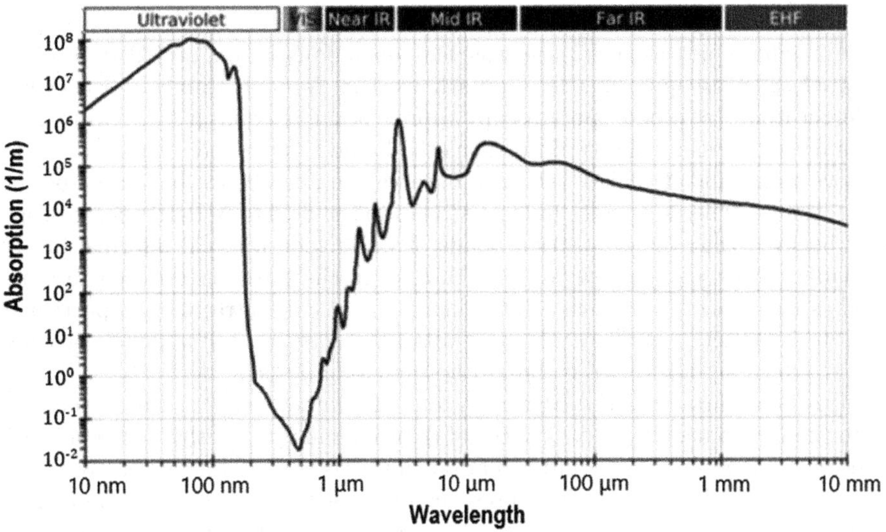

Fig. 1. Electromagnetic absorption by water [12]

Liquid water has no rotational spectrum, so the main part of the absorption is in the mid-infrared and near-infrared regions. Water absorption in the near-infrared (NIR) is much weaker than in the mid- and far-infrared regions of the spectrum. It offers the possibility of analyzing thicker samples and objects rapidly, in a completely non-destructive and non-invasive manner, and with none or little sample preparation [13]. In the NIR region, the water spectrum shows four main bands located approximately around 970, 1190, 1450 and 1940 nm, which are attributed to the second overtone of the OH stretching band ($3v_{1,3}$), a combination of the first overtone of the OH stretching and OH bending band ($2v_{1,3} + v_2$), the first overtone of the OH stretching band ($2v_{1,3}$) and a combination of the OH stretching and OH bending band ($2v_{1,3} + v_2$), respectively [14].

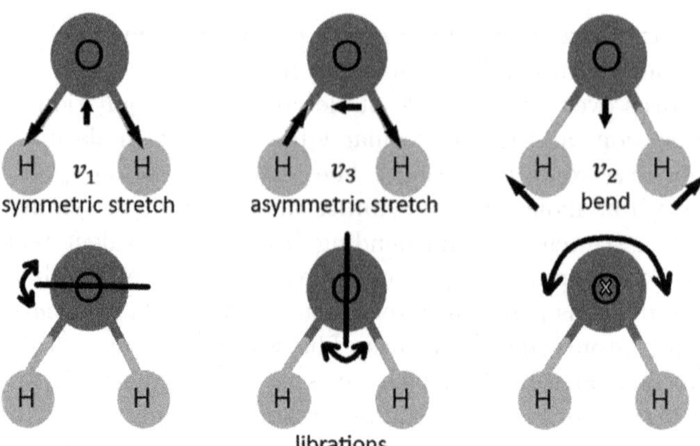

Fig. 2. Water vibration modes

Aquaphotomics as a science was laid on a foundation provided by near infrared spectroscopy [7]. The approach used in Aquaphotomics is somewhat different from traditional spectroscopy approaches. For example, to measure proteins or sugars using the traditional method, the samples are usually dried to remove water and it makes better to observe the absorbance bands of specific biomolecules. This is because in most studies in the field of NIR-IR spectroscopy it is believed that the absorption bands of water hide the real information. In Aquaphotomics, on the contrary, the changes in the water spectral pattern are used as a source of information. The change in the concentration of a particular analyte is reflected in the changes of absorbance at several water absorbance bands, which are then used to build the prediction model.

The breakthrough knowledge regarding the importance of water stemmed from the observation that NIR spectral data for milk of healthy and dairy animals with mammary gland inflammation (mastitis) differed at water absorbing bands (1440 and 1912 nm). The presence of disease in an organism influenced many biomolecules (fat, lactose, proteins, etc.); these changes were subtle and sometimes not even visible in the spectra at absorbance bands related to those compounds. However, all these components exerted an influence on the water structure, and this cumulative effect was observable and measurable at multiple water absorbance bands corresponding to different water molecular species. In other words, the water molecular network changed when the composition of the aqueous system was altered, and this was reflected in water spectral pattern.

This innovative knowledge changed the approach in spectral analysis and paved way for the development of Aquaphotomics [13]. Changes in the water spectrum accurately and sensitively reflect the changes of water molecular species, hydrogen bonding and charges of the solvated and solvent molecules. In liquid water, each water molecule forms bonds with neighboring molecules, and can also establish dipoles and induce dipole interactions with other molecules, which gives the water molecular systems a heterogeneous character responsive to physical and environmental conditions [15]. Water changes its absorbance pattern every time it adapts to a physical or chemical change in the system itself or its environment. This fact allows to use water absorbance bands for the indirect quantitative determination of specific analytes using the Aquaphotomics method. Any changes in analyte concentrations affect many water molecules and their absorption characteristics, what gives a definite advantage. Traditional NIRS methods are based on direct measurement of the absorption bands of the corresponding analytes. A comparison of the traditional and Aquaphotomics approaches and the resulting quantitative accuracy was performed in one of the proofs of the concept works using the measurement of the concentration of polystyrene particles in water [16].

Water is much more transparent to 'visible' light. This property is well used in photosynthesis and allows the production of both biomass and oxygen. However, some absorption exists in visible range of spectrum. Water has a pale blue color, since the intensity of the overtone and combined vibrational absorption is minimal in the blue region and increases towards the red part of the visible spectrum.

Table 1. Assignment of the VIS-IR vibrational absorption spectrum of liquid water (Raman picks are given in [21])

Wavelength	Assignment
200000 nm	Hydrogen bond bend
55000 nm	Hydrogen bond stretch
25000 nm	L_1, librations
15000 nm	L_2, librations
6080 nm	v_2, bend
4650 nm	$v_2 + L_2$
3050 nm	v_1, symmetric stretch
2870 nm	v_3, asymmetric stretch
1900 nm	$av_1 + v_2 + bv_3; a + b = 1$
1470 nm	$av_1 + bv_3; a + b = 2$
1200 nm	$av_1 + v_2 + bv_3; a + b = 2$
970 nm	$av_1 + bv_3; a + b = 3$
836 nm	$av_1 + v_2 + bv_3; a + b = 3$
739 nm	$av_1 + bv_3; a + b = 4$
660 nm	$av_1 + v_2 + bv_3; a + b = 4$
606 nm	$av_1 + bv_3; a + b = 5$ [20]
514 nm	$av_1 + bv_3; a + b = 6$ [20]
449 nm	$av_1 + bv_3; a + b = 7$ [19]
401 nm	$av_1 + bv_3; a + b = 8$ [19]
Note that a and b are integers, ≥ 0	

There is a small peak at 739 nm and shoulder at 836 nm, plus a smaller fourth overtone band of the $v_1 : v_3$ stretch at 606 nm, a very small fifth overtone band at 514 nm, and a combined overtone band at 660 nm (Table 1). These overtone and combination vibrational bands increase and sharpen somewhat with increasing temperature [17] in line with the expectation from the two-state water model. This absorption spectrum of water (red light absorbs 100 time more than blue light), together with the five-times greater scattering of blue light over reg light, contributes to the blue color of lake, river and ocean waters [18].

The clear absorption by the pure water without scattering effect was measured and examined by Pope and Fry in 1997 [19]. For their experiments they used an integrating cavity technique to measure all the light energy that is removed from the incident light field. The integrating cavity absorption meter (ICAM) permits the measurement of very small optical absorption coefficients (0.001 m^{-1}), virtually independent of scattering effect in sample. Briefly, the sample was isotropically illuminated in a cavity whose walls have a very high diffuse reflectivity, typically >99%. In addition to the described above overtones and combined vibration bands, these researchers confirmed shoulders at 449 and 401 nm, which are due to the 7th and 8th harmonic of the OH stretch (Table 1). They made the first observations of the combination mode between the fundamental frequency of the scissors motion and harmonics of the OH stretch. From their work it is also seen that the absorption of electromagnetic radiation by water in the visible range of the spectrum never reaches zero. The minimum absorption coefficient is at a wavelength of about 415 nm and is equal to 0.004 m^{-1}.

Although the absorptions of water's overtone bands within the visible spectrum are quite small (0.3–0.01 m^{-1}), they are sufficient to create spectral niches amongst photosynthetic organisms; thus directing water ecology and evolution [22].

3 Extension of Aquaphotomics Approach to the Visible Range and Preliminary Results

Each chemical element has a unique pattern in the absorption of electromagnetic radiation, called 'fingerprint'. Such bands are presented in a wide range of spectrum, including visible part. Based on this, it is assumed that changes of water spectral characteristics in the visible range provides the information about the changes in water composition. To characterize liquid water using a classic laboratory spectrophotometer, various powder or liquid reagents are used, which, when reacted with a specific element dissolved in water, color the sample. After that, the absorption of one specific wavelength of visible light is measured, since the maximum light absorption of many colored compounds lies in the visible region of the spectrum. However, we suggest that using the Aquaphotomics approach for the visible range of the spectrum should provide more information about the elements presented in the water.

In one of our previous works, we investigated the relationships between some values of water parameters and the spectral characteristics of the sample in the visible range of the spectrum. In that experiment the following water parameters were measured: dissolved oxygen (DO), temperature (T), electrical conductivity (EC), pH, and concentrations of chlorine (Cl), ammonia (NH3), ammonium (NH4). The results presented in that paper prove the existence of such dependencies. For example, a statistical analysis for the correlation between the spectral characteristics and the concentration of NH3 gave the number for the correlation coefficient $R = 0.6513$ and for p-value $= 0.0013$ [23].

Our next study pursued a similar goal to investigate the relationship of the spectral characteristics of water in the visible range with values of crucial water parameters. This time we used pH, electrical conductivity and temperature, as one of the most basic parameters. During the experiment, the parameters varied in such ranges: pH from 2.56 to 10.5; EC from almost 0 to 6.51 mS/cm; temperature from 2 to 50.5 °C. Samples were prepared in the way, where only one parameter was changed, while the changes of remaining parameters were close to 0. As a result, a partial least square regression model was created that should predict the values of parameters based on the spectral characteristics of water samples. The training results of regression model were very promising, with very small deviation, which does not exceed the value $4 * 10^{-8}$. Fitting showed that dependence of the spectral characteristics of water on tested parameters can be modeled by linear combinations of the spectral values [24].

In spectral measurements of liquid samples, it is necessary to remember such an important aspect as the path length of light. Most experiments using the Aquaphotomics method are performed with transmittance mode using the cuvette with 1 mm optical path length [3,25]. This path length was chosen as optimal for operation in the near infrared region of the spectrum. However, based on the fact that the absorption in the visible region of the spectrum is much weaker, we can conclude that the path length should be longer. This paper discusses the results of water spectra measurements using different thicknesses of the cuvette. We investigated the effect of the path length on the water absorption in the visible range.

4 Experimental Setup

In our experiment, an X-Rite ColorMunki spectrophotometer was used to collect transflectance spectra. This spectrophotometer works in the visible range 360–740 nm with step in 10 nm. To test the influence of the path length on the measurements in visible range Mili-Q water was used. As a holder we used reflectance cuvette from the instrument metri-NIR (Fig. 3). This cuvette has a circular shape and consists of a 'bath' for the sample and a 'head' with a reference white reflector. The light passes through the glass located at the bottom of the cuvette, through the sample, is reflected from the white surface of the reflector and returns back to the receiver. The thickness of the cuvette can be changed by using reflectors with different heights. In our experiment, 1 mm, 2 mm, 4.2 mm cuvette thickness were tested. A 10 mm square plastic cuvette was also tested using the same reflector behind it. For each measurement 5 consecutive scans were conducted.

Fig. 3. metriNIR cuvette in the original box

5 Results and Discussion

The absorbance is directly proportional to the length of the light path, which is in our case with transflectance mode is equal to the double cuvette thickness. Thus, in our experiment, absorption was measured with technical path lengths of 2 mm, 4 mm, 8.4 mm, and 20 mm, respectively.

Logically, we can assume that the greatest amount of information can be obtained from data with higher absorption. However, we can see that measurements with a 10 mm thick cuvette (20 mm path length) have poor repeatability, which makes it impossible to see small changes in spectral characteristics. On the other hand, water absorption in the visible spectrum is very weak and when using a cuvette with a short path length, the useful signal may be lost among the noise.

As can be seen from the Fig. 4, the influence of the path length strongly affects the absorption and the measured spectra are far from each other along the Y axis. To determine the character of the spectrum and the repeatability of measurements, we need to look at the spectra 'closer'. Figure 5 shows 5 successively measured water absorption spectra using a cuvette with a thickness of 4.2 mm. As expected, the changes in absorption over wavelengths in the range from 420 to 730 nm are quite small. However, measurements of the absorption of pure water with the same path length have good repeatability. The part of the spectrum after a wavelength of 650 nm has strong noises, which is most likely due to the sensitivity of the device at the edge of the range.

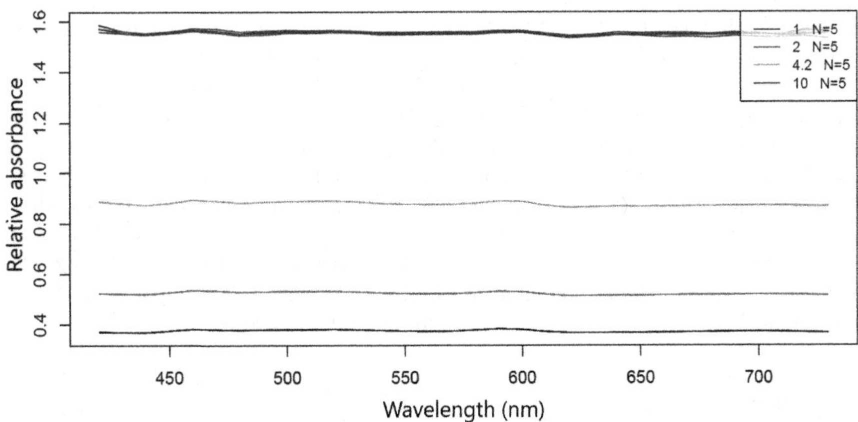

Fig. 4. Absorption spectra of Mili-Q water with different cuvette thicknesses (where numbers 1, 2, 4.2 and 10 represent different cuvette thicknesses in mm; N represents number of consecutive scans)

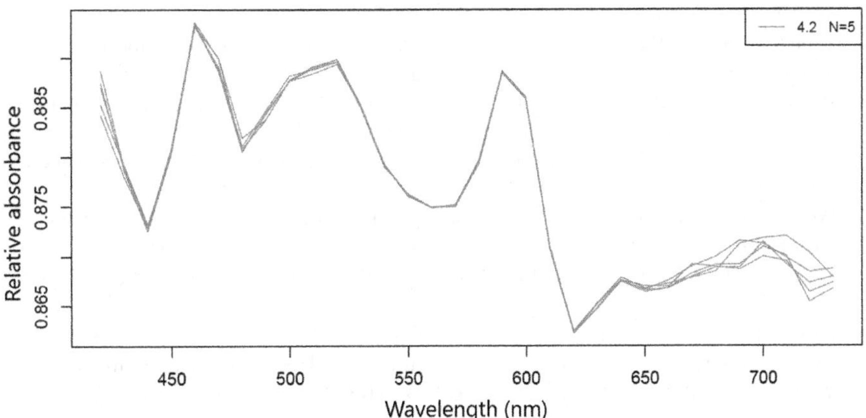

Fig. 5. Absorption spectra of Mili-Q water with 4.2 mm cuvette thickness (N represents number of consecutive scans)

6 Conclusion

The results presented in this work show that the path length has a huge effect on the absorption of visible light by water. Even using a low-cost device with quite small number of measured bands, we see good stability of the spectral characteristics of the same sample.

Water is changing its spectral characteristics as a response to the changes of water molecular species, hydrogen bonding and charges of the solvated and solvent molecules. However, the changes in the spectral pattern can be very small in the visible region. Therefore, to apply the aquaphotomics approach in the visible range of the spectrum, a good spectrophotometer is required, with a smaller step and good repeatability of the measurements.

Acknowledgments. The study was financially supported by the Ministry of Education, Youth and Sports of the Czech Republic - project 'CENAKVA' (LM2018099), the CENAKVA Centre Development [No. CZ.1.05/2.1.00/19.0380] and GAJU 013/2019/Z.

We are grateful to Jan Urban from the Institute of Complex Systems, Faculty of Fisheries and Protection of Waters, University of South Bohemia in Ceske Budejovice for the supervising of this project, as well as to Zsanett Bodor, John-Lewis Zinia Zaukuu and the entire staff of the Department of Physics and Control, Faculty of Food Science, Szent Istvan University for the assistance throughout the project.

References

1. Choukrouna, M.: Thermodynamic model for water and high-pressure ices up to 2.2 GPa and down to the metastable domain. J. Chem. Phys. **127**, 124506 (2007)
2. Tsenkova, R.: Visible-near infrared perturbation spectroscopy: water in action seen as a source of information. In: 12th International Conference on Near-Infrared Spectroscopy (Auckland), pp. 607–612 (2005)
3. Tsenkova, R., Muncan, J., Pollner, B., Zoltan, K.: Essentials of aquaphotomics and its chemometrics approaches. Front. Chem. **6**, 363 (2018)
4. Weber, J.M., Kelley, J.A., Nielsen, S.B., Ayotte, P., Johnson, M.A.: Isolating the spectroscopic signature of a hydration shell with the use of clusters: superoxide tetrahydrate. Science **287**, 2461–2463 (2000). https://doi.org/10.1126/science.287.5462.2461
5. Weber, J.M., Kelley, J.A., Robertson, W.H., Johnson, M.A.: Hydration of a structured excess charge distribution: infrared spectroscopy of the O-2·(H2O)n, ($1 \leq n \leq 5$) clusters. J. Chem. Phys. **114**, 2698–2706 (2001). https://doi.org/10.1063/1.1338529
6. Smith, J.D., Cappa, C.D., Wilson, K.R., Cohen, R.C., Geissler, P.L., Saykally, R.J.: Unified description of temperature-dependent hydrogen-bond rearrangements in liquid water. Proc. Natl. Acad. Sci. U.S.A. **102**, 14171–14174 (2005). https://doi.org/10.1073/pnas.0506899102
7. Tsenkova, R.: Aquaphotomics: dynamic spectroscopy of aqueous and biological systems describes peculiarities of water. J. Near Infrared Spectrosc. **17**, 303–313 (2009). https://doi.org/10.1255/jnirs.869
8. Tsenkova, R., Kovacs, Z., Kubota, Y.: Aquaphotomics: near infrared spectroscopy and water states in biological systems. In: Disalvo, E.A. (ed.) Membrane Hydration. SB, vol. 71, pp. 189–211. Springer, Cham (2015). https://doi.org/10.1007/978-3-319-19060-0_8
9. Pegau, W., Gray, D., Zaneveld, J.: Absorption and attenuation of visible and near-infrared light in water: dependence on temperature and salinity. Appl. Opt. **36**(24), 6035–6046 (1997)
10. Hall, R.T., Dowling, J.M.: Pure rotational spectrum of water vapor. J. Chem. Phys. **47**, 2454–2461 (1967)
11. Hall, R.T., Dowling, J.M.: Erratum: pure rotational spectrum of water vapor. J. Chem. Phys. **54**, 4968 (1971)
12. Electromagnetic absorption by water. https://en.wikipedia.org/wiki/Electromagnetic_absorption_by_water

13. Muncan, J., Tsenkova, R.: Aquaphotomics—from innovative knowledge to integrative platform in science and technology. Molecules **24**(15), 2742 (2019)
14. Luck, W.A.: Structure of water and aqueous solutions. Verlag Chemie (1974)
15. Chaplin, M.: Do we underestimate the importance of water in cell biology? Nat. Rev. Mol. Cell Biol. **7**, 861–866 (2006). https://doi.org/10.1038/nrm2021
16. Tsenkova, R., Iso, E., Parker, M., Fockenberg, C., Okubo, M.: Aqua-photomics: a NIRS investigation into the perturbation of water spectrum in an aqueous suspension of mesoscopic scale polystyrene spheres. In: 13th International Conference on Near Infrared Spectroscopy, vol. 72, p. A-04. Umea-Vasa, Sweden & Finland (2007)
17. Langford, V.S., McKinley, A.J., Quickenden, T.I.: Temperature dependence of the visible-near-infrared absorption spectrum of liquid water. J. Phys. Chem. A **105**, 8916–8921 (2001)
18. Chaplin, M.: Water structure and science. http://www1.lsbu.ac.uk/water/water_structure_science.html
19. Pope, R.M., Fry, E.S.: Absorption spectrum (380–700 nm) of pure water. II. Integrating cavity measurements. Appl. Opt. **36**, 8710–8723 (1997)
20. Yakovenko, A.A., Yashin, V.A., Kovalev, A.E., Fesenko, E.E.: Structure of the vibrational absorption spectra of water in the visible region. Biophysics **47**, 891–895 (2002)
21. Walrafen, G.E., Pugh, E.: Raman combinations and stretching overtones from water, heavy water and NaCl in water at shifts to *ca* 7000 cm^{-1}. J. Solution Chem. **33**, 81–97 (2004). https://doi.org/10.1023/B:JOSL.0000026646.33891.a8
22. Stomp, M., Huisman, J., Stal, L.J., Matthijs, H.C.P.: Colorful niches of phototrophic microorganisms shaped by vibrations of the water molecule. ISME J. **1**, 271–282 (2007)
23. Bozhynov, V., Soucek, P., Barta, A., Urbanova, P., Bekkozhayeva, D.: Visible aquaphotomics spectrophotometry for aquaculture systems. In: Rojas, I., Ortuño, F. (eds.) IWBBIO 2018. LNCS, vol. 10813, pp. 107–117. Springer, Cham (2018). https://doi.org/10.1007/978-3-319-78723-7_9
24. Bozhynov, V., Soucek, P., Barta, A., Urbanova, P., Bekkozhayeva, D.: Dependency model for visible aquaphotomics. In: Rojas, I., Valenzuela, O., Rojas, F., Ortuño, F. (eds.) IWBBIO 2019. LNCS, vol. 11465, pp. 105–115. Springer, Cham (2019). https://doi.org/10.1007/978-3-030-17938-0_10
25. Muncan, J., Matovic, V., Nikolic, S., Askovic, J., Tsenkova, R.: Aquaphotomics approach for monitoring different steps of purification process in water treatment systems. Talanta **206**, 120253 (2020)

Automatic Calibration, Acquisition, and Analysis for Color Experiments

Jan Urban(✉)

Laboratory of Signal and Image Processing, Institute of Complex Systems, Faculty of Fisheries and Protection of Waters, South Bohemian Research Center of Aquaculture and Biodiversity of Hydrocenoses, University of South Bohemia in Ceske Budejovice, Zamek 136, 37 333 Nove Hrady, Czech Republic
urbanj@frov.jcu.cz

Abstract. This article is presenting a device for color experiments with automatic setup. The device is designed to carry on measurements of color of semi-homogenous objects. The light conditions are controlled by mikroPc and standardized for the experiments. The capturing camera setup and calibrations are done automatically using Gray World theory for white balance and defined background. The calibration is adjusted by brightness and contrast calibration, and difference between black and white versus light and dark. The device is connected with the software for automatic color analysis. The object is segmented from the background and transformed into several color space representations. The color channel distributions are statistically evaluated.

The device should serve in the experiment with color analysis, stability, changes, comparison in fish or food production. Moreover, extension of the analysis cold be used in biometric or diseases tasks.

Keywords: Color · Fish skin color · Automatic calibration · White balance · Gray World · Retinex · Automatic contrast

1 Introduction

Color is a primary sense in our perception of the world. The same is natural for wide range of species. The electromagnetic radiation is an information rich source. In biology, we often estimate the state of the object by its color. The colorful meat, vegetable, fruits, or herbs are more likely to be sold [1,2]. The welfare of the fish, plants, or other beings is more or less expressed in the color attributes [3–5]. The defects, contamination, and diseases are also affecting the color characteristics [6].

One of the main focus is in investigation of the affection of the fish color by several different causes, including photoperiod changes, food supplements, parameters of the environment [7–10]. The classical spectrophotometric methods have a disadvantage of the point measurement, where only small area of the fish skin could be evaluated. Such method is invasive, since there is a direct contact.

I. Rojas et al. (Eds.): IWBBIO 2020, LNBI 12108, pp. 298–309, 2020.
https://doi.org/10.1007/978-3-030-45385-5_27

On the other, the correctly set camera could give a valuable color characteristic across the whole fish body, if image processing methods are applied [3,11,12]. With our previous software applications were already carried on case studies on determination of the color changes on aquatic organisms. The analysis resulted into justification of the chromatic colors approach and informational value of the hue color attribute [3,11,13–15].

To obtain the image of accurate color values, two conditions are required: the light, and the white balance. The typically used light profiles in the colormetry are $D65$ and $D50$, noon light and horizontal light respectively [16,17]. The $D50$ is equivalent to the industrial ICC color profile, while the $D65$ is more used in commercials for the more saturated colors. For example, the $D50$ fluorescent bulb provides standardized light conditions for basic color measurements [18]. Since the observing RGB camera has usually three channels (red, green, and blue), given by the Bayer mask [19]. Therefore, the white balance simply means, that the gains of each channel are tune to capture the same, like define white shade. There exist variant methods for automatic white balance in digital photography [16,20,21].

However, proper light and camera calibration are two related, but separated tasks. The setting of scene illumination could be time consuming, not always is the standard light available. Fortunately, if the light has enough brightness, the camera can adjust own gains using white balance algorithm. Some of the modern cameras have settings for the manual or automatic white balance [17]. Unfortunately, the practical experiences expressed the it is difficult to keep in mind and proceed all steps accurately, quickly, and during fish manipulation [13,14]. To improve the measurement acquisition, we developed a simple device, a box or chamber, with standardized light conditions, automatic camera calibration, environmental sensors, weighting scale, and software applications for color analysis and evaluation.

2 Setup

The devise [22] is illustrated at the Fig. 1. The chamber is sitting on the weighting scales for weighting living animals. Box itself consist of the black walls, and white bottom. The white serves to represent standard background, and helps in the image segmentation [23]. As a light source are implemented ordinary LED stripes. The camera looks at the bottom form the top, in the middle of light stripes. It has switchable filter for changing VIS/NOIR mode of acquisition. The device is controlled by the microPC with *Linux* distribution and *Python* scripts [24].

2.1 Lights

The white LEDs are not equal to the standard illuminations $D50$ ($5000K$) or $D65$ ($6504K$), its chromatic temperature is somewhere between ($5500K$). When we look at the spectral measurements on Fig. 2 in the visible range, there is a

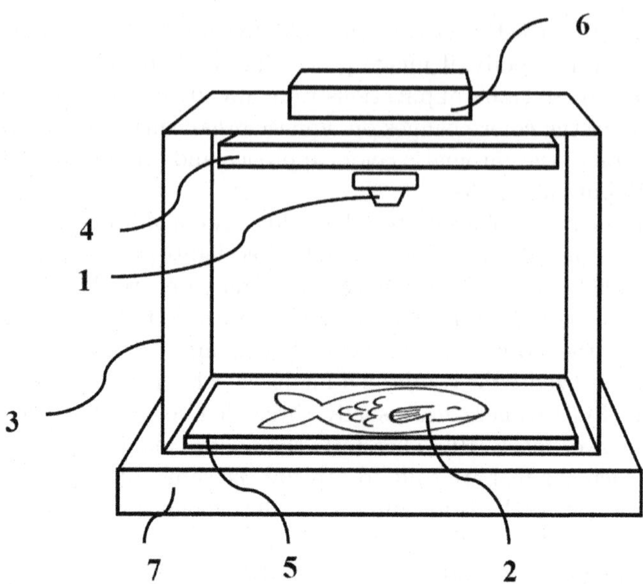

Fig. 1. Schematic description of the photochamber: 1-camera, 2-object (fish), 3-black walls of the chamber, 4-LED lights, 5-white background, 6-control microPC, 7-weighting scales.

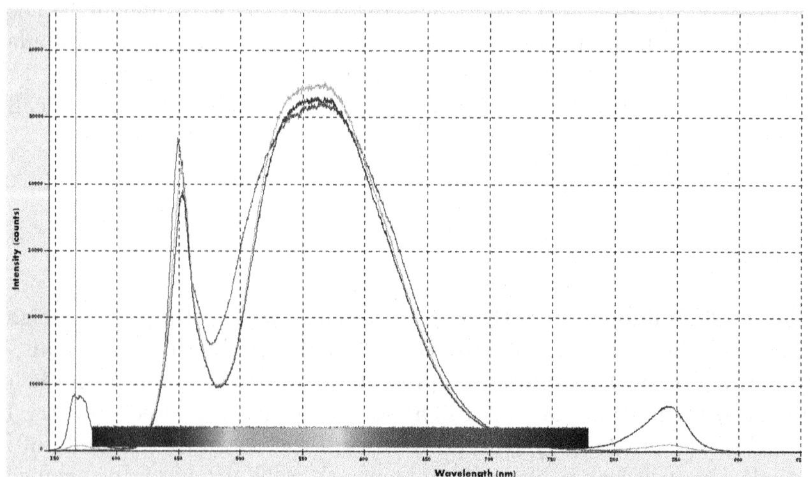

Fig. 2. Spectrum of the UV+white+NIR LEDs. (Color figure online)

sharper peak for the blue light and wider peak for the green light. During the experiments we also tested NIR (840 nm) and UVA (365 nm) LEDs, the complete spectral range was measured. As is clear from the spectral profile, there is missing a suitable red peak for accurate white calibration. Therefore, we improved the scene illumination by few red lights.

During the illumination, there is always a question of the direct or diffused light. Both settings have own advantages and disadvantages. The diffused light is not creating the shadows, however produces also weak edges for the object to background segmentation. On the other hand, the direct light has sharp edges, but produces shadows and reflections. In our setup we implemented the direct light illumination.

2.2 Control and Sensors

The lights, camera, and other sensors are controlled by the microcomputer RaspberryPi $3B+$, 4 core processor Broadcom $BCM2837B0$, 1.4 GHz, 1 GB RAM, under Linux distribution Raspbian [25].

The environment conditions are measured inside the box with Arduino sensors for temperature, pressure, and humidity. The whole box is sitting on the weighting scales with maximal load of 30 kg, and precision 0.5 g, see Fig. 1.

The device is automatically switching the lights, and calibrating the camera and scales.

2.3 Camera

The system could works with all versions of picamera, however we focused on the Waveshare products. The Cut type of the camera has IR with filter, which could be switched on or off. The gain of the green channel is given, therefore only gains of red and blue channels could be tuned. The camera offers a wide list of stable parameters, including brightness, contrast, ISO, and shutter speed (Fig. 3).

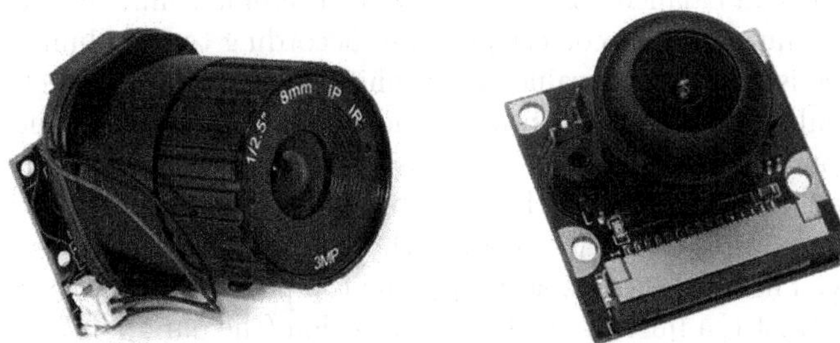

Fig. 3. PiCamera Waveshare Cut(B) and Cut(FE).

The camera is trying to calibrate gains of the red and blue channels, to see the background as white. The task is complicated by the experimental conditions, where fish are wet objects, and the reference white will also get wet. Such situation could produce reflexion and confuse the white balance algorithm.

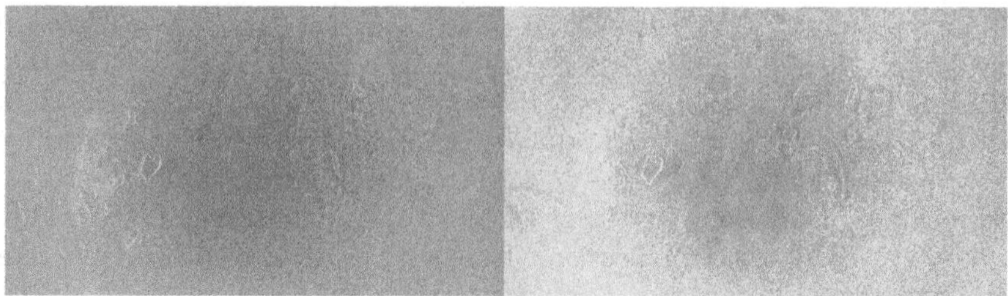

Fig. 4. Differences in calibration with the wet background, left Retinex, right Gray-World white balance method. (Color figure online)

For comparison of calibrated images, we were using the standard color checker with 24 colors (RGB, $CMYK$, gray shades), with known RGB and LAB values of the color [26]. However, it was reported, that the exact colors on the checker and provided table values do not match since November 2014 [27]. Therefore, we measured the values of each color from the color checker by XRite ColorMunki Photo [28,29].

3 Methods

The existing methods for the white balance were mostly developed for the corrections of the image taken with the incorrect settings. However, they are general enough to work directly on camera setting. Since the amount of light from the LEDs illumination is sufficient, two simplest methods of white balance algorithms could be used, the Retinex method, and GrayWorld method [16].

The white balance itself is just adjusting the gains for the red and blue channels. If the observed background is white, the responses of all three channels should be equal (in balance). Tuning the gains, therefore, shift the white point of the camera gamut [30] into correct position, according to the illuminating light.

This value is still not the value of the white respecting the reflection. Gamut calibration only preserves the captured colors to have the proper hue. The color representation of the RGB color space is tricky. The RGB values themselves do not represent the color, but the ratio between the values is representing the color. Therefore, after the white balance, the brightness and contrast corrections has to follow. The brightness is adjusting the top position in the dynamic range, while the contrast is adjusting the bottom position (the dark point). The red and blue channels are dependent on the green channel by the white balance gains, therefore, the brightness and contrast could be tuned for the green channel only.

3.1 White Balance

The Retinex theory assumes, that the white balance is given by the brightest points in the observed scene. The value of the maximal occupied level in the range (*8bits* usually) is therefore the brightest spot and assigned as a reference point. Gains of red and blue channels are evaluated from the maxima ratio:

$$Gain_{red} = \frac{G_{max}}{R_{max}}, \, and \, Gain_{blue} = \frac{G_{max}}{B_{max}}. \tag{1}$$

The GrayWorld theory assumes, that the most of the scene is usually gray, in other words, the colors and shades are distributed equally. Thus, the gains are computed from the average levels of each channel:

$$Gain_{red} = \frac{\mu_{green}}{\mu_{red}}, \, and \, Gain_{blue} = \frac{\mu_{green}}{\mu_{blue}}, \tag{2}$$

where $\mu_{channel}$ is average occupied level in the channel.

Both methods might be influenced by the noise, therefore reasonable amount of light is necessary.

3.2 Brightness and Contrast

Once the gains for the red and blue channels are set, the brightness of the green channel could be modified. The maximal occupied level of the green channel should have the green value of the calibration background. As a white reference is used standard photographic polypropylen background, with the reflection 0.7922 for two layers, and 0.8578 for 4 layers. Standard white checker has reflection 0.9529. On some image resolutions, the background might cause visible moire patterns, which are not affecting the color calibration nor color analysis.

The new brightness B_{new} value is obtained from the old brightness value B_{old}, background reflection in *8bits*, and maximal occupied level in the green level G_{max}.

$$B_{new} = \frac{255 * 0.7922 * B_{old}}{G_{max} - G_{std}}, \tag{3}$$

where G_{std} is the standard deviation in the green levels (*8bits*).

The contrast C is more complicated. The correction has to distinguish the high point value between emitted and reflected light, in other words between light and white, to avoid the saturation. In *8bits* representation between 255 and 243. The same is valid for the low point, to distinguish the dark from the black, 0 from 52. In chamber, we are capturing reflected light:

$$C = Black + (\mu_{green} - G_{min}) \times \frac{White - Black}{G_{max} - G_{min}}. \tag{4}$$

3.3 Analysis

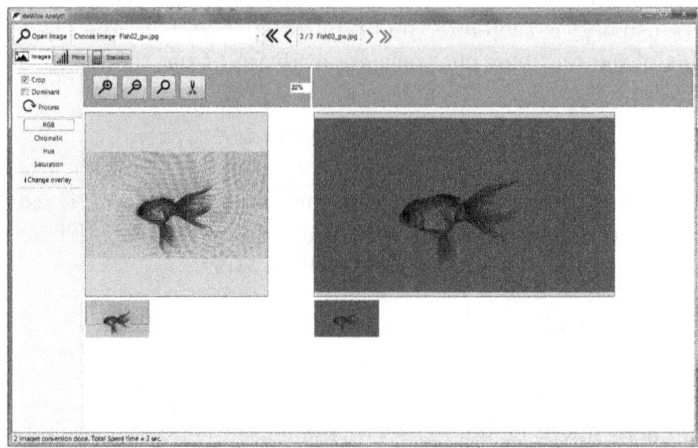

Fig. 5. The main window of deWise Analyst software application.

The captured images could be easily analysed with the software application for the segmentation (fish to background), color transformations and characteristics (sRGB, cRGB, LAB, HSV), image and set characteristics. The stand alone Win10 $C\#$ application is based on the previous research [11,13].

The application window consist of three tabs. The main tab allows to browse directories and images, view the images, and run the processing. The segmentation and color analysis is tuning automatically the parameters and thresholds. The result of segmentation is visible on the right image of the main tab, the background color could be chosen by user, see Fig. 5.

The second tab is showing the distributions of the various color space attributes across the object body:

- Standard Red, Standard Green, Standard Blue;
- Chromatic Red, Chromatic Green, Chromatic Blue;
- CIE Lightness, CIE a∗ (green-red), CIE b∗ (blue-yellow);
- Hue, Saturation, Value (Fig. 6).

The previous experiments and published results indicate, that the Hue color channel is representing the color attribute most accurately and is also one of the most relevant in the multivariate data analysis of fish skin color changes [3,11].

The last tab is showing the evaluated statistic (mean, standard deviation, median, mode) of current image, or whole set. The average position in the color gamut is also displayed, see Fig. 7.

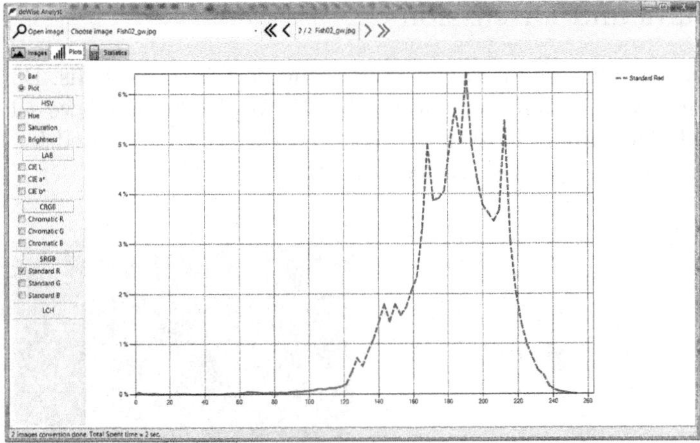

Fig. 6. The Plots window of deWise Analyst software application, with standard Red channel distribution.

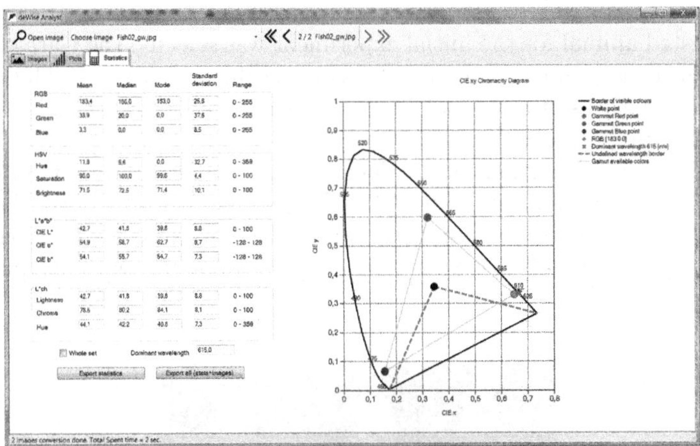

Fig. 7. The Statistics window of deWise Analyst software application, with color Gamut.

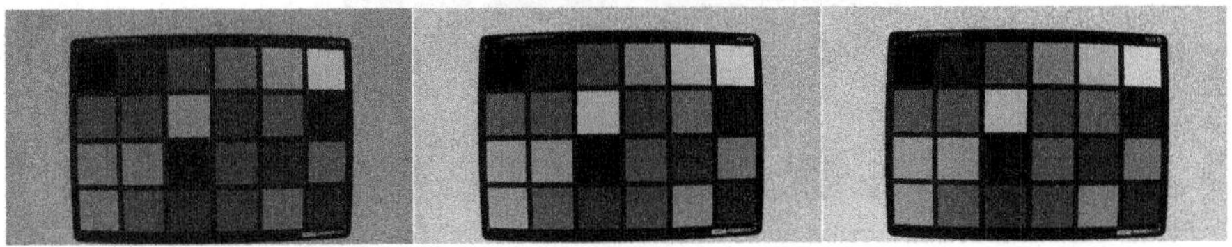

Fig. 8. Calibration chart, from left to right: Uncalibrated, Retinex, GrayWorld.

4 Results and Discussion

The camera is calibrated automatically, using described methods. Because the Retinex algorithm is the most affected by the wet background, we selected the GrayWorld algorithm. The standard color checker chart was used for the comparison of white balance calibration (Fig. 8).

Fig. 9. Carassius auratus in visible and infrared mode.

The tested animal for the initial experiment was selected the Carassius auratus (Goldfish) as a model organism for color evaluation [31–34]. The captured images passed the software analysis and a case study on the fish skin color changes is in preparation.

Several other applications of the device, using the near infrared mode, are in question, such us diseases and injuries analysis, or biometric analysis. For example, the human veins on the hand and fingers are currently in the investigation as biometric markers [35–37]. Such imaging is also possible with the introduced device, see Fig. 10.

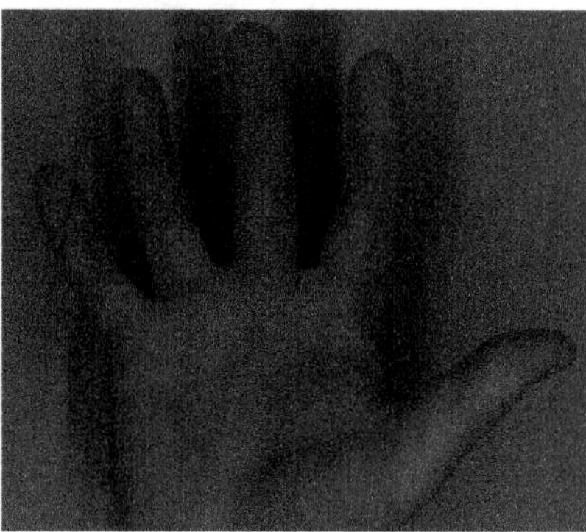

Fig. 10. Hand finger veins in near infrared mode.

While the calibration of the white balance is using the simple Gray World theory, more complicated methods are available [16], and could be implemented into the calibration. Generally, all the white balance methods suffers a bit with the reddish tendency, as it is also visible on the calibration on the wet surface see Fig. 4.

The more interesting is the connection of the image quality to the shutter speed of the camera. Since pinhole camera are primary video cameras, the shutter speed is related not only to the light on the scene, but also to the camera framerate, even if it is used as still camera.

Basically, the captured images could be used also for biometric analysis, in that case application of the adjustment of the lens distortions should be applied.

5 Conclusion

The device is standardizing the condition for the color measurements, automatically setup the camera parameters as white balance, brightness, and contrast to allows accurate color analysis from the captured images. The devise is easy to use, without advance user operation. It is connected with the analysing software for the segmentation, color transformation, and statistic. The device should help with the data acquisition as well as the analysis, comparison, and color evaluation.

Acknowledgments. The study was financially supported by the Ministry of Education, Youth and Sports of the Czech Republic - project CENAKVA (LM2018099), the CENAKVA Centre Development (No. CZ.1.05/2.1.00/19.0380) and project Biodiversity (CZ.02.1.01./0.0/0.0/16/025/0007370), as well as TACR GAMA (TG03010027 PoC02/23). Author thanks to P. Urbanova, J. Urban Jr., I. Koliada, O. Mashchenko, and P. Soucek for discussion and fish maintenance.

References

1. Fu, X., et al.: Comparative analysis of pigments in red and yellow banana fruit. Food Chem. **239**, 1009–1018 (2018)
2. Saad, A.M., Ibrahim, A., El-Bialee, N.: Internal quality assessment of tomato fruits using image color analysis. Agric. Eng. Int. CIGR J. **18**(1), 339–352 (2016)
3. Lundova, K., et al.: The effects of a prolonged photoperiod and light source on growth, sexual maturation, fin condition, and vulnerability to fungal disease in brook trout Salvelinus fontinalis. Aquac. Res. **50**(1), 256–267 (2019)
4. Shahjahan, M., Al-Emran, M., Islam, S.M., Baten, S.A., Rashid, H., Haque, M.M.: Prolonged photoperiod inhibits growth and reproductive functions of rohu Labeo rohita. Aquac. Rep. **16**, 100272 (2020)
5. Sacobie, C., Burke, H., Lall, S., Benfey, T.: The effect of dietary energy level on growth and nutrient utilization by juvenile diploid and triploid brook charr, Salvelinus fontinalis. Aquac. Nutr. **22**(5), 1091–1100 (2016)
6. Saberioon, M., Gholizadeh, A., Cisar, P., Pautsina, A., Urban, J.: Application of machine vision systems in aquaculture with emphasis on fish: state-of-the-art and key issues. Rev. Aquac. **9**(4), 369–387 (2017)

7. Wishkerman, A., Boglino, A., Darias, M.J., Andree, K.B., Estévez, A., Gisbert, E.: Image analysis-based classification of pigmentation patterns in fish: a case study of pseudo-albinism in Senegalese sole. Aquaculture **464**, 303–308 (2016)
8. Norazmi-Lokman, N.H., Purser, G., Patil, J.G.: Gravid spot predicts developmental progress and reproductive output in a livebearing fish, Gambusia holbrooki. PLoS ONE **11**(1), e0147711 (2016)
9. Jorjani, M., Sharifrohani, M., Mirhashemi Rostami, A., Tan Shau Hwai, A.: Effects of Hibiscus rosasiensis as a natural carotenoid on growth performance, body composition, pigmentation and carotenoid in blood plasma of blue gourami, trichogaster trichopterus at different stocking densities. Iran. J. Fish. Sci. **18**(4), 619–634 (2019)
10. Zenger, K.R., Khatkar, M.S., Jones, D.B., Khalilisamani, N., Jerry, D.R., Raadsma, H.W.: Genomic selection in aquaculture: application, limitations and opportunities with special reference to marine shrimp and pearl oysters. Front. Genet. **9**, 693 (2018)
11. Urban, J.: Colormetric experiments on aquatic organisms. In: Rojas, I., Ortuño, F. (eds.) IWBBIO 2017. LNCS, vol. 10208, pp. 96–107. Springer, Cham (2017). https://doi.org/10.1007/978-3-319-56148-6_8
12. Kouba, A., Sales, J., Sergejevová, M., Kozák, P., Masojídek, J.: Colour intensity in angelfish (Pterophyllum scalare) as influenced by dietary microalgae addition. J. Appl. Ichthyol. **29**(1), 193–199 (2013)
13. Urban, J., Štys, D., Sergejevová, M., Masojídek, J.: Expertomica Fishgui: comparison of fish skin colour. J. Appl. Ichthyol. **29**(1), 172–180 (2013)
14. Zat'ková, I., Sergejevová, M., Urban, J., Vachta, R., Štys, D., Masojidek, J.: Carotenoid-enriched microalgal biomass as feed supplement for freshwater ornamentals: albinic form of wels catfish (Silurus glanis). Aquac. Nutr. **17**(3), 278–286 (2011)
15. Urban, J., et al.: FISCEAPP: fish skin color evaluation application. In: 17th International Conference on Digital Image Processing, Dubai, UAE (2015)
16. Zapryanov, G., Ivanova, D., Nikolova, I.: Automatic white balance algorithms for digital still cameras–a comparative study. Inf. Technol. Control **1**, 16–31 (2012)
17. Johnston, W.M.: Color measurement in dentistry. J. Dent. **37**, e2–e6 (2009)
18. Mendelsohn, F.: Integrated fluorescent lamp device. US Patent 7,293,897, 13 November 2007
19. Knee, M.J.: Decoding a Bayer-mask or like coded image. US Patent App. 15/899,236, 23 August 2018
20. Liu, Y.C., Chan, W.H., Chen, Y.Q.: Automatic white balance for digital still camera. IEEE Trans. Consum. Electron. **41**(3), 460–466 (1995)
21. Lam, E.Y.: Combining gray world and Rtinex theory for automatic white balance in digital photography. In: 2005 Proceedings of the Ninth International Symposium on Consumer Electronics (ISCE 2005), pp. 134–139. IEEE (2005)
22. Urban, Bekkozhayeva, E.A.: Device for standardized photocapturing of living objects, mainly fish (2019). Utility model 32990
23. Chang, Y.C., Reid, J.F.: RGB calibration for color image analysis in machine vision. IEEE Trans. Image Process. **5**(10), 1414–1422 (1996)
24. Oliphant, T.E.: Python for scientific computing. Comput. Sci. Eng. **9**(3), 10–20 (2007)
25. Pajankar, A.: Introduction to single board computers and Raspberry Pi. In: Pajankar, A. (ed.) Raspberry Pi Supercomputing and Scientific Programming, pp. 1–25. Apress, Berkeley, CA (2017). https://doi.org/10.1007/978-1-4842-2878-4_1
26. Pascale, D.: A review of RGB color spaces... from xyY to RGB. Babel Color **18**, 136–152 (2003)

27. Pascale, D.: Colorchecker (2019). BabelColor.com
28. Bozhynov, V., Soucek, P., Barta, A., Urbanova, P., Bekkozhayeva, D.: Visible aquaphotomics spectrophotometry for aquaculture systems. In: Rojas, I., Ortuño, F. (eds.) IWBBIO 2018. LNCS, vol. 10813, pp. 107–117. Springer, Cham (2018). https://doi.org/10.1007/978-3-319-78723-7_9
29. Bozhynov, V., Soucek, P., Barta, A., Urbanova, P., Bekkozhayeva, D.: Dependency model for visible aquaphotomics. In: Rojas, I., Valenzuela, O., Rojas, F., Ortuño, F. (eds.) IWBBIO 2019. LNCS, vol. 11465, pp. 105–115. Springer, Cham (2019). https://doi.org/10.1007/978-3-030-17938-0_10
30. Smith, A.R.: Color gamut transform pairs. ACM SIGGRAPH Comput. Graph. **12**(3), 12–19 (1978)
31. Mizusawa, K., Yamamura, Y., Kasagi, S., Cerdá-Reverter, J.M., Takahashi, A.: Expression of genes for melanotropic peptides and their receptors for morphological color change in goldfish Carassius auratus. Gen. Comp. Endocrinol. **264**, 138–150 (2018)
32. Kumar, P.A., Sudhakaran, S., Mohan, T.C., Pamanna, D., Kumar, P.R., Shanthanna, P.: Evaluation of colour enhance potential of three natural plant pigment sources (African tulip tree flower, red paprika, pomegranate peel) in goldfish (Carassius auratus). Int. J. Fish. Aquat. Stud. **5**(6), 47–51 (2017)
33. Kasagi, S., Mizusawa, K., Takahashi, A.: The effects of chromatic lights on body color and gene expressions of melanin-concentrating hormone and proopiomelanocortin in goldfish (Carassius auratus). Gen. Comp. Endocrinol. **285**, 113266 (2020)
34. Liu, F., Zhang, J.W., Zhang, W.W.: Background color preference of Carassius auratus (goldfish). J. Hydroecol. (2019)
35. Jose, S., Bini, A.: Towards building a better biometric system based on vein patterns in human beings. In: 2019 IEEE International Conference on Electrical, Computer and Communication Technologies (ICECCT), pp. 1–4. IEEE (2019)
36. Walczak, T., Grabski, J.K., Michałowska, M., Szadkowska, D.: Application of artificial neural networks in the human identification based on thermal image of hands. In: Arkusz, K., Będziński, R., Klekiel, T., Piszczatowski, S. (eds.) BIOMECHANICS 2018. AISC, vol. 831, pp. 114–122. Springer, Cham (2019). https://doi.org/10.1007/978-3-319-97286-2_11
37. Badawi, A.M.: Hand vein biometric verification prototype: a testing performance and patterns similarity. IPCV **14**, 3–9 (2006)

Classification of Fish Species Using Silhouettes

Pavla Urbanova[1,2(✉)], Vladyslav Bozhynov[2], Petr Císař[2], and Miloš Železný[1]

[1] Department of Cybernetics, Faculty of Applied Sciences, University of West Bohemia in Pilsen, Univerzitní 8, 306 14 Plzeň, Czech Republic
urbanovp@kky.zcu.cz

[2] Laboratory of Signal and Image Processing, Institute of Complex Systems, Faculty of Fisheries and Protection of Waters, South Bohemian Research Center of Aquaculture and Biodiversity of Hydrocenoses, University of South Bohemia in Ceske Budejovice, Zamek 136, 37 333 Nove Hrady, Czech Republic

Abstract. The classification of the fish silhouettes allows a quick decision of the fish species presence and amount in the given scene. The classical approach of the machine learning is used to test the question of linear separability of fish species silhouettes classes. The preprocessing of images consisted of object to background segmentation and image registration. The classificator is trained using modified Rosenblatt algorithm for loss function of discriminant analysis.

This article is disseminating the preliminary results of training and testing of six fish species classification. The images were of different quality and light conditions. The classificator with the possibility to undecide is introduced and compared. The results are discussed from the point of view of usability of classical methods, preprocessing conditioning, and parametrization of loss function.

Keywords: Classification · Fish silhouettes · Linear separability

1 Introduction

In the fishery, various questions are related to the fish behaviour, tracking, classification, and identification. There are many types of tracking techniques to help you learn about fish, whether it be the needs of farming or smaller breeders [14,22]. The quality and original of data could also vary, from classical cameras, throught IR and multispectral sensors, to echolocation and sonars [2,8,10]. Often, the basic analysis works with corrupted and noised images, given by the nature of acquisition in real conditions. Obtained data is often misunderstood, images are of poor quality and in most cases there are also difficult conditions for data collection. Even with the poor signal, information relevant for tracking and classification are selected and extracted [14,16,22,25].

For these purposes, it is appropriate to recognize individual fish species. For the recognition itself, it is often enough to work only with the silhouettes of the fish [4,15,19]. The classification initialy starts with the assumption of linear separability of the fish species classes (Fig. 1).

I. Rojas et al. (Eds.): IWBBIO 2020, LNBI 12108, pp. 310–319, 2020.
https://doi.org/10.1007/978-3-030-45385-5_28

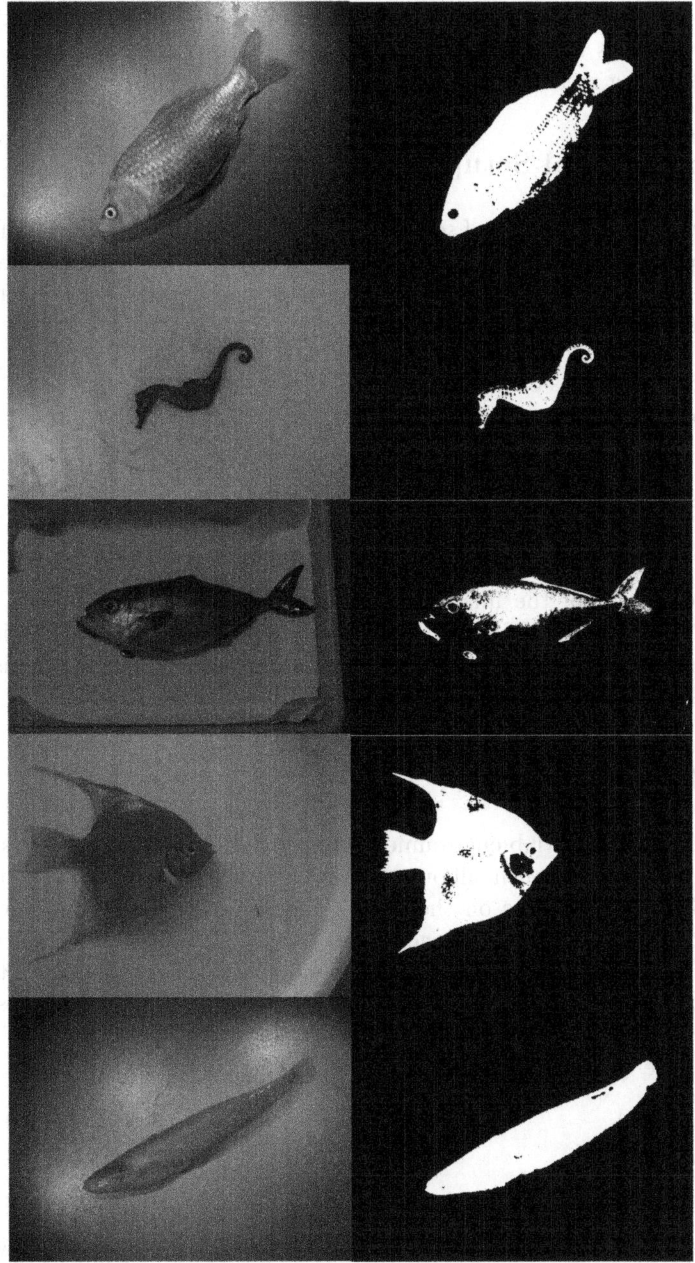

Fig. 1. Five fish species and black and white silhouettes. From top to down: Cyprinus carpio, Hippocampus algiricus, Caranx hippos, Pterophyllum scalare, Silurus glanis. Left fish images, right fish silhouettes.

In this article, we test a discrimination function for linear separability [13,17] of six fish species silhouettes, and discuss the perpetual usability of classical machine learning methods.

2 Experimental Setup

For the training and testing of selected method we used the silhouettes from real data from the color evaluation experiments [9,11,20,21,24]. The silhouettes as a results of segmentation are represented as black and white masks. For the basic evaluation were used 6 fish species:

- Coi carp (Cyprinus carpio),
- Sea horses (Hippocampus algiricus),
- Crevalle jack (Caranx hippos),
- Brook trout (Salvelinus fontinalis),
- Angelfish (Pterophyllum scalare),
- Wels catfish (Silurus glanis).

The resolution of the images varied from $640x480$ to $4700x1900$. In total we had 2132 silhouettes. The images are of various quality of acquisition: poor (Hippocampus algiricus, Caranx hippos), standard (Salvelinus fontinalis, Pterophyllum scalare), mixed (Cyprinus carpio, Silurus glanis).

3 Methods

We decided to use Matlab environment, especially for its Image processing toolbox. The images of the fish silhouettes were of different resolution, and the fish were in different positions on the scene. Therefore the image registration was applied to align the images on each other [3,12,23,26] for the comparison and classification. The reference image of fish silhouette was prepared in the resolution $60x60$ pixels. The black and white representation allows to consider the mask image as a matrix containing only values of 0 and 1.

The image registration consist of three basic geometric operations:

- Rotation,
- Translation,
- Scaling.

The silhouette images are represented in Cartesian coordinates, while the transformations are carried on in polar coordinates (Fig. 2).

Fig. 2. The reference silhouette for the image registration.

3.1 Linear Separability

For the classification in training period, it is expected that the two set X_1 (one group of fish silhouettes of one species) and X_2 (second group of fish silhouettes of other species) are linearly separable. Therefore, there exists a hyperplane representation of the set, where a distinct line could be drawn between the class areas [1,6,7,13,18]. In other words, two classes are linearly separable, if exist a linear discriminant function

$$g(x) = q_0 + q^T x : g(x) > 0, \forall x \in X_1; \quad (1)$$

$$g(x) < 0, \forall x \in X_2. \quad (2)$$

To prove, that the two given classes are separable, it is necessary to find a discriminant function which allows the classification of the images to the correct class [2,16,17,25]. The images are represented as a matrices. The distribution functions of the probabilities of each classes are apriori unknown. Therefore it is applied the method using direct loss minimization. To simplify the discriminant function, the vector of images is extended by the additional element $x_0 = +1$. Also the weighting vector is extended by additional threshold q_0. The discriminant function is therefore simplified to:

$$g(x) = q^T x. \quad (3)$$

Then, the decision rule $d(x, q)$ is possible to express by the signum function:

$$\omega = d(x, q) = sgn(q^T x), \quad (4)$$

where for dichotomy is $\omega_1 = 1$ and $\omega_2 = -1$.

Loss function:

$$Q(x, \Omega, q) = 0, \Omega = sgn(q^T x) \quad (5)$$

$$= 0, \Omega \neq (q^T x), \quad (6)$$

$$\Omega \in \{+1; -1\}. \quad (7)$$

Analyticaly:

$$Q(x, \Omega, q) = \frac{1}{4}(\Omega - sgn(q^T))^2 \quad (8)$$

$$= sgn(-Q^T x). \quad (9)$$

After the training, the classificator should decide:

$$q^T x > 0, x \in X_1 \tag{10}$$
$$q^T x < 0, x \in X_2. \tag{11}$$

Practically, the images of the separable classes are not necesarily neighbourhs, but their are separated by some distance 2δ. After such generalization, the classificator should decide:

$$q^T x \geq \delta, x \in X_1 \tag{12}$$
$$q^T x \leq -\delta x \in X_2. \tag{13}$$

Using the distance generalization, the loss function gets also modifications:

$$Q(x, \Omega, q) = sgn(-q^T x\Omega + \delta). \tag{14}$$

To avoid the non-zero gradient of the loss function, another modification is required:

$$\kappa = -q^T x\Omega + \delta; \tag{15}$$
$$Q(x, \Omega, q) = \kappa sgn(\kappa) = \kappa, \kappa \geq 0; \tag{16}$$
$$= 0, \kappa \leq 0. \tag{17}$$

Thus, the gradient of the function is defined as:

$$\nabla Q(x, \Omega, q) = 0, \Omega = \omega_1 \wedge q^T x \geq \delta \tag{18}$$
$$\vee \Omega = \omega_2 \wedge q^T x \leq -\delta \tag{19}$$
$$-x, \Omega = \omega_1 \wedge q^T x < \delta \tag{20}$$
$$x, \Omega = \omega_2 \wedge q^T x > \delta \tag{21}$$

Basic algorithm for loss minimization is:

$$q(k+1) = q(k) + C_{k+1} \nabla_q Q[x(k+1), \Omega(k+1), q(k)] \tag{22}$$

Therefore, the algorithm of training is:

$$q(k+1) = q(k), q(k)^T x(k+1)\Omega(k+1) > \delta \tag{23}$$
$$= q(k) + c_{k+1} x(k+1)\Omega(k+1), q(k)^T x(k+1)\Omega(k+1) \leq \delta \tag{24}$$

For different values of c_{k+1} and δ, we obtain different algorithms (Rosenblatt, Constant increase, Relaxation, $\cdots$). The Rosenblatt algorithm uses:

$$c_{k+1} = 1 \tag{25}$$
$$delta = 0. \tag{26}$$

and training:

$$q(k+1) = q(k), q(k)^T x(k+1)\Omega(k+1) \geq 0 \tag{27}$$
$$= q(k) + c_{k+1} x(k+1)\Omega(k+1), q(k)^T x(k+1)\Omega(k+1) \leq 0 \tag{28}$$

3.2 Modification of Discrimination Function

However, in our case, we do not have only two classes, but six. To simplify the output vector of class discrimination, the expect decision is:

$$qTx > 1; x2X1 \tag{29}$$

$$qTx < -1; x2X2 : \tag{30}$$

The distance interval δ was actually extended:

$$\delta = 1.5. \tag{31}$$

4 Results and Discussion

Described methods were programmed and tested in the Matlab environment. The training was stopped, if there were no changes of the weighting vector during the two consecutive iterations. The Rosenblatt algorithm required for the finding of the separating hyperplan about 50 iterations.

We evaluated 2132 images of fish silhouettes, which were separated into training testing set in ratio approximately $2 : 1$ $(1406 : 726)$. In the analysis, we distinquished and tested two classificators, considering the level of certainity for the classification, and the class strictness. The first is dichotomic in its decision, for each class decides only between object belongs to the class and object does not belong in the class. The result is vector of class coordinates for the tested image (1 for class membership, -1 otherwise). The second classificator is designed to expect imperfect images, or unknown class. Therefore, its decision is extended by the possibility not classified the object (undecide).

The results of the classification depends on the tested species. Purposely, we chosed images from different experiments and acquisition conditions, even poor. As the results reveals, the image preprocessing is conditioning the classification certainity.

4.1 Classifier Training According to Discrimination Function

For the training were used approxiamtely 2/3 of the available dataset. After training, each group of fish species silhouettes was classified by the classificator. The amounts of correct and false classification are listed in the Table 1.

In total, approximately 2/3 of the silhouettes were classified correctly. The seahorses (Hippocampus algiricus) classification failed. The obvious reason is in the seahorse body shape deviance, with is too distinct form the reference fish silhouettes 2, and the problem lies in the improper image registration. The Caranx images were also of poor quality, and again the classification failed. Such results were expected, the poor condition images were completing the set in case of classification possibility. The results, unfortunately, showed the conditionality of preprocessing methods (segmentation, silhouettes, registration).

Table 1. Table of correctly classified and missclassified silhouettes of each fish species in training dataset (direct classification).

Training	Correct	False	$\sum$
Cyprinus carpio	125	67	192
Hippocampus algiricus	0	32	32
Caranx hippos	1	6	7
Salvelinus fontinalis	80	6	86
Pterophyllum scalare	74	5	79
Silurus glanis	665	345	1010
$\sum$	945	461	1406

The standardised acquisition conditions were achieved during the Angelfish (Pterophyllum scalare) and trout (Salvelinus fontinalis) experiments. The results of classification of these two species are significantly proving the linear separability. The rest fish species were of mixed conditions and their correct ratio is again approximately 2/3.

Table 2. Table of correctly classified and missclassified silhouettes of each fish species in training dataset, unclassification possible.

Training	Correct	False	Undecided	$\sum$
Cyprinus carpio	92	39	61	192
Hippocampus algiricus	0	18	14	32
Caranx hippos	0	6	1	7
Salvelinus fontinalis	74	0	12	86
Pterophyllum scalare	38	2	39	79
Silurus glanis	560	236	214	1010
$\sum$	764	301	341	1406

In Table 2 are disseminated results of the classification, where the classificator had a possibility to undecide. As is visible, such undecision happened often with the poor silhouettes (Hippocampus, Caranx). However, the undecision in the standardised and mixed is also of high rate. The certainity of the classification is not strong, therefore additional tuning of δ distance and c_{k+1} weigh parameters is required.

4.2 Classifier Testing

The testing group was smaller than the training. Usually, the results of the classification of the testing group are worst than in the training, since the classificator never dealed with this data before. However, both Tables 3 and 4 shows the similar results as in the case of training.

Therefore, the limits of the linear separability are not in the higher amount of data. The necessary steps are proper preprocessing to obtain quality silhouettes, and loss function parametrization.

Table 3. Table of correctly classified and missclassified silhouettes of each fish species in testing dataset (direct classification)

Testing	Correct	False	$\sum$
Cyprinus carpio	64	37	101
Hippocampus algiricus	0	20	20
Caranx hippos	0	5	5
Salvelinus fontinalis	44	2	46
Pterophyllum scalare	33	3	36
Silurus glanis	334	184	518
$\sum$	475	251	726

Table 4. Table of correctly classified and missclassified silhouettes of each fish species in testing dataset, unclassification possible.

Testing	Correct	False	Undecided	$\sum$
Cyprinus carpio	55	23	23	101
Hippocampus algiricus	0	13	7	20
Caranx hippos	0	3	2	5
Salvelinus fontinalis	40	0	6	46
Pterophyllum scalare	17	1	18	36
Silurus glanis	274	125	119	518
$\sum$	386	165	175	726

5 Conclusion

The preliminary results shows that there exist linear separability between the fish silhouettes (Angelfish, trout). The modification of the algorithm requires parametrization tuning of the δ distance and c_{k+1} weigh [7]. The ability of the classification solution depends on the training datasets, accurate and precis silhouettes mask are necessary. Therefore, additional preprocessing has to be involved. Novadays, most of the image processing task are solved by the neural network and deep learning force [5]. Such approaches requires huge amount of training data, usually in tens of thousands. The powerful hardware is also often required. In the age of microPCs, classical machine learning approaches are still useful methods, since they required significantly lower amount of training data.

Acknowledgments. This research was supported by the Ministry of Education, Youth and Sports of the Czech Republic project No. LO1506. The study was financially supported by the Ministry of Education, Youth and Sports of the Czech Republic - project CENAKVA (*LM*2018099), the CENAKVA Centre Development (*No.CZ*.1.05/2.1.00/19.0380). Authors thank to J.Urban for discussion and consultation.

References

1. Balakrishnama, S., Ganapathiraju, A.: Linear discriminant analysis-a brief tutorial. Inst. Signal Inf. Process. **18**, 1–8 (1998)
2. Bothmann, L., Windmann, M., Kauermann, G.: Realtime classification of fish in underwater sonar videos. J. R. Stat. Soc. Ser. C (Appl. Stat.) **65**(4), 565–584 (2016)
3. Brown, L.G.: A survey of image registration techniques. ACM Comput. Surv. (CSUR) **24**(4), 325–376 (1992)
4. Cadieux, S., Michaud, F., Lalonde, F.: Intelligent system for automated fish sorting and counting. In: Proceedings of the 2000 IEEE/RSJ International Conference on Intelligent Robots and Systems (IROS 2000) (Cat. No. 00CH37113), vol. 2, pp. 1279–1284. IEEE (2000)
5. Dodge, S., Karam, L.: Understanding how image quality affects deep neural networks. In: 2016 Eighth International Conference on Quality of Multimedia Experience (QoMEX), pp. 1–6. IEEE (2016)
6. Elizondo, D.: The linear separability problem: some testing methods. IEEE Trans. Neural Netw. **17**(2), 330–344 (2006)
7. Fainzilberg, L., Matushevych, N.: Comparative evaluation of convergence's speed of learning algorithms for linear classifiers by statistical experiments method. Kibernetika i vychislitelnaya technika (2018)
8. Haghighat, M., Li, X., Fang, Z., Zhang, Y., Negahdaripour, S.: Segmentation, classification and modeling of two-dimensional forward-scan sonar imagery for efficient coding and synthesis. In: OCEANS 2016 MTS/IEEE Monterey, pp. 1–8. IEEE (2016)
9. Kouba, A., Sales, J., Sergejevová, M., Kozák, P., Masojídek, J.: Colour intensity in angelfish (p terophyllum scalare) as influenced by dietary microalgae addition. J. Appl. Ichthyol. **29**(1), 193–199 (2013)
10. Li, D., Hao, Y., Duan, Y.: Nonintrusive methods for biomass estimation in aquaculture with emphasis on fish: a review. Rev. Aquac. (2019). https://doi.org/10.1111/raq.12388
11. Lundova, K., et al.: The effects of a prolonged photoperiod and light source on growth, sexual maturation, fin condition, and vulnerability to fungal disease in brook trout salvelinus fontinalis. Aquac. Res. **50**(1), 256–267 (2019)
12. Maintz, J.A., Viergever, M.A.: A survey of medical image registration. Med. Image Anal. **2**(1), 1–36 (1998)
13. Murty, M.N., Raghava, R.: Linear discriminant function. Support Vector Machines and Perceptrons. SCS, pp. 15–25. Springer, Cham (2016). https://doi.org/10.1007/978-3-319-41063-0_2
14. Saberioon, M., Gholizadeh, A., Cisar, P., Pautsina, A., Urban, J.: Application of machine vision systems in aquaculture with emphasis on fish: state-of-the-art and key issues. Rev. Aquac. **9**(4), 369–387 (2017)
15. Shortis, M.: Camera calibration techniques for accurate measurement underwater. In: McCarthy, J.K., Benjamin, J., Winton, T., van Duivenvoorde, W. (eds.) 3D

Recording and Interpretation for Maritime Archaeology. CRL, vol. 31, pp. 11–27. Springer, Cham (2019). https://doi.org/10.1007/978-3-030-03635-5_2

16. Shortis, M.R., Ravanbakhsh, M., Shafait, F., Mian, A.: Progress in the automated identification, measurement, and counting of fish in underwater image sequences. Mar. Technol. Soc. J. **50**(1), 4–16 (2016)
17. Siddiqui, S.A., et al.: Automatic fish species classification in underwater videos: exploiting pre-trained deep neural network models to compensate for limited labelled data. ICES J. Mar. Sci. **75**(1), 374–389 (2018)
18. Sklansky, J., Wassel, G.N.: Linearly separable classes. In: Sklansky, J., Wassel, G.N. (eds.) Pattern Classifiers and Trainable Machines, pp. 31–78. Springer, New York (1981). https://doi.org/10.1007/978-1-4612-5838-4_2
19. Strachan, N.J.C., Nesvadba, P., Allen, A.R.: Fish species recognition by shape analysis of images. Pattern Recogn. **23**(5), 539–544 (1990)
20. Urban, J.: Colormetric experiments on aquatic organisms. In: Rojas, I., Ortuño, F. (eds.) IWBBIO 2017. LNCS, vol. 10208, pp. 96–107. Springer, Cham (2017). https://doi.org/10.1007/978-3-319-56148-6_8
21. Urban, J., Štys, D., Sergejevová, M., Masojídek, J.: Expertomica fishgui: comparison of fish skin colour. J. Appl. Ichthyol. **29**(1), 172–180 (2013)
22. Verschae, R., Kawashima, H., Nobuhara, S.: A multi-camera system for underwater real-time 3D fish detection and tracking. In: OCEANS 2017-Anchorage, pp. 1–5. IEEE (2017)
23. Viergever, M.A., Maintz, J.A., Klein, S., Murphy, K., Staring, M., Pluim, J.P.: A survey of medical image registration-under review (2016)
24. Zat'ková, I., Sergejevová, M., Urban, J., Vachta, R., Štys, D., Masojidek, J.: Carotenoid-enriched microalgal biomass as feed supplement for freshwater ornamentals: albinic form of wels catfish (silurus glanis). Aquac. Nutr. **17**(3), 278–286 (2011)
25. Zhang, D., Lee, D.J., Zhang, M., Tippetts, B.J., Lillywhite, K.D.: Object recognition algorithm for the automatic identification and removal of invasive fish. Biosyst. Eng. **145**, 65–75 (2016)
26. Zitova, B., Flusser, J.: Image registration methods: a survey. Image Vis. Comput. **21**(11), 977–1000 (2003)

E-Health Technology, Services and Applications

Spa-neg: An Approach for Negation Detection in Clinical Text Written in Spanish

Oswaldo Solarte-Pabón(✉), Ernestina Menasalvas(✉), and Alejandro Rodriguez-González(✉)

Centro de Tecnología Biomédica, Universidad Politécnica de Madrid, Madrid, Spain
oswaldo.solartep@alumnos.upm.es,
{ernestina.menasalvas,alejandro.rg}@upm.es

Abstract. Electronic health records contain valuable information written in narrative form. A relevant challenge in clinical narrative text is that concepts commonly appear negated. Several proposals have been developed to detect negation in clinical text written in Spanish. Much of these proposals have adapted the Negex algorithm to Spanish, but obtained results indicating lower performance than NegEx implementations in other languages. Moreover, in most of these proposals, the validation process could be improved using a shared test corpus focused on negation in clinical text. This paper proposes Spa-neg, an approach to improve negation detection in clinical text written in Spanish. Spa-neg combines three elements: (i) an exploratory data analysis of how negation is written in the clinical text, (ii) use of regular expressions best adapted to the way in which negation is expressed in Spanish, (iii) experiments, and validation using a shared annotated corpus focused on negation. Our findings suggest that the combination of these elements improves the process of negation detection. The tests performed have shown 92% F-Score using IULA Spanish, an annotated corpus for negation in clinical text.

Keywords: Negation detection · Electronic health records · Clinical Natural Language Processing

1 Introduction

Negation detection is a challenging problem in the information extraction field. This is particularly important in systems aimed to extract knowledge from clinical information, where the detection of negation is key to understand symptoms, diagnoses, or treatments [4].

Negation detection is typically divided into two subtasks: cue identification and scope recognition. The cues are words or terms that express negation (e.g., without, not, nothing) [8]. The expressions *negation terms* and *negation phrases* can also be used to refer to negation cues. The scope is a text fragment affected by the corresponding negation cue in a sentence [10].

I. Rojas et al. (Eds.): IWBBIO 2020, LNBI 12108, pp. 323–337, 2020.
https://doi.org/10.1007/978-3-030-45385-5_29

One of the most commonly used algorithms to detect negation in medical records is NegEx [5]. This algorithm has been recognized as one of the most useful approaches for the detection of negated medical concepts. However, it has been studied that it can present deficiencies when terms that express negation appear contiguously several times, or when multiple instances of the negation affect the same medical concept [12]. Despite the acceptance that NegEx has had, it could be improved. In the case of the Spanish language, several studies have been proposed to detect negation in clinical texts [7,13,27]. These proposals adapted the NegEx algorithm to Spanish but obtained lower results than Negex implementations in English. Additionally, in these proposals, the validation process could be improved using a shared test corpus focused on negation in clinical texts.

This paper proposes Spa-neg, an approach to detect negation in clinical texts written in Spanish. Spa-neg combines three elements to improve negation detection: (i) an exploratory data analysis to understand how negation appears in clinical texts; (ii) adaptation of regular expressions based on data analysis; and (iii) validation using a corpus annotated by experts and focused on negation in clinical texts. The results obtained suggest that the combination of these elements improves the process of detecting negation. When performing tests, we obtain a 92% in the F-Score measure using "UILA Spanish" [24], a shared corpus and focused on the negation.

The remainder of this paper is organized as follows: Sect. 2 describes proposals that address negation detection, with an emphasis on proposals for the Spanish language. Section 3 shows an exploratory data analysis of the negation. The Spa-neg proposal is described in detail in Sect. 4. Section 5 describes the tests that were carried out to measure the performance of the Spa-neg proposal. Finally, Sect. 6 includes conclusions and future work.

2 Related Works

In the field of clinical text, several proposals have been developed for negation detection. One of the most relevant is NegEx [5], an algorithm which has been widely used and adapted for several languages [3,21,26]. This algorithm uses two regular expressions and a set of negation terms that activate the negation. The Negex algorithm also uses a set of termination terms to indicate the negation scope [6]. Negex has been implemented in several clinical information extraction tools such as MetaMap [1] or Apache cTAKES [25].

In [2], a strategy is proposed that uses the syntactic properties of the sentence to calculate the scope. A similar study to the previous one was proposed in [17], where the authors described an algorithm that incorporates the use of a dependency tree within Negex.

On the other hand, [12] describes NegMiner, a proposal that aims to solve some of the weaknesses of the Negex algorithm. For example, when contiguous negation terms and multiple negation expressions appear in the same sentence. The author argues that NegEx algorithm is still not sufficiently robust because many sentences are too complex to be correctly processed by just a couple of regular expressions. To solve these shortcomings, NegMiner proposes new rules to deal with contiguous negation terms and to detect various expressions of negation within the scope of a medical concept. Experimental results showed a higher performance than the Negex algorithm.

According to [8], machine learning approaches have also been used as a technique in detecting negation in medical texts. For instance, in [9,18,22] machine learning-based classifiers were proposed to detect negations. Moreover, algorithms such as Support Vector Machines and Conditional Random Fields, were used. Tests were performed using the Bioscope corpus [29], which is focused on the English language.

Although the proposals mentioned above showed significant advances and improvements in negation detection, most of these approaches have focused on the English language. According to [19], information extraction in the medical domain also represents its own challenges in languages other than English.

2.1 Negation Detection in Clinical Text Written in Spanish

One of the proposals to detect negation on clinical texts in Spanish was described in [7]. This proposal adapts Negex using an approach that first translates negation terms from Negex to Spanish, and then calculates the frequency of negated terms. Reported results showed that when calculating the frequency of the terms that activate the negation, large differences were found between the terms used in English and Spanish. When Negex adaptation was evaluated, a large number of false positives were found, and an F-score value of 84% was obtained. This value was lower than the value obtained by Negex implementations in English. The authors suggest that one of the reasons for the high number of false positives might be because the structure in which medical texts are written in Spanish differs from English. Therefore, the rules implemented in NegEx do not always work properly for negation in Spanish. Other Negex adaptations to Spanish were also developed in [13,27]. These proposals define a wider set of negation terms appropriate for the Spanish language while adapting the rules proposed by NegEx to Spanish.

In [20], an adaptation of Negex is proposed by adding syntactic properties such as Part of Speech (POS) tagging and syntactic dependency trees. In this proposal, the syntactic properties were used to perform a manual identification of patterns that are used to calculate the negation scope. Reported results show an improvement in efficiency when combining NegEx with Pos Tagging information. However, this adaptation only used the original rules proposed in Negex. This may represent a disadvantage in certain cases, such as those reported in [12].

In addition to syntactic properties, [15] proposes the use of pragmatic properties and grammar rules previously created to detect negation in radiology reports. Although they showed promising results, one disadvantage is that, the performed tests lack the use of a shared annotated corpus focused on negation.

Finally, to address the lack of annotated corpus focused on the negation in Spanish, several studies have been carried out in [11,14,16]. In particular, annotated corpora for negation detection in the Spanish medical texts have been presented in [23,24]. In [28], is highlighted the importance of shared annotated corpus for developing Natural Language Processing tools in the medical domain.

3 Exploratory Data Analysis of the Negation

The data analysis aims to obtain indicators to understand how negation is expressed in clinical texts written in Spanish. It describes extracted indicators such as the length of sentences, number of negation terms by sentence, types of negation, and frequency.

Length is the number of tokens within the sentence. A *token* is the result of the tokenization of the sentence text in atomic elements such as words, numbers, or acronyms. *Negation types* are different ways to express the negation in clinical texts. *Negation terms* are words that express negation (e.g., *"no, sin, nunca, negativo para"*)

3.1 Datasets

- ***Dataset 1:*** a random sample of 3000 medical reports, which have been previously pseudo-anonymized. This sample represents 20% of a database that contains around 15.000 medical reports from the *"Hospital Universitario Puerta de Hierro"*, in Madrid, Spain. This dataset is used in a real-life research project to support medical data analysis of lung cancer patients.
- ***Dataset 2:*** the corpus *IULA Spanish*[1], proposed by [24]. This corpus is a shared dataset, in which experts have manually annotated the negation in clinical text written in Spanish. This corpus contains 3194 sentences, each annotation includes the negation term and their scope.

3.2 Results from Dataset 1

- **Length of sentences:** Figure 1 reports the distribution of the length, measured as the number of tokens in the sentences in which negation appears. The length of sentences is distributed between 1 and 198 tokens. The first quartile corresponds to sentences with a length of 6 tokens, the second quartile to 9 tokens, and the third quartile to 17 tokens.
  This distribution is positive asymmetric since the higher frequencies are below the mean. In other words, to express the negation, the use of short sentences rather than long sentences, is more frequent. For example, only the range between 1 and 9 tokens contains 50% of the negated sentences. In addition, after ten tokens, the frequency decreases rapidly, and sentences of greater length are rare.

[1] http://eines.iula.upf.edu/brat/#/NegationOnCR_IULA/.

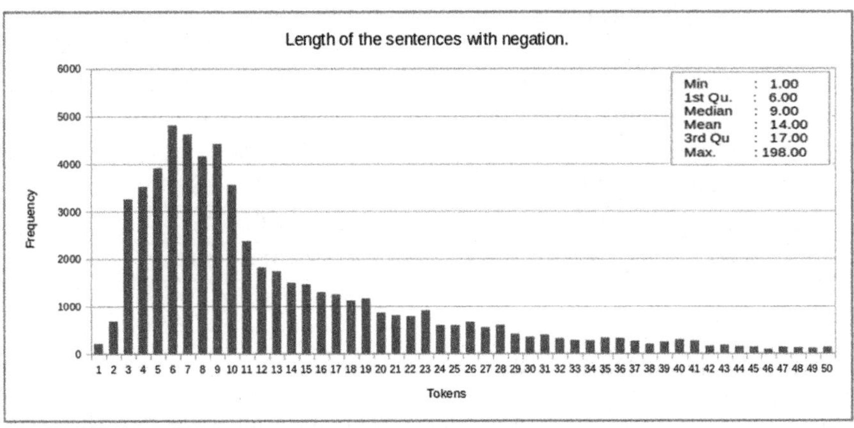

Fig. 1. Length of sentences with negation (Dataset 1)

– **Negation types:** The number of sentences that match each type of negation was obtained under the definitions shown in Table 1. In Sect. 4.2 there are examples of sentences related to these types.

Table 1. Different ways to express the negation and their frequency (Freq)

Negation type	Description	Freq
Contiguous negation	When the same negation term is repeated several times consecutively on the sentence	28%
Not contiguous negation	When the sentence contains one or more different negation terms	43%
Short sentence negation	When the sentence contains a single negation term, and the number of tokens in the sentence is in the first quartile	25%
Double negation	Sentences where the double negation occurs	4%

– **Number of negation terms:** Table 2 shows the number of negation terms that appear in a Contiguous way compared with Not contiguous way. The results are shown in 4 ranges, separated by the length of the sentences and the quartile (Q1, Q2, Q3) to which they belong. According to Table 2, the distribution of negation terms in the *Contiguous negation* is different, in comparison with the *Not contiguous negation*.

Table 2. Number of negation terms.

Tokens range	Not contiguous negation							Contiguous negation		
	1	2	3	4	5	6	7	1	2	3
1. [1–Q1]		99%	1%					100%		
2. (Q1–Q2]		77%	23%					95%	5%	
3. (Q2–Q3]		61%	32%	5%	4%			93%	7%	
4. >Q3		48%	27%	12%	8%	3%	2%	91%	9%	

3.3 Results from Dataset 2

Figure 2 shows the distribution of sentences where negation appears in the *"IULA Spanish"* dataset. The length is distributed between 1 and 130 tokens. The first quartile corresponds to sentences with a length of 7 tokens, the second quartile to 11 tokens, and the third quartile to 20 tokens. Similar to results obtained from dataset 1, this distribution is positive asymmetric since the higher frequencies are below the mean. This data set also shows that to express negation, the use of short sentences rather than long sentences is more frequent.

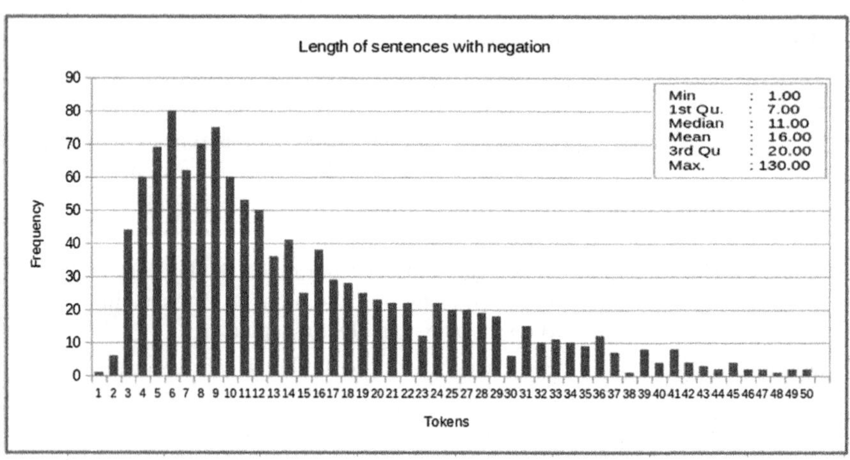

Fig. 2. Length of sentences with negation (Dataset 2)

Table 3 shows a summary of the indicators obtained from the exploratory data analysis for both analyzed datasets. There are appreciable similarities between these datasets. For example in both cases, the use of short sentences instead of long sentences for expressing negation, is more frequent. Moreover, in both cases, the negation is expressed in different ways, such as double negation, contiguous, and not contiguous negation.

Table 3. Summary of negation indicators from exploratory data analysis.

Indicator	Dataset 1	Dataset 2
Negation frequency	27%	32%
First quartile	6.00	7.00
Median	9.00	11.00
Mean	14.00	16.00
Third quartile	17.00	20.00
Contiguous negation	28%	30%
Not contiguous negation	43%	40%
Short sentence negation	25%	27%
Double negation	4%	3%

4 Proposal for Negation Detection in Clinical Texts

Spa-Neg proposal aims to improve negation detection in clinical texts written in Spanish. For this purpose, Spa-neg takes advantage of statistical information extracted from exploratory data analysis of the negation. Spa-neg is divided into three components: negation indicators, negation detection, and scope calculation.

4.1 Negation Indicators

This component contains indicators extracted from exploratory data analysis which are used to improve negation detection, as shown below:

- **Types of negation indicator** revealed that there are different ways of expressing negation in clinical texts. For this reason, our proposal includes rules that are better adapted to the way in which negation is expressed in Spanish. These rules are shown in Sect. 4.2.
- **The number of negation terms indicator** showed that the way in which contiguous negation occurs is different from not contiguous negation. This indicator is used to calculate the negation scope. Spa-neg first checks if negation happens in a contiguous way, and depending on the outcome, calculates the negation scope. The scope calculation is explained in Sect. 4.3.
- **The sentence length indicator** is used to estimate the value of the short sentence heuristic. This value is estimated based on the first quartile position in the length distribution of sentences. This value indicates that a sentence is considered as a *short sentence* if its length belongs to the first quartile, and it has only one negation term. Short sentence heuristic is also used to calculate the scope. An example of short sentence is: *"**No** se palpan masas"*.

4.2 Negation Detection Component

Spa-neg uses five regular expressions (Regex) to detect negation, as described below: Regex 1 and 2 are adapted from the Negex proposal. Regex 3 and 4 are an adaptation for Spanish based on [12] proposal. Moreover, we add the fifth Regex to deal with cases where double negation is presented in clinical texts written in Spanish:

1. <pre-negation term> * <UMLS term>
2. <UMLS term> * <post-negation term>

The symbol * represents an unspecified number of tokens in the sentence. The UMLS (Unified Medical Language System) term, represents medical concepts affected by the pre-negation or post-negation terms which are also included in the Spa-neg dictionary.

In the sentence *"**No** lesiones cutaneas relevantes"*, the negation is detected using the first regular expression because the word *"No"* is considered as a pre-negation term.

In the sentence *"Urocultivos de control* **negativos**.", the negation is detected using the second Regex because the word *"Negativos"* is considered as a post-negation term. Regular expressions 1 and 2 best fit in cases of not contiguous negation.

3. <pre-contiguous negation term> * <UMLS term>
4. <UMLS term> * <post-contiguous negation term>

The Regex 3 improves negation detection in sentences that contain multiple contiguous pre-negation terms. This case occurs when the same negation term is repeated several times consecutively, as it is shown in the example below:

*"**No** dolor en el tórax, **no** tos **ni** expectoración, **no** dolor abdominal".*

The Regex 4 improves negation detection in sentences that contain several contiguous post-negation terms, as the next example shows.

*"Análisis de proteínas 0.2 g/l **negativo**, c.cetonicos **negativo**, bilirrubina **negativo**, urobilinogeno +- mg/dl, **negativo**, leucocitos pendiente realización."*

Finally, we add the fifth Regex to detect double negation in clinical text written in Spanish.

5. <pre-negation term> * <pre-negation term> * <UMLS term>

Double negation happens when two negation terms have been detected and they change the meaning of what is being negated. For example, the word *"descartar"* is often used to negate concepts within medical texts. However, this word can also be used to change the meaning of negation if it is combined with other terms that also activate the negation.

In the sentence: *"**No** se puede **descartar** tumor en el pulmón."*, there are two negation terms: *"No"* and *"descartar"*. In this case, these two terms should not be considered separately but should be analyzed together. Therefore, this sentence should not be detected as negated. Rule 5 allows us to identify these cases.

4.3 Scope Calculation

When negation is detected with a pre-negation term, the scope is to the right of that term (forward in the sentence). If the negation is detected with a post-negation term, the scope is to the left of the term (backwards in the sentence).

When negation is detected with a pre-negated term, the scope is calculated using the algorithm shown in Fig. 3. This algorithm receives two inputs: the sentence where negation is detected and metadata about negation detection (NegData). This metadata contains the conditions in which negation was detected. The algorithm also requires that the sentence has been previously tokenized and POS (*Part of speech*) tagged.

First, the algorithm checks whether negation was detected in a contiguous way. In this case, the negation scope will be given by the next negation term. The position of the next negation term indicates the end of the negation scope being analyzed at that point.

Next, the algorithm checks if negation was detected in a short sentence. In this case, the *short sentence heuristic* is used, and the scope is given by the end of the sentence. This heuristic improves negation detection because it avoids possible errors in searching for a termination term.

Afterwards, the algorithm searches for a termination term, which indicates the end of the negation scope. Termination terms have been previously defined in the Spa-neg dictionary.

Finally, if none of the above conditions are true, the algorithm uses POS tagging properties to calculate the negation scope. In this case, the scope is determined by a token labeled with any of the following categories: conjunction, punctuation symbol, or a verb. POS tagging is useful when negation is detected in a sentence that does not contain a termination term.

In cases when the negation is detected using a post-negated term, the scope is determined using an algorithm similar to the one shown in Fig. 3, but in this case the scope is to the left of that term (backwards in the sentence).

5 Experiments and Validation

To validate our proposal, we used the "IULA Spanish" corpus, proposed by [24]. This corpus was described previously in Sect. 3.1. The results obtained were

```
Algorithm 1: Scope Calculation
inputs: sentence, Neg-Data;
output: scope;

if (Neg-Data.is-contiguos = true) then
    scope=Neg-Data.next-position;
else
    if (sentence = shortSentence) then
        scope = sentence.end;
    else
        stopTerm = findTerminationTerm()
        if (isValid(stopTerm) = true) then
            scope = stopTerm.end;
        else
            token= findTokenUsingPOS();
            scope = token.end;
        end
    end
end
```

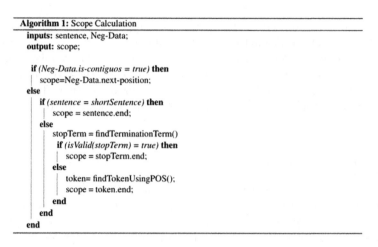

Fig. 3. Algorithm used to calculate negation scope.

measured using Precision, Recall and F-score for the task of negation detection and their scope calculation.

$$\textbf{Precision} = \frac{\text{Negations and their scope correctly detected}}{\text{Number of detected negations}} \quad (1)$$

$$\textbf{Recall} = \frac{\text{Negations and their scope correctly detected}}{\text{Total negations in the corpus}} \quad (2)$$

$$\textbf{F-score} = 2 * \frac{\text{Precision} * \text{Recall}}{\text{Precision} + \text{Recall}} \quad (3)$$

To validate our approach, we carried out four experiments that we describe below. Table 4 shows the results obtained.

- ***Experiment 1:*** This experiment consisted of an adaptation of the Negex algorithm to Spanish using only regular expressions 1 and 2 (see Sect. 4.2).
- ***Experiment 2:*** In this execution, rules 3 and 4 were added to the Negex adaptation that was carried out in Experiment 1.
- ***Experiment 3:*** Rule 5 is added to detect double negation cases.
- ***Experiment 4:*** Finally, we evaluated the use of the five rules mentioned above in addition to the use of POS Tagger labeling, as shown in Fig. 3. This experiment includes all the ideas proposed in this paper.

Table 4. Negation detection and its scope.

	Experiment 1: Negex rules 1, 2	Experiment 2: Rules: 1, 2, 3, 4	Experiment 3: Rules: 1, 2, 3, 4, 5	Experiment 4: Rules: 1, 2, 3, 4, 5 + POS Tagger
Precision	0.76	0.86	0,90	0.91
Recall	0.82	0.90	0.93	0.95
F score	0.78	0.87	0.90	0.92

In experiment 1, an F-score value of 78% was obtained, which is the lowest of all experiments. It is because, this experiment only takes into account rules 1 and 2, as proposed in Negex. These rules are not sufficient to correctly detect cases with multiple contiguous negation terms. The sentence:

> *"Análisis de proteínas 0.2 g/l* ***negativo****, c.cetonicos* ***negativo****, bilirrubina* ***negativo****, urobilinogeno +– mg/dl,* ***negativo****, leucocitos pendiente realización."*,

is an example of how experiment 1 fails to calculate the scope because there are multiple post-negation terms, and there is not a term that indicates scope termination for each instance of the detected negation.

In experiment 2, rules 3 and 4 were added to detect cases where contiguous negation terms appear, as in the previous example. By adding these rules, the results were significantly improved, and an 87% F-score was obtained. These rules are useful when negation terms are expressed contiguously. This type of negation is very common in clinical texts written in Spanish.

In experiment 3, we added rule 5, to allow detecting cases where double negation occurs. By adding rule 5, an F-score of 90% was obtained in the experiments performed. It indicates that, by correctly detecting the double negation, the results improved by 3% compared to the previous experiment.

Results obtained in experiment 4, as shown in Table 4, show 91% Precision, 95% Recall, and a 92% F-score. These results are superior to those obtained in the previous tests and were achieved by the use of 5 regular expressions and the algorithm shown in Fig. 3.

We have also compared the behavior of our approach with other approaches in the literature. In fact, the UILA Spanish corpus has been used for the experiments. Table 5 shows the results where one can see that the proposed approach outperforms other approaches in terms of F-Score. These proposals have only taken into account the rules proposed by NegEx. The results indicate that the NegEx rules are not sufficient to detect all negation cases in Spanish, such as *contiguous negation* and *double negation*.

6 Conclusions and Future Work

We proposed Spa-neg, an approach to improve negation detection in clinical texts written in Spanish. This approach used three elements: an exploratory

Table 5. Comparison between Spa-neg and other proposals

Proposal	NegEx by [7]	NegEx by [27]	NegEx by [13]	Spa-neg
Precision	0.71	0.58	0.72	**0.91**
Recall	0.78	0.81	0.86	**0.95**
F-score	0.74	0.67	0.78	**0.92**

data analysis to understand how negation is expressed in clinical texts; regular expressions best adapted to the way in which negation is expressed in Spanish, and a shared test corpus focused on negation in clinical texts.

The use of additional regular expressions improved negation detection because they are better adapted to the way negation is written in clinical texts. It is important to mention that using both, contiguous negation and double negation detection, improved results obtained in cases where Negex adaptations to Spanish can present deficiencies.

To calculate the negation scope, Spa-neg has taken into account: the regular expressions, the indicators obtained from an exploratory data analysis, termination terms that indicate the end of the scope, and the POS tagger properties of the sentence. Negation detection in clinical texts is difficult to achieve since it can be expressed in different ways. For this reason, it is important to use an annotated and shared corpus for improving the validation and testing process. In our case, the "UILA Spanish" corpus was used. With regard to future work, we are planning to explore other approaches to negation detection in medical texts. One example might be to include the use of a semantic properties of the sentence to improve results.

Acknowledgements. This paper is supported by European Union's Horizon 2020 research and innovation program under grant agreement No. 727658, project IASIS (Integration and analysis of heterogeneous big data for precision medicine and suggested treatments for different types of patients).

References

1. Aronson, A.R., Lang, F.M.: An overview of MetaMap: historical perspective and recent advances. J. Am. Med. Inform. Assoc. **17**(3), 229–236 (2010). https://doi.org/10.1136/jamia.2009.002733
2. Ballesteros, M., Francisco, V., Díaz, A., Herrera, J., Gervás, P.: Inferring the scope of negation in biomedical documents. In: Gelbukh, A. (ed.) CICLing 2012, Part I. LNCS, vol. 7181, pp. 363–375. Springer, Heidelberg (2012). https://doi.org/10.1007/978-3-642-28604-9_30
3. Barigou, B.N., Barigou, F., Atmani, B.: Handling negation to improve information retrieval from French clinical reports. J. E-Learning Knowl. Soc. **14**(1), 11–31 (2018). https://doi.org/10.20368/1971-8829/1455
4. Budrionis, A., Dalianis, H., Yigzaw, K.Y., Makhlysheva, A., Chomutare, T.: Negation detection in Norwegian medical text: porting a Swedish NegEx to Norwegian. Work in progress (2018)
5. Chapman, W.W., Bridewell, W., Hanbury, P., Cooper, G.F., Buchanan, B.G.: A simple algorithm for identifying negated findings and diseases in discharge summaries. J. Biomed. Inform. **34**(5), 301–310 (2001). https://doi.org/10.1006/jbin.2001.1029
6. Chapman, W.W., et al.: Extending the NegEx lexicon for multiple languages. Stud. Health Technol. Inform. **192**(1–2), 677–681 (2013). https://doi.org/10.3233/978-1-61499-289-9-677
7. Costumero, R., Lopez, F., Gonzalo-Martín, C., Millan, M., Menasalvas, E.: An approach to detect negation on medical documents in Spanish. In: Ślęzak, D., Tan, A.-H., Peters, J.F., Schwabe, L. (eds.) BIH 2014. LNCS (LNAI), pp. 366–375. Springer, Cham (2014). https://doi.org/10.1007/978-3-319-09891-3_34
8. Cruz Díaz, N.P., Maña López, M.J.: Negation and Speculation Detection. Editorial Assistant (2019). https://doi.org/10.1075/nlp.13
9. Cruz Díaz, N.P., Maña López, M.J., Vázquez, J.M., Álvarez, V.P.: A machine-learning approach to negation and speculation detection in clinical texts. J. Am. Soc. Inform. Sci. Technol. **63**(7), 1398–1410 (2012). https://doi.org/10.1002/asi.22679
10. De Albornoz, J.C., Plaza, L., Diaz, A., Ballesteros, M.: UCM-I: a rule-based syntactic approach for resolving the scope of negation. In: *SEM 2012–1st Joint Conference on Lexical and Computational Semantics, vol. 1, pp. 282–287 (2012)
11. Donatelli, L.: Cues, scope, and focus: annotating negation in Spanish corpora. In: CEUR Workshop Proceedings, vol. 2174, pp. 29–34 (2018)
12. Elazhary, H.: NegMiner: an automated tool for mining negations from electronic narrative medical documents. Int. J. Intell. Syst. Appl. **9**(4), 14–22 (2017). https://doi.org/10.5815/ijisa.2017.04.02
13. GitHub: NegEX-MES: NegEX para textos médicos en ESpanol. https://octoverse.github.com/. (Santamaria, J)

14. Jiménez-Zafra, S.M., Cruz Díaz, N.P., Morante, R., Martín-Valdivia, M.T.: Neges 2018: workshop on negation in Spanish. Procesamiento de Lenguaje Natural **62**, 21–28 (2019). https://doi.org/10.26342/2019-62-2
15. Koza, W., Filippo, D., Cotik, V., Vanessa, S., Ricardo, M.G.: Automatic detection of negated findings in radiological reports for Spanish language: methodology based on lexicon-grammatical information processing. J. Digit. Imaging **1**, 19–29 (2019)
16. Martí Antonín, M.A., Taulé Delor, M., Nofre, M., Marsó, L., Martín Valdivia, M.T., Jiménez Zafra, S.M.: La negación en español: análisis y tipología de patrones de negación (2016). http://rua.ua.es/dspace/handle/10045/57750
17. Mehrabi, S., et al.: DEEPEN: a negation detection system for clinical text incorporating dependency relation into NegEx. J. Biomed. Inform. **54**, 213–219 (2015). https://doi.org/10.1016/j.jbi.2015.02.010
18. Morante, R., Blanco, E.: SEM 2012 shared task: resolving the scope and focus of negation. In: SEM 2012–1st Joint Conference on Lexical and Computational Semantics, vol. 1, pp. 265–274 (2012)
19. Névéol, A., Dalianis, H., Velupillai, S., Savova, G., Zweigenbaum, P.: Clinical Natural Language Processing in languages other than English: opportunities and challenges. J. Biomed. Semant. **9**(1), 1–13 (2018). https://doi.org/10.1186/s13326-018-0179-8
20. Syntactic methods for negation detection in radiology reports in Spanish. In: Proceedings of the 15th Workshop on Biomedical Natural Language Processing, BioNLP 2016, Berlin, Germany, 12 August 2016 (2016). https://doi.org/10.18653/v1/w16-2921
21. Negation detection in clinical reports written in German. In: Proceedings of the 5th Workshop on Building and Evaluating Resources for Biomedical Text Mining (BioTxtM 2016) (2016). http://www.aclweb.org/anthology/W16-5113
22. Detecting the scope of negations in clinical notes. In: Proceedings of the Second Italian Conference on Computational Linguistics CLiC-IT 2015 (2016)
23. Annotating negation in Spanish clinical texts. In: Proceedings of the Workshop Computational Semantics Beyond Events and Roles (2017). https://doi.org/10.18653/v1/w17-1808
24. Annotation of negation in the IULA Spanish clinical record corpus. In: Proceedings of the Workshop Computational Semantics Beyond Events and Roles, Valencia, Spain (2017). https://doi.org/10.18653/v1/w17-1807
25. Savova, G.K., et al.: Mayo clinical text analysis and knowledge extraction system (cTAKES): architecture, component evaluation and applications. J. Am. Med. Inform. Assoc. **17**(5), 507–513 (2010). https://doi.org/10.1136/jamia.2009.001560
26. Tanushi, H., Dalianis, H., Duneld, M., Kvist, M., Skeppstedt, M., Velupillai, S.: Negation scope delimitation in clinical text using three approaches: NegEx, PyConTextNLP and SynNeg. In: Proceedings of the 19th Nordic Conference of Computational Linguistics (NODALIDA 2013), vol. 1, no. 1, pp. 387–397 (2013)
27. TIJCAI 2015: negated findings detection in radiology reports in Spanish: an adaptation of NegEx to Spanish (2015)

28. Velupillai, S., et al.: Using clinical natural language processing for health outcomes research: overview and actionable suggestions for future advances. J. Biomed. Inform. **88**, 11–19 (2018). https://doi.org/10.1016/j.jbi.2018.10.005
29. Vincze, V., Szarvas, G., Farkas, R., Móra, G., Csirik, J.: The BioScope corpus: biomedical texts annotated for uncertainty, negation and their scopes. BMC Bioinform. **9**(11), 38–45 (2008). https://doi.org/10.1186/1471-2105-9-S11-S9

In-Bed Posture Classification from Pressure Mat Sensors for the Prevention of Pressure Ulcers Using Convolutional Neural Networks

Aurora Polo Rodríguez[1], David Gil[2], Chris Nugent[3], and Javier Medina Quero[1](✉)

[1] Department of Computer Science, University of Jaen, Jáen, Spain
{apolo,jmquero}@ujaen.es
[2] Computer Technology Department, University of Alicante, Alicante, Spain
david.gil@ua.es
[3] School of Computing, Ulster University, Newtownabbey, Northern Ireland, UK
cd.nugent@ulster.ac.uk

Abstract. Due to the current population aging around the world, it is a fact that a good amount of the technology should be focused on the care of these people, improving their living conditions. In this work, we propose a methodology to classify in-bed human posture using pressure mat sensors for the prevention of pressure ulcers. First, we provide a visual representation using fuzzy processing from raw pressure data to grayscale. Second, we enable the generation of a large dataset from a limited dataset using ad hoc data augmentation, generating new synthetic sleeping positions. Third, we define 2 CNN models to evaluate the impact of layers on the performance of in-bed posture classification. The results show an encouraging performance in a small dataset using a leave-one-participant-out cross-validation.

Keywords: In-bed posture classification · Pressure mat sensor · Prevention of pressure ulcers · Convolutional neural networks

1 Introduction

Currently, 703 million people over 65 years of age inhabit the world. The number of elderly people is projected to double up to 1.5 billion in 2050. Globally, the share of the population aged over 65 has increased from 6% in 1990 to 9% in 2019. This proportion is projected to rise further to 16% by 2050, so that one in six people in the world will be aged 65 years or older [1]. Given the existence of advanced technologies that could improve the living conditions and independence of these people, we face the challenge of creating new models of healthcare technology.

As the average age of the population continues to increase, a large number of associated diseases are becoming more prominent, such as dementia, hypertension, diabetes, gait problems, etc., which mainly affect elderly people. This work

I. Rojas et al. (Eds.): IWBBIO 2020, LNBI 12108, pp. 338–349, 2020.
https://doi.org/10.1007/978-3-030-45385-5_30

has focused on the Prevention of Pressure Ulcers (PPU), an age-related complication in people with low or no mobility which is defined as injuries located in the skin or underlying dermal tissue, usually over a bony prominence, as a result of pressure [2]. They deeply affect the quality of life of patients due to reduction of independence and self-esteem, and even causing death in extreme cases [2].

Changing posture and maintaining a correct body position is the best and most efficient tool to prevent the appearance of PPUs [3]. In any case, a given in-bed position must not be held for more than two hours [4]. Change of posture is the main method of prevention and control. However, carrying out these practices continuously for a long time is an arduous task for caregivers, causing physical and emotional stress [5]. Regarding the cost of treatment, a study on the cost analysis of PUs [6] concluded that cost increases with the severity of the ulcer because it requires a greater number of healing processes, in addition to expenditure on materials, nursing time and hospitalization costs for the healthcare system. Investing in techniques to prevent these situations before they occur is widely accepted to be of paramount importance among the health and technology community.

The contribution of our approach is focused on the detection of in-bed positions by means of a smart system where convolutional neural networks (CNN) learn from the fuzzy visual representation of data from pressure mat sensors. Namely, non-intrusive pressure mat sensors are embedded in a *smart-blanket* within a smart home environment. This device is a more attractive option than other kinds of devices for recognizing posture because it enables the privacy of the person to be preserved at all times. Moreover, the body of the patient can be covered with sheets and blankets given that the sensor is deployed under the patient.

The remainder of the paper is organized as follows: in Sect. 1.1 we offer a review of works related to our proposal, Sect. 2 presents the proposed methodology to classify in-bed human posture for the prevention of pressure ulcers using pressure mat sensors, and Sect. 3 introduces the results of a dataset evaluated using our approach. Finally, in Sect. 4, conclusions and ongoing works are discussed.

1.1 Related Works

In recent years, academic and industrial research initiatives on smart systems have increased rapidly worldwide [7]. In order to improve quality of life for the elderly, different home-based detection technologies are used to monitor their activity. In this way, we can provide personalized services and support future health care demands, complementing specific medical services [8].

In the context of PU prevention, in [9] authors analyze the effectiveness of the use of special pressure management surfaces in the prevention and treatment of PU patients via authorized access to patient photographs and records. In [10], an integrative literature review is carried out by identifying documents in the main databases related to health sciences using reverse search in the identified articles, including prospective studies, systematic reviews or other types of studies that evaluate the effectiveness of postural changes.

In [11], a commercial pressure mapping system is used to create a time-stamped, whole-body pressure map of the patient. An ad hoc image-based processing algorithm is proposed to keep an unobtrusive and informative record of the in-bed posture of patients over time. In [12], a bedsore (PU) monitoring method using Pictorial Structure models is introduced to localize pressure distributions of the body. A pilot study including 12 subjects reveals that the proposed method enables reliable localization of body parts with 89.8% accuracy in common lying postures. In [13], a sensor matrix made of a multi-walled carbon nanotube (MWCNT)-polydimethylsiloxane (PDMS)-composite was fully printed to enable pressure distribution measurements. A final application was a printed insole manufactured with six single MWCNT-PDMS pressure sensors that were situated on characteristic points of the insole to detect unhealthy rollover patterns. Another specific software application for PU management [14] was developed and used for assessing its acceptability, usefulness and applicability by professional nurses from three residential homes for the elderly over a one year period. Three centres and 69 residents took part in this project. During this process, 27 nutritional status screens, and 22 PU risk assessments, as well as the monitoring of 230 PUs, were performed.

In another study conducted by Dresch [15], the measured area of venous ulcers was compared using the software AutoCAD (r) and Image Tool. It was concluded that both software applications are suitable to measure ulcers; however, their accuracy decreased dramatically when the wounds had an $area < 10$ cm^2. In [16], the authors present an electronic prototype to assist patients in the process of PU rehabilitation. The system identifies body movements and positions using a video device located in front of the bed. The results indicated that the prototype has 95% reliability but makes mistakes and activates false alarms in low lighting conditions or vibrations.

The proposed methodology aims to gather the best features of previous works, and in turn, as mentioned earlier, to offer a degree of privacy which is not provided by traditional camera methods, thus providing more positive acceptance than visible spectrum cameras [17].

2 Methodology

In this section, we detail the methodology proposed to classify in-bed human posture for the prevention of pressure ulcers using pressure mat sensors. To this end, we propose a straightforward data collection method to reduce system deployment time in the sensitive context of patients with pressure ulcers.

From the data collected from the pressure mat sensors, we first provide a visual representation using fuzzy processing from raw data to grayscale. Second, we include ad hoc data augmentation techniques to increase the dataset, generating new synthetic images by means of geometric transformations. Third, we evaluate 2 types of CNN to analyze the impact of the number of layers and kernel size on learning in-bed human posture. Finally, the classification of in-bed human posture enables real-time computation of the time each position is maintained, which allows caregivers to be notified when the time limits are reached.

In Fig. 1 we show the architecture of components described in the approach, which are addressed more in depth in the next sections.

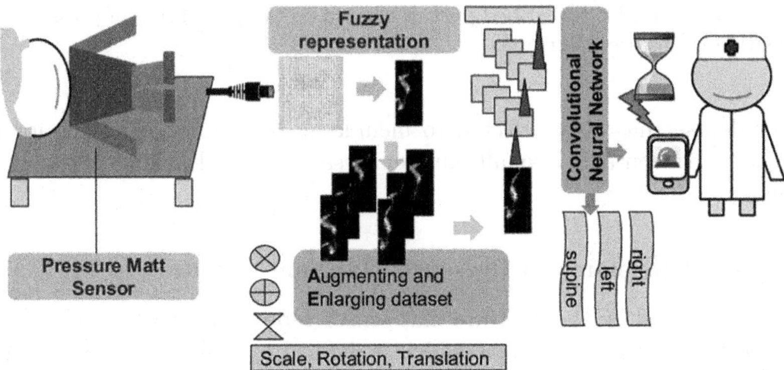

Fig. 1. Architecture of the components proposed in the methodology: limited dataset from pressure mat sensors, fuzzy visual representation, data augmentation and learning from CNNs.

2.1 Limited Dataset from Pressure Mat Sensors

The use of Deep Learning approaches requires a large amount of data [18]. However, in many contexts, obtaining a labelled dataset for learning purposes is an arduous task which interferes with the real deployment and configuration of intelligent systems in home-based health solutions. To overcome this limitation, we propose the agile collection of a limited amount of data that will be processed using augmentation methods to provide high performance in deep learning approaches.

The dataset evaluated in this work has been obtained from [19], based on data collected in experiment II. The data collected proceeds from the pressure mat sensor *Vista Medical BodiTrak BT3510*. This device provides a pressure data matrix of points $M^{w,h}$ whose size is $w = 27, h = 64$. Each value $m_{i,j}$ of the matrix $M^{w,h}$ represents a point of pressure in the range $[0, 500]$. A picture of *Vista Medical BodiTrak BT3510* is provided in Fig. 2.

In this limited dataset, only 28 positions were collected for each of the eight participants. Three positions were labeled in the dataset: supine, left and right, together with the data matrix for each experiment from the pressure mat sensor. Moreover, the dataset includes several configurations for each basic posture based on the prevention of pressure ulcers, which is shown in Fig. 2.

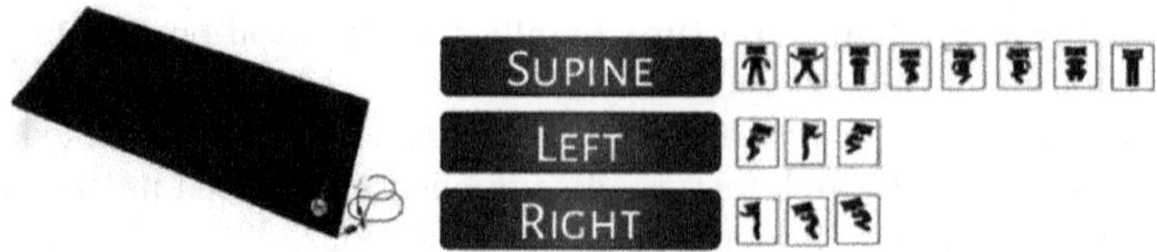

Fig. 2. Left, the Vista Medical BodiTrak pressure mat sensor selected to collect the dataset is shown. Right, the in-bed postures based on the prevention of pressure ulcers and position labels are described.

This dataset has been selected to include ad hoc in-bed positions for pressure ulcers and contains a small number of samples for learning purposes (232 samples).

2.2 Fuzzy Processing of Pressure Mat Sensor Data

The data collected by the pressure mat sensor represents human body pressure on the surface of the sensor mat which is defined by a matrix of points $M^{w,h}$. In order to provide a visual representation from the raw data, fuzzy processing into grayscale values has been proposed.

Thus, we define a fuzzy set to represent *relevant body pressure* in fuzzy color [20] by means of a membership function $\mu_M(m_{i,j})$, which relates the pressure values $m_{i,j}$ to a degree of relevance between 0 and 1 $\mu_M(m_{i,j}) : R \rightarrow [0,1]$, where 0 represents absence of pressure and 1 maximal pressure. A trapezoidal right function has been selected to determine the shape of the membership function which is defined by a lower limit l_1 and an upper limit l_2.

$$\mu_M(m_{i,j}) = TR([l_1, l_2], m_{i,j})$$
$$TR([l_1, l_2], x) = \begin{cases} 0 & \text{if } x < l_1 \\ (l_2 - x)/(l_2 - l_1) & \text{if } l_1 \leq x \leq l_2 \\ 1 & \text{if } x > l_2 \end{cases}$$

In addition, a fuzzy modifier α is proposed to model the progression of the linear function $TR([l_1, l_2], x)^{\alpha}$ [21]. If $\alpha_m < 0$, we obtain a weak modifier, such as *light*; and a heavy modifier when $\alpha_m > 0$, such as *strong*.

The aim of including fuzzy data processing in pressure values from the sensor mat is to provide: (i) a filter for non-relevant information and (ii) the reduction of noise from non-feasible values [22,23].

In Sect. 3, we describe the parameters and integration of fuzzy processing with the rest of the system components. In Fig. 3, we show an example of fuzzy representation of the pressure data matrix from the pressure mat sensor.

2.3 Data Augmentation

Collecting data on different orientations and positions in patients with low or no mobility with the aim of increasing learning performance is inappropriate due to

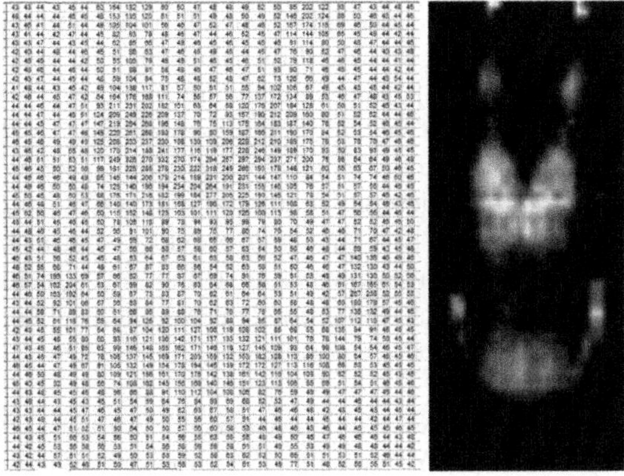

Fig. 3. Left, example of data matrix for supine position. Right, visual representation of the left data using fuzzy representation in grayscale.

the sensitive health conditions of the patients. Fortunately, the data augmentation method in [24] provides a solution to enlarge the number of learning cases from a limited dataset [25] to generate longer synthetic images and therefore reduce over-fitting [26].

In this work, we have applied the following geometric transformations to augment and enlarge the image data from the original dataset:

- *Translation.* The original image is relocated within a maximal window size $[t_x, t_y]^+$ using a random process which generates a random translation transformation $[t_x, t_y], t_x \in [0, t_x^+], t_y \in [0, t_y^+]$.
- *Rotation.* A rotation transformation is defined by a maximal rotation angle α^+, which generates a random rotation within an angle $\alpha \in [0, \alpha^+]$ which is applied in the center of the image.
- *Scale.* A maximal scale factor s^+ is defined to generate random scale $s \in [1 - s^+, 1 + s^+]$, reducing the impact of the height of the training sample.

We note that flipping the images horizontally is not suitable in this context, due to the need to differentiate between left and right positions in the classification carried out by the convolutional neural networks. Likewise, as the pressure sensor mat is oriented in a given position on the patient's bed, vertical flipping is also not recommended.

2.4 Design of the Convolutional Neural Network

In this section we describe 2 types of Convolutional Neural Networks (CNN) to classify the in-bed posture of patients. In the dataset there are three target classes for the CNN to learn: supine, left and right positions.

Based on the visual information of the images, the CNNs learn kernels which are related to key visual patterns, whose similarity with source visual regions is defined by a convolutional operation. They enable us to summarize and reduce the spatial information defined by a bi-dimensional kernel size whose convolutional size is defined by $[K_x, K_y]$. So each convolutional layer i is defined by the number of kernels L and its size $[K_x, K_y]^l$, represented as $K_i = [K_x, K_y] \times L$. In addition, some methods/sub-layers are usually included to configure the network and reduce the number of parameters: (i) *dropout* reduces the number of network nodes to reduce over-fitting [27], (ii) *pooling* provides spatial reduction in the size of the outputs within the layers, which is defined by a window size $[P_x, P_y]$ and an aggregation function, such as maximal or average, [25] and (iii) *activation function* filters the last output layer to train the neural network several times faster [26].

In this work, two types of CNN configurations are evaluated to classify in-bed human posture: (i) X and (ii) Y. In Table 1, we describe the layers of the two CNN models.

Table 1. Convolutional Neural Network configurations to classify in-bed human posture from augmented pressure mat sensor data

Model A	Model B
Conv2D:[5,5] × 32	Conv2D:[5,5] × 32
maxpooling:[2,2]	maxpooling:[2,2]
Conv2D:[5,5] × 64	dropout:0.25
maxpooling:[2,2]	Conv2D:[5,5] × 64
denselayer(1024)	maxpooling:[2,2]
soft max	dropout:0.25
cross-entropy	Conv2D:[5,5] × 128
	dropout:0.25
	denselayer(1024)
	denselayer(1024)
	soft max
	cross-entropy

3 Results

In this section, we describe the results obtained from the proposed methodology applied to a dataset of in-bed posture derived from a pressure ulcer prevention program to classify sleeping positions.

3.1 Dataset Description

For the purposes of evaluating the proposed methodology, we start with the dataset developed in [19] (experiment II), which was collected by the device *Vista Medical BodiTrak BT3510.*

This experiment was carried out with 8 participants aged between 19,34. The height and weight of the participants were in the range of [169,63] and [186,100], respectively. In experiment II, a sponge pressure sensor mat was used to collect data on the in-bed posture of the participants. The sampling rate was 1 Hz and each file includes the average pressure of around 20 2-min frames (around 120 frames). Supine posture was defined by 8 different positions. Left posture included 3 different positions and right posture also included 3.

For evaluating purposes, we include a leave-one-participant-out cross-validation which leads to arduous testing given that unseen participant data are used to evaluate models generated for other participants, without including personalized learning.

3.2 Dataset Pre-processing: Fuzzy Visual Representation and Data Augmentation

In this section, we describe the data processing from raw values as points of pressure on the mat sensor in order to generate visual augmented images which configure the learning of convolutional neural networks.

First, a trapezoidal function has been used to define the membership degree of *relevant body pressure*. We have defined the membership function based on expert criteria using the minimal and maximal threshold $l_1 = 50, l_2 = 400$. To smooth the impact of body and joints on pressure values, a fuzzy modifier $\alpha = 1/4$ is applied to compute the final membership function: $TR([l_1, l_2], m_{i,j})^{\alpha}$. In Fig. 3, we show an example using this fuzzy visual representation.

Second, we have applied the following geometric transformations for augmenting and enlarging the image data from the original dataset: a *translation* defined by the window size $[t_x, t_y]^+ = [5, 5]$, a *rotation* defined by a maximal rotation angle $\alpha^+ = \pi/5$ and, a *scale* defined by a random scale in the range $s \in [1 - s^+, 1 + s^+] = [0.8, 1.2]$. An augmentation ratio of 25 images per original one (232 images) provides a suitable dataset (6.032 images) for deep learning purposes.

3.3 Evaluation of Convolutional Neural Networks

In this section, we evaluate the two proposed convolutional neural network models. Thesss configuration of the two CNN models was detailed in Sect. 2.4. The learning stage was configured over 50 steps defining a non-extensive learning process with an average duration of 5m43s in model A and 8 m 27 s in model B (using a i5 CPU and 8 GB RAM computer).

In Table 2, we show the results of evaluating the convolutional neural network models, where precision, recall, f1-score and accuracy metrics were computed for each participant and model. In addition, in 4 we show the confusion matrices of the aggregated results obtained from participants for each model.

Based on the results described in Sect. 3.3, we observe that both models provide encouraging results with accuracy and f1-score of up to 98%. This is

Table 2. Table summarizing the results of single and multi-occupancy data with raw and fuzzy representation for the best configuration CNN_3. In Fig. 4, we also include a confusion matrix for the best models in single and multi-occupancy.

Participant	CNN	F1-Score	Precision	Recall	Accuracy (%)
User1	Model A	0.926	0.926	0.926	0.931
User2	Model A	1.00	1.00	1.00	1.00
User3	Model A	0.938	0.961	0.917	0.931
User4	Model A	1.000	1.000	1.000	1.000
User5	Model A	0.963	0.944	0.982	0.965
User6	Model A	1.000	1.000	1.000	1.000
User7	Model A	1.000	1.000	1.000	1.000
User8	Model A	1.000	1.000	1.000	1.000
Total	**Model A**	**0.987**	**0.988**	**0.985**	**0.988**
User1	Model B	0.967	0.952	0.980	0.965
User2	Model B	1.000	1.000	1.000	1.000
User3	Model B	0.967	0.980	0.952	0.965
User4	Model B	1.000	1.000	1.000	1.000
User5	Model B	0.963	0.944	0.9815	0.965
User6	Model B	1.000	1.000	1.000	1.000
User7	Model B	1.000	1.000	1.000	1.000
User8	Model B	1.000	1.000	1.000	1.000
Total	**Model B**	**0.989**	**0.989**	**0.989**	**0.990**

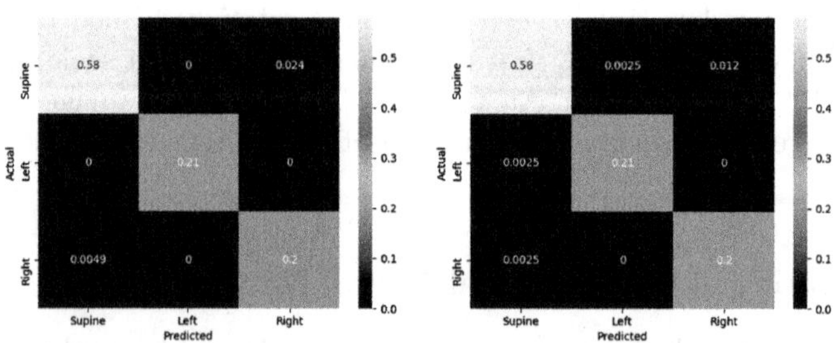

Fig. 4. Confusion matrix for aggregated data from participant in models A (left) and B (right).

sterling performance given the highly demanding learning context and validation process: (i) a small number of samples was used as training data, (ii) a leave-one-participant-out cross-validation with unseen user data was used for evaluation.

There are no significant differences between the performance of models A and B, which both describe an agile CNN model with quick learning capabilities which can also be integrated into embedded devices [28] to provide real-time evaluation in the edge-computing of smart mat devices.

4 Conclusions and Ongoing Works

In this work, in-bed posture classification models from non-invasive pressure mat sensor data have been proposed and evaluated for the prevention of pressure ulcers using Convolutional Neural Networks. First, fuzzy processing from raw values provided a straightforward visual representation. Second, we enabled the generation of a large dataset from limited data using ad hoc data augmentation.

Two convolutional neural network models were evaluated from a dataset which included ad hoc in-bed positions for pressure ulcers and contained a small number of samples for learning purposes. Based on the results, data processing with fuzzy logic and augmentation has enabled suitable data learning from agile CNNs with 2 and 3 convolutional layers.

In future works, we will focus on collecting a dataset with a wide range of participants with low mobility to evaluate the approach in a real context. In addition, we will integrate the classification into a fuzzy rule-based system to define the temporal limits for each in-bed position of patients in an interpretable and flexible way, enabling real-time notifications to caregivers.

Acknowledgments. Funding for this research is provided by EU Horizon 2020 Pharaon Project 'Pilots for Healthy and Active Ageing', Grant agreement no. 857188. Moreover, this research has received funding under the REMIND project Marie Sklodowska-Curie EU Framework for Research and Innovation Horizon 2020, under grant agreement no. 734355. Furthermore, this contribution has been supported by the Andalusian Health Service by means of the project PI-0387-2018.

References

1. World Health Organization: World Population Ageing Report. https://www.un.org/en/development/desa/population/publications/pdf/ageing/WorldPopulationAgeing2019-Highlights.pdf. Accessed 14 Nov 2019
2. Ministerio de Salud y de la Protección Social: Herramientas Para Promover la Estrategia de la Seguridad del Paciente en el Sistema Obligatorio de Garantía de Calidad de la Atención en Salud; Ministerio de Salud y de la Protección Social, Bogotá, Colombia (2007)
3. Vanderwee, K.: Pressure ulcer prevention and repositioning. In: Romanelli, M., Clark, M., Cherry, G., Colin, D., Defloor, T. (eds.) Science and Practice of Pressure Ulcer Management, pp. 67–73. Springer, London (2006). https://doi.org/10.1007/1-84628-134-2_8
4. González-Consuegra: 2 Caring for the skin through a weblog 2015, Universidad Javeriana de Colombia. https://integridaddelostejidosun.wordpress.com. Accessed 13 Nov 2019
5. Anders, J., Heinemann, A., Leffmann, C., Leutenegger, M., Pröfener, F., von Renteln-Kruse, W.: Decubitus ulcers: pathophysiology and primary prevention. Deutsches Ärztebl. Int. **107**, 371 (2010)

6. Zuo, X.L., Meng, F.J.: A care bundle for pressure ulcer treatment in intensive care units. Int. J. Nurs. Sci. **2**, 340–347 (2015)
7. Gjoreski, H., Piltaver, R., Gams, M.: Person identification by analyzing door accelerations in time and frequency domain. In: De Ruyter, B., Kameas, A., Chatzimisios, P., Mavrommati, I. (eds.) AmI 2015. LNCS, vol. 9425, pp. 60–76. Springer, Cham (2015). https://doi.org/10.1007/978-3-319-26005-1_5
8. Sundaravadivel, P., Kougianos, E., Mohanty, S.P., Ganapathiraju, M.K.: Everything you wanted to know about smart health care: evaluating the different technologies and components of the Internet of Things for better health. IEEE Consum. Electron. Mag. **7**, 18–28 (2007)
9. Herrero Boil, L.: Las superficies especiales de manejo de presión en la prevención y tratamiento las úlceras por presión. Revisión de la literatura (2015)
10. López-Casanova, P., Verdú-Soriano, J., Berenguer-Pérez, M., Soldevilla-Agreda, J.: Prevención de las úlceras por presión y los cambios de postura. Revisión integrativa de la literatura. Gerokomos **29**(2), 92–99 (2018)
11. Yousefi, R., et al.: Bed posture classification for pressure ulcer prevention. In: 2011 Annual International Conference of the IEEE Engineering in Medicine and Biology Society, pp. 7175–7178. IEEE, September 2011
12. Liu, J.J., Huang, M.C., Xu, W., Sarrafzadeh, M.: Bodypart localization for pressure ulcer prevention. In: 2014 36th Annual International Conference of the IEEE Engineering in Medicine and Biology Society, pp. 766–769. IEEE, August 2014
13. Gerlach, C., Krumm, D., Illing, M., Lange, J., Kanoun, O., Odenwald, S., Hübler, A.: Printed MWCNT-PDMS-composite pressure sensor system for plantar pressure monitoring in ulcer prevention. IEEE Sens. J. **15**(7), 3647–3656 (2015)
14. Yáñez, O.B., Arrieta, J.R., Bafaluy, M.I.B., Aguirre, J.J.C.: Evaluación e impacto del uso de las tecnologías de la información y comunicación para la gestión clínica y seguimiento compartido y consensuado de las úlceras por presión. Revista Española de Geriatría y Gerontología **50**(4), 179–184 (2015)
15. Eberhardt, T.D., Lima, S.B.S.D., Lopes, L.F.D., Borges, E.D.L., Weiller, T.H., Fonseca, G.G.P.D.: Measurement of the area of venous ulcers using two software programs. Revista latino-americana de enfermagem **24**, e2862 (2016)
16. Pilataxi, A., Daniel, H.: Sistema electrónico para asistir a pacientes en proceso de rehabilitación de úlceras por presión (Bachelor's thesis, Universidad Técnica de Ambato. Facultad de Ingeniería en Sistemas, Electrónica e Industrial. Carrera de Ingeniería en Electrónica y Comunicaciones) (2018)
17. Aguagüiña, H. Sistema Electrónico Para Asistir A Pacientes en Proceso de Rehabilitación de Úlceras Por Presión; Universidad Técnica de Ambato. Facultad de Ingeniería en Sistemas, Electrónica e Industrial. Carrera de Ingeniería en Electrónica y Comunicaciones, Ambato, Ecuador 2018
18. Yamashita, T., Watasue, T., Yamauchi, Y., Fujiyoshi, H.: Improving quality of training samples through exhaustless generation and effective selection for deep convolutional neural networks. In: VISAPP, vol. 2, pp. 228–235 (2015)
19. Pouyan, M.B., Birjandtalab, J., Heydarzadeh, M., Nourani, M., Ostadabbas, S.: A pressure map dataset for posture and subject analytics. In: 2017 IEEE EMBS International Conference on Biomedical Health Informatics (BHI), pp. 65–68. IEEE, February 2017
20. Han, J., Ma, K.K.: Fuzzy color histogram and its use in color image retrieval. IEEE Trans. Image Process. **11**(8), 944–952 (2002)
21. Medina Quero, J., Fernández Olmo, M., Peláez Aguilera, M., Espinilla Estevez, M.: Real-time monitoring in home-based cardiac rehabilitation using wrist-worn heart rate devices. Sensors **17**(12), 2892 (2017)

22. Schulte, S., Morillas, S., Gregori, V., Kerre, E.E.: A new fuzzy color correlated impulse noise reduction method. IEEE Trans. Image Process. **16**(10), 2565–2575 (2007)
23. Morillas, S., Gómez-Robledo, L., Huertas, R., Melgosa, M.: Method to determine the degrees of consistency in experimental datasets of perceptual color differences. JOSA A **33**(12), 2289–2296 (2016)
24. Medina-Quero, J., Burns, M., Razzaq, M., Nugent, C., Espinilla, M.: Detection of falls from non-invasive thermal vision sensors using convolutional neural networks. In: Multidisciplinary Digital Publishing Institute Proceedings, vol. 2, no. 19, p. 1236, October 2018
25. Ciresan, D.C., Meier, U., Masci, J., Gambardella, L.M., Schmidhuber, J.: High-performance neural networks for visual object classification. arXiv preprint arXiv:1102.0183 (2011)
26. Krizhevsky, A., Sutskever, I., Hinton, G.E.: Imagenet classification with deep convolutional neural networks. In: Advances in Neural Information Processing Systems, pp. 1097-1105 (2012)
27. Srivastava, N., Hinton, G., Krizhevsky, A., Sutskever, I., Salakhutdinov, R.: Dropout: a simple way to prevent neural networks from overfitting. J. Mach. Learn. Res. **15**, 1929–1958 (2014)
28. Zhang, Y., Suda, N., Lai, L., Chandra, V.: Hello edge: keyword spotting on microcontrollers. arXiv preprint arXiv:1711.07128 (2017)

Pin-Code Authentication by Local Proximity Based Touchstroke Classifier

Orcan Alpar and Ondrej Krejcar(✉)

Faculty of Informatics and Management, Center for Basic and Applied Research, University of Hradec Kralove, Rokitanskeho 62, 500 03 Hradec Kralove, Czech Republic
orcanalpar@hotmail.com, ondrej.krejcar@uhk.cz

Abstract. Most of the recently released touchscreen devices enable fingerprint authentication; while pin-codes connected to the fingerprints are still in common usage. Among various biometric feature extractors, such as time-based, frequency-based or even pressure-based, the most reliable and implementable with mathematical infrastructure is location-based approach for enhancing security of touchscreen devices. Therefore, in this paper, we propose fundamentals of a novel feature extraction protocol to strengthen pin-codes by calculating local proximity of the touches on the screen without long training sessions. We presented a fuzzy-like area methodology for finding outputs for each input and also conducted experiments to show the discretization of the outputs per real and fraud attempts.

Keywords: Biometrics · Security · Pin-code · Authentication · Proximity

1 Introduction

Emerging touchscreen technology leads to several enhancements on the personal security of the devices containing unlimited personal data including social media accounts and even bank accounts connected to the device. Recently implemented and indeed very efficient finger print authentication; however the majority of the new touchscreen devices still ask for pin-codes after each restart. Therefore, be they are enhanced by fingerprint or not, every phone still could be accesses by pin-codes.

Pin-codes mostly consist of 4 numeric digits which makes any kind of key-time extraction implausible including key-times or inter-key times due to low number of inputs. It is similar with frequency extraction as well since there would be very limited data for determining high frequency trajectories. On the contrary, the most promising solution as we had already presented an instance of it very recently in [1] is the proximity; yet this approach actually requires intentional designation of a secondary password.

A secondary or the ghost password, as we named after, is very irrelevant from the traditional passwords predetermined touch locations for each key. In the research [1], we deliberately defined the ghost password as "touch right" for each key in the password. The new ghost password is definitely not causing burden to the users, since it could be very simple that remembering any kind of passwords; however it provides very high security for the touchscreen password. We used global positioning and global proximity

I. Rojas et al. (Eds.): IWBBIO 2020, LNBI 12108, pp. 350–361, 2020.
https://doi.org/10.1007/978-3-030-45385-5_31

calculation to classify the attempts which also means that the features extracted from the password entering sequence is the coordinates. The coordinates extracted through two enrollment steps are averaged and stored as the sole training session for further classification. In testing phase, the touch coordinates are also extracted to compare with the stored one and the algorithm is designed to give a score as outputs. The results, if compared with the literature, seems to have one of the lowest equal error rate 1.61% with 0% false reject rate (FRR) and 1.56% false accept rate (FAR).

Among the papers presented in recent years on touchscreen authentication like [2–10], Roh et al. [11] worked on enhancing pin-codes like we did; yet with Euclidean and Manhattan distance based classifiers and with gyroscope to identify postures of the users. The Table 1 below summarizes the relevant papers and kernels of each paper recently published on enhancing touchscreen authentication.

Table 1. Kernel of the papers focused on touchscreen authentication

Author/s	Protocol	Features
This paper	*Pin-code*	*Local proximity*
Alpar [1]	Text password	Global proximity
Alpar [12]	Tap password	Frequency
Alpar [6]	Text password	Frequency
De Luca et al. [13]	Text password	Speech
Sae-Bae et al. [14]	Multi-touch	Gestures
Chang et al. [15]	Text password	Pressure
Alsultan and Warwick [16]	Text password	Inter-key times
Ahmed and Traore [17]	Text password	Key relations
Alpar [18]	Pattern password	Durations
Alpar and Krejcar [19]	Swipe	Coordinates
Alpar and Krejcar [20]	Pattern password	Touch locations
Buschek et al. [21]	Text password	Touch locations
Roh et al. [11]	Pin-code	Hand posture
Rzecki et al. [22]	Pattern password	Gestures
Alsultan et al. [23]	Text password	Inter-key times

Despite the very promising results of the global proximity based authentication we proposed, the emulated screens are designed for touchscreen tablets and text passwords only. The coordinates are extracted globally without taking the key places into consideration; therefore the hidden interface was standalone operating totally independently from the real interface. The biggest drawback emerged due to alternatives of some buttons or existence of different entering choices; which lowered the EER and FAR indeed as a positive resulted drawback. For instance, there were two shift buttons on the emulated screen and selection of the wrong button was drastically changing the results. The pin-code screens, however, don't have any kind of alternatives and smaller in area, which made us consider more precise alternatives.

Local proximity, in this paper, means the distance of the touch coordinate through an attempt on a key to the corresponding interpolated coordinate derived from the enrollment step. On the other hand, global proximity corresponds to the similar concept; while the coordinates are extracted globally though. Moreover, one of the important reasons is the variety of key sizes on the touchscreen keyboard. On the other hand, key areas are very standard on pin-code entering screens, therefore the whole system starts with touching the circles while entering a pin code, which is universally assumed to have 4 digits. The circles could be squares on some touchscreen and even might be borderless depending on the operating system and brand of the device; yet we implemented circles for our interface for ease of operations, as presented in Fig. 1, taken from Samsung mobile.

Fig. 1. Pin-code screen of a touchscreen device

The registration phase is similar with the most common one, which is entering the same pin-code twice; while in this phase, it is plausible to warn or inform the user about the infrastructure of the authentication enhancement. Every touch on the screen in the limits of a key is locally extracted in enrollment phase and the coordinates are linearly interpolated for find the mid-point. The distances for each key are calculated and sent to mathematical inference system for classification of attempts which will give a score; yet could be evaluated with binary decision as reject or accept by thresholding. The summary of the system we propose is shown in Fig. 2.

The system summarized in Fig. 2 is explained in detail in following sections starting from touch point extraction. Afterwards, mathematical foundations of the local proximity classifier are presented with the experiments, results and conclusion sections at the end of the paper.

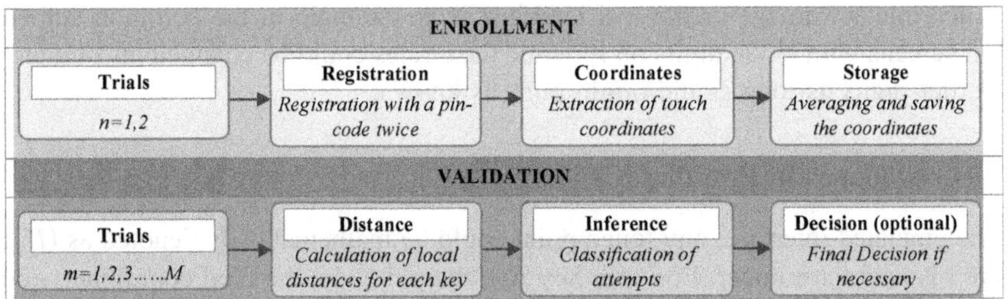

Fig. 2. Basic flowchart

2 System Design

A Samsung mobile pin-code interface is emulated by Matlab 2017a on Dell Inspiron 15 N-7577-N2-713 K i7 with 16 GB RAM and 4xprocessors as seen in Fig. 4. The interface is in 410 × 720 resolution where the circles are identical with diameter R = 90 px. The algorithm stealthily working beneath the emulated interface is collecting the coordinates; yet for research purposes we made the touch points and the coordinates visible for this research. Each touch on the interface is arbitrarily circled to show points and the coordinates on the interface for storing as seen in Fig. 3 below.

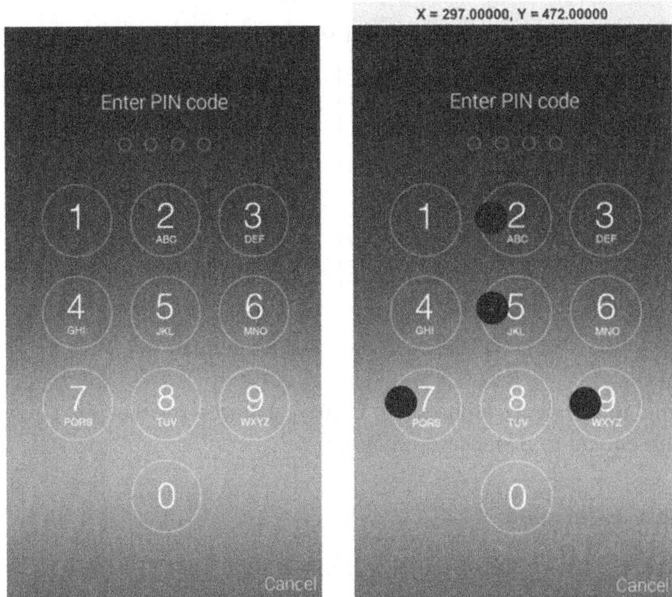

Fig. 3. Blank interface on the left, visible pin-code on the right.

The emulated image of the real interface is an example of the common authentication screens with circle digits on it; while the circles could be changed into square or no-border digits as long as the origin point is known.

2.1 Coordinates in Training Session

On the emulated interface, any touch point could be mathematically denoted as (I_i^x, I_i^y) where i is attempt number. For each key p in the pin-code, the final coordinates could be linearly interpolated on the analytical plane as:

$$I_e^x(p) = \frac{1}{2}\sum_{i=1}^{2} I_i^x \tag{1}$$

$$I_e^y(p) = \frac{1}{2}\sum_{i=1}^{2} I_i^y \tag{2}$$

which is very simple by analytical geometry as seen in Fig. 4 where Touch 1 has the coordinates of (I_1^x, I_1^y) while Touch 2 has (I_2^x, I_2^y) for each digit of a pin-code.

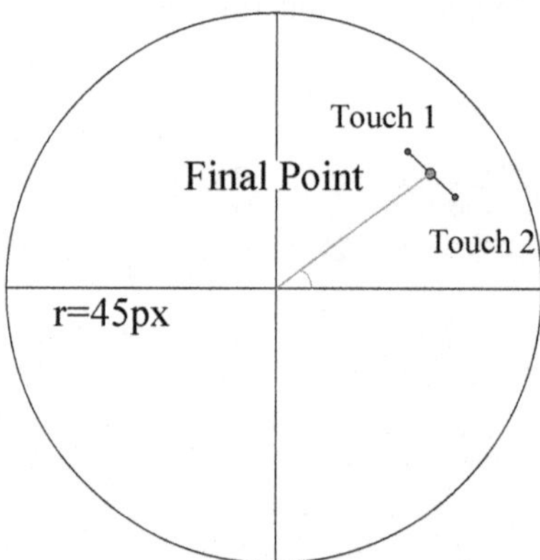

Fig. 4. Enlarged circle and touch locations

According to the final points, the further attempts on the pin circle could be evaluated subsequent to distance estimation.

2.2 Distance Estimation

When the final points are calculated, the distance of further touches on the circle could be analytically computed by:

$$D^{x,y}(p) = \sqrt{\left(I_a^x(p) - I_e^x(p)\right)^2 + \left(I_a^y(p) - I_e^y(p)\right)^2} \tag{3}$$

where $p \in 1, 2, 3, 4$ is the digit of a pin-code and $D^{x,y}(p)$ is the measured distance. For the digit p.

2.3 Proximity Evaluation

There actually are many methods to evaluate, from binary to gradual, and also to fuse the inputs gathered for each digit to reach a final output. However, it is very likely to state that touching exactly the same points on a small screen is nearly impossible; therefore, the selection of the methodology should be gradual whatsoever. In other words, without rejecting the attempt at once for lower false reject rate, all further coordinates should be evaluated according to the closeness to the center points calculated in training gradually. In addition, there are numerous types of fusion of the inputs and outputs to finalize the decision. In this case with four digits, the logical operator could be AND to force the user stay inside the area, where one attempt outside would result in immediate rejection.

Given the requirements of a flexible but robust evaluation, it is necessary to define the acceptable proximities. Above all, in a circle with the diameter of R = 90 px, the maximum distance would be $D^{x,y}(p) \leq 90$ as well, though it is not likely to come about. Considering that the minimum absolute difference $D^{x,y}(p) \geq 0$, the inference system should be defined between these borders and still gradually. The gradual structure could be linear or non-linear as well; yet we prefer a nonlinear and gradual evaluation. Therefore, we defined fuzzy like areas by mathematical basis which are all implementable to the interface design.

The first triangle membership function is mathematically denoted as:

$$\begin{gathered} U^{x,y}(p) = 0, \mu_3 = 1 \\ 0 < U^{x,y}(p) \leq 30, \mu_3 = 1 - U^{x,y}(p)/30 \end{gathered} \tag{4}$$

producing the first area of:

$$A^3(p) = \frac{1 - (1 - \mu_3)^2}{8}, C^3(p) = 1 - 0.25/3 \tag{5}$$

which gives the 10-pixel proximity named as “close”. The second triangular membership function is defined as “intermediate” distance, represented by:

$$\begin{gathered} 10 < U^{x,y}(p) \leq 30, \mu_2 = (U^{x,y}(p) - 10)/20 \\ 30 < U^{x,y}(p) \leq 90, \mu_2 = (1 - (U^{x,y}(p) - 30)/60 \end{gathered} \tag{6}$$

triggering the area of:

$$A^2(p) = \frac{1 - (1 - \mu_2)^2}{4}, C^2(p) = 0.5 \tag{7}$$

The third and the last triangular membership function is defined as "far" which is stated as:

$$\begin{aligned} 30 < U^{x,y}(p) \leq 90, \mu_1 &= (U^{x,y}(p) - 30)/60 \\ U^{x,y}(p) = 90, \quad \mu_1 &= 1 \end{aligned} \tag{8}$$

and the corresponding area as:

$$A^1(p) = \frac{1 - (1 - \mu_1)^2}{8}, C^1(p) = 0.25/3 \tag{9}$$

The final area as well as the final output of the inference system could be found by:

$$D_p = \sum_{m=1}^{3} A^m(p)C^m(p) / \sum_{m=1}^{3} A^m(p) \tag{10}$$

for $\forall p \in 1, 2, 3, 4$ while it is still possible to find another way of fusion. The boundaries of membership functions are 10 and 30 are arbitrarily selected to create a left-leaning inference system giving more importance to very close attempt for better discrimination, as shown in Fig. 5.

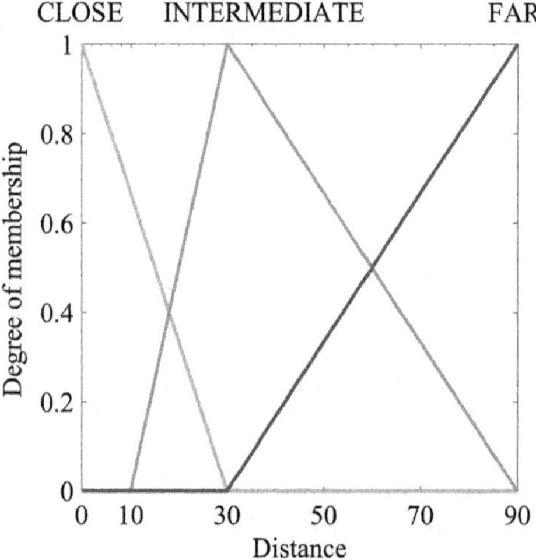

Fig. 5. Triangular membership functions

The training set and experimental results will be presented in following section.

3 Experimental Results

The secondary password for this case is predefined as touch-left of the circles of the pin-code 2579, like in the Fig. 4 right, which is very easy to remember. The two-step registration is applied and the following Table 2 is achieved.

Table 2. The training set

Pin	2		5		7		9	
Step	x	y	x	y	x	y	x	y
1	176	480	173	367	57	249	290	246
2	175	481	175	362	57	248	290	247
Final	175.5	480.5	174	364.5	57	248.5	290	246.5

The data collection process is indeed a real-world application; yet not by an android application but emulated touchscreen interface written on MATLAB. Before the experiments, a testing phase is realized for comparing the expected outcomes and the real outputs for extreme and very common cases.

3.1 Testing Phase

As seen in previous sections, the algorithm seems a bit tangled; yet we may test the outputs very easily by putting arbitrary values to check max and min values as well as the most probable expectation, which is pressing the middle of the circles.

Table 3. Testing data

Pin		2	5	7	9	Output
Test	Scenario	$D^{x,y}(1)$	$D^{x,y}(2)$	$D^{x,y}(3)$	$D^{x,y}(4)$	D_p
1	Max distance	90	90	90	90	0.083
2	Min distance	0	0	0	0	0.917
3	Touching middle	35	35	35	35	0.382

Although the proximity evaluation is nonlinear, the areas and final output equation make the outputs stuck in the middle values like all kind of fuzzy systems. Therefore, without binary classification, an experiment is conducted to find the outputs.

3.2 Visualization

Given the 40 real and fraud attempts, we present the touching points in Fig. 6 with imaginary circles of the touching points for better visualization.

Fig. 6. Real set on the left, fraud set on the right

As seen in the figure, the real set includes very consistent touching locations; while the fraud set consists of very disordered attempts with quite scattered points. Lack of information regarding the ghost password, in this case: "touch-left" disables the users to press any designated place on the circles and keep them focus on the pin-code itself. It is very likely to see a complete discretization between the outputs of real and fraud set indeed; although there is no binary classification involved. According to the outputs, the diagram consisting of real attempts in ascending and fraud attempts in descending order is plotted and presented in Fig. 7.

It is obvious that there is no intersection point of real and fraud attempts for 40 trials each, which makes EER calculation not possible. On the other hand, we didn't aim to find finalized output for the experiment since the results are very differentiative. However, although to be fair, there should be false accepts like in every biometric classifier, when the sample size is increasing. We presume that the final FAR would be around $1/4^4$ considering there are four sides of circles to press if the fraud team is aware of location-based classifier and while the trial number goes to infinity as well. In this case. On the contrary, if there had been a thresholding for giving a final decision and the threshold had been decided as T = 0.5 as the most plausible scenario, there would have been no FAR; but one FRR in the sample set which will create a 2.5% FAR with 0% FRR and obviously 0% EER due to inexistence of intersection point regardless of the thresholding.

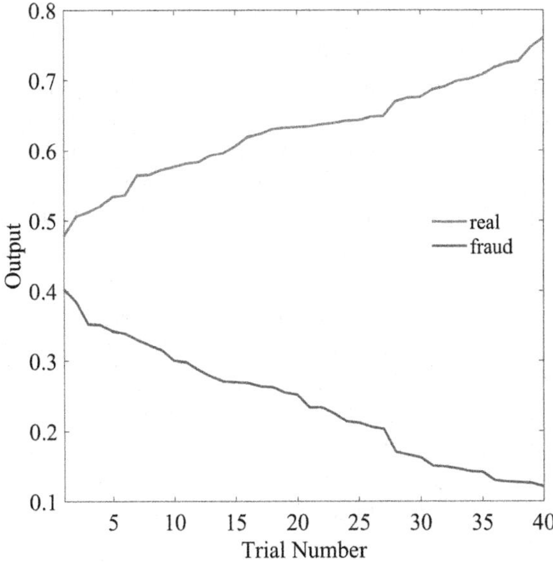

Fig. 7. Outputs of the experiments

4 Conclusion and Discussion

In this paper, we proposed a very promising and implementable enhancements for pin-code authentication protocol by stealthily collecting the locations and evaluating the proximity. It is slightly harder than text passwords due to digit limit; however, the results seem to have a potential. According to the results, the outputs are very consistent and inside of the limits of $0.083 \leq D_p \leq 0.917$ revealed by the extreme scenario analysis presented in Table 3. In addition, without any kind of information on the protocol, the fraud set attempts are very spread; while the real set attempts are more or less on the same spot of the circle. It is obviously possible to make authentication harder by selecting a variable ghost password unlike "touch-left"; however, we don't suggest to put more burden on the users to remember a harder password.

There is no disadvantage or drawback worth mentioning indeed; however, touching same locations is mandatory for this kind of location and proximity-based protocols, which is really difficult. On the contrary, the benefits of the system are significantly more than the drawbacks; since the extra protection of the pin-code even stolen is promotive. On the other hand, despite 0% EER we reached, the framework is expected to cause <1% EER in reality, considering the key areas are divided in four. Therefore, the projected EER would be one of the lowest among the relevant researches thanks to the proximity kernel. The Table 4 includes some EER results from relevant papers only for providing insight.

Table 4. EER comparison

Author/s	Method	EER
This paper	*Local fuzzy proximity*	*<1% (expected value)*
Alpar [12]	mSTFT + SVM	1.40%–2.12%
Alpar [12]	mSTFT + SVM	2.01%–3.21%
Alpar [12]	STFT + SVM	6.93%–10.12%
Alpar [12]	STFT + SVM	7.49%–11.95%
Alpar [1]	Global fuzzy proximity	1.61%
Alpar [6]	GN-ANN	4.1%
Alshanketi et al. [5]	Random forest	2.3%–9%
Roh et al. [11]	Statistical	6.93%–12.3%
Alpar [18]	RGB Histogram + LM	7.5%
Alpar [18]	ANFIS	2.5%
Alpar [18]	BP-ANN	8.75%
Alpar and Krejcar [19]	GN-ANN	31.8%
Alpar and Krejcar [19]	LM-ANN	14.75%
Alpar and Krejcar [20]	ANFIS	5.4%
Alpar and Krejcar [20]	LM-ANN	2.2%
Sae-bae [14]	Statistical	5%–10%
Chang [15]	Statistical	6.9%–14.6%

As future research, we suggest to implement the framework to real devices to understand the robustness. In addition, fuzzy or any kernel-based proximity is key to differentiating the attempts of any authentication systems collecting location; which would be investigated further. Changing inputs is also an option to find biomedical applications of the framework, like eye-hand coordination investigation of the patients suffering Parkinson's disease, Balint's syndrome, optic apraxia or ataxia.

Acknowledgement. The work and the contribution were supported by the SPEV project "Smart Solutions in Ubiquitous Computing Environments", University of Hradec Kralove, Faculty of Informatics and Management, Czech Republic. We are also grateful for the support of Ph.D. students of our team (Ayca Kirimtat and Sebastien Mambou) in consultations regarding application aspects.

References

1. Alpar, O.: Biometric touchstroke authentication by fuzzy proximity of touch locations. Future Gener. Comput. Syst. **86**, 71–80 (2018)
2. Sarier, N.D.: Multimodal biometric identity based encryption. Future Gener. Comput. Syst. (2017). https://doi.org/10.1016/j.future.2017.09.078
3. Kroeze, C.J., Malan, K.M.: User authentication based on continuous touch biometrics. S. Afr. Comput. J. **28**(2), 1–23 (2016)
4. Mondal, S., Bours, P.: A study on continuous authentication using a combination of keystroke and mouse biometrics. Neurocomputing **230**, 1–22 (2017)
5. Alshanketi, F., Traore, I., Ahmed, A.A.: Improving performance and usability in mobile keystroke dynamic biometric authentication. In: Security and Privacy Workshops (SPW). IEEE (2016)

6. Alpar, O.: Frequency spectrograms for biometric keystroke authentication using neural network based classifier. Knowl.-Based Syst. **116**, 163–171 (2017)
7. Chang, B., Li, Y., Wang, Q., Zhu, W.T., Deng, R.H.: Making a good thing better: enhancing password/PIN-based user authentication with smartwatch. Cybersecurity **1**(1), 7 (2018)
8. Suraj, Sarma, P., Yadav, A.K., Barma, S.: Keystroke rhythm analysis based on dynamics of fingertips. In: Tanveer, M., Pachori, R. (eds.) Machine Intelligence and Signal Analysis. Advances in Intelligent Systems and Computing, pp. 555–567. Springer, Singapore (2019). https://doi.org/10.1007/978-981-13-0923-6_48
9. Saini, B.S., Kaur, N., Bhatia, K.S.: Authenticating mobile phone users based on their typing position using keystroke dynamics. In: Krishna, C.R., Dutta, M., Kumar, R. (eds.) Proceedings of 2nd International Conference on Communication, Computing and Networking. LNNS, vol. 46, pp. 25–33. Springer, Singapore (2019). https://doi.org/10.1007/978-981-13-1217-5_3
10. Alpar, O.: Keystroke recognition in user authentication using ANN based RGB histogram technique. Eng. Appl. Artif. Intell. **32**, 213–217 (2014)
11. Roh, J.H., Lee, S.H., Kim, S.: Keystroke dynamics for authentication in smartphone. In: International Conference on Information and Communication Technology Convergence (ICTC). IEEE (2016)
12. Alpar, O.: TAPSTROKE: a novel intelligent authentication system using tap frequencies. Expert Syst. Appl. **136**, 426–438 (2019)
13. De Luca, A., Hang, A., Brudy, F., Lindner, C., Hussmann, H.: Touch me once and i know it's you!: implicit authentication based on touch screen patterns. In: CHI 2012 Proceedings of the 2012 ACM Annual Conference on Human Factors in Computing Systems, New York (2012)
14. Sae-Bae, N., Ahmed, K., Isbister, K., Memon, N.: Biometric-rich gestures: a novel approach to authentication on multi-touch devices. In: CHI 2012 Proceedings of the 2012 ACM Annual Conference on Human Factors in Computing Systems, New York (2012)
15. Chang, T.Y., Tsai, C.J., Lin, J.H.: A graphical-based password keystroke dynamic authentication system for touch screen handheld mobile devices. J. Syst. Softw. **85**(5), 1157–1165 (2012)
16. Alsultan, A., Warwick, K.: User-friendly free-text keystroke dynamics authentication for practical applications. In: 2013 IEEE International Conference on Systems, Man, and Cybernetics (SMC). IEEE (2013)
17. Ahmed, A.A., Traore, I.: Biometric recognition based on free-text keystroke dynamics. IEEE Trans. Cybern. **44**(4), 458–472 (2014)
18. Alpar, O.: Intelligent biometric pattern password authentication systems for touchscreens. Expert Syst. Appl. **42**(17), 6286–6294 (2015)
19. Alpar, O., Krejcar, O.: Biometric swiping on touchscreens. In: Computer Information Systems and Industrial Management (2015)
20. Alpar, O., Krejcar, O.: Pattern password authentication based on touching location. In: Intelligent Data Engineering and Automated Learning–IDEAL 2015 (2015)
21. Buschek, D., De Luca, A., Alt, F.: Improving accuracy, applicability and usability of keystroke biometrics on mobile touchscreen devices. In: Proceedings of the 33rd Annual ACM Conference on Human Factors in Computing Systems. ACM (2015)
22. Rzecki, K., Pławiak, P., Niedźwiecki, M., Sośnicki, T., Leśkow, J., Ciesielski, M.: Person recognition based on touch screen gestures using computational intelligence methods. Inf. Sci. **415–416**, 70–84 (2017)
23. Alsultan, A., Warwick, K., Wei, H.: Non-conventional keystroke dynamics for user authentication. Pattern Recogn. Lett. **89**, 53–59 (2017)

Behavioral Risk Factors Based Cancer Prediction Model Utilizing Public and Personal Health Records

Emil Saweros and Yeong-Tae Song(✉)

Department of Computer and Information Sciences, Towson University, 8000 York Rd, Towson, MD 21252, USA
esawer1@students.towson.edu, ysong@towson.edu

Abstract. Cancer has become one of the major public health problems worldwide while the etiology of cancer remains largely unknown. Even with advanced cancer research, prediction of it has not been as practical as those of other chronic diseases such as diabetes. However, behavioral risk factors (BRF) may be used to monitor and predict cancer diseases. Such factors can be used to demonstrate and educate the general public on potential cancer pathways and possible outcomes. For that purpose, we have analyzed public health data and personal health records and discovered some histological features related to behavioral risk factors in the cancer diseases. Such characteristics are then used to assess each individual's BRFs for classification and prognosis of the diseases. It plays a key role in many health-related realms, including increasing patient awareness on BRFs, developing related medical procedures, the way of handling patients' records and the treatment of chronic diseases. In this paper, we presented predictive analysis based on some BRFs that might contribute to increase the chances of developing cancer disease.

Keywords: Data science · Behavioral risk factors · Health care · Personal health record (PHR) · Electronic health record (EHR) · Cross-sectional analysis

1 Introduction

Cancer is considered as one of the major international health problems [1]. Several studies have shown that there are significant variations on the influences of the behavioral risk factors (BRFs) to the recovery outcomes [2–5]. Epidemiology studies identified most of cancer risks and protective factors [6]. Many risk factors such as age, family history, race, geographical location, smoking, diet, and alcohol consumption may have affected the chances of developing cancer. However, it is usually hard to know exactly why one person develops cancer, and another does not. As the number of cancer survivors continues to grow, it is important to understand and monitor patients' current physical and health behaviors thoroughly so we may know how to improve the survival rate systematically. The American Cancer Society (ACS) estimated the numbers of new cancer cases and related deaths that will occur in the United States and compiled the most recent data on cancer incidence, mortality, and survival [7].

I. Rojas et al. (Eds.): IWBBIO 2020, LNBI 12108, pp. 362–377, 2020.
https://doi.org/10.1007/978-3-030-45385-5_32

According to ACS research in 2017, about 1.7 million individuals in the US will be diagnosed with cancer, and over 600,000 deaths will result from cancer. A significant number of those cases can be easily prevented with behavior changes, including dietary and smoking habits.

It is widely agreed upon that early detection of cancer is critical. Some forms of cancer such as breast and prostate cancer have survival rates of nearly 100% if detected and treated early, which is at or before stage I, but survival rate dropped to below 30% if left undetected until at stage IV, the most severe stage.

Various factors and complex interactions among them are involved in developing cancer. These factors fall under different categories: the environment, genetics, individual behaviors, and preexisting medical conditions. There are aspects in predicting cancer, but in our study, we are focusing on the behavioral risk factors. Through our paper, we examined the need to find methods to identify the potential of developing cancer with the hopes of improving survival rates by understanding their behavioral risk factors. Different types of cancer have varying risk factors relationships, and we examined some factors that may affect a person's chance of developing cancer disease.

In general, most causes of cancer fall into two categories: genetic and behavioral risk factors [8]. Specific genes changes that promote cancer are inherited, which, unfortunately, cannot be prevented. However, cancer can also develop from one's behavioral lifestyle, such as with exposure to carcinogenic like smoking and excessive UV radiation, as these promote unfavorable mutations to DNA. In our study, we are focusing on behavioral risk factors. We used the behavioral risk factors surveillance system (BRFSS) [9] to collect data in 2018 and studied different risk factors like alcohol consumption, body mass index (BMI), weight, physical activity, smoking, race, level of education, age, and level of physical activity.

Cancer diagnosis, treatment procedures, and outcomes have improved over time because of medical advances. Despite these advances, the risk of cancer is still prevalent [10]. Fortunately, many preventative measures can be taken to reduce the risk of cancer. Advances in cancer prediction have not been as practical as those for other chronic diseases; effective screening methods are available for only a few types of cancer. Prevention through lifestyle and environmental interventions remains the most effective way to reduce the burden of cancers [6].

There are disagreements about the importance of risk factors as there is no clear evidence about which factors may or not have a potential impact on developing diseases. For example, as explained in the related work section, some studies showed that alcohol consumption is a high-risk factor for prostate cancer, and other studies do not. There is a need for a transparent understanding model for uncertain or combined risk factors that cause cancer.

Most of the current support models in public and personal health care are based on past health issues and not to be used for prediction. We are aiming to proactively raise patient's awareness rather than react to issues as they pop up. Instead of addressing issues in a traditional and reactionary way, we would like to control the health issues before they occur, using cross-sectional analysis and multidimensional algorithms to find correlation and causation.

Continuity of care and patient awareness of the associated risk factors are essential parts of cancer prevention. In our approach, we connected our analysis outcomes to a personal healthcare application to raise awareness of the factors that predispose people to cancer and enable early identification of disease and tailored treatment plans to ensure optimal results.

There has not been much work reported in any disease prediction model utilizing behavioral risk factors. We incorporated using data science algorithms, as they play a crucial role in decision support. A few data science tools were used to normalize patient-specific workflows to find potential disease(s). Our analytic tools were also used to identify noncompliant access, pass audits with ease, and proactively monitor and improve patient care.

The remainder of the paper is organized as follows: we provided the basic concepts needed to understand the behavioral risk factors. We highlighted the goal of using the descriptive analyses and the relationship among exposure, confounders, and outcomes. In the related work, we have introduced articles concerning analytics. Our main ideas are discussed in subsequent sections. Finally, we summarize ad give the final thoughts of our study in the conclusion section.

2 Background

In our approach, we examined 29 different types of cancer against various risk factors using the Behavioral Risk Factor Surveillance System (BRFSS) [9] with the data collected from 2018. The objective of the BRFSS is to collect uniform, state-specific data on health risk behaviors, clinical preventive health practices, and health care access that is associated with the leading causes of morbidity and mortality in the United States [11]. We are expanding the study of the surveillance data by implementing descriptive surveillance analyses using the data set of 2018. BRFSS represents a collaboration between the federal Center for Disease Control and Presentation (CDC) and local state public health authorities/state health departments. The CDC's role is to organize the effort. The CDC helps the states with their landline and cell phone sampling, and they also make core and module questionnaires and associated resources available so the states can use them.

In USA, the risk factors surveillance data sets mainly come from two different sources:

1. **National Health and Nutrition Examination Survey (NHANES)** [9]: Conducted by the U.S. Centers for Disease Control and Prevention (CDC). In the NHANES, neighborhoods, households, and individuals are sampled. Then data collectors contact respondents using a mobile examination center (MEC). These respondents provide answers to questionnaires and clinical measurements data such as weight, height, and blood pressure. The NHANES is done every two years and its dataset is publicly available to the researchers but there are some challenges in using the dataset.

   Drawbacks:

- The datasets from each form are stored separately, so some assemblies are required when developing an analytic dataset.
- Compared to the BRFSS, there are relatively few records, around 10 thousand total.
- Low participation rates and high refusal rates.

2. **The Behavioral Risk Factor Surveillance System (BRFSS)** is done yearly. CDC organizes the data and provides support to the states for the data collection. In this method, the BRFSS does anonymous phone surveys by using randomly generated phone numbers. Unlike NHANES, BRFSS compiles the dataset annually. In the BRFSS, there is a concept of core questions and questions from the modules used. Because the feds organize the BRFSS, there are specific questions that states are obligated to ask. This way, the feds can capture the trend rates such as smoking. Since the states are doing the survey, their own needs may be satisfied by imposing the state specific modules. To accommodate those, they use different sets of validated BRFSS modules each year so they can keep tabs on their state-specific problems. For example, some states have cities with smog problems, and those states may choose to include asthma/adult asthma history. The answers to the core questions are available publicly in a vast dataset that can be downloaded.

   Drawbacks:

- Some researchers don't trust the BRFSS because people used self-report conditions such as having diabetes.
- Lack of clinical validation due to the nature of the survey, which is phone-based.
- Lack of clinical evidence of self-reported conditions used in other metrics even though the results from the BRFSS is considered accurate.
- Only the results from the core questions are available publicly but the answers from state-specific modules may not be available. The availability is determined by the states.

   The BRFSS questionnaire consists of three parts:

A. Core questions: The core questions include demographic information, health status, health-related quality of life, health care access, hypertension awareness, cholesterol awareness, chronic health conditions, tobacco use, consumption of fruits and vegetables, physical activity, disability (limited activity, use of special equipment), arthritis burden, seat belt use, immunization (seasonal influenza and pneumococcal vaccination), alcohol consumption, and issues regarding human virus/acquired immunodeficiency syndrome (HIV and AIDS).
B. Optional modules: The optional modules are proposed by CDC Programs and other agencies (such as SAMHSA and Veteran's Affairs). They include information concerning other issues such as diabetes, visual impairment and access to eye care, inadequate sleep, secondhand smoke, anxiety and depression, and access to preventive cancer screenings. The states may add or remove modules depending on their needs. If selected by a state or grantee, optional modules are implemented by following a standardized protocol.
C. State-added questions: State-added questions address state-specific health issues or track a state's health objective.

3 Related Work

Philips-Salimi [12] performed a study based on The Childhood Cancer Cohort Study or CCSS. It is a longitudinal study that follows the same patient through time, unlike the BRFSS, which is cross-sectional at one point in time. Specific exposures did precede a particular outcome, but the study included siblings who don't have cancer disease as a comparison group.

Mukherjeea et al. [13] claimed that the prostate specific antigen (PSA) test is not accurate enough to diagnose prostate cancer and tends to lead men to get overtreated for prostate cancer, which causes its own problems. Guidelines were released by the US Preventive Service's task force, advising doctors to discuss with their patients avoiding the unnecessary cancer treatment. Our study focuses on 29 different types of cancer to find out how the outcomes are connected to personal healthcare applications.

Wiener and et al. [14] researched about the relationship between oral health and cardiovascular disease. They evaluated the association of cardiovascular disease and the number of missing teeth as a risk indicator using the BRFSS data collected in 2010.

Paul M. Faestel, M.D. conducted a research about perceived insufficient rest or sleep among veterans using behavioral risk factor surveillance system 2009 [15]. The study found out that veterans have high burden of sleep problems and also have subgroups that need interventions and enhanced education regarding insufficient sleep. The study stratified veterans into two categories: newly transitioned and longer-term, depending on how recently they left the service.

The alcohol consumption contributed to overall cancer incidences in the western world. In a meta-analysis [16] by Hendriks HFJ, it is estimating the impact of alcohol consumption on the risk distribution of the 20 most common cancer types among men and women in the Western world. The study considered only the alcohol consumption risk factor.

Buck et al. [17] researched the modeling of geographic cancer risk factor disparities in US counties. The goal of this research is to create a theoretical framework for the identification of cancer risk factor disparities and address the recognition of geographic patterns in these factors.

Mukamal et al. [18] worked on a population-based cross-sectional survey about alcohol consumption, physical activity, and chronic disease risk factors. These researchers studied the association of physical activity with alcohol consumption and the association of physical activity with asthma. They did not associate alcohol consumption with cancer.

A survey reaserch was conducted in Jefferdon medical college by Craig J. Newschaffer: "Validation of behavioral risk factor surveillance system (BRFSS) Health-Related Quality of Life (HRQOL) measures in a statewide sample" [19]. The study evaluated the validity of the BRFSS core and supplemental HRQOL survey measures in a statewide sample of 588 Missouri adults using the medical outcomes study (MOS) short form 36 (SF-36) HRQOL assessment as a gold standard. The study appears to be a good criterion validity between individual BRFSS HRQQL items and component SF-36 scales in the general population sample. Some of the shortcomings can be:

- The findings from the study may not have external validity of other specific population groups. For example, certain ethnic minorities, e.g., Hispanics and Asians, were poorly represented in the study samples.
- Exploration of the validity of the BRFSS measures in other populations defined by age, ethnicity, and health or functional status.
- The study covered the descriptive and relative validity analyses for chronic disease in general, but not to a specific disease like prostate cancer.

J. Zhao et al. investigated alcohol consumption as a risk factor for prostate cancer [20]. The study focuses on the influence of risk factors on estimates of the relationship between alcohol consumption and prostate cancer.

4 Methods

In our approach, we implemented a logistic regression model by building regression class where the independent variable is used to predict the dependent variable. Logistic Regression is used when the data is linearly separable or classifiable and the outcome is Binary or Dichotomous. This can be further extended when the dependent has more than 2 categories. Logistic regression models the probability of the membership to a particular group or category without directly modeling the values of the dependent variable. If the dependent variable consists of only two categories, logistic regression estimates the odds outcome of the dependent variable given a set of quantitative and/or categorical independent variables (Fig. 1).

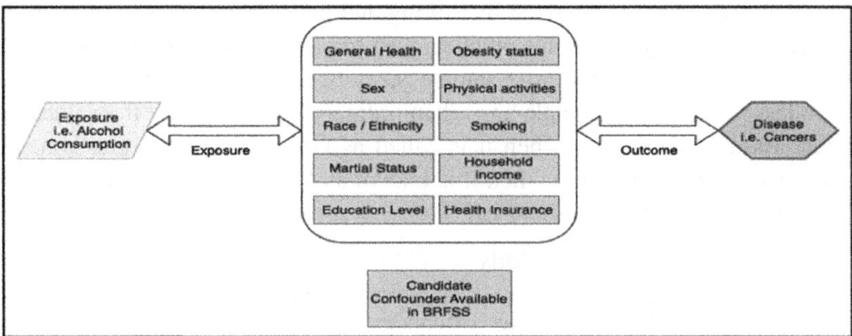

Fig. 1. Exposures & outcomes

Dependent Variable: is the presence of cancer disease (yes/no). The response to the posed questions in the BRFSS survey: "With your most recent diagnoses of cancer, what type of cancer was it? ".

Independent Variable: measures the independent risk factor. If it has a significant contribution to an outcome in a statistical model that includes established risk factors. As such, independence is based on a specific mathematical model and depends on the set of established risk factors involved in that model. Even when strong statistical evidence indicates that a variable is an independent risk factor for an outcome, this does not necessarily suggest that the risk factor causally contributes to the outcome. The opposite is correct, too: risk factors that have causal relationships with the outcome will not necessarily prove to be independent. These are basic statistical principles that are too often given short shrift in medical research [21].

Chi-Square Statistic p-Value: There are two types of chi-square tests. Both use the chi-square statistic and distribution for different purposes:

1. Chi-Square Goodness of fit test determines if a sample data matches a population.
2. A chi-square test for independence compares two variables in a contingency table to see if they are related. In a more general sense, it tests to see whether distributions of categorical variables differ from each other.

A minimal chi-square test statistic means that observed data fit the expected data exceptionally well. In other words, there is a relationship.

A huge chi-square test statistic result means that the data does not fit very well, or there isn't a relationship.

$$x_c^2 = \sum \frac{(O_i - E_i)^2}{E_i} \quad (1)$$

where O = Observed result, E = Expected result

Logistic regression is used for problem classification to find the probability of cancer disease, where the dependent variable is binary (0/1 or True/False). It doesn't require a linear relationship between dependent and independent variables. It can handle various types of relationships because it applies a non-linear log transformation to the predicted odds ratio. To avoid overfitting and underfitting, we should include all significant variables. To ensure this practice, we used a stepwise method to estimate the logistic regression. It requires large sample sizes because maximum likelihood estimates are less potent at low sample sizes than ordinary least square. If the values of the dependent variable are ordinal, then it is called as Ordinal logistic regression. If the dependent variable is multi-class, then it is known as Multinomial Logistic regression. The following Eq. (2) can represent it:

$$\mathrm{Odds} = \mathrm{p}/(1 - \mathrm{p}), \quad (2)$$

where p is the probability of presence of cancer disease

$$\ln(\mathrm{odds}) = \ln(\mathrm{p}/(1 - \mathrm{p})) \quad (3)$$

where:

ln is the natural logarithm, logexp, where exp = 2.71828…

p is the probability that the event Y occurs, p(Y = 1)

p/(1-p) is the "odds ratio" ln(p/(1-p)) is the log odds ratio, or "logit"

$$\mathrm{logit(p)} = \ln(\mathrm{p}/(1 - \mathrm{p})) = \mathrm{b0} + \mathrm{b1X1} + \mathrm{b2X2} + \mathrm{b3X3} \ldots. + \mathrm{bkXk} \quad (4)$$

The above Eq. (4) calculates changes in the log odds of the dependent variable and the parameters are chosen to maximize the likelihood of observing the sample values rather than minimizing the sum of squared errors, Eq. (4)

where;

B's in logistic regression are analogous to b's in ordinary least squares (OLS)

B1 is the average change in logit per one unit increase in X1, controlling for the other predictors

Odd Ratio - Confidence Interval (CI): An odds ratio is a measure of association between the presence or absence of two properties. It can also be defined as a type of interval estimate, computed from the statistics of the observed data, that might contain the real value of an unknown population parameter. The interval has an associated confidence level or coverage that, loosely speaking, quantifies the level of confidence that the range captures the deterministic setting. In our study, we used a 95% confidence level for modeling the upper and lower bounds of cancer disease.

5 Descriptive Statistical Analyses

We conducted descriptive analyses and population-based percentages, as shown in Tables 1 and 2. The results are split into two parts: non-manageable and behavioral characteristics risk factors. The study included 436,323 participants, where (17%) reported they have a different type of cancer. Statistically significant associations ($P < 0.0001$) were observed between cancer disease and sex, race, ethnicity, age, education, income, smoking, physical activity, marital status, body mass index, and general health status.

Table 1. Non-manageable risk factors characteristics of the 436323 with cancer disease in the BRFSS, 2018 (N,17% with cancer).

Category	Sub-Category	Total n, %	Has Cancer n, %	No Cancer n, %	Chi-square p-value
	All	436323, 100%	74199, 17%	362124, 83%	NA
Sex	Male	197412, 45%	31396, 7%	166016, 38%	<0.0001
	Female	238911, 55%	42803, 10%	196108, 45%	
Age	Age 18 to 24	25945, 6%	273, 0%	25672, 6%	<0.0001
	Age 25 to 34	46516, 11%	1134, 0%	45382, 10%	
	Age 35 to 44	52345, 12%	2540, 1%	49805, 11%	
	Age 45 to 54	67566, 15%	6521, 1%	61045, 14%	
	Age 55 to 64	90406, 21%	15471, 4%	74935, 17%	
	Age 65 or older	153545, 35%	48260, 11%	105285, 24%	
Hispanic	Hispanic	36849, 8%	2160, 0%	34689, 8%	<0.0001
	Non-Hispanic	395138, 91%	71416, 16%	323722, 74%	
	Not reported	4336, 1%	623, 0%	3713, 1%	
Race	White	345132, 79%	66412, 15%	278720, 64%	<0.0001
	African American	37769, 9%	3048, 1%	34721, 8%	
	American Indian	9102, 2%	981, 0%	8121, 2%	
	Asian	10220, 2%	428, 0%	9792, 2%	
	Hawaiian/ Pacific	2605, 1%	182, 0%	2423, 1%	
	Other Race/Multi-racial	11584, 3%	889, 0%	10695, 2%	
	Multiracial	9549, 2%	1169, 0%	8380, 2%	
	Not reported	10362, 2%	1090, 0%	9272, 2%	

Females are represented by (238911, 55%) from the total participants, while males (197412, 45%). Cancer frequencies in females are considered high than males, (42803, 10%) compared to (31396, 7%). Ages are divided into six groups with participation rate of: Age 18 to 24 (25945, 6%), Age 25 to 34 (46516, 11%), Age 35 to 44 (52345, 12%), Age 45 to 54 (67566, 15%) Age 55 to 64 (90406, 21%) and Age 65 or older (153545, 35%). Participants' ages and their weighted cancer percentage is getting higher as much as people get older.

Cancer's percentage of people less than 55 years old is about 1% while the percentage is getting higher with Age 55 to 64 (15471, 4%) and Age 65 or older (48260, 11%). Hispanic represented by (36849, 8%) compared to (395138, 91%) non-Hispanic and non-reported (4336, 1%). Non-Hispanic group cancer percentage (71416, 16%) is considered high, compared to the Hispanic group. The race was categorized into six groups (non-Hispanic white, Non- Hispanic Black, Hispanic, Asian, American

Table 2. Behavioral characteristics risk factors of 436323 participants with cancer disease in the BRFSS, 2018 (N,17% with cancer)

Category	Sub-Category	Total n, %	Has Cancer n, %	No Cancer n, %	Chi-square p-value
	All	436323, 100%	74199, 17%	362124, 83%	NA
Alcohol Consumption	Weekly drinker	153521, 35%	24691, 6%	128830, 30%	<0.0001
	Monthly drinker	60792, 14%	9937, 2%	50855, 12%	
	Nondrinker	222010, 51%	39571, 9%	182439, 42%	
Smoking	Smoker	180077, 41.2%	35544, 19.7%	53061, 12%	<0.0001
	Non-smoker	240029, 55%	36479, 15.2%	294672, 68%	
	Not reported	16217, 3.7%	2231, 13.8%	14391, 3%	

Category	Sub-Category	Total n, %	Has Cancer n, %	No Cancer n, %	Chi-square p-value
	All	436323, 100%	74199, 17%	362124, 83%	NA
Exercise	Exercised last month	325731, 75%	52875, 12%	272856, 63%	<0.0001
	Not exercise last month	109949, 25%	21197, 5%	88752, 20%	
	Not reported	643, 0%	127, 0%	516, 0%	
Marital status	Currently married	223019, 51%	39988, 9%	183031, 42%	<0.0001
	Divorced, widowed, separated	120710, 28%	27578, 6%	93132, 21%	
	Never married	74503, 17%	5080, 1%	69423, 16%	
	Not reported	18091, 4%	1552, 0%	16539, 4%	
Highest Education Level	Less than high school	32423, 7%	4640, 1%	27783, 6%	<0.0001
	High school graduate	118784, 27%	18931, 4%	99853, 23%	
	Some college/technical	119748, 27%	20290, 5%	99458, 23%	
	4+ years of college	163881, 38%	30157, 7%	133724, 31%	
	Not reported	1487, 0%	181, 0%	1306, 0%	
Annual household income	<$10k	16702, 4%	2203, 1%	14499, 3%	<0.0001
	$10k - <$15k	17988, 4%	3234, 1%	14754, 3%	
	$15k - <$20k	25779, 6%	4143, 1%	21636, 5%	
	$20k - <$25k	32129, 7%	5532, 1%	26597, 6%	
	$25k - <$35k	37748, 9%	6715, 2%	31033, 7%	
	$35k - <$50k	49485, 11%	9076, 2%	40409, 9%	
	$50k - <$75k	58033, 13%	10030, 2%	48003, 11%	
	$75k or more	122806, 28%	19476, 4%	103330, 24%	
	Not reported	75653, 17%	13790, 3%	61863, 14%	
Obesity	Underweight	6749, 2%	1198, 0%	5551, 1%	<0.0001
	Normal	123297, 28%	21435, 5%	101862, 23%	
	Overweight	143621, 33%	26015, 6%	117606, 27%	
	Obese	127774, 29%	21054, 5%	106720, 24%	
	Not reported	34882, 8%	4497, 1%	30385, 7%	
General health	Excellent	71726, 16%	7973, 2%	63753, 15%	<0.0001
	Very Good	141930, 33%	21611, 5%	120319, 28%	
	Good	137942, 32%	23919, 5%	114023, 26%	
	Fair	60607, 14%	13391, 3%	47216, 11%	
	Poor	23019, 5%	7035, 2%	15984, 4%	
	Not reported	1099, 0%	270, 0%	, 0%	

Indian/Alaskan native, and other). The white race was represented by (345132, 79%) from the total participants which cancer weighted percentage of (66412, 15%), which is considered high compared to other races.

Behavioral characteristics and manageable risk factors are grouped into nine: alcohol consumption, smoking status, exercise, marital status, education level, income, Obesity, and General health condition. Weekly drinkers have cancer higher rate (24691, 6%) compared to monthly drinkers (9937, 2%), while non-drinkers with cancer represent (39571, 9%). Cancer disease is tied with smoking status as smokers with cancer are higher (35544, 19.7%) compared to (36479, 15.2%) non-smoker and non-reported (2231, 13.8%). Participants who exercised during the past 30 days have (52875, 12%) cancer rate compared to (21197, 5%) of people who not exercise regularly. Married people have a high cancer percentage (39988, 9%) compared to another marital status, as well as highly educated people who have (30157, 7%) cancer rate.

6 Adjusted Binary and Multinomial Logistic Regression Findings

We carried the sample data forward to conduct a multivariable logistic regression model analysis. It was used to evaluate the association between the lifestyle factors and cancer diseases after controlling for other risk factors described above. Each behavioral risk factors was examined as an independent variable or a series of independent indicator variables when multiple categories were defined. We split the result into two parts: manageable and non-manageable risk factors, as shown in Tables 3 and 4, which represent the Adjusted odds ratios (AOR) and 95% confidence intervals (CI) from the multivariable logistic regression model. AOR indicated a significant relationship between dependent exposure variables with other independent potential risk factors variables.

Table 3. Non-manageable risk factors - calculated Adjusted Odds Ratios (AOR) and the 95% confidence intervals according to cancer diseases of the final logistic regression analysis behavioral risk factor surveillance system, 2018.

Category	Sub - Category	Odds Ratio (AOR)	Confidence Interval (CI) 95%
Sex	Male vs. Female	0.87	0.85 - 0.88
Age	Age 35 to 44 vs. Age 25 to 34	0.19	0.18 – 0.20
	Age 45 to 54 vs. Age 25 to 34	0.41	0.40 – 0.42
	Age 55 to 64 vs. Age 25 to 34	0.87	0.85 – 0.88
	Age 65 or older vs. Age 25 to 34	3.91	3.84 – 3.97
Hispanic	Hispanic	0.37	0.33 -0.41
	Non-Hispanic	1.31	1.21 – 1.43
Race	White vs. Asian	2.38	2.32 – 2.44
	Black/African American vs. Asian	0.40	0.39 - 0.42
	American Indian/Alaskan Native vs. Asian	0.58	0.55 - 0.62
	Native Hawaiian/ Pacific Islander vs. Asian	0.37	0.31 - 0.42
	Other Race/Multi-racial vs. Asian	0.40	0.37 - 0.43
	Multiracial vs. Asian	0.68	0.64 - 0.72
	Not reported vs. Asian	0.57	0.53 - 0.6

AOR and 95% CI from multivariable logistic regression of the number of cancer disease categories, sex, race/ethnicity, and age are displayed in the Table 3. Males are less likely to report cancer disease with AOR 0.87 (95% CI, 0.85–0.88). The AOR for cancer disease for Hispanic participants is very low compared to non-Hispanic 0.37 (95% CI, 0.33–0.41) vs. (95% CI, 1.21–1.43). White American race is more likely to report cancer disease compared to Asian race with AOR 2.38 (95% CI, 2.32–2.44).

In the Table 4, AOR and 95% CI from multivariable logistic regression of the number of cancer disease categories, alcohol consumption, marital status, smoking, education level, household income, BMI, exercise behavior, and general health status. Highlighting significant results in Table 4: Participants who drink weekly are more likely to report cancer disease compared to non-drinker with AOR 1.17 (95% CI, 1.15–1.19). While the monthly drinker is less likely to have cancer with AOR 0.85 (95% CI, 0.85–0.87). Smokers are facing a highly AOR cancer disease risk AOR 1.59 (95% CI, 1.51–1.66) compared to a non-smoker. Divorced, widowed, or separated participants subject to cancer disease more likely versus another marital status AOR 1.42 (95% CI, 1.40–1.45). Excellent general health indicates a low cancer disease AOR 0.6 (95% CI, 0.59–0.62).

Table 4. Behavioral characteristics risk factors - Adjusted odds ratios (AOR) and the 95% confidence intervals according to cancer diseases of the final logistic regression analysis behavioral risk factor surveillance system, 2018.

Category	Sub - Category	Adjusted Odds Ratio (AOR)	Confidence Interval (CI) 95%
Alcohol Consumption	Drink Weekly vs. Non-Drinker	1.17	1.15 - 1.19
	Drink Monthly vs. Non-Drinker	0.85	0.84 - 0.87
Smoking	Smoker vs. Non-Smoker	1.59	1.51 - 1.66
	Not reported vs. Non-Smoker	0.90	0.81 - 1.00
Marital status	Currently married vs. Never married	0.82	0.81 – 0.83
	Divorced, widowed, vs Never married	1.42	1.40 - 1.45
	Not reported vs. Never married	0.38	0.36 - 0.40
Highest education level	High school vs. Less High School Grad.	0.88	0.862 - 0.894
	Some college vs. Less High School Grad.	0.97	0.955 - 0.990
	4+ college vs. Less High School Grad.	1.15	1.13 - 1.17
	Not reported vs. Less High School Grad.	0.66	0.569 - 0.777

Category	Sub - Category	Adjusted Odds Ratio (AOR)	Confidence Interval (CI) 95%
Annual household income	$10k - <$15k vs. <$10k	1.07	1.03 – 1.11
	$15k - <$20k vs. <$10k	0.92	0.89 – 0.96
	$20k - <$25k vs. <$10k	1.01	0.98 – 1.04
	$25k - <$35k vs. <$10k	1.05	1.03 – 1.08
	$35k - <$50k vs. <$10k	1.1	1.08 – 1.13
	$50k - <$75k vs. <$10k	1.02	0.99 – 1.04
	$75k or more vs. <$10k	0.88	0.87 – 0.9
	Not reported vs. <$10k	1.14	1.12 – 1.17
Obesity	Underweight vs. Obese	1.04	0.97 - 1.11
	Normal vs. Obese	1.02	1.0 – 1.04
	Overweight vs. Obese	1.12	1.1 – 1.14
Exercise status	Exercised in the last month vs. not exercised	0.79	0.65 – 0.96
General health	Excellent vs. Poor	0.6	0.59 – 0.62
	Very Good vs. Poor	0.9	0.88 – 0.91
	Good vs. Poor	1.13	1.11 – 1.15
	Fair vs. Poor	1.58	1.55 0 1.62

7 Improving Health Information Exchange and Connecting Analysis Results to Personal Health Applications

Personal health record (PHR) is proposed as an innovative solution to the problems of fragmented records and a lack of interoperability issues among diverse electronic health record (EHR) systems. The components of public health surveillance are ongoing data collection, regular and frequent data analysis and the provision of the results of these analyses to those who need to know [22] (Fig. 2).

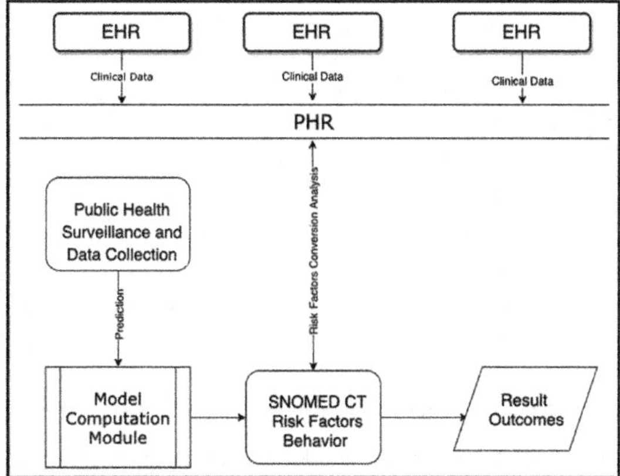

Fig. 2. Risk factors health information exchange

In this study, the analyses of surveillance data include cross-sectional descriptions of the population, outcomes, and risk factors, which can be further analyzed for the trends over time. These kinds of analyses are useful for estimating the burden of the disease in the population, determining whether this burden is increasing or decreasing in the population as well as making assessments about whether certain segments of the population are more at risk for the disorder or its complications. Health data can be collected as part of surveys that are population-based such as from BRFSS. Sentinel surveillance systems can be established in health care provider sites such as hospitals, clinics to monitor key health events such as cancer. The primary purpose of such provider-based surveillance systems is to obtain timely information on changes in the occurrence of a disease or condition that can inform preventive public health activities.

Tidyverse [23] can be applied to PHR, which is a coherent system of packages for data manipulation, exploration and visualization that share a common design philosophy. Tidyverse packages are intended to make statisticians and data scientists more productive by guiding them through workflows that facilitate communication and result in reproducible work products. Fundamentally, the tidyverse is about the connections between the tools that make the workflow possible (Figs. 3, 4 and 5).

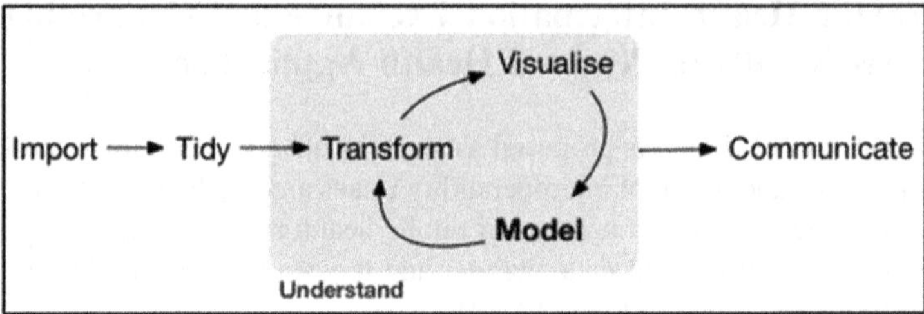

Fig. 3. Tidyverse workflow

```
macroTidyModal <- defmacro(InputVar ,
expr = {
    LogModel <- glm(CancerFlag ~    InputVar  , data=analytic, family = "binomial")
    summary(LogModel)
    Tidy_LogModel <- tidy(LogModel)
    Tidy_finalModel <- Tidy_LogModel

    #Add calculations
    # 1.96 is the margin of error
    Tidy_finalModel $OR <- exp(Tidy_finalModel $estimate)
    Tidy_finalModel $LL <- exp(Tidy_finalModel $estimate - (1.96 * Tidy_finalModel $std.error))
    Tidy_finalModel $UL <- exp(Tidy_finalModel $estimate + (1.96 * Tidy_finalModel $std.error))
    Tidy_finalModel
})
```

Fig. 4. Tidyverse model implementation A

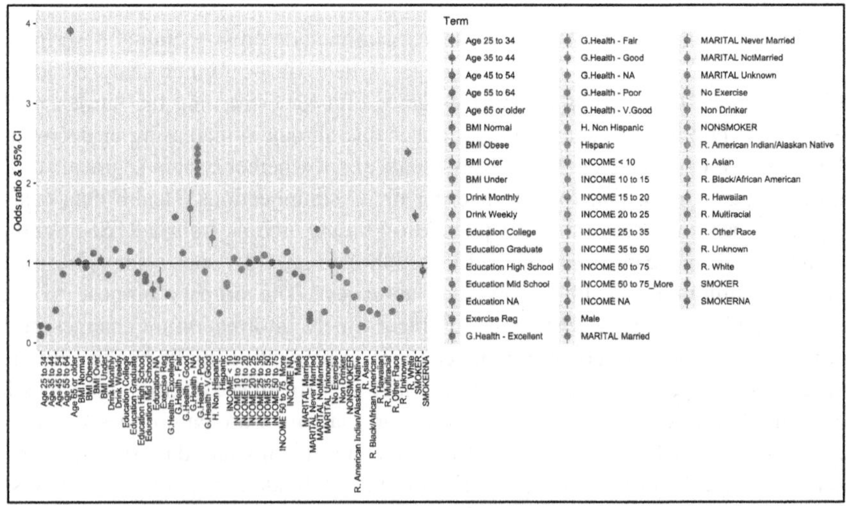

Fig. 5. Tidyverse model implementation - plot diagram B

8 Conclusion

In this study, we have used BRFSS dataset from 2018 as part of a public health surveillance system to estimate the magnitude of a problem of cancer disease. We examined the relationships between risk factors and outcomes. We also examined several risk factors and extended previous epidemiological researches by highlighting the association between lifestyle factors and 29 different types of cancer diseases. We created a logistic regression cancer model that provides a cancer prediction. The results were utilized with personal healthcare applications for the prediction. We developed continued monitoring to assess the effectiveness of the interventions to modify the complications or outcomes. Some of these, such as measures of socioeconomic status or general health, are apt to be correct confounders, as they appear to influence both exposures (such as alcohol consumption or physical activity) and outcome (cancer disease). The study indicated a significant relationship between dependent exposure variables with other independent potential risk factor variables, as it provided more confidence about the relationship between the two. We expanded the possibility of how these factors could contribute to cancer.

Future Direction

Even for those who have one or more of the risk factors mentioned above, it is hard to know for sure if these factors contribute to cancer. In other words, it is usually difficult to know exactly why one person develops cancer while others don't unless we combine the behavioral risk factors with many other factors such as cancer genomics dataset. Current work can be extended by applying to other diseases or other behavioral risk factors. Risk factor dataset can be translated into useful information that can be used to predict diseases and extract useful information to make decisions. For example, according to cBioPortal for Cancer Genomics, which was originally developed at Memorial Sloan Kettering Cancer Center (MSK) [24], we examined the gene CDK12 Mutation, which can be responsible for 35 categories of cancer types. As shown in Fig. 6 which was based on the study of 10953 patients with 10967 samples.

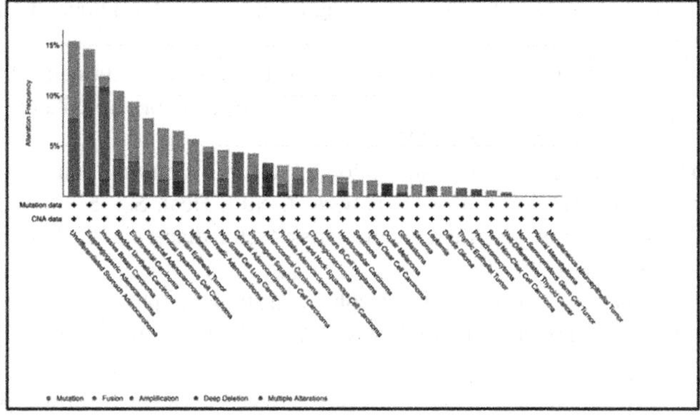

Fig. 6. Gene CDK12 sample future study

References

1. Shah, S.I.A.: An update on the risk factors for prostate cancer. World Cancer Res. J. **3**(2), e711 (2016)
2. Dwyer-Lindgren, L., Flaxman, A.D., Ng, M., Hansen, G.M., Murray, C.J.L., Mokdad, A.H.: Drinking patterns in US counties from 2002 to 2012. Am. J. Public Health **105**(6), 1120–1127 (2015)
3. Dwyer-Lindgren, L., et al.: Prevalence of physical activity and obesity in US counties, 2001–2011: a road map for action. Popul. Health Metr. **11**(1), 1–11 (2013)
4. Dwyer-Lindgren, L., Mokdad, A.H., Srebotnjak, T., Flaxman, A.D., Hansen, G.M., Murray, C.J.L.: Cigarette smoking prevalence in US counties: 1996–2012. Popul. Health Metr. **12**(1), 1–13 (2014)
5. Mokdad, A.H., Marks, J.S., Stroup, D.F., Gerberding, J.L.: Actual causes of death in the United States, 2000. J. Am. Med. Assoc. **291**(10), 1238–1245 (2004)
6. Danaei, G., Vander Hoorn, S., Lopez, A.D., Murray, C.J.L., Ezzati, M.: Causes of cancer in the world: comparative risk assessment of nine behavioural and environmental risk factors. Lancet 366(9499), 1784–1793 (2005)
7. Cancer.Net Editorial Board, Prostate Cancer: Statistics. https://www.cancer.net/cancer-types/prostate-cancer/statistics. Accessed 01 Feb 2019
8. National Cancer Institute, The Genetics of Cancer. https://www.cancer.gov/about-cancer/causes-prevention/genetics
9. Centers for Disease Control and Preventation (CDC): Behavioral Risk Factor Surveillance System. https://www.cdc.gov/brfss/index.html
10. Utah Environmental Epidemiology Program: Cancer: Risk Factors and Prevention. https://epht.health.utah.gov/epht-view/topic/Cancer.html
11. Mokdad, A.H.: The behavioral risk factors surveillance system: past, present, and future. Annu. Rev. Public Health **30**(1), 43–54 (2009)
12. Phillips-Salimi, C.R., Lommel, K., Andrykowski, M.A.: Physical and mental health status and health behaviors of childhood cancer survivors: Findings from the 2009 BRFSS survey. Pediatr. Blood Cancer **58**(6), 964–970 (2012)
13. Mukherjee, K., Segal, R.: Discussions with healthcare providers about prostate-specific antigen testing: evidence from the behavioral risk factor surveillance system in the USA. J. Pharm. Heal. Serv. Res. **6**(1), 47–52 (2015)
14. Wiener, R.C., Sambamoorthi, U.: Cross-sectional association between the number of missing teeth and cardiovascular disease among adults aged 50 or Older: BRFSS 2010. Int. J. Vasc. Med. **2014**, 6 (2014)
15. Faestel, P.M., Littell, C.T., Vitiello, M.V., Forsberg, C.W., Littman, A.J.: Perceived insufficient rest or sleep among veterans: behavioral risk factor surveillance system 2009. J. Clin. Sleep Med. **9**(6), 577–584 (2013)
16. Hendriks, H., Calame, W.: The contribution of alcohol consumption to overall cancer incidence in the western world: a meta-analysis. J. Nutr. Heal. Sci. **5**(3), 308 (2018)
17. Buck, K.D.: Modelling of geographic cancer risk factor disparities in US counties. Appl. Geogr. **75**, 28–35 (2016)
18. Mukamal, K.J., Ding, E.L., Djoussé, L.: Alcohol consumption, physical activity, and chronic disease risk factors: a population-based cross-sectional survey. BMC Public Health **6**, 1–9 (2006)
19. Newschaffer, C.J.: Jefferson Medical College - Center for Research in Medical Education and Health Care. Validation of behavioral risk factor surveillance system (BRFSS) HRQOL measures in a statewide sample (1998)

20. Zhao, J., Stockwell, T., Roemer, A., Chikritzhs, T.: Is alcohol consumption a risk factor for prostate cancer? A systematic review and meta-analysis. BMC Cancer **16**(1), 1–13 (2016)
21. Brotman, D.J., Walker, E., Lauer, M.S., O'Brien, R.G.: In search of fewer independent risk factors. Arch. Intern. Med. **165**(2), 138–145 (2005)
22. Soucie, J.M.: Public health surveillance and data collection: general principles and impact on hemophilia care. Hematology **17**(1), 1–6 (2015)
23. R for Data Science. https://www.tidyverse.org/
24. Center for Molecular Oncology: cBioPortal for Cancer Genomics. https://www.cbioportal.org/

IoMT-Driven eHealth: A Technological Innovation Proposal Based on Smart Speakers

David Domínguez[1], Leticia Morales[1(✉)], Nicolas Sánchez[1,2], and Jose Navarro-Pando[3]

[1] University of Seville, Escuela Técnica Superior de Ingeniería Informática. Web Engineering and Early Testing (IWT2) Group, Avda. Reina Mercedes S/N, 41012 Seville, Spain
davdomvaz@alum.us.es, {leticia.morales,nicolas.sanchez}@iwt2.org
[2] G7Innovations Company, Seville, Spain
[3] Inebir Clinic, Seville, Spain
jose.navarro@inebir.com

Abstract. Internet of Medical Things (IoMT) is a technological concept applied in healthcare contexts to achieve the digital interconnection of everyday objects with the Internet in order to make life easier for people. IoMT can help monitor, inform and notify not only caregivers, but provide healthcare providers with actual data to identify issues before they become critical or to allow for earlier invention. In this sense, this paper is contextualized in Assisted Reproduction Treatment (ART) processes to reduce the number of hospital visits, reduce healthcare costs and improve patientcare, as well as the productivity of the healthcare professional. So, we present an IoMT-based technological proposal to manage and control the prescription of pharmacological treatments to patients who are carried out ART processes. In this context, we propose the integration of iMEDEA (modular system specialized in the management of electronic clinical records for ART unit) and smart speaker devices (specifically, Amazon's Alexa), as well as the validation of our proposal in the real environment offered by Inebir clinic.

Keywords: Internet of Medical Things (IoMT) · iMEDEA · Alexa · Patientcare improvement

1 Introduction

Internet of Things (IoT) is a technological concept that emerged in the 90's in the field of sensor and radiofrequency technologies. Today, IoT aims to achieve the digital interconnection of everyday objects with the Internet in order to make life easier for people [1]. When the IoT concept is applied in healthcare contexts, it takes the name of Internet of Medical Things (IoMT) [2]. Also known as healthcare IoT, the IoMT comprises the medical devices and applications connected to healthcare information technology systems via the Web. Wi-Fi enabled devices facilitate machine-to-machine communication and link to cloud platforms for data storage. In short, IoMT is a concept that combines medical devices and software applications that can connect to healthcare information

I. Rojas et al. (Eds.): IWBBIO 2020, LNBI 12108, pp. 378–386, 2020.
https://doi.org/10.1007/978-3-030-45385-5_33

technology systems using networking technologies. The IoMT can help monitor, inform and notify not only caregivers, but provide healthcare providers with actual data to identify issues before they become critical or to allow for earlier invention.

In addition, the use of this technology allows to reduce unnecessary hospital visits and the burden on healthcare systems by connecting patients to their physicians and allowing the transfer of medical data over a secure network. IoMT also could reduce healthcare costs in the coming years.

In this context, this paper describes an IoMT-based technological proposal to manage and control the ingestion of pharmacological treatments to patients. More specifically, it is contextualized with the Assisted Reproduction Treatment (ART) processes [3], which have become a very used health service by more and more sentimental couple around the world because of problems such as fertility limiting pathologies, delay in the maternity age, single-parent couples, couples and women who wish to face maternity individually [4], among others. In fact, some epidemiological studies conclude that Infertility pathologies affect 15% of the population of reproductive age in Western countries (i.e., one in six couples) and this percentage is gradually increasing every year [5]. However, these data can be extrapolated to other countries.

Despite upward trends in the use of ARTs, these ones are expensive processes whose success depends on many factors [6]. One of them is the assimilation of pharmacological treatments that patients (usually women) have to take before, during and after carrying out the ART process.

In this context, we propose the integration of: (*i*) Hospital Information Systems (HIS), which are used by healthcare professionals to carry out the monitoring and control of ART processes, as well as the medication of the patients; and (*ii*) smart speaker devices, which is going to be located in the patient's home, it is going to notify when exactly each medication must be ingested, and it is going to receive the patient's response, storing it in the system to be checked by the healthcare professional. In addition, it is important to highlight that our technological proposal has been applied and validated in the real environment offered by Inebir Clinic [19] (Spanish assisted reproduction clinic). This collaboration has allowed us to obtain valuable feedback to improve our proposal and propose future work.

Finally, this paper is structured as follows. After this introduction, Sects. 2 and 3 explain the methodology used and the results obtained, respectively. Section 4 provides further discussion, and Sect. 5 states final conclusions and some future works.

2 Materials and Methods

As mentioned above, our IoMT-based technological proposal aims to improve the control and productivity of ART professionals when they prescribe pharmacological treatments to their patients. For this purpose, our proposal has been: (*i*) designed using model-driven methodologies and collaborative work techniques for product design; and (*ii*) carried out by integrating smart speakers with commercial HIS.

On the one hand, we have used the agile version of NDT (Navigational Development Techniques) [7] which is enriched with collaborative work techniques for product design (e.g., design thinking [8], sprint design [9], among others), providing a flexible, dynamic and powerful methodological environment. In addition, NDT is framed under the MDE paradigm (Model Driven Engineering) and it also offers its software toolkit (NDT-Suite [10]) to successfully apply NDT in practical environments. In fact, NDT-Suite has been satisfactorily applied in numerous contexts: aeronautics [11], software requirement management [12, 20], healthcare [13], software process management [14], functional software testing [21], among others.

On the other hand, our IoMT-based proposal has used iMEDEA [15] (innovative MEDical Engineering Assistance) system as data source and the integrated development environment offered by Amazon. iMEDEA is a HIS solution designed and developed by G7Innovations company [16] that provides a modular technological environment with advanced mechanisms for managing ART unit whereas Amazon provides smart speaker devices (Alexa [17]), Amazon's cloud-based voice services and toolkits to develop virtual assistant solutions using the Alexa Skills Kit (ASK) [18].

3 Results

This section describes our solution proposal to control and manage of pharmacological treatments to patients who are carried out ART processes. For this purpose, Sect. 3.1 describes the architecture of our IoMT-based proposal and Sect. 3.2 describes the workflow and communications when our proposal is used in practical environments.

3.1 Architecture of Our Technological Proposal

The proposal presented in this paper has been designed with a two-layer architecture (see Fig. 1): (*i*) «client/device layer»; and (*ii*) «cloud layer» . On the one hand, «client/device layer» contains patient's IoT devices (smart speakers) and client application (web browsers) of the healthcare professional.

On the other hand, cloud layer contains: (1) «Skill Alexa4iMEDEA» , which is am integration module between Alexa and the HIS used in our proposal (i.e., iMEDEA) that is deployed in Amazon's cloud (i.e., Amazon Web Services or AWS in Fig. 1); and (2) a submodule within iMEDEA and its «Integration and Interoperability Module» , which allows synchronizing the patient's instance with his/her user account on Amazon (this submodule is represented as a yellow box in Fig. 1 to avoid complications in the graphic representation of our architecture).

Regarding «Skill Alexa4iMEDEA», this one has been designed and developed with different cloud-based components which are coded in two different levels. The first one is the *client level* where the different interactions (i.e., voice commands) are created associated with our Alexa's skill. These voice commands are interpreted by Alexa engine (*server level*). The second level is the *server level* which could be hosted in AWS or in our server. It supports Node.js and Python languages. At *server level*, voice commands are managed in order according to the main configuration file (see Table 1) defined in our skill.

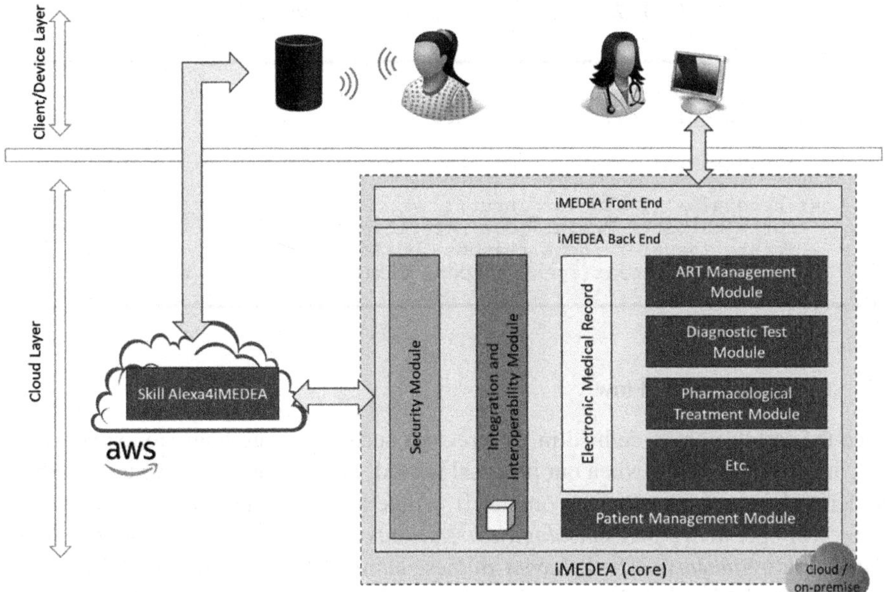

Fig. 1. Architecture of our IoMT-based proposal. (Color figure online)

Table 1. Main configuration file to manage each interaction (voice command) in our skill.

```
sb = SkillBuilder()

sb.add_request_handler(LaunchRequestHandler())
sb.add_request_handler(GeneralInteractionIntentHandler())
sb.add_request_handler(reminderInteractionIntentHandler())
sb.add_request_handler(CancelOrStopIntentHandler())
sb.add_request_handler(SessionEndedRequestHandler())
sb.add_request_handler(HelpIntentHandler())

sb.add_exception_handler(CatchAllExceptionHandler())
lambda_handler = sb.lambda_handler()
```

Each mentioned instruction in Table 1 represents the definition of a Python class in our skill to manage each voice command. For example, Table 2 shows the Python class associated with the first interaction which allows initiating the communication of our solution for Alexa.

These class contains two main functions. The first one is *can_handle* and its objective is to check if this class has to be executed. The second function is *handle*, which contains the logic of the interaction. This function returns a set of actions predefined by Alexa: speak, that is a phrase to be reproduced by Alexa; *ask*, which allows to activate our Skill (listening mode) to identify any command indicated by the user; *response*, that returns the *response object* to be sent to the Alexa device; *AskForPermissionsConsentCard*, that manages request permissions.

Table 2. Code to start communication with Alexa

```
class LaunchRequestHandler(AbstractRequestHandler):
   def can_handle(self, handler_input):
      return
      ask_utils.is_request_type("LaunchRequest")(handler_input)

   def handle(self, handler_input):
      speak_output = "Hola, ¿Que necesitas?"
      return (handler_input.response_builder.
                  speak(speak_output).ask(speak_output).response)
```

3.2 Communication Flow

Once the architecture is defined in the previous section, we are going to explain what the communication flow when our proposal is used. In this sense, we have created three on-demand interactions (voice command) to interact with Alexa: (1) *«start interaction»* ; (2) *«get active pharmacological treatments»*; and (3) *«create reminders associated with treatments»*. The behavior of these commands is shown in Fig. 2 using an UML (Unified Modeling Language) sequence diagram. However, Fig. 2 only shows the first and last interaction because the second one is very similar, and the sequence diagram could be very extensive.

It is important to mention that, before using our «Skill Alexa4iMEDEA» , it is necessary a configuration step (see at the top of Fig. 2) which is performed by the healthcare professional and consists of enabling the communication of the patient with iMEDEA using Alexa (this action automatically generates a security token by IMEDEA; this token is used in subsequent transactions). Once the patient is enabled, s/he can configure his/her Alexa device with his/her own iMEDEA's security token and start interacting with Alexa.

Once the user has been activated, patient can interact with Alexa and IMEDEA using voice commands. As mentioned above, the first interaction shown in Fig. 2 is *«start interaction»* which allows to initiating communications and, subsequently, interact using next commands. In this sense, Alexa communicates with «Skill Alexa4iMEDEA» module (into AWS) and these one communicates with «Security Module» of iMEDEA to authenticate the patient. This security module responds with rejected or successful authentication (the communication flow continues if authentication is successful).

Moreover, the second interaction shown in Fig. 2 is *«create reminders associated with treatments»* which allows creating automatically reminders. For this purpose, the patient only has to say: *«create reminders for my treatments»* (voice command). It is necessary that the patient indicates the number of days in which reminders should be created and the time of the first dose (if this is not done, Alexa ask for this information). Subsequently, «Skill Alexa4iMEDEA» module (into AWS) checks if the user is authenticated («Security Module» of iMEDEA) and obtains the list of their active treatments («Integration and Interoperability» and «Pharmacological Treatment» modules of iMEDEA).

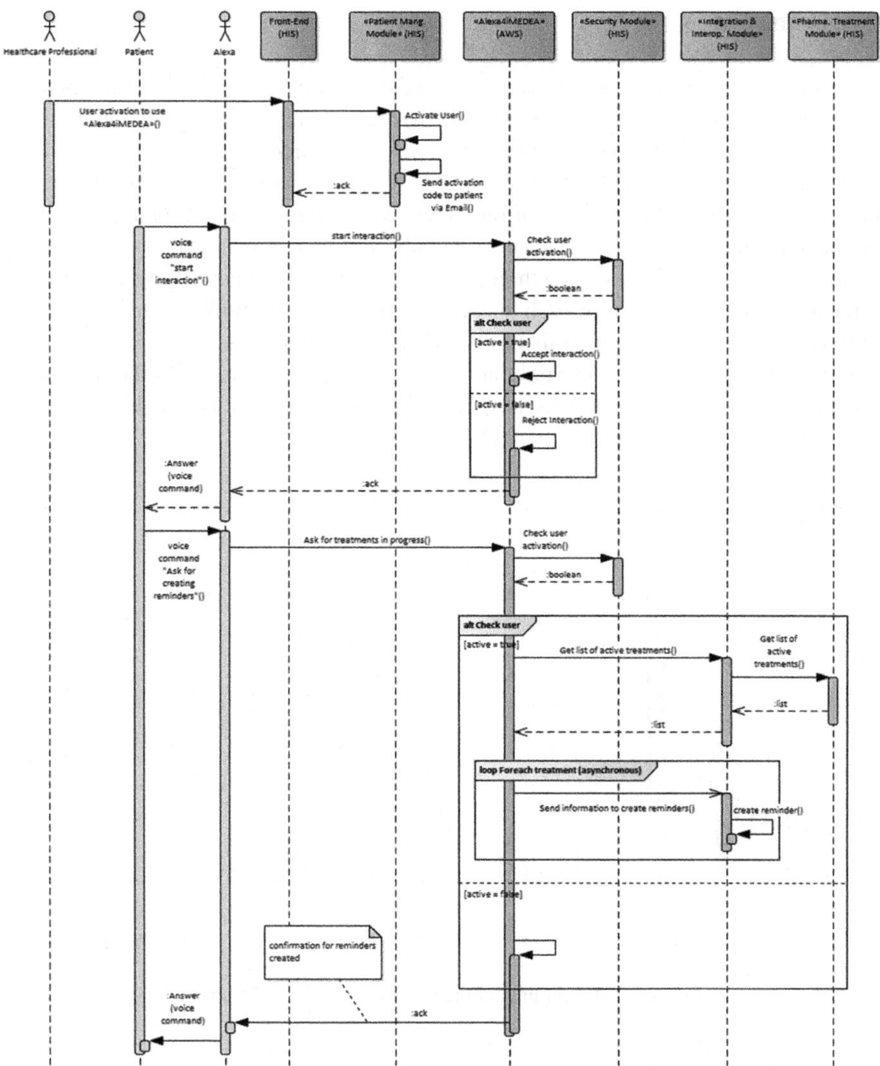

Fig. 2. Communication flow of our IoMT-based proposal and representation.

Once the request is completed, «Skill Alexa4iMEDEA» retrieves the patient's active treatments. Finally, it sends an order with all the information to create the reminders in an asynchronous way and tells the patient that soon they will be created.

4 Discussion

Once our proposal has been designed and developed, we have managed to apply and validate it in the real environment offered by Inebir clinic [19]. This validation has been carried out using the case-studies method as *proof-of-concept*.

In this sense, we have designed 7 cases of study to evaluate the performance and efficacy of our skill in the creation of reminders according to different pharmacological treatment settings. Specially, for each case study, we have conducted tests varying the number of treatments from one to three; and for these treatments we have changed the frequency of the doses between 2 h and 12 h. Also, we have modified the end date of the treatments in order to finish them during the requested days.

Figure 3 shows all cases of study and their variations, according to the number of reminders created in each case (X-axis represents the combination of the amount of treatments with their dosage frequency).

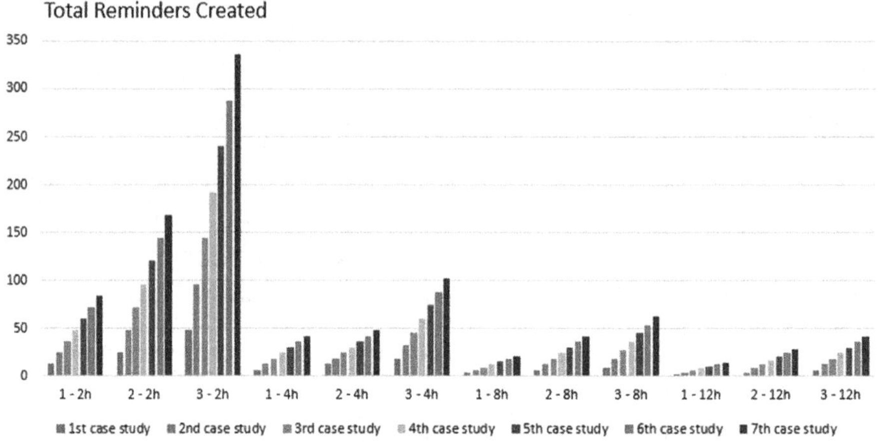

Fig. 3. Total reminders created in each case of study.

Figure 3 shows that cases where the dosage frequency is 2 h, a lot of reminders can be created. However, for all other frequencies it does not exceed 100 reminders because of issues of our preliminary design. Although user experience has been successful, we have received comments to improve the usability of voice commands between patient-Alexa to promote more human communication (question-answer). From a technical perspective, we have identified some limitations. The main one is related to the existence of limitations in the number of transactions that can be issued by our Skill.

5 Conclusions and Future Works

This paper describes an IoMT-based technological proposal to manage and control the prescription of pharmacological treatments to patients who are carried out ART processes. Our proposal aims to reduce the number of hospital visits, reduce healthcare costs and improve patient care, as well as the productivity of the healthcare professional. In this context, we propose the integration of iMEDEA (modular system specialized in the management of electronic clinical records for ART unit) and smart speaker devices (specifically, Amazon's Alexa), as well as the validation of our proposal in the real environment offered by Inebir clinic.

Finally, after carrying out this proposal, some future works are proposed: optimization of our Skill Alexa for iMEDEA through concurrent algorithms; mechanisms to facilitate the daily work of health professionals when they manually enter information into their HIS (we will consider using voice commands with Alexa); alert notifications (via voice commands from Alexa) when an critical error has been detected that could compromise the success of the ART processes; integrate our proposal into the design and development of ART processes using process modeling languages [22, 23], among others.

However, we have already started new research lines related to our proposal. Specifically, we are defining generic and abstract models that allow the design of technological solutions that are independent of the IoT device. In this sense, we could define abstract models and automatically (using model-to-text transformations) generate code associated to specific technologies (such as, Alexa, LG smart speakers[1], among others). In addition, from perspective of software product design, we plan to improve the NDT methodology when this one is used to design products with IoT device. These improvements will be related to the incorporation of prototype-driven mechanisms to facilitate the communication of users and software engineers during the design of these technological solutions.

Acknowledgments. This research has been supported by POLOLAS project (TIN2016-76956-C3-2-R) of the Spanish Ministry of Economy and Competitiveness (Spain) under ERD funds and SocietySoft project (AT17_5904_USE) of the Regional Ministry of Economy, Knowledge, Business and University (Andalucía, Spain).

References

1. Qian, Z., Wang, Y.: IoT technology and application. Acta Electronica Sinica **5**, 026 (2012)
2. Joyia, G., Liaqat, R., Farooq, A., Rehman, S.: Internet of Medical Things (IOMT): applications, benefits and future challenges healthcare domain. J. Commun. **12**(4), 240–247 (2017)
3. Zegers-Hochschild, F., et al.: The international committee for monitoring assisted reproductive technology (ICMART) and the world health organization (WHO) revised glossary on ART terminology, 2009. Hum. Reprod. **24**(11), 2683–2687 (2009)

[1] https://www.lg.com/us/smart-speakers

4. Matzuk, M.M., Lamb, D.J.: The biology of infertility: research advances and clinical challenges. Nat. Med. **14**(11), 1197 (2008)
5. Skakkebaek, N.E., et al.: Male reproductive disorders and fertility trends: influences of environment and genetic susceptibility. Physiol. Rev. **96**(1), 55–97 (2015)
6. Vaegter, K., Lakic, T.G., Olovsson, M., Berglund, L., Brodin, T., Holte, J.: Which factors are most predictive for live birth after in vitro fertilization and intracytoplasmic sperm injection (IVF/ICSI) treatments? Analysis of 100 prospectively recorded variables in 8,400 IVF/ICSI single-embryo transfers. Fertil. Steril. **107**(3), 641–648 (2017)
7. Escalona, M.J., Aragón, G.: NDT. A model-driven approach for web requirements. IEEE Trans. Software Eng. **34**(3), 377–390 (2008)
8. Design thinking (2020). http://www.designthinking.es/inicio/
9. Banfield, R., Lombardo, C. T., Wax, T.: Design Sprint: A Practical Guidebook for Building Great Digital Products. O'Reilly Media, Inc. (2015)
10. García-García, J.A., Escalona, M.J., Domínguez-Mayo, F.J., Salido, A.: NDT-Suite: a methodological tool solution in the model-driven engineering paradigm. J. Softw. Eng. Appl. **7**(04), 206 (2014)
11. Salido, A., García, J.A.G., Ponce, J., Gutierrez, J.: Tests management in CALIPSOneo: a MDE solution. J. Softw. Eng. Appl. **7**(06), 506 (2014)
12. García-García, J.A., Escalona, M.J., Ravel, E., Rossi, G., Urbieta, M.: NDT-merge: a future tool for conciliating software requirements in MDE environments. In: 14th International Conference Information Integration and Web-based Applications Services, pp. 177–186 (2012)
13. García-García, J.A., Escalona, M.J., Martínez-García, A., Parra, C., Wojdyński, T.: Clinical process management: a model-driven tool-based proposal (2015)
14. Garcia-Garcia, J.A., Enríquez, J.G., Garcia-Borgoñon, L., Arévalo, C., Morillo, E.: A MDE-based framework to improve the process management: the EMPOWER project. In: IEEE 15th International Conference on Industrial Informatics, pp. 553–558 (2017)
15. IMEDEA Suite (2020). http://g7innovation.com/imedea-suite/
16. G7Innovations company (2020). http://g7innovation.com/
17. Alexa (2020). https://developer.amazon.com/en-US/blogs/alexa
18. Alexa Skills Kit (2020). https://developer.amazon.com/es-ES/alexa/alexa-skills-kit
19. Inebir clinic (2020). https://inebir.com/
20. Escalona, M.J., Urbieta, M., Rossi, G., Garcia-Garcia, J.A., Luna, E.R.: Detecting web requirements conflicts and inconsistencies under a model-based perspective. J. Syst. Softw. **86**(12), 3024–3038 (2013)
21. Cutilla, C., et al.: Model-driven test engineering: a practical analysis in the AQUA-WS project. In: 7th International Conference Software Paradigm Trends, pp 111–119 (2012)
22. García-García, J.A., García-Borgoñón, L., Escalona, M.J., Mejías, M.: A model-based solution for process modeling in practice environments: PLM4BS. J. Softw. Evol. Proc. **30** (12), e1982 (2018)
23. Garcia-Garcia, J.A., Meidan, A., Carreño, A.V., Risoto, M.M.: A model-driven proposal to execute and orchestrate processes: PLM 4 BS. In: International Conference on Software Process Improvement and Capability Determination, pp. 211–225 (2017)

Evolving Towards Digital Twins in Healthcare (EDITH)

Epileptic Seizure Detection Using a Neuromorphic-Compatible Deep Spiking Neural Network

Pouya Soltani Zarrin[1(✉)], Romain Zimmer[2], Christian Wenger[1,3], and Timothée Masquelier[2,4]

[1] IHP–Leibniz-Institut fuer innovative Mikroelektronik, 15236 Frankfurt (Oder), Germany
soltani@ihp-microelectronics.com
[2] CNRS–CERCO UMR 5549, 31300 Toulouse, France
[3] Brandenburg Medical School, 16816 Neuruppin, Germany
[4] Paul Sabatier University (Université Toulouse 3), 31330 Toulouse, France

Abstract. Monitoring brain activities of Drug-Resistant Epileptic (DRE) patients is crucial for the effective management of the chronic epilepsy. Implementation of machine learning tools for analyzing electrical signals acquired from the cerebral cortex of DRE patients can lead to the detection of a seizure prior to its development. Therefore, the objective of this work was to develop a deep Spiking Neural Network (SNN) for the epileptic seizure detection. The energy and computation-efficient SNNs are well compatible with neuromorphic systems, making them an adequate model for edge-computing devices such as healthcare wearables. In addition, the integration of SNNs with neuromorphic chips enables the secure analysis of sensitive medical data without cloud computations.

Keywords: Epileptic seizure detection · Deep spiking neural networks · Bio-neuromorphics · Surrogate gradient · Precision medicine · Edge computing

1 Introduction

Epilepsy is a common chronic neurological disorder, affecting millions of people worldwide [1]. High mortality rate of epilepsy—due to its direct and indirect consequences such as accidents, drowning, falling injuries, and sudden unexpected death due to long-term brain damages—necessitates the adequate management and monitoring of the disease for reducing its potential risks. Although the development of antiepileptic drugs have significantly improved the treatment quality of the disease, more than 30% of patients still suffer from a particular type of epilepsy known as Drug-Resistant-Epilepsy (DRE) [1]. In the absence of a curative therapy for DRE, surgical treatment might be the only viable option for reducing the seizure frequency in patients. However, considering the complex mechanism of DRE, achieving radical improvements through surgical

I. Rojas et al. (Eds.): IWBBIO 2020, LNBI 12108, pp. 389–394, 2020.
https://doi.org/10.1007/978-3-030-45385-5_34

operations, alone, is not feasible [1]. Therefore, tracking the electrical activities of the cerebral cortex, by implanting electrode grids known as intracranial electroencephalography (iEEG) into the skull, provides important information on the treatment progress of DRE; while enabling the accurate prediction of a seizure prior to its development [2]. The availability of long duration iEEG recordings, acquired from DRE patients in clinical settings, has facilitated the adequate statistical analysis for the real-time seizure forecasting, thus transforming the epilepsy care [2,3]. Various Machine Learning (ML) techniques, or more specifically deep learning methods, have been applied in recent studies for predicting seizures in drug-resistant epileptic patients [3,4]. Despite the remarkable performance of the developed Deep Neural Networks (DNNs) for forecasting epileptic seizure, their implementation on the real-world mobile medical devices for point-of-care (PoC) applications is still not practical. This is due to the fact that the astonishing performance of DNNs comes at the cost of immense energy consumption and enormous computational power, thus, requiring cloud computations [3]. On the other hand, complexities associated with cloud communications such as robustness against interference, wide bandwidth requirements, low latency, and data security limit the application of DNN-based methods in sensitive fields like healthcare. On the contrary, hardware-based neuromorphic systems address these limitations by bringing the data-processing from the back-end onto the chip, offering an energy-efficient platform for the real-time analysis of acquired medical data in a secure manner with less time delay [5,6]. However, the conversion of DNN's sophisticate architecture into a rudimentary neuromorphic structure often impairs the accuracy and performance of the network [3]. As an alternative, biologically-plausible Spiking Neural Networks (SNNs) comply better with the specifications of neuromorphic systems considering their incomplex network structure [7]. Although, development of deep SNNs for performing complex tasks is still challenging (due to the discrete nature of spikes), recent attempts in using surrogate gradients for the backpropagation calculations have shown promising results for simplifying the algorithmic complexities associated with training these models [7,8]. Therefore, the objective of this work was to develop a neuromorphic-compatible deep SNN for the epileptic seizure detection using a surrogate gradient-based learning algorithm. The implementation of the developed SNN model on IHP's HfO2-based Resistive Random Access Memory (RRAM) neuromorphic chip will enable the real-time detection of diseases in the future [6]. The inherent stochasticity of CMOS-integrated RRAM devices enables the on-chip learning possibilities using various ML models including SNNs [5]. As a result, advancements in developing neuromorphic-compatible SNNs for medical applications will pave the way towards the better integration of Artificial Intelligence (AI) with PoC medical devices and biosensors [9–11]. In addition, the integration of the surrogate gradient model with novel training algorithms such as a few-shot learning, will enable the on-chip training of the SNN-based neurmorphic chips in medical applications with limited data availability [12].

2 Methods

The open access chronic ambulatory iEEG data, provided for the Kaggle seizure detection-prediction competition (https://msel.mayo.edu/data.html), were used in this study for training and evaluating the developed model. The dataset contains information on three classes of seizure (ictal), pre-seizure (preictal), and seizure-free (interictal) signals. The ictal segment of the signal is a representative of the period when a patient experiences a seizure, while the preictal segment represents the 1-hour time window prior to a seizure development. The interictal segment represents any signal period at least 4 hours before or after a seizure has been recorded. The provided data clips for the seizure prediction task were 10-minutes in duration with a sampling frequency of 400 Hz. The iEEG data were collected from canine subjects using surgically implanted electrodes with 15 channels. The similar seizure mechanism between human and dogs, make the acquired data from canine subjects very valuable for clinical applications. On the other hand, the provided data clips for the seizure detection task were 1 s in duration with a sampling frequency of 400 Hz. The iEEG data were collected from human subjects using surgically implanted electrodes with 55 channels. For training our network, 100 iEEG recordings (30–seizure (ictal) and 70–seizure-free (interictal)) of a single patient were split into the training and validation datasets with 70 to 30 percent ratios, respectively. In addition, 41 data points (27–seizure (ictal) and 14–seizure-free (interictal)) were used as the unseen test dataset for the network performance evaluations. Prior to the conversion of iEEG signals into spikes, spectrograms of the recorded data were calculated using the short-time Fourier transform in order to extract the time-frequency representations of the signals in the range of 0–200 Hz with 155 time-steps. The spectrogram transformation was done using the Scipy library of Python on the Jupyter Lab environment. As shown in Fig. 1, a deep spiking neural network with two convolutional hidden layers was developed using the PyTorch library. The conversion of the analog iEEG spectrograms into spikes has been done at the first input layer of the network. The weighted sum of the generated output spikes are the inputs of the following hidden layers. The readout layer with a softmax activation function has two output neurons, representing the seizure and seizure-free categories. The hidden layers are two-dimensional convolutional spiking layers with 32 neurons and a kernel size of 4×3. It is noteworthy that, the temporal dimension of the convolution in the time-frequency domain is a representative of the propagation delays of the input spikes. Considering the discrete nature of spikes, the surrogate gradient method was used for the backpropagation calculations. For this purpose, a Sigmoid function (with a scale of 8) was used to approximate the derivative of the Heaviside step function. Rectified-Adam optimizer, with a 0.0001 learning rate, and the cross entropy error function were used for training and optimizing the network parameters. Further details of the SNN model are available at the following repository: https://github.com/Pouya-SZ/DSCONN. After modeling the SNN, the pre-processed iEEG data were fed into the network for 20 training epochs with a batch size of 70. Finally, the trained network was used to predict the labels of the unseen test data.

3 Results and Discussions

The developed deep SNN model provided a validation accuracy of 93.3% for the epileptic seizure detection task, after 20 cycles of training. In addition, the network predicted the correct label of the unseen test signals with an accuracy of 97.6%. As illustrated in the confusion matrix of Fig. 2(a), the SNN provided precision and sensitivity values of 100% and 96.3%, respectively, on 41 unseen test data with only one false-negative prediction. The high performance of the developed SNN makes it a reliable model for edge-computing devices capable of real-time detection of seizure episodes. Figure 2(b) shows an example of such a wearable device which could be used as an epileptic seizure detector in a PoC setting. In such a setup, the iEEG signals acquired from patient's cerebral cortex can be transmitted by a portable transducer to the healthcare wearable such as a smart watch. The obtained data by the wearable device can be processed locally using a neuromorphic chip, prior to sending to a smartphone-based user interface for patient records.

As presented in Table 1, the introduced deep SNN was able to perform a complex classification task, the epileptic seizure detection, in an accuracy range comparable to the performance of the well-established DNNs. Furthermore, the biologically-inspired structure of SNNs comply better with the hardware-based neuromorphic systems, while requiring less energy and computational power, thus making them an adequate approach for edge-computing applications such as mobile medical devices. As a result, the implementation of the SNN-based ML techniques on the healthcare technologies and medical wearables will revolutionize the PoC medicine in the upcoming years.

Preliminary results of the network performance for the seizure prediction task provided validation and testing accuracies of 87.5% and 93.05%, respectively. However, the repeatability of the results were questionable due to the over-fitting issue experienced during training the network. The over-fitting problem could be due to the small number of data points used for training. Moreover, the prediction task is, without a doubt, a more challenging and complex task

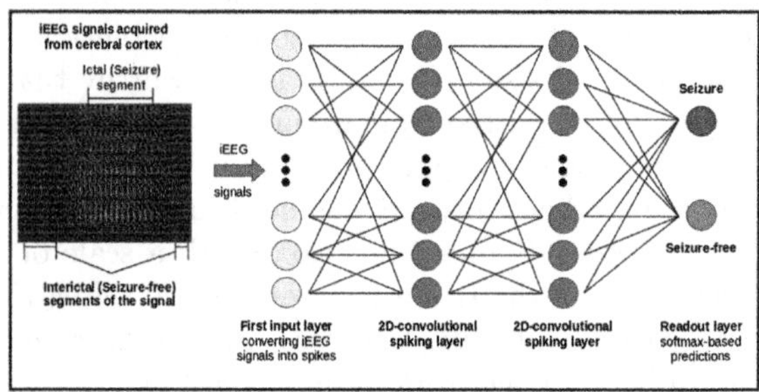

Fig. 1. Architecture of the developed deep SNN for the epileptic seizure detection.

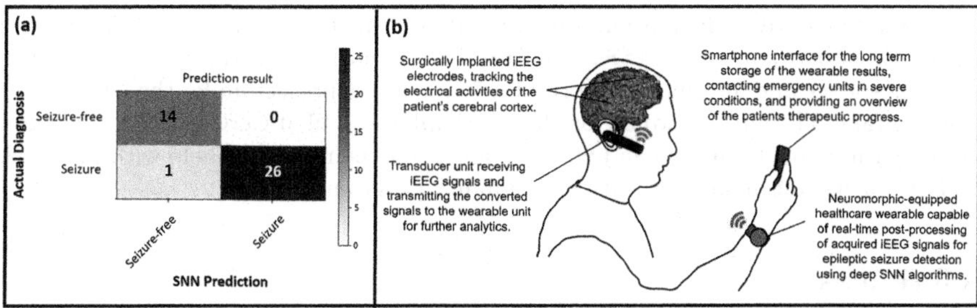

Fig. 2. (a) Confusion matrix for the SNN performance on the unseen test data; (b) Sketch of a PoC healthcare setup for the epileptic seizure detection using a healthcare wearable equipped with neuromorphic chips and a smartphone user interface.

compared to the seizure detection, considering the slight differences between two signal categories. Therefore, further investigation on a vast dataset are required for improving the network performance in the future and to make the results more generalizable and reliable. In addition, taking advantage of the phase information for the spectrogram transformation could possibly improve the network performance.

AI-equipped medical devices will bridge the gap between patients in remote locations and the medical staff by accurate monitoring of patients' health status. Moreover, AI will remarkably improve the management of chronic and degenerative conditions such as epileptic seizure by predicting the critical and emergency conditions. Additionally, collection of further health-related data from patients through edge-computing technologies, such as the one introduced in this work, will facilitate the statistical analysis of medical conditions with better therapeutic outcome for patients. Nonetheless, the trade-off between the mentioned benefits and the risks related to securing sensitive medical data is still a significant concern challenging governments and policy makers today. Therefore, investments for developing precise data safety regulations as well as patient-oriented secure technologies is of great importance. Among these technologies, AI-enabled neuromorphic devices will most likely provide the best platform for patients to take advantage of the AI-based medicine, while having control over their personal data and medical privacy. Therefore, the integration of the presented SNN model, for the epileptic seizure detection, on our previously developed neuromorphic platform is the next goal of this work.

Table 1. Performance of the introduced SNN compared to DNNs.

	Accuracy (%)
SNN	97.6
DNN-classifier [3]	95
Convolutional-DNN [4]	99.6

Acknowledgement. The authors thank the department of science and technology of the French embassy in Berlin (SST) and the French national institute for research in computer science and automation (Inria) for funding this project under the AI-Procope mobility grant. The authors would also like to thank the staff at CerCo-CNRS Toulouse, especially Emmanuel Barbeau and Simon Thorpe, for their precious help with this work and IHP for its initial support with the mobility program.

References

1. Sheng, J., Liu, S., Qin, H., Li, B., Zhang, X.: Drug-resistant epilepsy and surgery. Curr. Neuropharmacol. **16**, 17–28 (2018). https://doi.org/10.2174/1570159X15666170504123316
2. Cook, M.J., et al.: Prediction of seizure likelihood with a long-term, implanted seizure advisory system in patients with drug-resistant epilepsy: a first-in-man study. The Lancet Neurol. **12**, 563–571 (2013). https://doi.org/10.1016/S1474-4422(13)70075-9
3. Kiral-Kornek, I., et al.: Epileptic seizure prediction using big data and deep learning: toward a mobile system. EBioMedicine **27**, 103–111 (2018). https://doi.org/10.1016/j.ebiom.2017.11.032
4. Daoud, H., Bayoumi, M.A.: Efficient epileptic seizure prediction based on deep learning. IEEE Trans. Biomed. Circuits Syst. **13**, 804–813 (2019). https://doi.org/10.1109/TBCAS.2019.2929053
5. Wenger, C., et al.: Inherent stochastic learning in CMOS-integrated HfO 2 arrays for neuromorphic computing. IEEE Electron Device Lett. **40**, 639–642 (2019)
6. Soltani Zarrin, P., Wenger, C.: Pattern recognition for COPD diagnostics using an artificial neural network and its potential integration on hardware-based neuromorphic platforms. In: Tetko, I.V., Kůrková, V., Karpov, P., Theis, F. (eds.) ICANN 2019. LNCS, vol. 11731, pp. 284–288. Springer, Cham (2019). https://doi.org/10.1007/978-3-030-30493-5_29
7. Neftci, E.O., Mostafa, H., Zenke, F.: Surrogate gradient learning in spiking neural networks. arXiv preprint, 1901, 09948 (2019). https://arxiv.org/abs/1901.09948v2
8. Zimmer, R., Pellegrini, T., Singh, S.F., Masquelier, T.: Technical report: supervised training of convolutional spiking neural networks with PyTorch. arXiv preprint, 1911, 10124 (2019). https://arxiv.org/abs/1911.10124
9. Zarrin, P.S., et al.: Development of a 2-DOF sensorized surgical grasper for grasping and axial force measurements. IEEE Sens. J. **18**, 2816–2826 (2018). https://doi.org/10.1109/JSEN.2018.2805327
10. Zarrin, P.S., et al.: Design and fabrication of a BiCMOS dielectric sensor for viscosity measurements: a possible solution for early detection of COPD. Biosensors **8**, 78 (2018). https://doi.org/10.3390/bios8030078
11. Zarrin, P.S., Jamal, F.I., Roeckendorf, N., Wenger, C.: Development of a portable dielectric biosensor for rapid detection of viscosity variations and its in vitro evaluations using saliva samples of COPD patients and healthy control. Healthcare **7**, 11 (2019). https://doi.org/10.3390/healthcare7010011
12. Stewart, K., Neftci, E., Orchard, G.: On-chip few-shot learning with surrogate gradient descent on a neuromorphic processor. arXiv preprint, 1910, 04972 (2019). https://arxiv.org/abs/1910.04972

Anonymizing Personal Images Using Generative Adversarial Networks

Esteban Piacentino and Cecilio Angulo(✉)

IDEAI-UPC, Universitat Politècnica de Catalunya, Barcelona, Spain
cecilio.angulo@upc.edu

Abstract. This paper introduces a first approach on using Generative Adversarial Networks (GANs) for the generation of fake images, with the objective of anonymizing patients information in the health sector. This is intended to create valuable images that can be used both, in educational and research areas, while avoiding the risk of a sensitive data leakage. For this purpose, firstly a thorough research on GAN's state of the art and available databases has been developed. The outcome of the research is a GAN system prototype adapted to generate personal images that imitates provided samples. The performance of this prototype has been checked and satisfactory results have been obtained. Moreover, a novel research pathway has been opened so further research can be developed.

Keywords: GAN · Anonymization · Image generation

1 Introduction

The recent Generative Adversarial Networks (GANs) [4] algorithms have been highlighted as potential alternatives for data augmentation [7] and missing data problems [6], among others, due to their outstanding capabilities on generating realistic image instances.

In particular, the purpose of this paper is to assess the feasibility of using GAN systems to generate fake images, that imitates the attributes of a private dataset. If possible, this generated machine would be a very useful tool as it will enable unlimited similar-to-the-original images without compromising the privacy of the original elements, avoiding any potential leakage risk of sensitive information [1,3]. The applications of this tool could range from educational purposes to scientific simulations and researches, as sensitive data from any field could be available without a risk of private data leakage.

Hence, general objective of this research is developing a system based on GAN for the creation of believable new images from image datasets in the healthcare domain.

This research has been partially supported by the EDITH Research Project (PGC2018-102145-B-C22 (AEI/FEDER, UE)), funded by the Spanish Ministry of Science, Innovation and Universities – State Research Agency.

I. Rojas et al. (Eds.): IWBBIO 2020, LNBI 12108, pp. 395–405, 2020.
https://doi.org/10.1007/978-3-030-45385-5_35

This paper is organized as follows. In the next Section, an introduction to the Generative Adversarial Networks is provided. Moreover, some available databases to be employed in the research are displayed. Next, the proposed GAN-based system is developed. Then, the GAN system is trained for each of the datasets and results are analysed. Finally, conclusions and further steps of the investigation are provided.

2 Generative Adversarial Networks

In order to answer the question exposed, first of all it would be necessary to understand how a GAN works. Generative Adversarial Networks (GANs) are systems based on a min-max strategy where two algorithms are confronted: one algorithm generates data (the generator) and the other discriminates between fake and real data (the discriminator).

The generator's objective is to maximize the discriminator error while the discriminator wants to minimize it. This is an iterative process that ends when the discriminator fails to recognise generated fake data, approximating the baseline error. As described, in order to generate a fake image, we always need a source of "creativity" that in this case comes from a random noise vector (*seed*). On the other side, in order to be able to discriminate between real and fake images, so that the discriminator model can send to the generator model what is doing wrong, a database of real images is needed.

Hence, the objective function of the complete network is the following:

$$\min_G \max_D V(D,G) = E_{x \sim P_{data}(x)}[\log D(x)] + E_{z \sim P_z(z)}[\log(1 - D(G(z)))] \quad (1)$$

This expression represents value (V), which is a function of both, discriminator D and generator G. The goal is to maximize the discriminator (D) loss and minimize the generator (G) loss. Value V is the sum of expected log likelihood for real and generated data. Likelihoods (probabilities) are the discriminator outputs for real or generated images. Note that the discriminator output for a generated image is subtracted from 1 before taking the logarithmic value. Maximizing the resulting values leads to optimization of the discriminator parameters such that it learns to correctly identify both real and fake data.

It is also necessary to explain that:

- P_{data} represents the distribution of real data.
- P_z represents the distribution of noise, usually a Gaussian distribution, from which we can generate a fake image.
- x and z represent the samples from each corresponding space.
- E_x and E_z represent the expected log likelihood from the different outputs of both real and generated images.
- D function outputs a real number ranged between 0 and 1 representing the probability for data being real (1) or fake (0). On the other hand, G function outputs a generated sample or instance.

Besides, in order to train generator and discriminator, errors on their outputs are propagated back into the models. These errors are propagated as gradients of the following loss functions.

Update rule for the discriminator:

$$\nabla_{\theta_d} \frac{1}{m} \sum_{i=1}^{m} [\log D(x^{(i)}) + \log(1 - D(G(z^{(i)})))] \tag{2}$$

Update rule for the generator:

$$\nabla_{\theta_g} \frac{1}{m} \sum_{i=1}^{m} \log(1 - D(G(z^{(i)}))) \tag{3}$$

where m represents the total number of samples tested in batch before updating both models, and θ_d and θ_g represents the weights of each model. It is worth to note that on following sections we will be referring to these errors that we are calculating the gradient as *losses*.

As a GAN is just a system structure, the user will be able to choose their elements to compose the system (generator and discriminator) according to their preferences. In this case, it is going to be used the most popular option: using a convolutional neural network (CNN) for the discriminator and a transposed CNN for the generator. In order to keep this article focused on the GAN structure, CNNs will not be explained in detail.

3 Available Databases

In order to test the hypothesis of generating usable anonymized personal data, databases of personal data are selected. The main features used to choose the datasets have been the number of samples and the available information about the data.

The analysed databases can be organised in two different groups: *Image* directories and *Data* directories. As a first approach, GAN anonymization will be focused on image generation, which is the most common usage. The second type of databases on general raw data generation is left for further research. This way, it will be possible to focus entirely in the source of innovation of this research: how (image) data can be feed into a GAN system in order to yield good results on anonymization for personal data.

3.1 Fingerprints Database

This is a set of high-definition auto generated fingerprints from the Anguli generator used as ground truth samples for inpainting and denoising tools (see Fig. 1(Left)). In this case, it will be used as an example of private information that can be reproduced through a GAN. Database source is ChaLearn (Anguli: Synthetic Fingerprint Generator[1]) and the number of available samples is 75,600.

[1] http://chalearnlap.cvc.uab.es/dataset/32/description/.

3.2 Iris Database

This is a database with 2,224 instances of left-and-right iris images collected from the students and staff at IIT Delhi, India[2] (see Fig. 1(Right)). This database is available in the public domain as a tool given the recent popularity of iris based personal identification systems. In this case, just like the fingerprint database, it will be used as an example of private information that can be reproduced through a GAN as well. Unlike fingerprints, these images contain more information and complexity.

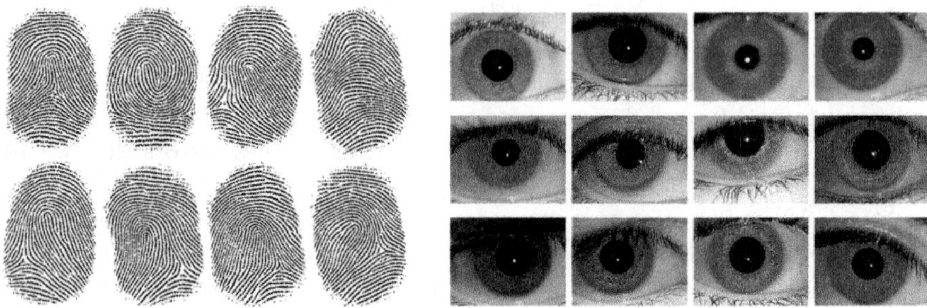

Fig. 1. (Left) Data samples from the Fingerprint Database. Source: http://dsl.cds.iisc.ac.in/projects/Anguli/. (Right) Data samples from the Iris Database. Source: https://www4.comp.polyu.edu.hk/~csajaykr/IITD/.

4 GAN-based Anonymization System

In this section, the setup for the implementation of a GAN in a specific environment will be explained. The execution environment chosen to carry out this project has been Google Colab, using Python 3.6 and Pytorch for coding. Google Colab offers free cloud processing capacity with dedicated GPU graphics cards for training and inference tasks. As far as we are not concerned on the GAN study, but its application for anonymization, the default code and structure for the starting GAN script has been obtained from a third party [5]. The modules in the code include:

- *Dataset Class.* After importing the required libraries, an extension of the `Dataset` class from Pytorch is implemented in order to define how database is indexed, how many samples there are and how to read each instance.
- *Database Loading.* The dataset is instanced and fed into the `DataLoader` class with a specific batch to train the discriminator and the generator. Besides that, it converts the image to a *tensor* object and normalise its values.

[2] https://www4.comp.polyu.edu.hk/~csajaykr/IITD/Database_Iris.htm.

- *Discriminator and Generator Models.* The discriminator and generator models are configured and instanced. The number of layers, its size and the type of network will depend on the test. In all tests, however, the discriminator model always starts with an image-sized input and a single value output ranging between 0 and 1, which is the one that specifies if the image fed is real or fake. The generator starts with a noise vector, the seed for the generated image, of n dimensions, chosen by the user. It outputs a fake image of the same size as the original one. In order to constraint the output of the discriminator between 0 and 1 the sigmoid activation function is used. Similarly, the hyperbolic tangent activation function is used in the generator model to range all pixel values between -1 and 1, just as the original images do.
- *Noise Generator Function.* The function for generating noise vectors is defined. This random vector is used as a seed for creating a new generated image. Each random number of the seed is normal distributed with mean 0 and variance 1 and the dimension of each seed vector is defined by the user.
- *Model Optimizer.* Optimizers are defined for both, the generator and the discriminator. These optimizer models are the ones responsible of updating the net weights in order to improve the output results of both generator and discriminator through the error gradient.
- *Training Loop.* Here, the previously listed elements are used altogether to form the GAN iterative system. In this case, the training loop is set to 100 epochs. In each of them, all the real images will be feed in random batches to the discriminator and train both generator and discriminator models.
- *Saving Step Results.* Both models and their respective current losses are saved in a specified rate (every 5 epochs by default). This way the evolution of the losses can be then studied over time and a back-up copy of their models can be accessed.
- *Generating Final Results.* A 3-by-3 grid is rendered with final generated results.

5 Testing the GAN-Based Anomymization Systems

Now that the GAN system and its implementation in the working environment have been presented along with the image databases that will be used, it is time to demonstrate how powerful using Generative Adversarial Networks is for anonymizing image-like private health data.

For both experiments below, the only changes that have been made to the default code are the following:

- Mounting a Google Drive directory in the work environment to host training images on the cloud.
- An extension of the `Dataset` class to enable the correct reading of the specific datasets enabling the possibility of working directly from a .zip file of all the images.
- Add-ons for visualizing and saving results live during the optimization process in order to see the evolution of discriminator and generator losses and reuse the models for further image generation.

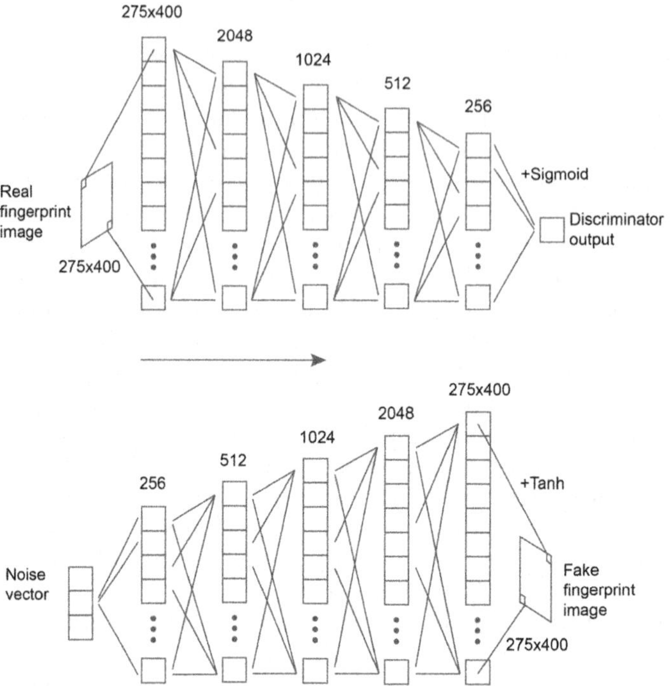

Fig. 2. Schematic representation of the FCN models used for the Fingerprint test for both discriminator (top) and generator (bottom).

- Specific generator and discriminator models for each database: both Fully Connected Network (FCN) and Convolutional Neural Network (CNN) models.

5.1 Fingerprints Dataset

Initially, sample images have been transformed to a grey-scale format where pixel values are transformed from [0:255,0:255,0:255] (RGB breakout) to [−1:1].

In this first test, the chosen model for the discriminator has been a FCN model with linear transfer functions. The fingerprint images, with original size 275×400 are mapped to an output ranging from 0 to 1 by using a final sigmoid layer. For the generator, from a 100-dimension noise vector a 275×400 image is obtained through an FCN model. The batch size is 52, as in the original code of the GAN system. Both models are depicted in Fig. 2.

The first findings of this test showed that trained FCN models are heavier than expected given the high number of links needed to connect all pixels from one layer to another ($\sim$ 1–2 GB). This was an important limitation, as layer's dimensions were highly limited to avoid excessive training times and because of hardware limitations. That's why, as seen in Fig. 2, the first dimension reduction for the discriminator goes from 275×400 to 2048.

After a 100 epoch training process, first iterations of the problem showed that losses tend to stagnate after some epochs. This is a concurrent problem with GAN systems [2], and it will be found again in the next tests. For the moment, however, our main goal is to get used to the system and get a reasonably good first fake generated image, so this problem won't be further inquired.

Regarding the output results seen in Fig. 3, it can be perceived how in the first epoch there is already a defined contour of the fingerprint, where the outside of it is purely black, as in the original figures, but the inside is just noise without any kind of grooves. On following epochs, these grooves start to be defined but fingerprints are still very bright as there is not a clear separation between finger lines. Finally, between 60 and 100 epochs, results have improved significantly: fingerprints are darker, because of more defined grooves, and some finger patters can be identified. However, results are still blurry and finger lines are not as defined as the real samples. These problems could be caused by the nature of FCN models: as fully connected layers are based on the aggregation of linear regressions, results tend to resemble more to an average of all real samples rather than a brand new generated sample.

In the next section, similar experiments will be carried out for the Iris dataset. In order to mitigate this problem, CNN models will be used as well as the already known FCN ones. CNN models are non-linear and, because of its methods to extract features (in the case of discriminator) and create patterns (in the case of the generator) they tend to give better results. Plus, as it's not a fully connected architecture, models are significantly lighter ($\sim$ 30 MB).

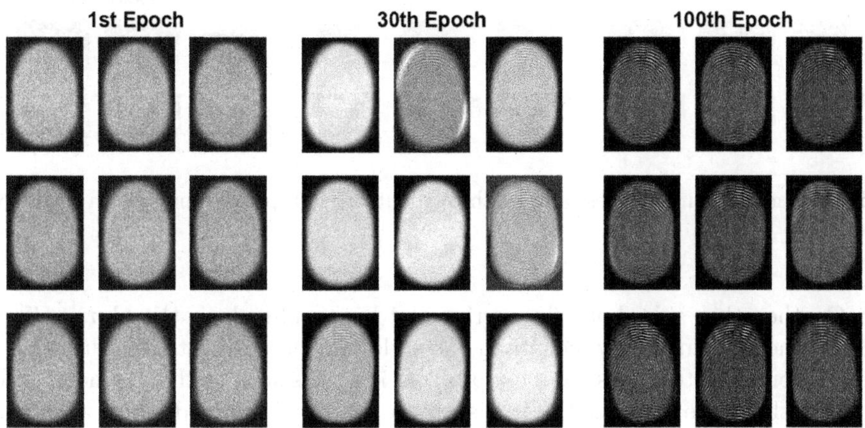

Fig. 3. Generated fingerprint images samples throughout the 100 epoch training. 30 epoch has been chosen as a middle point due to loss stagnation around the 60th epoch.

5.2 Iris Dataset

For the case of Iris dataset, the procedure has been the same as in the previous Fingerprints dataset: Images have been transformed and fed into the model aiming to observe the output performance of fake images. This time, however, tests have been carried out for both, FCN and CNN models, to compare results between them.

FCN Model. For the linear model, the main change from the fingerprint one has been the batch size, which has been reduced from 52 to 20 as the total database is significantly smaller (from 75,600 to 2,224). Besides from that, as the image size of the samples has changed as well (from 275×400 to 320×240), FCN model has slightly changed from last test to fit input and output images. The structure, however, remains the same from Fig. 2.

Comparing losses between Fingerprint and Iris test, it is checked that in this case the model doesn't stagnate so much.

Regarding the visual results, after 100 epochs, fake samples have some interesting attributes (see Fig. 4): Images seem to be more unique between them than fingerprint results; each eye has a slightly different orientation, eyelids are sometimes closer than others and the light source changes position between samples.

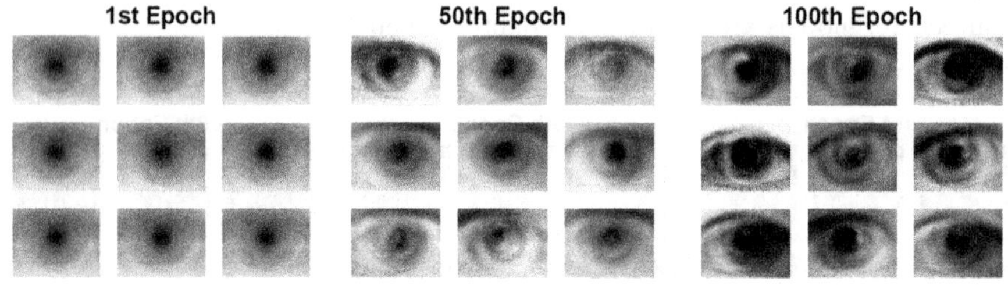

Fig. 4. Generated iris images samples throughout the 100 epoch training with the FCN model.

On the other side, both fingerprint and iris results share the blurry effect due to the FCN model, which gives the style of a brush painted picture. As a medical oriented test, this can be a problem if details such as the iris membrane or pupil shape are important. That is why, a "pattern" oriented model as CNNs could be more suitable for this kind of task.

CNN Model. A CNN model for the Iris dataset was created. The structure of it, both for the discriminator and the generator is displayed in Fig. 5. Due to the non-square nature of the Iris database, CNN layers should be set up meticulously to smoothly shift from a square image (noise vector) to a rectangular one (generated image) or vice versa. CNN models are lighter than FCN, which makes the training process significantly faster. Because of that, the model has been trained for 200 epochs instead of 100. Visually, nice results seemed to take longer to rise than FCN models.

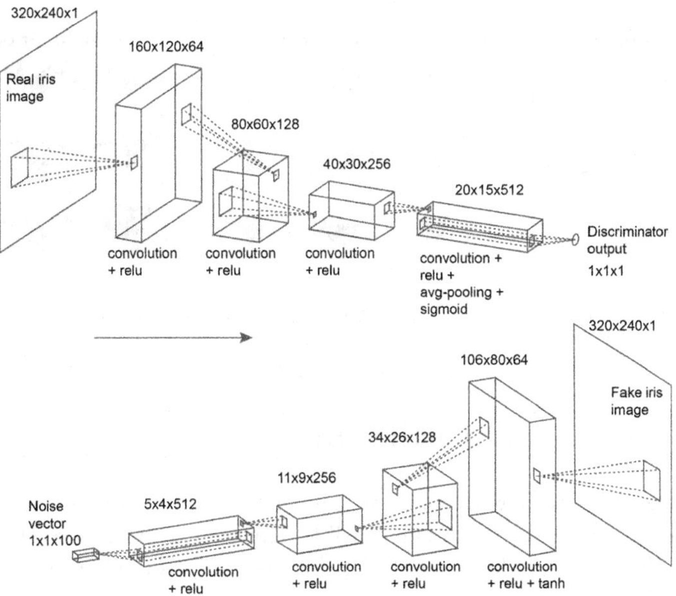

Fig. 5. Schematic representation of the CNN models used for the Iris test for both discriminator (top) and generator (bottom). Sigmoid and hyperbolic tangent functions have the same functionality as in FCN models. Regarding ReLU's, they are used to increase the non-linearity on generated images, which makes them more natural. Lastly, the avg-pooling function has been used to average the last output matrix into a single value ($1 \times 1 \times 1$).

Regarding losses, it is shown here one of the popular problems about GAN systems [2], the discriminator getting too successful so that the generator gradient vanishes and stop learning.

However, throughout the training process eyes kept turning more realistic (see Fig. 6). One of the key improvements over the 200 epochs has been the renderization of a single pupil in an image: as seen on the 100th epoch samples, the pupil was still split in two or even nonexistent in some of the generated images. On the final results, it is important to observe that fake images are remarkably more detailed than the ones from Fig. 4. However, the overall shape of the eye seems less natural than on the previous iteration, which leads us to the main problems of the CNN model: as a patterned model, all samples are less unique between them. One example of this can be found on the eyelashes of the final fake images, which are mostly all made of the exact same pattern. Just like the blurriness of the FCN samples, having the same patterns for the iris membrane or the pupil shape is neither good. Actually, another of GAN's problems is the *mode collapse* [2], where the generator collapses producing a very narrow variety of samples, which could be an important problem for health environments.

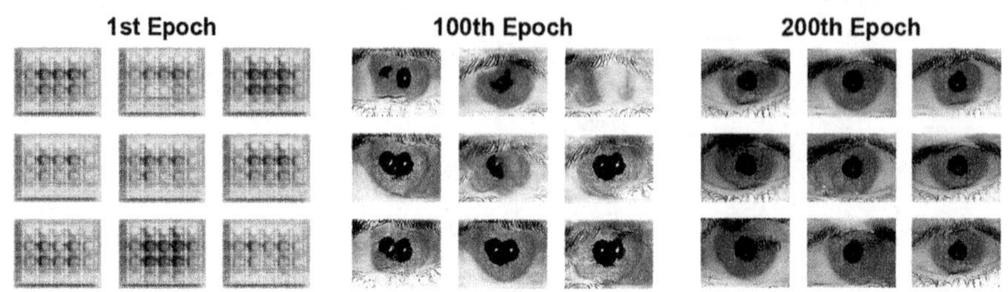

Fig. 6. Generated iris images samples throughout the 200 epoch training with the CNN model.

6 Conclusions and Further Research

On the whole, results show that image-like personal data anonymization through Generative Adversarial Networks is feasible. However, further investigations will determine the accuracy levels that the data output can get and whether it is useful for health issues or not.

On the objectives side, it has been surprising to observe the ease of conversion from images to data for the GAN system and the results obtained in a small amount of time, both for fully connected and convolutional models.

Regarding the elements from the investigation that can be improved or studied further, it is important to highlight the following ones:

- On a general level, a recurrent problem that has been encountered is the non-convergence of results, eventough they are bounded in admissible ranges. Although all tests had a first valid output, losses graphs seemed not to be converging to stable values. This could be caused by a short number of training epochs or a bad system configuration. In any case, new iterations of the training process with longer computing periods and more powerful machines would be necessary.
- A more mature system version would be appreciated. This means fine-tuning the configuration and standardizing its code to yield more solid and reliable results. This also entails further investigation on the creation of GANs.
- Finally, these methodologies could also be tested when working with other image formats like tissue slides or tumoral moles.

References

1. Bae, H., Jung, D., Yoon, S.: AnomiGAN: generative adversarial networks for anonymizing private medical data. arXiv (2019). https://arxiv.org/abs/1901.11313
2. Barnett, S.A.: Convergence problems with generative adversarial networks (GANs) (2018). https://arxiv.org/abs/1806.11382
3. Feutry, C., Piantanida, P., Bengio, Y., Duhamel, P.: Learning anonymized representations with adversarial neural networks. arXiv (2018). https://arxiv.org/abs/1802.09386
4. Goodfellow, I., et al.: Generative adversarial nets. In: Ghahramani, Z., Welling, M., Cortes, C., Lawrence, N.D., Weinberger, K.Q. (eds.) Advances in Neural Information Processing Systems, vol. 27, pp. 2672–2680. Curran Associates, Inc., New york (2014). http://papers.nips.cc/paper/5423-generative-adversarial-nets.pdf
5. Lakhey, M.: Generative adversarial networks demystified. Medium, Data Driven Investor (2019). https://medium.com/datadriveninvestor/gans-demystified-f057f5e32fc9
6. Li, S.C.X., Jiang, B., Marlin, B.: MisGan: learning from incomplete data with generative adversarial networks. arXiv https://arxiv.org/abs/1902.09599 (2019)
7. Wang, P., Shao, S., Yan, R.: Generative adversarial networks for data augmentation in machine fault diagnosis. Comput. Ind. **106**, 85–93 (2019). https://doi.org/10.1016/j.compind.2019.01.001

Generating Fake Data Using GANs for Anonymizing Healthcare Data

Esteban Piacentino and Cecilio Angulo(✉)

IDEAI-UPC, Universitat Politècnica de Catalunya, Barcelona, Spain
cecilio.angulo@upc.edu

Abstract. EDITH is a project aiming to orchestrate an ecosystem of manipulation of reliable and safe data, applied to the field of health, proposing the creation of digital twins for personalised healthcare. This paper elaborates on a first approach about using Generative Adversarial Networks (GANs) for the generation of fake data, with the objective of anonymizing users information in the health sector. This is intended to create valuable data that can be used both, in educational and research areas, while avoiding the risk of a sensitive data leakage. Meanwhile GANs are mainly exploited on images and video frames, we are proposing to process raw data in the form of an image, so it can be managed through a GAN, then decoded back to the original data domain. The performance of this prototype has been demonstrated. Moreover, a novel research pathway has been opened so further developments are expected.

Keywords: GAN · Anonymization · Healthcare data · Data transformation

1 Introduction

In recent years there has been a huge proliferation of solutions that store and process personal health data and infer knowledge, from mobile health apps to smart wearable sensors [9]. In [1] a proposal is introduced to orchestrate an ecosystem of manipulation of reliable and safe data, applied to the field of health, proposing the creation of digital twins for personalised healthcare [3].

One of the elements to be considered in health-related projects is *Data privacy for ethical issues.* Sources of medical data in health services are causing important concerns, the main one being privacy and legal issues when sharing and reporting health information of patients. However, an accurate diagnosis depends on the quantity and quality of the information about a patient, as well as extensive medical knowledge. In this context, anonymization arises as a tool to mitigate the risks of obtaining and massively processing personal data [4]. We

This research has been partially supported by the EDITH Research Project (PGC2018-102145-B-C22 (AEI/FEDER, UE)), funded by the Spanish Ministry of Science, Innovation and Universities.

I. Rojas et al. (Eds.): IWBBIO 2020, LNBI 12108, pp. 406–417, 2020.
https://doi.org/10.1007/978-3-030-45385-5_36

propose an initial GAN-based anonymization [5] phase, so a seedbed would be obtained from the training data that allow not only to capture information from the original data, but to generate new information with a similar behaviour to the original one.

Generative Adversarial Network (GAN) algorithms have arisen in 2014 [6] and, since then, have been highlighted as potential alternatives for data augmentation [11] and missing data problems [8], among others, due to their outstanding capabilities on generating realistic data instances, mostly images. In particular, a question raised in the EDITH project is about the feasibility of using GAN systems to generate fake data, not necessarily images, that imitates the attributes of a private data-set. If possible, this generated machine would be a very useful tool as it is enabling unlimited similar-to-the-original data without compromising the privacy of the original elements. The applications of this tool could range from educational purposes to scientific simulations and investigations, as sensitive data from any field could be available without a risk of private data leakage.

This article is the very first approach on using GANs for the generation of fake data in the health domain avoiding as far as possible images as original samples, but usual raw data. We are extending our previous work in [10], where it was demonstrated how GANs can be used for an anonymization process on personal biometric image data (fingerprints and iris). Hence, we intend to open new lines of investigation and do not aim to produce a final solution based on accuracy metrics and similar, but rather get first evidences of what this enabling technology can obtain on raw data.

Specific objectives for this proposal include the study of (i) pre-processing datasets for its correct manipulation; (ii) training several GAN systems for each of the datasets, and (iii) analyze the obtained results and define further steps in the research.

This paper is organized as follows. In the next section, the problem setup is settled from the point of view of the overall project, the GAN structures to be analysed, and the databases to be considered for the study. Next, the experimental part is developed on both, static and dynamic data, and the obtained results are analyzed. Finally, some conclusions and further research are displayed.

2 Problem Definition

The problem setup is defined from the point of view of the overall project, the GAN structures (two) to be analysed, and the databases (two) to be considered for the study.

The general environment where our anomymization system is working corresponds to the one defined in the EDITH project, an ecosystem of manipulation of reliable and safe data, applied to the field of health, proposing the creation of digital twins for personalised healthcare [1]. Hence, one of the main objectives is the use of Generative Adversarial Networks on sensitive health data information allowing both, anonymizing data in the form of a 'fake' dataset and generating fake patients that health professionals can use for study.

The execution environment to work with GANs is Google Colab, using Python 3.6 and Pytorch for coding. Google Colab offers free cloud processing capacity with dedicated GPU graphics cards for training and inference tasks. As far as we are not concerned on the GAN study, but its application for anonymization, the default code and structure for the starting GAN script is obtained from a third party [7]. Further information about the implemented modules can be found in [1].

For experimentation, specific generator and discriminator models for each database, both Fully Connected Network (FCN) with linear transfer function and Convolutional Neural Network (CNN), were implemented.

In order to test the hypothesis of generating usable anonymized personal data, databases of personal data are selected. The main features used to choose the datasets have been the number of samples and the available information about the data.

The analysed databases can be organised in two different groups: *Image* directories and *Data* directories. As a first approach, GAN anonymization was primarily focused in [1] on image generation, which is the most common usage. The second type of databases on general raw data generation is the one to be considered in this research.

Thyroid Database. The thyroid database contains user features that are relevant for thyroid illnesses detection. All its variables are static, meaning that for each patient there's only one value per feature without contemplate its evolution. This 7,200 instances database from KEEL[1] has been released to identify if a given patient suffers from hyperthyroidism, hypothyroidism, or not. The data contains both continuous and binary features, and they are all being imitated trough a GAN for a specific type of thyroid illnesses, hypothyroidism in this case. These features are:

- *Continuous* (6): Age, TSH, T3, TT4, T4U, FTI.
- *Binary* (15): Sex, On thyroxine, Query on thyroxine, On antithyroid medication, Sick, Pregnant, Thyroid surgery, I131 treatment, Query hypothyroid, Query hyperthyroid, Lithium, Goitre, Tumor, Hypopituitary, Psych.
- *Class (label)* (3): normal values (1), hyperthyroidism (2), hypothyroidism (3).

Cardiogram Database. In contrast with the previous dataset, the cardiogram database shows the evolution of its variables throughout time. The National Metrology Institute of Germany has provided this compilation of digitized ECGs for research, algorithmic benchmarking or teaching purposes to the users of PhysioNet[2]. The ECGs were collected from healthy volunteers and patients with different heart diseases by Professor Michael Oeff, M.D., at the Department of Cardiology of University Clinic Benjamin Franklin in Berlin, Germany.

[1] https://sci2s.ugr.es/keel/dataset.php?cod=67.

[2] https://physionet.org/physiobank/database/ptbdb/.

Each record includes 15 simultaneously measured signals: the conventional 12 leads placements (i, ii, iii, avr, avl, avf, v1, v2, v3, v4, v5, v6) together with the 3 Frank lead ECGs (vx, vy, vz). Each signal is digitized at 1000 samples per second, with 16 bit resolution over a range of ± 16.384 mV. Available samples are 549, expandable by splitting each sample into multiple segments.

The main objective of the usage of this database is to simulate one of the ECG leads (i) for a specific range of time feeding the GAN previously with all the samples available from this dataset.

3 Fake Static Data Generation

Experimentation in the generation of fake data using GANs in this research moves its starting focus from images domain to raw data generation. This movement is not trivial, however. Data, unlike images, can have many different dimensions and contain values within many different ranges. Images, on the other side, are mainly represented in a range value of 0 to 255 for every pixel and with just 2 or 3 dimensions depending if it is RGB or not.

Hence, in order to use the same tools as for image samples, changes are needed to uniform data and represent them in a *visual* way to the GAN system. This issue is divided in two tasks:

- **Data standardization**: Bringing all features of the data-set to the same range value, which are from 0 to 255, and trimming all samples to same same amount of features if needed.
- **Data arrangement**: Deciding the layout of the data, meaning how features are placed, in a square shaped space.

A domestic parallelism of this problem could be how humans visualize data in order to understand it themselves better and quicker. Feeding the original data to the GAN system in the correct way could be as important as representing an electrocardiogram data to a doctor in a proper –and visual– way.

The following sections are divided in two: static and dynamic data. This separation is necessary to differentiate the type of data it is being simulated. On the first section, static data, each feature is an independent variable that it is supposed, within the scope of the project, to be constant over time. Opposed to that, the dynamic data section contains features that are different values over time of the same variable. In other words, on dynamic data each row is the sequence of values from a time-series sample. While on static data each row is a list of independent attributes that describes the sample itself.

The first dataset to be imitated is Thyroids, from KEEL's repository. This database contains both continuous and binary features from patients thyroid-related health status. The main objective of using a GAN on this repository is to generate new anonymous users with the same conditions as the original patients. In order to do so, a method to translate the data into an image format should be designed.

3.1 Data Standardization

All units are standardized to a common range to unify the weight of each variable range. This action is also called feature scaling or normalization. The distribution of all continuous variables has been studied to check its extreme values and evaluate anomalous ones (*outliers*) to be removed to avoid losing resolution.

The GAN system is trained only with hypothyroidism patients in order to simulate just one type of diagnostic. It was selected because the number of samples in the data-set (6,666) in contrast with hyperthyroidism (368) and normal condition (166). After removing outliers, the total remaining samples are 6,330.

The normalization formula to be applied is

$$\frac{x - \min(x)}{\max(x) - \min(x)} \cdot (255 - 1) + 1 \qquad (1)$$

This equation outputs every feature between 1 and 255, which is the usual range for image files. The number 0 is excluded from the range so that can be used exclusively as a NULL value.

3.2 Data Arrangement

Now we can proceed to the arrangement of normalized data in an image format. Taking into account the two types of features –binary and continuous– and their number –6 and 15 respectively– many arrangements can be done in a 7×7 grid. In Fig. 1(left) are displayed some of them. The reason why the arrangement of all features should be done in a square area is to avoid complications in the system configuration if models such as CNN are used.

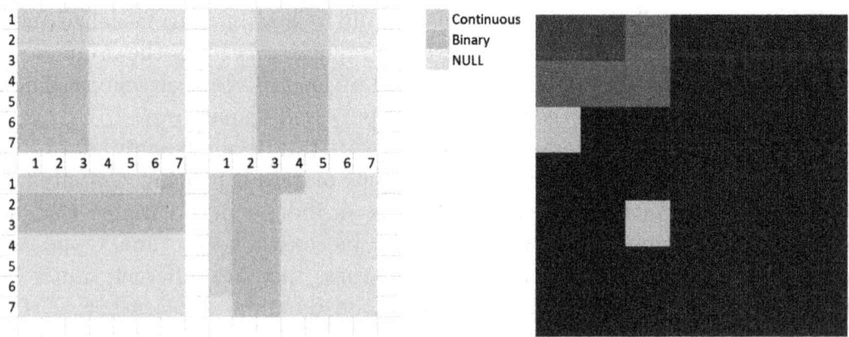

Fig. 1. (Left) Possible Thyroid's features arrangements. (Right) Sample from the Thyroid's data-set converted into an image.

The selected arrangement is the first one (left, top scheme). In Fig. 1(right), there is an example of real thyroid sample turned into image. It is important to note that for the NULL area, all values are set to 0, this way it is easier for the neural network to distinguish between feature areas and NULL areas.

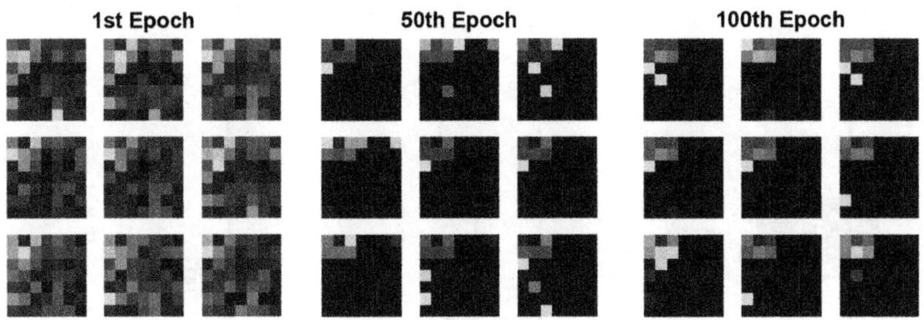

Fig. 2. Thyroid's fake images evolution throughout 100 epochs on a FCN model.

3.3 Model, Training and Results

For this case, as a first test, the Thyroid images are feed into a Fully Connected Network with linear activation functions. It is trained for 100 epochs. Batch sizes are of 20 images. Regarding FCN layers, just one hidden layer of size 64 between the input and the output is considered for both the discriminator and the generator. The size of the noise vector for the generator is five.

After training, the generator overtook the discriminator from the beginning. There seems to be a diminished gradient [2] on the discriminator side that is causing it an inability to improve because the generator is too strong.

On the output results side, it can be seen a great improvement between epochs on Fig. 2. It is perceived how between epoch 1 and 50, the values on the binary zone (bottom left) start to get contrasted values –around 1 or around 255– and on the continuous values there is still a variety of values, which is correct. However, on epoch 50 there are yet values on the NULL side (right side). Finally, on epoch 100 this problem is solved, all values of the NaN side being 0.

Next, in order to understand whether fake generated data is following the same distributions as the original, 6330 data samples are generated and compared to the original ones. After generating these samples and converting the image files into numeric data, all continuous features data –both original one and generated– have been visualized through box-plots in Fig. 3.

3.4 Discussion

In all cases, the generated samples are positioned inside the ranges of the ground truth values for all continuous features. However, the dispersion of the values is different. Medians does not match neither Q1 and Q3 percentiles or min and max values. The feature that could be more in-line with ground truth samples is T3.

This difference in the distribution of the features might be explaining that a simple GAN with FCN linear models is not enough to replicate this kind of data-set. This rises the possibility of future lines of investigation related with this project around the study of new indicators to be used as loss values for

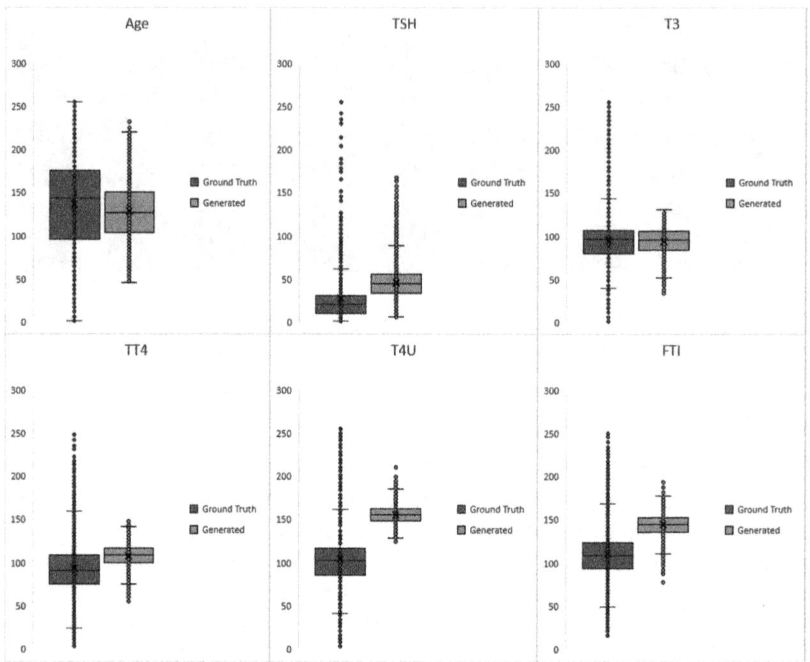

Fig. 3. Thyroid's continuous data features box-plots: comparison between fake generated data and original data.

the discriminator and generator. One example could be comparing standard deviations between ground truth batch samples and generated samples for each of the continuous features.

On the side of binary variables, it has been observed that, for the same amount of samples of fake and real data, the total amount of positive and negative values in all features is similar between both groups.

In conclusion, results are satisfactory like a very first state of the investigation. Hence, the data-set is not to be tested on more complicated CNN models, as it is thought that for the goals of the project dynamic data is much more interesting.

4 Fake Dynamic Data Generation

The second data-set to be imitated is the Cardiogram database from Physionet. As explained in Sect. 2, this database contains records of 15 different signals from patient's electrical impulses from the heart for a certain amount of time. The main objective using a GAN on this repository is to generate new anonymous cardiograms samples that look similar to the original ones. Specifically, in this case it is simulated a single signal from the 15 available, lead "i". Same as on static data, a method to translate the data into an image format should be designed. This way it would be possible to pass all patients information to the GAN system and then receive the generated patient samples accordingly.

4.1 Data Standardization

The Cardiogram data-set, as an example of dynamic data, has a single variable –the "i" lead chosen– but as many features as sequential temporal values are available for each patient. Similar to the static data section, for this cardiogram signal it is necessary to know which are the minimum and maximum values it can get in order to standardize the features values into the [0,255] range[3].

Due to the size of the database (1GB, ~59,000,000 values), it has been analyzed using Python and Pandas' library. Just as for the static data section, a min-max normalization is used. Now, however, as the output range should be from 0 to 255, the formula used is

$$\frac{x - \min(x)}{\max(x) - \min(x)} \cdot 255 \tag{2}$$

Unlike the static data, however, the Cardiogram data-set has another issue that needs to be tackled: the number of features is not the same for all samples –as not all patients recordings have the same length.

A solution is trimming each user sample into equal-sized features pieces. This way the number of samples is greater and they have all the same amount of features. The choice of what size –and therefore number of features– should have each sample needs to be balanced between enough duration length and a good amount of total samples. In this case it has been decided to trim each patient recording into blocks of 2025 features –removing the tail if needed–. In this form, the number of samples goes from 549 to 28,902 while maintaining around 2 seconds of recording in each sample, which represent between 2 and 3 heart beats most of the times. The reason of choosing 2025 features is related with the preferred squared images (45×45) when dealing with some models such as CNNs.

4.2 Data Arrangement

This time there is not a second type of features such as the binary group on the static data, hence all the square area available for the data to image transformation can be filled up with features. The only factor to be determined is the path that follow consecutive features in the image. Many options are possible. For this test is has been decided to follow a "Z" movement from left to right. In Fig. 4 there is an example of a ground truth cardio sample turned into image with the chosen arrangement.

[3] For this case it is not necessary to isolate the 0 value to use it as a NULL element.

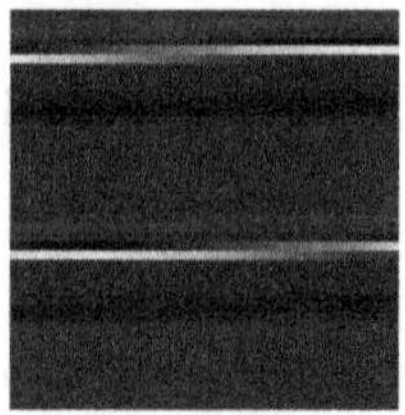

Fig. 4. Original sample from the Cardio's data-set processed into an image.

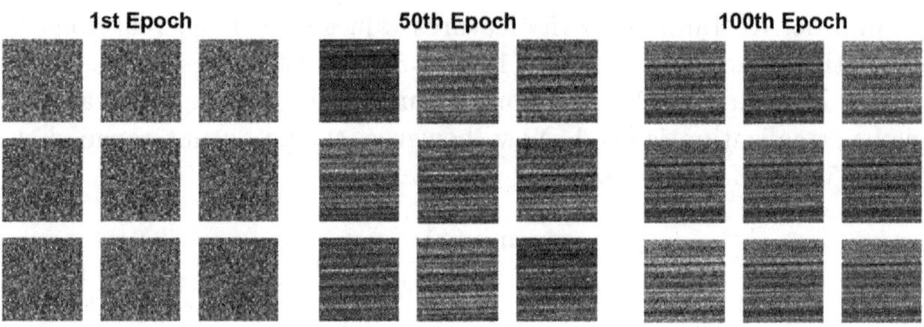

Fig. 5. Generated Cardio images samples throughout the 100 epoch training with FCN models as discriminator and generator.

4.3 Model, Training and Results

Same as for the static data, the Cardio data-set is first feed into a FCN linear model training it for 100 epochs. Compared to the 6,330 samples available for the Thyroids database, now for the Cardio database there are available 28,902 samples. Hence, both the batch size and the hidden layers of the model are larger than in the previous configuration: the batch size is 52 and there are 3 hidden layers of size 1024, 512 and 256 respectively for both the discriminator and the generator. The noise vector is sized 100.

After training, the losses for both the discriminator and the generator seemed to be more unstable than previous cases: values were similar at some epochs between models and both had positive trends along the first 100 epochs. Moreover, the system is not able to reproduce a cardiogram signal. As seen in Fig. 5, around the 50th epoch and beyond, all generated images were very similar and far away from the original samples. Fake outputs did not have coherent values between contiguous features and there were not identifiable pulse signals, just very noisy waves.

In this situation, a more complex pattern based model –such as CNN– could work better. At the end, for this experiment there is a need of a very defined chain of values with different patterns for both the heart beat and the steady state of the electric signal and not a sequence of diffused mean values throughout the recording.

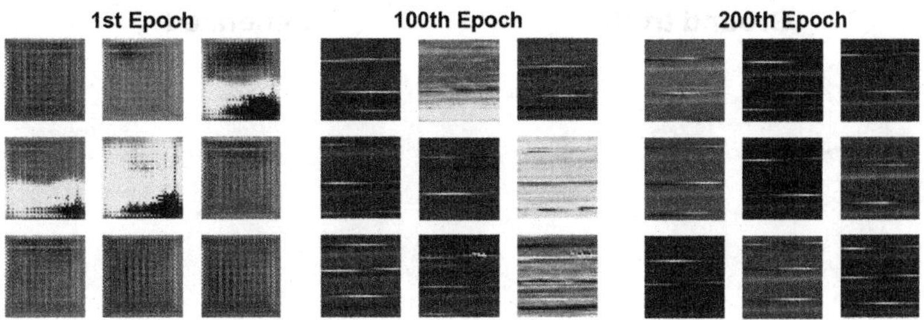

Fig. 6. Generated Cardio images samples throughout the 200 epoch training with CNN models as discriminator and generator.

Hence, a CNN model have been configured for the Cardio database: the GAN is trained for 200 epochs with a batch size of 30. Regarding the CNN configuration, as images have a squared aspect ratio, the settings are easy. For the structure of the CNN, there are 3 hidden layers of 64, 128 and 256 dimensions respectively. The noise vector remains of size 100.

On the losses side, there is again a problem of *vanished gradient* [2] as the discriminator gets too successful very quickly.

However, this time, to avoid a major saturation of the model, a threshold value is set up to avoid training discriminator more time when its loss is already very low. Gradients are propagated to the discriminator in order to train the model only when its loss is above a specific value. The threshold value has been set up to 0.01.

Now, after a few epochs the output images started to contain some patterns similar to the ones on ground truth samples. As shown in Fig. 6, after the 100th epoch, some of the samples were already resembling to the original ones, however there were still some strange patters such as indefinite heart beats (mid bottom sample) or very high pitched images (mid and bottom right samples). On the 200th epoch, however, these problems were gone.

4.4 Discussion

Given that now results are not static data, instead of analyzing the distribution of the studied variable, the output data is visually compared to the original one –just how a doctor would do for this kind of information–. This way, it is possible to see if signal samples seem to have the same patters, sizes and frequencies as the original ones. A random sub-group of real and fake cardiogram data can be observed in Fig. 7. These results are very interesting on a first sight as both could seem real from a non-professional perspective.

In a detailed comparison, there are some differences and similarities between both groups. Before mention them however, it is important to highlight that these evaluations are purely based on the visual differences between fake and real data. We are not aware if the fake data patters that seem unreal because they are

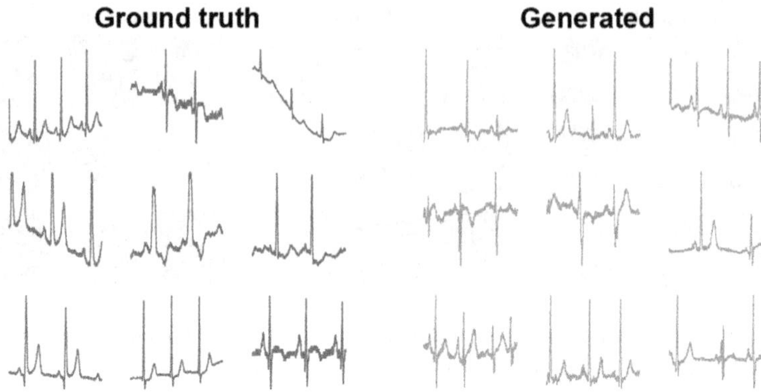

Fig. 7. Ground truth Cardio signals vs generated samples after 200 epoch training on a GAN system with CNN models as discriminator and generator.

not presented in the real data sample, could indeed resemble real conditions on human cardiograms. In order to make a better study of the results the consultant of a doctor would be required.

That being said, if we compare both groups, we can see that the generated cardiograms have quite equidistant heart pulses just as the real data does. Furthermore, overall patterns are very similar. Another similarity is that on all ground truth signals, the base slope is constant during all the time range. Same trend is observed on generated images.

Regarding differences, there are mainly two elements. There is a clear difference on spike lengths. Ground truth heart pulses have consistently the same length, however this consistency is not solid on the generated side. Sometimes spikes are smaller or taller than before. On the other side, the spike pattern within the same patient seems to be always the same but on the generated group patters have slightly variations throughout the sample.

5 Conclusions and Further Research

This paper elaborates on a first approach about using Generative Adversarial Networks (GANs) for the generation of fake data, with the objective of anonymizing users information in the health sector. As a first result, a general procedure is provided to convert original usual raw data into images, which are more fitted to work with GANs. Data under consideration include static data (binary and continuous features) and time-series data. As a second result, simple linear fully connected networks can deal with static data in order to obtain data with similar behavior. Finally, dynamic data needs of more complicated structures into the GAN architecture, but results are demonstrating that convolutional neural networks could deal with this kind of problems.

This study being an exploratory research, a lot of improvement is still possible: networks models into the GAN architecture, losses definition according to the databases, data organization in the form of an image, training times for discriminator and generator.

References

1. Angulo, C., Ortega, J.A., Gonzalez-Abril, L.: Towards a healthcare digital twin. In: Sabater-Mir, J., Torra, V., Aguiló, I., González-Hidalgo, M. (eds.) Frontiers in Artificial Intelligence and Applications, vol. 319, pp. 312–315. IOS Press, Oxford (2019)
2. Barnett, S.A.: Convergence problems with generative adversarial networks (GANs) (2018). https://arxiv.org/abs/1806.11382
3. Bruynseels, K., Santoni de Sio, F., van den Hoven, J.: Digital twins in health care: ethical implications of an emerging engineering paradigm. Front. Genet. **9**, 31 (2018). https://doi.org/10.3389/fgene.2018.00031. https://www.frontiersin.org/article/10.3389/fgene.2018.00031
4. El Emam, K., Arbuckle, L.: Anonymizing Health Data: Case Studies and Methods to Get You Started, 1st edn. O'Reilly Media, Inc., Newton (2013)
5. Feutry, C., Pablo Piantanida, Y.B., Duhamel, P.: Learning anonymized representations with adversarial neural networks. arXiv (2018). https://arxiv.org/abs/1802.09386
6. Goodfellow, I., et al.: Generative adversarial nets. In: Ghahramani, Z., Welling, M., Cortes, C., Lawrence, N.D., Weinberger, K.Q. (eds.) Advances in Neural Information Processing Systems, vol. 27, pp. 2672–2680. Curran Associates, Inc., New York (2014). http://papers.nips.cc/paper/5423-generative-adversarial-nets.pdf
7. Lakhey, M.: Generative adversarial networks demystified. Medium, Data Driven Investor (2019). https://medium.com/datadriveninvestor/gans-demystified-f057f5e32fc9
8. Li, S.C.X., Jiang, B., Marlin, B.: MisGan: learning from incomplete data with generative adversarial networks. arXiv (2019). https://arxiv.org/abs/1902.09599
9. Morillo, L.M.S., Gonzalez-Abril, L., Ramirez, J.A.O., De la Concepcion, M.A.A.: Low energy physical activity recognition system on smartphones. Sensors **15**(3), 5163–5196 (2015). https://doi.org/10.3390/s150305163. https://www.mdpi.com/1424-8220/15/3/5163
10. Piacentino, E., Angulo, C.: Anonymizing personal images using generative adversarial networks. In: Rojas, I., Guzman, F.M.O. (eds.) International Work-Conference on Bioinformatics and Biomedical Engineering, IWBBIO 2020, Granada, Spain, 6–8 May 2020. Copicentro Editorial (2020, submitted)
11. Shao, S., Wang, P., Yan, R.: Generative adversarial networks for data augmentation in machine fault diagnosis. Comput. Ind. **106**, 85–93 (2019). https://doi.org/10.1016/j.compind.2019.01.001

A Proposal to Evolving Towards Digital Twins in Healthcare

Cecilio Angulo[1(✉)], Luis Gonzalez-Abril[2], Cristóbal Raya[1], and Juan Antonio Ortega[2]

[1] IDEAI-UPC, Universitat Politècnica de Catalunya, Barcelona, Spain
{cecilio.angulo,cristobal.raya}@upc.ede

[2] Universidad de Sevilla, Seville, Spain
{luisgon,jortega}@us.es

Abstract. The main objective in this proposal is to orchestrate an ecosystem of manipulation of reliable and safe data, applied to the field of health, specifically lung cancer, by introducing the creation of digital twins for personalised healthcare about the behaviour of this disease on patients. Digital twins is a very popular and novel approach in digitisation units in industry which will be used by both kind of experts: (i) data analysts, who will design expert recommender systems and extract knowledge – explainable Artificial Intelligence (AI); and (ii) professionals in medicine, who will consume that knowledge generated with their research for better diagnosis. This knowledge generation/extraction process will work in the form of a lifelong learning system by iterative and continuous use. The produced software platform will be abstracted so it can be applied like a general purpose service tool in other domains of knowledge, specially health and industry. Furthermore, a rule extraction module will be made available for explainability issues.

Keywords: Digital twin · Healthcare · GAN · Proposal

1 Introduction

Data, data, data... In recent years there has been a huge proliferation of companies and research groups working with different volumes of data. There exist solutions that store and process these data and from them infer knowledge and/or know better about our experience, invading even privacy when manipulating or extracting this information. Thus, mobile phone's geolocation allows knowing about our position, and people we interact with. Furthermore, new technologies in smart wearable sensors [1] allow continuous monitoring on people of physiological functions – heart rate, oxygen saturation in blood, temperature, movement, rest periods, etc. –, adding to diagnostic tests and clinical information, a third

This research has been partially supported by the EDITH Research Project (PGC2018-102145-B-C21,C22 (AEI/FEDER, UE)), funded by the Spanish Ministry of Science, Innovation and Universities.

I. Rojas et al. (Eds.): IWBBIO 2020, LNBI 12108, pp. 418–426, 2020.
https://doi.org/10.1007/978-3-030-45385-5_37

source of continuous information: the patient himself through mobile devices (mHealth) [2].

In order to carry out a study about these topics, the elements to be considered are:

- *Data privacy for ethical issues.* It is appropriate to put some coherence, limitations on data use, data quality, and a long list of factors and aspects on which there is now a broad social and political debate, establishing criteria on this new science that it is created around the data.
  Hence, in particular, sources of medical data in health services are causing important concerns, the main one being privacy and legal issues when sharing and reporting health information of patients. However, an accurate diagnosis will depend on the quantity and quality of the information about a patient, as well as extensive medical knowledge. These data will be treated taking into account that our objective is to generate patterns, this is to perform their analysis and structuring them through mathematical, statistical, mining techniques of data and machine learning. In this context, anonymization arises as a tool to mitigate the risks of obtaining and massively processing personal data [5].
  Statistical methods protecting sensitive information or the identity of the data owner have become critical to ensure privacy of individuals as well as of organizations. In [6], anonymization methods are investigated based on representation learning and deep neural networks. The training procedure aims at learning representations that preserve the relevant part of the information (about regular labels) while dismissing information about the private labels which correspond to the identity of a person.
  We propose an initial GAN-based [7] anonymization phase, so a seedbed would be obtained from the training data that allow not only to capture information from the original data, but to generate new information with a similar behaviour to the original one.
  Generative Adversarial Networks will be designed and developed to anonymize original data for both objectives, privacy-preserving and data synthesis. Privacy is in the origin of the ethical and legal dimension.
- *Knowledge generation (in the health domain).* "To generate information and knowledge that are valid for the user and her/his environment" . This is very important in the field of health since it allows measurement of the immediate advantage it brings to the user and the rest of the actors involved around: family, doctors, administration and society.
  At this point, it is worth to note that during the last few years important advances have been experienced in applying new information analysis technologies and their introduction in different aspects of society, including, of course, medicine and health. Most of these technologies are coming from the social media domain due to the huge volume of information to deal. Medical information from a patient can imply also a large volume of data (not ever), however the nature and purpose of this information seems more aligned with dealing critical industrial processes and devices that social media.

How data should be structured, stored and analyzed the information, with the aim of extracting knowledge form it, is highly correlated with industrial issues about data protection, safety, regulations, expert knowledge, and so on [3].
Hence, the industrial concept of *Digital Twin* as just a digital representation of the actual physical product [8] can be proposed for the health domain. One of the most important advantages of digital twins is to test decision in a simulated "real" environment to check how the simulated environment behaves or obtain some kind of feedback about how good the decision was. Hence a bidirectional (dyadic) communication is established between medical doctors and data analysts in a lifelong learning system.

- *Lifelong learning.* A digital twin is defined as a digital representation of an entity, including attributes and behaviors, sufficient to meet the requirements of a set of use cases, that is, they are virtual representations of physical assets. Differently to physics or mathematical models, as the digital twin model represents more of the object's behaviors, covering more of its life cycle, it becomes a digital twin of the real-world object.
Digital Twins, a concept from the "industrial internet of things" or IIoT, is the discipline of devising highly capable simulation models, especially those that consume streaming data from sensors to anticipate maintenance issues, impending failure of components and improving performance. Devising a simulation model of clinical behavior in front a disease, such as the classical propensity models, is much more difficult because humans are so unpredictable and engineering approaches obviously don't apply.
In our case, we are not worried about modelling artificial pancreas for diabetic patients or artificial lungs in the case of lung cancer, but to model the behaviour of these diseases in the patients; how patients' measures drift along the evolution of the disease.
This approach means a continuous learning and reshape of the behavioural model, as well as continuous bidirectional interaction between data analysts and professionals in medicine.
- *General purpose service.* The complete system should be designed as a general purpose service to be used in multiple domains. As a general purpose approach, it would facilitate the process of abstraction of the knowledge embedded into a bidirectional recommender system [9], being approached by an explainable AI module able to extract rules from the dialogue between professionals in medicine and data scientists, avoiding lack of accountability [4].

2 Our Proposal

The goals pursued in this proposal are multiple. We can summarise them by observing the diagram in the Fig. 1.

Hence, the complete system depicted in Fig. 1 is designed as a general purpose service to be used in multiple domains, from health to industry. As a general purpose approach, it will facilitate the process of abstraction of the knowledge embedded into the bidirectional recommender system, hence could being

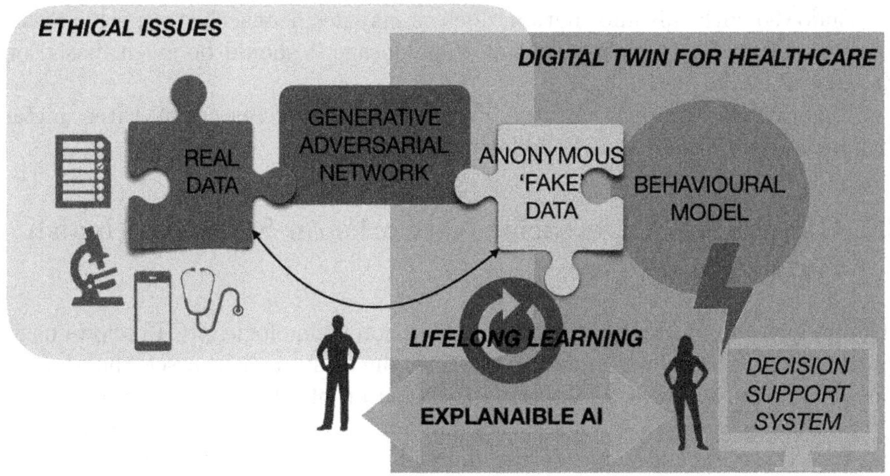

Fig. 1. Diagram of the elements of the proposal for a healthcare digital twin

approached by an explainable AI system able to extract rules from the dyadic dialogue between professionals in medicine and data scientists.

The overall aim of this project is to research in the following three meta-hypotheses and associated general objectives:

- Hypothesis 1: The use of Generative Adversarial Networks on sensitive health data information will allow:
  - anonymizing data in the form of a 'fake' dataset;
  - to generate a seedbed along with the GAN machine for generating fake patients that health professionals can use to perform a deeper study on the disease.

  Let us indicate that in our context 'fake' is not negative aspect since we sought this dataset in order to improve the capacity of the doctor in your work.
- Hypothesis 2: The use of the digital twins approach, extrapolated from the industrial domain, will lead to a behavioural model of the disease (lung cancer) that allows:
  - experimenting new health treatments with simulated 'real' patients before to be applied in hospitals;
  - extracting knowledge from regular data science research to be implemented in the form of a decision support system.
- Hypothesis 3: A decision support system developed in a bidirectional form will allow:
  - a dyadic dialogue between health professionals and data scientists in order to work in a lifelong learning paradigm, that means an iterative and adaptive process;
  - this dialogue will eventually drive to an AI explainable system able to generate decision rules.

Endowed with this information, doctors may decide whether a specific treatment would be likely to help and at what dosage it should be given, based on the digital model.

The overall approach of this proposal implies research in three meta-hypotheses as displayed in the following sections.

3 Generative Adversarial Networks on Sensitive Health Data

The progress in information and communication technologies (ICT) allows us to promote a new model where data is the core, the most precious asset, the support on which it must pivot and orienting the solution of information systems.

Sources of medical data are very heterogeneous, so technological barriers exist in the communication of the data of the same patient between health services causing important difficulties when it comes to collecting and harmonising patient data. Several reasons can be adduced, the main one being privacy and legal concerns when sharing and reporting health information of patients. However, an accurate diagnosis will depend on the quantity and quality of the information about a patient, as well as extensive medical knowledge.

In this context, anonymization arises as a tool to mitigate the risks of obtaining and massively processing personal data, consisting of a process that allows identifying and hiding the sensitive information contained in the documents, allowing its disclosure without imply to violate the rights to the protection of data of the people and organisations that can be referenced in them[1].

Anonymisation of information, as a method protecting sensitive information or the identity of the data owner, for legal or ethical issues, is usually seen as a major problem in data analytic because it could lead to reduce the explainability of the dataset. However, new training procedures, like Generative Adversarial Networks (GANs), aim at learning representations that preserve the relevant part of the information (about regular labels) while dismissing information about the private labels which correspond to the identity of a person. The success of this approach has been demonstrated, in [10] for instance. A diagram to the architect to GAN can be seen in Fig. 2.

As a result of this GAN-based anonymization phase, a seedbed is obtained from the training data that allows not only to capture information from the original data, but to generate new information with a similar behaviour to the original one. This result is currently being applied in generative applications on speech, vision or natural language, but we want to demonstrate that it can be also applied in the health domain.

Medical knowledge implies an experience acquired through learning, detecting signs, looking for symptoms, assessing risks, until reaching a diagnosis and being able to propose a treatment indicated for each patient. However, often,

[1] https://www.aepd.es/media/guias/guia-orientaciones-procedimientos-anonimizacion.pdf.

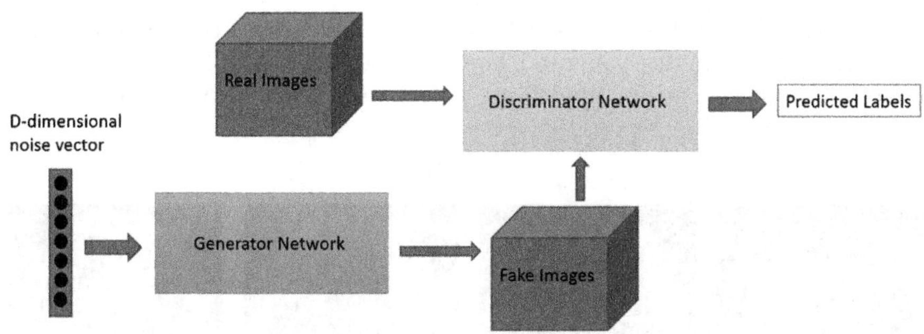

Fig. 2. Overview of a Generative Adversarial Network structured. Source: towards datascience.com/generative-adversarial-networks-gans-a-beginners-guide-5b38eceece24

physicians are unable to fully consider the large amount of data obtained from a patient and use it to make diagnostic decisions. If we consider the total set of patients, even for a single disease, and generate 'fake' experiences from a seedbed emerged from real patients, we expect that they can benefit from this valuable information better than buried within huge amounts of data.

On the other hand, this volume of data is obviously interesting for the data science community. Many approaches can be considered in this point that will not be discused here because we have a limited space. From our perspective, the nature and purpose of medical information from a patient seems more aligned with dealing critical industrial processes and devices than social media. How data should be structured, stored and analyzed, with the aim of extracting knowledge form it, is highly correlated with industrial issues about data protection, safety, regulations, expert knowledge, and so on.

In order to see as the GAN can provide some help, the Fig. 3 is shown as an illustration.

4 Digital Twins in Healthcare

The concept of *Digital Twin* in industry exists since 2003: it should be just a digital representation of the actual physical product [11]. According to [12], digital twins play three distinct roles when extrapolated to healthcare: hospital design, hospital management and patient care. Digital twins for hospital design and management exists and are selled by GE Healthcare Camed Group. For patient care, Dassault Systèmes claims to have one of the first realistic model of a human heart, including the electricity, mechanics and blood flow of the heart. Also, Philips sees the potential of digital twins in healthcare, especially a digital twin of devices and humans. Philips breaks down a digital twin of a device into four components. Firstly, you need real device data and secondly there must be some kind of artificial intelligence (AI) or data analytics. Those two components could be described as the basic components. To understand the outcome of the AI or the data analytics you need human knowledge. The last component is about physics-based device modelling, therefore no special AI has to be used here.

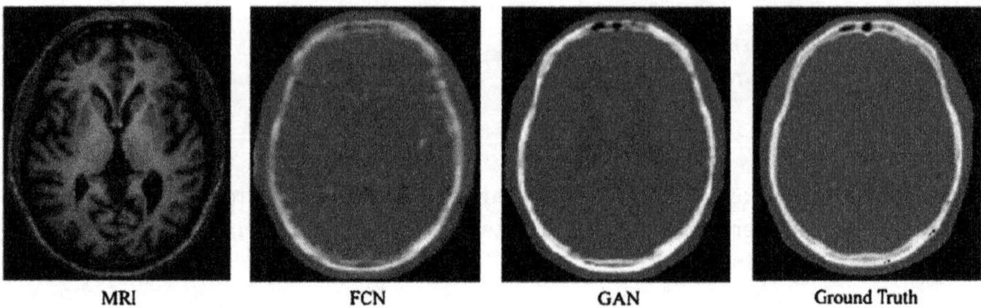

Fig. 3. Generated CT images from an MRI scan. Second image has been generated with a Fully Connected Network (FCN) and third by a GAN. Last image is the original CT image of the patient. Source: https://www.researchgate.net/figure/Conversion-of-MRI-to-CT-using-GAN-38-Adapted-with-permission-Fig-5-Example-of-a_fig3_322657913

One of the most important advantages of digital twins is to test decision in a simulated "real" environment [2]. Then it is possible to see how the simulated environment behaves, also the digital twin could give some kind of feedback of how good the decision was. Maybe it can also tell how to change the initial decision to make the outcome even better. Especially the last aspect can be in healthcare very useful. An ideal example would be, if a doctor wants to treat a patient, but the doctor tests the treatment on the patient's digital twin first. The digital twin will then return a feedback of how effective the treatment was and optimally returns an alternative treatment with a better outcome result. Hence a bidirectional (dyadic) communication is established between medical doctors and data analysts in a lifelong learning system.

Therefore, the Digital Twins approach will lead to behavioural models that allows both, experimenting new health treatments with simulated 'real' patients before to be applied in hospitals and extracting knowledge from regular data science research to be implemented in the form of a decision support system. Figure 4 shows a pictured of the Digital Twins.

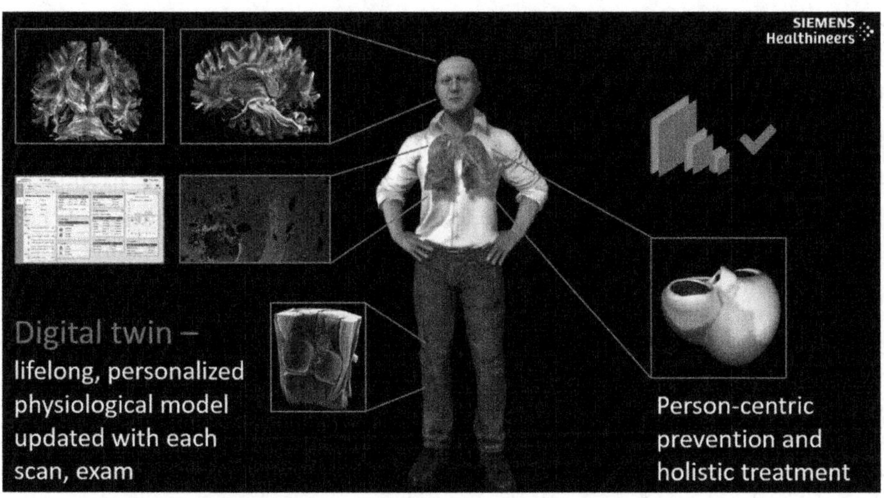

Fig. 4. Digital twins for a patient. From European society of radiology

5 Decision Support System

The anonymized GAN-generated information will allow creating repositories from the seedbed from which the digital twins will generate a behavioural model of the disease, and, from here, provide the data as needed by both kind of analysts: develop a decision support system for data analysts, and generate fake patients' data for clinic professionals, in a lifelong learning system that integrates a dyadic iterative interaction between both kind of professionals, health professionals and data scientists.

Moreover, this dyadic interaction should help to develop explainable reasoning from the behavioural model of the disease, leading to explainable AI in the form of generated decision rules.

6 Discussion and Conclusion

The proposed architecture aims to provide a clinical information integration model in the form of a digital twin of the behavior of the lung cancer in patients under treatment. Thus, there is research, in the medical field, on the adequacy of treatments to patients, based mainly on clinical data. However, in order to achieve improvements in the diagnosis as well as in the treatments, the combination of the clinical data and the diagnostic tests seems appropriate, eventually with other data coming from the outpatient setting of the patient and obtained from intelligent sensors.

The generation of digital twins will allow the use of data in a manner adapted to the needs of each researcher or scientist in particular, and also incorporate tools from the field of ICTs to analysis, study, validation, visualization, etc. of these data. These virtual patients will become a powerful ICT tool that allows the proposal of new biomarkers of diseases, made up of the aggregation of data, and in addition, the visualization and interpretation of the results by doctors and researchers.

Data from patients will be approached from a novel perspective, the GAN machines, that allows a complete anonymization of health records, hence this technique will impact on the EU data protection laws. Nonetheless, flexible and interpretable models will be obtained that will lead to the generation of 'fake' patients serving as both, training patients for novel doctors and a source of new insights about the disease for expert doctors.

Finally, on a different matter, the possibility of generating an infinite number of samples through a GAN is also very coveted. This virtue could allow the continuous simulation of certain variables from a patient for research purposes. This could help as well in the training process of other types of models by augmenting the number of samples, which are usually scarce in private datasets. It could also be convenient in educational areas to avoid misconceptions in the subject because of a scarcity in examples.

References

1. Soria, L.M., Gonzalez-Abril, L., Ortega-Ramirez, J.A., Alvarez, M.A.: Low energy physical activity recognition system on smartphones. Sensors **15**, 5163–5196 (2015)
2. Bruynseels, K., Santoni de Sio, F., van den Hoven, J.: Digital twins in health care: ethical implications of an emerging engineering paradigm. Front. Genet. **9**, 31 (2018)
3. Raghupathi, W., Raghupathi, V.: Big data analytics in healthcare: promise and potential. Health Inf. Sci. Syst. **2**, 3 (2014)
4. Ford, R.A., Price II, W.N.: Privacy and accountability in black-box medicine. Mich. Telecommun. Technol. Law Rev. **23**(1) (2017)
5. El Emam, K., Arbuckle, L.: Anonymizing Health Data: Case Studies and Methods to Get You Started. O'Reilly Media, Inc., Cambridge (2013)
6. Feutry, C., Piantanida, P., Bengio, Y., Duhamel, P.: Learning anonymized representations with adversarial neural networks. https://arxiv.org/abs/1802.09386. Accessed 12 Dec 2019
7. Goodfellow, I., et al.: Generative adversarial nets. Adv. Neural Inf. Process. Syst. **27**, 2672–2680 (2014)
8. Kharat, R., Bavane, V., Jadhao, S., Marode, R.: Digital twin: manufacturing excellence through virtual factory replication. Glob. J. Eng. Sci. Res. [**NC–Rase 18**], 6–15 (2018)
9. Nguyen, J., Sanchez-Hernandez, G., Armisen, A., Agell, N., Rovira, X., Angulo, C.: A linguistic multi-criteria decision-aiding system to support university career services. Appl. Soft Comput. **67**, 933–940 (2018)
10. Feutry, C., Piantanida, P., Bengio, Y., Duhamel, P.: Learning anonymized representations with adversarial neural networks. https://arxiv.org/pdf/1802.09386.pdf (2018)
11. Grieves, M.: Digital twin: manufacturing excellence through virtual factory replication (2014). http://www.apriso.com
12. Hempel: Digital Twins in healthcare. https://www.dr-hempel-network.com/digital-health-technolgy/digital-twins-in-healthcare/

High Performance in Bioinformatics

Role of Homeobox Genes in the Development of *Pinus Sylvestris*

Tatiana Guseva[1], Vladislav Biriukov[1,2], and Michael Sadovsky[1,3(✉)]

[1] Institute of Fundamental Biology and Biotechnology, Siberian Federal University, Svobodny prosp., 79, 660049 Krasnoyarsk, Russia
dianema2010@mail.ru, biryukov.vv@ksc.krasn.ru

[2] Laboratory of Genomic Research and Biotechnology, Federal Research Center "Krasnoyarsk Science Center of the Siberian Branch of the Russian Academy of Sciences", 660036 Krasnoyarsk, Akademgorodok, Russia

[3] Institute of Computational Modelling of SB RAS, 660036 Krasnoyarsk, Akademgorodok, Russia
msad@icm.krasn.ru
http://icm.krasn.ru

Abstract. Comprehensive gene expression profiling of homeobox gene family members allows to retrieve the role in *Pinus sylvestris* growth and development. Homeobox genes encode transcriptional factors playing important role in the development of organism. Homeodomains are common in a vast amount of species. Therefore, they can be identified even in non-model organisms. Understanding of homeobox genes functions supports the investigation of tissues development and yields the ways to regulate it. Homeobox genes are understudied for Scots pine. Hence, we assembled *de novo* transcriptome of *Pinus sylvestris* obtained from five tissues. The transcriptome comprises 775 502 transcripts. 243 homeobox-containing transcripts were found and DE analysis was carried out using these sequences. We have obtained 5 clusters of homeobox DE genes (visualized as a heatmap of gene expression). DE genes were annotated. The obtained results give some insights into the development of bud and mature tissues of *Pinus sylvestris*.

Keywords: Differential expression · Evolution · *de novo* transcriptome, Gymnosperm, Clustering

1 Introduction

Homeobox genes play an important role in the processes of the organism development and are discovered in plants, fungi, and vertebrates [1]. Homeobox genes act as regulatory genes, it controls the cascades of reactions, so the study of expression patterns of these genes is essential for understanding the process of organism development. Homeobox genes encode transcriptional factors; these latter play important roles in the development of multicellular organisms [2,3].

I. Rojas et al. (Eds.): IWBBIO 2020, LNBI 12108, pp. 429–437, 2020.
https://doi.org/10.1007/978-3-030-45385-5_38

Homeodomain proteins of different plant species have been classified over the years into different families and subfamilies; currently, researcher identify 14 distinct classes [1,4]. Earlier, the WUSCHEL-related homeobox gene family in *Pinus pinaster* was analyzed [13], moreover expression of the WUSCHEL-related homeobox gene family in the conifer *Picea abies* during somatic embryogenesis and in adult tissues was investigated [5,6].

Pinus sylvestris is widely distributed in Russia and Europe and is of great economic value. Also, Scots pine (*P. sylvestris*) plays an essential role in forest ecosystems [7,8]. A tight sight on the genes involved in the development of the tissues of Scots pine may provide a tool to control it [9–11]. Expression and function of genes regulating development in *P. sylvestris* are of interest from an evolutionary point of view [12]. Development processes are more studied for angiosperms [13]; for gymnosperms, transcriptional profiling of Scots pine embryo [12], *P. sylvestris* heart-wood formation [12] and involvement of the plant growth regulator ethylene in somatic embryo maturation of *P. sylvestris* is studied [14,15]. Bioinformatic analysis of forest tree species can help to understand the development processes that occur in these species better.

Here we study the process of organism development exploring the differential expression of homeobox genes. It should be stressed that the analysis of RNA-seq data for evaluation of the differential expression is quite hard, since there is no annotated reference genome [16]. The aim of the work is to examine the development of Scots pine at the homeobox-containing genes level using the differential gene expression approach.

2 Materials and Methods

2.1 RNA-seq Source

P. sylvestris sequencing data deposited in the NCBI BioProject database under accession number PRJNA531617 (SRR8996768-SRR8996761) [17] provided by the Norwegian Institute of Bioeconomy Research was used as a source for this study. The material comprises five tissues (needle, phloem, vegetative bud, embryo, and megagametophyte) collected from six non-related individuals of P. sylvestris growing in a forest study site located in the Punkaharju, Southern Finland on May 26th–27th, 2016.

2.2 Pre-processing of Sequences and *de novo* Transcriptome Assembly

Read quality was analyzed with FastQC and low-quality reads were removed with Trimmomatic 0.33 [19] using the following parameters: ILLUMINACLIP: TruSeq3-PE-2.fa: 2:30:10:1: true TRAILING:3 SLIDINGWINDOW:4:25 AVGQUAL:30. Firstly, Trimmomatic will look for initial matches (16 bases) within the adapters library allowing a maximum of **2** mismatches. These seeds will be expanded and trimmed if, in the case of a paired-end reading, a quality score of **30** (about 50 bases) is reached, or in the case of a single-end reading, a quality score of **10** (about 17 bases) is obtained, the **true** parameter allows to save reverse read. In case the quality value of the last bases below **3** Trimmomatic will cut these ones. Sliding window with size **4** bases starts scanning at the 5′ end and clips the read once the average quality within the window falls below **25**. Finally, Trimmomatic will drop the read if the average quality is below **30**.

Reads were assembled into transcriptome using Trinity software (version 2.8.4) [18] and transcriptome completeness was estimated with BUSCO software using the embryophyta odb9 dataset [19].

2.3 Selection of Homeobox-Containing Transcripts

Homeobox is highly conserved and its domains can be easily identified at non-model organisms. HMMER software (version 3.2.1) [20,21] was used for the homeobox domain identification in the assembled transcripts using a hidden Markov model of the homeodomain, which was downloaded from the PFAM database (Homeodomain accession number PF00046) [22].

2.4 Differential Expression Analysis and Functional Annotation

To estimate transcript abundance and carry out differential expression analysis Trinity differential gene expression analysis module (align_and_estimate_abundance Perl script), RSEM, as well as Bowtie programs (version 1.2.3), were used. Also, cross-sample TMM normalization was performed. Further, the EdgeR package (R version 3.5.0, Bioconductor version 3.8) was used for statistical analysis and identification of significantly differentially expressed transcripts. Further, to perform functional analysis OmicsBox (version 1.2.4) workflow was used. Gene annotation was provided based on sequence homologies with the proteins deposed in the SwissProt/UniProt database [23]. Gene Ontology (GO) categories represented in the transcripts were grouped into three categories: molecular function, biological process, and cellular component.

3 Results and Discussion

Assembled transcriptome comprises of 775 502 transcripts with the mean GC content of 40.19 %. The N50 value for transcripts was 1,273 bp, while the median contig length was 360 bp. (Table 1). Transcriptome completeness was assessed based on six parameters calculated in BUSCO (Benchmarking Universal Single-Copy Orthologs): C:complete [S:Single, D:duplicated], F:fragmented, M:missed, n:number of genes. These parameters are the metric of transcriptome completeness and show the percentage of Completed Single, Completed Duplicated, Fragmented and Missed genes from the BUSCO sets of single-copy orthologs in the transcriptome [19]. High values of completed genes percentage represent the good quality of assembled transcriptome. In summary, completeness scores were counted resulting C:85.9% [S:27.3%, D:58.6%] F:2.2%, M:11.9%, n:1440 (Fig.1).

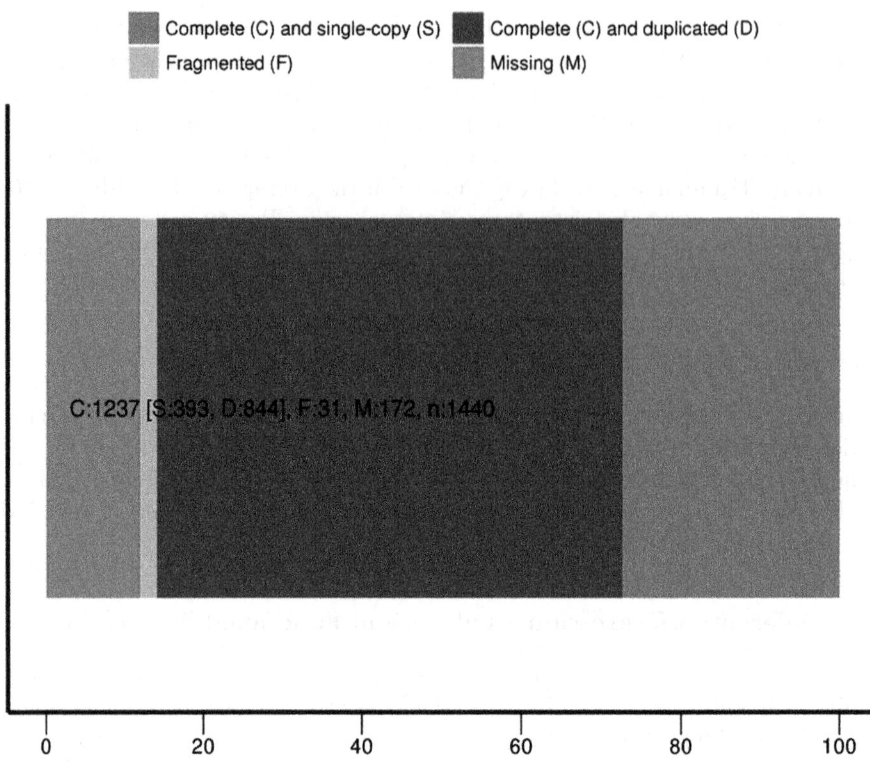

Fig. 1. Percentage of completeness on the core set of genes in BUSCO of the *P. sylvestris* transcriptome assembly.

These results show a slightly higher value of transcriptome completeness than in the previous assembly [17].

243 homeobox-containing transcripts were selected for further analysis and then were annotated (*e*-value $<10^{-3}$) using OmicsBox software.

Here is presented the distribution of identified homeobox genes at *P. sylvestris* transcriptome in 14 classes (Table 2). The most represented classes of homeobox genes were HD-ZIP I, HD-ZIP II, WOX, and HD-ZIP IV. HD-ZIP I class of homeobox genes was found to be the most abundant and homeodomains of this class generally involved in responses related to abiotic stress, abscisic acid (ABA), blue light, de-etiolation and embryogenesis [24]. HD-ZIP II transcription factors initially known for their role in shade avoidance, moreover, they regulate apical embryo development and meristem function [25]. Homeodomains of WOX class are known to be an essential part of numerous developmental processes, namely, embryo patterning, organ formation, stem cell maintenance [26], members of HD-ZIP IV class involved in the shoot and reproductive developmental processes besides maintenance of epidermal cell layer [27]. It should be emphasized that some of the transcripts were not classified, which is interesting and needs further research related to studying their functions.

Table 1. Transcriptome statistics

Total trinity 'genes'	488 116
Total trinity transcripts	775 502
Percent GC	40.19
Stats based on ALL transcript contigs	
Contig N50 (bp)	1 273
Median contig length (bp)	360
Average contig (bp)	713.6
Total assembled bases	553 398 248
Stats based on ONLY LONGEST ISOFORM per 'gene'	
Contig N50 (bp)	596
Median contig length (bp)	313
Average contig (bp)	513.56
Total assembled bases	250 675 880

To gain insights into the putative functions of homeobox genes in *P. sylvestris* its expression patterns were analyzed in various tissues. 46 statistically significantly differentially expressed trinity "genes" were identified (adjusted p-value < 0.03) (Fig. 2) and visualized as a heatmap. Five resulting clusters of DE transcripts were analyzed.

In the first cluster, two transcripts were found encoding proteins WUSCHEL-related homeobox 9 (WOX9) and late embryogenesis abundant protein D-34 involved in early development, meristem growth, and late embryo development respectively, which were up-regulated at embryo and megagametophyte stages and down-regulated at other stages. It was previously indicated that WOX2 and WOX8/9 are involved in conifer embryo formation and differentiation [28].

The second cluster comprises transcripts encoding transcriptional factors (TF), namely Zinc-finger homeodomain protein 1, Homeobox-leucine zipper protein ROC (1,2,8), Homeobox-leucine zipper protein PROTODERMAL FACTOR 2 involved in cotyledon development, seed germination and epidermal cell differentiation, down-regulated in phloem tissue. Recently, there were no reports about down-regulated genes encoding Homeobox-leucine zipper protein PROTODERMAL FACTOR 2 transcription factors in the phloem tissue.

Table 2. Distribution of homeobox-containing transcripts across the classes of homeobox genes; N is transcripts abundance.

Class	N	Class	N	Class	N	Class	N
HD-ZIP I	67	PLINC	1	DDT	11	NDX	0
HD-ZIP II	29	WOX	29	PHD	4	SAWADEE	11
HD-ZIP III	15	BEL	21	PINTOX	0	Unclassified	14
HD-ZIP IV	26	KNOX	11	LD	4	Total	243

In the third cluster, transcripts annotated as proteins WUSCHEL-related homeobox (1,4 and 8) responsible for plant organ development, cell division, multicellular organism development, Homeobox protein knotted-1-like (1 and 2) playing role in cell fate commitment, regulation of transcription, Homeotic protein knotted-1 appears to be involved in meristem formation and in the regulation of leaf morphology and finally Homeobox-leucine zipper protein (2 and 14) responsible auxin-mediated morphogenesis was observed. These transcripts are down-regulated in needle and megagametophyte tissues. Previously it was reported that Picea abies WOX8A expression could be detected in young needles although this expression was extremely low. Also, WOX2, WOX8A, and WOX8/9 are all more or less embryo-specific [5].

The fourth cluster comprises the proteins such as BEL1-like homeodomain 4 that establishes leaf shape by repressing growth in specific subdomains of the leaf, homeobox leucine zipper protein, homeobox protein knotted-1-like 3 (*KNAT3*) involved in the detection and cellular response to cytokine stimulus, response to light stimulus. Up-regulated at needle, bud, phloem and down-regulated at embryo and megagametophyte, therefore we can suggest the specified role of these transcriptional factors in the postembryonic development. *KNAT3* was mainly expressed in early organ development of leaves, buds [29]. Although at the moment there is no information about their role in the development of young tissues of *Pinus sylvestris*, also there is no data referring to the regulation of development of phloem tissue.

Transcripts in the fifth cluster determine proteins including Homeobox-leucine zipper protein, involved in the cotyledon morphogenesis (the cotyledon is the modified leaf (seed leaf), found as part of the embryo in plant seeds), positive regulation of transcription, and protein WUSCHEL involved in cell differentiation. Transcripts were found to be up-regulated in the bud.

For deeper analysis, the expression profiles of each class of homeobox genes were studied. Two classes of homeobox genes show a significant difference in expression patterns between groups of tissues, namely, HD-ZIP IV and BEL. Transcripts included HD-ZIP IV family of homeobox genes were down-regulated in needle and phloem tissue and up-regulated at megagametophyte, bud, and embryo.

Simultaneously, BEL family members were up-regulated in phloem, bud, needle tissues and found down-regulated at megagametophyte and embryo, thereby suggesting their role in the development of tissues of the mature tree. BEL1-like homeodomain (BLH) proteins have significant roles in the range processes of organism development, especially of meristem development. Their functions are often overlapping and redundant [30].

After analysis of differential expression profiles of homeobox genes, it can be estimated which of the homeobox genes or set of genes are crucial for different tissues development. Transcripts of cluster 5th were found to be significantly up-regulated at bud tissue, hence assuming the importance of the roles of these genes in the development of that tissue. Transcripts of this class mostly include members of HD-ZIP I class genes and also one transcript annotated as a member

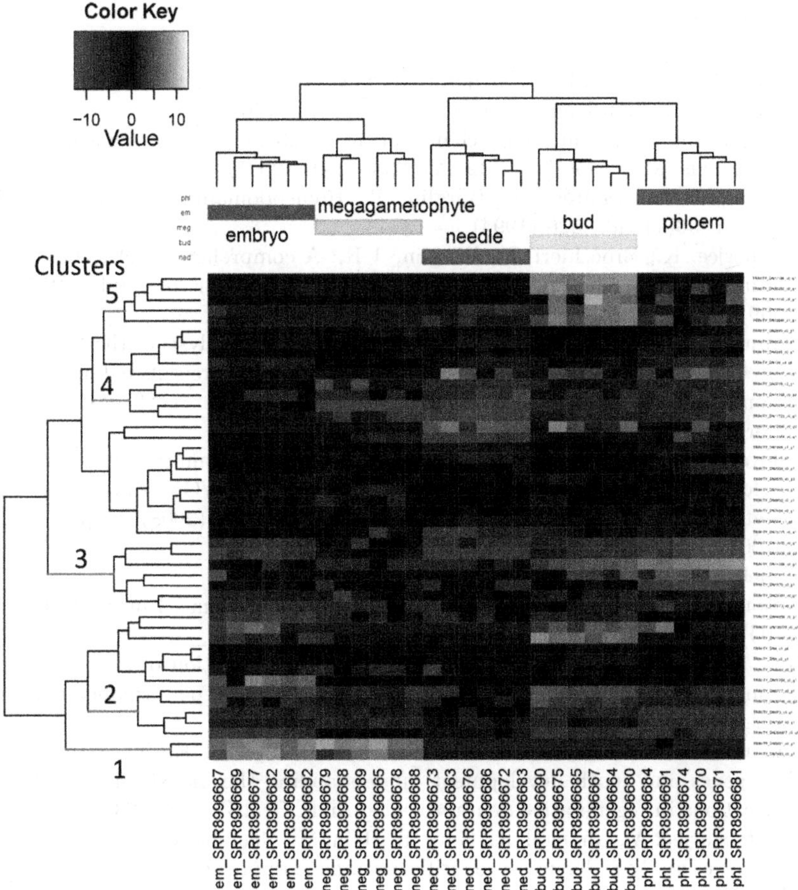

Fig. 2. Heatmap of gene expression, five tissues of *P. sylvestris*. Horizontal axis presents tissues, and right vertical axis presents "genes" identified by Trinity.

of the WOX class. Also, genes of the BEL class presumably involved in the development of mature tissues of the *P. sylvestris.*

Clusters show the specific groups of genes that appear to be a cascade. It means that regulating a small number of specific homeobox genes one can affect the huge number of developmental processes. Future plans connected with this work are oriented to more detailed studying of clusters of DE genes across tissues of *P. sylvestris*, including new tissues like shoot and xylem.

Finally, obtained results can be used in future, for example in regulating the growth of desirable tissue, working with and studying stress tolerance and abiotic and biotic stress response. These suggest that homeobox genes may prove to be suitable candidates for engineering stress tolerance in Scots pine, but these ideas need further study [9–11]. Thus, the results bring a more comprehensive understanding of the *P. sylvestris* development process.

References

1. Viola, I.L., Gonzalez, D.H.: Structure and evolution of plant homeobox genes. In: Plant Transcription Factors, pp. 101–112. Elsevier (2016)
2. Nam, J., Nei, M.: Evolutionary change of the numbers of homeobox genes in bilateral animals. Mol. Biol. Evol. **22**(12), 2386–2394 (2005)
3. Gehring, W.J., Affolter, M., Bürglin, T.: Homeodomain proteins. Annu. Rev. Biochem. **63**(1), 487–526 (1994)
4. Mukherjee, K., Brocchieri, L., Bürglin, T.R.: A comprehensive classification and evolutionary analysis of plant homeobox genes. Mol. Biol. Evol. **26**(12), 2775–2794 (2009)
5. Hedman, H., Zhu, T., von Arnold, S., Sohlberg, J.J.: Analysis of the WUSCHEL-related homeobox gene family in the conifer *Picea abies* reveals extensive conservation as well as dynamic patterns. BMC Plant Biol. **13**(1), 89 (2013). https://doi.org/10.1186/1471-2229-13-89
6. Palovaara, J., Hakman, I.: Conifer wox-related homeodomain transcription factors, developmental consideration and expression dynamic of WOX2 during Picea abies somatic embryogenesis. Plant Mol. Biol. **66**(5), 533–549 (2008). https://doi.org/10.1007/s11103-008-9289-5
7. Frelich, L.E.: Boreal and taiga biome (2019)
8. Farjon, A.: Pines: Drawings and Descriptions of the Genus Pinus. Brill, Leiden (2005)
9. Guo, M., Niu, X., Rupe, M., Schussler, J.: Down-regulation of a homeodomain-leucine zipper I-class homeobox gene for improved plant performance US Patent 9,677,084, 13 June 2017
10. Ramanathan, A., Srijaya, T.C., Sukumaran, P., Zain, R.B., Kasim, N.H.A.: Homeobox genes and tooth development: understanding the biological pathways and applications in regenerative dental science. Arch. Oral Biol. **85**, 23–39 (2018)
11. Bhattacharjee, A., Ghangal, R., Garg, R., Jain, M.: Genome-wide analysis of homeobox gene family in legumes: identification, gene duplication and expression profiling. PLoS One **10**(3), e0119198 (2015)
12. Merino, I., Abrahamsson, M., Sterck, L., Craven-Bartle, B., Canovas, F., von Arnold, S.: Transcript profiling for early stages during embryo development in Scots pine. BMC Plant Biol. **16**(1), 255 (2016). https://doi.org/10.1186/s12870-016-0939-5
13. Tandre, K., Svenson, M., Svensson, M.E., Engström, P.: Conservation of gene structure and activity in the regulation of reproductive organ development of conifers and angiosperms. Plant J. **15**(5), 615–623 (1998)
14. Lim, K.J., et al.: Developmental changes in Scots pine transcriptome during heartwood formation. Plant Physiol. **172**(3), 1403–1417 (2016)
15. Lu, J., Vahala, J., Pappinen, A.: Involvement of ethylene in somatic embryogenesis in Scots pine (*Pinus sylvestris* L.). Plant Cell, Tissue Organ Cult. (PCTOC) **107**(1), 25 (2011). https://doi.org/10.1007/s11240-011-9952-4
16. De Heredia, U.L., Vázquez-Poletti, J.L.: RNA-seq analysis in forest tree species: bioinformatic problems and solutions. Tree Genet. Genomes **12**(2), 30 (2016). https://doi.org/10.1007/s11295-016-0995-x
17. Ojeda, D.I., et al.: Utilization of tissue ploidy level variation in de novo transcriptome assembly of Pinus sylvestris. G3 Genes Genomes Genet. **9**(10), 3409–3421 (2019)

18. Haas, B., et al.: De novo transcript sequence reconstruction from RNA-seq using the trinity platform for reference generation and analysis. Nat. Protoc. **8**(8), 1494 (2013)
19. Simão, F.A., Waterhouse, R.M., Ioannidis, P., Kriventseva, E.V., Zdobnov, E.M.: BUSCO: assessing genome assembly and annotation completeness with single-copy orthologs. Bioinformatics **31**(19), 3210–3212 (2015)
20. Finn, R.D., Clements, J., Eddy, S.R.: HMMER web server: interactive sequence similarity searching. Nucleic Acid Res. **39**(suppl_2), W29–W37 (2011)
21. Eddy, S.: HMMER user's guide. Department of Genetics, Washington University School of Medicine 2(1), 13 (1992)
22. Bateman, A., et al.: The PFAM protein families database. Nucleic Acids Res. **32**(suppl_1), D138–D141 (2004)
23. Bairoch, A., et al.: The universal protein resource (UniProt). Nucleic Acids Res. **33**(suppl_1), D154–D159 (2005)
24. Elhiti, M., Stasolla, C.: Structure and function of homodomain-leucine zipper (HD-Zip) proteins. Plant Signal. Behav. **4**(2), 86–88 (2009)
25. Turchi, L., et al.: Arabidopsis HD-Zip II transcription factors control apical embryo development and meristem function. Development **140**(10), 2118–2129 (2013)
26. He, P., et al.: Comprehensive analysis of WOX genes uncovers that WOX13 is involved in phytohormone-mediated fiber development in cotton. BMC Plant Biol. **19**(1), 312 (2019). https://doi.org/10.1186/s12870-019-1892-x
27. Chew, W., Hrmova, M., Lopato, S.: Role of homeodomain leucine zipper (HD-Zip) IV transcription factors in plant development and plant protection from deleterious environmental factors. Int. J. Mol. Sci. **14**(4), 8122–8147 (2013)
28. Palovaara, J., Hallberg, H., Stasolla, C., Hakman, I.: Comparative expression pattern analysis of WUSCHEL-related homeobox 2 (WOX2) and WOX8/9 in developing seeds and somatic embryos of the gymnosperm Picea abies. New Phytol. **188**(1), 122–135 (2010)
29. Huang, Z., Meilan, R., Woeste, K.: A *KNAT3*-like homeobox gene from *Juglans nigra* L., *JnKNAT3*-like, highly expressed during heartwood formation. Plant Cell Rep. **28**(11), 1717–1724 (2009). https://doi.org/10.1007/s00299-009-0771-6
30. Sharma, P., Lin, T., Grandellis, C., Yu, M., Hannapel, D.J.: The BEL1-like family of transcription factors in potato. J. Exp. Bot. **65**(2), 709–723 (2014)

Function vs. Taxonomy: Further Reading from Fungal Mitochondrial ATP Synthases

Victory Fedotovskaya[2], Michael Sadovsky[1,2,4](✉), Anna Kolesnikova[2,3], Tatiana Shpagina[2], and Yulia Putintseva[2]

[1] Institute of Computational Modelling of SB RAS, 660036 Akademgorodok, Krasnoyarsk, Russia
msad@icm.krasn.ru

[2] Institute of Fundamental Biology and Biotechnology, Siberian Federal University, Svobodny prosp., 79, 660049 Krasnoyarsk, Russia
viktoriia.fedotovskaia@gmail.com, kolesnikova.denovo@gmail.com, shpagusa@mail.ru, yaputintseva@mail.ru

[3] Federal Research Center RAS, Laboratory of Genomics and Biotechnology, Krasnoyarsk, Russia

[4] V.F. Voino-Yasenetsky Krasnoyarsk State Medical University, P. Zheleznyaka str., 1, 660022 Krasnoyarsk, Russia
http://icm.krasn.ru

Abstract. We studied the relations between triplet composition of the family of mitochondrial *atp*6, *atp*8 and *atp*9 genes, their function, and taxonomy of the bearers. The points in 64-dimensional metric space corresponding to genes have been clustered. It was found the points are separated into three clusters corresponding to those genes. 223 mitochondrial genomes have been enrolled into the database.

Keywords: Order · Clustering · *K*-means · Elastic map · Stability · Evolution

1 Introduction

Despite significant success in up-to-date molecular biology and bioinformatics, the problem of the interplay of structure of biological macromolecules and functions encoded in them still brings a lot of news. However, rapid growth of sequenced genetic data makes another look at the problem and raises new questions. The problem of relationships between structure and function requires special analysis and discussions. The question is, whether it is true that various genetic texts (these can be genes, genomes, fragments of both, and individual fragments of DNA sequences) form relatively distinctive clusters (dense groups) in the triplet frequency space, or not, and if so, do these clusters unevenly comprise the entities with close functions defined by these genetic texts? To answer

I. Rojas et al. (Eds.): IWBBIO 2020, LNBI 12108, pp. 438–444, 2020.
https://doi.org/10.1007/978-3-030-45385-5_39

this question precisely and clearly, one must define what is structure and function. The point is that the diversity and abundance of structure identified in nucleotide sequences is great enough [1–6]), and those structure are quite different and may not be reduced one to another.

We stipulate that within this paper **structure** is a frequency dictionary of some symbol sequence corresponding to biological macromoleculae. We shall consider two types of symbol sequences: the former are nucleotide sequence, and the latter are amino acid sequences. As soon, as the alphabet of a sequence is fixed, one must set up two parameters to develop a frequency dictionary:

(1) the length q of window identifying a string in a sequence (often called *word*), and
(2) the length t of the step of the window shift when moving along a sequence in order to develop a dictionary.

Thus, a dictionary is the list of all the words found within a sequence, where each word is supplied with its frequency (1).

For nucleotide sequences, we shall consider triplet dictionaries, only (that means $q = 3$). Two kinds of triplet frequencies will be studied; they differ in reading frame shift t. For a triplet frequency dictionary $W_{(3,1)}$ the shift t is set up to one ($t = 1$), and for a triplet frequency $W_{(3,3)}$ the shift t is the set to three ($t = 3$). Frequency is defined in standard way

$$f_\omega = \frac{n_\omega}{N}, \tag{1}$$

where N is the total number of words. It coincides to the length of a sequence, for $W_{(3,1)}$, but it is less, for other frequency dictionaries.

223 mitochondrial genomes of five fungal division: *Basidiomycota* (24 entries), *Ascomycota* (185 entries), *Blastocladiomycota* (2 entries), *Chytridiomycota* (6 entries) and *Zygomycota* (6 entries) have been studied. We used the genes *atp*6, *atp*8 and *atp*9 belonging to ATP synthase genes family, to reveal the relation between structure, taxonomy and function. With CLC Genomic Workbench v.10 the annotated sequences of three standard mitochondrial protein encoding genes involved into the oxidative phosphorylation (these are *atp*6, *atp*8, *atp*9) were retrieved. Next, the sequence for each gene has been prepared in two versions:

(1) *gene* is a sequence containing exons and introns as it is presented in a genome, and
(2) *CDS (coding DNA sequence)* is a sequence free from introns, in fact, it corresponds to a mature RNA ready for protein translation.

Besides, ATP synthase genes are quite often used to trace phylogeny [7–9].

The frequency dictionary $W_{(3,1)}$ or $W_{(3,3)}$, respectively, were developed with *ad hoc* software. Next, we used *VidaExpert*[1] freeware to study the distribution of the points corresponding to genetic entities. The transformation of sequences

[1] http://bioinfo-out.curie.fr/projects/vidaexpert/.

into frequency dictionaries makes an implementation of powerful and efficient tools of up-to-date statistical analysis and multidimensional data visualization.

CDS is the mRNA ready for protein translation. Hence, $W_{(3,3)}$ is the dictionary of codons, since the shift of the reading frame is equal to ribosomal step in protein synthesis process (translation). Thereby it is possible to study the distribution of genes in the other space with reduced dimension. To change the space we combined the synonymous codons into one group, so the sum of the frequencies of synonymous codons makes the frequency of amino acid. Thus, we changed the 64-dimensional Euclidean space for 21-dimensional one, where the frequencies of amino acids plus stop signal are the coordinates.

1.1 Clustering Techniques

Clustering plays the key role in this research; we used K-means and elastic map technique to cluster the data. K-means is well known and exhaustively described method of clustering, hence we shall not describe the method here in detail (see [10] for more details).

Also, the elastic map technique has been used to cluster and analyze data distribution, in triplets frequency space. Since this method is quite new, we describe it here in few details. To start, one must find out the first and the second principal components, and develop a plane over them (as on axes); next, each data point must be projected on this plane. Secondly, each data point must be connected to its projection with a mathematical spring. That latter has infinite expansibility and the elasticity coefficient remains permanent, for any expansion. Thirdly, figure out the minimal square comprising all the projections, and change it with the elastic membrane. That latter is supposed to be homogeneous, so that it may bend and expand. Next, release the system to reach the minimum of the total deformation energy. The elastic membrane would transform into a jammed surface, and this is the two-dimensional manifold approximating the data set. Fourthly, redefine each point on the jammed surface through the orthogonal projection. Finally, cut-off all the springs, so that the jammed surface comes back to a plane. That is the elastic map representing the cluster structuredness, if any, in the data set [11–13].

To identify clusters, we used the local density of points. That latter is defined as following. Supply each point of an elastic map (in so called inner coordinates, when the jammed surface is already flattened) with a bell-shaped function, e. g.

$$f(r) = \mathcal{A} \cdot \exp\left\{-\frac{(r - r_j)^2}{\sigma^2}\right\}. \tag{2}$$

Here r_j is the coordinate vector of j-th point, and σ is an adjusting parameter (that is a specific width of the bell-shaped function). Then the sum function

$$F(r) = \mathcal{A} \cdot \sum_{j=1}^{N} \exp\left\{-\frac{(r - r_j)^2}{\sigma^2}\right\}, \tag{3}$$

is calculated; the function $F(r)$ is then shown in elastic map.

2 Results

We start from the clustering obtained due to elastic map technique and then consider the structuredness provided by K-means classification. Here we present the results of study of the distribution of genes of the mitochondrial ATP synthase family in the space of reduced dimension (in the space of amino acid frequencies). Figure 1 shows the distribution of the ATP family genes on the soft elastic map (16×16 grid) in the context of three genes: *atp*6, *atp*8 and *atp*9 (left) and the distribution of the same genes obtained with K-means classification, 4 classes (right). Also, this figure shows local density function, in green scale (left) and in grey scale (right). It is clearly seen that there is three distinct clusters, and the clusters are gene specific with a high accuracy: the upper left cluster gathers mainly *atp*6 genes (shown in blue), the right cluster gathers *atp*8 genes (shown in red) and the bottom left cluster gathers *atp*9 genes (shown in yellow). This distribution is substantially more apparent in comparison to that one developed in the 64-dimensional space of triplet frequencies [14]. The classification of genes obtained with K-means is rather weakly stable: for $K = 3$ the level of stability is very low (about 0.50), for $K = 4$ the stability level increases to 0.78.

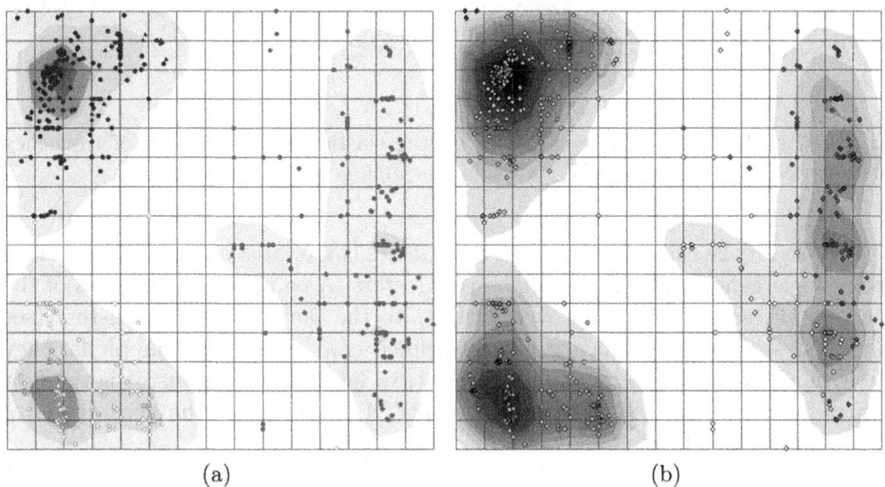

Fig. 1. The distribution of *atp* genes over elastic map: *atp*6 is in blue, *atp*8 is in red and *atp*9 is in yellow (left). Right is the same distribution with K-means classification, 4 classes. (Color figure online)

2.1 Taxonomy vs. Function: The Case of a Single Gene

Previously, all three ATP genes of 223 mitochondrial genomes of fungi were considered. Now we analyze the distribution of genes converted to $W_{(3,1)}$ and $W_{(3,3)}$ dictionaries, separately. It means that the distribution has been studied for genes *atp*6, *atp*8 and *atp*9 individually. In other words, previously a prevalence of function (i. e. the type of a gene from the ATP synthase family) over taxonomy for the gene family was found [14]. Now we aim to examine what is the effect of taxonomy, if one analyzes the single type of genes (say, *atp*6, only).

An analysis of the data presented in Figs. 2 and 3 shows that for the case of clustering by triplet frequencies for one gene only (regardless the specific gene) the distribution is close to homogeneous.

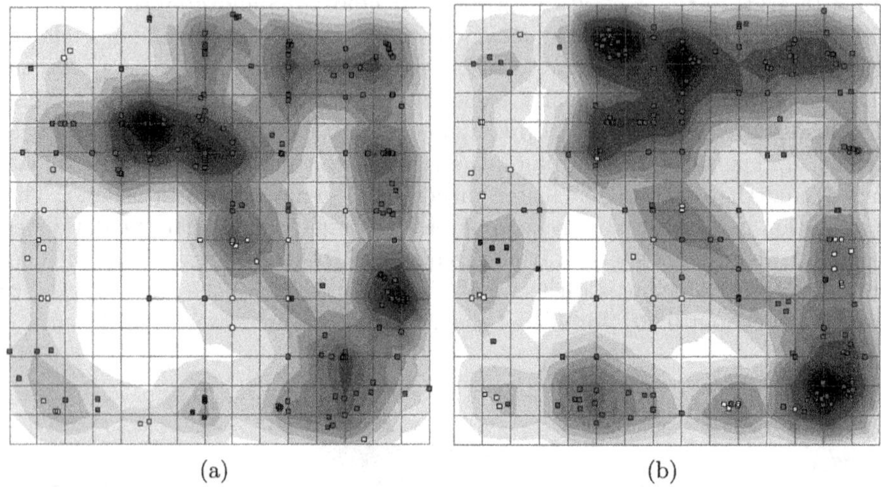

Fig. 2. Distribution of different entries on the elastic map on the set of frequency dictionaries $W_{(3,1)}$ (left) and $W_{(3,3)}$ (right) for *atp*6 genes.

Unlike for the case of analysis all three genes (*atp*6, *atp*8 and *atp*9), clustering for a single gene yields larger number of clusters. A comparative analysis of the clusters (Figs. 1, 2 and 3) proves it. Despite the fact that these clusters (see Figs. 1, 2 and 3) do not have a clearly defined connection with the phyla, they show more expressed connection to lower taxa level. If it happens, it is the first contradiction to the results reported earlier [4,6]. However, the verification of this hypothesis is beyond the scope of this article.

3 Discussion

Here we present further studies of the interplay of three basic genetic entities (these are *structure*, *function* and *taxonomy*) started by paper [14]. First of all, the reduction of the dimension space due to biological issues improves the clustering, both by elastic map, and K-means. The reduction has been achieved through the conversion of the triplet nucleotide frequencies into the frequencies of corresponding amino acids. Such transformation improved the clustering patter.

Obviously, this improvement of the pattern seems quite natural: the space dimension is three times less for amino acids, in comparison to nucleotides. One might expect some destroy of the pattern due to the growth of specific entropy

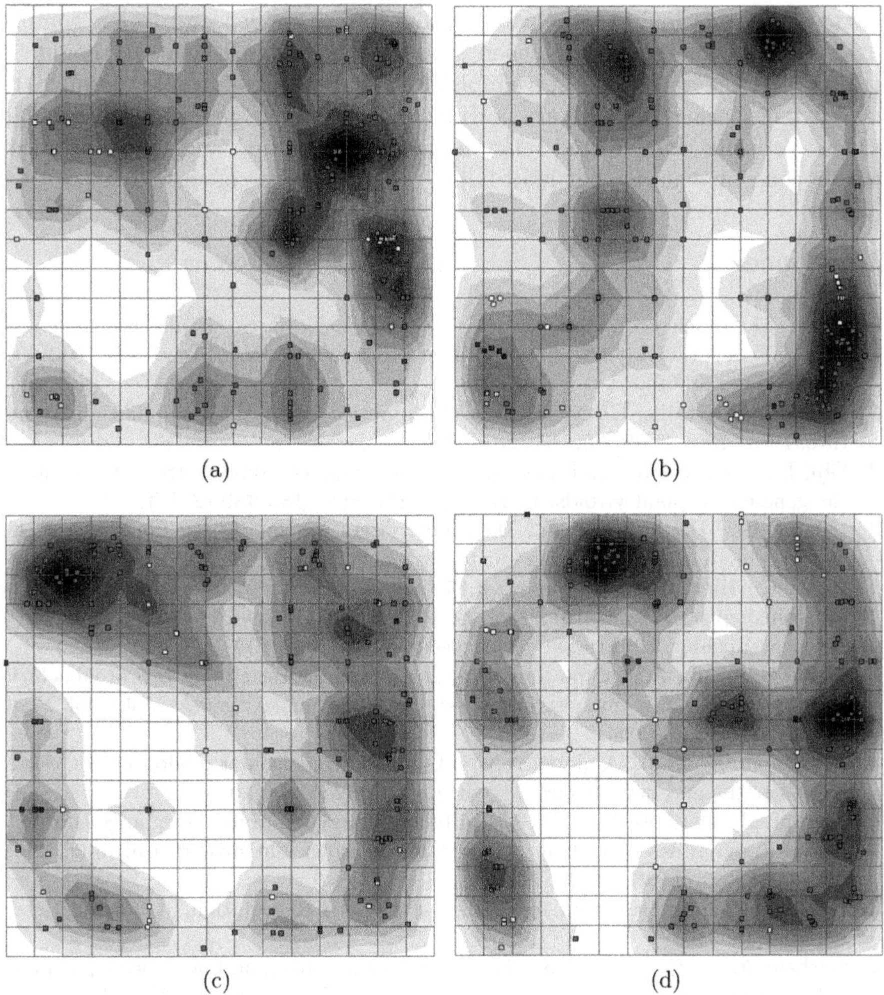

Fig. 3. Distribution of genes *atp*8 (above) and genes *atp*9 (below) over the elastic map, for $W_{(3,1)}$ (left) and $W_{(3,3)}$ (right).

per symbol determined for nucleotides, in comparison to that latter determined for amino acids. Meanwhile, such growth, if any, does not affect the pattern.

Figure 1 shows the distribution of three different (while closely related) genes for *atp* family; function takes evident advantage over the taxonomy. Obviously, this pattern is provided by the simultaneous analysis of three types of genes; hence, one might want to check what happens, if a single gene is taken into consideration. Figures 2 and 3 answer this question.

It should be said that the species composition in the database is rather biased: there are 182 organisms in one division, and only 2 ones at the other. Thus, the multicluster pattern seen in Figs. 2 and 3 might result from this discrepancy.

Furthermore, this multicluster pattern might be an evidence of rather complicated interplay of the species when studied over a single gene. It should be stressed that the patterns observed for all three different *atp* genes resemble, to some extent, each other, but are not identical. This divergence may also be an evidence of some complicated relations between structure and taxonomy. Yet, more specific analysis of that issue falls beyond the scope of this paper.

References

1. Molla, M., Delcher, A., Sunyaev, S., Cantor, C., Kasif, S.: Triplet repeat length bias and variation in the human transcriptome. Proc. Nat. Acad. Sci. **106**(40), 17095–17100 (2009)
2. Provata, A., Nicolis, C., Nicolis, G.: DNA viewed as an out-of-equilibrium structure. Phys. Rev. E **89**, 052105 (2014)
3. Qin, L., et al.: Survey and analysis of simple sequence repeats (SSRs) present in the genomes of plant viroids. FEBS Open Bio **4**(1), 185–189 (2014)
4. Moghaddasi, H., Khalifeh, K., Darooneh, A.H.: Distinguishing functional DNA words; a method for measuring clustering levels. Sci. Rep. **7**, 41543 (2017)
5. Bank, C., Hietpas, R.T., Jensen, J.D., Bolon, D.N.: A systematic survey of an intragenic epistatic landscape. Mol. Biol. Evol. **32**(1), 229–238 (2015)
6. Albrecht-Buehler, G.: Fractal genome sequences. Gene **498**(1), 20–27 (2012)
7. Esser, C., et al.: A genome phylogeny for mitochondria among α-proteobacteria and a predominantly eubacterial ancestry of yeast nuclear genes. Mol. Biol. Evol. **21**(9), 1643–1660 (2004)
8. Davoodian, N., et al.: A global view of Gyroporus: molecular phylogenetics, diversity patterns, and new species. Mycologia **110**, 985–995 (2018)
9. Nadimi, M., Daubois, L., Hijri, M.: Mitochondrial comparative genomics and phylogenetic signal assessment of mtDNA among arbuscular mycorrhizal fungi. Mol. Phylogenet. Evol. **98**, 74–83 (2016)
10. Fukunaga, K.: Introduction to Statistical Pattern Recognition. Academic Press, London (1990)
11. Gorban, A.N., Zinovyev, A.Y.: Fast and user-friendly non-linear principal manifold learning by method of elastic maps. In: IEEE International Conference on Data Science and Advanced Analytics, DSAA 2015, Campus des Cordeliers, Paris, France, 19–21 October 2015, pp. 1–9 (2015)
12. Gorban, A.N., Zinovyev, A.: Principal manifolds and graphs in practice: from molecular biology to dynamical systems. Int. J. Neural Syst. **20**(03), 219–232 (2010). PMID: 20556849
13. Gorban, A.N., Kégl, B., Wünsch, D., Zinovyev, A.Y. (eds.): Principal manifolds for Data Visualisation and Dimension Reduction. Lecture Notes in Computational Science and Engineering, vol. 58, 2nd edn, pp. 153–176. Springer, Heidelberg (2007). https://doi.org/10.1007/978-3-540-73750-6
14. Sadovsky, M., Fedotovskaya, V., Kolesnikova, A., Shpagina, T., Putintseva, Y.: Function vs. taxonomy: the case of fungi mitochondria ATP synthase genes. In: Rojas, I., Valenzuela, O., Rojas, F., Ortuño, F. (eds.) IWBBIO 2019. LNCS, vol. 11465, pp. 335–345. Springer, Cham (2019). https://doi.org/10.1007/978-3-030-17938-0_30

Discovering the Most Characteristic Motif from a Set of Peak Sequences

Ginés Almagro-Hernández[1,2(✉)] and Jesualdo Tomás Fernández-Breis[1,2(✉)]

[1] Department of Informatics and Systems, Faculty of Computer Science Campus de Espinardo, University of Murcia, 30100 Murcia, Spain
{gines.almagro,jfernand}@um.es

[2] Murcian Bio-Health Institute (IMIB-Arrixaca), Campus de Ciencias de la Salud, 30120 Murcia, Spain

Abstract. Chromatin immunoprecipitation experiments and the subsequent sequencing of these fragments (ChIP-Seq) are subject to great uncertainty, due to execution errors, technical and calculation limitations and the inherent complexity of the biological systems to be studied. Therefore, one of the challenges that researchers face when analyzing the results of ChIP-Seq experiments is to elucidate the pattern behind the obtained sequences (peaks), facing a huge amount of data and noise. A significant amount of statistical tools and algorithms have been proposed to solve this issue in the last years. The method presented in this paper innovates by taking advantage of both the structure of the data obtained in these experiments (peaks) and the existing resources. The motif or pattern obtained by this procedure from these peaks is considered the most characteristic motif. This method also allows to obtain the quality metrics of the analyzed experiment. The method has been validated with data retrieved from public repositories.

Keywords: ChIP-Seq experiment · Motif · Peaks sequences

1 Introduction

The field of computational genomics exists to improve knowledge in the areas of genomics and genetics, through the integration of information obtained from a series of families of experiments based on next-generation sequencing technology (NGS), such as DNA-seq for sequencing *de novo* genomes or identifying variants in the sequence of known genomes or RNA-seq to determine expression levels of different transcripts, or ChIP-Seq. ChIP-Seq [1] experiments identify regions of the genome that interact specifically with certain individual proteins or protein

This work has been funded by the Spanish Ministry of Economy, Industry and Competitiveness, the European Regional Development Fund (ERDF) Programme through grant TIN2017-85949-C2-1-R and by the Spanish Ministry of Education, Culture and Sports through fellowship FPU014/06303.

I. Rojas et al. (Eds.): IWBBIO 2020, LNBI 12108, pp. 445–456, 2020.
https://doi.org/10.1007/978-3-030-45385-5_40

complexes, in order to regulate the proper functioning of the cellular machinery as well as the structure and conformation of the genome within the cell nucleus.

In this work, we focus on the type of experiments called ChIP-Seq, which consist of a first phase of immunoprecipitation of chromatin fragments followed by a phase of sequencing these fragments. This type of experiments is carried out for a certain protein, called the target protein (TP), in a certain cell line or biological tissue, subject to a specific biological condition. The main steps of ChIP-Seq experiments are: (i) Cross-linking between TP and DNA molecule; (ii) Cell lysis to release the DNA molecules; (iii) Sonicate the chromatin, since the TP protects the sites to which it is attached; (iv) Inmunoprecipitate of TP-DNA complexes using antibody against that TP; (v) Reverse-crosslink to dissociate the TP-DNA complex and further purify the double-stranded DNA fragments; (vi) Sequence the ends of the two strands of the DNA fragments (reads); (vii) Align sequenced reads to reference genome (mapped step); (viii) Peak calling. At this point in the experiment, a set of regions with length ranging between 150 and 1500 bp is obtained, called peaks. The binding between the TP and the DNA molecule that makes up the genome of the cell line under study is expected to happen in these regions; (ix) Functional analyses or peak annotation, which aims at assigning a biological meaning to each individual peak, thus inferring the role of the TP in specific biological conditions; (x) Motif discovery, that is, identification of the model of the sequence or pattern of sequences (with small variations) to which the TP binds. It is important to note that each of these stages has uncertainty associated with potential execution errors, technical limitations, limitations of the algorithms used, or the complexity of the biological systems studied.

Defining the characteristic motif of the target protein from the peaks obtained generally consists of finding a series of sequences, ranging from 5 to 20 nucleotides, that are very similar to each other and which are present in most of these peaks, and which are statistically more enriched in the peaks than in the set of sequences known as background, whose composition and distribution of nucleotides is similar to the genome of the cell line under study.

This process faces the following challenges: (i) there is a large amount of noise because the length of the binding site is shorter than the length of the peak; (ii) the sequence recognized by the TP usually has small variations; (iii) motifs recognized by other proteins may co-localize with the motif of interest; (iv) the experiments may have artefacts, so not all the peaks include the motif of interest; and (v) the different algorithms and tools usually produce different results for the same set of peaks.

In this work, the above mentioned challenges are addressed by a reproducible, reliable method which standardizes the process of obtaining the most representative motif from a set of peaks. We have validated this procedure using the peaks corresponding to the GSE36354 [2] experiment collected from the Remap 2018 v1.2 database [3].

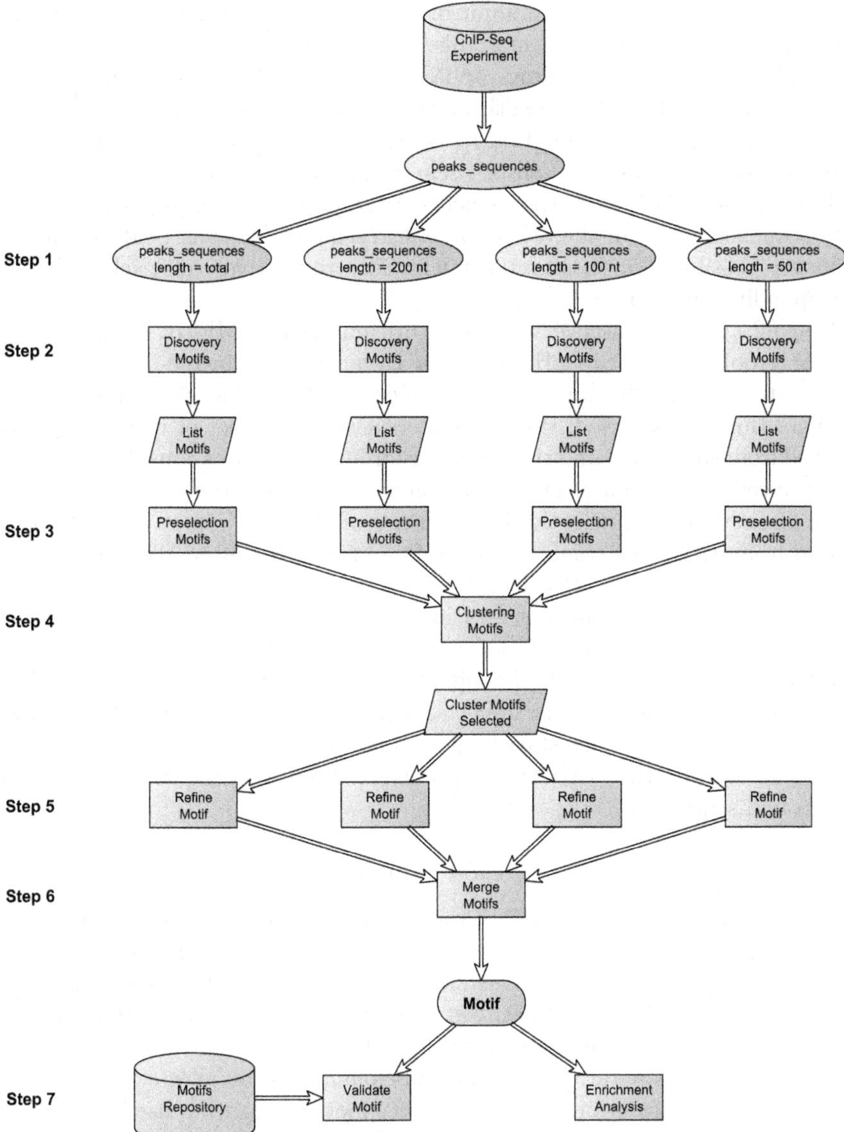

Fig. 1. Overview of the pipeline, whose stages are marked

2 Methods

Our method consists of several stages (see Fig. 1). We start from a file, usually in BED format (https://genome.ucsc.edu/FAQ/), where the start, end and summit coordinates of every peak obtained in a given ChiP-Seq experiment are shown.

Stage 1 assumes that the summit of each peak is the site where the binding site between PT and DNA is most likely to occur according to the read mapping and peak calling algorithms applied. For each peak we do four independent searches, one on the whole length of the sequence and the other three using different window sizes centered on its corresponding peak. In this way, we generate four sets of sequences, all of them containing the summit of each initial peak. In the set called *Raw*, the sequence corresponding to each peak is its complete sequence, while in the other three, the sequence of each peaks comprises, whenever possible, 25, 50 and 100 nucleotides respectively on each side of its corresponding summit.

Stage 2 applies a discovery motif algorithm such as MEME (http://meme-suite.org/tools/meme-chip), Homer [5] or Dreme (http://meme-suite.org/tools/dreme), to each of the four sets of sequences. Note that you must indicate the algorithm or tool used, the parameters setting, the set of target sequences (derived from the peaks) and the set of background sequences considered (derived from the cell line genome). Depending on the algorithm, the latter can be used either directly or the nucleotides frequencies of order "n" (first, second,...) calculated from it. At this stage, we generally obtain a list of possible motifs, with more or less information attached.

Stage 3 is optional and consists in making a pre-analysis and filtering of motifs to reduce the potential noise. We propose to use a metric (see Eq. 1) that takes into account both the significance of the motif obtained (*p_value*) and the number of hits in the target sequences (*num.hits.target*). In this case, the *p_value* represents the statistical significance of the enrichment analysis, taking into account the histograms obtained for the target sequences and for the background sequences.

$$score = -log(p\_value) * log(num.hits.target) \quad (1)$$

Stage 4 consists in clustering all the pre-selected motifs belonging to all the sets. This stage is the first time where the data previously obtained separately are integrated. Later, we select the cluster that fulfills the two following conditions: (i) it contains one element of each set of sequences (raw, 25, 50, 100); and (ii) the distance between all its members is the shortest.

Stage 5 refines separately every motif belonging to the selected cluster. Normally, during the execution of the "discovery motif" algorithm used in the stage 2, the search area is restricted due to the presence of more than one possible motif. Now we scan the motif obtained in stage 2 on the target sequences of the corresponding set, after setting a threshold to consider positive a match. The sequences matching the motif that exceed the established threshold are used to generate the new refined motif. Enrichment analysis is applied for this new motif with the corresponding set of target and background sequences used in stage 2.

Stage 6 generates a compendium motif from the four already refined motifs belonging to each of the sets. To do this, first the four motifs have to be aligned, since their lengths are likely to be different. Then the probability of each base is calculated for each position. In this stage it is necessary to configure both the algorithm of alignment between the motifs and the method to calculate this probability. We propose using the arithmetic mean or the weighted mean according to the metric defined in Eq. 1. An optional trimming step can be performed, to eliminate positions with a very low amount of information content. Finally, we carry out an enrichment analysis using the number of hits in both the whole sequences target (set Raw) and the background sequences set. The merged motif obtained is considered to be the characteristic motif of the set of peaks.

Stage 7 evaluates the characteristic motif obtained. On one hand, we conducted a search for similar motifs in repositories such as Jaspar [9], Hocomoco (http://hocomoco11.autosome.ru/), etc. In case a protein already has a defined motif, this stage serves to validate the characteristic motif. Otherwise the function of the protein can be inferred by identifying similar motifs. On the other hand, when we have more than one sample for the same TP and cell line, replica or not, we make a clustering, represented by a heatmap, to observe if the characteristic motifs of each sample are more similar to each other than to the rest of refined motifs. And if so, to determine the height of that cluster as a measure of similarity between the motifs that constitute it.

3 Results

3.1 The Use Case

Remap 2018 v1.2 [3] is a catalogue of 2829 ChIP-Seq experiments on real biological data from ENCODE (https://www.encodeproject.org) and the public sources GEO (https://www.ncbi.nlm.nih.gov/geo) and ArrayExpress (https://www.ebi.ac.uk/arrayexpress). Such experiments have been subjected to a high quality filtering process according to four different metrics based on ENCODE ChIP-seq guidelines. From this database we downloaded the file in BED format with the peaks corresponding to the study GSE36354, which consists of three experiments in three different conditions. Those experiments study the behaviour of the protein MYC in the P4936 cell line under three different conditions of protein concentration. The experiments according to the increase in concentration are CMCY_0H, CMCY_1H y CMYC_24H respectively.

MYC is an active oncogene in numerous types of cancer, whose protein product forms a heterodimer with the transcription factor MAX. This complex binds to the DNA consensus sequence E-box. Under normal conditions its expression is induced by growth factor signalling, which is thought to induce expression of genes involved in cellular proliferation. Cell line **P493-6** (RRID:CVCL_6783) is a Human Burkitt's lymphoma cell line transfected with a tetracycline (Tet)-repressible MYC transgenes through a Epstein-Barr virus (EBV) transformant system. This cell line expressed high levels of MYC (WT).

3.2 Use Case Results

Stage 1. As a set of background sequences, we obtain a random sample of sequences corresponding to the human reference genome GRCh38.p13 from Ensembl [4] release 99 database. This sample is representative of all types of sequences with different biological roles, such as promoter regions, exons, introns, etc. From the peaks file for each biological condition, we use the Ensembl API to obtain the four sets of sequences detailed in the previous section (50, 100, 200 and Raw). For the conditions CMYC_OH, CMYC_1H and CMYC_24H we collect a dataset of 3936, 7256 and 5933 peaks respectively.

Stage 2. We use Homer [5] for the motif discovery stage, which implements a differential algorithm that uses ZOOPS scoring (zero or one occurrence per sequence) coupled with the hypergeometric enrichment calculations to determine motif enrichment. That is, taking the target and the background sets of sequences, it tries to identify the motifs that are specifically enriched in the target set with respect to the background set. We have executed the *findMotifs.pl* script in Perl with the default parameters except for: (i) "*human*" to compare each motif discovered with those existing in several databases corresponding only to humans. (ii) "*-fastaBg*" where the background sequence file is indicated in FASTA format. (iii) "*-len 8,10,12*" indicating the width of the motifs to be searched. For the biological condition CMYC_OH 6, 11, 18 and 29 motifs are obtained for the sets 50, 100, 200 and Raw respectively. In the case of CMYC_1H we obtained 4, 11, 25 and 37 motifs, and for CMCY_24H 8, 9, 34 and 31 motifs were obtained.

Stage 3. The motifs obtained in the previous stage are ordered according to the metric of the Eq. 1. Initially we select for each set of sequences the three motifs with the highest score (see Fig. 2). If in the following stage we do not obtain a cluster, we take from each set one by one the next motif in the corresponding ordered list and repeat this process until a cluster meets the selection conditions.

Stage 4. We use the package "*Universalmotif*" v1.4.6 [6] from the Bioconductor repository, which contains different functionalities for the manipulation of motifs with the R language. More concretely, we use the function "*compare_motifs*" with the parameters: (i) "*use.type = ICM*". This package does pairwise alignments of the motifs pre-selected in the previous stage by using the information contained matrix (ICM) of each motif. (ii) "*method = PCC*", to generate an alignment score matrix using the Pearson correlation coefficient (PCC) metric. (iii) "*tryRC = F*", which prevents the use of the reverse and complementary sequence for the alignment.

This alignment score matrix is used to perform a hierarchical cluster analysis with the R package "*ggheatmap* [7]", that implements from the R package "*stats*" [8] the functions "*hclust = ward.D2*" with the agglomeration method that implements Ward's clustering criterion selection and "*dist = euclidean*" to compute the distance matrix with the measure "euclidean" used in the generation of the dendrogram. Finally, for each biological condition we select the cluster according to the two conditions exposed above. For CMYC_0H we select

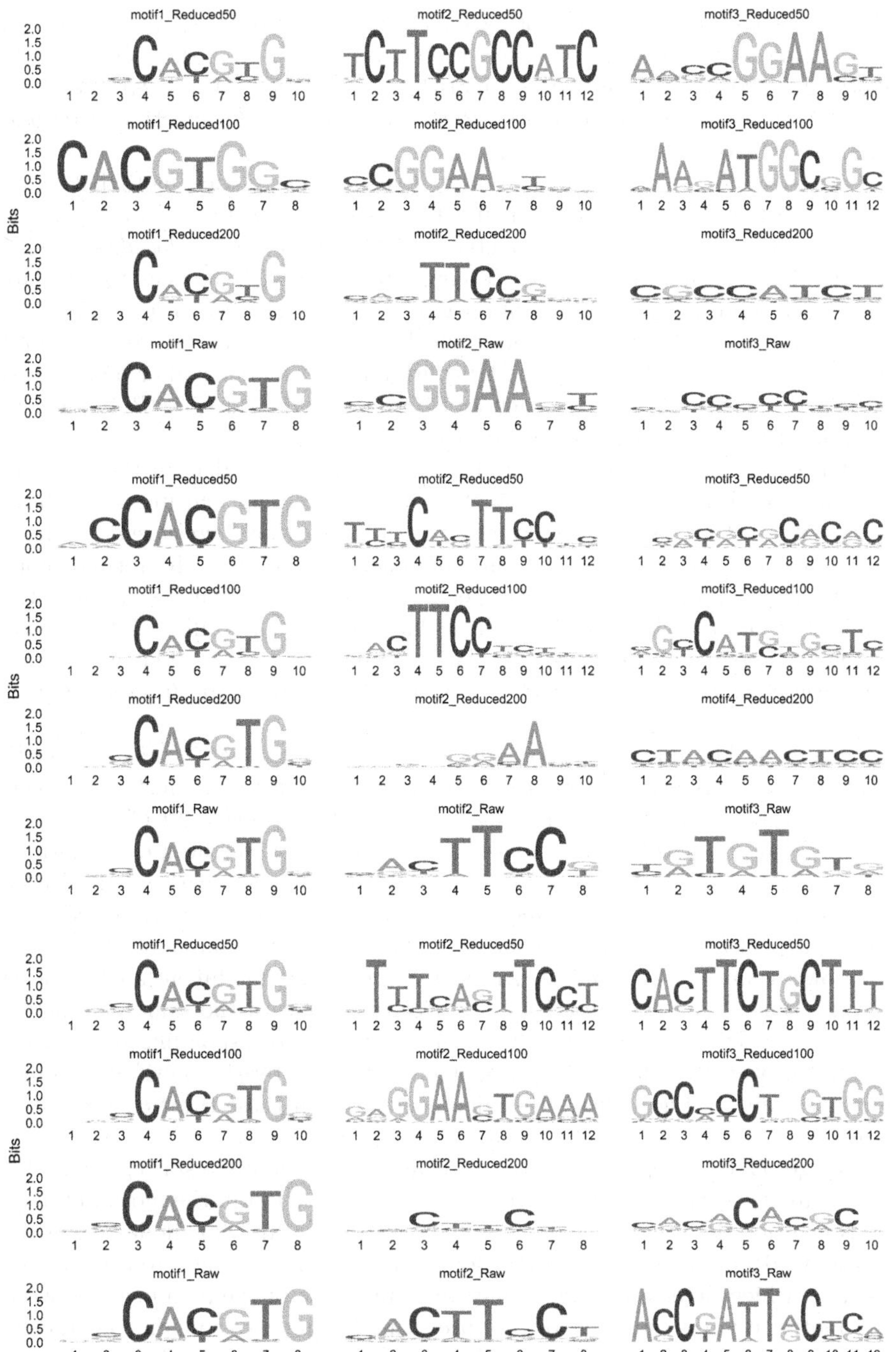

Fig. 2. Sequences logo for the three motifs with the highest score selected for each set of each biological condition. The first four rows correspond to CMCY_0H. The next four rows correspond to CMYC_1H and the last four rows correspond to CMYC_24H.

the cluster composed of the motif1_Rec50, motif1_Rec100, motif1_Rec200 and motif1_Raw. For CMYC_1H we select the cluster composed of the motif1_Rec50, motif1_Rec100, motif1_Rec200 and motif1_Raw. And for CMYC_24H we select the cluster composed of the motif1_Rec50, motif1_Rec100, motif1_Rec200 and motif1_Raw (see Fig. 3).

Stage 5. We scan the set of target sequences using each motif belonging to the selected cluster, through the function "*scan_sequences*" from the package "*Universalmotif*", with the parameters: (i) "*threshold.type = logodds*", which uses the log of each probability correcting for background frequencies to calculate the match score between the position weight matrix (PWM) of the motif and a sequence; (ii) "*threshold = 0.80*", which is applied to the score of a motif according to its PWM, so only the hits with a match score equal or higher than 80% of the maximum score of each motif are selected; and (iii) "*RC = T*", to scan also the complementary and reverse sequence.

Then, the sequences corresponding to the hits obtained from the scan are used for creating the new refined motif with the function "*create_motif*" from the package "*Universalmotif*". Finally with the function "*enrich_motifs*" from this same package, we carry out an enrichment analysis for the refined motif against the same sequences of the peaks. This is to get the *p_value* and the number of hits match to be able to calculate the score according to the metric of the Eq. 1 to use in further stages. The parameters used in the latter function are "*qval.method = BH*", "*RC = T*", "*threshold = 0.80*" and "*threshold.type = logodds*".

Stage 6. The function "*merge_motifs*" from the package "*Universalmotif*" is applied to merge the four motifs that make up the selected cluster for a certain biological condition. The parameters used are "*method = PCC*", "*use.type = PPM*" and "*tryRC = F*". In this case, we have not weighted each motif as a function of the metric in the Eq. 1. This function simply averages the PPMs according to the alignment obtained. Later, with the function "*trim_motifs*" from the same package, we trim the columns (positions) with an amount of information lower than 0.25 bits. Subsequently, we perform an enrichment analysis with the functions "*scan_sequences*" and "*enrich_motifs*" with the same parameters setting as in the stage 5, but only on the sequences corresponding to the Raw set. In this way, we achieve the considered most characteristic motif of each biological condition. Fig. 4 shows the alignment between these three characteristic motifs.

Stage 7. In order to validate the characteristic motif resulting from this procedure, we carry out a search for the characteristic motif, the motif obtained by Homer for the Raw set and the refined motif derived from the latter, in the Jaspar v2010 database [9] with the Stamp [10] toolkit. Taking into account the E-value, which determines the statistical significance of the alignment between two motifs, it turns out that for the three samples the corresponding characteristic motif is more similar to the MYC protein motif stored in this repository (MA0147.1_Myc), than the other two motifs, Raw and refined Raw. Finally, we performed a clustering between the twelve refined motifs (four from each

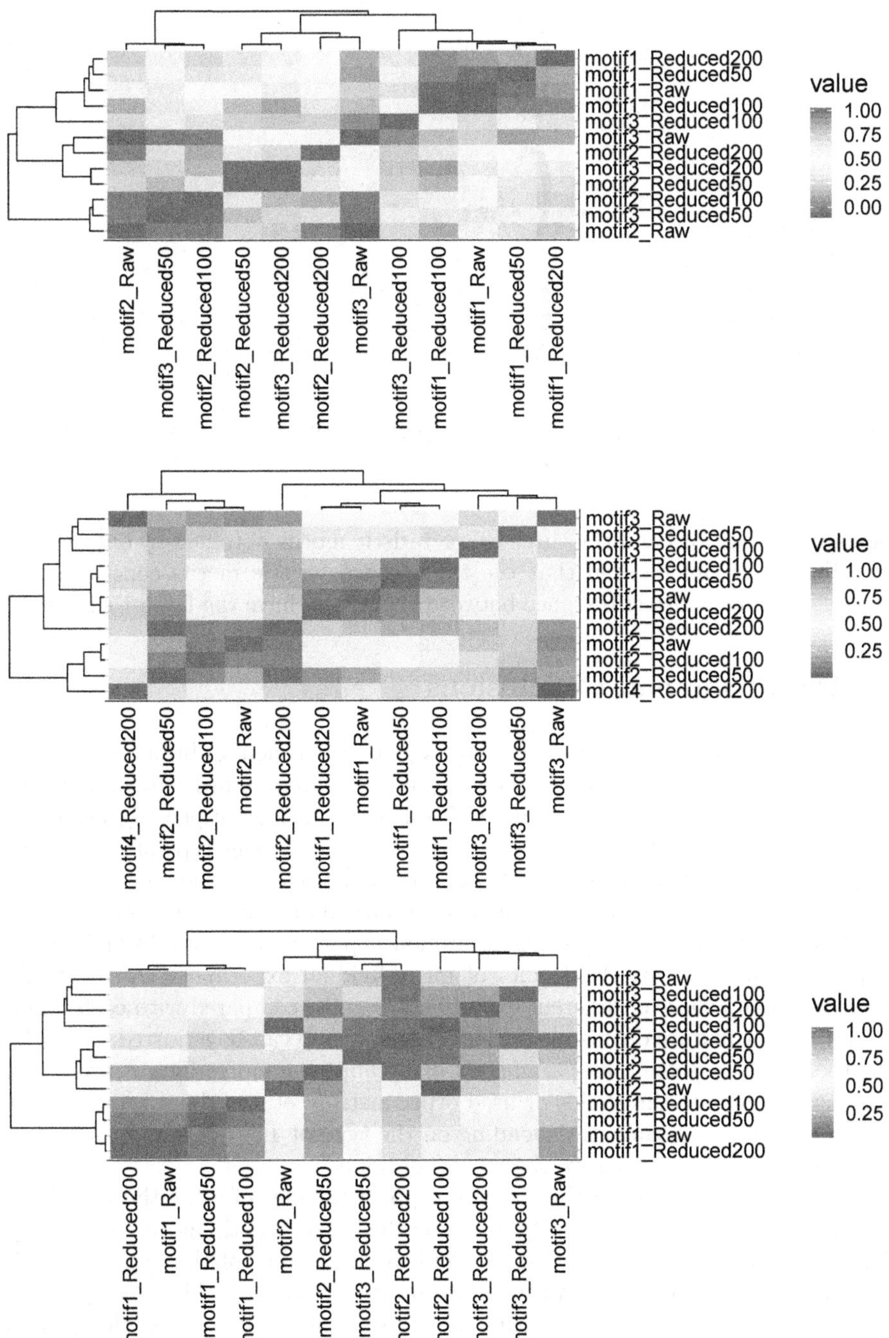

Fig. 3. Heatmaps and dendrograms for the twelve motifs selected for each biological condition. The first one corresponds to CMCY_0H. The next one corresponds to CMYC_1H and the last corresponds to CMYC_24H.

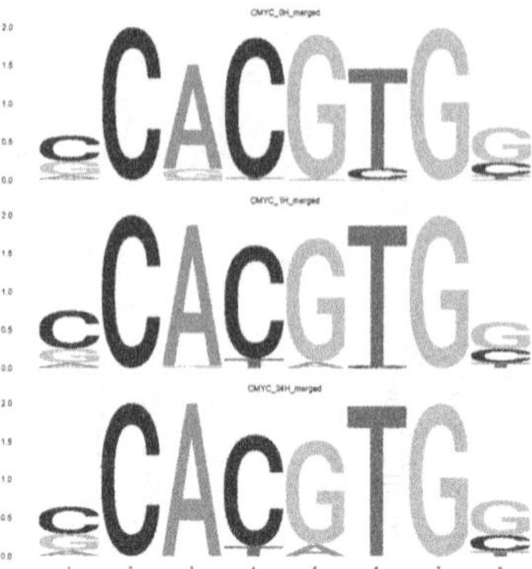

Fig. 4. Alignment between the most characteristic motifs for each biological condition

biological condition) and the three characteristic motifs obtained by our method (see Fig. 5). It can be seen that the three characteristic motifs constitute the cluster with the shortest distance between them, and have the largest similarity.

4 Discussion and Conclusions

We have worked directly with data from real experiments obtained from the Remap database. We have chosen a well-studied protein in order to validate the results obtained. These are in line with our expectations, especially given the large amount of uncertainty involved in the execution of this type of experiment and the subsequent processing and analysis of the results. The contribution of this work consists in the design of a procedure that standardizes the process of obtaining the most characteristic sequence pattern or motif from a set of sequences. In this way, the results of an individual experiment can be easily reproduced and those of different experiments can be compared with each other. An important feature of this method is that each step can be adjusted, either by the tool used, by setting its parameters or by applying more efficient processes, such as to calculate thresholds or used other metrics, etc, to the specific characteristics of each experiment, depending on the type of TP, cell line or biological condition, in order to improve the results obtained.

The results obtained for the use case support the idea of using the summit of the peaks obtained as a reference to define the characteristic motif (see Fig. 3). This criterion could also be used as proof of the quality of the experiment. If no cluster meets the two conditions set in step 4, this would be a sign that the peaks do not accurately capture the true binding site between the protein and the DNA. The height at which the first cluster is achieved could also be considered a measure of quality, since the lower the height is, the higher the accuracy is. In this case study, in the three biological conditions, the 4 motifs that make up the selected cluster correspond to the most significant motif of

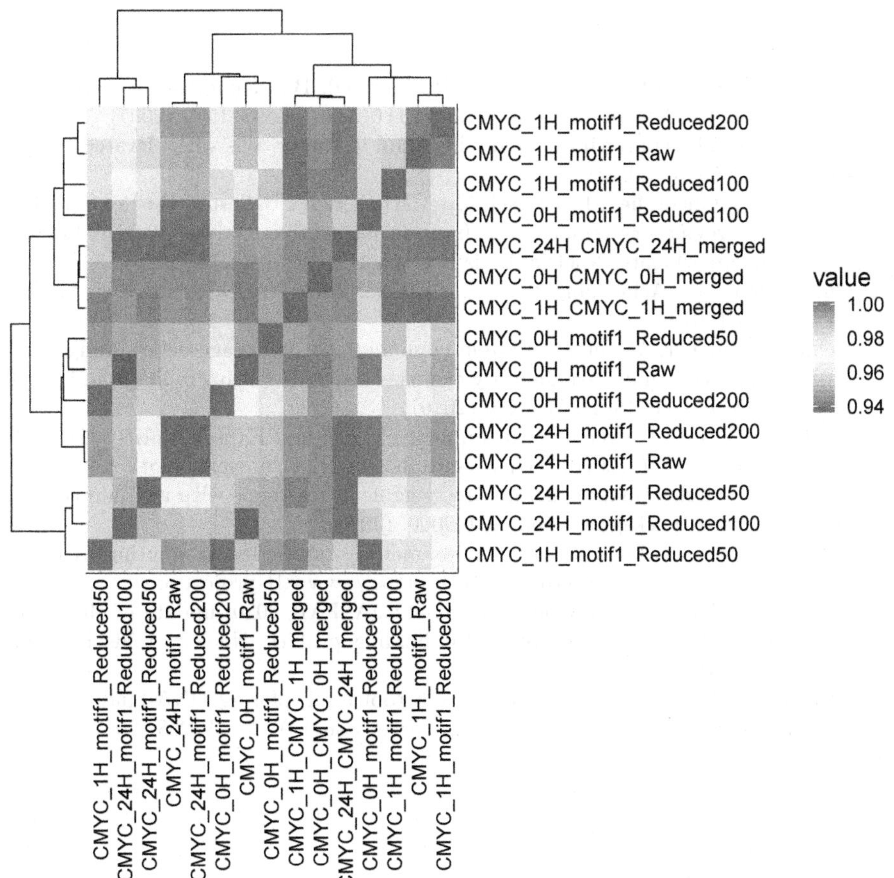

Fig. 5. Heatmap and dendrogram corresponding to the 12 refined motifs (4 for each bio-condition) and the three characteristic motifs derived from them

each set discovered by the Homer tool in stage two. In CMYC_1H there is a second cluster, but it presents a larger distance than the one selected.

There are subtle differences between the three characteristic motifs of each biological condition (see Fig. 4), mainly because when there is a low concentration of MYC protein, it chooses the sites for which it has the highest affinity, while when there is a higher concentration, sites with a lower affinity are also chosen, which generates small variations in the recognized sequence with respect to those of higher affinity.

Data Availability. The data generated in this work is available at https://github.com/gines-almagro/ChIP-Seq-motif.

References

1. Johnson, D.S., Mortazavi, A., Myers, R.M., Wold, B.: Genome-wide mapping of in vivo protein-DNA interactions. Science **316**(5830), 1497–1502 (2007)
2. Lin, C.Y., et al.: Transcriptional amplification in tumor cells with elevated c-Myc. Cell **1**(151), 56–67 (2012)
3. Cheneby, J., Gheorghe, M., Artufel, M., Mathelier, A., Ballester, B.: ReMap 2018: an updated regulatory regions atlas from an integrative analysis of DNA-binding ChIP-Seq experiments. Nucleic Acids Res. **46**(DI), D267–D275 (2018)
4. Cunningham, F., Achuthan, P., et al.: Ensembl 2019. Nucleic Acids Res. **47**(DI), D745–D751 (2019)
5. Heinz, S., Benner, C., et al.: Simple combinations of lineage-determining transcription factors prime cis-regulatory elements required for macrophage and B cell identities. Mol. Cell **38**(4), 576–589 (2010)
6. Tremblay, B.J.M.: Universalmotif: Import, Modify, and Export Motifs with R. R package version 1.4.6 (2020). https://github.com/bjmt/universalmotif
7. Leonardi, T.: ggheatmap: generate pretty ggplot2 heatmaps with row and column dendrograms. R package version 0.0.0.9000. (2020)
8. R Core Team: R: a language and environment for statistical computing. R Foundation for Statistical Computing (2019). https://www.R-project.org/
9. Fornés, O., Castro-Mondragon, J.A., et al.: JASPAR 2020: update of the open-access database of transcription factor binding profiles. Nucleic Acids Res. **48**, D87–D92 (2019)
10. Mahony, S., Benos, P.V.: STAMP: a web tool for exploring DNA-binding motif similarities. Nucleic Acids Res. **35**(Web Server issue), W253–W258 (2007)

An Overview of Search and Match Algorithms Complexity and Performance

Maryam Abbasi[1] and Pedro Martins[2(✉)]

[1] Department of Computer Sciences, University of Coimbra, Coimbra, Portugal
maryam@dei.uc.pt

[2] Department of Computer Sciences, Polytechnic Institute of Viseu, Viseu, Portugal
pedromom@estgv.ipv.pt

Abstract. DNA data provide us a considerable amount of information regarding our biological data, necessary to study ourselves and learn about variant characteristics. Even being able to extract the DNA from cells and sequence it, there is a long way to process it in one step.

Over past years, biologists evolved attempting to "decipher" the DNA code. Keyword search and string matching algorithms play a vital role in computational biology. Relationships between sequences define the biological functional and structural of the biological sequences. Finding such similarities is a challenging research area, comprehending BigData, that can bring a better understanding of the evolutionary and genetic relationships among the genes. This paper studied and analyzed different kinds of string matching algorithms used for biological sequencing, and their complexity and performance are assessed.

Keywords: DNA · Patterns · Genome assembly · Graph · BigData · Assemblers · Algorithms · Matching algorithms · Keyword search · DNA sequence · Distance measurements

1 Introduction

Keyword search and matching are techniques to discover patterns inside specific strings. Algorithms for matching, are used to discover matches between patterns and input strings. For instance, V represents an alphabet; in V there are characters or symbols. Assuming, $V = \{A, G\}$, then $AAGAG$ is a string. Patterns are labeled by $P(1...M)$, while the string is labeled as $T(1...N)$. Pattern can occur inside a string by using a shifting operation.

Text-editing applications can also benefit from the aid of string matching algorithms, aiding and improving responsiveness while writing. There are two main approaches for string matching, first is exact matching, for instance: Smith-Waterman (SW); Needleman Wunsch (NW); Boyer Moore Horspool (BMH); Dynamic Programming; Knuth Morris Pratt (KMP). Second approach, is approximate matching, also known by Fuzzy string searching, for instance: Rabin Karp; Brute Force.

I. Rojas et al. (Eds.): IWBBIO 2020, LNBI 12108, pp. 457–471, 2020.
https://doi.org/10.1007/978-3-030-45385-5_41

Many algorithms try to give solutions for the string matching problems like, pattern matching using wide window, approximate matching, polymorphic matching, minimize mismatches, prefix/suffix matching, similarity measure, longest commons sub-sequence (using dynamic programming algorithms), BHM, Brute Force, KMP, Quick search, Rabin Karp (Singla and Garg 2012).

In this paper is analyzed the similarity measures on Protein, DNA and RNA, using for that effect, different types of string matching algorithms, like: NW algorithm, Boyer Moore (BM), SW algorithm, Hamming Distance, Levenshtein Distance, AhoCorasick (AC), KMP, Rabin Karp, and CommentZwalter (CZW).

This paper is organized as follows, Sect. 2, reviews the related work in the field, Sect. 3 compares selected algorithms in therms of complexity. Section 4, presents experimental results comparing the different algorithms. Finally, Sect. 5, concludes the study and presents some future research lines.

2 Related Work

In pattern recognition problems it is essential to measure distance or similarity. Given the following example:

```
String  T:   A C C T C G A G T
                     | | |
Pattern P:   _ _ _ _ C G A _ _
```

Pattern P can be matched in String T by adding four empty spaces before the pattern and two after.

Authors in (Yeh and Cheng 2008), use Levenshtein distance applied to images and videos to determine feature vectors. For instance:

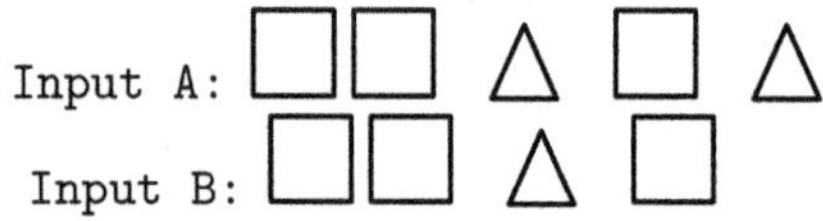

The objective is to find the maximum matches between Input A and B. By removing the last triangle in Input A the maximum match is reached.

In (Amir et al. 2004), the authors propose a new distance for string matching, similar to Levenshtein distance, with K-Mismatches on the given string. This proposed approach was implemented with Message Passing Interface (MPI), and proved to be useful to establish similarity between strings.

Authors in (Knuth et al. 1977), proposed an algorithm for pattern matching in strings, with running time proportional to the sum of the length of the strings. This traditional algorithm is now known as KMP string matching algorithm.

Other classical string pattern matching algorithm was proposed in (Hussain et al. 2013), named Bidirectional Exact Pattern Matching (BDEPM). This algorithm introduces the idea to compare strings using pointers in simultaneous, one from the left other from the right. For example:

```
String   T:  A C C T C G A G T
                     ↑|  |  |↑
Pattern P:   _ _ _ _ C G A _ _
```

In (Alsmadi and Nuser 2012), they evaluated two algorithms for DNA string comparison in terms of accuracy and performance. The Longest Common Substring (LCS) algorithm, and Longest Common Sub-Sequence (LCSS) algorithms. In the following example, the highlighted letters, CTCT, in the sequences is LCSS of the specified sequences.

```
String   T:  A C G T C G A G T
               |   | |       |
Pattern P:   _ C _ T C _ _ _ T
```

Different types of string matching algorithms are explored in (Singla and Garg 2012), concluding that for string matching, Boyer Moore algorithm is the best.

In (Pandey), authors test many algorithms for string pattern match. These algorithms are tested and compared based on multiple parameters, such as execution time, matching order, the number of comparisons, shift factor, and accuracy. Conclusions show that Boyer Moore algorithm is the more efficient when applied to a heterogeneous system for pattern matching.

Aho-Corasick and CommentZ-Walter algorithms (Vidanagamachchi et al. 2012) are two types of multiple patterns matching algorithms, authors in (Vidanagamachchi et al. 2012) implemented these two algorithms and worked with peptide sequences to study their accuracy and execution time. Results show that Aho-Corasick performs better than the CommentZ-Walter algorithm.

3 Algorithms Analysis

In this section, we analyze the proposed matching algorithms mentioned in Sect. 2 (Related work).

3.1 Hamming Distance

Hamming distance was introducing to measure, detect and correct codes in 1950. This distance can be applied to biological sequences. This algorithm measures the minimum number of substitutions required to transform one sequence into another.

Definition 1 *(Hamming Distance). Consider two sequences* $A = (a_1, \ldots, a_n)$ *and* $B = (b_1, \ldots, b_n)$ *with sizes n over an alphabet* Σ*. The Hamming distance between two sequences A and B is denoted by* $\delta_{ham}(A, B)$*.*

$$\delta_{ham}(A, B) = \sum_{i=1}^{n} s(\varphi_i) \tag{1}$$

where φ_i *is the pairing variable and* $s(\varphi_i)$ *is equal to 1 when* $a_i \neq b_i$*.*

From Eq. 1, it is possible to calculate the minimum number of substitutions required to transform one sequence into another. Hamming distance fundamentally assumes that the input sequence have the same length. We can generalize the hamming distance to allow for insertions and deletions and calculate the Levenshtein distance.

3.2 Levenshtein Distance

Levenshtein distance between two sequences is defined as the minimum number of substitutions required to transform one sequence into another. It allowed to compare sequences with different lengths, by considering the operations insertion, deletion and substituting characters.

Definition 2 *(Levenshtein Distance). Consider two sequences* $A = (a_1, \ldots, a_{n_1})$ *and* $B = (b_1, \ldots, b_{n_2})$ *over the alphabet* Σ. *The Levenshtein distance between two sequences A and B of length* n_1 *and* n_2*, respectively, is given by* $\delta_{lev}(n_1, n_2)$ *where*

$$\delta_{lev}(i,j) = \begin{cases} max(i,j) & \text{if } min(i,j) = 0, \\ \Delta(i,j) & \text{otherwise} \end{cases} \tag{2}$$

where

$$\Delta(i,j) = min \begin{cases} \delta_{lev}(i-1,j)+1 \\ \delta_{lev}(i,j-1+1 \\ \delta_{lev}(i-1,j-1)+s(a_i,b_j) \end{cases}$$

and $s(a_i, b_j) = 1$ *when* $a_i \neq b_j$ *and* 0 *otherwise. The first element in the minimum function corresponds to deletion from A to B, the second to insertion and the third to match or mismatch (substitution).*

For instance, assuming that the Levenshtein distance between "CCGTCG" and "CGGTTGA" is three, then it is not possible to transform one into the other with less than three edits:

1. C**G**GTTGA → C**C**GTTGA (replace 'C' for 'G');
2. CGGT**T**GA → CCGT**C**GA (replace 'T' for 'C');
3. CGGTTG**A** → CCGTCG~~**A**~~ (remove 'A' from the end).

3.3 Damerau–Levenshtein

Damerau–Levenshtein distance includes transpositions among operations, additionally to the three classical single-character operations (insertions, deletions and substitutions) (Levenshtein 1966; Bard 2007). Damerau–Levenshtein distance is also applied in biology to measure the variation between protein sequences (Majorek et al. 2014).

To express the Damerau–Levenshtein distance between two strings a and b a function $d_{a,b}(i,j)$ is defined, where the result is the distance between an i-symbol prefix (initial sub-string) of string a and a j–symbol prefix of b.

The restricted distance function is defined as follows in the equation:

$$d_{a,b}(i,j) = min \begin{cases} 0 & \text{if } i = j = 0, \\ d_{a,b}(i-1,j)+1 & \text{if } i > 0, \\ d_{a,b}(i,j-1)+1 & \text{if } j > 0, \\ d_{a,b}(i-1,j-1)+1_{(a_i \neq b_j)} & \text{if } i,j > 0, \\ d_{a,b}(i-2,j-2)+1 & \text{if } *, \end{cases} \tag{3}$$

$*\ i,j > 1$ and $a[i] = b[j-1]$ and $a[i-1] = b[j]$

Where $1_{(a_i \neq b_j)}$ is the indicator function equal to 0 when $a_i = b_j$ and equal to 1 otherwise.

Each recursive call matches one of the cases covered by the Damerau–Levenshtein distance:

- $d_{a,b}(i-1,j)+1$, corresponds to a deletion (from a to b);
- $d_{a,b}(i,j-1)+1$, corresponds to an insertion (from a to b);
- $d_{a,b}(i-1,j-1)+1_{(a_i \neq b_j)}$, corresponds to a match or mismatch, depending on whether the respective symbols are the same;
- $d_{a,b}(i-2,j-2)+1$, corresponds to a transposition between two successive symbols;

The Damerau–Levenshtein distance between a and b is then given by the function value for the full strings $d_{a,b}(|a|,|b|)$, where $i = |a|$ is the length of string a and $j = |b|$ is the length of b.

3.4 Needleman Wunsch Algorithm

The Needleman-Wunsch (NW) algorithm (Needleman and Wunsch 1970) is a Dynamic Programming (DP) algorithm that solves the problem of sequence alignment. It was one of the first applications of DP to compare biological sequences. To determine the degree of similarity (distance) between two sequences, an score function as given in Definition 3 is required.

Definition 3 *(Score of a pairwise alignment). Let $A = (a_1, \ldots, a_{n_1})$ and $B = (b_1, \ldots, b_{n_2})$ be two sequences over an alphabet Σ and "$-$" indicate the indel (insertion or deletion) character. Let $\varphi = (\varphi_1, \ldots, \varphi_\ell)$ be an alignment with length ℓ. For $a, b \in \Sigma$, let $s(\varphi_j)$ indicate the score of a pair such as $((a,-)$, $(-,b)$ or $(a,b))$ in the alignment, $1 \leq j \leq \ell$. let M be a substitution matrix for aligning two characters and d be the score for a pair that contains $(a,-)$ or $(-,b)$. The score function $\delta(\varphi)$ of the alignment φ is given by:*

$$\delta(\varphi) = \sum_{j=1}^{\ell} s(\varphi_j) \tag{4}$$

	0	1	2	3	4
	-	A	G	T	A
0 -	0	-2	-4	-6	-8
1 A	-2	↖1	←-1	-3	-5
2 T	-4	-1	0	↖0	-2
3 A	-6	-3	-2	-1	↖1

Fig. 1. Illustration of the DP matrix of the Needleman-Wunsch algorithm and the trace-back of the alignment (red arrows) (Color figure online)

where,

$$s(\varphi_j) = \begin{cases} M[a,b] & \text{if } \varphi_j = (a,b), \\ d & \text{otherwise} \end{cases} \quad (5)$$

Therefore, for finding the optimal alignment between two sequences, the maximum score of this function is needed to compute and the alignment that yields it. The working principle for solving the sequence alignment problem with DP is to compute the optimal alignment for all pairs of prefixes of the given sequences. The DP algorithm consists of four parts: (i) a recursive definition of the score; (ii) a dynamic programming matrix for storing the optimal scores of sub-problems; (iii) a bottom-up approach to complete the matrix starting from the smallest subproblems, and (iv) a traceback method to recover the optimal alignment (Kleinberg and Tardos 2006). The recursive definition of the score is as follows:

$$\delta(i,j) = \begin{cases} i \cdot d & \text{if } j = 0 \\ j \cdot d & \text{if } i = 0 \\ \Delta(i,j) & \text{if } i \neq 0 \text{ and } j \neq 0 \end{cases} \quad (6)$$

where

$$\Delta(i,j) = \max \begin{cases} \delta(i-1, j-1) + M[a_i, b_j] \\ \delta(i-1, j) + d \\ \delta(i, j-1) + d \end{cases}$$

M is the substitution matrix and d is the score of an indel.

The recurrence is applied repeatedly to fill a score matrix and once it is filled, the last element of the matrix, (n_1, n_2), holds the score of the optimal alignment. Figure 1 shows the score matrix for the nucleotide sequences `AGTA` and `ATA` with match reward 1 ($a = b$), mismatch penalty -1 ($a \neq b$) and indel penalty ($d = -2$). From the bottom-right cell, a route is traced back to the top-left cell, which gives the alignment. By following the path in the matrix, an optimal alignment, with score 1, is:

```
AGTA
A-TA
```

3.5 Smith Waterman Algorithm

Global alignment methods force alignments to span the entire length of the sequences by attempting to align every character of each sequence. They are useful when two sequences are similar and have roughly equal length. Local alignments are more useful to identify discrete regions of similarity between otherwise divergent sequences. The algorithm for finding an optimal local alignment is called the Smith-Waterman algorithm (Smith and Waterman 1981). It is closely related to the algorithm for global alignment as described in the previous section. The two main differences are:

(i) In each cell in the score matrix can take the value zero if all the three options have negative values. This option allows the algorithm to start a new alignment, which might result in a better score of the prefixes' alignment than continuing an existing one. This translates into resetting the current score of the prefixes' alignment to zero.
(ii) In order to reconstruct the alignment, the trace back must start from the highest value in score matrix. The trace-back ends when a cell with value zero is found.

The recurrence equation for local alignment is given as follows:

$$\delta(i,j) = \max \begin{cases} 0 & \text{for } i \geq 0 \text{ or } j \geq 0, \\ \delta(i-1,j)+d & \text{for } i > 0, \\ \delta(i,j-1)+d & \text{for } j > 0, \\ \delta(i-1,j-1)+M[a_i,b_j] & \text{for } i > 0 \text{ or } j > 0. \end{cases} \tag{7}$$

with $1 \leq i \leq n_1$, $1 \leq j \leq n_2$. A bottom-up DP algorithm can also be derived from the above recursions, analogously to the Needleman-Wunsch algorithm.

3.6 Knuth Morris Pratt Algorithm

Knuth Morris Pratt (KMP) algorithm is a linear time algorithm for string matching, where the longest prefix or suffix called core is represented by, $u = t\,[l'...r]$, $v = t\,[l...r]$, where, u represents to longest prefix and suffix of v (Knuth et al. 1977). KMP works left to right processing the pattern P, important to note that it uses a failure function. The KMP algorithm prepossess the pattern P by computing a failure function f that indicates the largest possible shift s using previously performed comparisons. Specifically, the failure function f(j) is defined as the length of the longest prefix of P that is a suffix of P[i . . j]. When a match is found the current index is increased, if not the failure function determines the new index, and P is again checked again against T. This process is repeated until a match P in text T or index for T reached n (the size of T). The main part of KMP algorithm is a loop which compares a character in T and P for each iteration. In KMP there is no backtrack and the shifting is only one position. The algorithm in Listing 1.1 exemplifies how the algorithm works in practice, as input there is the text T with size n and pattern P of size m, as output, the index of the string of T matching P.

Listing 1.1. KMP algorithm for string match

```
F = failureFunction(P);
i = 0;
j = 0;
while (i < n){
    if(T[i] == P[j]){
        if (j == m-1){
            return i - j; \\match found
        }else{
            i = i + 1;
            j = j + 1;
        }
    }else{
        if (j > 0){
            j = F[j-1];
        }else{
            i = i + 1;
        }
    }
}
```

For better understanding the algorithm, lets assume the following example, where, W = "APCDAPD" and S = "APC APCDAP APCDAPCDAPDE". The state of the algorithm can be identified, at any given time, by two integer values:

1. m, representing the position in S, which is the start of a match for W.
2. i, the position in W, identifying the character being matched.

For each step of the algorithm, $S[m+i]$ is compared with $W[i]$, and moved forward if there is a match.

```
Pattern   = ACCGTT
String    = ... ACCGTGCGAT
                |||||
        B =     ACCGTT
```

3.7 Boyer Moore Algorithm

Boyer Moore algorithm (BM) for string search and match is a standard benchmark algorithm, considered one of the most efficient when the alphabet comprises a small size of characters, used on standard editors to perform string search. SO this algorithm is often used in bioinformatics for disease detection. This algorithm works right to left by matching two sequences, thins method consists on a backward approach. When there is any mismatch it means that the patter was found, otherwise the sequence is moved to right (shifted) and a new match attempt is performed (Martin et al. 2005). The pseudo code in Listing 1.2 illustrates how the Boyer Moore algorithm works. Where as input, the text T of size n and pattern P of size m, and as output, the first index of the string T equal to P or −1 if no match is found.

Listing 1.2. Boyer Moore algorithm for string match

```
i = m - 1;
j = m - 1;
do{
    if (P[j] == T[i]){
        if (j==0){
            return i; //match found
        }else{
            i = i - 1;
            j = j - 1;
        }
    }else{
        i = i+m - Min(j, 1+last[T[i]]);
        j = j - 1;
    }
}while(i > n - 1);
return -1; //no match found
```

Lets consider pattern P in the text T, with mismatches in text character $T[i] = c$, then, the corresponding text pattern search $P[j]$ is performed as follows; If c is within P, then completely shift the pattern P past i, else, shift P until c is in P and aligned with $T[i]$. For example:

```
Input   = MNNQRKKTARPSFNMLLRAR
Pattern = KKT

After BM execution

Input   = MNNQRKKTARPSFNMLLRAR
                 |||
Pattern =        KKT
i       =          ^
```

3.8 Brute Force

This algorithm is the simplest method, it checks all patterns with the text, position by position, until matching characters are found. The algorithm works from left to right without the need for prepossessing. There are two steps in this algorithm, which consist on two nested loops (Rajesh et al. 2010; Dudas 2006). An example of implementation is as follows in Listing 1.3, where the input consists on the text T of size n and pattern P of size m, and the output is the index start of the string T equal to P or −1 if no match found.

Listing 1.3. Brute force basic algorithm for string match

```
for (i=0; i<n; i++){
    j=0;
    while (j<m && T[i+j] == P[j]){
        j=j+1;
        if (j==m){
            return i; //match at i
        }else{
            return -1; //no match
        }
    }
}
```

The algorithm can be set to find the entire pattern or stop with just part of it. Example:

```
Text :  ABRAKADABRA
Trace:  AKA
         AKA
          AKA
           AKA
```

3.9 Rabin Karp Algorithm

Rabin Karp (RK) algorithm is used to look for similarities in two sequences, proteins, i.e. a high sequence similarity means significant structural or functional similarity. RK utilizes a hash function to make the string searching faster. The hash value for the pattern is calculated, used then to compare with sub-sequences of the text. When the hash values are different, RK algorithm estimates the hash for the next matching sequence of characters. If hash values are equal, RK algorithm uses brute-force to compare sequence pattern with the text. RK algorithm efficiency is based on the computation of hash values of text sub-strings.

Rolling hash functions analyze sub-strings as a number, the base of this functions, usually is a large prime number. For instance, considering the sub-string “AC” and the base 1011, the hash would be $65 \times 10111 + 67 \times 10110 = 65782$, where “A” is 65 and “C” is 67 in the ASCII table.

Lets consider a *M-character* sequence with *M-digit* number, base b, where b is the number of letters in the alphabet, the text mapped into sub-sequence $t\left[1...i + M - 1\right]$.

$$X\left(i\right) = t\left[i\right] \times b^{M} - 1 + t\left[i+1\right] \times b^{M} - 2 + ... + t\left[i + M - 1\right] \tag{8}$$

Equation 8 is used to compute sub-sequences of specific sequences.

Given $x\,(i)$ it is possible to compute $x\,(i+1)$ for the next sub-sequence $t\,[i+1...i+M]$ as in Eq. 9

$$\begin{aligned} X\,(i+1) = t\ \ [i+1] \times b^{M} - 1 \\ +t\,[i+2] \times b^{M} - 2 \\ +... \\ +t\,[i+M] \end{aligned} \tag{9}$$

Equation 9 shows how to discover the next sub-sequence for the predecessor.

$$\begin{aligned} h(i) = ((t[i] \times b^{M} - 1 modq) + (t[i+1] \times b^{M} - 2modq) \\ + \ldots + (t\ [i+M-1]modq)) \end{aligned} \tag{10}$$

Equation 10 is used to calculate hash values for the sub sequences. Where:

- $x\,(i)$ represents the text sub-sequence $t\,[i]$;
- $h\,(i)$ represents the hash function;
- b represents the base of the string;
- q is the prime number;

3.10 Aho-Corasick Algorithm

Aho-Corasick (AC) algorithm is widely used for multi-pattern matching, and for exact string matching (Vidanagamachchi et al. 2012). This algorithm is divided into two stages. First, finite machine construction stage used to backtrack failures and remove them to the root node where there is presence of failure. Second, matching step is used to find patterns in the given string.

3.11 CommentZ Walter Algorithm

CommentZ-Walter (CZW) algorithm, used for multi-pattern matching, combines shifting techniques of BM with AC algorithm. CZW has three stages: finite state machine construction; shift calculation; and machining stage Note that, in this algorithm, the finite state machine is built in reverse order to use the shifting methods of BM algorithm.

After the result of CZW algorithm first stage, then the shift is calculated using BM. Finally, it is compared with string sequences.

3.12 Jaro and Jaro–Winkler

The Jaro distance between two sequences consists on the minimum number of single-character transpositions required to change one word into the other.

This approach gives more relevance to words with similar prefixes. Starting from the beginning with the Jaro distance formula, the Jaro distance between two sequences s1 and s2 is defined by Eq. 11 (Jaro distance formula):

$$d_j = \frac{1}{3}\left(\frac{m}{|s_1|} + \frac{m}{|s_2|} + \frac{m-t}{m}\right) \tag{11}$$

Where in Eq. 11:

- dj is the Jaro distance;
- m is the number of matching characters (characters that appear in s1 and in s2);
- t is half the number of transpositions (compare the i-th character of s1 and the i-th character of s2 divided by 2)
- |s1| is the length of the first string;
- |s2| is the length of the second string;

Considering the following example: the word “martha” and the word “marhta”. Then we have:

```
m = 6
t = 2/2 = 1
(two characters do not match,
position 4, position 5)
{t/h; h/t}
|s1| = 6
|s2| = 6

Applying the given formula:
dj = (1/3) ( 6/6 + 6/6 + (61) / 6)
   = 1/1 . 17/6
   = 0,944

Jaro distance = 94,4%
```

Jaro-Winkler similarity distance algorithm, Eq. 12, uses a prefix scale p which gives a better rating to strings which start matching from the beginning, for a set prefix length l.

p is a constant scaling factor for how much the score is adjusted upwards for having common prefixes. The standard value for this constant in Winkler’s work is p = 0.1, while l is a prefix, up to a maximum of 4 characters, at the start of the string.

$$d_e = d_j + (lp\,(1 - d_j)) \tag{12}$$

Using again the example of “martha” and “marhta”, the prefix length of l is equal 3 (refers to “mar”).

```
dw = 0,944 + ((0,1*3)(10,944))
   = 0,944 + 0,3*0,056
   = 0,961

Jaro-Winkler distance = 96,1%
```

Thus applying the Jaro-Winkler formula, the Jaro distance of 94% similarity increases to 96%.

4 Comparison Study

In this section all string matching algorithms are compared regarding complexity, accuracy and execution time until pattern matching.

Table 1. Online tools and manual algorithms analysis

Algorithm	Preprocessing	Execution time	Accuracy
Hamming	–	$O(N^2)$	99%
Levenshtein	–	$O(N+M)$	65%
Needleman wunsch	–	$O(MN)$	53%
Smith waterman	–	$O(MN)$	85%
Knuth Morris Pratt	$O(M)$	$O(M+N)$	84%
Brute Force	–	$O(MN)$	40%
Boyer Moore	$O(M+N)$	$O(MN)$	91%
Rabin Karp	$O(N)$	$O(MN)$	85%
AhoCorasick	–	$O(N+M+Z)$	78%
CommentZ Walter	–	$O(N+M+Z)+O(MN)$	78%
Damerau-Levenshtein	–	$O(MN.max(M,N))$	75%
Jaro–Winkler	–	$O(N^2)$	80%

First test consists on comparing only the three main matching algorithms for sequence matching, Knuth Morris Pratt, Brute Force, and Boyer Moore. The data-set used was two DNA sequences, a normal one, and the other with a disease to be checked. The three algorithms were implemented and tested in JAVA. Moreover, pattern matching techniques is used to optimize the time and to analyze the vast amount of data in a short span of time. Table 2 shows the result of the algorithms execution, where N and M are two strings. Where, Boyer Mores algorithm was the best, with 91% accuracy and 61 s of processing time. On the other hand, Brute Force algorithm was the worst, with 40% accuracy and 147 s of processing time.

Table 2. Knuth Morris Pratt, Brute Force, and Boyer Moore

Algorithm	Matches	Size	Similarity	Processing time (s)
Knuth Morris Pratt	39	46	85%	123
Boyer Moore	39	55	85%	61
Brute Force	39	60	64%	147

Second, the complexity of each algorithm is studied and compared. Table 1, shows resumes study results. Results show the different string matching algorithms regarding accuracy and execution time until pattern matching, using online tools such as EMBOSS, GENE Wise, and manually implemented. For this comparison study the Genbank Accession No. JN222368 was used, which belongs to Marine Sponge. Sequence size was 1321 characters.

5 Conclusions and Future Work

In this survey are analyzed different string matching algorithms in the context of biological sequence, DNA and Proteins.

Algorithms like Knuth Morris Pratt are easier to implement, because they never need to back-reanalyze in the sequence, however, requires more space. Rabin Karp algorithm requires extra space for matching. Brute Force, has the advantage of not needing any pre-processing. However, it is slow. AhoCorasick algorithm is commonly used for a multi-pattern string match. CommentZ-Walter is slower to reach a result, Boyer More is faster when using large sequences, avoiding many comparisons. Boyer More in best case scenario complexity is sub-linear. As future work, it is proposed a parallel algorithm for fuzzy string matching, using artificial intelligence neural networks for better performance and accuracy.

Acknowledgements. "This work is funded by National Funds through the FCT - Foundation for Science and Technology, I.P., within the scope of the project Refa UIDB/05583/2020. Furthermore, we would like to thank the Research Centre in Digital Services (CISeD) and the Polytechnic of Viseu for their support."

References

Alsmadi, I., Nuser, M.: String matching evaluation methods for DNA comparison. Int. J. Adv. Sci. Technol. **47**(1), 13–32 (2012)

Amir, A., Lewenstein, M., Porat, E.: Faster algorithms for string matching with k mismatches. J. Algorithms **50**(2), 257–275 (2004)

Bard, G.V.: Spelling-error tolerant, order-independent pass-phrases via the Damerau-Levenshtein string-edit distance metric. In: Proceedings of the Fifth Australasian Symposium on ACSW Frontiers, vol. 68, pp. 117–124. Citeseer (2007)

Dudas, L.: Improved pattern matching to find DNA patterns. In: IEEE International Conference on Automation, Quality and Testing, Robotics, vol. 2, pp. 345–349. IEEE (2006)

Hussain, I., Kausar, S., Hussain, L., Khan, M.A.: Improved approach for exact pattern matching. Int. J. Comput. Sci. Issues **10**, 59–65 (2013)

Kleinberg, J., Tardos, É.: Algorithm Design. Pearson Education India, Bangalore (2006)

Knuth, D.E., Morris Jr., J.H., Pratt, V.R.: Fast pattern matching in strings. SIAM J. Comput. **6**(2), 323–350 (1977)

Levenshtein, V.I.: Binary codes capable of correcting deletions, insertions, and reversals. Sov. Phys. Dokl. **10**, 707–710 (1966)

Majorek, K.A., et al.: The RNase H-like superfamily: new members, comparative structural analysis and evolutionary classification. Nucleic Acids Res. **42**(7), 4160–4179 (2014)

Martin, D.P., Posada, D., Crandall, K.A., Williamson, C.: A modified bootscan algorithm for automated identification of recombinant sequences and recombination breakpoints. AIDS Res. Hum. Retroviruses **21**(1), 98–102 (2005)

Needleman, S.B., Wunsch, C.D.: A general method applicable to the search for similarities in the amino acid sequence of two proteins. J. Mol. Biol. **48**, 443–453 (1970)

Jain, P., Pandey, S.: Comparative study on text pattern matching for heterogeneous system. Citeseer (2008)

Rajesh, S., Prathima, S., Reddy, L.S.S.: Unusual pattern detection in DNA database using KMP algorithm. Int. J. Comput. Appl. **1**(22), 1–5 (2010)

Singla, N., Garg, D.: String matching algorithms and their applicability in various applications. Int. J. Soft Comput. Eng. **1**(6), 218–222 (2012)

Smith, T.F., Waterman, M.S.: Identification of common molecular subsequences. J. Mol. Biol. **147**(1), 195–197 (1981)

Vidanagamachchi, S.M., Dewasurendra, S.D., Ragel, R.G., Niranjan, M.: CommentZ-Walter: any better than Aho-Corasick for peptide identification? Int. J. Res. Comput. Sci. **2**(6), 33 (2012)

Yeh, M.-C., Cheng, K.-T.: A string matching approach for visual retrieval and classification. In: Proceedings of the 1st ACM international conference on Multimedia information retrieval, pp. 52–58. ACM (2008)

Highly Parallel Convolution Method to Compare DNA Sequences with Enforced In/Del and Mutation Tolerance

Anna Molyavko[3], Vladimir Shaidurov[1,2], Eugenia Karepova[1,3], and Michael Sadovsky[1,3(✉)]

[1] Institute of computational modelling of SB RAS, Akademgorodok, 660036 Krasnoyarsk, Russia
shaidurov04@mail.ru, {e.d.karepova,msad}@icm.krasn.ru

[2] Tianjin University of Finance and Economics, Zhujiang Road, 25, Tianjin 300222, China

[3] Siberian federal university, Svobodny prosp., 79, Krasnoyarsk 660041, Russia
okvaylom@gmail.com
http://icm.krasn.ru

Abstract. New error tolerant method for the comparison and analysis of symbol sequences is proposed. The method is based on convolution function calculation, where the function is defined over the binary numeric sequences obtained by the specific transformation of original symbol sequence. The method allows highly parallel implementation and is of great value for insertion/delition mutations search. To calculate the convolution function, fast Fourier transform is used in the method implementation.

Keywords: Fast Fourier transform · Parallel computing · Order · Pattern · Error tolerant search

1 Introduction

Incredible growth of genetic data challenges researchers to develop and implement a number of new and more effective of the analysis of symbol sequences corresponding to DNA moleculae. The classic problem of search common subsequence in two (or several) symbol sequences still is far for a completion in spite of a long story. Here we propose new approach in the problem based on the smart combination of parallel computation technique, convolution implementation of two functions, and fast Fourier transformation. Further we consider four-letter alphabet $\aleph = \{\mathsf{A}, \mathsf{C}, \mathsf{G}, \mathsf{T}\}$ only, since we aim to deal with genetic data.

Let now concentrate on the rigorous statement of the problem. Consider 2 sequences $\mathfrak{T}_1$, $\mathfrak{T}_2$ from a finite alphabet $\aleph$. Find all sufficiently long strings $\mathfrak{S}_j$, $1 \leqslant j \leqslant K$ that occur at least once in $\mathfrak{T}_1$ and $\mathfrak{T}_2$; here index j enlists such strings. Obviously, the answer depends on the length $L = |\mathfrak{S}_j|$: longer strings are less

I. Rojas et al. (Eds.): IWBBIO 2020, LNBI 12108, pp. 472–481, 2020.
https://doi.org/10.1007/978-3-030-45385-5_42

abundant than shorter ones. There are two versions of the problem: the former means a search for **exactly** matching substrings, and the latter is a search with some tolerable mismatches. Practically, the second version is of greater interest, especially in bioinformatics; besides, the first version is the special case of the second one.

Exact matching search might be considered as a complete problem; of course, some new and advanced algorithms appear [1,2] thus providing the acceleration and efficiency growth of the exact matching problem solution. The situation is getting worse, as soon as one changes for an error tolerant search solution. Currently, the most popular tool for the comparison of sequences with (minor) mismatches is BLAST [2]. The popularity of this tool competes to its inadequacy. Indeed, the method is divergent and one has to kill the divergence artificially. It makes alignment inapplicable for the comparison of long (longer than $\sim 10^3$ symbols) sequences. Moreover, no one contemporary BLAST version is free from an arbitrariness in penalty function determination. A divergence of the method is not the only disadvantage; penalty function system is also arbitrary, and one always is able to find some papers where *ad hoc* penalty system has been introduced just to confirm the expected results.

New error tolerant non-alignment method providing the genome-wide comparison is present here. It takes the special advantage in insertions/delitions search. The method is based on implementation of the convolution of a set of polynomials derived from the sequences under comparison accompanied by the fast Fourier transformation (FFT). The idea to implement FFT for sequence analysis has quite a story [3–8], starting from the classic paper [9]. To decrease the number of arithmetic operations, one usually implements the wrapped convolutions and relative FFT. We believe, a regular (not wrapped) convolution is more effective, for two reasons. Firstly, the calculations are carried out with binary sequences; such calculations with binary digits are expectedly more effective, since it has happened with integers multiplication in regular convolution [10–12]. Secondly, as we see further, FFT responds on mismatches in compared sequences, but fails to provide localization of them.

2 Core Idea

Let $\mathfrak{L}$ be a sequence of the length N from a finite alphabet $\aleph$; everywhere further we stipulate $\aleph = \{\mathsf{A}, \mathsf{C}, \mathsf{G}, \mathsf{T}\}$. Practically, $N \sim 10^{10}$ to 10^{11}. Let also $\mathfrak{T}$ be a sequence of the length $N_{\mathfrak{T}} < N$ (called *template*) from the same alphabet. Find all embedments of $\mathfrak{T}$ into $\mathfrak{L}$ provided that each embedment may have not more than δ mismatches, $0 \leqslant \delta < l$. Obviously, $\delta = 0$ means exact matching.

At the first step a symbol sequence $\mathfrak{L}$ from the alphabet $\aleph$ of the capacity $|\aleph| = 4$ is transformed into a set of four binary sequences. This transformation plays the key role in the algorithm providing algorithmic parallelization in $|\aleph|$ times. Similarly, the template $\mathfrak{T}$ must be transformed into $|\aleph|$ binary sequences. To transform an original symbol sequence, one must execute the following:

(1) Change all symbols A in $\mathfrak{L}$ for 1 while all the other ones for 0 thus getting the first transformed sequences (denoted as $\mathfrak{L}_\mathsf{A}$) of the same length N.
(2) Change all symbols C in $\mathfrak{L}$ for 1 while all the other ones for 0 thus getting the second transformed sequences $\mathfrak{L}_\mathsf{C}$.
(3) Do this transformation for two other symbols (G and T, respectively), thus getting two more sequences ($\mathfrak{L}_\mathsf{G}$ and $\mathfrak{L}_\mathsf{T}$, respectively).

The same transformation of a template into four binary templates $\mathfrak{T}_\mathsf{A}$, $\mathfrak{T}_\mathsf{C}$, $\mathfrak{T}_\mathsf{G}$ and $\mathfrak{T}_\mathsf{T}$ must be carried out.

Let it be sequences $\mathfrak{T}_\mathsf{A} = \{\nu_0, \nu_1, \nu_2, \ldots, \nu_{N_\mathfrak{T}-1}\}$ and $\mathfrak{L}_\mathsf{A} = \{t_0, t_1, t_2, \ldots, t_{N-1}\}$ for definiteness. To define the similarity index, first invert $\mathfrak{T}_\mathsf{A}$:

$$\overleftarrow{\mathfrak{T}}_\mathsf{A} = \{z_0, z_1, z_2, \ldots, z_{N_\mathfrak{T}-1}\} = \{\nu_{N_\mathfrak{T}-1}, \ldots, \nu_2, \nu_1, \nu_0\}.$$

Second, consider the binary sequences $\overleftarrow{\mathfrak{T}}_\mathsf{A}$ and $\mathfrak{L}_\mathsf{A}$ be the coefficients of polynomials of degree $N_\mathfrak{T} - 1$ and $N - 1$, respectively:

$$p_\mathsf{A}(x) = \sum_{i=0}^{N_\mathfrak{T}-1} z_i x^i \quad \text{and} \quad q_\mathsf{A}(x) = \sum_{i=0}^{N-1} t_i x^i.$$

Multiplication of these polynomials yields the polynomial

$$r_\mathsf{A}(x) = \sum_{j=0}^{L} w_j^\mathsf{A} x^j$$

of the degree $L = N + N_\mathfrak{T} - 2$. The coefficients of $r(x)$ are the following scalar products:

$$w_j^\mathsf{A} = \sum_{0 \le s \le j} t_s z_{j-s} = \sum_{0 \le s \le j} t_s \nu_{s-j+N_\mathfrak{T}-1} \qquad \text{if} \qquad 0 \le j \le N_\mathfrak{T} - 1, \tag{1}$$

$$w_j^\mathsf{A} = \sum_{s=j-N_\mathfrak{T}+1}^{N_\mathfrak{T}-1} t_{s-N+1} z_{j-s} = \sum_{s=j-N_\mathfrak{T}+1}^{N_\mathfrak{T}-1} t_{s-N+1} \nu_{s-j+N_\mathfrak{T}-1} \text{ if } N_\mathfrak{T} \le j \le L. \tag{2}$$

Then two identical subsequences (comprising the symbol A only) will manifest in apparent outburst of some coefficient w_J^A clearly seen against the possible random coincidence for $j \ne J$.

Fast multiplication of two polynomials is provided by Fast Fourier Transformation [10,14,15]. For the sake of optimality, it requires that number of elements both in $\overleftarrow{\mathfrak{T}}_\mathsf{A}$ and $\mathfrak{L}_\mathsf{A}$ is equal to a power of 2. To avoid this constraint, zero symbols must be added to both sequences in the positions exceeding $N_\mathfrak{T} - 1$ and $N - 1$, respectively, up to the nearest power of 2.

Algorithmically it means that $N_\mathfrak{T} = N = 2^m$, for some integer m, for the augmented sequences. Then Fast Fourier Transformation must be carried out implying the roots of the power 2^{m+1} from -1 for the augmented sequences.

Corresponding values of both transformations are to be multiplied and yield the sequence of length 2^{m+1} since the polynomial of multiplication is of twice greater order. Finally, the Back Fast Fourier Transformation gives us the coefficients of the polynomial $r(x)$.

Note that the first coefficient of the discrete Fourier transformation is equal to the sum of units in sequences. It simplifies the calculation of the probability $p_{\mathsf{A}}^{\mathfrak{T}}$ and $p_{\mathsf{A}}^{\mathfrak{L}}$ for symbol A through division of this sum by the total number of elements in a sequence. Obviously, the calculations with complex numbers result in rounding and calculation errors. Meanwhile, keeping in mind the integer result of the calculations, at the last stage, rounding to the nearest integer is applied for elimination the accumulated error.

Next, applying this algorithm to each letter A, C, G and T and summing up, one gets

$$w_j = w_J^{\mathsf{A}} + w_J^{\mathsf{C}} + w_J^{\mathsf{G}} + w_J^{\mathsf{T}}. \tag{3}$$

The sum (3) yields rather precise evaluation for w_j against the possible random coincidence for $j \neq J$, in comparison to each individual w_j^* due to lower impact of possible random coincidences.

The mathematical expectation of a coincidence is described by the formula

$$p = p_{\mathsf{A}}^{\mathfrak{T}} p_{\mathsf{A}}^{\mathfrak{L}} + p_{\mathsf{C}}^{\mathfrak{T}} p_{\mathsf{C}}^{\mathfrak{L}} + p_{\mathsf{G}}^{\mathfrak{T}} p_{\mathsf{G}}^{\mathfrak{L}} + p_{\mathsf{T}}^{\mathfrak{T}} p_{\mathsf{T}}^{\mathfrak{L}}. \tag{4}$$

Thus, the coefficients calculated through (1–3) characterize the level of discordance between two symbol sequences, including indels. Besides, there are no theoretical constraint on the length of the sequences under comparison (see Sect. 4 below). Computational capacities provide the major limitation on the method feasibility: e. g. RAM necessary for computations.

3 Preliminary Results

To begin with, we should discuss in few detail the testing sequences used to illustrate the method feasibility. We used surrogate nucleotide sequences of various lengths from the alphabet $\aleph$. The surrogate sequences were the realization of Bernoulli process, i. e. no correlations have been implemented. Such sequences are well known for their strong deviation from any real genetic sequence, meanwhile they seem to be rather good to test the method. Moreover, to avoid effects of degeneracy, we eliminated Chargaff's parity rule implementation in those sequences. In particular, we use the following frequencies of the symbols: $p_{\mathsf{A}} = 0.1$, $p_{\mathsf{C}} = 0.2$, $p_{\mathsf{G}} = 0.3$, $p_{\mathsf{T}} = 0.4$ in both sequences.

Totally, we have carried out a series of computational experiments described below.

3.1 Random Sequences

We tried a series of random non-correlated sequence couples of equal length. The length of sequences within a couple grew up from $N = 10^5$ to $3 \cdot 10^6$ symbols;

totally 100 test runs in the couples of various length falling within the given range have been executed. These experiments were aimed to evaluate the *ad hoc* software feasibility, and estimate the computation time. Typical pattern observed in these experiments looks like a piece-wise linear function with maximum observed at the configuration of the sequences corresponding to the complete coincidence in length.

Typical computation time was equal to 0.299 s for the couple of the sequences of ten thousand length, while the time was equal to 81.115 s for the sequences of $3 \cdot 10^6$ length. This, the computation time grows up almost linearly, with slight deviations resulted from the intermittent approximation of the length of concatenation of two sequences by the nearest upper length of power two.

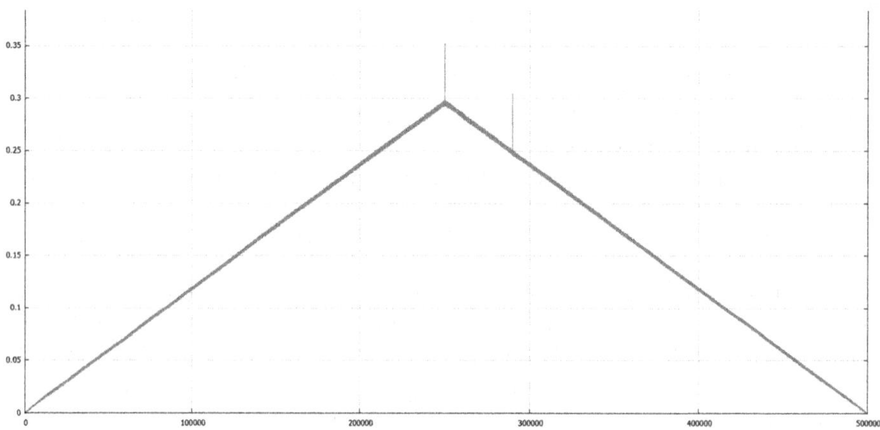

Fig. 1. Typical pattern of the convolution (1, 2) determined over two sequences of the same length, with two perfectly matching insertions.

3.2 Random Sequences with Common Substrings

Next, we have generated a family of random non-correlated sequences (with similar frequencies of the symbols occurrence), so that a perfectly matching substring takes place in two sequences. The key idea of this experimental series was identification of the sensitivity threshold. To do that, we embedded a copy of a part of the first sequence into the other; the relative length of the embedded string was the key factor under investigation.

The point is that there is a "natural noise" in the convolution function (1, 2) calculation resulted from a number of shorter coincidences. These latter vary in length from one to tens of symbols, while take place in a relatively significant number of couples. Indeed, all 64 triplets are present in a sequence under consideration, so the number of coincidences is quite high. These occasional coincidences (matching of short and shorter fragments) yield the function (1, 2) value, while the pattern of their impact resembles to some extent a random noise. Such noise absorbs a signal coming from the longer perfectly matching substrings; this problem is discussed below.

Let now focus on Fig. 1. First of all, the piece-wise linear pattern of the convolution function is evident in it. Next, the figure presents the case of the comparison of two sequences (10^6 each) containing two exactly matching substrings; the former is of the length 10 000, and the latter is of the length 7 000 symbols. The scale in this figure does not allow to reveal the difference in the height of the peaks, while they differ in size. The outreach level of a peak depends on the length of the site of the perfect matching: the size depends on the ratio of the site length L and the sequence length N.

Again, we executed a series of computational experiments where the length of embedded substring grows up, while the length of the sequences under comparison remains the same. Here are two variables: the former is the length of a common substring, and the latter is the length of sequences. Briefly speaking, we found that there is a critical length L of a common string still detectable with no supplementary tools or measures. The typical threshold of the length is about 0.001; in other words, if

$$\frac{L}{N} \sim 0.001, \tag{5}$$

then the peak of convolution function (1, 2) falls into the set of ten greatest deviations from the mean figure of the function. Further shortening of the substring results in a loss of the "signal" in a bulky noise.

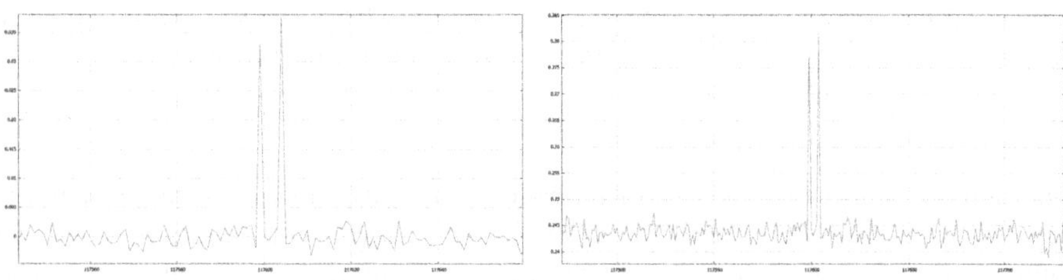

Fig. 2. Insertion and deletion detection. Left is the raw graph (original figures of convolution (1, 2)), and right is flatten pattern of convolution, see text for details.

Surprisingly, the number of peaks to be observed in a convolution function (1) (see Fig. 1) is not equal to the number of exactly matching sites to be found within two sequences. The number of observed peaks is the lower estimation of the perfectly matching sites; the point is that if there are two (or more) couples of the perfectly matching sites located **at the same** (or very close) **distance** in two sequences under comparison, the convolution (1, 2) glues them into a couple of peaks. This effect is also discussed further in the section devoted to localization problem solution.

3.3 Sequences of Different Length

Comparison of two sequences of the lengths N_1 and N_2 yields similar results. Actually, the length of a shorter sequence is here the key factor, both for detection of a matching site, and its localization. In other words, the selection criterion (5) holds true, and the shorter sequences must be used to implement it. This observation stands behind the idea of localization tool implementation, see below.

3.4 In\Del Detection

The proposed method is very effective in InDel detection. Indeed, this type of mismatches is a kind of a headache for researchers. The problem is that it may not be effectively detected by the local comparison techinques; e. g. BLAST fails to detect them properly, requiring some additional information towards these mismatches. To reveal the efficiency of convolution (1, 2) technique in detection of such type mismatches[1], we have carried out a series o computational experiments, where small (not exceeding 12 in length) insertion was embedded into a site on one sequence. Figure 2 illustrates this point. First of all, the patterns shown in Fig. 2 evidently show the high efficiency in localization of the mismatch of InDel type. Moreover, the distance between two peaks in this figure unambiguously determines the length of the insertion.

Few words should be said towards the flattening procedure. Convolution (1, 2) depends on the length of a common intersecting part of two sequences; that is why it looks like linear piece-wise function (see Fig. 1). We used special procedure to remove this effect: stipulating a sequence to be random, or complex enough to be indistinguishable from a random one, first calculate the frequency p_* of each symbol (A, C, G and T, in our case). Then find the value

$$\rho = p_{\mathsf{A}}^2 + p_{\mathsf{C}}^2 + p_{\mathsf{G}}^2 + p_{\mathsf{T}}^2. \tag{6}$$

Let then M denotes the length of intersection of two sequences, and L denotes the length of the shorter one. To normalize the convolution function (1, 2), we change the value of that latter in each point from the "raw" one z_j for the normalized:

$$\widehat{z}_j = z_j - \rho \frac{M}{L}. \tag{7}$$

This procedure allows to eliminate the hill-like pattern of convolution function, thus contrasting some details; the pay-off of this contrasting approach is a decrease (in absolute values) of the normalized convolution figures; cf. left and right subfigures in Fig. 2.

[1] Actually, there is no difference between insertion and deletion: changing a reference sequence, one always is able to convert the situation to a single mutation, e. g. to insertion.

4 Discussion

Here we proposed newly developed method to compare and retrieve structural elements (short subsequences and their combination, in fact) in symbol sequences. The method may be implemented regardless a nature of a sequence. Some preliminary result unambiguously prove the efficiency and feasibility of the method; however, some further problems still await the resolution, and we discuss them here in detail.

4.1 Noise and Shorter Fragments Detection

This is number one problem, in current version of the method. Indeed, we found that the "brute force" version of the method effectively identifies common strings, if their length is not less than 0.001 from the length of a shorter sequence. Since the basic applicability of the proposed method is expected for genome-wide analysis, then one must develop the version that is sensitive for shorter fragments (e. g., as short, as 0.00001 from the length of a shorter sequence).

The detection of such short exactly (or with minor mismatches) matching strings is deteriorated by the noise resulted from numerous coincidences of short and very short strings. Thus, a number of contrasting techniques must be developed; one of them is described above, see Subsect. 3.4. However, there might be other techniques and approaches still awaiting for realization.

4.2 Localization

Yet, the greatest disadvantage of the method consists in the very poor localization of the coinciding fragments within two (or greater) sequences. The problem is that the location of a peak manifesting the coincidence over a sufficiently long subsequence within the convolution function (1, 2) does not reveal the real localization of the coincided strings within two sequences under comparison.

More exactly, localization of the peak close to the edge of convolution tells more towards the localization; ultimately, peak localized at the very end is unambiguously localized at the end of a sequence. On the contrary, a drift of the peak to the center of the convolution function kills the information towards the real location of matching sites within the sequences under comparison. This ambiguity results from the peculiarities of fast Fourier transform. Probably, the simplest (while not the most efficient) method to overcome this problem is the approach based on sequential bisection of original sequence into smaller parts, in geometry progression. Our preliminary tests show this method to work rather satisfactory.

4.3 Strong Imbalance in Compared Sequences

Since the sensitivity of the method to identification of the shortest visible site depends on the length of a shorter sequence, only, we implemented this feature into analysis practice. Suppose, two sequences under comparison are of a proximal length, thus providing calamities in the localization of common sites. Hence, the idea is to cut-off a sequence into a set of slightly overlapping considerably short fragments with further conveyer-like processing of them. Remarkable fact is that such conveyer could be run in parallel. Overlapping is necessary to avoid the loss of common sites located at the ends of the fragments.

4.4 Parallelism and Visualization

The greatest advantage of the method is its high potential for parallelism. Indeed, the transformation of original symbol sequence into a set of binary ones provides their parallel processing. There are some other ways to run the computations in parallel mode: the above mentioned fragmentation of one sequence from a couple is among them. Another option for parallel computing implementation is bisection of a sequence targeted to localize common sites in them.

Parallel computing implementation actually causes a list of related (technical) problems to be resolved, and visualization is among them. Indeed, parallel computing is expected to be applied for the analysis of genomes and similar biological entities; these latter are billion-long entities, thus making a problem of presentation of immediately calculated convolution functions, as is. Hence, proper implementation of the method requires development of a number of service tools and auxiliary software for visualization and presentation of the results of the comparison and pattern recognition in genetic sequences. All these problems should be discussed in more detail, before any activities to be done.

Finally, we stress one more advantage of the proposed method: its efficiency grow up, as the capacity of alphabet of the sequences under analysis grows up. The main reason for that is parallelism implementation strongly supported by the higher alphabet capacity. This issue makes the method very highly potential for the tasks of amino acid sequences analysis.

References

1. Tsarev, S.P., Sadovsky, M.G.: New error tolerant method for search of long repeats in DNA sequences. In: Botón-Fernández, M., Martín-Vide, C., Santander-Jiménez, S., Vega-Rodríguez, M.A. (eds.) AlCoB 2016. LNCS, vol. 9702, pp. 171–182. Springer, Cham (2016). https://doi.org/10.1007/978-3-319-38827-4_14
2. Altschul, S.F., Gish, W., Miller, W., Myers, E.W., Lipman, D.J.: Basic local alignment search tool. J. Mol. Biol. **215**(3), 403–410 (1990)
3. Freschi, V., Bogliolo, A.: A faster algorithm for the computation of string convolutions using lz78 parsing. Inform. Process. Lett. **110**(14), 609–613 (2010)
4. Freschi, V., Bogliolo, A.: Longest common subsequence between run-length-encoded strings: a new algorithm with improved parallelism. Inform. Process. Lett. **90**(4), 167–173 (2004)
5. Keogh, E., Chakrabarti, K., Pazzani, M., Mehrotra, S.: Dimensionality reduction for fast similarity search in large time series databases. Knowl. Inf. Syst. **3**(3), 263–286 (2001)
6. Katoh, K., Misawa, K., Kuma, K.I., Miyata, T.: MAFFT: a novel method for rapid multiple sequence alignment based on fast Fourier transform. Nucleic Acids Res. **30**(14), 3059–3066 (2002)

7. Janacek, G.J., Bagnall, A.J., Powell, M.: A likelihood ratio distance measure for the similarity between the Fourier transform of time series. In: Ho, T.B., Cheung, D., Liu, H. (eds.) PAKDD 2005. LNCS (LNAI), vol. 3518, pp. 737–743. Springer, Heidelberg (2005). https://doi.org/10.1007/11430919_85
8. Hetland, M.L.: A survey of recent methods for efficient retrieval of similar time sequences. In: Data Mining in Time Series Databases, pp. 23–42. World Scientific (2004)
9. Benson, D.C.: Fourier methods for biosequence analysis. Nucleic Acids Res. **18**(21), 6305–6310 (1990)
10. Aho, A.V., Hopcroft, J.E.: The Design and Analysis of Computer Algorithms. Pearson Education India, Bengaluru (1974)
11. Baase, S.: Computer Algorithms: Introduction to Design and Analysis. Pearson Education India, Bengaluru (2009)
12. Kozen, D.C.: The Design and Analysis of Algorithms. Springer, Heidleberg (2012)
13. Levenshtein, V.I.: Bounds for deletion/insertion correcting codes. In: Proceedings IEEE International Symposium on Information Theory, p. 370. IEEE (2002)
14. Merhi, S., Zhang, R., Iwen, M.A., Christlieb, A.: A new class of fully discrete sparse fourier transforms: faster stable implementations with guarantees. J. Fourier Anal. Appl. **25**(3), 751–784 (2019)
15. Karam, C., Sugimoto, K., Hirakawa, K.: Fast convolutional distance transform. IEEE Signal Process. Lett. **26**(6), 853–857 (2019)

A Mini Review on Parallel Processing of Brain Magnetic Resonance Imaging

Ayca Kirimtat[1], Ondrej Krejcar[1(✉)], Rafael Dolezal[1], and Ali Selamat[1,2]

[1] Faculty of Informatics and Management, Center for Basic and Applied Research, University of Hradec Kralove, Rokitanskeho 62, 500 03 Hradec Kralove, Czech Republic
a.kirimtat@gmail.com,
{ondrej.krejcar, rafael.dolezal}@uhk.cz
[2] Malaysia Japan International Institute of Technology (MJIIT), Universiti Teknologi Malaysia, Jalan Sultan Yahya Petra, Kuala Lumpur, Malaysia
aselamat@utm.my

Abstract. Parallel processing is an execution of processes that make computation and calculation on many things simultaneously. In addition, parallel processing methods are applied extensively to the examination of MR imaging in treatment. As parallel computer systems become larger and faster at the present time; scientists, researchers and engineers are eventually able to find solutions to the problems in medicine, which had been taken too long to run before. Therefore, various fields including medicine and bioinformatics have already taken the advantages of parallel processing. In this review study, we deal with analyzing key concepts and eminent parallel processing methods that have been used to analyze the brain MRI images. In addition to this, we indicate great number of examples from the current literature in a comprehensive literature matrix. Based on the literature matrix that is created according to the Web of Science analysis, information graphics are presented in a comprehensive manner. As a result, parallel processing methods in brain magnetic resonance imaging offer powerful replacements to computer clusters in order to run large, disseminated solicitations.

Keywords: Parallel processing · Magnetic resonance imaging · Brain · Review

1 Introduction

Through increasing complexity of magnetic resonance imaging (MRI) techniques in handling machines, a large amount of data processed in MRI is expanded. [1–3] Furthermore, MRI is a well-known medical modality, which generates 2D, 3D and 4D images in medicine, and these images also leads to medical diagnosis and specialized treatment [4–8]. A classical MRI examination of head involves several scanning regimens (e.g. T1 weighted, T2 weighted, diffusion weighted imaging (DWI), fluid attenuated inversion recovery (FLAIR), etc.) producing hundreds of gigabytes of greyscale pictures that must be analyzed in detail to achieve reliable medical diagnosis.

I. Rojas et al. (Eds.): IWBBIO 2020, LNBI 12108, pp. 482–493, 2020.
https://doi.org/10.1007/978-3-030-45385-5_43

However, digital MRI image analysis in general is computationally costly, and imaging data sizes in biomedicine is extremely increasing [9]. For these reasons, parallel processing has revealed as a novel technology that is capable for providing new solutions to the computational complexity and its problems in both biomedicine and engineering fields. Moreover, this review study mainly focuses on parallel processing methods for solving computational complexity in brain MRI images apart from other medical images [2].

On the other hand, the analysis speed of image segmentation techniques becomes quite important since the safety of patients gains higher priority through the technological developments. In the current literature, there are many proposals for increasing the rapidity of image analysis procedures by integrating the imperative information to image reconstruction. The most of the image analysis methods mentioned in the recent literature were trying to find the fast way in comparison with the traditional sampled image analyzing [10].

In the continuation of this review study, we show the overall contextual of parallel processing and its methods in Sect. 2. Moreover, Sect. 3 explains the importance of parallel processing for MRI analysis; such as trendy methods and algorithms used for MRI analysis. The detailed literature matrix based on the Web of Science search analysis is given in Sect. 3. Moreover, we debate the outcomes of the literature survey by information graphics in Sect. 5, whereas future trends are presented in Sect. 6. Finally, we give conclusion remarks about this review study in the last section.

2 Overview of Parallel Processing

Parallel processing technology has been being developed since early research prototype was created as a clinical tool. In history, parallel computers as clinical tools were used for scientific purposes and the scientific problem simulation, particularly in the engineering sciences, such as biomedicine. Moreover, several parallel processing methods have been developed over the last decade. However, most of these methods use the same approach for data acquisition, they are separated from each other in terms of generating the final image.

Additionally, there are two classes of parallel processing methods differing in the technique they create the reconstruction. The first session includes the approaches that necessitate obvious information of the coil sensitivity functions with the aim of separating aliased signals; for instance sensitivity encoding (SENSE) method, improved SENSE method, simultaneous acquisition of spatial harmonics (SMASH) and sensitivity profiles from an array of coils for encoding and reconstruction in parallel (SPACE RIP) [11] in comparison with other methods [12, 13]. Therefore, the first class of parallel processing methods is named as "physically-based" reconstruction, since those methods carefully model the primary physical process, which arises from image procurement. On the other hand, the second class does not necessitate explicit coil sensitivity information; instead of this, it requires a data fitting approach with the aim of calculating the linear combination weights, thus the name of this second approach is "data-driven" reconstruction.

3 Methodology: Literature Matrix

Prior to the citation count of the previous studies in the Web of Science, we created a comprehensive literature matrix for the applications of parallel processing [14, 15] in brain MRI image analysis [16]. A complete organization of pertinent scientific works is achieved based on some criteria, which are proposed methods, imaging parameters, materials and results. A great amount of 47 publications issued between 1995 and 2019 are gathered in Table 2 with the aim of presenting a comprehensive matrix. Predominantly in the current time intervals, the number of studies on parallel processing in brain MRI image analysis has increased, revealing technological developments. Consequently, and based on Table 2, info graphics of earlier works on parallel processing of brain MRI image analysis are provided, and a meticulous discussion stating the relevant articles is provided in the subsequent section.

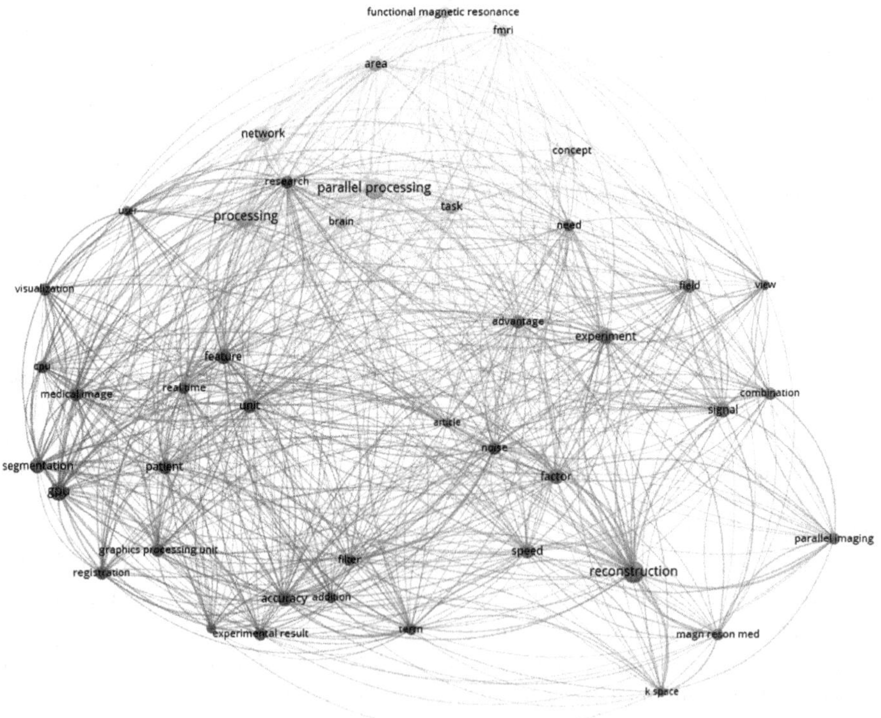

Fig. 1. The network visualization of the Web of Science data using VOSviewer software. (Color figure online)

On the other hand, for Fig. 1, we used VOSviewer software to visualize the networks [17] between keywords on parallel processing in brain MRI image analysis. In order to generate Fig. 1, we performed a detailed literature survey in the Web of Science through some strings, such as “parallel processing”, “brain” and “MRI”.

In total, 43 items, 4 clusters, and 725 links were extracted from the network visualization that belongs to the 216 articles in the Web of Science. Figure 1 displays the most imperative keywords from red cluster, such as reconstruction and parallel imaging, yet segmentation, medical image and GPU are the most important ones from blue cluster. Parallel processing, processing, area and network are eye-catching keywords from yellow cluster. Lastly, the most used keywords from green cluster are patient, accuracy, and registration with parameters are presented in Table 1, which explains which item belongs to which cluster color and how many links and occurrences the items have.

Table 1. The items with clusters, links and occurrences from VOSviewer software.

Item (Keyword)	Cluster	Links	Occurrences
Reconstruction	Red	40	51
Parallel imaging	Red	23	17
Segmentation	Blue	32	27
Medical image	Blue	32	22
GPU	Blue	36	36
Parallel processing	Yellow	41	53
Processing	Yellow	41	58
Area	Yellow	36	26
Network	Yellow	37	31
Patient	Green	35	24
Accuracy	Green	39	24
Registration	Green	30	21

Table 2. The existing works on parallel programming in MRI image analysis according to the citation count.

Author (s)	Method	Imaging parameters	Journal/Conference	Citation
[18]	SPIRIT (parallel image reconstruction)	Echo time (ET) = 8 ms, pulse repetition time (PRT) = 17.6 ms, flip = 20°, BW = 6.94 kHz	Magnetic Resonance in Medicine	348
[19]	Image visualization	–	Audiology & Neuro-Otology	262
[20]	Brain mapping	–	NeuroImage	223
[21]	fMRI	ET = 300 ms, PRT = 150 ms, BW = 0.44 kHz	The Journal of Neuroscience	141
[14]	MR image reconstruction	ET = 5.172 ms, PRT = 25 ms	IEEE Transactions in Medical Imaging	130
[22]	fMRI	ET = 14 ms, PRT = 600 ms	NeuroImage	128

(*continued*)

Table 2. (*continued*)

Author (s)	Method	Imaging parameters	Journal/Conference	Citation
[11]	Coil-by-coil data-driven reconstruction	ET = 13 ms, PRT = 400 ms, BW = 16 kHz	Magnetic Resonance in Medicine	122
[23]	The GRAPPA reconstruction	ET = 10 ms, PRT = 300 ms, BW = 16 kHz	Magnetic Resonance in Medicine	60
[15]	Object recognition	ET = 3.93 ms, PRT = 1960 ms, flip = 15°	Brain	53
[24]	GPU-based parallelisation	ET = 111 ms, PRT = 4.9 s	PLOS One	50
[25]	Restoration and enhancement of MRI	ET = 25, 50, 75, 100 ms, PRT = 2500 ms	IEEE Transactions on Image Processing	47
[13]	pMRI	ET = 12 ms, PRT = 450 ms	Magnetic Resonance in Medicine	46
[26]	Efficient parallelization of mutual information (MI) computation	–	Computer Methods and Programs in Biomedicine	42
[27]	MRI reconstruction	ET = 85 ms, PRT = 3000 ms	Magnetic Resonance in Medicine	37
[28]	BROCCOLI: Software for fast fMRI	–	Frontiers in Neuroinformatics	36
[29]	A 7-tesla magnetic resonance imaging	ET = 1.54 ms, PRT = 2500 ms, flip = 7°	Experimental Brain Research	31
[1]	Parallel MRI reconstruction	ET = 17.8 ms, PRT = 500 ms, BW = 10 kHz	Magnetic Resonance in Medicine	31
[16]	A fast reconstruction	ET = 85 ms, PRT = 3000 ms	IEEE Transactions in Medical Imaging	31
[30]	A generalized autocalibrating partially parallel acquisitions	ET = 4.5 ms, PRT = 13000 ms	Magnetic Resonance in Medicine	29
[31]	fMRI	ET = 66 ms, PRT = 5 s, flip = 90°	NeuroImage	28
[32]	A calibrationless method for parallel magnetic resonance imaging	ET = 11 ms, PRT = 700 ms	International Conference on Medical Image Computing and Computer-Assisted Intervention	28

(*continued*)

Table 2. (*continued*)

Author (s)	Method	Imaging parameters	Journal/Conference	Citation
[33]	Functional magnetic resonance imaging	ET = 62 ms, PRT = 3500 ms, flip = 90°	Human Brain Mapping	27
[34]	Single-Shot Magnetic Resonance Spectroscopic Imaging with Partial Parallel Imaging	ET = 11 ms, PRT = 2 s	Magnetic Resonance in Medicine	27
[35]	Image reconstruction	–	Journal of Parallel and Distributed Computing	25
[36]	fMRI BOLD	ET = 4.38 ms, PRT = 2000 ms	Brain & Language	24
[37]	Calibrationless parallel imaging reconstruction	ET = 5 ms, PRT = 15 ms, flip = 20°	IEEE 2011 Conference Record of the Forty Fifth Asilomar Conference on Signals, Systems and Computers	20
[38]	Multilayer perceptron (MLP) algorithm	ET = 10 ms, PRT = 558 ms	Medical Physics	20
[39]	3D reconstructions of highly under sampled MR angiograms	ET = 2 ms, PRT = 4.4 ms, flip = 30°	2009 IEEE International Symposium on Biomedical Imaging: From Nano to Macro	19
[40]	Probabilistic tractography through diffusion-weighted MRI	ET = 30 ms, PRT = 3000 ms, flip = 90°	NeuroImage	16
[41]	Image reconstruction	ET = 45 ms, PRT = 1000 ms, flip = 45°	Magnetic Resonance in Medicine	15
[42]	A point-based 'fast' non-rigid registration	–	Computers in Biology and Medicine	14
[43]	3D registration	–	Magnetic Resonance Imaging	13
[44]	fMRI	ET = 85 ms, PRT = 3000 ms, flip = 83°	NeuroImage	13
[45]	A parallel adaptive segmentation	–	Neurocomputing	13
[46]	Image reconstruction	ET = 99 ms, PRT = 5000 ms	Computing in Science & Engineering	11

(*continued*)

Table 2. (*continued*)

Author (s)	Method	Imaging parameters	Journal/Conference	Citation
[47]	A multiagent-consensus-MapReduce-based attribute reduction algorithm	–	Neurocomputing	11
[48]	3D image registration	–	Computer Methods and Programs in Biomedicine	10
[49]	fMRI	ET = 33.1 ms, PRT = 720 ms, flip = 52°	Medical Engineering & Physics	10
[50]	Deep Residual Learning for Accelerated MRI using Magnitude and Phase Networks	ET = 420 ms, PRT = 3000-4000 ms, flip = 90°	IEEE Transactions on Biomedical Engineering	10
[51]	parallel imaging reconstruction	ET = 16 ms, PRT = 500 ms, flip = 18°	Magnetic Resonance in Medicine	7
[52]	Robust GRAPPA reconstruction	ET = 14 ms, PRT = 400 ms, BW = 33.3 kHz	Magnetic Resonance Imaging	6

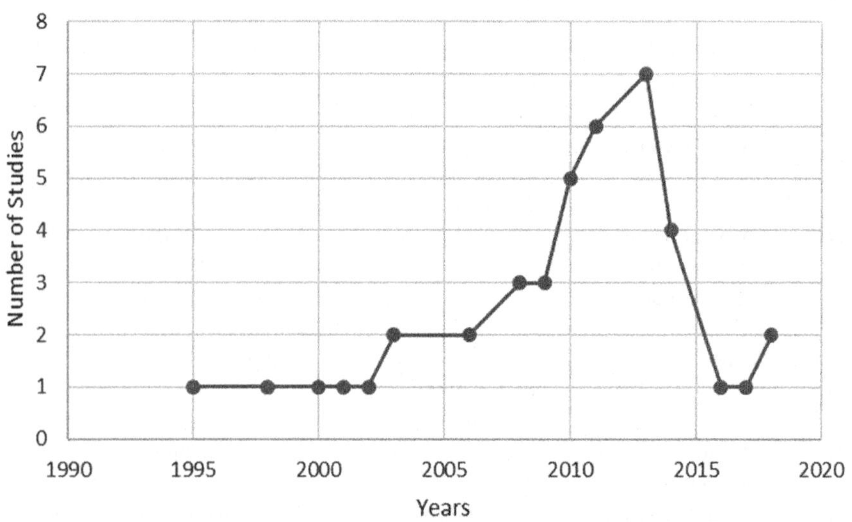

Fig. 2. The number of studies into years based on citation count from Table 2.

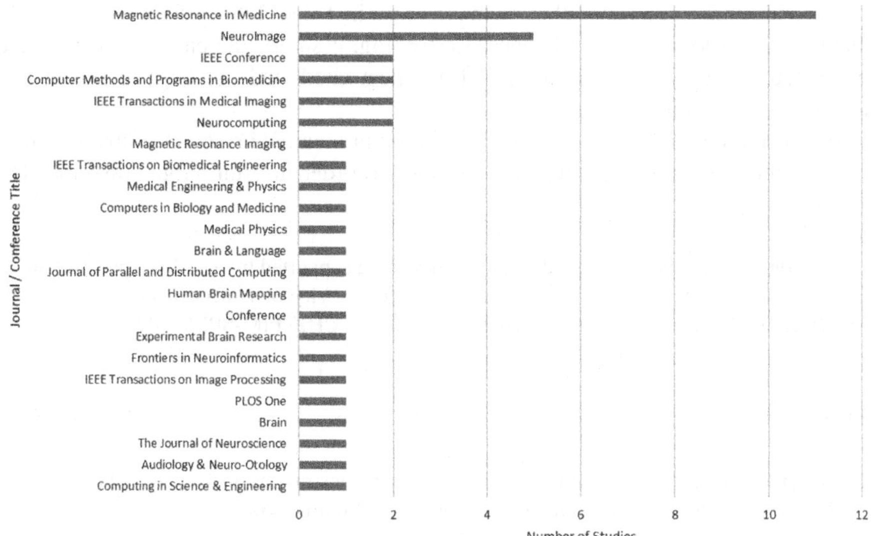

Fig. 3. The number of studies in journals/conferences from Table 2.

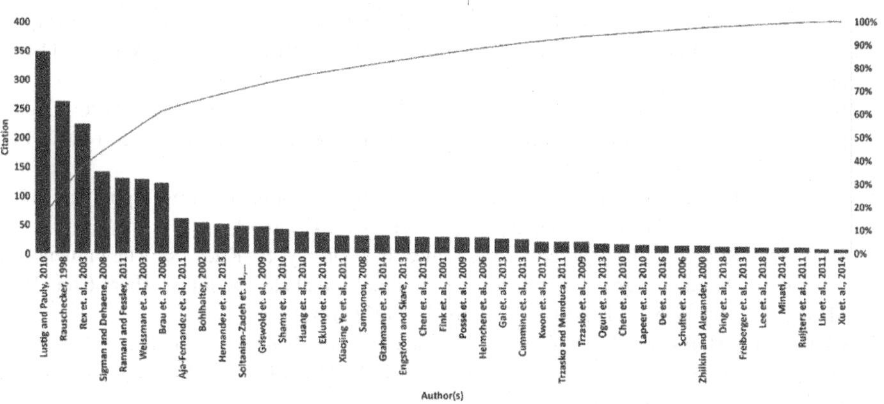

Fig. 4. The citation count and the author(s) from Table 2.

4 Conclusion and Discussion

In this review study, we present key concepts and eminent parallel processing methods that have been used to analyze the brain MRI images. Moreover, we indicate great number of examples from the current literature in a comprehensive literature matrix. The detailed literature matrix is indicated in Table 2, after that the information graphics are created according to Table 2 and Web of Science analysis. Figures 2, 3 and 4 represent our analysis on Table 2, for instance, we try to gather the number of studies into specific years in Fig. 2 and the number of studies had been increased after 2010 until 2015. On the other hand, Fig. 3 represent the number of studies in important journals and conferences, and all of them are given in Table 2, for instance which study belong to which journal or conference. Lastly, Fig. 4 shows the citation count of the previous studies in Web of Science, and the most cited study belongs to Lustig and Pauly with 348 citations.

As a result, parallel processing methods in brain magnetic resonance imaging offer powerful replacements to computer clusters in order to run large, disseminated solicitations.

Acknowledgement. The work and the contribution were supported by the SPEV project "Smart Solutions in Ubiquitous Computing Environments", University of Hradec Kralove, Faculty of Informatics and Management, Czech Republic (under ID: UHK-FIM-SPEV-2020).

References

1. Samsonov, A.A.: On optimality of parallel MRI reconstruction in k-space. Magn. Reson. Med. **59**(1), 156–164 (2008). https://doi.org/10.1002/mrm.21466
2. Kubicek, J., et al.: Autonomous segmentation and modeling of brain pathological findings based on iterative segmentation from MR images. In: Nguyen, N.T., Gaol, F.L., Hong, T.-P., Trawiński, B. (eds.) ACIIDS 2019. LNCS (LNAI), vol. 11432, pp. 324–335. Springer, Cham (2019). https://doi.org/10.1007/978-3-030-14802-7_28
3. Kubicek, J., et al.: Design and analysis of LMMSE filter for MR image data. In: Nguyen, N. T., Gaol, F.L., Hong, T.-P., Trawiński, B. (eds.) ACIIDS 2019. LNCS (LNAI), vol. 11432, pp. 336–348. Springer, Cham (2019). https://doi.org/10.1007/978-3-030-14802-7_29
4. Kalaiselvi, T., Sriramakrishnan, P., Somasundaram, K.: Survey of using GPU CUDA programming model in medical image analysis. Inform. Med. Unlocked **9**, 133–144 (2017). https://doi.org/10.1016/j.imu.2017.08.001
5. Cerna, L., Maresova, P.: Modern technologies in diabetes treatment. J. Eng. Appl. Sci. **11**(7), 1475–1479 (2016). https://doi.org/10.3923/jeasci.2016.1475.1479
6. Bužga, M., Maresova, P., Seidlerova, A., Zonča, P., Holéczy, P., Kuča, K.: The influence of methods of bariatric surgery for treatment of type 2 diabetes mellitus. Ther. Clin. Risk Manag. **12**, 599–605 (2016). https://doi.org/10.2147/tcrm.s96593
7. Cimler, R., Maresova, P., Kuhnova, J., Kuca, K.: Predictions of Alzheimer's disease treatment and care costs in European countries. PLoS ONE **14**(1) (2019). https://doi.org/10.1371/journal.pone.0210958
8. South-Paul, J.E., Matheny, S.C., Lewis, E.L.: Current Diagnosis & Treatment in Family Medicine, 3rd edn. McGraw-Hill Medical, New York (2011)
9. Rodger, J.A.: Discovery of medical Big Data analytics: improving the prediction of traumatic brain injury survival rates by data mining Patient Informatics Processing Software Hybrid Hadoop Hive. Inform. Med. Unlocked **1**, 17–26 (2015). https://doi.org/10.1016/j.imu.2016.01.002
10. Hamilton, L.H., et al.: "PINOT": time-resolved parallel magnetic resonance imaging with a reduced dynamic field of view. Magn. Reson. Med. **65**(4), 1062–1074 (2011). https://doi.org/10.1002/mrm.22696
11. Brau, A.C.S., Beatty, P.J., Skare, S., Bammer, R.: Comparison of reconstruction accuracy and efficiency among autocalibrating data-driven parallel imaging methods. Magn. Reson. Med. **59**(2), 382–395 (2008). https://doi.org/10.1002/mrm.21481

12. Pruessmann, K.P., Weiger, M., Börnert, P., Boesiger, P.: Advances in sensitivity encoding with arbitrary k-space trajectories. Magn. Reson. Med. **46**(4), 638–651 (2001). https://doi.org/10.1002/mrm.1241. SENSE with Arbitrary k-Space Trajectories
13. Griswold, M.A., Jakob, P.M., Nittka, M., Goldfarb, J.W., Haase, A.:Partially parallel imaging with localized sensitivities (PILS). Magn. Reson. Med.**44**(4), 602–609 (2000). https://doi.org/10.1002/1522-2594(200010)44:4<602::aid-mrm14>3.0.co;2-5. https://www.researchgate.net/publication/12297882_Partially_parallel_imaging_with_localized_sensitivities_PILS. PMID: 11025516
14. Ramani, S., Fessler, J.A.: Parallel MR image reconstruction using augmented Lagrangian methods. IEEE Trans. Med. Imaging **30**(3), 694–706 (2011). https://doi.org/10.1109/tmi.2010.2093536
15. Bohlhalter, S.: Hierarchical versus parallel processing in tactile object recognition: a behavioural-neuroanatomical study of aperceptive tactile agnosia. Brain **125**(11), 2537–2548 (2002). https://doi.org/10.1093/brain/awf245
16. Ye, X., Chen, Y., Lin, W., Huang, F.: Fast MR image reconstruction for partially parallel imaging with arbitrary *k*-space trajectories. IEEE Trans. Med. Imaging **30**(3), 575–585 (2011). https://doi.org/10.1109/tmi.2010.2088133
17. Maresova, P., et al.: Consequences of industry 4.0 in business and economics. Economies **6**(3), 46 (2018). https://doi.org/10.3390/economies6030046
18. Lustig, M., Pauly, J.M.: SPIRiT: iterative self-consistent parallel imaging reconstruction from arbitrary k-space. Magn. Reson. Med. (2010). https://doi.org/10.1002/mrm.22428
19. Rauschecker, J.P.: Parallel processing in the auditory cortex of primates. Audiol. Neurotol. **3**(2–3), 86–103 (1998). https://doi.org/10.1159/000013784
20. Rex, D.E., Ma, J.Q., Toga, A.W.: The LONI pipeline processing environment. NeuroImage **19**(3), 1033–1048 (2003). https://doi.org/10.1016/s1053-8119(03)00185-x
21. Sigman, M., Dehaene, S.: Brain mechanisms of serial and parallel processing during dual-task performance. J. Neurosci. **28**(30), 7585–7598 (2008). https://doi.org/10.1523/jneurosci.0948-08.2008
22. Weissman, D.H., Giesbrecht, B., Song, A.W., Mangun, G.R., Woldorff, M.G.: Conflict monitoring in the human anterior cingulate cortex during selective attention to global and local object features. NeuroImage **19**(4), 1361–1368 (2003). https://doi.org/10.1016/s1053-8119(03)00167-8
23. Aja-Fernández, S., Tristán-Vega, A., Hoge, W.S.: Statistical noise analysis in GRAPPA using a parametrized noncentral Chi approximation model. Magn. Reson. Med. **65**(4), 1195–1206 (2011). https://doi.org/10.1002/mrm.22701
24. Hernández, M., et al.: Accelerating fibre orientation estimation from diffusion weighted magnetic resonance imaging using GPUs. PLOS One **8**(4), e61892 (2013)
25. Soltanian-Zadeh, H., Windham, J.P., Yagle, A.E.: A multidimensional nonlinear edge-preserving filter for magnetic resonance image restoration. IEEE Trans. Image Process. **4**(2), 147–161 (1995). https://doi.org/10.1109/83.342189
26. Shams, R., Sadeghi, P., Kennedy, R., Hartley, R.: Parallel computation of mutual information on the GPU with application to real-time registration of 3D medical images. Comput. Methods Programs Biomed. **99**(2), 133–146 (2010). https://doi.org/10.1016/j.cmpb.2009.11.004
27. Huang, F., et al.: A rapid and robust numerical algorithm for sensitivity encoding with sparsity constraints: self-feeding sparse SENSE. Magn. Reson. Med. **64**(4), 1078–1088 (2010). https://doi.org/10.1002/mrm.22504
28. Eklund, A., Dufort, P., Villani, M., LaConte, S.: BROCCOLI: software for fast fMRI analysis on many-core CPUs and GPUs. Front. Neuroinform. **8** (2014). https://doi.org/10.3389/fninf.2014.00024

29. Gathmann, B., et al.: Stress and decision making: neural correlates of the interaction between stress, executive functions, and decision making under risk. Exp. Brain Res. **232**(3), 957–973 (2014). https://doi.org/10.1007/s00221-013-3808-6
30. Engström, M., Skare, S.: Diffusion-weighted 3D multislab echo planar imaging for high signal-to-noise ratio efficiency and isotropic image resolution. Magn. Reson. Med. **70**(6), 1507–1514 (2013). https://doi.org/10.1002/mrm.24594. Diffusion-Weighted 3DMS-EPI
31. Fink, G.R., et al.: Deriving numerosity and shape from identical visual displays. NeuroImage **13**(1), 46–55 (2001). https://doi.org/10.1006/nimg.2000.0673
32. Chen, C., Li, Y., Huang, J.: Calibrationless parallel MRI with joint total variation regularization. In: Mori, K., Sakuma, I., Sato, Y., Barillot, C., Navab, N. (eds.) MICCAI 2013. LNCS, vol. 8151, pp. 106–114. Springer, Heidelberg (2013). https://doi.org/10.1007/978-3-642-40760-4_14
33. Helmchen, C., Mohr, C., Erdmann, C., Binkofski, F., Büchel, C.: Neural activity related to self-versus externally generated painful stimuli reveals distinct differences in the lateral pain system in a parametric fMRI study. Hum. Brain Mapp. **27**(9), 755–765 (2006). https://doi.org/10.1002/hbm.20217
34. Posse, S., Otazo, R., Tsai, S.-Y., Yoshimoto, A.E., Lin, F.-H.: Single-shot magnetic resonance spectroscopic imaging with partial parallel imaging. Magn. Reson. Med. **61**(3), 541–547 (2009). https://doi.org/10.1002/mrm.21855
35. Gai, J., et al.: More IMPATIENT: a gridding-accelerated Toeplitz-based strategy for non-Cartesian high-resolution 3D MRI on GPUs. J. Parallel Distrib. Comput. **73**(5), 686–697 (2013). https://doi.org/10.1016/j.jpdc.2013.01.001
36. Cummine, J., et al.: Manipulating instructions strategically affects reliance on the ventral-lexical reading stream: converging evidence from neuroimaging and reaction time. Brain Lang. **125**(2), 203–214 (2013). https://doi.org/10.1016/j.bandl.2012.04.009
37. Trzasko, J.D., Manduca, A.: Calibrationless parallel MRI using CLEAR. In: 2011 Conference Record of the Forty Fifth Asilomar Conference on Signals, Systems and Computers (ASILOMAR), Pacific Grove, CA, USA, pp. 75–79 (2011). https://doi.org/10.1109/acssc.2011.6189958
38. Kwon, K., Kim, D., Park, H.: A parallel MR imaging method using multilayer perceptron. Med. Phys. **44**(12), 6209–6224 (2017). https://doi.org/10.1002/mp.12600
39. Trzasko, J., Haider, C., Manduca, A.: Practical nonconvex compressive sensing reconstruction of highly-accelerated 3D parallel MR angiograms. In: 2009 IEEE International Symposium on Biomedical Imaging: From Nano to Macro, Boston, MA, USA, pp. 274–277 (2009). https://doi.org/10.1109/isbi.2009.5193037
40. Oguri, T., et al.: Overlapping connections within the motor cortico-basal ganglia circuit: fMRI-tractography analysis. NeuroImage **78**, 353–362 (2013). https://doi.org/10.1016/j.neuroimage.2013.04.026
41. Chen, Z., Zhang, J., Yang, R., Kellman, P., Johnston, L.A., Egan, G.F.: IIR GRAPPA for parallel MR image reconstruction. Magn. Reson. Med. **63**(2), 502–509 (2010). https://doi.org/10.1002/mrm.22197
42. Lapeer, R.J., Shah, S.K., Rowland, R.S.: An optimised radial basis function algorithm for fast non-rigid registration of medical images. Comput. Biol. Med. **40**(1), 1–7 (2010). https://doi.org/10.1016/j.compbiomed.2009.10.002
43. Zhilkin, P., Alexander, M.E.: 3D image registration using a fast noniterative algorithm. Magn. Reson. Imaging **18**(9), 1143–1150 (2000). https://doi.org/10.1016/s0730-725x(00)00209-5

44. Schulte, T., Chen, S.H.A., Müller-Oehring, E.M., Adalsteinsson, E., Pfefferbaum, A., Sullivan, E.V.: fMRI evidence for individual differences in premotor modulation of extrastriatal visual–perceptual processing of redundant targets. NeuroImage **30**(3), 973–982 (2006). https://doi.org/10.1016/j.neuroimage.2005.10.023
45. De, A., Zhang, Y., Guo, C.: A parallel adaptive segmentation method based on SOM and GPU with application to MRI image processing. Neurocomputing **198**, 180–189 (2016). https://doi.org/10.1016/j.neucom.2015.10.129
46. Freiberger, M., Knoll, F., Bredies, K., Scharfetter, H., Stollberger, R.: The agile library for biomedical image reconstruction using GPU acceleration. Comput. Sci. Eng. **15**(1), 34–44 (2013). https://doi.org/10.1109/mcse.2012.40
47. Ding, W., Lin, C.-T., Chen, S., Zhang, X., Hu, B.: Multiagent-consensus-MapReduce-based attribute reduction using co-evolutionary quantum PSO for big data applications. Neurocomputing **272**, 136–153 (2018). https://doi.org/10.1016/j.neucom.2017.06.059
48. Ruijters, D., ter Haar Romeny, B.M., Suetens, P.: GPU-accelerated elastic 3D image registration for intra-surgical applications. Comput. Methods Programs Biomed. **103**(2), 104–112 (2011). https://doi.org/10.1016/j.cmpb.2010.08.014
49. Minati, L.: Fast computation of voxel-level brain connectivity maps from resting-state functional MRI using l_1-norm as approximation of Pearson's temporal correlation: proof-of-concept and example vector hardware implementation. Med. Eng. **36**, 1212–1217 (2014)
50. Lee, D., Yoo, J., Tak, S., Ye, J.C.: Deep residual learning for accelerated MRI using magnitude and phase networks. IEEE Trans. Biomed. Eng. **65**(9), 1985–1995 (2018). https://doi.org/10.1109/tbme.2018.2821699
51. Lin, W., Börnert, P., Huang, F., Duensing, G.R., Reykowski, A.: Generalized GRAPPA operators for wider spiral bands: rapid self-calibrated parallel reconstruction for variable density spiral MRI. Magn. Reson. Med. **66**(4), 1067–1078 (2011). https://doi.org/10.1002/mrm.22900. Generalized GRAPPA Operator for Wider Spiral Bands (GROWL)
52. Xu, L., Feng, Y., Liu, X., Kang, L., Chen, W.: Robust GRAPPA reconstruction using sparse multi-kernel learning with least squares support vector regression. Magn. Reson. Imaging **32**(1), 91–101 (2014). https://doi.org/10.1016/j.mri.2013.10.001

Watershed Segmentation for Peak Picking in Mass Spectrometry Data

Vojtěch Bartoň[1,2(✉)], Markéta Nykrýnová[1], and Helena Škutková[1]

[1] Department of Biomedical Engineering, Brno University of Technology, Brno, Czech Republic
barton@vutbr.cz

[2] RECETOX Centre, Masaryk University, Brno, Czech Republic
https://www.ubmi.feec.vutbr.cz/en/
https://www.recetox.muni.cz/en

Abstract. Mass spectrometry with gas chromatography is one of the emerging high-resolution instruments. This technology can be used to discover the composition of the chemical compounds. It is used for targeted detection or for untargeted screening. As such, this technology is providing a large volume of measurements. These data are also in high precision. There are emerging need to efficiently process these data and be able to identify and extract all possible information. There are numerous tools to do that, using common steps. One of the steps is peak picking, usually carried by signal processing methods. We are proposing a two-dimensional approach to identify the peaks and extract their features for further analysis. This method can be easily adaptable to fit the current pipelines and to perform the computation efficiently. We are proposing a method to preprocess the data onto a grid of required precision. After that, we are applying an image processing method watershed, to extract the region of interest and the peaks.

Keywords: Mass spectrometry · Peak picking · Image segmentation

1 Introduction

Mass spectrometry with gas chromatography is an analytical method used to identify compounds in the chemical sample. It is also used to quantify the compounds and discover the composition of the samples. It is widely used in environmental studies to discover toxic compounds and monitor their paths in the environment. Other usages include medical sciences, biological studies for proteomics, and forensic sciences [3].

Modern instruments like Orbitrap are using ion traps to capture fragmented ions and analyze them with mathematical methods. It is using Fourier transform to identify individual ions a determine their signal intensity as a measure of their abundance in the sample [12].

I. Rojas et al. (Eds.): IWBBIO 2020, LNBI 12108, pp. 494–502, 2020.
https://doi.org/10.1007/978-3-030-45385-5_44

This computational instrumentation allows measuring in high resolution. It allows us to identify the mass-to-charge ratio with a precision of above ten decimal places. This is making requirements to adapt the algorithms to process large amounts of data. Also, the databases used to compare the spectra need to be updated or recomputed to fit the high-resolution data [4].

Mass spectrometry experiments could be held in two modes: targeted and untargeted. During the targeted experiments, the operator can choose specific values for known chemicals. These values are then verified in the instrument if there is a signal prooving the occurrence of the substance. This mode is used if there is a list of suspected compounds that may occur in the sample [11].

The real challenge is to process untargeted data. During this mode, the instrument is scanning across a wide continuous range of values and recording all the signals from the sample. This type of experiment is used for screening purposes. It could be widely used in environmental screening studies to map the complex impact of pollution in the environment [5].

Using this type of experiment, it emerges the need to process complex samples of unknown compounds. Also, it is raising the need to process the samples from acquisition to compound identification automatically. The data processing in mass spectrometry experiments includes several steps from preprocessing, data filtration, noise removal, peak picking, deconvolution, and compound identification and quantification. Most of these steps are right now carried by signal processing methods and statistical techniques and working by scans. The example workflow of such processing is illustrated by Fig. 1 [2,9].

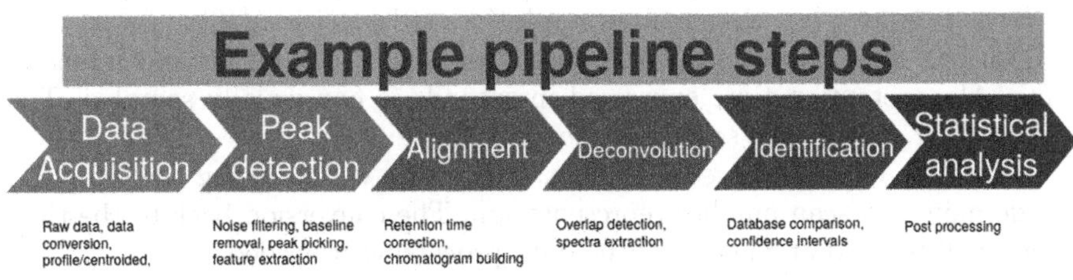

Fig. 1. Processing steps for mass spectrometry data.

One of the key parts of the workflow is the peak picking part. During this step, we reduce the data matrix to only a few points. Each point should represent a fragmented ion from the sample. This method should be robust enough to identify all ions data and not to be confused by a noise. There could be several types of noise added to the sample signal. One type of noise is contamination or partial fragmentation of the ions. Also, there could be a signal that originated in chemicals used to process the experiment. Another type of noise is an electric interference noise caused by parts of the measurement instrument [7].

One of the bottlenecks of the algorithms is the volume of data itself. As the precision of the instrument is so high, there is a need to represent all the scans in the same discrete scope. Ideally, to project all data point onto the same data grid. If there is a defined discrete grid of the data, we could use a known image processing methods to treat the data and process them all in one, and not by individual scans.

As a mass spectrometry imaging is a known method to produce microscopy-like images of samples based on their composition, using an image processing algorithm as a part of the processing pipeline for gas chromatography-mass spectrometry is not widely spread [6].

2 Experiment Processing

The raw data obtained from the instrument contain a lot of information. For our purpose, we only need to extract a three-column matrix of data point retention time, mass-to-charge ratio, and measured intensity of the signal. To be able to manipulate the data, it often needs to convert the vendor data format to some open alternative, such as *mzML*.

For a testing purpose, we were working with a gas chromatography-mass spectrometry experiment measured at orbitrap instrument with settings to produce profile data. This experiment showing flame retardants mixture. The processing pipeline is described in general, not optimized for this only experiment.

We transform the data into a matrix with coordinates in retention time and mass-to-charge ratio axis and the value represented as the intensity of the signal. Intensity can be expressed as a double format. Retention time can be shown in the time domain, or as integers of the ordering of the scans. The mass-to-charge axis format depends on the required resolution and precision [10].

With the first inspection of the data, we could see a lot of zero intensity points. Also, retention time expressed in seconds is non-equally sampled. The gaps between consecutive scans are shown in Fig. 2.

To have an equally spaced grid for the data, we will be using the retention time domain as a scan number representation. The conversion back to the time domain will be held at the end of the data processing if needed.

To get an equally spaced mass-to-charge axis, we need to resample the data. Datapoint in the mass-to-charge axis is sparsely distributed, producing an enormously large vector. The new sampling frequency will determine the precision of the measurement, and it is reducing the data sparsity and volume. There are numerous resampling techniques, including interpolation. To illustrate the influence of interpolation, look at Fig. 3.

The B-spline interpolation is producing unwanted artifacts forming undulation in the regions with zero intensity signals. These waves are sometimes even higher than some original signals. Based on this fact, we decided to use the basic linear interpolation for the resampling step.

After zero intensity values removal and resampling of the scans on the desired precision, we can construct the data matrix. The matrix building is about placing the scans vectors consecutively onto the same grid. To decrease the memory

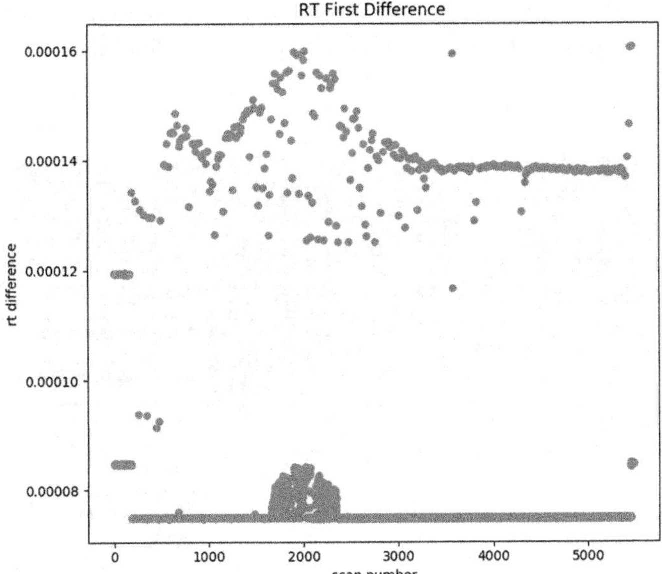

Fig. 2. First difference of consecutive scans in time domain.

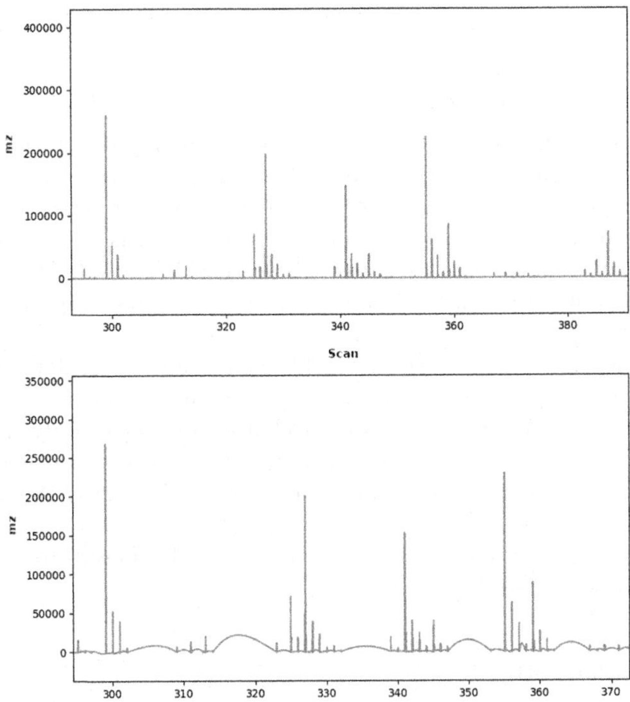

Fig. 3. Interpolation of scans. (Top - linear interpolation method, bottom - B-spline interpolation)

consumption of our dataset, we convert the matrix to a store it sparse matrix format. As the grid contain a lot of blank space. The final matrix is shown in Fig. 4.

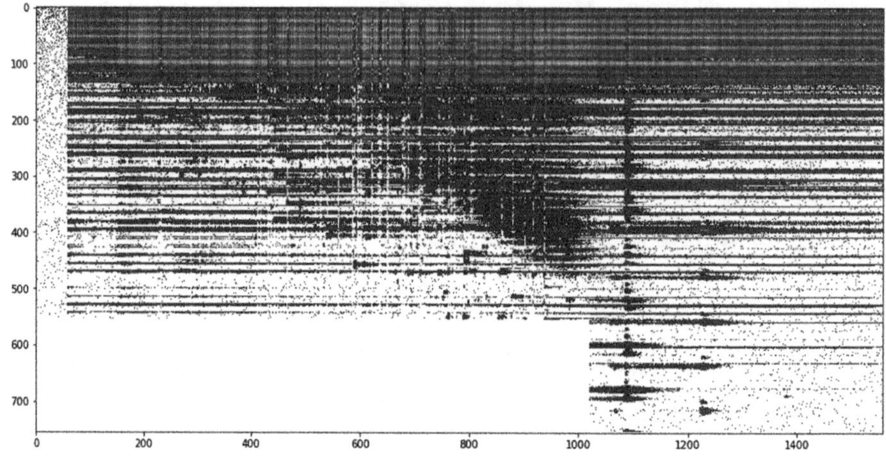

Fig. 4. Constructed data matrix.

3 ROIs

We use the procedure described above to obtain our input data matrix of signal intensity. This matrix is still quite large to be processed at once. We could divide the matrix into regions for more efficient processing. The region of interest is defined as a connected set of points. Each region is then extracted to a separate matrix, so none of the regions will overlap. It is needed to preserve the information about retention time values and the mass-to-charge ratio for each of the points.

We can then filter all the regions with a small number of data points, thus they are not able to form a valid peak. Also, we omitted for further processing the regions which are not variable enough. That means having only one retention time value, so unable to form a two-dimensional peak. These in-place filters help to decrease the volume of the data to process and to clear away the meaningless data.

Each of the regions is considered to be an image, which needs to be segmented into individual peaks areas.

4 Segmentation

Each region is processed separately to enable parallelization of whole pipeline. For the segmentation we choose to use watershed algorithm [1].

If there is still prevented a lot of noise in the sample, we can smoothen the surface. We use convolution with smoothening kernel, to remove a small oscilation of the surface.

To illustrate the method, we are attaching Fig. 5, showing a small regions. In first column is the raw data points, their interpolation in second column and the result after convolution with smoothening kernel in the last column.

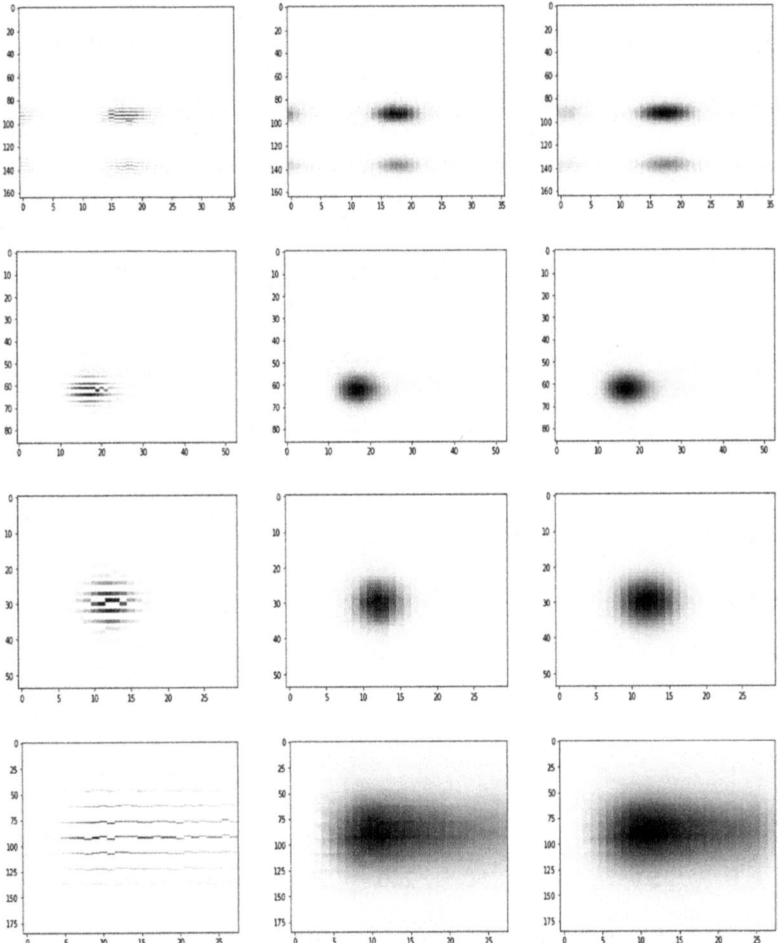

Fig. 5. Example of the regions for watershed segmentation. Each row contain the same peak. Raw data in first column. Second column contain interpolated data and last column showing the region after smoothening.

Resulted image is used as an input to watershed algorithm. To prevent over-segmentation we can use a marker-based algorithm. We set markers as a local maximas of the image, if its smoothened enough, or h-maximas if there is still some noise presented. The coordination of these markers are then provided to watershed algorithm. As an input image we need to transform the region image so the peaks will be presented as valleys. So the image is inverted.

Watershed segmentation provide as a certain number of regions, ideally each can be considered as one peak area.

5 Peak Picking

The labeled region from the watershed segmentation step is considered to contain one peak each. The maxima of the region are identified as a peak value. From the region, there is then computed several features to help identify and classify the peak. Example of one region with marked peaks is shown on Fig. 6. We compute peak area, kurtosis as a measure of the sharpness of the peak, center of mass, which should not be distant from the peak value of the region. An important feature is also eccentricity because there is an assumption of the Gaussian shape of all the peaks. If this criterion is not met, we can classify this peak for further confirmation as it is not a standard peak.

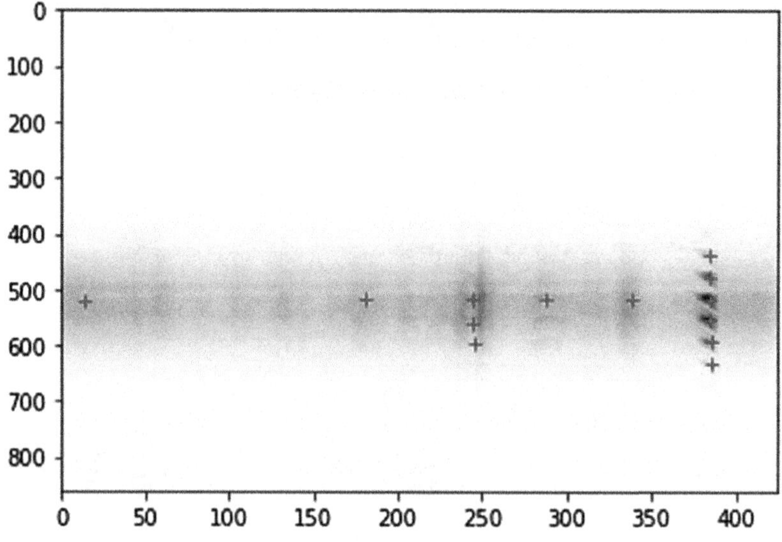

Fig. 6. Example of the regions with marked peaks.

6 Discussion

Presented algorithms for mass spectrometry data processing are dealing with a key part of a whole processing pipeline, peak picking. The proposed procedure is dealing with two main problems of spectrometric data obtained from high-resolution instruments like Orbitrap. First is the non-equality of the sampling rate, thus the non-existence of a natural grid for the measured data. This can be solved by resampling the data. This produces the equally distant grid and thus enabling the processing by an image processing algorithms.

The second problem is the volume of the data. This is overcome by using a sparse matrix data format for storing the experiment data. Then the data is divided into smaller regions, which can be processed individually at the desired precision. Also, the division into the separate regions enabling parallelization of the whole method.

Nevertheless, the peak picking part is only one step in the whole complex mass spectrometry data processing pipelines, including further steps like a peaks deconvolution, identifications, quantization, and more, depending on the selected application.

Most of the tools are working by scans, with signal processing methods. The hands of the analyst still hold most of the work in processing mass spectrometry data. Such as there are emerging many tools to automatize this process [8].

Our presented algorithm will still need to be tested on the complex samples to determine the right parameters, but as such, it is designed to be easily incorporated into the existing pipelines, representing only one of the complex tasks series.

7 Conclusion

We are presenting a possible way to deal with a peak picking step of mass spectra processing. Our approach is using simple image processing and such as can work in two dimensions. This approach can identify the peaks and their features, bypassing the traditional signal processing methods and the need for spectra alignment and their post-processing. Our peaks identified as a three-element vector of retention time, mass-to-charge ratio, and signal intensity can be easily adapted to be used in other known tools for mass spectrometry data processing.

Our approach is also adaptable to different mass-to-charge precision needs, which means that it could be used both for high and low-resolution instruments. It is also easily parallelizable to facilitate computation. This method works in 2D and so it is easy to identify and annotate the peaks by their feature in space. We also presented a simple way of adapting to the desired precision, and effectively storing the data, reducing the storage and computational demands.

Acknowledgment. Computational resources were provided by the CESNET LM2015042 and the CERIT Scientific Cloud LM2015085, provided under the programme "Projects of Large Research, Development, and Innovations Infrastructures".

This work was carried out with the support of the RECETOX (LM2018121) research infrastructures funded by the Ministry of Education, Youth and Sports of the Czech Republic.

References

1. Bieniek, A., Moga, A.: An efficient watershed algorithm based on connected components. Pattern Recogn. **33**(6), 907–916 (2000). https://doi.org/10.1016/S0031-3203(99)00154-5. https://linkinghub.elsevier.com/retrieve/pii/S0031320399001545
2. Castillo, S., Gopalacharyulu, P., Yetukuri, L., Orešič, M.: Algorithms and tools for the preprocessing of LC-MS metabolomics data. Chemometr. Intell. Lab. Syst. **108**(1), 23–32 (2011). https://doi.org/10.1016/j.chemolab.2011.03.010. https://linkinghub.elsevier.com/retrieve/pii/S0169743911000608
3. Considine, E.C., Thomas, G., Boulesteix, A.L., Khashan, A.S., Kenny, L.C.: Critical review of reporting of the data analysis step in metabolomics. Metabolomics **14**(1), 1–16 (2017). https://doi.org/10.1007/s11306-017-1299-3. http://link.springer.com/10.1007/s11306-017-1299-3
4. Dunn, W.B., Bailey, N.J.C., Johnson, H.E.: Measuring the metabolome. Analyst **130**(5) (2005). https://doi.org/10.1039/b418288j, http://xlink.rsc.org/?DOI=b418288j
5. Han, T.L., Yang, Y., Zhang, H., Law, K.P.: Analytical challenges of untargeted GC-MS-based metabolomics and the critical issues in selecting the data processing strategy. F1000Research **6** (2017). https://doi.org/10.12688/f1000research.11823.1, https://f1000research.com/articles/6-967/v1
6. He, J., et al.: Massimager. Anal. Chim. Acta **1015**, 50–57 (2018). https://doi.org/10.1016/j.aca.2018.02.030. https://linkinghub.elsevier.com/retrieve/pii/S0003267018302459
7. Johnsen, L.G., Skou, P.B., Khakimov, B., Bro, R.: Gas chromatography - mass spectrometry data processing made easy. J. Chromatogr. A **1503**, 57–64 (2017). https://doi.org/10.1016/j.chroma.2017.04.052
8. Pluskal, T., Castillo, S., Villar-Briones, A., Orešič, M.: Mzmine 2. BMC Bioinform. **11**(1) (2010). https://doi.org/10.1186/1471-2105-11-395, https://bmcbioinformatics.biomedcentral.com/articles/10.1186/1471-2105-11-395
9. Sturm, M., et al.: Openms – an open-source software framework for mass spectrometry. BMC Bioinform. **9**(1) (2008). https://doi.org/10.1186/1471-2105-9-163, https://bmcbioinformatics.biomedcentral.com/articles/10.1186/1471-2105-9-163
10. Treviño, V., et al.: Gridmass. J. Mass Spectrom. **50**(1), 165–174 (2015). https://doi.org/10.1002/jms.3512. http://doi.wiley.com/10.1002/jms.3512
11. Wei, X., et al.: Metsign. Anal. Chem. **83**(20), 7668–7675 (2011). https://doi.org/10.1021/ac2017025
12. Zubarev, R.A., Makarov, A.: Orbitrap mass spectrometry. Anal. Chem. **85**(11), 5288–5296 (2013). https://doi.org/10.1021/ac4001223. https://pubs.acs.org/doi/10.1021/ac4001223

High-Throughput Genomics: Bioinformatic Tools and Medical Applications

LuxHS: DNA Methylation Analysis with Spatially Varying Correlation Structure

Viivi Halla-aho(✉) and Harri Lähdesmäki

Aalto University, 00076 Aalto, Finland
{viivi.halla-aho,harri.lahdesmaki}@aalto.fi

Abstract. Bisulfite sequencing (BS-seq) is a popular method for measuring DNA methylation in basepair-resolution. Many BS-seq data analysis tools utilize the assumption of spatial correlation among the neighboring cytosines' methylation states. While being a fair assumption, most existing methods leave out the possibility of deviation from the spatial correlation pattern. Our approach builds on a method which combines a generalized linear mixed model (GLMM) with a likelihood that is specific for BS-seq data and that incorporates a spatial correlation for methylation levels. We propose a novel technique using a sparsity promoting prior to enable cytosines deviating from the spatial correlation pattern. The method is tested with both simulated and real BS-seq data and compared to other differential methylation analysis tools.

Keywords: DNA methylation · Bayesian analysis · Spatial correlation

1 Introduction

DNA methylation is an epigenetic modification of the DNA where a methyl group is attached to a cytosine of the DNA. This phenomenon is essential for normal function of eukaryotic cells, and abnormal DNA methylation levels have been linked to diseases and cancer. DNA methylation is known to be a spatially correlated phenomena. In some cases, however, one or more cytosines in a local neighbourhood can deviate from the spatial correlation pattern due to e.g. transcription factor binding [4].

Many of the tools for differential methylation analysis assume spatial correlation without allowing cytosines to deviate from a common spatial correlation pattern. This inflexibility can lead us to not detecting all the possibly differentially methylated cytosines and could muddle the evidence for the non-deviating cytosines as well. For example RADMeth [3], which uses beta-binomial regression and weighted Z test and M^{3}D [8] where maximum mean discrepancies over the regions are used for p-value calculation do not support finding deviating cytosines. One of the tools that could take such deviation into account is BiSeq [7] which has a hierarchical procedure, where defined CpG clusters are first tested by taking the spatial correlation into account and then trimming the found differentially methylated regions (DMRs) by removing the not differentially methylated cytosines from the regions. Even though spatial correlation is assumed in

I. Rojas et al. (Eds.): IWBBIO 2020, LNBI 12108, pp. 505–516, 2020.
https://doi.org/10.1007/978-3-030-45385-5_45

the first testing phase and preprocessing of the data includes smoothing, the second step allows for controlling location-wise false discovery rate (FDR). Also, BiSeq tool divides a DMR into smaller regions if the sign of the methylation difference changes.

In [5] we proposed a novel method LuxUS, that assumes spatial correlation for cytosines in a genomic window of interest. However, the method does not support detecting deviating cytosines and it calculates one Bayes factor for the whole genomic window. Here we present a different formulation of the spatial correlation that enables the analysis of deviating cytosines by introducing weight variables d_i for each cytosine i in the genomic window. The weight variable will tell whether the corresponding cytosine follows the general spatial correlation pattern or not. Horseshoe priors [2] are often used to enhance sparsity of the coefficients in generalized linear models, where the number of covariates in the model is very high and it is assumed that many of them have little effect on the predicted variable. Here we utilize horseshoe prior in the definition of the weight variables d_i. The statistical testing, i.e. calculation of Bayes factors, is done for each cytosine separately.

2 Methods

In this section the LuxHS model and analysis workflow is described. The model consists of a data generating process and a generalized linear mixed model, which models the methylation proportions by taking into account covariates, replicate effects and spatial correlation. After this the fitting of the model parameters and the method for testing for differential methylation is explained.

The first step of workflow in LuxHS analysis is to divide the data set of interest into genomic windows, which are then analysed one at a time with possibility of parallelisation. A simple preanalysis method for this purpose was proposed by Halla-aho and Lähdesmäki [5]. The cytosines are divided into genomic windows based on their genomic distance and a maximum number of cytosines in a window while filtering out cytosines with low coverage. Genomic windows with too low average coverage can also be filtered out. For windows with high enough coverage, an F-test is performed to quantify the significance for the variable of interest. The F-test p-value threshold is set to a moderate value to refrain from filtering out too many prospective genomic windows. The windows that passed the F-test phase are further processed into LuxHS input format. The model parameters are fitted, after which statistical testing is performed. Finally, the found differentially methylated cytosines can be combined into DMRs for which a follow-up analysis, such as gene-enrichment analysis, can be performed.

2.1 Model

Plate diagram of the model is presented in Fig. 1. The analysis of an experiment with N_R samples is performed for a genomic window with N_C cytosines at a time. The total sequencing read counts for each cytosine are stored in $\mathbf{N}_{\mathrm{BS,tot}}$

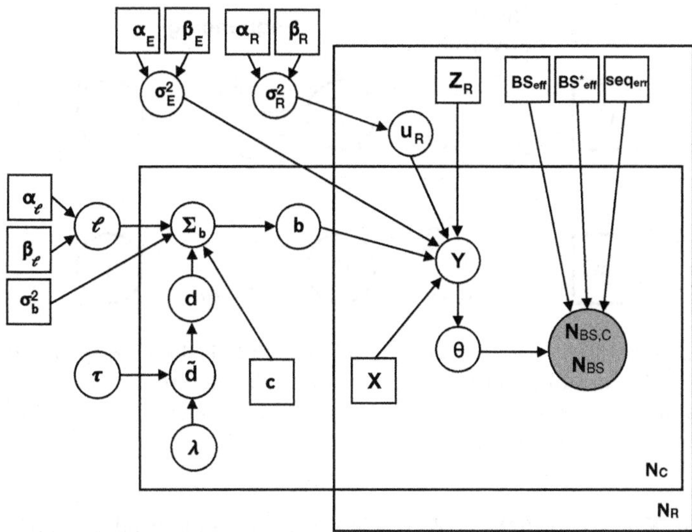

Fig. 1. Plate diagram of the LuxHS model. Rectangles represent input data such as design matrices or fixed hyperparameters. White and grey circles represent latent and observed variables respectively.

out of which $\mathbf{N}_{\mathrm{BS,C}}$ (both vectors of length $N_C \cdot N_R$) were methylated. If the experimental parameters for each sample are available, they can be stored in vectors $\mathbf{BS}_{\mathrm{eff}}$, $\mathbf{BS}^*_{\mathrm{eff}}$ and $\mathbf{seq}_{\mathrm{err}}$, each of length N_R, which correspond to bisulfite conversion efficiency, incorrect bisulfite conversion efficiency and sequencing error. If the experimental parameters are not known, they can be set to correspond to a perfect experiment with no sequencing error and perfect bisulfite conversion efficiency.

The methylated cytosine count $N_{\mathrm{BS,C},i}$ for observation i, $i = 1, ..., N_R \cdot N_C$, follows binomial distribution

$$N_{\mathrm{BS,C},i} \sim \mathrm{Binomial}(N_{\mathrm{BS,tot},i}, p_{\mathrm{BS,C},i}) \tag{1}$$

with success probability, e.g. probability of observing a C in bisulfite sequencing experiment, $p_{\mathrm{BS,C},i}$, which is calculated as

$$\begin{aligned} p_{\mathrm{BS,C},i} = \;& \theta_i((1 - \mathrm{seq}_{\mathrm{err},i})(1 - \mathrm{BS}_{\mathrm{eff},i}) + \mathrm{seq}_{err}\mathrm{BS}_{\mathrm{eff},i}) \\ &+ (1 - \theta_i)((1 - \mathrm{seq}_{\mathrm{err},i})(1 - \mathrm{BS}^*_{\mathrm{eff},i}) + \mathrm{seq}_{err}\mathrm{BS}^*_{\mathrm{eff},i}), \end{aligned}$$

where θ_i is the methylation proportion for the observation i, $i = 1, ..., N_C \cdot N_R$. $\mathrm{seq}_{\mathrm{err},i}$, $\mathrm{BS}_{\mathrm{eff},i}$ and $\mathrm{BS}^*_{\mathrm{eff},i}$ are the experimental parameters for the replicate corresponding to index i. The equation follows the probability tree in Fig. 2. This is the same data generating process as in LuxGLM [1] for non-methylated and methylated cytosines. Methylation proportions are estimated using the generalized linear mixed model of the form

$$\mathbf{Y} = \mathbf{X}\mathbf{b} + \mathbf{Z}_R\mathbf{u}_R + \mathbf{e}, \tag{2}$$

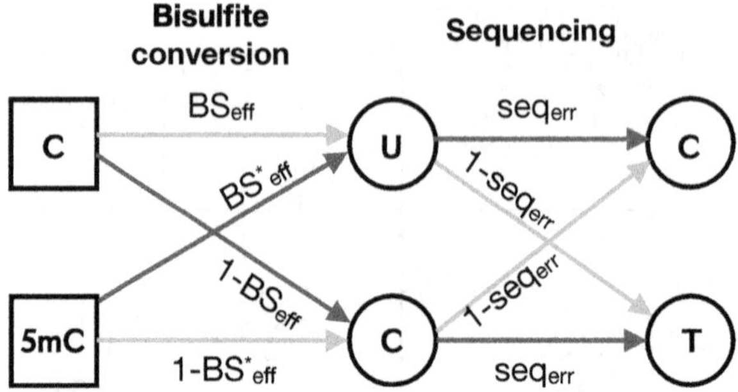

Fig. 2. The probability tree for observing a C or T in bisulfite sequencing data when the true methylation state is methylated or unmethylated. Green and red edges lead to correct and incorrect outcome nodes of the bisulfite conversion and sequencing steps, respectively. (Color figure online)

where term $\mathbf{Xb}$ is fixed effect, $\mathbf{Z}_R\mathbf{u}_R$ is replicate random effect and $\mathbf{e}$ is noise term with distribution $\mathbf{e} \sim N(0, \sigma_E^2 \mathbf{I})$ and prior $\sigma_E^2 \sim \text{Gamma}(\alpha_E, \beta_E)$. The number of covariates in the fixed effect term is N_P. Each of the cytosines has its own set of fixed effect coefficient vector $\mathbf{b}_j$ of length N_P, $j = 1, ..., N_C$, and thus $\mathbf{b} = [\mathbf{b}_1^T, \ldots, \mathbf{b}_{N_C}^T]^T$ has length $N_C \cdot N_P$. The design matrix $\mathbf{X}$ size is $(N_C \cdot N_R) \times (N_C \cdot N_P)$ and it has the individual cytosine design matrices as block matrices in the diagonal. The fixed effect coefficients have prior distribution $\mathbf{b} \sim N(0, \boldsymbol{\Sigma}_\mathbf{b})$, where $\boldsymbol{\Sigma}_\mathbf{b}$ is a covariance matrix. Matrix $\mathbf{Z}_R$ is the random effect design matrix of size $(N_C \cdot N_R) \times N_R$ and the vector $\mathbf{u}_R$ of length N_R contains the effects for each replicate. The effects have a normal prior distribution $\mathbf{u}_R \sim N(0, \sigma_R^2 \mathbf{I})$, where $\sigma_R^2 \sim \text{Gamma}(\alpha_R, \beta_R)$ is the variance term for the replicate random effect.

The spatial correlation structure is brought to the model through the fixed effect coefficients' covariance matrix $\boldsymbol{\Sigma}_\mathbf{b}$. Using indexing notation $b_{j,k}$, $j = 1, ..., N_C$, $k = 1, ..., N_P$, to distinguish coefficients for each cytosine and covariate, $\boldsymbol{\Sigma}_\mathbf{b}$ can be expressed as

$$\boldsymbol{\Sigma}_\mathbf{b} = \begin{pmatrix} \sigma_b^2 & \text{cov}(b_{1,1}, b_{1,2}) & \cdots & \text{cov}(b_{1,1}, b_{N_C,N_P}) \\ \text{cov}(b_{1,2}, b_{1,1}) & \sigma_b^2 & \cdots & \text{cov}(b_{1,2}, b_{N_C,N_P}) \\ \vdots & \vdots & \ddots & \vdots \\ \text{cov}(b_{N_C,N_P}, b_{1,1}) & \text{cov}(b_{N_C,N_P}, b_{1,2}) & \cdots & \sigma_b^2 \end{pmatrix}, \tag{3}$$

where the covariance terms are

$$\text{cov}(b_{j,k}, b_{j',k'}) = \begin{cases} \sigma_b^2 \cdot \exp\left(\frac{-|c_j - c_{j'}|}{\ell^2}\right) \cdot d_j \cdot d_{j'} & \text{, if } k = k' \\ 0 & \text{, if } k \neq k', \end{cases}$$

which gives the coefficients of different covariates zero covariance to fulfill linear model requirements. In the computation of the covariance terms, the cytosine locations c_j and $c_{j'}$ and the lengthscale parameter ℓ with prior $\ell \sim$

Gamma$(\alpha_\ell, \beta_\ell)$ are used. The coefficient variance σ_b^2 is set to the value 15. Weight variables d_j and $d_{j'}$ tell whether the corresponding cytosine follows the correlation pattern along with its neighboring cytosines. The weight variables can have values ranging from 0 to 1, and they have the ability to scale down the covariance terms $\text{cov}(b_{j,k}, b_{j',k'})$.

The correlation weight variable d_j for cytosine $j = 1, ..., N_C$ is calculated through transformation

$$d_j = 1 - f(\tilde{d}_j), \tag{4}$$

where transformation function $f(x)$ is a generalized logistic function

$$f(x) = A + \frac{K - A}{(C + Q \cdot \exp(-B \cdot x))^{\frac{1}{\nu}}}, \tag{5}$$

where $A = 0$, $K = 1$, $C = 1$, $Q = 10$, $B = 5$ and $\nu = 0.5$. This transformation ensures that the resulting d_j have values from range $[0, 1]$. The auxiliary variable $\tilde{d}_j$ has a horseshoe prior with the modification of the normal priors for $\tilde{d}_j$ being restricted to the positive side, defined as

$$\tilde{d}_j \sim N^+(0, \tau^2 \cdot \lambda_j^2), \tag{6}$$

where the global shrinkage parameter τ and local shrinkage parameters λ_j have positive Cauchy hyperpriors $\tau \sim C^+(0, 1)$, and $\lambda_j \sim C^+(0, 1)$. The level of sparsity of vector $\tilde{\mathbf{d}} = [\tilde{d}_1, \ldots, \tilde{d}_{N_C}]^T$ containing $\tilde{d}_j$, $j = 1, ..., N_C$, can be controlled with the choice of hyperprior for τ.

Finally, the methylation proportions θ_i in Eq. 2 are calculated with the sigmoid function

$$\theta_i = \frac{1}{1 + \exp(-Y_i)}. \tag{7}$$

2.2 Fitting the Model Parameters with Stan and Testing Differential Methylation

The model is implemented with probabilistic programming language Stan, and the Stan program is used for sampling from the posterior distribution. Stan offers both Hamiltonian Monte Carlo (HMC) and automatic differentation variational inference (ADVI) approaches for obtaining posterior samples and either one can be used for LuxHS. As variational inference approaches are often faster than Markov chain Monte Carlo (MCMC) methods such as HMC, they are a potential alternative to MCMC in computationally heavy tasks.

After obtaining samples for the model parameters, Bayes factors can be calculated for each cytosine to describe the evidence for two alternative models. The testing is done cytosine-wise, which enables deviating Bayes factor values inside a genomic window. There are two versions of the differential methylation test, with the type 1 test having a base model $M_0 : b_{j,k} = 0$ and an alternative model $M_1 : b_{j,k} \neq 0$, subscript j corresponding to the cytosines $j = 1, ..., N_C$ and subscript k corresponding to the covariate of interest. The type 2 test has a base model $M_0 : b_{j,k} - b_{j,k'} = 0$ and an alternative model $M_1 : b_{j,k} - b_{j,k'} \neq 0$, subscripts k and k' corresponding to the covariates of interest. Corresponding Bayes factors (BF) are used for the testing. As exact Bayes factors are intractable, Savage-Dickey estimates of the BFs are used instead. S-D estimate for the type 1 test is

$$BF \approx \frac{p(b_{i,j} = 0|M_1)}{p(b_{i,j} = 0|M_1, \mathcal{D})}, \tag{8}$$

where $\mathcal{D}$ is the data. The numerator is calculated using the normal prior for $\mathbf{b} \sim N(\mathbf{0}, \Sigma_b)$ and the denominator is estimated from the obtained samples using kernel density estimation. The type 2 test S-D estimate is formed similarly.

3 Results

In this section we present the results for real and simulated BS-seq data sets. We first analyze whole genome bisulfite sequencing (WGBS-seq) data from [6] and demonstrate that LuxHS can identify differentially methylated cytosines as well as individual cytosines whose methylation state deviate from the general spatial correlation pattern. With simulated data (for which we know the ground truth) we quantitatively evaluate LuxHS performance and compare with other state-of-the-art methods.

3.1 Real Bisulfite Sequencing Data

The colon cancer data set by Hansen [6] was used for testing LuxHS. The data set consists of six paired colon cancer and healthy colon tissue samples. The preanalysis step was run on data from chromosome 22 with the same settings as for LuxUS [5], and it resulted with 4728 genomic windows that passed the coverage and F-test criteria. Those genomic windows covered 86189 cytosines in total. For these windows, LuxHS analysis was performed. The LuxHS BF value distribution consisting of all 86189 cytosines is shown in Fig. 3. The histogram demonstrates that large majority of the Bayes factors had value smaller than 10 (or $\log(BF) \leq 1$), but there are also a few cytosines with high BF values indicating differential methylation. In total 5334 cytosines had BF$>$ 3. To filter the results even further, a threshold for the minimum average difference between the case and control sample methylation states can be applied. In comparison, LuxUS analysis resulted in 593 windows (covering 10324 cytosines) with BF$>$ 3, more detailed description of the results can be found from [5].

The number of cytosines for which the weight variables d were below 0.5 was 464. The Fig. 4 demonstrates the differences between LuxUS and LuxHS results for a genomic window chr22:27014415-27015343. LuxUS gives one BF value (1.480) for the whole window, which suggests that there is no statistically significant differential methylation in the region. In contrary, LuxHS gives a Bayes factor for every cytosine separately while at the same time achieving two important goals: utilizing spatial correlation across the whole window of interest, and simultaneously detecting individual cytosines that deviate from

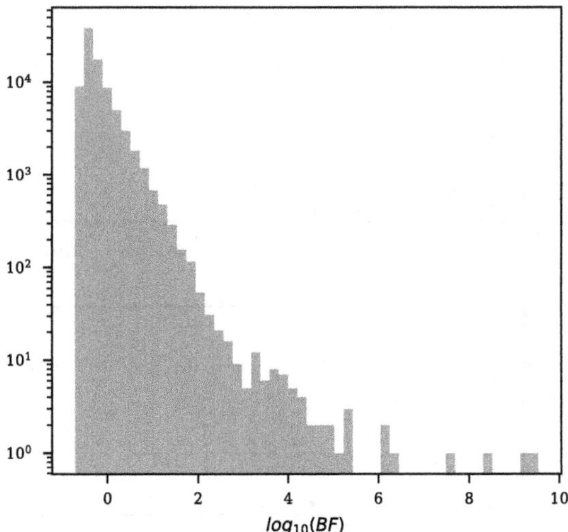

Fig. 3. Histogram of the log(BF) values for the colon cancer data set. The y-axis of the histogram is in log-scale.

this correlation pattern. Consequently, LuxHS is able to adapt to changes in the data swiftly. In the lowest panel of Fig. 4 it can be seen how LuxHS finds the cytosines for which the methylation states especially for the case samples are lower than in general in the window, and gives those cytosines lower weight parameter d values.

3.2 Simulated Data

The data simulation was done using the LuxHS model, using variances $\sigma_E^2 = 1$, $\sigma_B^2 = 0.25$ and $\sigma_R^2 = 0.69$. The experimental design of the simulations included an intercept term and a case-control binary covariate. The used coefficient mean μ_B values were $[-1.4, 1]$, $[-1.4, 1.8]$,$[-1.4, 2.3]$ and $[-1.4, 2.8]$, corresponding to methylation state differences between the case and control groups $\Delta\theta$ values 0.2, 0.4, 0.5 and 0.6 respectively. The data is generated for type 1 tests. The number of total reads $N_{\text{BS,tot}}$ for the methylated counts generation and the number of replicates N_R both had values 6, 12 and 24. For each combination of μ_B, $N_{\text{BS,tot}}$ and N_R we generated 100 data sets (each containing a genomic window of width 1000bp with 10 cytosines at randomly chosen locations) with and without differential methylation. The deviating cytosines had both opposite differential methylation status and deviating methylation state. We simulated data sets with 0, 1 and 2 deviating cytosines per data set. In this section we will refer to the number of deviating cytosines as N_D.

LuxHS model was compared to four other models and tools: LuxUS [5], LuxUS applied separately to every cytosine (cytosine random effect removed from the model), RADMeth [3] and BiSeq [7]. Also, LuxHS models estimated

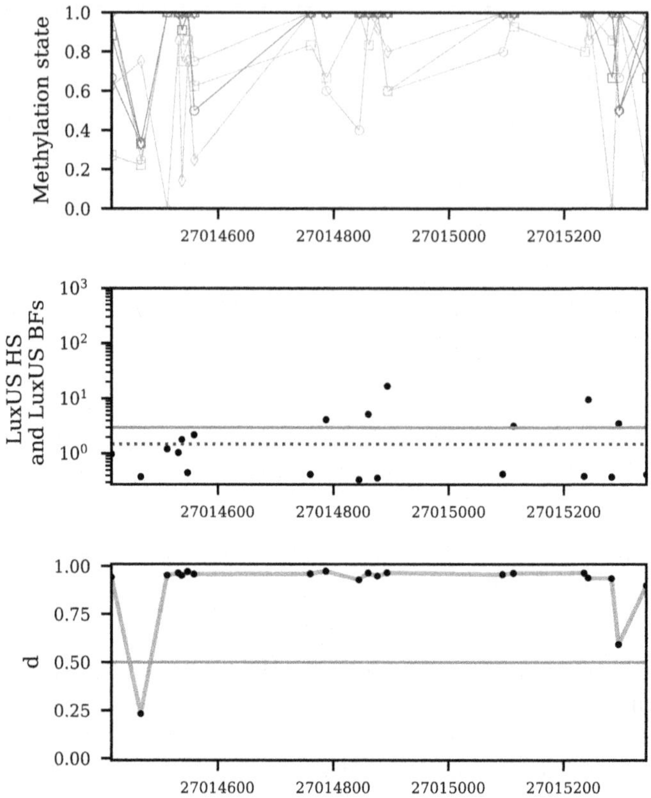

Fig. 4. Results for a genomic region chr22:27014415-27015343. The top panel shows the methylation state data (as fractions $N_{\mathrm{BS,tot}}/N_{\mathrm{BS,C}}$) for the cytosines included in this genomic region. The cases have been plotted with purple and controls with orange, each replicate pair with a marker of its own. In the middle panel the LuxUS BF for the same region is plotted with the dashed blue line. The red line shows the threshold of BF value 3. The black dots are the LuxHS Bayes factors for each cytosine. The lowest panel shows the posterior mean of the samples for d, red line is plotted at value $d = 0.5$. (Color figure online)

with HMC and ADVI approaches are compared. BiSeq and RADMeth were ran with default settings. We decided not to present the BiSeq results, as BiSeq did not perform very well with the simulated data. This is perhaps due to the small size of the simulated genomic regions. The comparison was done with Receiver Operating Characteristic (ROC) curve statistics for all method. RADMeth runs resulted in a few NaN p-values, which were removed from the AUROC and TPR calculation. Area Under ROC curve (AUROC) value tables for $N_D = 1$ and $N_D = 2$ in Tables 1 and 2 show that when the magnitude of differential methylation $\Delta\theta$ is smaller, LuxUS performs the best. When $\Delta\theta$ is higher, LuxHS and LuxUS for each cytosine separately have the highest AUROC values.

Table 1. AUROC values for the simulated data set with one deviating cytosine ($N_D = 1$) with best value for each simulation setting in bold.

		$\mu_B = [-1.4, 1]$					$\mu_B = [-1.4, 2.3]$				
		LuxHS	LuxHS	LuxUS		RADMeth	LuxHS	LuxHS	LuxUS		RADMeth
N_R	$N_{\text{BS,tot}}$	HMC	ADVI	sep	LuxUS	(NaN values)	HMC	ADVI	sep	LuxUS	(NaN values)
6	**6**	0.528	0.532	0.488	**0.587**	0.565 (29)	0.821	0.809	0.747	**0.836**	0.808 (46)
12	**6**	0.622	0.62	0.592	**0.654**	0.648 (0)	**0.894**	0.874	0.856	0.872	0.839 (31)
24	**6**	0.682	0.674	0.666	**0.732**	0.676 (20)	**0.959**	0.947	0.947	0.893	0.887 (30)
6	**12**	0.539	0.543	0.522	0.565	**0.569** (0)	0.835	0.811	0.783	**0.836**	0.796 (10)
12	**12**	0.612	0.601	0.588	**0.66**	0.614 (10)	**0.917**	0.904	0.899	0.883	0.871 (10)
24	**12**	0.708	0.704	0.699	**0.714**	0.698 (0)	**0.975**	0.967	0.967	0.896	0.899 (40)
6	**24**	0.59	0.584	0.569	**0.618**	0.59 (10)	**0.828**	0.812	0.792	0.812	0.791 (10)
12	**24**	0.664	0.656	0.641	**0.688**	0.651 (30)	**0.906**	0.894	0.894	0.852	0.839 (10)
24	**24**	0.75	0.747	0.74	**0.767**	0.727 (10)	**0.974**	0.969	0.97	0.891	0.884 (30)

Table 2. AUROC values for the simulated data set with two deviating cytosines ($N_D = 2$) with best value for each simulation setting in bold.

		$\mu_B = [-1.4, 1]$					$\mu_B = [-1.4, 2.3]$				
		LuxHS	LuxHS	LuxUS		RADMeth	LuxHS	LuxHS	LuxUS		RADMeth
N_R	$N_{\text{BS,tot}}$	HMC	ADVI	sep	LuxUS	(NaN values)	HMC	ADVI	sep	LuxUS	(NaN values)
6	**6**	0.554	0.544	0.537	**0.568**	**0.568**(36)	**0.759**	0.73	0.742	0.712	0.685 (53)
12	**6**	0.618	0.607	0.61	**0.622**	0.599 (20)	**0.858**	0.823	0.845	0.75	0.742 (20)
24	**6**	**0.702**	0.687	0.697	0.679	0.678 (30)	**0.952**	0.934	0.95	0.782	0.797 (30)
6	**12**	0.563	0.538	0.556	**0.579**	0.564 (1)	**0.796**	0.769	0.779	0.722	0.721 (30)
12	**12**	0.599	0.585	0.6	**0.606**	0.586 (20)	**0.897**	0.88	0.896	0.757	0.751 (10)
24	**12**	0.686	0.68	**0.692**	0.635	0.639 (20)	0.956	0.945	**0.958**	0.783	0.802 (10)
6	**24**	0.557	0.555	0.553	**0.565**	0.538 (30)	**0.835**	0.808	0.825	0.738	0.729 (10)
12	**24**	0.648	0.641	**0.651**	0.622	0.588 (30)	0.905	0.889	**0.906**	0.75	0.774 (10)
24	**24**	0.696	0.695	**0.702**	0.658	0.639 (30)	**0.965**	0.957	**0.965**	0.785	0.787 (10)

Based on the AUROC values, HMC version of LuxHS performs consistently slightly better than ADVI. The strength of ADVI is its computational efficiency. The mean runtime (over the 200 generated genomic windows) of the HMC version ranged from 40 to 971 s (for $\mu_B = [-1.4, 1]$, $N_{\text{BS,tot}} = [6, 12, 24]$ and $N_R = [6, 12, 24]$), while for ADVI the range is $5 - 47$ s. The computations were run on a computation cluster.

The accuracy of estimating whether a cytosine is deviating or non-deviating from the common spatial correlation pattern was assessed using the estimated weight variable values d_j. The posterior means of all weight variables were computed, and AUROC and TPRs were determined. The results in Table 3 show, that overall LuxHS can determine the deviance status accurately, but it seems not to be able to find all of the deviating cytosines. This indicates, that LuxHS rather gives too high d values than too low.

To investigate how LuxHS behaves when there are no deviating cytosines, such data sets were simulated and LuxHS analysis was performed along with

Table 3. AUROC and true positive rates (TPR) for detecting the deviating cytosines in simulated data sets for LuxHS (HMC). AUROC was calculated using the posterior means for each d_j. For the TPR calculation the jth cytosine is considered deviating if the posterior mean of d_j is smaller than a threshold value. The results for two weight value thresholds 0.5 and 0.75 are shown in separate columns.

	AUROC			TPR (0.5)			TPR (0.75)		
N_R	$N_{\text{BS,tot}}$								
	6	12	24	6	12	24	6	12	24
	$N_D = 1$, $\mu_B = [-1.4, 1]$								
6	0.788	0.832	0.858	0.095	0.12	0.065	0.37	0.295	0.23
12	0.877	0.882	0.905	0.09	0.105	0.07	0.255	0.29	0.295
24	0.935	0.935	0.938	0.1	0.035	0.055	0.33	0.31	0.25
	$N_D = 1$, $\mu_B = [-1.4, 2.3]$								
6	0.774	0.853	0.888	0.14	0.09	0.125	0.315	0.36	0.34
12	0.885	0.930	0.939	0.145	0.13	0.18	0.38	0.345	0.46
24	0.965	0.967	0.983	0.175	0.17	0.19	0.455	0.45	0.535
	$N_D = 2$, $\mu_B = [-1.4, 1]$								
6	0.751	0.775	0.763	0.138	0.093	0.073	0.435	0.35	0.218
12	0.791	0.842	0.829	0.095	0.09	0.07	0.305	0.3075	0.268
24	0.869	0.846	0.864	0.075	0.078	0.065	0.275	0.29	0.278
	$N_D = 2$, $\mu_B = [-1.4, 2.3]$								
6	0.741	0.786	0.804	0.103	0.11	0.118	0.36	0.318	0.358
12	0.833	0.863	0.869	0.153	0.145	0.11	0.423	0.408	0.313
24	0.893	0.899	0.937	0.15	0.16	0.183	0.458	0.458	0.5

the other methods it was compared to earlier. The data was simulated with $\Delta\theta = 0.5$. Out of the compared methods, LuxUS had the best AUROC values (see Table 4). LuxHS showed relatively good performance, demonstrating that the added flexibility of modeling cytosines that can deviate from the general spatial correlation pattern does not significantly decrease the performance of differential methylation analysis in the case of all cytosines following the same correlation pattern. Recall that for the cases where one or more of the cytosines deviate from the spatial correlation pattern LuxHS can reach state-of-the-art performance (see Tables 1 and 2). Moreover, LuxHS does not impose small values of weight variables d_j where it is not appropriate. There were no d_j values smaller than 0.5 for any of the generated genomic windows in any of the simulation settings.

4 Discussion

The analysis of real and simulated BS-seq data shows that LuxHS model can detect loci where the methylation state deviates from the surrounding cytosines.

Table 4. AUROC values for the simulated data set with zero deviating cytosines. $\mu_B = [-1.4, 2.3]$ was used for the simulations. The best AUROC for each simulation setting is shown bolded.

N_R	$N_{\mathrm{BS,tot}}$	LuxHS HMC	LuxHS ADVI	LuxUS sep	LuxUS	RADMeth (NaN values)
6	**6**	0.865	0.875	0.755	**0.943**	0.896 (3)
12	**6**	0.925	0.93	0.863	**0.972**	0.945 (0)
24	**6**	0.965	0.965	0.935	**0.994**	0.977 (30)
6	**12**	0.874	0.879	0.794	**0.941**	0.885 (21)
12	**12**	0.964	0.962	0.915	**0.992**	0.972 (40)
24	**12**	0.967	0.961	0.948	**0.99**	0.973 (10)
6	**24**	0.848	0.846	0.787	**0.906**	0.869 (10)
12	**24**	0.925	0.92	0.889	**0.967**	0.936 (40)
24	**24**	0.982	0.978	0.971	**0.998**	0.986 (20)

The tests with the simulated data show that the way LuxHS calculates Bayes factors separately for each cytosine can improve the accuracy when compared to LuxUS or other state-of-the-art methods, especially if the proportion of deviating cytosines is high.

The proportion of deviating cytosines that can be found in a genomic window could be further tweaked through the choice of hyperprior for global horseshoe prior τ. For example, the recommendations in [9] could be used if the default prior does not match the user's beliefs about the number of deviating cytosines.

The covariance structure with possibility of breaking the correlation pattern might also be advantageous in other bioinformatic modeling purposes, where a spatial correlation pattern with possibility of deviation is needed. The spatial correlation structure proposed in here can be easily applied in a general or generalized linear model setting. Another application could be time series analysis, where consecutive time points are often correlated, but some of the time points may deviate from the expected correlation pattern e.g. due to an outlier value.

5 Conclusion

In this work we propose a novel method for differential methylation analysis, LuxHS. The tool supports detecting cytosines, which do not follow the same methylation pattern as its neighboring cytosines. This could happen because of e.g. transcription factor binding. The results with simulated and real BS-seq data show, that LuxHS is able to detect such cytosines and that this feature increases the accuracy of differential methylation analysis, especially when the number of deviating cytosines or the amount of differential methylation is higher. The tool and usage instructions are available in GitHub repository in https://github.com/hallav/LuxUS-HS.

Acknowlegements. The calculations presented above were performed using computer resources within the Aalto University School of Science "Science-IT" project.

Funding. This work has been supported by the Academy of Finland (project numbers: 292660 and 314445).

References

1. Äijö, T., Yue, X., Rao, A., Lähdesmäki, H.: LuxGLM: a probabilistic covariate model for quantification of DNA methylation modifications with complex experimental designs. Bioinformatics **32**(17), i511–i519 (2016)
2. Carvalho, C.M., Polson, N.G., Scott, J.G.: Handling sparsity via the horseshoe. In: Artificial Intelligence and Statistics, pp. 73–80 (2009)
3. Dolzhenko, E., Smith, A.D.: Using beta-binomial regression for high-precision differential methylation analysis in multifactor whole-genome bisulfite sequencing experiments. BMC Bioinform. **15**(1), 215 (2014)
4. Domcke, S., Bardet, A.F., Ginno, P.A., Hartl, D., Burger, L., Schübeler, D.: Competition between dna methylation and transcription factors determines binding of NRF1. Nature **528**(7583), 575 (2015)
5. Halla-aho, V., Lähdesmäki, H.: LuxUS: detecting differential DNA methylation using generalized linear mixed model with spatial correlation structure. bioRxiv, p. 536722 (2019)
6. Hansen, K.D.: bsseqData: example whole genome bisulfite data for the bsseq package. R package version 0.12.0. (2016)
7. Hebestreit, K., Dugas, M., Klein, H.U.: Detection of significantly differentially methylated regions in targeted bisulfite sequencing data. Bioinformatics **29**(13), 1647–1653 (2013)
8. Mayo, T.R., Schweikert, G., Sanguinetti, G.: M3D: a kernel-based test for spatially correlated changes in methylation profiles. Bioinformatics **31**(6), 809–816 (2014)
9. Piironen, J., Vehtari, A.: On the hyperprior choice for the global shrinkage parameter in the horseshoe prior. arXiv preprint arXiv:1610.05559 (2016)

Unravelling Disease Presentation Patterns in ALS Using Biclustering for Discriminative Meta-Features Discovery

Joana Matos[1], Sofia Pires[1,2], Helena Aidos[1], Marta Gromicho[2], Susana Pinto[2], Mamede de Carvalho[2,3], and Sara C. Madeira[1(✉)]

[1] LASIGE, Departamento de Infomática, Faculdade de Ciências, Universidade de Lisboa, Lisbon, Portugal
sacmadeira@ciencias.ulisboa.pt

[2] Instituto de Medicina Molecular, Instituto de Fisiologia, Faculdade de Medicina, Universidade de Lisboa, Lisbon, Portugal

[3] Department of Neurosciences and Mental Health, Hospital de Santa Maria CHLN, Lisbon, Portugal
https://imm.medicina.ulisboa.pt/

Abstract. Amyotrophic Lateral Sclerosis (ALS) is a heterogeneous neurodegenerative disease with a high variability of presentation patterns, impacting patient care and survival. Given the heterogeneous nature of ALS patients and targeting a better prognosis, clinicians usually estimate disease progression at diagnosis using the rate of decay computed from the Revised ALS Functional Rating Scale (ALSFRS-R). In this context, we aim at unravelling disease presentation patterns by proposing a new Biclustering-based approach, termed Discriminative Meta-features Discovery (DMD). These patterns (Meta-features) are composed of discriminative subsets of features together with their values, allowing them to distinguish and characterize subgroups of patients with similar disease presentation patterns. The proposed methodology was used to characterize groups of ALS patients with different progression rates (Slow, Neutral and Fast) using Biclustering-based Classification and Class Association Rule Mining. The patterns found for each of the three progression groups (described either as important features used by a Random Forest or as interpretable Association Rules) were validated by ALS expert clinicians, who were able to recognize relevant characteristics of slow, neutral and fast progressing patients. These results suggest that our general Biclustering approach is a promising way to unravel disease presentation patterns and can be applied to similar problems and other diseases.

Keywords: Amyotrophic Lateral Sclerosis · Disease presentation patterns · Pattern Mining-based Biclustering · Biclustering-based classification · Discriminative Meta-features · Discriminative biclusters

I. Rojas et al. (Eds.): IWBBIO 2020, LNBI 12108, pp. 517–528, 2020.
https://doi.org/10.1007/978-3-030-45385-5_46

1 Introduction

Amyotrophic Lateral Sclerosis (ALS) is an idiopathic and heterogeneous neurodegenerative disease affecting the upper and lower human motor system. Although the origin onset area of the body may vary, within weeks or months progressive motor deficits ensue, culminating in respiratory failure, appointed as the leading cause of death. Survivability is highly variable, averaging around 3 to 4 years. Thus it is crucial to unravel specific diagnostic tests or biomarkers to help clinicians make a fast and precise diagnosis for ALS. Currently, the Revised ALS Functional Rating Scale (ALSFRS-R) is used to assess the progression of the disease [7]. However, it is believed that distinct mechanisms cause neurodegeneration in ALS patients [13], such as the high degree of variability in phenotype, family history, genes involved, molecular pathways and environmental factors.

Nevertheless, studies regarding prognostic prediction in ALS are still limited and focused on finding biomarkers associated with patient survival [15,17], exploring the impact of diagnosis delay [9], or finding diagnostic/prognostic predictors [6]. Carreiro et al. [2] proposed prognostic models based on patient snapshots and time windows to predict disease progression to assisted ventilation in ALS. While Pires et al. [16] proposed specialized prognostic models to assisted ventilation using stratified disease progression groups.

Biclustering [10] has been used successfully to find groups of patients with correlated clinical features from Electronic Health Records (EHR) data and to generate class-conditional profiles for computer-aided diagnosis. Nezhad et al. [14] proposed a supervised biclustering method to detect and prioritize risk factors for hypertense patients. Moreover, biclustering-based classification has also been used to classify clinical gene expression time series [3,4].

In this context, we propose a new biclustering-based approach, Discriminative Meta-features Discovery (DMD), integrating supervised and unsupervised learning to find disease presentation patterns in two-dimensional EHR data. These patterns, here called Meta-features, are composed of discriminative subsets of features and their values, which allow to distinguish and characterize different groups/classes. The proposed methodology was used to characterize groups of patients with different progression rates (Slow, Neutral and Fast) in ALS. The promising results in ALS motivate its use as a promising way to unravel disease presentation patterns that can be applied to similar problems and other diseases.

2 Data

EHR come from the Lisbon ALS database, where clinical features and relevant information were recorded prospectively by applying a structured questionnaire developed in the ONWebDUALS (ONTology-based Web Database for Understanding ALS) JPND project [1]. This dataset was compiled to investigate the interplay between demographics, genetic mutations, clinical features and survival to discover causal relationships linking the patients' specific risk factors and ALS genotype-phenotype and contains data from five ALS centres from four European countries. The data considered for each patient has a set of static features (demographics, disease severity, co-morbidities, medication, genetic information, habits, trauma/surgery information and occupations) together with temporal features (collected repeatedly at each follow-up), such as disease progression tests (ALSFRS-R scale, etc) and clinical laboratory investigations. Controls present have the same features except for disease-related information. Given the main goal is to characterize patient progression groups, we used only patient data (not controls) and restricted the analysis to data from the Lisbon centre ($n = 473$) to ensure data quality (less missing information per subject).

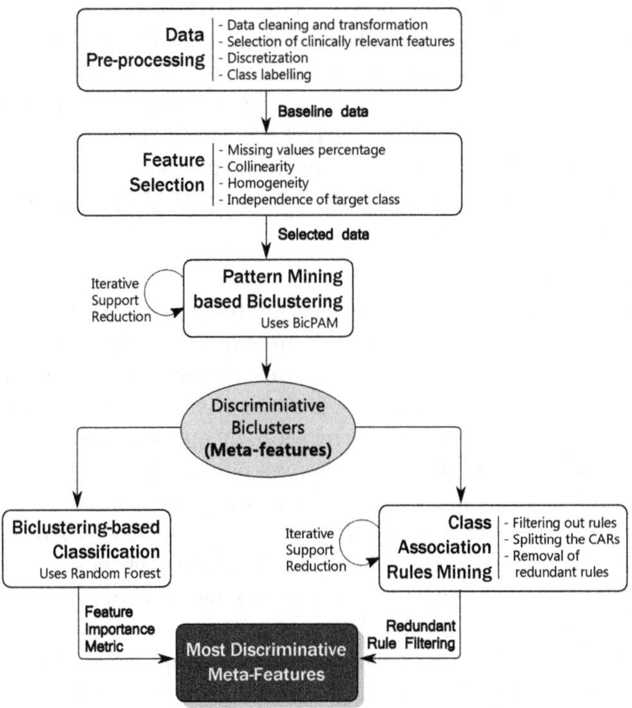

Fig. 1. Detailed workflow of the DMD approach.

3 Discriminative Meta-Features Discovery Methodology

The Discriminative Meta-feature Discovery (DMD) approach integrates unsupervised and supervised learning to obtain discriminative, understandable and intuitive descriptions of medical concepts (Meta-features), allowing to distinguish and characterize different groups/classes in the data. Figure 1 shows the workflow of DMD approach, whose steps are described below. Pattern Mining-based Biclustering is applied over discretized and class-labelled data to find discriminative patterns in the form of biclusters, which are then used to:

1. Learn biclustering-based classification models (classifiers) from discriminative features/subsets of features;
2. Find class association rules in order to discover the subsets of features (and respective values) that show higher association with each class label.

Data Preprocessing. Data was initially preprocessed to remove uninformative or erroneous values. ONWebDUALS dataset contains questionnaire answers with over 600 features, from which the clinical experts picked the most relevant features ($d = 198$) for this analysis. Also, continuous features were discretized according to criteria defined by the clinicians, and features regarding ALS metrics were discretized according to the literature. No missing values imputation was deemed necessary since the chosen biclustering algorithm (BicPAM [12]) is able to deal with them. Finally, each patient was classified into one of the three progression groups according to their ALSFRS-R scale rate of decay: Slow, Neutral or Fast, using an Expectation-Maximization approach. The class distribution between the 473 patients was as follows: 150 Slow (≈32%), 190 Neutral (≈40%) and 133 Fast (≈28%).

Feature Selection. Several feature selection techniques were applied to obtain the most relevant features and remove features with a high percentage of missing values or highly correlated with other features. Hence, the feature selection stage ensues the following steps: (1) Remove features with over 70% of missing values; (2) Remove features with over 70% correlation, by applying Pearson's Chi-Square test with Cramer's V normalization, removes one per pair; (3) Remove features with very high homogeneity, corresponding to $< 10\%$ maximum entropy for the given features; and (4) Remove features less associated (more independent) with the class, according to the Chi-Square statistic between each feature and the class. This allowed keeping the k features most associated with the class (highest Chi-Square statistic values).

In this context, the 198 features obtained from preprocessing ONWebDUALS dataset were reduced to 20 by feature selection. Since "Gender" and "Age (1st Symptoms)" were not chosen, we decided to add them due to their clinical relevance, leading to 22 features in total, which were used for further analysis.

Pattern Mining-Based Biclustering. BicPAM [12] algorithm was used to perform this task since it is a flexible and robust approach to discover biclustering solutions with multiple coherencies under relaxed conditions, such as an arbitrary number and structure of biclusters. It has several advantages: works with real-valued and nominal data; discovers all the maximal biclusters efficiently, while validating their homogeneity and statistical significance; and, handles medium-to-high levels of missing values and noise. BicPAM is further free to use through BicPAMS (Biclustering based on PAttern Mining Software) tool [11], with an Application Programming Interface (API) mode for integration in Java code. Table 1 shows that the Stopping Criteria Value (%) was the only parameter to vary, meaning the stopping criteria of the search algorithm (Minimum Support) was iteratively lowered to find the discriminative biclusters with the highest number of rows. It started at 40% given the largest portion of patients between all classes (Neutral class). In this work, a bicluster was considered discriminative if at least 75% of the patients in it belonged to the same class (purity $\geq$ 75%), the one with the largest precision.

Table 1. BicPAMS parameter values [11].

Parameter	Values
Coherency assumption	Constant biclusters
Coherency strength	50 items
Quality (%)	100 (No noise)
Pattern representation	Closed patterns
Orientation	Pattern on rows
Normalization	No
Discretization	No
Noise handler	No
Missings handler	Remove
Remove uninformative elements	None
Stopping criteria	Minimum support
Stopping criteria value (%)	40, 35, 30, 25, 20, 15, 10, 5, 2.5
Minimum bicluster columns	3
Pattern miner	CharmDiffsets
Scalability	No
Merging procedure	Heuristic
Filtering procedure	Dissimilar elements
Filtering procedure Value (%)	25

Biclustering-Based Classification. Random Forests (RF) were chosen as the classifier for their robustness, for being fast to train and able to return Feature Importance metrics, used to determine the most important features (or a subset of features). Since our data had features with varying numbers of categories, the Permutation Importance metric was used to prevent biases. The number of tree instances in each RF classifier was set to 300, and the Permutation Importance values (MLxtend library [18]) were calculated by computing the mean of 10 runs.

Class Association Rule (CAR) Mining. The Association Rules (AR) were generated from frequent closed itemsets using the SPMF library [8]. Since the number of rules was large, in order to facilitate interpretation, a few steps were performed: (1) filtering out rules without the class as sole consequent; (2) splitting CARs according to class; and (3) removing of redundant rules per class.

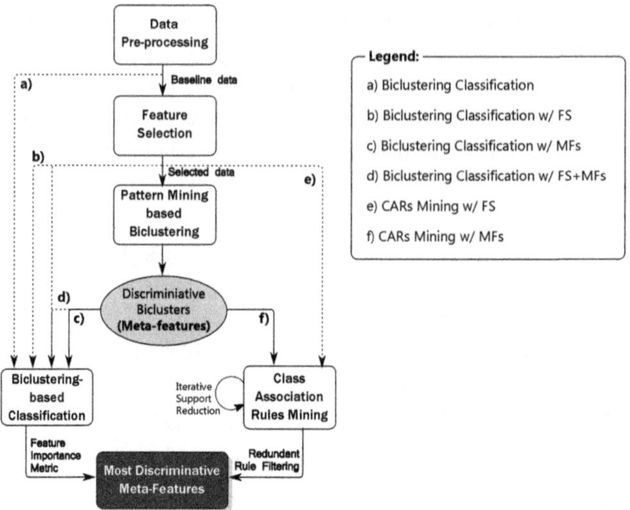

Fig. 2. Set of experiments performed to evaluate the DMD methodology.

4 Results and Discussion

Figure 2 shows the set of experiments performed to evaluate the DMD methodology. For Biclustering-based Classification, the baseline experiments (a) and (b) considered only individual features, before and after feature selection, respectively. While, for CARs mining, the baseline experiment (e) was performed only with the subset of 22 features, resulting from feature selection, since it was time-consuming to calculate the baseline from all 198 original features. For the experiments involving biclusters (c), (d) and (e), random sampling was used on the most frequent class(es) to consider the same number of discriminative biclusters for all classes. Finally, for each experiment (e) and (f) the Minimum Support threshold was also iteratively lowered until a significant number of CARs for all classes was found. Furthermore, the Biclustering-based Classification evaluation metrics were obtained using stratified 10-fold cross-validation (CV). Average accuracy, precision, recall, F-measure and specificity were computed.

4.1 Pattern Mining-Based Biclustering

As described in Sect. 3 and depicted in Fig. 3, the minimum support was iteratively lowered until a considerable number of discriminative biclusters was found. Figure 3 shows that the largest number of biclusters corresponds to 2.5% Relative Support, and for the same support, a significant amount of discriminative biclusters for each class were present, as seen in Fig. 4. At this point, we can observe that more discriminative biclusters were found for the Slow and Fast classes than for the Neutral. Below we consider only the sampled discriminative biclusters for the 2.5% Relative Support.

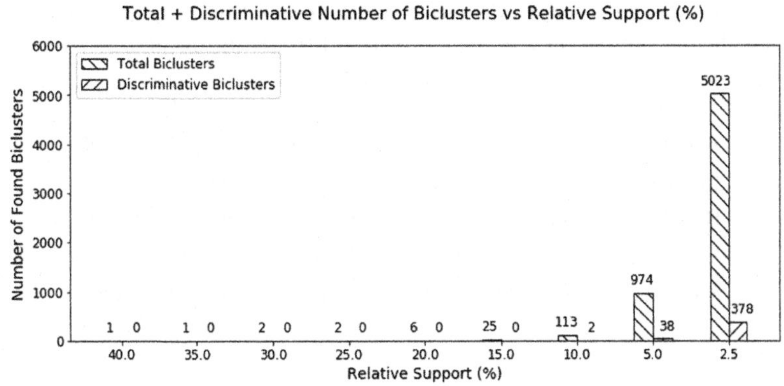

Fig. 3. Number of total/discriminative biclusters vs Relative Support (%).

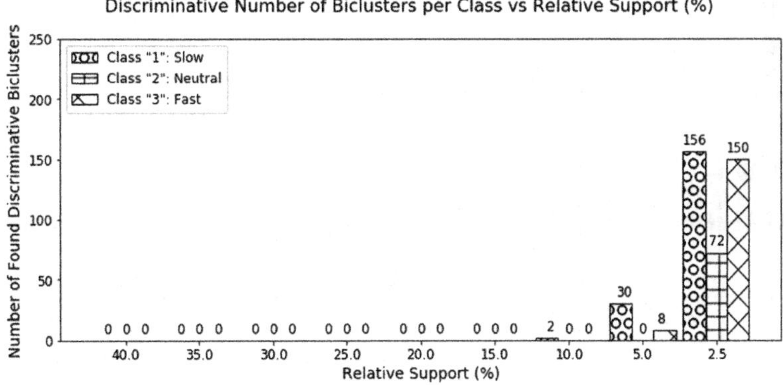

Fig. 4. Number of discriminative biclusters per class vs Relative Support (%).

4.2 Biclustering-Based Classification

Table 2 presents the results for Biclustering-based Classification, corresponding to experiments (a) to (d) in Fig. 2. As can be seen, feature selection alone (experiment (b)) improved the classification over the baseline with all features (experiment (a)). Moreover, the use of meta-features (experiment (c)) also improved over the baseline (experiment (a)). Finally, merging the individual feature space with the meta-features space (experiment (d)) led to an improvement in the results in all metrics. Figure 5 shows the 30 most important features, according to the Permutation Importance metric for the best case (experiment (d)). Besides individual features, some bicluster patterns were considered important for a good classification. Table 3 reports the patterns of the five most important biclusters in Fig. 5.

Table 2. Average and standard deviation for the evaluation metrics for the Random Forest classifier (corresponding to experiments (a) to (d) in Fig. 2).

Metric	(a)	(b)	(c)	(d)
Accuracy	0.65 ± 0.07	0.72 ± 0.06	0.70 ± 0.05	0.74 ± 0.05
Precision	0.67 ± 0.07	0.74 ± 0.06	0.73 ± 0.05	0.76 ± 0.06
Recall	0.65 ± 0.07	0.72 ± 0.06	0.68 ± 0.06	0.74 ± 0.04
F-measure	0.65 ± 0.07	0.73 ± 0.06	0.69 ± 0.06	0.74 ± 0.05
Specificity	0.82 ± 0.04	0.86 ± 0.03	0.84 ± 0.03	0.86 ± 0.02

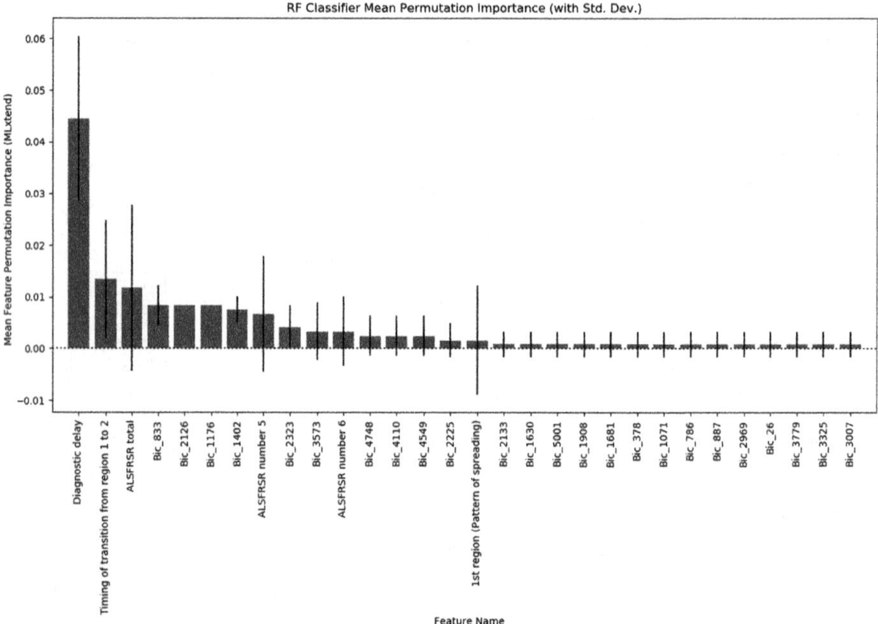

Fig. 5. Top-30 most important features according to mean Permutation Importance for the experiment (d) in Fig. 2.

4.3 Class Association Rule Mining

The experiments with Class Association Rules outlined in Fig. 2 were able to find rules to characterize all the classes (the three progression groups). Table 4 shows the levels of Support used, the size of the transaction database and the number of rules found (before and after filtering the redundant rules).

The minimum confidence and lift thresholds (see [8] for details) used for all experiments were 90% and 1, respectively. All non-redundant rules for all classes on both experiments had lift values above 2. Given the limited space, Table 5 presents the most clinically relevant rules per class (progression group) and experiment, as chosen by the clinicians in the team. The rules obtained in the baseline experiment (e) showed higher lift values for the Slow and Fast classes, while the discriminative bicluster experiment (f) showed higher values for the Neutral and Fast classes. The most relevant rules for the Fast class in both experiments are very similar, implying a higher discriminative power of that pattern. Furthermore, as shown in Table 6, the non-redundant rules obtained in experiment (f) had smaller, more condensed patterns with higher relative support, indicating higher discriminative power than those found on experiment (e).

Table 3. Top-5 most important bicluster patterns.

Id	Class	Pattern
Bic_833	Fast	{Diagnostic delay = [0, 6] months, Timing of transition from region 1 to 2 = [0, 3] months, ALSFRS-R number 1 = 3, ALSFRS-R number 2 = 3}
Bic_2126	Slow	{1st region (Pattern of spreading) = 5a>, ALSFRS-R number 1 = 4, ALSFRS-R number 2 = 4, ALSFRS-R number 3 = 4, Main Occupation in the last 5 years (level 1) = 10 Pensioner / Out of job}
Bic_1176	Fast	{Diagnostic delay = [12, 18] months, ALSFRS-R number 5 = 1, Time gap between first medical observation and diagnosis = [12, 18] months}
Bic_1402	Slow	{1st region (Pattern of spreading) = 5a>, ALSFRS-R number 1 = 4, ALSFRS-R number 3 = 4, ALSFRS-R number 4 = 4, Main Occupation in the last 5 years (level 1) = 10 Pensioner / Out of job}
Bic_2323	Fast	{Diagnostic delay = [0, 6] months, Timing of transition from region 1 to 2 = [0, 3] months, ALSFRS-R number 6 = 3}

Table 4. Metrics of class Association Rule mining experiments.

Exp./Class	Support (%)	Transactions	Rules	Non-redundant rules
(e)/Slow	2.0%	473	75	36
(e)/Neutral	2.0%	473	22	14
(e)/Fast	2.0%	473	73	49
(f)/Slow	2.5%	3064	94	34
(f)/Neutral	2.5%	3064	15	15
(f)/Fast	2.5%	3064	12	12

Table 5. Most clinically relevant Class Association Rules.

Exp./Class	Rule	Sup. (%)	Lift
(e)/Slow	ALSFRS-R number 6 = 4 $\wedge$ ALSFRS-R number 7 = 4 $\wedge$ ALSFRS-R total = 46 $\Rightarrow$ Class = Slow	≈3.38	≈3.15
(e)/Neutral	ALSFRS-R number 7 = 4 $\wedge$ Diagnostic delay = [6, 12] months $\wedge$ Time gap between first medical observation and diagnosis = [6, 9] months $\Rightarrow$ Class = Neutral	≈2.75	≈2.49
(e)/Fast	Diagnostic delay = [0, 6] months $\wedge$ Timing of transition from region 1 to 2 = [0, 3] months $\wedge$ Timing of transition from region 2 to 3 = [0, 3] months $\Rightarrow$ Class = Fast	≈3.59	≈3.56
(f)/Slow	ALSFRS-R number 3 = 4 $\wedge$ ALSFRS-R number 4 = 4 $\Rightarrow$ Class = Slow	≈17.3	≈2.46
(f)/Neutral	ALSFRS-R number 2 = 4 $\wedge$ ALSFRS-R number 5 = 3 $\Rightarrow$ Class = Neutral	≈5.35	≈3.47
(f)/Fast	Diagnostic delay = [0, 6] months $\wedge$ Timing of transition from region 1 to 2 = [0, 3] months $\Rightarrow$ Class = Fast	≈7.73	≈3.28

Table 6. Average relative support of non-redundant rules per experiment and class.

Experiment/Class	Average support (%)
(e)/Slow	≈2.7
(e)/Neutral	≈2.36
(e)/Fast	≈2.57
(f)/Slow	≈8.42
(f)/Neutral	≈3.32
(f)/Fast	≈4.68

5 Conclusions

We propose a new biclustering-based approach, Discriminative Meta-features Discovery (DMD), combining supervised and unsupervised machine learning to find disease presentation patterns, and used it to characterize ALS patients targeting the identification of different disease progression patterns: Fast, Neutral and Slow progression groups. Our results suggest that our biclustering-based approach is a promising tool to unravel disease presentation patterns and can be applied to similar problems and other diseases.

ALS is an inevitably progressive disease, but the individual rate of clinical deterioration is quite variable. The "Diagnostic Delay" that is the delay from first symptoms till diagnosis is a recognized prognostic factor in ALS (shorter delay associated with faster progression) [19]. Moreover, it has been observed that shorter times of transition between body regions (disease spreading, in short periods of 0–3 months) are also associated with faster progression.

The ALSFRS-R scale was developed to assess functionality in ALS and has been shown to track the progression of patients' disability accurately [5]. The individual ALSFRS-R questions assessing salivation (Q2), swallowing (Q3), handwriting (Q4), cutting food and handling utensils (Q5), dressing and personal hygiene (Q6) and turning on bed and adjusting bedclothes (Q7) were found to be important features, in particular for the Slow and Neutral progression groups.

In this context, our experimental results regarding biclustering-based classification using discriminative biclusters are very promising, corroborating the expert knowledge regarding prognostic factors described above, and highlighting the potential of Discriminative Meta-features Discovery in finding disease presentation patterns able to characterize and distinguish different disease progression groups. Furthermore, the most important individual features found to distinguish between the groups are "Diagnostic Delay", "Timing of transition from region 1 to 2" and "ALSFRS-R Total", confirmed as clinical indicators of different progression patterns by the clinical experts in the team. Moreover, the Association Rules considered as more relevant by expert clinicians for each progression group, since they identified key combinations of the individual ALSFRS-R questions characteristics of each progression group described above, showed high positive values of lift, meaning the Meta-features found on their antecedents were highly associated with each class. In particular, for the Fast group, the association rules were consistent with the patterns characterizing the most relevant biclusters, indicating higher discriminative power.

Acknowledgements. This work was supported by FCT funding to Neuroclinomics2 (PTDC/EEI-SII/1937/2014) and iCare4U (LISBOA-01-0145-FEDER-031474 + PTDC/EME-SIS/31474/2017) research projects, and LASIGE Research Unit (UIDB/00408/2020).

References

1. ONWebDUALS - ONtology-based Web Database for Understanding Amyotrophic Lateral Sclerosis (2015). https://www.encals.eu/onwebduals-web-database/. Accessed 25 July 2019
2. Carreiro, A.V., Amaral, P.M., Pinto, S., Tomás, P., de Carvalho, M., Madeira, S.C.: Prognostic models based on patient snapshots and time windows: predicting disease progression to assisted ventilation in amyotrophic lateral sclerosis. J. Biomed. Inform. **58**, 133–144 (2015)
3. Carreiro, A.V., Anunciação, O., Carriço, J.A., Madeira, S.C.: Prognostic prediction through biclustering-based classification of clinical gene expression time series. J. Integr. Bioinform. **8**(3), 73–89 (2011)

4. Carreiro, A.V., Ferreira, A.J., Figueiredo, M.A., Madeira, S.C.: Towards a classification approach using meta-biclustering: impact of discretization in the analysis of expression time series. J. Integr. Bioinform. **9**(3), 105–120 (2012)
5. Cedarbaum, J.M., et al.: Complete listing of the BDNF Study Group, A., et al.: The ALSFRS-R: a revised ALS functional rating scale that incorporates assessments of respiratory function. J. Neurol. Sci. **169**(1–2), 13–21 (1999)
6. Creemers, H., Grupstra, H., Nollet, F., van den Berg, L.H., Beelen, A.: Prognostic factors for the course of functional status of patients with ALS: a systematic review. J. Neurol. **262**(6), 1407–1423 (2015)
7. van Es, M.A., et al.: Amyotrophic lateral sclerosis. Lancet **390**(10107), 2084–2098 (2017)
8. Fournier-Viger, P., et al.: The SPMF open-source data mining library version 2. In: Berendt, B., et al. (eds.) ECML PKDD 2016. LNCS (LNAI), vol. 9853, pp. 36–40. Springer, Cham (2016). https://doi.org/10.1007/978-3-319-46131-1_8
9. Gupta, P., Prabhakar, S., Sharma, S., Anand, A.: A predictive model for amyotrophic lateral sclerosis (ALS) diagnosis. J. Neurol. Sci. **312**(1–2), 68–72 (2012)
10. Henriques, R., Antunes, C., Madeira, S.C.: A structured view on pattern mining-based biclustering. Pattern Recogn. **48**(12), 3941–3958 (2015)
11. Henriques, R., Ferreira, F.L., Madeira, S.C.: BicPAMS: software for biological data analysis with pattern-based biclustering. BMC Bioinform. **18**(1), 82 (2017)
12. Henriques, R., Madeira, S.C.: BicPAM: pattern-based biclustering for biomedical data analysis. Algorithms Mol. Biol. **9**(1), 27 (2014)
13. Kiernan, M.C., et al.: Amyotrophic lateral sclerosis. Lancet **377**(9769), 942–955 (2011)
14. Nezhad, M.Z., Zhu, D., Sadati, N., Yang, K., Levi, P.: SUBIC: a supervised biclustering approach for precision medicine. In: 2017 16th IEEE International Conference on Machine Learning and Applications (ICMLA), pp. 755–760. IEEE (2017)
15. Pfohl, S.R., Kim, R.B., Coan, G.S., Mitchell, C.S.: Unraveling the complexity of amyotrophic lateral sclerosis survival prediction. Front. Neuroinform. **12**, 36 (2018)
16. Pires, S., Gromicho, M., Pinto, S., Carvalho, M., Madeira, S.C.: Predicting non-invasive ventilation in ALS patients using stratified disease progression groups. In: 2018 IEEE International Conference on Data Mining Workshops (ICDMW), pp. 748–757. IEEE (2018)
17. Polkey, M.I., Lyall, R.A., Yang, K., Johnson, E., Leigh, P.N., Moxham, J.: Respiratory muscle strength as a predictive biomarker for survival in amyotrophic lateral sclerosis. Am. J. Respir. Crit. Care Med. **195**(1), 86–95 (2017)
18. Raschka, S.: MLxtend: providing machine learning and data science utilities and extensions to Python's scientific computing stack. J. Open Source Software **3**(24), 638 (2018)
19. Westeneng, H.J., et al.: Prognosis for patients with amyotrophic lateral sclerosis: development and validation of a personalised prediction model. Lancet Neurol. **17**(5), 423–433 (2018)

Patient Stratification Using Clinical and Patient Profiles: Targeting Personalized Prognostic Prediction in ALS

Sofia Pires[1,2], Marta Gromicho[2], Susana Pinto[2], Mamede de Carvalho[2,3], and Sara C. Madeira[1(✉)]

[1] LASIGE, Departamento de Infomática, Faculdade de Ciências, Universidade de Lisboa, Lisbon, Portugal
sacmadeira@ciencias.ul.pt

[2] Instituto de Medicina Molecular, Instituto de Fisiologia, Faculdade de Medicina, Universidade de Lisboa, Lisbon, Portugal

[3] Department of Neurosciences and Mental Health, Hospital de Santa Maria CHLN, Lisbon, Portugal

Abstract. Amyotrophic Lateral Sclerosis (ALS) is a severe neurodegenerative disease with highly heterogeneous disease presentation and progression patterns. This hampers effective treatments targeting all patients and finding a cure is still a challenge. In this scenario, patient stratification is believed to be a key tool to deal with the heterogeneous nature of the disease, promoting the discovery of more homogeneous groups of patients, that can then be used to improve patient prognosis and care. In this work, we propose to use clustering to stratify patient observations in accordance with clinically defined subsets of features (Clinical Profiles). The groups obtained by clustering patients using the Clinical Profiles are called Patient Profiles. Each patient profile is then used to learn specialized prognostic models to predict the need for Non-Invasive Ventilation (NIV) within a time window of 90 days. Each patient profile specific prognostic model is then used in ensemble learning. We used three clinical profiles (prognostic, respiratory and functional) based on complementary clinically relevant views of disease presentation and progression. These clinical profiles yielded two, four, and two patient profiles, respectively. The specialized prognostic models learned from these clinical and patient profiles show overall improvements when compared to the baseline models, where patients are not stratified. These promising results highlight the need for patient stratification for prognostic prediction in ALS. Furthermore, this innovative approach for prognostic prediction, where clinical profiles and patient profiles are integrated to enhance patient stratification, can be used to improve predictions for other disease outcomes in ALS or applied to other diseases.

Keywords: Amyotrophic Lateral Sclerosis · Patient stratification · Prognostic prediction · Clinical profiles · Patient profiles

I. Rojas et al. (Eds.): IWBBIO 2020, LNBI 12108, pp. 529–541, 2020.
https://doi.org/10.1007/978-3-030-45385-5_47

1 Introduction

Amyotrophic Lateral Sclerosis (ALS) is an aggressive neurodegenerative disease, characterized by progressive degeneration of upper and lower motor neurons, resulting in paralysis and death from respiratory failure [10]. The survival average for ALS patients is usually 3 to 5 years [2]. The short survival time allied with the lack of available cure means the prognosis for ALS patients is not usually the best for these patients. Therefore, it is key to develop prognostic models allowing to anticipate the treatments that may extend survival and improve patients' quality of life. Prognostic studies in ALS have mostly been focused on finding discriminatory prognostic features for survival prediction [3]. However, far less was done to promote earlier treatment administration. Currently, there are only two available treatments proved to extend survival in ALS the Riluzole drug [4], and Non-Invasive Ventilation (NIV) [5].

Since respiratory failure is the most common cause of death [6], prognostic models able to anticipate the need for NIV prescription can have a positive impact in quality of life and extend survival. However, the heterogeneity of the disease presents as an obstacle to ALS studies [7]. In fact, ALS is now considered a syndrome due to its high variability in presentation, progression and genetics [8]. To tackle this problem, patient stratification has been lighted as a promise by finding subgroups of patients that may help the understanding of ALS, providing a new perspective on how to plan clinical trials and better manage disease progression [3]. In this scenario, we propose a patient stratification approach based on different sets of prognostic markers (Clinical Profiles) and different groups of patients (Patient Profiles) used to learn specialized prognostic models able to predict the need for NIV, within a time window of 90 days (since ALS patients are usually followed every three months).

Stratification approaches in ALS are usually patient-based. This means that patients belong to a single group and all their observations are associated with that group. However, ALS patients' condition always worsens as time goes by, thus a patient's condition is better at disease onset when compared to later stages of the disease. Furthermore, different patients can have very distinct observations in the same stages of the disease. This means patient observations are highly heterogeneous. As such, we need patient stratification to aggregate heterogeneous patient observations into smaller and more homogeneous groups.

In this context, our aim is to cluster similar observations, thus reducing the variability in data and potentially enhance the classifier's performance. An akin approach proposed to stratify ALS patients according to their progression rate, resulting in specialized models that outperformed the baseline models when predicting the need for NIV [1]. We used three sets of clinically relevant features (Prognostic, Respiratory and Prognostic sets), called Clinical Profiles, composed by a set of features that are focused on different aspects of the disease:

1. Prognostic Profile: set of features described in the literature as good prognostic features for ALS;
2. Respiratory Profile: set of features describing the respiratory status of the patient;

3. Functional Profile: ALS-FRS and ALS-FRS-R scales and sub-scales assessing the functional status of the patient.

The groups obtained by clustering data using each Clinical Profile, we termed Patient Profiles, are further used to learn specialized models to predict the need for NIV within a given time window. Figure 1 states the problem and presents an overview of the proposed prognostic prediction methodology based of patient stratification using Clinical and Patient Profiles.

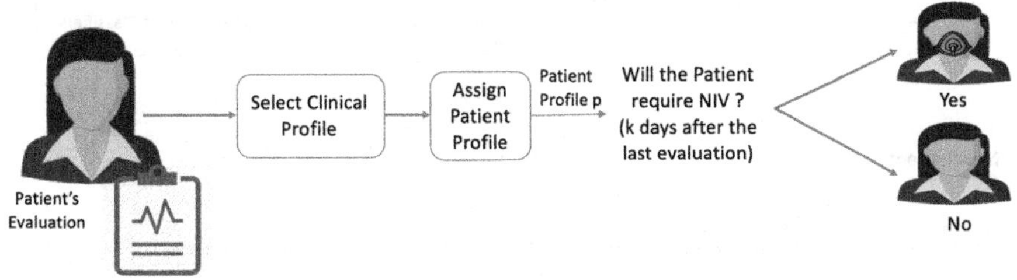

Fig. 1. Problem Formulation: given the patient's current state, together with the corresponding profile according to a predefined clinical profile, can we predict the need for NIV in a given time window?

This paper is organized as follows: Sect. 2 describes data used the proposed methods for prognostic prediction. Section 3 presents and discusses the results regarding the prediction of NIV need in a time window of 90 days (before next appointment). Finally, Sect. 4 draws conclusions.

2 Data and Methods

We first present data (Sect. 2.1). Then, we describe the temporal preprocessing steps needed to obtain a class-labeled dataset with patient observations that can then be used for both the stratification and classification steps of the proposed approach (Sect. 2.2). Follows the presentation of the proposed patient stratification methodology using Clinical and Patient Profiles (Sect. 2.3). Finally, Sect. 2.4 describes the methodology used to build the specialized prognostic models. Figure 2 presents the workflow.

2.1 Data

We use data from a cohort of 1360 Portuguese ALS patients, followed between 1992 and March 2019. For each patient, we gathered demographic and genetic features, as well as results from multiple clinical exams and tests, performed at each appointment. Table 1 describes the features available in the dataset.

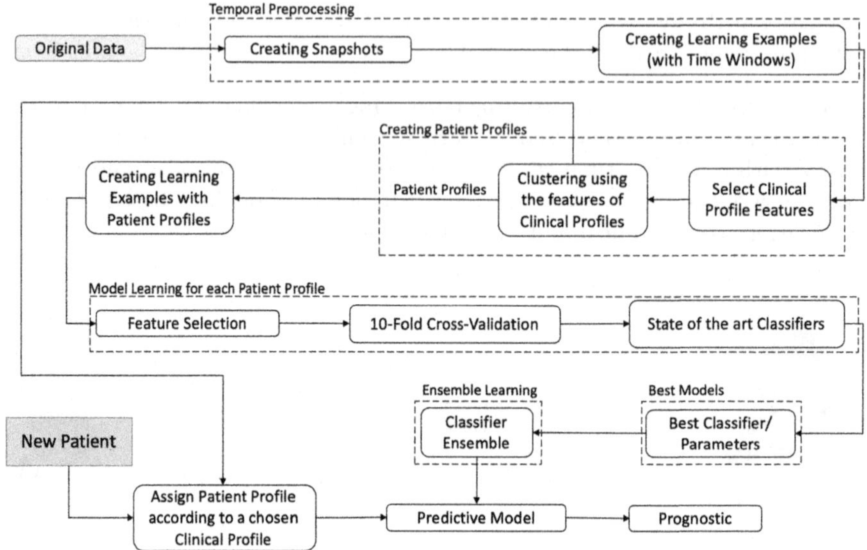

Fig. 2. Workflow of the proposed approach using Patient Stratification using Clinical and Patient Profiles. First, the original data is preprocessed to create patient snapshots. Then, an Evolution Class that takes into an account the chosen time windows, turning the snapshots into learning examples. For the chosen Clinical Profile a particular set of features is extracted. Next, clustering uses only these features to create Patients Profiles. New datasets are created for each Patient Profile, and are further used to build the personalized prognostic models. The models are evaluated using a stratified cross-validation scheme, and the best parameters are chosen. The best models (set of classifiers trained with the best parameters) are then combined in a Classifier Ensemble. After the models are trained, when a new patient arrives at an appointment his/her observation is compared with the centroids for each Patient Profile (according to the chosen Clinical Profile) and assigned to the most similar. The patient observation is then fed to the final model outputing a prediction for early NIV prescription.

2.2 Temporal Data Preprocessing

Due to the rapid progression of the disease, ALS patients need frequent clinical follow-up and therefore have medical appointments regularly. Thus, our baseline dataset is composed of multiple patient observations, one for every appointment. Each observation is a representation of the status of the patient (at a certain point in time), called snapshot. Additionally, we computed an Evolution Class (E), indicating if the patient will need NIV ($E = 1$) or not ($E = 0$), 90 days from the time of the observation. This creates learning instances with information about the patients' status at a given point in time and the need for NIV, k days after. The creation of snapshots and derivation of Evolution Class follows the work in [9].

Table 1. Features in the Portuguese ALS dataset, where * identifies scores and subscores of the ALS Functional Rating Scale (ALSFRS).

Name	Temporal/Static	Type	SubGroup	Mean/Mode
Gender	Static	Categorical	Demographics	Male
Body Mass Index (BMI)	Static	Numeric	Demographics	25.08
Family History of Motor Neuron Disease (MND)	Static	Categorical	Medical and Family History	No
UMN vs LMN	Static	Categorical	Onset Evaluation	LMN
Age at Onset	Static	Numeric	Onset Evaluation	58.97
Onset Form	Static	Categorical	Onset Evaluation	Spinal
Diagnostic Delay	Static	Numeric	Onset Evaluation	21.45
El Escorial Reviewed Criteria (EERC)	Static	Categorical	Onset Evaluation	Probable
Expression of C9orf72 Mutations	Static	Categorical	Genetic	Unknown
ALS-FRS*	Temporal	Numeric	Functional Scores	29.74
ALS-FRS-R*	Temporal	Numeric	Functional Scores	37.55
ALS-FRSb*	Temporal	Numeric	Functional Scores	10.07
ALS-FRSsUL*	Temporal	Numeric	Functional Scores	8.24
ALS-FRSsLL*	Temporal	Numeric	Functional Scores	7.71
ALS-FRSr*	Temporal	Numeric	Functional Scores	3.71
R*	Temporal	Numeric	Functional Scores	11.49
Vital Capacity (VC)	Temporal	Numeric	Respiratory Tests	85.8
Forced VC (FVC)	Temporal	Numeric	Respiratory Tests	86.51
Airway Occlusion Pressure (P0.1)	Temporal	Numeric	Respiratory Tests	58.46
Maximal Sniff Nasal Inspiratory Pressure (SNIP)	Temporal	Numeric	Respiratory Tests	66.2
Maximal Inspiratory Pressure (MIP)	Temporal	Numeric	Respiratory Tests	97.34
Maximal Expiratory Pressure(MEP)	Temporal	Numeric	Respiratory Tests	64.59
Date of Non-Invasive Ventilation	Temporal	Date	Respiratory Status	-
Phrenic Nerve Response amplitude (PhrenMeanAmpl)	Temporal	Numeric	Neurophysiological Tests	8.36
Phrenic Nerve Response latency (PhrenMeanLat)	Temporal	Numeric	Neurophysiological Tests	0.52
Cervical Extension	Temporal	Numeric	Other Physical Values	4.43
Cervical Flexion	Temporal	Numeric	Other Physical Values	4.83

2.3 Creating Patient Profiles: Patient Stratification Using Clinical and Patient Profiles

To create Patient Profiles we first need to define the Clinical Profiles (clinically defined subsets of features). These clinical profiles are sets of features describing specific patient conditions, and were thus defined in close collaboration with clinical experts. For each Clinical Profile, we create a new version of the dataset by selecting the specific features. These datasets are then used in Clustering to create the Patient Profiles. In this work, we defined three Clinical Profiles (Prognostic, Respiratory, and Functional) and created sets of Patient Profiles for each of them. Table 2 shows the set of features used for each of them.

Table 2. Set of Features used to perform Clustering for each Clinical Profile.

Clinical profile	Features used
Prognostic	Gender, BMI, MND, Age at Onset, Diagnostic Delay, EERC, UMN vs LMN, Onset form, C9orf72, ALS-FRS, ALS-FRS-R, FVC
Respiratory	FVC, PhrenMeanAmpl, ALS-FRSr, R
Functional	ALS-FRS, ALS-FRS-R, ALS-FRSb, ALS-FRSsUL, ALS-FRSsLL, ALS-FRSr, R

Each Clinical Profile uses the specific dataset as input to Expectation-Maximization (EM) clustering algorithm [11]. The silhouette score [12] is used to determine the number of clusters for each profile and the clustering solution with the best score is chosen [12]. The dataset used in each Clinical Profile is then split in several new datasets: one for each group (Patient Profile). These datasets are then used to learn specialized prognostic models for NIV prediction.

2.4 Learning Specialized Predictive Models: Learning Using Each Patient Profile

We use a 5 × 10-fold cross-validation scheme, followed by a combination of random undersampling [13] and SMOTE [14] to deal with class imbalance (train only). The majority class is undersampled until its distribution percentage hits 60%. Then SMOTE is used to oversample the minority class until the class distribution is balanced. Then a collection of classifiers is trained, and grid search is performed to optimize parameters. The classifiers used are: Decision Trees (DT), K-Nearest Neighbor (kNN), Support Vector Machines (SVM) with both Polynomial (P) and Gaussian (G) kernels, Naive Bayes (NB), Random Forests (RF) and Logistic Regression (LR). Table 3 shows the parameters and respective ranges used to perform grid search for each classifier. After classifier optimization, the best models (set of classifiers trained with the best parameters) are used in a Classifier Ensemble (CE) [15]. Since RF are already an Ensemble Classifier, their prediction is not used inside the first CE created for the predictive model. Instead RF and CE predictions are then combined to obtain a final prediction. We compute AUC, Sensitivity and Specificity measures to evaluate the classification performance.

Table 3. Parameters and corresponding ranges tested for each classifier.

Classifier	Parameter	Range
DT	Confidence factor	{0.15, 0.20, 0.25, 0.30}
kNN	Nr of Neighbours	{1, 3, 5, 7, 9, 11}
SVM P/G	Complexity	$\{e^{-2}, e^{-1}, e^{0}, e^{1}, e^{2}\}$
SVM P	Polynomial degree	{1, 2, 3}
SVM G	Gamma	$\{e^{-3}, e^{-2}, e^{-1}, e^{0}, e^{1}, e^{2}, e^{3}\}$
NB	Kernel	{True, False}
RF	Nr of trees	{5, 10, 15, 20}
LR	Ridge factor	$\{e^{-9}, e^{-8}, e^{-7}, e^{-5}, e^{-4}, e^{-2}, e^{-3}, e^{-4}\}$

3 Results and Discussion

This section presents and discusses the results obtained by the proposed approach using stratification and specialized prognostic models when predicting the need for NIV in ALS patients in a time window of 90 days. First, we look into the creation of Clinical and Patient Profiles (Sect. 3.1). Then, we show the classification results for each specialized prognostic model (Sect. 3.2).

3.1 Creating Clinical and Patient Profiles

The first step was to create patient profiles for each clinical profile. We ran the EM algorithm multiple times using a different number of clusters (ranging from two to five) and computed the silhouette score for each solution. The clustering with the best score was used to create the dataset for each group. Other clustering algorithms, such as k-means and DBSCAN, were tested but EM outperformed them. This could be explained by the nature of data, as there is no clear separation of groups and this algorithm dealt better with this problem. The final number of patient profiles created for each clinical profile was: 2 for Prognostic, 4 for Respiratory, and 2 for Functional.

Table 4 reports the statistics and class distribution of the baseline and resulting patient profiles datasets. On one hand, for the Prognostic and Functional groups, the clustering algorithm finds a small group (with only a few snapshots), and a much larger group (with the remaining snapshots). On the other hand, the Respiratory Profile results in two small and two large groups.

Regarding class distribution, we can further observe some differences between groups of the same clinical profile. Since clustering should group the snapshots by the patients' condition at a certain time point, we expected patients in better condition to be in the same group, and the same for patients in worse condition. This can be most observable for the respiratory profiles, as r1 to r3 show more than doubled percentage of evolution's when compared to r4, suggesting r4 is probably composed of patient observations in better condition, as patients in worse condition tend to evolve more rapidly.

Table 4. Baseline and patient profiles statistics and class distribution.

Clinical profile	Patient profile	Snapshots Nr	Evolution (E = 1)	No evolution (E = 0)
Baseline	-	3343	17.76%	82.24%
Prognostic	p1	2668	18.52%	81.48%
	p2	675	14.81%	85.19%
Respiratory	r1	243	25.51%	74.49%
	r2	1339	22.40%	77.60%
	r3	228	24.56%	75.44%
	r4	1533	11.48%	88.52%
Functional	f1	2992	17.21%	82.79%
	f2	351	22.51%	77.49%

To better understand the characteristics of the patients in each Patient Profile, we computed the means/modes of each feature used for clustering. Tables 5, 6 and 7 present the results for the Prognostic, Respiratory, and Functional Clinical Profiles, respectively.

In the Prognostic Profiles, the main difference between the two groups is in the Diagnostic Delay feature, which more than doubles in p2. Thus, the difference between groups means that patients with a late diagnosis are in the same group. The same happens for patients with a faster diagnosis. Other difference is in the UMN vs LMN feature where the two groups are opposite.

Regarding the Respiratory Profiles, the feature values tend to increase, specially for the FVC, as we progress from Patient Profile r1 to r4. For these four

Table 5. Differences in prognostic patient profiles (means/modes for each feature).

Feature	p1	p2
Gender	Male	Male
BMI	25.15	24.8
Family History MND	No	No
Age at Onset	59.81	55.66
Diagnostic Delay	16.26	41.95
EERC	Probable	Probable
UMN vs LMN	LMN	UMN
Onset Form	Spinal	Spinal
C9orf72	Unknown	Unknown
ALS-FRS	29.7	29.9
ALS-FRS-R	37.53	37.65
FVC	87.04	84.07

features, higher values are associated with better patient condition. Thus, looking at each group we can infer that from group r1 to r4 the overall patients' condition goes from worse to better.

Finally, the Functional Profiles show similarities to the Respiratory Profiles. In a similar fashion, for all the features the higher the score, the better the patient's condition. Considering all the scores and sub-scores of the ALS functional scales we can see that in f1 profile all features have higher mean values. This suggests that patients in f1 are more functionally capable than in f2, whose patients show a greater functional loss.

3.2 Learning Predictive Models

After creating the datasets for each patient profile, we proceeded to build the specialized prognostic models. For comparison reasons we also built a model for the baseline dataset. Table 8 shows the results with no stratification. There we can see that the baseline kNN, SVM P and SVM G were outperformed by the other classifiers. Moreover, their lower performance could hinder Ensemble performance. Therefore, these three classifiers were removed from subsequent tests. This contributes to simpler models with better performance and less time-consuming model training. Furthermore, we tested multiple methods to combine the classifiers in the ensemble: Product of Probabilities, Majority Voting, Minimum Probability, Maximum Probability, and Average of Probabilities. Average rule had the best results and thus it was further used in all models.

Table 6. Differences in respiratory patient profiles (means for each feature).

Feature	r1	r2	r3	r4
FVC	78.9	84.99	87.09	88.95
PhrenMeanAmpl	0.47	0.51	0.63	0.53
ALS-FRSr	3.2	3.7	3.73	3.78
R	10.69	11.5	11.4	11.59

Table 7. Differences between functional patient profiles (means for each feature).

Feature	f1	f2
ALS-FRS	30.13	26.23
ALS-FRS-R	37.96	33.13
ALS-FRSb	10.17	9.20
ALS-FRSsUL	8.37	7.01
ALS-FRSsLL	7.82	6.73
ALS-FRSr	3.75	3.32
R	11.56	10.68

Next, we learned the specialized models for all Clinical and respective Patient Profiles, using only the best classifiers from the previous test. The model for the baseline dataset was also rebuilt.

Tables 9, 10 and 11 show the classification results for the personalized prognostic models as well as the baseline. Overall, the results of our stratification approach suggest that using specialized prognostic models in a subset of the data outperform the baseline models. In a related work, using disease progression groups [1], where ALS patients where stratified according to their progression rate, the specialized model for each disease progression group also outperformed the baseline models. This reinforces the idea that patient stratification is key to fight the heterogeneity problem in ALS (Table 12).

Table 8. AUC, Sensitivity and Specificity using all classifiers for the baseline dataset. Ensemble is the combination of DT, NB and LR classifiers and Final Decision the combination of the Ensemble and RF classifier.

Metric	DT	kNN	SVM Poly	SVM Gaus	NB	LR	Ensemble	RF	Final decision
AUC	74.38	68.08	64.71	60.26	80.19	79.59	80.98	79.84	81.99
Sensitivity	62.53	44.38	61.72	62.09	70.40	67.00	69.80	67.07	69.66
Specificity	75.96	77.96	67.69	58.41	74.12	77.27	76.25	75.99	76.97

Table 9. AUC results for all patient profiles datasets and baseline dataset. The classifiers used were: Decision Trees (DT), Naive Bayes (NB), Logistic Regression (LR) and Random Forests (RF). Ensemble is the combination of the DT, NB and LR classifiers and Final Decision is the combination of the Ensemble and RF classifier.

Clinical profile	Patient profile	DT	NB	LR	Ensemble	RF	Final decision
Baseline	-	73.78	80.65	78.34	80.96	80.77	82.01
Prognostic	p1	74.16	80.02	78.81	80.77	79.72	81.87
	p2	78.41	84.63	83.73	86.50	83.01	86.85
Respiratory	r1	57.99	70.11	68.06	71.26	65.31	71.66
	r2	74.97	82.03	80.93	80.93	80.43	83.37
	r3	72.23	84.32	78.63	83.14	78.12	83.64
	r4	73.31	79.90	77.6	80.76	79.15	81.90
Functional	f1	76.46	82.41	81.66	83.11	81.20	83.74
	f2	61.48	68.64	72.39	73.09	70.17	74.78

Table 10. Sensitivity results for all patient profiles datasets and baseline dataset. The classifiers used were: Decision Trees (DT), Naive Bayes (NB), Logistic Regression (LR) and Random Forests (RF). Ensemble is the combination of the DT, NB and LR classifiers and Final Decision is the combination of the Ensemble and RF classiifer.

Clinical profile	Patient profile	DT	NB	LR	Ensemble	RF	Final decision
Baseline	-	61.99	75.42	64.44	72.15	66.94	71.41
Prognostic	p1	60.69	71.30	65.30	70.32	64.25	70.20
	p2	72.40	78.00	80.20	73.80	78.40	81.60
Respiratory	r1	48.06	68.71	59.68	62.26	50.32	60.00
	r2	59.47	71.27	67.80	69.47	66.27	69.40
	r3	63.21	70.36	67.14	68.21	65.36	68.93
	r4	62.39	70.80	66.02	70.91	70.45	72.61
Functional	f1	63.38	70.76	67.92	71.38	69.05	71.61
	f2	54.43	71.39	62.03	63.54	55.44	63.29

Table 11. Specificity results for all patient profiles datasets and baseline dataset. The classifiers used were: Decision Trees (DT), Naive Bayes (NB), Logistic Regression (LR) and Random Forests (RF). Ensemble is the combination of the DT, NB and LR classifiers and Final Decision is the combination of the Ensemble and RF classifier.

Clinical profile	Patient profile	DT	NB	LR	Ensemble	RF	Final decision
Baseline	-	76.24	70.63	77.26	74.74	77.51	76.78
Prognostic	p1	76.14	73.76	77.90	76.25	77.41	77.85
	p2	72.59	75.69	77.98	77.25	71.17	76.56
Respiratory	r1	64.09	57.24	69.17	66.85	70.17	69.39
	r2	79.75	78.21	80.65	80.69	78.42	80.79
	r3	74.07	81.74	76.86	82.33	74.53	80.35
	r4	75.42	74.93	76.54	76.80	70.92	75.87
Functional	f1	76.88	77.41	79.48	78.72	76.62	79.09
	f2	66.69	54.71	69.56	67.79	73.38	71.76

Table 12. AUC, Sensitivity and Specificity of the final models for each Clinical and respective Patient profiles, as well as baseline datasets.

Clinical profile	Patient profile	Sensitivity	Specificity	AUC
Baseline	-	70.41	76.78	82.01
Prognostic	p1	70.20	77.85	81.87
	p2	81.60	76.56	86.85
Respiratory	r1	60.00	69.39	71.66
	r2	69.40	80.79	83.37
	r3	68.93	80.35	83.64
	r4	72.61	75.87	81.90
Functional	f1	71.61	79.09	83.74
	f2	63.29	71.76	74.78

4 Conclusion

We propose a patient stratification approach using Clinical and Patient Profiles to tackle the heterogeneity problem associated with ALS. We use clustering to group patients' observations according to predefined clinical profiles (Prognostic, Respiratory and Functional), resulting in homogeneous groups ,which are then used to learn specialized prognostic models.

Our proposed approach resulted in three sets of ALS Patient Profiles that were then used to create specialized prognostic models capable of predicting early administration of NIV. Some of these models outperformed the baseline model, highlighting the importance of patient stratification to improve prognostic prediction in this heterogeneous disease.

Since Patient Profiles were created in an unsupervised fashion, the emerging groups are not specific to NIV prediction, and can thus be used to predict other outcomes, such as when the patient will need to use a wheelchair or when the patient will lose the ability to speak. Likewise, the whole pipeline described in this work can be adapted for different disease end-points and diseases.

In future work, we would like to combine the predictions of the three Clinical Profiles to check whether we can further improve the classification performance by learning an overall prognostic ensemble. We plan also to use clustering ensembles to obtain the groups used to learn the prognostic models.

As an end note, we would like to draw the attention to the importance of further research in patient stratification and specialized prognostic models in heterogeneous diseases. In the case of ALS, much needs to be done to help in the understanding of thiss complex disease and promote personalized medicine. Unravelling clinically relevant of patient profiles and disease progression patterns would allow for more personalized care, ultimately leading to extended survival and a better quality of life for the patients, as well as their caregivers.

Acknowledgements. This work was partially supported by FCT funding to Neuroclinomics2 (PTDC/EEI-SII/1937/2014) and iCare4U (LISBOA-01-0145-FEDER-031474 + PTDC/EME-SIS/31474/2017) research projects, and LASIGE Research Unit (UIDB/00408/2020). We are grateful to Genomed for performing the genetic tests in a subset of the included patients.

References

1. Pires, S., Gromicho, M.: Predicting non-invasive ventilation in ALS patients using stratified disease progression groups. In: 2018 IEEE International Conference Data Mining Workshops, pp. 748–757 (2018)
2. Lechtzin, N., et al.: Respiratory measures in amyotrophic lateral sclerosis. Amyotroph. Lateral Scler. Front. Degener. **19**(5–6), 1–10 (2018)
3. Grollemund, V., Pradat, P., Querin, G., Delbot, F.: Machine learning in amyotrophic lateral sclerosis: achievements, pitfalls, and future directions. Front. Neurosci. **13**, 1–28 (2019)

4. Fang, T., et al.: Stage at which riluzole treatment prolongs survival in patients with amyotrophic lateral sclerosis: a retrospective analysis of data from a dose-ranging study. Lancet Neurol. **17**(5), 416–422 (2018)
5. Bourke, S.C., Tomlinson, M., Williams, T.L., Bullock, R.E., Shaw, P.J., Gibson, G.J.: Effects of non-invasive ventilation on survival and quality of life in patients with amyotrophic lateral sclerosis: a randomised controlled trial. Lancet Neurol. **5**(2), 140–147 (2006)
6. Westeneng, H.J., et al.: Prognosis for patients with amyotrophic lateral sclerosis: development and validation of a personalised prediction model. Lancet Neurol. **17**(5), 423–433 (2018)
7. Pfohl, S.R., Kim, R.B., Coan, G.S., Mitchell, C.S.: Unraveling the complexity of amyotrophic lateral sclerosis survival prediction. Front. Neuroinform. **12**(36), 36 (2018)
8. van Es, M.A., et al.: Amyotrophic lateral sclerosis. Lancet **390**(10107), 2084–2098 (2017)
9. Carreiro, A.V., Amaral, P.M.T., Pinto, S., Tomás, P., de Carvalho, M., Madeira, S.C.: Prognostic models based on patient snapshots and time windows: predicting disease progression to assisted ventilation in Amyotrophic Lateral Sclerosis. J. Biomed. Inform. **58**, 133–144 (2015)
10. Martin, S., Al Khleifat, A., Al-Chalabi, A.: What causes amyotrophic lateral sclerosis? F1000Research **6**, 371 (2017)
11. Do, C.B., Batzoglou, S.: What is the expectation maximization algorithm? Nat. Biotechnol. **26**(8), 897–899 (2008)
12. Rousseeuw, P.J.: Silhouettes: a graphical aid to the interpretation and validation of cluster analysis. J. Comput. Appl. Math. **20**, 53–65 (1987)
13. He, H., Garcia, E.A.: Learning from imbalanced data. IEEE Trans. Knowl. Data Eng. **21**(9), 1263–1284 (2009)
14. Chawla, N.V., Bowyer, K.W., Hall, L.O., Kegelmeyer, W.P.: SMOTE: synthetic minority over-sampling technique. J. Artif. Intell. Res. **16**, 321–357 (2002)
15. Zhou, Z.H.: Ensemble learning. In: Li, S.Z., Jain, A.K. (eds.) Encyclopedia of Biometrics, pp. 411–416. Springer, Boston (2015). https://doi.org/10.1007/978-1-4899-7488-4

Micro-Variations from RNA-seq Experiments for Non-model Organisms

Elena Espinosa[1], Macarena Arroyo[1,2], Rafael Larrosa[3,4], Manuel Manchado[5], M. Gonzalo Claros[1,4](✉), and Rocío Bautista[4]

[1] Department of Molecular Biology and Biochemistry, Universidad de Málaga, Malaga, Spain
claros@uma.es

[2] Unidad de Gestión Clínica de Enfermedades Respiratorias, Hospital Regional Universitario de Málaga, Avda Carlos Haya s/n, Malaga, Spain
macarroyo@uma.es

[3] Departamento de Arquitectura de Computadores, Universidad de Málaga, 29071 Malaga, Spain
rlarrosa@uma.es

[4] Plataforma Andaluza de Bioinformática, Universidad de Málaga, 29590 Malaga, Spain
rociobm@uma.es

[5] IFAPA Centro El Toruño, Consejería de Agricultura y Pesca, 11500 El Puerto de Santa María, Cadiz, Spain
manuel.manchado@juntadeandalucia.es

Abstract. RNA-based high-throughput sequencing technologies provide a huge amount of reads from transcripts. In addition to expression analyses, transcriptome reconstruction, or isoform detection, they could be useful for detection of gene variations, in particular micro-variations (single nucleotide polymorphisms [SNPs] and indels). Gene variations are usually based on homogenous (one single individual) DNA-seq data, but this study aims the usage of heterogeneous (several individuals) RNA-seq data to obtain clues about gene variability of a population. Therefore, new algorithms or workflows are required to fill this gap, usually disregarded. Here it is presented an automated workflow based on existing software to predict micro-variations from RNA-seq data using a genome or a transcriptome as reference. It can deal with organism whose genome sequence is known and well-annotated, as well as non-model organism where only draft genomes or transcriptomes are available. Mapping is based on *STAR* in both cases. Micro-variation detection relies on *GATK* (combining *Mutect2* and *HaplotypeCaller*) and *VarScan* since they are able to provide reliable results from RNA-seq reads. The workflow has been tested with reads from normal and diseased lung from patients having small-cell lung carcinoma. Human genome, as well as human transcriptome, were used as reference and then compared: from the initial 120 000 micro-variations, only 267 were predicted by at least two algorithm in the exome of patients. The workflow was tested in non-model organisms such as Senegalese sole, using its transcriptome as reference, to determine micro-variations in sole larvae exposed to different salinities.

I. Rojas et al. (Eds.): IWBBIO 2020, LNBI 12108, pp. 542–549, 2020.
https://doi.org/10.1007/978-3-030-45385-5_48

Therefore, the workflow seems to produce robust and reliable micro-variations in coding genes based on RNA-seq, irrespective of the nature of the reference sequence. We think that this paves the way to correlate micro-variations and differentially expressed genes in non-model organisms with the aim of foster breeding plans.

Keywords: RNA-seq · SNPs · Variations · Indels · Sole · Human · Transcriptome

1 Introduction

Next-generation sequencing enables the obtention of millions of transcriptomic reads at an unprecedented rate. New algorithms have the been developed to analyse this information, thus converting NGS technologies into a powerful tool capable of providing molecular basis to genetic issues. Among the NGS technologies, RNA sequencing (RNA-seq) is commonly used for gene expression studies and only recently has been considered a source of genetic variation [5] in spite of gene splicing isoforms [16]. Therefore, it is now feasible the detection of micro-variations (mainly single nucleotide polymorphisms [SNPs] and indels) within a population to determine its genetic variability. Correlation of micro-variations with expression patterns can be used as a source of new putative biomarkers in gene-wide association studies [2].

Although variation detection has been widely used in model organisms such as human, it also an interest in non-model organisms since they may help in breeding programs and any other individual screening [17,19]. For example, *Solea senegalensis* has become in an important cultivated flatfish species last years producing more than 8 700 M$ in Spain [1]. Its genome sequencing is an on-going process [12] ant its transcriptome has been *de novo* assembled [4] and recently refined based on its genome draft [6]. Hence, a workflow to detect micro-variations from RNA-seq data using as reference a genome or a transcriptome is described in this chapter. Variation callers such as *VarScan* [11], *Mutect2* [3] y *HaplotypeCaller* [7] were benchmarked to provide differential variations. The workflow has been tested with reads from normal and diseased lung from patients having small-cell lung cancer, mapping them both on human genome and transcriptome. It was also tested with reads from Senegalese sole larvae exposed to normal and high salinity.

2 Materials and Methods

2.1 Sequence Data

Human RNA-Seq samples were from Bioproject EGAS00001000334 in the EGA (*European Genome-phenome Archive*) database, containing 2 × 75 bp paired-reads from 17 patients with SCLC (small-cell lung carcinoma) generated with an Illumina HiSeq2000 [15]. For benchmarking, only the first three patients were used. Usage authorisation requirements were fulfilled. Sole RNA-seq samples were from 1 day old *Solea senegalensis* larvae from SRS663634 (exposed to low salinity, 10 ppt) and SRS663635 (exposed to high salinity, 36 ppt). Human genome version hg38.p1 (GCA_000001405.16) was used as reference for mapping SCLC reads. As human transcriptome, the corresponding cDNA sequences were downloaded from UCSC Genome Browser Gateway. *S. senegalensis* transcriptome v5.0 [6] corresponded to an improved version of the one described in [4]. It consists of 55 440 transcripts of which 22 683 code for 17 570 different proteins.

2.2 Bioinformatic Analysis

The bioinformatic workflow has been tested, implemented and executed on Picasso supercomputer of the University of Málaga, consisting of a OpenSUSE LEAP 42.3 with Slurm queue system and Infiniband network (54/40 Gbps) containing 216 nodes with Intel E5-2670 2.6 GHz cores for a total of 3,456 cores and 22 TB of RAM. It requires installation of: (1) *SeqTrimBB* (an evolution of *SeqTrimNext* [9]) for read-preprocessing, (2) *STAR* (v 2.5) [8] for read mapping, (3) *HaplotypeCaller* (v 3.5) [7], *Mutect2* (v 3.5) [3] from *GATK* (v 3.5) [5] as variant detectors, (4) *VarScan* (v 2.3.6) [11] as the third variant detector, (5) *VCFtools, BEDtools, BCFtools* (v 1.4) for result combination and comparison, and other manipulations. There are also in-house scripts to parse results and tools, as well as to provide a consistent workflow integration.

The resulting automated workflow can detect both all possible micro-variations as well as the differential variations between two experimental conditions. For illustrative purposes, it can be divided into several main blocks: data trimming and mapping, processing, variant calling, and comparative analysis (Fig. 1).

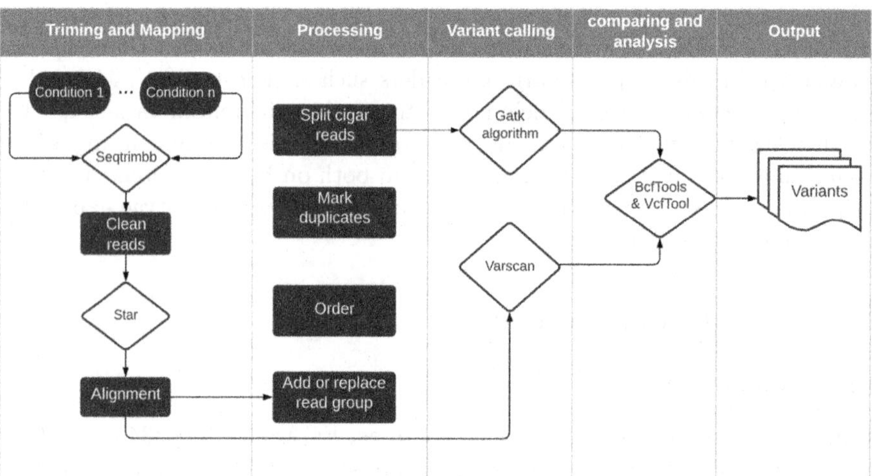

Fig. 1. Schematic description of the automated workflow designed in this study to detect micro-variations from RNA-seq datasets.

Fragments containing low quality nucleotides, contaminants or any other artefactual sequence were removed with *SeqTrimBB*. Clean, useful reads were mapped against a genome reference using *STAR* with the following parameters:

```
--genomeLoad NoSharedMemory
--runThreadN 16 $arg_read
--outSAMstrandField intronMotif ${GTFS}
--genomeDir ${STAR_INDEX}
--readFilesIn $file1 $file2
--outFilterMismatchNmax 6
--outFileNamePrefix align_STAR_sorted
--outSAMtype BAM SortedByCoordinate
--twopassMode Basic
--outReadsUnmapped None
--chimSegmentMin 12
--chimJunctionOverhangMin 12
--alignSJDBoverhangMin 10
--alignMatesGapMax 200000
--alignIntronMax 200000
--chimSegmentReadGapMax parameter 3
--alignSJstitchMismatchNmax 5 -1 5 5
```

When the reference is a transcriptome, `alignIntronMax` is set to zero.

The resulting alignment in BAM format is direclty analysed with *VarScan*, while requiring some processing before use for *GATK* tools *HaplotypeCaller* and *Mutect2* (Fig. 1). Any micro-variation is filtered out when minimal frequency <10% and minimal coverage <10.

In the next step, the VCF files obtained (one per paired sample) were submitted to *BCFtools* and *VCFtools* to detect micro-variations inferred by at least two of the algoritms in the complete sample population. To do so, options `-isec` in *BCFtools* and `-merge` in *VCFtools* were used.

2.3 Functional Annotation

VCF files containing the predicted micro-variations were submitted to *VE!P* (Variant Effect Predictor) [13] and *wANNOVAR* [18] for annotation of functional consequences on genes, transcripts, and protein sequence, as well as regulatory regions. Gene lists afected by micro-variations were analysed and classified with *Panther* (v 14.1) [14].

3 Results and Discussion

Since the final goal of our algorithm is to detect differential micro-variations in non-model organisms, it must be first validated on well-known models of genome and transcriptome, such as human. The comprehensive summary of this analysis is shown in Table 1, where it can be observed that *HaplotypeCaller* produces more differential micro-variations when human genome is the reference, while *Mutect2* is leading the ranking when a transcriptome is used as reference. Moreover, the number of micro-variations using the transcriptome is about 10-fold lower with *HaplotypeCaller* and 3-fold with *Mutect2*. Interestingly, *VarScan* is the most restrictive algorithm and provides closer amount of micro-variations (8 201/5 505 for patient 1, 11 762/10 617 for patient 2, and 9 029/8 017 for patient 3; Table 1).

In-house scripts were used to split and compare SNPs and indels between the three algorithms, considering 'common' variations those that were predicted by at least two algorithms, following the rule of all-but-one that our laboratory previously demonstrated as appropriate [10]. It worths mention that (i) patient 1 seems to present less differential micro-variations than the other two, and (ii) differential micro-variations are less numerous in transcriptome than in genome. However, this fall is less pronounced than expected taking into account that the transcriptome represents a scarce 2% of the genome. In summary, common micro-variations in Table 1 (last row) are expected to be reliable, differential variations among patients.

Table 1. Differential micro-variations per SCLC patient when genome or transcriptome is used as reference.

Algorithm	Variation type	Genome ref.			Transcriptome ref.		
		Pat. 1	Pat. 2	Pat. 3	Pat. 1	Pat. 2	Pat. 3
Varscan	SNPs + indels	8201	11762	9029	4505	10617	8017
HaplotypeCaller	SNPs + indels	119184	160135	48186	12233	17026	6364
Mutect2	SNPs + indels	76149	84858	46530	22484	26035	11082
Common	SNPs	3780	6208	6823	1543	3350	2767
	Indels	3769	6252	6852	803	1064	593

In order to determine differential variations related to the disease (SCLC) and not mere polymorphisms, the common variations of Table 1 were prioritised for presence in the three patients (column Genome in Table 2). Next, only those present in the exome (column Exome in Table 2) were retained with the aim of comparison with transcriptome micro-variations. Differential micro-variations of the transcriptome in Table 1 were also filtered to retain only those present in the three patients (column Transcriptome in Table 2). Even though the important differences in the number of indels in exome and transcriptome (211 vs. 46), the number of SNPs in both references is very close (267 and 231, respectively), suggesting that the workflow is consistent and not excessively depending on the reference used.

The reliable exomic SNPs were studied in detail. A total of 186 (69.7%) were already known but 81 (30.3%) were new variants. The most abundant were frameshift mutations (30%), and 29 regulatory features were affected, in particular regulatory regions (6%), transcription factor binding sites (11%) and

Table 2. Differential micro-variations in all patients per genome, exome and transcriptome that are expected to be related with the disease (SCLC) and not a polymorphisms.

Variation type	Genome	Exome	Transcriptome
SNP	439	267	231
Indels	421	211	46

other upstream regions (13%). With respect to variants on coding sequences, 75% produce a frameshift, 20% produce missense mutations, and as low as 5% were synonymous mutations. Hence, most SNPs seem to produce altered proteins. Since the 267 SNPs map on 87 genes (producing 255 transcripts) their cellular function was inspected in detail. Twenty five genes were related to binding, regulation and signal transduction; these genes are mainly involved in immune processes (35%), biological regulation (15%) and response to stimulus (12%). It is not surprising that none of the common SNPs is directly mapped to cancer genes, but it must be taken into account that the three patients will have the same driver and somatic mutations for SCLC, which is, additionally, a poorly studied lung cancer. In fact, the common micro-variations are expected to conform a gene context where growing of cells having SCLC is allowed. Although confirmation that SNPs in exome and transcriptome are referring to mostly the same micro-variations is pending, we think that the workflow can be executed with non-model organisms where no other confirmatory information is available.

Table 3. Micro-variation summary in sole per algorithm and replicate

Replicate	Algorithm	Var. type	10 ppt	36 ppt
#1	Varscan	SNPs + indels	95328	79827
	HaplotypeCaller	SNPs + indels	244046	214278
	Common	SNPs	60094	49573
		Indels	60222	49688
#2	Varscan	SNPs + indels	88265	104465
	HaplotypeCaller	SNPs + indels	225566	257148
	Common	SNPs	55250	65729
		Indels	55371	65883
#3	Varscan	SNPs + indels	105420	103456
	HaplotypeCaller	SNPs + indels	246991	253578
	Common	SNPs	66221	64736
		Indels	66373	64883
All	Common	SNPs	55666	56418
		Indels	55875	56619

Senegalese sole (*Solea senegalensis*) was selected as the non-model organism to test the workflow. Version 5.0 of its transcriptome [6] was used as reference to detect all possible micro-variations, without taking into account the treatment, therefore not providing any differential variation. This assumption precludes *Mutect2*, that is only able to produce differential variations. It can be seen in Table 3 that the numbers are clearly higher than in Table 1 due to the lack of differential variation analysis. Once again, *HaplotypeCaller* is producing more variations than *VarScan*. More interestingly, the numbers of common variations in all samples are very close to the common micro-variations per replicate, suggesting that replicates revealed approximately the same variations.

4 Conclusions

Micro-variations have been widely used from genome sequencing (DNA-seq) while the detection from RNA-seq experiments, although being an important source of variability, has been largely disregarded. Here it is presented that an automated workflow (Fig. 1) for the identification of consistent variations from RNA-Seq data can provide reliable results when analysing three patients with SCLC (Table 1). Part of the reliability of the algorithm relies on filtering out micro-variations detected only by one algorithm. An added robustness is guaranteed by filtering for micro-variations present in all patients or samples considered. *VarScan* seems the most restrictive algorithm, while *HaplotypeCaller* is the one providing the higher number of possible variations. It is also shown that the workflow is consistent, robust and not excessively depending on the reference used, since the amounts of SNPs detected in exome and transcriptome are very close (Table 2). Since the number of indels is less consistent, it is a pending task their verification. The final list of common micro-variations in all patients of SCLC must be regarded as the gene context allowing the growth of cancer cells and should not be considered cancer-specific or driving mutations. The automated workflow has also been tested with Senegalese sole (Table 3), a non-model organism where no other confirmatory information is available. This will pave the way to correlate micro-variations and differentially expressed genes in non-model organisms with the aim of foster breeding plans.

Acknowledgments. This work was funded by the NeumoSur grants 12/2015 and 14/2016 as well as projects RTA2017-00054-C03-03, AGL2017-83370-C3-3-R and TIN2017-88728-C2-1-R co-funded by MCIU/AEI/FEDER (Spanish Ministerio de Ciencia, Innovación y Universidad, Spanish Agencia Estatal de Investigación, and European Regional Development Fund 2014–2020). The authors also thankfully acknowledge the computer resources and the technical support provided by the Andalusian Platform for Bioinformatics of the University of Malaga.

References

1. APROMAR: Asociación Empresarial de Acuicultura de España: La Acuicultura en España 2018. Technical report, Ministerio de Agricultura y Pesca, Alimentación y Medioambiente (2018)
2. Arroyo, M., Bautista, R., Larrosa, R., Cobo, M.Á., Claros, M.G.: Biomarker potential of repetitive-element transcriptome in lung cancer. PeerJ **7**, e8277 (2019)

3. Benjamin, D., Sato, T., Cibulskis, K., Getz, G., Stewart, C., Lichtenstein, L.: Calling somatic snvs and indels with mutect2. BioRxiv (2019). https://doi.org/10.1101/861054
4. Benzekri, H., et al.: De novo assembly, characterization and functional annotation of Senegalese sole (Solea senegalensis) and common sole (Solea solea) transcriptomes: integration in a database and design of a microarray. BMC Genomics **15**, 952 (2014)
5. Brouard, J.S., Schenkel, F., Marete, A., Bissonnette, N.: The GATK joint genotyping workflow is appropriate for calling variants in RNA-seq experiments. J. Anim. Sci. Biotechnol. **10**, 44 (2019)
6. Córdoba-Caballero, J., Seoane-Zonjic, P., Manchado, M., Gonzalo Claros, M.: *De novo* Transcriptome Assembly of *Solea senegalensis* v5.0 Using TransFlow. In: Rojas, I., Valenzuela, O., Rojas, F., Ortuño, F. (eds.) IWBBIO 2019. LNCS, vol. 11465, pp. 48–59. Springer, Cham (2019). https://doi.org/10.1007/978-3-030-17938-0_5
7. DePristo, M.A., et al.: A framework for variation discovery and genotyping using next-generation DNA sequencing data. Nat Genet **43**(5), 491–8 (2011)
8. Dobin, A., et al.: STAR: ultrafast universal RNA-seq aligner. Bioinformatics **29**(1), 15–21 (2013)
9. Falgueras, J., Lara, A.J., Fernández-Pozo, N., Cantón, F.R., Pérez-Trabado, G., Claros, M.G.: SeqTrim: a high-throughput pipeline for pre-processing any type of sequence read. BMC Bioinf. **11**, 38 (2010)
10. González Gayte, I., Bautista Moreno, R., Seoane Zonjic, P., Claros, M.G.: DEgenes Hunter - A Flexible R Pipeline for Automated RNA-seq Studies in Organisms without Reference Genome. Genomics Comput. Biol. **3**(3), e31 (2017)
11. Koboldt, D.C., et al.: Varscan 2: somatic mutation and copy number alteration discovery in cancer by exome sequencing. Genome Res. **22**(3), 568–76 (2012)
12. Manchado, M., Planas, J.V., Cousin, X., Rebordinos, L., Claros, M.G.: Genetic and genomic characterization of soles. In: Muñoz-Cueto, J.A., Mañanós-Sánchez, E.L., Sánchez-Vázquez, F.J. (eds.) The Biology of Sole. Number B6.1, pp. 361–379. CRC Press (2019)
13. McLaren, W., et al.: The ensembl variant effect predictor. Genome Biol. **17**(1), 122 (2016)
14. Mi, H., Muruganujan, A., Thomas, P.D.: Panther in 2013: modeling the evolution of gene function, and other gene attributes, in the context of phylogenetic trees. Nucleic Acids Res. **41**((Database issue)), D377–D386 (2013)
15. Rudin, C.M., et al.: Comprehensive genomic analysis identifies SOX2 as a frequently amplified gene in small-cell lung cancer. Nature Gen. **44**(10), 1111–1116 (2012)
16. Stein, S., Bahrami-Samani, E., Xing, Y.: Using RNA-Seq to Discover genetic polymorphisms that produce hidden splice variants. Methods Mol. Biol. **1648**, 129–142 (2017)
17. Wang, W., et al.: Genetic structure of six cattle populations revealed by transcriptome-wide SNPs and gene expression. Genes Genomics **40**(7), 715–724 (2018)
18. Yang, H., Wang, K.: Genomic variant annotation and prioritization with annovar and wannovar. Nat. Protoc. **10**(10), 1556–66 (2015). https://doi.org/10.1007/s13258-018-0677-1
19. Yuan, Y., et al.: Genome-wide association and differential expression analysis of salt tolerance in gossypium hirsutum l at the germination stage. BMC Plant Biol. **19**(1), 394 (2019)

Network-Based Variable Selection for Survival Outcomes in Oncological Data

Eunice Carrasquinha[1,2(✉)], André Veríssimo[2,5], Marta B. Lopes[3,4], and Susana Vinga[2,5]

[1] Center of the Unknown, Champalimaud Foundation, Av. Brasília, 1400-038 Lisbon, Portugal
[2] INESC-ID, Instituto Superior Técnico, Universidade de Lisboa, R. Alves Redol, 9, 1000-029 Lisbon, Portugal
eunice.trigueirao@tecnico.ulisboa.pt
[3] NOVA Laboratory for Computer Science and Informatics (NOVA LINCS), FCT, UNL, 2829-516 Caparica, Portugal
[4] Centro de Matemática e Aplicações (CMA), FCT, UNL, 2829-516 Caparica, Portugal
[5] IDMEC, Instituto Superior Técnico, Universidade de Lisboa, Av. Rovisco Pais, 1, 1049-001 Lisbon, Portugal

Abstract. The accessibility to "big data" sets down an ambitious challenge in the medical field, especially in personalized medicine, where gene expression data are increasingly being used to establish a diagnosis and optimize treatment of oncological patients. However, the high-dimensionality nature of the data brings many constraints, for which several approaches have been considered, with regularization techniques in the cutting-edge research front. Additionally, the network structure of gene expression data has fostered the development of network-based regularization techniques to convey data into a low-dimensional and interpretable level. In this work, classical elastic net and two recently proposed network-based methods, HubCox and OrphanCox, are applied to high-dimensional gene expression data, to model survival data. An oncological transcriptomic dataset obtained from The Cancer Genome Atlas (TCGA) is used, with patients' RNA-seq measurements as covariates. The application of sparsity-inducing techniques to the dataset enabled the selection of relevant genes over a range of parameters evaluated. Comparable results were obtained for the elastic net and the network-based OrphanCox regarding model performance and genes selected.

Keywords: High-dimensional data · Regularized optimization · Gene expression data · Network-based regularization

Partially funded by H2020 (No. 633974) and the Portuguese Foundation for Science & Technology FCT (UIDB/00297/2020, UIDB/04516/2020, UIDB/50021/2020, UIDB/50022/2020, PTDC/CCI-CIF/29877/2017, PTDC/CCI-INF/29168/2017 and SFRH/BD/97415/2013).

I. Rojas et al. (Eds.): IWBBIO 2020, LNBI 12108, pp. 550–561, 2020.
https://doi.org/10.1007/978-3-030-45385-5_49

1 Introduction

One of the challenges faced nowadays by several areas of research concerns extracting knowledge from high-dimensional data. In this type of data, the number of covariates (p) is often much larger than the number of observations (n), i.e., $p \gg n$, which may hamper the application of standard statistical methods due to the inherent ill-posed inverse problem of parameter estimation. An example of high-dimensional data regards survival analysis based on gene expression experiments. The identification of relevant genes has gained significant importance in the medical field, especially in the study of cancer and the identification of biomarkers with prognostic value.

A solution to cope with this dimensionality problem is the use of additional constrains in the optimization of the cost function. Regularized optimization techniques [10–15] are widely applied in regression models, particularly in survival analysis, by constraining the Cox's proportional hazards model. Lasso, elastic net and other sparsity-inducing methods have been successfully applied under this rationale. Although leading to more interpretable models, these methods still do not fully profit from the relationships between the features, especially when these can be represented through graphs [13]. Following these ideas, the DegreeCox [13], HubCox, and OrphanCox [11] were proposed as methods rooted in network-based regularization, in order extend Cox proportional hazards models when the features are gene expression values and the outcome is patient survival.

The main goal of the present work is to evaluate the predictive performance of survival analysis in a gene expression dataset using different regularization techniques, namely, the elastic net and model extensions based on network-based regularization. A gene expression dataset obtained from The Cancer Genome Atlas (TCGA) (http://cancergenome.nih.gov/) was used to illustrate the performance of those techniques, with and without accounting for network information.

2 Survival Analysis

Survival analysis is one of the most widely used techniques in the medical field to analyse the follow-up time until a given event of interest occurs. In most cases the event of interest is death, but also can be a disease relapse or complications after surgery. The main difference between survival analysis and other statistical techniques is the fact that the response variable, called *survival time*, may be censored, i.e., not observed on all individuals present in the study, due to, e.g., patients lost to follow-up or because the study ended.

Different approaches (parametric or non-parametric) can be used in the context of survival analysis; however, the most common regression technique used is the Cox model [3]. The Cox regression model is very flexible and can deal with censored data, mostly due to its semi-parametric likelihood function. Before introducing the semi-parametric likelihood function, an essential notion in survival analysis must be first defined, the hazard function, $h(t)$ at time t, given by:

$$h(t; \mathbf{x}) = h_0(t) \exp(\mathbf{x}^T \boldsymbol{\beta}), \tag{1}$$

where $\boldsymbol{\beta} = (\beta_1, ..., \beta_p)$ are the (unknown) regression coefficients, which represent the covariate effect in the survival, $\mathbf{x} = (x_1, ..., x_p)$ is the covariate vector associated to an individual and $h_0(t)$ represents the baseline hazard, which does not need to be specified, thus conferring high flexibility to the Cox model.

The semi-parametric likelihood function is given by:

$$L(\boldsymbol{\beta}) = \prod_{i=1}^{n} \left[\frac{\exp(\mathbf{x}_i^T \boldsymbol{\beta})}{\sum_{j \geq i} \exp(\mathbf{x}_j^T \boldsymbol{\beta})} \right]^{\delta_i}, \tag{2}$$

where δ_i is the censored indicator, and the unknown regression coefficients, $\boldsymbol{\beta}$, are obtained by maximizing the semi-parametric log-likelihood function given by

$$l(\boldsymbol{\beta}) = \sum_{i=1}^{n} \delta_i \left\{ \mathbf{x}_i^T \boldsymbol{\beta} - \log \left[\sum_{j \geq i} \exp(\mathbf{x}_j^T \boldsymbol{\beta}) \right] \right\}. \tag{3}$$

In the presence of high-dimensional data ($p \gg n$), the estimation procedure in the Cox model may bring severe identifiable problems, leading to multiple possible solutions with a large number of non-zero parameters. One possible solution to overcome this challenge is to use regularized optimization, which includes the most widely Lasso and elastic net [15] functions. More recently, penalizers based on the underlying network structure of the features have provided promising results to improve model identifiability and enhance the overall interpretability of the obtained parameters [11,13]. This is especially relevant in the discovery of biomarkers for diagnosis and prognostic assessment.

3 Variable Selection Methods

3.1 Classical Regularization Techniques

A vast number of different approaches is available in the literature to reduce the dimensionality of high-dimensional datasets. One of the most common approaches is the application of sparsity-inducing regularizers [10]. In the context of survival analysis, the regularization is applied by adding a constraint to the semi-parametric log-likelihood function given by expression (3).

The most common regularizers are based on the Ridge, Lasso, and elastic net penalties. The difference between them lies in the combinations of the L_p norms used. Lasso regression shrinks features coefficient to zero, which works well for feature selection in case of high-dimensional data. The elastic net [15] is the result of combining the L_1 (Lasso) and L_2 (Ridge) norms, which is further detailed next.

Elastic Net was proposed by Zou and Hastie [15] as a regularization technique combining the L_1 and L_2 norms, to restrict the solution space by imposing sparsity and small coefficients to the parameters. This framework is used in different types of regression models, and particularly in the Cox regression model for survival data by penalizing the semi-parametric log-likelihood function.

The penalized semi-parametric log-likelihood function (Eq. 3) with a weighted sum of the L_1 and L_2 norms is given by summing a penalization function $\Psi(\boldsymbol{\beta})$ to $l(\boldsymbol{\beta})$, where

$$\Psi(\boldsymbol{\beta}) = \lambda\{\alpha||\boldsymbol{\beta}||_1 + (1-\alpha)||\boldsymbol{\beta}||_2^2\} \tag{4}$$

with $\lambda > 0$ and $0 \leq \alpha \leq 1$. The λ controls the penalization of the weights, and α gives the balance between L_1 and L_2 norms, with the L_1 part being responsible for achieving sparsity. The Ridge and Lasso are particular cases of the elastic net. For $\alpha = 0$, Eq. 4 leads to the Ridge regression, for $\alpha = 1$ it corresponds to the Lasso regression.

One important issue when dealing with regularization is the decision on the α value that should be considered, with no closed-form solution. For instance, in the presence of a group of correlated features in the data, the Lasso ($\alpha = 0$) tends to arbitrarily select only one feature of the group, regardless of their role in the overall network. Even though a sparse solution is obtained by using the classic approach defined before, the use of network information in the regularization term is not considered. Recently proposed network-based regularization techniques are presented next.

3.2 Network-Based Regularization

Lasso, elastic net and other sparsity-inducing methods have been successfully applied to high-dimensional survival data. To explore the usefulness of accounting for network information in classical regularization, [13] and [11] proposed a method that applies network-based regularizers to different regression models, in particular to Cox regression models.

Since the features that are considered here correspond to gene expression values, there is an inherent network that can be represented as a graph G, with a set of nodes V and a set of edges that connect pairs of nodes E, given by

$$G := (V, E). \tag{5}$$

For this particular case, the features considered are genes, and the graph, G, represents a relationship between expressed genes, where V are the genes (nodes), and E represents a weighted relation between two genes (edges).

The idea of using the graph methodology in a gene network is to take advantage of topological measures, in particular, the centrality of a node [6]. Among all of the possible approaches, we will only explore the degree of the node, d_i, defined as

$$d_i = \sum_{j=1, j \neq i}^{P} W_{ij}, \tag{6}$$

where $\mathbf{W}$ represents a positively weighted adjacency matrix, of dimension $p \times p$, associated to G.

Depending on the value of the degree, two types of nodes are considered: *hubs*, or high degree nodes, and *orphans*, those with a small degree. The network itself can be built in two different ways: (1) it can be directly estimated from the data, or (2) built independently based on external knowledge and *a priori* information.

In the present work, a data-dependent network was considered, where the edge weights are directly calculated from the Pearson's correlation matrix. In order to consider only edges with significant values, thus filtering edges that have negligible weights and may introduce some noise in the procedures, a threshold for the cut-off was used. This approach corresponds to considering edge weights equal to zero for those not reaching a pre-specified threshold value. The degree vector obtained was then scaled and transformed by a double exponential heuristic function, to rise the difference between the nodes with small and those with a high degree. Nevertheless, this transformation maintains the ranking of the degree. For more details and the full description of the methodology and associated options, see [11].

The scaled and transformed degree vector obtained is then used as a penalty factor Ψ, given by

$$\Psi(\beta) = \lambda \left(\alpha \|\mathbf{w} \circ \beta\|_1 + (1 - \alpha) \|\mathbf{w} \circ \beta\|_2^2 \right), \tag{7}$$

with $\mathbf{w}$ representing the degree centrality information to be included. Note that $\circ$ corresponds to the Hadamard product (or element-wise product) between two vectors.

In [13] the DegreeCox was proposed, which is a network-based regularization technique for the Cox regression model, that combines the semi-parametric log-likelihood function (3) with degree regularization, which conveys a vertex centrality information of the network. However, no sparsity was induced. As mentioned before, two types of nodes can be considered in the network-based regularization (hubs and orphans).

The HubCox [11], which penalizes nodes with small degree, is an extension of the DegreeCox that includes the L_1 norm, which allows the model inference to find the coefficients that minimize Eq. (7) and thus performs feature selection. Network-based regularization aims to identify a set of genes that correlate with survival and also have a key role as a hub in the underlying network.

On the other hand, OrphanCox [11] promotes nodes that are disconnected or with few edges in a network, by penalizing nodes with a higher degree.

In the recently developed `glmSparseNet` R BioConductor package [12], all of these network-based regularization methods are available, in order to estimate sparse survival models from high dimensional cancer datasets. The network used when penalizing the models can be either inferred from the dataset using Pearson

Correlation matrix, or defined externally from other literature or other sources, such as the STRING database.

The available `glmSparseNet` package also can be applied to any generalized linear model, extending elastic net to network-based penalization. In our survival study, the available R scripts further allow to build Kaplan-Meier curves for high vs. low-risk patients and perform external validation of the biomarkers retrieved using the Cancer Hallmarks Analytics Tool (CHAT) available at http://chat.lionproject.net/ [2].

4 Dataset

To illustrate the challenges associated when handling high-dimensional survival data, an oncological dataset available at The Cancer Genome Atlas (TCGA) was used. The TCGA collects information on high-quality tumor samples from clinical studies and makes the annotated datasets available for the scientific community. By providing this information, it allows the study of new biomarkers aiming at improving patient survival. The oncological dataset chosen was the Melanoma cancer dataset (skcm).

The skcm dataset used corresponds to gene expression data, i.e., RNA-Seq data, from metastatic tissue of oncological patients. This dataset is constituted by 351 observations (patients) measured over 19, 844 features (gene expression). A first pre-processing step was undertaken by eliminating missing values and repeated features. Also, the clinical data was cleaned, with only cases for which the number of "days of follow-up" and "days to death" matched being considered for further analysis. The same process was performed for "days to death" and "vital status", eliminating cases with a status deceased, but a missing "days to death". For the survival data, the "days to follow up" were determined by subtracting the "date of last follow up" and "days to submitted specimen". The "days to death" were determine based on the subtraction of "date to death" and "days to submitted specimen". The gene expression data were filtered as mentioned before, and then pre-processed with a $\log_2$ and z-score transformation.

The dimensionality reduction was performed in two steps. First, a univariate survival analysis for each gene expression was performed, and the log-rank test [7] applied, with only genes considered significant for a level of significance of 20% being kept for further analysis and thus avoiding to be too stringent in the first selection; for the log-rank test, the individuals were divided into two groups, high and low-risk, based on their median risk value. Second, for the genes selected, three regularization techniques were subsequently evaluated: elastic net, HubCox, and OrphanCox.

The choice of the parameters used for regularization was performed as follows. A cross-validation procedure was used to optimize λ, considering a training set composed of 80% of samples and 10 folds. For the α parameter, 0.1, 0.15, 0.2, 0.3, 0.4, 0.5 and 0.6 values were considered. Note that for the illustrative representation of the results obtained, only $\alpha = 0.1$ is shown. For the network-based regularization, the correlation matrix was used to obtain the network, and a cut-off of 0.3 was used.

All the analysis were performed in R [9]. The libraries used for the analysis were: `survival`, for the log-Rank test, `glmnet`, for elastic net regularization, and `glmSparseNet` [12], to conduct the network-based dimensionality reduction.

5 Results

The classical elastic net and the recently proposed network-based regularizers, namely, HubCox and OrphanCox, were evaluated in the survival analysis of the TCGA skcm transcriptomic dataset based on the Cox regression model. The skcm dataset after pre-processing kept 351 samples and a total of 19, 844 gene expressions measured. After the univariate log-rank test, the number of gene expressions dropped to 6, 997, which were further used in regularized Cox regression. Different results were obtained, depending on the regularized technique used and the parameter chosen. The results presented are those considering $\alpha = 0.1$.

Different numbers of features (genes) selected were obtained for each dimensionality reduction method: 156 for elastic net; 91 for HubCox and 147 for OrphanCox (Fig. 1).

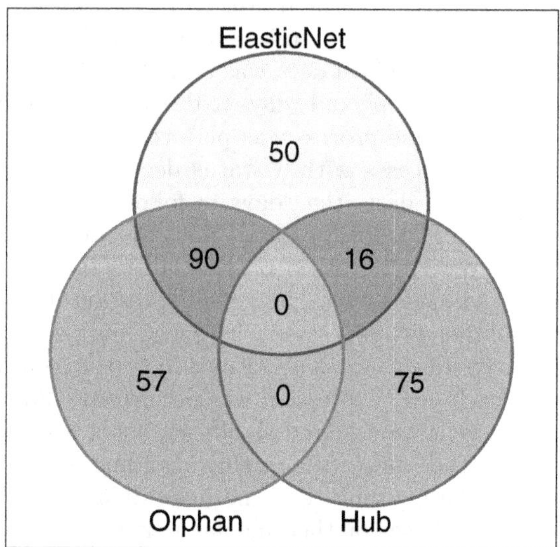

Fig. 1. Venn diagram representing the number of features selected by elastic net, HubCox and OrphanCox.

Several genes were selected in common by the different techniques used. The elastic net and the OrphanCox shared 90 genes selected. From these common genes we point out: *BCL7A*, *GPC3* and *Pole*. *BCL7A* is a protein expression in normal and malignant lymphoid tissues. Also *BCL7A* point mutations, deletions

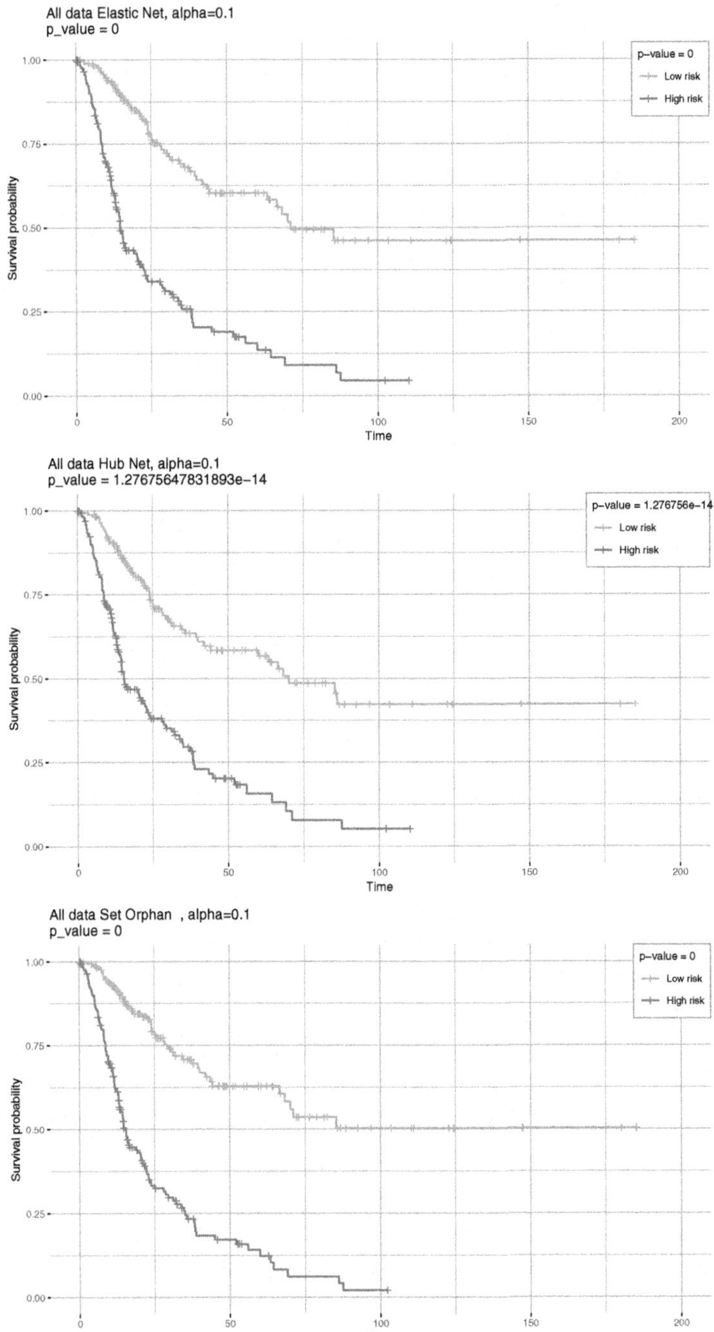

Fig. 2. Kaplan Meier curves obtained for each regularization technique considering $\alpha = 0.1$, considering whole dataset after training.

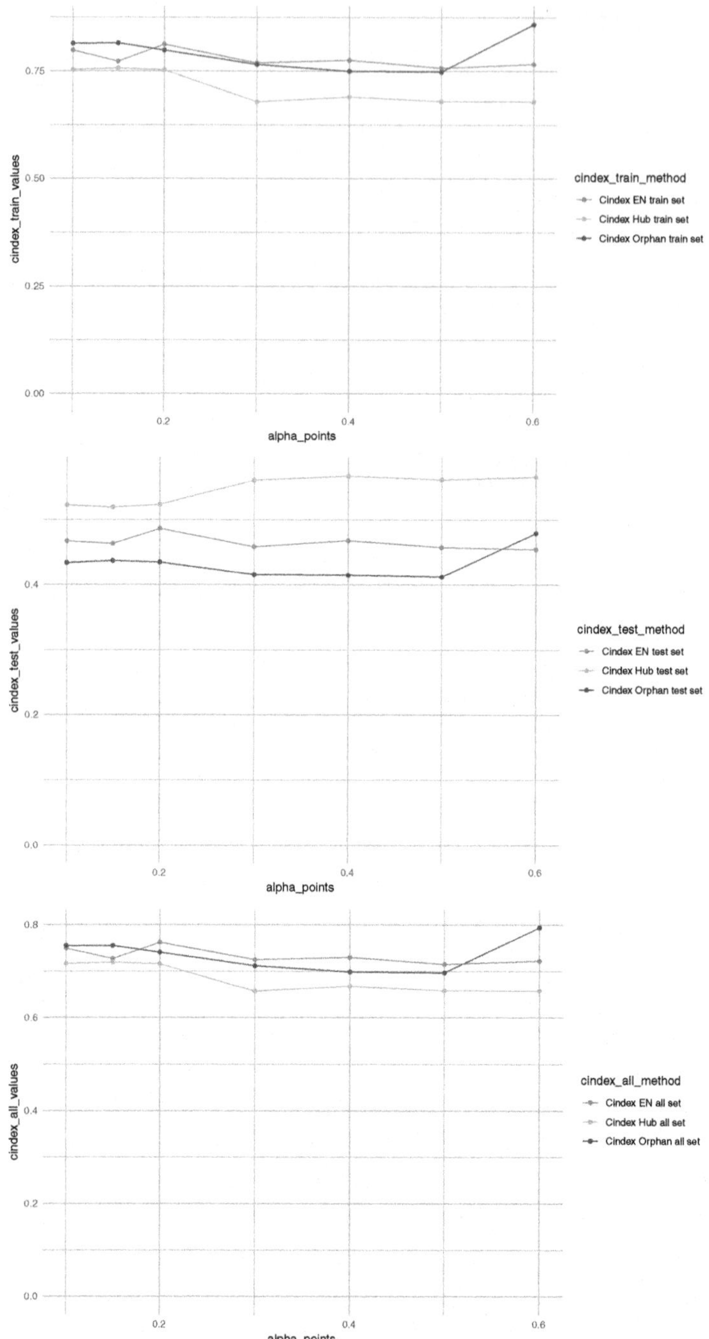

Fig. 3. Values of the concordance c-index for the different regularization techniques considering different values of α, for the training, test and whole dataset, respectively.

and/or rearrangements of other cancer-related genes have been associated with chronic myeloid leukemia (CML) [14]. The *GPC3* gene provides instructions for making a protein called glypican 3. This protein is one of several glypicans in humans, and are involved in numerous cell functions, including regulating cell growth and division (cell proliferation) and cell survival. Recent study show that *GPC3* are tumor markers used in Hepatocellular carcinoma, [5]. Finally, *Pole* gene encodes the catalytic subunit of DNA polymerase epsilon. The enzyme is involved in DNA repair and chromosomal DNA replication, and its mutations might predispose to cutaneous melanoma, as proposed by [1].

Regarding the elastic net and the HubCox, 16 genes were shared by the two methods. We analysed three of these common genes: *CIITA*, *HLA-DQB1* and *HLA-DQA1*. The *CIITA* gene provides instructions for making a protein that primarily helps control the activity (transcription) of genes called major histocompatibility complex (MHC) class II genes. In this sense, *CIITA* is critical for the production of specialized immune proteins called MHC class II proteins from these genes. In [4] found that the master transactivator of MHC genes, i.e., *CIITA*, was also significantly down-regulated in metastatic melanomas when compared to vertical growth phase melanomas. The *HLA-DQB1* and *HLA-DQA1* genes are part of a family of genes called the human leukocyte antigen (HLA) complex, providing instructions for making a protein that plays a critical role in the immune system. The association of melanoma with HLA is present in the literature in many studies, e.g., [8].

Finally regarding HubCox and OrphanCox, no genes were selected in common, which penalize highly and poorly connected genes in the gene network, respectively.

In order to clinically validate the biological role of the variables selected by elastic net, OrphanCox, and HubCox, the survival curves for the three datasets composed of the variables selected by each regularization technique were obtained, considering high and low-risk patients (Fig. 2). It should be noticed that for all cases a difference between high and low-risk patients was statistically significant, as assessed by the log-rank test, meaning that the three sets of genes selected are relevant in the disease.

The concordance c-index was also evaluated as a measure for model performance and comparison. The results for all α values considered are presented in Fig. 3. The elastic net and the OrphanCox showed comparable concordance c-index values, although a similar behaviour was obtained for the training and whole datasets across the different techniques.

6 Conclusions

The goal of this work was to evaluate the performance of network-based regularizers, compared to the classical elastic net, under the scope of survival analysis of high-dimensional cancer transcriptomic data. The elastic net, OrphanCox, and HubCox were applied to the Melanoma RNA-Seq dataset available from The Cancer Genome Atlas (TCGA). The results showed comparable model performance for the three methods regarding the concordance c-index and statistically significant difference for high and low-risk survival curves, with the elastic net and OrphanCox presenting similar results. Even though different combinations of genes are selected depending on the technique used, with no loss of model performance, the main contribution of this work lies in the disclosure of (also relevant) peripherical genes other than those playing a central role (hubs) in the gene network. Simultaneously evaluating different methods promoting the selection of different gene functional interrelationships might be seen as a valuable tool towards increased complex disease understanding and biomarker discovery in cancer.

References

1. Aoude, L.G., et al.: Pole mutations in families predisposed to cutaneous melanoma. Fam. Cancer **14**(4), 621–628 (2015). https://doi.org/10.1007/s10689-015-9826-8
2. Baker, S., et al.: Cancer Hallmarks Analytics Tool (CHAT): a text mining approach to organize and evaluate scientific literature on cancer. Bioinformatics **33**(24), 3973–3981 (2017). https://doi.org/10.1093/bioinformatics/btx454
3. Cox, D.R.: Regression models and life-tables. J. Roy. Stat. Soc. Ser. B (Methodol.) **34**(2), 187–220 (1972). http://www.jstor.org/stable/2985181
4. Degenhardt, Y., et al.: Distinct MHC gene expression patterns during progression of melanoma. Genes Chromosom. Cancer **49**(2), 144–154 (2010). https://doi.org/10.1002/gcc.20728. https://onlinelibrary.wiley.com/doi/abs/10.1002/gcc.20728
5. El-Wahab, N., et al.: Glypican-3 and melanoma antigen genes 1 and 3 as tumor markers for hepatocellular carcinoma. Egypt. J. Immunol. **24**(2), 187–200 (2017)
6. Nieminen, J.: On the centrality in a graph. Scand. J. Psychol. **15**(1), 332–336 (1974). https://doi.org/10.1111/j.1467-9450.1974.tb00598.x. http://onlinelibrary.wiley.com/doi/10.1111/j.1467-9450.1974.tb00598.x/abstract
7. Peto, R., Peto, J.: Asymptotically efficient rank invariant test procedures. J. Roy. Stat. Soc. Ser. A (Gen.) **135**(2), 185–207 (1972). http://www.jstor.org/stable/2344317
8. Planelles, D., et al.: HLA class II polymorphisms in Spanish melanoma patients: homozygosity for HLA-DQA1 locus can be a potential melanoma risk factor. Br. J. Dermatol. **154**(2), 261–266 (2006). https://doi.org/10.1111/j.1365-2133.2005.06896.x. https://onlinelibrary.wiley.com/doi/abs/10.1111/j.1365-2133.2005.06896.x
9. Team, R.C.: R: A Language and Environment for Statistical Computing. R Foundation for Statistical Computing, Vienna, Austria (2012). http://www.R-project.org/
10. Tibshirani, R.: Regression shrinkage and selection via the lasso. J. Roy. Stat. Soc. Ser. B **58**(1), 267–288 (1996)
11. Veríssimo, A., Carrasquinha, E., Lopes, M., Oliveira, A., Sagot, M.F., Vinga, S.: Sparse network-based regularization for the analysis of patientomics high-dimensional survival data. bioRxiv (2018). https://doi.org/10.1101/403402
12. Veríssimo, A., Carrasquinha, E., Lopes, M.B., Vinga, S.: glmSparseNet - network centrality metrics for elastic-net regularized models. Bioconductor (2018). https://bioconductor.org/packages/release/bioc/html/glmSparseNet.html
13. Veríssimo, A., Oliveira, A.L., Sagot, M.F., Vinga, S.: DegreeCox - a network-based regularization method for survival analysis. BMC Bioinformatics **17**(16), 449 (2016). https://doi.org/10.1186/s12859-016-1310-4

14. Yu, N., Shin, S., Choi, J., Kim, Y., Lee, K.: Concomitant AID expression and BCL7A loss associates with accelerated phase progression and imatinib resistance in chronic myeloid leukemia. Ann. Lab. Med. **37**(2), 177–179 (2017). https://doi.org/10.3343/alm.2017.37.2.177
15. Zou, H., Hastie, T.: Regularization and variable selection via the elastic net. J. Roy. Stat. Soc. Ser. B **67**(2), 301–320 (2005)

Evaluating Basic Next-Generation Sequencing Parameters in Relation to True/False Positivity Findings of Rare Variants in an Isolated Population from the Czech Republic South-Eastern Moravia Region with a High Incidence of Parkinsonism

Radek Vodicka[1], Kristyna Kolarikova[1], Radek Vrtel[1(✉)], Katerina Mensikova[2], Petr Kanovsky[2], and Martin Prochazka[1]

[1] Department of Medical Genetics, University Hospital Olomouc, Faculty of Medicine and Dentistry, Palacky University, I.P. Pavlova 6, 77900 Olomouc, Czech Republic
{vodickar, vrtel, Martin.Prochazka}@fnol.cz, Kolarikovakristyna@seznam.cz

[2] Department of Neurology, University Hospital Olomouc, Faculty of Medicine and Dentistry, Palacky University, Olomouc, Czech Republic
katmen@centrum.cz, Petr.Kanovsky@fnol.cz

Abstract. Next-generation sequencing in 16 genes known to be associated with parkinsonism, including coding DNA, intron/exon boundaries, and UTRs loci, was used to find rare variants in 30 patients and 12 healthy controls from an isolated population of South-Eastern Moravia in the Czech Republic where epidemiological data has proved a significantly increased prevalence of parkinsonism (2.9%). The aim of the study is to evaluate the true/false positivity ratio in relation to the basic sequencing parameters (coverage, type of mutation – SNV/INDEL, percentage of rare variants in heterozygosity, ± strand bias, and length of homopolymers). The final filtered rare variants were obtained from the Ion Torrent platform with the following workflow: Torrent Suite Base calling and BAM mapping, Ion Reporter Variant calling, and rare variant filtering. True positivity findings were distinguished from false by Sanger confirmation sequencing. In total, 36 rare variants (MAF < 1%) were found, of which 50% were confirmed as true positive. For SNV, the probability of false positivity is 12%; for INDEL, the false positivity proportion is 84%. A high correlation in strand biases of reference and rare variants in heterozygous findings could be a very strong indicator for true positive variants.

Keywords: Next generation sequencing · Target sequencing · Data analysis · Rare variant · Variant false positivity · Analysis parameters · Bioinformatics · Parkinsonism

I. Rojas et al. (Eds.): IWBBIO 2020, LNBI 12108, pp. 562–568, 2020.
https://doi.org/10.1007/978-3-030-45385-5_50

Highlights

Rare variants found by next-generation sequencing (Ion Torrent platform) show relatively high levels of false positive results.

Basic statistics of next-generation sequencing reads can be very helpful for deciding whether a variant is a true or false positive.

1 Introduction

The search for rare genetic variants with next-generation sequencing (NGS) technology is a part of routine DNA diagnostic laboratory practices [1].

This technology currently includes sequencing by commonly used optical readings of the fluorescent labeled incorporated nucleotides – Illumina platform [2–5] and sequencing by semiconductor measurements of pH changes after nucleotide incorporation – Ion Torrent platform [6–8].

The primary goal of scanning sequencing technologies is the conclusive finding of variants associated with the genetic load. Evaluation algorithm settings should minimize the loss of any potentially pathogenic changes that may cause a greater degree of false positives [9].

The NGS method was introduced in the Department of Medical Genetics at the University Hospital in Olomouc to search for variants that could be associated with parkinsonism in South-Eastern Moravia in the Czech Republic in the selected genes that are most often reported to be connected with the development of parkinsonism [10, 11]. An extensive epidemiological study was carried out in this region, identifying a significantly higher incidence of parkinsonism [12].

The aims of the study are:

(1) to evaluate the rare variant true/false positivity ratio after minor allele frequency (MAF < 0.01) filtering in relation to the basic NGS parameters: coverage, type of mutation – SNV/INDEL, percentage of rare variants in case of heterozygosity, $\pm$ strand bias, and length of homopolymers.
(2) to set the power of particular parameters to be able reliably assess the probability of true/false findings.

2 Methods

The study was approved by the ethics committee of the University Hospital Olomouc, Czech Republic. The patients were informed about the study and signed informed consent forms. Target sequencing (Ion Torrent platform) in 16 genes known to be associated with parkinsonism, including coding DNA, intron/exon boundaries, and UTRs loci, was used to find rare variants in 30 patients and 12 healthy controls from an isolated population of South-Eastern Moravia in the Czech Republic. The sequencing method was described more in detail in a previous study [13]. Briefly, raw electrical signals arising from pH changes from a particular well and flow was transferred to a number and then converted into the base sequences and aligned to the reference using Torrent Suite software. Variant calling, variant annotation, and final rare variant

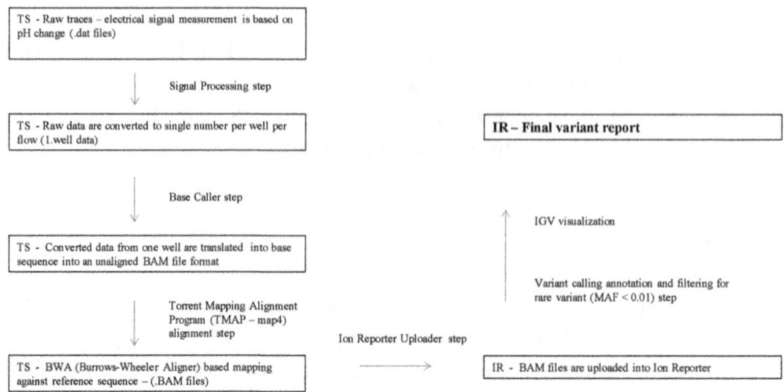

Fig. 1. Flowchart of the NGS data analysis process from raw electrical signal measurement to final rare variant report by Torrent Suite (TS) and Ion Reporter (IR) pipeline. (Legend: TS – Torrent Suite; BAM - Binary Alignment Map; MAF – minor allele frequency; IR – Ion Reporter; IGV – Integrative Genomics Viewer)

filtering were done using Ion Reporter software (Fig. 1). True positivity findings were distinguished from false by Sanger confirmation sequencing.

3 Results

In total, 36 rare variants were found – 18 SNP and 18 INDELs (MAF < 0.01); 50% of them were confirmed as true positive. Almost all the variants were found in a heterozygous state; variant c.421G > T in *HTRA2* gene was found in a homozygous state. A comparison between true and false positivity is shown in Table 1. For SNV, the probability of false positivity is 11.7%; for INDEL, the false positivity proportion is 84%. One very interesting indicator of true positivity could be the high correlation in strand biases of reference (wild type) and rare variants in heterozygous findings (Table 1). In the heterozygous variant, the minimum depth of coverage for particular variant was 4.

Table 1. Basic NGS statistics between 18 confirmed and 18 false positive rare variants

	True positives	False positives
Coverage median	337	277
Min	10	51
Max	1007	805
Type of mutation SNV	15	2
Type of mutation INDEL	3	16
Average ratio of heterozygous variants	0.474	0.41
Min	0.16	0.16
Max	0.7	0.93
Average of strand bias coverage ratio ref+/ref−	2.2	5
Min	0.3	0
Max	18.1	22

(continued)

Table 1. (*continued*)

	True positives	False positives
Average of strand bias coverage ratio var+/var−	1.2	3.9
Min	0.2	0.34
Max	3.1	4.8
Correlation of coverage ratio ref+/var+	0.95	−0.15
Correlation of coverage ratio ref−/var−	0.94	0.02
Length of homopolymers	1.7	3.6
Min	1	1
Max	5	7

Legend: SNV – single nucleotide variants; INDEL – short insertion or deletion variant; ref – wild type variant; var – rare variant; "+" – sense DNA strand; "–" – antisense DNA strand

Table 2. Description of rare variants (MAF < 0.01) from this study

Coordinate (hg19)	Gene	Variant	Number of individuals: patients/controls	Confirmed/ unconfirmed
1:20960385	*PINK1*	c.344A > T	4	4/0
1:155214640	*GBA*	c.-395_-394delTC	13/3	0/16
2:74757189	*HTRA2*	c.59_60delTG	14/10	0/24
2:74757554	*HTRA2*	c.421G > T	3/0	3/0
2:233620929	*GIGYF2*	c.268-4G > T	8/0	0/8
2:233641208, 233641209	*GIGYF2*	c.533-10651_533-10650delAG	6/2	8/0
2:233620907	*GIGYF2*	c.268-26CT > TT	19/9	0/28
2:233721959	*GIGYF2*	c.*389CT > TC	6/1	0/7
3:184032388	*EIF4G1*	c.-109G > A	6/0	6/0
3:184037539	*EIF4G1*	c.509_509delT	7/0	0/7
3:184053042	*EIF4G1*	c.*347delG	9/1	0/10
3:184053097	*EIF4G1*	c.*408delG	8/2	0/10
3:194159730	*ATP13A3*	c.1711-29delG	11/0	0/11
4:41270217	*UCHL1*	c.*127CC > CCCT	6/0	0/6
4:90758280	*SNCA*	−26 + 1123delC	3/0	0/3
6:161770322	*PARK2*	c.*802delG	10/2	0/12
12:40634203	*LRRK2*	c.572-82A > G	6/0	6/0
12:40645097	*LRRK2*	c.1023_1023delG	6/2	0/8
12:40668752	*LRRK2*	c.1898C > T	3/0	3/0
12:40671989	*LRRK2*	c.2167A > G	5/1	6/0
12:40677655	*LRRK2*	c.2242-22C > T	6/0	6/0
12:40703046, 40703047	*LRRK2*	c.4317 + 12delT	6/0	6/0
12:40707861	*LRRK2*	c.4624C > T	1/1	2/0

(*continued*)

Table 2. (*continued*)

Coordinate (hg19)	Gene	Variant	Number of individuals: patients/controls	Confirmed/ unconfirmed
12:40713899	*LRRK2*	c.4937T > C	4/1	5/0
12:40740686	*LRRK2*	c.6241A > G	6/0	6/0
12:40760764	*LRRK2*	c.7391-44T > C	6/0	6/0
16:46702740	*VPS35*	c.1647 + 102A > G	5/0	5/0
16:46714512	*VPS35*	c.506 + 71A > G	6/1	7/0
16:46717387	*VPS35*	c.102 + 33G > A	4/1	5/0
17:44055844	*MAPT*	c.373 + 37delT	4/1	0/5
17:44060859	*MAPT*	c.689A > G	6/1	7/0
17:44061168	*MAPT*	c.999_999delG	3/0	0/3
17:44103454	*MAPT*	c.*1917G > A	5/5	0/10
17:44104449	*MAPT*	c.*2912delG	3/0	0/3
22:32880006	*FBXO7*	c.540A > G	4/0	4/0
22:38507696	*PLA2G6*	c.*472delG	4/1	0/5

Legend: The coordinate is the location of the individual nucleotide in the genome (it is related to hg 19); the variant is the nucleotide change in the genome, its position in the coding sequence is described using HGVS nomenclature; the number of individuals is the number of patients or controls in whom the variant was found; confirmed/unconfirmed variants are based on variant confirmation used Sanger sequencing

4 Discussion

All analyses of sequencing (Torrent Suite and Ion Reporter) data were made in the default mode recommended by Ion Reporter Software 5.10 User Guide Pub. No. MAN0017605 C.0 and Torrent Suite Software 5.10 User Guide Pub. No. MAN0017598 A.0 for Ampliseq amplicon sequencing.

Total coverage of the variants was very variable, as is typical for amplicon sequencing, where the different amplifiability of particular sections is mainly influenced by factors affecting the final amount of PCR amplicons. Most important is the different representation of GC in individual amplicons and the different sensitivity of primer hybridization (hundreds of primers hybridize at the same temperature). Despite the coverage variability, there is no difference between true and false positives.

The average number of unfiltered variants was 70 per sample from a minimum of 48 to a maximum of 101 [13]. Most of the variants were with a frequency of more than 1% in the population. For these "common" variants, the assumption is that they were sequenced properly.

Taking into account all the variants, the total false positivity is very low and can be estimated at 0.5%–1% working on an assumption of an average of roughly 1 rare variant (MAF < 0.01) per 1 sample (36 rare variants/42 samples versus 18 true rare variants/42 samples).

On the other hand, when detecting rare INDEL variants, it is necessary to expect a higher than 80% probability that this is a sequencing artifact.

The value of an unbalanced ratio of the sense/antisense amplicon proportion itself (±strand biases) did not influence the increase in false positive findings. Even the variants with a very unbalanced ratio of + and – reads (0.2 and 18) have been confirmed as truly present. If a strand bias for variants and wild types was similar for both strands, there is a high probability that it will be a real variant. Predictably, a higher number of nucleotides in homopolymers was present in false positives.

5 Conclusion

Basic statistics of reads can be very helpful for deciding whether the finding of a rare variant is reliable based on NGS analysis itself, whether to choose Sanger sequencing for confirmation, and whether it is possible to reliably exclude the variant as a false positive. Our results indicate that it is possible to optimize the analysis parameters in Torrent Suite and Ion Reporter software to filter out sequencing artifacts without increasing the risk of false negative results.

Acknowledgement. This study was funded by a grant from the Ministry of Health of the Czech Republic, grant no. 15-32715A; by a grant from the Palacky University Medical School Internal Grant Agency—IGA LF 2018-009; and by a grant from the Ministry of Health, Czech Republic, conceptual development of a research organization, MH CZ – DRO (FNOL,00098892) 2018; and by the OP VVV (Czech Republic) project "Molecular, cellular and clinical approach to the healthy aging – ENOCH", reg. no. CZ.02.1.01/0.0/0.0/16_019/0000868.

Conflicts of Interest

All the authors declare that there is no conflict of interest.

References

1. Di Resta, C., Galbiati, S., Carrera, P., Ferrari, M.: Next-generation sequencing approach for the diagnosis of human diseases: open challenges and new opportunities. EJIFCC **29**, 4–14 (2018)
2. Merriman, B., Ion Torrent R&D Team, Rothberg, J.M.: Progress in ion torrent semiconductor chip based sequencing. Electrophoresis **33**, 3397–3417 (2012). https://doi.org/10.1002/elps.201200424
3. Liu, L., Li, Y., Li, S., Hu, N., He, Y., Pong, R., et al.: Comparison of next-generation sequencing systems. J. Biomed. Biotechn., 251364 (2012). https://doi.org/10.1155/2012/251364
4. Van Hoorde, K., Butler, F.: Use of next-generation sequencing in microbial risk assessment. EFSA J. **16**(S1), e16086 (2018). https://doi.org/10.2903/j.efsa.2018.e16086
5. Kuo, F.C.: Next generation sequencing in hematolymphoid neoplasia- Illumina. Semin. Hematol. **56**, 2–6 (2019). https://doi.org/10.1053/j.seminhematol.2018.05.006
6. Rusk, N.: Torrents of sequence. Nat. Methods **8**, 44 (2011). https://doi.org/10.1038/nmeth.f.330

7. Rothberg, J.M., Hinz, W., Rearick, T.M., Schultz, J., Mileski, W., Davey, M., et al.: An integrated semiconductor device enabling non-optical genome sequencing. Nature **475**, 348–352 (2011). https://doi.org/10.1038/nature10242
8. Guerra, S.G., Chong, W., Brown, C.J., Navarrete, C.V.: Evaluation of Ion Torrent sequencing technology for rapid clinical human leucocyte antigen typing. Int. J. Immunogenet. **45**, 230–235 (2018). https://doi.org/10.1111/iji.12378
9. Wu, W., Lu, L., Xu, W., Liu, J., Sun, J., Zheng, L., et al.: Whole exome sequencing identifies a novel pathogenic RET variant in hirschsprung disease. Front. Genet. **9**, 752 (2019). https://doi.org/10.3389/fgene.2018.00752
10. Bartonikova, T., Mensíkova, K., Kolarikova, K., Vodicka, R., Vrtel, R., Otruba, P., et al.: New endemic familial parkinsonism in south Moravia, Czech Republic and its genetical background. Medicine (Baltimore) **97**, e12313 (2018). https://doi.org/10.1097/md.0000000000012313
11. Bartonikova, T., Mensikova, K., Mikulicova, L., Vodicka, R., Vrtel, R., Godava, et al: Familial atypical parkinsonism with rare variant in VPS35 and FBXO7 genes: a case report. Medicine (Baltimore) **95**(46), art. no. e5398 (2016). https://doi.org/10.1097/MD.0000000000005398
12. Mensikova, K., Kanovsky, P., Kaiserova, M., Mikulicova, L., Vastik, M., Hlustik, P., et al.: Prevalence of neurodegenerative parkinsonism in an isolated population in south-eastern Moravia. Czech Rep. Eur. J. Epidemiol. **28**, 833–836 (2013). https://doi.org/10.1007/s10654-013-9823-x
13. Vodicka, R., Vrtel, R., Mensikova, K., Kanovsky, P., Dolinova, I., Kolarikova, K., et al.: Next generation sequencing data analysis evaluation in patients with parkinsonism from a genetically isolated population. Genomics Comput. Biol. **3**, e44 (2017). https://doi.org/10.18547/gcb.2017.vol3.iss3.e44

Detection of Highly Variable Genome Fragments in Unmapped Reads of *Escherichia coli* Genomes

Marketa Nykrynova[1(✉)], Vojtech Barton[1], Matej Bezdicek[2], Martina Lengerova[2], and Helena Skutkova[1]

[1] Department of Biomedical Engineering, Brno University of Technology, Technicka 12, 616 00 Brno, Czech Republic
{nykrynova,barton,skutkova}@vutbr.cz

[2] Department of Internal Medicine - Hematology and Oncology, University Hospital Brno, Brno, Czech Republic
{Bezdicek.Matej,Lengerova.Martina}@fnbrno.cz

Abstract. Whole-genome sequencing becomes a powerful tool in the study of closely related bacterial population as a single nucleotides changes can be detected. However, the postprocessing of obtained data still remains problematic. Reference-based assembly of genomes only allows identification of shared parts of genomes. Here, we show a pipeline for *de novo* assembly of unmapped reads and locating variable regions in it. Identified regions can be used as new markers for bacterial genotyping.

Keywords: Genome assembly · Unmapped reads · Genotyping

1 Introduction

Bacterial typing is a process which is used for distinguishing between different strains within one species [20]. Typing is an essential tool in epidemiology as it helps to find sources of infection, how they are transmitted, and it is also used for epidemiological surveillance [15,21].

In the past, typing methods were based on phenotyping, but in these days genotyping systems are used more often due to their resolution power [15].

Typing methods such as pulsed-field electrophoresis (PFGE) or multilocus sequence typing (MLST) are used in clinical practice. Unfortunately, the discriminatory power of these methods is not sufficient for discrimination of closely-related bacterial strains, and it should be combined with methods such as whole-genome sequencing (WGS) that is capable to find even single nucleotide variants [4]. As the cost of sequencing is dropping and the speed of sequencing is increasing the WGS has the potential to become a routine microbiological tool for typing [10,12].

Unfortunately, in these days, the postprocessing of NGS data remains problematic as there are no standards protocols for data processing [11] and also the

I. Rojas et al. (Eds.): IWBBIO 2020, LNBI 12108, pp. 569–578, 2020.
https://doi.org/10.1007/978-3-030-45385-5_51

assembly of genomes remains problematic for clinical practice. Nowadays, two approaches for genome assembly exist. The first one is *de novo* assembly which is based on de Bruijn graphs or overlaps. Unfortunately, this method is time and computationally demanding, and high-quality reads are essential. The second method is reference-based assembly, where reads are assigned to the reference sequence. As *de novo* assembly also reference-based assembly have some drawbacks. The reference sequence can vary from the sequenced genome, and during assembly, the unmapped reads are discarded from further analysis [8].

The goal of our project is to use *de novo* assembly of unmapped reads and in obtained scaffolds find regions with high variability which can be used for genotyping of closely-related bacterial strains.

2 Materials and Methods

Our project for the location of variable regions in unmapped reads consists of several steps which are described in the following paragraphs.

Before genome assembly, the quality of reads is examined. Then reads are mapped to the reference genome, and unmapped reads are extracted. The discarded reads are assembled *de novo*. Via BLAST scaffolds from different genomes which correspond to the same genome regions are extracted and then aligned. In the following step, the variable parts in the aligned sequences are detected. Finally, the phylogenetic trees of variable sequences are created, and the discrimination power of these sequences is established. Diagram of the proposed method is depicted in Fig. 1.

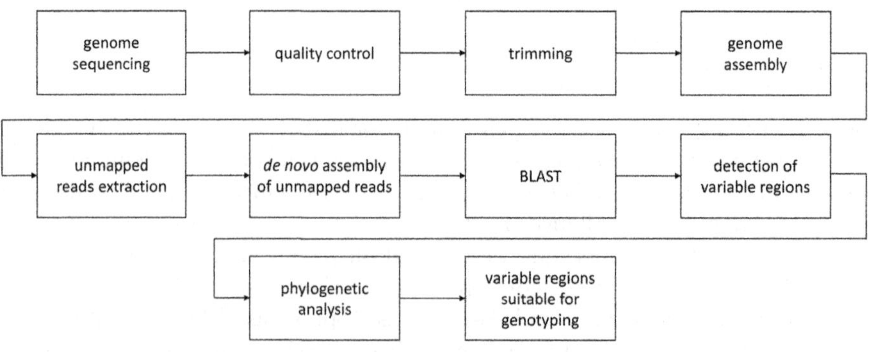

Fig. 1. Block diagram of the proposed method.

2.1 Genome Assembly

The genomes of *Escherichia coli* were sequenced using Illumina Miseq, and paired-end sequencing was performed. Before reads mapping the quality of raw data was examined via FastQC [2] and MultiQC [7]. Firstly, the number of unique and duplicate reads was calculated. Then for each base position in the read, the mean quality value was determined. In the next part, the read length distribution, GC content, N content and adapter content were inspected. The output from MultiQC for genome EC163 is depicted in Fig. 2. Then Trimmomatic [5] was used to trim, and crop reads and to remove adapters.

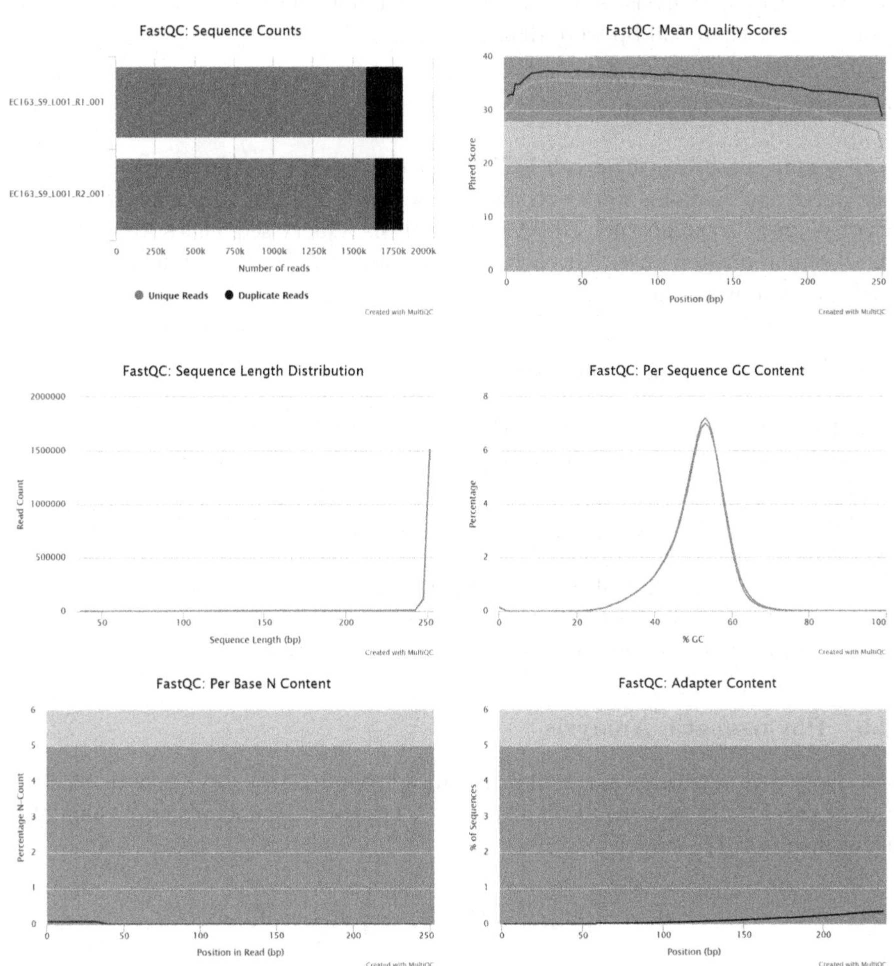

Fig. 2. Output from MultiQC for genome EC163.

In the next step, reads were mapped to human genome GRCh38.p13 to remove contamination which can emerge during library preparation. Reads which did not map to the human genome were assembled by Burrows-Wheeler Aligner [13]. The reference-based assembly was used and as the reference genome Escherichia coli O157:H7 str. Sakai (NC_002695.2) was chosen.

2.2 Unmapped Reads Assembly

In the next part of the project, for each genome reads which remain unmapped were extracted to specific files and from these files reads with poor quality and optical and PCR duplicates were removed via Samtools [14].

After that, *de novo* assembly of unmapped reads was performed via SPAdes [3]. For further analysis, scaffolds of each genome were used, and these which were shorter than 500 bp were discarded.

2.3 BLAST Analysis

The genome of *Escherichia coli* EC155 was chosen as the reference one. From it, the particular scaffolds were extracted to separate FASTA files which then were used as query sequences for BLAST [1] analysis. Query sequences were searched in all remaining genomes. For each output from BLAST, the sequences with the highest score were chosen.

2.4 Variable Regions Detection

Sequences which corresponded to the same scaffolds were aligned. If particular scaffold was not found in all genomes of *E.coli* it was discarded from further analysis.

From aligned scaffolds, parts which were presented in all genomes were selected.

As a variable fragments were labelled aligned sequences where more than 10% of all nucleotide positions were variable.

Example of the proposed process is depicted on Fig. 3.

2.5 Phylogenetic Analysis

For every region which was labelled as variable enough, the phylogenetic analysis takes part. Firstly, the evolution distances d between all genomes were calculated using Kimura [17] model:

$$d = -\frac{1}{2}\ln(1 - 2P - Q) - \frac{1}{4}\ln(1 - 2Q), \tag{1}$$

where P is number of transitions and Q is number of transversion. From obtained evolution distances the phylogenetic tree was constructed by UPGMA (Unweighted Pair Group Method with Arithmetic Mean) method, and in the created tree the number of clusters was determined [18, 19].

2.6 Dataset

Escherichia coli belongs to *Enterobacteriaceae* family and it is Gram-negative bacterium. Naturally, it can be found in the gastrointestinal tract of human,

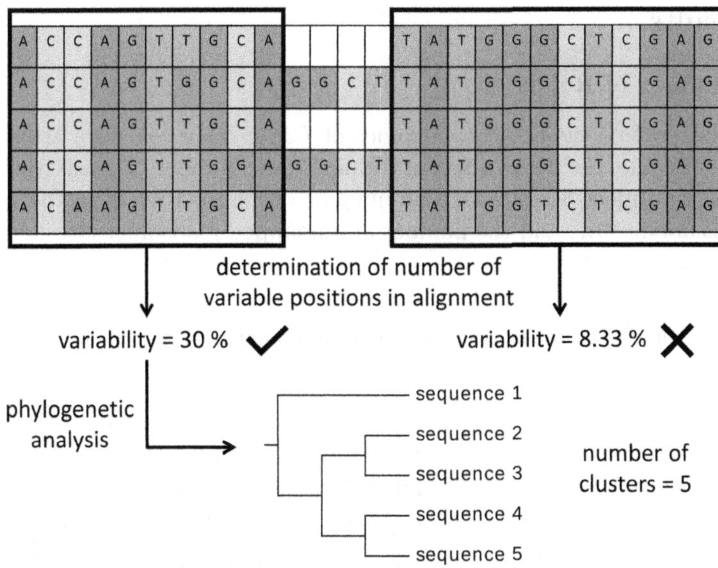

Fig. 3. Example of variable fragments detection from aligned scaffolds.

but some strains can be pathogenic and cause urinary tract infection, sepsis or diarrhoea [16]. The average size of genome varies from 4.5 to 5.5 Mbp [9] and the core genome of *Escherichia coli* contains about 2200 genes [6].

In this project, we worked with 21 genomes of *Escherichia coli*, which were collected in University Hospital Brno. In silico multilocus sequence typing identified eleven sequence types which are mentioned in Table 1.

Table 1. Genomes of *Escherichia coli* and their sequence types.

Genome	Sequence type	Genome	Sequence type	Genome	Sequence type
EC155	UNW	EC162	404	EC169	69
EC156	131	EC163	58	EC170	95
EC157	131	EC164	131	EC171	297
EC158	38	EC165	517	EC172	1049
EC159	38	EC166	404	EC173	1049
EC160	58	EC167	58	EC174	101
EC161	58	EC168	131	EC1773	101

3 Results

3.1 Number of Reads

In the first part of the project, genomes of *Escherichia coli* were assembled to reference genome. As we can see in Table 2 total number of reads varies from 2 400 000 to almost 5 000 000. The number of mapped reads to the reference genome is about 80%, and the number of unmapped reads fluctuates about 20% of all reads.

Table 2. Number of all reads, mapped reads and unmapped reads of analyzed genomes of *Escherichia coli.*

Genome	Number of reads	Number of mapped reads	Number of unmapped reads
EC155	3 841 125	3 040 071 (79.15%)	801 054 (20.85%)
EC156	3 370 881	2 464 761 (73.12%)	906 120 (26.88%)
EC157	3 114 528	2 363 526 (75.89%)	751 002 (24.11%)
EC158	3 777 378	3 093 514 (81.90%)	683 864 (18.10%)
EC159	3 596 972	2 964 713 (82.42%)	632 259 (17.58%)
EC160	3 021 626	2 428 258 (80.36%)	593 368 (19.64%)
EC161	3 119 012	2 383 653 (76.42%)	735 359 (23.58%)
EC162	3 315 868	2 400 666 (72.40%)	915 202 (27.60%)
EC163	3 470 408	2 795 610 (80.56%)	674 798 (19.44%)
EC164	3 151 029	2 310 384 (73.32%)	840 645 (26.68%)
EC165	2 926 253	2 455 510 (83.91%)	470 743 (16.09%)
EC166	2 944 953	2 137 699 (72.59%)	807 254 (27.41%)
EC167	4 939 016	3 876 828 (78.49%)	1 062 188 (21.51%)
EC168	2 904 579	2 160 490 (74.38%)	744 089 (25.62%)
EC169	3 122 161	2 354 572 (75.41%)	767 589 (24.59%)
EC170	2 974 925	2 241 301 (75.34%)	733 624 (24.66%)
EC171	3 010 427	2 609 824 (86.69%)	400 603 (13.31%)
EC172	2 454 326	2 089 502 (85.14%)	364 824 (14.86%)
EC173	2 818 059	2 409 003 (85.48%)	409 056 (14.52%)
EC174	2 499 576	2 151 030 (86.06%)	348 546 (13.94%)
EC1773	2 847 507	2 433 779 (85.47%)	413 728 (14.53%)

3.2 *De novo* Assembly

The unmapped reads were assembled *de novo* via SPAdes algorithm. The number of created scaffolds varied from 150 to almost 300 and the average size of scaffolds was approximately 4400 bp. The exact value are shown in Table 3.

Table 3. Number of created scaffolds and their mean length of genomes of *Escherichia coli.*

Genome	Number of scaffolds	Mean length of scaffold [bp]	Genome	Number of scaffolds	Mean length of scaffold [bp]	Genome	Number of scaffolds	Mean length of scaffold [bp]
EC155	212	3742	EC162	266	5093	EC169	268	4491
EC156	221	5001	EC163	177	4563	EC170	273	4651
EC157	288	3813	EC164	246	5233	EC171	171	3683
EC158	296	3287	EC165	238	2818	EC172	206	3459
EC159	243	3877	EC166	255	5279	EC173	153	4476
EC160	154	5189	EC167	196	4916	EC174	151	4945
EC161	166	6131	EC168	262	4946	EC175	224	3273

3.3 BLAST Analysis

After *de novo* assembly scaffolds of genome EC155 were searched in obtained scaffolds of remaining genomes. Totally, 161 scaffolds (51 scaffolds were removed because of insufficient length) were analysed. From them, 26 scaffolds were found in all genomes of *Escherichia coli* and were aligned.

3.4 Variable Fragments Evaluation

In aligned scaffolds, nine fragments which were labelled as variable were located. Obtained fragments are described in Table 4.

For each identified fragment with high variability, the phylogenetic analysis was conducted. As a result, phylogenetic trees were obtained, and in each one, the number of clusters was calculated, and it is also shown in Table 4.

Table 4. Identified variable fragments in scaffolds of *Escherichia coli* genomes.

Variable fragment	Length [bp]	Number of clusters	Number of variable positions in alignment
1	48	4	7
2	23	5	10
3	38	5	9
4	291	5	81
5	153	5	46
6	10	2	4
7	1158	9	276
8	64	2	12
9	4762	11	557

One out of nine variable fragments is capable of distinguishing between the sequence types and its phylogenetic tree is depicted on Fig. 4.

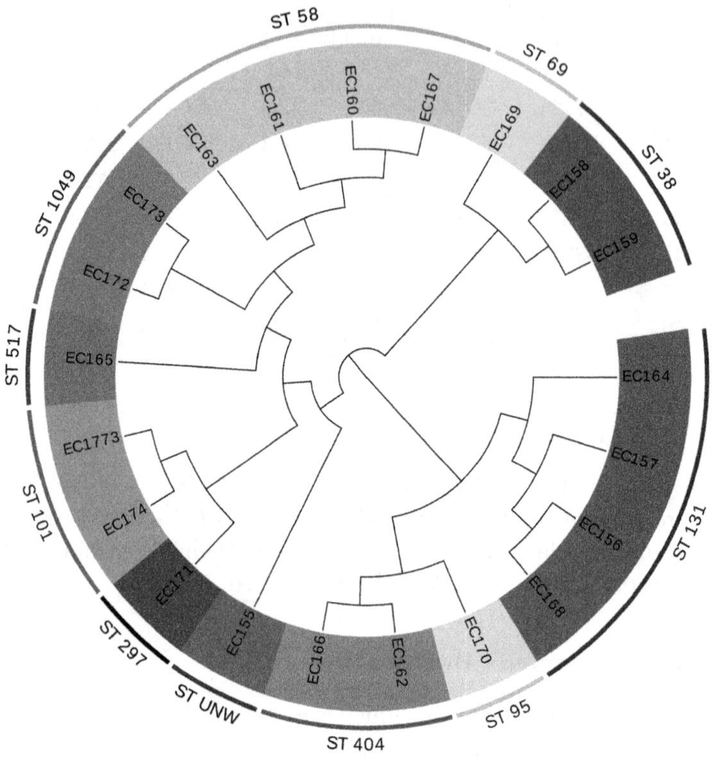

Fig. 4. Phylogenetic tree of variable fragment for 21 genomes of *Escherichia coli* with sequence types created by Evolview [22].

4 Conclusion

In this paper, we present a new method for identification of highly variable sequences in unmapped reads of *Escherichia coli*, which can be used for genotyping. Based on identified sequences, we are able to distinguish between sequence types using only one nucleotide sequence instead of seven housekeeping genes.

The variable sequence was located in *de novo* assembly of unmapped reads which were not assigned during reference-based assembly. The obtained results were compared to *in silico* multilocus sequence typing and validated via phylogenetic analysis. One variable region which is capable of distinguishing between eleven present sequence types of genomes of *Escherichia coli* was found. The located variable fragment can be used in MLST for precise bacterial genotyping.

Our approach for *de novo* assembly of unmapped reads can be used to find genes and other genome regions which are not present in the reference genome and can be specific to the analysed group of genomes. Also, it can be used in the case of having low-quality NGS data with short reads length where *de novo* assembly of whole-genome gives insufficient results.

The drawback of proposed methods is uncertainty in the *de novo* assembled data. The assembly of scaffolds can be affected by the small length of the reads (about 250 bp). Thus, laboratory verification of variable fragments is necessary.

Acknowledgments. This work was supported by grant project of the Czech Science Foundation [GACR 17-01821S].

References

1. Altschul, S.F., Gish, W., Miller, W., Myers, E.W., Lipman, D.J.: Basic local alignment search tool. J. Mol. Biol. **215**(3), 403–410 (1990). https://doi.org/10.1016/S0022-2836(05)80360-2. https://linkinghub.elsevier.com/retrieve/pii/S0022283605803602
2. Andrews, S., Krueger, F., Segonds-Pichon, A., Biggins, L., Krueger, C., Wingett, S.: FastQC. Babraham Institute (2012)
3. Bankevich, A., et al.: Spades. J. Comput. Biol. **19**(5), 455–477 (2012). https://doi.org/10.1089/cmb.2012.0021. http://www.liebertpub.com/doi/10.1089/cmb.2012.0021
4. Bezdicek, M., et al.: Application of mini-MLST and whole genome sequencing in low diversity hospital extended-spectrum beta-lactamase producing Klebsiella pneumoniae population. PLoS ONE **14**(8) (2019). https://doi.org/10.1371/journal.pone.0221187. http://dx.plos.org/10.1371/journal.pone.0221187
5. Bolger, A.M., Lohse, M., Usadel, B.: Trimmomatic. Bioinformatics **30**(15), 2114–2120 (2014). https://doi.org/10.1093/bioinformatics/btu170. https://academic.oup.com/bioinformatics/article-lookup/doi/10.1093/bioinformatics/btu170
6. Croxen, M.A., Finlay, B.B.: Molecular mechanisms of Escherichia coli pathogenicity. Nat. Rev. Microbiol. **8**(1), 26–38 (2010). https://doi.org/10.1038/nrmicro2265. http://www.nature.com/articles/nrmicro2265
7. Ewels, P., Magnusson, M., Lundin, S., Käller, M.: MultiQC. Bioinformatics **32**(19), 3047–3048 (2016). https://doi.org/10.1093/bioinformatics/btw354. https://academic.oup.com/bioinformatics/article-lookup/doi/10.1093/bioinformatics/btw354
8. Iqbal, Z., Caccamo, M., Turner, I., Flicek, P., McVean, G.: De novo assembly and genotyping of variants using colored de Bruijn graphs. Nat. Genet. **44**(2), 226–232 (2012). https://doi.org/10.1038/ng.1028. http://www.nature.com/articles/ng.1028
9. Kolisnychenko, V.: Engineering a reduced Escherichia coli genome. Genome Res. **12**(4), 640–647 (2002). https://doi.org/10.1101/gr.217202. http://www.genome.org/cgi/doi/10.1101/gr.217202
10. Köser, C.U., et al.: Routine use of microbial whole genome sequencing in diagnostic and public health microbiology. PLoS Pathog. **8**(8) (2012). https://doi.org/10.1371/journal.ppat.1002824. http://dx.plos.org/10.1371/journal.ppat.1002824
11. Kwong, J., Mccallum, N., Sintchenko, V., Howden, B.: Whole genome sequencing in clinical and public health microbiology. Pathology **47**(3), 199–210 (2015). https://doi.org/10.1097/PAT.0000000000000235. https://linkinghub.elsevier.com/retrieve/pii/S003130251630126X

12. Leopold, S.R., Goering, R.V., Witten, A., Harmsen, D., Mellmann, A.: Bacterial whole-genome sequencing revisited. J. Clin. Microbiol. **52**(7), 2365–2370 (2014). https://doi.org/10.1128/JCM.00262-14. http://jcm.asm.org/cgi/doi/10.1128/JCM.00262-14
13. Li, H., Durbin, R.: Fast and accurate short read alignment with Burrows-Wheeler transform. Bioinformatics, pp. 1754–1760. (2009). https://doi.org/10.1093/bioinformatics/btp324. https://academic.oup.com/bioinformatics/article-lookup/doi/10.1093/bioinformatics/btp324
14. Li, H., et al.: The sequence alignment/map format and Samtools. Bioinformatics **25**(16), 2078–2079 (2009). https://doi.org/10.1093/bioinformatics/btp352. https://academic.oup.com/bioinformatics/article-lookup/doi/10.1093/bioinformatics/btp352
15. Li, W., Raoult, D., Fournier, P.E.: Bacterial strain typing in the genomic era. FEMS Microbiol. Rev. **33**(5), 892–916 (2009). https://doi.org/10.1111/j.1574-6976.2009.00182.x. https://academic.oup.com/femsre/article-lookup/doi/10.1111/j.1574-6976.2009.00182.x
16. Nataro, J., Kaper, J.: Diarrheagenic Escherichia coli. Clin. Microbiol. Rev. **11**(1), 142–201 (1998)
17. Nei, M., Kumar, S.: Molecular Evolution and Phylogenetics. Oxford University Press, New York (2000)
18. Nykrynova, M., Maderankova, D., Barton, V., Bezdicek, M., Lengerova, M., Skutkova, H.: Entropy-based detection of genetic markers for bacteria genotyping. In: Rojas, I., Valenzuela, O., Rojas, F., Ortuño, F. (eds.) IWBBIO 2019. LNCS, vol. 11466, pp. 177–188. Springer, Cham (2019). https://doi.org/10.1007/978-3-030-17935-9_17
19. Nykrynova, M., Maderankova, D., Bezdicek, M., Lengerova, M., Skutkova, H.: Bioinformatic tools for genotyping of Klebsiella pneumoniae isolates. In: Pietka, E., Badura, P., Kawa, J., Wieclawek, W. (eds.) ITIB 2018. AISC, vol. 762, pp. 419–428. Springer, Cham (2019). https://doi.org/10.1007/978-3-319-91211-0_37
20. Sabat, A.J., et al.: Overview of molecular typing methods for outbreak detection and epidemiological surveillance. Eurosurveillance **18**(4) (2013). https://doi.org/10.2807/ese.18.04.20380-en. http://www.eurosurveillance.org/content/10.2807/ese.18.04.20380-en
21. Struelens, M.J.: Molecular epidemiologic typing systems of bacterial pathogens. Memórias do Instituto Oswaldo Cruz **93**(5), 581–586 (1998). https://doi.org/10.1590/S0074-02761998000500004
22. Subramanian, B., Gao, S., Lercher, M.J., Hu, S., Chen, W.H.: Evolview v3. Nucleic Acids Res. **47**(W1), W270–W275 (2019). https://doi.org/10.1093/nar/gkz357. https://academic.oup.com/nar/article/47/W1/W270/5494715

Machine Learning in Bioinformatics

Clustering Reveals Common Check-Point and Growth Factor Receptor Genes Expressed in Six Different Cancer Types

Shrikant Pawar[1], Aditya Stanam[2], and Chandrajit Lahiri[3(✉)]

[1] Yale University, New Haven, CT 06519, USA
[2] University of Iowa, UI Research Park, Iowa City, IA, USA
[3] Sunway University, 47500 Petaling Jaya, Selangor, Malaysia
chandrajitl@sunway.edu.my

Abstract. Cancer diagnosis and prognosis has been significantly impacted by understandings of gene expression data analysis. Several groups have utilized supervised and unsupervised machine learning tools for classification and predictions on gene expression data sets. Clustering, principal component analysis, regression are some important and promising tools for analyzing gene expression data. The complex and multi-dimensions of this data with limited samples makes it challenging to understand common patterns. Several features of high dimensional data contributing to a cluster generated by a finite mixture of underlying probability distributions can be implemented with a model-based clustering method. While some groups have shown that projective clustering and ensemble techniques can be effective to combat these challenges, we have employed clustering on 6 different cancer types to address the problem of multi-dimensionality and extracting common gene expression patterns. Our analysis has provided an expression pattern of 42 genes common throughout all cancer types with most of the genes involved in important check-point and growth factor receptor functions associated with cancer pathophysiology.

Keywords: Cancer diagnosis · Gene expression · Clustering analysis

1 Introduction

Cancer gene expression data can be efficiently clustered through single clustering algorithms [1]. Several features of high dimensional data contributing to a cluster generated by a finite mixture of underlying probability distributions can be implemented with a model-based clustering method [2, 3]. However, it is difficult to integrate clustering solutions as they only address the multi-view nature of clustering and may not consider multi-dimensional issue [4, 5]. In this paper, we have investigated gene expression patterns common among 5 different cancer types using model-based clustering technique on gene expression data.

I. Rojas et al. (Eds.): IWBBIO 2020, LNBI 12108, pp. 581–589, 2020.
https://doi.org/10.1007/978-3-030-45385-5_52

2 Methods and Materials

2.1 Data Collection

Microarray data for 5 different cancer types (1629 patients) was retrieved from Gene Expression Omnibus (GEO) database. The GSE ID's and number of samples is provided in Table 1. Libraries GEOquery, Biobase, preprocessCore, and multiClust were used for Mas5.0 normalization.

2.2 Clustering Analysis

Hierarchical clustering analysis was performed on patients with gene expression values. Gap statistic technique was implemented to identify optimum number of clusters for feeding into Hierarchical clustering. With gap statistic technique, 5 clusters were found to be optimal for clustering all the patient samples. Bootstrapping, b was performed till 100. Libraries ctc, gplots, dendextend, graphics, grDevices, and amap were used for implementing clustering. For Hierarchical clustering parameters like cluster_type = "Hierarchical", seed = 5, distance = NULL, linkage_type = NULL, gene_distance = NULL, num_clusters = 5, data_name = "Cancer type", probe_rank = "SD_Rank", probe_num_selection = "Fixed_Probe_Num", and cluster_num_selection = "Fixed_Clust_Num" were applied. The analysis pipeline can be found at: https://github.com/spawar2/Clustering_Analysis_Cancer (Table 2).

2.3 Functional Annotation of Significant Genes

Microarray data for patients identified from clustering analysis was further analyzed Annotation of significant genes was performed using DAVID functional annotation tool and was further validated with gene set enrichment analysis (GSEA) from cytoscape (Cytohubba).

3 Results

3.1 Clustering Analysis Identified Groups of Patients with Similar Gene Expression Changes

Microarray data for patients (2117 total) with breast, colon, lung, multiple myeloma, esophageal and ovarian cancers were clustered hierarchically for identifying similarities amongst them. By utilizing gap statistic technique optimal number of clusters (5) was identified for this sample set. With this optimal number, patients within different cancer types were clustered and clusters with maximal patient count was considered for further analysis. Cluster numbers 2, 1, 1, 1, and (1, 2, 3) were chosen for breast, colon, lung, multiple myeloma, esophageal and ovarian cancer types respectively. Figures 1, and 2 depicts the clustering results for these cancer types.

3.2 Identification of Significant Expression Patterns

Microarray data for patients identified from clustering analysis was further analyzed for identifying significant gene expression changes. From approximately 20,000 probe ids, 42 genes were found to have significant expression levels (fold change >1.5 and <−1.5) across all the cancer types when compared to the normal breast, colon, lung, multiple myeloma, esophageal and ovarian tissue samples. Figure 3 depicts the heat map for these genes amongst different cancer types.

4 Discussion and Future Scope

The purpose of this study was to identify common gene expression changes amongst 5 different cancer types. We found 42 genes to have a significant expression levels across all the cancer types with only 5 genes being upregulated while the rest reflected down regulation. Notable among the former comprise genes like SDF2, YIPF2, COLL11A1, while the latter category has CHEK2, NRG1, TU3A, GCAT and AMT among others. These genes have been known to have adverse effects in different types of cancer as discussed hereunder.

It has been found that some important genes like CHEK2 (checkpoint kinase 2) are significant in all cancer types. In fact, the protein encoded by CHEK2 is a regulator for the control of the cell cycle and a putative suppressor of tumors. Essentially, this contains a fork head-associated protein interaction domain being necessary for the activation through phosphorylation, in response to DNA damage and replication blocks. Such responses evoke critical cell cycle regulators like CHEK2 which can be controlled to stop the progression of cell cycle [6]. Moreover, CHEK2 protein inhibits CDC25C phosphatase, thereby preventing its entry into mitosis and in turn, stabilizing tumor suppressor protein p53, leading to cell cycle arrest in G1. Furthermore, CHEK2 also phosphorylates BRCA1 allowing it to restore survival after DNA damage. To this end, mutations in CHEK2 gene are thought to cause sarcomas, breast cancer, and brain tumors a predisposition besides being diagnosed with Li-Fraumeni syndrome, an extremely penetrant cancer phenotype, usually associated with inherited TP53 mutations [6].

The NRG1 gene encodes neuregulin-1, a signaling protein mediating cell-cell interactions and playing a critical role in the growth of organ systems. Neuregulin, also known as heregulin or NEU differentiation factor (NDF), was first identified as a ligand for the NEU/ERBB2 protooncogene [7]. NEU/ERBB2 is closely related to epidermal growth factor receptor (EGFR) but binds none of the EGFR ligands. Notably, of the three Nrg1, type I and type II, both containing an Ig domain, are expressed preferentially by Trkc positive dorsal root ganglion (DRG) sensory neurons at a developmental stage when proprioceptive afferents first invade muscles. In contrast, the type III Nrg1, containing a cysteine-rich domain, was expressed broadly by DRG neurons and motor neurons [7]. Elimination of all Nrg1 isoforms from DRG and motor neurons have shown adverse effects like impairment of muscle spindle differentiation resulting in the failure of proprioceptive afferents to elaborate annulospiral terminals. NRG1 signaling, thus, is critical in the early induction of muscle spindle differentiation [7].

Among the other important downregulated genes, TU3A, GCAT and AMT are mentionable. Of these, TU3A was originally identified as a candidate tumor suppressor gene in renal cell carcinoma (RCC). Besides RCC, a down-regulation of its expression has also been reflected in other types of cancers [8]. In fact, an epigenetic inactivation of TU3A in human cancers and promoter hypermethylation has been shown to have an association with TU3A expression as revealed through bisulfite sequencing of the TU3A promoter [8]. GCAT (Glycine C-Acetyltransferase) has glycine C-acetyltransferase and pyridoxal phosphate binding activity and affects the glycine, serine and threonine metabolism pathways probably giving rise to diseases like Leber Optic Atrophy. Gene Ontology (GO) annotations reflect ALAS2 as an important paralog of GCAT [9]. The AMT gene provides instructions for making an enzyme called aminomethyltransferase. This enzyme is one of four components (subunits) that make up a large complex called glycine cleavage enzyme. The glycine cleavage enzyme processes a molecule called glycine by cutting it into smaller pieces. The breakdown of excess glycine is necessary for the normal development and function of nerve cells in the brain and spinal cord. A novel intronic homozygous mutation in the AMT gene of a patient with non-ketotic hyperglycinemia and hyperammonemia [10].

The COL11A1 gene codes for the pro-alpha1(XI) chain of type XI collagen. Collagens are molecules giving the connective tissue structure and strength to sustain the muscles, joints, organs, and skin of the body. Type XI collagen is normally found in cartilage, a tough but flexible tissue covering much of skeleton during early developmental stages. Some of the cartilages are later converted to bone, with the exception of those which tends to cover and protect the bone ends and is found in the external ears and nose. Type XI collagen also forms part of the inner ear known as the vitreous, which is the clear gel filling up the eyeball and forms the nucleus pulposus, which is the central part of the discs between the spine bones. COL11A1 has been identified as a potential metastasis-associated gene in lung and breast cancers. Notably, a high expression levels of COL11A1 mRNA in patients related to significantly lower values of the 5-year recurrence-free and overall survival rates ($P = 0.006$ and $P = 0.018$, respectively) compared to those with low expression. Furthermore, COL11A1 has been reported to induce tumor aggressiveness through the TGF-β1-MMP3 axis and as predictive clinical outcomes in patients with ovarian cancer [11].

To this end, genes like SDF2 and YIPF2 has been reported in few important cases. For instance, SDF2 gene is perceived to be an important regulatory factor by which trophoblast cells can control cell survival under ER stress [12]. In fact, the downregulation of SDF2 is interfered with C/EBP homologous protein expression, one of the highest inducible genes during ER stress. Again, YIPF2 is reported as essential for CD147 glycosylation and transport, serving as the new trafficking determinant. As such, reports of CD147-medated malignant phenotypes in HCC have been recorded to be promoted by YIPF2-controlled ER-Golgi trafficking signature [13]. Real time PCR validations of these signature genes in selected cancer types is presently being validated.

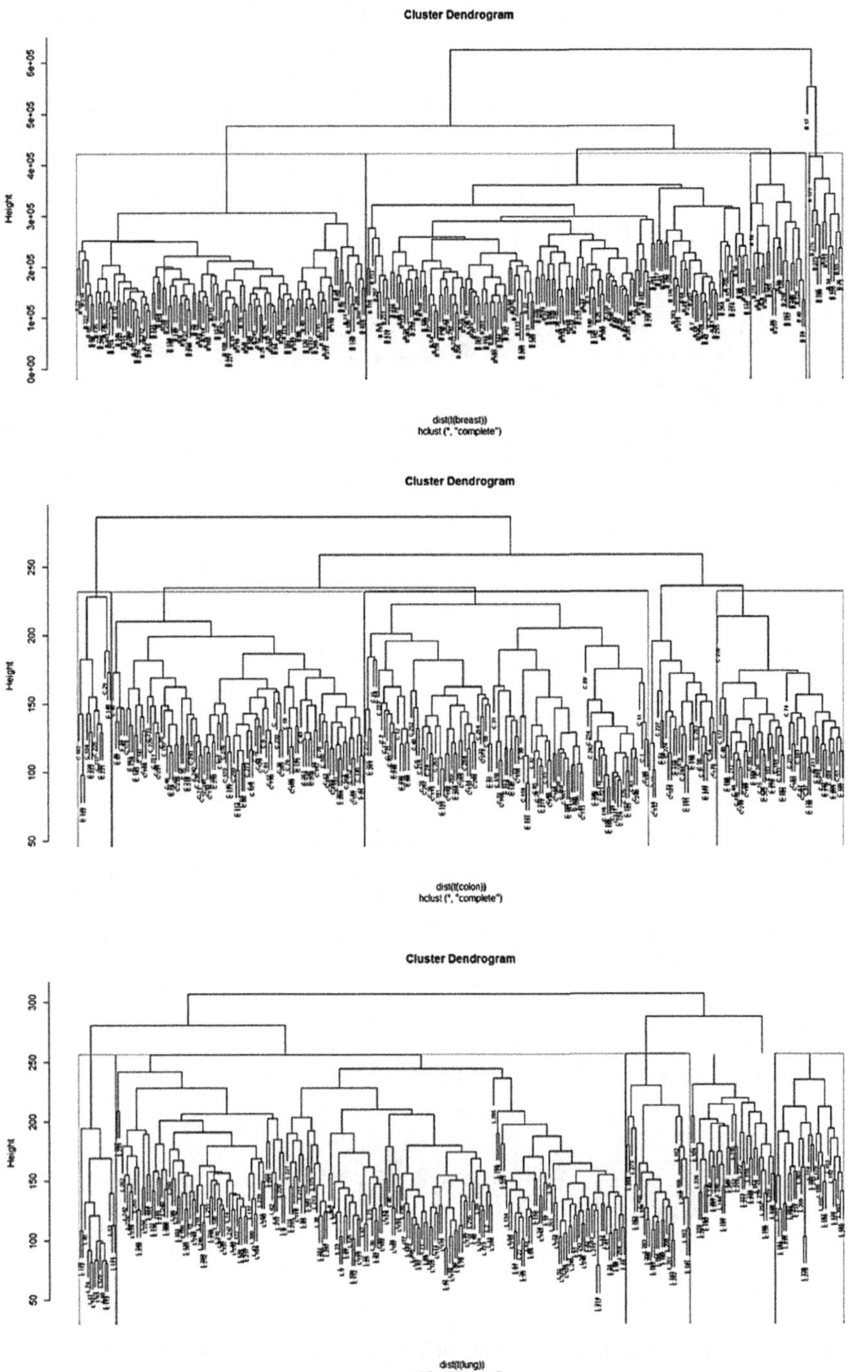

Fig. 1. Hierarchical clustering of breast, colon and lung cancer samples.

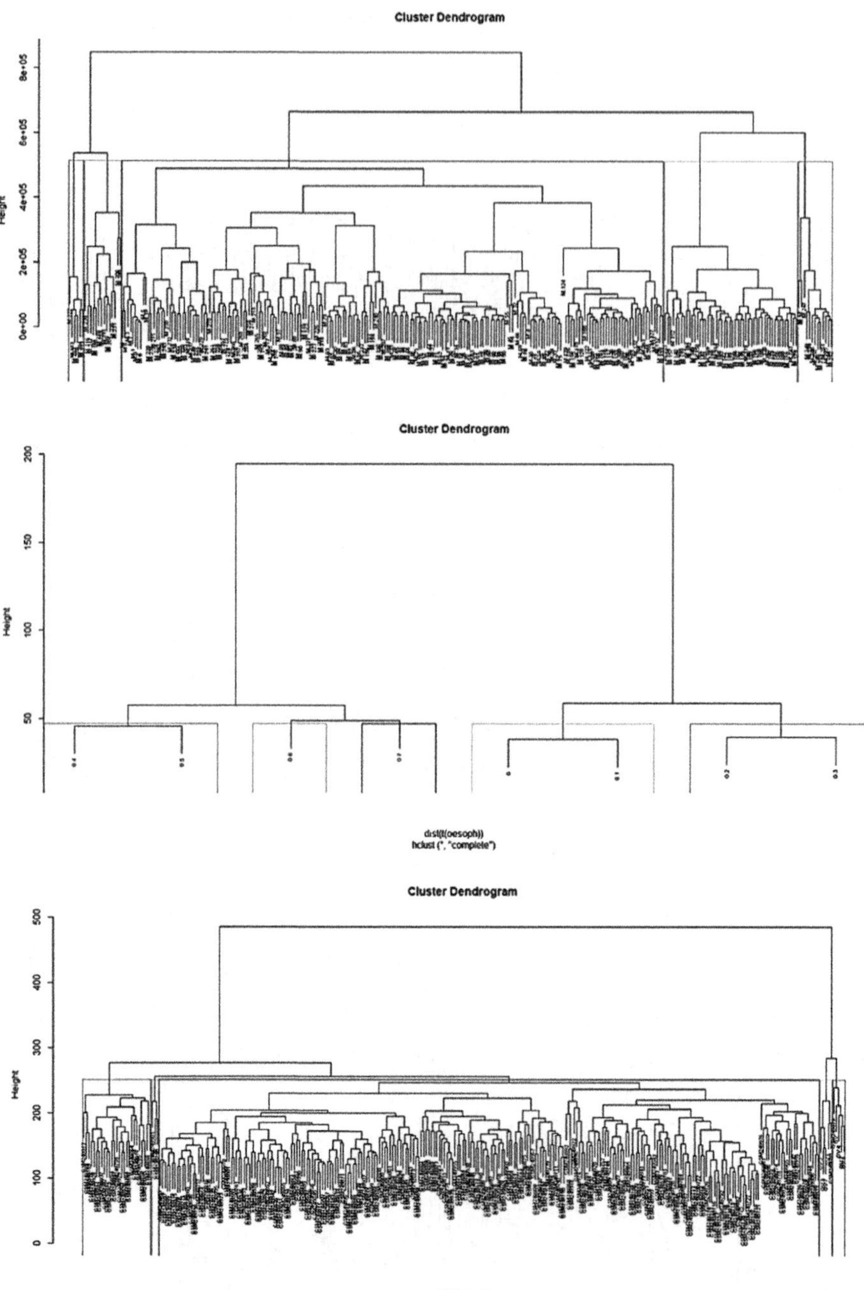

Fig. 2. Hierarchical clustering of multiple myeloma, esophageal and ovarian cancer samples

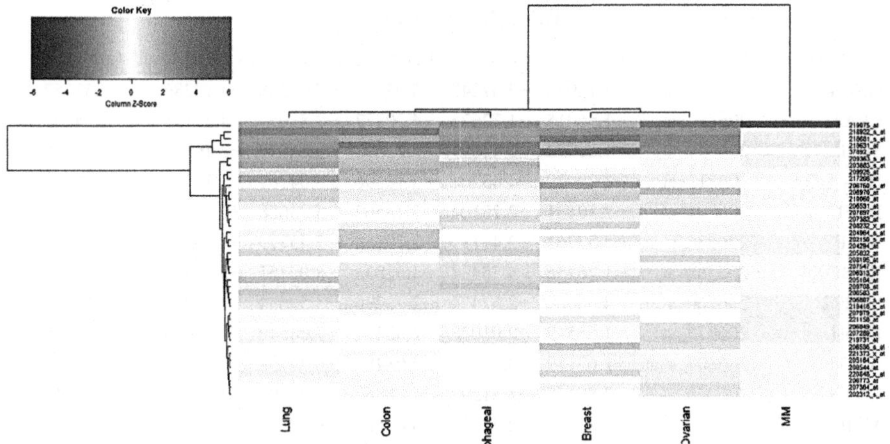

Fig. 3. Heat map with significant up and down regulated genes amongst 6 different cancer types.

Table 1. GSE ID's and number of samples.

Cancer type	GEO GSE ID	Number of samples
Breast	GSE2034 GSE25066	286
Ovarian	GSE9899 GSE26712-14764	295
Colon	GSE39582 GSE14333	585
Lung	GSE30219 GSE68465	307
Esophageal squamous cell	GSE130078	46
Multiple myeloma	GSE106218	488

Table 2. Gene expression levels of significant genes.

Gene symbol	ID	Breast	Colon	Lung	MM	Oesophageal	Ovarian
NF1	210631_at	1.69347	6.350963	3.125725	16.67207	8.116301	2.712491
SDF2L1	218681_s_at	5.432635	2.157724	2.431058	11.82592	4.951206	2.968049
CERS4	218922_s_at	3.471062	5.942869	4.80933	13.16954	4.688574	2.209344
YIPF2	219075_at	1.770018	2.347111	1.935586	179.6526	5.672229	3.81938
COL11A1	37892_at	6.01297	4.373462	4.702482	1.728933	6.446241	2.291404
NEDD9	202150_s_at	−2.31384	−5.02241	−2.58892	−8.7418	−2.03586	−1.82448
COL1A1	202312_s_at	−1.67868	−1.77813	−2.17125	−6.87774	−2.24777	−2.08029
RAB11FIP2	203883_s_at	−1.57136	−5.5875	−6.22016	−10.3276	−5.60564	−1.71155
AMT	204294_at	−1.8828	−5.70143	−3.28635	−9.18884	−3.59656	−1.54854
SSPN	204964_s_at	−1.69751	−5.01715	−1.70746	−6.37156	−2.21703	−1.78067
GCAT	205164_at	−1.83864	−2.69826	−2.35081	−7.47086	−1.64096	−1.66766

(*continued*)

Table 2. (*continued*)

Gene symbol	ID	Breast	Colon	Lung	MM	Oesophageal	Ovarian
GNG4	205184_at	−3.12953	−4.37248	−5.03798	−7.00338	−4.13286	−2.53757
CPA4	205832_at	−1.56015	−1.72675	−4.20877	−8.8805	−4.21155	−1.94806
SELP	206049_at	−1.87072	−2.42697	−2.23078	−9.66977	−2.46162	−2.27798
HLA-DOA	206313_at	−1.99939	−4.0376	−3.10596	−8.04767	−3.78779	−2.3789
DPF1	206531_at	−2.19131	−2.78104	−3.33567	−5.33628	−1.7256	−2.12663
XIAP	206536_s_at	−3.57761	−2.4111	−2.20852	−7.45779	−1.5666	−2.29722
KRBOX4	206583_at	−1.76256	−4.55434	−4.62833	−8.02751	−3.87438	−1.69943
FCER2	206760_s_at	−4.66086	−2.67474	−2.20296	−3.59694	−2.64826	−1.50192
LY6H	206773_at	−1.65519	−2.01028	−2.82221	−7.04549	−1.79833	−1.94412
ADD2	206807_s_at	−1.63179	−3.59577	−4.08482	−8.29738	−3.324	−1.59468
CNTN2	206970_at	−2.89158	−3.31292	−4.06862	−5.22497	−2.51538	−3.1511
MMP25	207289_at	−1.80877	−2.42813	−3.05528	−9.10957	−2.31049	−2.37912
TEX28	207364_at	−2.10535	−1.82339	−2.26262	−6.37036	−1.89691	−2.35267
TP63	207382_at	−2.03927	−2.20692	−2.96645	−4.96809	−4.00363	−1.50285
FAM107A	207547_s_at	−1.90349	−3.60144	−2.91124	−7.17193	−3.48931	−1.64393
CRHR2	207897_at	−2.7409	−2.05522	−2.2837	−4.50462	−2.70095	−3.25137
CD8B	207979_s_at	−1.54218	−2.90109	−2.2646	−8.63807	−1.92759	−1.58261
TTN	208195_at	−1.61456	−2.6675	−2.59303	−7.94114	−2.9698	−2.43016
NRG1	208232_x_at	−2.77548	−3.2994	−2.46721	−5.55459	−3.34708	−1.61954
ADRA2B	208544_at	−2.05858	−2.54114	−2.93358	−7.23529	−1.50859	−1.90857
MED21	209363_s_at	−1.64732	−5.15966	−5.59623	−9.8889	−3.03477	−1.61962
MOXD1	209708_at	−1.60386	−4.26768	−3.14269	−7.73064	−4.92881	−1.72301
OCLN	209925_at	−1.895	−6.10725	−3.73528	−5.92513	−5.03456	−1.77762
PDE6G	210060_at	−3.13624	−3.44968	−4.52738	−6.29829	−2.90946	−2.14823
CHEK2	210416_s_at	−1.78101	−3.99216	−3.61726	−8.23458	−3.26291	−1.82161
RPL15	217266_at	−2.39996	−5.37204	−6.23782	−4.65231	−4.63599	−1.89968
ENTPD1-AS1	219731_at	−1.77641	−3.02203	−3.22506	−9.24227	−3.05526	−2.52669
OBP2A	220848_x_at	−2.77257	−1.76244	−3.19578	−6.96	−2.05005	−1.97285
PAXBP1	221158_at	−2.33324	−2.71188	−1.99124	−9.4028	−1.75456	−1.52342
PSPN	221373_x_at	−2.05656	−2.94195	−2.67975	−6.67225	−1.97516	−1.66317

References

1. Yeung, K.Y., Fraley, C., Murua, A., Raftery, A.E., Ruzzo, W.L.: Model-based clustering and data transformations for gene expression data. Bioinformatics **17**(10), 977–987 (2001). https://doi.org/10.1093/bioinformatics/17.10.977
2. Domeniconi, C., Gunopulos, D., Ma, S., Yan, B., Al-Razgan, M., Papadopoulos, D.: Locally adaptive metrics for clustering high dimensional data. Data Min. Knowl. Disc. **14**(1), 63–97 (2007). https://doi.org/10.1007/s10618-006-0060-8
3. Parsons, L., Haque, E., Liu, H.: Subspace clustering for high dimensional data: a review. ACM SIGKDD Explor. Newsl. **6**(3), 90–105 (2004). https://doi.org/10.1145/1007730.1007731

4. Agrawal, R., Gehrke, J., Gunopulos, D., Raghavan, P.: Automatic subspace clustering of high dimensional data. Data Min. Knowl. Disc. **11**(1), 5–33 (2005). https://doi.org/10.1007/s10618-005-1396-1
5. Gullo, F., Domeniconi, C., Tagarelli, A.: Projective clustering ensembles. Data Min. Knowl. Disc. **26**(3), 452–511 (2013). https://doi.org/10.1007/s10618-012-0266-x
6. Gao, Y., Yin, J., Tu, Y., Chen, Y.C.: Theaflavin-3,3′-digallate suppresses human ovarian carcinoma OVCAR-3 cells by regulating the checkpoint kinase 2 and p 27 kip1 pathways. Molecules **24**(4) (2019). https://doi.org/10.3390/molecules24040673
7. Hippenmeyer, S., Shneider, N.A., Birchmeier, C., Burden, S.J., Jessell, T.M., Arber, S.: A role for neuregulin 1 signaling in muscle spindle differentiation. Neuron **36**, 1035–1049 (2002)
8. Awakura, Y., Nakamura, E., Ito, N., Kamoto, T., Ogawa, O.: Methylation-associated silencing of TU3A in human cancers. Int. J. Oncol. **33**(4), 893–899 (2008)
9. Jacquot, C., et al.: Effect of four genes (ALDH1, NRF1, JAM and KBL) on proliferation arrest in a non-small cell bronchopulmonary cancer line. Anticancer Res. **22**(4), 2229–2235 (2002)
10. Silverstein, S., Veerapandiyan, A., Hayes-Rosen, C., Ming, X., Kornitzer, J.: A novel intronic homozygous mutation in the *AMT* gene of a patient with nonketotic hyperglycinemia and hyperammonemia. Metab. Brain Dis. **34**(1), 373–376 (2018). https://doi.org/10.1007/s11011-018-0317-0
11. Wu, Y.H., Chang, T.H., Huang, Y.F., Huang, H.D., Chou, C.Y.: COL11A1 promotes tumor progression and predicts poor clinical outcome in ovarian cancer. Oncogene **33**(26), 3432–3440 (2014). https://doi.org/10.1038/onc.2013.307
12. Lorenzon-Ojea, A.R., Guzzo, C.R., Kapidzic, M., Fisher, S.J., Bevilacqua, E.: Stromal cell-derived factor 2: a novel protein that interferes in endoplasmic reticulum stress pathway in human placental cells. Biol. Reprod. **95**(2), 41 (2016)
13. Qi, S., et al.: YIPF2 is a novel Rab-GDF that enhances HCC malignant phenotypes by facilitating CD147 endocytic recycle. Cell Death Dis. **10**, 462 (2019)

Predicting Infectious Diseases by Using Machine Learning Classifiers

Juan A. Gómez-Pulido[1(✉)], José M. Romero-Muelas[1], José M. Gómez-Pulido[2], José L. Castillo Sequera[2], José Sanz Moreno[3], María-Luz Polo-Luque[4], and Alberto Garcés-Jiménez[5]

[1] Department of Technology of Computers and Communications, University of Extremadura, Cáceres, Spain
{jangomez,jromeroaj}@unex.es

[2] Department of Computer Sciences, University of Alcala, Alcala de Henares, Spain
{jose.gomez,jluis.castillo}@uah.es

[3] Infectious Diseases Unit, University Hospital Príncipe de Asturias, Alcala de Henares, Spain
josesanzm@gmail.com

[4] Department of Nursering, University of Alcalá, Alcala de Henares, Spain
mariluz.polo@uah.es

[5] Center for Research and Innovation in Knowledge Management, University of Francisco de Vitoria, Madrid, Spain

Abstract. The change and evolution of certain health variables can be an evidence that makes easier the diagnosis of infectious diseases. In this kind of diseases, it is important to monitor some patients' variables along a particular period. It is possible to build a prediction model from registers previously stored with this information. This model can give the probability to develop the disease from input data. Machine learning algorithms can generate these prediction models, which can classify samples composed of clinical parameters in order to predict if an infectious disease will be developed. The prediction models are trained from the patients' registers previously collected and stored along the time. This work shows an experience of applying machine learning techniques for classifying samples of different infectious diseases. Besides, we have studied the influence on the classification of the different clinical parameters, which could be very useful for the medical staff in order to monitor carefully certain parameters.

Keywords: Infectious diseases · Machine learning classification

1 Introduction

The evolution of an infectious process is characterized by the change of certain medical parameters over time. It is interesting to be able to analyze these data in order to determine the probability that a patient may develop an infectious disease, anticipating its possible treatment. In this way, the monitoring of the

I. Rojas et al. (Eds.): IWBBIO 2020, LNBI 12108, pp. 590–599, 2020.
https://doi.org/10.1007/978-3-030-45385-5_53

most relevant medical parameters gives us very valuable information on the evolution of the disease once detected [9].

One way of approaching predictive analysis is to apply Machine Learning (ML) [2]. There are a large number of algorithmic techniques, grouped around the term ML, that facilitate the data processing and analysis for predictive purposes. ML provides features as pattern recognition and forecasting, very attractive from a health point of view, because the prediction of the evolution of a disease can improve the protocols of control and care of patients.

Machine learning is an area of knowledge in computer sciences that, coming from artificial intelligence, groups algorithmic techniques from which computers learn using previous data and behaviour, even in real time. These techniques have been widely applied, with very satisfactory results, particularly in health and medicine [4]. In this paper, we present an approach to predict the development of infectious diseases using ML techniques, which use certain medical data previously collected from patients using custom-designed sensor devices.

2 Methodology

To address the problem of analyzing infectious diseases data for predictive purposes, it is necessary to sample patients who developed the disease over time. For this purpose, we considered patients in two nursing homes, where we monitored both people who developed an infectious disease and those who did not.

In this study, we considered three types of infectious diseases: acute respiratory infection (IRA), urinary tract infection (ITU) and skin and soft tissue infection (PB). There are different features as incubation time, evolution and relationship among the clinical parameters, etc. For this reason, it is important to monitor patients over time, preferably daily.

2.1 Clinical Parameters

The main clinical parameters measured for this study are listed in Table 1. These parameters were carefully selected not only for their interest in identifying the disease, but to be measured from the available sensors and devices.

2.2 Population

The process begins with the identification and collection of data from potential patients: elderly people living in nursing homes, who are susceptible to developing infectious diseases. Table 2 lists the main data of this population.

2.3 Data Acquisition and Storage

The medical staff was responsible for monitoring the patients. Due to the casuistry of real environments and unforeseen circumstances, the samples were not always collected following a regular time pattern.

Table 1. Clinical parameters regarding the infectious disease.

Label	Parameter
Temperature	Body temperature
SPO2.Min	Minimum peripheral oxygen saturation
SPO2.Max	Maximum peripheral oxygen saturation
BPMmin	Minimum heart rate (beats/minute)
BPMmax	Maximum heart rate (beats/minute)
BPMavg	Average heart rate (beats/minute)
Sys	Systole
Dias	Diastole
EDA.min	Minimum electrodermal activity
EDA.max	Maximum electrodermal activity
EDA.avg	Average electrodermal activity
Date	Date of the sample

Table 2. Information about the population for data acquisition.

	Nursing home		
	Cardenal Cisneros	Francisco de Vitoria	Total
Residents	127	316	443
Residents participating	20 (16%)	40 (13%)	60 (14%)
Above, who developed disease	7	33	40
Medical staff participating	4	14	18
Average age	87.7	87.6	87.6
First sample	24/3/2018	4/4/2018	24/3/2018
Last sample	11/3/2019	11/3/2019	11/3/2019

The sampling process was carried out by means of a wireless electronic device equipped with different sensors. The selected biosensors were developed by BiosignalsPlux [1] for this project. The hardware device (Fig. 1) is composed of a sensors, wireless controller and a tablet. It is characterized by enough energy autonomy (10 h), robustness (protection of the wires), data consistency (predefined ranges of compatibility of the medical variables), latency (data are stabilized for collecting in a few seconds) and storage resources (double precision floating point data, 84 MB memory), among other factors.

This device communicates with a software application developed specifically for this project, installed in a mobile device (tablet) under Android OS. This application controls the entire data collecting process: patient identification, date and time of capture, parameter values, etc. In order to guarantee privacy, the patient's identity is anonymized by assigning a number.

One aspect to highlight in the data collecting was the training of the staff in charge of this task. Personnel tackled the data collection voluntarily. They were trained to know the process, place the sensors, set up the mobile device and send the data to the server. On average, the time for learning the collecting process was 7 min, whereas the time for reading vital signs was 4.2 min.

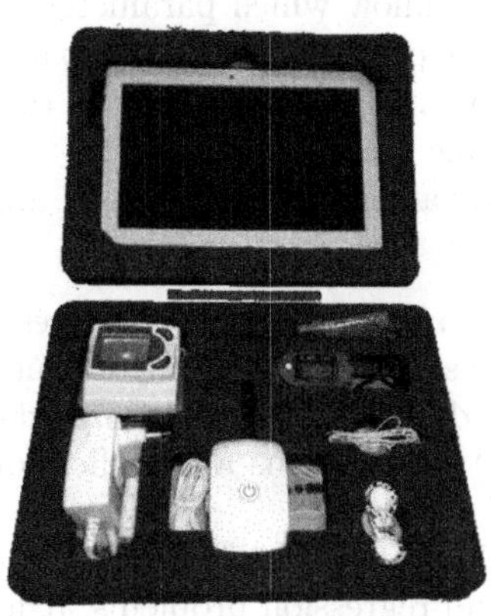

Fig. 1. Kit composed of biosensors, wireless controller and tablet for data collecting.

2.4 Data Storage and Analysis in Remote Servers

The data stored in the mobile application are exported in CSV format to a database in the cloud. These data are available for different micro-services hosted in servers, which were developed for data analysis purposes. The micro-services [6] are small programs of specific purpose with user interfaces that allow to connect them with applications of third parties. One of these applications applied ML algorithms for predictive analysis, as we will see later.

3 Machine Learning Approaches

We have considered two approaches to the problem: time and spatial.

- The time approach takes into account the evolution of data over time. This approach requires an analysis based on time series.
- The spatial approach takes into account the relationship among the medical parameters of a sample, to find patterns and make classifications according to all samples.

In this work, we show the approach and results of the spatial approach. The absence of the time component prevents a predictive approach, but the spatial dimension allows a more precise pattern recognition analysis. In this way, it is possible to classify a sample measured from an individual as a sample recognized as possibly belonging to an infectious disease. In addition, the information obtained with this approach will allow us in the future a better predictive analysis based on time series.

On the other hand, an important feature that can be analyzed by pattern recognition is to determine the weight of each of the medical parameters in the classification, that is, to know which parameters are most important in the classification of a sample as a possible sample of a patient with infectious disease. This knowledge would allow medical personnel to take more care in measuring and monitoring these specific parameters.

In this work, three ML algorithms have been applied to process the data from the infection database:

- *Naive Bayes* (NB) [8] is an algorithm that makes use of the Bayes theorem to classify data instances. It is easy to implement, and has been applied to many works of medical diagnosis and disease prediction.
- *Filtered Classifier* (FC) [3] performs a classification of previously filtered or pre-processed data.
- *Random Forest* (RF) [10] is a supervised classifier that builds decision trees to solve classification and regression problems. It has been applied under the *Random Tree* (RT) technique in this work.

They allow to modify the weight of an attribute so that it has more importance at the time of making a prediction. For example, we can assign more importance to body temperature than to other parameters in the classification, and see how the corresponding result improves or not other cases. Therefore, the assignation of weights may be of interest to medical personnel when improving diagnosis based on observation of clinical parameters.

These algorithms are included in the API of *Waikato Environment for Knowledge Analysis* (WEKA) [11]. WEKA is a specialized ML software environment written in Java under GNU-GPL license.

We have used the *Apache Spark* [12] development environment to implement the software applications based on WEKA, which allows massive data processing. Apache Spark converts the medical data stored in CSV files into instances handled by WEKA. Also, we have used *Java Servlets* (JS) and *Java Server Pages* (JSP) [5] to manage data entry and other features of a web service (micro-service), which allows to evaluate the model trained by the ML algorithms. Finally, we have used *Apache Maven* [7] to build and manage the web service in Java. In this way, Apache Spark and WEKA tools could be used easily.

4 Developments

In this section, we describe two developments for experimenting with the ML algorithms. First, a web service was designed to apply NB and FC, as a first approach for data classification. Next, a software application based on RF was developed to experiment with the weights of the clinical parameters in order to check their influence on the classification.

4.1 Data Processing

Figure 2 shows an example of three patients who developed IRA, ITU and PB infections. A time sample (the set composed of the values of 11 clinical parameters measured from a patient in a particular time) is the work unit (instance) for the classifiers.

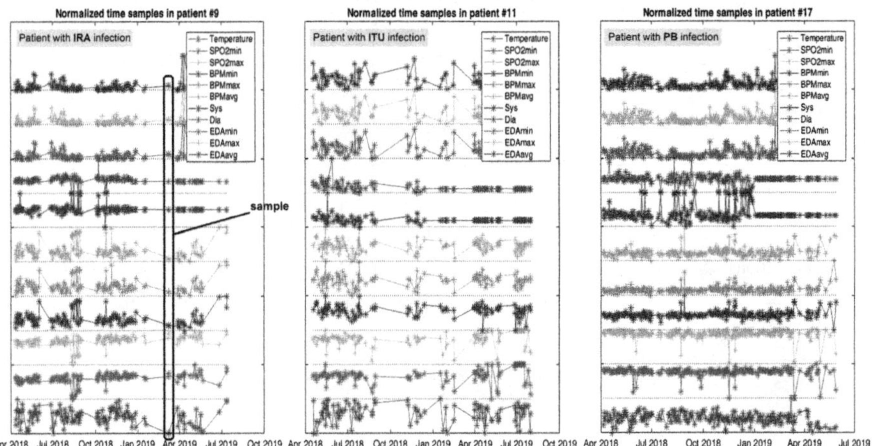

Fig. 2. Example of three patients whit IRA, ITU and PB infections. Each sample is the work unit for the ML classifiers.

In our work, the ML algorithms are trained from a training dataset, composed of all the samples from all the patients who developed an infectious disease. A classifier model is then generated capable of indicating the percentage of matching of any sample to belong to a possible case of IRA, ITU or PB infection.

4.2 Web Service for NB and FC Classifiers

The micro-service running NB and FC was developed for predictive purposes: it classifies an input sample as a possible IRA, ITU or PB infection.

The tool was developed using JS and JSP, implementing an interface based on Apache Spark, through which the user communicates with the algorithms included in WEKA. First, the user chooses the algorithm to use. Then, he enters the clinical data of a sample measured from a patient and orders its processing. The model previously trained is now executed to classify the input sample.

The result is given as a percentage of the probability that the patient is or is not in an infectious process, and what type of infection it is, if applicable. This can be useful to medical personnel as an aid to diagnosis.

This development was validated by predicting test data: real data of which it is previously known whether they correspond to patients who have developed the disease or not. Qualitatively, the results are satisfactory in may cases. However, the prediction is not precise enough yet, mainly because the training dataset is very small for the usual sizes of the classification problems.

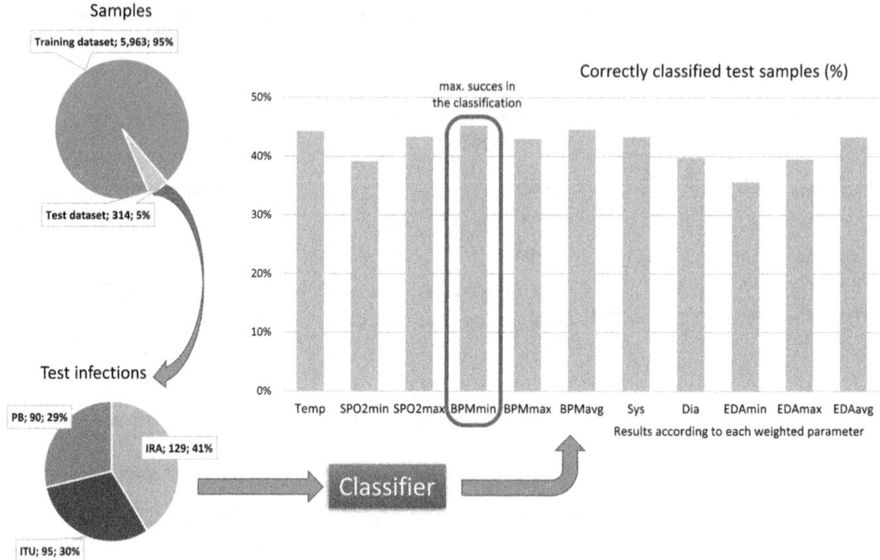

Fig. 3. Classification of test samples according to the weight given to each clinical parameter.

4.3 Influence of the Clinical Parameters on the Classification

Random Tree predicts the dependent variable (type of infectious disease) from independent variables or attributes (the 11 medical parameters). The algorithm addresses the classification problem considering low entropy: the amount of information disorder or the amount of data randomness is as low as possible.

As Fig. 3 shows, we have split for this experiment all available samples (6,277) from all patients (60) into the training set (5,963) and test set (314), following a proportion of 95% and 5% respectively.

We know the infectious diseases to which each of the test data corresponds. Specifically, we have 129, 95 and 90 samples for IRA, ITU and PB infections, respectively. The model of the classifier previously trained takes the test samples and classifies them into these three types of infection, giving the percentage of success in the classification (correctly classified samples in relation to the total number of test samples, for each type of infection) as a result, among other relevant information.

The classification of the test dataset was repeated 11 times, where each execution selected a different clinical parameter with a weight higher than the remainder with regard to its importance or influence on the classification. The purpose of this experiment was to determine which of the 11 parameters can affect more

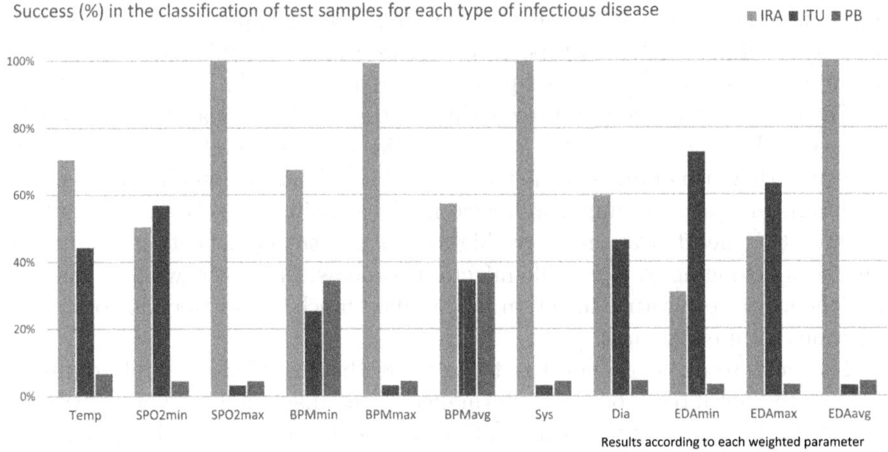

Fig. 4. Classification results considering the infectious disease.

positively on the classification, allowing the medical personnel to consider it when monitoring the patients. In this way, after the 11 executions were carried out, we checked that BPMmin gives the highest percentage of success in the classification, followed by BPMavg, as Fig. 3 shows. This indicates that heart rate monitoring may be more interesting from a medical point of view when making the diagnosis.

Notwithstanding the above, the results in Fig. 3 do not offer high success rates. However, analyzing these percentages according to the type of infection, we found very interesting information. Thus, as can be seen in Fig. 4, the classification of IRA infection is very successful, in some cases reaching 100% success. On the contrary, classifying PB infection is more difficult. There may be two reasons for this result. On the one hand, from a computational point of view, there are more samples of IRA than PB, so that the algorithm is better trained to recognize IRA samples. On the other hand, from a medical point of view, each infectious disease can be more or less difficult to be identified from clinical parameters, which is also reflected in the results of the classification algorithm. We believe that a larger number of samples for the training dataset would substantially improve the classification results.

Analyzing both figures together, we can conclude that giving more weight to BPMavg the classifier works better. In other words, heart rate can influence more in the diagnosis of the infectious disease.

5 Conclusions

This work shows some experiences based on ML for the classification of samples corresponding to three types of infectious diseases. The real environment where the samples were collected conditions the classification results, due to the number of patients, the measuring devices, the training of medical personnel and the type of infection, among other factors. However, we think that this study is valuable and offers an interesting starting point for further research.

The main contribution of this work lies in the analysis of the weight or importance of each clinical parameter in the identification of the infectious disease. In this sense, there is not any parameter standing out from the remainder too much, or parameters with minimum influence in the classification. However, we have observed that heart beat may have high impact in the classification of an input sample as belonging to a possible infectious process. Moreover, we have checked that the acute respiratory infection is identified much better than the other two infections in most of cases.

The next research proposal is to increase the size of the sample database in order to guarantee a better performance of the machine learning algorithms. This could be a slow task, as it implies the collaboration of medical personnel of different institutions and more hardware resources. Furthermore, we want to undertake a study that addresses the time nature of the samples, linking their classification with the evolution of the disease over time.

Acknowledgements. This work was funded by the European Union under the project ELAC2015/T09-0819 "*Design and Implementation of a Low Cost Smart System for Pre-Diagnosis and Telecare of Infectious Diseases in Elderly People*" (SPIDEP) and by the Government of Extremadura (Spain) under the project IB16002.

References

1. Wearable body sensing platform. https://www.biosignalsplux.com
2. Alpaydin, E.: Introduction to Machine Learning, 2nd edn. The MIT Press, Cambridge (2010)
3. Chandrika, G., Reddy, E.: An efficient filtered classifier for classification of unseen test data in text documents, pp. 1–4, December 2017. https://doi.org/10.1109/ICCIC.2017.8524416
4. Deo, R.: Machine learning in medicine. Circulation **132**(20), 1920–1930 (2015)
5. Genender, J.M.: Enterprise Java Servlets with Cdrom. Addison-Wesley Longman Publishing Co., Inc., Boston (2001)
6. Krämer, M., Frese, S., Kuijper, A.: Implementing secure applications in smart city clouds using microservices. Future Gener. Comput. Syst. **99**, 308–320 (2019). https://doi.org/10.1016/j.future.2019.04.042
7. Miller, F.P., Vandome, A.F., McBrewster, J.: Apache Maven. Alpha Press, Indianapolis (2010)
8. Murty, M.N., Susheela Devi, V.: Pattern Recognition: An Algorithmic Approach. UTiCS, 1st edn. Springer, London (2011). https://doi.org/10.1007/978-0-85729-495-1
9. Nishiura, H.: Early efforts in modeling the incubation period of infectious diseases with an acute course of illness. Emerg. Themes Epidemiol. **4**, 2 (2007). https://doi.org/10.1186/1742-7622-4-2
10. Ho, T.K.: The random subspace method for constructing decision forests. IEEE Trans. Pattern Anal. Mach. Intell. **20**(8), 832–844 (1998)

11. Witten, I.H., Frank, E., Hall, M.A., Pal, C.J.: Data Mining, Fourth Edition: Practical Machine Learning Tools and Techniques, 4th edn. Morgan Kaufmann Publishers Inc., San Francisco (2016)
12. Zaharia, M., et al.: Apache spark: a unified engine for big data processing. Commun. ACM **59**, 56–65 (2016). https://doi.org/10.1145/2934664

Bayesian Optimization Improves Tissue-Specific Prediction of Active Regulatory Regions with Deep Neural Networks

Luca Cappelletti[1], Alessandro Petrini[1], Jessica Gliozzo[1,4], Elena Casiraghi[1], Max Schubach[2,3], Martin Kircher[2,3], and Giorgio Valentini[1(✉)]

[1] AnacletoLab, Dipartimento di Informatica, Università degli Studi di Milano, Milan, Italy
valentini@di.unimi.it
[2] Berlin Institute of Health (BIH), Berlin, Germany
[3] Charité – Universitätsmedizin Berlin, Berlin, Germany
[4] Department of Dermatology, Fondazione IRCCS Ca' Granda - Ospedale Maggiore Policlinico, Milan, Italy

Abstract. The annotation and characterization of tissue-specific cis-regulatory elements (CREs) in non-coding DNA represents an open challenge in computational genomics. Several prior works show that machine learning methods, using epigenetic or spectral features directly extracted from DNA sequences, can predict active promoters and enhancers in specific tissues or cell lines. In particular, very recently deep-learning techniques obtained state-of-the-art results in this challenging computational task. In this study, we provide additional evidence that Feed Forward Neural Networks (FFNN) trained on epigenetic data and one-dimensional convolutional neural networks (CNN) trained on DNA sequence data can successfully predict active regulatory regions in different cell lines. We show that model selection by means of Bayesian optimization applied to both FFNN and CNN models can significantly improve deep neural network performance, by automatically finding models that best fit the data. Further, we show that techniques applied to balance active and non-active regulatory regions in the human genome in training and test data may lead to over-optimistic or poor predictions. We recommend to use actual imbalanced data that was not used to train the models for evaluating their generalization performance.

1 Introduction

Non-coding DNA regions, which include 98% of the human genome, are that part of DNA that does not encode for structural proteins and enzymes. A subset of those regions, so-called cis-regulatory elements (CREs) determine spatiotemporal patterns of gene expression [1,2] and therefore play a key role in the control of transcription. CREs are involved in the development of different cell

I. Rojas et al. (Eds.): IWBBIO 2020, LNBI 12108, pp. 600–612, 2020.
https://doi.org/10.1007/978-3-030-45385-5_54

types/tissues, in the timing and intensity of gene expression during the cell life, in the dynamical response to changes in physiological conditions through interactions with DNA-binding transcription factors (TFs), and in the focal alteration of chromatin structure [3]. Genome-wide association studies (GWAS) discovered thousands of variants associated with diseases and traits enriched in non-coding sequences, and several lines of research show that genetic variants in regulatory regions may be deleterious or directly involved in genetic diseases [4,5].

A great deal of research work has been devoted to the identification of CREs and to their cell-specific activation status. Such studies are essential to dissect the mechanisms underlying the modulation of gene expression and to understand the functional impact of genetic variants on human diseases. Indeed, the effect of genetic variants in non-coding regions is strongly related to the prediction of active regulatory regions (e.g. nucleosome-free regions that are accessible by TFs). Conversely, if a genetic variant, even if potentially deleterious/functionally constrained (e.g. high conservation), is located in an inactive DNA region, it is less likely to be pathogenic.

Thus, great effort has been undertaken to map TF binding sites and histone modifications across cell types and tissues [6–10]. In particular, the ENCODE project [8] identified promoters and enhancers in 147 cell types using a wide range of high-throughput technologies, while the FANTOM project employed CAGE (Cap Analysis of Gene Expression) technologies to broaden the spectrum of considered samples, including 1,816 human and 1,016 mouse samples [11,12]. The Roadmap Epigenomics Consortium [13] studied the epigenomic landscape of 111 representative primary human tissues and cell-lines. However, the experimental identification of CREs is still expensive and time consuming, and, despite the great deal of research effort devoted to this task, the problem is still open.

The use of computational methods, and in particular machine learning approaches, can be a crucial tool to identify the location and activation status of these regions. To this aim, initial approaches, due to the reduced set of reliable annotations, applied unsupervised learning techniques [14,15] to data from the ENCODE project [8]. However, their low accuracy (around 26%) in predicting enhancer [16], pushed the development of more sophisticated supervised learning models, such as random-forest methods [17] and AdaBoost-based models [18]. The subsequent availability of large-scale and high-resolution CREs provided by the FANTOM5 Consortium [11] enabled the development of ensembles of both support vector machines [19] and deep learning models [20–23], which model complex systems and capture high-level patterns from data, when an underlying, non-obvious structures are present. Examples of promising deep learners applied in regulatory genomics [24] for identifying CREs from sequence data, are DeepEnhancer [20] (Sect. 3) and BiRen [25]. On the other side, PEDLA [26], a deep hybrid method, achieve high generalization performance across different samples by learning on heterogeneous datasets (i.e. epigenomic, sequence, and conservation data). DECRES [21] is a notable FFNN model that out-performs state-of-the-art unsupervised works when predicting enhancers, promoters, and their activity in a specific human cell-line. Exploiting annotation data from

FANTOM [27] and epigenomic features from ENCODE [8], it extends the FANTOM enhancer atlas of 16,988 bidirectionally transcribed loci, therefore providing the most complete annotation of CREs in the human genome so far. However, the experimental setup used to train and test DECRES distorts the actual distribution of the data. Indeed, authors not only balance the training set, which is quite common when dealing with highly-unbalanced data, but they also compute performance on a balanced test set, which may provide a biased evaluation. In this work, we concentrate on the prediction of the activity state of CREs (Sect. 2), and we present results (Sect. 4) obtained by two deep neural network models, a FFNN and a CNN (Sect. 3), whose optimal hyper-parameters have been selected by Bayesian optimization. Moreover, we provide a comparative evaluation to highlight the effects of different balancing schemes (Sect. 4).

2 Dataset

The models were trained and tested on genomic regions of transcriptionally active enhancer and promoters downloaded from FANTOM5 [11] and matched features collected by Li et al. [21] from ENCODE [8] for four cell lines (GM12878, HelaS3, HepG2, K562).

Li et al. [21] defined six different classes, active enhancers (A-E), active promoters (A-P), active exons (A-X) and their inactive counterparts (I-E, I-P, I-X), using thresholds on tags per million (TPM) values of the Cap Analysis of Gene Expression (CAGE) data set downloaded from the FANTOM5 database. Classes of active and inactive exons were defined based on exon transcription levels from RNA-seq data downloaded from ENCODE[1]. Finally, an unknown class (UK) labels regions sampled from the genome, but excluding those regions overlapping FANTOM CAGE tags, exons and DNaseI peaks. The employed genomic regions and thresholds, as well as the considered features, are the same as those used in [21]. To train and test FFNN methods (see Sect. 3), the feature set consisted of histone modification and TF binding ChIP-seq, DNase-seq, FAIRE-seq, and ChIA-PET data from ENCODE [8][2]. Further, CpG islands and phastCons scores were included in the feature set by computing the mean value of the feature signal which falls within 200-bps bins centered at each labeled region.

To train and test CNN methods (see Sect. 3), we used sequence data obtained from the human reference genome GRCh37/hg19[3] from the UCSC repository data set[4]. In particular, each genomic region is represented by a sequence of 200 one-hot encoded nucleotides. To automate the coding process we developed an UCSC genome downloader[5]. Thus, for each cis-regulatory element, we have two

[1] ENCODE Data at ftp://hgdownload.cse.ucsc.edu/goldenPath/hg19/encodeDCC.

[2] ENCODE Data at ftp://hgdownload.cse.ucsc.edu/goldenPath/hg19/encodeDCC; ENCODE fold-change values are described here https://sites.google.com/site/anshulkundaje.

[3] https://www.ncbi.nlm.nih.gov/assembly/GCF_000001405.13/.

[4] https://genome.ucsc.edu/.

[5] https://github.com/LucaCappelletti94/ucsc_genomes_downloader.

different representations: the (1) a set of numeric features suitable for training FFNN models [28], and (2) nucleotide sequences to be processed with CNN models [29]. To provide some insights into the data distributions, we show projections of the training matrix for one of the cell lines (GM12878) with the two principal components computed by t-SNE [30] for the epigenomic data set (Fig. 1A,B) and MCA [31][6] for sequence data (Fig. 1C,D). A high level of entanglement among classes is shown in the t-SNE decomposition for task "IE vs IP" (column A in Fig. 1), therefore we expect that CNNs will provide better predictions for this task. t-SNE and MCA plots for tasks "AE+AP vs ELSE" (shown, respectively, in columns B and D in Fig. 1) show that the classes are relatively well separated. Hence, we expect that our models will reach good performance in such classification tasks.

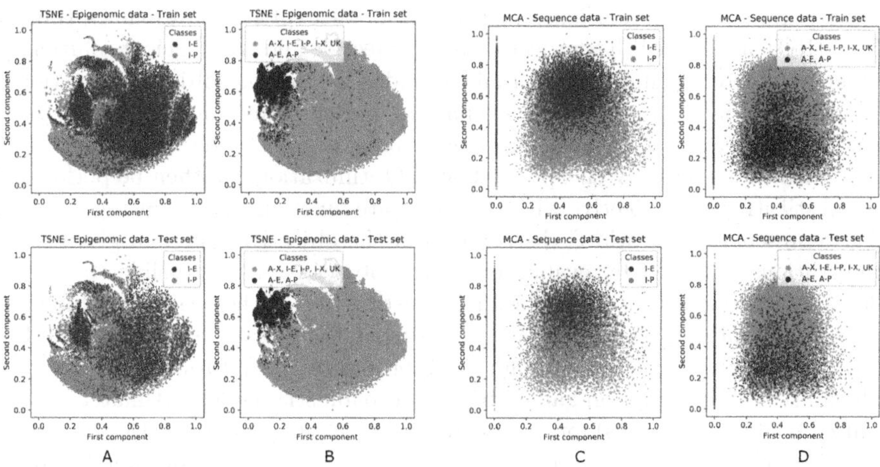

Fig. 1. Decomposition of one of the hold-outs of cell line GM12878. A, B: epigenomic data projected on the two principal components computed by TSNE; C, D: sequence data projected on the two principal components computed by MCA. Top row: training set; bottom row: test set. A, C: Inactive Enhancers vs Inactive Promoters classification task; B, D: Active Enhancers and Promoters vs anything else classification task.

3 Methods

The identification of active regulatory regions can be modeled as a binary classification task. To perform our experiments, we used FFNN [28] for processing epigenomic data, while sequence data were analyzed using CNN [29]. For each method (FFNN and CNN) we developed a "fixed" baseline model, and an

[6] For computing Multiple Correspondence Analysis we used the python package available at https://github.com/esafak/mca.

"optimized" model, with hyper-parameters selected by Bayesian optimization[7]. Therefore, we obtained four different models, which we call *fixed-FFNN*, *fixed-CNN*, *Bayesian-FFNN* and *Bayesian-CNN* (the presented models were developed using Keras [32] with the TensorFlow backend [33].).

Bayesian Optimization. When designing a neural network (NN) for a given classification task, the choice of architecture (number of layers, neurons and activation functions) and setting of learning hyper-parameters (e.g. optimizer algorithm, batch size, learning rate) are critical for achieving reliable and high performances. At the state-of-the-art, no well-accepted nor unified method for finding the appropriate hyper-parameters for a given task has been defined, and model selection is generally performed either manually or automatically by methods such as "Grid search", which exhaustively searches in the hyper-parameter space, or "random search" [34], which evaluates only a random sequence of hyper-parameter combinations. In this work, we exploit "Bayesian Optimization" (BO) [35], since it has proven to be an effective and cost efficient solution to hyper-parameter optimization. Briefly, the idea is that the "objective function", characterized by high cost for the evaluation of each point of a bounded domain, can be approximated by building a probabilistic model (the "surrogate function") which is relatively cheaper to query. Optimization can then be performed by substituting the objective with the surrogate function. As the surrogate function represents an "a priori" distribution of the objective function, given some observations obtained by evaluation of the objective, it is possible to exploit Bayes's rule to generate an "a posteriori" estimation of the (objective) function and then update the probabilistic model (surrogate function). Candidates for the observations are suggested through an appropriate "Acquisition function" [36] which uses the information gained by the probabilistic model (estimated by the n already observed points) for suggesting the next $n+1$ candidate. Depending on the task, it is possible to select the most appropriate acquisition function from a wide array of choices. A common trait of these functions is that they all act upon the criteria of "exploration versus exploitation", so that the sequence of suggested points will provide a better overlook of the objective function (exploration) or a better identification of its maximum/minimum (exploitation).

Fixed-FFNN and Bayesian-FFNN. We designed a baseline *fixed-FFNN*whose architecture is composed by three cascading fully-connected layers (with 16, 4 and 2 neurons, respectively) with the Rectified Linear Unit (ReLU) [37] activation function. A final layer structured as a single neuron with sigmoid activation function acts as output layer, computing the final binary predictions. During network training, weight values were adjusted using a Stochastic Gradient Descent technique with a relatively small value for the batch size hyper-parameter (32), learning rate 0.5, learning rate decay of 0.1, l_2 regularizer of 0.0, no momentum, and a maximum of 64 epochs.

[7] https://scikit-optimize.github.io/.

Table 1. The architecture (left) and learning parameters (right) of the *fixed-FFNN* and the *Bayesian-FFNN* models. The hyper-parameter space explored by BO is shown in square brackets (continuous interval) or curly brackets (finite set). Selected values are in bold. LR stands for learning rate.

fixed-FFNN		*Bayesian-FFNN*
Units	Activation	Units hyper-parameters
16	ReLU	{**256**, 128, 64, 32, 16, 8, 4, 2}
4	ReLU	{**128**, 64, 32, 16, 8, 4, 2}
2	ReLU	{**64**, 32, 16, 8, 4, 2}
1	Sigmoid	1

Parameters	*fixed-FFNN*	*Bayesian-FFNN*
LR	0.5	[**0.1**, 0.5]
LR decay	0.1	[**0.01**, 0.2]
L2 reg.	0.0	[0, .., **0.001**, .., 0.1]
Batch size	32	[32, .., **100**, .., 256]
Optimizer	SGD	SGD
Max no. epochs	64	[32, **1000**]

Starting from *fixed-FFNN*, we developed *Bayesian-FFNN* by automatic model selection. Instead of using the computationally expensive grid search as in [21], where it is used to set the number of hidden layers - from 0 to 3, the number of their units - from 0 to a maximum of 256, 128, 64 neurons in the first, second and third layer, respectively, the initial learning rate, and the l_2-regularization amount in continuous intervals not reported by the authors, we use Bayesian optimization [38] to maximize the mean AUPRC computed over the validation sets of 10 internal hold-outs (see Sect. 4). More precisely, Bayesian optimization chooses the network architecture from the same search space as that used in [21], while the other hyper-parameters are equal to those of *fixed-FFNN*. The *fixed-FFNN* and *Bayesian-FFNN* models are summarized in Table 1. In particular, we note that the chosen number of layers in *Bayesian-FFNN* was often equal to that of *fixed-FFNN*, the number of chosen units was always bigger than that of *fixed-FFNN*, and the learning parameters were often selected in the lower spectrum of the continuous search interval, except for the maximum number of epochs.

Fixed-CNN and Bayesian-CNN. To analyze raw DNA sequence data, we used 1D Convolutional Neural Networks. Like for FFNN models, we firstly developed a fixed model to assess whether this approach effectively recognizes active regulatory regions. After obtaining promising results, we aimed at improving performance by automatically selecting the CNN model parameters through Bayesian optimization. The *fixed-CNN* model is outlined in the left of Table 2. The core of the network is composed of three consecutive blocks, each consisting of three (consecutive) convolutional layers followed by one 1-dimensional max/average pooling layer. The number of units in the three convolutional layers of each block, as well as the filter sizes, are fixed. A filter size of 5 for the first three convolutional layers was chosen as this represents a reasonable motif size. As for the FFNN models, all neurons in each layer have ReLU activation function with the exception of the output layer, where the output neuron has sigmoid activation. The Nadam algorithm [39] was used to adjust weight values, learning rate was set to 0.002, and batch size set to 100 examples.

Table 2. Architecture of the *fixed-CNN* (left)and *Bayesian-CNN* (right) models. Square brackets show the explored hyper-parameter space. Selected values are in bold. MP refers to max-pooling 1D layer, AP refers to average-pooling 1D layer and CBM refers to a convolutional layer with batch normalization.

fixed-CNN						*Bayesian-CNN*				
Layers	Type	Units	Kernel	Activation	Notes	Layers	Type	Units	Kernel	Notes
3	Conv	64	5	ReLU	–	3	CBM	64	5	–
1	MP	–	–	–	Size 2	1	MP	–	–	Size 2
3	Conv	128	3	ReLU	–	1	CBM	{32, **64**, 128}	{5, **10**}	–
1	MP	–	–	–	Size 2	1	MP	–	–	Size 2
3	Conv	128	3	ReLU	–	1	Flatten	–	–	–
1	AP	–	–	–	–	1	Dense	{10, 32, **64**}	–	–
1	Dropout	–	–	–	P. 0.5	1	Dropout	–	–	P. 0.1
2	Dense	10	–	ReLU	–	1	Dense	{10, 32, **64**}	–	–
1	Dropout	–	–	–	P. 0.5	1	Dropout	–	–	P. 0.1
1	Dense	1	–	Sigmoid	–	1	Dense	1	–	–

Considering that the *fixed-CNN* architecture has many weights that need to be set, we applied Bayesian optimization to simplify its architecture. We maximized the mean AUPRC computed over the validation sets of 10 internal hold-outs to choose the number of blocks from 1 to 3, and to choose, for each layer, a number of units lower than that of the *fixed-CNN* model. In Table 2, the architecture of the *fixed-CNN* model is shown, together with the meta-structure of the *Bayesian-CNN* model. Again, the Nadam algorithm was used to estimate the weight values, the learning rate is set to 0.002, and the batch size to 100.

DeepEnhancer. We compared our *Bayesian-CNN* model with the five DeepEnhancer networks [20], which are 1D-CNNs with one-hot encoded sequence data for distinguishing enhancers from background sequences. With DeepEnhancer, the best performing model is 4conv2pool4norm [20] which consists of four convolutional layers, each one followed by a batch normalization operation. In the second and fourth layer, batch normalization is followed by a max-pooling layer. The first two convolutional layers contain 128 kernels of shape 1×8, while the other convolutional layers contain 64 kernels with shape 1×3. They are followed by two dense layers, with 256 and 128 neurons respectively, interleaved with a dropout layer (ratio 0.5), while a final 2-way softmax layer computes the classification probability results. The ReLU activation function is employed in the dense layers. To distinguish the activity state of enhancers versus promoters we used the network structure and hyper-parameters of the 4conv2pool4norm model [20], but modified the output layer by substituting the 2 output neurons (with softmax activation) with one single output neuron with a sigmoid activation function to generate the final binary predictions, in line with our FFNN and CNN models.

4 Experimental Results

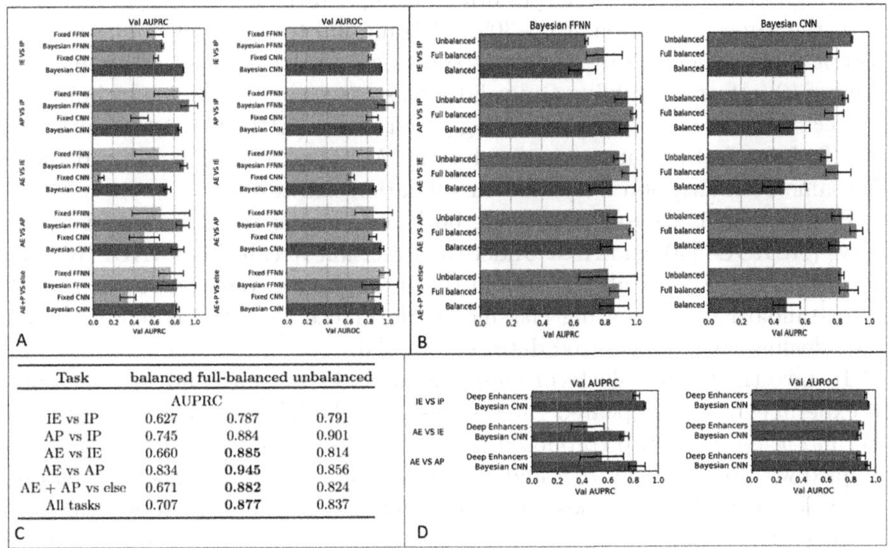

Task	balanced	full-balanced	unbalanced
	AUPRC		
IE vs IP	0.627	0.787	0.791
AP vs IP	0.745	0.884	0.901
AE vs IE	0.660	**0.885**	0.814
AE vs AP	0.834	**0.945**	0.856
AE + AP vs else	0.671	**0.882**	0.824
All tasks	0.707	**0.877**	0.837

Fig. 2. A: Comparison of deep neural network models with fixed parameters and Bayesian optimized parameters. The plotted AUPRC (left) and AUROC (right) are averaged over cell lines. Black bars represent standard deviations. B: Comparison of the mean AUPRC obtained by *Bayesian-FFNN* (left) and *Bayesian-CNN* (right) among the three different balancing setups for each the five classification tasks. C: Average AUPRC compared across the different experimental setups. For each experimental setup (columns) and task (rows), we report the AUPRC averaged with respect to the Bayesian optimized FFNN and CCN models and the four cell lines. Bold text highlights significantly best results according to Wilcoxon rank sum tests at 0.01 significance level between full-balanced and unbalanced experimental settings; both unbalanced and full-balanced significantly outperform the balanced setting. D: Comparison between *Bayesian-CNN* and DeepEnhancer. The plotted AUPRC (Left) and AUROC (Right) are averaged across multiple hold-out.

Experimental Setup. For each of the cell lines described in Sect. 2, we tested our methods on the five dichotomic tasks introduced in [21]: Inactive Enhancers vs Inactive Promoters (IE vs IP), with average imbalance ratio (AIR) equal to 2.57 (the imbalance ratio is measured as the ratio of the cardinalities of the higher represented and the lower represented class); Active Promoters vs Inactive Promoters (AP vs IP), with AIR = 7.70; Active Enhancers vs Inactive Enhancers (AE vs IE) with AIR = 22.32; Active Enhancers vs Active Promoters (AE vs AP) with AIR = 7.17; Active Enhancers and Promoters vs anything else ((AE + AP) vs ELSE) with AIR = 18. Note that the five classification tasks have different class imbalance ratios, with ratios ranging from 2.5 to 38.5.

All classification tasks are executed using 10 randomly generated (external) hold-outs, each composed by splitting the data set into training (containing 70% of samples) and test set (containing 30% of samples). Classification tasks involving model selection were performed using additional 10 internal hold-outs (with the same proportion, 70%–30%, of train and test samples). The internal hold-outs are generated by randomly splitting each training set 10 times, thus forming 10 (internal) training and validation sets, used in Bayesian Optimization to select the best model by maximizing performance (AUPRC) on the validation sets. Training features are normalized using "MinMax" scaling between 0 and 1. The same normalization is applied on validation and test sets.

Performance is measured by using both Area Under the Receiver-Operating Curve (AUROC) [40] and Area Under the Precision-Recall Curve (AUPRC) [41] metrics computed over all test sets in the 10 hold-outs. While AUROC is a de-facto standard for evaluating classifier performance, AUPRC is more suitable when dealing with unbalanced data sets [42–44].

To investigate the effects of class balancing in training and test set data, all experiments were repeated three times with the following balancing setups: (1) *"full-balanced"* setup (proposed in [21]): training and test set are randomly sampled with respectively 70% and 30% of samples. The training set is then randomly downsampled to at most 3000 samples per class. This provides a balanced training set. The 30% of samples in the test set are also randomly downsampled to generate a corresponding test set with proportion of A-E:A-P:A-X:I-E:I-P:I-X:UK = 1:1:1:2:2:1:10, according to the setup proposed in [21]. Note that the described test set subsampling greatly reduces class imbalance for all available cell lines. (2) *"balanced"* setup: only the training set is balanced as described in (1); (3) *"unbalanced"* setup: any balancing is avoided, maintaining the imbalance that characterizes the original class distribution.

Bayesian Optimization Improves Prediction Performance of FFNN and CNN Models. To investigate whether automatic model selection can improve performance we assessed the two FFNN learning models (using epigenomic features) and the two CNN models (based only on sequence) for the five classification tasks, by using the unbalanced setup. For each combination of model/task/data set, mean AUPRC and AUROC computed over the 10 repetitions and over the cell lines are shown in Fig. 2A. Performance of "fixed" and "Bayesian" models on each task were compared by applying Wilcoxon signed rank tests (at 0.01 significance level) [45–47] to detect statistically significant differences in the mean values of the classifiers' AUPRC and AUROC distributions. For AUPRC, Wilcoxon test showed a statistically significant difference in means between *Bayesian-FFNN* and *fixed-FFNN* in all tasks. We remark that *Bayesian-FFNN* achieved a better AUPRC value than *fixed-FFNN* for all AUPRCs computed over all hold-outs, tasks, and cell lines, i.e. *Bayesian-FFNN* outperformed *fixed-FFNN* in 200 out of 200 comparisons.

Comparing performance of the two CNN models, *Bayesian-CNN* significantly outperformed *fixed-CNN*. Indeed, when looking again at the full list of AUPRC values across hold-outs, tasks, and cell lines, *Bayesian-CNN* always outperformed *fixed-CNN*. Our results show that model selection by Bayesian optimization improves AUPRC results.

Regarding AUROC results, *Bayesian-FFNN* scores better average ratings than *fixed-FFNN* in all tasks with the exception of "AE+AP vs else". Also, Wilcoxon tests detected a statistically significant difference in mean between *Bayesian-FFNN* and *fixed-FFNN* in all tasks but one ("AE+AP vs else"). Considering all AUROC values computed over the 10 hold-outs, five tasks, and four cell lines, *Bayesian-FFNN* outperformed the *fixed-FFNN* 93% of the times (186 out of 200). Comparing CNN models, we note again that *Bayesian-CNN* always outperforms *fixed-CNN*. These results suggest that Bayesian model selection is a valid aid for improving both AUPRC and AUROC values of CNN models. This is also true for *Bayesian-FFNN*, as model selection improved the results in both AUPRC and AUROC for almost all tests.

The Bayesian FFNNs outperform Bayesian CNNs in tasks where we need to predict active versus inactive regulatory regions, i.e A-E vs I-E or A-P vs I-E, (Fig. 2B). This is not surprising as epigenetic features are more informative than pure sequence in predicting whether a regulatory region is active or not in a specific cell-type. On the contrary, when we need to discriminate between different types of regulatory regions (i.e. I-E vs I-P or A-E vs A-P) Bayesian CNNs outperform Bayesian FFNNs, as CNNs seem to extract DNA sequence motifs or characteristics (like GC or CpG content) that distinguish enhancers from promoters.

Bayesian CNN Models Show Comparable Results with State-of-the-Art Methods. Due to the very good performance achieved by *Bayesian-CNN*, we decided to further assess its capability for detecting active regulatory regions from raw DNA sequences by comparing it with 4conv2pool4norm net, the best performing DeepEnhancer neural network model (Sect. 3, [20]). Precisely, we used the unbalanced setup and the four cell lines to perform the three classification tasks involving enhancers ("IE vs IP", "AE vs IE" and "AE vs AP"). Using 4conv2pool4norm for these classification tasks is appropriate, as DeepEnhancer networks have been developed for recognizing enhancers against the background genome, and the original authors [20] state that it can be used for similar tasks.

Both models were assessed using multiple hold-outs. In Fig. 2–D we show, for each of the three tasks, the mean AUPRC (left) and the mean AUROC (right). Wilcoxon tests confirmed that the difference in means of the computed AUPRC and AUROC distributions are statistically significant. Looking at individual AUPRC results, *Bayesian-CNN* outperforms the DeepEnhancer 4conv2pool4norm model 199 times out of 200. For AUROC values, 4conv2pool4norm outperforms *Bayesian-CNN* in only one task. These results suggest that Bayesian optimization is able to select models competitive with state-of-the-art CREs classifiers. Moreover, we confirm that a CNN model trained on sequence data may achieve accurate results in the prediction of cis-regulatory element activity.

Test Set Balancing May Lead to Over-Optimistic Results. In [21], to deal with the data imbalance that characterizes the prediction of active regulatory regions, the authors balanced both training and test data. We reproduced this experimental setup that we name "full-balanced". In addition, we test a "balanced" setup where we only balance the training set, and we compare both with the "unbalanced" experimental setup, for which results have been presented so far (see Sect. 4).

Figure 2C reports the average AUPRC across Bayesian FFNN and CCN models for the three different balancing techniques. In the last row, average AUPRC values over all tasks are reported for each balancing setup. Comparing the AUPRCs in Fig. 2C and in Fig. 2B, we note that the balanced experimental setup is the one with the worst performance in all tasks. Wilcoxon tests confirm that, on average, the full-balanced setup produces the highest AUPRC scores.

We hypothesize that a reduced performance of the balanced setup may be due to sub-sampling of the training set for balancing, which requires to discard a relatively large amount of training samples. This ultimately affects data coverage during training and the neural network may not be able to effectively learn the intra-class variability, which results in a reduced generalization capability.

In contrast, the better performance obtained by the full-balanced experimental setup (Fig. 2B) could be the result of a distortion in the distribution of the test data (i.e. artificial increment of the ratio minority/majority class), thus leading to an over-optimistic estimation of the generalization capabilities of the predictor. Furthermore, test set balancing is not always feasible or possible, for instance when predicting the activity of not previously annotated CREs, since in this application the true labeling is not known.

5 Conclusion

This work showed that Bayesian optimization has the potential of increasing the performance of deep neural networks trained for predicting active regulatory regions in specific cell lines. Further, results show that balancing the test set may lead to an over-optimistic estimation of the generalization performance of the model, while naive balancing of the training data may lead to poor generalization results. To improve the achieved performance, in future works we aim at enlarging the spectrum of the optimized learning parameters, as well as their exploration space.

References

1. Latchman, D.S.: Transcription factors: an overview. Int. J. Exp. Pathol. **74**, 417–422 (1993)
2. Mora, A., Sandve, G.K., Gabrielsen, O.S., Eskeland, R.: In the loop: promoter-enhancer interactions and bioinformatics. Brief. Bioinform. **17**, 980–995 (2016)
3. Lambert, S.A., et al.: The human transcription factors. Cell **172**, 650–665 (2018)
4. Schubach, M., Re, M., Robinson, P.N., Valentini, G.: Imbalance-aware machine learning for predicting rare and commondisease-associated non-coding variants. Sci. Rep. **7**(1), 1–2 (2017)

5. Rentzsch, P., Witten, D., Cooper, G., Shendure, J., Kircher, M.: CADD: predicting the deleteriousness of variants throughout the human genome. Nucleic Acids Res. **47**, D886–D894 (2019)
6. Javierre, B., et al.: Lineage-specific genome architecture links enhancers and non-coding disease variants to target gene promoters. Cell **167**, 1369–1384 (2016)
7. Bernstein, B., et al.: The NIH roadmap epigenomics mapping consortium. Nat. Biotechnol. **28**, 1045 (2010)
8. Dunham, I., et al.: An integrated encyclopedia of DNA elements in the human genome. Nature **489**, 57–74 (2012)
9. Shen, Y., et al.: A map of the cis-regulatory sequences in the mouse genome. Nature **488**, 116 (2012)
10. Zhu, J., et al.: Genome-wide chromatin state transitions associated with developmental and environmental cues. Cell **152**, 642–654 (2013)
11. Noguchi, S., et al.: FANTOM5 CAGE profiles of human and mouse samples. Sci. Data **4**, 170112 (2017)
12. Lizio, M., et al.: Gateways to the FANTOM5 promoter level mammalian expression atlas. Genome Biol. **16**, 22 (2015)
13. Kundaje, A., et al.: Integrative analysis of 111 reference human epigenomes. Nature **518**, 317 (2015)
14. Ernst, J., Kellis, M.: ChromHMM: automating chromatin-state discovery and characterization. Nat. Methods **9**(3), 215–216 (2012)
15. Hoffman, M.M., Buske, O.J., Wang, J., Weng, Z., Bilmes, J.A., Noble, W.S.: Unsupervised pattern discovery in human chromatin structure through genomic segmentation. Nat. Methods **9**, 473 (2012)
16. Kwasnieski, J.C., Fiore, C., Chaudhari, H.G., Cohen, B.A.: High-throughput functional testing of encode segmentation predictions. Genome Res. **24**, 1595–1602 (2014)
17. Yip, K.Y., et al.: Classification of human genomic regions based on experimentally determined binding sites of more than 100 transcription-related factors. Genome Biol. **13**, R48 (2012)
18. Lu, Y., Qu, W., Shan, G., Zhang, C.: DELTA: a distal enhancer locating tool based on AdaBoost algorithm and shape features of chromatin modifications. PLoS ONE **10**, e0130622 (2015)
19. Kleftogiannis, D., Kalnis, P., Bajic, V.: DEEP: a general computational framework for predicting enhancers. Nucleic Acids Res. **43**(1), e6 (2014)
20. Min, X., Zeng, W., Chen, S., Chen, N., Chen, T., Jiang, R.: Predicting enhancers with deep convolutional neural networks. BMC Bioinformatics **18**, 478 (2017). https://doi.org/10.1186/s12859-017-1878-3
21. Li, Y., Shi, W., Wasserman, W.W.: Genome-wide prediction of cis-regulatory regions using supervised deep learning methods. BMC Bioinformatics **19**, 202 (2018)
22. Hinton, G., Salakhutdinov, R.: Reducing the dimensionality of data with neural networks. Science **313**(5786), 504–507 (2006)
23. Bengio, Y., Courville, A., Vincent, P.: Representation learning: a review and new perspectives. IEEE Trans. Pattern Anal. Mach. Intell. **35**(8), 1798–1828 (2013)
24. Park, Y., Kellis, M.: Deep learning for regulatory genomics. Nat. Biotechnol. **33**, 825 (2015)
25. Yang, B., et al.: BiRen: predicting enhancers with a deep-learning-based model using the DNA sequence alone. Bioinformatics **33**(13), 1930–1936 (2017)
26. Liu, F., Li, H., Ren, C., Bo, X.C., Shu, W.: PEDLA: predicting enhancers with a deep learning-based algorithmic framework. Sci. Rep. **6**, 28517 (2016)

27. Andersson, R., et al.: An atlas of active enhancers across human cell types and tissues. Nature **507**, 455–461 (2014)
28. Schmidhuber, J.: Deep learning in neural networks: an overview. Neural Netw. **61**, 85–117 (2015)
29. Fukushima, K.: Neocognitron: a self-organizing neural network model for a mechanism of pattern recognition unaffected by shift in position. Biol. Cybern. **36**, 193–202 (1980). https://doi.org/10.1007/BF00344251
30. van der Maaten, L., Hinton, G.: Visualizing data using t-SNE. J. Mach. Learn. Res. **9**, 2579–2605 (2008)
31. Hierlemann, A., Schweizer-Berberich, M., Weimar, U., Kraus, G., Pfau, A., Göpel, W.: Pattern recognition and multicomponent analysis. Sens. Update **2**, 119–180 (1996)
32. Chollet, F., et al.: Keras (2018). https://github.com/fchollet/keras
33. Abadi, M., et al.: TensorFlow: large-scale machine learning on heterogeneous distributed systems. arXiv preprint arXiv:1603.04467 (2016)
34. Bergstra, J., Bengio, Y.: Random search for hyper-parameter optimization. J. Mach. Learn. Res. **13**, 281–305 (2012)
35. Swersky, K., Snoek, J., Adams, P.: Multi-task Bayesian optimization. In: Burges, C.J.C., Bottou, L., Welling, M., Ghahramani, Z., Weinberger, K.Q. (eds.) Advances in Neural Information Processing Systems 26, pp. 2004–2012. Curran Associates, Inc., Red Hook (2013)
36. Shahriari, B., Swersky, K., Wang, Z., Adams, R.P., de Freitas, N.: Taking the human out of the loop: a review of Bayesian optimization. Proc. IEEE **104**, 148–175 (2016)
37. Nair, V., Hinton, G.E.: Rectified linear units improve restricted Boltzmann machines. In: Proceedings of the 27th International Conference on Machine Learning (ICML 2010), pp. 807–814 (2010)
38. Snoek, J., Larochelle, H., Adams, R.P.: Practical Bayesian optimization of machine learning algorithms. In: Proceedings of the 25th International Conference on Neural Information Processing Systems - Volume 2, NIPS 2012, pp. 2951–2959. Curran Associates, Inc., Red Hook (2012)
39. Dozat, T.: Incorporating Nesterov momentum into Adam. In: International Conference on Learning Representations, Workshop (ICLRW), pp. 1–6 (2016)
40. Bewick, V., Cheek, L., Ball, J.R.: Statistics review 13: receiver operating characteristic curves. Crit. Care **8**, 508–512 (2004)
41. Boyd, K., Eng, K.H., Page, C.D.: Area under the precision-recall curve: point estimates and confidence intervals. In: Blockeel, H., Kersting, K., Nijssen, S., Železný, F. (eds.) ECML PKDD 2013. LNCS (LNAI), vol. 8190, pp. 451–466. Springer, Heidelberg (2013). https://doi.org/10.1007/978-3-642-40994-3_29
42. Fawcett, T.: An introduction to ROC analysis. Pattern Recogn. Lett. **27**, 861–874 (2006)
43. He, H., Garcia, E.A.: Learning from imbalanced data. IEEE Trans. Knowl. Data Eng. **21**, 1263–1284 (2009)
44. Saito, T., Rehmsmeier, M.: The precision-recall plot is more informative than the ROC plot when evaluating binary classifiers on imbalanced datasets. PLoS ONE **10**, 1–21 (2015)
45. Wilcoxon, F.: Individual comparisons by ranking methods. Biom. Bull. **1**, 80–83 (1945)
46. Pratt, J.W.: Remarks on zeros and ties in the Wilcoxon signed rank procedures. J. Am. Stat. Assoc. **54**, 655–667 (1959)
47. Derrick, B., Paul W.: Comparing two samples from an individual Likert question. Int. J. Math. Stat. **18**(3) (2017)

DiS-TSS: An Annotation Agnostic Algorithm for TSS Identification

Dimitris Grigoriadis[1,2(✉)], Nikos Perdikopanis[1,3,4], Georgios K. Georgakilas[4,5], and Artemis Hatzigeorgiou[1,2,4(✉)]

[1] Hellenic Pasteur Institute, 11521 Athens, Greece
[2] Department of Computer Science and Biomedical Informatics, University of Thessaly, 35131 Lamia, Greece
{digrigoriadis, arhatzig}@uth.gr
[3] Department of Informatics and Telecommunications, National and Kapodistrian University of Athens, 15784 Athens, Greece
[4] Department of Electrical and Computer Engineering, University of Thessaly, 38221 Volos, Greece
[5] Central European Institute of Technology, Masaryk University, Kamenice 735/5, 62500 Brno, Czech Republic

Abstract. The spread, distribution and utilization of transcription start sites (TSS) experimental evidence within promoters are poorly understood. Cap Analysis of Gene Expression (CAGE) has emerged as a popular gene expression profiling protocol, able to quantitate TSS usage by recognizing the 5′ end of capped RNA molecules. However, there is an increasing volume of studies in the literature suggesting that CAGE can also detect 5′ capping events which are transcription byproducts. These findings highlight the need for computational methods that can effectively remove the excessive amount of noise from CAGE samples, leading to accurate TSS annotation and promoter usage quantification. In this study, we present an annotation agnostic computational framework, DIANA Signal-TSS (DiS-TSS), that for the first time utilizes digital signal processing inspired features customized on the peculiarities of CAGE data. Features from the spatial and frequency domains are combined with a robustly trained Support Vector Machines (SVM) model to accurately distinguish between peaks related to real transcription initiation events and biological or protocol-induced noise. When benchmarked on experimentally derived data on active transcription marks as well as annotated TSSs, DiS-TSS was found to outperform existing implementations, by providing on average $\sim$11k positive predictions and an increase in performance by $\sim$5% based on in the experimental and annotation-based evaluations.

Keywords: GSP · TSS · DSP · Bioinformatics · CAGE · Transcription · Promoter · Machine Learning

D. Grigoriadis and N. Perdikopanis—Equal contribution.

I. Rojas et al. (Eds.): IWBBIO 2020, LNBI 12108, pp. 613–623, 2020.
https://doi.org/10.1007/978-3-030-45385-5_55

1 Introduction

Cap Analysis of Gene Expression (CAGE) is a high-throughput experimental protocol for transcriptome analysis, specifically developed to recognize, capture and quantify the 5′ end of capped RNA molecules. Since the introduction of the initial methodology in 2003 [1], CAGE has undergone an extensive refinement procedure that lead to the gradual improvement into the most popular transcription start site (TSS) identification protocol enabling genome-wide promoter usage/expression quantification. During the past two decades, CAGE has been extensively applied by the FANTOM consortium [2] resulting in the accumulation of thousands of human and mouse (among other species) CAGE datasets. The transcriptomics research community has long been utilizing this wealth of information to study the promoterome and refine gene expression regulatory networks in physiological and pathological conditions.

Despite the widespread usage of CAGE, there is increasing evidence in the literature [3–5] that unveil alarming levels of noise embedded in CAGE datasets, raising issues related to the specificity of CAGE as a TSS identification protocol. These studies suggest that CAGE also identifies capping events involving diverse locations of transcribed loci such as different splicing products which may be classified as transcriptional noise. Therefore, even the most meticulously generated CAGE datasets typically suffer from noisy signal entirely unrelated to transcription initiation events.

To overcome this restriction, several in silico techniques have been developed in the past two decades, providing pipelines for peak identification in CAGE datasets. Since 2007, three major algorithms are reported as TSS identification frameworks. CAGER [3] introduced a method for differential TSS usage by addressing variability in the choice of TSSs within the same promoter across different experimental conditions. RECLU [4] is an extension of PARACLU [1] that can also account for replicated experiments using the irreproducible discovery rate (IDR) [4, 5]. TSRchitect [6] is a more versatile implementation that is able to analyze data from a spectrum of transcriptome profiling techniques including CAGE, RAMPAGE, PEAT and STRIPE-Seq among others, while being able to also handle replicated experiments.

The common denominator across all the aforementioned methods is that they can directly be applied on CAGE alignments without any additional input prerequisites such as the underlying DNA sequence, other experimental evidence or in silico derived features. These algorithms essentially provide basic pipelines that can efficiently process large-scale CAGE data without involving Machine Learning (ML) or any other prediction accuracy optimization technique.

Genomic signal processing (GSP) is an intriguing field that introduces features in the space (the equivalent of time in the traditional signal processing field) and frequency domains. GSP refers to signal processing techniques and well-established mathematical methods for analyzing time-series data [7], summarizing an engineering field that aims to utilize digital signal processing (DSP) tools and mathematical models for analyzing and processing a wide spectrum of genomic data. The main challenge in GSP is to transform the DNA sequence underlying Next Generation Sequencing (NGS) data into usable formats, such as numerical single or multiple vectors. There are many GSP-based approaches in the literature, developed for different applications aiming to solve a diverse compendium of biological problems, such as repeat element characterization [8], identification of protein-coding DNA sequences [9], exons [10] and sequence structure prediction [11].

In this study, we present DIANA Signal-TSS (DiS-TSS) an in silico TSS identification approach that combines CAGE data with DSP-derived features and ML to provide highly accurate and single-nucleotide resolution predictions (Fig. 1). To this end, CAGE reads are represented in the time series domain as signal vectors, after basic pre-processing takes place based on mapping quality and tag-cluster aggregation. DiS-TSS extracts signal features inspired by the DSP field that are related to the signal's structural properties and are able to accurately distinguish real transcription initiation events from biological and protocol-induced noise (Fig. 2). These features are subsequently combined into a Support Vector Machines (SVM) model that has been trained on CAGE signal from annotated TSSs (positive set) and non-promoter regions (negative set). DiS-TSS was found to outperform existing algorithms in all benchmarks that were based on both experimental data and annotated genomic loci of protein-coding genes. DiS-TSS is a Python framework freely accessible at https://github.com/DimitrisGrig/DiS_TSS.git.

2 Materials and Methods

2.1 Utilized Experimental Data and Annotation

Bam formatted CAGE datasets were downloaded from FANTOM public repository [2] (GRCh38 assembly), derived from H9 (CNhs11917 identification code) and K562 (CNhs12334) cells. DiS-TSS and TSRchitect can directly work on bam files. However, for applying RECLU and CAGER we downloaded the 5′ end collapsed CAGE alignments, denoted as ctss files, in FANTOM repository for CNhs11917 and CNhs12334 samples.

Polymerase II (ENCSR000BMR) and H3K4me3 (ENCSR000EWA) ChIP-Seq samples in bed narrowpeak format were obtained from the ENCODE [12] repository and converted in GRCh38 coordinates using the UCSC liftover tool. The human genome annotation was downloaded from Ensembl v98 [13].

Genomic coordinates for transcription factor binding sites (TFBS) were downloaded from the ENCODE 'Txn Factor' track. This track incorporates a large collection of ChIP-Seq derived TFBSs from 161 TFs in 91 cell types.

2.2 Overview of DiS-TSS

DiS-TSS algorithm has two different operating modes (Fig. 1). In the first mode, users can provide bam formatted CAGE alignments as input and undertakes to score all candidate TSSs. In the second mode of operation, users can also provide BED formatted genomic loci in addition to the bam alignments. DiS-TSS will utilize the file to focus the aforementioned analysis in the selected loci instead of the whole genome. Initially, CAGE tags with mapping quality less than 10 are removed and the remaining tags are aggregated into clusters/peaks using a distance parameter cutoff (default = 25).

Peaks are further filtered based on the normalized (tags per million - tpm) expression level threshold (default = 1). For each peak, DiS-TSS identifies the position with the highest 5′ end tag coverage and flags it as the peak's representative for future use. The following step involves DSP-based feature extraction that captures the characteristics of each peak's signal. Subsequently, the features are vectorized and forwarded to a SVM model that has been trained to distinguish between CAGE signal from transcription initiation events and biological or technical noise.

Detailed information regarding the feature extraction/selection and training process of DiS-TSS can be found in the following sections.

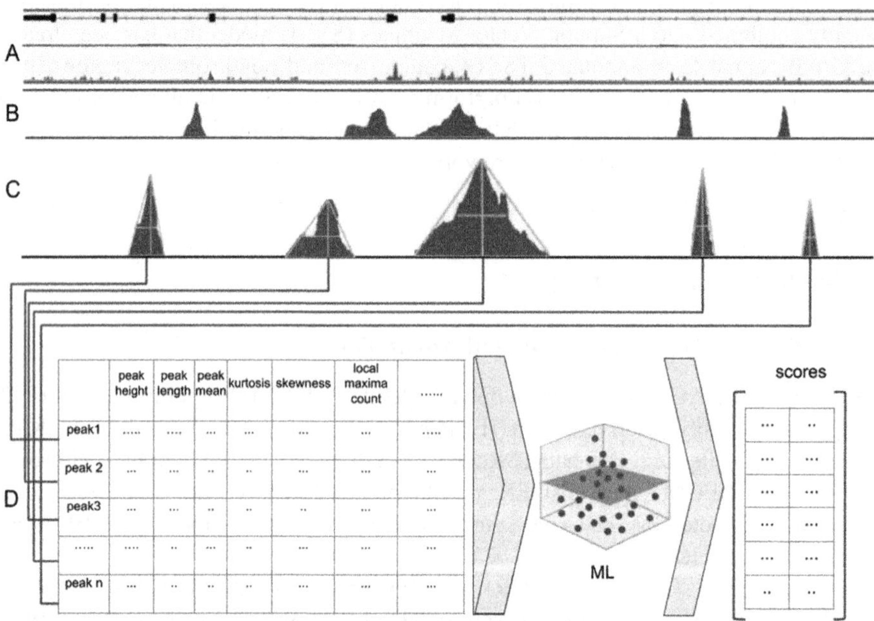

Fig. 1. Overview of DiS-TSS pipeline. (A) Genome browser view of raw CAGE signal. (B) Initial step that summarizes the aggregation of CAGE tags into clusters/peaks. (C) Extraction of features related to peak properties. (D) Assembly of feature vectors prior to using the DiS-TSS ML model (SVM) that produces the final score for each peak.

2.3 Feature Analysis and Selection

Inspired by the DSP field, we extracted the 13 most popular features for analyzing and unveiling patterns embedded in digital signals. These features are tightly related to the signal's structural properties [9] and as our exploratory analysis showed, they can highlight structural differences between transcriptional noise and TSS-associated CAGE signal (Fig. 2). The list of features includes peak length, width, height, kurtosis, skewness, peak area, local maxima mean and variance, count of local maximum peaks and prominence. Additionally, after transferring the signal from space to frequency domain with fast Fourier transform (FFT module from numpy), mean and variance of the frequency amplitudes is calculated as well as the frequency carrying more energy inside the power spectrum (also known as dominant frequency) [14].

To assess the importance of each feature and retain only those with high predictive power, we employed the Recursive Feature Elimination (RFE) [15] method. RFE fits a model using different combinations of features and eliminates the weak ones until a performance limit is reached. In this study, we utilized Python's scikit-learn library and applied RFE using a radial basis function (RBF) SVM model (13 iterations) to score different feature subsets. With this technique, 8 features were selected as the best performing collection which includes peak length, peak height, kurtosis, skewness, peak area, mean and count of local maxima as well as the dominant frequency (Fig. 2). The contribution of the remaining features to the algorithm's performance was found to be negligible and were therefore removed from any subsequent analysis. Features that do not correlate with improved model performance are typically removed prior to the training procedure to improve the model's generalisation capacity and reduce the overall computational overhead.

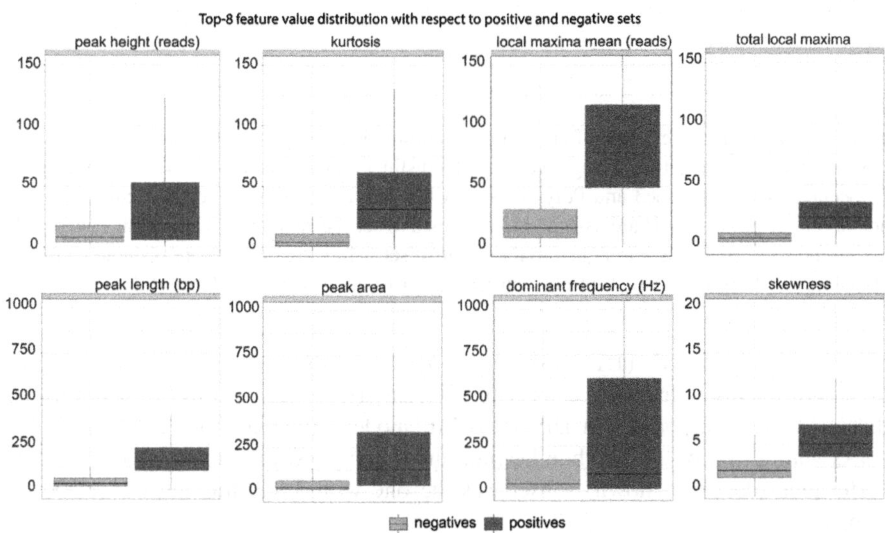

Fig. 2. Distribution of the top-8 feature values in the positive and negative sets.

2.4 DiS-TSS Training

Peaks (N = 38,439) were extracted from CAGE H9 cell sample, as described in the Overview of DiS-TSS section, and formed the basis for training our algorithm (Fig. 3). CAGE peaks that were localized closer than 1 kb from annotated protein-coding TSSs and overlapped H3K4me3 and Polymerase II ChIP-Seq enriched regions, formed the positive set (N = 11,304). To avoid the inclusion of promoter-proximal genomic loci that are rich in functional information (i.e. promoters), CAGE peaks that were found in regions flanking promoters (up to 9 kb in each direction from the 1 kb window mentioned above) were removed entirely from the dataset. Intergenic peaks that did not overlap any H3K4me3 and Polymerase II ChIP-Seq enriched regions were selected as the negative set (N = 11,579). The same pipeline was used for generating a benchmarking set of 75,127 CAGE peaks (32,310 positives and 42,817 negatives) in K562 cells which was used to compare the performance of DiS-TSS with existing algorithms outside the biological context of DiS-TSS training. The importance of utilizing an evaluation dataset from a cell line (K562) with an entirely different expression profile than the samples used for training is paramount for exploring the possibility of overfitting our model on putative cell-specific structural properties of CAGE signal or sequencing batch effects.

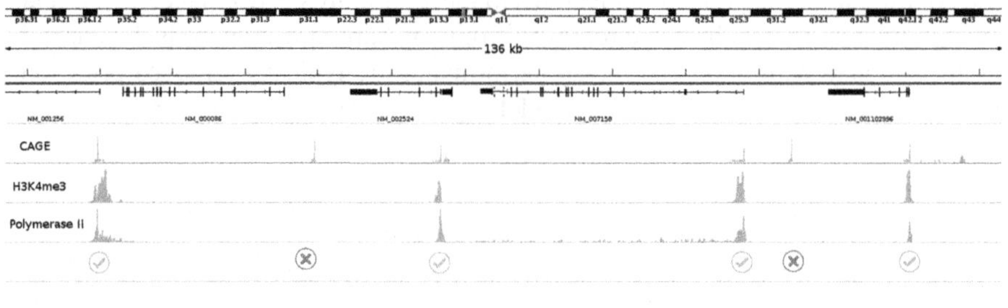

Fig. 3. Genome browser view of an example genomic locus depicting the process of assigning CAGE peaks to the positive or negative sets. The distinction between the two sets depends on the co-occupancy of H3K4me3 and Polymerase II ChIP-Seq peaks. CAGE peaks occupied by both active transcription signals are assigned to the positive set. Peaks that do not exhibit coverage by any of the two signals were assigned to the negative set, while peaks that were occupied either by H3K4me3 or Polymerase II were not considered for training or for the labeled data evaluation.

Multiple balanced (1:1 positive to negative ratio) and randomly selected training/test subsets from H9 cells with different sizes were used to evaluate the candidate (to be incorporated in DiS-TSS) ML models, ranging from 2,000 to 12,000 peaks with a step of 2,000 while keeping the training/test ratio fixed to 3/1. The best performing (data not shown) subset was the one with 3,000 training and 1,000 test samples.

SVM with Radial Basis Function (RBF) kernel was selected as the best performing DiS-TSS model (data not shown) and was incorporated into DiS-TSS pipeline after being compared to commonly used classification algorithms such as Random Forests, K-Nearest Neighbors, Decision Trees, Naive Bayes and linear/polynomial kernel based SVM flavors.

2.5 Application of Existing Algorithms

Existing implementations do not include any ML component in their pipelines. Therefore, by applying them with default settings, we considered the output as their positive set of predictions. Also, there is a mismatch on the accepted input format of each algorithm. For example, RECLU requires 5′ end collapsed CAGE alignments, denoted as ctss files in the FANTOM repository. In contrast, the starting point of DiS-TSS analysis is based on BAM formatted CAGE alignments. These minor discrepancies combined with the algorithmic design of each implementation might cause differences across the final sets of CAGE enriched regions.

TSRchitect was applied with parameters 'tagCountThreshold = 25 clustDist = 20', RECLU with 'number_of_reads = 30 density = 2' and CAGER with 'threshold = 0.5 method = paraclu max_distance = 20'.

3 Results

We employed two distinct types of evaluation strategies for benchmarking the performance of CAGE-oriented TSS predictors, including DiS-TSS, RECLU, CAGER and TSRchitect. The first strategy is purely experimentally-driven and utilizes H3K4me3, Polymerase II and transcription factor ChIP-Seq occupancy. The second evaluation approach is based only on gene annotations that were used to segment the genome into positive and negative zones in terms of promoter functionality. Both evaluation processes were applied on K562 datasets to further explore the generalisation capacity of our algorithm and provide a benchmarking environment outside the cell type context of DiS-TSS training. Table 1 summarizes all evaluation results.

3.1 Experimentally-Driven Evaluation

For the purposes of the evaluation process presented in this section, we utilized ChIP-Seq datasets based on known marks of active transcription such as H3K4me3 [16–18] and Polymerase II in H9 and K562 cells. After applying a DiS-TSS score cutoff of 0.5, we calculated the overlap of positive predictions with H3K4me3 and Polymerase II ChIP-Seq peaks. The same overlap was also calculated for RECLU, CAGER and TSRchitect predictions. 87.95% (9,616 out of 10,937) of positive DiS-TSS predictions were found enriched in H3K4me3 (Fig. 4A) and 87.53% (9,574) in Polymerase II ChIP-Seq signal (Fig. 4B), 81.1% and 83.48% of positive CAGER predictions, 81.07% and 79.49% for RECLU and 57.14% and 57.98% for TSRchitect respectively.

An additional evaluation approach was also employed, based on the cross-tissue compendium of transcription factor ChIP-Seq binding sites (TFBS) provided by ENCODE (Txn Factor track). We calculated the number of TFBSs overlapping with the positive predictions set provided by each algorithm in K562 cells (Fig. 4C). 92.57% (10,125 out of 10,937) of DiS-TSS predictions were found to overlap at least one TFBS, while 87.66%, 86.67% and 64.16% were the results for CAGER, RECLU and TSRchitect respectively.

3.2 Evaluation Based on Protein-Coding Transcript Annotation

To further explore the performance limits of CAGE-oriented TSS predictors, we adopted an evaluation approach purely relied on annotated protein-coding transcripts. The region surrounding each transcript start (± 1 kb) was considered as the positive zone and the flanking region, up to 50 kb in both directions, as the negative zone. For every algorithm, positive predictions within the positive zone were considered true positives (TP) while those found in the negative zone were flagged as false positives (FP). DiS-TSS achieved the highest performance (Fig. 4D, E) with 81.51% TP (8,915 out of 10,937), followed by RECLU with 76.69% (9,420 out of 12,282), CAGER with 74.79% (7,479 out of 14,465) and TSRchitect with 56.69% (4,128 out of 7,281).

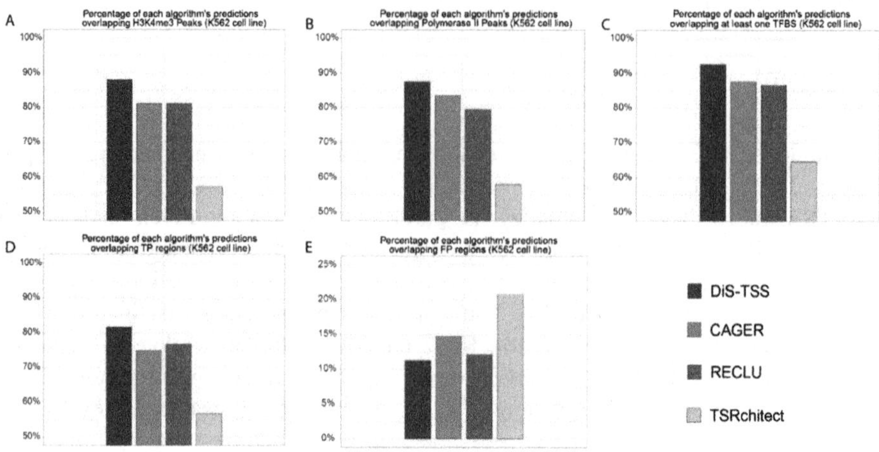

Fig. 4. Experimental evaluation of algorithms based on annotated protein-coding TSSs and H3K4me3, Polymerase II and TF ChIP-Seq peaks in K562 cells. Percentage of each algorithm's predictions overlapping (A) H3K4me3 and (B) Polymerase II enriched regions as well as (C) at least one TFBS. (D) Percentage of predictions that were found in promoters (±1 kb around annotated TSSs, true positive regions) and (E) outside of promoters (flanking true positive regions and up to ±50 kb from the TSSs, false positive regions).

Table 1. Summarized evaluation results in K562 cells, based on experimental data and annotated protein-coding TSSs. From left to right, each column shows the number of predictions overlapping with at least one TFBS, H3K4me3 and Polymerase II peaks, the true positive and false positive zones (as defined by annotated protein-coding TSSs). DiS-TSS results are based on a 0.5 score cutoff.

Algorithm	Total positive predictions	Number of predictions overlapping with:			
		TFBS (%)	H3K4me3 (%)	Polymerase II (%)	TP zone (%)
DiS-TSS	10,937	10,125 (92.57)	9,619 (87.94)	9,574 (87.53)	8,915 (81.51)
CAGER	14,465	12,681 (87.66)	11,732 (81.1)	12,076 (83.48)	10,819 (74.79)
RECLU	12,282	10,646 (86.67)	9,958 (81.07)	9,763 (79.49)	9,420 (76.69)
TSRchitect	7,281	4,705 (64.62)	4,161 (57.14)	4,222 (57.98)	4,128 (56.69)

4 Discussion

Multicellular organisms exhibit remarkable cell functional variability, a feature that fundamentally derives from the underlying diverse gene expression patterns. Understanding the transition from physiological to pathological states requires developing experimental methods that are able to probe the transcription mechanism and unveil hidden patterns responsible for cell-specific gene expression regulation.

CAGE is an experimental technique that was developed more than a decade ago, specifically to assist in quantifying the abundance of 5′ end capped RNA molecules. Since then, the continuous improvement of CAGE lead to a gradually increased popularity, and to this date, CAGE is considered as the golden standard technique for studying promoter usage and transcriptional mechanics. Despite its popular status, reliability and the availability of thousands CAGE samples in the FANTOM and ENCODE public repositories, there is alarming evidence in the literature regarding the increased biological and technical noise levels in these samples. This limitation brings Computational Biology to the spotlight and highlights the need for robust in silico methodologies that can effectively remove noise without compromising the sensitivity of CAGE in capturing transcription initiation events.

There are several computational frameworks, RECLU, CAGER and TSRchitect, that have attempted to address this issue, since they were specifically developed to process CAGE data. These algorithms incorporate simple heuristics to aggregate sequenced reads into clusters/peaks and utilize arbitrarily selected cutoffs, related to peak size and expression, to filter the final results. These algorithms aim to provide basic computational steps for processing large-scale CAGE datasets efficiently. There is no Machine Learning involved in the pipelines of these algorithms, thus their functionality and applicability is severely limited.

The algorithm presented here attempts to overcome the aforementioned limitations, and provide a breakthrough in CAGE-oriented TSS identification. DiS-TSS is annotation-agnostic and the first algorithm to combine digital signal processing, on CAGE data for extracting peak shape related features, and Machine Learning for effectively distinguishing real TSS-related CAGE enriched regions from biological/technical noise. Additionally, through this study, the field of digital signal processing will be introduced to the transcriptomics community as a powerful arsenal that can be effectively combined with Machine Learning to provide answers to complex and diverse biological questions.

The evaluation process of algorithms with different underlying functionalities is far from straightforward and requires meticulous planning. Our 2-fold strategy involved, (a) an evaluation based on the enrichment of the algorithms' predictions with H3K4me3, Polymerase II and TFBS ChIP-Seq signal separately, and (b) a benchmarking approach solely based on annotated protein-coding transcripts and their promoters. The key point here is that each comparison has its own advantages and disadvantages while they are able to complement one another. They also provide a spherical view of the algorithms' performance and unveil critical components of their applicability and functional limitations. We chose to train and evaluate the performance of our algorithm in two cell types with fundamentally different gene expression profiles, to test its robustness against overfitting on cell-specific signal structural properties or sequencing batch effects. H9 is one of the most widely distributed and well researched embryonic stem cell lines while K562 cells are extensively utilized as a myelogenous leukemia model. The aforementioned gene expression diversity was the primary reason for selecting these cell types, in addition to their popularity and widespread usage in Consortia such as the ENCODE and FANTOM. The availability of CAGE, H3K4me3, Polymerase II and TFBS ChIP-Seq data for both cell types, also played a decisive role for actively selecting them in this study.

The contribution of this study gravitates around the novel application of digital signal processing techniques on transcriptomic data and the extraction of features that when combined with a robustly trained Machine Learning model are able to provide a performance boost in the problem of CAGE-mediated TSS identification. Reliable algorithms, such as DiS-TSS, can play a fundamental role towards unveiling key regulators of gene expression and push the horizon of scientific knowledge even further.

Contributions. A.H. supervised the study. N.P. and D.G. envisioned and designed the algorithm and performed the unsupervised analysis. D.G. developed the algorithm. N.P performed all comparisons. A.H., D.G., N.P. and G.K.G. made the figures and wrote the manuscript.

Funding. We acknowledge the support of this work by projects "ELIXIR-GR: The Greek Research Infrastructure for Data Management and Analysis in Life Sciences" (MIS 5002780) which is implemented under the Action "Reinforcement of the Research and Innovation Infrastructure", and "Metalasso: A platform for computational meta-analysis of Genome Wide Association Studies-GWAS" (MIS 5032832) which is implemented under the Action "Research-Create-Innovate", both funded by the Operational Program "Competitiveness, Entrepreneurship and Innovation" (NSRF 2014–2020) and co-financed by Greece and the European Union (European Regional Development Fund).

Conflict of Interest. None declared.

References

1. Frith, M.C., Valen, E., Krogh, A., Hayashizaki, Y., Carninci, P., Sandelin, A.: A code for transcription initiation in mammalian genomes. Genome Res. **18**, 1–12 (2008)
2. The FANTOM Consortium and the RIKEN PMI and CLST (DGT): A promoter-level mammalian expression atlas. Nature **507**, 462–470 (2014)
3. Haberle, V., Forrest, A.R.R., Hayashizaki, Y., Carninci, P., Lenhard, B.: CAGEr: precise TSS data retrieval and high-resolution promoterome mining for integrative analyses. Nucleic Acids Res. **43**, e51 (2015)
4. Ohmiya, H., et al.: RECLU: a pipeline to discover reproducible transcriptional start sites and their alternative regulation using capped analysis of gene expression (CAGE). BMC Genom. **15**, 269 (2014)
5. Li, Q., Brown, J.B., Huang, H., Bickel, P.J.: Measuring reproducibility of high-throughput experiments. Ann. Appl. Stat. **5**, 1752–1779 (2011)
6. Taylor Raborn, R., Brendel, V.P., Sridharan, K.: TSRchitect: promoter identification from large-scale TSS profiling data

7. Mendizabal-Ruiz, G., Román-Godínez, I., Torres-Ramos, S., Salido-Ruiz, R.A., Alejandro Morales, J.: On DNA numerical representations for genomic similarity computation. PLoS ONE **12**, e0173288 (2017)
8. Sharma, D., Issac, B., Raghava, G.P.S., Ramaswamy, R.: Spectral repeat finder (SRF): identification of repetitive sequences using Fourier transformation. Bioinformatics **20**, 1405–1412 (2004)
9. Morgan, D.P., Scofield, C.L.: Signal processing and feature extraction. In: Neural Networks and Speech Processing. SECS, vol. 130, pp. 163–201. Springer, Boston (1991). https://doi.org/10.1007/978-1-4615-3950-6_6
10. Kotlar, D.: Gene prediction by spectral rotation measure: a new method for identifying protein-coding regions. Genome Res. **13**(8), 1930–1937 (2003)
11. Lio, P., Vannucci, M.: Wavelet change-point prediction of transmembrane proteins. Bioinformatics **16**, 376–382 (2000)
12. The ENCODE Project Consortium: An integrated encyclopedia of DNA elements in the human genome. Nature **489**, 57–74 (2012)
13. Zerbino, D.R., et al.: Ensembl 2018. Nucleic Acids Res. **46**, D754–D761 (2017)
14. Telgarsky, R.: Dominant frequency extraction. arXiv [cs.NA] (2013)
15. Guyon, I., Weston, J., Barnhill, S., Vapnik, V.: Gene selection for cancer classification using support vector machines. Mach. Learn. **46**, 389–422 (2002). https://doi.org/10.1023/A:1012487302797
16. Bernstein, B.E., et al.: Methylation of histone H3 Lys 4 in coding regions of active genes. Proc. Natl. Acad. Sci. U.S.A. **99**, 8695–8700 (2002)
17. Santos-Rosa, H., et al.: Active genes are tri-methylated at K4 of histone H3. Nature **419**, 407–411 (2002)
18. Guenther, M.G., Levine, S.S., Boyer, L.A., Jaenisch, R., Young, R.A.: A chromatin landmark and transcription initiation at most promoters in human cells. Cell **130**, 77–88 (2007)

LM-Based Word Embeddings Improve Biomedical Named Entity Recognition: A Detailed Analysis

Liliya Akhtyamova and John Cardiff(✉)

Social Media Research Group, Technological University Dublin, Dublin, Ireland
akhtyamova@phystech.edu, john.cardiff@tudublin.ie

Abstract. Recent studies have shown that contextualized word embeddings outperform other types of embeddings on a variety of tasks. However, there is little research done to evaluate their effectiveness in the biomedical domain under multi-task settings.

We derive the contextualized word embeddings from the Flair framework and apply them to the task of biomedical NER on 5 benchmark datasets, yielding major improvements over the baseline and achieving competitive results over the current best systems. We analyze the sources of these improvements, reporting model performances over different combinations of word embeddings, and fine-tuning and casing modes.

Keywords: Deep learning · Biomedical named entity recognition · Contextualized word embeddings

1 Introduction

Named entity recognition (NER) is a fundamental basis for many applications such as speech recognition [6], question answering [13], knowledge base population [14], query. One of the areas in which NER and its applications are most useful is the biomedical domain.

However, as the labeling of a corpus for biomedical NER requires domain knowledge, the preparation of high-quality training corpora is usually quite expensive and time-consuming. *Transfer learning* introduced in NLP through the concept of pretrained word embeddings allows us to leverage knowledge about the language semantics more accurately. One of the recent advances of it is *contextualized language modeling* based concept representations.

The release of contextualized word embeddings [3,7,21] has substantially advanced the state-of-the-art in many NLP tasks. It has become possible by learning the *contextual* representations of terms and training of models based on fragments of *contiguous* text that typically span multiple sentences thus capturing long distance relationships within the text fragments better.

Models based on contextualized word embeddings due to the more complex structure of latter in comparison to the standard word embeddings such as

I. Rojas et al. (Eds.): IWBBIO 2020, LNBI 12108, pp. 624–635, 2020.
https://doi.org/10.1007/978-3-030-45385-5_56

Word2vec [19], Glove [20], FastText [4] are better at capturing information from domain-restricted corpora or even the unrelated or general nature corpora.

These advantages of contextualized word embeddings motivate us to apply them to biomedical NER tasks. The identification of biomedical instances in texts can lead to an improvement in the structuring of biomedical and medical knowledge (e.g., biomedical knowledge bases' population) and revealing hidden or unknown previously phenomena from biomedical texts to help clinicians and medical professionals in their routine (e.g., medical database query, decision support systems).

While the most popular version of language representation – BERT [7] is well investigated and has yielded state-of-the-art results on many biomedical benchmark datasets [16], the capabilities of Flair language model (LM) [3] have not yet been researched comprehensively for biomedical NER. Although, Sharma and Daniel [24] in their paper present the BioFlair system learnt over the part of benchmark datasets from Lee et al. [16], they do not learn the model extensively over a variety of combinations of word embeddings and different model architectures.

In this work, we aim to close this gap by (1) incorporating pre-trained contextualized embeddings in a state-of-the-art NER multi-task system [27], obtaining major performance improvements over previous state-of-the-art and competitive to other systems result; (2) for comparability of single-task models, we also experiment with contextualized embeddings integrated into the of-the-shelf Flair NER system[1]; (3) we test model performances over different combinations of the standard, character and contextualized word embeddings as well as parameter settings (casing, fine-tuning).

2 Materials and Methods

The following sections present the technical details of the NER architectures used in this study [1,27]. We first briefly give the problem definition, then describe single-task and multi-task learning systems. We also describe word embeddings and datasets used in the experiments. And finally, we give details on the evaluation metric.

2.1 Problem Definition

The problem of biomedical NER is a sequence labeling task where the goal is to detect the correct spans of entities and assign them the right labels.

To be in line with the results of the original work, to classify entities in Wang's model [27], we used a BIO schema. These classify entities in a document as [B]eginning, [I]nside, [O]utside.

For the Flair NER system, we used the default best settings which include BIOES tagging schema, where B stands for Beginning, I for Inside, O for Out, E for End, and S for Single entity.

[1] https://github.com/zalandoresearch/flair.

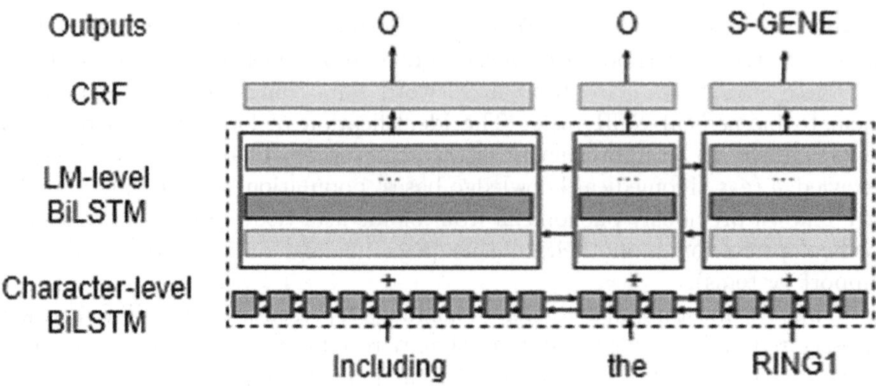

Fig. 1. Architecture of modified Wang et al. deep multi-task learning system. Instead of the original word embeddings, concatenated LM-based word embeddings are used.

2.2 Single-Task Learning

The single-task model (STM) learns on one task at a time. In this work, we experiment with two STMs. The first is the model of Wang et al [27] who in turn adopted their model from Liu et al. [17]. It is the bi-LSTM-CRF model with integrated character-level embeddings to be combined with the word level embedding representations. The character-level embeddings in their models are learned through another bi-LSTM model. As stated by authors, the advantage of their architecture from vanilla bi-LSTM is that its character level word representations allow capturing out-of-vocabulary (OOV) terms and context around words, thus being "contextualized" in some degree. In their architecture, we expanded the word embedding layer with other types of embeddings including contextualized word embeddings. The augmented architecture is presented in Fig. 1.

Another part of experiments was conducted using the Flair NER framework (see Footnote 1) which goes on top of Theano providing a convenient way to experiment with the combination of different types of word embeddings. It consists of a bidirectional Long Short Term Memory (bi-LSTM) network of Huang et al. [12] with the options to select and tune its parameters. We trained it with Conditional Random Fields (CRF) using the default best parameter settings: one LSTM layer, hidden state dimension 256, initial learning rate 0.1 with subsequent halving if the loss does not decrease for 5 epochs, mini-batch size 8, and Adam objective function optimizer.

2.3 Multi-Task Learning

Multi-task learning (MTL) is the task of learning on many tasks in *parallel* by sharing some part of learning model representation between tasks. This approach became popular in NLP [5], computer vision [18], speech recognition [6], simulation of electrocardiogram signals [23] and other tasks [22] outperforming results gained with STL model architectures.

For our MTL experiments, we utilize again the MTL architecture of Wang et al. [27]. Authors using the single-task based model of Liu et al. [17] built the competitive multi-task model for solving biomedical NER tasks. Using 15 benchmark datasets they showed the substantially better performance of their approach in comparison to STL and other baseline systems.

We took their best-performed MTL architecture - with shared both word and character-level layers - as a foundation for comparison with STL while integrating contextualized, standard and character-level word embeddings.

2.4 Flair Embeddings

In our experiments, we consider the variant of LM-based word embeddings called Flair [3] and ELMo [21]. As in Wang et al. [27] these embeddings are also character-level and trained using the bi-LSTM network. The principal difference of them from Wang et al. [27] is that they are trained in a separate task of LM with next character in a text being the target to predict, while in the model of Wang et al. [27] the character-level embeddings are trained *jointly* as part of NER model with the word label to be the final target to predict.

In comparison to, for example, BERT language representation which allows after pre-training it further fine-tune it for the downstream task, Flair, ELMo and other similar LM architectures do not allow to do it and should be used in a pre-trained form to *embed* sentences of the downstream task's input to form contextualized embeddings.

In this work, we use the *pooled* version of Flair embeddings which keeps the information on each encountered word and reduces the word representation bias when the same word occurs in noisy, under specified context [2]. For example, the biomedical term "hemoglobin" is not ambiguous and its word embedding should not vary heavily in different contents.

We chose Flair and ELMo embeddings both pre-trained on in-domain English PubMed articles[2].

2.5 Additional Embeddings

In numerous papers, it was shown that stacking different types of embeddings mostly improves the quality of NLP models [3,21]. In this work, we integrate the following types of additional embeddings:

[2] http://evexdb.org/pmresources/language-models/.

Table 1. Statistics on biomedical NER datasets

Dataset	Size	Entity types and counts
BC2GM	20,000 sentences	Gene/Protein (24,583)
BC4CHEMD	10,000 abstracts	Chemical (84,310)
BC5CDR	1,500 articles	Chemical (15,935), Disease (12,852)
NCBI-Disease	793 abstracts	Disease (6,881), Gene/Protein (35,336)
JNLPBA	2,404 abstracts	Cell Line (4,330), DNA (10,589), Cell Type (8,649), RNA (1,069)

1. **General-domain word2vec embeddings.**[3] These embeddings are trained over news and Wikipedia data.
2. **Biomedical word2vec embeddings.**[4] These embeddings were trained on 5.5M terms over PubMed, PubMed Central and Wikipedia texts with the window size 200.
3. **Byte-pairwise encoded embeddings (BPE).** They are statistically calculated based on occurrences of sub-word tokens of words [11].
4. **Character-level word embeddings** are trained in the model of Wang et al. [27] using the methodology developed by Lample et al. [15].

2.6 Datasets

For comparative purposes, we test our models on the same datasets as used by [27] (Table 1). Here, NER on BC2GM, BC4CHEMD and NCBI-Disease are *binary classification* problems, and NER on JNLPBA and BC5CDR are *multi-classification* ones.

These datasets cover major biomedical entity types (genes, proteins, chemicals, diseases) and thus were chosen as a standalone set of biomedical datasets by many researchers. All datasets could be downloaded from the GitHub repository of MTL Bioinformatics Lab[5].

In line with Wang et al. [27], below we also briefly mention the origin of datasets and state-of-the-art results on them to the current moment for the systems similar to ours.

BC2GM This dataset was used in the BioCreative II gene mention recognition task. The best result to the moment are holded by to the moment are holded by [26] and Lee et al. [16] (with insignificant difference). Lee et al. [16] utilized LM-based BERT system. They trained a large BERT system on relevant corpora and fine-tuned on a downstream tasks. Wang et al. [26] applied the multi-task learning techniques cross-sharing structure for their neural-network based model.

[3] https://github.com/flairNLP/flair/blob/master/resources/docs/embeddings/CLASSIC_WORD_EMBEDDINGS.md.

[4] http://evexdb.org/pmresources/vec-space-models/wikipedia-pubmed-and-PMC-w2v.bin.

[5] https://github.com/cambridgeltl/MTL-Bioinformatics-2016.

Table 2. Comparative evaluation of proposed STM systems against state-of-the-art systems on five NER tasks.

	NCBI-disease	JNLPBA	BC5CDR	BC4CHEMD	BC2GM
STM_LM	86.47	75.17	88.98	89.34	81.66
STM_Flair	87.13	76.81	90.33	–	82.89
Best published					
STM, Wang et al. [27]	83.92	72.17	86.96	88.75	80.00
Collabonet, Yoon et al. [29]	84.69	–	–	88.19	78.56
BiLM, Sachan et al. [25]	87.34	75.03	89.28	–	81.69
FullyNER, Gupta et al. [10]	88.31	76.20	88.64	–	82.06
BioBERT, Lee et al. [16]	–	–	–	91.41	84.40
BioFlair, Sharma and Daniel [24]	–	–	89.42	–	–
TransferSM, Giorgi and Bader [9]	87.66	–	–	88.98	80.65

BC4CHEMD used in BioCreative IV shared task on chemical entity mention recognition. The state-of-the-art is again belongs to Lee et al. [16] with BioBERT system and Watanabe et al. [28] with multi-task paraphrasing neural network model to utilize paraphrase pairs.

BC5CDR used in BioCreative V challenge on chemical and disease mention recognition. The state-of-the-art for STM is obtained by Sharma and Daniel [24] with their BioFlair system. They combined Flair embeddings with ELMo embeddings trained both over the biomedical corpora using the FLair framework. For MTM, we did not find publicly available recent results on 3 class problem.

NCBI-Disease A collection of 793 fully annotated PubMed abstracts obtained by Doğan et al. [8]. It was widely used by researchers and the current state-of-the-art result belongs again to Wang et al. [26] for SMT and for MTM to Zhao et al. [30] with their jointly performed NER and normalization tasks.

JNLPBA is the 2004 year shared task on biomedical entity recognition of wide range of entities (5 classes). The best STM belongs to Gupta et al. [10] who trained their own version of contextualized word embeddings.

2.7 Evaluation Metric

All datasets are provided with training, development and test data. In our experiments, we merge training and development data, shuffle it and select 10% of it for evaluation of results.

We compared all methods in terms of macro-averaged F-score. It is computed as the harmonic mean of precision and recall. Here, precision is computed as the percentage of the predicted entities that are gold ones, and recall as the percentage of the gold entities that are correctly predicted. The exact entity span match is used for evaluation.

Table 3. Comparative evaluation of proposed MTM systems against state-of-the-art systems on five NER tasks.

	NCBI-disease	JNLPBA	BC5CDR	BC4CHEMD	BC2GM
MTM_LM	86.56	76.01	89.33	89.52	81.82
Best published					
MTM, Wang et al. [27]	86.14	73.52	88.78	89.37	80.74
CollabonetMulti, Yoon et al. [29]	86.36	–	–	88.85	79.73
CompParaph, Watanabe et al. [28]	–	–	–	92.57	–
CrossSharing, Wang et al. [26]	86.50	–	–	–	84.40
TransferMM, Giorgi and Bader [9]	86.89	–	–	88.81	79.60
JointNER, Zhao et al. [30]	87.43	–	–	87.63	–

3 Results and Discussion

In this section, we provide details of the NER results for STMs and MTMs. The section is divided into two broad parts – the first presenting the results of the NER task and comparison with other works, and the second providing comparative, selective results over different variants of word embedding stacking and parameter settings.

3.1 NER Results

The experimental results of the baseline models, models with integrated LM-based word embeddings and current state-of-the-art models are provided in Tables 2 and 3, respectively. Table 2 shows the comparison between the existing state-of-the-art STMs and STM of Wang et al. [27] with and without integrated LM-based word embeddings as well as Flair STM trained using the Flair NER framework [1]. For the MTM, in Table 3 we present the comparison of the MTM system of Wang et al. [27] with and without integrated LM-word embeddings and best published MTM systems.

Note that we do not report results on the BC4CHEMD dataset using the Flair NER framework due to limited computation sources (BC4CHEMD dataset is around four times larger than the next largest dataset used in our analysis). Also, it should be noted that some authors solved only binary entity classification problems, i.e. with one biomedical entity to be predicted. In these cases, we do not report results for these evaluations (missing BC5CDR and JNLPBA datasets' result entries).

Overall, for both STM and MTM the NER performances in all cases using Wang et al. [27] model architecture significantly benefit from incorporating additional embeddings with the maximum gain of 2.4% achieved by MTM on the JNLPBA dataset.

Moreover, for STM in all cases *STM_Flair* results outperform *STM_LM* results. It is probably due to the fact that in Flair NER, the default hyperparam-

Table 4. Results of experiments over different combinations of word embeddings

	Combination	F-score
BC2GM	embeddings pubmed	78.96
	embeddings pubmed+pubmed Flair	81.05
	embeddings pubmed+pubmed Flair+bpe	81.66
	embeddings pubmed+ELMo+bpe	81.40
NCBI	embeddings pubmed+pubmed Flair+bpe	86.40
	embeddings pubmed+pubmed Flair+ELMo+bpe	85.10
	embeddings pubmed+ELMo+bpe	86.42
	ELMo+bpe	86.30

Table 5. Case sensitivity of model

	Combination	F-score (caseless)	F-score (case-sensitive)
NCBI	embeddings pubmed+pubmed Flair+bpe	85.46	86.07
BC2GM	embeddings pubmed+pubmed Flair+bpe	80.28	81.66

eters values were more thoughtfully selected and some additional mechanisms of Flair NER model such as learning rate annealing, gradient clipping, etc.

Overall, the constructed STM and MTM achieve higher F1-score than most other models of similar complexity on all datasets.

With relation to *BioBERT*, we can only compare results on BC2GM dataset (1.8% lower) as for BC4CHEMD dataset we did not calculate *STM_Flair* results however *STM_LM* results stand not far from *BioBERT* ones on the BC4CHEMD dataset. This is good results taking into account the complexity of the BERT model (large BERT consists of 24 layers, 1024 hidden layers, and total of 340 M parameters).

3.2 Discussion

Combination of Word Embeddings. We wanted to compare the results over different combinations of word embeddings to evaluate the performance gain while increasing the complexity of embedding layer. The results over two benchmark datasets using the single-task model of Wang et al. [27] are presented in Table 4.

It should be noted that for experiments where Flair embeddings are used we did not fine tune the model, however for ELMo model we fine-tune the model as from our observations fine-tuning for model with ELMo embeddings works the best.

From the results, presented in Table, it could be seen that overall increasing the complexity of word level representation by adding more different types of

Table 6. Results of fine-tuning the model

	Combination	F-score (no fine-tuning)	F-score (fine-tuning)
NCBI	embeddings pubmed+pubmed Flair+bpe	86.40	86.07
	embeddings pubmed+pubmed ELMo+bpe	86.33	86.47

embeddings improves results. However, two complex similarly constructed word embeddings such as ELMo and Flair coupled together in one model deteriorate results. Overall, Flair embeddings usually give on par or better results.

Case Sensitivity. The results of experiments with lower-casing the words and without lower-casing on two benchmark datasets are presented in Table 5.

Lower-casing always positively influences the performance of model. Indeed, many biological terms are upper-cased or start with upper-cased letter. In addition to the formal nature of benchmark datasets, all these requires leaving the textual data "as it is".

Fine Tuning. The results of experiments with and without fine-tuning the model for NCBI dataset are presented in Table 6.

While fine-tuning process works better for ELMo embeddings, it deteriorates results when using Flair embeddings. The reason for that should be investigated further.

4 Conclusion

In this paper, we focused on the problem of biomedical NER. In particular, we attempted to investigate approaches by which LM-based word embeddings can be applied to improve the automatic NER on textual data containing biomedical entities. Our particular focus was on scientific literature texts. Our results strongly suggest that integrating contextualized embeddings and combining them with other types of embeddings can improve sequence labeling accuracy. As such, there is a strong motivation to explore other ways to integrate contextualized information into the current state-of-the-art NER models to further boost their performance. types of advances in language representation such as transformers, etc.

We explored the incorporation of LM-based embeddings in the strong multi-task learning framework. The incorporation of such embeddings has shown to improve the baseline on all tasks. We suggest investigating further the behavior of LM-based embeddings under multi-task learning settings.

Lastly, we conducted a comparative analysis of different model architectures, text preprocessing techniques, and model parameter settings. Simple off-shelf Flair NER architecture turned out giving better performance rather than the more sophisticated architecture of Wang et al. [27]. Preprocessing in terms of lower-casing and fine-tuning the model deteriorates results. However, fine-tuning showed to work well on ELMo embeddings for Wang et al. [27] architecture.

In the future, we would like to explore other combinations of word embeddings and different NN architectures. Moreover, as mostly NER tasks in the biomedical domain are unbalanced problems, future research on improving model parameter settings to handle this problem should improve the results of biomedical sequence labeling as well.

References

1. Akbik, A., Bergmann, T., Blythe, D., Rasul, K., Schweter, S., Vollgraf, R.: FLAIR: an easy-to-use framework for state-of-the-art NLP. In: Proceedings of the 2019 Conference of the North, pp. 54–59. Association for Computational Linguistics, Stroudsburg (2019). https://doi.org/10.18653/v1/N19-4010, http://aclweb.org/anthology/N19-4010
2. Akbik, A., Bergmann, T., Vollgraf, R.: Pooled contextualized embeddings for named entity recognition. In: NAACL (2019). https://github.com/zalandoresearch/flair
3. Akbik, A., Blythe, D., Vollgraf, R.: Contextual string embeddings for sequence labeling. In: COLING (2018). https://github.com/zalandoresearch/flair
4. Bojanowski, P., Grave, E., Joulin, A., Mikolov, T.: Enriching word vectors with subword information. Trans. Assoc. Comput. Linguist. **5**(2307–387X), 135–146 (2017). http://arxiv.org/abs/1607.04606
5. Collobert, R., Weston, J.: A unified architecture for natural language processing, pp. 160–167. Association for Computing Machinery (ACM) (2008). https://doi.org/10.1145/1390156.1390177
6. Deng, L., Hinton, G., Kingsbury, B.: New types of deep neural network learning for speech recognition and related applications: an overview. In: IEEE International Conference on Acoustics, Speech and Signal Processing - Proceedings, ICASSP, pp. 8599–8603, October 2013. https://doi.org/10.1109/ICASSP.2013.6639344, ISBN 9781479903566, ISSN 15206149
7. Devlin, J., Chang, M.W., Lee, K., Toutanova, K.: BERT: pre-training of deep bidirectional transformers for language understanding. arXiv preprint arXiv:1810.04805, October 2018. http://arxiv.org/abs/1810.04805
8. Doğan, R.I., Leaman, R., Lu, Z.: NCBI disease corpus: a resource for disease name recognition and concept normalization. J. Biomed. Inform. **47**, 1–10 (2014). https://doi.org/10.1016/j.jbi.2013.12.006. ISSN 15320464
9. Giorgi, J.M., Bader, G.D.: Towards reliable named entity recognition in the biomedical domain. Bioinformatics **36**(1), 280–286 (2020). https://doi.org/10.1093/bioinformatics/btz504. https://academic.oup.com/bioinformatics/article/36/1/280/5520946, ISSN 1367–4803
10. Gupta, A., Goyal, P., Sarkar, S., Gattu, M.: Fully contextualized biomedical NER. In: Azzopardi, L., Stein, B., Fuhr, N., Mayr, P., Hauff, C., Hiemstra, D. (eds.) ECIR 2019. LNCS, vol. 11438, pp. 117–124. Springer, Cham (2019). https://doi.org/10.1007/978-3-030-15719-7_15
11. Heinzerling, B., Strube, M.: BPEmb: Tokenization-free pre-trained subword embeddings in 275 languages. In: Proceedings of the Eleventh International Conference on Language Resources and Evaluation (LREC 2018), pp. 18–1473 (2018). https://aclweb.org/anthology/papers/L/L18/L18-1473/

12. Huang, Z., Xu, W., Yu, K.: Bidirectional LSTM-CRF Models for Sequence Tagging, August 2015. http://arxiv.org/abs/1508.01991
13. Jin, Q., Dhingra, B., Liu, Z., Cohen, W.W., Lu, X.: PubMedQA: a dataset for biomedical research question answering. In: Proceedings of the 2019 Conference on Empirical Methods in Natural Language Processing and the 9th International Joint Conference on Natural Language Processing, pp. 2567–2577, September 2019. http://arxiv.org/abs/1909.06146
14. Kim, D., et al.: A neural named entity recognition and multi-type normalization tool for biomedical text mining. IEEE Access **7**, 73729–73740 (2019). https://doi.org/10.1109/ACCESS.2019.2920708. https://ieeexplore.ieee.org/document/8730332/, ISSN 2169-3536
15. Lample, G., Ballesteros, M., Subramanian, S., Kawakami, K., Dyer, C.: Neural architectures for named entity recognition. In: Proceedings of the 2016 Conference of the North American Chapter of the Association for Computational Linguistics: Human Language Technologies, pp. 260–270. Association for Computational Linguistics, Stroudsburg (2016). https://doi.org/10.18653/v1/N16-1030, http://aclweb.org/anthology/N16-1030
16. Lee, J., et al.: BioBERT: a pre-trained biomedical language representation model for biomedical text mining. Bioinformatics (btz682) (2019). https://doi.org/10.1093/bioinformatics/xxxxxx, https://github.com/dmis-lab/biobert
17. Liu, L., et al.: Empower sequence labeling with task-aware neural language model, September 2017. http://arxiv.org/abs/1709.04109
18. Liu, S., Johns, E., Davison, A.J.: End-to-End Multi-Task Learning with Attention, March 2018. http://arxiv.org/abs/1803.10704
19. Mikolov, T., Chen, K., Corrado, G., Dean, J.: Distributed representations of words and phrases and their compositionality. In: Advances in neural information processing systems, pp. 3111–3119 (2013). https://arxiv.org/pdf/1310.4546.pdf
20. Pennington, J., Socher, R., Manning, C.D.: GloVe: global vectors for word representation. In: Proceedings of the 2014 Conference on Empirical Methods in Natural Language Processing (EMNLP) (2014). https://nlp.stanford.edu/pubs/glove.pdf
21. Peters, M.E., et al.: Deep contextualized word representations. arXiv preprint arXiv:1802.05365, February 2018. http://arxiv.org/abs/1802.05365
22. Ruder, S.: An overview of multi-task learning in deep neural networks, June 2017. http://arxiv.org/abs/1706.05098
23. Sarkar, P., Ross, K., Ruberto, A.J., Rodenburg, D., Hungler, P., Etemad, A.: Classification of cognitive load and expertise for adaptive simulation using deep multitask learning, July 2019. http://arxiv.org/abs/1908.00385
24. Sharma, S., Daniel, R.: BioFLAIR: pretrained pooled contextualized embeddings for biomedical sequence labeling tasks. arXiv preprint arXiv:1908.05760, August 2019. http://arxiv.org/abs/1908.05760
25. Sachan, D.S., Xie, P., Sachan, M., Xing, E.P.: Effective use of bidirectional language modeling for transfer learning in biomedical named entity recognition. Technical report (2018). https://arxiv.org/pdf/1711.07908.pdf
26. Wang, X., Lyu, J., Dong, L., Xu, K.: Multitask learning for biomedical named entity recognition with cross-sharing structure. BMC Bioinformatics **20**(1), 427 (2019). https://doi.org/10.1186/s12859-019-3000-5. ISSN 14712105
27. Wang, X., et al.: Cross-type biomedical named entity recognition with deep multi-task learning. Bioinformatics **35**(10), 1745–1752 (2018). https://doi.org/10.1093/bioinformatics/xxxxxx. https://github.com/yuzhimanhua/lm-lstm-crf

28. Watanabe, T., Tamura, A., Ninomiya, T., Makino, T., Iwakura, T.: Multi-task learning for chemical named entity recognition with chemical compound paraphrasing. In: Proceedings of the 2019 Conference on Empirical Methods in Natural Language Processing and the 9th International Joint Conference on Natural Language Processing, pp. 6243–6248 (2019). https://pubchem.ncbi.nlm.nih.gov/
29. Yoon, W., So, C.H., Lee, J., Kang, J.: CollaboNet: collaboration of deep neural networks for biomedical named entity recognition (2019). https://doi.org/10.1186/s12859-019-2813-6
30. Zhao, S., Liu, T., Zhao, S., Wang, F.: A Neural multi-task learning framework to jointly model medical named entity recognition and normalization. In: Proceedings of the AAAI Conference on Artificial Intelligence, vol. 33, pp. 817–824 (2019). https://doi.org/10.1609/aaai.v33i01.3301817, https://aaai.org/ojs/index.php/AAAI/article/view/3861, ISSN 2374-3468

Evaluating Mutual Information and Chi-Square Metrics in Text Features Selection Process: A Study Case Applied to the Text Classification in PubMed

José Párraga-Valle[1], Rodolfo García-Bermúdez[1](✉), Fernando Rojas[2], Christian Torres-Morán[1], and Alfredo Simón-Cuevas[3]

[1] Universidad Técnica de Manabí, Portoviejo, Ecuador
pepeparraga74@gmail.com, rodgarberm@gmail.com, christian.torres@fci.edu.ec
[2] Architecture and Technology, CITIC University of Granada, Granada, Spain
frojas@ugr.es
[3] Universidad Tecnológica de la Habana José Antonio Echeverría, Havana, Cuba
asimon@ceis.cujae.edu.cu

Abstract. The aim of this work was to compare the behavior of mutual information and Chi-square as metrics in the evaluation of the relevance of the terms extracted from documents related to "software design" retrieved from PubMed database tested in two contexts: using a set of terms retrieved from the vectorization of the corpus of abstracts and using only the terms retrieved from the vocabulary defined by the IEEE standard ISO/IEC/IEEE 24765. A search was conducted concerning the subject "software" in the last 6 years and we used Medical Subject Headings (Mesh) term "software design" of the articles to label them. Then mutual information and Chi-square metrics were computed as metrics to sort and select features. Chi-square obtained the highest accuracy scores in documents classification by using a multinomial naive Bayes classifier. Although these results suggest that Chi-square is better than mutual information in feature relevance estimation in the context of this work, further research is necessary to obtain a consistent foundation of this conclusion.

Keywords: Software design · Features selection · Natural language processing · Chi-square · Mutual information

1 Introduction

Feature selection is a fundamental step in document classification, usually it is necessary to reduce the length of term vectors obtained from a corpus of documents. The excess of non relevant terms used as input features for the classifiers increases the computational costs and reduce the performance of the classification [2].

I. Rojas et al. (Eds.): IWBBIO 2020, LNBI 12108, pp. 636–646, 2020.
https://doi.org/10.1007/978-3-030-45385-5_57

Filter models are usual techniques for this reduction of the dimensionality, they have less computation costs than other methods by evaluating only the association between a feature and the class [1]. These filters are based on the evaluation of the relevance of the feature by using some known metric in order to select a more convenient features subset for classification. Scoring values can be computed directly from terms and documents frequencies, among the most employed are term frequency, term frequency-inverse document frequency (TF-IDF) and term strength (TS). Also those based on information theory [3][2], among them Chi-squared can be useful to estimate statistical independence of a feature with respect to the class of a document [5], another metric widely used is the mutual information, which measures the mutual dependency between a feature and a class [10]. Related to probabilistic approaches to the feature selection, other indexes have been used. They include the so called "ambiguity measure" based on the confidence that a document belongs to only one class [8], also "information gain" which defines the information associated to the presence or not of a term. Also vocabulary based vectorization has been used to limit the dimensionality of the terms used as features [5].

Multinomial classifiers are based on term frequency and the basic naive Bayes assumption of independence of them respecting to their position and context in documents [7]. They have shown to have good results in document information retrieval tasks, consistent results in accuracy were achieved in classification on the Ling-spam corpus [1]. Also in sentiment analysis in hotel reviews, in a work where also two approaches to feature selection are compared [4]. These classifiers have been used also in automatic identification of argument structures in text documents [9], and they found that stop word removal produced an important decreasing in the classifier accuracy.

PubMed is a bibliographic database of health information that provides advanced search capabilities in more than 28 million articles in 2018 [11]. Relevant efforts are made in PubMed in order to offer a consistent classification of documents by means of the Medical Subject Headings (MeSH), assigned to each document by human indexers of the National Library of Medicine of the United States. The structured hierarchy of MeSH terms allows to estimate relationships between the subject headings [6].

The aim of this work was to compare the behavior of mutual information and Chi-square as metrics in the evaluation of the relevance of the terms extracted from documents related to "software design" retrieved from PubMed database tested in two contexts: using a set of terms retrieved from the vectorization of the corpus of abstracts and using only the terms retrieved from the vocabulary defined by the IEEE standard ISO/IEC/IEEE 24765.

2 Materials and Methods

2.1 Obtention of the Corpus from the Abstracts

In this work the corpus of documents was conformed from a bibliographic search carried out in PubMed, a database maintained by the National Center for Biotechnology Information (https://www.ncbi.nlm.nih.gov/pubmed/).

The search was performed by using the search strings S1 and S2 as seen in Table 1. As a result a PubMed structured XML file was obtained for each search. After a filtering step excluding the articles with no abstract, 877 documents were retrieved for S1 and 112288 documents for S2.

Table 1. Pubmed searches

Nr.	Search string
S1	(software) AND ("2018/01/01" [*Date – Publication*] : "2018/12/31" [*Date – Publication*])) AND software design [*MeSHTerms*]
S2	(software) AND ("2018/01/01" [*Date – Publication*] : "2018/12/31" [*Date – Publication*])) NOT software design [*MeSHTerms*]

Every document in the XML file is composed by a hierarchy of the fields usually found as part of scientific contributions. We have used the field corresponding to "Abstract". This field is an structured summary of the article, it includes the labels "ISSUE ADDRESSED", "BACKGROUND", "METHODS", "RESULTS" and "CONCLUSIONS".

The MeSH term "software design" was considered as a gold standard to label all the documents resulting from the search S1 as belonging to this class and those from S2 as not member of the class. This dataset was then balanced by means of a random sampling of the majority class, to equal its size to the minority class, resulting in a balanced corpus of 1754 documents, all of them related to software, but with equally amounts of them labeled by human experts as belonging or not to the class "software design" in its TermMesh attribute.

2.2 Vocabulary Retrieval

The glossary of terms we used in the further documents processing was the "ISO/IEC/IEEE 24765:2017(E) Systems and software engineering—Vocabulary. Second edition 2017-09". This is a glossary supported by a joint technical committee of ISO (the International Organization for Standardization) and IEC (the International Electrotechnical Commission) aiming to provide standard definitions for the terms related to the systems and software engineering.

In total 4633 terms are contained in a non structured pdf document. Repeated terms, abbreviations or clarifications of other related terms were present, so it was necessary to make the conversion of the document to a text format, the extraction of terms and the elimination of repeated term, abbreviations and other non useful information.

The entire process of experimentation was carried out using Python 3.7 in Jupyter Notebooks 5.5.0 as part of Anaconda integrated development environment. Below a detailed description of the experiments is given.

2.3 Detailed Description of the Experiments

1. Description of the bibliographic search
   (a) Database: Pubmed (https://www.ncbi.nlm.nih.gov/pubmed/)
   (b) Date: January 8, 2018
   (c) Search strings: S1 and S2 (see Sect. 2.1 above)
   (d) Search results were exported to single XML file
2. Corpus pre-processing
   (a) Conversion of the XML file to Pandas dataframe
   (b) Documents with no abstract were excluded
   (c) Segmentation of documents into sentences
   (d) Elimination of stop words, numbers and punctuation signs
3. Extraction and cleaning of the phrases of the glossary ("Systems and software engineering-Vocabulary. ISO/IEC/IEEE 24765:2017(E)")
   (a) Conversion of the file from portable document format (PDF) to plain text format
   (b) Extraction of terms and phrases
   (c) Elimination of abbreviations and clarifications (enclosed in parenthesis)
   (d) Elimination of duplicated items, some abbreviations have the terms they represent enclosed in parenthesis causing they appear more than once
   (e) Identification of items composed by more than one term and its encapsulation as an unique item
   (f) Manual classification of items whether they belong or not to the phase of analysis and design in software engineering
4. Computation of the features from the corpus of documents
   (a) Vectorization of the documents by means of scikit-learn feature extraction functions CountVectorizer (term frequency) and TfidfVectorizer (term frequency-inverse document frequency) using no vocabulary
   (b) Vocabulary based vectorization of the documents by means of the same methods above. As dictionary we used the glossary "Systems and software engineering-Vocabulary. ISO/IEC/IEEE 24765:2017(E)"
5. Processing of the features
   (a) Ranking of features based on their values of Chi-square respecting to the class of the document
   (b) Ranking of features based on their values of mutual information respecting to the class of the document
6. Comparison of the results of a multinomial naive Bayes classifier by using incremental subsets of ordered features

3 Experimental Results

3.1 Processing of the Corpus with No Vocabulary

The first processing did not consider the use of vocabulary. Vectorization of the corpus identified a total quantity of 20505 terms from 1749 documents. We selected term frequency (TF) and term frequency - inverse document frequency (TF-IDF) as features for all the further processing. Many terms were present only in a few documents or even in only one, while a few terms had significant higher frequencies causing that most of the values got for every metric are zero. The result is then a very sparse matrix, with a huge number of columns (features) in relation to the number of rows (documents).

Figure 1 plots the distribution and the cumulative of frequencies of the number of documents containing every term identified by vectorization. As seen in the graph, the distribution is close to normal. Cumulative graph shows that over 80% of the terms appears in less than 110 documents.

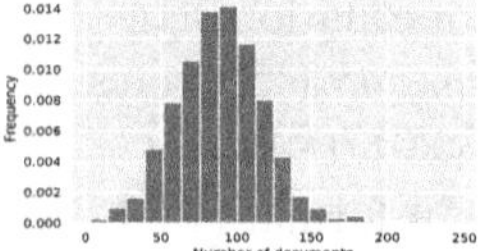

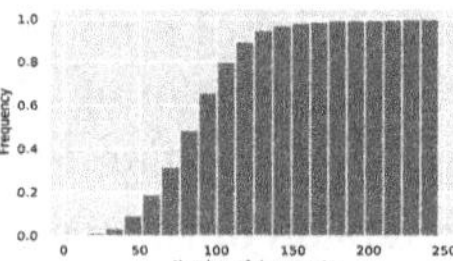

Fig. 1. Distribution (left) and cumulative (right) of the number of documents containing every term with no vocabulary

Concerning TF and TF-IDF, Fig. 2 shows also histograms resembling normal distributions of frequencies of the mean of every term. The p-values for Shapiro test were 0.029 for TF and 0.03 for TF-IDF, so they confirmed their normality.

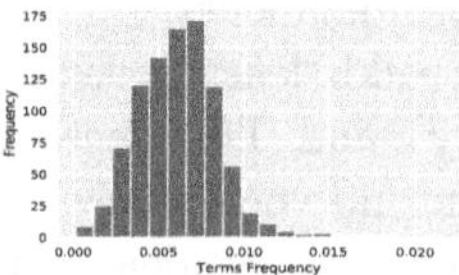

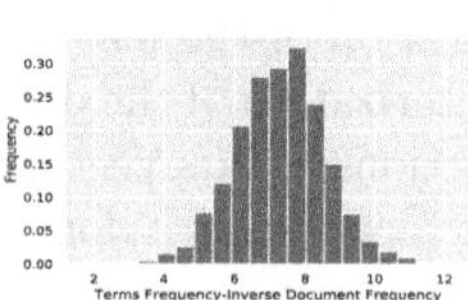

Fig. 2. Distribution of the mean of TF (left) and TF-IDF (right) of every term with no vocabulary

The next step was to compute the values of Chi-square and mutual information as estimators of the relevance of the values of TF and TF-IDF of every term in the corpus of documents.

The scatter plots of Chi-square versus mutual information shown in Fig. 3 clearly reveal the presence of no correlation between both estimators, computed for TF (left) and TF-IDF (right).

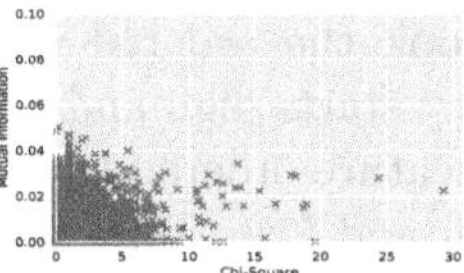
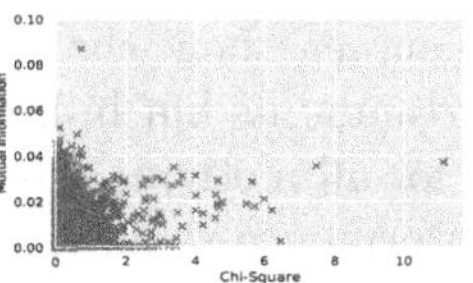

Fig. 3. Scatter plot of Chi-square vs Mutual information for TF (left) and TF-IDF (right) with no vocabulary

3.2 Classification Results with No Vocabulary

We ordered the terms in correspondence to the values of Chi-square and mutual information to use either bins of 20 or the correspondent cumulative amounts of features for classification, aiming to evaluate how the different strategies to select features affect the results of the classifier. To get the accuracy, we trained the classifier with 10-fold cross validation and used its mean as metrics. As we expected, the accuracy of the multinomial naive Bayes classifier behaved with significant differences according to the strategy used to order the terms. Figures 4 and 5 show the accuracy obtained for every case.

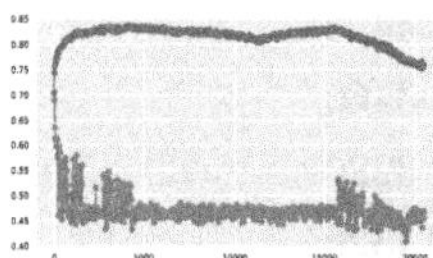
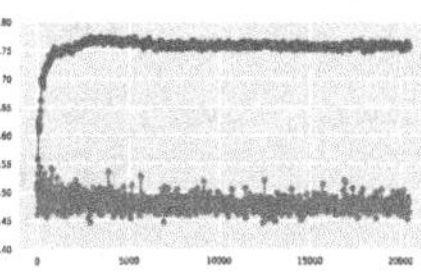

Fig. 4. Accuracy of the classifier, by using TF as feature with the terms ordered by Chi-square (left) and mutual information (right). Features were taken in bins of 20 (green) or the correspondent cumulative quantities (red) (Color figure online)

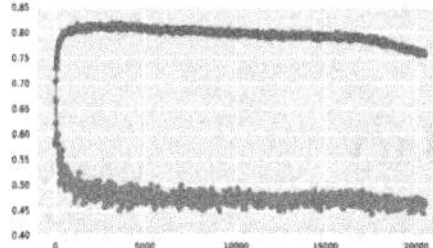
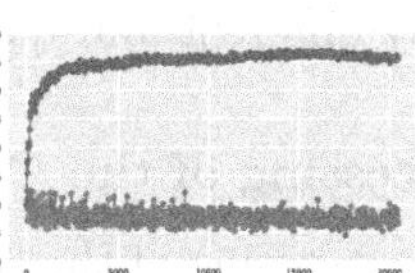

Fig. 5. Accuracy of the classifier, by using TF-IDF as feature with the terms ordered by Chi-square (left) and mutual information (right). Features were taken in bins of 20 (green) or the correspondent cumulative quantities (red) (Color figure online)

These graphs show that Chi-square performs better than mutual information by having a faster curve to achieve the maximum of the accuracy, and this maximum is greater than we got with mutual information. In consequence, a lower quantity of features are necessary to get a similar performance.

Green curves show the accuracy when we took the ordered features not cumulative amounts but in bunches of 20. Accuracy starts high and consistently decreased for all methods, except for TF used as feature ordered by Chi-square, with a performance some erratic by showing high and low values intercalated, with three zones more disturbed by this. The first just at the beginning, the second after a short zona less disturbed and a third one at the last part of the graph, corresponding to the worst-rated terms.

This conduct is showing a certain fail of Chi-square as metric to rank the relevance when term frequency is the descriptor of the terms. It also causes the oscillation observed in accuracy when the classifier uses cumulative amounts of the bunches of 20 terms. We observed the cumulative (red) curve shows the highest zones when the green curve is more disturbed (Fig. 4). However, Table 2 shows Chi-square behaved as a better score than mutual information to sort the terms, by achieving greater maximum values of accuracy for both TF (0.84 for the first 4420 terms) and TF-IDF (0.82 for the first 3220 terms).

Table 2. The maximum values and the amount of terms necessaries to achieve it with no vocabulary

Metric	Ordering	Max	Terms
TF	Chi-square	0.84	4420
	Mutual Inf.	0.77	3460
TF-IDF	Chi-square	0.82	3220
	Mutual Inf.	0.77	14320

Shapiro tests yielded results of non-normality for the distribution of the accuracy score of the multinomial naive Bayes classifier for every sorting strategy of the features TF and TF-IDF. So no-parametric Wilcoxon test was used to make the comparisons between different approaches. In all the cases the p-values were very close to 0, so we consistently concluded the results for every method were significantly different and not because of the chance.

3.3 Processing of the Corpus with Vocabulary

After this processing of the corpus by using no vocabulary we tested how well it could perform an approach based on the use of 4674 terms retrieved from a spe-

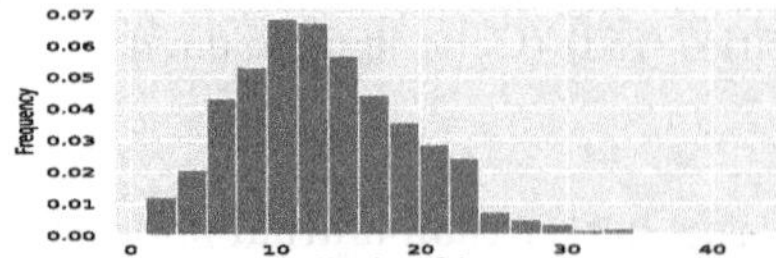

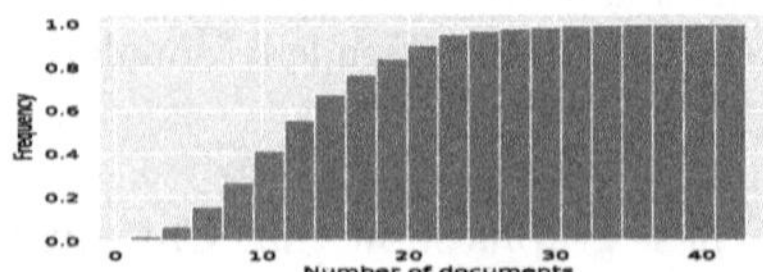

Fig. 6. Distribution (left) and cumulative (right) of the number of documents containing every term with vocabulary

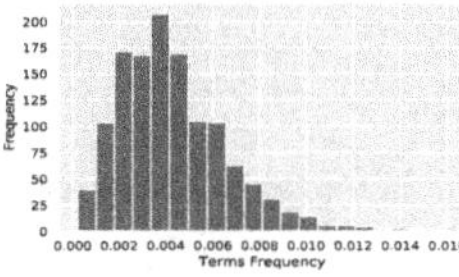

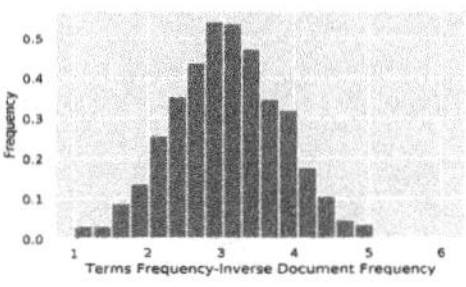

Fig. 7. Distribution of the mean of TF (left) and TF-IDF (right) of every term with vocabulary

cialized vocabulary aiming to reduce the amount of terms without a significant lost of the accuracy.

The histogram of Fig. 6 shows a normal distribution of the amount of documents where every term appears, some similar as we got with vocabulary concerning the number of documents containing every term identified by vectorization without the use of a dictionary, although in this case the distribution seems to be more skewed. As seen in the graph, the distribution is also close to normal, and cumulative graph shows that over 80% of the terms appears in 20 documents or fewer.

TF and TF-IDF, Fig. 7 shows also histograms resembling normal distributions of frequencies of the mean of every term. The p-values for Shapiro test were 0.019 for TF and 0.022 for TF-IDF, so they confirmed their normality.

3.4 Chi-Square and Mutual Information with Vocabulary

We computed again Chi-square and mutual information for the reduced subset of terms of the vocabulary. The scatter plots of them show, as with no vocabulary, the lack of correlation between both estimators, computed for TF (left) and TF-IDF (right) (Fig. 8).

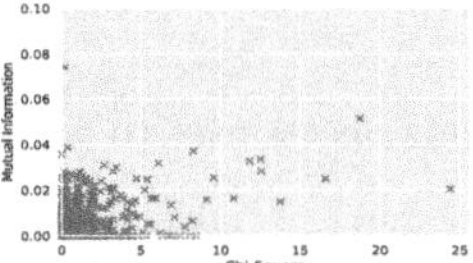

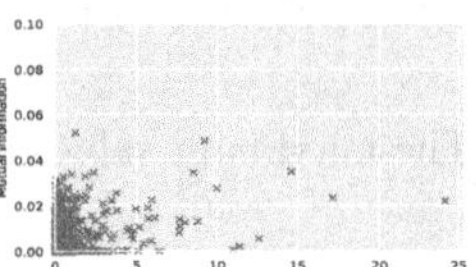

Fig. 8. Scatter plot of Chi-square vs Mutual information for TF (left) and TF-IDF (right) with vocabulary

We ordered again the terms of the vocabulary in correspondence to the values of Chi-square or mutual information grouped in bins of 20, then we computed the results of the classifier for every bunch of 20 terms or the correspondent cumulative amounts of terms, aiming to assess how the different strategies to select features affect these results.

To get the accuracy, we trained the classifier with 10-fold cross validation and used its mean as metrics. As it happened with no vocabulary, the accuracy of the

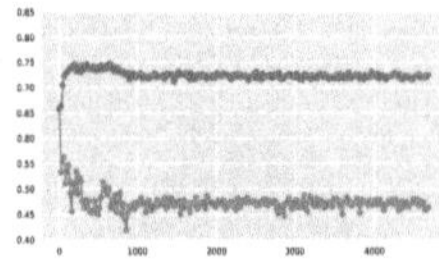

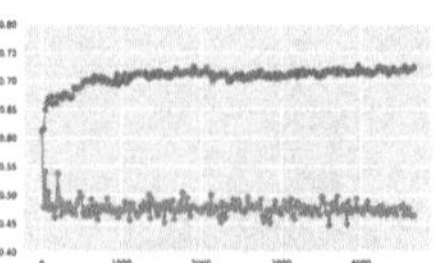

Fig. 9. Accuracy of the classifier, by using TF as feature with the terms ordered by Chi-square (left) and mutual information (right). Features were taken in bins of 20 (green) or the correspondent cumulative quantities (red) (Color figure online)

multinomial naive Bayes classifier behaved with significant differences according to the strategy used to order the terms (Figs. 9 and 10).

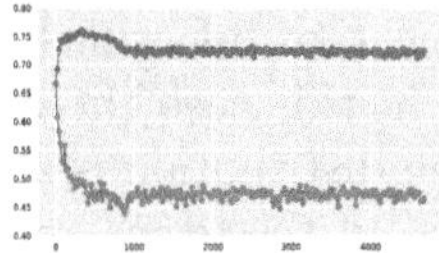

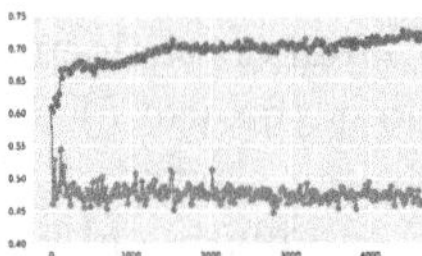

Fig. 10. Accuracy of the classifier, by using TF-IDF as feature with the terms ordered by Chi-square (left) and mutual information (right). Features were taken in bins of 20 (green) or the correspondent cumulative quantities (red) (Color figure online)

These graphs show that again Chi-square performs better than mutual information by having a faster curve to achieve the maximum of the accuracy, and this maximum is greater than we got with mutual information. The curves of the terms taken in bunches of 20 show a more consistent behaviour than those got with no vocabulary.

We got the maximum values of the accuracy when used Chi-square just with only 360 terms for TF-IDF (0.76) and 660 terms (0.75) when we used TF as the feature for classification (Table 3).

Table 3. The maximum values and the amount of terms necessaries to achieve it with vocabulary

Metric	Ordering	Max	Terms
TF	Chi-square	0.75	660
	Mutual Inf.	0.73	3980
TF-IDF	Chi-square	0.76	360
	Mutual Inf.	0.73	4420

As occurred with the no vocabulary approach, in this case also Shapiro tests yielded results of non-normality for the distribution of the accuracy score, and no-parametric Wilcoxon tests yielded p-values very close to 0, supporting then that the results for every method were significantly different.

3.5 Comparing Vocabulary and No Vocabulary Approaches

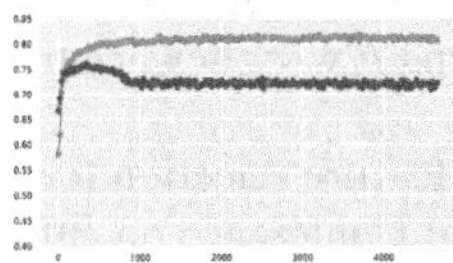

Fig. 11. Accuracy of the classifier, by using TF-IDF as feature with the terms ordered by Chi-square with no vocabulary (green) and with vocabulary (red). Features were taken cumulative bunches of 20 terms (red) (Color figure online)

Figure 11 shows the accuracy by using Chi-square computed from TF-IDF for both approaches, with and without a vocabulary for the first 4674 terms (the amount of terms retrieved from the dictionary). It is perceptible the better performance with no vocabulary. Its curve is running above for all the interval, with no significant disturbances. The maximum value of accuracy (0.82) is achieved with the first 3220 terms, very close to the highest value of 0.84 achieved by Chi-square computed from TF with 4420 terms and a more erratic behavior.

4 Conclusions

We have tested the use of Chi-square and mutual information as relevance metrics to retrieve documents related to the software design in Pubmed database, a huge set of documents labeled by human experts in a hierarchy of concepts given by MesH classification. Our experiments show that concerning feature selection Chi-square overcomes mutual information in all the tests we performed. Using a dictionary did not improve as we expected the results, neither allowing to achieve a higher accuracy nor to decrease the number or terms necessary to get the best accuracy. Despite of the "Systems and software engineering vocabulary" is a formal standard developed by a specialized board of theIEEE, we observed that this dictionary includes a lot of terms directly related to software design that are not specific only for this discipline. In our understanding it is a possiblecause of this result. But the use of the feature selection based on Chi-square allowed a consistent reduction of dimensionality that overcomes the reduction of terms achieved by the use of the dictionary.

Further work is necessary to asses more sophisticated features than term frequency and term frequency-inverse document frequency and also other methods to rank features not only considering their individual relevance but also when subsets of features are considered.

References

1. Cai, J., Luo, J., Wang, S., Yang, S.: Feature selection in machine learning: a new perspective. Neurocomputing **300**, 70–79 (2018). https://doi.org/10.1016/J.NEUCOM.2017.11.077. https://www.sciencedirect.com/science/article/pii/S0925231218302911
2. Chandra, A.: Comparison of feature selection for imbalance text datasets. In: Proceedings of 2019 International Conference on Information Management and Technology, ICIMTech, August 2019, vol. 1, pp. 68–72 (2019). https://doi.org/10.1109/ICIMTech.2019.8843773
3. Deng, X., Li, Y., Weng, J., Zhang, J.: Feature selection for text classification: a review. Multimedia Tools and Applications **78**(3), 3797–3816 (2018). https://doi.org/10.1007/s11042-018-6083-5. http://link.springer.com/10.1007/s11042-018-6083-5
4. Farisi, A.A., Sibaroni, Y., Faraby, S.A.: Sentiment analysis on hotel reviews using multinomial Naive Bayes classifier. J. Phys: Conf. Ser. **1192**, 12024 (2019). https://doi.org/10.1088/1742-6596/1192/1/012024. https://doi.org/10.1088%2F1742-6596%2F1192%2F1%2F012024
5. Forman, G.: An extensive empirical study of feature selection metrics for text classification. J. Mach. Learn. Res. **3**, 1289–1305 (2003). http://dl.acm.org/citation.cfm?id=944919.944974
6. Mao, Y., Lu, Z.: Mesh now: automatic mesh indexing at pubmed scale via learning to rank. J. Biomed. Semant. **8**(1), 15 (2017). https://doi.org/10.1186/s13326-017-0123-3
7. McCallum, A., Nigam, K.: A comparison of event models for Naive Bayes text classification (1998)
8. Mengle, S.S., Goharian, N.: Using ambiguity measure feature selection algorithm for support vector machine classifier. In: Proceedings of the 2008 ACM symposium on Applied computing, pp. 916–920 (2008)
9. Rohman, H.N., Asror, I.: Automatic detection of argument components in text using multinomial Nave Bayes clasiffier. J. Phys: Conf. Ser. **1192**, 12034 (2019). https://doi.org/10.1088/1742-6596/1192/1/012034. https://doi.org/10.1088%2F1742-6596%2F1192%2F1%2F012034
10. Sulaiman, M.A., Labadin, J.: Feature selection based on mutual information. In: 2015 9th International Conference on IT in Asia (CITA), pp. 1–6. IEEE, August 2015. https://doi.org/10.1109/CITA.2015.7349827, http://ieeexplore.ieee.org/document/7349827/
11. Tran, T., Kavuluru, R.: Distant supervision for treatment relation extraction by leveraging mesh subheadings. Artif. Intell. Med. **98**, 18–26 (2019). https://doi.org/10.1016/j.artmed.2019.06.002. http://www.sciencedirect.com/science/article/pii/S0933365718304913

Profiling Environmental Conditions from DNA

Sambriddhi Mainali[1(✉)], Max H. Garzon[1(✉)], and Fredy A. Colorado[2]

[1] Computer Science, University of Memphis, Memphis, TN 38152, USA
{smainali,mgarzon}@memphis.edu
[2] Biology, National University of Colombia, Bogotá, Colombia
facoloradog@unal.edu.co

Abstract. DNA is quintessential to carry out basic functions by organisms as it encodes information necessary for metabolomics and proteomics, among others. In particular, it is common nowadays to use DNA for profiling living organisms based on their phenotypic traits. These traits are the outcomes of the genetic makeup constrained by the interaction between living organisms and their surrounding environment over time. For environmental conditions, however, the conventional assumption is that they are too random and ephemeral to be encoded in the DNA of an organism. Here, we demonstrate that, to the contrary, genomic DNA may also encode sufficient information about some environmental features of an organism's habitat for a machine learning model to reveal them, although there seem to be exceptions, i.e. some environmental features do not appear to be coded in DNA, unless our methods miss that information. Nevertheless, we demonstrate that these features can be used to train better models for better predictions of other environmental factors. These results lead directly to the question of whether over evolutionary history, DNA itself is actually also a repository of information related to the environment where the lineage has developed, perhaps even more cryptically than the way it encodes phenotypic information.

Keywords: Noncrosshybridizing DNA chips · Genotype · Phenotype · Environmental conditions · Deep neural networks · Machine learning · Simuliidae · *A. thaliana*

1 Introduction

It is well known that, as the blueprint of life, DNA encodes for critical information required to develop and sustain life in each living organism (e.g., protein synthesis and self-organization) due to its hybridization properties [29]. In particular, it plays a major role in determining the morphological and metabolic behaviors of an organism. For example, genes BRCA1 and BRCA2 cause as many as 60% of all cases of hereditary breast and ovarian cancers in female *Homo sapiens* [6]. Further research has demonstrated that DNA hybridization can be leveraged to solve computational problems, for instance, its capability to serve as a substrate for molecular computers [1] and intelligent self-assembly of complex materials [24, 25].

More recently, models of the so-called DNA spaces of oligonucleotides [9, 10] have led to the discovery of a deep structure in DNA that made possible a next

I. Rojas et al. (Eds.): IWBBIO 2020, LNBI 12108, pp. 647–658, 2020.
https://doi.org/10.1007/978-3-030-45385-5_58

generation family of microarrays [9] to enable significant reductions in the dimensionality of genomic sequences into very compact but informationally rich features (so-called genomic signatures).

That have been effectively used to reproduce *ab-initio* standard biological phylogenies [10, 11, 13] from DNA sequences alone, without recourse to sequence alignments or morphological information. In fact, in a further step, we have shown that they can also be used to predict phenotypic features of an organism from DNA sequences alone [19] up to and excluding environmental conditions. We were able to predict the phenotypic features such as the *area* and *spot pattern* of the cephalic apotome and the *area of postgenal clefts* of blackfly larvae with relative error less than 15%, as well as the *life span* of *Arabidopsis thaliana* with relative error about 20%. In this work, we extend these results to demonstrate that DNA appears to be encoding even for environmental conditions where the expression of the genomic sequence into an organism took place, such as location (latitude, longitude) and average temperature.

This conclusion appears to be somewhat surprising since, according to the Darwinian theory of evolution, life on earth appears to be essentially determined by the occurrence of random phenomena, such as mutations and their consequent changes given a genotype and environmental conditions. The relative contribution of these components to a given organism has remained a matter of debate since the discovery of DNA [29]. But one cannot deny the fact that interaction between any given organism and its environment might be the outcome of rapid evolution (punctuated equilibrium) or the result of long-time evolution (gradualism) [7, 23, 26] as restricted by biological, chemical and physical conditions [4]. This adaptation/selection through the evolutionary process could be addressed by some mechanisms, such as natural selection, genetic drift, mass extinctions and adaptive radiations, among others. All these processes point towards the exceptional capacity of DNA as a memory structure of past and even present events witnessed by any given organism. Even more surprisingly, DNA molecules might be used to predict (at least with reasonable probability) the location of a species using Species Distribution Models (SDM) (hypothesizing the occurrence of species at unexplored areas on top of previously sampled areas). This is an important advance given that field work is expensive [8, 15], not to mention that such models can become a powerful tool to predict migrations and new habitats of species in a dynamic planet, where global warming is a major new player to reckon with [17]. Thus, it is at least conceivable that DNA might also keep temporal and spatial information like a "living storage device".

Darwin's evolutionary theory is well-supported by broad evidence in diverse areas, particularly genetics, as variations (genotypes) that are better adapted to given environment have a higher reproductive rate (number of fertile descendants) and their genomes become more represented (fixed) in each generation. Biologists have often interpreted the individual-environment relationship within this framework (environment selecting individuals), but in the context of DNA as a "living storage device". However, this line of reasoning leads directly into the question of whether DNA itself is actually storing information related to the environment where the lineage has developed, perhaps even more cryptically than the way it encodes phenotypic information. It is our purpose below to show evidence that this may be indeed the case.

2 Theoretical Framework for GenISs

A GenIS can be informally described as a universal coordinate system to extract few but information rich features from an arbitrary genomic sequence to reduce the dimension of the sequence (like over 600 nucleotides to 3D or 4D feature vectors as shown in Figs. 1 (right) and 2), along with a set of workflows to answer questions about the original organism based on those features alone. In prior work, we demonstrated that they can be used to build phylogenetic hypotheses nearly identical to standard biological phylogenies for bacteria [11] and to solve the problem of species identification of 80 strains representing 16 different species of very common hospital-acquired infections [12] using alignment-free methods on next generation microarrays (so-called nxh chips), as described in [10]. The theoretical background defining these bases have been already discussed in these sources. Nonetheless, we summarize these findings next in order to make this paper self-contained.

The design in nxh chips is based on the theoretical foundation set by a metric called hybridization (h-) distance, introduced in [14] and computed as illustrated in Fig. 1. (left) below. It is known that the h-distance affords a good approximation of the Gibbs energy of duplex formation [9].

Definition 1 (Hybridization distance, h-distance).

A *pmer* consists of an oligomer (n-mer, $n > 0$) and its Watson-Crick (WC) complement. A DNA space D_n consists of all pmers of length n. The h-distance $|xy|$ between a pair of pmers x, y in D_n is defined as the minimum of the h-measures, $h(x,y)$ and $h(x,y')$ between x and y, and x and y', where y' is the WC-complement of y and $h(x, y)$ is computed as follows:

1. align x and y^r (y reversed) in $2n - 1$ alignments shifted by k characters, $-n < k < n$;
2. count the total number c_k of WC complementary mismatches between facing nucleotide pairs (single nucleotides are counted as mismatches);
3. compute the h-measure $h(x,y) = min_k\{c_k\}$.

Table 1. Noncrossbhybridizing (nxh) bases, their total number of probes, their length and their hybridization threshold, used to compute genomic signatures.

Basis	Probe length	Probes	τ
3mE4b-2	3	4	1.1
4mP3-3	4	3	2.1

The h-distance was used in [11] to introduce a family of GenISs afforded by noncrosshybridizing (nxh) bases, as shown in Table 1. A n $\times$ h basis can be defined as a set of pmers of the same length n obtained after a judicious selection so that, ideally, it contains a sufficient number of oligos to guarantee that every random n-mer of the same length n in any target will hybridize with exactly one pmer (a basis oligo or its complement) in the set. Such a basis can then be used to arrange multiple copies of the oligo and their WC-complements in bundles (the probes) on a microarray chip (with a minimal separation on the chip so that none of the WC pairs hybridize with one another). Under appropriate reaction conditions (as determined by a stringency threshold τ), any genomic sequence of arbitrary length can be reduced to a feature vector x that can be processed as shown in Fig. 1 (right) to enable efficient computational analysis about the original source organism from the feature vector. The process was simulated using Perl and Python scripts for this paper, although it could be performed *in vitro* as well for longer sequences.

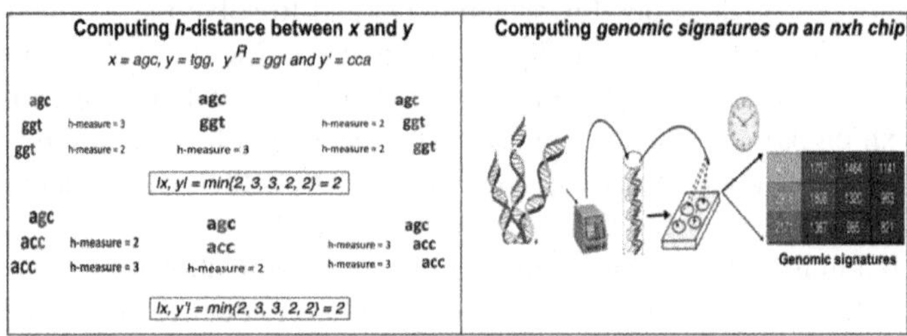

Fig. 1. (Left) Workflow for computing h-distances $|xy|$ [9] and (Right) for computing a genomic signature counting the number of hybridizing fragments in a sequence x to the probes on an nxh chip. The sequence x is shredded to obtain fragments of the same length as the probes (e.g., using sonication). After some relaxation time, a signal from each probe can be read for the components of a genomic signature.

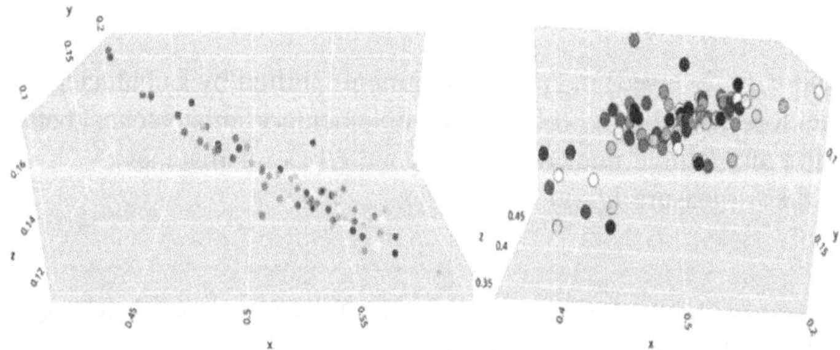

Fig. 2. Genomic signatures of specimens in sample A83 for *A. thaliana* on nxh basis 3mE4b-2 (left) and basis 4mP3-3 (right). The dimension of the signatures is the number of probes used in basis. For instance, the signatures on basis 3mE4b-2 are four dimensional vectors and the fourth dimension is coded by size of the dots/circles (although there is little variation).

3 Data Collection and Methods

In this section, we discuss the details about the data collection and the methodologies used in the models below for predicting latitude, longitude and temperature for a specimen in three samples. We also briefly discuss the methods used for the quality assessment of our proposed models.

3.1 Data Collection

Three data samples were selected to assess the quality of the models, as shown in Table 2. For *A. thaliana*, we extracted partial genomes of 83 specimens from the 1001 genome project [30] and the respective information about their habitat from the supplementary materials provided in [27]. Similarly, we used a dataset containing 46 larvae specimens in blackfly, that were curated for [5], along with their respective habitat information. The sequences we used in this sample were partial *Cytochrome c oxidase subunit I* (COI). Table 3 shows the corresponding features of the habitat where these specimens were grown. We introduced some randomization in the two samples in Table 2 in order to construct two larger samples to increase the generalization ability of the models trained on them. The details about the randomization of these samples are discussed below with the results.

Table 2. Description of data samples for predicting environmental features consisting of DNA for *A. thaliana* and blackfly in Simuliidae. The field observations about environmental conditions for Simuliidae were recorded by the authors for the research reported in the source.

ID	Organism	# of Specimens	Sequences	Source
A83	*A. thaliana*	83	Partial genomes	[30]
A2656	*A. thaliana*	2656	Partial genomes	[30]
S46	Simuliidae (blackfly)	46	Partial COIs	[5]
S1216	Simuliidae (blackfly)	1216	Partial COIs	[5]

Table 3. Description of environmental features defining the habitat of the specimens along with the working definition used in their collection.

Features	Sample	Feature description
Latitudes (degrees) (Standard deviation (std) on A83 = 5.58, S46 = 1.36)	A83, A2656, S1216	The angular distance of the location (where a specimen grew) north of the earth's equator
Longitudes (degrees) (Std on A83 = 16.63, on S46 = 0.83)		The angular distance of the location (where a specimen grew) west of the prime meridian
Annual Mean temperature (°C) (std = 3.19)	A83, A2656	Annual mean temperature of the location where a specimen grew
Temperature (°C) (std = 1.52)	S1216	Temperature of the location at the time and day where a specimen of blackfly was found
Isothermal (std = 0.42)	A83, A2656	A derived feature obtained as *(Mean of monthly (max temp – min temp))/(Max Temp of warmest month – Min Temp of coldest month) * 100*
Annual Precipitation (AnPn) (mm) (std = 253.46)		Annual precipitation of the location where a specimen grew

3.2 Predicting Environmental Features

For a predictive model, we trained deep neural networks to estimate certain environmental conditions in the organisms' habitats, namely latitude, longitude and average temperature during their lifetime. Deep neural networks do not require hardwired feature selection but can be fine-tuned using a learning algorithm. These networks are based on an extreme approach that a learning model can extract all necessary features from data itself with no assumption being made about the underlying domain.

Recent literature shows that learning everything directly from the data might not always lead to an effective learning algorithm, especially when data is limited, has low quality, or the labels of the data change with time [20]. This finding has been addressed by integrating some domain knowledge to statistical/machine learning models in order to increase their efficiency and effectiveness [18, 22, 28, 31]. Hence, in this paper, features extracted by the $n \times h$ basis from the sequences defining the specimens afford some domain knowledge for deep networks as an appropriate solution in order to predict environmental features, as will become evident below.

We experimented with several neural network topologies with layers of various sizes following common heuristics [16] and using the machine learning package h2o [3] available in R. The simplest architectures with NN[m k 1] neurons giving better predictions for all two GenISs are reported in Figs. 3, 4, 5, 6 7 in the Results section. These models were trained using genomic signatures as predictors in 70% of the data corpus from each sample and were then tested and validated using the remaining data points, held out during the training phase. As is customary in the field for continuous variables, the performance of these networks was assessed using the measure of the deviation of the predictions from the actual observations given by relative error (RE) in the specimens in each sample i.e.

$$RE = \frac{|Observed\ Value - Predicted\ Value|}{Observed\ Value}$$

We have used average RE as a metric for the quality assessment in this paper. In other words, *a model is considered to be good enough if the average RE given by the model is less than the standard deviation* of the actual observations.

4 Results

We first trained a network to predict the latitude of the habitat where a specimen in the data set A83 grew using genomic signatures as predictors. We found that these models predicted the latitudes with average relative error about 0.09 (9%) on the training dataset and about 0.10 (10%) on the testing dataset. We observed that these scores are below the standard deviation in the actual observations, which is about 5.58, as shown in Fig. 3 (left side). Similar kinds of results were obtained for the networks predicting the features longitudes and annual mean temperatures, as shown in Fig. 3 (middle) and (right). It did not go unnoticed to us that there were only 83 specimens in the sample, so it was still possible that these networks may not be robust enough, i.e. they might lack generalization ability. To address this issue, we randomized the data set and obtained a sample A2656 with 2656 data points by mutating the sequence for each specimen 32 times with a rate typical for this species, about 4%. Likewise, we randomized the environmental features such that each observation for each specimen was used to generate 32 observations with a normal distribution with the same mean and standard deviation as the observed values in the original specimen(s) for data set A83. Now, it is possible that these features might not follow a normal distribution in the actual population. The same type of networks produced similar predictions with the data generated with a uniform distribution with the similar parameters implying that they will be able to scale to the actual distribution in the population.

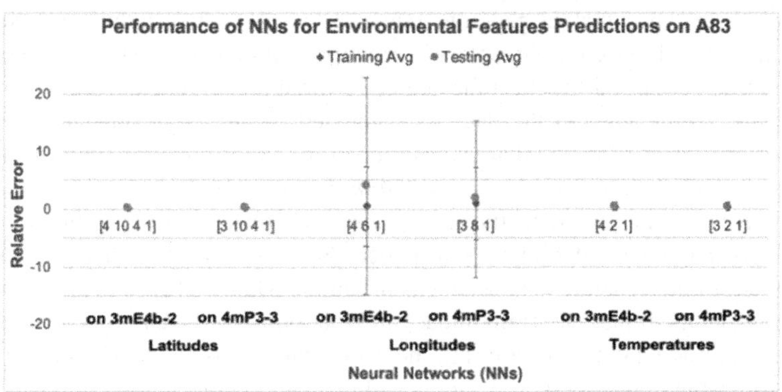

Fig. 3. The performance assessment of two best performing deep networks for predicting latitudes (left), longitudes (middle) and annual mean temperature (right) of *A. thaliana* from sample A83 on two GenISs based on nxh bases. (The standard deviations between all relative errors are so small that they are hardly visible).

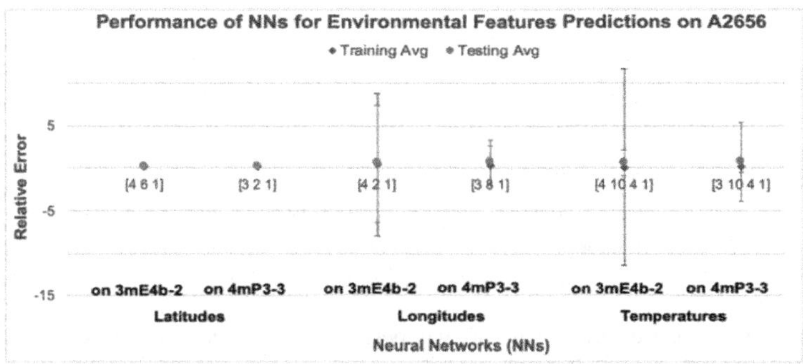

Fig. 4. The performance assessment of two best performing deep networks for predicting latitudes (left), longitudes (middle) and annual mean temperature (right) of *A. thaliana* from sample A2656 in two GenISs based on nxh bases. The standard deviations between all relative errors while making predictions for latitude are so small that they are not distinguishable.

Figure 4 shows the performance of the model on randomized data, as described above. The models are more robust because the standard deviation of the predictions in longitude on both bases decreased substantially on both the training and testing datasets (roughly, from 23 to 9 and from 15 to 7) while maintaining the quality of the predictions for latitude. On the other hand, the standard deviation of the predictions for temperature increased in the training phase for basis 3mE4b-2 and in the testing phase for basis 4mP3-3, although they remained about the same for the other phases.

The question arises as to whether these predictions are accurate enough to be of acceptable quality. As mentioned above, we are assuming that if the average RE is less than the standard deviation, the quality is acceptable. The standard view in biology, however, is that an organism follows the genetic blueprint within the constraints imposed by environment, relatively independent of one another. Therefore, it might appear unreasonable to expect that the genomic sequences would contain enough information to allow a model to infer environmental information from an organism. However, these predictions do not appear to reflect the degree of variability and randomness concerning location and temperature in the data, as witnessed by the large standard deviations. Therefore, one must conclude that, as mentioned in the Introduction, *natural selection must have encoded some environmental information to make these predictions possible.*

We were also interested in trying our approach on an entirely different type of organism to gauge the scalability of our models. So, we trained the same type of model using the genomic signatures of specimens in sample S1216. This sample was obtained by mutating COIs of blackfly (Simuliidae) and randomizing the environmental features (latitude, longitude and temperature) in the same manner discussed above. The trained models were able to predict these features within an acceptable margin of relative error, as shown in Fig. 5.

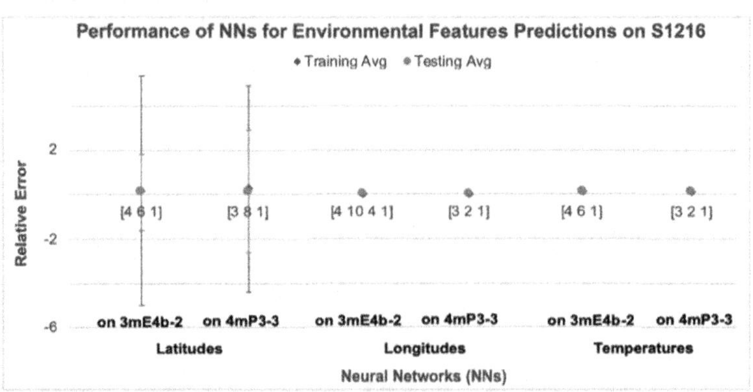

Fig. 5. The performance assessment of two best performing deep networks for predicting latitude (left), longitude (middle) and annual mean temperature (right) of blackfly in sample S1216 on two nxh bases. The standard deviations between all relative errors while making predictions for longitude and temperature are so small that they are not distinguishable.

The same method produces results of comparable quality for feature *Isothermal*, the mean of the monthly range of temperatures compared to the annual range of temperature during growth. Interestingly, despite efforts, we were unable to train a model to make a prediction for feature Annual Precipitation of high enough quality. Therefore, only information about certain environmental factors seem to be encoded into DNA.

These results are consistent with the results in [2] demonstrating that DNA sequences can act as means to estimate the spatial distributions for specimens implying that there are some features that describe the environment of the specimens but are not encoded by DNA.

Nevertheless, they are somewhat informative when used as features for better predictions of other features such as longitude, as can be observed by Figs. 3 and 6 (roughly from 22 to 4 in statistically significance units) and Figs. 4 and 7 (roughly from 9 to 4 in statistically significance units), where the model used Isothermal and Annual Precipitation as predictors along with genomic signatures. The corresponding improvement for latitude was not as significant, however.

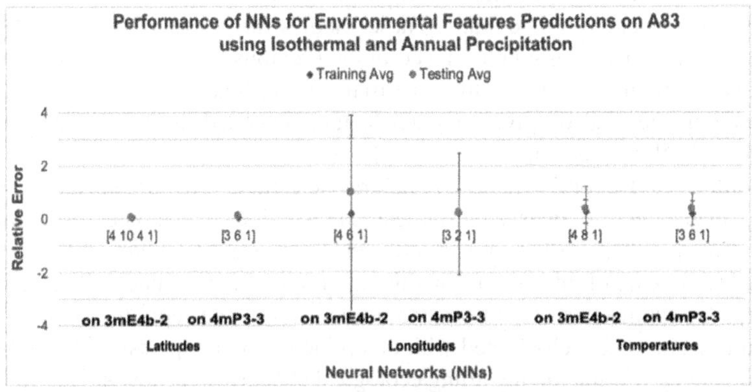

Fig. 6. The performance assessment of two best performing deep networks calibrated with Isothermal and Annual Precipitation for predicting latitudes (left), longitudes (middle) and annual mean temperature (right) of *A. thaliana* from sample A83 on two GenISs based on nxh bases.

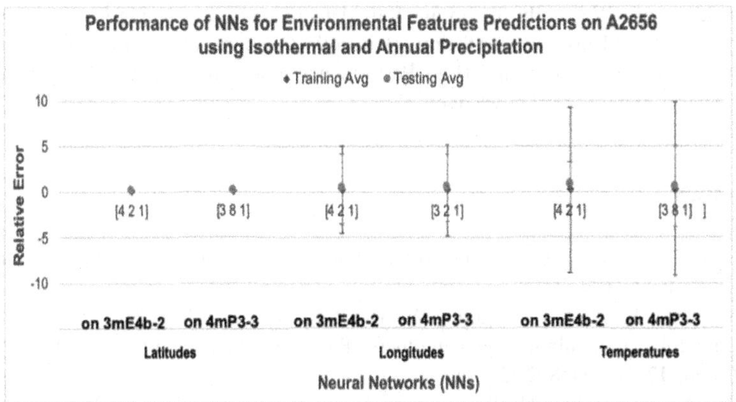

Fig. 7. The performance assessment of two best performing deep networks calibrated with Isothermal and Annual Precipitation for predicting latitudes (left), longitudes (middle) and annual mean temperature (right) of *A. thaliana* from sample A2656 on two GenISs based on nxh bases.

5 Conclusion and Future Research

Ever since Darwin proposed his theory of natural selection and Watson and Crick demonstrated that DNA is a blueprint of life, many works have been done as evidence of DNA being capable of encoding crucial information about living organisms. The recent advances show that this information can become quintessential to test hypotheses related to speciation processes, host-parasite relationships, endogamy, reproductive isolation, species delimitation, evolutionary relationships, and population dynamics. In this paper, we have demonstrated that, contrary to conventional wisdom that the influence of environmental conditions is too random to actually be encoded in genomic DNA, it contains enough information to make possible some determination of the conditions of the habitat where an organism grows, such as location (latitude and longitude) and average temperature. These models are made possible by Genomic Information Systems (GenISs) introduced in the previous works [9, 11] to extract low-dimensional and informative features to train and validate such predictive models. Characterizing the kind of environmental features encoded in DNA is an interesting problem for further research.

According to Darwin's theory of natural selection, only organisms capable of adapting themselves to their environment can survive. Much later, Maturana and Varela went one step further and introduced the concept of *autopoietic systems* to characterize the kind of interactions that living organisms effect internally and possibly with their environment in order to maintain themselves and reproduce (survive) [21]. Our results seem to be well-aligned with this principle of autopoiesis. If so, DNA may be accumulating information regarding ecological changes somehow similar to the way the layers of soil and ice record certain environmental conditions and geological time on earth, including fossil records. Therefore, DNA may actually be, in addition to its genetic role, a living repository of information about the environment where its lineage has developed over evolutionary history.

Acknowledgement. We would like to thank the labs of professors Nubia Matta and Fernando Garcia at the National University for their work in collecting some of the sample data for blackfly used in this paper. The use of the High Performance Computing Center (HPC) at the U of Memphis is also gratefully acknowledged.

References

1. Adleman, L.M.: Molecular computation of solutions to combinatorial problems. Science **266** (5), 1021–1024 (1994)
2. Barberán, A., Ramirez, K.S., Leff, J.W., Bradford, M.A., Wall, D.H., Fierer, N.: Why are some microbes more ubiquitous than others? Predicting the habitat breadth of soul bacteria. Ecol. Lett. **17**(7), 794–802 (2014)
3. Candel, A., Parmar, V., LeDell, E., Arora, A.: Deep learning with H2O. H2O. ai Inc (2016)
4. Chuine, I.: Why does phenology drive species distribution? Philos. Trans. R. Soc. B Biol. Sci. **365**(1555), 3149–3160 (2010)

5. Colorado-Garzón, F.A., Adler, P.H., García, L.F., Muñoz de Hoyos, P., Bueno, M.L., Matta, N.E.: Estimating diversity of black flies in the Simulium ignescens and Simulium tunja complexes in Colombia: chromosomal rearrangements as the core of integrative taxonomy. J. Hered. **108**(1), 12–24 (2017)
6. Cook-Deegan, R., DeRienzo, C., Carbone, J., Chandrasekharan, S., Heaney, C., Conover, C.: Impact of gene patents and licensing practices on access to genetic testing for inherited susceptibility to cancer: comparing breast and ovarian cancers with colon cancers. Genet. Med. **12**, S15–S38 (2010)
7. Darlington, P.J.: The cost of evolution and the imprecision of adaptation. Proc. Natl. Acad. Sci. **74**(4), 1647–1651 (1977)
8. Elith, J., Leathwick, J.R.: Species distribution models: ecological explanation and prediction across space and time. Annu. Rev. Ecol. Evol. Syst. **40**, 677–697 (2009)
9. Garzon, M.H., Bobba, K.C.: A geometric approach to gibbs energy landscapes and optimal DNA codeword design. In: Stefanovic, D., Turberfield, A. (eds.) DNA 2012. LNCS, vol. 7433, pp. 73–85. Springer, Heidelberg (2012). https://doi.org/10.1007/978-3-642-32208-2_6
10. Garzon, M.H., Mainali, S.: Towards reliable microarray analysis and design. In: The 9th International Conference on Bioinformatics and Computational Biology, ISCA (2017)
11. Garzon, M.H., Mainali, S.: Towards a universal genomic positioning system: phylogenetics and species IDentification. In: Rojas, I., Ortuño, F. (eds.) IWBBIO 2017. LNCS, vol. 10209, pp. 469–479. Springer, Cham (2017). https://doi.org/10.1007/978-3-319-56154-7_42
12. Garzon, M.H., Pham, D.T.: Genomic solutions to hospital-acquired bacterial infection identification. In: Rojas, I., Ortuño, F. (eds.) IWBBIO 2018. LNCS, vol. 10813, pp. 486–497. Springer, Cham (2018). https://doi.org/10.1007/978-3-319-78723-7_42
13. Garzon, M.H., Wong, T.Y.: DNA chips for species identification and biological phylogenies. Nat. Comput. **10**, 375–389 (2011)
14. Garzon, M., Neathery, P., Deaton, R., Murphy, R.C., Franceschetti, D.R., Stevens Jr., S.E.: A new metric for DNA computing. In: Proceedings of the 2nd Genetic Programming Conference, pp. 472–478. Morgan-Kaufmann (1997)
15. Guisan, A., et al.: Predicting species distributions for conservation decisions. Ecol. Lett. **16** (12), 1424–1435 (2013)
16. Haykin, S.: Neural Networks and Learning Machines. Prenctice-Hall, New Jersey (2018)
17. Hoegh-Guldberg, O., et al.: Assisted colonization and rapid climate change. Science **321**, 345–346 (2008)
18. Li, X., Qian, B., Wei, J., Zhang, X., Chen, S., Zheng, Q.: Domain knowledge guided deep atrial fibrillation classification and its visual interpretation. In: Proceedings of the 28th ACM International Conference on Information and Knowledge Management, pp. 129–138. ACM (2019)
19. Mainali, S., Colorado, F.A., Garzon, M.H.: Foretelling the phenotype of a genomic sequence. In: IEEE Transactions on Computational Biology and Bioinformatics, revision under review (2020)
20. Marcus, G.: Innateness, alphazero, and artificial intelligence. arXiv preprint arXiv:1801. 05667 (2018)
21. Maturana, H.R., Varela, F.J.: Autopoiesis and Cognition. BSPHS, vol. 42. Springer, Dordrecht (1980). https://doi.org/10.1007/978-94-009-8947-4
22. Radovanović, S., Delibašić, B., Jovanović, M., Vukićević, M., Suknović, M.: Framework for integration of domain knowledge into logistic regression. In: Proceedings of the 8th International Conference on Web Intelligence, Mining and Semantics, p. 24. ACM (2018)
23. Ricklefs, R.: Phyletic gradualism vs. punctuated equilibrium: applicability of neontological data. Paleobiology **6**(3), 271–275 (1980). https://doi.org/10.1017/s0094837300006795
24. Seeman, N.C.: Nucleic acid junctions and lattices. J. Theor. Biol. **99**(2), 237–247 (1982)

25. Seeman, N.C.: DNA in a material world. Nature **421**(6921), 427 (2003)
26. Sober, E.: What is wrong with intelligent design? Q. Rev. Biol. **82**(1), 3–8 (2007)
27. Vasseur, F., et al.: Adaptive diversification of growth allometry in the plant Arabidopsis thaliana. PNAS 115:13 3416-3421 (2018)
28. Wang, J.X., Wu, J.L., Xiao, H.: Physics-informed machine learning approach for reconstructing Reynolds stress modeling discrepancies based on DNS data. Phys. Rev. Fluids **2**(3), 034603 (2017)
29. Watson, J.D., Crick, F.: A structure for deoxyribose nucleic acid. Nature **171**, 737–738 (1953)
30. Weigel, D., Mott, R.: The 1001 genomes project for Arabidopsis thaliana. Genome Biol. **10** (5), 107 (2009)
31. Yin, C., Zhao, R., Qian, B., Lv, X., Zhang, P.: Domain Knowledge guided deep learning with electronic health records. In: IEEE International Conference on Data Mining (ICDM) (2019)

Stability of Feature Selection Methods: A Study of Metrics Across Different Gene Expression Datasets

Zahra Mungloo-Dilmohamud[1(✉)], Yasmina Jaufeerally-Fakim[1], and Carlos Peña-Reyes[2]

[1] University of Mauritius, Reduit, Mauritius
{z.mungloo,yasmina}@uom.ac.mu
[2] School of Business and Engineering Vaud (HEIG-VD), Swiss Institute of Bioinformatics (SIB), CI4CB, Computational Intelligence for Computational Biology Group, University of Applied Sciences Western Switzerland (HES-SO), Yverdon-les-Bains, Switzerland
carlos.pena@heig-vd.ch

Abstract. Analysis of gene-expression data often requires that a gene (feature) subset is selected and many feature selection (FS) methods have been devised. However, FS methods often generate different lists of features for the same dataset and users then have to choose which list to use. One approach to support this choice is to apply stability metrics on the generated lists and selecting lists on that base. The aim of this study is to investigate the behavior of stability metrics applied to feature subsets generated by FS methods. The experiments in this work explore a plethora of gene expression datasets, FS methods, and expected number of features to compare several stability metrics. The stability metrics have been used to compare five feature selection methods (SVM, SAM, ReliefF, RFE + RF and LIMMA) on gene expression datasets from the EBI repository. Results show that the studied stability metrics display a high amount of variability. The reason behind this is not clear yet and is being further investigated. The final objective of the research, that is to define how to select a FS method, is an ongoing work whose partial findings are reported herein.

Keywords: Stability · Stability metrics · FS methods · Gene expression data

1 Introduction

Recent advancement in high-throughput technologies have resulted in the generation of huge amounts of data. These data can be very expensive to analyse in terms of the required computational resources and therefore various means have been devised to decrease costs. One such means is feature selection (FS). Feature selection in machine learning is the process of choosing relevant or important features from a large set of features to be used in the construction of a model. The aim of performing feature selection is three-fold: enhancing the prediction performance of the predictors, offering more rapid and more economical predictors, and providing a better understanding of

I. Rojas et al. (Eds.): IWBBIO 2020, LNBI 12108, pp. 659–669, 2020.
https://doi.org/10.1007/978-3-030-45385-5_59

the underlying process that generated the data [1]. However there exists a large number of FS methods [2] and they may produce very different results for the same data [3–5]. Therefor the robustness or stability of the FS methods need to be looked into. Various attempts have been made to measure the variability of the subset of features produced when running an FS method and a number of stability metrics have been proposed as shown in Table 1. The aim of the work here is to investigate some of the existing stability metrics when applied to results produced by FS methods.

It should be noted that, in literature, robustness and similarity have often been used interchangeably. However, in the context of our research, a robust FS method is one which is able to find stable subsets of features while enabling a good performance of the classifier or the predictive model.

2 Materials and Methods

2.1 Stability Metrics

A very natural way to represent the output of feature selection is as a subset of all the features. FS methods may produce outputs in 3 different ways: (1) all features are ranked, example method: Recursive Feature Elimination–RFE [1], (2) a score or weight is provided to all features, as done by the Mutual Information FS method [6] and (3) a feature subset is produced, as is the case for any wrapper method like RFE with RF [7]. Given that FS methods produce outputs in these 3 different ways, stability measures have been devised for each type of output produced.

A literature survey of publications on stability measures/metrics has shown that they can be categorized according to either the approach they use, as defined by [8] or the results they produce, as defined by [9]. The approaches used by the metrics can either be similarity-based or frequency-based. In similarity-based approaches, the similarity, or commonality, between various feature sets is computed. Stability is often calculated as the average similarity over all pairs of feature subsets. In frequency-based approaches the frequency with which a feature or a feature set occurs is calculated. Here, the output of the FS method is often represented as a binary string (1 for selected and 0 for not selected) as opposed to a subset and stability can be calculated by looking at the frequencies of selection of each feature over M feature sets. Following the literature survey, a comprehensive list of stability metrics categorized according to both the approach they use and the results they produce has been constructed and shown in Table 1.

This study explores, besides a simple commonality percentage, the following six stability metrics. The *Jaccard similarity* is calculated by the intersection of the sets divided by the union of the sets and is based on pairwise comparison. Its value ranges from 0 to 1. *Dice's coefficient* is related to the Jaccard Similarity Coefficient and is calculated as 2 times the union of the sets divided by the sum of the number of elements in each set. It also uses pairwise comparison and has values in the range 0 to 1. *CWrel* uses property-based analysis and is non-pairwise. It suppresses the effect of the size of subsets in a system and its value ranges from 0 to 1. *Lustgarten's Measure* is derived from the Kuncheva, caters for changing number of features and has correction for chance. It is based on pairwise comparison and its value ranges from −1 to 1. *Stability Measure Novovičová* is based on the Shannon entropy and is non-pairwise. Its value ranges from 0 to 1. *Nogueira Stability Index* is also non-pairwise, is based on the 5 properties that the authors have found important for stability measures [8]. It ranges from −1 to 1.

Table 1. Feature-selection stability measures

FS Measures	Approach	Type of stability
Robustness Index [4]	Similarity-based	Index
*Jaccard Similarity Coefficient [10]		Index
Tanimoto Distance [11]		Index/Subset
Spearman's rank correlation coefficient/Spearman's Rho [11]		Rank
Pearson Correlation		Weight
Stability based on Jensen-Shannon Divergence [12]		Rank
Canberra Distance [9]		Rank
*Lustgarten Stability Measure [13]		Index/Subset
Average Normal Hamming Distance (ANHD) [14]		Index/Subset
Kuncheva stability index [15].		Index/Subset
Percentage of Overlapping Gene (POG) [16]		Index/Subset
*Dice Coefficient [17]		Index/Subset
Ochiai's Index [18]		Index
*Relative Weighted Consistency Measure (CWrel) [19]	Frequency-based	Index/Subset
*Stability Measure Novovičová [20]		Index/Subset
Entropy of Feature Sets [21]		Index/Subset
Average Frequency of Selection [22]		Index/Subset
Corrected Frequency of Selection [23]		Index/Subset
Lausser's Measure [24]		Index/Subset
Entropy of the Selection of Each Feature based on Jensen-Shannon Divergence [12]		Rank
*Nogueira Stability Index [8]		Index/Subset

2.2 Datasets

For the purpose of the empirical work, nine high dimensional datasets from the field of transcriptomics are selected. As shown in Table 2, these gene-expression datasets are quite diverse, with the classes being binary or multiclass, with sample sizes in the range of 16 to 190, and with their number of features ranging between 7,000 and 55,000.

Table 2. Datasets used for running the FS methods

Datasets	Source	Samples	# of Features	Classes
Leukemia (GOLUB)	[25]	72	7129	Binary
Leukemia 2	[26]	104	22283	Binary
Leukemia 3	[27]	190	22277	Multiclass
Breast cancer 1	[26]	50	22283	Multiclass
Prostate cancer 1	[27]	22	22153	Multiclass
9-cancers Dataset	[26]	174	54674	Multiclass
MELAS 1	[26]	16	22214	Binary
Ulcerative colitis 1	[26]	16	54675	Binary
Pregnancy Stages Dataset	[26]	48	33297	Multiclass

2.3 Feature-Selection Methods

To run the various experiments, five different methods are selected (see Table 3): SAM, LIMMA, ReliefF, RFE + RF and SVM. This is a diversity-driven choice, as these methods use different model representations and are either deterministic or nondeterministic. Non-deterministic methods usually produce different subsets of candidate biomarkers at each run for the same dataset [28].

Table 3. Selected feature-selection methods

FS Methods	Selection management	Deterministic	Class dimensionality
SAM [29]	Filter	Yes	Multiclass
LIMMA [30]	Filter	Yes	Multiclass
ReliefF [31]	Filter	No	Multiclass
SVM [1]	Embedded	No	Binary
RFE + RF [7]	Wrapper	No	Multiclass

2.4 Empirical Study of Stability Metrics

To widely study the stability metrics, the five selected FS methods (Table 3) are run on the nine different datasets (Table 2). The experiments are conducted as follows: the deterministic methods are run once while non-deterministic methods are run 20 times and a consensus list is generated [32]. These runs are performed for an increasing number of features to be selected (i.e., 50, 100, 500, 1000, 5000, and 10000). The resulting feature subsets are then analyzed for their similarity as in [32] and [33] and then their stability is assessed using the selected list of metrics (Table 4) as explained in sections E and F below. Summarizing: the stability metrics are compared across a total of 270 feature subsets (i.e., 5 FS methods, 9 datasets, and 6 subset sizes). Additionally, each one of the 54 lists obtained by the RFE-RF method is the result of a consensus among 20 subsets, for a total of 1080 additional subsets.

2.5 Intra-method Similarity of Feature Subsets

A simple and intuitive way to assess the robustness or stability of features selected by various FS methods is to measure the difference/similarity between features present in various lists of features obtained under different conditions. In this empirical work, the results obtained between the different runs of the non-deterministic wrapper method (RFE with RF) are analyzed. As mentioned before, this method is run 20 times, each time with a different seed value and this is repeated for different values of the number of features. This intra-method analysis pursues two aims: (1) investigating the stability of the feature subsets produced by non-deterministic methods across various runs and for different number of selected features and (2) comparing the behavior of several different stability metrics across diverse conditions. The lists produced by this method for the "9-cancers" dataset are compared in terms of percentage of common features as well as using the similarity measures highlighted in Table 1.

2.6 Inter-methods Similarity of Feature Subsets

Some preliminary work on the inter-method similarity of feature subsets has already been reported in [32, 33] where 7 FS methods were applied to 9 different datasets to study the similarity between the various lists obtained. The effect of FS methods, the specificity of the datasets as well as the size of the feature subset produced were investigated. However, the work focused mostly on percentage similarity and no stability metric was investigated. To complement that work, the feature subsets produced in that work by four of the selected methods on the nine datasets were further analyzed by using six stability metrics. These inter-method experiments compare the lists of features (i) between pairs of methods, (ii) across four different methods and (iii) as the size of the feature subsets increase.

3 Results

3.1 Intra-method Similarity

Figure 1 shows the results obtained with the selected stability metrics on feature lists produced by an increasing number of runs (from 1 to 20) of the RFE + RF method on the 9-cancers dataset. The analysis is performed for different number of selected features.

Table 4. Selected Stability Metrics

Name	Measure calculation	Values	Range
% Similarity	$\frac{r_{i,j}}{\lvert s_i \rvert}$	$r_{i,j}$ is the size of the intersection between feature sets s_i and s_j $\lvert s_i \rvert$ and $\lvert s_j \rvert$ are normalized subset and are equal for all cases	[0,1]
Jaccard	$\frac{r_{i,j}}{\lvert s_i \cup s_j \rvert}$	$\lvert s_i \cup s_j \rvert$ is the size of the union of s_i and s_j	[0,1]
Dice	$\frac{2r_{i,j}}{\lvert s_i \rvert + \lvert s_j \rvert}$		[0,1]
Lustgarten	$\frac{\text{Observed}\, r_{i,j} - \text{Expected}\, r_{i,j}}{\text{Maximum}\, r_{i,j} - \text{Minimunm}\, r_{i,j}} = \frac{r_{i,j} - \frac{k_i k_j}{d}}{\min(k_i, k_j) - \max(0, k_i + k_j - d)}$	$\frac{k^2}{d}$ is the expectation of the size of the set intersection $r_{i,j}$ where k = size of a fixed feature subset	[−1,1]
CW_{rel}	$\hat{\Phi}(\mathcal{Z}) = \frac{d\left(M\bar{k} - D + \sum_{f=1}^{d} M\hat{p}_f\left(M\hat{p}_f - 1\right)\right) - (M\bar{k})^2 + (D)^2}{d(H^2 + M(M\bar{k} - H) - D) - (M\bar{k})^2 + (D)^2}$ where $D = (M\bar{k}) mod\, d$ and $H = (M\bar{k})\ mod\, M$	M is the number of feature subsets. $\hat{p}_f = \frac{1}{M}\sum_{i=1}^{M} z_{i,f}$ is the frequency of selection of the fth feature	[0,1]
Novovicova	$\frac{1}{q \log_2(m)} \sum_{j:X_j \in V} h_j \log_2(h_j)$ where $q = \sum_{j=1}^{p} h_j$ and $V = \bigcup_{i=1}^{m} V_i$	h_j denotes the number of sets V_i that contain feature X_j so that h_j is the absolute frequency with which feature X_j is chosen. m is the number of subsets	[0,1]
Nogueira	$\frac{2}{m(m-1)} \sum_{i=1}^{m-1} \sum_{j=i+1}^{m} \mathrm{Cor}(z_i, z_j)$	$\mathrm{Cor}(z_i, z_j)$ denotes the Pearson correlation between z_i and z_j	[−1,1]

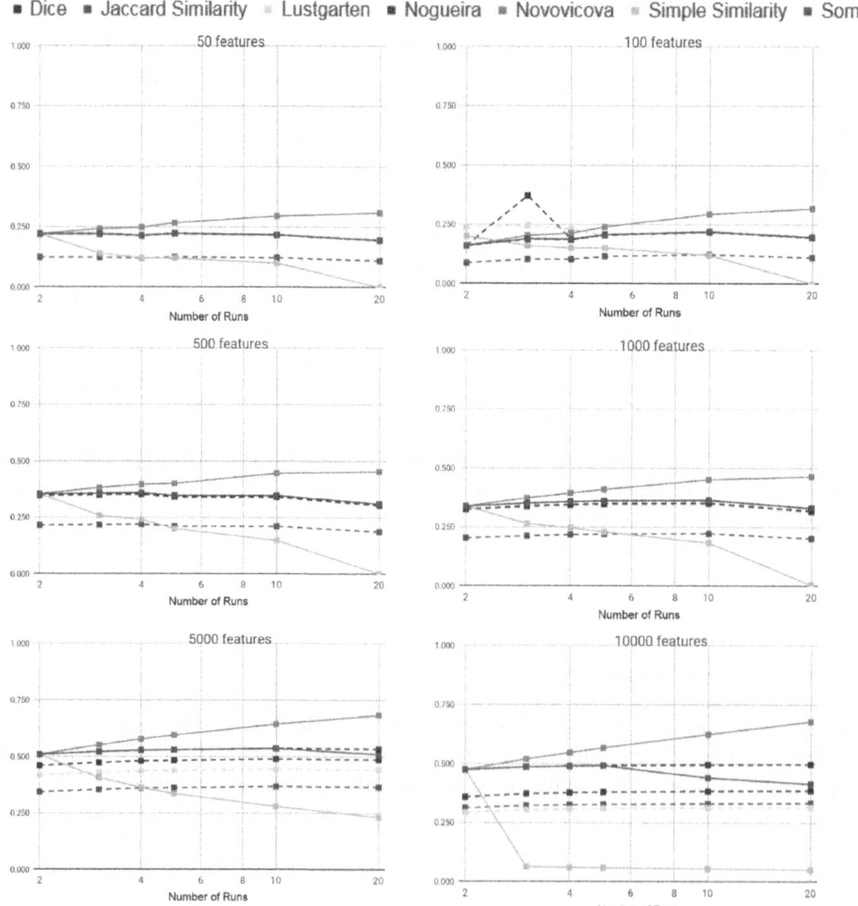

Fig. 1. Comparison of stability measures applied to lists obtained from applying RFE-RF to 9-cancers dataset as number of selected features increases

Intuitively, one would expect that the stability increases with both the number of selected features (as the more features are selected, the more probable that different FS methods select similar subsets) and the number of runs (as across runs the most relevant features should be repeatedly selected). From the graphs, it is noted that the values of the stability metrics tend to be similar for lower number of features and for lower number of runs and, in general all the metrics behave similarly excepting for the simple similarity metrics. We deduce that this metric might not be indicative of the stability. On the other side, Novovičová's metric seems to be the closest to the expected behavior.

3.2 Similarity of Feature Subsets Inter-methods

1. *Pairwise comparison.* Figure 2 shows the comparison of stability metrics for different number of selected features computed across 6 pairs of 4 methods applied on the Golub dataset. In this case, as the stability metrics are computed on the base of only two feature subsets, we may expect them to behave very similarly capturing the similarity of lists from both methods at different subset sizes. As it can be seen in Fig. 2, while this is the case for small feature sets, the metrics diverge for bigger lists. In this former case, Dice and simple similarity metrics behave close to the expected higher stability for bigger feature sets, while Nogueira is the most counterintuitive. Concerning the methods, two pairs appear to produce lists of relatively-higher similarity: RFE-RF with SVM and SAM with ReliefF.

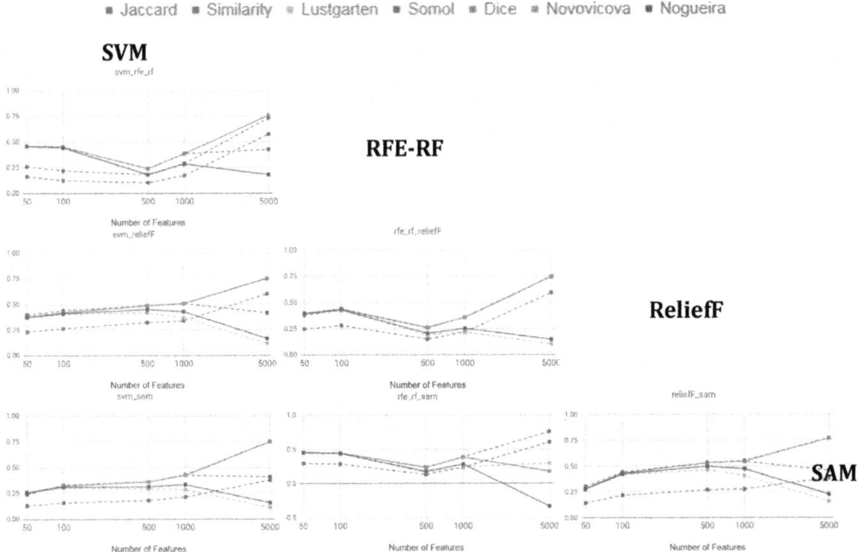

Fig. 2. Percentage Commonality and 6 stability metrics between SVM, ReliefF, SAM and RFE_RF for the Golub (Leukemia 1) Dataset

2. *Comparison of stability metrics across 8 datasets.* Figure 3 shows the stability metrics computed, using a single pair of FS methods (RFE + RF and LIMMA), for the remaining 8 datasets. Akin to the previous experiment, the metrics behave similarly for short lists of features and diverge for bigger sets. Simple similarity and Somol's metric being the closest to the expected behavior of higher stability for bigger feature sets and Nogueira and Lustgarten metrics the farthest. With respect to the behavior of the stability metrics across the different sets, it is clear that it depends strongly on the dataset. While in half of the datasets the stability changes significantly with the number of selected features, in the other half the stability metrics requires a relatively high number of features to become relevant.
3. *Comparison of lists of features obtained across 4 different FS methods.* Figure 4 shows the results obtained when the Jaccard, Lustgarten, Nogueira and Novovicova metrics were calculated for the lists produced by the 4 FS (SVM, ReliefF, SAM and RFE_RF) methods applied to the Leukemia 1 dataset with the number of selected features increasing from 20 to all features. In this case a fine-grained analysis was done with comparisons at 20, 50, 100, 250, 500, 1000, 2500, 5000 and 7219(all) features. These 4 stability metrics were selected since they were found to behave either as expected (Novovicova and Jaccard) or unexpectedly (Lustgarten and Nogueira) for the pairwise comparisons above. Results obtained confirm the divergent behavior of these 2 metrics. It is found that although the stability measure increases for Novovicova and Jaccard, the stability between the lists produced by the 4 methods remain quite stable and quite low (around 0.25) for Jaccard and a bit higher for Novovicova (around 0.47) from 20 to 2500 features.

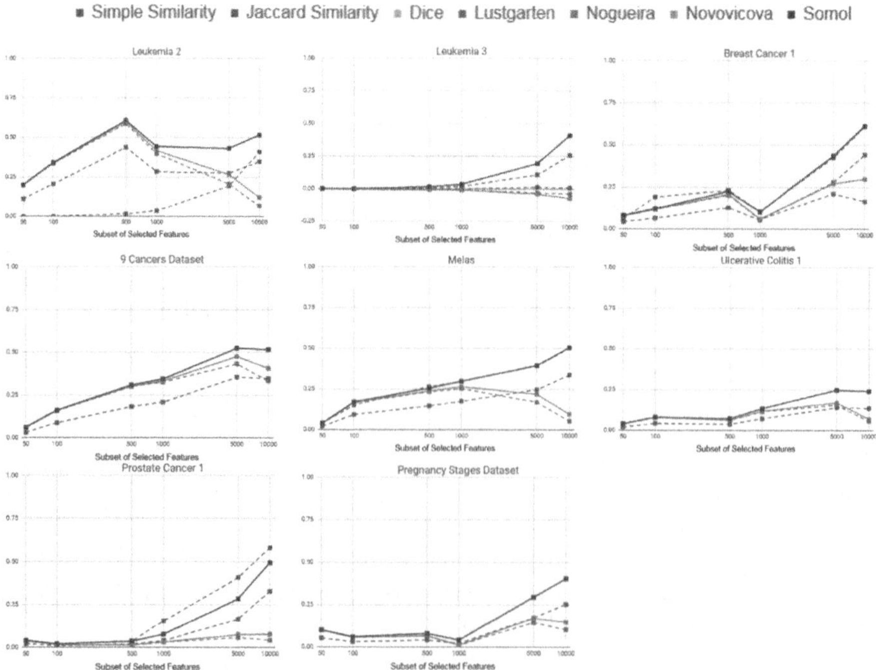

Fig. 3. Various stability measures applied to lists produced by FS methods RFE and LIMMA for 8 different datasets.

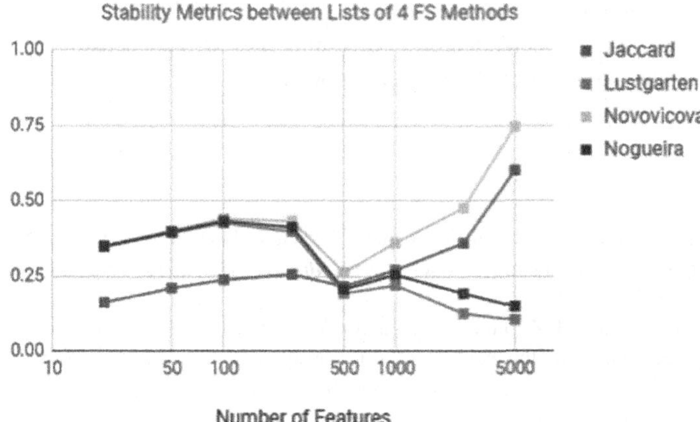

Fig. 4. Evolution of 4 stability metrics applied to lists produced by 4 different FS methods (Leukemia 1 dataset)

4 Conclusion

This work analyzes the stability metrics applied to lists produced by running various FS methods on gene expression data. Among a plethora of existing stability metrics, we study 6 such metrics applied to feature subsets obtained by different FS methods on diverse gene expression datasets. Upon analysis of the results, a first conclusion is that for pairwise comparison (i.e., comparing lists from single pairs of methods) all the metrics behave similarly. Their main difference is that some metrics may be more "sensitive" as they seem to amplify the differences.

For both the inter-methods and the intra-method analyses, the stability is expected to improve (or at least not to worsen) as the number of subsets increases or for longer feature lists. However, our results show that this is not always the case. We find that the stability metrics Somol and Novovicova behave as expected while Nogueira's and Lustgarten's metrics do not. Possible hypotheses to explain this unforeseen behavior can be the randomness factor used by both Lustgarten and Nogueira, as well as their use of a range of values from −1 to 1 instead of 0 to 1. These hypotheses need to be further explored by extending the analysis to more datasets and multiple FS methods. Finally, in this same sense, the simple-similarity should be avoided as a metrics as it does not scale satisfactorily with the number of sets being considered.

The final objective of our research in the subject is to use stability metrics as a support and a tool to define how to best combine different FS methods so as to produce stable feature subsets. So, the work presented herein makes part of an ongoing effort. Currently more FS methods, datasets and metrics are being looked into. Some issues that call for further investigation are whether the size of the feature subset impact on the metrics and secondly what causes the value of the metrics to decrease at some point and then increase again.

It should be emphasized that the stability does not provide any information about the performance of the selected features but simply indicates the sensitivity of a feature selection method output to random perturbations in the input data.

References

1. Guyon, I., Weston, J., Barnhill, S., Vapnik, V.: Gene Selection for Cancer Classification using Support Vector Machines. Mach. Learn. **46**, 389–422 (2002). https://doi.org/10.1023/A:1012487302797
2. Mungloo-Dilmohamud, Z., Jaufeerally-Fakim, Y., Peña-Reyes, C.: A meta-review of feature selection techniques in the context of microarray data. In: Rojas, I., Ortuño, F. (eds.) IWBBIO 2017. LNCS, vol. 10208, pp. 33–49. Springer, Cham (2017). https://doi.org/10.1007/978-3-319-56148-6_3
3. Abeel, T., Helleputte, T., Van deaaa Peer, Y., Dupont, P., Saeys, Y.: Robust biomarker identification for cancer diagnosis with ensemble feature selection methods. Bioinformatics **26**, 392–398 (2010). https://doi.org/10.1093/bioinformatics/btp630
4. He, Z., Yu, W.: Stable feature selection for biomarker discovery. Comput. Biol. Chem. **34**, 215–225 (2010). https://doi.org/10.1016/j.compbiolchem.2010.07.002
5. Bolón-Canedo, V., Sánchez-Maroño, N., Alonso-Betanzos, A., Benítez, J.M., Herrera, F.: A review of microarray datasets and applied feature selection methods. Inf. Sci. (N.Y.) **282**, 111–135 (2014). https://doi.org/10.1016/j.ins.2014.05.042
6. Cover, T.M., Thomas, J.A.: Elements of Information Theory. Wiley-Interscience, Hoboken (1991)
7. Kuhn, M.: Building predictive models in *R* using the caret Package. J. Stat. Softw. **28**(5), 1–26 (2008)
8. Nogueira, S., Brown, G.: Measuring the stability of feature selection. In: Frasconi, P., Landwehr, N., Manco, G., Vreeken, J. (eds.) ECML PKDD 2016. LNCS (LNAI), vol. 9852, pp. 442–457. Springer, Cham (2016). https://doi.org/10.1007/978-3-319-46227-1_28
9. Mohana, C.: A Survey on feature selection stability measures. International Journal of Computer and Information Technology **05**(1), 98–103 (2016)
10. Saeys, Y., Abeel, T., Van de Peer, Y.: Robust feature selection using ensemble feature selection techniques. In: Daelemans, W., Goethals, B., Morik, K. (eds.) ECML PKDD 2008. LNCS (LNAI), vol. 5212, pp. 313–325. Springer, Heidelberg (2008). https://doi.org/10.1007/978-3-540-87481-2_21
11. Kalousis, A., Prados, J., Hilario, M.: Stability of feature selection algorithms: a study on high-dimensional spaces. Knowl. Inf. Syst. **12**, 95–116 (2007)
12. Guzmán-Martínez, R., Alaiz-Rodríguez, R.: Feature selection stability assessment based on the jensen-shannon divergence. In: Gunopulos, D., Hofmann, T., Malerba, D., Vazirgiannis, M. (eds.) ECML PKDD 2011. LNCS (LNAI), vol. 6911, pp. 597–612. Springer, Heidelberg (2011). https://doi.org/10.1007/978-3-642-23780-5_48
13. Lustgarten, J.L., Gopalakrishnan, V., Visweswaran, S.: Measuring stability of feature selection in biomedical datasets. AMIA Annu. Symp. Proc. **2009**, 406–410 (2009)
14. Dunne, K., Cunningham, P., Azuaje, F.: Solutions to instability problems with sequential wrapper-based approaches to feature selection. J. Mach. Learn. Res., 1–22 (2002)
15. Kuncheva, L.I.: A stability index for feature selection. In: Proceedings of the 25th IASTED International Multi-Conference: artificial intelligence and applications, pp. 390–395. ACTA Press (2007)

16. Shi, L., Reid, L.H., Jones, W.D., Shippy, R., et al.: The MicroArray Quality Control (MAQC) project shows inter- and intraplatform reproducibility of gene expression measurements. Nat. Biotechnol. **24**, 1151–1161 (2006). MAQC Consortium
17. Yu, L., Ding, C., Loscalzo, S.: Stable feature selection via dense feature groups. In: Proceeding of the 14th ACM SIGKDD international conference on Knowledge discovery and data mining - KDD 08, p. 803. ACM Press, New York (2008)
18. Zucknick, M., Richardson, S., Stronach, E.A.: Comparing the characteristics of gene expression profiles derived by univariate and multivariate classification methods. Stat. Appl. Genet. Mol. Biol. **7** (2008). Article7
19. Somol, P., Novovicová, J.: Evaluating stability and comparing output of feature selectors that optimize feature subset cardinality. IEEE Trans. Pattern Anal. Mach. Intell. **32**, 1921–1939 (2010)
20. Novovicová, J., Somol, P., Pudil, P.: A new measure of feature selection algorithms' stability. In: 2009 IEEE International Conference on Data Mining Workshops, pp. 382–387. IEEE (2009)
21. Křížek, P., Kittler, J., Hlaváč, V.: Improving stability of feature selection methods. In: Kropatsch, Walter G., Kampel, M., Hanbury, A. (eds.) CAIP 2007. LNCS, vol. 4673, pp. 929–936. Springer, Heidelberg (2007). https://doi.org/10.1007/978-3-540-74272-2_115
22. Goh, W.W.B., Wong, L.: Evaluating feature-selection stability in next-generation proteomics. J. Bioinform. Comput. Biol. **14**, 1650029 (2016)
23. CA, D.: Reliable gene signatures for microarray classification: assessment of stability and performance. Bioinformatics **22**, 2356–2363 (2006)
24. Lausser, L., Müssel, C., Maucher, M., Kestler, H.A.: Measuring and visualizing the stability of biomarker selection techniques. Comput Stat. **28**, 51–65 (2013)
25. Cancer Program Legacy Publication Resources. http://portals.broadinstitute.org/cgi-bin/cancer/datasets.cgi
26. ArrayExpress < EMBL-EBI. https://www.ebi.ac.uk/arrayexpress/
27. Home - GEO – NCBI. https://www.ncbi.nlm.nih.gov/geo/
28. Hira, Z.M., Gillies, D.F.: A review of feature selection and feature extraction methods applied on microarray data. Adv. Bioinform. **2015**, 198363 (2015)
29. Tusher, V.G., Tibshirani, R., Chu, G.: Significance analysis of microarrays applied to the ionizing radiation response. Proc. Natl. Acad. Sci. U.S.A. **98**, 5116–5121 (2001)
30. Smyth, G.K.: Limma: linear models for microarray data. In: Gentleman, R., Carey, V.J., Huber, W., Irizarry, R.A., Dudoit, S. (eds.) Bioinformatics and Computational Biology Solutions Using R and Bioconductor, pp. 397–420. Springer, New York (2005). https://doi.org/10.1007/0-387-29362-0_23
31. Kononenko, I.: Estimating attributes: Analysis and extensions of RELIEF. In: Bergadano, F., De Raedt, L. (eds.) ECML 1994. LNCS, vol. 784, pp. 171–182. Springer, Heidelberg (1994). https://doi.org/10.1007/3-540-57868-4_57
32. Mungloo-Dilmohamud, Z., Marigliano, G., Jaufeerally-Fakim, Y., Pena-Reyes, C.: A comparative study of feature selection methods for biomarker discovery. In: 2018 IEEE International Conference on Bioinformatics and Biomedicine (BIBM), pp. 2789–2791. IEEE (2018). https://doi.org/10.1109/bibm.2018.8621267
33. Mungloo-Dilmohamud, Z., Jaufeerally-Fakim, T., Peña-Reyes, C.: Exploring the Stability of Feature Selection Methods across a Palette of Gene Expression Datasets. Proceedings of the 2019 6th International Conference on Biomedical and Bioinformatics Engineering, ICBBE 2019. ACM (2019)

Medical Image Processing

Influence of Sarcopenia on Bone Health Parameters in a Group of Elderly Lebanese Men

Amal Antoun[1,2], Hayman Saddick[1,3], Antonio Pinti[4(✉)], Riad Nasr[1], Eric Watelain[2], Eric Lespessailles[3,5], Hechmi Toumi[3,5], and Rawad El Hage[1]

[1] Department of Physical Education, Faculty of Arts and Social Sciences, University of Balamand, El-Koura, Lebanon
[2] Laboratoire IAPS, Université de Toulon, Toulon, France
[3] Laboratoire I3MTO EA 4708, University of Orléans, 45067 Orléans, France
[4] Design, Visuel, Urbain, EA 2445, UPHF, Valenciennes, France
antonio.pinti@uphf.fr
[5] Plateforme Recherche Innovation Médicale Mutualisée d'Orléans, Centre Hospitalier Régional d'Orléans, 14 Avenue de l'Hôpital, 45100 Orléans, France

Abstract. Sarcopenia is a disease characterized by the loss of muscle mass and strength. The aim of the current study was to explore the influence of sarcopenia on bone health parameters in a group of elderly Lebanese men. To do so, we compared bone health parameters (Bone Mineral Content (BMC), Bone Mineral Density (BMD) and femoral neck geometry indices) in a group of elderly men with sarcopenia and a group of elderly men with normal Skeletal Muscle mass Index (SMI). 23 sarcopenic men (SMI < 7 kg/m^2) and 23 men with normal SMI (>7 kg/m^2) participated in our study. Body composition and bone variables were measured by Dual-energy X-ray Absorptiometry (DXA). DXA measurements were completed for the Whole Body (WB), Lumbar spine (L1–L4), Total Hip (TH) and Femoral Neck (FN). Hip geometry parameters including Cross-Sectional Area (CSA), Cross-Sectional Moment of Inertia (CSMI), section modulus (Z), Strength Index (SI) and Buckling Ratio (BR) were derived by DXA. Age and height were not significantly different between the two groups. Weight, Body Mass Index (BMI), lean mass, fat mass, appendicular lean mass, SMI, WB BMC, TH BMD, FN BMD, CSA, CSMI and Z were significantly higher in non-sarcopenic men compared to sarcopenic men. In the whole population, lean mass was the strongest determinant of bone health parameters. After adjusting for lean mass, there were no significant differences regarding bone health parameters between the two groups. In conclusion, the present study suggests that sarcopenia negatively influences bone health parameters in elderly Lebanese men.

Keywords: Bone strength · Lean mass · Males · Prevention of osteoporosis

A. Antoun and H. Saddick—The first two authors contributed equally to this manuscript.

I. Rojas et al. (Eds.): IWBBIO 2020, LNBI 12108, pp. 673–682, 2020.
https://doi.org/10.1007/978-3-030-45385-5_60

1 Introduction

Bone Mineral Density (BMD) measured by Dual-energy X-ray Absorptiometry (DXA) is a surrogate of bone strength and a predictor of fracture risk in elderly people [1–4]. Research has shown that BMD is influenced by several factors including genetics, ethnicity, gender and mechanical factors [5–13]. For instance, previous studies conducted in the Lebanese population showed that mean BMD values are lower than American and European values [14–24]. The reasons are not completely elucidated. However, low daily calcium intake and serum vitamin D levels as well as inactivity may in part explain this result [25–31]. Although osteoporosis affects much more women than men, low BMD values can lead to osteoporotic fractures in both sexes [11–13]. Previous studies conducted on the Lebanese population showed strong connections between lean mass and BMD values especially in males [32–35]. The decrease in muscle mass associated with ageing can lead to sarcopenia [36–39]. Sarcopenia is a progressive and generalized skeletal muscle disorder that is associated with increased likelihood of adverse outcomes including falls, fractures, physical disability and mortality [36–39]. We have previously shown that maximal strength, power and maximum oxygen consumption are positive predictors of BMD in adults [40–47]. Based on all of the above, we hypothesized that sarcopenia would be associated with decreased BMD values in elderly Lebanese men. Thus, the aim of the current study was to explore the influence of sarcopenia on bone health parameters in a group of elderly Lebanese men. To do so, we compared bone health parameters (Bone Mineral Content (BMC), BMD and femoral neck geometry indices) in a group of elderly Lebanese men with sarcopenia and a group of elderly Lebanese men with normal Skeletal Muscle mass Index (SMI).

2 Materials and Methods

2.1 Subjects and Study Design

The present study was carried out in accordance with the declaration of Helsinki (regarding human experimentation developed for the medical community by the World Medical Association). Forty six elderly Lebanese men whose ages range from 66 to 85 years participated in our study. They were randomly selected from Tripoli, Lebanon and were then divided into two groups according to their SMI. Accordingly, 23 elderly men with sarcopenia (SMI < 7 kg/m^2) and 23 elderly men with normal SMI (SMI > 7 kg/m^2) were included. Subjects with any medical condition likely to affect bone metabolism, including history of a chronic disease with vital organ involvement or intake of medications that may affect bone metabolism (i.e. steroid intake for more than six months, treatment with bisphosphonates or other bone antiresorptive drugs) were excluded. Also were excluded subjects with a history of radiotherapy or chemotherapy, or bed rest for more than one month within six months prior to the study. An informed written consent was obtained from the participants.

2.2 Anthropometrical Measurements and Body Composition

Height and body weight were measured using a mechanic scale (precision of 100 g) and a standard stadiometer (upright position to the nearest 1 mm). The participants were weighed wearing light clothing and had their shoes removed. BMI was calculated as body weight divided by height squared (kg/m^2). Body composition (lean mass, fat mass and BMC) was evaluated by DXA (GE Healthcare, Lunar iDXA System, version 13.60). We used the SMI (appendicular lean mass/height^2) to define sarcopenia as previously described [36]. An SMI < 7 kg/m^2 was defined as the cut point for sarcopenia [36].

2.3 Bone Variables

BMD measurements were completed for the Whole Body (WB), the Lumbar spine (L1–L4), the Total Hip (TH) and the Femoral Neck (FN) using the DXA medical imaging instrument described earlier. Geometric indices of FN strength [Cross-Sectional Area (CSA), Cross-Sectional Moment of Inertia (CSMI), section modulus (Z), Strength Index (SI) and Buckling Ratio (BR)] were derived by DXA. The same certified technician (holder of a Bachelor of Science in medical imaging sciences) performed all analyses using the same technique for all measurements. The coefficients of variation were $<1\%$ for BMC and BMD in our laboratory [42–47].

2.4 Handgrip Strength

Handgrip strength was measured using a valid device (CAMRY Model: EH101 – Fig. 1). The Southampton protocol has been used to evaluate handgrip strength [48].

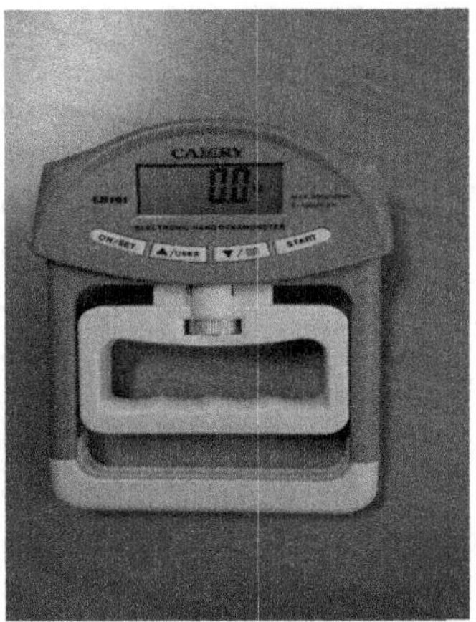

Fig. 1. A Camry digital hand dynamometer.

2.5 Statistical Analysis

The means and standard deviations were calculated for all clinical data and for the bone measurements. Comparisons between the 2 groups (sarcopenic men and non-sarcopenic men) were made after checking for Gaussian distribution. If Gaussian distribution was found, parametric unpaired *t*-tests were used. In other cases, Mann-Whitney *U*-tests were used. Correlations between clinical characteristics and bone data were given as Pearson correlation coefficients. Multiple linear regressions were used to test the relationships of BMD with age, lean mass and fat mass, and r^2 were reported. Bone variables were compared between the 2 groups (sarcopenic men and non-sarcopenic men) after adjustment for age and lean mass, and age and Appendicular Lean Mass (ALM) using a one-way analysis of covariance. Data were analyzed with Number Cruncher Statistical System (NCSS, 2001; NCSS, Kaysville, UT). A level of significance of $p < 0.05$ was used.

3 Results

3.1 Clinical Characteristics and Bone Variables of the Two Groups

Age, height, ALM/BMI, WB BMD, L1–L4 BMD and SI were not significantly different between the two groups. Weight, lean mass, fat mass, fat mass percentage, ALM, SMI, WB BMC, TH BMD, FN BMD, CSA, CSMI, Z, BR and handgrip were significantly higher in non-sarcopenic men compared to sarcopenic men (Table 1).

Table 1. Clinical characteristics and bone variables oft he study population

	Sarcopenic men (n = 23)	Non-sarcopenic men (n = 23)	
	Mean ± SD	Mean ± SD	p-value
Age (years)	77.087 ± 6.614	74.287 ± 4.960	p = 0.11
Weight (kg)	73.217 ± 12.157	86.913 ± 13.235	p < 0.001
Height (m)	1.66 ± 0.06	1.68 ± 0.06	p = 0.53
BMI (kg/m²)	26.3 ± 3.8	30.9 ± 5.2	p = 0.001
Lean mass (kg)	42.383 ± 5.182	49.421 ± 6.568	p < 0.001
Fat mass (kg)	24.879 ± 8.475	32.167 ± 8.830	p = 0.007
Fat mass (%)	32.8 ± 7.0	36.6 ± 5.1	p = 0.04
ALM (kg)	18.214 ± 1.553	22.306 ± 2.898	p < 0.001
SMI (kg/m²)	6.51 ± 0.39	7.98 ± 1.06	p < 0.001
ALM/BMI (m²)	0.701 ± 0.0865	0.731 ± 0.111	p = 0.31
WB BMC (kg)	2.199 ± 0.338	2.447 ± 0.441	p = 0.03
WB BMD (g/cm²)	1.037 ± 0.0893	1.076 ± 0.120	p = 0.213
L1–L4 BMD (g/cm²)	0.989 ± 0.146	1.028 ± 0.252	p = 0.53
TH BMD (g/cm²)	0.817 ± 0.100	0.929 ± 0.124	p = 0.002
FN BMD (g/cm²)	0.760 ± 0.101	0.865 ± 0.142	p = 0.006

(continued)

Table 1. *(continued)*

	Sarcopenic men (n = 23)	Non-sarcopenic men (n = 23)	
CSA (mm^2)	119.9 ± 17.2	140.5 ± 26.1	p = 0.003
CSMI $(mm^2)^2$	9.987 ± 3.224	12.795 ± 3.082	p = 0.004
Z (mm^3)	603.8 ± 147.7	694.7 ± 123.1	p = 0.02
Strength index	1.33 ± 0.34	1.25 ± 0.35	p = 0.40
Buckling ratio	4.4 ± 2.1	6.4 ± 3.8	p = 0.03
Handgrip (Kg)	25.3 ± 5.3	32.7 ± 8.4	p < 0.001

SD: Standard Deviation; BMI: Body Mass Index; FM %: Fat Mass percentage; ALM: Appendicular Lean Mass; SMI: Skeletal Muscle mass Index; WB: Whole Body; BMC: Bone Mineral Content; BMD: Bone Mineral Density; L1–L4: Lumbar spine; TH: Total Hip; FN: Femoral Neck; CSA: Cross-Sectional Area; CSMI: Cross-Sectional Moment of Inertia; Z: section modulus; SI: Strength Index; BR: Buckling Ratio.

3.2 Correlations Between Clinical Characteristics and Bone Variables in the Whole Population

Age was negatively correlated to TH BMD, FN BMD, CSA, Z and BR. Lean mass was positively correlated to WB BMC, WB BMD, L1–L4 BMD, TH BMD, FN BMD, CSA, CSMI, Z and BR. ALM was positively correlated to WB BMC, WB BMD, TH BMD, FN BMD, CSA, CSMI, Z and BR. Handgrip was positively correlated to WB BMC, TH BMD, FN BMD, CSA, CSMI, Z and BR (Table 2).

Table 2. Correlations between clinical characteristics and bone variables in the whole population

	WB BMC (kg)	WB BMD (g/m^2)	L1–L4 BMD (g/cm^2)	TH BMD (g/cm^2)	FN BMD (g/cm^2)	CSA (mm^2)	CSMI $(mm^2)^2$	Z (mm^3)	SI	BR
Age (years)	−0.11	−0.10	−0.01	−0.36*	−0.39**	−0.35*	−0.28	−0.37*	−0.03	−0.33*
Weight (kg)	0.28	0.21	0.05	0.34*	0.28	0.24	0.16	0.24	−0.30*	0.18
Height (m)	0.41**	0.17	0.09	−0.07	0.02	0.27	0.40**	0.30*	0.15	0.05
BMI (Kg/m^2)	0.08	0.13	0.01	0.38**	0.28	0.12	0.00	0.12	−0.37**	0.19
Lean mass (kg)	0.75***	0.55***	0.45**	0.53***	0.48***	0.66***	0.55***	0.36*	0.05	0.40**
Fat mass (kg)	−0.13	−0.21	−0.08	−0.15	−0.12	0.09	0	−0.12	0.21	0.15
Fat mass (%)	0.11	0.16	0.06	0.23	0.17	0.09	0	0.29*	−0.44**	−0.07
ALM (kg)	0.54***	0.45**	0.26	0.53***	0.52***	0.57***	0.48***	0.41**	−0.17	0.42**

(continued)

Table 2. (*continued*)

	WB BMC (kg)	WB BMD (g/m²)	L1–L4 BMD (g/cm²)	TH BMD (g/cm²)	FN BMD (g/cm²)	CSA (mm²)	CSMI (mm²)²	Z (mm³)	SI	BR
SMI (kg/m²)	0.32*	0.31*	0.18	0.53***	0.46**	0.43**	0.27	0.21	−0.24	0.39**
ALM/BMI (m²)	0.45**	0.26	0.24	0.06	0.18	0.43**	0.51***	0.27	0.31*	0.27
Handgrip (kg)	0.51***	0.27	0.27	0.38**	0.39**	0.54***	0.50***	0.32*	0.07	0.31*

BMI: Body Mass Index; ALM: Appendicular Lean Mass; SMI: Skeletal Muscle mass Index; WB: Whole Body; BMC: Bone Mineral Content; BMD: Bone Mineral Density; L1–L4: Lumbar spine; TH: Total Hip; FN: Femoral Neck; CSA: Cross-Sectional Area; CSMI: Cross-Sectional Moment of Inertia; Z: section modulus; SI: Strength Index; BR: Buckling Ratio; * $p < 0.05$; ** $p < 0.01$; *** $p < 0.001$.

3.3 Multiple Linear Regression Models

Lean mass was the strongest predictor of WB BMD and L1–L4 BMD. Lean mass and age remained correlated to TH BMD and FN BMD after controlling for fat mass (Table 3).

Table 3. Multiple linear regression models

	Coefficient ± SE	*t*-value	*p*-value
Dependent variable: WB BMD (R^2 = 0.296)			
Constant	0.774 ± 0.207	3.731	p < 0.001
Age (years)	−0.001 ± 0.002	−0.548	p = 0.587
Lean mass (kg)	0.008 ± 0.001	4.219	p < 0.001
Fat mass (kg)	−0.000 ± 0.000	−1.482	p = 0.146
Dependent variable: L1–L4 BMD (R^2 = 0.156)			
Constant	0.290 ± 0.436	0.666	p = 0.509
Age (years)	0.001 ± 0.004	0.256	p = 0.799
Lean mass (kg)	0.013 ± 0.004	3.294	p = 0.002
Fat mass (kg)	−0.000 ± 0.000	−0.382	p = 0.705
Dependent variable: TH BMD (R^2 = 0.363)			
Constant	1.003 ± 0.231	4.336	p < 0.001
Age (years)	−0.006 ± 0.002	−2.731	p = 0.009
Lean mass (kg)	0.008 ± 0.002	3.999	p < 0.001
Fat mass (kg)	−0.000 ± 0.000	−1.504	p = 0.140
Dependent variable: FN BMD (R^2 = 0.325)			
Constant	1.053 ± 0.253	4.168	p < 0.001
Age (years)	−0.008 ± 0.002	−2.922	p = 0.006
Lean mass (kg)	0.008 ± 0.002	3.463	p = 0.001
Fat mass (kg)	−0.000 ± 0.000	−1.245	p = 0.220

WB: Whole Body; BMC: Bone Mineral Content; BMD: Bone Mineral Density; L1–L4: Lumbar spine; TH: Total Hip; FN: Femoral Neck.

3.4 Adjusted Bone Variables in the Two Groups

After adjusting for age and lean mass or for age and ALM, there were no significant differences between the two groups regarding bone variables (Table 4).

Table 4. Bone variables adjusted for covariates in the two groups

	Adjusted for age and lean mass		Adjusted for age and ALM	
	Sarcopenic men (n = 23)	Non-sarcopenic men (n = 23)	Sarcopenic men (n = 23)	Non sarcopenic men (n = 23)
	Mean ± SE	Mean ± SE	Mean ± SE	Mean ± SE
WB BMC (kg)	2.373 ± 0.057	2.272 ± 0.057	2.365 ± 0.073	2.281 ± 0.073
WB BMD (g/cm^2)	1.072 ± 0.018	1.040 ± 0.018	1.079 ± 0.020	1.033 ± 0.020
L1–L4 BMD (g/cm^2)	1.047 ± 0.038	0.969 ± 0.038	1.038 ± 0.042	0.978 ± 0.042
TH BMD (g/cm^2)	0.850 ± 0.020	0.894 ± 0.020	0.858 ± 0.021	0.887 ± 0.021
FN BMD (g/cm^2)	0.796 ± 0.022	0.828 ± 0.022	0.809 ± 0.022	0.814 ± 0.022
CSA (mm^2)	128.9 ± 3.6	131.6 ± 3.6	129.4 ± 4.0	131.0 ± 4.0
CSMI (mm^2)^2	10.9 ± 0.5	11.8 ± 0.5	10.9 ± 0.6	11.7 ± 0.6
Z (mm^3)	634.2 ± 26.5	664.2 ± 26.5	646.9 ± 26.2	651.5 ± 26.2
SI	1.37 ± 0.07	1.21 ± 0.07	1.30 ± 7.3	1.28 ± 7.3
BR	5.19 ± 0.61	5.62 ± 0.61	5.45 ± 0.61	5.36 ± 0.61

SE: Standard Error; ALM: Appendicular Lean Mass; WB: Whole Body; BMC: Bone Mineral Content; BMD: Bone Mineral Density; L1–L4: Lumbar spine; TH: Total Hip; FN: Femoral Neck; CSA: Cross-Sectional Area; CSMI: Cross-Sectional Moment of Inertia; Z: section modulus; SI: Strength Index; BR: Buckling Ratio.

4 Discussion

The aim of this study was to explore the influence of sarcopenia on bone mineral density and hip geometry parameters in a group of elderly men. Herein, we showed that sarcopenia is associated with lower BMC, BMD and hip strength indices values. Body weight, BMI, lean mass, appendicular lean mass and handgrip were significantly higher in non-sarcopenic men compared to sarcopenic men. In fact, sarcopenia is not only characterized by decreased lean mass but also with a decreased muscular strength which leads to consequences on mobility and autonomy [36–38]. Previous studies have also shown significant relations between sarcopenia and decreased bone mass, and several mechanisms have been suggested to explain this relationship [49–52]. In our study, WB BMC, TH BMD, FN BMD, CSA, CSMI and Z were significantly higher in non-sarcopenic men compared to sarcopenic men. However, lumbar spine BMD was not significantly different between the two groups. In fact, the cortical bone of the femoral neck is much more affected by mechanical factors than the trabecular bone of the lumbar spine [12, 13]. Importantly, the differences between the two groups regarding bone variables disappeared after adjustment for age and lean mass or age and appendicular lean mass. These results suggest a causal relationship between lean mass or ALM and BMD in our studied population. Lean mass was the strongest determinant of bone variables as revealed by the correlations and the multiple linear regression models. This result is in line with those of many studies conducted on elderly men [21, 22, 34]. Appendicular lean mass and handgrip were also positively correlated to most of bone variables. Accordingly, increasing appendicular lean mass and muscular strength seems to be beneficial to prevent osteoporosis. The present study has several limitations such as its cross-sectional nature, the relatively low number of subjects, the two-dimensional nature of the DXA measurement, and the lack of measurement of many bone determinants (hormones, vitamin D and nutritional intakes). However, up tour knowledge, it is one of very few studies that aimed at studying the influence of sarcopenia on bone health parameters in the Lebanese elderly.

5 Conclusion

In conclusion, the present study suggests that sarcopenia negatively influences bone parameters in elderly men. Strategies to prevent osteoporosis in elderly sarcopenic men should be implemented. More precisely, resistance training should be advised in order to prevent the loss of lean mass that occurs with ageing.

Conflicts of Interest. The authors state that they have no conflicts of interest.

References

1. Beck, T.J.: Extending DXA beyond bone mineral density: understanding hip structure analysis. Curr. Osteoporos Rep. **5**(2), 49–55 (2007). https://doi.org/10.1007/s11914-007-0002-4
2. Friedman, A.W.: Important determinants of bone strength: beyond bone mineral density. J. Clin. Rheumatol. **12**(2), 70–77 (2006)
3. Ammann, P., Rizzoli, R.: Bone strength and its determinants. Osteoporos. Int. **14**(Suppl 3), S13–S18 (2003)
4. Fonseca, H., Moreira-Gonçalves, D., Coriolano, H.-J., Duarte, J.A.: Bone quality: the determinants of bone strength and fragility. Sports Med. **44**(1), 37–53 (2013). https://doi.org/10.1007/s40279-013-0100-7
5. Rizzoli, R., Bonjour, J.P., Ferrari, S.L.: Osteoporosis, genetics and hormones. J. Mol. Endocrinol. **26**(2), 79–94 (2001)
6. Beck, B.R., Snow, C.M.: Bone health across the lifespan–exercising our options. Exerc. Sport Sci. Rev. **31**(3), 117–122 (2003)
7. Petit, M.A., Beck, T.J., Kontulainen, S.A.: Examining the developing bone: What do we measure and how do we do it? J. Musculoskelet. Neuronal Interact. **5**(3), 213–224 (2005)
8. Goltzman, D.: The Aging Skeleton. Adv. Exp. Med. Biol. **1164**, 153–160 (2019)
9. Min, S.K., et al.: Position statement: exercise guidelines to increase peak bone mass in adolescents. J. Bone Metab. **26**(4), 225–239 (2019)
10. Monge, M.C.: Optimizing bone health in adolescents. Curr. Opin. Obstet. Gynecol. **30**(5), 310–315 (2018)
11. Bonjour, J.P., Chevalley, T., Rizzoli, R., Ferrari, S.: Gene-environment interactions in the skeletal response to nutrition and exercise during growth. Med. Sport Sci. **51**, 64–80 (2007)
12. Bonjour, J.P., Chevalley, T., Ferrari, S., Rizzoli, R.: The importance and relevance of peak bone mass in the prevalence of osteoporosis. Salud Publica Mex. **51**(Suppl 1), S5–S17 (2009)
13. Bonjour, J.P., Chevalley, T.: Pubertal timing, bone acquisition, and risk of fracture throughout life. Endocr. Rev. **35**(5), 820–847 (2014)

14. El Hage, R., Jacob, C., Moussa, E., Jaffré, C., Baddoura, R.: Bone mass in a group of Lebanese girls from Beirut and French girls from Orleans. J. Med. Liban. **59**(3), 131–135 (2011)
15. El Hage, R., Baddoura, R.: Anthropometric predictors of geometric indices of hip bone strength in a group of Lebanese postmenopausal women. J Clin Densitom. **15**(2), 191–197 (2012)
16. El Hage, R., Jacob, C., Moussa, E., Baddoura, R.: Relative importance of lean mass and fat mass on bone mineral density in a group of Lebanese postmenopausal women. J. Clin. Densitom. **14**(3), 326–331 (2011)
17. Ayoub, M.L., et al.: DXA-based variables and osteoporotic fractures in Lebanese postmenopausal women. Orthop. Traumatol. Surg. Res. **100**(8), 855–858 (2014)
18. Hage, R.E., Bachour, F., Sebaaly, A., Issa, M., Zakhem, E., Maalouf, G.: The influence of weight status on radial bone mineral density in lebanese women. Calcif. Tissue Int. **94**(4), 465–467 (2013). https://doi.org/10.1007/s00223-013-9822-7
19. El Hage, R., et al.: Influence of age, morphological characteristics, and lumbar spine bone mineral density on lumbar spine trabecular bone score in Lebanese women. J. Clin. Densitom. **17**(3), 434–435 (2014)
20. Maalouf, G., et al.: Epidemiology of hip fractures in Lebanon: a nationwide survey. Orthop. Traumatol. Surg. Res. **99**(6), 675–680 (2013)
21. El Hage, R., Mina, F., Ayoub, M.L., Theunynck, D., Baddoura, R.: Relative importance of lean mass and fat mass on bone mineral density in a group of Lebanese elderly men. J. Med. Liban. **60**(3), 136–141 (2012)
22. El Hage, R., Theunynck, D., Rocher, E., Baddoura, R.: Geometric indices of hip bone strength in overweight and control elderly men. J. Med. Liban. **62**(3), 150–155 (2014)
23. El-Hajj Fuleihan, G., Baddoura, R., Awada, H., Salam, N., Salamoun, M., Rizk, P.: Low peak bone mineral density in healthy Lebanese subjects. Bone **31**(4), 520–528 (2002)
24. Arabi, A., et al.: Bone mineral density by age, gender, pubertal stages, and socioeconomic status in healthy Lebanese children and adolescents. Bone **35**(5), 1169–1179 (2004)
25. El Hage, R., Jacob, C., Moussa, E., Jaffré, C., Benhamou, C.L.: Daily calcium intake and body mass index in a group of Lebanese adolescents. J. Med. Liban. **57**(4), 253–257 (2009)
26. Salamoun, M.M., et al.: Low calcium and vitamin D intake in healthy children and adolescents and their correlates. Eur. J. Clin. Nutr. **59**(2), 177–184 (2005)
27. Gannagé-Yared, M.H., Chemali, R., Yaacoub, N., Halaby, G.: Hypovitaminosis D in a sunny country: relation to lifestyle and bone markers. J. Bone Miner. Res. **15**(9), 1856–1862 (2000)
28. Gannagé-Yared, M.H., Chemali, R., Sfeir, C., Maalouf, G., Halaby, G.: Dietary calcium and vitamin D intake in an adult Middle Eastern population: food sources and relation to lifestyle and PTH. Int. J. Vitam. Nutr. Res. **75**(4), 281–289 (2005)
29. Fazah, A., Jacob, C., Moussa, E., El-Hage, R., Youssef, H., Delamarche, P.: Activity, inactivity and quality of life among Lebanese adolescents. Pediatr. Int. **52**(4), 573–578 (2010)
30. Nasreddine, L., et al.: Dietary, lifestyle and socio-economic correlates of overweight, obesity and central adiposity in Lebanese children and adolescents. Nutrients **6**(3), 1038–1062 (2014)
31. Naja, F., Hwalla, N., Itani, L., Karam, S., Sibai, A.M., Nasreddine, L.: A Western dietary pattern is associated with overweight and obesity in a national sample of Lebanese adolescents (13–19 years): a cross-sectional study. Br. J. Nutr. **114**(11), 1909–1919 (2015)
32. El Hage, Z., et al.: Bone mineral content and density in obese, overweight and normal weight adolescent boys. J. Med. Liban. **61**(3), 148–154 (2013)

33. El Hage, R.: Geometric indices of hip bone strength in obese, overweight, and normal-weight adolescent boys. Osteoporos. Int. **23**(5), 1593–1600 (2012)
34. Arabi, A., Baddoura, R., Awada, H., Salamoun, M., Ayoub, G., El-Hajj, F.G.: Hypovitaminosis D osteopathy: is it mediated through PTH, lean mass, or is it a direct effect? Bone **39** (2), 268–275 (2006)
35. Arabi, A., Baddoura, R., El-Rassi, R., El-Hajj, F.G.: Age but not gender modulates the relationship between PTH and vitamin D. Bone **47**(2), 408–412 (2010)
36. Cruz-Jentoft, A.J., et al.: Writing group for the European working group on Sarcopenia in older people 2 (EWGSOP2), and the extended group for EWGSOP2. Sarcopenia: revised European consensus on definition and diagnosis. Age Ageing **48**(4), 601 (2019)
37. Beaudart C, et al.: Sarcopenia in daily practice: assessment and management. BMC Geriatr. 16(1):170 (2016)
38. Dhillon, R.J., Hasni, S.: Pathogenesis and management of Sarcopenia. Clin. Geriatr. Med. **33**(1), 17–26 (2017)
39. Hirschfeld, H.P., Kinsella, R., Duque, G.: Osteosarcopenia: where bone, muscle, and fat collide. Osteoporos. Int. **28**(10), 2781–2790 (2017)
40. Khawaja, A., et al.: Does muscular power predict bone mineral density in young adults? J. Clin. Densitom. **22**(3), 311–320 (2019)
41. Berro, A.J., et al.: Physical performance variables and bone parameters in a group of young overweight and obese women. J Clin Densitom. **22**(2), 293–299 (2019)
42. Al Rassy, N., et al.: The relationships between bone variables and physical fitness across the BMI spectrum in young adult women. J. Bone Miner. Metab. **37**(3), 520–528 (2019)
43. Nasr R, et al: Muscular maximal strength indices and bone variables in a group of elderly women. J. Clin. Densitom. 2018 pii: S1094–6950(18)30014-3. https://doi.org/10.1016/j.jocd.2018.03.003
44. El Khoury, G., et al.: Bone Variables in active overweight/obese men and sedentary overweight/obese men. J. Clin. Densitom. **20**(2), 239–246 (2017)
45. El Khoury, C., et al.: Physical performance variables and bone mineral density in a group of young overweight and obese men. J. Clin. Densitom. **21**(1), 41–47 (2018)
46. Zakhem, E., et al.: Performance physique et densité minérale osseuse chez de jeunes adultes libanais. J. Med. Liban. **64**(4), 193–199 (2016)
47. El Hage, R., et al.: Maximal oxygen consumption and bone mineral density in a group of young Lebanese adults. J. Clin. Densitom. **17**(2), 320–324 (2014)
48. Roberts, H.C., et al.: A review of the measurement of grip strength in clinical and epidemiological studies: towards a standardised approach. Age Ageing **40**(4), 423–429 (2011)
49. Reiss, J., et al.: Sarcopenia and osteoporosis are interrelated in geriatric inpatients. Z. Gerontol. Geriatr. **52**(7), 688–693 (2019)
50. Qi, H., et al.: Bone mineral density and trabecular bone score in Chinese subjects with sarcopenia. Aging Clin. Exp. Res. **31**(11), 1549–1556 (2019)
51. Wong, R.M.Y., et al.: The relationship between sarcopenia and fragility fracture-a systematic review. Osteoporos. Int. **30**(3), 541–553 (2019)
52. Nasr, R., Watelain, E., Pinti, A., Maalouf, G., Berro, A.J., El Hage, R.: Sarcopenia and hip structure analysis variables in a group of elderly men. J Clin Densitom. **21**(2), 312–313 (2018)

Novel Thermal Image Classification Based on Techniques Derived from Mathematical Morphology: Case of Breast Cancer

Sebastien Mambou[1], Ondrej Krejcar[1(✉)], Ali Selamat[1,2], Michal Dobrovolny[1], Petra Maresova[1], and Kamil Kuca[1]

[1] Center for Basic and Applied Research, Faculty of Informatics and Management, University of Hradec Kralove, Rokitanskeho 62, 500 03 Hradec Kralove, Czech Republic
{jean.mambou, ondrej.krejcar, michal.dobrovolny, petra.maresova, kamil.kuca}@uhk.cz

[2] Faculty of Computing, Universiti Teknologi Malaysia, 81310 Johor Baharu, Johor, Malaysia
aselamat@utm.my

Abstract. Image processing (IP) is a method of converting an image to digital form by performing operations on it to obtain an improved image or to extract useful information from it. It is a type of signal distribution in which the input is an image such as a video image or a photograph, and the output can be an image or associated characteristics. Besides, this system includes the processing of images in the form of two-dimensional signals, while applying signal processing methods already defined for them. One of the essential steps in IP is a combined application of erosion and dilation procedures, which is part of the mathematical morphology. This article presents a novel thermal image classification based on techniques derived from mathematical morphology. In the processing of grayscale breast cancer images, this method reveals the region of interest as the whitest area.

Keywords: Image processing · Morphology · Breast cancer

1 Introduction

Thermal imaging is a technique using infrared energy (IRE) which does not appear to the naked eye, the IRE emitted by the object, is then converted into a visual image [1]. Every object above a temperature of absolute 0 emits thermal energy in infrared form; thus, each object can be identified using a thermal imaging camera. The same rules applied to a given subject undertaking a thermography diagnosis, as well as the entire region where the creation, evolution, and end of cells behave abnormally. Once the growth of the cells is no longer regulated in a favorable proportion of cell growth to cell death is observed, which is a primary means of cancer [1, 2]. Moreover, this abnormal growth of cells causes an increase of temperature in the area surrounding the tumor, as shown (see Fig. 1). One of the difficulties of breast cancer study is the adoption of the model (spherical, cylindrical …) as breasts do not have a static shape. It is, therefore,

I. Rojas et al. (Eds.): IWBBIO 2020, LNBI 12108, pp. 683–694, 2020.
https://doi.org/10.1007/978-3-030-45385-5_61

crucial to choose a model close to the breast you intend to examine. Several authors such as [1, 3, 4] have already contributed to this vast field, although there is still a lot to do. This article will emphasize on the preprocessing phase of grayscale breast cancer images, with the ultimate goal of revealing the region of interest (ROI) as the whitest area [5, 6], which can be potentially inputted to a given the convolutional neural network model. Saying that, the first part of this article will be a related work, followed by the proposed model, then a slight discussion and a satisfactory conclusion.

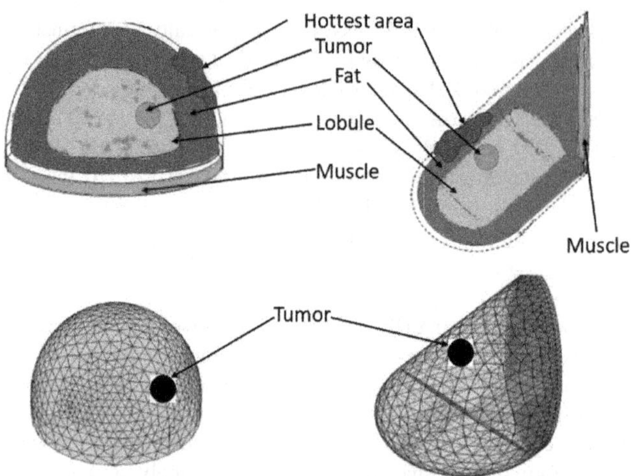

Fig. 1. The first row of images illustrates an annotation diagram of the spherical and cylindrical representation of a cancerous breast. The second row shows a 3D grayscale representation of the two breast models with a black spot as the area of the tumor.

2 Related Work

Although image preprocessing can be done using several techniques, one of the most common is morphology. Its application on the prerequisite dataset can increase the execution time of an entire computer vision system and contributes to its performance. Taking into consideration few variances of the image morphology, authors in [1, 7–11] exhibit an algorithm that performed binary morphology on images described by a quadtree. They also reveal that their approach considerably decreases the execution time of many images. The latter is due to the fact, a considerable number of images and the number of nodes in their representation in a quadtree, is insignificant compared to the number of pixels. Overall, the use of a quadtree algorithm in the resolution of problems in d-dimensional space runs overtime proportionally to the algorithm based on a similar array in space (d − 1) of the d original dimensional image [12]. Many states exist in which a corrupt additive element (noise) must be extracted from an unnamed digital signal; An example can be a two-dimensional image. Although this intricacy does not have a general solution, real and synthetic images have enough varied characteristics from regular noise to allow the rise of many practically valuable noise compression algorithms [13–15]. The achievement and features of these algorithms strongly depend on how people separate represent the discrepancy when they have to separate "noise" from "signal." In this context, the signal can be considered as anything that contains a height or a least over an assigned spatial area. This representation is fundamentally self-sufficient, taking into account the information classification data. Therefore, it is also applied to smooth and disjoint signals.

A filter can be developed as an aggregation of operators based on classification and linear (Gaussian filtering), which find its application in the elimination of noise on damaged signals, also in medical computed tomography [16–19]. Furthermore, such filter has been found to perform well, give a various range of noise levels; it also transcends other morphology-based options. In addition, such filter can be compared to similar linear filters, for instance, non-local means or anisotropic diffusion [20], especially for images where a considerable level of noise is detected. The structurally remodeling morphological procedures (adaptive morphology) gained some interest in modern studies [21] with a strong arithmetical base [9]. There are many methods for adjusting the mask shape; however, the degree to which each mask can be shaped based on the data depends on the performance of the noise reduction [21].

The definitions of the other forms are necessary if a significant attenuation of the noise is required. If not the case, each mask should be readjusted to deal with the noise level properly. Considering the predefined plane masks [22], which are suitable enough to include in the filter, the ellipses being the most straightforward extension of a circle. After defining the structurally varying type of mask, its specific adjustment and form must be adequate to adjust to the image data.

Having a closer look at the preprocessing of thermal images (TI) [2, 23], it appears through literature the correct use of TI can lead to an impressive outcome, as shown by [24]. As mentioned in the author's paper [24], current methods of detecting ships by thermal infrared (TI) potentially face a substantial decrease in performance, in the event of significant marine congestion. To cope with this dilemma, [24] introduced a new way of detecting ships based on morphological remodeling and multifunctional study. First, the TIR image is processed by a morphological reconstruction of the gray levels based on the opening or closing to smooth the complex bulk of the background while retaining the intensity, shape, and contour characteristics of the target of the ship. Then, taking into account the features of intensity and contrast, the fusion saliency apprehension approach comprising a foreground warmth saliency map and a shine contrast saliency map is given to highlight possible objectives of ships and remove congestion from the Wed. After that, an elective contour representation, specifically the mean eigenvalue of the structure tensor, is created to discriminate the objectives of candidate ships, including knowledge of the statistical form is introduced to identify the actual targets of ships from residual targets not related to boats. Lastly, the binary method is used to concurrently distinguish light and dark targets of vessels in the TI image. An illustration of the results of the preprocessing of a synthetic TI ship image is shown (see Fig. 1), and was based on the opening or closing of the morphological reconstruction. Their corresponding 3D mesh plots are shown in the second line [14, 25]. Shiny ship targets are labeled in boxes, and dark ship targets are labeled in circles. The authors [26] had for purpose to promote an equation to determine the breast reference heat as a function of the variation in ambient and central body temperature; for their experiments, four asymptomatic ladies were assessed during three continuous menstrual cycles. They have considered breast and eye temperatures as an indirect allusion to kernel body and room temperatures. To assess the thermal behavior of the breasts during the cycle, the essence body and room heats were normalized using a precise equation [2, 17, 27] (Fig. 2).

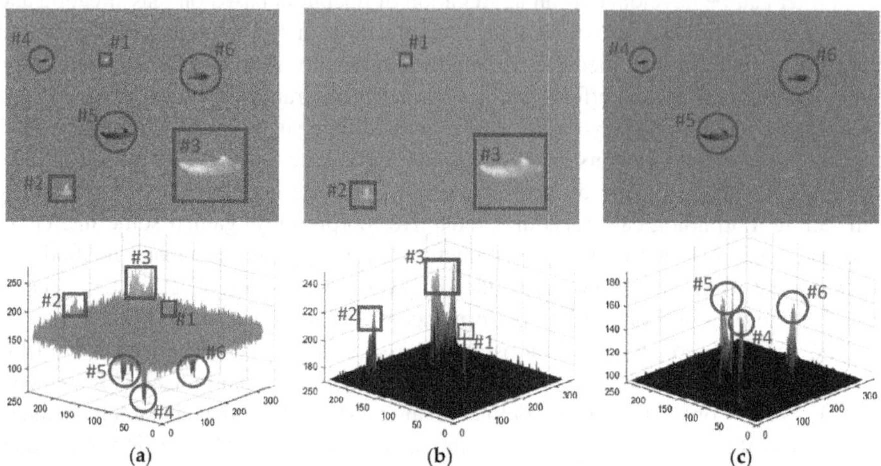

Fig. 2. The illustration of the preprocessing results of a synthetic TI ship image based on the morphological reconstruction of the gray levels. (a) Original artificial TI image, which includes three lighted ship objectives and three obscure ship targets buried in massive white Gaussian noise at a conventional deviation of 10. (b) The result of preprocessing the target image of shiny ships filtered by gray level based on morphological closure reconstruction. (c) The result of the preprocessing of the specific image of the dark ship refined by gray-based morphological reconstruction with aperture base [24].

As a result, [26] did 180 illustrations, including the inside temperature, which had the most active association with breast heat, accompanied by room temperature. The suggested forecast model could reveal 45.3% of the variation in breast temperature, with a changeable room temperature; it can be considered as a method for determining the reference breast heat at various ambient temperatures [28]. Overall, [26] found that the common breast heat in healthy ladies was directly linked to core and room temperature and can be estimated mathematically. It was suggested that an equation could be used in clinical practice to estimate the normal reference breast temperature in young women, despite the time of the cycle, thereby assisting in the evaluation of anatomical studies.

3 Extraction of Region of Interest

Bearing in mind our goal, which is to reveal the region of interest as the whitest area of the grayscale image. Several parts of image morphology processing must be followed (see Fig. 3).

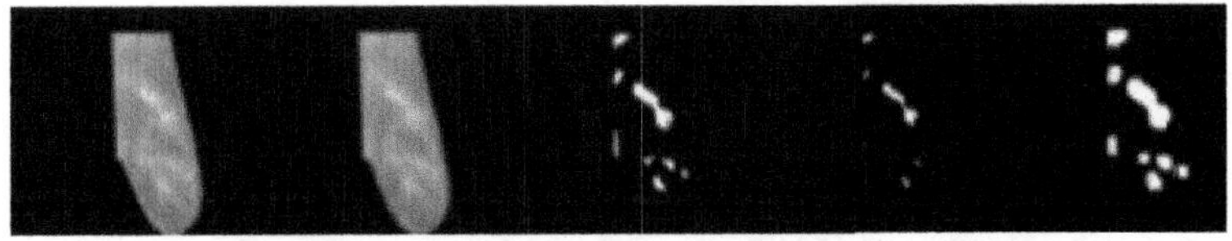

Fig. 3. Result of a list of sequential operations applied to an image. As input, a grayscale image is thresholded to reveal bright regions. Besides, the resulting image is blurred, and a set of erosions and expansions are performed to remove small spots of noise.

3.1 A Threshold-Based Method

The threshold-based approach is manageable and popularly used in the segmentation method. It brings into account the variation in gray value between the target objects and the background, then determines one or more image thresholds using certain main parties to divide the image into one or more parts. The gray pixel value above the threshold is organized in a region class, while the gray pixel value below the threshold is classified in another region class. It can not only compress a large amount of data but also considerably simplify the analysis and image processing steps. Hence, in various circumstances, the segmentation of the threshold is quite significant before pattern recognition, feature extraction, and model analysis. It is especially relevant to the circumstances where the targets and the background have distinct gray levels. The benefits are high efficiency and simple operations. There are many ways of threshold segmentation. Depending on the field of application of the information, it can be divided into two classes, one is the global threshold, and another is the method based on edge detection. The global limit gains the benefit of information from the entire image. It then determines the optimal threshold for the whole image, which can be a unique value or multiple thresholds. The "Ostu" process takes the gray value, which can cause the variance within the classes to reach the highest amount as the optimal threshold.

Let's assume $1 - g$ the gray value scale of an image, p a pixel value, and T is the number of pixels.

$$T = \sum_{i=1}^{g} x_i \tag{1}$$

Also, a probability resulting of each pixel is computed as

$$P_p = \frac{x_p}{T} \tag{2}$$

In addition, a division into 2 set S of the gray values is required

$$S_0 = \{1, 2, 3, \ldots v\} \tag{3}$$

$$S_1 = \{v+1, v+2, v+3, \ldots g\} \tag{4}$$

Where $v \in \mathbb{N}$

Furthermore, a probability $\mathcal{O}$ of each group can be computed as

$$\mathcal{O}_0 = \sum_{j=1}^{v} \left(\frac{x_i}{T}\right)_j => \mathcal{O}_0 = \sum_{j=1}^{v} (P_p)_j = \mathcal{O}(v) \tag{5}$$

$$\mathcal{O}_1 = \sum_{j=v+1}^{g} \left(\frac{x_i}{T}\right)_j => \mathcal{O}_1 = \sum_{j=v+1}^{g} (P_p)_j = 1 - \mathcal{O}(v) \tag{6}$$

Besides, the average value A of each set can be found with

$$A_0 = \sum_{i=1}^{v} p\left(\frac{P_p}{\mathcal{O}_0}\right) => A_0 = \frac{A(v)}{\mathcal{O}(v)} \tag{7}$$

$$A_1 = \sum_{j=v+1}^{g} p\left(\frac{P_p}{\mathcal{O}_1}\right) => A_1 = \frac{A - A(v)}{1 - \mathcal{O}(v)} \tag{8}$$

Going back to the whole image, its average value A is

$$A = \sum_{p=1}^{g} p(P_p) \tag{9}$$

Considering Eqs. (1) to (9), the good threshold value can be found adjusting the value v in the equation below:

$$Var(v) = \mathcal{O}_0(A_0 - A)^2 + \mathcal{O}_1(A_1 - A)^2 \tag{10}$$

3.2 Blur, Erosion and Dilation Extension of Morphological Operators

A blurred area is defined based on the fuzzy map of unique value constructed, and a blur mask is created based on the threshold achieved in the preceding subsection (see Fig. 3). The precise amount of the area extraction is defined as the ratio of correctly segmented pixels to the entire number of pixels in the image. Two aspects influence the blur level of an image: the first one is the blur intensity of the full picture, which is assessed by the single value feature; another is the ratio of the size of the blur area for the entire picture region.

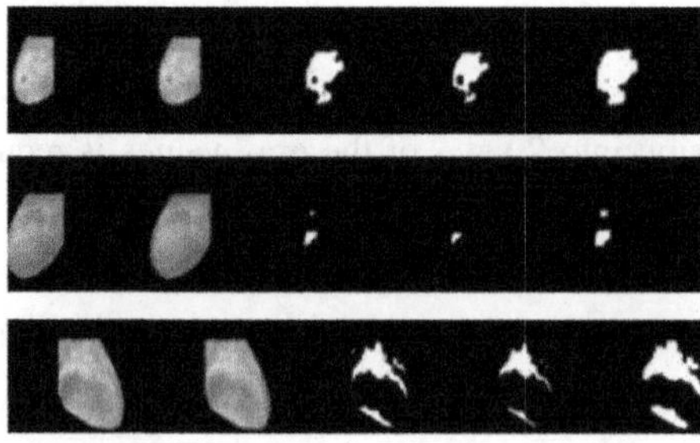

Fig. 4. A series of respective operations: blurring, erosion, and dilation on thresholded images.

On the other hand, the erosion and dilation techniques extend the morphological operators a Cartesian grid where real-valued or integer signals are defined. The descriptions of binary operation increase consistently to the field of digital grayscale signals with inversion and translation following a stead processing. At the same time, union and intersection become respectively point maximum and point minimum operators. Hence, considering point-wise maximum denoted by w, the dilatation of grayscale image denoted $f \circ i$ can be computed as:

$$f \circ i = W_{x \in \mathbb{D}_i} f_x \tag{11}$$

A result of the above technique is given in Fig. 4.

3.3 Workflow and Algorithm Involve in the Described Model

Workflow

Considering the workflow below and the given problem of breast Cancer thermal images. Any preprocessing of grayscale images dataset can be covered by Mask generation one image per iteration to guaranty an optimal result (see Fig. 5).

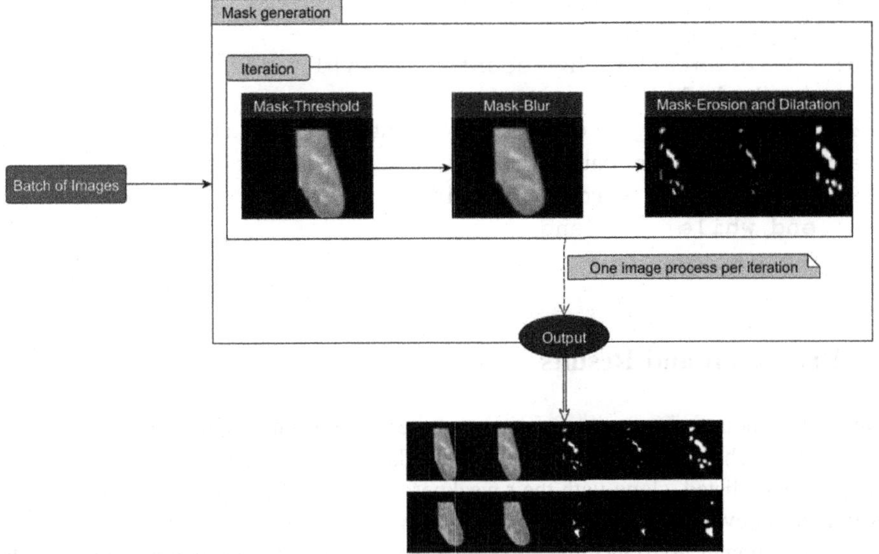

Fig. 5. The illustration of the different stages requires to obtain an effective mask generation. The latter is defined as revealing the region of interest as the whitest area of the grayscale image.

Algorithm

Adopting the respective functions threshold (), Blur(), and dilat_Eros() as the mains actors described in the above workflow, any given a grayscale thermal image of a breast cancer dataset, the algorithm below describes how well our method will compute a "Mask generation."

```
Input: Image_Dataset
Input: Number_Image
Output:  mask_Generation
Batch [10]← 0, counterBatch ← 0, counter10 ← 0, counter-
Img ← 0, Total_Image_Dataset[Number_Image]← Image_Dataset
//Initialization
while counter10 < Number_Image do //beginning
    counterBatch← 0
   while counterBatch < 10 do
      Batch[counterBatch]←Total_Image_Dataset[counter-
Img]
      counterBatch←counterBatch+1
   end while
   counterBatch← 0
   while counterBatch < 10 do
      image_Threshold = Threshold(Batch[counterBatch])
      image_Blur = Blur(image_Threshold)
      image_dilat_Eros = dilat_Eros(image_Blur)
      mask_Generation[counterBatch]
 ← image_dilat_Eros
      counterBatch← counterBatch+1
   end while
   counterImg ← counter10  // next time count after
value content in counter10
   counter10 ← counter10 + 10
end while    //end
```

4 Discussion and Results

Given the amount of image processing and the name of other applications that can be run above each “mask generation.” The standard methods applied to identify breast cancer can be listed, along with their weaknesses and strengths; However, one appears with a bright eventuality due to its non-immersive quality. Infrared imagery, joined by a robust computer assistance device (CAD), such as an estimate or comparison of the whitest area, can lead to an exact tumor detector (See Fig. 6).

A brain neoplasm happens if unusual cells grow in the brain. Two categories of neoplasms can be identify: cancerous (malignant) and benign (non-cancerous) tumors. Given the recent data set published in [29], the algorithm described is applied to it, and the region of interest (cancerous area) is determined as indicated below (See Fig. 7).

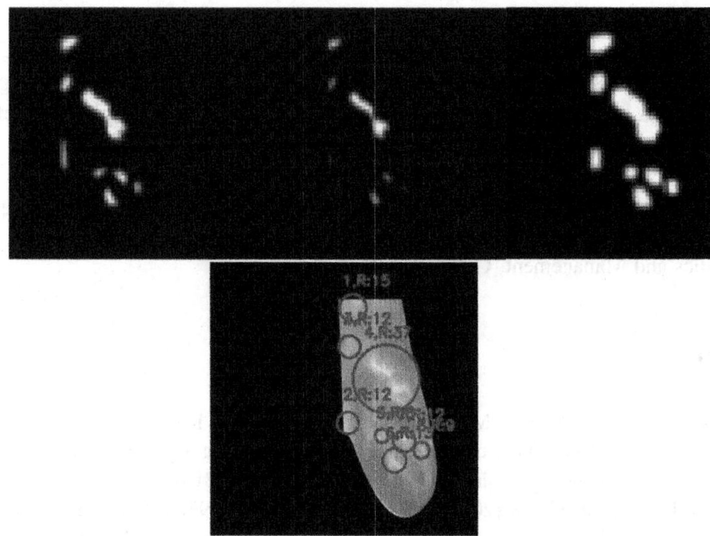

Fig. 6. An estimation or comparison of the whitest area can lead to an exact tumor detector.

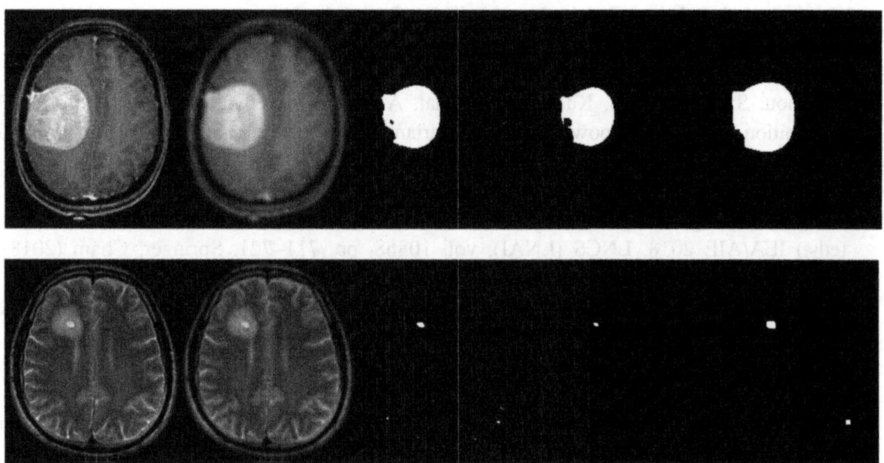

Fig. 7. From left to right, continuous blurring, erosion, and expansion operations are carried out according to the algorithm described a few lines above. In the rightest images, the regions of interest are determined [29].

5 Conclusions

A new method based on morphological grayscale processing is proposed in this article to reveal the region of interest as the whitest area of a thermal image of grayscale breast cancer. The intended image (IP) processing method can automatically segment the image using average breast temperature, and the study suggests that the use of techniques derived from mathematical morphology on thermography in medical practice is feasible. Furthermore, this system includes the processing of images in the form of two-dimensional signals while applying for the already defined signal processing methods. One of the essential steps in IP is a combined application of erosion and dilation procedures, which is part of mathematical morphology.

Acknowledgment. The work and the contribution were supported by the SPEV project "Smart Solutions in Ubiquitous Computing Environments", 2019, University of Hradec Kralove, Faculty of Informatics and Management, Czech Republic.

References

1. Mambou, S., Krejcar, O., Maresova, P., Selamat, A., Kuca, K.: Novel four stages classification of breast cancer using infrared thermal imaging and a deep learning model. In: Rojas, I., Valenzuela, O., Rojas, F., Ortuño, F. (eds.) IWBBIO 2019. LNCS, vol. 11466, pp. 63–74. Springer, Cham (2019). https://doi.org/10.1007/978-3-030-17935-9_7
2. Mambou, S.J., Maresova, P., Krejcar, O., Selamat, A., Kuca, K.: Breast Cancer detection using infrared thermal imaging and a deep learning model. Sensors (Basel) **18** (2018). https://doi.org/10.3390/s18092799
3. Mambou, S., Krejcar, O., Selamat, A.: Approximate outputs of accelerated Turing machines closest to their halting point. In: Nguyen, N.T., Gaol, F.L., Hong, T.-P., Trawiński, B. (eds.) ACIIDS 2019. LNCS (LNAI), vol. 11431, pp. 702–713. Springer, Cham (2019). https://doi.org/10.1007/978-3-030-14799-0_60
4. Mambou, S., Krejcar, O., Kuca, K., Selamat, A.: Novel cross-view human action model recognition based on the powerful view-invariant features technique. Future Internet **10**, 89 (2018). https://doi.org/10.3390/fi10090089
5. Alpar, O., Krejcar, O.: A comparative study on chrominance based methods in dorsal hand recognition: single image case. In: Mouhoub, M., Sadaoui, S., Ait Mohamed, O., Ali, M. (eds.) IEA/AIE 2018. LNCS (LNAI), vol. 10868, pp. 711–721. Springer, Cham (2018). https://doi.org/10.1007/978-3-319-92058-0_68
6. Samuel, T., Assefa, D., Krejcar, O.: Framework for effective image processing to enhance tuberculosis diagnosis. In: Nguyen, N.T., Hoang, D.H., Hong, T.-P., Pham, H., Trawiński, B. (eds.) ACIIDS 2018. LNCS (LNAI), vol. 10752, pp. 376–384. Springer, Cham (2018). https://doi.org/10.1007/978-3-319-75420-8_36
7. Zhang, X., et al.: Cancer cell membrane-coated rare earth doped nanoparticles for tumor surgery navigation in NIR-II imaging window. Chem. Eng. J. **385**, 123959 (2020). https://doi.org/10.1016/j.cej.2019.123959
8. Nobel, T.B., et al.: Incidence and risk factors for isolated esophageal cancer recurrence to the brain. Ann. Thorac. Surg. **109**, 329–336 (2020). https://doi.org/10.1016/j.athoracsur.2019.09.028
9. Bouaynaya, N., Schonfeld, D.: Theoretical foundations of spatially-variant mathematical morphology Part II: gray-level images. IEEE Trans. Pattern Anal. Mach. Intell. **30**, 837–850 (2008). https://doi.org/10.1109/TPAMI.2007.70756
10. Devarriya, D., Gulati, C., Mansharamani, V., Sakalle, A., Bhardwaj, A.: Unbalanced breast cancer data classification using novel fitness functions in genetic programming. Expert Syst. Appl. **140**, 112866 (2020). https://doi.org/10.1016/j.eswa.2019.112866

11. Peter, S.C., et al.: Combination of an ultrafast TWIST-VIBE Dixon sequence protocol and diffusion-weighted imaging into an accurate easily applicable classification tool for masses in breast MRI. Eur. Radiol. (2020). https://doi.org/10.1007/s00330-019-06608-8
12. Samet, H.: Applications of Spatial Data Structures: Computer Graphics, Image Processing, and GIS. Addison-Wesley Longman Publishing Co., Inc., Boston (1990)
13. Asem, M.M., Oveisi, I.S., Janbozorgi, M.: Blood vessel segmentation in modern wide-field retinal images in the presence of additive Gaussian noise. J. Med. Imaging **5** (2018). https://doi.org/10.1117/1.JMI.5.3.031405
14. Alpar, O., Krejcar, O.: Virtual road condition prediction through license plates in 3D simulation. In: Nguyen, N.-T., Manolopoulos, Y., Iliadis, L., Trawiński, B. (eds.) ICCCI 2016. LNCS (LNAI), vol. 9875, pp. 269–278. Springer, Cham (2016). https://doi.org/10.1007/978-3-319-45243-2_25
15. Alpar, O., Krejcar, O.: Detection of irregular thermoregulation in hand thermography by fuzzy C-means. In: Rojas, I., Ortuño, F. (eds.) IWBBIO 2018. LNCS, vol. 10814, pp. 255–265. Springer, Cham (2018). https://doi.org/10.1007/978-3-319-78759-6_24
16. Alpar, O., Krejcar, O.: Frequency and time localization in biometrics: STFT vs. CWT. In: Mouhoub, M., Sadaoui, S., Ait Mohamed, O., Ali, M. (eds.) IEA/AIE 2018. LNCS (LNAI), vol. 10868, pp. 722–728. Springer, Cham (2018). https://doi.org/10.1007/978-3-319-92058-0_69
17. Alpar, O., Krejcar, O.: Thermal imaging for localization of anterior forearm subcutaneous veins. In: Rojas, I., Ortuño, F. (eds.) IWBBIO 2018. LNCS, vol. 10814, pp. 243–254. Springer, Cham (2018). https://doi.org/10.1007/978-3-319-78759-6_23
18. Fernandez, J.-J.: Computational methods for electron tomography. Micron **43**, 1010–1030 (2012). https://doi.org/10.1016/j.micron.2012.05.003
19. Agulleiro, J.I., Vazquez, F., Garzon, E.M., Fernandez, J.J.: Hybrid computing: CPU+GPU co-processing and its application to tomographic reconstruction. Ultramicroscopy **115**, 109–114 (2012). https://doi.org/10.1016/j.ultramic.2012.02.003
20. Buades, A., Coll, B., Morel, J.M.: A review of image denoising algorithms, with a new one. Multiscale Model. Simul. **4**, 490–530 (2005). https://doi.org/10.1137/040616024
21. Legaz-Aparicio, Á.-G., Verdu-Monedero, R., Angulo, J.: Adaptive morphological filters based on a multiple orientation vector field dependent on image local features. J. Comput. Appl. Math. **330**, 965–981 (2018). https://doi.org/10.1016/j.cam.2017.05.001
22. Landström, A., Thurley, M.J.: Adaptive morphology using tensor-based elliptical structuring elements. Pattern Recogn. Lett. **34**, 1416–1422 (2013). https://doi.org/10.1016/j.patrec.2013.05.003
23. Mambou, S., Krejcar, O., Maresova, P., Selamat, A., Kuca, K.: Novel hand gesture alert system. Appl. Sci. **9**, 3419 (2019). https://doi.org/10.3390/app9163419
24. Li, Y., Li, Z., Zhu, Y., Li, B., Xiong, W., Huang, Y.: Thermal infrared small ship detection in sea clutter based on morphological reconstruction and multi-feature analysis. Appl. Sci. **9**, 3786 (2019). https://doi.org/10.3390/app9183786
25. Marek, T., Krejcar, O., Selamat, A.: Possibilities for development and use of 3D applications on the android platform. In: Nguyen, N.T., Trawiński, B., Fujita, H., Hong, T.-P. (eds.) ACIIDS 2016. LNCS (LNAI), vol. 9622, pp. 519–529. Springer, Heidelberg (2016). https://doi.org/10.1007/978-3-662-49390-8_51
26. de Souza, G.A.G.R., Brioschi, M.L., Vargas, J.V.C., Morais, K.C.C., Dalmaso Neto, C., Neves, E.B.: Reference breast temperature: proposal of an equation. Einstein (Sao Paulo) **13**, 518–524 (2015). https://doi.org/10.1590/S1679-45082015AO3392

27. Mesicek, J., Zdarsky, J., Dolezal, R., Krejcar, O., Kuca, K.: Simulations of light propagation and thermal response in biological tissues accelerated by graphics processing unit. In: Nguyen, N.-T., Manolopoulos, Y., Iliadis, L., Trawiński, B. (eds.) ICCCI 2016. LNCS (LNAI), vol. 9876, pp. 242–251. Springer, Cham (2016). https://doi.org/10.1007/978-3-319-45246-3_23
28. Kubicek, J., Penhaker, M., Augustynek, M., Cerny, M., Oczka, D., Maresova, P.: Detection and dynamical tracking of temperature facial distribution caused by alcohol intoxication with using of modified OTSU regional segmentation. In: Nguyen, N.T., Hoang, D.H., Hong, T.-P., Pham, H., Trawiński, B. (eds.) ACIIDS 2018. LNCS (LNAI), vol. 10752, pp. 357–366. Springer, Cham (2018). https://doi.org/10.1007/978-3-319-75420-8_34
29. Brain MRI Images for Brain Tumor Detection. https://kaggle.com/navoneel/brain-mri-images-for-brain-tumor-detection. Accessed 9 Feb 2020

Data Preprocessing via Multi-sequences MRI Mixture to Improve Brain Tumor Segmentation

Vladimir Groza[1(✉)], Bair Tuchinov[2], Evgeniy Pavlovskiy[2], Evgeniya Amelina[2], Mihail Amelin[2,3], Sergey Golushko[2], and Andrey Letyagin[2]

[1] Median Technologies, Valbonne, France
vladimir.groza@mediantechnologies.com
[2] Novosibirsk State University, Novosibirsk, Russia
bairt@nsu.ru, pavlovskiy@post.nsu.ru, amelina.evgenia@gmail.com, amelin81@gmail.com, s.k.golushko@gmail.com, letyaginay@bionet.nsc.ru
[3] FSBI "Federal Neurosurgical Center", Novosibirsk, Russia

Abstract. Automatic brain tumor segmentation is one of the crucial problems nowadays among other directions and domains where daily clinical workflow requires to put a lot of efforts while studying computer tomography (CT) or structural magnetic resonance imaging (MRI) scans of patients with various pathologies. The MRI is the most common method of primary detection, non-invasive diagnostics and a source of recommendations for further treatment. The brain is a complex structure, different areas of which have different functional significance.

In this paper, we propose a robust pre-processing technique which allows to consider all available information from MRI scans by composition of T1, T1C and FLAIR sequences in the unique input. Such approach enriches the input data for the automatic segmentation process and helps to improve the accuracy of the segmentation performance.

Proposed method demonstrates significant improvement on the binary segmentation problem with respect to Dice and Recall metrics compare to similar training/evaluation procedure based on any single sequence regardless of the chosen neural network architecture.

Obtained results demonstrates significant evaluation improvement while combining three MRI sequences either as weighted mixture to get 1-channel mixed up image or in the 3-channel RGB like image for both considered problems - binary brain tumor segmentation with and without inclusion of edema in the region of interest (ROI). Final improvements on the test part of data set are in the range of 5.6–9.1% on the single-fold trained model according to the Dice metric with the best value of 0.902 without considering a priori "empty" slides. We also demonstrate strong impact on the Recall metric with the growth up to 9.5%. Additionally this approach demonstrates significant improvement according to the Recall metric getting the increase by up to 11%.

Keywords: Medical imaging · Deep learning · Neural network · Segmentation · Brain · MRI

I. Rojas et al. (Eds.): IWBBIO 2020, LNBI 12108, pp. 695–704, 2020.
https://doi.org/10.1007/978-3-030-45385-5_62

1 Introduction

According to the data published in global cancer statistics the death rate from oncological diseases in the world currently estimated at 100–150 people per 100 thousand people. At the same time, 65–80% of those who died from cancer have brain tumors. The problem of diagnosing and monitoring the dynamics of neuro-oncological diseases in patients with primary and secondary brain tumors is a hot issue [1–3]. Early detection of cancer significantly improves the efficiency of targeted therapy (operative, radiotherapy, chemotherapeutic, and immunological).

The MRI is the most common method of primary detection, non-invasive diagnostics and a source of recommendations for further treatment. The brain is a complex structure, different areas of which have different functional significance. As a result, another problem arises related to the assessment of the influence of the stage of tumor growth and/or surgical damage to brain structures on the patient's health and quality of life, including the clinical severity of neurological deficiency.

One of the possible approaches to solving the above-mentioned problems is the development of new artificial intelligence based diagnostic methods. The current level of diagnostic tools based on technologies of artificial intelligence can allow doctors to more effectively and efficiently detect and predict the condition of patients with minimizing the factor of "human error". But such a development requires the involvement of highly qualified specialists in various fields: radiation diagnosticians, neurologists, neuro-oncologists, mathematicians, computer scientists, software developers. Usually in the medical imaging applied problems it is necessary to collect and create datasets with specially marked images (CT/X-Ray/MRI/MRE scans) in order to develop and implement automatic numerical solution and solve applied math tasks (segmentation, classification and etc.).

Segmentation of the malignant brain tumors with its edema around turns out as tricky problem due to its highly heterogeneous shape, weekly visual differentiation from healthy matter and requires domain knowledge paired with strong expertise from experienced radiologists. Within the recent achievements and announcements this problem can be solved successfully enough with the use of 2D and 3D deep learning (DL) based methods [4–6,8]. Moreover, DL algorithms demonstrate its capacity and power in many applied topics in the medical image processing being considered as robust and powerful tool.

Brain tumors are usually very heterogeneous in their structure and may have multiple components (tissue, edema, cysts, necrosis etc.). Some of those can mimic healthy brain tissue or could be very hard to distinguish between them. None of single sequences of structural MRI such as T1, T1C, FLAIR or other permits to observe and identify all tumor composition elements and edema by eyes or with the use of existing (semi-)automated techniques.

However, in the daily workflow radiologists rely not only on their competencies, but also on the every accessible data regarding to each particular case. The most problematic situation arise being limited in the use of single sequence by the choice or extracting information from them separately, since there is significant information in each of the available MRI sequence.

The research paper is organized as follows: Sect. 2 presents the description of the designed dataset, Sect. 3 presents the methods and information of experiments, Sect. 4 presents the experimental results with the steps and cases used in the proposed technique, and finally Sect. 5 contains the conclusion and future scope.

2 Dataset Description

The private dataset used in this work consists of 31 brain MRI volume scans in the format of NIfTI files and totally resulting in 5146 2D slices. This limited dataset comprise only two different subtypes of the brain tumors - meningioma and neurinoma and describe several acquisition sequences such as (a) per-contrast T1-weighted (T1), (b) post-contrast T1-weighted (T1C), (c) T2-weighted (T2), (d) T2 Fluid Attenuated Inversion Recovery (FLAIR) volumes and (e) diffusion weighted images (DWI). All separate scans were acquired with different clinical protocols and scanners from Federal Center for Neurosurgery, co-registered to the same anatomical template and interpolated to the same pixel spacing and resolution ($1\,\text{mm}^3$).

All the MRI scans have been segmented manually, by two raters, following the same annotation (labels) protocol. In the progress of segmentation labels were checked (approved) were independently by two experienced board-certified neuro-radiologist and any label misclassification was manually corrected by an expert.

Annotations comprise labels of the peritumoral edema (Ed – label 4), the non-enhancing tumor (NenTu – label 3), GD-enhancing tumor (EnTu – label 2) and the necrotic tumor core (Necr – label 1).

Later for the particular binary segmentation problem, this labeling format was modified according to each requirement by assigning all labeled regions (or except peritumoral edema "Ed" label) to value 1.

3 Methods

In the recent works there were a number of applications and approaches how to better use different modalities and sequences of brain MRI scans in order to produce more stable solutions, increase its performance or synthesize missing data [11–14].

Proposed pre-processing data mixture technique was introduced and evaluated within the pure and light in terms of additional post-processing or complications binary segmentation pipeline. We consider two different sub problems as segmentation of the brain tumor with the surrounding peritumoral edema and segmentation only the tumor itself.

In the core of this framework we use the "LinkNet-like" networks [7] with two different backbones from Se-Resnext50 (SxLink50) and Se-Resnext101 (SxLink101) [9,10,15]. Additionally to that we also implemented three other neural networks (including the "U-Net like" [16]) for the complete numerical comparison and to generalize results.

To avoid overfitting and increase generalization, multiple data augmentation methods such as flipping, shifting and random brightness/contrast from the specialized python library [17] were used in the training.

We trained all networks on the minibatches of 24 samples for 100 epochs with the Adam optimizer and initial learning rate of 0.0001 using the "ReduceLROnPlateau" scheduling for more precise weights optimization via the Pytorch framework. After each epoch training process was evaluated on the validation part of the dataset. In order to get the binarized predictions we use the Sigmoid activation and binarization threshold of 0.6 being selected on the validation subset.

Proposed pre-processing technique in the first case consists of the weighted combination of the T1, T1C and FLAIR sequences in the single 1-channel image of the same dimension. Moreover and more efficient way is to use the various sequence information to construct the RGB-like 3-channel input image by assigning each channel to each sequence. None of the additional manipulation was done.

4 Results

Results presented in this work was obtained on the private and limited in size sub-dataset in order to demonstrate how is it important to consider all available information which is possible to extract to construct the automatic segmentation solution. Our dataset initially contained 31 full brain volumes comprising only two different subtypes of the brain tumors - meningioma and neurinoma. This first version of available data resulted in 5146 2D slices which was randomly split on training/validation/test parts with the sizes of 3828/957 and 361 slices respectively. All data was resized to 448 * 448 pixels without any additional compression. Additionally, we consider a holdout test set as 2 separate full brain volumes (named "B057" and "P019", represented in total by 314 slices) for the independent evaluation.

In this work we present two different approaches of the binary tumor segmentation while including or excluding edema from the ROI. Since edema is very unclear structure on the images, it is very challenging to segment it properly; moreover excluding it from the ROI leads to significant improvement in the accuracy metrics.

Calculating the mean Dice score with the consideration of the "empty" slices where Dice is assigned equal to 1 is very common approach nevertheless not really fair. It allows better understand if the model perform correctly outside the ROI without high false positive (FP) and true negative (TN). After observing very high results, we decided to calculate mean Dice metric for each particular experiment only on the slices where ground truth (GT) or segmentation output is present. Additionally, in order to better control and observe behavior of the given methods we compute Recall and Precision metrics.

4.1 Including Edema in the Segmentation ROI

Segmentation of the tumor including the edema demonstrates good accuracy performance itself achieving the Dice of 0.733 and 0.727 on the test subset for SxLink50 and SxLink101 respectively being trained for binary case only on the T1C sequence. Introduction of the multimodal mixture for the single 1-channel input ("3-mixture") leads to average improvement by 3% and achieving Dice scores of 0.765 and 0.754. Moreover, the preferred method of the multimodal data transformation by assigning each of T1, T1C and FLAIR sequence to each of 3-channels of "RGB" like image ("3-channel") demonstrate increase of the Dice scores by 10.8% and 9.3% with the values of 0.822 and 0.802 (Table 1).

Table 1. DICE scores of test subset wrt the input data type and pipeline backbone for brain tumor segmentation including edema in the ROI.

Input type	SxLink50	SxLink101
T1C (contrast)	0.7334	0.7266
3-mixture	0.7653	0.7538
3-channel	**0.8221**	**0.8017**

Additionally, one could notice from the obtained results that the most significant improvement of proposed approach is observed on edema region and leads to more accurate results and significant decrease of the TN regions in tumor segmentation as demonstrated on the Fig. 1.

4.2 Excluding Edema from the Segmentation ROI

Even if edema is very complex structure for the automatic segmentation and poorly visible and hard-to-separate image region, in this subsection we propose binary segmentation results only for the tumor area.

All experiment details are absolutely equal to the ones from previous subsection. Additionally to the Dice metric we calculate Recall and Precision values in order to demonstrate the strengths of our approach from the clinical side of view (Table 2).

From the obtained results we can notice that significant improvement of the Dice accuracy score, given by the proposed method to combine the input data, is mostly aligned with very strong increase of the Recall values. These results show the importance of the including the multimodal data in the training process and how it can lead to the performance amelioration (Fig. 2).

In order to evaluate the robustness and generalization of the proposed method, we provide similar metrics comparison in Table 3 on the two independent full brain volumes from the cases named "B057" and "P019" as the holdout test set.

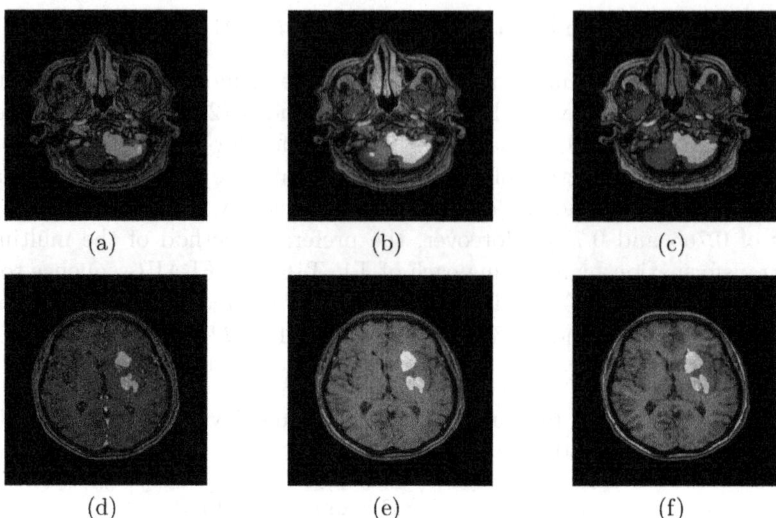

Fig. 1. (a, d) - GT [dark pink] vs Prediction of the tumor with edema [yellow] based on T1C, (b, e) - Prediction of the tumor with edema [yellow] on "3-mixture" and (c, f) - on "3-channel" inputs respectively. (Color figure online)

Table 2. Dice, Recall, Precision scores of test subset wrt input data type and pipeline backbone for brain tumor segmentation excluding edema from the ROI. Values in the brackets obtained with the use of "3-channel" inputs.

Metric	SxLink50	SxLink101
Dice	0.8335 (**0.8975**)	0.8501 (**0.9020**)
Recall	0.8297 (**0.9177**)	0.8652 (**0.9065**)
Precision	**0.9415** (0.9263)	0.9323 (**0.9478**)

4.3 Impact on Models Architecture and Ensembling

Architecture of the neural network can be considered as one of the parameters to solve the problem. Selecting the best model is always somehow the trade-off between the size, performance quality and speed. There are exist several methods to improve the final results by considering several neural network architectures such as K-fold training and average prediction from each of them, or different techniques of ensembling.

In this subsection we investigate the behavior of the proposed pipeline and provide results of the numerical comparison of different network architectures as well as different backbones used as encoders. The main focus of this part is to demonstrate certain independence of the proposed multimodal mixture technique on selected neural network structure.

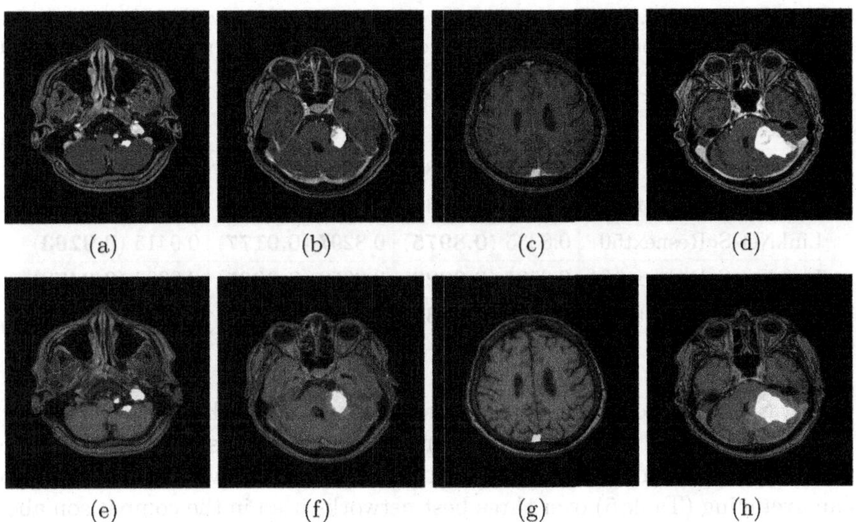

Fig. 2. (a - d) - Segmentation results based on the T1C inputs only, (e - h) - corresponding segmentation outputs in case of "3-channel" input type [GT - dark pink, Prediction - light blue; Intersection - white]. (Color figure online)

Table 3. Dice, Recall, Precision scores for independent patients "B057" and "P019" on brain tumor segmentation excluding edema from the ROI. Values in the brackets obtained with the use of "3-channel" inputs.

Metric	SxLink50 [B057]	SxLink101 [B057]	SxLink50 [P019]	SxLink101 [P019]
Dice	0.8758 (**0.9196**)	0.9073 (**0.9299**)	0.8071 (**0.8444**)	0.7985 (**0.8573**)
Recall	0.9162 (**0.9514**)	0.9168 (**0.9433**)	0.7855 (**0.8238**)	0.8113 (**0.8334**)
Precision	0.9086 (**0.9101**)	**0.9339** (0.9260)	**0.9768** (0.9392)	0.9161 (**0.9556**)

There Dice, Recall and Precision metrics are given in the Table 4 for chosen set of the network. These results report the performance on the binary tumor segmentation excluding the edema from the ROI for two cases - trained only on the T1C sequence inputs and trained on "3-channel" type inputs.

First, it is possible to notice that on this particular problem the difference in the backbones architecture and size is not so sufficient and all models lead to the similar results, except that more complex networks from the "SeResnext" family perform slightly better.

Additionally to that, we observe that regardless of the model and neural network architecture the multimodal "3-channel" approach always improves the segmentation performance by 5.6–9.1% in Dice metric. Another very strong improvement concerns Recall metric where the boost is in range of 4.9–9.5% what is finally complemented by small gain in Precision.

Table 4. Dice, Recall, Precision scores for different neural network architectures. Values in the brackets obtained with the use of "3-channel" multimodal mixture inputs.

Model	Dice	Recall	Precision
UNet-Resnet34	0.8199 (**0.8686**)	0.8302 (**0.8726**)	0.9269 (**0.9471**)
LinkNet-Resnet34	0.8159 (**0.8965**)	0.8560 (**0.9047**)	0.8956 (**0.9330**)
LinkNet-SeResnext50	0.8335 (**0.8975**)	0.8297 (**0.9177**)	0.9415 (**0.9263**)
LinkNet-SeResnext101	0.8501 (**0.9020**)	0.8652 (**0.9065**)	0.9323 (**0.9478**)
LinkNet-SeResnet152	0.8260 (**0.8833**)	0.8347 (**0.8877**)	0.9432 (**0.9461**)

As was mentioned above, some improvement can be achieved by ensembling either of some model over K-fold split or of different models from same or different folds. To give an overview of the possible gain we provide results of simple mean averaging (Table 5) over three best networks used in the comparison above only on one fold from 5-fold split.

Table 5. Dice, Recall, Precision scores for mean averaging ensembling over 3 best models on one fold over 5.

Metric	T1C input	"3-channel" input
Dice	0.8565	0.9026
Recall	0.8559	0.9058
Precision	0.9555	0.9494

And as final experiment in order to complete all possible comparisons, we provide corresponding results for the mean averaging of the best performed model (LinkNet-SeResnext101) over all 5 folds in Table 6.

Table 6. Dice, Recall, Precision scores for mean averaging ensembling over all 5 folds for LinkNet-SeResnext101 model.

Metric	T1C input	"3-channel" input
Dice	0.8796	0.9036
Recall	0.8907	0.9096
Precision	0.9367	0.9504

5 Conclusions

This work presents efficient approach to combine multimodal data in order to significantly improve the quality of the particular applied numerical problem of binary brain tumor segmentation. Stability and robustness of this method was confirmed with various numerical experiments and can be extended to any kind of applied problem with very high probability.

Our results demonstrate strong impact on the Recall metric in both considered subproblems what can be interpreted as significant improvement in the segmentation of the relevant pixels. These particular results are very important from the clinical point of view and can strongly increase quality of the computer-aided systems where similar solutions are deployed.

Automatic brain tumor segmentation can be used to generate computer-aided and manually-revised labels enable quantitative computational and clinical studies without the need to repeat manual annotations whilst allowing for comparison across studies.

One of the possibilities for the future research directions is investigation of the behavior of the proposed pipeline and multimodal technique through the inclusion of the samples with additional tumors types (glioblastoma and etc.). Such continuation of this work will allow to explore clinical parameters such as radiomic and imaging features (including intensity, volumetric, morphologic, histogram-based and textural parameters), as well as spatial information and diffusion properties extracted from tumor growth models.

The provided dataset with radiomic features may facilitate integrative research of the molecular characterization and hence allow associations with molecular markers, clinical outcomes, treatment responses and other endpoints, by researchers without sufficient computational background to extract such features.

Acknowledgement. The reported study was funded by RFBR according to the research project No 19-29-01103.

References

1. Bray, F., Ferlay, J., Soerjomataram, I., Siegel, R.L., Torre, L.A., Jemal, A.: Global cancer statistics 2018: GLOBOCAN estimates of incidence and mortality worldwide for 36 cancers in 185 countries. CA Cancer J. Clin. **68**, 1–31 (2018)
2. Bobinski, M., Greco, C.M., Schrot, R.J.: Giant intracranial medullary thyroid carcinoma metastasis presenting as apoplexy. J. Skull Base **19**, 359–362 (2009)
3. Chrastina, J., Novak, Z., Riha, I., et al.: Diagnostic value of brain tumor neuroendoscopic biopsy and correlation with open tumor resection. J. Neurolog. Surg. Part A **75**(2), 110–115 (2012)
4. Kamnitsas, K., et al.: Ensembles of multiple models and architectures for robust brain tumour segmentation. In: Crimi, A., Bakas, S., Kuijf, H., Menze, B., Reyes, M. (eds.) BrainLes 2017. LNCS, vol. 10670, pp. 450–462. Springer, Cham (2018). https://doi.org/10.1007/978-3-319-75238-9_38
5. Li, C., Wang, S., Serra, A., Torheim, T., Yan, J.L., et al.: Multi-parametric and multi-regional histogram analysis of MRI: modality integration reveals imaging phenotypes of glioblastoma. Eur. Radiol. **29**, 1–12 (2019)

6. Myronenko, A.: 3D MRI brain tumor segmentation using autoencoder regularization. In: Crimi, A., Bakas, S., Kuijf, H., Keyvan, F., Reyes, M., van Walsum, T. (eds.) BrainLes 2018. LNCS, vol. 11384, pp. 311–320. Springer, Cham (2019). https://doi.org/10.1007/978-3-030-11726-9_28
7. Chaurasia, A., Culurciello, E.: LinkNet: exploiting encoder representations for efficient semantic segmentation, CoRR, vol. abs/1707.03718 (2017)
8. Milletari, F., et al.: V-Net: fully convolutional neural networks for volumetric medical image segmentation. In: 2016 Fourth International Conference on 3D Vision, pp. 565–571. IEEE (2016)
9. Xie, S., Girshick, R., Dollár, P., Tu, Z., He, K.: Aggregated residual transformations for deep neural networks. In: Proceedings - 30th IEEE Conference on Computer Vision and Pattern Recognition, CVPR 2017, vol. 1, pp. 5987–5995 (2017)
10. Hu, J., Shen, L., Sun, G.: Squeeze-and-excitation networks, CoRR abs/1709.01507 (2017). https://arxiv.org/abs/1709.01507
11. Ge, C., Gu, I.Y., Store Jakola, A., Yang, J.: Cross-modality augmentation of brain MR images using a novel pairwise generative adversarial network for enhanced glioma classification. In: 2019 IEEE International Conference on Image Processing (ICIP), pp. 559–563 (2019)
12. Havaei, M., Guizard, N., Chapados, N., Bengio, Y.: HeMIS: hetero-modal image segmentation. In: Ourselin, S., Joskowicz, L., Sabuncu, M.R., Unal, G., Wells, W. (eds.) MICCAI 2016. LNCS, vol. 9901, pp. 469–477. Springer, Cham (2016). https://doi.org/10.1007/978-3-319-46723-8_54
13. Varsavsky, T., Eaton-Rosen, Z., Sudre, C.H., Nachev, P., Cardoso, M.J.: PIMMS: permutation invariant multi-modal segmentation, CoRR, vol. abs/1807.06537 (2018). http://arxiv.org/abs/1807.06537
14. Dorent, R., Joutard, S., Modat, M., Ourselin, S., Vercauteren, T.: Hetero-modal variational encoder-decoder for joint modality completion and segmentation, arXiv e-prints. arXiv:1907.11150, July 2019
15. Roy, A.G., Navab, N., Wachinger, C.: Recalibrating fully convolutional networks with spatial and channel 'squeeze & excitation' blocks, CoRR abs/1808.08127 (2018). https://arxiv.org/abs/1808.08127
16. Ronneberger, O., Fischer, P., Brox, T.: U-Net: convolutional networks for biomedical image segmentation. In: Navab, N., Hornegger, J., Wells, W.M., Frangi, A.F. (eds.) MICCAI 2015. LNCS, vol. 9351, pp. 234–241. Springer, Cham (2015). https://doi.org/10.1007/978-3-319-24574-4_28
17. Buslaev, A., Parinov, A., Khvedchenya, E., Iglovikov, V., Kalinin, A.: Albumentations: fast and flexible image augmentations. ArXiv e-prints, 1809.06839 (2018)

Brain MRI Modality Understanding: A Guide for Image Processing and Segmentation

Ayca Kirimtat[1], Ondrej Krejcar[1(✉)], and Ali Selamat[1,2]

[1] Faculty of Informatics and Management, Center for Basic and Applied Research, University of Hradec Kralove, Rokitanskeho 62, 500 03 Hradec Kralove, Czech Republic
a.kirimtat@gmail.com, ondrej.krejcar@uhk.cz, aselamat@utm.my

[2] Malaysia Japan International Institute of Technology (MJIIT), Universiti Teknologi Malaysia, Jalan Sultan Yahya Petra, Kuala Lumpur, Malaysia

Abstract. Medical image processing is a highly challenging research area, thus medical imaging techniques are used to make diagnosis in human body. Moreover, as tumor in the brain is a critical and medical complaint, segmentation of the images has an important role to make segmentation of the brain tumor and it provides suspicious region diagnosis from the medical images. By the help of MRI scanners, signals generated by the human body tissues could be detected and determined spatially. Thus, we in this paper try to propose basics of MRI image modalities as a guide for understanding the processes and methods. Since original brain image is not appropriate for the examination, segmentation of the images could be very useful method for partition of the digital image into similar regions. This research also presents a guide for understanding the brain MRI sequences in other words modalities.

Keywords: MRI · Brain · Image processing · Image segmentation

1 Introduction

Brain images are mostly noisy and inhomogeneous; therefore, it is quite challenging to make accurate segmentation on these images. In order to make correct segmentation and reduce noise on those images, there are various imaging methods including magnetic resonance imaging (MRI) [1, 2]. In recent years, the implementation of image processing techniques has been rapidly increasing, and also storing and capturing of medical images are done in a digital way [3–5]. Moreover, to make interpretation on the medical images in an easy and effective way in other words to make image segmentation, there are different computer vision applications. These applications are used for abnormalities in brain areas that are recognized by the help of radiologists. In addition to these, given the criteria for future processes, image segmentation is highly recommended to partition the images into several regions [6–8].

In several medical applications such as abnormality detection, medical image segmentation is used, and there are a lot of techniques for the segmentation of the

I. Rojas et al. (Eds.): IWBBIO 2020, LNBI 12108, pp. 705–715, 2020.
https://doi.org/10.1007/978-3-030-45385-5_63

images automatically or semi-automatically, some of them do not work and some of them work due to low image contrast or unknown noise [9]. As segmentation of the brain images is rather complex and thought-provoking, it is useful for distinguishing tumors, edema and necrosis, and precise diagnosis of the diseases is highly significant [3, 10, 11].

Basically, segmentation means partition of the medical image into several areas. Furthermore, the main challenges of the segmentation could be noisiness, the bias field and the partial-volume effect. Sometimes, it is very difficult to get rid of noise in MRI images, thus there are several filtering techniques to remove these noises from MRI images, and they are linear and nonlinear filtering methods, anisotropic nonlinear diffusion filtering, a Markov random field models, wavelet models, non-local means models and analytically correction schemes. All of the techniques own both rewards and drawbacks, this means any of them is not healthier than other methods regarding quality, computational rate, denoising etc. [3, 12].

As MRI scanners are quite sensitive to detect abnormalities in human brain, careful determination should be made on imaging features and patterns in other words careful diagnosis should be made on brain lesions. Explicit lesion characteristics and patterns must be identified by supporting with differential diagnosis [13–15]. Therefore, the main aim of this study is to formulate real-world guidelines for the accurate interpretation and classification of brain lesions and to lead scientific era about this topic by making more correct diagnosis.

In the existing literature, there are several studies on brain MRI lesion diagnosis by trying to make accurate diagnosis. For instance, Loizou et al. [16] proposed MR images with an integrated scheme for the register ion and 3D reconstruction. Those MRI images were attained from MS patients, and the doctor of the patients will be accurately aided by following up to disease. The stages of the whole process involve 6 different phases. As a result, the proposed method provided high accuracy in the results and would lead the future clinical practices.

Another MRI brain lesion segmentation study by Qiao et al. [17] showed that there were no difference between K-means and Gaussian Mixture Model-Expectation Maximization in the estimation of performance metrics, which are false positive rate, sensitivity, accuracy etc. Moreover, sensitivity and accuracy of both methods were not affected by the lesion size. However, as a result, both of the method easily segmented the lesion area of the brain MRI.

Xue et al. [18] provided a fully-automated method, which outperformed the previous studies even for small lesions, in order to make stroke brain lesion segmentation. Moreover, it reveals the lesion from given MRI image without any intervention by human. The model that was presented in this study achieved higher efficiency in comparison with the previous machine learning methods. Also, the model presented in this study has faster real-time use thanks to its usability.

Wang et al. proposed a new method to make instinctive segmentation of MS laceration in MRI brain image in T1-weighted, T2-weighted and FLAIR sequences. First, an adaptive sparse Bayesian decision theorem (ASBDT) algorithm was developed, after that a probabilistic label fusion algorithm was developed regarding local weighted voting method. In final, the proposed approaches were evaluated by 20 different brain MRI images. As a result, TPR, PPV, and DSC parameters indicated that the method was quite better than other methods in terms of the number and volume, which are key points in defining the disease.

In the study of Mohr et al. [19], the connection between traumatic life events and the consequent enhancement of brain lesions was examined. Since psychological life traumas are generally associated with MS in the brain, this study aimed to investigate the relationship between these two aspects for human. Therefore, in the present study, the observations that examined the relationships between monthly standardized measures of traumatic life events and the presence of Gd (Gadolinium enhancing) and MRI lesion. As a result, the provided data from samples supported the notion, which conflict and disrupt the relation to the disease in human brain with MS.

According to the study of Stankiewicz [2], the relationship between the brain lacerations and the medical position of 1.5T and 3T MRI was assessed. Therefore, FLAIR sequences were carried out in 32 MS subjects. In conclusion, the FLAIR laceration volume with 3T was significantly more advanced than 1.5T and regarding the patients' ages and depressions relationship between FLLV and cognitive procedures was noteworthy at 1.5T.

In the continuation of this paper, we present various cardinal imaging features and different modalities in the subcategories of Sect. 2. Moreover, Sect. 3 gives the differential features in lesion subclassification, for instance how they look like etc. We finish this paper by giving conclusion remarks on brain MRI image modalities in Sect. 4.

2 Brain MRI Lesion Diagnosis

An optimal imaging sequence changes for each lesion type, thus careful attention should be given while deciding on the correct sequence. Also, in order to guide neurologists and neuroradiologists on the interpretation of the lesions in an adequate way, some guidelines should be specified as it is in our study. Therefore, in the first subsection of this section, we present four cardinal imaging features and in the second subsection, we mention four different modalities by giving example images in Sect. 3.

2.1 Modalities

As MRI imaging method is extensively used in neurology and neurosurgery, it provides exclusive details of human brain, spinal cord or vascular autonomy. Additionally, there are very common MRI sequences namely T1 and T2 (two different relaxation time). These are also called T1 and T2 weighted scans and they are quite relevant with Repetition Time (TR) and Echo Time (TE). Along with the TR and TE times, for instance, T1 weighted images are generated from short TR and TE times, and the contrast and the brightness of the MRI images are defined by the characteristics of the T1 tissue. On the other hand, T2 weighted images are produced from longer TE and TR times, and again the contrast and the brightness of the MRI images are defined by the characteristics of the T2 tissue [20].

However, there is the third very common sequence namely FLAIR (Fluid Attenuated Inversion Recovery) and it is quite similar to T2 weighted image, but it is produced from very longer TE and TR times. The most common MRI sequences are summarized as TI-weighted, T2-weighted and FLAIR as seen in Table 1 [14, 20].

Table 1. Very common MRI sequences as T1, T2 and FLAIR with TR and TE times [20].

	TR (ms)	TE (ms)
T1-weighted	500	14
T2-weighted	4000	90
FLAIR	9000	114

Table 1 shows the TR and TE times of three different MRI sequences, which are T1-weighted, T2-weighted and FLAIR. T1-weighted image is one of the MRI sequences and it shows differences in the T1 relaxation times of tissues. As we compare it with other sequences, it has the shortest TE and TR times.

2.2 Cardinal Imaging Features

Since brain has a very complicated structure, it is very difficult to differentiate the rate of casualties. In addition to this, brain tissues are connected to each other in a complicated way so that efficient segmentation of human brain is quite difficult [21]. Moreover, there are various brain lesions caused by disease or traumas, and they are namely as non-enhanced tumor, enhanced tumor, necrosis and edema.

Basically, lesion is defined as irregular change in the tissue of the brain or organism, and it often reveals in animal's or human's brain. On the other hand, tumor is a mass found in the brain tissue and it is generated from abnormal cells. As one stage further of tumor, necrosis reveals in the dying phase of cells, in other words the act of killing. Lastly, edema means swelling in medicine and it can be also found in the human brain, and it has a little effect on the human body rather than other lesions. Table 2 shows the lesion differentiation by colors in the human brain in T1-weighted, T1 contrast, T2-weighted and FLAIR sequences. For instance, non-enhanced tumor is less bright in T2 weighted and FLAIR sequences. On the other hand, necrosis is dark in T1-weighted and FLAIR, whereas it is bright in T2-weighted sequence.

Table 2. Key features of T1, T1-contrast, T2, and FLAIR sequences.

		T1	T1 contrast	T2	FLAIR
Whole lesion	Non-enhanced tumor	-	-	Less bright	Less bright
	Enhanced tumor	-	Brighter areas than T1	-	-
	Necrosis	Dark	-	Bright	Dark
	Edema	-	-	-	Bright

3 Differential Features in Lesion Subclassification

A lesion visible in MRI is consisting of edema, enhanced and non-enhanced tumor and in some cases necrosis. Whole area could be identified by FLAIR sequence. Figure 1 displays the whole lesion in FLAIR sequence. The example images in Fig. 1 were acquired from the Department of Radiology, University Hospital of Hradec Kralove, consists of MRI axial FLAIR sequence of a patient diagnosed as having a brain tumor [15, 22].

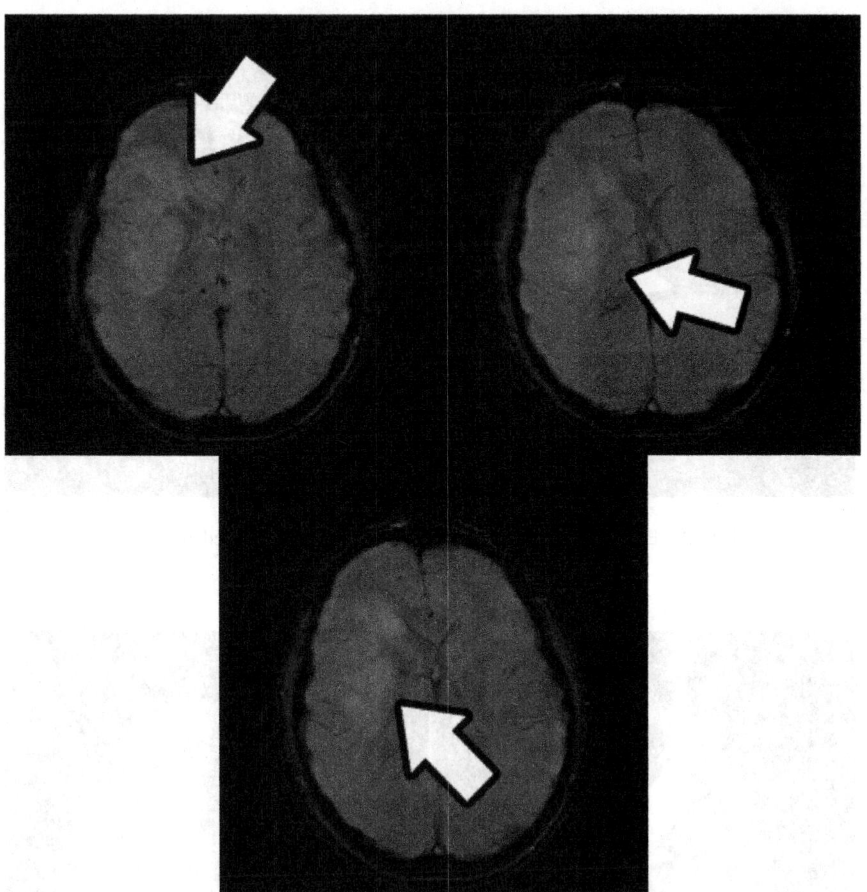

Fig. 1. A figure that shows the whole lesion in FLAIR sequence.

3.1 Enhanced Tumor

Enhanced tumor could be identified as lesions discovered on a brain MRI image growths in contrast at a precise rate over a short-time, which designates enlarged vascularity to the lesion area. Enhanced tumor is generally identified in T1 contrast sequence, and it has brighter areas than T1-weighted. T1-weighted sequence namely as T1WI is a basic pulse sequence in MRI and it basically shows the variances in the T1 relaxation times of tissues. T1weighted sequence tends to have shorter TE and TR times once it is compared with other sequences. On the contrary, T1 contrast can also be performed injecting Gadolinium (Gad). Basically, Gad is an agent that has a non-toxic paramagnetic contrast enhancement, also during the scanning, Gad changes the intensities of the signals by decreasing T1 time [20]. In Figs. 2 and 3, enhanced tumor is shown in both T1 contrast and T1-weighted sequences.

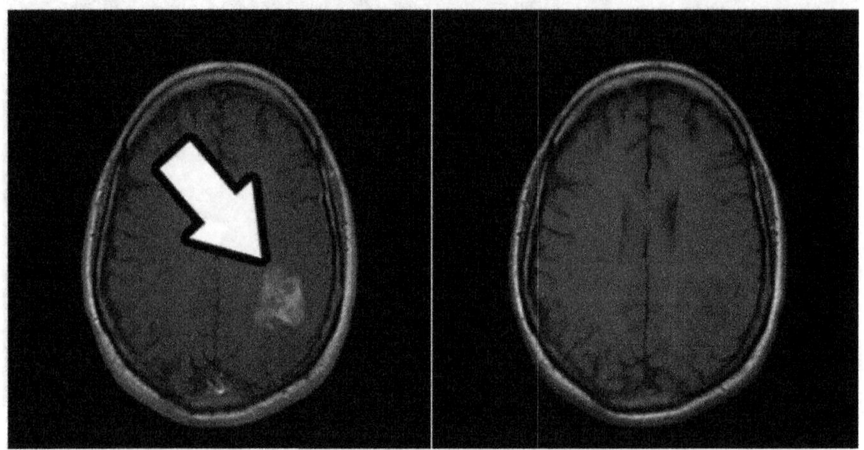

Fig. 2. Enhanced tumor in T1 contrast and T1-weighted images.

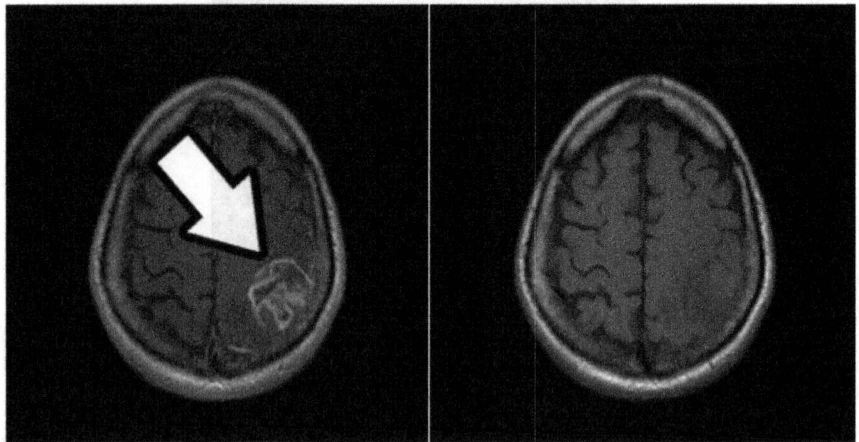

Fig. 3. Enhanced tumor in T1 contrast and T1-weighted images.

3.2 Necrosis

Necrosis could be caused by external or internal reasons and different specific forms of necrosis could exist; for instance Coagulative necrosis, Liquefactive necrosis, Gangrenous necrosis, Caseous necrosis, Fat necrosis, and Fibrinoid necrosis. Necrosis is a basically form of cell injury which is premature death of cells that live in the tissues. Also, the external factors that cause necrosis are trauma, infection, and toxins which are all irregular digestion of cell components. Figure 4 demonstrates the examples of necrosis in T2-weighted and FLAIR sequences from the same patient's brain.

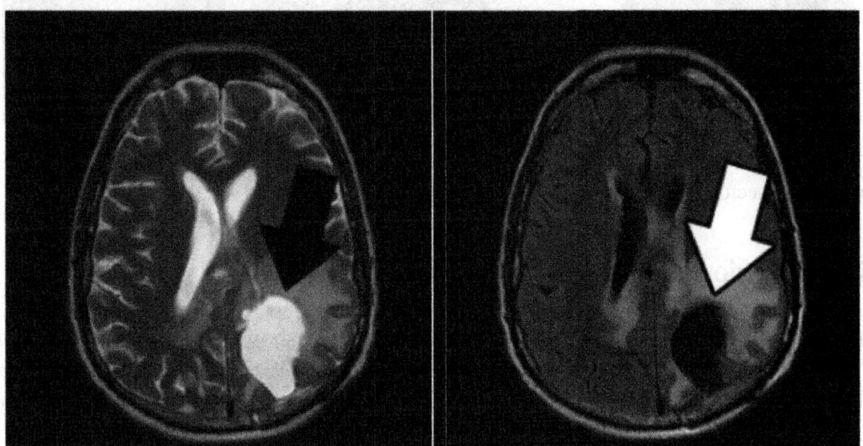

Fig. 4. Necrosis in T2-weighted on the left and FLAIR sequences on the right.

3.3 Edema

Edema [23], also known as swelling or fluid retention, is gathering of fluid in the body tissue. There are a lot of specific examples of edema in the human body such as Pedal edema, Cerebral edema, Pulmonary edema, etc. The edema that occurs in the human brain is Cerebral edema, which the fluid is accumulated in the brain. In Fig. 5, edema could be seen around the necrosis in brighter color in T2-weighted and FLAIR sequences respectively.

Cerebral edema [24] could be caused by many diseases and events in human brain such as traumatic brain injury mostly caused by fall or traffic accident, Ischemic stroke caused by lack of oxygen, brain tumor, infection, brain hemorrhage, high altitude. Moreover, there could be some symptoms of edema such as a headache, loss of consciousness, difficulty in speaking, vision loss, vomiting, memory problems, dizziness, seizures, neck pain and nausea.

Diagnosis of edema basically consists of a physical exam of the head, MRI scan of the whole head, neurological tests and blooding tests. Also, there are various treatments of edema such as medication, surgery, hypothermia and osmotherapy.

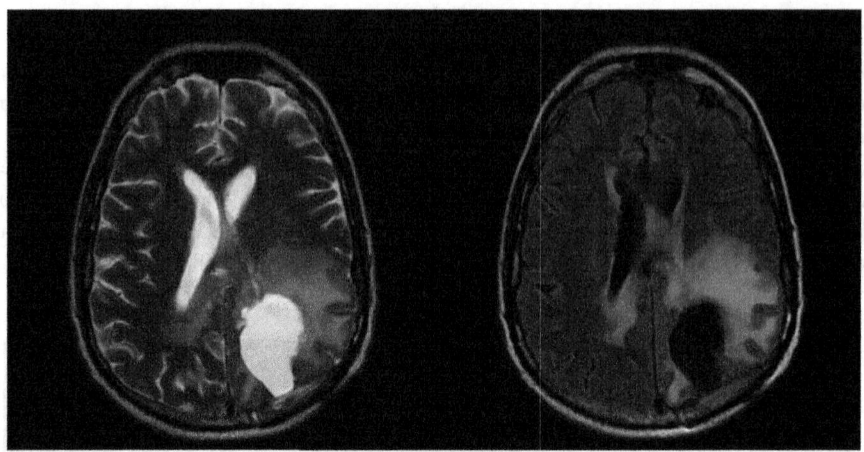

Fig. 5. Edema in T2-weighted on the left and FLAIR sequences on the right (brighter areas around the necrosis).

4 Discussion

As seen in above figures between Figs. 1 and 5, we show the real examples from different patients diagnosed as having a brain tumor. We could see that there are contrast differences in each figure like in some of them we see the necrosis in bright or dark depending on the sequence type.

There are 4 different sequence types studied in this paper namely as T1-weighted, T1 contrast, T2-weighted and FLAIR. Above MRI images shows us whole lesion, enhanced tumor, necrosis, and edema with various sequence types. For instance, in Fig. 1 whole lesion could be diagnosed in FLAIR sequence in very bright color, and this whole lesion consists of enhanced tumor, necrosis and edema. In Fig. 2, enhanced tumor could be identified in T1 contrast in bright color whereas we can see the whole brain area in the same color without any contrast difference in T1-weighted sequence. In addition to Fig. 2, another example of enhanced tumor demonstration could be seen in Fig. 3 in T1 contrast and T1-weighted sequences. On the other hand, a necrosis could be detected in both T2-weighted and FLAIR sequences respectively in Fig. 4, but it is brighter in T2-weighted sequence while it is in dark color in FLAIR sequence. Finally, we can see edema example around the necrosis in brighter color on the left in Fig. 5, whereas the edema area is again in brighter color on the right. Also, Table 3 shows the comparison among each lesion appearance in each sequence type that means which sequence type is the best for recognizing the appropriate lesion. For instance, the best recognition of enhanced tumor belongs to T1 contrast sequence type.

These above figures prove us and lead the scientific era that lesions could be recognized in MRI images with different sequences by understanding the contrast differences between the areas in the brain. Moreover, various studies have shown that by choosing the accurate sequence type, any brain lesion could be easily recognized. Even though, MRI scanners are quite sensitive to determine brain lesions accurately, important

Table 3. Comparison of each lesion appearance in each sequence type (+: best -: worst).

	T1-weighted	T1 contrast	T2-weighted	FLAIR
Enhanced tumor	+	-	-	-
Edema	+	+	+	+
Necrosis	-	-	+ (bright)	+ (dark)
Whole lesion	-	-	-	+

decision should be made on the modality and sequence type. Basically, we compared 4 different cardinal imaging features in this study and they are the most preferred ones in the previous studies in the existing literature as we show in the first section of this paper.

5 Conclusion

As we understood from this study that understanding the brain MRI image modalities is quite significant for further processes which are image segmentation and image processing. In addition to this, the accurate sequence type will provide useful segmentation on MRI images by presenting precise contrast differences.

We, in this paper, present and compare 4 different cardinal imaging features and brain lesion types by also indicating various studies from the existing literature. Our research will guide future studies to make more accurate image segmentation on MRI images. Moreover, since each lesion type has a different presence in each sequence, which are mainly T1-weighted, T1 contrast, T2-weighted and FLAIR. For example, necrosis has both bright and dark appearance in T2-weighted and FLAIR sequences respectively. On the other hand, while enhanced tumor is seen in T1 contrast sequence in brighter, it is not recognized in T1 weighted sequence.

In the light of this study, physicians and scientific era will be guided to easily recognize the patients' diseases in their brains by using accurate sequence type for the specified lesion. Furthermore, since brain images are mostly noisy and inhomogeneous, it is quite challenging to make accurate segmentation on these images. In order to make correct segmentation and reduce noise on those images, there are various imaging methods including magnetic resonance imaging (MRI) which also contains various sequence type for accurate lesion diagnosis.

Acknowledgement. This work is partially supported by the project of SPEV 2020, University of Hradec Kralove, Faculty of Informatics and Management, Czech Republic (under ID: UHK-SPEV-2020) and project of the Ministry of Education, Youth and Sports of Czech Republic (project ERDF no. CZ.02.1.01/0.0/0.0/18_069/0010054).

References

1. Kubicek, J., et al.: Design and analysis of LMMSE filter for MR image data. In: Nguyen, N. T., Gaol, F.L., Hong, T.-P., Trawiński, B. (eds.) ACIIDS 2019. LNCS (LNAI), vol. 11432, pp. 336–348. Springer, Cham (2019). https://doi.org/10.1007/978-3-030-14802-7_29

2. Stankiewicz, J.M., et al.: Brain MRI lesion load at 1.5T and 3T versus clinical status in multiple sclerosis. J. Neuroimaging **21**(2), e50–e56 (2011). https://doi.org/10.1111/j.1552-6569.2009.00449.x
3. Balafar, M.A., Ramli, A.R., Saripan, M.I., Mashohor, S.: Review of brain MRI image segmentation methods. Artif. Intell. Rev. **33**(3), 261–274 (2010). https://doi.org/10.1007/s10462-010-9155-0
4. Alpar, O., Krejcar, O.: A comparative study on chrominance based methods in dorsal hand recognition: single image case. In: Mouhoub, M., Sadaoui, S., Ait Mohamed, O., Ali, M. (eds.) IEA/AIE 2018. LNCS (LNAI), vol. 10868, pp. 711–721. Springer, Cham (2018). https://doi.org/10.1007/978-3-319-92058-0_68
5. Alpar, O., Krejcar, O.: Quantization and equalization of pseudocolor images in hand thermography. In: Rojas, I., Ortuño, F. (eds.) IWBBIO 2017. LNCS, vol. 10208, pp. 397–407. Springer, Cham (2017). https://doi.org/10.1007/978-3-319-56148-6_35
6. Chang, P.-L., Teng, W.-G.: Exploiting the self-organizing map for medical image segmentation. Presented at the Twentieth IEEE International Symposium on Computer-Based Medical Systems (CBMS 2007), Maribor, Slovenia (2007). https://doi.org/10.1109/CBMS.2007.48
7. Marek, T., Krejcar, O., Selamat, A.: Possibilities for development and use of 3D applications on the android platform. In: Nguyen, N.T., Trawiński, B., Fujita, H., Hong, T.-P. (eds.) ACIIDS 2016. LNCS (LNAI), vol. 9622, pp. 519–529. Springer, Heidelberg (2016). https://doi.org/10.1007/978-3-662-49390-8_51
8. Novotny, J., Dvorak, J., Krejcar, O.: User based intelligent adaptation of five in a row game for android based on the data from the front camera. In: De Paolis, L.T., Mongelli, A. (eds.) AVR 2016. LNCS, vol. 9768, pp. 133–149. Springer, Cham (2016). https://doi.org/10.1007/978-3-319-40621-3_9
9. Hall, L.O., Bensaid, A.M., Clarke, L.P., Velthuizen, R.P., Silbiger, M.S., Bezdek, J.: A comparison of neural network and fuzzy clustering techniques in segmenting magnetic resonance images of the brain. IEEE Trans. Neural Netw. **3**, 672–682 (1992)
10. Kubicek, J., et al.: Autonomous segmentation and modeling of brain pathological findings based on iterative segmentation from MR images. In: Nguyen, N.T., Gaol, F.L., Hong, T.-P., Trawiński, B. (eds.) ACIIDS 2019. LNCS (LNAI), vol. 11432, pp. 324–335. Springer, Cham (2019). https://doi.org/10.1007/978-3-030-14802-7_28
11. Alpar, O., Krejcar, O.: Thermal imaging for localization of anterior forearm subcutaneous veins. In: Rojas, I., Ortuño, F. (eds.) IWBBIO 2018. LNCS, vol. 10814, pp. 243–254. Springer, Cham (2018). https://doi.org/10.1007/978-3-319-78759-6_23
12. Dolezal, R., et al.: Variable elimination approaches for data-noise reduction in 3D QSAR calculations. In: Pereira, F., Machado, P., Costa, E., Cardoso, A. (eds.) EPIA 2015. LNCS (LNAI), vol. 9273, pp. 313–325. Springer, Cham (2015). https://doi.org/10.1007/978-3-319-23485-4_33
13. Filippi, M., et al.: Assessment of lesions on magnetic resonance imaging in multiple sclerosis: practical guidelines. Brain **142**(7), 1858–1875 (2019). https://doi.org/10.1093/brain/awz144
14. Samuel, T., Assefa, D., Krejcar, O.: Framework for effective image processing to enhance tuberculosis diagnosis. In: Nguyen, N.T., Hoang, D.H., Hong, T.-P., Pham, H., Trawiński, B. (eds.) ACIIDS 2018. LNCS (LNAI), vol. 10752, pp. 376–384. Springer, Cham (2018). https://doi.org/10.1007/978-3-319-75420-8_36
15. Kunes, M., et al.: Imaging and evaluating method as part of endoscopical diagnostic approaches. In: Nguyen, N.T., Attachoo, B., Trawiński, B., Somboonviwat, K. (eds.) ACIIDS 2014. LNCS (LNAI), vol. 8398, pp. 605–614. Springer, Cham (2014). https://doi.org/10.1007/978-3-319-05458-2_62

16. Loizou, C.P., et al.: Brain image and lesions registration and 3D reconstruction in DICOM MRI images. In: 2017 IEEE 30th International Symposium on Computer-Based Medical Systems (CBMS), Thessaloniki, pp. 419–422 (2017). https://doi.org/10.1109/CBMS.2017.53
17. Qiao, J., et al.: Data on MRI brain lesion segmentation using K-means and Gaussian mixture model-expectation maximization. Data Brief **27**, 104628 (2019). https://doi.org/10.1016/j.dib.2019.104628
18. Xue, Y., et al.: A multi-path 2.5 dimensional convolutional neural network system for segmenting stroke lesions in brain MRI images. NeuroImage Clin. **25**, 102118 (2020). https://doi.org/10.1016/j.nicl.2019.102118
19. Mohr, D.C., et al.: Psychological stress and the subsequent appearance of new brain MRI lesions in MS. Neurology **55**(1), 55–61 (2000). https://doi.org/10.1212/WNL.55.1.55
20. Preston, D.C.: Magnetic resonance imaging (MRI) of the brain and spine: basics. Magnetic Resonance Imaging (MRI) of the Brain and Spine: Basics (2006). https://casemed.case.edu/clerkships/neurology/Web%20Neurorad/MRI%20Basics.htm. Accessed 04 Jan 2020
21. Usman, K., Rajpoot, K.: Brain tumor classification from multi-modality MRI using wavelets and machine learning. Patt. Anal. Appl. **20**(3), 871–881 (2017). https://doi.org/10.1007/s10044-017-0597-8
22. Novozámský, A., Flusser, J., Tachecí, I., Sulík, L., Bureš, J., Krejcar, O.: Automatic blood detection in capsule endoscopy video. J. Biomed. Opt. **21**(12) (2016). https://doi.org/10.1117/1.jbo.21.12.126007
23. Chen, X., et al.: A prediction model of brain edema after endovascular treatment in patients with acute ischemic stroke. J. Neurol. Sci. **407**, 116507 (2019). https://doi.org/10.1016/j.jns.2019.116507
24. Nakano, T., et al.: Goreisan prevents brain edema after cerebral ischemic stroke by inhibiting Aquaporin 4 upregulation in mice. J. Stroke Cerebrovasc. Dis. **27**(3), 758–763 (2018). https://doi.org/10.1016/j.jstrokecerebrovasdis.2017.10.010

Computer-Aided Breast Cancer Diagnosis from Thermal Images Using Transfer Learning

Çağrı Cabıoğlu[1] and Hasan Oğul[2](✉)

[1] Department of Computer Engineering, Başkent University, 06790 Ankara, Turkey
[2] Faculty of Computer Sciences, Østfold University College, 1757 Halden, Norway
hasan.ogul@hiof.no

Abstract. Breast cancer is one of the prevalent types of cancer. Early diagnosis and treatment of breast cancer have vital importance for patients. Various imaging techniques are used in the detection of cancer. Thermal images are obtained by using the temperature difference of regions without giving radiation by the thermal camera. In this study, we present methods for computer aided diagnosis of breast cancer using thermal images. To this end, various Convolutional Neural Networks (CNNs) have been designed by using transfer learning methodology. The performance of the designed nets was evaluated on a benchmarking dataset considering accuracy, precision, recall, F1 measure, and Matthews Correlation coefficient. The results show that an architecture holding pre-trained convolutional layers and training newly added fully connected layers achieves a better performance compared with others. We have obtained an accuracy of 94.3%, a precision of 94.7% and a recall of 93.3% using transfer learning methodology with CNN.

Keywords: Deep learning · Transfer learning · AlexNet · Thermal image · Image processing · Convolutional neural network · Breast cancer

1 Introduction

Cancer is a disease caused by uncontrolled and rapid growth of abnormal cells beyond the normal growth limits. These abnormal cells also can spread to other part of the body, which is called metastasis. There are many types of cancer. Most common types are lung, prostate, stomach, colorectal and breast. Cancer is the one of the dangerous diseases that causes 9.6 million death in 2018 [1].

Breast cancer is one of the common cancers among women. Each year, affect 2.1 million women, and also approximately 627,000 women died due to breast cancer worldwide in 2018 [1]. These statistics shows the importance of research about breast cancer. According to The Health Insurance Plan of Greater New York (HIP) trial, with early diagnosis and treatments can reduce deaths caused by breast cancer [2].

I. Rojas et al. (Eds.): IWBBIO 2020, LNBI 12108, pp. 716–726, 2020.
https://doi.org/10.1007/978-3-030-45385-5_64

The incidence of breast cancer has increased in the last few years, but the mortality rate is decreasing [3]. This reduction is because of new imaging methodologies to diagnose breast cancer. These techniques help doctors to make an accurate diagnoses and localization.

There are several techniques to diagnose breast cancer. One of them is mammography which uses low-dose x-rays to detect cancer. However, cancer can be hidden under fibroglandular tissue at dense breasts, this situation decreases sensitivity of mammography [4]. The other technique is Magnetic Resonance Imaging. Imaging with MRI has more detailed information also its sensitivity higher than other techniques. This procedure mostly used to patients who are in high risk group or their cancer tissue could not find at mammography [5]. But it is expensive and time consuming. Ultrasound is another medical imaging technique. It uses sound waves for detecting cancer. This technique is safe and inexpensive. Using all these methods together provide good visualization. Because of that, these are complementary methods [6].

Nowadays, infrared (IR) thermography has a rising popularity to detecting breast cancer. Thermography captures heat radiation over selected surface of the region. Human body would give up heat radiation in any situation. Especially in areas where the tumor is located, temperature is higher than other normal areas caused by the high metabolic activity of cancer cells [7]. Thermography has an ability to visualize this heat changing on the human skin and also on breast. Thermography is fast, non-contact and it is not sending harmful radiation through the human body.

Computer aided detection or diagnosis (CAD) systems has an important role to produce meaningful data and accurate diagnosis automatically from images [8]. CAD systems for breast cancer diagnoses using image processing techniques are improving in last years and current researches contribute on three main perspectives: automatic segmentation approaches, smart image enhancement and restoration algorithms, and feature extraction and classification [7].

Initial stage of CAD systems is image acquisition and storage. There are two common acquisition protocol: static and dynamic. In static protocol, single images taken at room temperature. On the other hand, images taken by using dynamic protocol contains time data. The specific area of the body is cooled first and the images are taken until body recover that cooling effect [9].

This paper makes the following contributions. First, we develop supervised learning methodology based on transfer learning using CNN architecture. Next, we show how selection of transferred layers affect performance that evaluate using cross validation technique. Last, we compare results using five metric which are accuracy, precision, recall, F1 measure and Matthews correlation coefficient (MCC).

2 Related Work

Araújo et al. [10] developed non-automatic segmentation and three stage feature extraction methodology to classify breast cancer. First stage is extracting maximum and minimum temperature value from morphologically processed IR image. At second stage is extracting interval features and produce continues features. Using Fisher's criterion continues features mapped on new feature space for the last stage. Parzen-window, linear discriminant and distance-based classifiers applied on these new feature spaces. They achieved 85.7% sensitivity and 86.5% specificity.

Krawczyk and Schaefer [11] developed another methodology for detecting breast cancer. Their approach based on obtaining image features which describes asymmetry of normal and abnormal breast. For feature extraction, they extract basic statistical features, histogram features, image moments, and various texture features. In pattern classification part, they combine multiple classifier using neural network fusion approach and evolutionary computing. This method tested on 146 static IR breast image which 29 of them are sick and 177 of them are healthy. They reported an 90.03% accuracy, 80.35% sensitivity and 90.15% specificity.

Another paper is written by Gaber et al. [12] Their approach has two stage: automatic segmentation and classification. In segmentation part, they used Neutrosophic sets (NS) and optimized Fast Fuzzy c-mean (F-FCM) algorithm. Support vector machine (SVM) used for classification of normal and abnormal breast and tested on 29 healthy and 34 malignant images. They reported an 92.06% accuracy, 96.55% recall and 87.50% precision.

Baffa and Lattari [6] developed another methodology based on convolutional neural networks. They used static and dynamic IR images. Data set tested on their CNN architecture. Data augmentation, mean subtraction and gray to RGB transformation applied on IR images separately. For static protocol, they reported 98% accuracy, 97% sensitivity and 100% specificity.

3 Materials and Methods

3.1 Convolutional Neural Networks

Convolution neural network (CNN) is a class of deep neural network [13]. CNN is consisting of trainable filters and local neighborhood pooling operations. These are used in the layers. Number of layers has an important impact on the network performance [14]. So, CNN capabilities are depending on their depth and breadth. About performance, CNN achieves higher success compared to standard feed forward neural network. Because CNN have less connection and parameters then standard feed-forward neural network despite of same network depth [13].

Generally, CNN models composed of five parts. The first part is convolution layer. Convolution Layer is the most important part of CNN. It has trainable filters and each iteration its parameters updated. Rectified Linear Activation Function (RELU) layer mostly preferred in CNN architectures because of it speed up training process. Max pooling layer reduces parameter size and control overfitting. Neurons in fully connected layer is a regular neural network. Some CNN architectures use dropout to prevent overfitting.

3.2 Transfer Learning

Machine learning and deep learning methods work according to the feature space and feature distribution. If training data and test data has the same feature space and the same distribution, these methods work very well. But newly collected data has different from an available feature distribution, we have to adjust static models with newly collected data. Achievement a new data can be expensive, time-consuming or impossible. In such a case, transfer learning is beneficial methods [15].

Transfer learning is the machine learning methods. The main purpose of transfer learning is to create a framework for a new feature distribution data using accumulated data previously to solve different feature distribution problem faster and more effectively [16]. Transfer learning focuses on classification and labeling problems. For classification problems, learning performance increase in direct proportion to success of knowledge transfer [15].

Transfer learning is popular approach in deep learning area where pretrained deep neural network models used for a starting point. Training a deep neural network and finding an optimum value of the weight of the layers is time consuming, even with modern hardware. Transfer learning works well if the network trained with large dataset and generalize the dataset sufficient enough.

3.3 AlexNet

Alex Kriztevesky proposed AlexNet that is the winner of ImageNet Large Scale Visual Recognition Challenge (ILSVRC) at 2012 [13]. This net is different from traditional convolutional neural network. Because, AlexNet is wider and deeper convolutional neural network. Thus, it provided a different perspective to classification and recognition problems. It has an important place in the deep learning as it achieves very successful results in solving these problems.

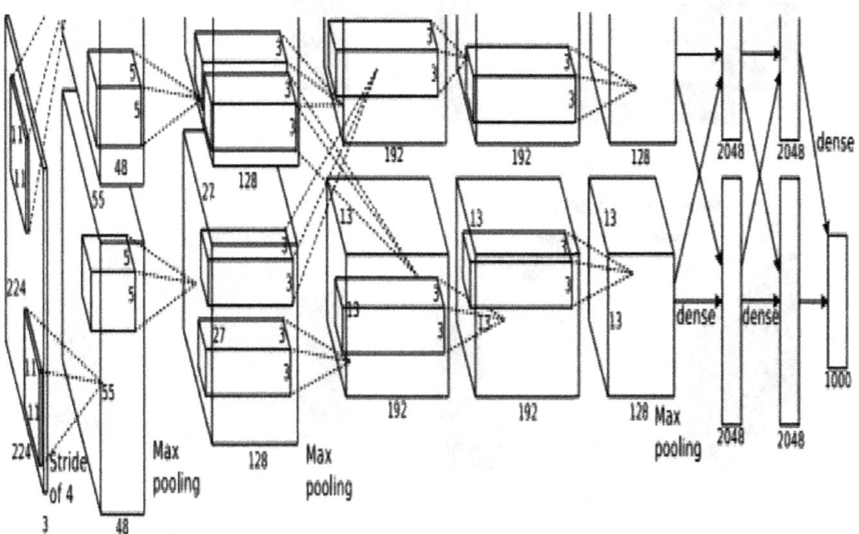

Fig. 1. An illustration of the architecture of AlexNet [13].

AlexNet has a relatively simple layout compared to other modern architectures and starts with data input layer. The input data dimension is 227 × 227 × 3. The net consists of five convolutional layers, three fully-connected layer and one soft-max layer. The neuron numbers of fully-connected layer are 4096, 4096 and 1000 [13]. AlexNet was trained using stochastic gradient descent, momentum of 0.9, weight decay of 0.0005, and with 0.5 dropout rate. Also, they used rectified linear unit (ReLU) that is computationally efficient activation function. They used ImageNet dataset that contains 1000 categories and total number of images is 1.2 million. AlexNet CNN architecture is shown in Fig. 1.

3.4 Dataset

Database for Mastology Research (DMR) is used for evaluating performance parameters such as precision, accuracy and recall. DMR contains breast thermogram images and these can be accessed online [17]. The thermal images belong to patients of the Antonia Pedro University Hospital [18]. FLIR SC-620 Thermal camera used for acquisition of thermograms with spatial resolution of 640 × 480 pixels. In our work, we use 147 thermograms of healthy individuals and 34 thermograms belong to sick individuals.

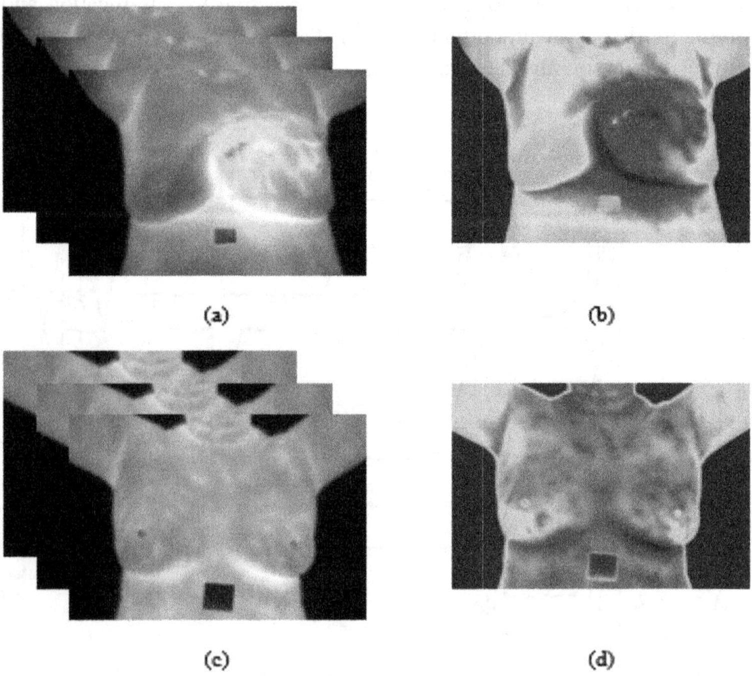

Fig. 2. Example of prepared images. In (a) shows duplicated gray image belongs to sick patient, (b) represents RGB jet image belongs to sick patient, (c) shows duplicated gray image belongs to healthy patient and (d) is an example of RGB jet image belongs to healthy patient. (Color figure online)

4 Experiments and Results

4.1 Data Preparation

In this study, public DMR image library used for training and validation. We use 181 patients image has spatial resolution of 640 × 480. All the images taken by using static protocol. 34 images belong to sick patients and 147 image belongs to healthy patients. We use only thermal matrixes which contains temperature values.

Two different strategies applied on thermal matrixes. First one is converting the matrix to the gray image. The main purpose of the first strategies is trying to preserve thermal matrix originality but AlexNet was trained with colored images and also its input layer was designed for three dimensional images. So, All the values at thermal matrix were scaled to between 0 to 255. The content of every gray scale image copied into 3 channels. The second strategy is converting thermal matrix to RGB image just like AlexNet was trained before. For this methodology, we use MATLAB jet colormap functionality. At last, all the images were resized to 227 × 227 × 3, which is the input layer size of AlexNet. The sample demonstration of two strategies is shown in Fig. 2.

DMR dataset has small amount of data to train deep neural network. Because of this, in this study we use data augmentation techniques for increasing amount of data to use in training phase and also to avoid overfitting problem. Translation and reflection methods are the most common way to produce synthetic data from original dataset. In this study, reflection was applied on only vertical axis because the tumor can be seen on the other breast and translation was performed to avoid dependency of the localization using randomly selected pixel range between −30 to 30.

4.2 Network Architectures

We designed four different Convolutional Neural Network (CNN) based on transfer learning to classify images and show the effect of the layers. We chose AlexNet as a base model because it successfully completed a large and challenging image classification task such as the ImageNet 1000 class photograph classification competition.

In the first model named Net1, AlexNet was transferred to all layers except the last three layers. These are trained for 1000 class classification but our aim is only to classify thermogram images as healthy or sick. So, fully connected layer with 2 neurons, softmax layer and output layer was added to the first model. In this model, we only trained last newly added fully connected layer and other layers were transferred from AlexNet including convolutional layers and fully connected layers. Net2 is the second model in our work. Net2 has one extra fully connected layer with 1024 neurons according to Net1 and only convolution layers were transferred from AlexNet. Therefore, AlexNet was used only for feature extractor. Third model is Net3. Layer transfer strategy is different from Net1 and Net2. At this model, fifth convolution layer was extracted and four fully connected layer added with 4096, 4096, 1024 and 2 neurons. The main purpose of the Net3 is evaluating the effect of the last convolutional layer because early convolutional layers has a more generic features and in later layers features are become data specific. Net4 is the last model designed to see how the number of fully connected layer changes performance in our work. The difference of

Net4 from Net3 is one fully connected layer with 4096 neurons has been extracted. All the architectures of models are shown in Fig. 3.

In the training phase, we use learning rate 0.0001 for the transferred layers to slow down learning and for the newly added fully connected layers, learning rate was set at 20 to speed up learning. Dropout rate is 0.5 and Adam Optimizer was used. To stop the training of CNN, custom stop function is defined. Training was stopped when if consecutively five iteration had training accuracy was 100%. We also use leave-one-out cross-validation to ensure every image is used in train and test sets.

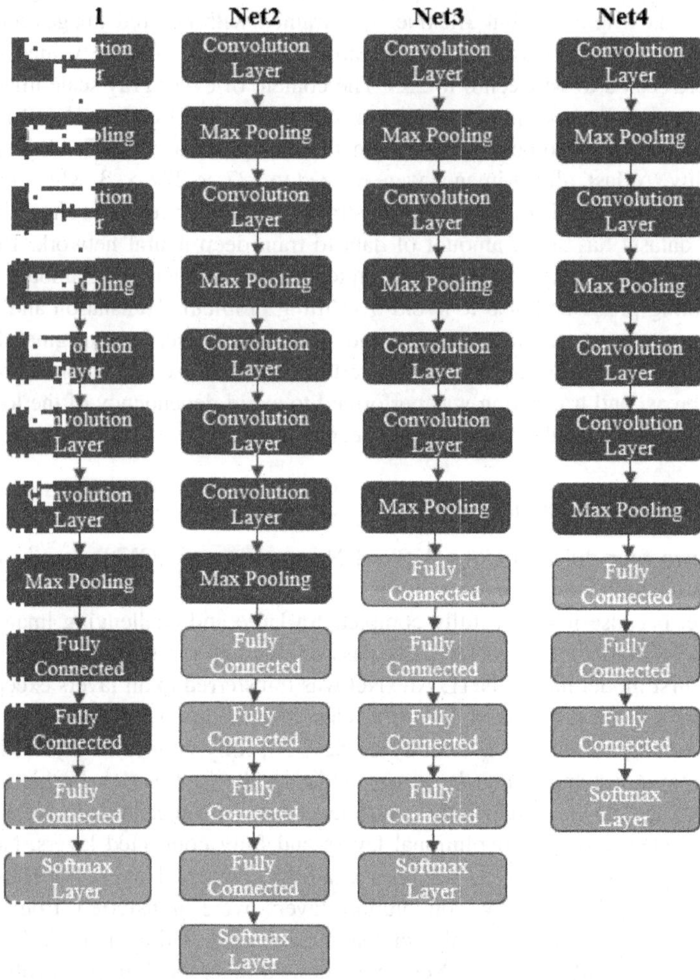

Fig. 3. The graphical pipeline of the proposed CNN models. The transferred layers are shown in blue and green ones are newly added layers. (Color figure online)

4.3 Empirical Results

CNN models were evaluated using leave-one-out cross-validation. In test and training phase, 181 images which 34 of them are sick and 147 of them are healthy of DMR dataset were used. We trained all the networks using 180 images and the network was tested on a sample which was not included at the training data. Also, we did this process for every sample of the dataset. That means, each network was trained 181 times.

In addition, we produced balanced dataset using RGB images. We increased the amount of sick patients images with data augmentation techniques. We applied random translation and reflection to 34 sick patients images to generate 135 number of image. As a result, we obtained 135 patient images and 147 healthy patient images in the data set.

Results were calculated according to five metrics considering leave-one-out cross-validation. These are considering accuracy (Acc), precision, recall, F1 measure (F1), and Matthews Correlation coefficient (MCC).

We tested all the CNN models with 2 different input. One of them is RGB image was given as input and gray image with 3 channel which all the channels have duplicated version of original gray image. All the results are showed in Tables 1, 2, 3, 4 and 5. We trained Net1 with augmentation and without augmentation. Also, we gave two different image type as an input which is RGB image and duplicated gray image (Tables 1 and 2). Results shows that to train with augmentation and giving RGB image as an input gives good performance in comparison with training without augmentation. Moreover, Net3 and Net4 performs worst performance than Net1 and Net2. That's because we extract last convolutional layer and feature vectors produced by other convolutional layers could not achieve a good generalization of the problem compared to other networks. Therefore, these nets have lots of parameters to learn and update. Furthermore, giving RGB image as input and to train Net2 with augmentation performs best performance among the other CNN models (Tables 3 and 4). Net2 uses AlexNet as feature extractor and we trained fully connected layers according to features that comes from pre-trained convolutional layers. All these additions improve its performance because AlexNet trained with RGB images and its parameters were updated according to this input type. Net1 architecture also has pre-trained fully connected layers and this is the main difference of Net1 from Net2. The weights of the transferred fully connected layers were trained and updated according to ImageNet dataset. Therefore, the performance of Net1 remained low compared to Net2.

At last, we train our designed networks with balanced RGB dataset (Table 5). Net2 has the highest score compared to other networks. Results show that training the networks with a balanced dataset increased the performance significantly. Our best result with the unbalanced dataset is %89,5, and with the balanced dataset, Net2 achieves %94,3 accuracy.

We also compared our results with other studies using DMR dataset to detect breast cancer (Table 6). In most of the studies, statistical features were used to extract the features, also SVM, ANN and CNN were used for classification [6, 12, 19–21]. Two study performed better than our work [6, 21]. That's because their dataset is more balanced than ours. But it is not fair to make an empirical comparison of these methods since each used a different number of images with an independent experimental setup.

Table 1. Result of Net1 trained with RGB image

Net1	Accuracy	Precision	Recall	F1	MCC
With Aug.	0.8729	0.7037	0.5588	0.623	0.553
Without Aug.	0.8674	0.6786	0.5588	0.6129	0.5375

Table 2. Result of Net1 trained with duplicated gray image

Net1	Accuracy	Precision	Recall	F1	MCC
With Aug.	0.8564	0.6429	0.5294	0.5806	0.4984
Without Aug.	0.85	0.6538	0.5	0.5667	0.4886

Table 3. Result of CNN models trained with RGB image and augmentation

CNN model	Accuracy	Precision	Recall	F1	MCC
Net1	0.8729	0.7037	0.5588	0.623	0.553
Net2	0.895	0.7143	0.7353	0.7246	0.6599
Net3	0.8177	0.5185	0.4118	0.459	0.3545
Net4	0.7956	0.4286	0.2647	0.3273	0.2233

Table 4. Result of CNN models trained with duplicated gray image and augmentation

CNN model	Accuracy	Precision	Recall	F1	MCC
Net1	0.8564	0.6429	0.5294	0.5806	0.4984
Net2	0.8287	0.5429	0.5588	0.5507	0.445
Net3	0.8398	0.619	0.3824	0.4727	0.4
Net4	0.8287	0.5652	0.3824	0.4561	0.3686

Table 5. Result of CNN models trained with a balanced RGB image dataset

CNN model	Accuracy	Precision	Recall	F1	MCC
Net2	0.943463	0.947761	0.933824	0.940741	0.886781
Net3	0.915194	0.91791	0.904412	0.911111	0.830122

Table 6. Comparison with other studies on detection of breast cancer.

Paper	Features/Classifiers	Acquisition protocol	Number of images	Accuracy
Gaber et al. [12]	Gabor coefficients/SVM RBF	Static	63 (29 healthy and 34 malignant)	88.41%
Lessa and Marengoni [19]	Statistical features/Artificial neural networks	Static	94 (48 normal and 46 abnormal)	85%
Borchartt et al. [20]	Statistical features/Genetic algorithm	Static	51 (14 abnormal and 37 normal)	88.2%
Sathish et al. [21]	Statistical texture features/SVM RBF	Static	80 (40 normal and 40 abnormal)	90%
Baffa and Lattari [6]	CNN features/CNN	Static	300 images (126 abnormal and 174 normal)	98%
Our work	CNN features/CNN using transfer learning	Static	282 (135 sick and 147 healthy)	94.3%

5 Conclusion

Breast cancer is one of the most common types of cancer among women. Early detection of breast cancer plays an important role to save patients. For this purpose, we designed a CNN model using transfer learning techniques. We changed the type and number of the transferred layer to find their effects. The result of Net2 has the best performance metrics and it indicates that using all convolutional layers of AlexNet as a feature extractor and training the newly added fully connected layers is a good way than other strategies. Also, results show that AlexNet the feature vectors of the fifth convolutional layer is necessary for improving the performance of classification.

In addition, the balanced and unbalanced dataset was created, and its contribution to the performance was examined. The results show that using balanced dataset improves the performance of the CNN models.

As a result, the feature level of the transferred convolutional layer and the number of the newly added fully connected layer have changed the performance of the CNN model.

Potential contribution of other pre-trained CNN models is left as a future work. Transfer learning with other models can improve the performance.

References

1. World Health Organization Homepage. http://www.who.int/mediacentre/factsheets/fs297/en/. Accessed 21 Mar 2019
2. Nyström, L., et al.: Breast cancer screening with mammography: overview of Swedish randomised trials. The Lancet. **341**, 973–978 (1993)
3. Griffiths, C., Brock, A.: Twentieth century mortality trends in England and Wales. Health Stat Q. **18**, 5–17 (2003)
4. Kandlikar, S., et al.: Infrared imaging technology for breast cancer detection – current status, protocols and new directions. Int. J. Heat Mass Transf. **108**, 2303–2320 (2017)
5. Saslow, D., et al.: American cancer society guidelines for breast screening with MRI as an adjunct to mammography. CA Cancer J. Clin. **57**, 75–89 (2007)
6. Baffa, M., Lattari, L.: Convolutional neural networks for static and dynamic breast infrared imaging classification. In: 31st Conference on Graphics, Patterns and Images (SIBGRAPI), Brazil, pp. 174–181. IEEE (2018)
7. Faust, O., Rajendra Acharya, U., Ng, E., Hong, T., Yu, W.: Application of infrared thermography in computer aided diagnosis. Infrared Phys. Technol. **66**, 160–175 (2014)
8. Oğul, H., Oğul, B., Ağıldere, A., Bayrak, T., Sümer, E.: Eliminating rib shadows in chest radiographic images providing diagnostic assistance. Comput. Methods Programs Biomed. **127**, 174–184 (2016)
9. Silva, L., et al.: A new database for breast research with infrared image. J. Med. Imaging Health Inf. **4**, 92–100 (2014)
10. Araújo, M., Lima, R., de Souza, R.: Interval symbolic feature extraction for thermography breast cancer detection. Expert Syst. Appl. **41**, 6728–6737 (2014)
11. Krawczyk, B., Schaefer, G.: Breast thermogram analysis using classifier ensembles and image symmetry features. IEEE Syst. J. **8**, 921–928 (2014)

12. Gaber, T., et al.: Thermogram breast cancer prediction approach based on neutrosophic sets and fuzzy C-means algorithm. In: 37th Annual International Conference of the IEEE Engineering in Medicine and Biology Society (EMBC), pp. 4254–4257 (2015)
13. Krizhevsky, A., Sutskever, I., Hinton, G.E.: ImageNet classification with deep convolutional neural networks. In: Advances in Neural Information Processing Systems, pp. 1097–1105 (2012)
14. Ji, S., Xu, W., Yang, M., Yu, K.: 3D convolutional neural networks for human action recognition. IEEE Trans. Pattern Anal. Mach. Intell. **35**, 221–231 (2013)
15. Pan, S., Yang, Q.: A survey on transfer learning. IEEE Trans. Knowl. Data Eng. **22**, 1345–1359 (2010)
16. Lu, J., Behbood, V., Hao, P., Zuo, H., Xue, S., Zhang, G.: Transfer learning using computational intelligence: a survey. Knowl. Based Syst. **80**, 14–23 (2015)
17. Gogoi, U.R., Majumdar, G., Bhowmik, M.K., Ghosh, A.K., Bhattacharjee, D.: Breast abnormality detection through statistical feature analysis using infrared thermograms. In: 2015 Fifth International Conference on Advanced Computing & Communication Technologies (ISACC), India, pp. 258–265. IEEE (2015)
18. Silva, L.F., et al.: A new database for breast research with infrared image. J. Med. Imaging Health Inf. **4**(1), 92–100 (2014)
19. Lessa, V., Marengoni, M.: Applying artificial neural network for the classification of breast cancer using infrared thermographic images. In: Chmielewski, L.J., Datta, A., Kozera, R., Wojciechowski, K. (eds.) ICCVG 2016. LNCS, vol. 9972, pp. 429–438. Springer, Cham (2016). https://doi.org/10.1007/978-3-319-46418-3_38
20. Borchartt, T., et al.: Combining approaches for early diagnosis of breast diseases using thermal imaging. Int. J. Innovative Comput. Appl. **4**, 163 (2012)
21. Sathish, D., Kamath, S., Prasad, K., Kadavigere, R., Martis, R.: Asymmetry analysis of breast thermograms using automated segmentation and texture features. SIViP **11**, 745–752 (2016). https://doi.org/10.1007/s11760-016-1018-y

Blood Cell Types Classification Using CNN

Ishpreet Singh, Narinder Pal Singh, Harnoor Singh, Saharsh Bawankar(✉), and Alioune Ngom

School of Computer Science, University of Windsor, 5113, Lambton Tower, Windsor, ON N9B 3P4, Canada
{singh1vb,singh1vj,singh1vp,bawanka,angom}@uwindsor.ca

Abstract. White Blood Cells also known as leukocytes plays an important role in the human body by increasing the immunity by fighting against infectious diseases. The classification of White Blood Cells, plays an important role in detection of a disease in an individual. The classification can also assist with the identification of diseases like infections, allergies, anemia, leukemia, cancer, Acquired Immune Deficiency Syndrome (AIDS), etc. that are caused due to anomalies in the immune system. This classification will assist the hematologist distinguish the type of White Blood Cells present in human body and find the root cause of diseases. Currently there are a large amount of research going on in this field. Considering a huge potential in the significance of classification of WBCs, we will be using a deep learning technique Convolution Neural Networks (CNN) which can classify the images of WBCs into its subtypes namely, Neutrophil, Eosinophil, Lymphocyte and Monocyte. In this paper, we will be reporting the results of various experiments executed on the Blood Cell Classification and Detection (BCCD) dataset using CNN.

Keywords: CNN · Blood cell classification · Basophils · Eosinophil · Monocytes · Lymphocytes · Neutrophils · Tensorflow · Keras · Softmax function · Relu function · White blood cell google colab

1 Introduction

White Blood cells are key players in the immune system of the human body. There are three broad classifications of blood cells-Red Blood Cells (RBC) that transport oxygen, White Blood Cells (WBC) the face of immune system and platelets that trigger blood clotting in damaged tissues [1]. White Blood Cells makes up 1% of the human blood in a healthy human adult. They are present throughout the body and each type of White Blood Cells have a certain functionality in the human body and serves by protecting human body against various infections and diseases. If they detect any of these in the blood, they attack them to counter any potential damage these elements can cause in the body [2,6]. The structure of the WBC, predominantly, comprises of a large lobed nucleus that

I. Rojas et al. (Eds.): IWBBIO 2020, LNBI 12108, pp. 727–738, 2020.
https://doi.org/10.1007/978-3-030-45385-5_65

can be used to distinguish a WBC from other blood cell types. Apart from a nucleus, WBC consists of cytoplasm and cell wall.

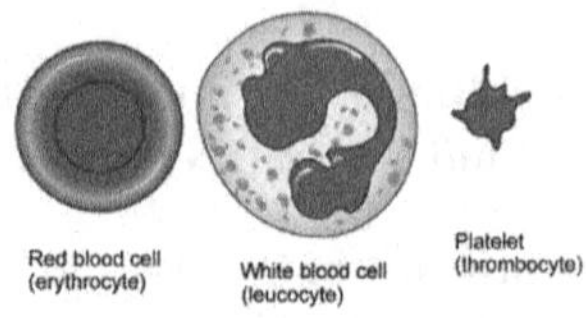

Fig. 1. Types of blood cells.

There are major five categories of WBC in human body. However due to data set constraints we have classified data into four categories: Basophils (0.4% approximately), Eosinophil (2.3% approximately), Monocytes (5.3% approximately), Lymphocytes (30% approximately) [2,7] and Neutrophils (62% approximately) (Fig. 1).

1.1 Eosinophil

The exact count of the Eosinophil in body keeps on changing during the day depending on the season and during different phases of the human body. On an average, Eosinophil amount to 2–4% of the total WBC count and can persist in the blood circulation for 8–12 days. These are found in the medulla, cortex region, lower gastrointestinal region and lymph nodes [2]. For recognizing the Eosinophil from the images, the cell is rounded in shape of skin-red color with a purple-colored bi-lobed nucleus. The lobes of the nucleus are connected by a thin strand.

1.2 Monocytes

The count of Monocytes present in a healthy human body varies between 6–9% of total WBC count. The lifetime of Monocyte varies from hours to a day. Monocytes are also responsible for presenting these pathogens to T cells so that they can be easily killed and it helps reduce the response time of antibodies in humans. Monocytes can be recognized in the BCCD image dataset using certain features, the nucleus in it is a kidney shaped-roundish cell with skin red color and some purple color in it without any lobe [2].

1.3 Lymphocytes

Lymphocytes count present in a healthy human body is around 25–30% of total WBC count. These cells are present in lymphatic system than in blood. Lymphocytes consists of two types of cells, namely B-cells and T-cells. These cells responsible for directly killing virus infected cells in human [3] body and also eliminating cancer cells. Lymphocytes can be easily identified in the BCCD dataset by looking at the nucleus as it is clearly round purple colored potato and eccentric.

1.4 Neutrophils

Neutrophils are a part of the innate immune system. The WBCs consists of almost 60–70% of Neutrophils making it largest component of WBCs. The main targets of Neutrophils are bacteria and fungal pathogens. Neutrophils can be recognized as purple colored multi-lobed groundnut-shaped nucleus inside the skin-red colored cells. Generally, there are three to five lobes in the nucleus with a transparent looking cytoplasm (Figs. 2 and 3).

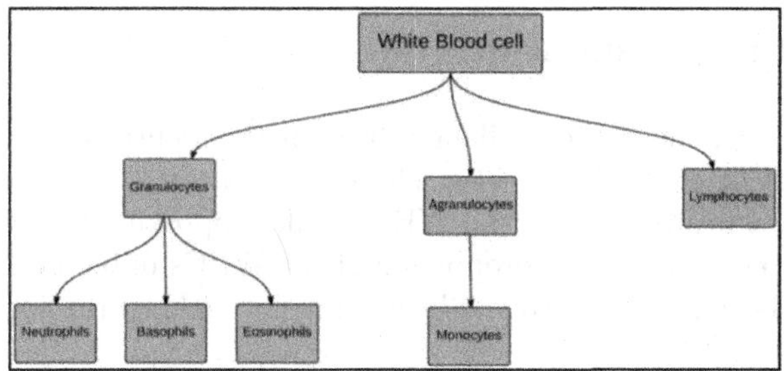

Fig. 2. Classification of WBCs.

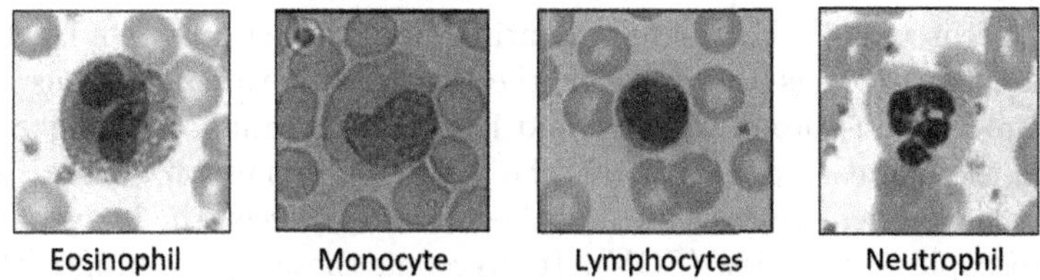

Fig. 3. Types of blood cells

2 Application of WBC Classification

Hematologist can use this classification process to diagnose the patients in an effective manner. For instance, this classification can be used to check if a person's blood sample consists of a particular type of WBC. Generally in the laboratory to classify WBC some instruments are used namely, flow cytometry.

However, this instrument is not very accurate so to overcome this disadvantage an automatic system using image processing, feature extraction and some deep learning techniques needs to be implemented for more accurate classification.

The lower level of Monocytes can be due to a lower number or lack of WBC in human body which can be due to chemotherapy, bone marrow disorder or bloodstream infection. The increase number of Monocytes classification means that the cells are increasing in response to infections, sarcoidosis and Langerhans [6]. B cells and T cells present in the WBC are also deficient which means that chances inhibiting cancer cells is very low. If the chance of classifying blood cells into Lymphocytes is more that means that the body is suffering from infection (bacterial, viral or other) or Cancer of the blood and lymphatic system. Deficiency of Neutrophils means that a person is suffering from a problem known as Neutropenia. Without these cells human body cannot resist from infections.

3 Problem Statement

In medical science, one of the challenges faced is the identification and determining the number of white blood cells. The major reason is the abundance of red blood cells. In a healthy adult, the WBCs make approximately 1% of the total blood volume. Due to this low proportion of the WBCs in blood, the recognition of the WBCs become a challenge which further toughens the job of classifying the subtypes of WBCs.

The change in number of any subtype of classification means that there is a problem in the body and the body is responding to a type of pathogen. The further prognosis of the disease can be determined by the disease type and can help in prescription of treatment for that specific ailment. The traditional method of classifying the WBC types includes studying the blood smeared slides under light and electron microscope. The blood cells are stained prior to studying them under a microscope [7]. For perfect identification, the pathologists need to look for the shape of nucleus and compare the size relative to RBCs. Since this is a manual process it is prone to error and is time consuming. The biggest drawback with the manual classification is the aspect of human error associated with mechanical scanning of glass slide and the tradeoff between the image resolution and microscopic field of view (FOV). To overcome these disadvantages, there is a need for an automated method to classify the white blood cells using an images of stained blood cells.

4 Blood Cell Count and Detection Dataset

For training the algorithm and performing the validations and experiments, we used the Blood Cell Count and Classification (BCCD) data set. The data set comprises of augmented images of the blood cells in JPEG format. Apart from the blood cell images, it is accompanied by cell type labels in a .csv file. There are a total of 12,500 labelled images of the blood cells with approximately 3000 images for 4 classes of WBCs namely Eosinophil, Lymphocyte, Monocyte and Neutrophil [3].

There are two main folders in the data set called "dataset-master" and "dataset2-master". The "dataset-master" contains 410 subtype labelled and augmented images while the "dataset2-master" contains 2500 augmented images. In total, "dataset2-master" contains 3000 images for each sub classes while "data-master" contains 88, 33, 21 and 207 images of the subtypes. In addition to this, the data set contains xml files corresponding to each image which contains the attributes that can be used to create bounding boxes on the images to highlight the RBC and WBC in the cell image. We are not using this aspect of the data set as our research is restricted to classifying the cell image on the basis of the WBC present in the image.

5 Techniques Used

5.1 Convolution Neural Networks (CNN)

For image classification, the CNN algorithm converts the image into an array of pixels called a feature map depending on the resolution of image. The CNN network generally consists of multiple hidden layers that convolve with a multiplication or dot product of the inputs from the previous layer. The image, transformed into a feature map can be combined with a filter/kernel to perform operations over the image to deduce some meaningful output. Using these filters, operations like edge detection, sharpening the image, blurring whole/partial image and identification can be performed [14]. After the convolution procedure is complete, we perform pooling on the result for dimension reduction to reduce the number of parameters. After pooling, we have a 3D resultant matrix which we pass through a fully connected ANN architecture. In order to converge out 3D input to a 1D array, we apply flattening on the resultant matrix which arranges the 3D volume of numbers into a 1D vector [9] (Fig. 4).

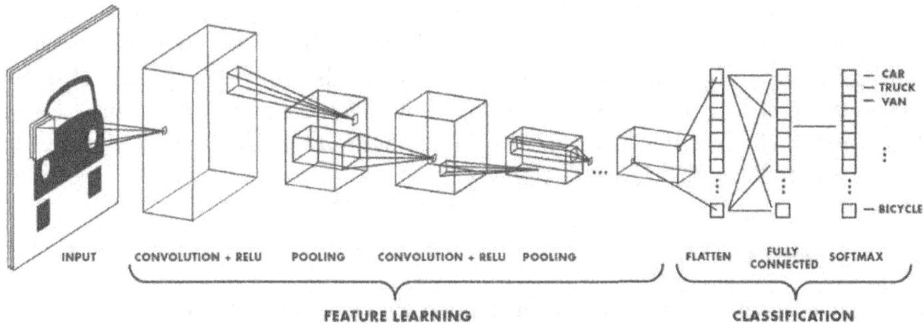

Fig. 4. A figure illustrates basic flow of CNN network.

5.2 Rectified Linear Unit (ReLU)

ReLU is a type of activation function which can be mathematically defined as y = max(0, x). It is used to extract only the positive part of the argument. ReLU is used to introduce non linearity in the training of the network. In this problem, we want our algorithm to get trained only on positive values. As compared to other activation functions, ReLU is inexpensive in terms of complexity as it does not have any complex computations.

5.3 Softmax Activation Function

The softmax function is another type of activation function used in training the CNN for this problem. Using the softmax function, we can perform logistic regression on the inputs and can normalize the input value to a vector of values. The vector of values are modelled as per a probability distribution where the sum of all vectors is equal to 1. The sigmoid function can be mathematically represented as:

$$\mathrm{P}(\mathrm{y}=\mathrm{j}) \mid \theta^{j} = \frac{e^{\theta^{(j)}}}{\sum_{j=0}^{k} e^{\theta_k^{(j)}}}$$

5.4 Keras

Keras is an open-source neural network library capable of running on top of TensorFlow. Keras is used in implementation for the blood cell training model as it provides the implementations of the convolution neural networks and filters, as required for the model construction. Using Keras, other CNN concepts are implemented like pooling, connecting to a highly connected network, dense and so on by using the inbuilt function os Keras framework.

5.5 TensorFlow

TensorFlow is also a computational network for constructing machine learning models. As Keras, it consists of end-to-end flexible ecosystem of tools which can be implemented into an algorithm in the form of libraries and build machine learning related applications. Similar to Keras, it also provides specific abstract methods which can be extended and optimised for usage in algorithms. Using TensorFlow, the architecture can also be configured on which the program has to be executed like CPU, TPU, GPU etc.

5.6 Google Colab

Due to computational limitations of the personal systems, we executed the training and testing of the algorithms on Google Colab. Colab is a Google project which provides a free Jupyter notebook environment that executes entirely on the cloud. Due to high intensity of the computations required for training the CNN network.

6 Implementation

In the implementation part, batch size is initialized as 128. Once all the images are passed through the network for one time, it marks the end of an epoch. The mean and standard image is generated using numpy by combining all the images in the training set and normalizing every pixel location and performing the mean and standard deviation functions on the images. After computation of the images, the mean image is subtracted from every image in the batch. The resultant image is then divided by the standard image (Fig. 5).

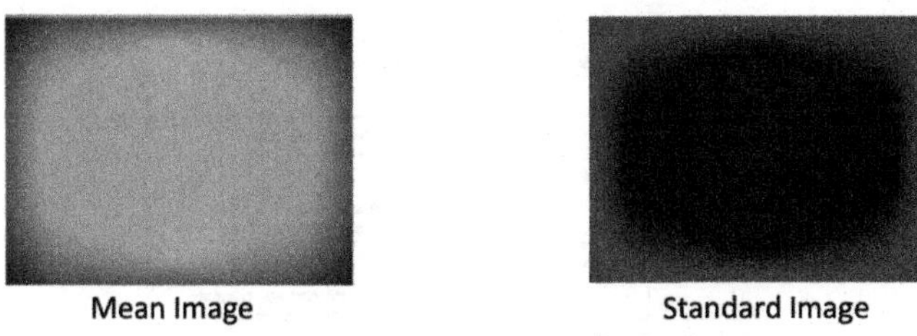

Fig. 5. Images of mean and standard deviation

After this our data set is divided into training dataset, validation dataset and test data set. The training data is of size 8961 and output data corresponding to this data is of size 8961 * 4 matrix (size of training data * number of classes). The validation set is of size 996 and output data corresponding to this data is of size 996 * 4 (size of training data * number of classes). In the CNN model, one input layer, three hidden layers and one output layer are created. For the input layer, the model is initialized using Input function and input is fed to Conv2D function of Keras, which created a convolution kernel that is convolved with the layer input to produce a tensor of outputs. In this layer features are extracted from the image using convolution, RELU, Batch Normalization, Dropout and performing pooling. After performing normalization, the Dropout is used which randomly sets a fraction rate of input units to zero at each update during training, which somehow helps prevent overfitting. Four Convolution layer are created using three different filters for feature extraction with 16, 8 and 4 layers respectively.

After performing flattening step, we create three dense hidden layers of 32, 16 and 8 dimensions using the Dense function of Keras and along with these layers an output layer of 4 dimension is created where each dimension corresponds to each class [15]. After initializing the model, the next step is to train the model. The model is trained using fit_generator() function of Keras. After feeding the training data to model summary is generated for the model that is optimized using Root mean square using RMSProp function which is an optimizer used to change the attributes of your neural network such as weights and learning rate in order to reduce losses (Fig. 6).

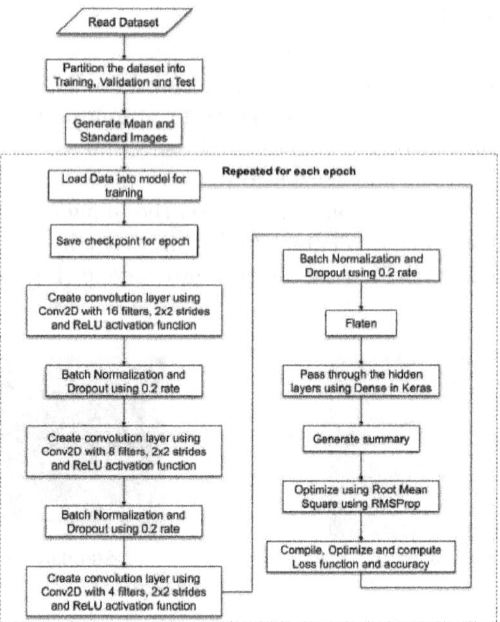

Fig. 6. Flowchart for training the algorithm.

7 Results and Discussions

7.1 Experiment

For performing the experiments, we trained and tested the model on three different epoch values i.e. 10, 100 and 200 on Google Cola using the GPU processor. The test was carried out on approximately 16000 parameters and trained on 9957 images and tested on 2487 images. The images are 240×320 pixel size.

```
Training samples:
Cell: EOSINOPHIL        num samples: 2497
Cell: LYMPHOCYTE        num samples: 2483
Cell: MONOCYTE          num samples: 2478
Cell: NEUTROPHIL        num samples: 2499
Total training samples: 9957

Test samples:
Cell: EOSINOPHIL        num samples: 623
Cell: LYMPHOCYTE        num samples: 620
Cell: MONOCYTE          num samples: 620
Cell: NEUTROPHIL        num samples: 624
Total test samples: 2487
```

Fig. 7. Summary of dataset

7.2 Selection of Metrics

For evaluating the performance of the model, we recorded three major performance metric namely train performance, validation performance and test performance from every time we trained the model and tested the trained model. As being a multi-class problem with multiple labels. The loss and accuracy of whole training and testing of the program is calculated using an in-built Keras function called categorical crossentrophy. The output value for loss and accuracy value obtained is in the range of 0 to 1. For each performance metric recorded, we analysed loss and accuracy and is represented as a tuple in the following format: Performance: [Loss, Accuracy] (Fig. 7).

7.3 Results

10 Epochs: In training analysis for 10 epochs, we can see that the loss function gives a value of 0.85 which signifies a high loss. A perfect model would have a log loss entropy of 0. An accuracy of 64.5% is observed. Similarly, a loss of 0.82 and 0.80 was observed for validation and test loss, respectively. The validation and test accuracy was evaluated as 66.9% and 66.98%. On a general, we can see that we are getting a very high value for the loss function and a low accuracy. The main reason is the low amount of training provided to the model since the number of iterations is only 10 (Figs. 8 and 9).

```
Train error:  [0.8489277419624053, 0.6459778347406514]
Validation error:  [0.8246554594994742, 0.6696697828709288]
Test error:  [0.8013397489790114, 0.6698833936469643]
```

Fig. 8. Result of 10 epochs

100 Epochs: We can see that the metrics improved when we increased the number of epochs to 100 from 10. The loss function for training dropped down to 0.165. The accuracy increased significantly to 93.48% for training. Similarly, a significant improvement can be seen in validation and test part as the loss function value dropped to 0.17 and 1.02, respectively. The accuracy is evaluated as 93.5% for validation and 80.9% for test. The test performance is relatively poor due to low number of epochs used for training (Fig. 10).

```
Train error:  [0.16513286295201243, 0.9348801266586249]
Validation error:  [0.17981732740644762, 0.935728287092883]
Test error:  [1.0293043496378786, 0.8090068355448331]
```

Fig. 9. Result of 100 epochs

200 Epochs: On further training till 200 epochs, the loss function value decreased that shows that with more number of epochs the quality of training improved significantly. For test performance, we can see that the value of loss function is 0.06 which is very close to 0 which shows that with further training the model is coming close to being a perfect model. The accuracy also increased to 97.7% for testing. Similarly, the validation performance also got better with the loss function value reaching to 0.11 and the accuracy elevated to 96.1%. However, we do not see much improvement in test performance as the value of loss function decreased slightly to 0.94 and accuracy increased by 6% to 86% as compared to 100 epochs.

```
Train error:  [0.06925135199018018, 0.9774200844390832]
Validation error:  [0.11224683812902929, 0.9618610524728589]
Test error:  [0.9430864831911208, 0.860876558102131]
```

Fig. 10. Result of 200 epochs

7.4 Comparison of Recorded Metrics

On analyzing the above graph plotted for loss value it can be deduced that when the value of epochs was increased, training and validation loss decreases as we increase the number of epochs. However, while using the model for testing on new images, we can see that the value of loss function increased as compared to lower number of iterations. However, due to high computation complexity, there is a need of better GPU processor to experiment using more number of epochs. On the analysis of the accuracy metric for all the count of epochs, it can be observed from the graph that on increasing the number of epochs, the accuracy improves. The accuracy improved significantly when the epochs were increased from 10 to 100. A small improvement in accuracy can be observed for train, test and validation when the epochs were elevated from 100 to 200. From this trend, it can be ascertained that the accuracy increases when the number of epochs are increased (Fig. 11).

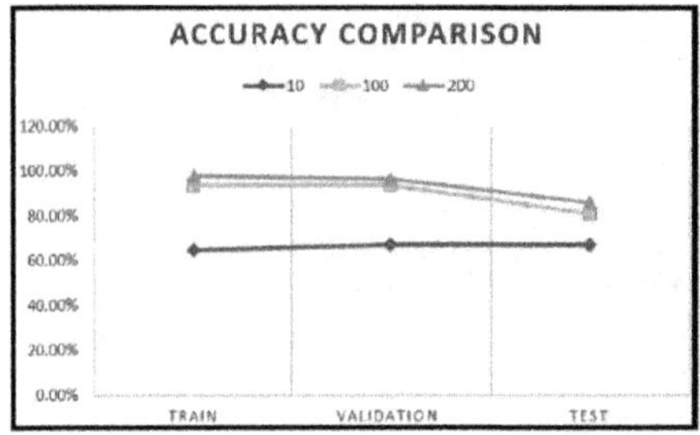

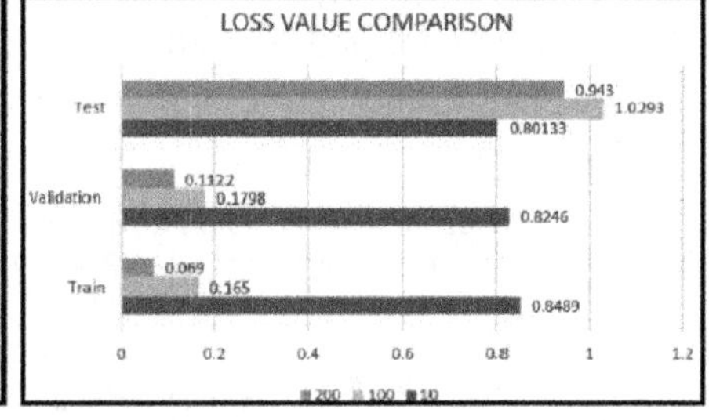

Fig. 11. Comparison of accuracy and loss function value for 10, 100 and 200 epochs

8 Challenges Faced

The biggest concern was that while training and testing the model the time taken by the system was very high due to shortage of RAM in the system. At first the model was executed for around 1000 epochs which would have taken around 8 to 10 h just to train the model and the testing would have taken even more time. So to reduce the time the number of epochs was decreased to around 200 and Google Colab platform was used, which provides Jupyter platform for python development completely on cloud.

9 Future Work

On analyzing the dataset, there are attribute files attached with the dataset corresponding to each image. In that xml file, the attributes specify the dimensions of bounding boxes. Based on that, every cell present in the image can be classified as a WBC, RBC or platelet. The cell image count helps in diagnosis of various diseases as an elevation or depreciation in the count of WBC, RBC and platelets can be a pointer to identify an ailment. The main reason for this diagnosis is that during a dengue infection, the number of platelets start decreasing.

10 Conclusion

This research helps the hematologist to classify White Blood Cells into their subtypes with the help of microscopic images of cell using Convolutional Neural Network techniques. This classification helps to distinguish the cells and check what type of disease a patient is suffering from. The results obtained from this experiment helps identify images in a robust way as compared to the orthodox lab methods. The good level of accuracy above 90 for the test set. Hence, when the model is trained with high computational abilities present, a perfect model can be trained and can be applied in the medical analysis and applications dealing with the number of white blood cells and sub types of white blood cells.

References

1. Maton, A.: Human Biology and Health. Prentice Hall, Englewood Cliffs (1993)
2. LaFleur-Brooks, M.: Exploring Medical Language: A Student-Directed Approach, 7th edn, p. 398. Mosby Elsevier, St. Louis Missouri (2008). ISBN 978-0-323-04950-4
3. Alberts, B., Johnson, A., Lewis, J., Raff, M., Roberts, K., Walter, P.: Molecular Biology of the Cell, p. 1367. Garland Science, New York (2002)
4. Kampbell, N.A.: Biology. Benjamin Cummings, San Francisco (n.d.)
5. NCI Dictionary of Cancer Terms (n.d.). https://www.cancer.gov/publications/dictionaries/cancer-terms/
6. Macawile, M.J., Quinones, V.V., Ballado, A., Cruz, J.D., Caya, M.V.: White blood cell classification and counting using convolutional neural network. In: 2018 3rd International Conference on Control and Robotics Engineering (ICCRE) (2018)

7. Al-Dulaimi, K., Chandran, V., Banks, J., Tomeo-Reyes, I., Nguyen, K.: Classification of white blood cells using bispectral invariant features of nuclei shape. In: 2018 Digital Image Computing: Techniques and Applications (DICTA) (2018)
8. Dertat, A.: Applied Deep Learning - Part 4: Convolutional Neural Networks, Medium, 13 November 2017. https://towardsdatascience.com/applied-deep-learning-part-4-convolutional-neural-networks-584bc134c1e2
9. Prabhu: Understanding of Convolutional Neural Network (CNN) - Deep Learning, Medium, 21 November 2019. https://medium.com/@RaghavPrabhu/understanding-of-convolutional-neural-network-cnn-deep-learning-99760835f148
10. Dernoncourt, F.: What is batch size in neural network? Cross Validated, 01 June 1965. https://stats.stackexchange.com/questions/153531/what-is-batchsize-in-neural-network
11. Daniel: What's is the difference between train, validation and test set, in neural networks? Stack Overflow, 01 July 1960. https://stackoverflow.com/questions/2976452/whats-is-the-difference-between-train-validation-and-test-set-in-neural-netwo
12. LNCS Home Page. http://www.springer.com/lncs. Accessed 4 Oct 2017
13. A Comprehensive Guide to Convolutional Neural Networks - the ELI5 way. https://towardsdatascience.com/a-comprehensive-guide-to-convolutional-neural-networks-the-eli5-way-3bd2b1164a53. Accessed 17 Dec 2018
14. ReLU. https://www.tinymind.com/learn/terms/relu. Accessed 30 Oct 2017
15. Di Ruberto, C., Putzu, L.: Accurate blood cells segmentation through intuitionistic fuzzy set threshold. In: 2014 Tenth International Conference on Signal-Image Technology and Internet-Based Systems, pp. 57–64, November 2014. https://doi.org/10.1109/SITIS.2014.43
16. Blood Cell Images. https://www.kaggle.com/paultimothymooney/blood-cells. Accessed 21 Apr 2018
17. Srivastava, N., Hinton, G., Krizhevsky, A., Sutskever, I., Salakhutdinov, R.: Dropout: a simple way to prevent neural networks from overfitting. J. Mach. Learn. Res. **15**(1), 1929–1958 (2014)

Medical Image Data Upscaling with Generative Adversarial Networks

Michal Dobrovolny[1], Karel Mls[1], Ondrej Krejcar[1(✉)], Sebastien Mambou[1], and Ali Selamat[1,2,3]

[1] Faculty of Informatics and Management, Center for Basic and Applied Research, University of Hradec Kralove, Hradec Kralove, Czech Republic
{michal.dobrovolny,karel.mls,ondrej.krejcar,jean.mambou}@uhk.cz

[2] Malaysia Japan International Institute of Technology (MJIIT), Universiti Teknologi Malaysia Kuala Lumpur, Jalan Sultan Yahya Petra, 54100 Kuala Lumpur, Malaysia
aselamat@utm.my

[3] School of Computing, Faculty of Engineering, Universiti Teknologi Malaysia (UTM), 81310 Skudai, Malaysia

Abstract. Super-resolution is one of the frequently investigated methods of image processing. The quality of the results is a constant problem in the methods used to obtain high resolution images. Interpolation-based methods have blurry output problems, while non-interpolation methods require a lot of training data and high computing power. In this paper, we present a supervised generative adversarial network system that accurately generates high resolution images from a low resolution input while maintaining pathological invariance. The proposed solution is optimized for small sets of input data. Compared to existing models, our network also provides faster learning. Another advantage of our approach is its versatility for various types of medical imaging methods. We used peak signal-to-noise ratio (PSNR) and structural similarity (SSIM) as the output image quality evaluation method. The results of our test show an improvement of 5.76% compared to optimizer Adam used in the original paper [10]. For faster training of the neural network model, calculations on the graphic card with the CUDA architecture were used.

Keywords: Super-resolution · Deep neural network · CUDA · Parallel processing · Adam · RMSprop

1 Introduction

The use of super-resolution (SR) images may vary, but the main reason to get them is always the same. We need a low resolution (LR) image in high resolution (HR). Mathematical methods (interpolation-based) are commonly used for super-resolution. They are not computationally demanding, but fast; on the other hand, they only provide limited output quality.

I. Rojas et al. (Eds.): IWBBIO 2020, LNBI 12108, pp. 739–749, 2020.
https://doi.org/10.1007/978-3-030-45385-5_66

Algorithms of deep learning (DL) can search and represent both structured and not structured data - for instance natural language processing (NLP), time series or image data [1,17,27]. In the image data processing can be found examples like fixing an image [22,24], compression [19], super-resolution [10] or image classification [3,4,8,12]. Image processing is currently a highly developed field. Most current deep learning algorithms use convolution theory. In many competitions, DL algorithms are ranked more often at the forefront. The most common applications include image understanding, old image damage repair, styling image, and false image generation.

If we look at the Web of Knowledge database, the topic of medical super-resolution has a growing trend here. Since 2015, almost twice as many articles have been published than in the previous period. Most of them specialize in Magnetic Resonance Imaging (MRI) [23,25,26,28].

This paper is divided into five chapters. Chapter 2 - Problem Definition - describes the need to improve medical image data. The third chapter describes the previous general methods based on interpolation. The fourth chapter describes the proposed and used method. It also contains a description of the training process and the results achieved. The last chapter provides a brief overview of the results and the possibility of future work.

2 Problem Definition

High resolution has a significant benefit for physicians. With the images in HR, they can better diagnose. That is mainly due to the better details in the image.

Many interpolation and non-interpolation methods are used for super-resolution [23,25,26,28]. For example, edge directed interpolation (NEDI) promises to sharpen edges, but it also causes some new artefacts [28]. Some deep neuron networks also promise great results [11]. All of these methods generally specialize in one type of image or require huge datasets to learn.

Capsule endoscopy has shown significant benefits in the diagnosis of gastrointestinal diseases. There are different types of endoscopy - in our article, we discuss wireless capsule endoscopy [14]. Wireless capsule endoscopy is a small pill with a camera that the patient swallows. This camera will later send LR images to a portable tracking device [6]. LR image quality may cause the doctor to overlook the disease.

3 Previous Techniques and Comments

Using basic mathematical methods leads to distortion of the resulting image. That is due to the loss of high frequencies. Neural networks, on the other hand, have less fuzzy and distorted results.

3.1 Basic Methods of Super-Resolution

As a basic method, we consider the nearest neighbour and bilinear interpolation. More advanced methods are bicubic interpolation and convolutional neural networks.

Nearest Neighbour. The first method is the nearest neighbor. This method replaces the missing value by the value of the nearest pixel. A significant disadvantage of this method is the final image quality in case of a significant upscale factor. The result will be blurred.

Linear Interpolation. Linear interpolation uses two nearest neighbors to calculate a missing value. We calculate the missing value from a line between two nearest neighbors. Missing value Y is a point on the graph corresponding to the line.

Bilinear Interpolation. The more advanced method is a bilinear interpolation. This method uses four nearest neighbors to calculate a missing value. At first, we create a line between two similar pixels. Then we take these lines and create a line between them at the missing point. The last step is to take a value from the third line at the missing pixel.

Bicubic Interpolation. The method of bicubic interpolation is computationally demanding. The calculation is based on 14 neighbours and five cubic curves. Bicubic interpolation has excellent results, but computational demands do not meet expectations.

3.2 Related Studies

Image quality in HR is essential. Image interpolation leads to increased input data. There are many methods for interpolating medical images [13]. It has been shown that generative models have a great result in super-resolution [20]. Generally, neural networks are dependent on the data set, which is their disadvantage.

The SR methods, based on a single image, create a downscaled image that feeds the network as input and tries to learn the mapping between the original and LR image. The network learns from this method, the mapping between LR and HR images that generate HR images.

3.3 Related Topics

The methods described below evaluate the results. These methods commonly evaluate the quality of super-resolution output.

Peak Signal-to-Noise Ratio. The mathematical formula PSNR expresses the ratio between signal and noise. It is based on mean squared error (MSE). This method is more often used as a measure of image compression quality [16]. The Eq. 1 was used to calculate PSNR with the result:

$$PSNR[n] = 10 \log_{10} \frac{255^2}{MSE[n]} \tag{1}$$

where MSE is the mean square error [16].

Structural Similarity. Result of the SSIM formula is a similarity value from interval `<0,1>` between two images. The method is based on the way the human eye works [21]. Equation 2 was used to calculate SSIM:

$$SSIM[x,y] = \frac{(2\mu_x\mu_y + C_1)(2\sigma_{xy} + C_2)}{(\mu_x^2 + \mu_y^2 + C_1)(\sigma_x^2 + \sigma_y^2 + C_2)} \tag{2}$$

where:

- μ_x is average of x,
- μ_y average of y,
- σ_{xy} is covariance of x and y,
- μ_x^2 is variance of x,
- μ_y^2 is variance of y [21].

Optimizer. In mathematics, the optimizer is used to select the best element from a set using some criteria. In the field of neural networks, the optimizer is a function used to calculate the weights of neurons with the lowest loss function. The best case is to find a global minimum.

In term of deep convolution neuron networks is optimizer used for calculation of weights and error propagation (backpropagation). Neuron network can solve many different tasks. Every framework already provides an implementation of many optimizers. A programmer has only to use them. Sometimes it is necessary to find the right one using the empiric method.

Adam. Optimizer Adam, full name Adaptive moment estimation, is a very popular and used optimizer. Adam builds up on Adadelta and RMSprop. Adam also uses values of the previous gradient and uses the momentum of previous gradients for his calculations [7].

RMSprop. Root Mean Square Propagation evaluates the sign of gradient. RMSprop compares the sign of the previous and current gradient. If the sign is the same, the step increases otherwise is decreased. This optimizer is mostly used for recurrent neural networks [15].

Dataset. We conducted training and testing on the dataset IDV2K [2]. This dataset contains 900 images. We divided the data into two groups at a ratio of 8:1. Data is 2 K resolution as HR. During the training process, images were transformed into LR.

Table of results 1 is calculated on dataset named "Set14" [9]. This dataset contains 14 images. We did transformed them to LR and generated new HR images.

4 Proposed Method

The need for a new approach is mainly based on the need for a general solution [28]. We have modified the super-resolution generative adversarial network (SRGAN) method to provide a model capable of enhancing any medical image.

We did the training, validation, and testing on IDV2K images [2]. The dataset contains a total of 900 images. Of these, 800 were training and 100 test images. Pictures are in HR. We converted the images to LR before being inserted into the network.

The proposed method focuses on the upscaling of medical images by a factor of two. Our method turns the original Adam optimizer into RMSprop. As a result of this change, we have obtained faster training and better results on a limited number of training data.

4.1 Model

The complexity of the Generative adversarial network (GAN) model complicates the training process. We divided the training into several steps. In the beginning, there is a trained generator (Fig. 2). After a few epochs, the training moved to the discriminator (Fig. 3). After we trained a discriminator using a few examples, we changed the training process to a combination of both networks. We train until our loss function is stable. With GAN, it is not clear when to stop the training process.

AThe ac SRGAN implementation used the `MathiasGruber/SRGAN-Keras` [5] github repository. It is an implementation of original paper Photo-Realistic Single Image Super-Resolution Using a Generative Adversarial Network [10].

Generator. Implementation of the generator is as proposed in the original paper. Contains input layer with arbitrary input size, next is the pre-residual block with convolution layer and core size nine. Then sixteen residual blocks described in Fig. 2. Next is the post-residual block with convolution layer with core size three and normalization. Next block is for upscaling. The last layer is the convolution layer with core size nine.

We rewrote the generator for performance reasons. The previous implementation did generate a batch and kept the latest image pointer. Implementation was working good, but rewriting to `yield` we got many times faster batch provider.

Discriminator. Discriminator is implemented as was proposed in original article [10]. The model contains the input layer with a resolution of HR image. Also contains eight convolution layers with a core size three, dense layer with activation function LeakyReLU.

We made two versions of generators, where every version have a different number of samples and optimizer. We marked generators as "G" + the number of input samples (Fig. 1).

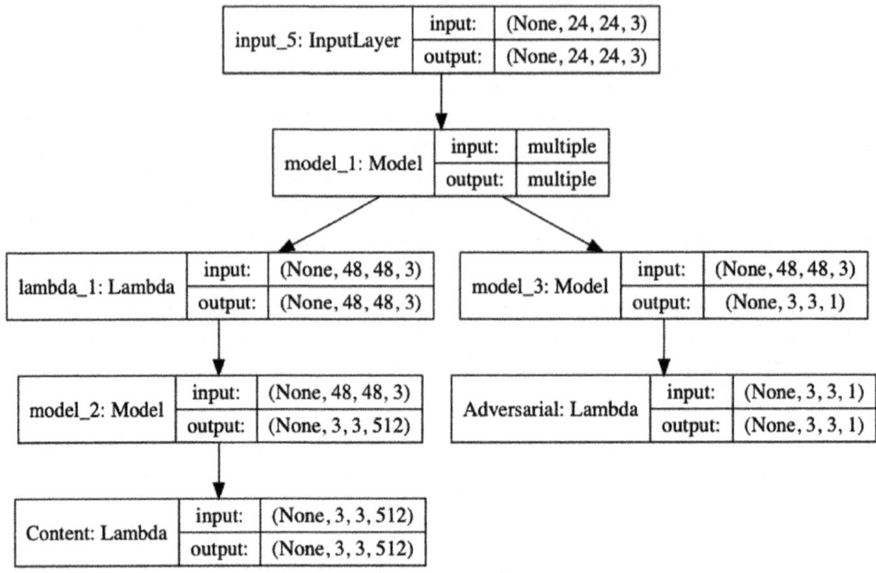

Fig. 1. Model of SRGAN

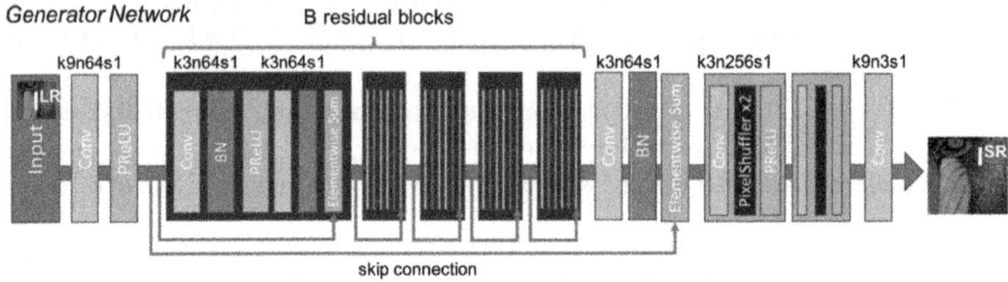

Fig. 2. SRGAN generator model [10]

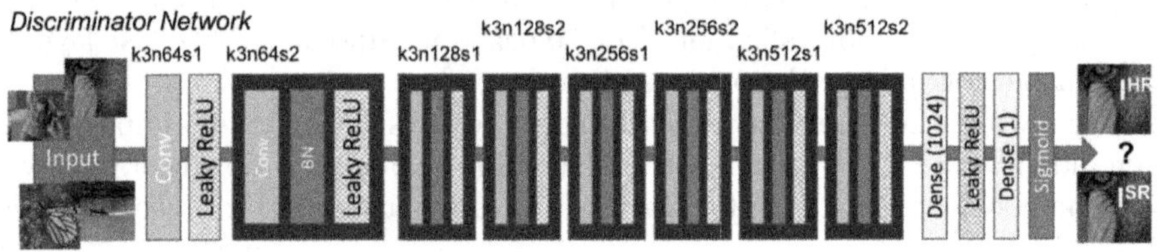

Fig. 3. Discriminator model [10]

G1600. Generator G1600 has got a small number of training samples. We provided training data as random two samples from the input image. This method of feeding needs to consider the possibility that every input image crop is different.

G90592. Generator with name G90592 is inspired by generator proposed by original article [10]. We provided training data to the generator in a batch of 16 crops. Each crop is part of the original image. This crop contains 50% of the same content. The generator generated exactly 90592 crops from 800 images from a data file (Fig. 4).

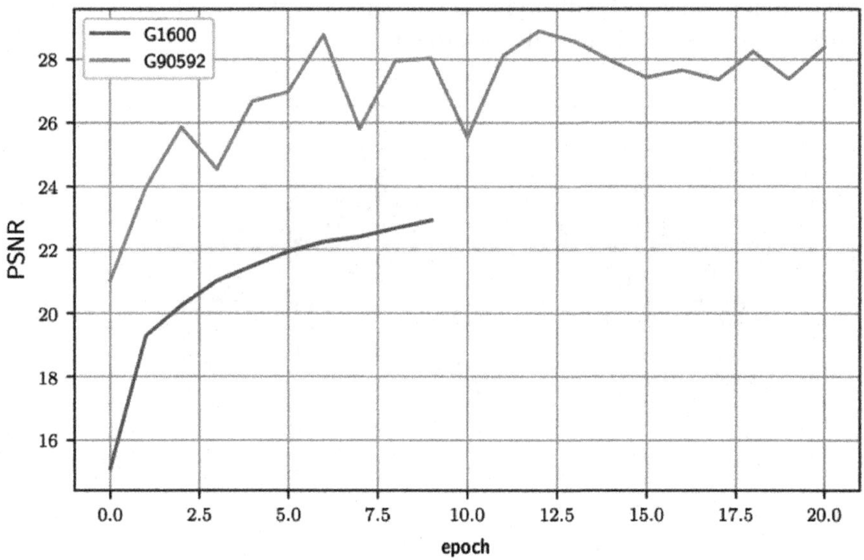

Fig. 4. PSNR of generators at pre-train stage GAN

VGG Net. We used the classification network Visual Geometry Group (VGG) for transfer learning. VGG comes from Google Labs in partnership with Oxford University. VGG was created for the image classification task [18]. It is possible to transfer weights from similar tasks.

Discriminator training is a simple task. There are two types of input images. One is a group of generated images, and the other one are real images. These data are feed-in batch. Every batch is based only on one type of input.

The discriminator is trained only during the GAN training. Discriminator has loss function cross-entropy.

GAN has two content and adversarial loss functions to measure during GAN training.

Authors of original discriminator did training on ImageNet. [10] We changed the dataset to IDV2K [2]. We also changed discriminator's optimizer to RMSprop (described 3.3). We got a faster learning process and stabilization of adversarial loss. Details are described in Sect. 4.2.

4.2 Results

This section describes differences in the training process with optimizer Adam and RMSprop. Also contains a table of the results generated by final networks.

The change of optimizer has an impact on adversarial loss. On Fig. 5 is rendered adversarial loss value during the training process. We compare NN1004 and NN1005 with the best results. The figure shows the RMSprop is stable since 5 000 inputs. Adam was diverging for a very long time and got stable after 90 000 inputs. The optional value is around 16.12.

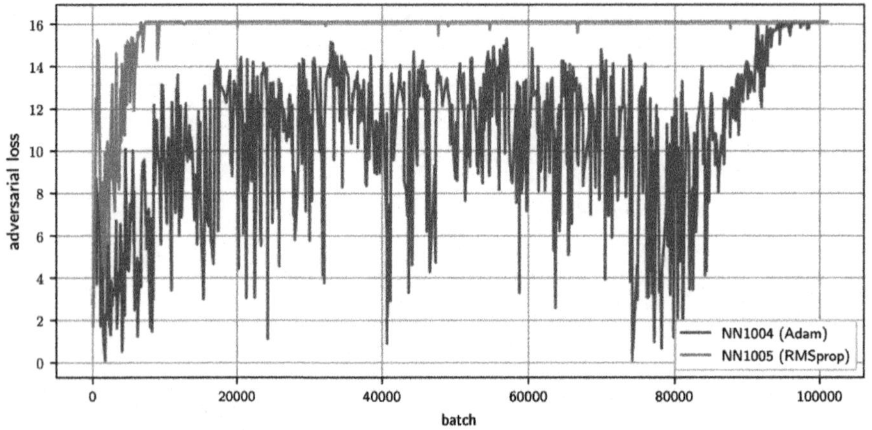

Fig. 5. Adversarial loss of NN1004 and NN1005

Table 1. PSNR and SSIM results

	Average			Median		
Model	PSNR	SSIM (db)	Time (s)	PSNR (db)	SSIM	Time (s)
NN1004	24.9772	0.7172	4.4367	25.4944	0.7229	4.9891
NN1005	**26.1629**	**0.8004**	**4.0475**	**26.9638**	**0.7979**	**4.3858**
NN1006	**27.9129**	**0.8438**	**4.0683**	**28.3415**	**0.8303**	**4.3482**
NN1007	27.5834	0.8360	4.2082	27.9748	0.8227	4.4687

Table 1 contains results of average and median of PSNR and SSIM. Bolted are the best networks. Networks are separated into two different groups by the number of input images. The best result differs in every group. In case of significant input, their optimizer Adam gets better results. In the case of the small dataset, RMSprop works better. We got 5,7% better results than with Adam. Also, there is a possibility to stop training at a sooner point and get the same results. The last column contains time consumed for model load info GPU and generating a single image.

5 Conclusion

The described solution is universal and does not need a specific type of input images. Wireless capsule endoscopy (WCE), MRI and others can benefit from our solution. We found an improvement for image super-resolution using GAN. Thanks to development on hardware Graphic processing unit (GPU) we can generate more precise outputs with less time consumed.

Part of this paper is describing fast but not optional interpolation-based methods. They are providing an excellent solution for computers with no computation power. The proposed method is high-performance demands. The proposed method uses convolutional networks in the concept of adversarial training. The main disadvantage of this method is the need for computation power and time consummation.

The proposed solution allows the possibility of upscaling the image even over a small dataset. RMPSprop provides a better solution and faster training over small dataset. The main benefit of our work is the improvement in the results of 5,76%.

Acknowledgement. The work and the contribution were supported by the SPEV project "Smart Solutions in Ubiquitous Computing Environments", University of Hradec Kralove, Faculty of Informatics and Management, Czech Republic.

Conflict of Interest. The authors declare that they have no conflicts of interest regarding the publication of this article.

References

1. Abdel-Nasser, M., Mahmoud, K.: Accurate photovoltaic power forecasting models using deep LSTM-RNN. Neural Comput. Appl. **31**(7), 2727–2740 (2017). https://doi.org/10.1007/s00521-017-3225-z
2. Agustsson, E., Timofte, R.: NTIRE 2017 challenge on single image super-resolution: dataset and study. In: 2017 IEEE Conference on Computer Vision and Pattern Recognition Workshops (CVPRW). IEEE, Honolulu, HI, USA, July 2017. https://doi.org/10.1109/CVPRW.2017.150, http://ieeexplore.ieee.org/document/8014884/
3. Anuar, S., Sallehuddin, R., Selamat, A.: Implementation of artificial neural network on graphics processing unit for classification problems. In: Nguyen, N.-T., Manolopoulos, Y., Iliadis, L., Trawiński, B. (eds.) ICCCI 2016, Part II. LNCS (LNAI), vol. 9876, pp. 303–310. Springer, Cham (2016). https://doi.org/10.1007/978-3-319-45246-3_29
4. Ciresan, D., Meier, U., Schmidhuber, J.: Multi-column deep neural networks for image classification. In: 2012 IEEE Conference on Computer Vision and Pattern Recognition (CVPR), pp. 3642–3649. IEEE, New York (2012). wOS:000309166203102
5. Gruber, M.: Implementation of SRGAN in Keras. Try at: www.fixmyphoto.ai: MathiasGruber/SRGAN-Keras, March 2019. https://github.com/MathiasGruber/SRGAN-Keras, original-date: 2018-04-08T13:19:38Z

6. Iddan, G., Meron, G., Glukhovsky, A., Swain, P.: Wireless capsule endoscopy. Nature **405**(6785), 417–417 (2000). https://doi.org/10.1038/35013140. http://www.nature.com/articles/35013140
7. Kingma, D.P., Ba, J.: Adam: A Method for Stochastic Optimization. arXiv:1412.6980 [cs], December 2014
8. Krizhevsky, A., Sutskever, I., Hinton, G.E.: ImageNet classification with deep convolutional neural networks. Commun. ACM **60**(6), 84–90 (2017). https://doi.org/10.1145/3065386. wOS:000402555400026
9. Lai, W.S., Huang, J.B., Ahuja, N., Yang, M.H.: Fast and accurate image super-resolution with deep laplacian pyramid networks. IEEE Trans. Pattern Anal. Mach. Intell. **41**, 2599–2613 (2018)
10. Ledig, C., et al.: Photo-Realistic Single Image Super-Resolution Using a Generative Adversarial Network. arXiv:1609.04802 [cs, stat], September 2016
11. Mahapatra, D., Bozorgtabar, B.: Progressive Generative Adversarial Networks for Medical Image Super resolution. arXiv:1902.02144 [cs], February 2019
12. Mambou, S.J., Maresova, P., Krejcar, O., Selamat, A., Kuca, K.: Breast cancer detection using infrared thermal imaging and a deep learning model. Sensors **18**(9), 2799 (2018). https://doi.org/10.3390/s18092799. https://www.mdpi.com/1424-8220/18/9/2799
13. Manjón, J.V., Coupé, P., Buades, A., Fonov, V., Louis Collins, D., Robles, M.: Non-local MRI upsampling. Med. Image Anal. **14**(6), 784–792 (2010). https://doi.org/10.1016/j.media.2010.05.010. http://www.sciencedirect.com/science/article/pii/S1361841510000630
14. Mohammed, A., Farup, I., Yildirim, S., Pedersen, M., Hovde, O.: Variational approach for capsule video frame interpolation. EURASIP J. Image Video Process. **2018**(1), 30 (2018). https://doi.org/10.1186/s13640-018-0267-9
15. Mukkamala, M.C., Hein, M.: Variants of RMSProp and Adagrad with Logarithmic Regret Bounds. arXiv:1706.05507 [cs, stat] June 2017
16. Nemethova, O., Ries, M., Zavodsky, M., Rupp, M.: PSNR-Based Estimation of Subjective Time-Variant Video Quality for Mobiles, p. 5 (2019)
17. Pena-Barragan, J.M., Ngugi, M.K., Plant, R.E., Six, J.: Object-based crop identification using multiple vegetation indices, textural features and crop phenology. Remote Sens. Environ. **115**(6), 1301–1316 (2011). https://doi.org/10.1016/j.rse.2011.01.009
18. Simonyan, K., Zisserman, A.: Very Deep Convolutional Networks for Large-Scale Image Recognition. arXiv:1409.1556 [cs] September 2014
19. Sun, Y., Chen, J., Liu, Q., Liu, G.: Learning image compressed sensing with sub-pixel convolutional generative adversarial network. Pattern Recognit. **98**, 107051 (2020). https://doi.org/10.1016/j.patcog.2019.107051
20. Wang, X., et al.: ESRGAN: Enhanced Super-Resolution Generative Adversarial Networks. arXiv:1809.00219 [cs] January 2018
21. Wang, Z., Bovik, A., Sheikh, H., Simoncelli, E.: Image quality assessment: from error visibility to structural similarity. IEEE Trans. Image Process. **13**(4), 600–612 (2004)
22. Wolterink, J.M., Leiner, T., Viergever, M.A., Isgum, I.: Generative adversarial networks for noise reduction in low-dose CT. IEEE Trans. Med. Imaging **36**(12), 2536–2545 (2017). https://doi.org/10.1109/TMI.2017.2708987. wOS:000417913600013
23. Wu, K., et al.: Image synthesis in contrast MRI based on super resolution reconstruction with multi-refinement cycle-consistent generative adversarial networks. J. Intell. Manuf. (2019). https://doi.org/10.1007/s10845-019-01507-7

24. Yang, Q., et al.: Low-dose CT image denoising using a generative adversarial network with wasserstein distance and perceptual loss. IEEE Trans. Med. Imaging **37**(6), 1348–1357 (2018). https://doi.org/10.1109/TMI.2018.2827462. wOS:000434302700006
25. Zhang, F., et al.: Super resolution reconstruction for medical image based on adaptive multi-dictionary learning and structural self-similarity. Comput. Assist. Surg. **24**, 81–88 (2019). https://doi.org/10.1080/24699322.2018.1560092. wOS:000486310400011
26. Zhao, X., Zhang, Y., Zhang, T., Zou, X.: Channel splitting network for single MR image super-resolution. IEEE Trans. Image Process. **28**(11), 5649–5662 (2019). https://doi.org/10.1109/TIP.2019.2921882
27. Zhou, Y., Chang, F.J., Chang, L.C., Kao, I.F., Wang, Y.S.: Explore a deep learning multi-output neural network for regional multi-step-ahead air quality forecasts. J. Clean. Prod. **209**, 134–145 (2019). https://doi.org/10.1016/j.jclepro.2018.10.243. wOS:000457351900013
28. Zhu, Q., Ren, Y., Qiu, Z., Wang, W.: Robust MR image super-resolution reconstruction with cross-modal edge-preserving regularization. Int. J. Imaging Syst. Technol. **29**(4), 491–500 (2019). https://doi.org/10.1002/ima.22327. wOS:000495457300009

Enhancing Breast Cancer Classification via Information and Multi-model Integration

J. C. Morales, Francisco Carrillo-Perez(✉), Daniel Castillo-Secilla, Ignacio Rojas, and Luis Javier Herrera

Department of Computer Architecture and Computer Technology, University of Granada, Granada, Spain
franciscocp@ugr.es

Abstract. The integration of different sources of information for proper classification is of utter importance, specially in the biomedical field. Many different sources of information can be collected from a patient and they all may contribute to an accurate diagnosis. For example in cancer disease these can include gene expression (RNA-Seq) or Tissue Slide Imaging, however, their integration in order to correctly train a classification model is not straightforward. Making use of Whole-Slide-Images, this work presents a novel information integration model when different sources of data from a patient are available, named as Multi-source integration model (MSIM). Using two different Convolutional Neural Networks architectures and a Feed Forward Neural Network, the potential of a multi-model integration process which combines the information of different sources is introduced and its results are presented for Breast Cancer classification.

Keywords: CNNs · WSI · Breast cancer

1 Introduction

Currently, cancer is the second leading cause of death worldwide following cardio vascular diseases [1,2], being Breast Cancer one of the most deadly ones and the most frequent among women. As a means to understand the scope of the disease, Fig. 1 shows a comparison between estimated cases and deaths of different types of cancer. The difficulty of treating it properly increases if an early diagnosis is not performed. Therefore, it is crucial to increase patient's probability of survival. When it comes to early diagnosis, the identification of biomarkers from biological data gathered from patients, and their use to identify the disease has shown to be of utter importance. There has been a rapid raise in the gathering of biological

J. C. Morales and F. Carrillo-Perez—These authors contributed equally to this work.

I. Rojas et al. (Eds.): IWBBIO 2020, LNBI 12108, pp. 750–760, 2020.
https://doi.org/10.1007/978-3-030-45385-5_67

information from a variety of technologies for diagnosing purposes, such as next-generation sequencing and digital image analysis. The advances within the fields of data analysis, machine learning and high performance computing have enabled researchers to take advantage of it and to present models for cancer classification [4–6]. Digital image analysis of histology images combined with the usage of Deep Learning (DL) has shown outstanding results in detecting, segmenting and classifying cancer, specifically in Whole-Slide-Images (WSI) [7–9]. WSI, also known as virtual microscopy, refers to scanning a complete microscope slide and creating a single high-resolution digital file. With it, different resolutions of the same image can be obtained and, for instance, an extraction of patches can be performed.

Different types of WSI may be available, presenting different resolutions or having undergone different preprocessing steps. The usage of different sources of information can be of great interest in order to improve models' performance and create a model with a larger generalization capability. In video classification it has already been proposed, combining the information of raw images and the generated optical flow from the video [10,11]. When it comes to the bioinformatics domain, the integration of information from different sources has been explored previously in literature for pancancer prognosis prediction [12] but, to the best of our knowledge, an integration of information has not been previously performed for breast cancer classification.

The aim of this work is to present a methodology for a multi-model integration for the task of breast cancer classification when multiple sources of information are available, specifically WSI, using Convolutional Neural Networks (CNN) and Feed Forward Neural Networks (FFNN). In this Section an introduction to the problem has been outlined. In Sect. 3, the methodology and data used for this work will be presented. In Sect. 4, results obtained for the proposed experiments will be shown and discussed. Finally, in Sect. 5 conclusions will be drawn.

2 Data Description

As aforementioned in Sect. 1, this work focused on the usage of WSI. Data were obtained from GDC Portal [13], selecting a total of 1093 patients of breast cancer, with a total of 3885 images obtained after applying the next exposed preprocessing steps. Specifically, data were selected from the TCGA program. Two classes are found for the samples considered, one of them being Primary Tumor (PT), which denotes a patient with Breast Cancer, and the other Solid Tissue Normal (STN), denoting a healthy patient. As it is usual in biomedical problems, data are imbalanced, having more samples from PT than from STN. It is important to note here that since this work aims to introduce a methodology for data integration, and since available datasets with similar WSI standards are not that common or publicly accessible, data were replicated to serve as input for each of the two CNN models considered in this work. The implications of this restriction will be later discussed in the discussion section.

Common Types of Cancer	Estimated New Cases 2019	Estimated Deaths 2019
1. Breast Cancer (Female)	**268,699**	**41,760**
2. Lung and Bronchus Cancer	228,150	142,670
3. Prostate Cancer	175,650	31,620
3. Prostate Cancer	175,650	31,620
4. Colorectal Cancer	145,600	51,020
5. Melanoma of the Skin	96,480	7,230
6. Bladder Cancer	80,470	17,670
7. Non-Hodking Lymphoma	74,200	19,970
8. Kidney and Renal Pelvis Cancer	73,820	14,770
9. Uterine Cancer	61,880	12,160
10. Leukemia	61,780	22,840

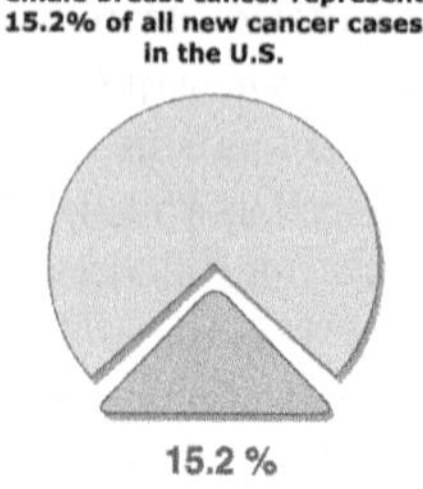
Female breast cancer represents
15.2% of all new cancer cases
in the U.S.
15.2 %

Fig. 1. A comparison of how common is female breast cancer against other types of cancer in the Unite States [3]. A it can be observed, it represents the 15.2% of total cases.

Some preprocessing steps need to be carried out in order to facilitate and enable working with the data. These steps will be explained in the following subsections.

2.1 Preprocessing

Tissue Slide data obtained from GDC, and specifically TCGA project, are in SVS format. In order to train our models, firstly several preprocessing steps need to be performed. A summary of them can be observed in Fig. 2.

Firstly, SVS images need to be read with an specific factor of magnification. In this work, a factor of 2.5x was chosen in order to obtain an adequate resolution without sacrificing computational cost. Once images were obtained, they were converted from SVS to PNG format in order to facilitate further manipulations.

For the gathering of the WSI, different histological sections of tissue can be performed to an organ of the patient. When a WSI is being obtained, more that one section can be placed in the slide, therefore, several tissue sections might appear in the final WSI. In order to help the classifier, an homogenization of the images used is therefore necessary. Thus, if several tissues were contained in one WSI, a separation of them in as many images as histological sections found was carried out, performing the following steps:

- The whole image is binarized using the Otsu threshold method [15].
- Multiple closing and opening operations with kernels of increasing size are applied to the binarized image to reduce noise.

- All values in the vertical direction are added to create a histogram in the x axis. For some images, the tissue slides are disposed vertically instead of horizontally, so for those, the image is rotated 90° before computing the histogram.
- A gaussian filter is applied to reduce noise in the histogram.
- A binary search algorithm is used to detect the number of peaks. for each detected peak, its area is computed and substracted from the total. Once the remaining area is below a certain threshold, the algorithm stops.
- The slides are obtained by splitting the whole image in the middle points of the end of a peak and the start of the next one.

Several models need to have the same shape for all their inputs. Since the images have been split, different widths and heights can be found. Reshaping all of them to an specific shape not only would enable the usage of specific DL algorithms but also would reduce the computing needs of the classification task. The images were reshaped to 299 × 299, maintaining the height-width ratio and the height or width excess obtained while reshaping them was filled with white background. In Fig. 3, an example of a preprocessed image can be observed.

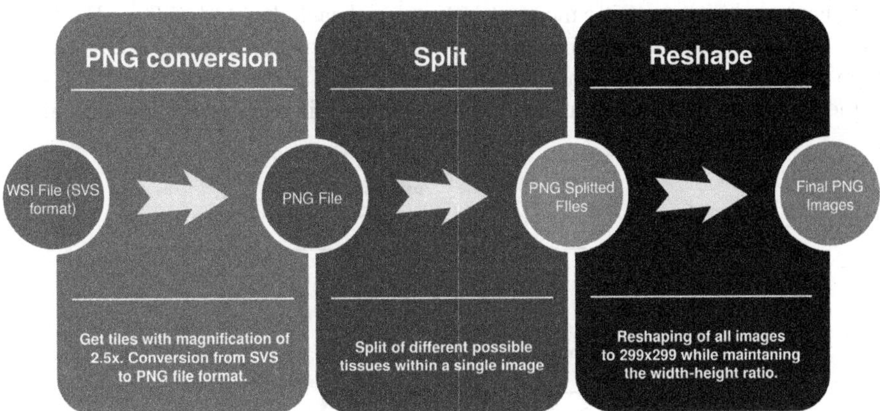

Fig. 2. Preprocessing steps performed in order to obtain the final images used for models training.

2.2 Database

Once the preprocessing has been applied to all image data, having an organized database for easy access and straightforward data information retrieval is crucial. This work make usage of a database formed by a three-level hierarchy of folders, as it can be observed in Fig. 4.

The root directory contains a folder for each patient. The folder name is a patient identifier, which in this work would be named as Patient ID. Inside the patient folder several folders can be found, each of them containing all patient

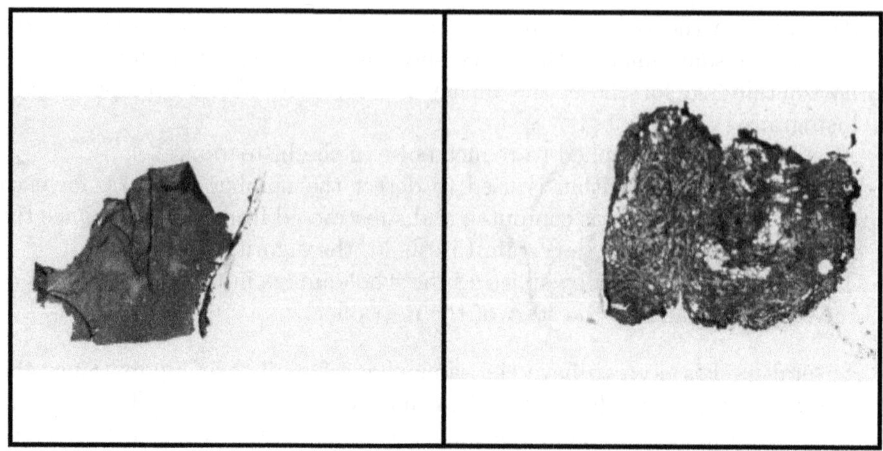

Fig. 3. Examples of images after performing all the aforementioned preprocessing steps. On the left side, an image which belongs to PT class, on the right side one which belongs to STN class.

data captured in an specific moment in time, and each denoted as Case ID. Inside each Case ID folder, and in order to provide with straightforward access to each type of data, each data type would have it's own folder with the exact same name across patients. Within that folder, the final files to be read are contained.

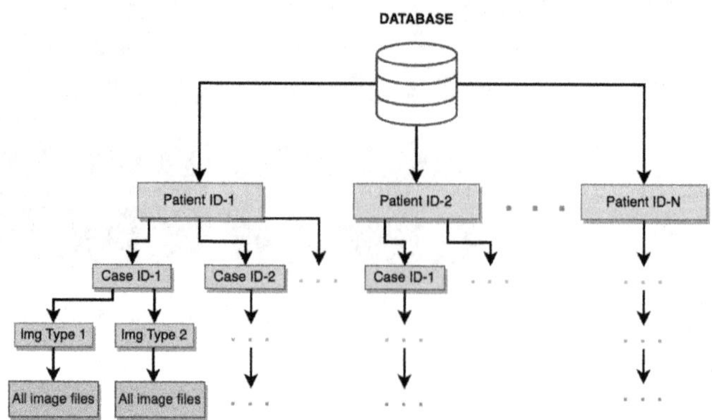

Fig. 4. Database organization for model training and prediction.

3 Materials and Methods

When working with data from various sources, the possibility of building different models for the same purpose is available. Nonetheless, not only contrasting the outcomes of different models may be desirable, but also joining their capabilities and integrating their results in an unique global model may be of interest. However, their integration must be consistent, taking into account the information that each model is providing for the training of a final model.

An ensemble model (which we will also name super classifier), for data integration classification is presented in this work, named as Multi-source integration model (MSIM). The main idea of MSIM is to enable the training of a classifier from various sources of information, making use of a variety of models within it. N + 1 models will be trained simultaneously, using a specific batch of information from different Case IDs, as explained in Subsect. 2.2. These models could be of any type, as could be the information fed to them. For a given input, feature vectors will be obtained from each model, and their concatenation will be used as the input for the ensemble model which will perform the final prediction. Therefore, the models will enhance the super classifier while improving themselves, being the ensemble model as good as the features provided by the models within it.

A detailed explanation of the training an prediction will be presented in Subsect. 3.1. A diagram of the MSIM architecture used in this work can be observed in Fig. 5.

3.1 MSIM Training and Predicting

Training and predicting must be sequentially performed for all models within the super classifier. Training will be performed using batches of data where each of them will contain all the information for an specific Case ID. For each iteration the training procedure would be as follows:

1. A batch is fed to each sub-model sequentially and training is performed.
2. Once each sub-model has been trained, a feature vector is obtained for a selected sample from the batch and for each sub-model. Feature vectors are concatenated to generate the input for the super classifier.
3. The super classifier is trained with the generated feature vector.

When performing the prediction, the methodology followed is the same as when training. The inputs are firstly passed through the sub-models to obtain the feature vectors and then the final feature vector is fed to the super classifier where the final prediction is obtained.

3.2 MSIM Submodels and Inputs

In this work WSI images from a set of patients are used. Based on the outstanding results obtained with Convolutional Neural Networks (CNNs) in the field of computer vision [14], they were the selected models to design the different classifiers. Nevertheless, a known CNNs drawback is that, if they wanted to be trained from scratch, a huge amount of data is needed to properly learn the features that describe them. Since in this work, and generally in biomedical

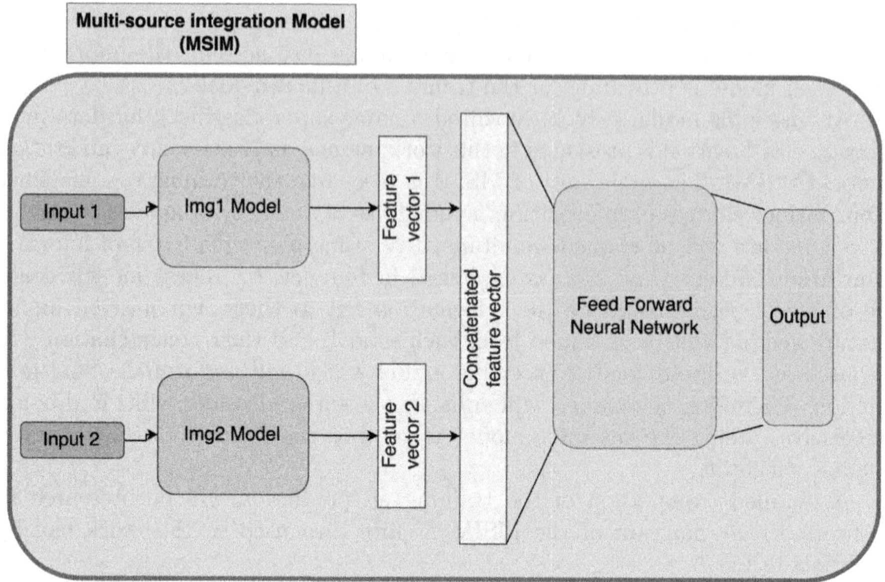

Fig. 5. MSIM architecture where there are two classifiers with two different input data. More models could be added with different inputs, concatenating the feature vectors for each input.

problems, not many data are available another approach need to be taken, i.e. Transfer Learning (TL). With TL, network weights trained in another problem domain are used as base weights for your network. Therefore, basic features are already learnt and the weights just need to be tuned for an specific problem. As the super classifier, a Feed Forward Neural Network (FFNN) was selected.

Two different CNNs models were used as image classifiers. The usage of two different models contributes to the diversity of the features obtained and subsequently used for the super classifier to learn and to predict. The models selected were a Resnet-18 architecture [16] and a VGG-16 architecture [17] both pre-trained on imagenet and whose weights where not freezed in order to fine tuning them. The two CNN architectures would be labeled as Img1 model and Img2 model respectively. For the super classifier, that from now on would be named as MSIM for the sake of clarity, a FFNN with two layers was used. The two layers were a fully connected (FC) layer formed by 1280 neurons, followed by a ReLU activation layer and another FC layer formed by 1280 neurons. FC layers' weights were initialized with the Xavier initialization [18].

Code for the MSIM model and submodels was written in Python 3.6. [19] and Pytorch [20] was used as the Deep Learning library. For preprocessing steps OpenCV [22], Numpy [21] and Scikit-learn [23] libraries were used (Fig. 6).

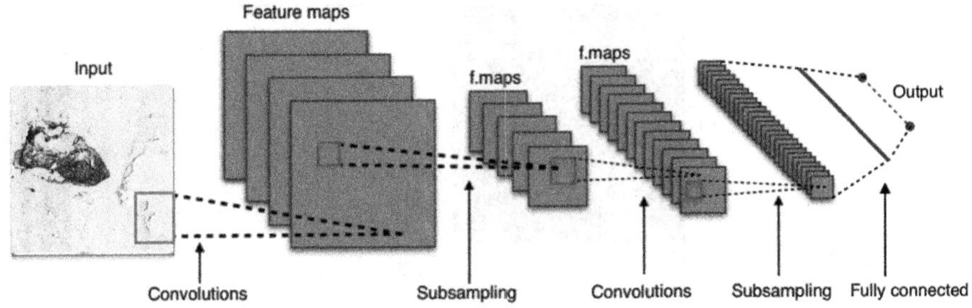

Fig. 6. Example of a typical Convolutional Neural Network architecture [24].

4 Results and Discussion

For the experiments, a Five-Fold Cross Validation (5-Fold CV) was performed to evaluate MSIM generalization, leaving each time a test set with 20% of the total data. In each execution, 20% of the training data was used for validation purposes. In order to avoid information leakage, all samples of the same patient can only belong to one of the splits, being it train, validation or test. Data augmentation was used for the CNN models, randomly applying vertical an horizontal flips and images were normalized with zero mean and unit variance. For models training Stochastic Gradient Descent (SGD) was used as the optimizer with a learning rate of 0.001, momentum equal to 0.9 and weight decay equal to 0.0001, and they were trained for 9 epochs using Cross-Entropy Loss as loss function. As performance metrics, accuracy and the Confusion Matrix (CM) were computed for each set and split.

In Table 1 mean accuracy and standard deviation among all splits can be observed for each model. In Fig. 7, the CM for MSIM model in the test set trained in the third split is presented.

Table 1. Mean accuracy and standard deviation in the validation and test sets for each model.

	Val Acc %	Test Acc %
MSIM	98.14(±0.82)	99.07(±0.62)
Img1 model	97.11(±0.94)	98.39(±0.31)
Img2 model	96.07(±0.02)	98.22(±0.01)

As it can be observed in Table 1, remarkable results are obtained for Breast Cancer classification. MSIM outperforms results obtained for each submodel separately for both validation and test sets. Therefore, it seems that the addition of features from different sources helps model generalization when unseen data is presented. Taking advantage of the features learnt from each model, which

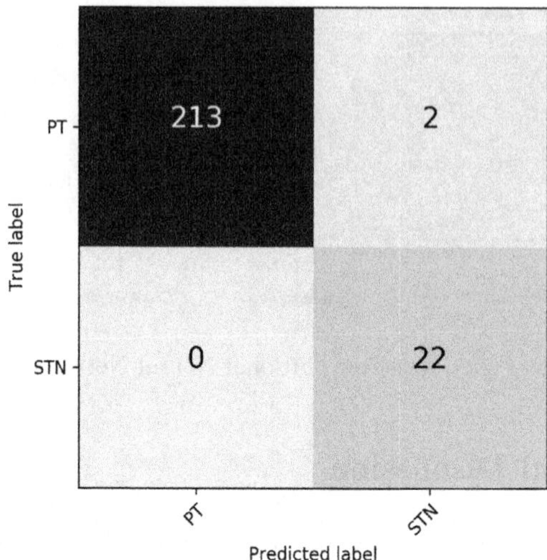

Fig. 7. CM for the test set in the fifth split for the MSIM. Primary Tumor class is labeled as PT and Solid Tissue Normal class as STN.

may be different, their combination enhanced the MSIM performance for the classification task.

In Fig. 7, the MSIM CM for the test set can be observed. Even though data are highly imbalanced, MSIM is able to properly handle it and correctly classify the underrepresented class.

5 Conclusions

In this work a new methodology for a Multi-source integration model has been presented, showing that the integration of information enhance model performance for Breast Cancer classification. Thus, it has been shown that the combination of features from different architectures helps model's generalization when new data is available, as it can be observed in results presented in Table 1. WSI were used as source of information, and their usefulness for Breast Cancer classification has been proven with the results presented in Sect. 4.

For future work, the addition of next-generation sequencing data (such as RNA-Seq) or patient's clinical information want to be carried out in order to improve MSIM performance and to test whether the integration of such variety of sources might help to classify in which stage of the disease may the patient be. Having this prediction would not only immensely help their treatment, but it would also hugely increase their lifespan.

Acknowledgements. The results shown here are in whole or part based upon data generated by the TCGA Research Network: https://www.cancer.gov/tcga.

This research has been supported by the project: RTI2018-101674-B-I00 (from the Spanish Ministry of Economy and Competitiveness –MINECO– and the European

Regional Development Fund. -ERDF). The funding body did not play any role in the design or conclusion of this study.

References

1. Siegel, R.L., Miller, K.D., Jemal, A.: Cancer statistics. CA: A Cancer J. Clin. **69**(1), 7–34 (2019)
2. Breast Cancer. World Health Organization. World Health Organization (2018). https://www.who.int/cancer/prevention/diagnosis-screening/breast-cancer/en. Accessed 17 Jan 2020
3. Number of new cases and deaths. National Cancer Institute (2018). https://seer.cancer.gov/statfacts/html/breast.html. Accessed 17 Jan 2020
4. Castillo, D., et al.: Leukemia multiclass assessment and classification from microarray and RNA-seq technologies integration at gene expression level. PloS One **14**(2), 1–25 (2019)
5. Öztürk, Ş., Akdemir, B.: HIC-net: a deep convolutional neural network model for classification of histopathological breast images. Comput. Electr. Eng. **76**, 299–310 (2019)
6. Gálvez, J.M., et al.: Towards improving skin cancer diagnosis by integrating microarray and RNA-seq datasets. IEEE J. Biomed. Health Inf. (2019)
7. Qaiser, T., Tsang, Y.W., Taniyama, D., Sakamoto, N., Nakane, K., Epstein, D., Rajpoot, N.: Fast and accurate tumor segmentation of histology images using persistent homology and deep convolutional features. Med. Image Anal. **55**, 1–14 (2019)
8. Gecer, B., Aksoy, S., Mercan, E., Shapiro, L.G., Weaver, D.L., Elmore, J.G.: Detection and classification of cancer in whole slide breast histopathology images using deep convolutional networks. Pattern Recogn. **84**, 345–356 (2018)
9. Benhammou, Y., Achchab, B., Herrera, F., Tabik, S.: BreakHis based breast cancer automatic diagnosis using deep learning: taxonomy, survey and insights. Neurocomputing **375**, 9–24 (2020)
10. Simonyan, K., Zisserman, A.: Two-stream convolutional networks for action recognition in videos. In: Advances in Neural Information Processing Systems, pp. 568–576 (2014)
11. Carreira, J., Zisserman, A.: Quo Vadis, action recognition? A new model and the kinetics dataset. In Proceedings of the IEEE Conference on Computer Vision and Pattern Recognition, pp. 6299–6308 (2017)
12. Cheerla, A., Gevaert, O.: Deep learning with multimodal representation for pancancer prognosis prediction. Bioinformatics **35**(14), i446–i454 (2019)
13. Grossman, R.L., Heath, A.P., Ferretti, V., Varmus, H.E., Lowy, D.R., Kibbe, W.A., Staudt, L.M.: Toward a shared vision for cancer genomic data. N. Engl. J. Med. **375**(12), 1109–1112 (2016)
14. LeCun, Y., Bengio, Y., Hinton, G.: Deep learning. Nature **521**(7553), 436–444 (2015)
15. Otsu, N.: A threshold selection method from gray-level histograms. IEEE Trans. Syst. Man Cybern. **9**(1), 62–66 (1979)
16. He, K., Zhang, X., Ren, S., Sun, J.: Deep residual learning for image recognition. In: Proceedings of the IEEE Conference on Computer Vision and Pattern Recognition, pp. 770–778 (2016)
17. Simonyan, K., Zisserman, A.: Very deep convolutional networks for large-scale image recognition (2014). arXiv preprint arXiv:1409.1556

18. Glorot, X., Bengio, Y.: Understanding the difficulty of training deep feedforward neural networks. In Proceedings of the Thirteenth International Conference on Artificial Intelligence and Statistics, pp. 249–256, March 2010
19. Python Software Foundation. Python Language Reference, version 3.6. http://www.python.org
20. Paszke, A., et al.: PyTorch: an imperative style, high-performance deep learning library. In: Advances in Neural Information Processing Systems, pp. 8024–8035 (2019)
21. Oliphant, T.E.: A Guide to NumPy, vol. 1. Trelgol Publishing, USA (2006)
22. Bradski, G., Kaehler, A.: Learning OpenCV: Computer Vision with the OpenCV Library. O'Reilly Media Inc., Newton (2008)
23. Pedregosa, F., et al.: Scikit-learn: machine learning in python. J. Mach. Learn. Res. **12**, 2825–2830 (2011)
24. Author: Aphex34, Date: 16 December 2015, Typical CNN Architecture. https://commons.wikimedia.org/wiki/File:Typical_cnn.png

Simulation and Visualization of Biological Systems

Kernel Based Approaches to Identify Hidden Connections in Gene Networks Using NetAnalyzer

Fernando Moreno Jabato[1], Elena Rojano[1], James R. Perkins[2,3], Juan Antonio García Ranea[1,2,3], and Pedro Seoane-Zonjic[2(✉)]

[1] Department of Molecular Biology and Biochemistry, University of Malaga, Bulevar Louis Pasteur, 31, 29010 Malaga, Spain
{jabato,elenarojano,ranea}@uma.es

[2] CIBER of Rare Diseases, Av. Monforte de Lemos, 3-5, Pabellon 11, Planta 0, 28029 Madrid, Spain
{jrperkins,seoanezonjic}@uma.es

[3] Institute of Biomedical Research in Malaga (IBIMA), C. Dr. Miguel Díaz Recio, 28, 29010 Malaga, Spain

Abstract. The latest advances in biotechnology are increasing the size and number of biological databases, specially those related to "omics" sciences. This data can be used to generate complex interaction networks, which analysis allows to extract biological information. Network analysis comprises a current bioinformatics challenge and the implementation of kernels offers a potential procedure to perform this analysis. Kernel algebraic functions have been used to study interaction networks and they are of major interest in new applications to improve machine learning studies. To manage these interaction networks, the NetAnalyzer tool was developed with the purpose of analysing multi-layer networks, calculating different probabilistic indices to establish the association between pairs of nodes. In this study we implement different kernel operations using several programming languages to inspect their reliability to perform these operations in different scenarios. Best performances have been included as a kernel functional module into NetAnalyzer, and we used them over gene interactions networks and gene-disease knowledge to identify disease causing genes.

Keywords: Kernel · Gene prioritization · Network

1 Background

In recent years, advances in Biology, Medicine and Informatics are producing an exponential increment of biological data, specially what concerns to "omics" science development [5]. To obtain knowledge from these large datasets, all data must go through computational processes that mostly encompass four main steps, including data generation, processing, integration and analysis. The first three steps correspond to well-known established protocols [11]. By its way, the

I. Rojas et al. (Eds.): IWBBIO 2020, LNBI 12108, pp. 763–774, 2020.
https://doi.org/10.1007/978-3-030-45385-5_68

analysis procedure to interpret the biological knowledge underlying this data offers more challenges [6], specially when integrating different types of information to explain complex relationships [8].

Kernel algebraic operations are a consistent mathematical method commonly used to integrate multi-dimensional data, as well as to study the elements relatedness in complex and huge networks – like Sensors Networks generates nowadays [3]. These kernel operations are popular because of their reliability to increase the prediction ability of data for machine learning (ML) problems [20]. The main problem with kernel operations is that different programming languages use specific algebraic modules implementations, which affect to results and resources consumption [15]. It is significantly sensible in approximation based operations – like several eigenvalues calculation do using power series. These differences must be considered for ML and network studies.

Kernels have been used to predict novel genes and their relations to disease [2,21], to analyse biological procedures like the mitotic chromosome condensation [7], to understand complex biological relations for drugs off-targets discovery [9] and to identify candidates in reverse vaccinology proteins studies [10]. In this study, we applied the use of kernels for biological network inference implementing them in NetAnalyzer, a tool for the analysis of multi-partite biological networks that has been used in different studies [12,13].

2 Materials and Methods

2.1 Description of Kernels

A kernel function can be defined mathematically as the inner product between vectors of a given Hilbert space ($\mathcal{H}$). The function does not necessarily perform a transformation of that space. A kernel k in $X \times X$ space can thus be formally defined as:

$$\begin{gathered} k : X \times X \to \mathbb{R} \\ \phi : X \to \mathcal{H} \\ k(x_1, x_2) = \langle \phi(x_1), \phi(x_2) \rangle \quad | \quad x_1, x_2 \in X \end{gathered} \tag{1}$$

Kernel functions must be:

$$\begin{aligned} (1) \quad & Continuous: && \lim_{x \to c} k(x) = k(c) \\ (2) \quad & Symmetric: && k(x_i, x_j) = k(x_j, x_i) \quad | \quad \forall i, j \in \mathbb{N} \leq N \\ (3*) \quad & Semi-definite: && a \geq 0 \quad | \quad \forall a \in \lambda_k \end{aligned}$$

With N being the kernel size and λ_k being the eigenvalues, as described below. The third property is not strictly mandatory to define a kernel, however the use of a positive definite kernel ensures convergence and unique solutions for kernel-based mathematical methods.

When a kernel operation is applied to an adjacency matrix, we obtain a kernel matrix. The values of this matrix can be used as similarity measures between adjacency elements, with k_{ij} representing the similarity value between the elements x_i and x_j from the original matrix.

Kernel functions can be deemed radial or lineal basis functions, based on how the features are related in the final kernelized results. They differ in how they integrate features: radial basis functions use hyperspheres; in contrast, linear basis functions use hyperplanes.

All kernels used in this study have been designed for use with adjacency matrices, which are necessarily square and symmetric. We will refer to the input adjacency matrix as (**A**) and the matrix element in row (i) and column (j) will be referred as (a_{ij}). A must be a square matrix of size (**n**). Several kernels used within this study are based on the Laplacian matrix (**L**) of a given adjacency matrix, defined as:

$$L = D - A \quad \text{where} \quad D = Diag(a_{i\bullet}) = [D]_{ij} \begin{cases} 0, & \text{if } i \neq j \\ \sum_{z=1}^{n} a_{iz}, & \text{if } i = j \end{cases} \tag{2}$$

Some kernels are based on matrix eigenvalues. The set of eigenvalues of a given matrix B will be referred as λ_B.

Using this nomenclature, we will now describe the 4 kernel methods that have been implemented in this work:

Kernelized Adjacency Matrix. Kernelized adjacency matrix (ka) is a simple strategy where an adjacency matrix is transformed to ensure that it is positive and semi-definite by shifting its eigenvalues [4]. This can be performed by adding a sufficiently large constant to adjacency matrix. In this case, we will use the smallest eigenvalues of A as the added constant:

$$K_{KA} = A + Diag(\lambda_\bullet) \quad | \quad \lambda_\bullet = min(\lambda_A) \tag{3}$$

Commute-Time Kernel. The commute time kernel (ct) [21] is a Markov chain based function which calculates the probability of a change from one state to another, such as moving from a node to an adjacent node. These probabilities are calculated using the random walk model on the network. As such, the transition probabilities depend only on current state and not on past states (first-order Markov chains).

This kernel is called commute-time because the distance between network nodes are used in a similar way to resistance in an electric circuit. It has been demonstrated mathematically that these resistances are meaningless when dealing with large graphs REF, as such the final kernel equation is:

$$K_{CT} = L^+ \tag{4}$$

where L^+ corresponds to the Moore-Penrose pseudoinverse of the Laplacian matrix (L).

Laplacian Exponential Diffusion Kernel. Exponential diffusion kernels [21] are mathematical functions based on the idea of the diffusion of *heat* throughout the network from a specific node, using connectivity as resistance. Exponential kernels are radial basis kernels; the Laplacian exponential diffusion Kernel (el) is an alternative to the exponential diffusion kernel, which substitute the adjacency matrix for the Laplacian (L) matrix:

$$K_{EL} = exp(-\alpha L) \tag{5}$$

The configurable parameter alpha (α), also known as the *exponential discounting rate* can significantly affect kernel performance. Overestimation can produce linear-like behaviour, causing loss of the non-linear power of this kernel. Underestimation can produce insufficient regularization, making results sensitive to noise in the source matrix.

Markov Exponential Diffusion Kernel. The Markov exponential diffusion kernel (me) [21] is another variation of the exponential diffusion kernel, for which the source of the *exponential discounting rate* is different:

$$K_{ME} = exp\Big(\frac{\beta}{n}(Diag(n) - D + A)\Big) \tag{6}$$

Its configurable value is beta (β), which exhibits similar effects to the alpha (α) value described above for the Laplacian exponential diffusion kernel.

2.2 Kernel Implementation

The kernels described above involve complex linear algebra operations, which have different implementations in different programming languages. These implementations contain subtle differences, which can affect the final output of the kernel functions. We therefore implemented the kernels in four distinct programming languages to compare their precision and performance.

We have previously developed the NetAnalyzer tool to process and analyse networks [13]. This tool was developed in Ruby, and we will use this language as one of the test cases. As such, if the kernel implementations in Ruby perform well in the benchmarks, they will be added to the NetAnalyzer software.

The choice of other programming languages was based on what we believe are the most widely used in terms of bioinformatics and network science. More specifically we chose: (i) R, (ii) Matlab, and (iii) Python.

Kernels operations were implemented following the theoretical definition of each kernel, using core language functionality where possible, and third parties packages for non-base implemented functionality.

Matlab contains core implementations of all necessary operations to implement all above-described kernels; the other three languages require specific third party packages to perform the exponential and pseudoinverse functions. In the case of R, the package *Matrix* [1] is used to perform the exponential function and *MASS* [18] for the Moore-Penrose pseudoinverse. For Python, *numpy* [17] is used to define matrices and perform pseudoinverse functions; *scipy* [19] is used to for the exponential function. For Ruby, it was necessary to import *Numo-narray* to handle matrices.

We were unable to find code capable of performing exponential operations in Ruby. Custom implementations were developed, however the results were not stable. Therefore, these operations were borrowed from Python implementations using the *Pycall* library, which allows connections between Ruby and Python.

2.3 Kernel Implementation Comparison in Different Platforms

The workflow to compare the performance of the implementations was developed using the workflow manager Autoflow [14]. It consists of three steps: (i) Creation of a random adjacency matrix of a given size, (ii) performance of the 4 above-described kernels for this adjacency matrix, separately for each programming language, (iii) for each kernel, the kernelized matrices generated by the different programming languages are compared, to calculate error rate. This is calculated as the mean difference between direct matrices after applying local min-max normalization.

The implemented kernels can be performed on binary or weighted adjacency matrices. Weighted matrices were used for this study, by generating random real number matrices with values between [0,100].

To measure resource consumption and performance, all kernel implementations were executed on one of two computational nodes: when the input matrix had 5,000 × 5,000 elements or fewer, a SL230/250 node was used (16 cores, 64 GB RAM, 500 GB SSD); when the matrix comprised 10,000 × 10,000 or more elements, a HP DL980 node was used (80 cores, 2TB RAM, 2TB HDD). Time, maximum memory and CPU usage were measured for each execution using the GNU linux time command.

2.4 Gene Prioritization

The kernelized matrices can be thought of as representing the similarity between each pair of nodes in a network, taking into account its structure. This property can be exploited to associate genes with biological processes, by measuring the similarity between a given gene and known gene sets, grouped according to some shared biological property. These sets can represent signalling or metabolomic pathways, disease relations or functional categories (i.e. GO terms). The genes in these sets can be thought of as seed genes, and the association of a given gene with the seed set can be computed by calculating the average score of this gene to all seeds in the set:

$$
\begin{aligned}
Rank(A, Seeds) =< k_1, ..., k_N > \mid \forall n \rightarrow k_n < k_{n+1} \;; \\
k_i = mean(a_{i,j}) \; with \; i \in \mathbb{N} \leq N, \\
j \in Seeds \subset \mathbb{N} \leq N \\
Ranking(A, Seeds, Target) = pos(Target, Rank(A, Seeds))
\end{aligned}
\tag{7}
$$

Once we have calculated the average scores of each non-seed gene to the seed set, the genes are sorted accordingly, in order of decreasing score. It is expected that the top genes, i.e. with the greatest average score, are involved in the same biological functions as the genes within the seed set. In this work, we have used groups of genes known to be related to diseases as the seed sets. We used these to obtain candidate genes using a gene interaction network as the input adjacency matrix for the prioritization process described above.

2.5 Testing the Prioritization of Disease Related Genes

The results of the kernel comparison showed a reasonable performance of the Ruby implementation. As such, it was incorporated into the NetAnalyzer software, and used for the gene prioritization process. To compare the ability of the different kernels to find novel genes related to a given gene set we have replicated the unbiased gene-disease association methodology of Zampieri et al. [21], based on the gene-disease association dataset of Börnigen et al. [2].

This dataset is composed of known gene-disease relations at a given point in time (15 May 2015), taken from various disease databases, and an additional 42 novel genes which were found to be related to these diseases during the subsequent six-month period [2].

We used these 42 new gene-disease relations to compare the performance of the different kernels, by comparing the ranking of these targets in the lists of sorted genes for each disease. More specifically, target gene positions were used to calculate the median, the true positive rate (TPR) at representative thresholds (5%, 10% and 30% top candidates) and AUC, by averaging over the 42 targets, as per Zampieri et al. [21].

In terms of the input data to the kernel functions, we limited ourselves to gene interaction data prior to 15 May 2015. More concretely, we build an adjacency matrix based on data from the String database version 8.2 [16], following [21]. We used the integrated channel, using the combined interaction scores as weights for the adjacency matrix.

3 Results

3.1 Platforms Benchmark Results

In order to compare error, performance and scalability between the different kernel implementations, all four kernels described in Sect. 2.1 were executed using matrices of four different sizes, generating a total of 64 kernelized matrices. Execution performance (time, CPU and memory consumption) and kernel results were compared between implementations for experiments of the same size and kernel type. The error was measured using the normalized matrices direct comparison as described in methods.

Results are shown in Figs. 1 and 2, grouped by kernel. The R executions have grey areas due to failed executions or excessive execution time. In the case of kernelized adjacency matrix (ka), the execution fails when matrix eigenvalues contains complex values and the algorithm tries to obtain the minimum eigenvalue.

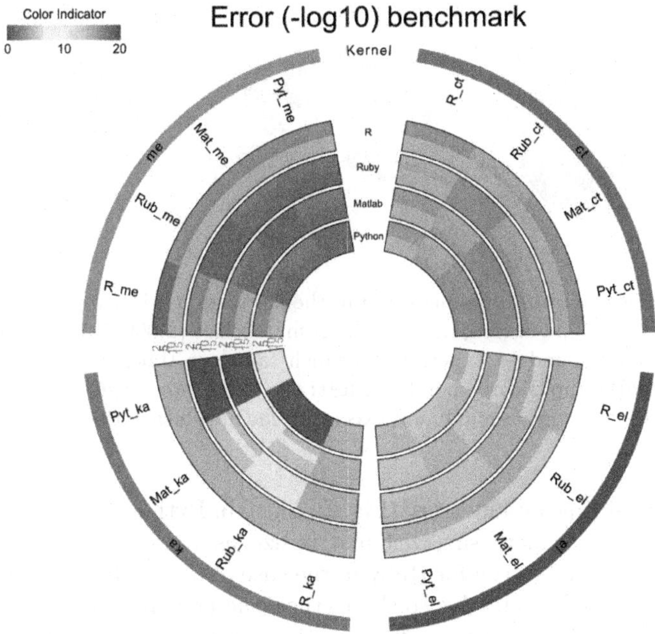

Fig. 1. Error rates obtained for all kernel executions. Grouped in **quarter-sections** by kernel type; in **rings** by platform used for comparison (R, Ruby [Rub], Matlab [Mat], Python [Pyt] from outer to inner rings); and in **inner ring lines** by input matrix size (coloured numbers, 2 for 2,000; 5 for 5,000; 10 for 10,000; and 15 for 15,000). Error rates are shown on a logarithmic scale. Where the results for a given platform is compared to itself, the smallest possible error for that section is used. The larger Grey values corresponds to experiments which have finished with errors or time out (24 h or more of execution time).

For other kernel types that use matrices greater than 5,000 × 5,000 elements, several that exceeded 24 h were halted.

By measuring error rates (Fig. 1) we can analyse how stable a method is across all platform implementations. Generally, very low error rates were obtained with orders of 10^{-14}, 10^{-16} and 10^{-18} for Laplacian Exponential Diffusion Kernel (el), Commute-Time Kernel (ct) and Markov Exponential Diffusion Kernel (me), respectively. Relatively high error rates were obtained for the *ka* kernel type; this method is based on changing the source matrix diagonal by adding the minimum eigenvalue. In most platforms, eigenvalues are calculated using power series, as such the convergence process leads to certain error rates, which would explain the observed results. In the case of the R platform, it may be that the eigenvalue calculation does not use the power series approximation, using exact calculation instead. These exact calculations generate complex eigenvalues, which is why the kernel implementation fails.

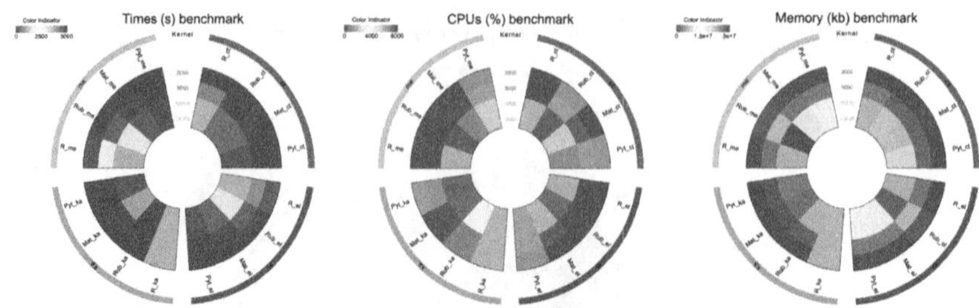

Fig. 2. Resource consumption measured in the kernel executions grouped in **quarter-sections** by kernel and in **ring lines** by input matrix size (2,000; 5,000; 10,000; 15,000). Grey values correspond to experiments which failed or timed out (24 h or more of execution time). Graphs corresponds to: **left:** execution time in seconds; **center:** CPU usage (percentage). **right:** maximum execution memory usage (kb).

Focusing on time and memory (Fig. 2), Matlab, Python and Ruby show similar values in general, increasing with matrix size, as would be expected. Markedly larger increases can be seen for Ruby in the case of the *me* and *el* kernels. These increments are likely to be due to the Python engine being called to execute the exponential matrix operations, affecting time and memory consumption. Also, we observe again the poor performance of R platform, which obtains similar times for $2{,}000 \times 2{,}000$ matrices that other platforms obtain for $15{,}000 \times 15{,}000$ matrices.

In terms of CPU consumption, R has a mono-core profile, whereas the other platforms have multi-core profiles. These CPU usage profiles may underlie the high execution time and poor performance of R. For the multi-core platforms, Matlab has a lower cpu percentage, which may be due to large mono-core execution stages, or low use of the active cores. On the other hand, Ruby and Python appear to use as many cores as available boosting their performance.

Given the results of the platform comparisons, Ruby and Python show the best performance: they show the least error, moreover they show multi-core CPU profiles and a memory usage which does not exceed 30gb for $15{,}000 \times 15{,}000$ matrices. Therefore, the Ruby kernel implementations, including the Python calls, were added to the NetAnalyzer network tool, which was applied to a real biological problem.

3.2 Kernel Performance in Prioritization of Disease Related Genes

String (v8.2) gene associations were used to generate an adjacency matrix of 17,078 elements, of which less than 1% are non-zero elements (Table 1). This connectivity density changes after kernel operations, except for *ka*, which is a simple kernelization operation, used to check the prediction performance of the input adjacency matrix.

Table 1 shows that the input matrix has an average degree of ~145 nodes, whereas the kernelized matrices can connect most of the elements to each other.

Table 1. String matrix and Kernel matrices summary statistics. All are 17,078 element squared matrices. The measured parameters are: (i) non-zero ratio, which corresponds to ratio of elements with non-zero values, (ii) average weight of the non-zero nodes (mean and standard deviation), and (iii) average connections per node.

Matrix	Non-zero ratio (%)	Non-zero node weights	Avg. connections per node
String v8.2	0.9	$3.8 \times 10^{2} \pm 2.4 \times 10^{-1}$	144.77 ± 1.10
el	99.3	$5.9 \times 10^{-5} \pm 1.4 \times 10^{-6}$	$16,957.22 \pm 0.46$
me	99.3	$6.1 \times 10^{-5} \pm 6.1 \times 10^{-5}$	$16,957.22 \pm 0.46$
ka	0.9	$5.4 \times 10^{2} \pm 1.5 \times 10^{1}$	144.77 ± 1.10
ct	100.0	$5.9 \times 10^{-25} \pm 3.1 \times 10^{-7}$	$17,077.00 \pm 0.00$

The generated kernels were used to prioritize 42 control genes whose association with disease gene sets are known. These gene sets were used to rank all other genes in the network, and the position of the control genes were used to measure the perormance of the different kernels. Results are shown in Table 2; metrics were computed as described in [21].

Table 2. Prioritization results for the four kernel methods. Measured parameters are: the median and mean with standard deviation of ranking positions obtained for the 42 control genes, the lowest ranking position obtained within the control genes, the true positives ratio (TPR) for different percentiles of the ranked gene list (at 5%, 10% and 30% of total ranked genes) and AUC when predicting control genes.

Kernel	Median	Mean ± s.d	Lowest	TPR in top 5%	TPR in top 10%	TPR in top 30%	AUC
el	67.5	65.02 ± 22.70	96	2%	4%	7%	0.35
me	14.0	21.52 ± 21.51	95	26%	42%	66%	0.78
ka	18.0	26.14 ± 24.54	80	26%	38%	64%	0.73
ct	11.0	18.74 ± 21.92	93	30%	45%	78%	0.81

It is clear that the *el* kernel shows poor performance in this experiment: only 7% of the control genes could be found among the top 30% of the total ranked genes. This was not the case for the other three kernels, which showed similar performance. Amongst these three kernels, there was a slight improvement with increasing kernel complexity. They can be ranked in increasing performance, in terms of TPR for all three measures, as *ka*, *me*, and *ct*. However, the difference between the three methods is small, showing that all three kernel operations can be used to prioritize novel disease genes using an interaction networks.

It is interesting to note that one of the kernels with lowest error rate, the *el*, resulted in the poorest prioritization result. Conversely, the *ka* kernel presented the highest error rate but obtained reasonably good rankings, although it should be taken into account that this kernel produces very large values in its kernelized matrix output, which may explain the apparently high error rate(Table 1).

4 Discussion and Conclusions

In this work we have studied the capability of different programming languages to perform kernel operations on adjacency matrices. Four different kernel operations were implemented: (i) kernelized adjacency matrix, (ii) commute-time kernel, (iii) Laplacian exponential diffusion kernel and (iv) Markov exponential diffusion kernel, coded using core language functionalities when they existed, and third parties packages when they did not. The languages were chosen based on their popularity in the bioinformatics and network science communities; more specifically we used R, Ruby, Matlab and Python. The code underlying the implementations are available from the repository https://github.com/seoanezonjic/kernels_testing.

Error rate, time, CPU and memory consumption were measured for all implementations. Python and Ruby showed the best performance for real number adjacency matrices and these implementations were thus included as a functional module of NetAnalyzer [13], a tool to handle and analyse biological networks.

This new NetAnalyzer module was used to test the performance of the different kernels for the discovery of new genes related to known gene sets. We used 42 gene-disease relations taken from [2], and compared the ability of the different kernels to discover these relations, ranking them among the other non-seed genes in the network. In this case, we use a gene interaction network from the String database (v8.2) that corresponded to a date before the gene-disease relations were discovered, meaning these relations could only be discovered based on kernel operations.

The kernelized adjacency matrix method was included among the kernels to inspect the prediction ability of the source matrix, i.e. the original interaction network, to discover the relations. Perhaps surprisingly, this kernel operation was able to infer new relations, performing almost as well as the Markov exponential diffusion kernel and commute-time kernel.

To conclude, we have shown that kernels can be used as mathematical consistent methods to study network structures and infer relationships for biologically-relevant multi-dimensional problems [4]. We have observed that different kernels obtain different performance in terms of identifying significant relationships between network elements. These differences confirm that each kernel operation shows different behaviour and the results depend on the details of the input matrix. For example, the most stable method for real number full-filled matrices (Laplacian exponential diffusion kernel), obtains the worst results for a sparse matrix.

Funding. This work was supported by The Spanish Ministry of Economy and Competitiveness with European Regional Development Fund [SAF2016-78041-C2-1-R], the Andalusian Government with European Regional Development Fund [CTS-486], the Ramon Areces foundation, which funds project for the investigation of rare disease (National call for research on life and material sciences, XIX edition) and the University of Malaga (Ayudas del I Plan Propio, Ramon y Cajal I3). The European Regional Development Fund (FEDER), Junta Andalucía, I+D+i, 2014–2020 Program (UMA18-

FEDERJA-102). The CIBERER is an initiative from the Institute of Health Carlos III and provides the funding with project ACCI2018 (ER192P1AC741). James Richard Perkins holds a research grant from the Andalusian Government (Fundacion Progreso y Salud)[PI-0075-2017]. Elena Rojano is a researcher from the Plan de Formacion de Personal Investigador (FPI) supported by the Andalusian Government.

References

1. Bates, D., Maechler, M.: Matrix: Sparse and Dense Matrix Classes and Methods (2015). http://cran.r-project.org/package=Matrix
2. Börnigen, D., et al.: An unbiased evaluation of gene prioritization tools. Bioinformatics **28**(23), 3081–3088 (2012). https://doi.org/10.1093/bioinformatics/bts581
3. Cheng, S., Cai, Z., Li, J., Gao, H.: Extracting kernel dataset from big sensory data in wireless sensor networks. IEEE Trans. Know. Data Eng. **29**(4), 813–827 (2017). https://doi.org/10.1109/TKDE.2016.2645212
4. Fouss, F., Francoisse, K., Yen, L., Pirotte, A., Saerens, M.: An experimental investigation of kernels on graphs for collaborative recommendation and semisupervised classification. Neural Netw. Official J. Int. Neural Netw. Soc. **31**, 53–72 (2012). https://doi.org/10.1016/j.neunet.2012.03.001
5. Gomez-Cabrero, D., et al.: Data integration in the era of omics: current and future challenges. BMCSyst. Biol. **8**, 11 (2014). https://doi.org/10.1186/1752-0509-8-S2-I1
6. Haas, R., Zelezniak, A., Iacovacci, J., Kamrad, S., Townsend, S.J., Ralser, M.: Designing and interpreting 'multi-omic' experiments that may change our understanding of biology. Curr. Opin Syst. Biol. **6**, 37–45 (2017). https://doi.org/10.1016/j.coisb.2017.08.009
7. Hériché, J.K.: Integration of biological data by kernels on graph nodes allows prediction of new genes involved in mitotic chromosome condensation. Mol. Biol. Cell **25**, 2522–2536 (2014). https://doi.org/10.1091/mbc.E13-04-0221
8. Huang, S., Chaudhary, K., Garmire, L.X.: More is better: recent progress in multi-omics data integration methods. Front. Genet. **8**, 84 (2017). https://doi.org/10.3389/fgene.2017.00084
9. van Laarhoven, T., Nabuurs, S.B., Marchiori, E.: Gaussian interaction profile kernels for predicting drug-target interaction. Bioinformatics **27**(21), 3036–3043 (2011). https://doi.org/10.1093/bioinformatics/btr500
10. Meunier, M., Guyard-Nicodème, M., Hirchaud, E., Parra, A., Chemaly, M., Dory, D.: Identification of novel vaccine candidates against campylobacter through reverse vaccinology. J. Immunol. Res **2016**, 9 (2016). https://doi.org/10.1155/2016/5715790
11. Pinu, F.R., et al.: Systems biology and multi-omics integration: Viewpoints from the metabolomics research community. Metabolites **9**(4), E76 (2019). https://doi.org/10.3390/metabo9040076
12. Rojano, E., Perkins, J.R., Sillitoe, I., Orengo, C., García Ranea, J.A., Seoane, P.: Associating protein domains with biological functions: a tripartite network approach. In: Rojas, I., Valenzuela, O., Rojas, F., Ortuño, F. (eds.) IWBBIO 2019, Part II. LNCS, vol. 11466, pp. 155–164. Springer, Cham (2019). https://doi.org/10.1007/978-3-030-17935-9_15

13. Rojano, E., Seoane, P., Bueno-Amoros, A., Perkins, J.R., Garcia-Ranea, J.A.: Revealing the relationship between human genome regions and pathological phenotypes through network analysis. In: Rojas, I., Ortuño, F. (eds.) IWBBIO 2017, Part I. LNCS, vol. 10208, pp. 197–207. Springer, Cham (2017). https://doi.org/10.1007/978-3-319-56148-6_17
14. Seoane, P., et al.: AutoFlow, a versatile workflow engine illustrated by assembling an optimised de novo transcriptome for a non-model species, such as Faba Bean (Vicia faba). Curr. Bioinform. **11**(4), 440–450 (2016). https://doi.org/10.2174/1574893611666160212235117
15. Si, S., Hsieh, C.J.: Memory Efficient Kernel Approximation. Technical report (2017). http://jmlr.org/papers/v18/15-025.html
16. Szklarczyk, D., et al.: STRING v11: protein-protein association networks with increased coverage, supporting functional discovery in genome-wide experimental datasets. Nucleic Acids Res. **47**(D1), D607–D613 (2019). https://doi.org/10.1093/nar/gky1131
17. Van Der Walt, S., Colbert, S.C., Varoquaux, G.: The NumPy array: a structure for efficient numerical computation. Comput. Sci. Eng. **13**(2), 22–30 (2011). https://doi.org/10.1109/MCSE.2011.37
18. Venables, W.N., Ripley, B.D.: Modern Applied Statistics with S, 4th edn. Springer, New York (2002). https://doi.org/10.1007/978-0-387-21706-2. http://www.stats.ox.ac.uk/pub/MASS4
19. Virtanen, P., et al.: SciPy 1.0-Fundamental Algorithms for Scientific Computing in Python, July 2019. http://arxiv.org/abs/1907.10121
20. Wilson, A.G., Hu, Z., Salakhutdinov, R., Xing, E.P.: Deep Kernel Learning, November 2015. http://arxiv.org/abs/1511.02222
21. Zampieri, G., et al.: Scuba: Scalable kernel-based gene prioritization. BMC Bioinformatics **19**(1), 23 (2018). https://doi.org/10.1186/s12859-018-2025-5

Comprehensive Analysis of Patients with Undiagnosed Genetic Diseases Using the Patient Exploration Tools Suite (PETS)

Elena Rojano[1], Pedro Seoane-Zonjic[2], Fernando M. Jabato[1], James R. Perkins[2,3], and Juan A. G. Ranea[1,2,3(✉)]

[1] Department of Molecular Biology and Biochemistry, University of Malaga, Bulevar Louis Pasteur 31, 29010 Malaga, Spain
{elenarojano,jabato,ranea}@uma.es

[2] CIBER of Rare Diseases, Av. Monforte de Lemos, 3-5, Pabellon 11, Planta 0, 28029 Madrid, Spain
{seoanezonjic,jimrperkins}@uma.es

[3] Institute of Biomedical Research in Malaga (IBIMA), C. Dr. Miguel Diaz Recio, 28, 29010 Malaga, Spain

Abstract. Systemic approaches based on network analysis have been successful in associating pathological phenotypes observed in patients with their affected genomic regions. Previously we have used phenotype-genotype associations to determine the genetic causes that lead to pathological phenotypes observed in patients with rare and complex disorders. However, these studies were limited as many of these associations had low specificity, frequently associating pathological phenotypes such as intellectual disability or growth abnormality with multiple regions of the genome. To help solve this problem, we propose that the phenotypic characterisation of patients using more specific terms will substantially improve the determination of the genetic causes that produce them. In this work we present the Patient Exploration Tools Suite (PETS), which includes three tools to: (1) determine the quality of information within a patient cohort; (2) associate genomic regions with their pathological phenotypes based on the cohort data; and (3) predict the possible genetic variants that cause the clinically observed pathological phenotypes using phenotype-genotype association values. This tool has been developed to be used by the clinical community, to facilitate patient characterisation, help identify where data quality can be improved within a cohort and help diagnose patients with complex disease.

Keywords: Rare diseases · PETS · DECIPHER · HPO · CNV

E. Rojano and P. Seoane-Zonjic—Equal contribution.

I. Rojas et al. (Eds.): IWBBIO 2020, LNBI 12108, pp. 775–786, 2020.
https://doi.org/10.1007/978-3-030-45385-5_69

1 Introduction

Rare diseases can be defined as those that affect at least one in 2000 people in a population [13]. Approximately 50% of those affected are children and 30% die in their first five years of life [15]. This high mortality is partly due to inadequate diagnosis, in fact the average time of diagnosis typically exceeds five years, resulting in poor treatment, often at a critical age. Data from the Spanish Federation of Rare Diseases (FEDER, https://enfermedades-raras.org) reveals that 26.7% of patients with a rare disease receive inadequate treatment and in more than 40% of cases they receive no treatment or support at all.

The correct diagnosis of rare diseases is complicated by the low number of patients who show similar pathological features, making characterisation by physicians difficult [6]. There are also technical limitations: 80% of rare diseases have a genetic basis, as such sequencing techniques are necessary to determine which variants are responsible [4]. In recent years, the costs of next-generation sequencing (NGS) have decreased and its use as a diagnostic tool for rare diseases has increased significantly [3].

Furthermore, there are resources to deepen our knowledge of rare disease and improve their diagnosis and treatment. These include the DatabasE of genomiC varIation and Phenotype in Humans using Ensembl Resources (DECIPHER), which contains genetic and phenotypic information for patients with rare undiagnosed diseases [2]. The latest version, 9.30, includes information from more than 30000 patients with genome variants, mostly copy number variations (CNVs) characterised using comparative genomic hybridization arrays (aCGH). More concretely, it provides information related to chromosome coordinates, mutation classification (deletion or duplication), genotype (heterozygous/homozygous) and inheritance mode (inherited or *de novo*). It also contains information on the clinically observed pathological phenotypes for these patients, annotated using the Human Phenotype Ontology (HPO) [9], a hierarchically organised vocabulary of standardised pathological phenotype terms [14].

Recent work has shown the utility of biological network analysis to integrate patient data and determine the genetic causes for undiagnosed rare diseases [1,16]. Previous work from our group used a tripartite network formed of phenotype-patient-genotype connections to infer the genetic causes of the pathological phenotypes of disease [1]. Here, we build on this work and present the Patient Exploration Tools Suite (PETS). This software suite comprises (1) the Cohort Analyzer tool to assess the data quality of patient cohort, (2) the Reg2Phen search engine that suggests pathological phenotypes likely to result from a given mutation, and (3) the Phen2Reg tool to predict affected genomic regions based on the pathological phenotypes observed in a patient. These tools have been developed to be used in clinical diagnosis by helping to characterise patients with undiagnosed disease. The suite is available from https://rubygems.org/gems/pets and https://bitbucket.org/elenarojano/pets.

2 Methods

2.1 Patient Data and Calculating Phenotype-Genotype Associations

The PETS software suite consists of three tools, which will be described in full detail below. They can be used to analyse any patient cohort for which the requisite information is available. In this work we have used data from DECIPHER (version 9.30) [2]. Of a total of 27887 patients with copy number variations (CNVs) characterised with comparative genomic hybridization arrays (aCGH), we selected 19997 with clinically observed pathological phenotypes that have been recorded using the Human Phenotype Ontology (HPO) [10]. The first tool, Cohort Analyzer, takes as input patient information, which must include all mutation data and full phenotypic profiles, recorded using the HPO. The two other tools, Reg2Phen and Phen2Reg, require a list of phenotype-genotype associations. These can be calculated using the NetAnalyzer tool, which implements various metrics to associate phenotypes with genomic regions based on their overlap among patients [11]. More concretely, a phenotype is associated with a short overlapping region (SOR) of the genome. These regions are found by decomposing the genome into discrete regions based on patient data, as described in [11]. Associations are then calculated between phenotypes and SORs using various association metrics: Jaccard, Simpson, geometric, cosine, hypergeometric index (HyI), Pearson correlation coefficient (PCC), Connection specificity index (CSI) and transference. Each phenotype-SOR relation must be shared by a minimum of two patients.

2.2 Patient Exploration Tools Suite (PETS) Tools

PETS is based on the idea of exploiting phenotype-SOR associations to understand the biological mechanisms underlying disease. To do this, we must first inspect the quality of the information of the patient cohort used to establish these associations. For this, PETS includes the Cohort Analyzer tool. If the quality of the data is appropriate, biological information can then be obtained from the phenotype-SOR associations using the other two PETS tools: Reg2Phen and Phen2Reg.

Cohort Analyzer produces an html report containing multiple tables and graphics to help assess the quality of patient cohort data. The main features that are analysed are described in Table 1. It can calculate and visualise the distribution of genome coverage across the entire cohort for both the original mutations (CNV) and the SORs. This allows the user to know the proportion of the genome covered by patients in the cohorts and how this is affected by the SOR decomposition. In addition, it analyses mutation length and frequency. At the patient level, it clusters patients in the cohort according to their phenotypic profiles. This can identify groups of patients with equivalent profiles and check profile information quality. Clustering is performed by creating a binary matrix of phenotypes and patients, calculating Euclidean distance between patients and performing general agglomerative hierarchical clustering [7]. For each cluster, the distribution of patients by chromosome can be visualised, moreover the information content of the phenotypes within each cluster can be calculated. This tool also generates a table containing the number of patients, phenotypes and their frequency in each cluster.

Table 1. Description of metrics calculated in the patient cohort analysis performed with Cohort Analyzer.

Metric name	Description
Unique HPOs	Number of unique HPO terms present in the whole cohort
Cohort size	Number of patients in the cohort
HPOs per patient	Average number of HPO terms per patient
Number of HPOs in the 90th patient percentile	Patients are ranked by increasing number of phenotypes in their profile and the number of phenotypes in the patient representing the first 10%
Percentage of HPOs with child terms	Percentage of HPOs in the patient profiles that have at least one child term in HPO ontology
Most frequent HPOs	Top 20 most frequent HPOs in the cohort, along with the percentage of patients that have been annotated with each

Reg2Phen is a search engine that returns the phenotypes associated with SORs within a genomic regions of interest (in the GRCh37 human assembly version) and their association values. As DECIPHER uses the GRCh37 human assembly, therefore PETS tools use this version when work with genomic coordinates. Reg2Phen can take as input genomic coordinates or a gene, which will in turn be converted to its genomic coordinates. We tested the different association metrics described above. In order to select the best performing method we calculated precision and recall (PR) using ten-fold cross-validation. For this, all the possible phenotype-patient-SOR connections in the dataset were partitioned into ten equal sized subsets. For each fold execution, nine subsets were selected to calculate association values using NetAnalyzer [11]. For the remaining subset we considered all connections between phenotypes and SORs as the ground truth. We then obtained PR values by comparing this ground truth to the associations calculated using the other nine subsets.

Phen2Reg analyses the pathological phenotypes observed in a patient (phenotypic profile) and predicts putative causal genomic regions. This tool performs two main functions: (1) a quality control of the phenotypes provided in the phenotypic profile and (2) a prioritisation of the genomic regions (SORs) associated with the profile.

Firstly, the HPO quality control step detects whether the pathological phenotypes in the profile have been previously associated with SORs. Then, it calculates the information content (IC) for each phenotype (defined as the negative logarithm of the relative frequency of each phenotype), showing how informative is each term in the DECIPHER patient cohort [10]. The phenotypic profile is also checked to determine if it includes terms with direct parent-child relationships amongst them, as this would lead to redundant phenotype-SOR associations that could reduce prediction accuracy. Likewise, to help the user select more specific terms within the HPO, this tool suggests all the possible child terms if available. This helps obtain more accurate clinical characterisation of the patient.

Secondly, Phen2Reg uses the phenotype-SOR associations to rank the putative causing regions and suggest which of them are most likely to cause such phenotypes. This ranking is made by combining association scores when several phenotypes are associated with the same SOR. From a profile of clinically observed HPOs in a patient, Phen2Reg locates all the SORs that have an association with one or more of the phenotypes within the profile. It then combines these association scores to produce a single value that represents the significance of the prediction for each SOR. One of two combination strategies are used, depending on the nature of the association method. The first is to transform the association values to P-values and integrate them through Fisher's combined probability test (Eq. 1).

$$\chi^2_{2k} \sim -2\sum_{i=1}^{k} ln(p_i) \tag{1}$$

Where p_i is the association value and k the degrees of freedom, calculated in accordance with the maximum number of phenotypes in the input profile. We use this procedure when associations are calculated with HyI, as they represent the minus log-transformed probability of having an equal or greater number of interactions between a pair of nodes (phenotype-SOR) than other given by chance [1,5].

The second strategy consists of standardising the association values to produce Z-scores and using Stouffer's combination method (Eq. 2).

$$Z \sim \frac{\sum_{i=1}^{k} Z_i}{\sqrt{k}} \tag{2}$$

Where Z_i is the Z-score transformed from the association value and k the number of degrees of freedom, calculated in the same way for Fisher's combined probability test. We applied this procedure to combine the association values calculated using the other indices (Jaccard, Simpson, geometric, cosine, PCC, CSI and transference). Additionally, we implemented a gene localisation module using Entrez identifiers using the GRCh37 human assembly coordinates. Furthermore, we included a module to detect in which pathways the genes associated with each each SOR are predicted to occur. For this, we incorporated information from the Kyoto Encyclopedia of Genes and Genomes (KEGG) [8].

Once the prediction has been performed, Phen2Reg returns an html report with the information gathered from the HPO quality control and a table with all predicted genomic regions, including (1) their genomic coordinates, (2) the HPOs from the profile associated with the predicted region, (3) the values for each phenotype-SOR associations, (4) the combined score, (5) the genes found within each predicted region, in terms of their NCBI Entrez Gene identifier, gene name, description and any available KEGG functional annotation.

We demonstrated the accuracy of Phen2Reg by predicting the CNVs for patients in the DECIPHER cohort based on their phenotypic profiles and building PR curves. For each patient we used their phenotypes as input to Phen2Reg and predicted their putative affected genomic regions. We then compared these regions to those in their original CNVs. Overlapping coordinates between predicted and original genomic regions were considered true positives, predicted areas outside of the original regions were considered false positives, and original regions that were not predicted were considered false negatives. Using this methodology, we tested Phen2Reg for the eight different methods used to associate phenotypes with SORs and determine which gave the best results.

3 Results

We present the results of PETS applied to the DECIPHER database. First, we characterized the data using Cohort Analyzer. We then calculated phenotype-SOR associations and used them as input for Reg2Phen and Phen2Reg.

Cohort Analyzer. Running Cohort Analyzer on the DECIPHER patient cohort returned the results shown in Table 2.

There are 3387 different HPO terms for the 19997 patients, and each phenotype profile has a mean of 6.74 terms. However, the 90th percentile patient has only one term, which means that at least 10% of the patients have only been annotated with one HPO term. Moreover, 63.82% of the HPO terms used to characterize the patients have more specific terms. In fact, the two most common HPO terms are *Intellectual disability* followed by *Global developmental delay*, two very general terms.

Table 2. Metrics for the DECIPHER patient cohort analysis. For the most frequent HPOs, the percentage indicates the proportion of the cohort annotated with the given HPO term.

Metric name	Result	
Unique HPOs	3387	
Cohort size	19997	
HPOs per patient	6.74	
Number of HPOs in the 90th patient percentile	1	
Percentage of HPOs with child terms	63.82%	
Most frequent HPOs	Intellectual disability	35.99%
	Global developmental delay	14.29%
	Delayed speech and language development	11.74%
	Microcephaly	8.87%
	Muscular hypotonia	7.44%

Results of the analysis of the pathological phenotypes within the patient cohort are shown in Fig. 1. In terms of the distribution of the informative content (IC) for the phenotypes included in the cohort (Fig. 1a), we have computed IC for each term using two different approaches: one using as reference the HP ontology structure itself (HP ontology IC) [12] and another one using the frequency of the individual phenotypes within the patient cohort (HP Frequency based IC). Most terms have a high IC value according to both metrics (IC $>$ 3). However, the distribution shown in Fig. 1b at the patient profile level demonstrates that the IC values are evidently lower at the level of ontology structure (HP ontology profile IC), but at the level of IC frequency based (HP ontology profile IC), the change to lower values is much more drastic. With respect to the clustering of patients by their HPO profile (Fig. 1c), for each cluster (named according to the total numbers patients in it, followed by an underscore and a sequential numerical identifier) we can see the number of patients that have mutations in the same chromosome. As can be seen, for most of clusters almost all chromosomes are represented. In terms of IC distribution by cluster (frequency based, Fig. 1d), the average does not exceed IC $=$ 1 for the two first clusters and barely reaches an IC of 1.5 for the others. The exception is cluster 14, with 117 patients, whose mean IC is 4.

The html file containing the information of the results for the analysis of the patient cohort is available at https://bitbucket.org/elenarojano/pets.

Reg2Phen. Regarding the 10-fold cross-validation performed to validate Reg2Phen, precision and recall (PR) values were calculated to select the best method to calculate the input phenotype-SOR associations (Fig. 2a). The area under the PR curve (AUCPR) of the geometric index ($\text{geometric}_{AUCPR} = 0.57$) is greater than that calculated for rest of methods ($\text{Jaccard}_{AUCPR} = 0.37$, $\text{Simpson}_{AUCPR} = 0.25$, $\text{cosine}_{AUCPR} = 0.35$, $\text{PCC}_{AUCPR} = 0.29$, $\text{HyI}_{AUCPR} = 0.47$, $\text{CSI}_{AUCPR} = 0.12$, $\text{transference}_{AUCPR} = 0.49$). We thus suggest Reg2Phen should use the phenotype-SOR associations calculated with this association method to perform its phenotype searches.

Phen2Reg. With respect to Phen2Reg validation, the most accurate predictions were obtained by combining the phenotypes-SOR association values calculated using the CSI (Fig. 2b). The degrees of freedom were set as the total number of phenotypes for each profile and the maximum number of predictions to be considered per run was 100.

4 Discussion

We have presented the Patient Exploration Tool Suite (PETS). This suite contains a tool for characterising the quality of a patient cohort containing phenotypic and genotypic information (Cohort Analyzer). It also contains tools that use this information to search for pathological phenotypes associated with a genomic region of interest (Reg2Phen) and predict the putative genomic regions that potentially underlie the pathological phenotypes observed in a patient (Phen2Reg).

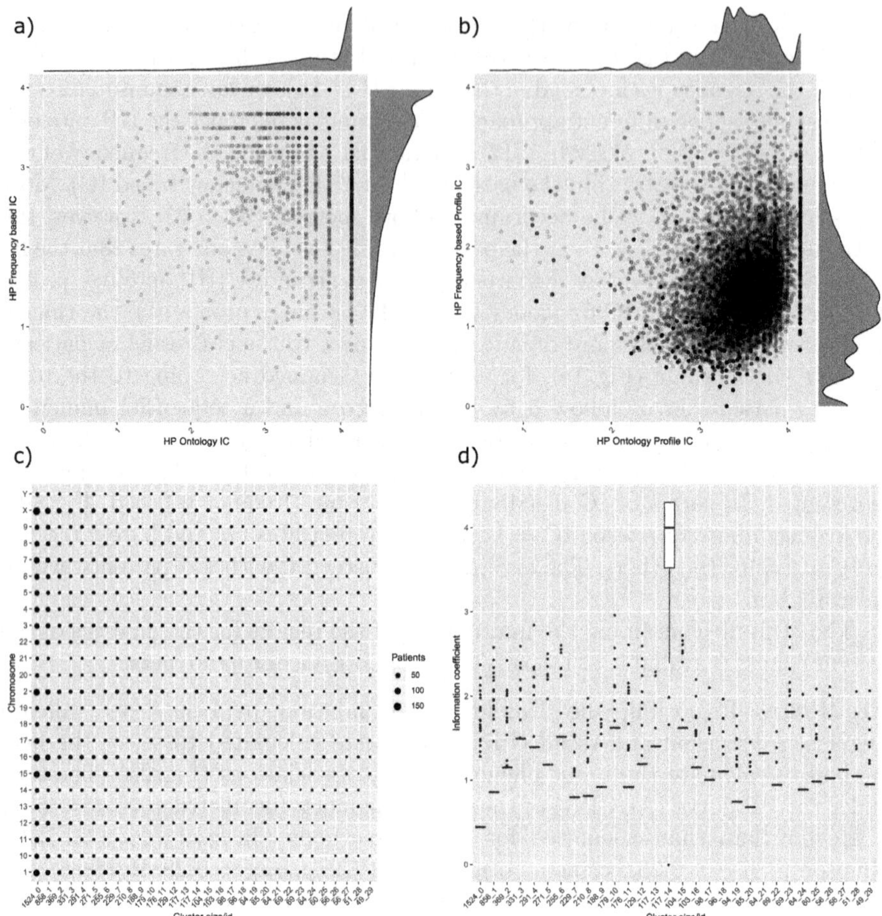

Fig. 1. Information collected with Cohort Analyzer for the analysis of the DECIPHER patient cohort. (a) Distribution of the informative content (IC) of the phenotypes included in the HPO based on ontology structure (HP ontology IC) and the frequency of the individual phenotypes belonging to the cohort (HP Frequency based IC). (b) Distribution of the IC of the phenotypic profiles based on ontology structure (HP ontology profile IC) and the frequency of the phenotypic profile (HP frequency based profile IC). (c) Affected chromosomes for the top 30 patient clusters analysed, circle width represents the number of patients with mutations in a specific chromosome. (d) Information content distribution for the top 30 clusters analysed.

We used PETS to analyse a cohort of 19 997 patients with undiagnosed diseases. We analysed this dataset with the Cohort Analyzer tool to characterise its quality. Despite having a substantial number of patients to establish phenotype-SOR associations (19997) and a large number of different phenotypic terms (3387), more than 10% of the patients were characterised with just a single phenotype. Moreover, the most frequent term was Intellectual disability, present

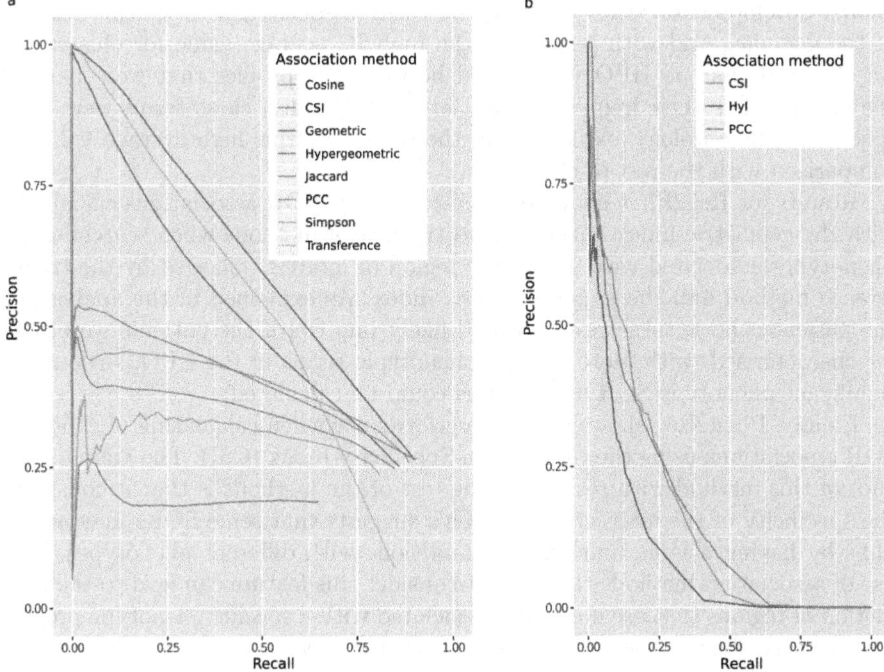

Fig. 2. Precision and recall curves to establish the best association method for Reg2Phen (a) and for Phen2Reg (b). The results for the three best association methods (CSI, HyI and PCC) are shown for this Phen2Reg for clarity. CSI: Connection specificity index, PCC: Pearson correlation coefficient, HyI: hypergeometric index.

in 35.99% of patients. This term actually has six child terms in the HPO, suggesting that more specific phenotypes could be ascribed to many of the DECIPHER patients.

The comparison of IC values shown in Fig. 1a suggests that the dataset contains highly informative phenotypes, necessary to perform a complete characterisation of the patients. However, when we analyse the IC calculations for the phenotypic profiles within the patient cohort (Fig. 1b) we observe that only general terms are used for many of the phenotypic annotations. We believe a deeper phenotypic characterisation using more specific HPO terms would improve our results when associating these phenotypes with the regions of the genome that cause them. With respect to the cluster analysis performed on the patient cohort, based on their phenotypic profiles, we observe that for each cluster all or most of the chromosomes are represented (Fig. 1c).

This indicates that the genetic causes that lead to a given profile can be numerous. Similarly, when we observe the quality of the phenotype profiles based on their IC for each cluster (Fig. 1d), we see that the IC distribution demonstrates that the profiles consisted of uninformative, unspecific HPO terms. Therefore, profiles with general HPO terms (such as Intellectual disability or

Global developmental delay) will not be easily associated with specific regions of the genome. And with respect to the high IC average value for cluster 14, we observed that no HPO was shared between the profiles that were part of the cluster, thus their frequency was the same. Besides, these terms were very specific in the ontology, explaining in the same way this high average value in comparison with the rest of clusters.

Results for Reg2Phen show that the phenotype-SOR associations calculated with the geometric index outperformed the rest of methods when searching for phenotypes associated with a genomic region of interest, followed by the transference method and the hypergeometric index. As explained in the analysis of the patient cohort, these results would likely improve if the patients were better characterised, with more specific phenotypic terms in the HPO, since more significant phenotype-SOR associations could be calculated.

Finally, Phen2Reg shows the best performance when calculating phenotype-SOR associations using the Connection Specificity Index (CSI). The main difference of this method with respect to the rest of the methods is that it considers the specificity of the interactions [5]. This suggests that some SORs may act as hubs by having a large number of connections with different phenotypes. The use of association methods that do not consider this feature can lead to the prediction of regions that are not really associated with a specific phenotype profile. Despite this, the validation results show that the predictions must be improved, since the error rate is high for all metrics. As per the case of the results obtained using Reg2Phen, we suspect we would obtain a higher success rate if the profiles were more complete in terms of the number of phenotypes per patient if more ontology specific terms were used.

We have developed PETS to improve the analysis of undiagnosed diseases by providing tools to extract useful information from cohorts of patients with a heterogeneous set of rare phenotypes, and to explore regions of the genome potentially involved in their manifestation. We believe that this tool could be useful for neonatal screening, analysing the possible phenotypes that may manifest in a patient in late stages of development. In future work, we will investigate groups of patients annotated with more specific HPO terms and mutations characterised using more specific methods (using sequencing data instead of aCGH) to check the behaviour of PETS.

Acknowledgements. This study makes use of data generated by the DECIPHER community. A full list of centres who contributed to the generation of the data is available from http://decipher.sanger.ac.uk and via email from decipher@sanger.ac.uk. Funding for the project was provided by the Wellcome Trust. The authors thank the Supercomputing and Bioinnovation Center (SCBI) of the University of Malaga for their provision of computational resources and technical support (http://www.scbi.uma.es/site).

Funding. This work was supported by The Spanish Ministry of Economy and Competitiveness with European Regional Development Fund [SAF2016-78041-C2-1-R], the Andalusian Government with European Regional Development Fund [CTS-486], the

Ramón Areces foundation, which funds project for the investigation of rare disease (National call for research on life and material sciences, XIX edition) and the University of Malaga (Ayudas del I Plan Propio). The CIBERER is an initiative from the Institute of Health Carlos III. James Richard Perkins holds a research grant from the Andalusian Government (Fundación Progreso y Salud) [PI-0075-2017]. Elena Rojano is a researcher from the Plan de Formación de Personal Investigador (FPI) supported by the Andalusian Government.

References

1. Bueno, A., et al.: Phenotype-loci associations in networks of patients with rare disorders: application to assist in the diagnosis of novel clinical cases. Eur. J. Hum. Genet. **26**, 1451–1461 (2018). https://doi.org/10.1038/s41431-018-0139-x
2. Corpas, M., et al.: DECIPHER: database of chromosomal imbalance and phenotype in humans using ensembl resources. Am. J. Hum. Genet. **84**, 1–17 (2009). https://doi.org/10.1016/j.ajhg.2009.03.010. http://linkinghub.elsevier.com/retrieve/pii/S0002929709001074doi.wiley.com/10.1002/0471142905.hg0814s72
3. Fernandez-Marmiesse, A., Gouveia, S., Couce, M.L.: NGS technologies as a turning point in rare disease research, diagnosis and treatment. Curr.t Med. Chem. **25**(3), 404–432 (2017). https://doi.org/10.2174/0929867324666170718101946
4. Field, M.J., Boat, T.F.: Rare Diseases and Orphan Products: Accelerating Research and Development (2011). https://doi.org/10.17226/12953
5. Fuxman Bass, J.I., Diallo, A., Nelson, J., Soto, J.M., Myers, C.L., Walhout, A.J.M.: Using networks to measure similarity between genes: association index selection. Nat. Methods (2013). https://doi.org/10.1038/nmeth.2728
6. Mueller, T., Jerrentrup, A., Bauer, M.J., Fritsch, H.W., Schaefer, J.R.: Characteristics of patients contacting a center for undiagnosed and rare diseases. Orphanet J. Rare Dis. **11**, 81 (2016). https://doi.org/10.1186/s13023-016-0467-2
7. Murtagh, F., Legendre, P.: Ward's hierarchical agglomerative clustering method: which algorithms implement ward's criterion? J. Classif. **31**(3), 274–295 (2014). https://doi.org/10.1007/s00357-014-9161-z
8. Ogata, H., Goto, S., Sato, K., Fujibuchi, W., Bono, H., Kanehisa, M.: KEGG: Kyoto encyclopedia of genes and genomes (1999). https://doi.org/10.1093/nar/27.1.29
9. Robinson, P.N., Mundlos, S.: The Human Phenotype Ontology (2010). https://doi.org/10.1111/j.1399-0004.2010.01436.x
10. Robinson, P.N., Köhler, S., Bauer, S., Seelow, D., Horn, D., Mundlos, S.: The human phenotype ontology: a tool for annotating and analyzing human hereditary disease. Am. J. Hum. Genet. **83**(5), 610–615 (2008). https://doi.org/10.1016/j.ajhg.2008.09.017
11. Rojano, E., Seoane, P., Bueno-Amoros, A., Perkins, J.R., Garcia-Ranea, J.A.: Revealing the relationship between human genome regions and pathological phenotypes through network analysis. In: Rojas, I., Ortuño, F. (eds.) IWBBIO 2017. LNCS, vol. 10208, pp. 197–207. Springer, Cham (2017). https://doi.org/10.1007/978-3-319-56148-6_17
12. Sánchez, D., Batet, M., Isern, D.: Ontology-based information content computation. Knowl.-Based Syst. **24**(2), 297–303 (2011). https://doi.org/10.1016/j.knosys.2010.10.001

13. Schieppati, A., Henter, J.I., Daina, E., Aperia, A.: Why rare diseases are an important medical and social issue. Lancet **371**(9629), 2039–2041 (2008). https://doi.org/10.1016/S0140-6736(08)60872-7
14. Shen, F., Wang, L., Liu, H.: Using human phenotype ontology for phenotypic analysis of clinical notes. In: Studies in Health Technology and Informatics, vol. 245, p. 1285. IOS Press (2017). https://doi.org/10.3233/978-1-61499-830-3-1285
15. The Lancet Diabetes & Endocrinology: Spotlight on rare diseases. Lancet Diab. Endocrinol. **7**(2), P75 (2019). https://doi.org/10.1016/S2213-8587(19)30006-3
16. Yan, J., Risacher, S.L., Shen, L., Saykin, A.J.: Network approaches to systems biology analysis of complex disease: Integrative methods for multi-omics data. Brief. Bioinf. **19**(6), 1370–1381 (2017). https://doi.org/10.1093/bib/bbx066

Method of Detecting Orientation of Red Blood Cells Based on Video Data

Kristina Kovalcikova(✉) and Michal Duracik

Cell-in-Fluid Biomedical Modeling & Computations Group,
Department of Software Technologies, Faculty of Management Science
and Informatics, University of Zilina, Žilina, Slovakia
kristina.kovalcikova@fri.uniza.sk

Abstract. This article propose a methodology to estimate the orientation of red blood cells flowing in laboratory microfluidic devices. Inputs for this methodology is a video output from the laboratory experiment, with an assumption that cells have a moderate deformation in the microfluidic device. This methodology is based on a hypothesis, that we can identify the position and inclination of the cell if we know the dimensions of its 2D projection. We applied the methodology to cells from numerical simulations. We compared the exact values of extremal cell point coordinates, with the values obtained only with a restricted knowledge about the bounding box of the 2D projection of the cell. We identified the accuracy of estimating the information about the 3D position of the cell from the 2D projection data. We found a good agreement mainly for estimation of the 3rd dimension of the cell's bounding box, when we know only the two dimensions of the bounding box of the 2D projection of the cell.

Keywords: Red blood cell · 3D rotation · Bounding box

1 Introduction

The motivation of this work is our ambition to evaluate the 3D rotation of the red blood cells in microfluidic devices. Usually, we do not have many information about motion of the cells from a laboratory experiment. In most of cases we have series of two-dimensional frames or a video, with captures of the cells in it [1].

A video from a simulation can be processed automatically, in order to identify the position of cells within one frame, with help of artificial intelligence. An example of such evaluation can be found in [2]. This method is able to find a cell and to draw a bounding box around it in each frame.

In this work we will try to propose a method of identifying the precise position of the cell and its inclination, if we know only the dimensions of the 2D bounding boxes during the simulation. The knowledge of the cell's inclination in each video frame would help us to identify its 3D rotation during the simulation.

This work was supported by the Slovak Research and Development Agency (contract number APVV-15-0751) and by the Ministry of Education, Science, Research and Sport of the Slovak Republic (contract No. VEGA 1/0643/17).

I. Rojas et al. (Eds.): IWBBIO 2020, LNBI 12108, pp. 787–799, 2020.
https://doi.org/10.1007/978-3-030-45385-5_70

2 Methodology

2.1 Cell Size and Definition of Its Bounding Box

In this part, we will explain how we can estimate the real position of the cell from the 2D picture of it.

Firstly, let's imagine the form of the red blood cell. It has a discoid shape, with diameter of approximately 7.82 μm and with thickness of approximately 2.55 μm, as depicted in Fig. 1.

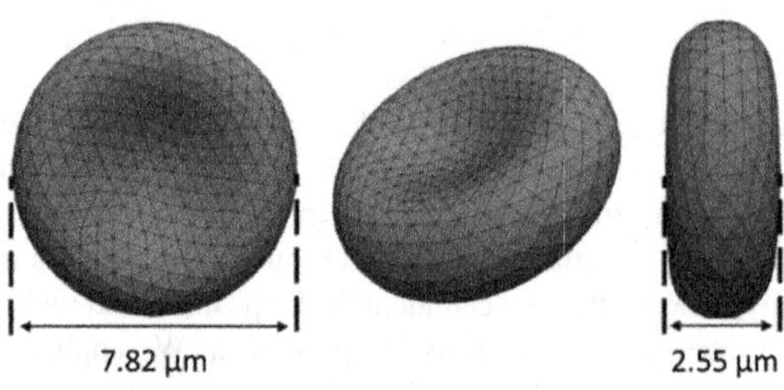

Fig. 1. Dimensions of normal red blood cell

A function that describe the form of the red blood cell has been estimated e.g. in [3]:

$$z = \pm 0.5 r_0 \left[1 - \frac{x^2 + y^2}{r_0^2}\right]^{\frac{1}{2}} \left[C_0 + C_1 \frac{x^2 + y^2}{r_0^2} + C_2 \left(\frac{x^2 + y^2}{r_0^2}\right)^2\right] \tag{1}$$

Here r_0 is the average cell radius in the axial direction; x, y and z are the Cartesian coordinates; and the constants are $C_0 = 0.207161$, $C_1 = 2.002558$ and $C_2 = -1.122762$.

Usually, the cell radius $r_0 = 3.91$ μm, which means the mean diameter D = 7.82 μm and the thickness d = 2.55 μm. In this article, we will consider a "normalized" cell, with $r_0 = 1$, D = 2 and d = 0.65.

Let's assume that the cell is not deformed. On a video-frame from a laboratory experiment, we can make for each cell its bounding box, as in Fig. 2. Bounding box is the smallest box, where the cell fits, and whose faces are parallel or perpendicular to x, y or z ax.

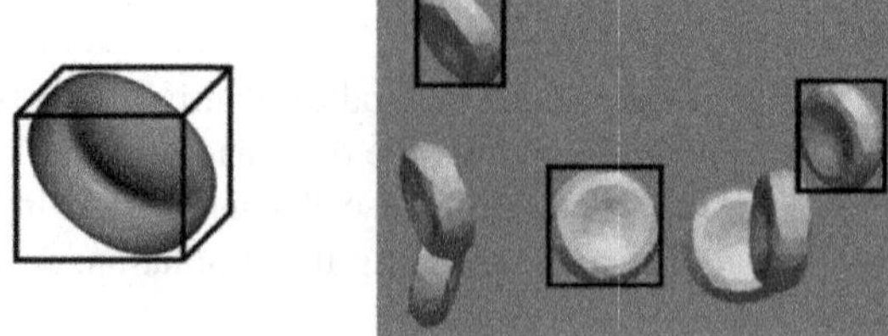

Fig. 2. Bounding box of a cell. Left: 3D bounding box of a cell. Right: 2D bounding box in a 2D picture.

By knowing the shape of the cell, which is defined by Eq. 1, we can deduce the third dimension of the bounding box – it is defined only by the given form of the cell and by the two dimensions of the bounding box.

The cell is touching its bounding box in 6 points: 2 extremal points in x-direction, than 2 extremal points in y-direction, and 2 extremal points in z-direction (Fig. 3). Among these 6 points, there are 3 couples, that have same coordinates, only multiplied by −1. These couples of points are points L and R, U and D, and B and F. For example, if the point U has coordinates (−2, 3, −1.2), than the point D will have coordinates (2, −3, 1.2). This is because the point D is the mirror of the point U in point reflection with respect to the center of the cell, which has coordinates (0, 0, 0). Therefore, we have information about 3 points, that are not linearly dependent from each other. In the following paragraph, we will consider only maximal extremal points in directions x, y and z. Nota – those points, even if they are "maximal" extremal points, can have some negative coordinates.

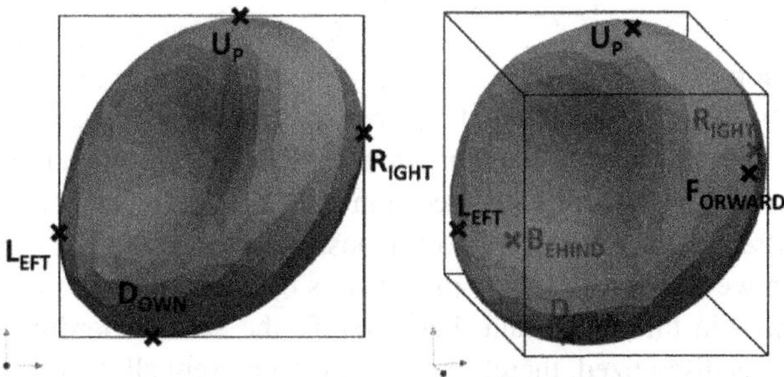

Fig. 3. Extremal bounding points of a cell – the points, where it is touching its bounding box. Left: 2D bounding box, with 4 extremal points. Right: 3D bounding box with 6 extremal points.

There is another interesting observation that let us simplify the coordinates even more. For each couple of x- and y- dimension of the bounding box, there is exactly 1 option to define the z- dimension of the bounding box, and 4 options to define the coordinates of extremal points (Fig. 4).

Let's consider the coordinates of the three maximal extremal points of the cells in each of the four positions. In the four different cases, the absolute numerical value of the coordinates of those extremal points will be the same – the only difference will be the sign. In other words, lets consider only the absolute values of the coordinates of the extremal bounding points – we will obtain the same values for all of the four possible positions of the cell in the bounding box. Therefore, in the rest of the article we will take into account only those absolute values, which are linked unambiguously with the dimensions of the bounding box.

To be absolutely correct, as the cell is symmetric around one of its local axes, there are actually an infinity of different positions within one bounding box, but we will neglect this. It would be important only in case, if the cell is really rotating for a considerably long time around this local axe, but we will assume that it will not happen very often.

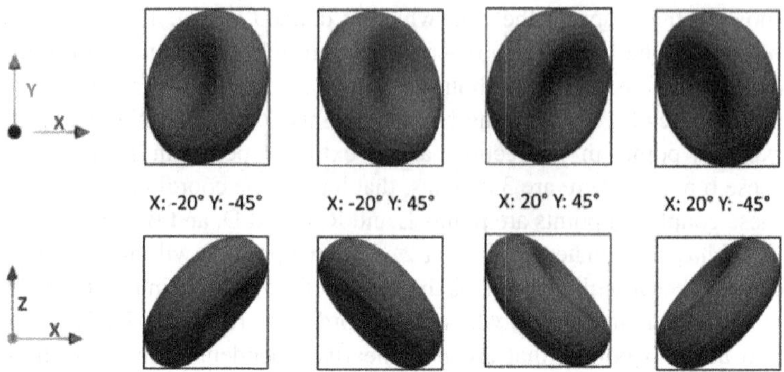

Fig. 4. Four possible positions of the cell inside of the defined bounding box

2.2 Identification of the Coordinates of the Cell's Bounding Extremal Points

Table of Rotation

In order to identify the coordinates of the extremal bounding points, we have prepared a table of all possible cell's positions of an undeformed cell. We run a routine, that made all possible rotations of the cell with precision of 2°, and that wrote down all possible positions of extremal points, related to all possible dimensions of bounding boxes. After that, when we have an x- and y- dimensions of the bounding box as an input, we can look for them in this table, and then identify the set of coordinates of extremal points. The table is discretized, therefore there are no present all the possible couples of x- and y- dimensions of the bounding box. For those, that are not present, we found the closest one and use this approximation, to estimate the coordinates of the bounding extremal points.

Analytical Continuous Functions

Another method, that we used for the estimation of the coordinates of the extremal bounding points, is to calculate them from an analytic function, where input is x- and y-dimensions of the bounding box, and output is a value of the specified coordinate of an extremal point. At all, there are 9 different functions: one function for each of the three coordinates of the three extremal bounding points.

In Fig. 5, we can see those functions. Each function is represented by a surface. The correct value of the searched parameter can be found as a point on this surface, whose position is defined by the x- and y- dimension of the bounding box.

All of those functions were made for a cell with $r_0 = 1$, where r_0 is the radius that define the form of the cell (Eq. 1).

Some of these functions are trivial. For example, if we want to find the x-coordinate of the x-extremal point, we just need to take the x-dimension of the bounding box and divide it by 2. But in most of the cases, we did not find an exact analytical way how to determine these functions. Instead of finding the exact formulae, we used the table mentioned in previous paragraph to draw the known values into 3D space, and then we tried to fit it with a continuous function.

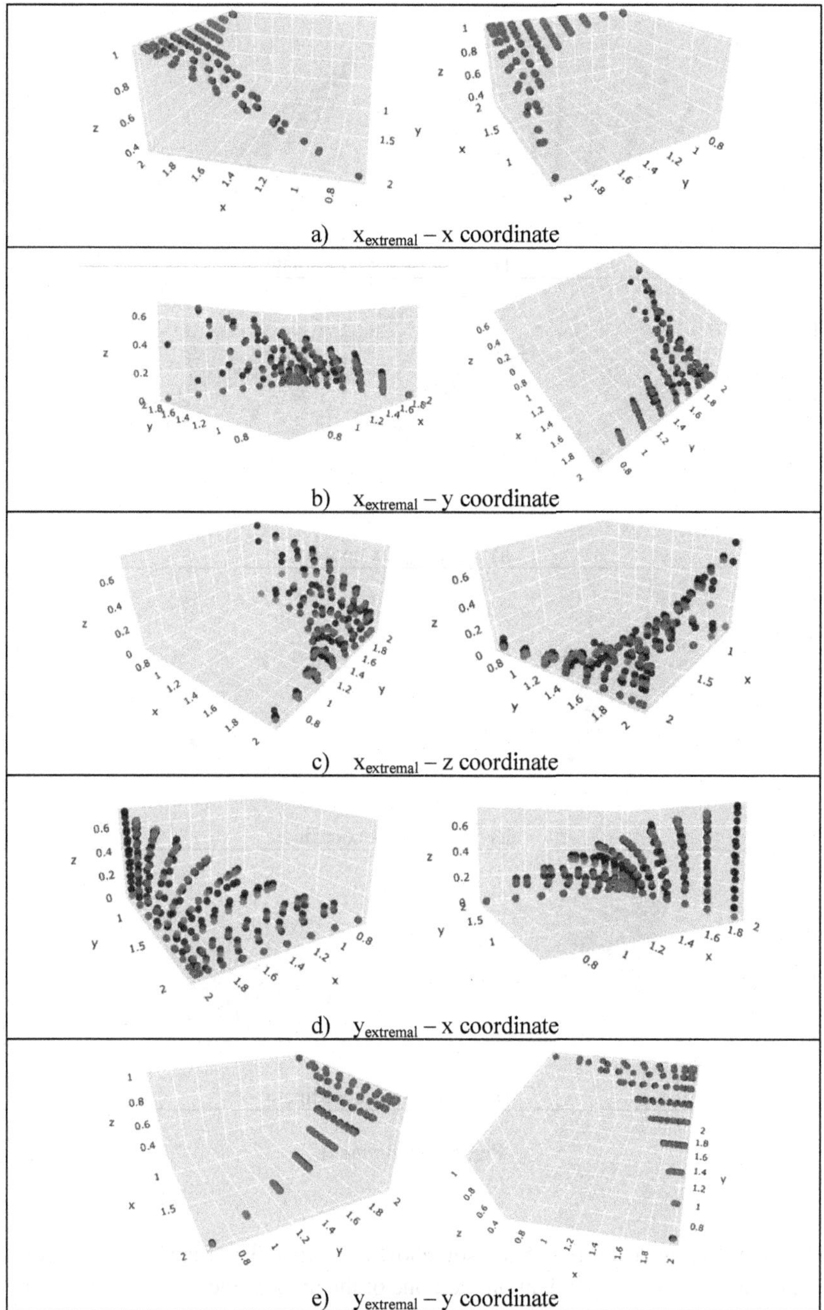

a) $x_{extremal}$ – x coordinate
b) $x_{extremal}$ – y coordinate
c) $x_{extremal}$ – z coordinate
d) $y_{extremal}$ – x coordinate
e) $y_{extremal}$ – y coordinate

Fig. 5. 3D spatial functions, that help us to determine the coordinates of the extremal bounding points. In each graph, the "x" is for x-dimension of the bounding box, the "y" is for y-dimension of the bounding box, and the "z" is for the searched parameter, one of coordinates of the extremal points. The blue points represent the measured values from table, the red points represent the continuous function that fits the measured values. (Color figure online)

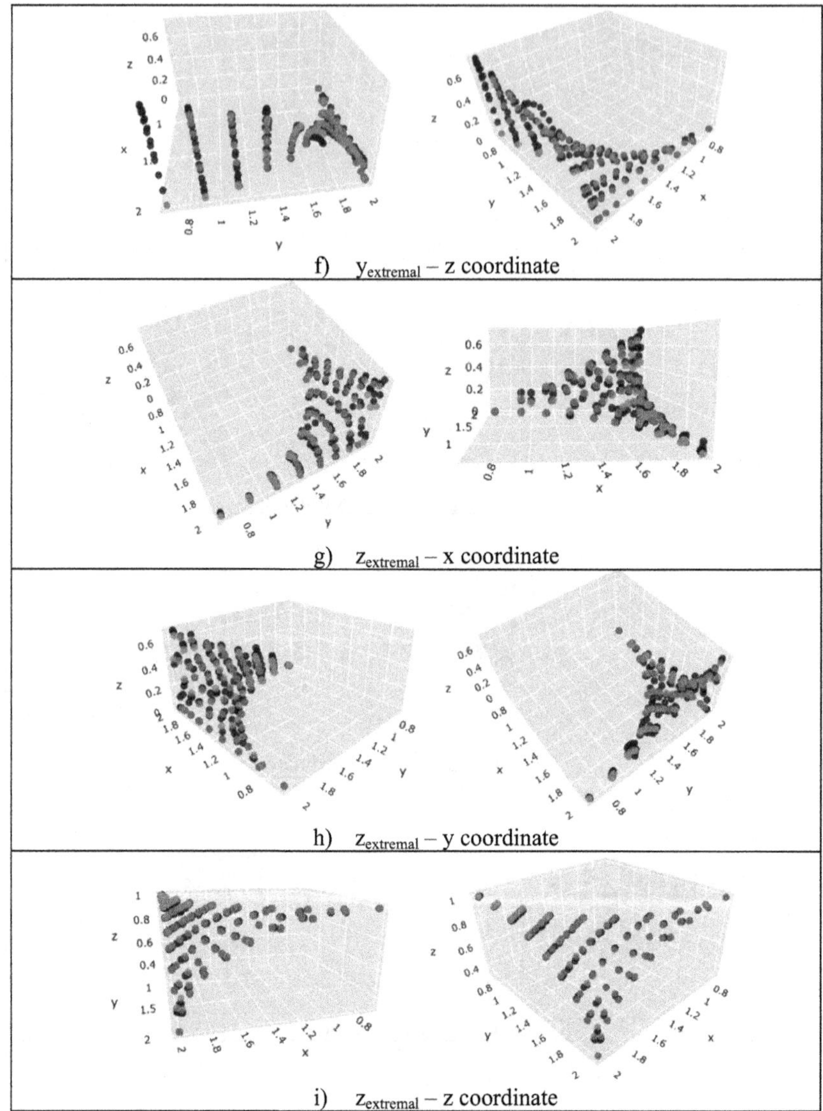

f) $y_{extremal}$ – z coordinate
g) $z_{extremal}$ – x coordinate
h) $z_{extremal}$ – y coordinate
i) $z_{extremal}$ – z coordinate

Fig. 5. *(continued)*

The nine surfaces from Fig. 5 are somehow repetitive. The functions (a) and (e) are trivial linear functions, dependent only on one of the input values. The functions (b) and (d) are alike and the function that we used for their estimation is the same one, with interchanged use of the input parameters. The function (c) and (f) are same as well.

Finally, the functions (g) and (h) are slightly different, but for their estimation, we used a different approach. Firstly, we calculated the value of z-bounding box dimension. Then, for the (g) function, we considered as an input the z- and the y- bounding box dimensions. With this approach, the estimated function had the same shape as the function from (c). Similarly, to estimate the shape of the function (h), we did not consider it as a function of x- and y- bounding box dimension, but as a function of x- and z- bounding box dimension. In this way, the function was the same as the one in (f).

But, where did we took the z-dimension of the bounding box? This parameter is twice the value of the z-coordinate of the z extremal bounding point, the function (i).

Estimation of the Analytical Functions to Calculate the Coordinates of the Cells Bounding Extremal Points

The functions (a) and (e) from Fig. 5 are trivial. It is because the x-coordinate of the x-extremal bounding point is the one who define the x-dimension of the bounding box, and similarly for the y-coordinate of the y-extremal bounding point. Their formulae are the following ones:

$$(a) \qquad x_{x_{ext}} = \frac{x_{bounding\ box}}{2} \tag{2}$$

$$(e) \qquad y_{y_{ext}} = \frac{y_{bounding\ box}}{2} \tag{3}$$

The functions (b) and (d) are alike, therefore we will explain into details only the estimation of the (d) function.

The projection of the surface to the xy-plane and to the yz-plane are presented in Fig. 6. We can notice, in the xy-projection, that all points are situated out of a circle, whose diameter could be estimated as D-d, where D is the big diameter of the cell, in our case D = 2, and d is the small diameter of the cell, in our case d = 0.65.

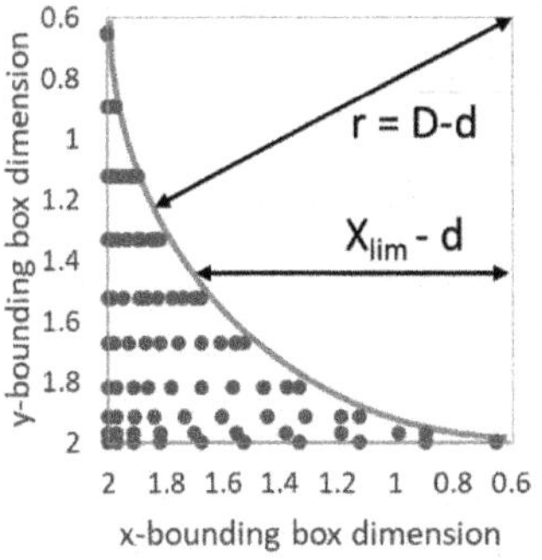

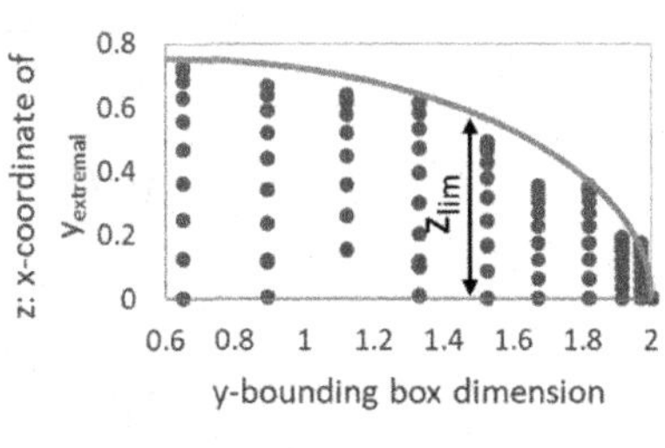

Fig. 6. Projection of the points representing the surface defined by the function. Left: projection to the xy-plane. Right: projection to je yz-plane, where z is, in this case, the x-coordinate of the y extremal bounding point.

For a given value of the y-bounding box dimension, we can thus calculate the local "width" of the circular part, which is denoted in Fig. 6 as $x_{lim} - d$.

The yz-projection from the Fig. 6 relieves that the projection of the surface to this plane form an ellipse, with the big diameter equal to D-d, and the small diameter equal to d. Here, for a given value of the y-bounding box dimension, we can calculate the value of the z_{lim}, that stands for a local "height" of the ellipsoid shape.

After that, lets concentrate on a cut through the surface, for a defined value of y-bounding box dimension = 1.53, for example. We will receive a blue-dotted line in Fig. 7. It is slightly curved and has an ellipsoidal shape. It relieves that the best approximation of the line is a combination of the elliptic shape and the straight line.

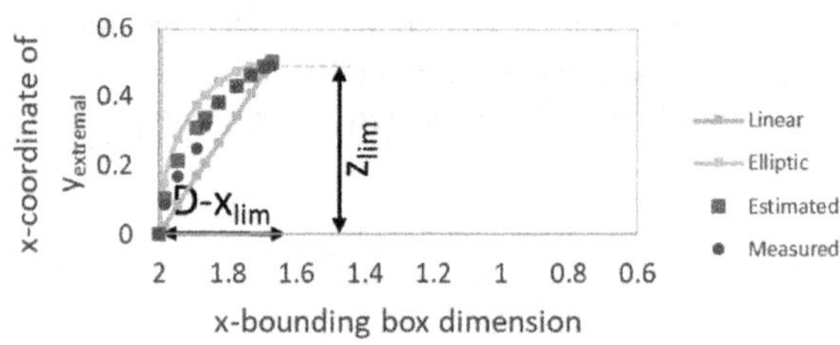

Fig. 7. Cut through the surface of the function for y-bounding box dimension = 1.53. Blue dots represent the original measured data, the yellow, orange and red lines represent different fits of the measured data. (Color figure online)

To obtain the value of x-coordinate of the y extremal bounding point, we need to use the following formulae:

$$x_{lim} = \sqrt{(D-d)^2 - (y-d)^2} + d \tag{4}$$

$$z_{lim} = \frac{\sqrt{(D-d)^2 - (y-d)^2} \cdot d}{D-d} \tag{5}$$

$$z_{elliptic} = \frac{\sqrt{(D-x_{lim})^2 - (x-x_{lim})^2} \cdot z_{lim}}{D-x_{lim}} \tag{6}$$

$$z_{linear} = \frac{(D-x) \cdot z_{lim}}{D-x_{lim}} \tag{7}$$

$$(d)\ x_{y_{ext}} = \frac{2 \cdot z_{elliptic} + 1 \cdot z_{linear}}{3} \tag{8}$$

To evaluate the function from Fig. 5(b), the y coordinate of x-extremal bounding point, the set of equations will be similar, with interchanged values of x- and y- input:

$$y_{lim} = \sqrt{(D-d)^2-(x-d)^2} + d \tag{9}$$

$$z_{lim} = \frac{\sqrt{(D-d)^2-(x-d)^2} \cdot d}{D-d} \tag{10}$$

$$z_{elliptic} = \frac{\sqrt{(D-y_{lim})^2-(y-y_{lim})^2} \cdot z_{lim}}{D-y_{lim}} \tag{11}$$

$$z_{linear} = \frac{(D-y) \cdot z_{lim}}{D-y_{lim}} \tag{12}$$

$$(b)\ y_{x_{ext}} = \frac{2 \cdot z_{elliptic} + 1 \cdot z_{linear}}{3} \tag{13}$$

Next functions to estimate are (c) and (f), estimation of z-coordinate of x- or y- extremal bounding points. The approach is similar to the approach applied previously. Let's start with the function (f). The Fig. 6 applies very well for this function, but the cut through the function surface for a fixed y-dimension of bounding box is different. The shape of the cut is presented in Fig. 8, for the fixed value of 1.53 for y-dimension of bounding box.

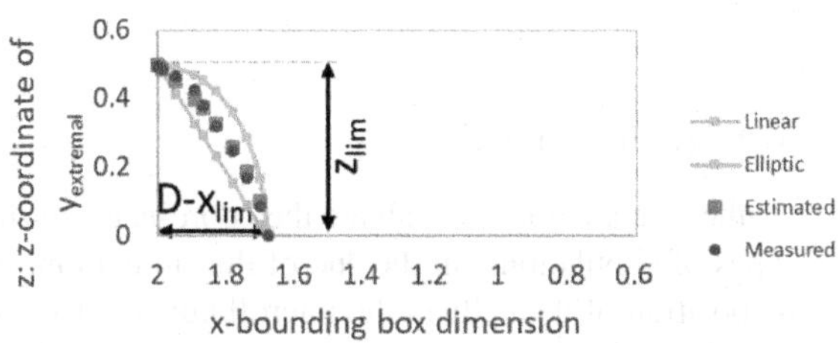

Fig. 8. Cut through the surface of the function for y-bounding box dimension = 1.53. Blue dots represent the original measured data, the yellow, orange and red lines represent different fits of the measured data. (Color figure online)

To estimate the value of z-coordinate of y-extremal bounding point, we will use the equations Eqs. 4 and 5, and for $z_{elliptic}$ and z_{linear} we will use the following formulae:

$$z_{elliptic} = \frac{\sqrt{(D-x_{lim})^2-(D-x)^2} \cdot z_{lim}}{D-x_{lim}} \tag{14}$$

$$z_{linear} = \frac{(x - x_{lim}) \cdot z_{lim}}{D - x_{lim}} \tag{15}$$

$$(f)\ z_{y_{ext}} = \frac{z_{elliptic} + z_{linear}}{2} \tag{16}$$

The (c) function, the estimation of the z-coordinate of the x-extremal bounding point, is calculated similarly, but with interchanged input values of x- and y- dimensions of the bounding box.

The (i) function, that define the z-coordinate of the z-extremal bounding box, is estimated as a surface of an ellipsoid, with the two main diameters equal to 2(D-d), and the small diameter equal to D-d. The value of the searched z-coordinate can be thus estimated as follows:

$$(i)\ z_{z_{ext}} = \frac{\sqrt{2 \cdot (D - d)^2 - (x - d)^2 - (y - d)^2} + d}{2} \tag{17}$$

$$z_{bounding\,box\,dimension} = 2 \cdot z_{z_{ext}} \tag{18}$$

The (g) and (h) functions are estimated in the same way as the (c) and (f) functions, but instead of using the x- and y- dimensions of the bounding box as input values, we use the combination of x- and z- dimensions for the (h) function, and z- and y- dimensions for the (g) function. The z-bounding box dimension are calculated with Eq. 18.

3 Results

3.1 Description of Numerical Simulations

In order to verify, whether we are able to evaluate the coordinates of the cells extremal points, we run two types of simulations. In the end of the simulation, we have detailed information about the position of the cells in the microfluidic device. On one hand, we know the exact values of the coordinates of the cells extremal bounding points. On the other hand, we can use only the information about the x- and y- dimension of the cells bounding box, and try to recalculate the missing information about the bounding point coordinates, and to compare it with the real values obtained directly from the simulation.

The first simulation was run with the cells, whose properties were similar to the properties of biological cells. The numerical cells were calibrated in order to fit the behavior of the biological cells, and they were situated in a microfluidic device, that is similar to devices in laboratory conditions. There were 60 cells in the simulation. The detailed description of the experiment can be found in [4].

The second simulation was run with only one cell, that was significantly more rigid than a biological cell. It was situated in a slow fluid flow, with obstacles that forced the cell to rotate slightly, but not to deform very much. This experiment was run in order to verify, whether the estimation of the extremal point coordinates will be more successful in those favorable conditions.

3.2 Obtained Values of Extremal Bounding Points Coordinates

In Fig. 9, we present the comparison of the real values of the extremal bounding points coordinates for the simulation of the stiff cell. We examined the position of the cell in 100 consecutive steps during the simulation. The blue values are the exact values obtained from the simulation. We can notice that the dimensions of the bounding box did not changed very much during the simulation, therefore it did not rotated very much, as well. The estimated values fit approximately the real values. The estimation based on the values from the table is approximately as good as the estimation based on the continuous functions.

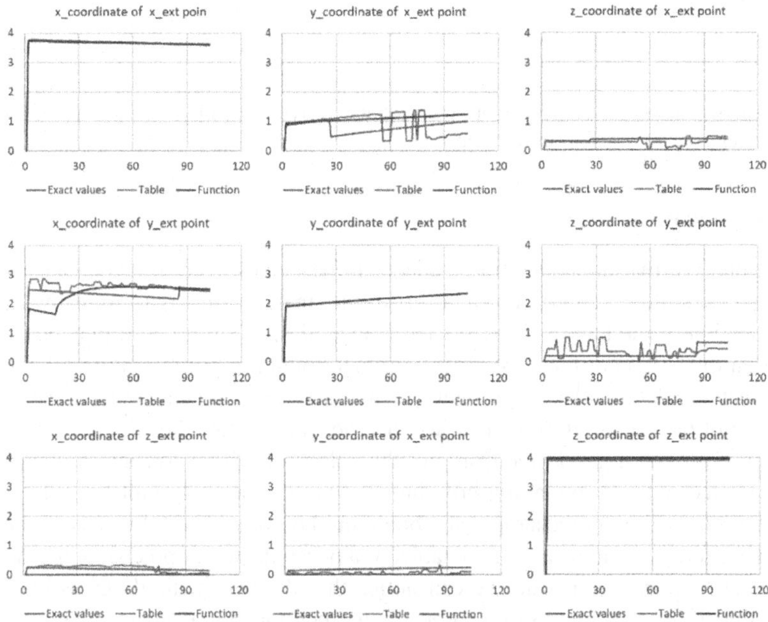

Fig. 9. Comparison of the real coordinates of the extremal points of cells bounding boxes, through 100 steps of simulation (on x-ax)

In Fig. 10, we present the comparison of the real values of the extremal bounding points coordinates for the simulation of the biological cell. We choose one of the 60 cells that were present in the simulation. The values are smoothed, on the graphs we can see the results of the floating average, in which we averaged 5 consecutive values. Here we can see that the dimensions of the bounding boxes are changing during the simulation, hence the cell was rotating considerably.

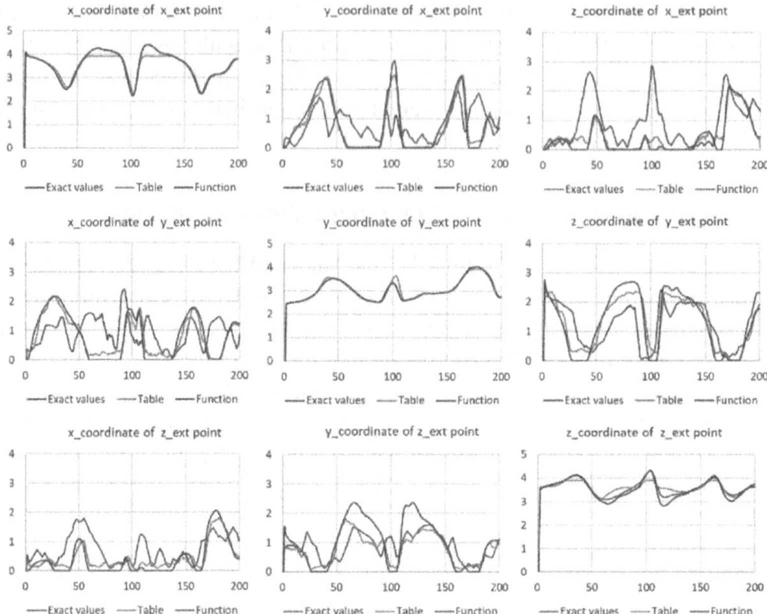

Fig. 10. Comparison of the real coordinates of the extremal points of cells bounding boxes, through 200 steps of simulation (on x-ax)

3.3 Discussion

We can observe that the estimation made with the values from the table and with the functions are similar. This is not a surprise, the analytic functions were made as an approximation of the table values. We can notice, despite of the used method, that the estimation of the z-coordinate of the z-extremal bounding point is more reliable than the estimation of the other coordinates. This variable is closely related with the z-dimension of the bounding box. It means that we can estimate the 3rd dimension of the bounding box with a good precision, but the values of other coordinates, that are not closely related with the bounding box dimensions, are more difficult to estimate.

The cause of the imprecision of the bounding box points coordinates estimation is the rough discretization in case of the table, or a possible lack of precision in estimation of the analytical function. But, we can notice that the two methods gives un similar results, therefore the imprecision caused by the mentioned reasons is smaller than the difference between the real values of coordinates and the estimated ones. It means that the main reason why we cannot estimate the values with a good precision is the deformation of the cells in the model.

Despite of this, the dimensions of the bounding box are estimated relatively good, therefore the orientation of the cell is well defined, and so we continue to look for a way how to define it, if we know value of any 2 dimensions of the bounding box.

4 Conclusion

In this article, we proposed a methodology to determine the position of a cell from a 2-dimensional information about cells. This methodology is based on an assumption, that the cells are undeformed. We saw that the method work better for a simulation with a rigid cell. For the simulation with the cells, whose parameters were close to the parameters of the biological cells, the estimation has lower precision. But, while we could not determine with a good accuracy the coordinates of extremal bounding points, we could estimate the 3rd dimension of the bounding box with a good accuracy. In our future work, we would like to find a way how to determine the precise orientation of the cell, if we know only 2 dimensions of its bounding box.

References

1. Tsai, C.H.D., et al.: An on-chip RBC deformability checker significantly improves velocity-deformation correlation. Micromachines **7**, 176 (2016)
2. Kajanek, F., Cimrak, I.: Evaluation of detection of red blood cells using convolutional neural networks. In: IDT 2019, Zilina, Slovakia, 25–27 June. IEEE (2019)
3. Evans, E., Fung, Y.-C.: Improved measurements of the erythrocyte geometry. Microvasc. Res. **4**(4), 335–347 (1972)
4. Jancigova, I.: Impact of an immersed large cell on red blood cell flow through asymmetric micro-bifurcation. In: 6th International Conference on Computational & Mathematical Biomedical Engineering, Sendai, Japan, 10.06.2019–12.06.2019, pp. 614–617 (2019)

Automated Tracking of Red Blood Cells in Images

František Kajánek(✉), Ivan Cimrák, and Peter Tarábek

Cell-in-fluid Biomedical Modelling and Computations Group,
Faculty of Management Science and Informatics,
University of Žilina, Žilina, Slovakia
frantisek.kajanek@fri.uniza.sk

Abstract. Computer simulations of processes inside microfluidic devices often require validation data from experiments with biological cells. Besides single cell experiments, data involving flow of many cells can be used to validate many-cell behaviour. Manual data gathering from such experiments, such as video sequence of cell flow, is inefficient and needs to be automated. Building on top of an automated detection of red blood cells, tracking of red blood cells is needed in order to provide physical data about each cell. In this work, we first describe our existing traditional algorithms for cell tracking. We assess the possible metrics for measuring their performance and iterate upon the flaws of our algorithm in order to design improvements and propose a neural network solution.

Keywords: Tracking · Red blood cell · Computer vision · Simulation

1 Introduction

Computational models are able to handle multiple dynamically interacting variables and parameters in modelled systems. In case of flow of biological cells, these parameters are different elastic properties of cells, different environmental factors, or various geometries in microfluidic channels. This ability enables the investigation of how individual components of a system contribute to its overall performance via systematic manipulation of these variables and parameters.

Foremost advantage of computer simulations lie in a simultaneous variation of the system parameters over a given set of values while analysis the system's response. This is in most cases impossible to achieve experimentally in an accurate and controlled fashion and it gives us an effective tool for example in optimization and design [6,9]. Computational modeling gives us a way to follow the behavior of the whole system as well as of individual cells.

Numerous computational models of red blood cells (RBC) have been recently used for microfluidic device design [5], to analyze the efficiency of tumor cell

This work was supported by the Slovak Research and Development Agency (contract number APVV-15-0751) and by the Ministry of Education, Science, Research and Sport of the Slovak Republic (contract number VEGA 1/0643/17).

I. Rojas et al. (Eds.): IWBBIO 2020, LNBI 12108, pp. 800–810, 2020.
https://doi.org/10.1007/978-3-030-45385-5_71

isolation [14], to perform computer-aided discovery [3,10,19]. Inherent part of such model development is the validation of the model by comparing the model behaviour to behaviour of cells in real biological experiments. Besides single cell experiments, such as the stretching cell experiment [13], data involving flow of many cells can be used to validate many-cell behaviour. In many-cell experiments, one can validate macroscopic behaviour of the model, for example by measuring the cell-free layer in simulations and in reality [15]. A different approach is to validate the model against individual cell behaviour by comparing for example distribution of cell velocities across the channel cross-section.

For the latter approach, the gathering of data about individual cells (e.g. positions and velocities of the cells) from the video recordings of experiments requires enhanced video processing. Manual data extraction is ineffective and this process needs to be automated. For high volumes of video data, we require an automated algorithm that takes videos and finds cells and connects them into tracks. This can be done through computer vision algorithms by separating them into two steps, detection and tracking. Cells in videos can for example provide information about velocity, shape, counting, regions of high occurrence etc. Detection provides us with easy counting and interesting regions, whereas tracking provides us with the rest. This means that any way to accelerate data gathering with as little manual work required for new experiments is of great benefit to any simulation software.

It is also critical to design algorithms with enough future proofing. With the advent of high-resolution high frame-rate cameras, and more processing power, many tasks can be extended to work with newer data, for example 1920×1080 resolutions. Not only does this provide more information and motion precision, but it also provides more challenges, as was noted in certain scenarios during the detection step research in [8].

The main goal of this article is to build upon our existing detection algorithms by devising a robust tracking algorithm, which will output validation data for RBC simulations. We take our existing detection algorithm, which was described more in detail in [8], that outputs bounding box data, and process this through our tracking algorithm, which will output connected tracks of RBCs. In Sect. 2 we will go over existing tracking approaches and highlight the work done in the field. Next in Sect. 3 we go over our existing physical model based approach and discuss its shortcomings. Section 4 deals with enhancements of tracking through information from RBC simulations. In Sect. 5 we propose a Convolutional Neural Network (CNN) to aid in tracking RBCs. And finally, in Sect. 6 we describe the approach to validation of simulations from acquired tracking data.

2 Related Work

Variety of methods already exist for the task of tracking cells. Our focus is specifically on RBCs, but generally certain types of cells share characteristics, making a plethora of approaches being valid for us as well. Existing cell tracking algorithms can be separated into two groups, either by contour matching methods, which segment cells in the first image and then continue to evolve their contours in subsequent images/frames. [4,7] This solves both the segmentation problem and the tracking problem simultaneously. Second group can be characterised by first detecting all cells and subsequently tracking found cells through images/frames through temporal information. [1,16,17]

Different approaches mainly exist due to the different niches and requirements of each task. Many issues common to general tracking can be disregarded when tracking cells. This includes issues like a moving camera, rapid changes in lighting or rapid movement of sought objects. Specifically for the case of cell tracking, data can very often be acquired through other means than just video and as such those imaging techniques are not transferable to our task. The most common approach is to track various if not all cell types [20]. Another complexity increase is from the lifetime of a normal cell. In general, cells can for example divide or die during the experiment. The tracking algorithm needs to adapt to these situations. This creates a more challenging task in comparison to just tracking RBCs, specifically during the creation of a dataset or during algorithm testing and the generalization has an impact on the algorithm performance. Adapting these approaches to a task with only one class and a fairly strict visual rule-set of cells characteristics means better results but makes the task more niche.

No matter what approach, it is critical to evaluate the performance of all tracking steps. For detection this is generally taken care of through Precision and Recall and/or Matthews correlation coefficient [11], both of which can be supplemented by using k-means cross-validation. Evaluating the tracking stage is less trivial, due to detection having an impact as well. Most approaches count the correct segments of a track after evaluating correct bounding boxes in each frame through some overlap scheme. In addition to that, incorrect connections need to be somehow penalized. Lastly, average track length is also a good indicator of performance for the tracking algorithm. Possible condensation of all these remarks can be seen for example in [12] where both detection and tracking contribute to a final score called AOGM (Acyclic oriented graphs matching) based on predefined weights adjusted according to their importance.

3 Existing Architecture

Our existing baseline architecture is a physical motion based temporal model. The input of our algorithm is a set of bounding boxes output from our detection step for each frame of a video. They contain x and y of the top-left corner and the width and height of the cell. While the tracking algorithm does not need the additional information, this is intended for future use where we can potentially use the shape information to determine cell rotation. For our task it is not necessary to process video in real-time and as such we are able to levy additional information during both the detection and tracking step. During detection this is equivalent to producing a better background and during tracking it enables us to adopt a multiple pass-through approach to video processing and be able to go back and fix certain errors. The tracking algorithm itself is composed of 4 steps:

1. Flow matrix creation
2. Initial naive cell seeking
3. First simple pass-through
4. Second complex pass-through

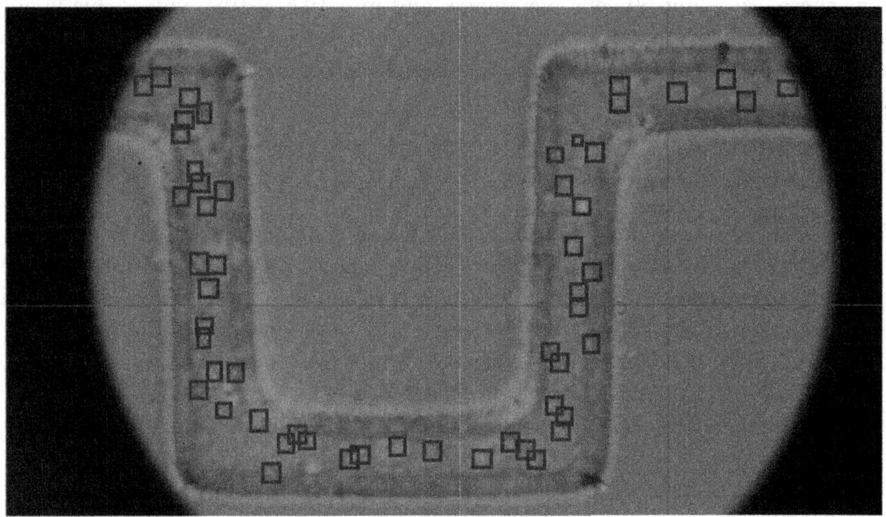

Fig. 1. Example of bounding box annotations used as input

3.1 Flow Matrix

The direction of a cell in our model is influenced by two factors. First factor is the previous history of a cell, i.e. its velocity over time and the second factor is the behaviour of a fluid. While the former is fairly trivial to compute from previous tracked bounding boxes, the latter can heavily change the predicted new position (Fig. 1).

The flow matrix serves two purposes. The first purpose is to be combined with existing cell movement to give us a better future estimate for the next video frame. The second purpose is during the initial cell seeking when no previous temporal information is available.

The source of our flow matrix is two-fold. The problem is that a flow matrix is not transferable. It is specific to each biological experiment. As such, we are able to obtain it from annotated track data. Our dataset currently has two parts, detection part and tracking part. The detection part are bounding boxes used for detection evaluation and as input for machine learning. The tracking part gives each bounding box a track ID which is equivalent to the output of the tracking algorithm. This can be then used for evaluation. Part of it however can be also used for the creation of a flow matrix. Second source of our flow matrix are subsequent enhanced tracks. The problem is that on frame 0 we have no previous information and as such we are not able to create a proper flow matrix. By combining both annotated flow matrix and subsequent track information we are able to create a better flow matrix. We have to note however that interpolation is required even with 100+ tracked frames. The reason is that there are about 50 cells per image, and in a 1920×1080 video, this is not enough to fill every pixel with information. The interpolation algorithm checks neighbouring pixel coordinates and creates a correct velocity from surrounding values.

3.2 Initial Tracking Step

In addition to having no flow matrix on frame 0 of detection, we also do not have any temporal information about the movement of a cell. As a result we are not able to tell the direction the cell will be heading immediately. If we have a flow matrix in the given point, we solve this problem by looking directly in the direction of the flow matrix velocity. While this is the best case scenario, this requires us to always have some sort of previous information. The other solution is to have a blind search around the original cell and pick the most likely candidate. The point of failure for this solution is when a lot of cells overlap, but it still does provide decent results.

3.3 First and Second Pass-Through

Both pass-throughs have one task, to connect cells into tracks. The major difference is in their capability to handle errors. Our first pass-through is setup so that the resulting tracks are almost always true. The downside is that the first step cannot compensate for missing detection or overlap of cells. In both cases there can be a gap between the previous frame and the next frame, which will cause fragmentation of tracks. The reason why we have this first step is in order to acquire correct data for future evaluation with almost 100% precision.

The second pass-through has a parameter, which tells it what the maximum gap can be between detections. This step is very sensitive to the quality of detection. Dealing with gaps in detection is pretty straightforward, we estimate the future position of a cell by computing its proposed position in the first missing gap, and then the next missing gap, up to the gap maximum. It has to be done iteratively in order to take feedback from the flow matrix.

3.4 Performance Evaluation

Mainly we would like to compare and illustrate the impact if our algorithm steps and the impact of quality detection. For this test we used our detection neural network to detect cells in the first 300 frames of our video. The resulting precision and recall of detection is about 99.5% and 94.7% respectively. Precision

Table 1. Tracking performance results

Average track length	Pass-through		
Data source	First	Second	Fragment per track
Annotated	41.602/355	59.552/248	1:2.3
Detected	36.243/399	48.5/298	1:2.9

Values in each cell represent the average track length/track count. Track dataset has average track length 139.7 and 73 tracks total. This amounts to about 2–3 holes per each track found by our algorithm.

can be calculated as: true positives/(true positives + false positives) and recall: true positives/(true positives + false negatives). We will be comparing it to our annotated bounding boxes in the same 300 frames.

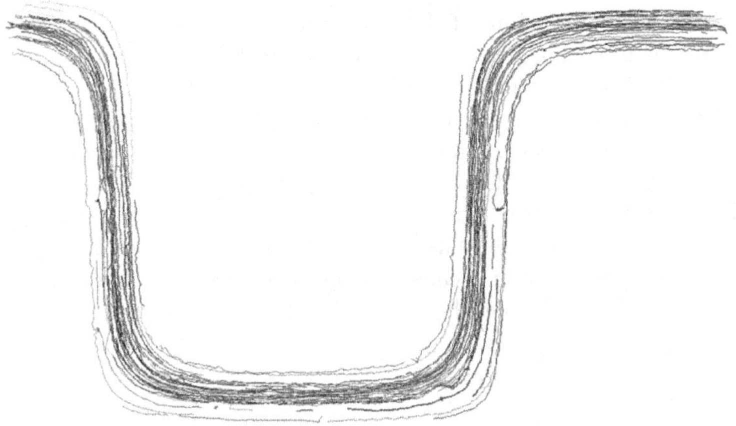

Fig. 2. Example of tracks found in first 300 frames

The results can be seen in Table 1. As we can see, both our first and second step have a big impact on the track fragmentation. If we compare our automated tracks to our dataset, we can see that on average our tracks have 2 or 3 holes in them, causing them to split apart. In Fig. 2 we can see visualized output of our algorithm.

4 Simulation Data Enhancement

The flow matrix as described above was obtained from the video data either by using annotated data or by subsequent tracks. There is another possibility to get a flow matrix - from computational fluid dynamics (CFD) simulation of flow in the channel. To setup a CFD simulation one needs to provide the geometry of the channel and inlet velocity conditions. The channel geometry is readily available and the averaged inlet velocity can be obtained from the information of maximal fluid velocity in the channel, or using the volumetric flow rate. The video data does not contain information about the volumetric flow rate, however, the maximal fluid velocity can be estimated using maximal velocities of the individual cells.

Our current results enabled us to extract this vital information. We extracted the maximum possible speed of cells inside our channel which turned out to be around 11 pixels per frame. This speed occurred in the direct middle of the channel.

We used the PyOIF module [2] within the ESPResSo package [18]. This module is capable of simulating the flow of red blood cells in a given microfluidic channels. We seeded the cell sizes roughly based on the occurrence of cell sizes in our dataset, which amounts to sizes between 25px and 35px.

The results of this simulation enabled us to gather a perfect flow matrix for experimentation within reasonable margin of error. In addition to a flow matrix we also gathered the positions of RBCs within the simulation with their cell size and velocity vector. This gives us the opportunity to supplement our dataset in case we need more data for machine learning.

In addition to gathering this data, we also evaluated our algorithm using the flow matrix acquired from a simulation. The resulting tracks were on average 1 frame longer than with the flow matrix gathered from annotated data and previous tracks. This tells us two things. Firstly, the flow matrix from the simulation in addition to being complete is also valid and does not degrade the performance of our algorithm. Secondly, it means that our tracking algorithm is mostly capable of finding correct tracks without complete flow matrix information.

5 Neural Network Tracking

As a next step in improving our tracking performance, we have designed a prototype using CNNs. The idea is to take the resulting tracks from our second pass-through and try to join them with other existing tracks together. The neural network is designed to predict the location in the next frame more accurately than our physical model would.

The initial step is to convert our tracking dataset into a manageable format for our neural network. We have created $30 \times 30 \times 5$ matrices out of our tracking dataset, centered at each given cell for which we are trying to find a segment in the future frame. First 2 channels contain the X and Y velocity of the cell respectively located at coordinates [15, 15] and the rest being 0. The 3rd channel contains locations of all cell centers in the 30px × 30px vicinity from our cell. The last 2 channels contain a flow matrix of X and Y velocities for each of the 30×30 points. The velocities of in the 4 channels share a similar magnitude and were calculated from a fluid-only simulation. Our dataset contains 10058 samples for training.

The output of the neural network is two values, predicted X and Y velocity between the current and the next frame. The structure of the neural network is

12 convolutional layers with 32 filters each with 3×3 convolutions and utilizing ReLu after each. Then we have 1 pooling layer and at the end we have 1 fully connected layer which outputs our two values. For the cost function we use mean square error and Adam Optimizer for the training. We measure the accuracy of our model through the sum of absolute values of all errors after each epoch of training.

We were able to train the neural network successfully and validated it after segmenting our dataset into 3 parts: 60% for training, 20% for testing and 20% for validation. The initial test took 60% sequential data and used only those for training. This has proven inefficient, because the neural network provided bad results on the other two parts of our dataset. We approached this issue through random sampling our dataset before segmenting it into parts. This increased the diversity of the data for the neural network and we were able to verify relatively the same performance on the latter two parts as well. Our current best performance is with error sum being at around 8 for a batch size of 32. The value is computed as a sum of all absolute values of differences between the predicted velocities and the dataset X and Y velocities. Going forward we will need to utilize this prototype in our tracking pipeline to see if the synthetic benchmark is indicative of being able to connect cells into segments using the CNN.

6 Comparing Acquired Data with Simulations

In previous sections we presented automated method for obtaining quantitative data about individual cells during their flow in microfluidic channels. In particular, we obtained positions of cells and their instant velocity.

Using this data, one can validate the model of flow of red blood cell using different approaches. There is too optimistic to require completely identical trajectories in simulations compared to those in experiments. This would for example require to seed the cells in the simulation identically to the experiment, which is impossible.

Therefore we rather focus on averaged quantities. We describe several quantities that may be used to compare model and the experiment.

6.1 Velocity Histogram

To capture correct reconstruction of cell's instant velocities in simulation versus the experiment, we define a channel cross-section (corresponding to a line in the video) and we create a histogram of velocities for all cells passing this cross-section. This cross-section may be defined on multiple places depending on the shape of the channel. In Fig. 3 left, two cross-sections are indicated with bold lines to include straight as well as curved channel.

To capture correct reconstruction of averaged velocities, we define a region and we calculate averaged velocity of cells by measuring the length of trajectory between points of cell entering and exiting that region, divided by time of cell located in that region. This can be the whole channel, or different parts of the channel. In Fig. 3 left, two regions are indicated by dashed areas. Again, we cover straight part as well as curved part of the channel.

6.2 Cell Density Heat Map

In biological experiments it is useful to identify regions with high density of flowing cells. To find out whether model reconstructs cell densities properly, one can define cell density heat map over the area of the whole channel. First of all, we divide the whole video image into squares with the same size. For each square we can enumerate how many cells are located in the square in each time instant and this number can be integrated over time. The result normalized by the whole time interval indicates how many cells on average are present in the given square, thus defining the cell density. Coloring all the squares by the corresponding cell density gives us a visual cell density map as depicted in Fig. 3 right.

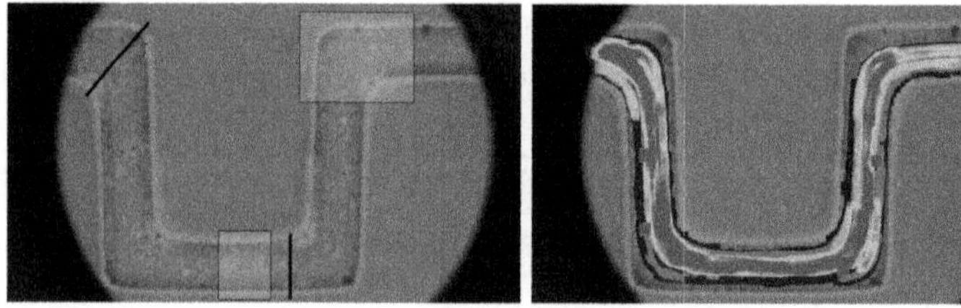

Fig. 3. Left: Two cross-sections (bold lines) and two regions (dashed) are indicated for evaluation of velocity histograms. Right: Heat map of the cell density in the channel. (Color figure online)

6.3 Cell Rotations Histograms

In addition to velocity histograms over cross-section or over a region, one can analyse rotation of the cell. Since the video sequence captures the cell from one view point, the shape of the cell may be an oval, circle, thick line, or, in case of severe cell deformation, an other undefined shape. The neural networks presented in previous sections do not provide which of these shapes are detected. We may however use the fact that the ouput of CNN gives the approximate bounding box of the detected cell in such matter that this bounding box may be considered as circumscribed rectangle.

7 Conclusion

Using simple physical model methods on the task of red blood cell tracking we managed to acquire the first data required for simulation validation. With the detection step being fairly robust towards different videos, we are now able to apply the same robustness in our tracking step, leading us to the automated processing of videos. We proposed a potential novel improvement for improving existing tracks of cells using CNNs, which could lead to further advancements and simplification of RBC tracking. The task of simulating real world applications with RBCs is fairly relevant for exploring scenarios which are hard to experiment with in the real world. With the prognosis of improving our tracking step, it will be possible for us to create a feedback loop on what information we might need so that we can improve the usefulness of our architecture.

References

1. Bensch, R., Ronneberger, O.: Cell segmentation and tracking in phase contrast images using graph cut with asymmetric boundary costs, vol. 2015, April 2015. https://doi.org/10.1109/ISBI.2015.7164093
2. Cimrák, I., Gusenbauer, M., Jančigová, I.: An ESPResSo implementation of elastic objects immersed in a fluid. Comput. Phys. Commun. **185**(3), 900–907 (2014)
3. Cimrák, I.: Collision rates for rare cell capture in periodic obstacle arrays strongly depend on density of cell suspension. Comput. Methods Biomech. Biomed. Eng. **19**(14), 1525–1530 (2016)
4. Dufour, A., Thibeaux, R., Labruyère, E., Guillen, N., Olivo-Marin, J.: 3-D active meshes: fast discrete deformable models for cell tracking in 3-D time-lapse microscopy. IEEE Trans. Image Process. **20**, 1925–1937 (2011). https://doi.org/10.1109/TIP.2010.2099125
5. Gleghorn, J.P., Smith, J.P., Kirby, B.J.: Transport and collision dynamics in periodic asymmetric obstacle arrays: Rational design of microfluidic rare-cell immunocapture devices. Phys. Rev. E **88**, 032136 (2013)
6. Janacek, J., Kohani, M., Koniorczyk, M., Marton, P.: Optimization of periodic crew schedules with application of column generation method. Transp. Res. Part C **83**, 165–178 (2017). https://doi.org/10.1016/j.trc.2017.07.008
7. Maška, M., DaněK, O., Garasa, S., Rouzaut, A., Muñoz-Barrutia, A., Ortiz-de Solorzano, C.: Segmentation and shape tracking of whole fluorescent cells based on the Chan-Vese model. IEEE Trans. Med. Imaging **32**, 995–1006 (2013). https://doi.org/10.1109/TMI.2013.2243463
8. Kajánek, F., Cimrák, I.: Evaluation of detection of red blood cells using convolutional neural networks. In: 2019 International Conference on Information and Digital Technologies (IDT), pp. 198–202, June 2019. https://doi.org/10.1109/DT.2019.8813664
9. Kleineberg, K.K., Buzna, L., Papadopoulos, F., Boguñá, M., Serrano, M.A.: Geometric correlations mitigate the extreme vulnerability of multiplex networks against targeted attacks. Phys. Rev. Lett. **118**, 218301 (2017). https://doi.org/10.1103/PhysRevLett.118.218301
10. Krüger, T.: Effect of tube diameter and capillary number on platelet margination and near-wall dynamics. Rheol. Acta **55**(6), 511–526 (2015). https://doi.org/10.1007/s00397-015-0891-6
11. Matthews, B.: Comparison of the predicted and observed secondary structure of T4 phage lysozyme. Biochim. Biophys. Acta (BBA) **405**(2), 442–451 (1975). https://doi.org/10.1016/0005-2795(75)90109-9

12. Matula, P., Maška, M., Sorokin, D., Matula, P., Ortiz-de Solorzano, C., Kozubek, M.: Cell tracking accuracy measurement based on comparison of acyclic oriented graphs. PloS One **10**, e0144959 (2015). https://doi.org/10.1371/journal.pone.0144959
13. Mills, J.P., Qie, L., Dao, M., Lim, C.T., Suresh, S.: Nonlinear elastic and viscoelastic deformation of the human red blood cell with optical tweezers. Mol. Cell. Biomech. **1**(3), 169–180 (2004)
14. Nagrath, S., et al.: Isolation of rare circulating tumour cells in cancer patients by microchip technology. Nature **450**, 1235–1239 (2007). https://doi.org/10.1038/nature06385
15. Pinho, D., Yaginuma, T., Lima, R.: A microfluidic device for partial cell separation and deformability assessment. BioChip J. **7**(4), 367–374 (2013). https://doi.org/10.1007/s13206-013-7408-0
16. Schiegg, M., Hanslovsky, P., Haubold, C., Köthe, U., Hufnagel, L., Hamprecht, F.: Graphical model for joint segmentation and tracking of multiple dividing cells. Bioinformatics (Oxford, England) **31**, 948–956 (2014). https://doi.org/10.1093/bioinformatics/btu764
17. Turetken, E., Wang, X., Becker, C., Haubold, C., Fua, P.: Network flow integer programming to track elliptical cells in time-lapse sequences. IEEE Trans. Med. Imaging **36**, 942–951 (2016). https://doi.org/10.1109/TMI.2016.2640859
18. Weik, F., et al.: ESPResSo 4.0 – an extensible software package for simulating soft matter systems. Eur. Phys. J. Spec. Top. **227**(14), 1789–1816 (2019). https://doi.org/10.1140/epjst/e2019-800186-9
19. Zhang, Z., Chien, W., Henry, E., Fedosov, D.A., Gompper, G.: Sharp-edged geometric obstacles in microfluidics promote deformability-based sorting of cells. Phys. Rev. Fluids **4**, 024201 (2019)
20. Zhong, B., et al.: Robust individual-cell/object tracking via PCANet deep network in biomedicine and computer vision. BioMed Res. Int. **2016**, 1–15 (2016). https://doi.org/10.1155/2016/8182416

A Novel Prediction Model for Discovering Beneficial Effects of Natural Compounds in Drug Repurposing

Suganya Chandrababu(✉) and Dhundy Bastola(✉)

School of Interdisciplinary Informatics,
University of Nebraska at Omaha, Omaha, USA
{schandrababu,dkbastola}@unomaha.edu

Abstract. Natural compounds are promising leads in drug discovery due to their low toxicity and synergistic effects existing in nature, providing efficient and low-cost therapeutic solutions. Synergistic effects are observed in highly similar or closely related compounds where the combined effect is much more significant than individual usage. However, multiple hurdles exist in the identification of similar compounds, in particular, accumulation of large volumes of compounds, procurement of authentic information, diversity and complexity of the compounds, convoluted mechanism of action, need of high-throughput screening and validation techniques, most importantly incompleteness of critical information like indications for the natural compounds. Currently, not many comprehensive computational pipelines are available for drug discovery using natural products. To overcome these challenges, in this study, we focus on predicting highly similar candidate compounds with synergistic effects useful in combinatorial/alternative therapies. We developed a molecular compound similarity prediction model for computing four different compound-compound similarity scores based on (i) bioactivity, (ii) chemical structure, (iii) target enzyme, and (iv) protein functional domain, using the data from public repositories. The calculated scores are combined efficiently for predicting highly similar compound pairs with similar biological or physicochemical properties. We evaluate the accuracy of our model with pharmacological and bioassay results, and manually curated literature from PubChem, NCBI, etc. As a use case, we selected 415 compounds based on 13 functional categories, out of which 66 natural compounds with 198 compound-compound similarity scores were identified as top candidates based on similar bioactivities, chemical substructures, targets, and protein functional sites. Statistical analysis of the scores revealed a significant difference in the mean similarity scores for all four categories. Twenty-eight closely interacting compounds, including Quercetin, Apigenin, etc. were identified as candidates for combinational therapies showing synergistic effects. Herbs, including Dill, Basil, Garlic, Mint, etc., were predicted as potential combinations for achieving synergistic effects. Twenty-four compounds with unknown pharmacological effects were associated with 58 potential new pharmacological effects/indications. If applied broadly, this model can address

I. Rojas et al. (Eds.): IWBBIO 2020, LNBI 12108, pp. 811–824, 2020.
https://doi.org/10.1007/978-3-030-45385-5_72

many problems in chemogenomics and help in identifying novel drug targets and indications, which is a critical step in natural drug discovery research and evidence for drug-repurposing.

Keywords: Natural compounds · Compound-similarity · New indications · Combinational therapies · Synergistic effects

1 Introduction

Phytochemicals in plants have always shown great promise as drug leads in natural product drug discovery. Herbal remedies are effective than their synthetic counterparts due to the combined effect of various constituents rather than a single entity [1]. The combined activity of the constituents may either be synergistic or antagonistic. So it is critical to identify compounds that can work synergistically to achieve safer and more efficient botanical mixtures with low toxicity, which underlies the natural drug discovery research. Compounds that are similar across various molecular descriptors possess identical functions, a fundamental fact which drives molecular similarity research [2]. Additionally, Chemogenomics is gaining greater interest among the researchers, paving the way for new novel drug discoveries based on the chemical and genomic information on various biological systems [3].

Natural product research demands multidisciplinary approaches for screening, procuring, and analyzing large volumes of complex chemical spaces. Natural product scientists encounter various challenges while trying to keep pace with the drug discovery pipeline and to prove its efficacy [4]. Some of the currently faced challenges include (1) large volumes of diverse chemical information, (2) complex chemical and molecular interactions, (3) lack of definite indications for a large number of compounds, (4) lack of computational approaches related to natural product research. Additionally, the rise of multi-drug resistant strains, not regulated by a single molecular target, demands a multi-targeted combinational therapeutic strategy rather than a single drug [5]. Therefore, identification of complex molecules having similar structural, biochemical, and physiological properties is of prime concern to address the problem due to multiple-disease resistant strains [6].

Identification of potential natural compounds that interact closely has always been a daunting task for both bioinformaticians and natural product scientists. Previously, similarity-based approaches focused on either structure or ligands. Structural similarity-based approaches do not take into account the molecular reactions and interactions that occur during the metabolism or biosynthesis of the compounds. Often compounds that are not structurally alike tend to have similar functions owing to the common targets or metabolizing pathways. Similarly, similarity approaches based on ligands alone tend to bypass the compounds which have no known targeting gene information [7]. Yamanishi *et al.*, have shown that similar molecular functions are governed by similar chemical substructures and protein functional sites [8]. In this study, we have developed a prediction model by

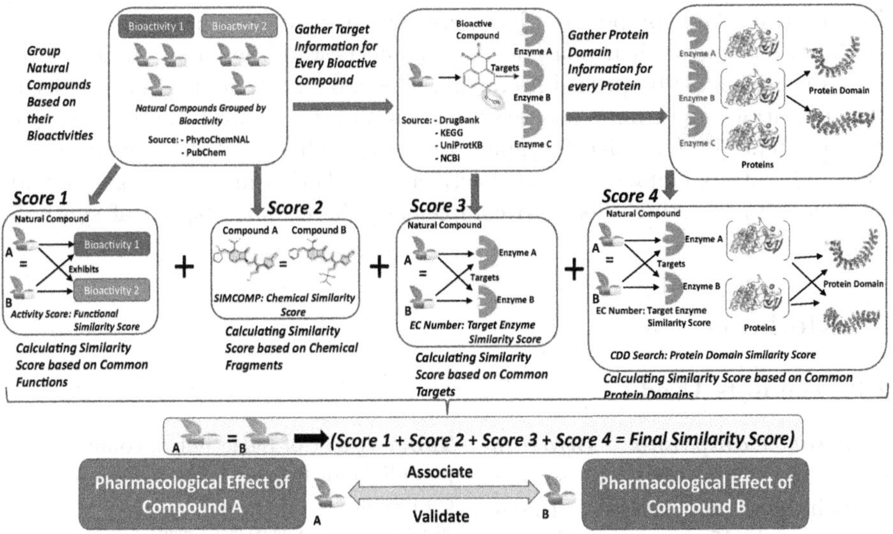

Fig. 1. Overview of the Model: compound-compound similarity prediction model.

combining information on chemical structure, bioactivities, target genes, and protein functional domain sites, for computing four different compound-compound similarity scores (Fig. 1). Our main goal is to obtain a final compound-compound similarity score by evaluating the similarity measures based on different descriptors and identify new pharmacological effects/indications for the compounds. The originality of the proposed model is that functionally similar compounds highly correlate chemical substructures similarity with target genes and protein domains similarity.

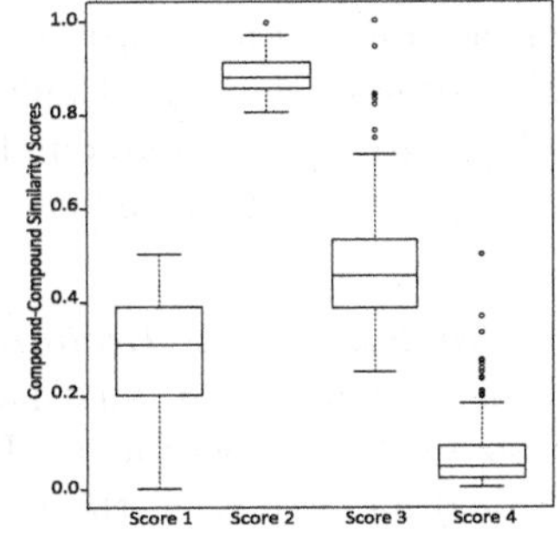

Fig. 2. Distribution plot for four types of similarity scores

Through our case study, we seek to answer whether compounds with similar functions also show similarity in chemical substructures, target genes, and protein domains. We considered 13 main functional categories (bioactivities), including antioxidant, anti-inflammatory, antibacterial, cancer-preventive, etc., and gathered 415 small molecules exhibiting these activities from 24 most commonly used culinary herbs. The data was obtained from various publicly available resources like Dr. Duke's Phytochemical and Ethnobotanical Database, PubChem, KEGG, UniProtKB, DrugBank, etc. We integrated bioactivity based similarity and target genes based similarity obtained through mathematical functions, with a chemical structure-based similarity obtained using SIMCOMP [9] and protein functional domain-based similarity obtained using CDD search [10].

The top candidate compounds that were similar were identified using the final similarity score, and their pharmacological effects were then associated and validated using manually queried literature. This model can be used for predicting new indications and compound-target associations for natural compounds, leading to potential alternative therapies for many multi-target drug-resistant diseases. This study emphasizes the effectiveness of herbal medicines that provide safer health-promoting effects to complement the chemical space of synthetic drugs.

2 Methods

2.1 Datasets Used

Natural Compounds Information: To begin with, we selected 13 main functional categories (bioactivities) and 415 compounds belonging to these categories from 24 culinary herbs (Table 1). Herbal compounds were chosen based upon the criteria that it should have at least one bioactive compound belonging to at least one of the 13 functional categories. The compound information was retrieved from Dr. Duke's Phytochemical and Ethnobotanical Database, and the activities for the compounds were extracted from ChEMBL database.

Table 1. List of bioactivites, count of compounds and list of herbs containing the compounds

Bioactivity	Compounds_Count	Herbs
Antibacterial	130	Cinnamon,Mint,
Antiinflammatory	115	Oregano,Majoram,
Antimutagenic	72	Dill,Ginger,Thyme,
Antioxidant	127	Sage,Ginseng,
Antiseptic	84	Fennel,Coriander,
Antispasmodic	73	French Tarragon,
Antitumor	76	Garlic,Cardamom,
Antiviral	70	Rosemary,Lemon
Cancer-Preventive	131	Balm,Basil,Parsley,
FLavor	94	Cumin,Lovage,
Fungicide	84	Cloves,Borage,
Perfumery	84	Chives, Chervil
Pesticide	235	

Compound-Target Information: Target proteins and enzyme information were retrieved from DrugBank and UniprotKB databases. 169 out of 415 compounds have known compound-target information. Three hundred fifty unique target genes and 2785 unique compound-target associations were retrieved.

Protein Functional Domain Information: For 350 target genes, 381 protein functional domain information was retrieved using the Conserved Domain Database (CDD) Search. CDD makes use of position-specific score matrices (PSSMs) for predicting the conserved domains in protein sequences via RPS-BLAST [10]. In total, 4263 unique compound:protein-domain associations were retrieved.

2.2 The Prediction Model

Score 1: Bioactivity-based Compound Similarity. We used the Jaccard similarity coefficient statistic to compute the similarity score between every pair of compounds (Compound A, Compound B). The activities (Table 1) for each compound is taken as finite sets, with every compound i having a vector of activities A_i.

$$A_i = \{a_{1,i}, a_{2,i}, ..., a_{n,i}\} \tag{1}$$

where $a_{n,i}$ is the bioactivity exhibited by the compound i and n, is an integer, taking values between $0 < n \leq 13$ (total number of activities), representing the nth activity of the ith compound. Then the similarity score is calculated as the size of the intersection of the activity sets divided by the size of the union of the activity sets.

$$B_{i,j} = \frac{Size(A_i \cap A_j)}{Size(A_i \cup A_j)} \tag{2}$$

$B_{i,j}$ is the similarity score (*Score 1*) (Fig. 1) calculated based on the bioactivities of every pair of compounds. $B_{i,j}$ takes a value between 0 and 1, 0 indicating no common activity between the compounds and 1 indicating all activities in common in the compound pair. A total of 86736 similarity scores were calculated between every pair of 415 compounds.

Score 2: Structure-based Compound Similarity. Here we used SIMCOMP (Simultaneous Comparisons for Multiple Endpoints) [9] from GenomeNet to compute the similarity score between pairs of compounds based on the chemical substructure similarity. The tool uses a 2D representation of the compounds to compute the graph matching between two compound structures. $S_{i,j}$ is the similarity score (*Score 2*) (Fig. 1) calculated based on the chemical substructure similarity for every pair of compounds. For maintaining the accuracy of the results, only highly similar compounds based on chemical structure were considered. And so, the cut-off or the threshold value was set to 0.8. Therefore, $S_{i,j}$ takes values only between 0.8 and 1. A total of 307 compounds yielded similarity scores between $0.8 \leq S_{i,j} \leq 1$, producing 755 scores between pairs of compounds.

Score 3: Target Enzyme-based Compound Similarity. The similarity between the compounds based on target enzymes was computed using the similarity between the Enzyme Commission Number (EC Number) [11]. The enzyme identifier number defines the type of chemical reaction catalyzed by that enzyme, using four digits. For every given pair of 169 compounds, the enzymes targeted by the compounds are taken as two finite sets. Next, the similarity score between each of the two set pairs is computed and combined as a weighted moving average (WMA). A score of 1 is given if all four digits of the enzyme pair's EC numbers match; a score of 0.75 is given if the first three digits from left to right match; a score of 0.5 is given if the first two digits from left to right match; a score of 0.25 is given if only the fist digit from left to right matches; a score of 0 is given if none of the digits match between the enzyme pair. For every enzyme in both the sets, the maximum score obtained from all the combinations is taken. And, the final enzyme-based similarity score for every compound pair is computed as a weighted moving average for every type of score by taking into account the number of occurrences of each of the five scores, as shown below.

$$E_{i,j} = \sum (\frac{C_{i,j}(x)}{n}) \times (x) \tag{3}$$

where n is the total number of unique enzyme-enzyme similarity scores obtained between each of two set pairs. $C_{i,j}(x)$ stands for the number/count of occurrences of the score x in both the sets of enzymes for a given compound pair, where $x = 0, 0.25, 0.5, 0.75, 1$. $E_{i,j}$ is the similarity score (*Score 3*) (Fig. 1) computed based on target enzyme similarity between a pair of compounds.

Score 4: Protein Domain-based Compound Similarity. Here we firstly obtain 381 protein functional domain information for 350 target genes. Next, the domains belonging to every compound are taken as a finite set, and the similarity scores $D_{i,j}$ is calculated in the same way as that of *Score 1* (Bioactivity-based compound similarity) using Jaccard Index.

Final Score: Homological Similarity Score. All four similarity scores provide information on highly alike or closely interacting compounds. However, computing a homological similarity score, $H_{i,j}$, based on all four similarity measures, requires combining the scores accurately and efficiently. The homological similarity score between a compound pair is calculated as below:

$$H_{i,j} = \alpha \times B_{i,j} + \beta \times S_{i,j} + \gamma \times E_{i,j} + \delta \times D_{i,j} \tag{4}$$

where the parameters α, β, γ, δ govern the balance of the equation between the weights of similarity scores $B_{i,j}$, $S_{i,j}$, $E_{i,j}$, $D_{i,j}$, respectively. For this study we choose the values of the parameters to be $\alpha = 0.1$, $\beta = 0.5$, $\gamma = 0.2$, $\delta = 0.2$.

After calculating the homological similarity scores, statistical analysis of the mean differences in the scores was made using ANOVA. And the results of the prediction model was evaluated using manually queried literature from various resources like NCBI, PubMed, etc.

3 Results and Discussion

3.1 Statistical Analysis

We obtained the homological similarity scores for 169 natural compounds. We then selected 66 compounds as the top candidates with similar structural, metabolic, or biosynthetic functions based on their structure, nature, and the similarity of the target-enzymes and protein functional sites. To see if the mean similarity scores for each of the four categories were different, ANOVA was performed. From the ANOVA results shown in Table 2, it can be seen that the *p-value*([$<$2.2e$-$16] $<$ 0.001) is much smaller than the alpha (0.001) showing a highly significant result. Also, pairwise comparison between all four types of scores shows a significant difference between the means. Therefore, we conclude that the mean similarity scores for all four similarity measures are different.

Table 2. ANOVA results showing mean differences in the scores of all four similarity measures

Response: similarity_score					
	Df	Sum Sq	Mean Sq	F value	*p value*
Score Type (1/2/3/4)	3	70.607	23.5356	2104.5	<2.2e−16 ***
Residuals	788	8.812	0.0112		
Signif. codes: '***' 0.001					
Pairwise comparison: with bonferroni adjustment					
	Difference	*p value*	Signif.	LCL	UCL
Score_1 - Score_2	−0.5917616	<2.2e−16	***	−0.6172602	−0.5662631
Score_1 - Score_3	−0.18256	<2.2e−16	***	−0.2080586	−0.1570614
Score_1 - Score_4	0.222099	<2.2e−16	***	0.1966004	0.2475975
Score_2 - Score_3	0.4092016	<2.2e−16	***	0.3837031	0.4347002
Score_2 - Score_4	0.8138606	<2.2e−16	***	0.788362	0.8393592
Score_3 - Score_4	0.404659	<2.2e−16	***	0.3791604	0.4301576

The similarity scores are not equally distributed across the compound pairs, as seen from the box plot (Fig. 2). Figure 2 shows the range and the distribution of the scores for all four types of similarity measures. The thickness and the weights on the edges correspond to the values of the similarity scores. A compound pair with a high substructure similarity score ($S_{i,j}$) might not always have high scores for other measures like target-enzymes or proteins too. Figure 3(b) shows how pairs of highly similar compounds (Rutin, Diosmin, and Cyanin) show a difference in similarity scores for each type of similarity measure. Compound pairs like Quercetin and Diosmetin have high structural similarity ($S_{i,j} = 0.90$), but very low protein functional site similarity ($D_{i,j} = 0.003$) and moderate target enzyme-based similarity ($E_{i,j} = 0.39$). These results emphasize the effectiveness of the model, which takes into account various factors including bioactivities, substructures, target enzymes, and protein domains for predicting the candidate compounds and their combinations for achieving synergistic effects instrumental in treating many drug-resistant chronic diseases.

3.2 Prioritizing Compounds for Combinatorial Therapies

Combinatorial therapies have been promising for treating chronic diseases like cancer due to their synergistic effects. It is advantageous to monotherapies mainly due to its capability to impact multiple biological processes simultaneously. Studies have shown that combining similar genomic information with structure-based similarity has led to better performance in successfully identifying promising combinations in a vast chemical space like natural products [12]. In this study, we systematically computed similarity scores between compounds based on four different similarity measures shown with different edges colors in the compound-compound similarity network (Fig. 3). From the figure (Fig. 3(a)) it is evident that network pharmacology allows us to systematically analyze the results by combining the features of multiple components and help in predicting the closely interacting compounds (the highly interconnected sub-network of the network in Fig. 3(a)). Twenty-eight compounds, including Quercetin, Apigenin, etc. were closely interacting, with higher similarity scores based on chemical substructures and target-enzymes. And, 158 compound-compound similarity scores were obtained from the highly connected network. Quercetin and Kaempferol have high similarity scores ($B_{i,j} = 0.48$, $S_{i,j} = 0.95$, $E_{i,j} = 0.5$, $D_{i,j} = 0.2$) as compared to other highly similar compounds based on the range of the scores for all four types of similarity measures. A study has shown that Quercetin and Kaempferol demonstrated a synergistic antiproliferative effect in cultured human cells providing an anti-cancer effect while working in concert [13]. Another study by Tang *et al.* [14], have shown that Quercetin exerts enhanced synergic anti-cancer effects when combined with other small molecules like 10-hydroxy camptothecin (HCPT). To evaluate the combined effect of these compound pairs, we further analyzed their pharmacological effects and then validated our results through manually queried available literature from NCBI, PubChem, etc. Table 3 shows some of the compound pairs from the highly interconnected sub-network of Fig. 3(a). All the compound pairs had similarity scores greater than or equal to 0.65. Also, the compound pairs did have identical pharmacological effects, as seen from the PubChem database, with much-supporting literature demonstrating the combinational or synergistic effects of these compounds. Combining these highly similar compounds with identical pharmacology may provide synergistic effects, required for multi-targeting therapeutics. Our findings through the model led to prioritizing compound combinations and paved the way for natural product drug discovery and repurposing.

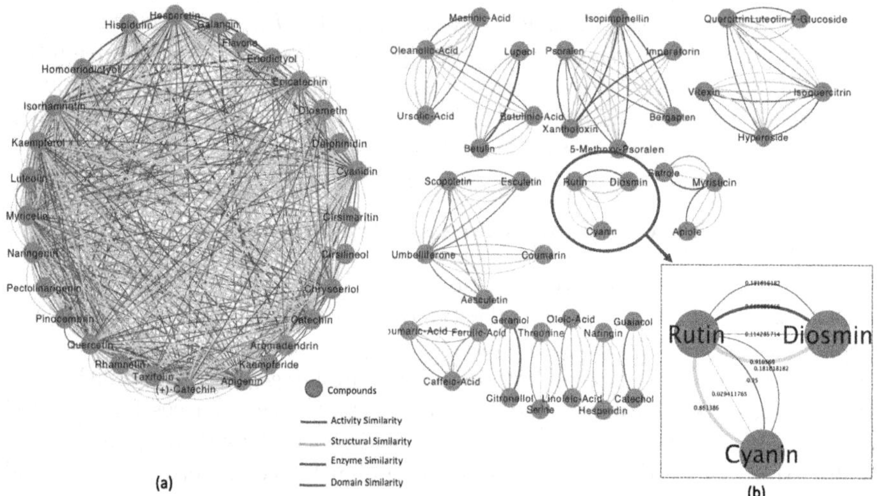

Fig. 3. (a) A Compound-Compound Similarity Network (b) A sub-network showing the similarity scores as edge weights for different similarity measures

3.3 Synergistic Effects Through Combinations of Herbs

Traditionally herbs were combined with other herbs or drugs for achieving the combined action of the bioactive compounds. Yet scientific evidence proving their therapeutic efficacy is still lacking. Most Chinese medicines are a combination of multiple plant products which they call a concoction (*fu-fang*) [15]. However, the vast diversity and the complexity of the herbal compounds pose challenges

Table 3. Synergistic effects and pharmacological validation of closely interacting compounds

Compound A	Compound B	Similarity Score	Synergistic Effects	Literature
Aromadendrin	Apigenin	0.6746	Oxidative Phosphorylation	The Effects of Flavonoid Compounds on Oxidative Phosphorylation and on the Enzymatic Destruction of Indoleacetic Acid. ***In Vivo** January-February 2005 vol. 19 no. 1 69-76*
Catechin	Apigenin	0.6525	Antioxidant, Free radical scavenger, Anti-Inflammatory, Carbohydrate Metabolism promoter, Immunity system modulater.	In vitro effects of myricetin, morin, apigenin, (+)-taxifolin, (+)-catechin, (−)-epicatechin, naringenin and naringin on cytochrome b5 reduction by purified NADH-cytochrome b5 reductase. ***Toxicology*** *Volume 308, 7 June 2013, Pages 34-40*
Myricetin	Epicatechin	0.6649		
Naringenin	Epicatechin	0.6671		
Catechin	Myricetin	0.6811		
Apigenin	Naringenin	0.734		
Catechin	Naringenin	0.6727		
Catechin	Taxifolin	0.7299		
Apigenin	Taxifolin	0.67		
Aromadendrin	Taxifolin	0.7109		
Myricetin	Taxifolin	0.7037		
Naringenin	Taxifolin	0.7058		
Luteolin	Apigenin	0.7562	Antiproliferative, Anti-Inflammatory, and Antimetastatic, Apoptosis-inducing and Chemopreventive activities, Scavenges free radicals	Pharmacokinetic study of luteolin, apigenin, chrysoeriol and diosmetin after oral administration of Flos Chrysanthemi extract in rats. ***Fitoterapia*** *Volume 83, Issue 8, December 2012, Pages 1616-1622*
Luteolin	Chrysoeriol	0.7198		
Apigenin	Diosmetin	0.6856		
Chrysoeriol	Diosmetin	0.6751		
Luteolin	Diosmetin	0.714		
Kaempferol	Quercetin	0.7498	Chemopreventive, anti-Inflammatory and Anti-Allergy effects.	Synergistic Antiproliferative Action of the Flavonols Quercetin and Kaempferol in Cultured Human Cancer Cell Lines. ***In Vivo** January-February 2005 vol. 19 no. 1 69-76*
Catechin	Quercetin	0.7126	Antioxidant, Chemopreventive, anti-Inflammatory and Anti-Allergy effects.	Antioxidant and iron-chelating activities of the flavonoids catechin, quercetin and diosmetin on iron-loaded rat hepatocyte cultures. ***Biochemical Pharmacology*** *Volume 45, Issue 1, 7 January 1993, Pages 13-19*
Cyanidin	Quercetin	0.7186	Chemopreventive, anti-Inflammatory and Anti-Allergy effects.	Antioxidant interactions of catechin, cyanidin, caffeic acid, quercetin, and ellagic acid on human LDL oxidation. ***Food Chemistry*** *Volume 61, Issues 1–2, January 1998, Pages 71-75*

for predicting the combinational effects of the herbs. Our model effectively overcomes this challenge and identifies herbal combinations through their closely interacting bioactive compounds. Based on the assumption that compounds with similar bioactive functional categories are more likely to have similar structural and molecular properties, in our case study, we began with grouping the compounds based on 13 main functions, as shown in Table 1. We constructed a compound-compound similarity network using the 66 highly similar compounds and also, mapped them to their respective functional categories and to the herbs they belong to (Fig. 4). The highly interconnected groups of compounds in the network represent the compounds that are alike or the candidates for combinational treatments. We could see that compounds having common activities are highly similar. Also, our result shows groups of herbs connecting these highly connected compound nodes, indicating the candidate herbs for investigating the synergistic interactions for new combinational therapy strategies (Fig. 4). The herbs, including Dill, French Tarragon, Fennel, Coriander, Parsley, Rosemary, Thyme, Oregano, Sage, Mint, and Basil, are some of the candidate herbs exhibiting multiple bioactivities and bioactive compounds (Fig. 4). Dill has the highest number of compounds: 26 out of 66 candidate compounds, and the compound Quercetin is present in 12 out of 24 herbs. This flavonoid is the mother of many other flavonoids with the highest activity, producing enhanced effects when combined with other bioactive compounds, in particular, other flavonoids [16]. Recently, Quercetin is widely used as an anticarcinogen in many cancer research due to its Chemopreventive, Anti-Inflammatory, Antioxidant, and Anti-Allergy effects. Quercetin, along with Kaempferol, inhibits oxidative stress, which otherwise leads to cell proliferation, a primary step in carcinogenesis [13]. Table 3 shows some of the highly similar compounds, their exerted synergistic effects, and pharmacological evidence through manually queried literature. The herbs identified through our results (Fig. 4) can be combined to exert combined or synergistic effects through various highly similar bioactive compounds that are capable of acting on acting on single or multiple targets associated with single or multiple disease conditions. Also, the notion of combining herbs with synthetic drugs for increasing the efficacy of the treatment is highly in practice, in particular in cancer treatments through drug repurposing strategies [16].

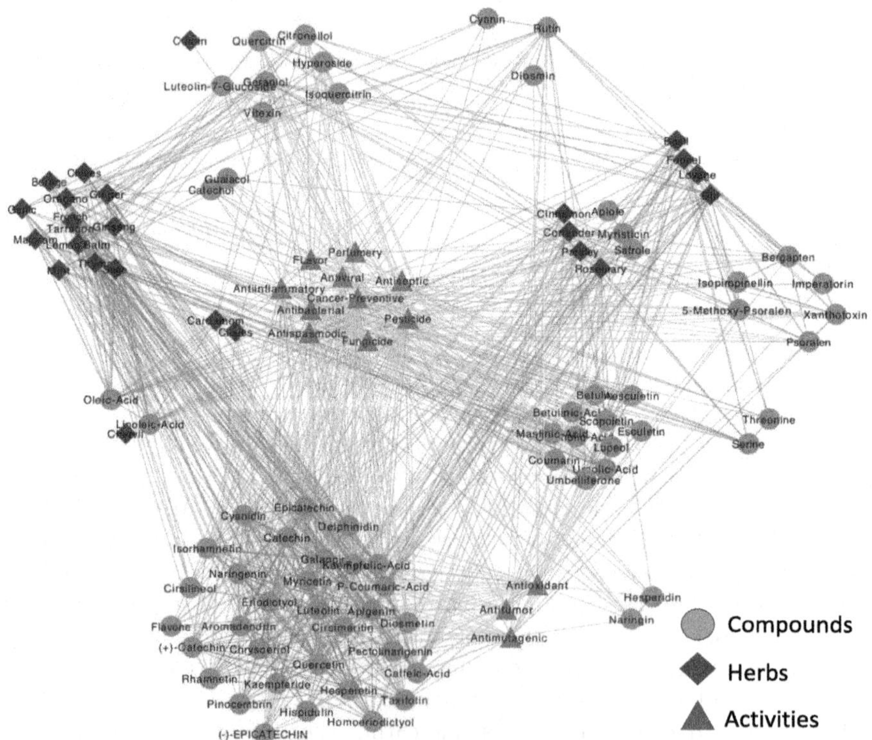

Fig. 4. A Compound-Compound Similarity Sub-network with Activity and Herb Nodes: Identifies herbal combinations for achieving the synergistic effects through highly interconnected regions of the network.

3.4 Identification of New Indications and Compound-Targets

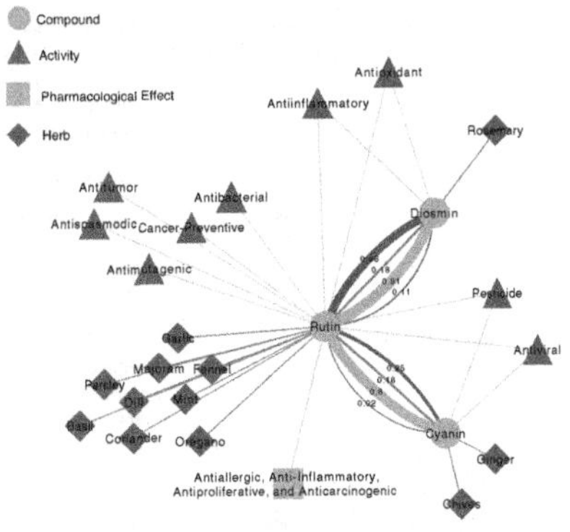

Fig. 5. Rutin showing high similarity with Diosmin and Cyanin

Repurposing herbal compounds has always been a daunting task owing to the large volumes of related information on the small molecules and their intricate mechanism of action. Bioinformaticians and data scientists still relied upon computational techniques for identifying potential new targets and novel indications, in particular for the identification of repurposing candidates. Along this direction, we used the prediction model proposed in this study for associating the indications and known targets of a compound in a highly similar compound pair to the other for which there are no known indications or target information. Out of the 66 candidate compounds, 42 compounds had known pharmacological effects and supporting literature retrieved from PubChem. Remaining 24 compounds do not have known indications. Figure 6 shows a compound-compound similarity network where the compounds are also mapped to their respective functional categories (activities) and pharmacological effects. It is evident from the figure (Fig. 6) that compounds with similar activities or functions are closely connected in the network, indicating high similarity between the compounds. However, it is also evident that not all compounds in the network have known pharmacological effect or indication (compounds near the center of the network). Through our findings, 24 compounds were associated with 58 pharmacological effects. We validated our results through manually queried potential literature from various resources like NCBI, PubMed, etc. Table 4 shows some of the results of the predicted novel pharmacological effects for the natural compounds with unknown indications.

Rutin was found to exhibit antiallergic, anti-inflammatory, antiproliferative, and anticarcinogenic properties through our model. It also acts as a quercetin deliverer to the large intestine. *Rutin's anti-inflammatory actions are mediated through a molecular mechanism that underlies the quercetin-mediated therapeutic effects: quercetin-mediated inhibition of tumor necrosis factor-alpha (TNF-alpha)-induced nuclear factor kappa B (NFkB) activation*[1]. From our results, Diosmin and Cyanin were identified as highly similar compounds to Rutin (Fig. 5). From Fig. 5, we can see that Rutin has similar functional categories with Diosmin and Cyanin. We associated the pharmacological effect of Rutin with Diosmin and Cyanin. A study has shown that Rutin and Diosmin demonstrated excellent anticarcinogenic, anti-varicose and vasoprotective activities, and also were a powerful captor of free radicals. Corsale *et al.*, have proven that the use

[1] National Center for Biotechnology Information. PubChem Database. Rutin, CID = 5280805, https://pubchem.ncbi.nlm.nih.gov/compound/Rutin (accessed on Feb. 4, 2020).

Table 4. Potential new indications for compounds

Query Compounds	Simlar Compounds	Predicted Pharmacological Effects	Literature Validation
Betulin	Betulinic-Acid	Agents used to treat AIDS and/or stop the spread of the HIV infection. Antineoplastic Agents, Phytogenic Agents obtained from higher plants that have demonstrable cytostatic or antineoplastic activity. Prostaglandin Antagonists Compounds that inhibit the action of prostaglandins. - *PubChem*	Pharmacological properties of the ubiquitous natural product betulin. ***European Journal of Pharmaceutical Sciences*** Volume 29, Issue 1, September 2006, Pages 1-13
	Lupeol	Suppress tumor growth but also to impair HNSCC cell invasion by reversal of the NF-kappaB-dependent epithelial-to-mesenchymal transition. - ***PubChem***	Betulin and lupeol in bark from four white-barked birches. ***Phytochemistry*** Volume 27, Issue 7, 1988, Pages 2175-2176
Aromadendrin	Apigenin	Exhibits antiproliferative, anti-inflammatory, and antimetastatic activities. This flavonoid provides selective activity to promote caspase-dependent-apoptosis of leukemia cells and uncover an essential role of PKCdelta during the induction of apoptosis by it(**PMID: 16844095**). - ***PubChem***	Aromadendrin, apigenin, and kaempferol from the wood of Pinus sibirica. ***Chemistry of Natural Compounds*** March 1971, Volume 7, Issue 2, pp 197–198.
	Epicatechin	Water soluble polyphenol and antioxidant that is easily oxidized. Sticks to proteins, blocking bacteria from adhering to cell walls and disrupting their ability to destroy them. - ***PubChem***	Phenolic Compounds from the Flower of Stewartia pseudo-camellia and Their Inhibitory Effects on the Release of β-Hexosaminidase in RBL-2H3 Cells. ***Planta Med 2013;*** 79 - PJ20 DOI: 10.1055/s-0033-1352224

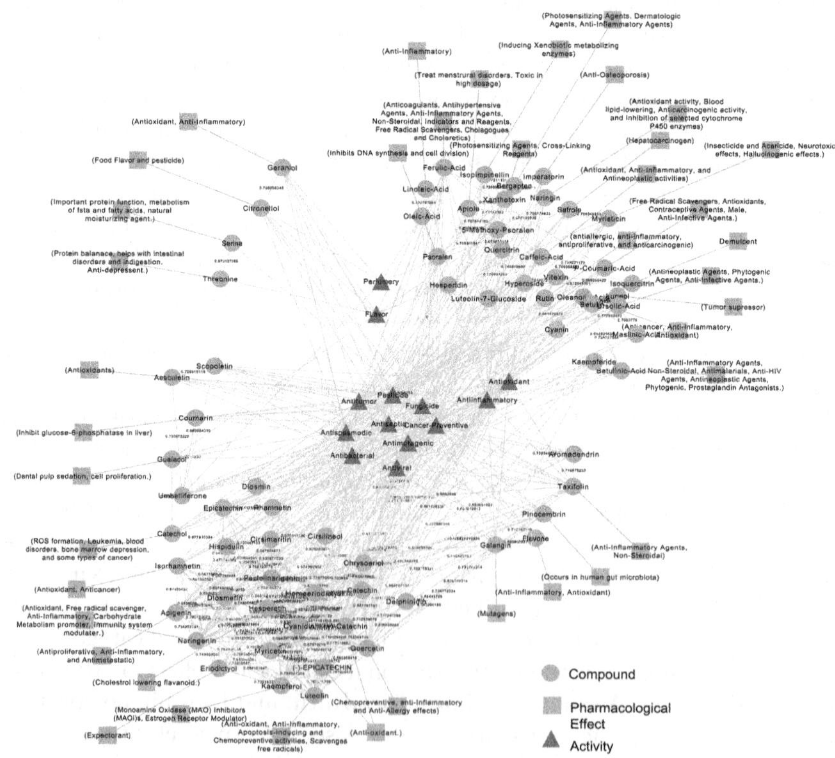

Fig. 6. A Compound-Compound Similarity sub-network with Activity and Pharmacological Effect Nodes: Closely interacting compounds are highly interconnected in the network.

of a mixture of flavonoids like Rutin, Diosmin, and Quercetin is a safe and effective alternative for controlling bleeding from hemorrhoidal disease with minimal adverse effects [17]. Also, we could see how the model was capable of predicting the combinations of herbs, like Basil, Coriander, Oregano, Dill, etc., for achieving synergistic effects through these compounds. These pieces of evidence prove the efficacy of the prediction model in the identification of new pharmacological effects or indications for herbal compounds. Not only the pharmacological effects but also we associated the known targets of the compounds for predicting new compound-target associations based on the similarity analysis.

4 Conclusion

In this study, we constructed a compound-similarity prediction model based on various descriptors like chemical structure, activities, target-enzymes, and protein domains. Four different compound-compound similarity scores were computed based on the descriptors mentioned above using publicly available datasets on herbs, compounds, target genes, and protein domains. Tools like SIMCOPM, CDD search, and measures like Jaccard Index, Weighted Moving Average were employed for calculating the scores. The final homological similarity score was used for predicting: (1) closely interacting compounds, (2) their synergistic effects, (3) potential combinations of herbs and compounds for combinatorial therapies, (4) new pharmacological effects/indications and compound-target associations. Our findings were evaluated using manually curated literature pieces of evidence from data resources like NCBI, PubMed, etc.

Five main reasons for why this study is important are (1) cost and time expensive new drug discovery process, (2) increasing costs of synthetic drugs and healthcare, (3) overwhelming population and demand for new solutions, (4) increasing drug-resistant chronic diseases, (5) increasing demand for multi-targeting therapeutics. However, this study currently has the following limitation. We did not include those compounds which are different but perform similar functions through different reaction sets and molecular pathways. A more accurate prediction model should also take into account the similarity based on the molecular functional component through reactions and pathways, which will be considered in our future work. We will also evaluate our model by comparing its performance with other existing prediction models.

References

1. Pezzani, R., et al.: Synergistic effects of plant derivatives and conventional chemotherapeutic agents: an update on the cancer perspective. Medicina **55**(4), 110 (2019)
2. Bender, A., Jenkins, J.L., Scheiber, J., Sukuru, S.C.K., Glick, M., Davies, J.W.: How similar are similarity searching methods? a principal component analysis of molecular descriptor space. J. Chem. Inf. Model. **49**(1), 108–119 (2009)
3. Gilissen, C., Hoischen, A., Brunner, H.G., Veltman, J.A.: Disease gene identification strategies for exome sequencing. Eur. J. Hum. Genet. **20**(5), 490–497 (2012)

4. Jachak, S.M., Saklani, A.: Challenges and opportunities in drug discovery from plants. Curr. Sci. **92**(9), 1251–1257 (2007)
5. Medina-Franco, J.L., Giulianotti, M.A., Welmaker, G.S., Houghten, R.A.: Shifting from the single to the multitarget paradigm in drug discovery. Drug Discov. Today **18**(9–10), 495–501 (2013)
6. Keri, R.S., Quintanova, C., Chaves, S., Silva, D.F., Cardoso, S.M., Santos, M.A.: New tacrine hybrids with natural-based cysteine derivatives as multitargeted drugs for potential treatment of Alzheimer's disease. Chem. Biolo. Drug Des. **87**(1), 101–111 (2016)
7. Öztürk, H., Ozkirimli, E., Özgür, A.: A comparative study of smiles-based compound similarity functions for drug-target interaction prediction. BMC Bioinform. **17**(1), 128 (2016)
8. Yamanishi, Y., Pauwels, E., Saigo, H., Stoven, V.: Identification of chemogenomic features from drug-target interaction networks by sparse canonical correspondence analysis. Mach. Learn. Syst. Biol. **28**(18), 87 (2011)
9. Kanehisa, M.: KEGG bioinformatics resource for plant genomics and metabolomics. In: Edwards, D. (ed.) Plant Bioinformatics. MMB, vol. 1374, pp. 55–70. Springer, New York (2016). https://doi.org/10.1007/978-1-4939-3167-5_3
10. Marchler-Bauer, A., et al.: CDD: NCBI's conserved domain database. Nucleic Acids Res. **43**(D1), D222–D226 (2015)
11. Heymans, M., Singh, A.K.: Deriving phylogenetic trees from the similarity analysis of metabolic pathways. Bioinformatics **19**(suppl-1), i138–i146 (2003)
12. Liu, Y., Zhao, H.: Predicting synergistic effects between compounds through their structural similarity and effects on transcriptomes. Bioinformatics **32**(24), 3782–3789 (2016)
13. Ackland, M.L., Van De Waarsenburg, S., Jones, R.: Synergistic antiproliferative action of the flavonols quercetin and kaempferol in cultured human cancer cell lines. Vivo **19**(1), 69–76 (2005)
14. Tang, Q., Ji, F., Wang, J., Guo, L., Li, Y., Bao, Y.: Quercetin exerts synergetic anti-cancer activity with 10-hydroxy camptothecin. Eur. J. Pharm. Sci. **109**, 223–232 (2017)
15. Che, C.-T., Wang, Z.J., Chow, M.S.S., Lam, C.W.K.: Herb-herb combination for therapeutic enhancement and advancement: theory, practice and future perspectives. Molecules **18**(5), 5125–5141 (2013)
16. HemaIswarya, S., Doble, M.: Potential synergism of natural products in the treatment of cancer. Phytotherapy Res. Int. J. Devoted Pharmacol. Toxicol. Eval. Natural Product Deriv. **20**(4), 239–249 (2006)
17. Corsale, I., et al.: Flavonoid mixture (diosmin, troxerutin, rutin, hesperidin, quercetin) in the treatment of I–III degree hemorroidal disease: a double-blind multicenter prospective comparative study. Int. J. Colorectal Dis. **33**(11), 1595–1600 (2018)

Assisted Generation of Bone Fracture Patterns

Gema Parra-Cabrera, Francisco Daniel Pérez-Cano, Adrián Luque-Luque, and Juan José Jiménez-Delgado(✉)

Graphics and Geomatics Group, Computer Science Department, University of Jaén, Campus Las Lagunillas s/n, Jaén, Spain
gpc00014@red.ujaen.es, {fdperez,alluque,juanjo}@ujaen.es

Abstract. We present a method for the generation of bone fracture patterns assisted by computer. A tool has been designed for the generation of a fracture pattern interactively and guided by the system, based on the study of real cases of fractures. This tool assists the specialist in obtaining fracture patterns according to certain rules taken from the statistical analysis of real cases. This tool can be used for the generation of biological databases of fractures. Another use of the fracture pattern could be the generation of virtual fractures, applying the fracture pattern to 3D osseous models.

Keywords: Automatic systems · Bone fracture database · Fracture pattern · Generation tools · Traumatology

1 Introduction

Generating validated fracture patterns allows to obtain different types of fractures including unusual cases and fracture cases that sometimes cannot be observed. In this paper, a tool based on forensic analysis is presented. This tool allows the generation of fracture patterns according to certain rules. These rules are established by studies of real fractures.

The research involved and the development of the tool proposed is essential for the creation and replication of fracture patterns, allowing to analyse fracture patterns without expensive preparations or experimentation.

The structure of this paper is as follows. First, a study of previous works is carried out about bone fracture representations, highlighting the existing tools for the design of bone fractures. Next, a description is made of the tool for the generation of fracture patterns. The results section shows several cases of generation of fracture patterns as well as a usability study for assessing its intuitive use. Finally, the conclusions objectively summarize the contributions and future work.

2 Fracture Pattern

A fracture pattern is a representation of the fracture zone of a bone. Normally fracture patterns are extracted from medical images of patients with some type of

I. Rojas et al. (Eds.): IWBBIO 2020, LNBI 12108, pp. 825–834, 2020.
https://doi.org/10.1007/978-3-030-45385-5_73

trauma. One possible use of the generated fracture patterns is their application to 3D geometric bone models, in order to simulate a geometric fracture with realistic aspect. Generating fracture patterns allows to obtain different types of fractures including unusual cases and fracture cases that sometimes cannot be observed. These fractures can serve as input to a simulator or tool for training specialists to perform a fracture reduction or for the generation of a bank of bone fractures.

A fracture pattern could be represented using spherical coordinates [6], using a 2D texture that includes the whole fractured area [1], or using a 3D representation through a map of heights [2]. Previous representations do not facilitate the entry or generation of new fracture patterns, but rather are representations of actual fracture patterns and as such they schematize or store fractures. The fracture patterns found in the literature, are formed by a projection on the plane of the four parts into which the bone is usually divided (anterior, posterior, lateral and medial) [3–5]. This approach to evaluating information facilitates the study of characteristics by specialists, as well as, to make a mental scheme of the fragments generated.

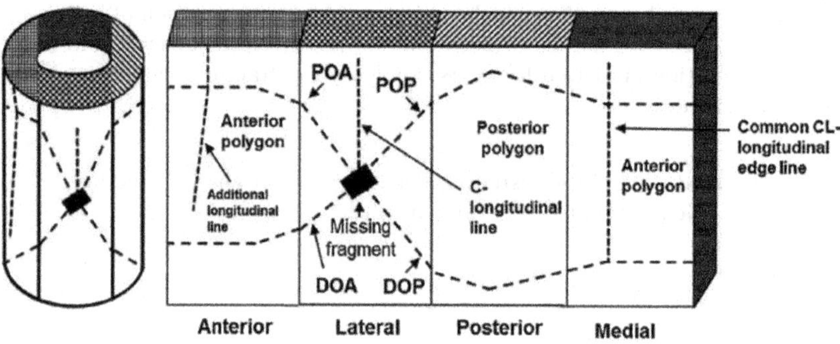

Fig. 1. Representation of a 3D fracture projection (left) to 2D plane (right) [3].

Regarding the existing tools for the generation of a fracture pattern using the proposed representation, no tool has been found that enables to obtain a representation of a fracture pattern in the terms of the representation proposed and used in this work. This is not the optimal situation because the drawing editors are not intended to draw a fracture pattern, so they are not adapted to it, not being guided, allowing multiple errors.

3 Fracture Pattern Generator Tool

The main functionalities of the proposed tool consist in the manual design of a fracture pattern as representation of real fractures. This form of representation allows the creation of different types of fracture patterns. The user can decide if the pattern will have fragment detachment or not, the shape, size and rotation of the fragment, the number of fracture lines that will be for each type of fracture line, as well as the position, inclination or branches of the main fracture line or other ramifications. In addition, the tool allows to change the thickness of the bone.

As far as the operation of the tool is concerned, it is very simple, since the user only has to worry about generating the pattern by selecting the type of brush (fragment or line) and its settings, clicking on the canvas to place this. In order to create a fracture pattern using the proposed tool, a set of factors must be taken into account as well as knowledge related to the generation of fractures must be acquired so that it can be carried out properly. For pattern generation, it is necessary to follow a number of steps. Each step implements a set of rules and guides the user with the design of the fracture pattern. These steps are as follows:

Step 1. Choose Whether the Fracture Pattern has or Not Chip-Loss. When the fracture has a chip detachment, it will be only necessary to select the shape of the detached fragment, followed by the selection of the place where the selected shape should be on the canvas (Fig. 2). Otherwise, if the fracture to be generated does not have a chip detachment, nothing has to be done in this step, just start to draw the fracture lines. In addition, it is possible to select different shapes of the detached fragment to place it, as well as to adjust the size, position and rotation through a panel on the side of the tool.

Step 2. Generation of Oblique Lines. This step focuses on drawing of oblique lines (Fig. 2). The number of lines of this type is limited. Once this maximum number of lines is reached, the tool goes automatically to step three. These lines come out from the fragment and extend with some horizontal inclination.

Step 3. Generation of Longitudinal Lines. In this step optional longitudinal lines are drawn (Fig. 3). The user can choose between drawing this type of lines or to move to the next step directly. In this type of lines it is important to know that they can appear either from the detached fragment or the initial fracture point. They also can appear in any part of the non impacted aspects, but only if the longitudinal line intersects with another line.

Step 4. Generation of Branches. Ramifications of the fracture (Fig. 3) can be created at this stage. An important factor in the creation of ramifications is to know that they can appear in any type of line except in longitudinal lines.

Additionally, traditional methods for editing have also been included in order to facilitate the use of the tool.

The fracture patterns generated are 2D patterns that are similar to the 2D images obtained in forensic articles related to bone fractures. The lower image (Fig. 4) represents the same fracture pattern as the fracture representation obtained from Cohen et al. study (Fig. 1). Therefore, not only does it enable the representation of new patterns, it is also possible to replicate the studies of other experts in the field.

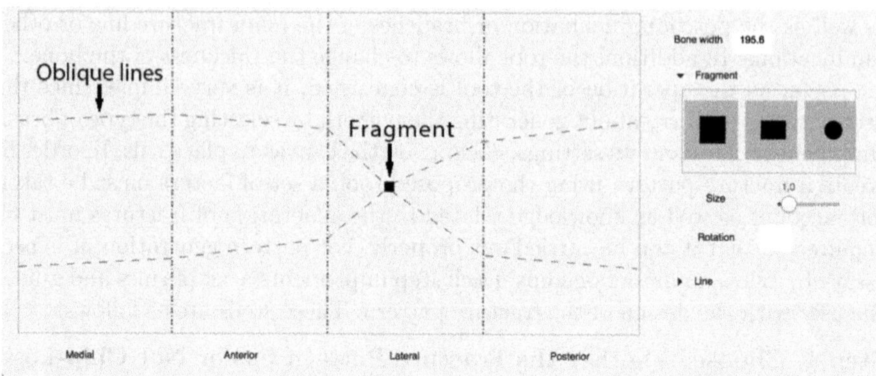

Fig. 2. Completion of the drawing of oblique lines in a fracture pattern and the use of a chip detachment in the fracture editor.

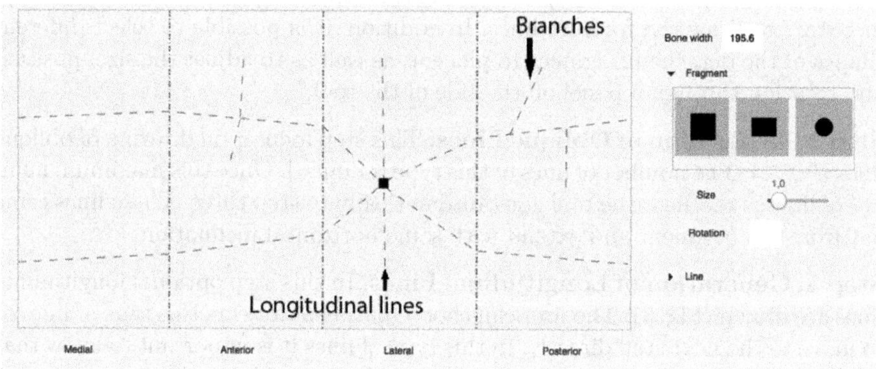

Fig. 3. Longitudinal lines and branches can also be drawn, according to certain rules, in order to represent the fracture pattern.

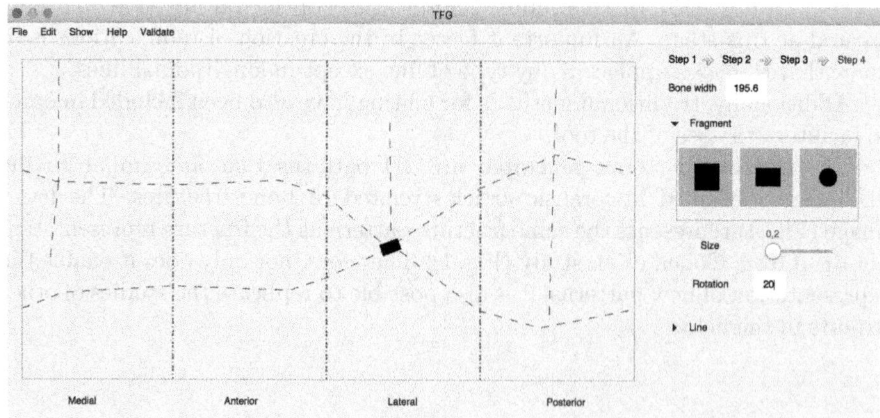

Fig. 4. Proposed 2D fracture pattern equivalent to the fracture pattern in Fig. 1

4 Results

This section shows the generation of several cases of fractures, keeping the forensic analysis studies of Cohen et al. [4]. For each of the bone fracture patterns, a description of the fracture and the process necessary for its generation with the tool is made. A usability study is also accomplished in this section, in order to evaluate the developed tool.

4.1 Fracture Pattern Generation

In this section a set of four cases has been designed in order to show the potential use of the generation tool for the generation of fracture patterns.

Pattern 1. The first fracture pattern (Fig. 5) is a lateral fracture pattern with chip detachment due to impact, which has an adequate size in relation to the existing line layout according to studies based on the forensic analysis carried out by Cohen et al. [5]. In addition, in the chip area there is presence of a longitudinal line and butterfly-shaped fractures lines emerging from the chip. There is also another longitudinal line that appears in the medial aspect.

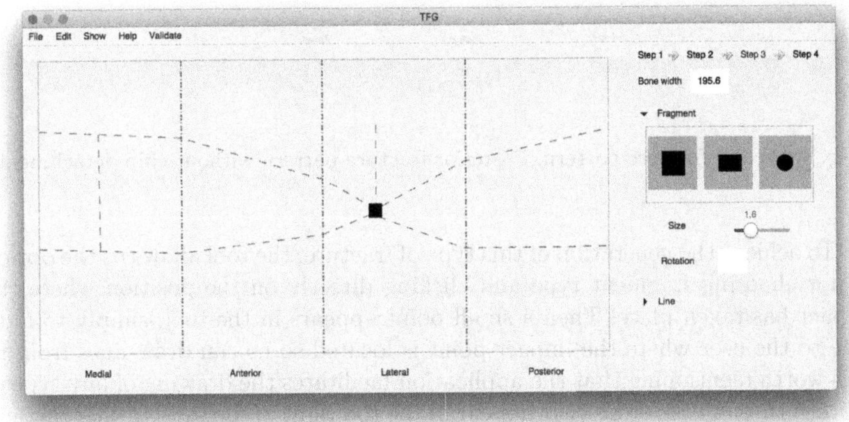

Fig. 5. First fracture pattern. Lateral fracture pattern with chip detachment

In order to generate this fracture pattern, it is necessary to select the impact position on the lateral aspect by including a square fragment, with a suitable rotation. The application then moves automatically to the next step, which restricts us to drawing oblique lines starting from the fragment and extending to the anterior, medial and posterior aspects. The application allows the drawing of the line to be correct limiting the inclination of the line by the previous line. Furthermore, the application allows to get a line that continues between the medial and posterior aspects, representing a shape that envelops the bone. Once the oblique lines have been drawn, the application automatically goes to the next step: drawing longitudinal lines. In this case, it is checked that the line starts from an oblique line or a fragment and that it is approximately vertical.

Pattern 2. The second case is a posterior fracture pattern (Fig. 6) in which there has been no chip detachment during impact. Despite this, oblique lines appear from the point of impact that extended horizontally to cover every aspect of the bone.

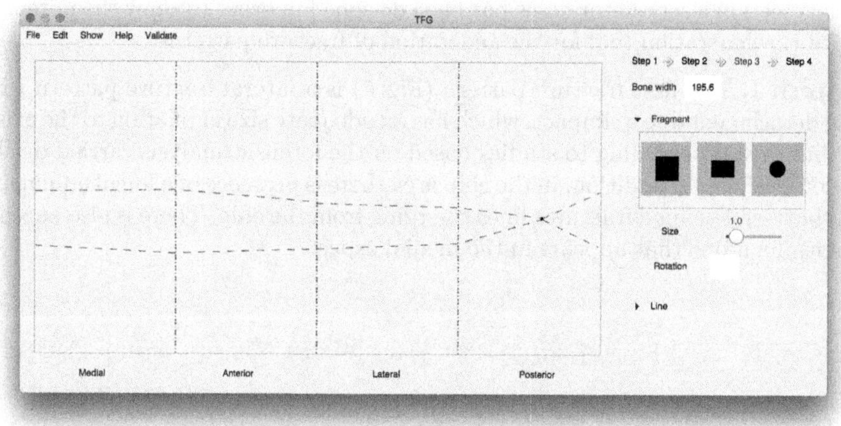

Fig. 6. Second fracture pattern. Posterior fracture pattern without chip detachment

To achieve the generation of this type of fracture, the tool allows us the option of not choosing fragment type and clicking directly on the position where the impact has taken place. Then a small point appears in the tool, simply to indicate to the user where the impact point is located so he can draw lines from it. It is worth mentioning that the application facilitates the drawing of any type of pattern through the steps that appear in the top right of the tool. In this particular case, when the impact point is placed, the first step is automatically completed and the application moving on to the next step: drawing obliques lines. To draw oblique lines you only have to create the lines by clicking on the point of impact and dragging to the nearby aspects (medial, anterior, lateral). After this step, the pattern would already be drawn, since no longitudinal lines or branches have been included in the fracture pattern.

Pattern 3. The third fracture pattern is an anterior fracture pattern (Fig. 7) with chip detachment due to impact, with an appropriate size according to the lines present in the fracture. Due to the impact, longitudinal lines have been produced from the fragment, which extend across the width of the bone. In this case no longitudinal lines have been produced, but some branching is present.

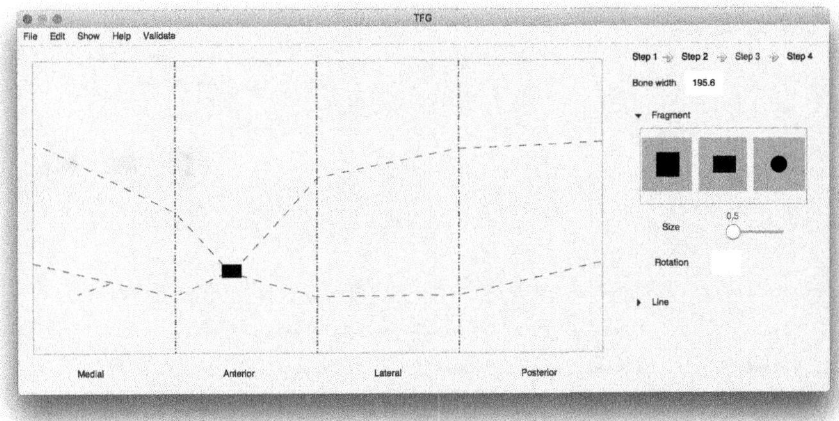

Fig. 7. Third fracture pattern. Anterior fracture pattern with chip detachment

To achieve this representation of the fracture pattern, the steps followed have been similar to the previous cases. The first step is the selection of type of fragment, its suitable size and position on the anterior aspect. After this, we proceed to draw the oblique lines in the same way as in the previous cases, but with the difference that at the end of drawing them, the tool leads to step 3 (for drawing longitudinal lines). In this fracture pattern no longitudinal lines have been produced, so we have to click on step 3 to indicate that in this occasion we are not going to create this type of lines, allowing us to draw the branches directly. When drawing branches, we only take into account that they always have to be created from another line, no matter if that line is longitudinal, oblique or another branch.

Pattern 4. The fourth fracture pattern (Fig. 8) is a medial fracture with chip detachment caused by impact. This pattern has oblique lines that begin at the fragment and extend across the various aspects of the bone, as well as a longitudinal line that also originates from the fragment. Finally, in the pattern we can appreciate a branch that begins in an oblique line of the anterior aspect.

The configuration of this fracture pattern is simple, since it uses all the indications proposed in the previous cases. First, the point of impact is selected and located with a corresponding chip fragment and located with the appropriate size and rotation. The oblique lines are then drawn, followed by longitudinal lines and branches.

4.2 Usability Study

Finally, experiments have been carried out related to the use of the tool, by means of an usability study. In the search for an intuitive and easy to use product, while the tool has been developed, it has been offered to different types of users, with different computer knowledge and age ranges to detect the least understandable

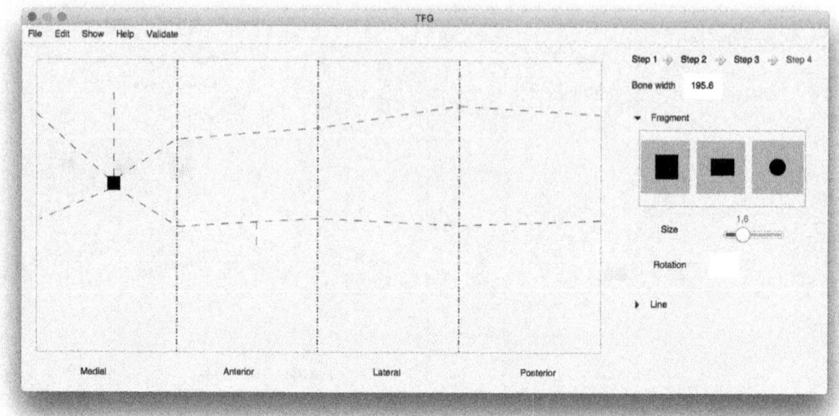

Fig. 8. Fourth fracture pattern. Medial fracture pattern with chip detachment

aspects of the application. With this information, the application has been modified to achieve a tool as intuitive as possible.

A sample of 10 users with different degrees of knowledge in traumatology and in the use of computer tools were selected. Two of them were experts in traumatology, additionally four were health professionals, three computer engineers and finally three users with limited knowledge about traumatology or computer tools. In order to detect these aspects, the tool has been tested by them without explaining how it is used. An image of a fracture pattern was provided to the users and they tried to reproduce this fracture pattern using the tool.

We exhibit some of the most relevant questions in the questionnaire composed of 12 questions. We show the questions with more deviated scores or scores below the optimal punctuation. Scores were in a Likert scale between 1 and 5, being 5 the best rating (Table 1).

1. **Question: Required help to perform the requested tasks.** The 24% of the users needed help in many cases to use the tool, mainly due to inexperience with computer equipment or inexperience in the area of fracture patterns.
2. **Question: I consider that it is not needed a previous knowledge for performing the required tasks.** The result was 72%, this means that users with lesser knowledge about the tasks performed requires a previous formation not for performing the tasks but for understanding the process of fracture.
3. **Question: I made mistakes while performing tasks because I didn't read a message or indication from the software product.** The results of this question were that 22% of the users do not read the indications given by the interface, so there are type errors, although in low proportion.
4. **Question: The software product has messages or instructions that are not clear to perform a task.** 98% of users concluded that the tool was clear, so this question reveal that the interface has no errors in their messages or while

performing tasks, as well as the interface is clear and makes the user feel comfortable.

5. **Question: The tool is simple to use.** It is concluded that it is not too complicated to use, as it has a score of 4 out of 5 for usability of the tool, that is, 80% of users believe that it is a simple tool to use.

Table 1. Summary of the statistical analysis obtained from the proposed usability questionnaire, with the most relevant questions.

Question	Mean	+/−SD
1	3.8	0.42
2	3.6	0.97
3	4.4	0.84
4	4.9	0.31
5	4	0.67

In general, the average obtained from the complete questionnaire is 4.6 with a deviation of 0.53, so we can affirm that the tool is completely usable and intuitive.

5 Conclusion

The tool proposed allows the generation of realistic fracture patterns. In addition to generating patterns manually, it is also possible to load other types of patterns and represent them cylindrically using the designed tool.

About the use of the tool, a usability study has been carried out. The results of this study conclude that the tool is simple and intuitive, so in the hands of experts it will be possible to make realistic fracture patterns that can be exported to other systems, establishing a new source for obtaining fracture patterns for ulterior studies.

Actually, the types of fracture patterns that the tool is able to generate are transversal, oblique or butterfly and longitudinal. The incorporation of spiral fracture patterns will be studied in the future because they are more complex. This fractures are caused by rotation forces in the bone or combination of torsion and flexion. Comminuted fractures, in which multiple fragments and multiple fracture lines are generated, will be also studied in future.

As future work, we propose the generation of a bank of validated fracture patterns that can be used in the generation of virtual fractures on bone geometric models, as a master pattern or definitive pattern. They can be used as input in simulators related to traumatology, such as training in fracture reduction.

Acknowledgements. This work has been supported by the Ministerio de Economía y Competitividad and the European Union (via ERDF funds) through the research project DPI2015-65123-R.

References

1. Pérez Cano, F.D., Jiménez Delgado, J.J.: Macroescale fracturation of osseous models. In: Tavares, J.M.R.S., Natal Jorge, R.M. (eds.) VipIMAGE 2019. LNCVB, vol. 34, pp. 492–500. Springer, Cham (2019). https://doi.org/10.1007/978-3-030-32040-9_50
2. Luque-Luque, A., Jiménez-Pérez, J.-R., Jiménez-Delgado, J.J.: Osseous fracture patterns: from CT to a plane representation. In: Tavares, J.M.R.S., Natal Jorge, R.M. (eds.) VipIMAGE 2019. LNCVB, vol. 34, pp. 474–481. Springer, Cham (2019). https://doi.org/10.1007/978-3-030-32040-9_48
3. Cohen, H., et al.: The effect of impact tool geometry and soft material covering on long bone fracture patterns in children. Int. J. Legal Med. **131**(4), 1011–1021 (2017). https://doi.org/10.1007/s00414-017-1532-7
4. Cohen, H., et al.: The impact velocity and bone fracture pattern: forensic perspective. Forensic Sci. Int. **266**, 54–62 (2016). https://doi.org/10.1016/j.forsciint.2016.04.035
5. Cohen, H., et al.: The influence of impact direction and axial loading on the bone fracture pattern. Forensic Sci. Int. **277**, 197–206 (2017). https://doi.org/10.1016/j.forsciint.2017.05.015
6. Winkelbach, S., Westphal, R., Goesling, T.: Pose estimation of cylindrical fragments for semi-automatic bone fracture reduction. In: Michaelis, B., Krell, G. (eds.) DAGM 2003. LNCS, vol. 2781, pp. 566–573. Springer, Heidelberg (2003). https://doi.org/10.1007/978-3-540-45243-0_72

Author Index

Printed in the United States
By Bookmasters